Lecture Notes in Artificial Intelligence   3559

Edited by J. G. Carbonell and J. Siekmann

Subseries of Lecture Notes in Computer Science

T0189881

Peter Auer   Ron Meir (Eds.)

Learning
Theory

18th Annual Conference on Learning Theory, COLT 2005
Bertinoro, Italy, June 27-30, 2005
Proceedings

 Springer

Series Editors

Jaime G. Carbonell, Carnegie Mellon University, Pittsburgh, PA, USA
Jörg Siekmann, University of Saarland, Saarbrücken, Germany

Volume Editors

Peter Auer
University of Leoben
Department of Mathematics and Information Technologies
Franz-Josef-Strasse 18, 8700 Leoben, Austria
E-mail: auer@unileoben.ac.at

Ron Meir
Technion, Israel Institute of Technology
Department of Electrical Engineering
Haifa 3200, P.O. Box, Israel
E-mail: rmeir@ee.technion.ac.il

Library of Congress Control Number: 2005927736

CR Subject Classification (1998): I.2.6, I.2.3, I.2, F.4.1, F.2, F.1.1

ISSN   0302-9743
ISBN-10   3-540-26556-2 Springer Berlin Heidelberg New York
ISBN-13   978-3-540-26556-6 Springer Berlin Heidelberg New York

Springer is a part of Springer Science+Business Media

springeronline.com

© Springer-Verlag Berlin Heidelberg 2005
Printed in Germany

Typesetting: Camera-ready by author, data conversion by Scientific Publishing Services, Chennai, India
Printed on acid-free paper   SPIN: 11503415   06/3142   5 4 3 2 1 0

Preface

This volume contains papers presented at the 18th Annual Conference on Learning Theory (previously known as the Conference on Computational Learning Theory) held in Bertinoro, Italy from June 27 to 30, 2005.

The technical program contained 45 papers selected from 120 submissions, 3 open problems selected from among 5 contributed, and 2 invited lectures. The invited lectures were given by Sergiu Hart on "Uncoupled Dynamics and Nash Equilibrium," and by Satinder Singh on "Rethinking State, Action, and Reward in Reinforcement Learning." These papers were not included in this volume.

The Mark Fulk Award is presented annually for the best paper co-authored by a student. The student selected this year was Hadi Salmasian for the paper titled "The Spectral Method for General Mixture Models" co-authored with Ravindran Kannan and Santosh Vempala.

The number of papers submitted to COLT this year was exceptionally high. In addition to the classical COLT topics, we found an increase in the number of submissions related to novel classification scenarios such as ranking. This increase reflects a healthy shift towards more structured classification problems, which are becoming increasingly relevant to practitioners. The large number of quality submissions placed a heavy burden on the Program Committee: Shai Ben David (University of Waterloo), Avrim Blum (Carnegie Mellon University), Peter Bartlett (University of California, Berkeley), Nader Bshouty (Technion), Ran El-Yaniv (Technion), Yoav Freund (Columbia University), Ralf Herbrich (Microsoft Research, Cambridge), Marcus Hutter (IDSIA, Switzerland), Tony Jebara (Columbia University), Balazs Kegl (University of Montreal), Vladimir Koltchinskii (University New Mexico), Phil Long (Columbia University), Gábor Lugosi (Pompeu Fabra University), Shie Mannor (McGill University), Shahar Mendelson (Australian National University), Massimiliano Pontil (University College London), Daniel Reidenbach (University of Kaiserslautern), Dan Roth (University of Illinois at Urbana-Champaign), Michael Schmitt (Ruhr University, Bochum), Rocco Servedio (Columbia University), Hans Ulrich Simon (Ruhr University, Bochum), Volodya Vovk (Royal Holloway), Manfred Warmuth (University of California, Santa Cruz), and Tong Zhang (IBM Research, Yorktown). We take this opportunity to thank all reviewers for the excellent job performed over a relatively short period of time. Some of them were even willing to review additional papers beyond those initially assigned. Their efforts led to the selection of an exceptional set of papers, which ensured an outstanding conference. We would like to have mentioned the sub-reviewers who assisted the Program Committee in reaching their assessments, but unfortunately space constraints do not permit us to include this long list of names and we must simply ask them to accept our thanks anonymously.

We are particularly grateful to Nicolò Cesa-Bianchi and Claudio Gentile, the conference local chairs. Together they handled the conference publicity and all the local arrangements to ensure a successful event. We would also like to thank Microsoft for providing the software used in the Program Committee deliberations, and Dori Peleg for creating the conference Web site. Jyrki Kivinen assisted the organization of the conference in his role as head of the COLT Steering Committee.

This work was also supported in part by the IST Programme of the European Community, under the PASCAL Network of Excellence, IST-2002-506778.

Finally, we would like to thank the Machine Learning Journal, Google Inc., the Bertinoro International Center for Informatics, and the Università degli Studi di Milano for their sponsorship of the conference.

April, 2005   Peter Auer,
                                                              Ron Meir
                                            Program Co-chairs COLT 2005

Sponsored by:

Table of Contents

Learning to Rank

Boosting

Unlabeled Data, Multiclass Classification

Online Learning I

Online Learning II

Support Vector Machines

Kernels and Embeddings

Inductive Inference

Unsupervised Learning

Generalization Bounds

Query Learning, Attribute Efficiency, Compression Schemes

Economics and Game Theory

Separation Results for Learning Models

Open Problems

Ranking and Scoring
Using Empirical Risk Minimization[*]

Stéphan Clémençon[1,3], Gábor Lugosi[2], and Nicolas Vayatis[3]

[1] MODALX - Université Paris X,
92001 Nanterre Cedex, France
sclemenc@u-paris10.fr
[2] Department of Economics, Universitat Pompeu Fabra,
Ramon Trias Fargas 25-27, 08005 Barcelona, Spain
lugosi@upf.es
[3] Laboratoire de Probabilités et Modèles Aléatoires - Université Paris VI,
4, place Jussieu, 75252 Paris Cedex, France
vayatis@ccr.jussieu.fr

Abstract. A general model is proposed for studying ranking problems. We investigate learning methods based on empirical minimization of the natural estimates of the ranking risk. The empirical estimates are of the form of a U-statistic. Inequalities from the theory of U-statistics and U-processes are used to obtain performance bounds for the empirical risk minimizers. Convex risk minimization methods are also studied to give a theoretical framework for ranking algorithms based on boosting and support vector machines. Just like in binary classification, fast rates of convergence are achieved under certain noise assumption. General sufficient conditions are proposed in several special cases that guarantee fast rates of convergence.

1 Introduction

Motivated by various applications including problems related to document retrieval or credit-risk screening, the ranking problem has received increasing attention both in the statistical and machine learning literature. In the ranking problem one has to compare two (or more) different observations and decide which one is "better". For example, in document retrieval applications, one may be concerned with comparing documents by degree of relevance for a particular request, rather than simply classifying them as relevant or not.

In this paper we establish a statistical framework for studying such ranking problems. We discuss a general model and point out that the problem may be approached by empirical risk minimization methods thoroughly studied in

---

[*] This research was supported in part by Spanish Ministry of Science and Technology and FEDER, grant BMF2003-03324, and by the PASCAL Network of Excellence under EC grant no. 506778.

P. Auer and R. Meir (Eds.): COLT 2005, LNAI 3559, pp. 1–15, 2005.

statistical learning theory with the important novelty that natural estimates of the ranking risk involve U-statistics. Therefore, the methodology is based on the theory of U-processes. For an excellent account of the theory of U-statistics and U-processes we refer to the monograph of de la Peña and Giné [9].

In this paper we establish basic performance bounds for empirical minimization of the ranking risk. We also investigate conditions under which significantly improved results may be given. We also provide a theoretical analysis of certain nonparametric ranking methods that are based on an empirical minimization of convex cost functionals over convex sets of scoring functions. The methods are inspired by boosting-, and support vector machine-type algorithms for classification.

The rest of the paper is organized as follows. In Section 2, the basic models and the two versions of the ranking problem we consider are introduced. In Sections 3 and 4, we provide the basic uniform convergence and consistency results for empirical risk and convex risk minimizers. In Section 5 we describe the noise assumptions which take advantage of the structure of the U-statistics in order to obtain fast rates of convergence.

2   The Ranking Problem

Let (X, Y) be a pair of random variables taking values in $\mathcal{X} \times \mathbb{R}$ where $\mathcal{X}$ is a measurable space. The random object X models some observation and Y its real-valued label. Let (X', Y') denote a pair of random variables identically distributed with (X, Y), and independent of it. Denote

$$Z = \frac{Y - Y'}{2} \ .$$

In the ranking problem one observes X and X' but not necessarily their labels Y and Y'. We think about X being "better" than X' if $Y > Y'$, that is, if $Z > 0$. The goal is to rank X and X' such that the probability that the better ranked of them has a smaller label is as small as possible. Formally, a *ranking rule* is a function $r : \mathcal{X} \times \mathcal{X} \to \{-1, 1\}$. If $r(x, x') = 1$ then the rule ranks x higher than x'. The performance of a ranking rule is measured by the *ranking risk*

$$L(r) = \mathbb{P}\{Z \cdot r(X, X') < 0\} \ ,$$

that is, the probability that r ranks two randomly drawn instances incorrectly. Observe that in this formalization, the ranking problem is equivalent to a binary classification problem in which the sign of the random variable Z is to be guessed based upon the pair of observations (X, X'). Now it is easy to determine the ranking rule with minimal risk. Introduce the notation

$$\rho_+(X, X') = \mathbb{P}\{Z > 0 \mid X, X'\} \ , \quad \rho_-(X, X') = \mathbb{P}\{Z < 0 \mid X, X'\} \ .$$

Then we have the following simple fact:

Proposition 1. *Define*

$$r^*(x, x') = 2\mathbb{I}_{[\rho_+(x,x') \geq \rho_-(x,x')]} - 1$$

and denote $L^* = L(r^*) = \mathbb{E}\{\min(\rho_+(X,X'), \rho_-(X,X'))\}$. *Then for any ranking rule* r, $L^* \leq L(r)$.

The purpose of this paper is to investigate the construction of ranking rules of low risk based on training data. We assume that given n independent, identically distributed copies of (X,Y), are available: $D_n = (X_1, Y_1), \ldots, (X_n, Y_n)$. Given a ranking rule r, one may use the training data to estimate its risk $L(r) = \mathbb{P}\{Z \cdot r(X, X') < 0\}$. The perhaps most natural estimate is the U-*statistic*

$$L_n(r) = \frac{1}{n(n-1)} \sum_{i \neq j} \mathbb{I}_{[Z_{i,j} \cdot r(X_i, X_j) < 0]} \quad \text{where } Z_{i,j} = \frac{Y_i - Y_j}{2}.$$

U-statistics have been studied in depth and their behavior is well understood. One of the classical inequalities concerning U-statistics is due to Hoeffding [14] which implies that, for all $t > 0$, if $\sigma^2 = \text{Var}(\mathbb{I}_{[Z \cdot r(X,X') < 0]}) = L(r)(1 - L(r))$, then

$$\mathbb{P}\{|L_n(r) - L(r)| > t\} \leq 2 \exp\left(-\frac{\lfloor (n/2) \rfloor t^2}{2\sigma^2 + 2t/3}\right). \tag{1}$$

It is important noticing here that the latter inequality may be improved by replacing σ^2 by a smaller term. This is based on the so-called Hoeffding's decomposition described below.

Hoeffding's Decomposition. Hoeffding's decomposition (see [21] for more details) is a basic tool for studying U-statistics. Consider the i.i.d. random variables $X, X_1, \ldots, X_n$ and denote by

$$U_n = \frac{1}{n(n-1)} \sum_{i \neq j} q(X_i, X_j)$$

a U-statistic of order 2 where q (the so-called *kernel*) is a symmetric real-valued function. Assuming that $q(X_1, X_2)$ is square integrable, $U_n - \mathbb{E}U_n$ may be decomposed as a sum T_n of i.i.d. r.v's plus a *degenerate* U-statistic W_n. In order to write this decomposition, consider the following function of one variable

$$h(X_i) = \mathbb{E}(q(X_i, X) \mid X_i) - \mathbb{E}U_n,$$

and the function of two variables

$$\tilde{h}(X_i, X_j) = q(X_i, X_j) - \mathbb{E}U_n - h(X_i) - h(X_j).$$

Then $U_n = \mathbb{E}U_n + 2T_n + W_n$, where

$$T_n = \frac{1}{n} \sum_{i=1}^{n} h(X_i), \quad W_n = \frac{1}{n(n-1)} \sum_{i \neq j} \tilde{h}(X_i, X_j).$$

W_n is called a *degenerate* U-statistic because $\mathbb{E}\left(\tilde{h}(X_i, X) \mid X_i\right) = 0$. Clearly,

$$\text{Var}(T_n) = \frac{\text{Var}(\mathbb{E}(q(X_1, X) \mid X_1))}{n}.$$

Note that $\mathrm{Var}(\mathbb{E}(q(X_1, X) \mid X_1))$ is less than $\mathrm{Var}(q(X_1, X))$ (unless q is already degenerate). Furthermore, the variance of the degenerate U-statistic W_n is of the order $1/n^2$. Thus, T_n is the leading term in this orthogonal decomposition. Indeed, the limit distribution of $\sqrt{n}(U_n - \mathbb{E}U_n)$ is the normal distribution $\mathcal{N}(0, 4\mathrm{Var}(\mathbb{E}(q(X_1, X) \mid X_1))$. This suggests that inequality (1) may be quite loose.

Indeed, exploiting further Hoeffding's decomposition, de la Peña and Giné [9] established a Bernstein's type inequality of the form (1) but with σ^2 replaced by the variance of the conditional expectation (see Theorem 4.1.13 in [9]). This remarkable improvement is not exploited in our "first-order" analysis (Sections 3 and 4) but will become crucial when establishing fast rates of convergence in Section 5.

Remark 1. (A MORE GENERAL FRAMEWORK.) One may consider a generalization of the setup described above. Instead of ranking just two observations X, X', one may be interested in ranking m independent observations $X^{(1)}, \ldots, X^{(m)}$. In this case the value of a ranking function $r(X^{(1)}, \ldots, X^{(m)})$ is a permutation π of $\{1, \ldots, m\}$ and the goal is that π should coincide with (or at least resemble to) the permutation $\bar{\pi}$ for which $Y^{(\bar{\pi}(1))} \geq \cdots \geq Y^{(\bar{\pi}(m))}$. Given a loss function ℓ that assigns a number in $[0, 1]$ to a pair of permutations, the ranking risk is defined as

$$L(r) = \mathbb{E}\ell(r(X^{(1)}, \ldots, X^{(m)}), \bar{\pi}) .$$

In this general case, natural estimates of $L(r)$ involve m-th order U-statistics. All results of this paper extend in a straightforward manner to this general setup. In order to lighten the notation, we restrict the discussion to the case described above, that is, to the case when $m = 2$ and the loss function is $\ell(\pi, \bar{\pi}) = \mathbb{I}_{[\pi \neq \bar{\pi}]}$.

Another formalization of this problem is the so-called *ordinal regression* approach (see Herbrich, Graepel, and Obermayer [13]) in which the relation between ranking and pairwise classification is also made clear. However, the fact that a sequence of pairs (X_i, X_j) of i.i.d. individual data (X_i) is no longer independent was not considered there.

Remark 2. (RANKING AND SCORING.) In many interesting cases the ranking problem may be reduced to finding an appropriate *scoring function*. These are the cases when the joint distribution of X and Y is such that there exists a function $s^* : \mathcal{X} \to \mathbb{R}$ such that

$$r^*(x, x') = 1 \quad \text{if and only if} \quad s^*(x) \geq s^*(x') .$$

A function s^* satisfying the assumption is called an *optimal scoring function*. Obviously, any strictly increasing transformation of an optimal scoring function is also an optimal scoring function. Below we describe some important special cases when the ranking problem may be reduced to scoring.

Example 1. (THE BIPARTITE RANKING PROBLEM.) In the bipartite ranking problem the label Y is binary, it takes values in $\{-1, 1\}$. Writing $\eta(x) = \mathbb{P}\{Y = 1 | X = x\}$, it is easy to see that the Bayes ranking risk equals

$$L^* = \mathbb{E} \min\{\eta(X)(1 - \eta(X')), \eta(X')(1 - \eta(X))\}$$

and also,

$$L^* = \mathrm{Var}\left(\frac{Y+1}{2}\right) - \frac{1}{2}\mathbb{E}\,|\eta(X) - \eta(X')| \leq 1/4$$

where the equality $L^* = \mathrm{Var}\left(\frac{Y+1}{2}\right)$ holds when X and Y are independent and the maximum is attained when $\eta \equiv 1/2$. Observe that the difficulty of the bipartite ranking problem depends on the concentration properties of the distribution of $\eta(X) = \mathbb{P}\{Y = 1 \mid X\}$ through the quantity $\mathbb{E}\{|\eta(X) - \eta(X')|\}$ which is a classical measure of concentration, known as *Gini's mean difference*. It is clear from the form of the Bayes ranking rule that the optimal ranking rule is given by a scoring function s^* which is any strictly increasing transformation of η. Then one may restrict the search to ranking rules defined by scoring functions s, that is, ranking rules of form $r(x, x') = 2\mathbb{I}_{[s(x) \geq s(x')]} - 1$. Writing $L(s) \overset{\text{def}}{=} L(r)$, one has

$$L(s) - L^* = \mathbb{E}\left(|\eta(X') - \eta(X)| \, \mathbb{I}_{[(s(X) - s(X'))(\eta(X) - \eta(X')) < 0]}\right) \ .$$

Observe that the ranking risk in this case is closely related to the AUC criterion which is a standard performance measure in the bipartite setting (see, e.g., [11]). More precisely, we have:

$$AUC(s) = \mathbb{P}\left(s(X) \geq s(X') \mid Y = 1, Y' = -1\right) = 1 - \frac{1}{2p(1-p)}L(s),$$

where $p = \mathbb{P}(Y = 1)$, so maximizing the AUC criterion is equivalent to minimizing the ranking risk.

Example 2. (A REGRESSION MODEL). Assume now that Y is real-valued and the joint distribution of X and Y is such that $Y = m(X) + \epsilon\sigma(X)$ where $m(x) = \mathbb{E}(Y|X = x)$ is the regression function and ϵ has a symmetric distribution around zero and is independent of X. Then clearly the optimal ranking rule r^* may be obtained by a scoring function s^* which may be taken as any strictly increasing transformation of m.

3 Empirical Risk Minimization

Based on the empirical estimate $L_n(r)$ of the risk $L(r)$ of a ranking rule defined above, one may consider choosing a ranking rule by minimizing the empirical risk over a class $\mathcal{R}$ of ranking rules $r : \mathcal{X} \times \mathcal{X} \to \{-1, 1\}$. Define the empirical risk minimizer, over $\mathcal{R}$, by

$$r_n = \arg\min_{r \in \mathcal{R}} L_n(r) \ .$$

(Ties are broken in an arbitrary way.) In a "first-order" approach, we may study the performance $L(r_n) = \mathbb{P}\{Z \cdot r_n(X, X') < 0 | D_n\}$ of the empirical risk minimizer by the standard bound (see, e.g., [10])

$$L(r_n) - \inf_{r \in \mathcal{R}} L(r) \leq 2 \sup_{r \in \mathcal{R}} |L_n(r) - L(r)| . \tag{2}$$

This inequality points out that bounding the performance of an empirical minimizer of the ranking risk boils down to investigating the properties of U-processes, that is, suprema of U-statistics indexed by a class of ranking rules. In our first-order approach it suffices to use the next simple inequality which reduces the problem to the study of ordinary empirical processes.

Lemma 1. *Let* $q_\tau : \mathcal{X} \times \mathcal{X} \to \mathbb{R}$ *be real-valued functions indexed by* $\tau \in T$ *where* T *is some set. If* $X_1, \ldots, X_n$ *are i.i.d. then for any convex nondecreasing function* ψ,

$$\mathbb{E}\psi\left(\sup_{\tau \in T} \frac{1}{n(n-1)} \sum_{i \neq j} q_\tau(X_i, X_j)\right) \leq \mathbb{E}\psi\left(\sup_{\tau \in T} \frac{1}{\lfloor n/2 \rfloor} \sum_{i=1}^{\lfloor n/2 \rfloor} q_\tau(X_i, X_{\lfloor n/2 \rfloor + i})\right),$$

assuming the suprema are measurable and the expected values exist.

The proof uses a similar trick Hoeffding's above-mentioned inequality are based on. The details are omitted.

Using the lemma with $\psi(x) = e^{\lambda x}$, we bound the moment generating function of the U-process by that of an ordinary empirical process. Then standard methods of handling empirical processes may be used directly. For example, the bounded differences inequality (see McDiarmid [20]) implies that

$$\log \mathbb{E} \exp\left(\lambda \sup_{r \in \mathcal{R}} |L_n(r) - L(r)|\right) \leq \lambda \mathbb{E} \sup_{r \in \mathcal{R}} |\tilde{L}_n(r) - L(r)| + \frac{\lambda^2}{4(n-1)},$$

where we have set $\tilde{L}_n(r) = \frac{1}{\lfloor n/2 \rfloor} \sum_{i=1}^{\lfloor n/2 \rfloor} \mathbb{I}_{[Z_{i,\lfloor n/2 \rfloor + i} \cdot r(X_i, X_{\lfloor n/2 \rfloor + i}) < 0]}$. The expected value on the right-hand side may now be bounded by standard methods. For example, if the class $\mathcal{R}$ of indicator functions has finite VC dimension V, then

$$\mathbb{E} \sup_{r \in \mathcal{R}} \frac{1}{\lfloor n/2 \rfloor} \left| \sum_{i=1}^{\lfloor n/2 \rfloor} \mathbb{I}_{[Z_{i,\lfloor n/2 \rfloor + i} \cdot r(X_i, X_{\lfloor n/2 \rfloor + i}) < 0]} - L(r) \right| \leq c\sqrt{\frac{V}{n}}$$

for a universal constant c (see, e.g., Lugosi [17]). By the Chernoff bound $P\{X > t\} \leq E \exp(\lambda X - \lambda t)$ we immediately obtain the following corollary:

Proposition 2. *Let* $\mathcal{R}$ *be a class of ranking rules of* VC *dimension* V. *Then for any* $t > 0$,

$$\mathbb{P}\left\{\sup_{r \in \mathcal{R}} |L_n(r) - L(r)| > c\sqrt{\frac{V}{n}} + t\right\} \leq e^{-(n-1)t^2} .$$

A similar result is proved in the bipartite ranking case by Agarwal, Har-Peled, and Roth ([1], [2]) with the restriction that their bound holds conditionally on a label sequence. Their analysis relies on a particular complexity measure called the rank-shatter coefficient but the core of the argument is the same (since they implicitly make use of the permutation argument to recover a sum of independent quantities).

The proposition above is convenient, simple, and, in a certain sense, not improvable. However, it is well known from the theory of statistical learning and empirical risk minimization for classification that the bound (2) is often quite loose. In classification problems the looseness of such a "first-order" approach is due to the fact that the variance of the estimators of the risk is ignored and bounded uniformly by a constant. However, in the above analysis of the ranking problem there is an additional weakness due to the fact that estimators based on U-statistics have an even smaller variance as we pointed it out above. Observe that all upper bounds obtained in this section remain true for an empirical risk minimizer that, instead of using estimates based on U-statistics, estimates the risk of a ranking rule by splitting the data set into two halves and estimate $L(r)$ by

$$\frac{1}{\lfloor n/2 \rfloor} \sum_{i=1}^{\lfloor n/2 \rfloor} \mathbb{I}_{[Z_{i,\lfloor n/2 \rfloor+i} \cdot r(X_i, X_{\lfloor n/2 \rfloor+i}) < 0]} .$$

(The same holds for the results of Section 4 as well.) Thus, in the analysis above one looses the advantage of using U-statistics. In Section 5 it is shown that under certain, not uncommon, circumstances significantly smaller risk bounds are achievable. There it will have an essential importance to use the sharp exponential bounds for U-statistics.

4 Convex Risk Minimization

Several successful algorithms for classification, including various versions of *boosting* and *support vector machines* are based on replacing the loss function by a convex function and minimizing the corresponding empirical convex risk functionals over a certain class of functions (typically over a ball in an appropriately chosen Hilbert or Banach space of functions). This approach has important computational advantages, as the minimization of the empirical convex functional is often computationally feasible by gradient descent algorithms. Recently significant theoretical advance has been made in understanding the statistical behavior of such methods see, e.g., Bartlett, Jordan, and McAuliffe [4], Blanchard, Lugosi and Vayatis [6], Breiman [8], Jiang [15], Lugosi and Vayatis [18], Zhang [23].

The purpose of this section is to extend the principle of convex risk minimization to the ranking problem studied in this paper. Our analysis also provides a theoretical framework for the analysis of some successful ranking algorithms such as the RANKBOOST algorithm of Freund, Iyer, Schapire, and Singer [11]. In what follows we adapt the arguments of Lugosi and Vayatis [18] (where a simple binary classification problem was considered) to the ranking problem.

The basic idea is to consider ranking rules induced by real-valued functions, that is, ranking rules of the form

$$r(x, x') = \begin{cases} 1 & \text{if } f(x, x') > 0 \\ -1 & \text{otherwise} \end{cases}$$

where $f : \mathcal{X} \times \mathcal{X} \to \mathbb{R}$ is some measurable real-valued function. With a slight abuse of notation, we will denote by $L(f) \overset{\text{def}}{=} \mathbb{P}\{\text{sgn}(Z) \cdot f(X, X') < 0\} = L(r)$ the risk of the ranking rule induced by f. (Here $\text{sgn}(x) = 1$ if $x > 0$, $\text{sgn}(x) = -1$ if $x < 0$, and $\text{sgn}(x) = 0$ if $x = 0$.) Let $\phi : \mathbb{R} \to [0, \infty)$ a convex *cost function* satisfying $\phi(0) = 1$ and $\phi(x) \geq \mathbb{I}_{[x \geq 0]}$. Typical choices of ϕ include the exponential cost function $\phi(x) = e^x$, the "logit" function $\phi(x) = \log_2(1 + e^x)$, or the "hinge loss" $\phi(x) = (1 + x)_+$. Define the *cost functional* associated to the cost function ϕ by

$$A(f) = \mathbb{E}\phi(-\text{sgn}(Z) \cdot f(X, X')).$$

We denote by $A^* = \inf_f A(f)$ the "optimal" value of the cost functional where the infimum is taken over all measurable functions $f : \mathcal{X} \times \mathcal{X} \to \mathbb{R}$.

The most natural estimate of the cost functional $A(f)$, based on the training data D_n, is the *empirical cost functional* defined by the U-statistic

$$A_n(f) = \frac{1}{n(n-1)} \sum_{i \neq j} \phi(-\text{sgn}(Z_{i,j}) \cdot f(X_i, X_j)).$$

The ranking rules based on *convex risk minimization* we consider in this section minimize, over a set $\mathcal{F}$ of real-valued functions $f : \mathcal{X} \times \mathcal{X} \to \mathbb{R}$, the empirical cost functional A_n, that is, we choose $f_n = \arg\min_{f \in \mathcal{F}} A_n(f)$ and assign the corresponding ranking rule

$$r_n(x, x') = \begin{cases} 1 & \text{if } f_n(x, x') > 0 \\ -1 & \text{otherwise}. \end{cases}$$

By minimizing convex risk functionals, one hopes to make the excess convex risk $A(f_n) - A^*$ small. This is meaningful for ranking if one can relate the excess convex risk to the excess ranking risk $L(f_n) - L^*$. This may be done quite generally by recalling a recent result of Bartlett, Jordan, and McAuliffe [4]. To this end, introduce the function

$$H(\rho) = \inf_{\alpha \in \mathbb{R}} (\rho\phi(-\alpha) + (1-\rho)\phi(\alpha))$$

$$H^-(\rho) = \inf_{\alpha : \alpha(2\rho-1) \leq 0} (\rho\phi(-\alpha) + (1-\rho)\phi(\alpha)).$$

Defining ψ over $\mathbb{R}$ by $\psi(x) = H^-((1+x)/2) - H((1+x)/2)$, Theorem 3 of [4] implies that for all functions $f : \mathcal{X} \times \mathcal{X} \to \mathbb{R}$,

$$L(f) - L^* \leq \psi^{-1}(A(f) - A^*)$$

where ψ^{-1} denotes the inverse of ψ. Bartlett, Jordan, and McAuliffe show that, whenever ϕ is convex, $\lim_{x \to 0} \psi^{-1}(x) = 0$, so convergence of the excess convex risk to zero implies that the excess ranking risk also converges to zero. Moreover, in most interesting cases $\psi^{-1}(x)$ may be bounded, for $x > 0$, by a constant multiple of $\sqrt{x}$ (such as in the case of exponential or logit cost functions) or even by x (e.g., if $\phi(x) = (1 + x)_+$ is the so-called *hinge loss*).

Thus, to analyze the excess ranking risk $L(f) - L^*$ for convex risk minimization, it suffices to bound the excess convex risk. This may be done by decomposing it into "estimation" and "approximation" errors as follows:

$$A(f_n) - A^*(f) \le \left(A(f_n) - \inf_{f \in \mathcal{F}} A(f) \right) + \left(\inf_{f \in \mathcal{F}} A(f) - A^* \right) .$$

To bound the estimation error, assume, for simplicity, that the class $\mathcal{F}$ of functions is uniformly bounded, say $\sup_{f \in \mathcal{F}, x \in \mathcal{X}} |f(x)| \le B$. Then once again, we may appeal to Lemma 1 and the bounded differences inequality which imply that for any $\lambda > 0$,

$$\log \mathbb{E} \exp \left(\lambda \sup_{f \in \mathcal{F}} |A_n(f) - A(f)| \right) \le \lambda \mathbb{E} \sup_{f \in \mathcal{F}} \left(\tilde{A}_n(f) - A(f) \right) + \frac{\lambda^2 B^2}{2(n-1)} ,$$

where $\tilde{A}_n(f) = \frac{1}{\lceil n/2 \rceil} \sum_{i=1}^{\lfloor n/2 \rfloor} \phi \left(- \operatorname{sgn}(Z_{i, \lfloor n/2 \rfloor + i}) \cdot f(X_i, X_{\lfloor n/2 \rfloor + i}) \right)$. Now it suffices to derive an upper bound for the expected supremum appearing in the exponent. This may be done by standard symmetrization and contraction inequalities. In fact, by mimicking Koltchinskii and Panchenko [16] (see also the proof of Lemma 2 in Lugosi and Vayatis [18]), the expectation on the right-hand side may be bounded by

$$4B\phi'(B) \mathbb{E} \sup_{f \in \mathcal{F}} \left(\frac{1}{\lfloor n/2 \rfloor} \sum_{i=1}^{\lfloor n/2 \rfloor} \sigma_i \cdot f(X_i, X_{\lfloor n/2 \rfloor + i}) \right)$$

where $\sigma_1, \ldots, \sigma_{\lfloor n/2 \rfloor}$ are i.i.d. Rademacher random variables independent of D_n. We summarize our findings:

Proposition 3. *Let f_n be the ranking rule minimizing the empirical convex risk functional $A_n(f)$ over a class of functions f uniformly bounded by $-B$ and B. Then, with probability at least $1 - \delta$,*

$$A(f_n) - \inf_{f \in \mathcal{F}} A(f) \le 8B\phi'(B)R_n(\mathcal{F}) + \sqrt{\frac{2B^2 \log(1/\delta)}{2(n-1)}}$$

where $R_n(\mathcal{F}) = \mathbb{E} \sup_{f \in \mathcal{F}} \left(\frac{1}{\lceil n/2 \rceil} \sum_{i=1}^{\lfloor n/2 \rfloor} \sigma_i \cdot f(X_i, X_{\lfloor n/2 \rfloor + i}) \right)$.

Many interesting bounds are available for the Rademacher average of various classes of functions. For example, in analogy of boosting-type classification problems, one may consider a class $\mathcal{F}_B$ of functions defined by

$$\mathcal{F}_B = \left\{ f(x, x') = \sum_{j=1}^{N} w_j g_j(x, x') : N \in \mathbb{N}, \sum_{j=1}^{N} |w_j| = B, g_j \in \mathcal{R} \right\}$$

where $\mathcal{R}$ is a class of ranking rules as defined in Section 3. In this case it is easy to see that

$$R_n(\mathcal{F}_B) \leq BR_n(\mathcal{R}) \leq \text{const.} \frac{BV}{\sqrt{n}}$$

where V is the VC dimension of the "base" class $\mathcal{R}$.

Summarizing, we have shown that a ranking rule based on the empirical minimization $A_n(f)$ over a class of ranking functions $\mathcal{F}_B$ of the form defined above, the excess ranking risk satisfies, with probability at least $1 - \delta$,

$$L(f_n) - L^* \leq \psi^{-1}\left(8B\phi'(B)c\frac{BV}{\sqrt{n}} + \sqrt{\frac{2B^2 \log(1/\delta)}{n}} + \left(\inf_{f\in\mathcal{F}_B} A(f) - A^*\right)\right).$$

This inequality may be used to derive the *universal consistency* of such ranking rules. For example, the following corollary is immediate.

Corollary 1. *Let $\mathcal{R}$ be a class of ranking rules of finite VC dimension V such that the associated class of functions $\mathcal{F}_B$ is rich in the sense that*

$$\lim_{B\to\infty} \inf_{f\in\mathcal{F}_B} A(f) = A^*$$

for all distributions of (X, Y). Then if f_n is defined as the empirical minimizer of $A_n(f)$ over $\mathcal{F}_{B_n}$ where the sequence B_n satisfies $B_n \to \infty$ and $B_n^2 \phi'(B_n)/\sqrt{n} \to 0$, then

$$\lim_{n\to\infty} L(f_n) = L^* \quad almost\ surely.$$

Classes $\mathcal{R}$ satisfying the conditions of the corollary exist, we refer the reader to Lugosi and Vayatis [18] for several examples.

Proposition 3 can also be used for establishing performance bounds for kernel methods such as support vector machines. The details are omitted for the lack of space.

5   Fast Rates

As we have mentioned at the end of Section 3, the bounds obtained there may be significantly improved under certain conditions. It is well known (see, e.g., §5.2 in the survey [7] and the references therein) that tighter bounds for the excess risk in the context of binary classification may be obtained if one can control the variance of the excess risk by its expected value. In classification this can be guaranteed under certain "low-noise" conditions combined with the fact that the optimal (Bayes) classifier is in the class of candidate classification rules (see, e.g., Massart and Nédélec [19], Tsybakov [22]).

The purpose of this section is to examine possibilities of obtaining such improved performance bounds for empirical ranking risk minimization. The main message is that in the ranking problem one also may obtain significantly improved bounds under some conditions that are analogous to the low-noise conditions in the classification problem, though quite different in nature.

Here we will greatly benefit from using U-statistics (as opposed to splitting the sample) as the small variance of the U-statistics used to estimate the ranking risk gives rise to sharper bounds.

Below we establish improved bounds for the excess risk for empirical ranking risk minimization introduced in Section 3 above. Similar results also hold for the estimator based on the convex risk $A(s)$ though some assumptions may be more difficult to interpret (see [6] for classification), and here we restrict our attention to the minimizer r_n of the empirical ranking risk $L_n(r)$ over a class $\mathcal{R}$ of ranking rules.

Set first

$$q_r((x,y),(x',y')) = \mathbb{I}_{[(y-y')\cdot r(x,x')<0]} - \mathbb{I}_{[(y-y')\cdot r^*(x,x')<0]}$$

and consider the following estimate of the *excess risk* $\Lambda(r) \stackrel{\text{def}}{=} L(r) - L^* = \mathbb{E}q_r((X,Y),(X',Y'))$ given by:

$$\Lambda_n(r) \stackrel{\text{def}}{=} \frac{1}{n(n-1)} \sum_{i \neq j} q_r((X_i, Y_i), (X_j, Y_j)),$$

which is a U-statistic of degree 2 with symmetric kernel q_r. Clearly, the minimizer r_n of the empirical ranking risk $L_n(r)$ over $\mathcal{R}$ also minimizes the empirical excess risk $\Lambda_n(r)$. To study this minimizer, consider the Hoeffding decomposition of $\Lambda_n(r)$:

$$\Lambda_n(r) = \Lambda(r) + 2T_n(r) + W_n(r),$$

where

$$T_n(r) = \frac{1}{n} \sum_{i=1}^{n} h_r(X_i, Y_i)$$

is a sum of i.i.d. random variables with $h_r(x,y) = \mathbb{E}q_r((x,y),(X',Y')) - \Lambda(r)$ and

$$W_n(r) = \frac{1}{n(n-1)} \sum_{i \neq j} \tilde{h}_r((X_i, Y_i), (X_j, Y_j))$$

is a degenerate U-statistic with symmetric kernel

$$\tilde{h}_r((x,y),(x',y')) = q_r((x,y),(x',y')) - \Lambda(r) - h_r(x,y) - h_r(x',y').$$

Now consider the estimator r_n obtained as the minimizer of

$$L_n(r) = \frac{1}{n(n-1)} \sum_{i \neq j} \mathbb{I}_{[(Y_i-Y_j)\cdot r(X_i,X_j)<0]}$$

over all $r \in \mathcal{R}$.

In this section we work under the following basic assumptions:

(a) The class $\mathcal{R}$ of ranking rules has a finite VC dimension V.
(b) The optimal ranking rule r^* is in the class $\mathcal{R}$.
(c) For all $r \in \mathcal{R}$,

$$\text{Var}(h_r(X,Y)) \leq c\Lambda(r)^\alpha$$

with some constants $c > 0$ and $\alpha \in [0,1]$.

The basic tools we need are an exponential inequality for U-processes indexed by a VC class of degenerate kernels due to Arcones and Giné [3] and a general inequality for empirical risk minimizers of Bartlett and Mendelson [5]. The Arcones-Giné inequality, simplified to the case we need states that there exists a universal constant C such that, with probability at least $1 - \delta$,

$$\sup_{r \in \mathcal{R}} |W_n(r)| \leq \frac{CV}{n-1} \log \left(\frac{1}{\delta} \right) . \qquad (3)$$

Theorem 1. *Consider the minimizer of the empirical ranking risk $L_n(r)$ over a class $\mathcal{R}$ of ranking rules and assume that conditions (a),(b), and (c) listed above hold. Then there exists a universal constant C such that, with probability at least $1 - \delta$, the ranking risk of r_n satisfies*

$$L(r_n) - L^* \leq C \left(\frac{V \log(n/\delta)}{n} \right)^{1/(2-\alpha)} .$$

SKETCH OF PROOF. Let A be the event on which $\sup_{r \in \mathcal{R}} |W_n(r)| \leq \rho$, where $\rho = \frac{CV}{n-1} \log \left(\frac{2}{\delta} \right)$ and C denotes the constant in (3). Then by (3), $\mathbb{P}[A] \geq 1 - \delta/2$. By the Hoeffding decomposition of the U-statistic $\Lambda_n(r)$, it is clear that, on A, r_n is an ρ-minimizer of $(1/n) \sum_{i=1}^{n} f_r(X_i, Y_i)$ over $r \in \mathcal{R}$ (in the sense that the average calculated for $r = r_n$ exceeds the minimum by not more than ρ) where, for every $r \in \mathcal{R}$, we write $f_r(x, y) = \mathbb{E} q_r((X, Y), (x, y))$. Define $\tilde{r}_n$ as r_n on A and an arbitrary minimizer of $(1/n) \sum_{i=1}^{n} f_r(X_i, Y_i)$ on A^c. Then clearly, with probability at least $1 - \delta/2$, $L(r_n) = L(\tilde{r}_n)$ and $\tilde{r}_n$ is a ρ-minimizer of $(1/n) \sum_{i=1}^{n} f_r(X_i, Y_i)$. Thus, we can use a general result of Bartlett and Mendelson [5] to bound the excess ranking risk $\Lambda(\tilde{r}_n) = \mathbb{E}(f_{\tilde{r}_n}(X, Y) | D_n)$ of $\tilde{r}_n$. To this end, we need an estimate on the L_2 covering numbers of the class of functions $\{f_r : r \in \mathcal{R}\}$. Now observe that for any pair $r, r' \in \mathcal{R}$, by Jensen's inequality,

$$d(f_r, f_{r'}) = \sqrt{\mathbb{E}(f_r(X, Y) - f_{r'}(X, Y))^2}$$
$$\leq \sqrt{\mathbb{E}(\mathbb{I}_{[(Y-Y') \cdot r(X,X')<0]} - \mathbb{I}_{[(Y-Y') \cdot r'(X,X')<0]})^2} .$$

Thus, the L_2 covering numbers of the class $\{f_r : r \in \mathcal{R}\}$ are not more than those of the class of indicator functions $\{\mathbb{I}_{[(y-y') \cdot r(x,x')<0]} : r \in \mathcal{R}\}$. However, since $\mathcal{R}$ has VC dimension V, by Haussler's inequality [12], the covering numbers of this class satisfy $\log N(\epsilon) \leq cV \log(1/\epsilon)$. Then an argument similar to Theorem 2.12 of [5] may be used to complete the proof. ∎

The Bipartite Ranking Problem. Next we derive a simple sufficient condition for achieving fast rates of convergence for the bipartite ranking problem. Recall that here it suffices to consider ranking rules of the form $r(x, x') = 2\mathbb{I}_{[s(x) \geq s(x')]} - 1$ where s is a scoring function. With some abuse of notation we write h_s for h_r.

Noise assumption. There exist constants $c > 0$ and $\alpha \in [0, 1]$ such that for all $x \in \mathcal{X}$,

$$\mathbb{E}_{X'}(|\eta(x) - \eta(X')|^{-\alpha}) \leq c. \qquad (4)$$

Proposition 4. *Under (4), we have, for all* $s \in \mathcal{F}$, $\mathrm{Var}(h_s(X, Y)) \le c\Lambda(s)^\alpha$.

PROOF.

$\mathrm{Var}(h_s(X, Y))$

$\le \mathbb{E}_X \left[\left(\mathbb{E}_{X'} (\mathbb{I}_{[(s(X) - s(X'))(\eta(X) - \eta(X')) < 0]}) \right)^2 \right]$

$\le \mathbb{E}_X \left[\mathbb{E}_{X'} \left(\mathbb{I}_{[(s(X) - s(X'))(\eta(X) - \eta(X')) < 0]} |\eta(X) - \eta(X')|^\alpha \right) \right.$

$\left. \times \left(\mathbb{E}_{X'}(|\eta(X) - \eta(X')|^{-\alpha}) \right) \right]$

(by the Cauchy-Schwarz inequality)

$\le c \left(\mathbb{E}_X \mathbb{E}_{X'} \left(\mathbb{I}_{[(s(X) - s(X'))(\eta(X) - \eta(X')) < 0]} |\eta(X) - \eta(X')| \right) \right)^\alpha$

(by Jensen's inequality and the noise assumption)

$= c\Lambda(s)^\alpha$. ∎

Condition (4) is satisfied under quite general circumstances. If $\alpha = 0$ then clearly the condition poses no restriction, but also no improvement is achieved in the rates of convergence. On the other hand, at the other extreme, when $\alpha = 1$, the condition is quite restrictive as it excludes η to be differentiable, for example, if X has a uniform distribution over $[0, 1]$. However, interestingly, for any $\alpha < 1$, poses quite mild restrictions as it is highlighted in the following example:

Corollary 2. *Consider the bipartite ranking problem and assume that* $\eta(x) = \mathbb{P}\{Y = 1 | X = x\}$ *is such that the random variable* $\eta(X)$ *has an absolutely continuous distribution on* $[0, 1]$ *with a density bounded by* B. *Then for any* $\epsilon > 0$,

$$\mathbb{E}_{X'}(|\eta(x) - \eta(X')|^{-1+\epsilon}) \le \frac{2B}{\epsilon}$$

and therefore, by Theorem 1 and Proposition 4, for every $\delta \in (0, 1)$ *there is a constant* C *such that the excess ranking risk of the empirical minimizer* r_n *satisfies*

$$L(r_n) - L^* \le CB\epsilon^{-1} \left(\frac{V \log(n/\delta)}{n} \right)^{1/(1+\epsilon)}$$

PROOF. The corollary follows simply by checking that (4) is satisfied for any $\alpha = 1 - \epsilon < 1$. The details are omitted. ∎

The condition (4) of the corollary requires that the distribution of $\eta(X)$ is sufficiently spread out, for example it cannot have atoms or infinite peaks in its density. Under such a condition a rate of convergence of the order of $n^{-1+\epsilon}$ is achievable for any $\epsilon > 0$.

Regression Model with Noise. Now we turn to the *general regression model with heteroscedastic errors* in which $Y = m(X) + \sigma(X)\epsilon$ for some (unknown) functions $m : \mathcal{X} \to \mathbb{R}$ and $\sigma : \mathcal{X} \to \mathbb{R}$, where ϵ has a Gaussian density and is independent of X. Set

$$\Delta(X, X') = \frac{m(X) - m(X')}{\sqrt{\sigma^2(X) + \sigma^2(X')}} .$$

We have again $s^* = m$ (or any strictly increasing transformation of it) and the optimal risk is $L^* = \mathbb{E}\Phi\left(-|\Delta(X, X')|\right)$ whose maximal value is attained when the regression function $m(x)$ is constant. Furthermore, we have

$$L(s) - L^* = \mathbb{E}\left(|2\Phi\left(\Delta(X, X')\right) - 1| \cdot \mathbb{I}_{[(m(x) - m(x')) \cdot (s(x) - s(x')) < 0]}\right)$$

where Φ is the distribution function of ϵ.

Noise Assumption. There exist constants $c > 0$ and $\alpha \in [0, 1]$ such that for all $x \in \mathcal{X}$,

$$\mathbb{E}_{X'}(|\Delta(x, X')|^{-\alpha}) \le c. \tag{5}$$

Proposition 5. *Under (5), we have, for all $s \in \mathcal{F}$, $\mathrm{Var}(h_s(X, Y)) \le (2\Phi(c) - 1)\Lambda(s)^{\alpha}$.*

PROOF. By symmetry, $|2\Phi\left(\Delta(X, X')\right) - 1| = 2\Phi\left(|\Delta(X, X')|\right) - 1$. Then, using the concavity of the distribution function Φ on $\mathbb{R}_+$, we have, by Jensen's inequality,

$$\mathbb{E}_{X'}\Phi(|\Delta(x, X')|^{-\alpha}) \le \Phi(\mathbb{E}_{X'}|\Delta(x, X')|^{-\alpha}) \le \Phi(c),$$

where we have used (5) together with the fact that Φ is increasing. Now the result follows following the argument given in the proof of Proposition 4. ∎

The preceding noise condition is fulfilled in many cases, as illustrated by the example below.

Corollary 3. *Suppose that $m(X)$ has a bounded density and the conditional variance $\sigma(x)$ is bounded over $\mathcal{X}$. Then the noise condition 5 is satisfied for any $\alpha < 1$.*

Acknowledgements. We thank Gilles Blanchard for his valuable comments on a previous version of this manuscript, and also Gérard Biau for his careful remarks.

References

1. S. Agarwal, T. Graepel, R. Herbrich, and D. Roth (2004). A large deviation bound for the area under the ROC curve. In Proceedings of the 18th Annual Conference on Neural Information Processing Systems, Vancouver, Canada.
2. S. Agarwal, S. Har-Peled, and D. Roth (2005). A uniform convergence bound for the area under the ROC curve. In Proceedings of the 10th International Workshop on Artificial Intelligence and Statistics, Barbados.

3. M.A. Arcones and E. Giné (1994). U-processes indexed by Vapnik-Chervonenkis classes of functions with applications to asymptotics and bootstrap of U-statistics with estimated parameters. Stochastic Processes and their Applications, **52**, pp. 17-38.

4. P.L. Bartlett, M.I. Jordan, and J.D. McAuliffe (2003). Convexity, classification, and risk bounds. Technical Report 638, Department of Statistics, U.C. Berkeley.

5. P.L. Bartlett and S. Mendelson (2003). Empirical minimization. Technical Report, Department of Statistics, U.C. Berkeley.

6. G. Blanchard, G. Lugosi, and N. Vayatis (2003). On the rate of convergence of regularized boosting classifiers. Journal of Machine Learning Research, 4:861-894.

7. O. Bousquet, S. Boucheron, and G. Lugosi (2004). Theory of classification: a survey of recent advances. ESAIM: Probability and Statistics, to appear.

8. L. Breiman (2004). Population theory for boosting ensembles. Annals of Statistics, **32**, pp. 1–11.

9. V. de la Peña and E. Giné (1999). *Decoupling: from dependence to independence.* Springer.

10. L. Devroye, L. Györfi, and G. Lugosi (1996). *A Probabilistic Theory of Pattern Recognition.* Springer-Verlag, New York.

11. Y. Freund, R. Iyer, R.E. Schapire, and Y. Singer (2003). An Efficient Boosting Algorithm for Combining Preferences. Journal of Machine Learning Research, **4**, pp. 933-969.

12. D. Haussler (1995). Sphere packing numbers for subsets of the boolean n-cube with bounded Vapnik-Chervonenkis dimension. Journal of Combinatorial Theory, Series A, **69**, pp. 217–232.

13. R. Herbrich, T. Graepel, and K. Obermayer (2000). Large margin rank boundaries for ordinal regression. In A. Smola, P.L. Bartlett, B.Schölkopf, and D.Schuurmans (eds.), *Advances in Large Margin Classifiers*, The MIT Press, pp. 115–132.

14. W. Hoeffding (1963). Probability inequalities for sums of bounded random variables. Journal of the American Statistical Association, **58**, pp. 13-30.

15. W. Jiang (2004). Process consistency for Adaboost (with discussion). Annals of Statistics, **32**, pp. 13–29.

16. V. Koltchinskii and D. Panchenko (2002). Empirical margin distribution and bounding the generalization error of combined classifiers. Annals of Statistics, **30**, pp. 1–50.

17. G. Lugosi (2002). Pattern classification and learning theory. In L. Györfi (editor), *Principles of Nonparametric Learning*, Springer, Wien, New York, pp. 1–56.

18. G. Lugosi and N. Vayatis (2004). On the Bayes-risk consistency of boosting methods (with discussion). Annals of Statistics, **32**, pp. 30–55.

19. P. Massart and E. Nédélec (2003). Risk bounds for statistical learning. Preprint, Université Paris XI.

20. C. McDiarmid (1989). On the method of bounded differences. In *Surveys in Combinatorics 1989*, pp. 148-188, Cambridge University Press.

21. R.J. Serfling (1980). Approximation theorems of mathematical statistics. John Wiley & Sons.

22. A. Tsybakov (2004). Optimal aggregation of classifiers in statistical learning. Annals of Statistics, **32**, pp. 135–166.

23. T. Zhang (2004). Statistical behavior and consistency of classification methods based on convex risk minimization (with discussion). Annals of Statistics, **32**, pp. 56–85.

Learnability of Bipartite Ranking Functions

Shivani Agarwal and Dan Roth

Department of Computer Science,
University of Illinois at Urbana-Champaign,
201 N. Goodwin Avenue, Urbana, IL 61801, USA
{sagarwal, danr}@cs.uiuc.edu

Abstract. The problem of ranking, in which the goal is to learn a real-valued ranking function that induces a ranking or ordering over an instance space, has recently gained attention in machine learning. We define a model of learnability for ranking functions in a particular setting of the ranking problem known as the bipartite ranking problem, and derive a number of results in this model. Our first main result provides a sufficient condition for the learnability of a class of ranking functions $\mathcal{F}$: we show that $\mathcal{F}$ is learnable if its bipartite rank-shatter coefficients, which measure the richness of a ranking function class in the same way as do the standard VC-dimension related shatter coefficients (growth function) for classes of classification functions, do not grow too quickly. Our second main result gives a necessary condition for learnability: we define a new combinatorial parameter for a class of ranking functions $\mathcal{F}$ that we term the rank dimension of $\mathcal{F}$, and show that $\mathcal{F}$ is learnable only if its rank dimension is finite. Finally, we investigate questions of the computational complexity of learning ranking functions.

1 Introduction

Two decades ago, Valiant [1] proposed a theory of learnability for binary classification functions defined on Boolean domains. His learning model (known now as the Probably Approximately Correct (PAC) learning model), and several variants and extensions thereof, have since been studied extensively, and have led to a rich set of theoretical results on classes of functions that can and cannot be learned, on algorithms that can be used to solve the learning problem, and on the computational complexity of learning various function classes. In particular, we now have a strong theoretical understanding of the learning problem for both classification (learning of binary-valued functions) and regression (learning of real-valued functions), two of the most well-studied problems in machine learning. Recently, a new learning problem, namely that of *ranking*, has gained attention in the machine learning community [2, 3, 4, 5]. In ranking, one learns a real-valued function that assigns scores to instances, but the scores themselves do not matter; instead, what is important is the relative ranking of instances induced by those scores. This problem is distinct from both classification and regression, and it is natural to ask whether a similar theoretical understanding can be developed for this problem. This paper constitutes a first step in that direction.

P. Auer and R. Meir (Eds.): COLT 2005, LNAI 3559, pp. 16–31, 2005.

1.1   Previous Results

In the binary classification problem, the learner is given a finite sequence of labeled training examples $\underline{z} = ((x_1, y_1), \ldots, (x_m, y_m))$, where the x_i are instances in some instance space X and the y_i are labels in $Y = \{-1, 1\}$, and the goal is to learn a binary-valued function $h : X \rightarrow Y$ that predicts accurately labels of future instances. In the PAC model, a learning algorithm for a class $\mathcal{H}$ of binary classification functions on X is a function $L : \bigcup_{m=1}^{\infty} (X \times Y)^m \rightarrow \mathcal{H}$ with the following property: given any $\epsilon, \delta \in (0, 1)$, there is an integer $m = m(\epsilon, \delta)$ such that for any distribution $\mathcal{D}$ on X and any target function $t \in \mathcal{H}$, given a random training sample $\underline{z} = ((x_1, t(x_1)), \ldots, (x_m, t(x_m)))$ of size m in which the x_i are drawn i.i.d. according to $\mathcal{D}$, with probability at least $1 - \delta$ the classification function $h = L(\underline{z})$ output by L has prediction error $\mathbf{P}_{x \sim \mathcal{D}}\{h(x) \neq t(x)\} < \epsilon$. The smallest such integer $m(\epsilon, \delta)$ is called the sample complexity of L. A class $\mathcal{H}$ is said to be learnable if there is a learning algorithm for $\mathcal{H}$.

In a classic paper, Blumer et al. [6] showed that the PAC learnability of a class of binary classification functions $\mathcal{H}$ is characterized by a single combinatorial parameter of $\mathcal{H}$, namely its Vapnik-Chervonenkis (VC) dimension, in the sense that $\mathcal{H}$ is learnable if and only if its VC dimension is finite. This characterization comprised two distinct results. The first made use of a uniform convergence result based on the work of Vapnik and Chervonenkis [7] to show the existence of a learning algorithm for $\mathcal{H}$ whose sample complexity could be upper bounded via the shatter coefficients (growth function) of $\mathcal{H}$, which in turn could be upper bounded in terms of the VC dimension of $\mathcal{H}$; this established that finiteness of the VC dimension is sufficient for learnability. The second result made use of the probabilistic method to show that the sample complexity of any learning algorithm for $\mathcal{H}$ is lower bounded by a linear function of the VC dimension of $\mathcal{H}$; this established that finiteness of the VC dimension is also necessary for learnability.

The PAC model assumes the existence of an underlying 'target function'; this assumption was removed in a generalization of the PAC model studied in [6, 8, 9], often referred to as the 'agnostic' model. In this general model, examples are generated according to an arbitrary joint distribution $\mathcal{D}$ over $X \times \{-1, 1\}$, and a learning algorithm is required to output with high probability a hypothesis $h \in \mathcal{H}$ with prediction error $\mathbf{P}_{(x,y) \sim \mathcal{D}}\{h(x) \neq y\}$ close to the best possible within the class $\mathcal{H}$. It has been shown that the VC dimension characterizes learnability also in this general model. Questions of the computational complexity of learning have been investigated for a large number of function classes in both models, leading to efficient algorithms in some cases and hardness results in others. For many common function classes, learning in the general model is hard, but polynomial-time algorithms exist for learning in the PAC model.

The regression problem is similar to the classification problem, except that the labels y_i in this case come from $Y = \mathbb{R}$ or $Y = [a, b]$ for some $a, b \in \mathbb{R}$, and the goal is to learn a real-valued function $f : X \rightarrow Y$ that approximates well labels of future instances. An analogous theory of learnability has been developed for this problem, starting with the work of Haussler [8] in which it was shown that finiteness of the pseudo-dimension of a class of (bounded) real-valued functions $\mathcal{F}$ is sufficient for learnability of $\mathcal{F}$ in the general learning model. As in the case of classification, this result made use of a uniform convergence result of [10] to show the existence of a learning algorithm for $\mathcal{F}$ whose sample complexity could be upper bounded via the covering numbers of $\mathcal{F}$, which in turn could be upper bounded in terms of the pseudo-dimension of $\mathcal{F}$. However, a lower bound on the sample complexity remained elusive. Later, Kearns and Schapire [11] introduced a new measure of the richness of a real-valued function class known now as the fat-shattering dimension. It was then shown [11, 12, 13] that the sample complexity of any learning algorithm for a real-valued function class $\mathcal{F}$ is lower bounded by a linear function of the fat-shattering dimension of $\mathcal{F}$, and that the covering numbers of $\mathcal{F}$ can also be upper bounded in terms of this dimension, thus establishing a characterization of learnability for real-valued functions in terms of the fat-shattering dimension. Questions of the computational complexity of learning have also been investigated for classes of real-valued functions, leading again to efficient algorithms in some cases and hardness results in others.

1.2   Our Results

In the bipartite ranking problem [5, 14], described in detail in Section 2, the learner is given a sequence of 'positive' training examples $\underline{x}^+ = (x_1^+, \ldots, x_m^+)$ and a sequence of 'negative' training examples $\underline{x}^- = (x_1^-, \ldots, x_n^-)$, the x_i^+ and x_j^- being instances in some instance space X, and the goal is to learn a real-valued ranking function $f : X \rightarrow \mathbb{R}$ that ranks future positive instances higher than negative ones, *i.e.*, that assigns higher values to positive instances than to negative ones. We define a model of learnability for ranking functions in the setting of the bipartite ranking problem, and derive a number of results in this model. Our first main result provides a sufficient condition for the learnability of a class of ranking functions $\mathcal{F}$: we show that $\mathcal{F}$ is learnable if its bipartite rank-shatter coefficients [14], which measure the richness of a ranking function class in the same way as do the standard VC-dimension related shatter coefficients for classes of classification functions, do not grow too quickly. As in the case of classification and regression, the proof of this result makes use of a uniform convergence result of [14] to show the existence of a learning algorithm for $\mathcal{F}$ whose sample complexity can be upper bounded via the bipartite rank-shatter coefficients of $\mathcal{F}$. Our second main result gives a necessary condition for learnability: we define a new combinatorial parameter for a class of ranking functions $\mathcal{F}$ that we term the rank dimension of $\mathcal{F}$, and show that $\mathcal{F}$ is learnable only if its rank dimension is finite. As in the case of classification, the proof of this result makes use of the probabilistic method to show that the sample complexity of any learning algorithm for $\mathcal{F}$ is lower bounded by a linear function of the rank dimension of $\mathcal{F}$. We use the above two results to give examples of both learnable and non-learnable classes of ranking functions. Finally, we investigate questions of the computational complexity of learning ranking functions. As in classification, we find that for some common ranking function classes, learning in a general 'agnostic' model is hard, but efficient algorithms can be found for learning in a PAC-type model.

1.3   Organization

We describe the bipartite ranking problem in greater detail in Section 2, and formulate our model of learnability for ranking functions in the setting of this problem in

Section 3. A sufficient condition for learnability in this model is derived in Section 4, and a necessary condition in Section 5. We consider the computational complexity of learning ranking functions in Section 6.

2   The Bipartite Ranking Problem

In the bipartite ranking problem [5, 14], the learner is given a training sample $(\underline{x}^+, \underline{x}^-)$ consisting of a sequence of 'positive' training examples $\underline{x}^+ = (x_1^+, \ldots, x_m^+)$ and a sequence of 'negative' training examples $\underline{x}^- = (x_1^-, \ldots, x_n^-)$, the x_i^+ and x_j^- being instances in some instance space X, and the goal is to learn a real-valued ranking function $f : X \rightarrow \mathbb{R}$ that ranks future positive instances higher than negative ones, *i.e.*, that assigns higher values to positive instances than to negative ones. Such problems arise, for example, in information retrieval, where one is interested in retrieving documents from some database that are 'relevant' to a given topic. In this case, the training examples given to the learner consist of documents labeled as relevant (positive) or irrelevant (negative), and the goal is to produce a list of documents that contains relevant documents at the top and irrelevant ones at the bottom; in other words, one wants a ranking of the documents such that relevant documents are ranked higher than irrelevant ones.

We assume that positive instances are drawn randomly and independently according to some (unknown) distribution $\mathcal{D}_+$ on X, and that negative instances are drawn randomly and independently according to some (unknown) distribution $\mathcal{D}_-$ on X. The quality of a ranking function $f : X \rightarrow \mathbb{R}$ is then measured by its *expected ranking error* with respect to $\mathcal{D}_+$ and $\mathcal{D}_-$, denoted by $R_{\mathcal{D}_+, \mathcal{D}_-}(f)$ and defined as follows:

$$R_{\mathcal{D}_+, \mathcal{D}_-}(f) = \mathbf{E}_{x^+ \sim \mathcal{D}_+, x^- \sim \mathcal{D}_-} \left\{ \mathbf{I}_{\{f(x^+) < f(x^-)\}} + \frac{1}{2} \mathbf{I}_{\{f(x^+) = f(x^-)\}} \right\}, \quad (1)$$

where $\mathbf{I}_{\{\cdot\}}$ denotes the indicator variable whose value is one if its argument is true and zero otherwise. The expected ranking error $R_{\mathcal{D}_+, \mathcal{D}_-}(f)$ is the probability that a positive instance drawn randomly according to $\mathcal{D}_+$ is ranked lower by f than a negative instance drawn randomly according to $\mathcal{D}_-$, assuming that ties are broken uniformly at random. A related quantity is the *empirical ranking error* of f with respect to a sample $(\underline{x}^+, \underline{x}^-) \in X^m \times X^n$, denoted by $\hat{R}_{\underline{x}^+, \underline{x}^-}(f)$ and defined as follows:

$$\hat{R}_{\underline{x}^+, \underline{x}^-}(f) = \frac{1}{mn} \sum_{i=1}^{m} \sum_{j=1}^{n} \left\{ \mathbf{I}_{\{f(x_i^+) < f(x_j^-)\}} + \frac{1}{2} \mathbf{I}_{\{f(x_i^+) = f(x_j^-)\}} \right\}. \quad (2)$$

This is simply the fraction of positive-negative pairs in $(\underline{x}^+, \underline{x}^-)$ that are ranked incorrectly by f, assuming again that ties are broken uniformly at random.

Although the bipartite ranking problem shares similarities with the binary classification problem, it should be noted that the two problems are in fact distinct. In particular, it is possible for binary functions obtained by thresholding different real-valued functions to have the same classification errors, while the ranking errors of the real-valued functions differ significantly. For a detailed discussion of this distinction, see [15, 14][1].

---

[1] In [15, 14], the performance of a ranking function is measured in terms of the area under the ROC curve (AUC); this quantity is simply equal to one minus the empirical ranking error.

3   Learnability

Since the goal of learning is to find a ranking function that ranks accurately future instances, we would like a learning algorithm to find a ranking function with minimal expected ranking error. More specifically, if a learning algorithm selects a ranking function from a class of ranking functions $\mathcal{F}$, we would like it to output a ranking function $f \in \mathcal{F}$ with expected error $R_{\mathcal{D}_+,\mathcal{D}_-}(f)$ close to the best possible within the class $\mathcal{F}$, i.e., close to

$$R^*_{\mathcal{D}_+,\mathcal{D}_-}(\mathcal{F}) = \inf_{g \in \mathcal{F}} R_{\mathcal{D}_+,\mathcal{D}_-}(g). \tag{3}$$

We formalize this idea below, following closely the notation and terminology of Anthony and Bartlett [16]. In what follows, $\mathbb{Q}$ denotes the set of rationals and $\mathbb{N}$ the set of positive integers.

Definition 1 (Learnability). *Let $\mathcal{F}$ be a class of real-valued ranking functions on X. A learning algorithm L for $\mathcal{F}$ is a function $L : \left(\bigcup_{m=1}^{\infty} X^m\right) \times \left(\bigcup_{n=1}^{\infty} X^n\right) \to \mathcal{F}$ with the following property: given any $\rho \in (0,1) \cap \mathbb{Q}$ and any $\epsilon, \delta \in (0,1)$, there is an integer $M = M(\epsilon, \delta, \rho)$ such that $m = \rho M \in \mathbb{N}$, $n = (1 - \rho)M \in \mathbb{N}$, and for any distributions $\mathcal{D}_+, \mathcal{D}_-$ on X,*

$$\mathbf{P}_{\underline{x}^+ \sim \mathcal{D}_+^m, \underline{x}^- \sim \mathcal{D}_-^n} \left\{ R_{\mathcal{D}_+,\mathcal{D}_-}(L(\underline{x}^+, \underline{x}^-)) - R^*_{\mathcal{D}_+,\mathcal{D}_-}(\mathcal{F}) \geq \epsilon \right\} \leq \delta.$$

The smallest such integer $M(\epsilon, \delta, \rho)$ is called the sample complexity of L, denoted $M_L(\epsilon, \delta, \rho)$. We say that $\mathcal{F}$ is learnable if there is a learning algorithm for $\mathcal{F}$.

Notice the introduction of the additional parameter ρ in the above definition, which was not required in classification. This parameter represents the 'positive skew', i.e., the proportion of positive examples. Its role will become clear in subsequent sections.

As in [16], our main model above corresponds to a general 'agnostic' model in which no assumption is made on the distributions $\mathcal{D}_+$ and $\mathcal{D}_-$; we refer to this as the *standard* model. We can also define a PAC-type model in which the distributions $\mathcal{D}_+$ and $\mathcal{D}_-$ are restricted to correspond to an underlying target function; following [16], we refer to this as the *restricted* model.

Definition 2 (Learnability in Restricted Model). *Let $\mathcal{F}$ be a class of real-valued ranking functions on X. A learning algorithm L for $\mathcal{F}$ in the restricted model is a function $L : \left(\bigcup_{m=1}^{\infty} X^m\right) \times \left(\bigcup_{n=1}^{\infty} X^n\right) \to \mathcal{F}$ with the following property: given any $\rho \in (0,1) \cap \mathbb{Q}$ and any $\epsilon, \delta \in (0,1)$, there is an integer $M = M(\epsilon, \delta, \rho)$ such that $m = \rho M \in \mathbb{N}$, $n = (1 - \rho)M \in \mathbb{N}$, and for any distributions $\mathcal{D}_+, \mathcal{D}_-$ on X for which there is a target function $t \in \mathcal{F}$ such that $R_{\mathcal{D}_+,\mathcal{D}_-}(t) = 0$,*

$$\mathbf{P}_{\underline{x}^+ \sim \mathcal{D}_+^m, \underline{x}^- \sim \mathcal{D}_-^n} \left\{ R_{\mathcal{D}_+,\mathcal{D}_-}(L(\underline{x}^+, \underline{x}^-)) \geq \epsilon \right\} \leq \delta.$$

The smallest such integer $M(\epsilon, \delta, \rho)$ is called the sample complexity of L, denoted $M_L(\epsilon, \delta, \rho)$. We say that $\mathcal{F}$ is learnable in the restricted model if there is a learning algorithm for $\mathcal{F}$ in this model.

Clearly, if a class of ranking functions $\mathcal{F}$ is learnable, then $\mathcal{F}$ is learnable in the restricted model. Note that learnability of $\mathcal{F}$ in the restricted model is equivalent to learnability of the class of classification functions $\mathcal{H} = \{h : X \to \{-1, 1\} \mid h(x) = \theta(f(x) + \tau)$ for some $f \in \mathcal{F}, \tau \in \mathbb{R}\}$, where $\theta(u) = 1$ for $u > 0$ and $\theta(u) = -1$ for $u \leq 0$, in the restricted (PAC) model for classification. However, this equivalence does *not* hold in the standard (agnostic) model.

4 Upper Bound on Sample Complexity

In this section we show that any algorithm that minimizes the empirical ranking error over a class of ranking functions $\mathcal{F}$ is a learning algorithm for $\mathcal{F}$ if the bipartite rank-shatter coefficients [14] of $\mathcal{F}$ do not grow too quickly, and obtain an upper bound on the sample complexity of such an algorithm.

Definition 3 (Bipartite Rank Matrix [14]). *Let* $f : X \to \mathbb{R}$ *be a ranking function on* X, *let* $m, n \in \mathbb{N}$, *and let* $\underline{x} = (x_1, \ldots, x_m) \in X^m$, $\underline{x}' = (x'_1, \ldots, x'_n) \in X^n$. *The bipartite rank matrix of* f *with respect to* $\underline{x}, \underline{x}'$, *denoted by* $\mathcal{B}_f(\underline{x}, \underline{x}')$, *is defined to be the matrix in* $\{0, 1/2, 1\}^{m \times n}$ *whose* (i, j)-*th element is given by*

$$[\mathcal{B}_f(\underline{x}, \underline{x}')]_{ij} = \mathbf{I}_{\{f(x_i) > f(x'_j)\}} + \frac{1}{2}\mathbf{I}_{\{f(x_i) = f(x'_j)\}}$$

for all $i \in \{1, \ldots, m\}, j \in \{1, \ldots, n\}$.

Definition 4 (Bipartite Rank-Shatter Coefficient [14]). *Let* $\mathcal{F}$ *be a class of real-valued functions on* X, *and let* $m, n \in \mathbb{N}$. *The* (m, n)-*th bipartite rank-shatter coefficient of* $\mathcal{F}$, *denoted by* $r(\mathcal{F}, m, n)$, *is defined as follows:*

$$r(\mathcal{F}, m, n) = \max_{\underline{x} \in X^m, \underline{x}' \in X^n} |\{\mathcal{B}_f(\underline{x}, \underline{x}') \mid f \in \mathcal{F}\}| .$$

Definition 5 (Empirical Error Minimization (EEM) Algorithm). *Let* $\mathcal{F}$ *be a class of ranking functions on* X. *Define an empirical error minimization (EEM) algorithm for* $\mathcal{F}$ *to be any function* $L : \left(\bigcup_{m=1}^{\infty} X^m\right) \times \left(\bigcup_{n=1}^{\infty} X^n\right) \to \mathcal{F}$ *with the property that for any* $m, n \in \mathbb{N}$ *and any* $(\underline{x}^+, \underline{x}^-) \in X^m \times X^n$,

$$\hat{R}_{\underline{x}^+, \underline{x}^-}(L(\underline{x}^+, \underline{x}^-)) = \min_{g \in \mathcal{F}} \hat{R}_{\underline{x}^+, \underline{x}^-}(g) .$$

Theorem 1. *Let* $\mathcal{F}$ *be a class of ranking functions on* X, *and let* L *be any EEM algorithm for* $\mathcal{F}$. *If there exist constants* $c_1 > 0$, $c_2 \geq 0$ *such that* $r(\mathcal{F}, m, n) \leq c_1(mn)^{c_2}$ *for all* $m, n \in \mathbb{N}$, *then* L *is a learning algorithm for* $\mathcal{F}$ *with sample complexity*

$$M_L(\epsilon, \delta, \rho) \leq \left\lceil \frac{64}{\rho(1-\rho)\epsilon^2} \left(4c_2 \ln\left(\frac{16}{\epsilon}\right) + c_2 \ln\left(\frac{c_2^2}{e^2\rho(1-\rho)}\right) + \ln\left(\frac{4c_1}{\delta}\right)\right)\right\rceil_\rho,$$

where $\lceil u \rceil_\rho$ *denotes the smallest integer* M *greater than or equal to* u *for which* $\rho M \in \mathbb{N}$.

The proof of this result makes use of the following uniform convergence result for the ranking error given in [14][2]:

Theorem 2 ([14]). *Let $\mathcal{F}$ be a class of ranking functions on X, and let $m, n \in \mathbb{N}$. Then for any distributions $\mathcal{D}_+, \mathcal{D}_-$ on X and for any $\epsilon > 0$,*

$$\mathbf{P}_{\underline{x}^+ \sim \mathcal{D}_+^m, \underline{x}^- \sim \mathcal{D}_-^n} \left\{ \sup_{f \in \mathcal{F}} \left| \hat{R}_{\underline{x}^+, \underline{x}^-}(f) - R_{\mathcal{D}_+, \mathcal{D}_-}(f) \right| \geq \epsilon \right\}$$
$$\leq 4 \cdot r(\mathcal{F}, 2m, 2n) \cdot e^{-mn\epsilon^2/8(m+n)} .$$

Proof (of Theorem 1). It can be shown using standard techniques [16] that for any $m, n \in \mathbb{N}$, any $(\underline{x}^+, \underline{x}^-) \in X^m \times X^n$ and any distributions $\mathcal{D}_+, \mathcal{D}_-$ on X,

$$R_{\mathcal{D}_+, \mathcal{D}_-}(L(\underline{x}^+, \underline{x}^-)) - R^*_{\mathcal{D}_+, \mathcal{D}_-}(\mathcal{F}) \leq 2 \sup_{f \in \mathcal{F}} \left| \hat{R}_{\underline{x}^+, \underline{x}^-}(f) - R_{\mathcal{D}_+, \mathcal{D}_-}(f) \right| .$$

Now, suppose there exist constants $c_1 > 0, c_2 \geq 0$ such that $r(\mathcal{F}, m, n) \leq c_1(mn)^{c_2}$ for all $m, n \in \mathbb{N}$. Let $\rho \in (0, 1) \cup \mathbb{Q}$ and $\epsilon, \delta \in (0, 1)$, and let $\mathcal{D}_+, \mathcal{D}_-$ be any distributions on X. For any $M \in \mathbb{N}$ for which $m = \rho M \in \mathbb{N}, n = (1 - \rho)M \in \mathbb{N}$, we then have

$$\mathbf{P}_{\underline{x}^+ \sim \mathcal{D}_+^m, \underline{x}^- \sim \mathcal{D}_-^n} \left\{ R_{\mathcal{D}_+, \mathcal{D}_-}(L(\underline{x}^+, \underline{x}^-)) - R^*_{\mathcal{D}_+, \mathcal{D}_-}(\mathcal{F}) \geq \epsilon \right\} \tag{4}$$

$$\leq \mathbf{P}_{\underline{x}^+ \sim \mathcal{D}_+^m, \underline{x}^- \sim \mathcal{D}_-^n} \left\{ \sup_{f \in \mathcal{F}} \left| \hat{R}_{\underline{x}^+, \underline{x}^-}(f) - R_{\mathcal{D}_+, \mathcal{D}_-}(f) \right| \geq \epsilon/2 \right\}$$

$$\leq 4 \cdot r(\mathcal{F}, 2\rho M, 2(1 - \rho)M) \cdot e^{-\rho(1-\rho)M\epsilon^2/32} \quad \text{(by Theorem 2)}$$

$$\leq 4 \cdot c_1(4\rho(1 - \rho)M^2)^{c_2} \cdot e^{-\rho(1-\rho)M\epsilon^2/32} .$$

Therefore, to make the probability in Eq. (4) smaller than δ, it is sufficient if

$$M \geq \frac{32}{\rho(1 - \rho)\epsilon^2} \left(2c_2 \ln M + c_2 \ln(4\rho(1 - \rho)) + \ln\left(\frac{4c_1}{\delta}\right) \right).$$

Since $\ln u \leq au - \ln a - 1$ for all $a, u > 0$, we have

$$\frac{64c_2}{\rho(1 - \rho)\epsilon^2} \ln M \leq \frac{64c_2}{\rho(1 - \rho)\epsilon^2} \left(\frac{\rho(1 - \rho)\epsilon^2}{128c_2} M - \ln\left(\frac{\rho(1 - \rho)\epsilon^2}{128c_2}\right) - 1 \right)$$
$$= \frac{M}{2} + \frac{64c_2}{\rho(1 - \rho)\epsilon^2} \ln\left(\frac{128c_2}{e\rho(1 - \rho)\epsilon^2}\right).$$

Using this and simplifying terms, we get that

$$M \geq \frac{64}{\rho(1 - \rho)\epsilon^2} \left(4c_2 \ln\left(\frac{16}{\epsilon}\right) + c_2 \ln\left(\frac{c_2^2}{e^2\rho(1 - \rho)}\right) + \ln\left(\frac{4c_1}{\delta}\right) \right)$$

suffices to make the probability in Eq. (4) smaller than δ. The result then follows from the definition of sample complexity (Definition 1).   □

---

[2] The uniform convergence result in [14] is given for the area under the ROC curve (AUC); as mentioned previously, this quantity is simply equal to one minus the empirical ranking error.

Notice that the upper bound on the sample complexity in ranking for given (ϵ, δ) grows larger as the positive skew ρ departs from $1/2$, $i.e.$, as the balance between positive and negative examples becomes more uneven. Similar observations regarding the role of the skew ρ in ranking have been made in different contexts in [15, 14]. Theorem 1 can be used to show learnability of any class of ranking functions whose bipartite rank-shatter coefficients can be bounded appropriately; we give some examples below.

Example 1 (Finite function classes). Let $\mathcal{F}$ be a finite class of ranking functions on some instance space X. Then $r(\mathcal{F}, m, n) \leq |\mathcal{F}|$ for all $m, n \in \mathbb{N}$. Thus we have from Theorem 1 that $\mathcal{F}$ is learnable; in particular, taking $c_1 = |\mathcal{F}|$, $c_2 = 0$, we have that any EEM algorithm L for $\mathcal{F}$ is a learning algorithm for $\mathcal{F}$ with sample complexity[3]

$$M_L(\epsilon, \delta, \rho) \leq \left\lceil \frac{64}{\rho(1-\rho)\epsilon^2} \ln\left(\frac{4|\mathcal{F}|}{\delta}\right) \right\rceil_\rho .$$

Example 2 (Linear ranking functions). Let $\mathcal{F}_{\mathrm{lin}(d)}$ be the class of linear ranking functions on $\mathbb{R}^d$. Then it can be shown [14] that $r(\mathcal{F}_{\mathrm{lin}(d)}, m, n) \leq (2emn/d)^d$ for all $m, n \in \mathbb{N}$. Thus we have from Theorem 1 that $\mathcal{F}_{\mathrm{lin}(d)}$ is learnable; in particular, taking $c_1 = (2e/d)^d$, $c_2 = d$, we have that any EEM algorithm L for $\mathcal{F}_{\mathrm{lin}(d)}$ is a learning algorithm for $\mathcal{F}_{\mathrm{lin}(d)}$ with sample complexity

$$M_L(\epsilon, \delta, \rho) \leq \left\lceil \frac{64}{\rho(1-\rho)\epsilon^2} \left(4d \ln\left(\frac{16}{\epsilon}\right) + d \ln\left(\frac{2d}{e\rho(1-\rho)}\right) + \ln\left(\frac{4}{\delta}\right) \right) \right\rceil_\rho .$$

Example 3 (Polynomial ranking functions). Let $q \in \mathbb{N}$, and let $\mathcal{F}_{\mathrm{poly}(d,q)}$ be the class of polynomial ranking functions on R^d with degree less than or equal to q. Then it can be shown [14] that $r(\mathcal{F}_{\mathrm{poly}(d,q)}, m, n) \leq (2emn/C(d,q))^{C(d,q)}$ for all $m, n \in \mathbb{N}$, where

$$C(d, q) = \sum_{i=1}^{q} \left(\binom{d}{i} \sum_{j=1}^{q} \binom{j-1}{i-1} \right) .$$

Thus we have from Theorem 1 that $\mathcal{F}_{\mathrm{poly}(d,q)}$ is learnable; in particular, taking $c_1 = (2e/C(d,q))^{C(d,q)}$, $c_2 = C(d,q)$, we have that any EEM algorithm L for $\mathcal{F}_{\mathrm{poly}(d,q)}$ is a learning algorithm for $\mathcal{F}_{\mathrm{poly}(d,q)}$ with sample complexity

$$M_L(\epsilon, \delta, \rho) \leq \left\lceil \frac{64}{\rho(1-\rho)\epsilon^2} \left(4C(d,q) \ln\left(\frac{16}{\epsilon}\right) + C(d,q) \ln\left(\frac{2C(d,q)}{e\rho(1-\rho)}\right) + \ln\left(\frac{4}{\delta}\right) \right) \right\rceil_\rho .$$

5   Lower Bound on Sample Complexity

In this section we define a new combinatorial parameter for a class of ranking functions $\mathcal{F}$ that we term the rank dimension of $\mathcal{F}$, and show that the sample complexity of any learning algorithm for $\mathcal{F}$ is lower bounded by a linear function of its rank dimension.

---

[3] It is in fact possible to obtain a slightly tighter upper bound in this case using a different uniform convergence result of [14] for finite function classes.

Definition 6 (Rank-Shattering). *Let $\mathcal{F}$ be a class of real-valued functions on X, let $r \in \mathbb{N}$, and let $S = \{(w_1, w_1'), \ldots, (w_r, w_r')\}$ be a set of r pairs of instances in X. For each $i \in \{1, \ldots, r\}$, $b \in \{0,1\}^r$, define*

$$w_i^{b+} = \begin{cases} w_i & \text{if } b_i = 1 \\ w_i' & \text{if } b_i = 0 \end{cases}, \qquad w_i^{b-} = \begin{cases} w_i' & \text{if } b_i = 1 \\ w_i & \text{if } b_i = 0 \end{cases}.$$

We say that $\mathcal{F}$ rank-shatters S if for each $b \in \{0,1\}^r$, there is a ranking function $f_b \in \mathcal{F}$ such that for all $i, j \in \{1, \ldots, r\}$, $f_b(w_i^{b+}) > f_b(w_j^{b-})$.

Definition 7 (Rank Dimension). *Let $\mathcal{F}$ be a class of real-valued functions on X. Define the rank dimension of $\mathcal{F}$, denoted by rank-dim$(\mathcal{F})$, to be the largest positive integer r for which there exists a set of r pairs of instances in X that is rank-shattered by $\mathcal{F}$.*

Theorem 3. *Let $\mathcal{F}$ be a class of ranking functions on X with rank-dim$(\mathcal{F}) = r$. Then for any function $L : \left(\bigcup_{m=1}^{\infty} X^m \right) \times \left(\bigcup_{n=1}^{\infty} X^n \right) \to \mathcal{F}$, any $m, n \in \mathbb{N}$ such that $m + n \geq 2r$, and any $\epsilon > 0$, there exist distributions $\mathcal{D}_+, \mathcal{D}_-$ on X such that*

$$\mathbf{E}_{\underline{x}^+ \sim \mathcal{D}_+^m, \underline{x}^- \sim \mathcal{D}_-^n} \left\{ R_{\mathcal{D}_+, \mathcal{D}_-}(L(\underline{x}^+, \underline{x}^-)) - R_{\mathcal{D}_+, \mathcal{D}_-}^*(\mathcal{F}) \right\}$$

$$\geq \frac{1}{2^{10}} \sqrt{\frac{r}{m+n}} \left(1 - \sqrt{1 - e^{-(2m/(m+n)+1)}} \right)^2 \left(1 - \sqrt{1 - e^{-(2n/(m+n)+1)}} \right)^2.$$

Proof (sketch). The proof makes use of ideas similar to those used to prove lower bounds in the case of classification; specifically, a finite set of distributions is constructed, and it is shown, using the probabilistic method, that for any function L there exist distributions in this set for which the above lower bound holds.

Let $S = \{(w_1, w_1'), \ldots, (w_r, w_r')\}$ be a set of r pairs of instances in X that is rank-shattered by $\mathcal{F}$. We construct a family of 2^r pairs of distributions $\{(\mathcal{D}_{b+}, \mathcal{D}_{b-}) : b \in \{0,1\}^r\}$ on X as follows. For each $b \in \{0,1\}^r$, define

$$\mathcal{D}_{b+}(w_i) = \begin{cases} (1+\alpha)/2r & \text{if } b_i = 1 \\ (1-\alpha)/2r & \text{if } b_i = 0 \end{cases} \qquad \mathcal{D}_{b-}(w_i) = \begin{cases} (1-\alpha)/2r & \text{if } b_i = 1 \\ (1+\alpha)/2r & \text{if } b_i = 0 \end{cases}$$

$$\mathcal{D}_{b+}(w_i') = \begin{cases} (1-\alpha)/2r & \text{if } b_i = 1 \\ (1+\alpha)/2r & \text{if } b_i = 0 \end{cases} \qquad \mathcal{D}_{b-}(w_i') = \begin{cases} (1+\alpha)/2r & \text{if } b_i = 1 \\ (1-\alpha)/2r & \text{if } b_i = 0 \end{cases}$$

$$\mathcal{D}_{b+}(x) = 0 \quad \text{for } x \neq w_i, w_i' \qquad\qquad \mathcal{D}_{b-}(x) = 0 \quad \text{for } x \neq w_i, w_i'$$

Here α is a constant in $(0,1)$ whose value will be determined later. Using the notation of Definition 6, it can be verified that for any $f : X \to \mathbb{R}$,

$$R_{\mathcal{D}_{b+}, \mathcal{D}_{b-}}(f) = \left(\frac{1-\alpha}{2} \right) + \frac{\alpha}{r^2} \sum_{i=1}^{r} \sum_{j=1}^{r} \left\{ \mathbf{I}_{\{f(w_i^{b+}) < f(w_j^{b-})\}} + \frac{1}{2} \mathbf{I}_{\{f(w_i^{b+}) = f(w_j^{b-})\}} \right\}.$$

Since S is rank-shattered by $\mathcal{F}$, for each $b \in \{0,1\}^r$ there is a function $f_b \in \mathcal{F}$ such that for all $i, j \in \{1, \ldots, r\}$, $f_b(w_i^{b+}) > f_b(w_j^{b-})$. From the above equation this gives

$$R_{\mathcal{D}_{b+}, \mathcal{D}_{b-}}^*(\mathcal{F}) = \left(\frac{1-\alpha}{2} \right).$$

Therefore, for any $f \in \mathcal{F}$, we have

$$R_{\mathcal{D}_{b+},\mathcal{D}_{b-}}(f) - R^*_{\mathcal{D}_{b+},\mathcal{D}_{b-}}(\mathcal{F}) = \frac{\alpha}{r^2}\sum_{i=1}^{r}\sum_{j=1}^{r}\left\{\mathbf{I}_{\{f(w_i^{b+})<f(w_j^{b-})\}} + \frac{1}{2}\mathbf{I}_{\{f(w_i^{b+})=f(w_j^{b-})\}}\right\}.$$

Now, let $L : \left(\bigcup_{m=1}^{\infty} X^m\right) \times \left(\bigcup_{n=1}^{\infty} X^n\right) \to \mathcal{F}$ be any function, and for any $\underline{x} = (\underline{x}^+, \underline{x}^-) \in X^m \times X^n$, denote by $f_{\underline{x}}$ the ranking function $L(\underline{x}^+, \underline{x}^-) \in \mathcal{F}$ output by L. Then we have for any $b \in \{0,1\}^r$,

$$\mathbf{E}_{\underline{x}^+\sim\mathcal{D}_{b+}^m,\underline{x}^-\sim\mathcal{D}_{b-}^n}\left\{R_{\mathcal{D}_{b+},\mathcal{D}_{b-}}(f_{\underline{x}}) - R^*_{\mathcal{D}_{b+},\mathcal{D}_{b-}}(\mathcal{F})\right\}$$

$$= \frac{\alpha}{r^2}\sum_{i=1}^{r}\sum_{j=1}^{r}\mathbf{E}_{\underline{x}^+\sim\mathcal{D}_{b+}^m,\underline{x}^-\sim\mathcal{D}_{b-}^n}\left\{\mathbf{I}_{\{f_{\underline{x}}(w_i^{b+})<f_{\underline{x}}(w_j^{b-})\}} + \frac{1}{2}\mathbf{I}_{\{f_{\underline{x}}(w_i^{b+})=f_{\underline{x}}(w_j^{b-})\}}\right\}.$$

We use the probabilistic method to show that the above quantity is greater than the stated lower bound for at least one pair of distributions $\mathcal{D}_{b+}, \mathcal{D}_{b-}$. In particular, we show that if $b \in \{0,1\}^r$ is chosen uniformly at random, then the expected value of the above quantity is greater than the stated lower bound; this implies that there is at least one $b \in \{0,1\}^r$ for which the bound holds. The techniques we use are similar to those used in the case of classification (see, for example, [16–Chapter 5]); the details are considerably more involved and are omitted for lack of space (see [17] for complete details). Denoting the uniform distribution over $\{0,1\}^r$ by $\mathcal{U}$, what we get is that for any $\alpha > 0$,

$$\mathbf{E}_{b\sim\mathcal{U}}\left\{\mathbf{E}_{\underline{x}^+\sim\mathcal{D}_{b+}^m,\underline{x}^-\sim\mathcal{D}_{b-}^n}\left\{R_{\mathcal{D}_{b+},\mathcal{D}_{b-}}(f_{\underline{x}}) - R^*_{\mathcal{D}_{b+},\mathcal{D}_{b-}}(\mathcal{F})\right\}\right\}$$

$$\geq \frac{\alpha}{2^{10}}\left(1 - \sqrt{1 - e^{-(2m/r+1)\alpha^2/(1-\alpha^2)}}\right)^2\left(1 - \sqrt{1 - e^{-(2n/r+1)\alpha^2/(1-\alpha^2)}}\right)^2.$$

Setting $\alpha^2 = r/(m+n)$ and assuming $m+n \geq 2r$ then gives

$$\mathbf{E}_{b\sim\mathcal{U}}\left\{\mathbf{E}_{\underline{x}^+\sim\mathcal{D}_{b+}^m,\underline{x}^-\sim\mathcal{D}_{b-}^n}\left\{R_{\mathcal{D}_{b+},\mathcal{D}_{b-}}(f_{\underline{x}}) - R^*_{\mathcal{D}_{b+},\mathcal{D}_{b-}}(\mathcal{F})\right\}\right\}$$

$$\geq \frac{1}{2^{10}}\sqrt{\frac{r}{m+n}}\left(1 - \sqrt{1 - e^{-(2m/(m+n)+1)}}\right)^2\left(1 - \sqrt{1 - e^{-(2n/(m+n)+1)}}\right)^2. \qquad \square$$

Corollary 1. *Let $\mathcal{F}$ be a class of ranking functions on X with* rank-dim$(\mathcal{F}) = r$, *and let L be any learning algorithm for $\mathcal{F}$. Then L has sample complexity*

$$M_L(\epsilon,\delta,\rho) \geq \frac{r}{2^{20}(\epsilon+\delta)^2}\left(1 - \sqrt{1 - e^{-(2\rho+1)}}\right)^4\left(1 - \sqrt{1 - e^{-(2(1-\rho)+1)}}\right)^4.$$

Proof. Let $\rho \in (0,1) \cup \mathbb{Q}$ and $\epsilon, \delta \in (0,1)$. Let $M = M_L(\epsilon,\delta,\rho)$, and let $m = \rho M$, $n = (1-\rho)M$. Then for all distributions $\mathcal{D}_+, \mathcal{D}_-$ on X,

$$\mathbf{P}_{\underline{x}^+\sim\mathcal{D}_+^m,\underline{x}^-\sim\mathcal{D}_-^n}\left\{R_{\mathcal{D}_+,\mathcal{D}_-}(L(\underline{x}^+,\underline{x}^-)) - R^*_{\mathcal{D}_+,\mathcal{D}_-}(\mathcal{F}) \geq \epsilon\right\} \leq \delta.$$

Using the fact that any $[0, 1]$-valued random variable Z satisfies $\mathbf{E}\{Z\} \leq \mathbf{P}\{Z \geq \epsilon\} + \epsilon$ for all $\epsilon \in (0, 1)$, we thus get that for all distributions $\mathcal{D}_+, \mathcal{D}_-$ on X,

$$\mathbf{E}_{\underline{x}^+ \sim \mathcal{D}_+^m, \underline{x}^- \sim \mathcal{D}_-^n} \left\{ R_{\mathcal{D}_+, \mathcal{D}_-}(L(\underline{x}^+, \underline{x}^-)) - R^*_{\mathcal{D}_+, \mathcal{D}_-}(\mathcal{F}) \right\} \leq \epsilon + \delta.$$

Theorem 3 then implies that

$$\epsilon + \delta \geq \frac{1}{2^{10}} \sqrt{\frac{r}{M}} \left(1 - \sqrt{1 - e^{-(2\rho+1)}}\right)^2 \left(1 - \sqrt{1 - e^{-(2(1-\rho)+1)}}\right)^2.$$

Solving for M gives the desired result. $\square$

As in the case of the upper bound, the lower bound on sample complexity grows larger as the proportion of positive examples ρ departs from $1/2$.

Corollary 2. *Let $\mathcal{F}$ be a class of ranking functions on X. If $\mathcal{F}$ is learnable, then* rank-dim$(\mathcal{F})$ *is finite.*

Proof. This follows directly from Corollary 1. $\square$

Example 4. Let $\mathcal{F}$ be the class of all ranking functions $f : \mathbb{R} \rightarrow \mathbb{R}$ on $\mathbb{R}$. Then clearly, $\mathcal{F}$ rank-shatters arbitrarily large sets of pairs of instances in $\mathbb{R}$. The rank dimension of $\mathcal{F}$ is therefore infinite, and hence by Corollary 2, $\mathcal{F}$ is not learnable.

Remark 1. We note that since the distributions constructed in the proof of Theorem 3 do not correspond to a target function, the lower bound on sample complexity and the necessary condition for learnability derived above do not apply to learning in the restricted model of Definition 2.

6   Computational Complexity

So far, we have viewed a learning algorithm as simply a function that maps training samples to ranking functions, and have focused only on the sample complexity of this function. However, in order to be of practical use, this function must also be *computable*, *i.e.*, the learning algorithm must truly be an *algorithm* that takes as input a training sample and returns as output a ranking function. Moreover, the learning algorithm must be computationally efficient.

In order to study the computational complexity of learning algorithms for ranking, we need to consider learning at a somewhat broader level than we have done above. In particular, a learning algorithm is usually defined for sets of ranking functions over domains of arbitrary dimension (*e.g.*, a learning algorithm for the class of linear ranking functions over $\mathbb{R}^d$ for any d), and it is then of interest to study how the computational complexity of the algorithm grows with the dimension. As in [16, 6], we formalize this by defining learning algorithms for *graded* function classes. For each $d \in \mathbb{N}$, let X_d be a subset of $\mathbb{R}^d$, and let $\mathcal{F}_d$ be a set of ranking functions on X_d. We refer to the union $\mathcal{F} = \bigcup \mathcal{F}_d$ as a *graded* class of ranking functions. A learning algorithm for $\mathcal{F}$ is then a function $L : \bigcup_{d=1}^{\infty} \left(\left(\bigcup_{m=1}^{\infty} X_d^m \right) \times \left(\bigcup_{n=1}^{\infty} X_d^n \right) \right) \to \mathcal{F}$ such that if $(\underline{x}^+, \underline{x}^-) \in X_d^m \times X_d^n$, then $L(\underline{x}^+, \underline{x}^-) \in \mathcal{F}_d$, and for each d, L is a learning algorithm for $\mathcal{F}_d$ (in the sense of Definition 1). Assuming that learning algorithms are computable functions, we can now ask how the computational complexity of a learning algorithm L for a graded class of ranking functions $\mathcal{F} = \bigcup \mathcal{F}_d$ grows with d.

Definition 8 (Efficient Learnability). *Let $\mathcal{F} = \bigcup \mathcal{F}_d$ be a graded class of ranking functions and let L be a learning algorithm for $\mathcal{F}$. We say that L is* efficient *if*

(i) *the worst-case time complexity $T_L(m, n, d)$ of L on samples $(\underline{x}^+, \underline{x}^-) \in X_d^m \times X_d^n$ is polynomial[4] in m, n and d, and*

(ii) *the sample complexity $M_L(\epsilon, \delta, \rho, d)$ of L on $\mathcal{F}_d$ is polynomial in $1/\epsilon$, $1/\delta$, $1/\rho(1 - \rho)$ and d (up to an $\lceil \cdot \rceil_\rho$ operation).*

We say $\mathcal{F}$ is efficiently learnable *if there is an efficient learning algorithm for $\mathcal{F}$.*

Efficient learnability in the restricted model can be defined in a similar manner. The sufficient and necessary conditions for learnability established in Sections 4 and 5 can be extended to efficient learnability as follows.

Definition 9 (Efficient EEM Algorithm). *Let $\mathcal{F} = \bigcup \mathcal{F}_d$ be a graded class of ranking functions. An* efficient EEM algorithm *for $\mathcal{F}$ is an algorithm that takes as input a sample $(\underline{x}^+, \underline{x}^-) \in X_d^m \times X_d^n$, and in time polynomial in m, n and d, returns a ranking function $f \in \mathcal{F}_d$ such that $\hat{R}_{\underline{x}^+, \underline{x}^-}(f) = \min_{g \in \mathcal{F}_d} \hat{R}_{\underline{x}^+, \underline{x}^-}(g)$.*

Theorem 4. *Let $\mathcal{F} = \bigcup \mathcal{F}_d$ be a graded class of ranking functions, and suppose that there exist functions $c_1 : \mathbb{N} \to \mathbb{R}^+$, $c_2 : \mathbb{N} \to \mathbb{R}^+ \cup \{0\}$ such that $r(\mathcal{F}_d, m, n) \le c_1(d)(mn)^{c_2(d)}$ for all $d, m, n \in \mathbb{N}$, and such that $c_2(d)$ is polynomial in d. Then any efficient EEM algorithm for $\mathcal{F}$ is an efficient learning algorithm for $\mathcal{F}$.*

Proof. Suppose that L is an efficient EEM algorithm for $\mathcal{F}$. Then

(i) by Theorem 1, L is a learning algorithm for $\mathcal{F}_d$ for each d and therefore a learning algorithm for $\mathcal{F}$,

(ii) by Definition 9, the time complexity $T_L(m, n, d)$ of L on $\mathcal{F}_d$ is polynomial in m, n and d, and

(iii) by Theorem 1, the sample complexity $M_L(\epsilon, \delta, \rho, d)$ of L on $\mathcal{F}_d$ is polynomial in $1/\epsilon$, $1/\delta$, $1/\rho(1 - \rho)$ and d (up to an $\lceil \cdot \rceil_\rho$ operation).

Thus, L is an efficient learning algorithm for $\mathcal{F}$. □

Theorem 5. *Let $\mathcal{F} = \bigcup \mathcal{F}_d$ be a graded class of ranking functions. If there is an efficient learning algorithm for $\mathcal{F}$, then $\mathrm{rank\text{-}dim}(\mathcal{F}_d)$ is polynomial in d.*

---

[4] In the logarithmic cost model of computation [18], the time complexity is also allowed to depend polynomially on the number of bits required to represent the input.

Proof. This follows directly from Definition 8 and Corollary 1. □

Next we define the following decision problem associated with a graded ranking function class $\mathcal{F} = \bigcup \mathcal{F}_d$. As in the case of classification [16], it can be shown that if this problem is NP-hard, then, assuming RP $\neq$ NP, $\mathcal{F}$ is not efficiently learnable. The proof is similar to that for classification; we omit the details.

$\mathcal{F}$-FIT

Instance: $(\underline{x}^+, \underline{x}^-) \in X_d^m \times X_d^n$ and an integer $k \in \{1, \ldots, mn\}$.
Question: Is there $f \in \mathcal{F}_d$ such that $\hat{R}_{\underline{x}^+, \underline{x}^-}(f) \leq k/mn$?

Theorem 6. *Let $\mathcal{F}$ be a graded class of ranking functions. If there is an efficient learning algorithm for $\mathcal{F}$, then there is a polynomial-time randomized algorithm for $\mathcal{F}$-FIT, i.e., $\mathcal{F}$-FIT is in* RP.

We now have the formal tools necessary to study the computational complexity of learning ranking functions. Below we use these tools to investigate the computational complexity of learning for the commonly used classes of linear and polynomial ranking functions. Our first result is a hardness result for linear ranking functions.

Theorem 7. *Let $\mathcal{F}_{\mathrm{lin}} = \bigcup \mathcal{F}_{\mathrm{lin}(d)}$, where $\mathcal{F}_{\mathrm{lin}(d)}$ is the class of linear ranking functions on $\mathbb{R}^d$. If* RP $\neq$ NP, *then $\mathcal{F}_{\mathrm{lin}}$ is not efficiently learnable.*

Proof. We show that $\mathcal{F}_{\mathrm{lin}}$-FIT is NP-hard; the result then follows by Theorem 6. To show that $\mathcal{F}_{\mathrm{lin}}$-FIT is NP-hard, we give a reduction from an NP-hard classification problem to $\mathcal{F}_{\mathrm{lin}}$-FIT. For each $d \in \mathbb{N}$, let $\mathcal{H}_{\mathrm{lin}(d)} = \{h : \mathbb{R}^d \to \{-1, 0, 1\} \mid h(\mathbf{x}) = \mathrm{sign}(\sum_{l=1}^d w_l x_l + \theta) \text{ for some } \mathbf{w} \in \mathbb{R}^d, \theta \in \mathbb{R}\}$. Given a function $h \in \mathcal{H}_{\mathrm{lin}(d)}$ and a sample $\underline{z} = ((\mathbf{x}_1, y_1), \ldots, (\mathbf{x}_m, y_m)) \in (\mathbb{R}^d \times \{-1, 1\})^m$, define the *empirical error* of h with respect to $\underline{z}$, denoted by $\hat{\mathrm{er}}_{\underline{z}}(h)$, as follows:

$$\hat{\mathrm{er}}_{\underline{z}}(h) = \frac{1}{m} \sum_{i=1}^m \left\{ \mathbf{I}_{\{h(\mathbf{x}_i) \neq 0\}} \mathbf{I}_{\{h(\mathbf{x}_i) \neq y_i\}} + \frac{1}{2} \mathbf{I}_{\{h(\mathbf{x}_i) = 0\}} \right\}.$$

Let $\mathcal{H}_{\mathrm{lin}} = \bigcup \mathcal{H}_{\mathrm{lin}(d)}$, and define the following decision problem associated with $\mathcal{H}_{\mathrm{lin}}$:

$\mathcal{H}_{\mathrm{lin}}$-FIT

Instance: $\underline{z} = ((\mathbf{x}_1, y_1), \ldots, (\mathbf{x}_m, y_m)) \in (\mathbb{R}^d \times \{-1, 1\})^m$ and an integer $k' \in \{1, \ldots, m\}$.
Question: Is there $h \in \mathcal{H}_{\mathrm{lin}(d)}$ such that $\hat{\mathrm{er}}_{\underline{z}}(h) \leq k'/m$?

Using exactly the same construction as that used to show the NP-hardness of a similar decision problem relating to linear threshold functions for binary classification [16], it can be shown that the problem $\mathcal{H}_{\mathrm{lin}}$-FIT defined above is NP-hard. We give now a reduction from $\mathcal{H}_{\mathrm{lin}}$-FIT to $\mathcal{F}_{\mathrm{lin}}$-FIT.

Let $\underline{z} = ((\mathbf{x}_1, y_1), \ldots, (\mathbf{x}_m, y_m))$, $k' \in \{1, \ldots, m\}$ be an instance of $\mathcal{H}_{\mathrm{lin}}$-FIT. We construct from $\underline{z}, k'$ an instance $(\underline{x}^+, \underline{x}^-) \in (\mathbb{R}^{d+1})^m \times (\mathbb{R}^{d+1})$, $k \in \{1, \ldots, m\}$ of $\mathcal{F}_{\mathrm{lin}}$-FIT as follows. For each $i \in \{1, \ldots, m\}$, define $x_i^+ = (\mathbf{x}_i, 1) \in \mathbb{R}^{d+1}$ if $y_i = 1$, and $x_i^+ = (-\mathbf{x}_i, -1) \in \mathbb{R}^{d+1}$ if $y_i = -1$. Define $x_1^- = \mathbf{0} \in \mathbb{R}^{d+1}$. Let $\underline{x}^+ = (x_1^+, \ldots, x_m^+)$, $\underline{x}^- = (x_1^-)$, and $k = k'$. We claim that there exists $h \in \mathcal{H}_{\text{lin}(d)}$ with $\hat{\text{er}}_{\underline{z}}(h) \leq k'/m$ if and only if there exists $f \in \mathcal{F}_{\text{lin}(d+1)}$ with $\hat{R}_{\underline{x}^+,\underline{x}^-}(f) \leq k/m$.

First, suppose there exists $h \in \mathcal{H}_{\text{lin}(d)}$ with $\hat{\text{er}}_{\underline{z}}(h) \leq k'/m$, given by $h(\mathbf{x}) = \text{sign}(\sum_{l=1}^{d} w_l x_l + \theta)$ for some $\mathbf{w} \in \mathbb{R}^d, \theta \in \mathbb{R}$. Define $f : \mathbb{R}^{d+1} \rightarrow \mathbb{R}$ as $f(\mathbf{x}) = \sum_{l=1}^{d} w_l x_l + \theta x_{d+1}$ for all $\mathbf{x} \in \mathbb{R}^{d+1}$. Then clearly, $f \in \mathcal{F}_{\text{lin}(d+1)}$, and it can be verified that $\hat{R}_{\underline{x}^+,\underline{x}^-}(f) = \hat{\text{er}}_{\underline{z}}(h) \leq k'/m = k/m$. Conversely, suppose there exists $f \in \mathcal{F}_{\text{lin}(d+1)}$ with $\hat{R}_{\underline{x}^+,\underline{x}^-}(f) \leq k/m$, given by $f(\mathbf{x}) = \sum_{l=1}^{d+1} w_l x_l + \theta$ for some $\mathbf{w} \in \mathbb{R}^{d+1}, \theta \in \mathbb{R}$. Define $h : \mathbb{R}^d \rightarrow \{-1,0,1\}$ as $h(\mathbf{x}) = \text{sign}(\sum_{l=1}^{d} w_l x_l + w_{d+1})$ for all $\mathbf{x} \in \mathbb{R}^d$. Then clearly, $h \in \mathcal{H}_{\text{lin}(d)}$, and it can be verified that $\hat{\text{er}}_{\underline{z}}(h) = \hat{R}_{\underline{x}^+,\underline{x}^-}(f) \leq k/m = k'/m$.

Since the time required to construct the instance $(\underline{x}^+, \underline{x}^-), k$ from $\underline{z}, k'$ is polynomial in the size of $\underline{z}, k'$, we conclude that $\mathcal{F}_{\text{lin}}$-FIT is NP-hard. □

Our next result shows that $\mathcal{F}_{\text{lin}}$ is efficiently learnable in the restricted learning model. We first specialize Definition 9 and Theorem 4 to the restricted model case.

Definition 10 (Efficient Consistent-Hypothesis-Finder). *Let* $\mathcal{F} = \bigcup \mathcal{F}_d$ *be a graded class of ranking functions. An efficient consistent-hypothesis-finder for* $\mathcal{F}$ *is an algorithm* L *such that, given any sample* $(\underline{x}^+, \underline{x}^-) \in X_d^m \times X_d^n$ *for which there exists a target function* $t \in \mathcal{F}_d$ *satisfying* $\hat{R}_{\underline{x}^+,\underline{x}^-}(t) = 0$, L *halts in time polynomial in* m, n *and* d *and returns a ranking function* $f \in \mathcal{F}_d$ *such that* $\hat{R}_{\underline{x}^+,\underline{x}^-}(f) = 0$.

Theorem 8. *Let* $\mathcal{F} = \bigcup \mathcal{F}_d$ *be a graded class of ranking functions, and suppose that there exist functions* $c_1 : \mathbb{N} \rightarrow \mathbb{R}^+$, $c_2 : \mathbb{N} \rightarrow \mathbb{R}^+ \cup \{0\}$ *such that* $r(\mathcal{F}_d, m, n) \leq c_1(d)(mn)^{c_2(d)}$ *for all* $d, m, n \in \mathbb{N}$, *and such that* $c_2(d)$ *is polynomial in* d. *Then any efficient consistent-hypothesis-finder for* $\mathcal{F}$ *is an efficient learning algorithm for* $\mathcal{F}$ *in the restricted model.*

Theorem 9. *The class of linear ranking functions* $\mathcal{F}_{\text{lin}} = \bigcup \mathcal{F}_{\text{lin}(d)}$ *is efficiently learnable in the restricted model.*

Proof (sketch). As discussed in Example 2 (Section 4), $r(\mathcal{F}_{\text{lin}(d)}, m, n) \leq (2emn/d)^d$ for all $d, m, n \in \mathbb{N}$. Therefore, by Theorem 8, it suffices to show the existence of an efficient consistent-hypothesis-finder for $\mathcal{F}_{\text{lin}}$. This can be done by formulating a linear program such that, given a training sample $(\underline{x}^+, \underline{x}^-) \in (\mathbb{R}^d)^m \times (\mathbb{R}^d)^n$ for which there exists a target function $t \in \mathcal{F}_{\text{lin}(d)}$ satisfying $\hat{R}_{\underline{x}^+,\underline{x}^-}(t) = 0$, the solution of the linear program gives a ranking function $f \in \mathcal{F}_{\text{lin}(d)}$ such that $\hat{R}_{\underline{x}^+,\underline{x}^-}(f) = 0$ (see [17] for details). Solving the linear program using a polynomial-time linear programming algorithm such as Karmarkar's [19] then constitutes an efficient consistent-hypothesis-finder for $\mathcal{F}_{\text{lin}}$. □

Remark 2. We note that since the polynomial time bound for linear programming algorithms such as Karmarkar's holds only in the logarithmic cost model of computation, the above proof establishes efficient learnability of $\mathcal{F}_{\text{lin}}$ in the restricted learning model only under this model of computation.

Remark 3. In the above proof, we could also have used a linear program that finds a classification function $h \in \mathcal{H}_{\text{lin}(d)}$ of the form $h(\mathbf{x}) = \text{sign}(\sum_{l=1}^{d} w_l x_l + \theta)$ such that $\hat{L}_S(h) = 0$, where $S = ((x_1^+, 1), \ldots, (x_m^+, 1), (x_1^-, -1), \ldots, (x_n^-, -1))$, and then taken f to be the linear function $f(\mathbf{x}) = \sum_{l=1}^{d} w_l x_l$.

Finally, we show that learning linear ranking functions over Boolean domains is hard even in the restricted model.

Theorem 10. *Let $\mathcal{F}_{\text{lin}}^b = \bigcup \mathcal{F}_{\text{lin}(d)}^b$, where $\mathcal{F}_{\text{lin}(d)}^b$ is the class of linear ranking functions on $\{0, 1\}^d$. If $\text{RP} \neq \text{NP}$, then $\mathcal{F}_{\text{lin}}^b$ is not efficiently learnable in the restricted model.*

Proof (sketch). Let, if possible, $\mathcal{F}_{\text{lin}}^b$ be efficiently learnable in the restricted model. Then there is an efficient randomized consistent-hypothesis-finder $\mathcal{A}$ for $\mathcal{F}_{\text{lin}}^b$ (see [16, 17]). Clearly, $\mathcal{A}$ can be used to construct an efficient randomized consistent-hypothesis-finder for $\mathcal{H}_{\text{lin}}^b = \bigcup \mathcal{H}_{\text{lin}(d)}^b$, where $\mathcal{H}_{\text{lin}(d)}^b$ is the class of Boolean threshold functions on $\{0, 1\}^d$. This, in turn, implies the existence of an efficient learning algorithm for $\mathcal{H}_{\text{lin}}^b$ in the restricted (PAC) model (see [16]). Since the problem of learning Boolean threshold functions in the PAC model is known to be NP-hard [20], this implies $\text{RP} = \text{NP}$. Thus, if $\text{RP} \neq \text{NP}$, then $\mathcal{F}_{\text{lin}}^b$ is not efficiently learnable in the restricted model. □

The techniques used above can be used also to establish that for any $q \in \mathbb{N}$, the class $\mathcal{F}_{\text{poly}(q)} = \bigcup \mathcal{F}_{\text{poly}(d,q)}$, where $\mathcal{F}_{\text{poly}(d,q)}$ is the class of polynomial ranking functions on $\mathbb{R}^d$ with degree at most q, is not efficiently learnable in the standard model, but is efficiently learnable in the restricted model, and that the class $\mathcal{F}_{\text{poly}(q)}^b = \bigcup \mathcal{F}_{\text{poly}(d,q)}^b$, where $\mathcal{F}_{\text{poly}(d,q)}^b$ is the class of polynomial ranking functions on $\{0, 1\}^d$ with degree at most q, is not efficiently learnable even in the restricted model.

7   Conclusion and Open Questions

Our goal in this paper has been to initiate a formal study of learnability for ranking functions. There are several questions to be answered. First, is there a single quantity that characterizes learnability of a class of ranking functions, analogous to the VC dimension for classification and the fat-shattering dimension for regression? For example, based on our results, an upper bound of the form $r(\mathcal{F}, m, n) = O((mn)^{\text{rank-dim}(\mathcal{F})})$ on the bipartite rank-shatter coefficients would establish the rank dimension as such a quantity. Second, can the rank dimension be related to previous quantities (such as the VC-dimension or pseudo-dimension), or is it a fundamentally new quantity? So far, we have not been able to find a relation to earlier dimensions. Third, for what other classes of ranking functions can efficient learning algorithms or hardness results be shown? Finally, for what other settings of the ranking problem can learnability be studied?

Acknowledgments

We would like to express warm thanks to Sariel Har-Peled for many valuable discussions. The exposition in this paper is influenced in large parts by the excellent text of Anthony and Bartlett [16]. This research was supported in part by NSF ITR grants IIS 00-85980 and IIS 00-85836 and a grant from the ONR-TRECC program.

References

1. Valiant, L.G.: A theory of the learnable. Communications of the ACM (1984) 1134–1142
2. Cohen, W.W., Schapire, R.E., Singer, Y.: Learning to order things. Journal of Artificial Intelligence Research **10** (1999) 243–270
3. Herbrich, R., Graepel, T., Obermayer, K.: Large margin rank boundaries for ordinal regression. Advances in Large Margin Classifiers (2000) 115–132
4. Crammer, K., Singer, Y.: Pranking with ranking. In Dietterich, T.G., Becker, S., Ghahramani, Z., eds.: Advances in Neural Information Processing Systems 14, MIT Press (2002) 641–647
5. Freund, Y., Iyer, R., Schapire, R.E., Singer, Y.: An efficient boosting algorithm for combining preferences. Journal of Machine Learning Research **4** (2003) 933–969
6. Blumer, A., Ehrenfeucht, A., Haussler, D., Warmuth, M.K.: Learnability and the Vapnik-Chervonenkis dimension. Journal of the ACM **36** (1989) 929–965
7. Vapnik, V.N., Chervonenkis, A.: On the uniform convergence of relative frequencies of events to their probabilities. Theory of Probability and its Applications **16** (1971) 264–280
8. Haussler, D.: Decision theoretic generalizations of the PAC model for neural net and other learning applications. Information and Computation **100** (1992) 78–150
9. Kearns, M.J., Schapire, R.E., Sellie, L.M.: Toward efficient agnostic learning. Machine Learning **17** (1994) 115–141
10. Pollard, D.: Convergence of Stochastic Processes. Springer-Verlag (1984)
11. Kearns, M.J., Schapire, R.E.: Efficient distribution-free learning of probabilistic concepts. Journal of Computer and System Sciences **48** (1994) 464–497
12. Alon, N., Ben-David, S., Cesa-Bianchi, N., , Haussler, D.: Scale-sensitive dimensions, uniform convergence, and learnability. Journal of the ACM **44** (1997) 615–631
13. Bartlett, P.L., Long, P.M., Williamson, R.C.: Fat-shattering and the learnability of real-valued functions. Journal of Computer and System Sciences **52** (1996) 434–452
14. Agarwal, S., Graepel, T., Herbrich, R., Har-Peled, S., Roth, D.: Generalization bounds for the area under the ROC curve. Journal of Machine Learning Research (2005) 393–425
15. Cortes, C., Mohri, M.: AUC optimization vs. error rate minimization. In: Advances in Neural Information Processing Systems 16, MIT Press (2004)
16. Anthony, M., Bartlett, P.L.: Learning in Neural Networks: Theoretical Foundations. Cambridge University Press (1999)
17. Agarwal, S.: A Study of the Bipartite Ranking Problem in Machine Learning. PhD thesis, University of Illinois at Urbana-Champaign (2005)
18. Aho, A.V., Hopcroft, J.E., Ullman, J.D.: The Design and Analysis of Computer Algorithms. Addison-Wesley (1974)
19. Karmarkar, N.: A new polynomial-time algorithm for linear programming. Combinatorica **4** (1984) 373–395
20. Pitt, L., Valiant, L.G.: Computational limitations on learning from examples. Journal of the ACM **35** (1988) 965–984

Stability and Generalization of Bipartite Ranking Algorithms

Shivani Agarwal[1] and Partha Niyogi[2]

[1] Department of Computer Science, University of Illinois at Urbana-Champaign,
201 N. Goodwin Avenue, Urbana, IL 61801, USA
sagarwal@cs.uiuc.edu
[2] Departments of Computer Science and Statistics, University of Chicago,
1100 E. 58th Street, Chicago, IL 60637, USA
niyogi@cs.uchicago.edu

Abstract. The problem of ranking, in which the goal is to learn a real-valued ranking function that induces a ranking or ordering over an instance space, has recently gained attention in machine learning. We study generalization properties of ranking algorithms, in a particular setting of the ranking problem known as the bipartite ranking problem, using the notion of algorithmic stability. In particular, we derive generalization bounds for bipartite ranking algorithms that have good stability properties. We show that kernel-based ranking algorithms that perform regularization in a reproducing kernel Hilbert space have such stability properties, and therefore our bounds can be applied to these algorithms; this is in contrast with previous generalization bounds for ranking, which are based on uniform convergence and in many cases cannot be applied to these algorithms. A comparison of the bounds we obtain with corresponding bounds for classification algorithms yields some interesting insights into the difference in generalization behaviour between ranking and classification.

1 Introduction

A central focus in learning theory research has been the study of generalization properties of learning algorithms. Perhaps the first work in this direction was that of Vapnik and Chervonenkis [1], who derived generalization bounds for classification algorithms based on uniform convergence. Since then, a large number of different tools have been developed for studying generalization, and have been applied successfully to analyze algorithms for both classification (learning of binary-valued functions) and regression (learning of real-valued functions), two of the most well-studied problems in machine learning. Recently, a new learning problem, namely that of *ranking*, has gained attention in the machine learning community [2, 3, 4, 5]. In ranking, one learns a real-valued function that assigns scores to instances, but the scores themselves do not matter; instead, what is important is the relative ranking of instances induced by those scores. This problem is distinct from both classification and regression, and it is natural to ask what kinds of generalization properties hold for algorithms for this problem, and in particular, whether tools that have been applied to study generalization properties of

P. Auer and R. Meir (Eds.): COLT 2005, LNAI 3559, pp. 32–47, 2005.

classification and regression algorithms can be adapted to study generalization properties of ranking algorithms. It has been shown recently that generalization bounds based on uniform convergence can be obtained for ranking algorithms in a particular setting of the ranking problem known as the *bipartite* ranking problem [5, 6]. In this paper, we ask whether such a result can be obtained using the notion of algorithmic stability, which has recently been used to derive generalization bounds for classification and regression algorithms, and which offers a different viewpoint than uniform convergence [7, 8].

1.1 Previous Results

The question of the generalization behaviour of ranking algorithms has only recently begun to be addressed. Generalization properties of algorithms for a distinct but closely related problem, namely that of ordinal regression, were considered in [3]. The first study of generalization in ranking was that of Freund et al. [5], in which generalization bounds for the bipartite RankBoost algorithm were derived. These bounds were derived from uniform convergence results for the classification error rate, and were expressed in terms of the VC-dimension of a class of binary classification functions derived from the class of ranking functions searched by RankBoost. More recently, Agarwal et al. [6] have derived a uniform convergence bound for the bipartite ranking error (see Section 2) which is expressed in terms of a new set of combinatorial parameters that measure directly the complexity of the class of ranking functions searched by an algorithm.

Uniform convergence requires the empirical errors of all functions in the searched class to converge to their expected errors. Generalization bounds based on uniform convergence are therefore necessarily loose, as they depend only on properties of the function class being searched, and do not take into account the manner in which the function class is actually searched by the algorithm. In addition, these bounds can be applied only to algorithms that search function classes of bounded complexity.

The notion of algorithmic stability, first studied for learning algorithms by Devroye and Wagner [9], has been used recently to directly obtain generalization bounds, without needing to show uniform convergence, for classification and regression algorithms that satisfy certain stability conditions [7, 8]. In particular, a stable learning algorithm is one whose output does not change much with small changes in the training sample; the above works have shown that classification and regression algorithms that satisfy this condition have good generalization properties. The stability-based bounds depend on properties of the algorithm rather than the function class that is searched, and can be applied also to algorithms that search function classes of unbounded complexity. Algorithms that have been shown to be stable include, for example, kernel-based classification and regression algorithms such as support vector machines (SVMs), which often cannot be analyzed using uniform convergence tools. In this paper, we show that the notion of algorithmic stability can be used also to analyze the generalization behaviour of (bipartite) ranking algorithms.

1.2 Our Results

We define notions of stability for bipartite ranking algorithms, and use these notions to analyze the generalization behaviour of such algorithms. In particular, we derive generalization bounds for bipartite ranking algorithms that exhibit good stability properties.

We show that kernel-based ranking algorithms that perform regularization in a reproducing kernel Hilbert space (RKHS) have such stability properties, and therefore our bounds can be applied to these algorithms; this is in contrast with previous generalization bounds for ranking, which are based on uniform convergence and in many cases cannot be applied to these algorithms. A comparison of the bounds we obtain with corresponding bounds for classification algorithms yields some interesting insights into the difference in generalization behaviour between ranking and classification. In particular, we find that for a training sample of M elements containing m positive and $n = M - m$ negative instances, the sample size M in the classification bounds is replaced with the quantity $mn/(m + n)$ in the ranking bounds. If we define the 'positive skew' of the sample as the proportion of positive examples $\rho = m/(m + n)$, then this means that the 'effective' sample size in ranking is reduced from M to $\rho(1 - \rho)M$, with the reduction being more drastic as ρ departs from $1/2$, i.e., as the balance between positive and negative examples becomes more uneven. This further corroborates previous observations about the importance of the skew ρ in ranking [10, 6, 11].

1.3   Organization

We describe the bipartite ranking problem in detail in Section 2, and define notions of stability for (bipartite) ranking algorithms in Section 3. Using these notions, we derive generalization bounds for stable ranking algorithms in Section 4. In Section 5 we show stability of kernel-based ranking algorithms that perform regularization in an RKHS, and apply the results of Section 4 to obtain generalization bounds for these algorithms. We conclude with a discussion in Section 6.

2   The Bipartite Ranking Problem

In the bipartite ranking problem [5, 6], instances come from two categories, positive and negative; the learner is given examples of instances labeled as positive or negative, and the goal is to learn a ranking in which positive instances are ranked higher than negative ones. Such problems arise, for example, in information retrieval, where one is interested in retrieving documents from some database that are 'relevant' to a given topic; in this case, the training examples given to the learner consist of documents labeled as relevant (positive) or irrelevant (negative), and the goal is to produce a list of documents that contains relevant documents at the top and irrelevant documents at the bottom – in other words, one wants a ranking of the documents such that relevant documents are ranked higher than irrelevant documents.

Formally, the setting of the bipartite ranking problem can be described as follows. There is an instance space $\mathcal{X}$ from which instances are drawn, and the learner is given a training sample $(S_+, S_-) \in \mathcal{X}^m \times \mathcal{X}^n$ consisting of a sequence of positive training examples $S_+ = (x_1^+, \ldots, x_m^+)$ and a sequence of negative training examples $S_- = (x_1^-, \ldots, x_n^-)$. The goal is to learn from these examples a real-valued ranking function $f : \mathcal{X} \to \mathbb{R}$ that ranks future positive instances higher than negative ones, where f is considered to rank an instance x higher than an instance x' if $f(x) > f(x')$ and is considered to rank x lower than x' if $f(x) < f(x')$. We assume that positive instances are drawn randomly and independently according to some (unknown) distribution

$\mathcal{D}_+$ on the instance space $\mathcal{X}$, and that negative instances are drawn randomly and independently according to some (unknown) distribution $\mathcal{D}_-$ on $\mathcal{X}$. The quality of a ranking function $f : \mathcal{X} \to \mathbb{R}$ is then measured by its *expected ranking error*, denoted by $R(f)$ and defined as follows:

$$R(f) = \mathbf{E}_{x^+ \sim \mathcal{D}_+, x^- \sim \mathcal{D}_-} \left\{ \mathbf{I}_{\{f(x^+) < f(x^-)\}} + \frac{1}{2} \mathbf{I}_{\{f(x^+) = f(x^-)\}} \right\}, \qquad (1)$$

where $\mathbf{I}_{\{.\}}$ denotes the indicator variable whose value is one if its argument is true and zero otherwise. The expected error $R(f)$ is the probability that a positive instance drawn randomly according to $\mathcal{D}_+$ is ranked lower by f than a negative instance drawn randomly according to $\mathcal{D}_-$, assuming that ties are broken uniformly at random. In practice, since the distributions $\mathcal{D}_+$ and $\mathcal{D}_-$ are unknown, the expected error of a ranking function f must be estimated from an empirically observable quantity such as its *empirical ranking error* with respect to a sample $(S_+, S_-) \in \mathcal{X}^m \times \mathcal{X}^n$, denoted by $\hat{R}(f; S_+, S_-)$ and defined as follows:

$$\hat{R}(f; S_+, S_-) = \frac{1}{mn} \sum_{i=1}^{m} \sum_{j=1}^{n} \left\{ \mathbf{I}_{\{f(x_i^+) < f(x_j^-)\}} + \frac{1}{2} \mathbf{I}_{\{f(x_i^+) = f(x_j^-)\}} \right\}. \qquad (2)$$

This is simply the fraction of positive-negative pairs in (S_+, S_-) that are ranked incorrectly by f, assuming that ties are broken uniformly at random.

Although the bipartite ranking problem shares similarities with the binary classification problem, it should be noted that the two problems are in fact distinct. In particular, it is possible for binary-valued functions obtained by thresholding different real-valued functions to have the same classification errors, while the ranking errors of the real-valued functions may differ significantly. For example, consider the following two rankings on a sample consisting of 4 positive and 4 negative examples:

In both cases, the error of the best classification function that can be obtained by applying a threshold is $2/8$. However, the ranking error of f_1 is $4/16$, whereas that of f_2 is $8/16$. For a detailed analysis of this distinction, see [10][1].

A bipartite ranking algorithm takes as input a training sample $(S_+, S_-) \in (\bigcup_{m=1}^{\infty} \mathcal{X}^m) \times (\bigcup_{n=1}^{\infty} \mathcal{X}^n)$ and returns as output a ranking function $f_{S_+,S_-} : \mathcal{X} \to \mathbb{R}$. For simplicity, we consider only deterministic algorithms. We are concerned in this paper with generalization properties of such algorithms; in particular, we are interested in bounding the expected error of a learned ranking function in terms of an empirically observable quantity such as its empirical error on the training sample from which it is learned. The following definitions will be useful in our study.

Definition 1 (Ranking loss function). *A ranking loss function is a function $\ell : \mathbb{R}^{\mathcal{X}} \times \mathcal{X} \times \mathcal{X} \to \mathbb{R}^+ \cup \{0\}$ that assigns, for each $f : \mathcal{X} \to \mathbb{R}$ and $x, x' \in \mathcal{X}$, a non-negative real number $\ell(f, x, x')$ interpreted as the loss of f in its relative ranking of x and x'.*

---

[1] In [10], the performance of a ranking function is measured in terms of the area under the ROC curve (AUC); this quantity is simply equal to one minus the empirical ranking error.

Definition 2 (Expected ℓ-error). *Let* $f : \mathcal{X} \to \mathbb{R}$ *be a ranking function on* $\mathcal{X}$. *Let* $\ell : \mathbb{R}^{\mathcal{X}} \times \mathcal{X} \times \mathcal{X} \to \mathbb{R}^+ \cup \{0\}$ *be a ranking loss function. Define the* expected ℓ-error *of* f, *denoted by* $R_\ell(f)$, *as follows:*

$$R_\ell(f) = \mathbf{E}_{x^+ \sim \mathcal{D}_+, x^- \sim \mathcal{D}_-} \left\{ \ell(f, x^+, x^-) \right\} .$$

Definition 3 (Empirical ℓ-error). *Let* $f : \mathcal{X} \to \mathbb{R}$ *be a ranking function on* $\mathcal{X}$, *and let* $(S_+, S_-) \in \mathcal{X}^m \times \mathcal{X}^n$ *be a finite sample. Let* $\ell : \mathbb{R}^{\mathcal{X}} \times \mathcal{X} \times \mathcal{X} \to \mathbb{R}^+ \cup \{0\}$ *be a ranking loss function. Define the* empirical ℓ-error *of* f *with respect to* S_+ *and* S_-, *denoted by* $\hat{R}_\ell(f; S_+, S_-)$, *as follows:*

$$\hat{R}_\ell(f; S_+, S_-) = \frac{1}{mn} \sum_{i=1}^{m} \sum_{j=1}^{n} \ell(f, x_i^+, x_j^-) .$$

Comparing with Eqs. (1-2), we see that the ranking error can be expressed as the ℓ_b-error, *i.e.*, $R \equiv R_{\ell_b}$ and $\hat{R} \equiv \hat{R}_{\ell_b}$, where ℓ_b is the *bipartite ranking loss* given by

$$\ell_b(f, x, x') = \mathbf{I}_{\{f(x) < f(x')\}} + \frac{1}{2} \mathbf{I}_{\{f(x) = f(x')\}} . \tag{3}$$

3   Stability of (Bipartite) Ranking Algorithms

A stable algorithm is one whose output does not change significantly with small changes in the input. The input to a ranking algorithm is a training sample of the form $(S_+, S_-) \in \mathcal{X}^m \times \mathcal{X}^n$ for some $m, n \in \mathbb{N}$; we consider changes to such a sample that consist of replacing a single element of the sample with a new instance. For any $i \in \{1, \ldots, m\}$ and $z \in \mathcal{X}$, we use $S_+^{i,z}$ to denote the sequence obtained from S_+ by replacing x_i^+ with z; similarly, for any $j \in \{1, \ldots, n\}$ and $z \in \mathcal{X}$, we use $S_-^{j,z}$ to denote the sequence obtained from S_- by replacing x_j^- with z.

Several different notions of stability have been used in the study of classification and regression algorithms [9, 12, 7, 8, 13]. The notions of stability that we define for ranking algorithms below are most closely related to those used by Bousquet and Elisseeff [7].

Definition 4 (Uniform loss stability). *Let* L *be a bipartite ranking algorithm whose output on a training sample* (S_+, S_-) *we denote by* f_{S_+, S_-}, *and let* $\ell : \mathbb{R}^{\mathcal{X}} \times \mathcal{X} \times \mathcal{X} \to \mathbb{R}^+ \cup \{0\}$ *be a ranking loss function. Let* $\alpha : \mathbb{N} \times \mathbb{N} \to \mathbb{R}$, $\beta : \mathbb{N} \times \mathbb{N} \to \mathbb{R}$. *We say that* L *has* uniform loss stability (α, β) *with respect to* ℓ *if for all* $m, n \in \mathbb{N}$, $(S_+, S_-) \in \mathcal{X}^m \times \mathcal{X}^n$, $z \in \mathcal{X}$, $i \in \{1, \ldots, m\}$ *and* $j \in \{1, \ldots, n\}$, *we have for all* $x^+, x^- \in \mathcal{X}$,

$$\left| \ell(f_{S_+, S_-}, x^+, x^-) - \ell(f_{S_+^{i,z}, S_-}, x^+, x^-) \right| \leq \alpha(m, n) ,$$

$$\left| \ell(f_{S_+, S_-}, x^+, x^-) - \ell(f_{S_+, S_-^{j,z}}, x^+, x^-) \right| \leq \beta(m, n) .$$

Definition 5 (Uniform score stability). *Let L be a bipartite ranking algorithm whose output on a training sample (S_+, S_-) we denote by f_{S_+,S_-}. Let $\mu : \mathbb{N} \times \mathbb{N} \rightarrow \mathbb{R}$, $\nu : \mathbb{N} \times \mathbb{N} \rightarrow \mathbb{R}$. We say that L has* uniform score stability (μ, ν) *if for all $m, n \in \mathbb{N}$, $(S_+, S_-) \in \mathcal{X}^m \times \mathcal{X}^n$, $z \in \mathcal{X}$, $i \in \{1, \ldots, m\}$ and $j \in \{1, \ldots, n\}$, we have for all $x \in \mathcal{X}$,*

$$\left| f_{S_+,S_-}(x) - f_{S_+^{i,z},S_-}(x) \right| \leq \mu(m,n),$$

$$\left| f_{S_+,S_-}(x) - f_{S_+,S_-^{j,z}}(x) \right| \leq \nu(m,n).$$

4   Generalization Bounds for Stable Ranking Algorithms

In this section we derive generalization bounds for ranking algorithms that exhibit good stability properties. Our methods are based on those of Bousquet and Elisseeff [7], who derived such bounds for classification and regression algorithms. We start with the following technical lemma.

Lemma 1. *Let L be a symmetric bipartite ranking algorithm[2] whose output on a training sample $(S_+, S_-) \in \mathcal{X}^m \times \mathcal{X}^n$ we denote by f_{S_+,S_-}, and let $\ell : \mathbb{R}^{\mathcal{X}} \times \mathcal{X} \times \mathcal{X} \rightarrow \mathbb{R}^+ \cup \{0\}$ be a ranking loss function. Then for all $i \in \{1, \ldots, m\}$, $j \in \{1, \ldots, n\}$, we have*

$$\mathbf{E}_{S_+,S_-} \left\{ R_\ell(f_{S_+,S_-}) - \hat{R}_\ell(f_{S_+,S_-}; S_+, S_-) \right\}$$
$$= \mathbf{E}_{S_+,S_-,x^+,x^-} \left\{ \ell(f_{S_+,S_-}, x^+, x^-) - \ell(f_{S_+^{i,x^+}, S_-^{j,x^-}}, x^+, x^-) \right\}.$$

Proof. We have,

$$\mathbf{E}_{S_+,S_-} \left\{ \hat{R}_\ell(f_{S_+,S_-}; S_+, S_-) \right\} = \frac{1}{mn} \sum_{i=1}^m \sum_{j=1}^n \mathbf{E}_{S_+,S_-} \left\{ \ell(f_{S_+,S_-}, x_i^+, x_j^-) \right\}.$$

By symmetry, the term in the summation is the same for all i, j. Therefore, for each $i \in \{1, \ldots, m\}$ and $j \in \{1, \ldots, n\}$, we get

$$\mathbf{E}_{S_+,S_-} \left\{ \hat{R}_\ell(f_{S_+,S_-}; S_+, S_-) \right\} = \mathbf{E}_{S_+,S_-} \left\{ \ell(f_{S_+,S_-}, x_i^+, x_j^-) \right\}$$
$$= \mathbf{E}_{S_+,S_-,x^+,x^-} \left\{ \ell(f_{S_+,S_-}, x_i^+, x_j^-) \right\}.$$

Interchanging the roles of x_i^+ with x^+ and x_j^- with x^-, we get

$$\mathbf{E}_{S_+,S_-} \left\{ \hat{R}_\ell(f_{S_+,S_-}; S_+, S_-) \right\} = \mathbf{E}_{S_+,S_-,x^+,x^-} \left\{ \ell(f_{S_+^{i,x^+}, S_-^{j,x^-}}, x^+, x^-) \right\}.$$

Since by definition

$$\mathbf{E}_{S_+,S_-} \left\{ R_\ell(f_{S_+,S_-}) \right\} = \mathbf{E}_{S_+,S_-,x^+,x^-} \left\{ \ell(f_{S_+,S_-}, x^+, x^-) \right\},$$

the result follows.   □

---

[2] A symmetric bipartite ranking algorithm is one whose output is independent of the order of elements in the training sequences S_+ and S_-.

Our main tool will be the following powerful concentration inequality of McDiarmid [14], which bounds the deviation of any function of a sample for which a single change in the sample has limited effect.

Theorem 1 (McDiarmid [14]). *Let $X_1, \ldots, X_N$ be independent random variables, each taking values in a set A. Let $\phi : A^N \to \mathbb{R}$ be such that for each $k \in \{1, \ldots, N\}$, there exists $c_k > 0$ such that*

$$\sup_{x_1,\ldots,x_N \in A, x'_k \in A} \left| \phi(x_1,\ldots,x_N) - \phi(x_1,\ldots,x_{k-1},x'_k,x_{k+1},\ldots,x_N) \right| \leq c_k .$$

Then for any $\epsilon > 0$,

$$\mathbf{P}\{\phi(X_1,\ldots,X_N) - \mathbf{E}\{\phi(X_1,\ldots,X_N)\} \geq \epsilon\} \leq e^{-2\epsilon^2 / \sum_{k=1}^N c_k^2} .$$

We are now ready to give our main result, which bounds the expected ℓ-error of a ranking function learned by an algorithm with good uniform loss stability in terms of its empirical ℓ-error on the training sample.

Theorem 2. *Let L be a symmetric bipartite ranking algorithm whose output on a training sample $(S_+, S_-) \in \mathcal{X}^m \times \mathcal{X}^n$ we denote by f_{S_+,S_-}, and let $\ell : \mathbb{R}^{\mathcal{X}} \times \mathcal{X} \times \mathcal{X} \to \mathbb{R}^+ \cup \{0\}$ be a ranking loss function such that $0 \leq \ell(f, x, x') \leq B$ for all $f : \mathcal{X} \to \mathbb{R}$ and $x, x' \in \mathcal{X}$. Let $\alpha : \mathbb{N} \times \mathbb{N} \to \mathbb{R}$, $\beta : \mathbb{N} \times \mathbb{N} \to \mathbb{R}$ be such that L has uniform loss stability (α, β) with respect to ℓ. Then for any $0 < \delta < 1$, with probability at least $1 - \delta$ over the draw of (S_+, S_-),*

$$R_\ell(f_{S_+,S_-}) < \hat{R}_\ell(f_{S_+,S_-}; S_+, S_-) + \alpha(m,n) + \beta(m,n)$$

$$+ \sqrt{\frac{\{n(2m\,\alpha(m,n) + B)^2 + m(2n\,\beta(m,n) + B)^2\} \ln(1/\delta)}{2mn}} .$$

Proof. Let $\phi : \mathcal{X}^m \times \mathcal{X}^n \to \mathbb{R}$ be defined as follows:

$$\phi(S_+, S_-) = R_\ell(f_{S_+,S_-}) - \hat{R}_\ell(f_{S_+,S_-}; S_+, S_-) .$$

We shall show that ϕ satisfies the conditions of McDiarmid's inequality (Theorem 1). Let $(S_+, S_-) \in \mathcal{X}^m \times \mathcal{X}^n$, and let $z \in \mathcal{X}$. For each $i \in \{1, \ldots, m\}$, we have

$$\left| R_\ell(f_{S_+,S_-}) - R_\ell(f_{S_+^{i,z},S_-}) \right| = \left| \mathbf{E}_{x^+,x^-}\{\ell(f_{S_+,S_-}, x^+, x^-) - \ell(f_{S_+^{i,z},S_-}, x^+, x^-)\} \right|$$

$$\leq \mathbf{E}_{x^+,x^-}\{|\ell(f_{S_+,S_-}, x^+, x^-) - \ell(f_{S_+^{i,z},S_-}, x^+, x^-)|\}$$

$$\leq \alpha(m,n) ,$$

and

$$\left| \hat{R}_\ell(f_{S_+,S_-}; S_+, S_-) - \hat{R}_\ell(f_{S_+^{i,z},S_-}; S_+^{i,z}, S_-) \right|$$

$$\leq \frac{1}{mn} \sum_{i' \neq i} \sum_{j=1}^n |\ell(f_{S_+,S_-}, x_{i'}^+, x_j^-) - \ell(f_{S_+^{i,z},S_-}, x_{i'}^+, x_j^-)|$$

$$+ \frac{1}{mn} \sum_{j=1}^n |\ell(f_{S_+,S_-}, x_i^+, x_j^-) - \ell(f_{S_+^{i,z},S_-}, z, x_j^-)|$$

$$\leq \alpha(m,n) + \frac{B}{m} .$$

This gives

$$\left|\phi(S_+, S_-) - \phi(S_+^{i,z}, S_-)\right| \le 2\alpha(m,n) + \frac{B}{m}.$$

Similarly, it can be shown that for each $j \in \{1, \ldots, n\}$,

$$\left|\phi(S_+, S_-) - \phi(S_+, S_-^{j,z})\right| \le 2\beta(m,n) + \frac{B}{n}.$$

Thus, applying McDiarmid's inequality to ϕ, we get for any $\epsilon > 0$,

$$\mathbf{P}_{S_+,S_-} \left\{ \left\{ R_\ell(f_{S_+,S_-}) - \hat{R}_\ell(f_{S_+,S_-}; S_+, S_-) \right\} \right.$$
$$\left. - \mathbf{E}_{S_+,S_-} \left\{ R_\ell(f_{S_+,S_-}) - \hat{R}_\ell(f_{S_+,S_-}; S_+, S_-) \right\} \ge \epsilon \right\}$$
$$\le e^{-2\epsilon^2 / (m(2\alpha(m,n)+B/m)^2 + n(2\beta(m,n)+B/n)^2)}$$
$$= e^{-2mn\epsilon^2 / (n(2m\alpha(m,n)+B)^2 + m(2n\beta(m,n)+B)^2)}.$$

Now, by Lemma 1, we have

$$\mathbf{E}_{S_+,S_-} \left\{ R_\ell(f_{S_+,S_-}) - \hat{R}_\ell(f_{S_+,S_-}; S_+, S_-) \right\}$$
$$= \mathbf{E}_{S_+,S_-,x^+,x^-} \left\{ \ell(f_{S_+,S_-}, x^+, x^-) - \ell(f_{S_+^{i,x^+}, S_-^{j,x^-}}, x^+, x^-) \right\}$$
$$= \mathbf{E}_{S_+,S_-,x^+,x^-} \left\{ \ell(f_{S_+,S_-}, x^+, x^-) - \ell(f_{S_+^{i,x^+}, S_-}, x^+, x^-) \right.$$
$$\left. + \ell(f_{S_+^{i,x^+}, S_-}, x^+, x^-) - \ell(f_{S_+^{i,x^+}, S_-^{j,x^-}}, x^+, x^-) \right\}$$
$$\le \mathbf{E}_{S_+,S_-,x^+,x^-} \left\{ \left| \ell(f_{S_+,S_-}, x^+, x^-) - \ell(f_{S_+^{i,x^+}, S_-}, x^+, x^-) \right| \right\}$$
$$+ \mathbf{E}_{S_+,S_-,x^+,x^-} \left\{ \left| \ell(f_{S_+^{i,x^+}, S_-}, x^+, x^-) - \ell(f_{S_+^{i,x^+}, S_-^{j,x^-}}, x^+, x^-) \right| \right\}$$
$$\le \alpha(m,n) + \beta(m,n).$$

Thus we get for any $\epsilon > 0$,

$$\mathbf{P}_{S_+,S_-} \left\{ R_\ell(f_{S_+,S_-}) - \hat{R}_\ell(f_{S_+,S_-}; S_+, S_-) - (\alpha(m,n) + \beta(m,n)) \ge \epsilon \right\}$$
$$\le e^{-2mn\epsilon^2 / (n(2m\alpha(m,n)+B)^2 + m(2n\beta(m,n)+B)^2)}.$$

The result follows by setting the right hand side equal to δ and solving for ϵ. □

Theorem 2 gives meaningful bounds when $\alpha(m,n) = o(1/\sqrt{m})$ and $\beta(m,n) = o(1/\sqrt{n})$. This means the theorem cannot be applied directly to obtain bounds on the expected ranking error, since it is not possible to have non-trivial uniform loss stability with respect to the bipartite ranking loss ℓ_b (except by an algorithm that picks the same ranking function for all training samples of a given size m, n). However, for any ranking loss ℓ that satisfies $\ell_b \le \ell$, Theorem 2 can be applied to ranking algorithms that have good uniform loss stability with respect to ℓ to obtain bounds on the expected ℓ-error; since in this case $R \le R_\ell$, these bounds apply also to the expected ranking error. We consider below a specific ranking loss that satisfies this condition.

For $\gamma > 0$, let the γ *ranking loss*, denoted by ℓ_γ, be defined as follows:

$$\ell_\gamma(f, x, x') = \begin{cases} 1 & \text{if } (f(x) - f(x')) \leq 0 \\ 1 - \frac{(f(x) - f(x'))}{\gamma} & \text{if } 0 < (f(x) - f(x')) < \gamma \\ 0 & \text{if } (f(x) - f(x')) \geq \gamma \end{cases} \tag{4}$$

Clearly, for all $\gamma > 0$, we have $\ell_b \leq \ell_\gamma$. Therefore, for any ranking algorithm that has good uniform loss stability with respect to ℓ_γ for some $\gamma > 0$, Theorem 2 can be applied to bound the expected ranking error of a learned ranking function in terms of its empirical ℓ_γ-error on the training sample. The following lemma shows that, for every $\gamma > 0$, a ranking algorithm that has good uniform score stability also has good uniform loss stability with respect to ℓ_γ.

Lemma 2. *Let L be a bipartite ranking algorithm whose output on a training sample (S_+, S_-) we denote by f_{S_+,S_-}. Let $\mu : \mathbb{N} \times \mathbb{N} \to \mathbb{R}$, $\nu : \mathbb{N} \times \mathbb{N} \to \mathbb{R}$ be such that L has uniform score stability (μ, ν). Then for every $\gamma > 0$, L has uniform loss stability $(\alpha_\gamma, \beta_\gamma)$ with respect to the γ ranking loss ℓ_γ, where for all $m, n \in \mathbb{N}$,*

$$\alpha_\gamma(m, n) = \frac{2\mu(m, n)}{\gamma}, \qquad \beta_\gamma(m, n) = \frac{2\nu(m, n)}{\gamma}.$$

Proof. By the definition of ℓ_γ in Eq. (4), we have that

$$\ell_\gamma(f, x, x') \leq 1 - \frac{(f(x) - f(x'))}{\gamma} \quad \text{if } (f(x) - f(x')) \leq 0, \tag{5}$$

$$\ell_\gamma(f, x, x') \geq 1 - \frac{(f(x) - f(x'))}{\gamma} \quad \text{if } (f(x) - f(x')) \geq \gamma. \tag{6}$$

Now, let $m, n \in \mathbb{N}$, $(S_+, S_-) \in \mathcal{X}^m \times \mathcal{X}^n$, $z \in \mathcal{X}$, $i \in \{1, \ldots, m\}$ and $j \in \{1, \ldots, n\}$, and let $x^+, x^- \in \mathcal{X}$. The case $\ell_\gamma(f_{S_+,S_-}, x^+, x^-) = \ell_\gamma(f_{S_+^{i,z},S_-}, x^+, x^-)$ is trivial. Assume $\ell_\gamma(f_{S_+,S_-}, x^+, x^-) \neq \ell_\gamma(f_{S_+^{i,z},S_-}, x^+, x^-)$. Then, using the observations in Eqs. (5-6), it can be verified that

$$\left| \ell_\gamma(f_{S_+,S_-}, x^+, x^-) - \ell_\gamma(f_{S_+^{i,z},S_-}, x^+, x^-) \right|$$

$$\leq \left| \left(1 - \frac{(f_{S_+,S_-}(x^+) - f_{S_+,S_-}(x^-))}{\gamma} \right) - \left(1 - \frac{(f_{S_+^{i,z},S_-}(x^+) - f_{S_+^{i,z},S_-}(x^-))}{\gamma} \right) \right|$$

$$\leq \frac{1}{\gamma} \left(\left| f_{S_+,S_-}(x^+) - f_{S_+^{i,z},S_-}(x^+) \right| + \left| f_{S_+,S_-}(x^-) - f_{S_+^{i,z},S_-}(x^-) \right| \right)$$

$$\leq \frac{2\mu(m, n)}{\gamma}.$$

Similarly, it can be shown that

$$\left| \ell_\gamma(f_{S_+,S_-}, x^+, x^-) - \ell_\gamma(f_{S_+,S_-^{j,z}}, x^+, x^-) \right| \leq \frac{2\nu(m, n)}{\gamma}.$$

The result follows. $\qquad \square$

Putting everything together, we thus get the following result which bounds the expected ranking error of a learned ranking function in terms of its empirical ℓ_γ-error for any ranking algorithm that has good uniform score stability.

Theorem 3. *Let L be a symmetric bipartite ranking algorithm whose output on a training sample $(S_+, S_-) \in \mathcal{X}^m \times \mathcal{X}^n$ we denote by f_{S_+,S_-}. Let $\mu : \mathbb{N} \times \mathbb{N} \to \mathbb{R}$, $\nu : \mathbb{N} \times \mathbb{N} \to \mathbb{R}$ be such that L has uniform score stability (μ, ν), and let $\gamma > 0$. Then for any $0 < \delta < 1$, with probability at least $1 - \delta$ over the draw of (S_+, S_-),*

$$R(f_{S_+,S_-}) < \hat{R}_{\ell_\gamma}(f_{S_+,S_-}; S_+, S_-) + \frac{2\mu(m,n)}{\gamma} + \frac{2\nu(m,n)}{\gamma}$$

$$+ \sqrt{\frac{\left\{ n\left(\frac{4m\,\mu(m,n)}{\gamma} + 1\right)^2 + m\left(\frac{4n\,\nu(m,n)}{\gamma} + 1\right)^2 \right\} \ln(1/\delta)}{2mn}}.$$

Proof. The result follows by applying Theorem 2 to L with the ranking loss ℓ_γ (using Lemma 2), which satisfies $0 \leq \ell_\gamma \leq 1$, and from the fact that $R \leq R_{\ell_\gamma}$. $\qquad\square$

We note that although our bounds above are derived for the case when a fixed number m of positive examples are drawn i.i.d. from $\mathcal{D}_+$ and a fixed number n of negative examples are drawn i.i.d. from $\mathcal{D}_-$, the bounds can be extended easily to the case when M examples are drawn i.i.d. from a joint distribution $\mathcal{D}$ over $\mathcal{X} \times \{-1, 1\}$. In particular, using exactly the same techniques as above, the same confidence intervals can be derived for a draw conditioned on any fixed label sequence that contains m positive and $n = M - m$ negative labels. The conditioning can then be removed using an expectation trick (see [6–Theorems 8 and 19]); in the resulting confidence intervals, the numbers m and n are replaced by functions of the (random) label sequence that correspond to the numbers of positive and negative labels drawn.

5   Stable Ranking Algorithms

In this section we show stability of certain ranking algorithms that select a ranking function by minimizing a regularized objective function. We start by deriving a general result for regularization-based ranking algorithms in Section 5.1. In Section 5.2 we use this result to show stability of kernel-based ranking algorithms that perform regularization in a reproducing kernel Hilbert space (RKHS). We show, in particular, stability of an SVM-like ranking algorithm, and apply the results of Section 4 to obtain a generalization bound for this algorithm. A comparison with the uniform convergence bound of [6] demonstrates the benefit of the stability analysis. Again, our methods are based on those of Bousquet and Elisseeff [7], who showed similar results for classification and regression algorithms.

5.1   General Regularizers

Given a ranking loss function $\ell : \mathbb{R}^\mathcal{X} \times \mathcal{X} \times \mathcal{X} \to \mathbb{R}^+ \cup \{0\}$, a class $\mathcal{F}$ of real-valued functions on $\mathcal{X}$, and a regularization functional $N : \mathcal{F} \to \mathbb{R}^+ \cup \{0\}$, consider the following regularized empirical ℓ-error of a ranking function $f \in \mathcal{F}$ (with respect to a sample $(S_+, S_-) \in \mathcal{X}^m \times \mathcal{X}^n$), with regularization parameter $\lambda > 0$:

$$\hat{R}_\ell^\lambda(f; S_+, S_-) = \frac{1}{mn} \sum_{i=1}^m \sum_{j=1}^n \ell(f, x_i^+, x_j^-) + \lambda N(f). \tag{7}$$

We consider bipartite ranking algorithms that minimize such a regularized objective function, *i.e.*, ranking algorithms that, given a training sample (S_+, S_-), output a ranking function $f_{S_+, S_-} \in \mathcal{F}$ that satisfies

$$
\begin{aligned}
f_{S_+, S_-} &= \arg\min_{f \in \mathcal{F}} \hat{R}_\ell^\lambda(f; S_+, S_-) \\
&= \arg\min_{f \in \mathcal{F}} \left\{ \hat{R}_\ell(f; S_+, S_-) + \lambda N(f) \right\},
\end{aligned}
\tag{8}
$$

for some fixed choice of ranking loss ℓ, function class $\mathcal{F}$, regularizer N, and regularization parameter λ. We derive below a general result that will be useful for showing stability of such regularization-based algorithms.

Definition 6 (σ-**admissibility**). *Let* $\ell : \mathbb{R}^{\mathcal{X}} \times \mathcal{X} \times \mathcal{X} \to \mathbb{R}^+ \cup \{0\}$ *be a ranking loss and* $\mathcal{F}$ *a class of real-valued functions on* $\mathcal{X}$. *Let* $\sigma > 0$. *We say that* ℓ *is* σ-admissible *with respect to* $\mathcal{F}$ *if for all* $f_1, f_2 \in \mathcal{F}$ *and all* $x, x' \in \mathcal{X}$, *we have*

$$
\left| \ell(f_1, x, x') - \ell(f_2, x, x') \right| \leq \sigma \left(\left| f_1(x) - f_2(x) \right| + \left| f_1(x') - f_2(x') \right| \right).
$$

Lemma 3. *Let* $\ell : \mathbb{R}^{\mathcal{X}} \times \mathcal{X} \times \mathcal{X} \to \mathbb{R}^+ \cup \{0\}$ *be a ranking loss such that* $\ell(f, x, x')$ *is convex in* f. *Let* $\mathcal{F}$ *be a convex class of real-valued functions on* $\mathcal{X}$, *and let* $\sigma > 0$ *be such that* ℓ *is* σ-admissible with respect to $\mathcal{F}$. *Let* $\lambda > 0$, *and let* $N : \mathcal{F} \to \mathbb{R}^+ \cup \{0\}$ *be a functional defined on* $\mathcal{F}$ *such that for all samples* $(S_+, S_-) \in \mathcal{X}^m \times \mathcal{X}^n$, *the regularized empirical* ℓ-error $\hat{R}_\ell^\lambda(f; S_+, S_-)$ *has a minimum (not necessarily unique) in* $\mathcal{F}$. *Let* L *be a ranking algorithm defined by Eq. (8), and let* $(S_+, S_-) \in \mathcal{X}^m \times \mathcal{X}^n$, $z \in \mathcal{X}$, $i \in \{1, \ldots, m\}$, *and* $j \in \{1, \ldots, n\}$. *For brevity, denote*

$$
f \equiv f_{S_+, S_-}, \qquad f_+^{i,z} \equiv f_{S_+^{i,z}, S_-}, \qquad f_-^{j,z} \equiv f_{S_+, S_-^{j,z}},
$$

and let

$$
\Delta f_+ = \left(f_+^{i,z} - f \right), \qquad \Delta f_- = \left(f_-^{j,z} - f \right).
$$

Then we have that for any $t \in [0, 1]$,

$$
N(f) - N(f + t\Delta f_+) + N(f_+^{i,z}) - N(f_+^{i,z} - t\Delta f_+)
$$
$$
\leq \frac{t\sigma}{\lambda mn} \sum_{j=1}^n \left(|\Delta f_+(x_i^+)| + 2|\Delta f_+(x_j^-)| + |\Delta f_+(z)| \right),
$$

$$
N(f) - N(f + t\Delta f_-) + N(f_-^{j,z}) - N(f_-^{j,z} - t\Delta f_-)
$$
$$
\leq \frac{t\sigma}{\lambda mn} \sum_{i=1}^m \left(|\Delta f_-(x_j^-)| + 2|\Delta f_-(x_i^+)| + |\Delta f_-(z)| \right).
$$

The proof of this result makes use of techniques similar to those used in [7], and is omitted for lack of space (see [15] for details). As we show below, this result can be used to establish stability of certain regularization-based ranking algorithms.

5.2 Regularization in Hilbert Spaces

Let $\mathcal{F}$ be an RKHS with kernel K. Then from the properties of an RKHS (see, for example, [16]), we have for all $f \in \mathcal{F}$ and all $x \in \mathcal{X}$,

$$|f(x)| \leq \|f\|_K \sqrt{K(x,x)}. \tag{9}$$

Let $N : \mathcal{F} \to \mathbb{R}^+ \cup \{0\}$ be the regularizer defined by

$$N(f) = \|f\|_K^2. \tag{10}$$

We show below that, if the kernel K is such that $K(x,x)$ is bounded for all $x \in \mathcal{X}$, then a ranking algorithm that minimizes an appropriate regularized error over $\mathcal{F}$, with regularizer N as defined above, has good uniform score stability.

Theorem 4. *Let $\mathcal{F}$ be an RKHS with kernel K such that for all $x \in \mathcal{X}$, $K(x,x) \leq \kappa^2 < \infty$. Let ℓ be a ranking loss such that $\ell(f,x,x')$ is convex in f and ℓ is σ-admissible with respect to $\mathcal{F}$. Let $\lambda > 0$, and let N be given by Eq. (10). Let L be a ranking algorithm defined by Eq. (8). Then L has uniform score stability (μ, ν), where for all $m, n \in \mathbb{N}$,*

$$\mu(m,n) = \frac{4\sigma\kappa^2}{\lambda m}, \qquad \nu(m,n) = \frac{4\sigma\kappa^2}{\lambda n}.$$

Proof. Let $m, n \in \mathbb{N}$, $(S_+, S_-) \in \mathcal{X}^m \times \mathcal{X}^n$, $z \in \mathcal{X}$, and $i \in \{1, \ldots, m\}$. Since $\mathcal{F}$ is a vector space, we have (using the notation of Lemma 3) that $\Delta f_+ \in \mathcal{F}$. Applying Lemma 3 with $t = 1/2$, we get that

$$\frac{1}{2}\|\Delta f_+\|_K^2 \leq \frac{\sigma}{2\lambda mn} \sum_{j=1}^n \left(|\Delta f_+(x_i^+)| + 2|\Delta f_+(x_j^-)| + |\Delta f_+(z)| \right).$$

By Eq. (9), we thus get that

$$\|\Delta f_+\|_K^2 \leq \frac{4\sigma\kappa}{\lambda m}\|\Delta f_+\|_K,$$

which gives

$$\|\Delta f_+\|_K \leq \frac{4\sigma\kappa}{\lambda m}. \tag{11}$$

Thus, by Eqs. (9) and (11), we have for all $x \in \mathcal{X}$,

$$\left| f_{S_+,S_-}(x) - f_{S_+^{i,z},S_-}(x) \right| = |\Delta f_+(x)| \leq \frac{4\sigma\kappa^2}{\lambda m}.$$

Similarly, for each $j \in \{1, \ldots, n\}$, we can show that

$$\left| f_{S_+,S_-}(x) - f_{S_+,S_-^{j,z}}(x) \right| \leq \frac{4\sigma\kappa^2}{\lambda n}.$$

The result follows. $\qquad\square$

Consider now the following ranking loss function, which we refer to as the *hinge ranking loss* due to its similarity to the hinge loss in classification:

$$\ell_h(f,x,x') = \begin{cases} 1 - (f(x) - f(x')) & \text{if } (f(x) - f(x')) < 1 \\ 0 & \text{if } (f(x) - f(x')) \geq 1 \end{cases}. \tag{12}$$

We consider a ranking algorithm L that minimizes the regularized ℓ_h-error in an RKHS $\mathcal{F}$. Specifically, let L be a ranking algorithm which, given a training sample (S_+, S_-), outputs a ranking function $f_{S_+,S_-} \in \mathcal{F}$ that satisfies (for some fixed $\lambda > 0$)

$$f_{S_+,S_-} = \arg\min_{f \in \mathcal{F}} \left\{ \hat{R}_{\ell_h}(f; S_+, S_-) + \lambda \|f\|_K^2 \right\}. \tag{13}$$

We note that this algorithm has an equivalent quadratic programming formulation similar to SVMs in the case of classification (see [17, 15]). It can be verified that $\ell_h(f, x, x')$ is convex in f, and that ℓ_h is 1-admissible with respect to $\mathcal{F}$. Thus, if $K(x, x) \leq \kappa^2$ for all $x \in \mathcal{X}$, then from Theorem 4 we get that L has uniform score stability (μ, ν), where for all $m, n \in \mathbb{N}$,

$$\mu(m, n) = \frac{4\kappa^2}{\lambda m}, \qquad \nu(m, n) = \frac{4\kappa^2}{\lambda n}.$$

Applying Theorem 3 with $\gamma = 1$, we then get that for any $0 < \delta < 1$, with probability at least $1 - \delta$ over the draw of $(S_+, S_-) \in \mathcal{X}^m \times \mathcal{X}^n$, the expected ranking error of the ranking function f_{S_+,S_-} learned by the above algorithm L is bounded by

$$R(f_{S_+,S_-}) < \hat{R}_{\ell_1}(f_{S_+,S_-}; S_+, S_-) + \frac{8\kappa^2}{\lambda}\left(\frac{m+n}{mn}\right) + \left(1 + \frac{16\kappa^2}{\lambda}\right)\sqrt{\frac{(m+n)\ln(1/\delta)}{2mn}}.$$
$$\tag{14}$$

In particular, for the RKHS corresponding to the linear kernel defined on the unit ball in $\mathbb{R}^d$, so that $K(\mathbf{x}, \mathbf{x}) \leq 1$ for all $\mathbf{x}$, we have that with probability at least $1 - \delta$ over the draw of $(S_+, S_-) \in \mathcal{X}^m \times \mathcal{X}^n$, the ranking function f_{S_+,S_-} learned by the above algorithm (defined by Eq. (13)) satisfies

$$R(f_{S_+,S_-}) < \hat{R}_{\ell_1}(f_{S_+,S_-}; S_+, S_-) + \frac{8}{\lambda}\left(\frac{m+n}{mn}\right) + \left(1 + \frac{16}{\lambda}\right)\sqrt{\frac{(m+n)\ln(1/\delta)}{2mn}}.$$

On the other hand, the confidence interval obtained for this algorithm using the uniform convergence bound of [6] gives that, with probability at least $1 - \delta$,

$$R(f_{S_+,S_-}) < \hat{R}(f_{S_+,S_-}; S_+, S_-) + \sqrt{\frac{8(m+n)\big(d(\ln(8mn/d) + 1) + \ln(4/\delta)\big)}{mn}}.$$

The above bounds are plotted in Figure 1 for $\delta = 0.01$, $\lambda = 1$, and various values of d and $m/(m+n)$. As can be seen, directly analyzing stability properties of the algorithm gives considerable benefit over the general uniform convergence based analysis. In particular, since the uniform convergence bound depends on the complexity of the function class that is searched, the bound quickly becomes uninformative in high dimensions; on the other hand, the stability bound is independent of the dimensionality of the space. In the case of kernel spaces whose complexity cannot be bounded, e.g., the RKHS corresponding to the Gaussian kernel, the uniform convergence bound cannot be applied at all, while the stability analysis continues to hold.

Comparing the bound derived in Eq. (14) to the corresponding bound for classification derived by Bousquet and Elisseeff [7], we find that if the total number of training examples is denoted by $M = m + n$, then the sample size M in their bound is replaced

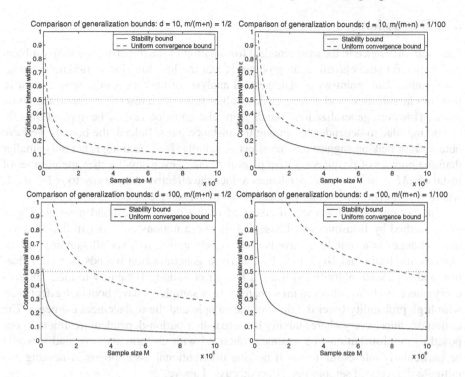

Fig. 1. A comparison of our stability bound with the uniform convergence bound of [6] for the kernel-based algorithm described in Section 5.2, with a linear kernel over the unit ball in $\mathbb{R}^d$. The plots are for $\delta = 0.01$, $\lambda = 1$, and show how the confidence interval size ϵ given by the two bounds varies with the sample size $M = m + n$, for various values of d and $m/(m + n)$

by the quantity $mn/(m+n)$ in our bound.[3] If we define the 'positive skew' of the sample as the proportion of positive examples $\rho = m/(m + n)$, then this is equivalent to replacing M in the classification bound with $\rho(1 - \rho)M$ in our bound. The 'effective' sample size in ranking is thus reduced from M to $\rho(1 - \rho)M$, the reduction being more drastic as the skew ρ departs from $1/2$. Interestingly, a similar observation holds for the uniform convergence and large deviation bounds for the ranking error derived in [6] when compared to corresponding bounds for the classification error.

As in the case of classification [7], the above results show that a larger regularization parameter λ leads to better stability and, therefore, a tighter confidence interval in the resulting generalization bound. In particular, one must have $\lambda \gg \sqrt{(m + n)/mn}$ in order for the above bound to be meaningful.

---

[3] The difference in constants in the two bounds is due in part to the difference in loss functions in ranking and classification, and in part to a slight difference in definitions of stability; in particular, our definitions are in terms of changes to a training sample that consist of replacing one element in the sample with a new one, while the definitions of Bousquet and Elisseeff are in terms of changes that consist of removing one element from the sample.

6 Discussion

The main difference in the mathematical formulation of the (bipartite) ranking problem as compared to the classification problem is that the loss function in ranking is 'pairwise' rather than 'point-wise'. The general analysis of ranking is otherwise similar to that for classification, and indeed, ranking algorithms often resemble 'classification on pairs'. However, generalization bounds from classification *cannot* be applied directly to ranking, due to dependences among the instance pairs. Indeed, the bounds we have obtained for ranking suggest that the effective sample size in ranking is not only smaller than the number of positive-negative pairs mn, but is even smaller than the number of instances $M = m + n$; the dependences reduce the effective sample size to $\rho(1 - \rho)M$, where $\rho = m/(m + n)$ is the 'positive skew' of the sample.

The notions of uniform stability studied in this paper correspond most closely to those studied by Bousquet and Elisseeff [7]. These notions are strict in that they require changes in a sample to have bounded effect uniformly over all samples and replacements. Kutin and Niyogi [8] have derived generalization bounds (for classification and regression algorithms) using a less strict notion of stability termed 'almost-everywhere' stability; this requires changes in a sample to have bounded effect only with high probability (over the draw of the sample and the replacement element). The notion of almost-everywhere stability leads to a distribution-dependent treatment as opposed to the distribution-free treatment obtained with uniform stability, and it would be particularly interesting to see if making distributional assumptions in ranking can mitigate the reduced sample size effect discussed above.

An open question concerns the analysis of other ranking algorithms using the algorithmic stability framework. It has been shown [18] that AdaBoost is stability-preserving, in the sense that stability of base classifiers implies stability of the final learned classifier. It would be interesting if a similar result could be shown for the bipartite RankBoost algorithm [5], which is based on the same principles of boosting as AdaBoost.

Finally, it is also an open question to analyze generalization properties of ranking algorithms in other settings of the ranking problem (*i.e.*, other than bipartite).

Acknowledgments

S. A. was supported in part through National Science Foundation (NSF) ITR grants IIS 00-85980 and IIS 00-85836. P. N. thanks the NSF for financial support.

References

1. Vapnik, V.N., Chervonenkis, A.: On the uniform convergence of relative frequencies of events to their probabilities. Theory of Probability and its Applications **16** (1971) 264–280
2. Cohen, W.W., Schapire, R.E., Singer, Y.: Learning to order things. Journal of Artificial Intelligence Research **10** (1999) 243–270
3. Herbrich, R., Graepel, T., Obermayer, K.: Large margin rank boundaries for ordinal regression. Advances in Large Margin Classifiers (2000) 115–132

4. Crammer, K., Singer, Y.: Pranking with ranking. In: Advances in Neural Information Processing Systems 14, MIT Press (2002) 641–647
5. Freund, Y., Iyer, R., Schapire, R.E., Singer, Y.: An efficient boosting algorithm for combining preferences. Journal of Machine Learning Research 4 (2003) 933–969
6. Agarwal, S., Graepel, T., Herbrich, R., Har-Peled, S., Roth, D.: Generalization bounds for the area under the ROC curve. Journal of Machine Learning Research 6 (2005) 393–425
7. Bousquet, O., Elisseeff, A.: Stability and generalization. Journal of Machine Learning Research 2 (2002) 499–526
8. Kutin, S., Niyogi, P.: Almost-everywhere algorithmic stability and generalization error. In: Proceedings of the 18th Conference on Uncertainty in Artificial Intelligence. (2002)
9. Devroye, L., Wagner, T.: Distribution-free performance bounds for potential function rules. IEEE Transactions on Information Theory 25 (1979) 601–604
10. Cortes, C., Mohri, M.: AUC optimization vs. error rate minimization. In: Advances in Neural Information Processing Systems 16, MIT Press (2004)
11. Agarwal, S., Roth, D.: Learnability of bipartite ranking functions. In: Proceedings of the 18th Annual Conference on Learning Theory. (2005)
12. Kearns, M., Ron, D.: Algorithmic stability and sanity-check bounds for leave-one-out cross-validation. Neural Computation 11 (1999) 1427–1453
13. Poggio, T., Rifkin, R., Mukherjee, S., Niyogi, P.: General conditions for predictivity in learning theory. Nature 428 (2004) 419–422
14. McDiarmid, C.: On the method of bounded differences. In: Surveys in Combinatorics 1989, Cambridge University Press (1989) 148–188
15. Agarwal, S.: A Study of the Bipartite Ranking Problem in Machine Learning. PhD thesis, University of Illinois at Urbana-Champaign (2005)
16. Evgeniou, T., Pontil, M., Poggio, T.: Regularization networks and support vector machines. Advances in Computational Mathematics 13 (2000) 1–50
17. Rakotomamonjy, A.: SVMs and area under ROC curves. Technical report, PSI- INSA de Rouen (2004)
18. Kutin, S., Niyogi, P.: The interaction of stability and weakness in AdaBoost. Technical Report TR-2001-30, Computer Science Department, University of Chicago (2001)

Loss Bounds for Online Category Ranking

Koby Crammer[1] and Yoram Singer[2,3]

[1] Dept. of Computer and Information Science,
Univ. of Pennsylvania, Philadelphia, PA 19104
[2] School of Computer Sci. & Eng., Hebrew University, Jerusalem 91904, Israel
[3] Google Inc., 1600 Amphitheatre Parkway, Mountain View CA 94043, USA
crammer@cis.upenn.edu, singer@{cs.huji.ac.il,google.com}

Abstract. Category ranking is the task of ordering labels with respect to their relevance to an input instance. In this paper we describe and analyze several algorithms for *online* category ranking where the instances are revealed in a sequential manner. We describe additive and multiplicative updates which constitute the core of the learning algorithms. The updates are derived by casting a constrained optimization problem for each new instance. We derive loss bounds for the algorithms by using the properties of the dual solution while imposing additional constraints on the dual form. Finally, we outline and analyze the convergence of a general update that can be employed with any Bregman divergence.

1 Introduction and Problem Setting

The task of category ranking is concerned with ordering the labels associated with a given instance in accordance to their relevance to the input instance. Category ranking often arises in text processing applications (see for instance [8]) in which the instances are documents and the labels constitute a list of topics that overlap with the subject matter of the document. The set of labels, or topics using the text processing jargon, is predefined and does not change along the run of the text processing and learning algorithm. A closely related problem studied by the machine learning community is called the multilabel classification problem. Few learning algorithms have been devised for the category ranking problem. Some notable example are a multiclass version of AdaBoost called AdaBoost.MH [12], a generalization of Vapnik's Support Vector Machines to the multilabel setting by Elisseeff and Weston [10], and a generalization of the Perceptron algorithm to category ranking [8]. This work employs hypotheses for category ranking that are closely related to the ones presented and used in [10, 8]. We generalize the algorithms presented in [10, 8] by providing both a more refined analysis as well as deriving and analyzing new algorithms for the same problem. First, we give online bounds for an additive algorithm which is a fusion of a generalization of the Perceptron for topic ranking [8] and the MIRA algorithm [9, 7]. We also derive a multiplicative algorithm and a general algorithm based on Bregman divergences that were not discussed in previous research papers. Last, but not least, previous work focused on feedback that takes a rather rigid structured form in which the set of labels is partitioned into relevant and non-relevant subsets. The framework presented here can be used with

P. Auer and R. Meir (Eds.): COLT 2005, LNAI 3559, pp. 48–62, 2005.

a rather general feedback which takes the form of a partial order. Experimental results [6] which unfortunately we do not have room to include in this paper indicate that the algorithms described in this paper outperform the previously published algorithms for topic ranking. Our algorithmic framework thus presents a viable practical and provably correct alternative to previous learning algorithms for the category ranking task.

Let us now describe the formal ingredients of the category ranking problem. As in supervised learning problems the learning algoritm is introduced to a set of instance-label pairs. For concreteness we assume that the instances are vectors in $\mathbb{R}^n$ and denote the instance received on round i by x^i. The labels that we examine in this paper may take a rather general form. Specifically, labels are preference relations over a set of k categories and is denoted by $\mathcal{C} = \{1, 2, \ldots, k\}$. That is, a label $y \subset \mathcal{C} \times \mathcal{C}$ is a relation, where $(r, s) \in y$ implies that category r is ranked above, or preferred over, category s. The only restriction we impose on a label y is that it does not contain any cycle. Put another way, we represent each label y as a graph. The set of vertices of the graph is defined as the set of categories in $\mathcal{C}$. Each preference pair $(r, s) \in y$ corresponds to a directed edge from the vertex r to the vertex s. Using this graph-based view, there is a one-to-one correspondence between relations which do not contain any cycle and directed acyclic graphs (DAGs). We refer to such relations as *semi-orders*.

A prediction function h maps instances $x \in \mathcal{X}$ to total-orders over $\mathcal{C}$ denoted by $\hat{\mathcal{Y}}$. We restrict ourselves to mappings based on linear functions which are parameterized by a set of k weight vectors $w_1, \ldots, w_k$ denoted by W. Formally, such mappings are defined as $h(x) = (\langle w^1, x \rangle, \ldots, \langle w^k, x \rangle) \in \mathbb{R}^k$, where $\langle \cdot, \cdot \rangle$ designates the inner-product operation. A prediction $\hat{y} \in \hat{\mathcal{Y}}$ naturally induces a total order where category r is ranked above category s iff $\langle w_r, x \rangle > \langle w_s, x \rangle$ and ties are broken arbitrarily. Throughout the paper, we overload the notation and denote by $\hat{y}$ both a k-dimensional vector and the total-order it induces.

Online algorithms work in rounds. On the ith round the algorithm receives an instance x^i and predicts a total-order $\hat{y}^i$ ($\in \mathbb{R}^k$). It then receives as feedback the semi-order y^i that is associated with x^i. We then suffer an *instantaneous* loss based on the discrepancy between the semi-order y^i and the total order $\hat{y}^i$. The goal of the online learning algorithm is to minimize a pre-defined *cumulative* loss. As in other online algorithms the collection of k weight vectors W is updated after receiving the feedback y^i. Therefore, we denote by W^i the set of parameters used for ranking the categories on round i. For brevity, we refer to W^i itself as the ranker.

As in other learning algorithms, proper loss functions should be defined in order to asses the quality of the prediction functions that are learned. In the problem of binary classification we are usually interested in the event of a misclassification, which induces the so called 0-1 loss. In the more complex category ranking problem there does not exist a unique and natural loss function. The lack of a natural loss function can be primarily attributed to the fact that the learning algorithm needs to take into consideration that some mistakes are less drastic than others. Nevertheless, the 0-1 loss can be also applied in category ranking problems, indicating whether the predicted total order is consistent with the preference represented by the semi-order received as feedback. This loss function is crude in the sense that it ignores completely how many preference pairs in y are in practice mis-ordered. Moving to the other extreme, we can define a loss

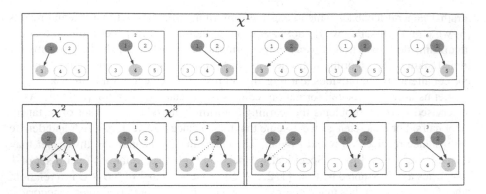

Fig. 1. Illustrations of various covers. The target semi-order in the example consists of six pairs (relations). These pairs constitute a bipartite graph with the "good" categories $\{1, 2\}$ on one side and the "bad" categories $\{3, 4, 5\}$ on the other side. The predicted total order is $\hat{y} = \{1 > 3 > 4 > 2 > 5\}$. Four different covers are depicted. Each subset within a cover is designated by a box. Pairs of categories for which the predicted order agrees with the target are depicted with bold edges while inconsistencies are designated by dashed edges. Thus, the induced loss is the number of boxes in which there is at least one dashed edge. **Top:** The all-pairs cover in which each subset is a pair of categories. **Bottom Left:** The 0-1 cover in which the entire set of edges reside in a single graph. **Bottom Center:** This cover counts the number of "good" categories that do not dominate all the "bad' categories. **Bottom Right:** The cover counts the number of "bad" categories that are not dominated by all of the "good" categories

function which is set to be equal to the number of preference relations in the semi-order which are not consistent with the predicted total-order. In this paper we chose a general approach which includes the above two choices of loss functions as special cases. Let $(\boldsymbol{x}^i, \boldsymbol{y}^i)$ be an instance-label pair. A loss function is parameterized by a partition or a cover χ of the semi-order $\boldsymbol{y}$ into finite disjoint sets, namely,

$$\cup_{\chi \in \boldsymbol{\chi}} \chi = \boldsymbol{y} \text{ and } \forall p \neq q : \chi_p \cap \chi_q = \emptyset .$$

Let $[\![\pi]\!]$ denote the indicator function, that is, $[\![\pi]\!]$ is 1 if the predicate π is true and is 0 otherwise. The loss suffered by a ranker W for a cover χ is defined to be,

$$\mathbb{I}(W; (\boldsymbol{x}, \boldsymbol{y}, \boldsymbol{\chi})) = \sum_{\chi \in \boldsymbol{\chi}} [\![\{(r, s) \in \chi : \langle \boldsymbol{w}_r, \boldsymbol{x} \rangle \leq \langle \boldsymbol{w}_s, \boldsymbol{x} \rangle\} \neq \emptyset]\!] , \qquad (1)$$

An illustration of four different covers and their associated loss is given in Fig. 1.

The effect of the specific cover χ that is being used may be crucial: a cover of a small number of (large) disjoint sets typically induces a loss function which is primarily sensitive to the *existence* of a mistake and is indifferent to the exact nature of the induced total-order. In contrast, a cover which includes many sets each of which has only a small number of elements induces a loss that may be too detailed. The natural question that arises is what cover to use. Unfortunately, there is no general answer as the specific choice is domain and task dependent. For example, in the problem of optical character recognition we merely interested in whether a prediction error occurred

Parameters: γ ; C
Initialize: $w_r^1 = 0$ $(1 \le r \le k)$
Loop: For $i = 1, 2, \ldots, m$

- Get a new instance: $x^i \in \mathbb{R}^n$
- Predict:
  $$\hat{y}^i = (\langle w_1^i, x^i \rangle, \ldots, \langle w_k^i, x^i \rangle)$$
- Get a target y^i and its cover χ^i
- Suffer loss: $\mathbb{I}\left(W^i; (x^i; y^i; \chi^i)\right)$
- Set $\alpha_{r,s}^i$ to be the solution $\alpha_{r,s}$
  of Eq. (9) and Eq. (10)

- Set for $r = 1 \ldots k$: $\tau_r^i = \sum_{s=1}^k \alpha_{r,s}^i$

- Update for $r = 1, \ldots, k$:
  $$w_r^{i+1} = w_r^i + \tau_r^i x^i$$

Output:
$$h(x) = (\langle w_1^{m+1}, x \rangle, \ldots, \langle w_k^{m+1}, x \rangle)$$

Fig. 2. The additive algorithm

Parameters: γ ; C
Initialize: $w_{r,l}^1 = \frac{1}{nk}$ $(1 \le r \le k, 1 \le l \le n)$
Loop: For $i = 1, 2, \ldots, m$

- Get a new instance: $x^i \in \mathbb{R}^n$
- Predict:
  $$\hat{y}^i = (\langle w_1^i, x^i \rangle, \ldots, \langle w_k^i, x^i \rangle)$$
- Get a target y^i and its cover χ^i
- Suffer loss: $\mathbb{I}\left(W^i; (x^i; y^i; \chi^i)\right)$
- Set $\alpha_{r,s}^i$ to be the solution $\alpha_{r,s}$
  of Eq. (13) and Eq. (14)

- Set for $r = 1 \ldots k$: $\tau_r^i = \sum_{s=1}^k \alpha_{r,s}^i$

- Update for $r = 1, \ldots, k$:
  $$w_{r,l}^{i+1} = w_{r,l}^i \frac{e^{\tau_r^i x_l^i}}{Z^i}$$
  where $Z^i = \sum_{s,l} w_{s,l}^i e^{\tau_s^i x_l^i}$

Output:
$$h(x) = (\langle w_1^{m+1}, x \rangle, \ldots, \langle w_k^{m+1}, x \rangle)$$

Fig. 3. The multiplicative algorithm

---

or not. In contrast, in the problem of document categorization, where each document is associated with a subset of relevant categories, it seems more natural to ask how many categories were mis-placed by the total order. To underscore the dependency on the cover, we slightly extend our definitions and denote an example by a *triplet* (x, y, χ): an instance x, a target semi-order y, and a cover χ of y. Thus the choice of a loss function is made part of the problem description and is not a sub-task of the learning algorithm. Since the loss functions are parameterized by a cover χ of the target y we call them *cover loss functions*. To derive our algorithms, we use a generalization of the hinge loss which depends on a predefined insensitivity parameter γ and is defined as,

$$\mathbb{H}_\gamma\left(W; (x, y, \chi)\right) = \sum_{\chi \in \chi} \max_{(r,s) \in \chi} \left[\gamma - (\langle w_r, x \rangle - \langle w_s, x \rangle)\right]_+ . \tag{2}$$

It is straightforward to verify the bound $\gamma \mathbb{I}(W; (x, y, \chi)) \le \mathbb{H}_\gamma((x, y, \chi))$. Note that if the loss is equal to zero then, independently of the form of the specific loss being used, $\langle w_r, x \rangle - \langle w_s, x \rangle \ge \gamma$ for all $(r, s) \in y$.

2   An Additive Algorithm

In this section we present the first algorithm for category ranking which is based on an additive update. The motivation for the algorithm as well as its analysis build on previous research, in particular the MIRA algorithm and the Passive-Aggressive algorithm [9, 7]. As discussed above, we generalize these algorithms by considering a general class of loss functions and provide tighter loss bounds by modifying the dual problem described in the sequel. Throughout the paper we denote the norm of the a category-ranker W by $\|W\|$. This norm is defined as the norm of the vector obtained by concatenating the vectors w_r, $\|W\| = \|(w_1, \ldots, w_k)\|$. The core of the online algorithm is an update rule that receives the current ranker, denoted W^i, along with the newly observed instance x^i, a feedback y^i, and a cover χ^i. The next ranker W^{i+1} is set to be the solution of the following optimization problem,

$$W^{i+1} = \underset{W}{\operatorname{argmin}} \ \frac{1}{2}\|W - W^i\|_2^2 + \frac{C}{k-1}\mathbb{H}_\gamma\left(W; (x^i; y^i; \chi^i)\right) \ , \qquad (3)$$

where $C > 0$. The new ranker is thus the solution to a problem that is composed of two opposing terms. The role of the first term is to try to keep the new ranker W^{i+1} as close as possible to the current one, W^i. The second term solely focuses on the hinge-loss achieved by the new ranker on the newest example. Thus, the constant C encapsulates the tradeoff between the two terms.

Expanding the hinge-loss, we rewrite the optimization problem of Eq. (3) as,

$$\min_W \ \frac{1}{2}\|W - W^i\|_2^2 + C\sum_{\chi \in \chi^i} \xi_\chi \qquad (4)$$

$$\text{subject to}: \ \forall \chi \in \chi^i \ , \ \forall (r,s) \in \chi \ : \quad \langle w_r, x^i \rangle - \langle w_s, x^i \rangle \geq \gamma - \xi_\chi$$

$$\forall \chi \in \chi^i \ : \quad \xi_\chi \geq 0 \ ,$$

where $\xi_\chi \geq 0$ are slack variables. To characterize the solution W^{i+1} we use the dual form of Eq. (3) and Eq. (4). We do so by introducing the Lagrangian of the problem,

$$\mathcal{L}(W; \alpha) = \frac{1}{2}\sum_{r=1}^{k} \|w_r - w_r^i\|^2 + C\sum_{\chi \in \chi^i} \xi_\chi$$

$$+ \sum_{(r,s) \in y^i} \alpha_{r,s}^i \left(\gamma - \langle w_r, x^i \rangle + \langle w_s, x^i \rangle\right) - \sum_{\chi \in \chi^i} \beta_\chi \xi_\chi \ , \qquad (5)$$

where $\alpha_{r,s}^i \geq 0$ (defined only for pairs $(r,s) \in y^i$) are the Lagrange multipliers. Mundane calculus yields that,

$$w_p = w_p^i + \sum_{s \ : \ (p,s) \in y^i} \alpha_{p,s}^i x^i - \sum_{r \ : \ (r,p) \in y^i} \alpha_{r,p}^i x^i \qquad \text{for } 1 \leq p \leq k \ . \quad (6)$$

To simplify Eq. (6) and the form of the optimal solution we extend $\alpha_{r,s}$ to be defined over *all* pairs r, s. For each $(r,s) \in y^i$ we define $\alpha_{s,r} = -\alpha_{r,s}$. We also set $\alpha_{r,s} = 0$ for all other values of r and s. Using this extension of the Lagrange multipliers, Eq. (6) can be rewritten as,

$$w_r^{i+1} = w_r^i + \sum_s \alpha_{r,s}^i x^i \qquad \text{for } 1 \leq r \leq k \ . \qquad (7)$$

Finally, we write $\tau_r^i \overset{\text{def}}{=} \sum_s \alpha_{r,s}^i$ yielding the following update

$$w_r^{i+1} = w_r^i + \tau_r^i x^i \qquad \text{for } 1 \le r \le k \ . \tag{8}$$

Summing up, the resulting dual is,

$$\min_{\{\alpha_{r,s}^i\}} \frac{1}{2} \|x^i\|^2 \sum_{r=1}^k \left(\sum_s \alpha_{r,s}^i \right)^2 + \sum_{(r,s) \in y^i} \alpha_{r,s}^i \left(\langle w_r^i, x^i \rangle - \langle w_s^i, x^i \rangle - \gamma \right)$$

$$\text{s. t.:} \begin{cases} \alpha_{r,s}^i \ge 0 & (r,s) \in y^i \\ \alpha_{s,r}^i = -\alpha_{r,s}^i & (r,s) \in y^i \\ \alpha_{s,r}^i = 0 & \text{Otherwise} \end{cases} \qquad \forall \chi \in \chi^i : \ \sum_{(r,s) \in \chi} \alpha_{r,s}^i \le \frac{C}{k-1} \tag{9}$$

The transformation from the primal to the dual form is standard. However, the resulting dual form given by Eq. (9) imposes a rather major difficulty whenever the optimal solution does not satisfy *any* of the inequality constraints with equality. In this case there is no way to distinguish between different covers from the values of $\alpha_{r,s}$. Since the proofs of our loss bounds are based on bounding first the cumulative sum of $\alpha_{r,s}$, this problem precludes the derivation of mistake bounds that are sensitive to the specific cover that is used. We illustrate this difficulty with the following toy example. Assume that there are only three different categories and the instance space is the reals, $\mathcal{X} = \mathbb{R}$. Assume further that the ith weight vectors are $w_1^i = -0.5$, $w_2^i = 0$, $w_3^i = 2.5$. Let the ith example be $x^i = 1$ and $y^i = \{(1,2),(1,3)\}$. If we now set $C = 3$, we get that the optimal solution of the dual is the same for two different covers, $\chi^i = \{\{(1,2)\},\{(1,3)\}\}$ and $\chi^i = \{(1,2),(1,3)\}$. Thus, it is impossible to unravel from $\alpha_{r,s}^i$ what cover was used and any analysis must unify the two covers into a single loss bound.

To overcome the problem above, we impose a lower bound on the total sum of the Lagrange multipliers in each cover. By construction, this lower bound depends on the particular cover that is being used. Specifically, we replace the constraints on $\alpha_{r,s}$ with the following constraints that bound the total sum from above *and* below,

$$\forall \chi \in \chi^i : \ \frac{c^i}{k-1} [\![\{(r,s) \in \chi : (s,r) \in \hat{y}\} \neq \emptyset]\!] \le \sum_{(r,s) \in \chi} \alpha_{r,s}^i \le \frac{C}{k-1} \ , \tag{10}$$

where $c^i = \min\{C, 1/\|x^i\|^2\}$. Put another way, if the predicted total-order is consistent with all the elements of a specific cover $\chi \in \chi^i$, then the lower bound is kept at zero. Alas, if the order of some pair in a cover is not predicted perfectly, then we aggressively set a lower bound on the sum of the Lagrange multipliers corresponding to the cover. We discuss briefly the implications of this construction at the end of next section. The pseudocode of the algorithm is given in Fig. 2.

To derive a loss-bound for the additive algorithm we first bound the cumulative sum $\sum_{i,r,s} |\alpha_{r,s}^i|$ as given in Lemma 1 below. We then draw a connection between this bound and the bound on the cumulative loss suffered by the algorithm.

Lemma 1. *Let* $(x^1, y^1), \ldots, (x^m, y^m)$ *be an input sequence for the algorithm described in Fig. 2 where* $x^i \in \mathbb{R}^n$ *and* $y^i \in \mathcal{Y} \times \mathcal{Y}$ *is a semi-order. Let* $W^* \in \mathbb{R}^{n \times k}$ *be* *a collection of k vectors and $\gamma^* > 0$. Assume that the algorithm of Fig. 2 is run with a parameter $C > 0$. Fix $\gamma > 0$, and let $\alpha^i_{r,s}$ be the optimal solution of Eq. (9) with a modified set of constraints given in Eq. (10). Then, the following bound holds,*

$$\sum_{i,r,s} |\alpha^i_{r,s}| \leq 4\frac{1}{\gamma^{*2}} \|W^*\|^2 + 4\frac{C}{(k-1)\gamma^*} \sum_i \mathbb{H}_{\gamma^*}\left(W^*; (x^i; y^i; \chi^i)\right) .$$

The proof is omitted due to the lack of space. The skeleton of the proof is similar to the proof of Lemma 2 which is given in the next section. Before stating the main theorem of this section, we would like to make a few comments in passing. First, whenever the category ranking is perfectly consistent with the feedback on all examples, then the right term of the bound above vanishes for a proper choice of W^*. Second, the bound still holds when solving the optimization problem given by Eq. (9) without the additional constraints provided in Eq. (10). However, as discussed above we incorporated the set of additional constraints since they enables us to cast the cumulative loss bound stated in the theorem below.

Theorem 1. *Assume that all the instances reside in a ball of radius R ($\forall i : \|x^i\|_2 \leq R$) and that $C \geq \gamma/R^2$. Then, under the same terms stated in Lemma 1 the cumulative cover loss the algorithm suffers is upper bounded by,*

$$\sum_i \mathbb{I}\left(W^i; (x^i; y^i; \chi^i)\right) \leq 2(k-1)\frac{R^2}{\gamma^{*2}} \|W^*\|^2 + 2\frac{C}{\gamma}\frac{R^2}{\gamma^*} \sum_i \mathbb{H}_{\gamma^*}\left(W^*; (x^i; y^i; \chi^i)\right) .$$

Thm. 1 tells us that the cumulative loss of the algorithm with respect to a given cover, is bounded by the hinge-loss suffered by *any* category plus a term that depends on the norm of ranker. The dependency on the number of different labels is distilled to a single factor: the multiplier of the ranker's norm, which is proportional to k. Furthermore, the dependency of the bound in the meta-parameters γ and C appears only through their ratio, and thus one of these parameters can be set to an arbitrary value, often we set $\gamma = 1$.

3   A Multiplicative Algorithm

In this section we describe a multiplicative algorithm for category ranking. As in the previous section, the algorithm maintains a collection of k weight vectors. In the case of the multiplicative update we add a constraint on the ranker by forcing the ℓ_1 norm of W^i to be one for all i. We further assume that all the components of W^i are non-negative. The resulting update incorporates these constraints for each new vector it constructs. On round i the new ranker W^{i+1} is again the minimizer of a constrained optimization problem which is similar to the one given in Eq. (3). The main difference is that we replace the Euclidean norm appearing in Eq. (3) with the Kullback-Leibler (KL) divergence [5]. The KL-divergence, also known as the relative entropy, is used in information theory and statistics to measure the discrepancy between information sources. The resulting constrained optimization that yields the multiplicative update is,

$$W^{i+1} = \underset{W}{\operatorname{argmin}} \, D_{\text{KL}}\left(W \,\|\, W^i\right) + \frac{2C}{k(k-1)}\mathbb{H}_{\gamma}\left(W; (x^i; y^i; \chi^i)\right) \quad \text{s.t.} \, \|W\|_1 = 1 .$$

$$(11)$$

We show in the sequel that the resulting update has a multiplicative form. As the additive update, the multiplicative update can be employed with any cover that satisfies the requirements listed above. The pseudocode of the algorithm is given in Fig. 3. Before proceeding to the derivation of the multiplicative update and its loss bound analysis we would like to underscore two important difference between the additive update of previous section and the multiplicative update. Setting $C = \infty$ puts all the emphasis on the empirical loss of the most recent example. In the additive case this results in a solution W^{i+1} such that $\mathbb{H}_\gamma \left(W^{i+1}; (\boldsymbol{x}^i; \boldsymbol{y}^i; \chi^i) \right) = 0$. However, due to the additional constraint that $\|W^i\|_1 = 1$ the inner products $\langle \boldsymbol{w}_r, \boldsymbol{x}^i \rangle$ are upper bounded by $\|\boldsymbol{x}^i\|_\infty$. Hence, depending on γ, it may be impossible to achieve a zero hinge-loss with W^{i+1} even when C is arbitrarily large. Second, note that the loss term is weighed differently in both algorithms: we use a factor of $1/(k-1)$ (Eq. (3)) for the additive algorithm and a factor of $2/(k(k-1))$ (Eq. (11)) for the multiplicative one. This difference is due to the conversion phase, described in the sequel, of the bounds on the weights into loss bounds.

To derive an update rule we use the dual form of Eq. (11). Similar to Eq. (3) we write the constraints explicitly, compute the corresponding Lagrangian, and get that the lth component of the optimal solution satisfies,

$$\log \left(\boldsymbol{w}_{p,l}\right) = \log \left(\boldsymbol{w}_{p,l}^i\right) + \sum_{s \,:\, (p,s)\in\boldsymbol{y}^i} \alpha_{p,s}^i x_l^i - \sum_{r \,:\, (r,p)\in\boldsymbol{y}^i} \alpha_{r,p}^i x_l^i - \beta \,. \qquad (12)$$

Taking the exponent of both sides of the above equation results in the multiplicative update described in Fig. 3 where $e^\beta = Z^i$. Similar to the line of derivation following Eq. (6) we simplify Eq. (12) by extending the definition of the Lagrange multipliers $\alpha_{r,s}^i$ to be defined over all r and s. The end result is the following dual problem,

$$\max_{\{\alpha_{r,s}^i\}} \; -\log \left(Z^i\right) + \gamma \sum_{(r,s)\in\boldsymbol{y}^i} \alpha_{r,s}^i$$

$$\text{subject to:} \; \begin{cases} \alpha_{r,s}^i \geq 0 & (r,s) \in \boldsymbol{y}^i \\ \alpha_{s,r}^i = -\alpha_{r,s}^i & (r,s) \in \boldsymbol{y}^i \\ \alpha_{s,r}^i = 0 & \text{Otherwise} \end{cases} \quad \forall \chi \in \chi^i : \sum_{(r,s)\in\chi} \alpha_{r,s}^i \leq \frac{2C}{k(k-1)} \,. \qquad (13)$$

Finally, as in the additive update we impose an additional set of constrains that cast a lower bound on each $\alpha_{r,s}^i$,

$$\forall \chi \in \chi^i \; : \; \frac{2c^i}{k(k-1)} [\![\{(r,s) \in \chi : (s,r) \in \hat{\boldsymbol{y}}\} \neq \emptyset]\!] \leq \sum_{(r,s)\in\chi} \alpha_{r,s}^i \,. \qquad (14)$$

where c^i depends on the ℓ_∞ norm of $\boldsymbol{x}^i$ and is equal to,

$$c^i = \min \left\{ \frac{\log \left(1 + \frac{\gamma}{\|\boldsymbol{x}^i\|_\infty}\right)}{\|\boldsymbol{x}^i\|_\infty}, C \right\} \,.$$

The technique for deriving a loss bound for the multiplicative update is similar the one used for the additive update, yet it is more involved. We first find a bound on the cumulative sum of coefficients $\alpha^i_{r,s}$. Then, we tie the cover loss with the value of the coefficients $\alpha^i_{r,s}$ which enables us to derive a loss bound.

Lemma 2. *Let* $(\boldsymbol{x}^1, \boldsymbol{y}^1), \ldots, (\boldsymbol{x}^m, \boldsymbol{y}^m)$ *be an input sequence for the algorithm described in Fig. 3 where* $\boldsymbol{x}^i \in \mathbb{R}^n$ *and* $\boldsymbol{y}^i \in \mathcal{Y} \times \mathcal{Y}$ *is a semi-order. Assume that the algorithm is run with a parameter* $C \geq 0$ *and a margin parameter* $\gamma > 0$. *Let* $\{\alpha^i_{r,s}\}$ *be the minimizer of Eq. (13) with the additional constraints given in Eq. (14). Let* $W^* \in \mathbb{R}^{n \times k}$ *be any collection of k vectors such that* $\|W^*\|_1 = 1$ *and fix* $\gamma^* > \gamma$. *Then, the cumulative sum of coefficients is upper bounded by,*

$$\sum_i \sum_{(r,s)} |\alpha^i_{r,s}| \leq 2 \frac{\log(kn)}{\gamma^* - \gamma} + 4 \frac{C}{k(k-1)(\gamma^* - \gamma)} \sum_i \mathbb{H}_{\gamma^*} \left(W^*; (\boldsymbol{x}^i; \boldsymbol{y}^i; \boldsymbol{\chi}^i) \right) .$$

Proof. Define $\Delta_i = D_{KL}\left(W^* \| W^i \right) - D_{KL}\left(W^* \| W^{i+1} \right)$. We prove the lemma by bounding $\sum_{i=1}^m \Delta_i$ from above and below. First note that $\sum_{i=1}^m \Delta_i$ is a telescopic sum and therefore,

$$\sum_{i=1}^m \Delta_i = D_{KL}\left(W^* \| W^1 \right) - D_{KL}\left(W^* \| W^{m+1} \right) \leq D_{KL}\left(W^* \| W^1 \right) .$$

Using the definition of D_{KL} and substituting the value of $\boldsymbol{w}^1_{r,l}$ with $1/(nk)$ we get,

$$\sum_{i=1}^m \Delta_i \leq \sum_{r,l} \boldsymbol{w}^*_{r,l} \log\left(\frac{\boldsymbol{w}^*_{r,l}}{1/nk} \right) = \log(nk) + \sum_{r,l} \boldsymbol{w}^*_{r,l} \log\left(\boldsymbol{w}^*_{r,l} \right) \leq \log(nk) , \quad (15)$$

where the last inequality holds since $\boldsymbol{w}^*_{r,l} \leq 1$. This provides an upper bound on $\sum_i \Delta_i$. In the following we prove a lower bound on Δ_i. Expanding Δ_i we get,

$$\begin{aligned}
\Delta_i &= D_{KL}\left(W^* \| W^i \right) - D_{KL}\left(W^* \| W^{i+1} \right) \\
&= \sum_{r,l} \left(\boldsymbol{w}^*_{r,l} \log \frac{\boldsymbol{w}^*_{r,l}}{\boldsymbol{w}^i_{r,l}} - \boldsymbol{w}^*_{r,l} \log \frac{\boldsymbol{w}^*_{r,l}}{\boldsymbol{w}^{i+1}_{r,l}} \right) \\
&= \sum_{r,l} \boldsymbol{w}^*_{r,l} \log\left(\frac{e^{\sum_s \alpha^i_{r,s} \boldsymbol{x}^i_l}}{Z^i} \right) \\
&= -\log(Z^i) \sum_{r,l} \boldsymbol{w}^*_{r,l} + \sum_{r,s,l} \alpha^i_{r,s} \boldsymbol{w}^*_{r,l} \boldsymbol{x}^i_l \\
&= -\log(Z^i) \sum_{r,l} \boldsymbol{w}^*_{r,l} + \sum_{r,s} \alpha^i_{r,s} \left\langle \boldsymbol{w}^*_r, \boldsymbol{x}^i \right\rangle .
\end{aligned} \quad (16)$$

We rewrite the right term of the last equality above as,

$$\sum_{r,s} \alpha^i_{r,s} \left\langle \boldsymbol{w}^*_r, \boldsymbol{x}^i \right\rangle = \sum_{(r,s) \in \boldsymbol{y}^i} \alpha^i_{r,s} \left(\left\langle \boldsymbol{w}^*_r, \boldsymbol{x}^i \right\rangle - \left\langle \boldsymbol{w}^*_s, \boldsymbol{x}^i \right\rangle \right) . \quad (17)$$

Substituting Eq. (17) in Eq. (16) while using the constraint that $\|W^*\|_1 = 1$ we get,

$$\begin{aligned}
\Delta_i &= -\log\left(Z^i \right) + \sum_{(r,s) \in \boldsymbol{y}^i} \alpha^i_{r,s} \left(\left\langle \boldsymbol{w}^*_r, \boldsymbol{x}^i \right\rangle - \left\langle \boldsymbol{w}^*_s, \boldsymbol{x}^i \right\rangle \right) \\
&= -\log\left(Z^i \right) + \gamma \sum_{(r,s) \in \boldsymbol{y}^i} \alpha^i_{r,s}
\end{aligned} \quad (18)$$

$$-\gamma \sum_{(r,s) \in \boldsymbol{y}^i} \alpha^i_{r,s} + \sum_{(r,s) \in \boldsymbol{y}^i} \alpha^i_{r,s} \left(\left\langle \boldsymbol{w}^*_r, \boldsymbol{x}^i \right\rangle - \left\langle \boldsymbol{w}^*_s, \boldsymbol{x}^i \right\rangle \right) . \quad (19)$$

We thus decomposed Δ_i into two parts denoted by Eq. (18) and Eq. (19). Note that Eq. (18) is equal to the objective of dual optimization problem given in Eq. (13). We now show that there exists a feasible assignment (not necessary the optimal one) of the variables $\alpha_{r,s}^i$ for which

$$-\log\left(Z^i\right) + \gamma \sum_{(r,s)\in\boldsymbol{y}^i} \alpha_{r,s}^i \geq 0 \ . \tag{20}$$

Therefore, the optimal solution of Eq. (13) should also satisfy the inequality above. We hence get that Δ_i is lower bounded solely by the term given in Eq. (19).

To describe a set of feasible values to the parameters $\alpha_{r,s}^i$ we assume that $\{(r,s) \in \chi : (s,r) \in \hat{\boldsymbol{y}}\}$ is not empty. That is, there is a mis-ordered pair in the set χ. We set $\alpha_{r,s}^i = 2c^i/(k(k-1))$ and set all other values $\alpha_{r',s'}^i$ to zero. For brevity we denote by $b^i = \|\boldsymbol{x}^i\|_\infty \sum_{(r,s)\in\boldsymbol{y}^i} \alpha_{r,s}^i$. We thus get

$$x_l^i \sum_s \alpha_{r,s}^i \leq \|\boldsymbol{x}^i\|_\infty \sum_{(r,s)\in\boldsymbol{y}^i} \alpha_{r,s}^i \leq b^i \ .$$

We upper bound Z^i as follows,

$$Z^i = \sum_{r,l} w_{r,l}^i e^{x_l^i \sum_p \alpha_{r,p}}$$

$$\leq \sum_{r,l} w_{r,l}^i \left(\frac{b^i + x_l^i \sum_p \alpha_{r,p}}{2b^i} e^{b^i} + \frac{b^i - x_l^i \sum_p \alpha_{r,p}}{2b^i} e^{-b^i} \right)$$

$$= \sum_{r,l} w_{r,l}^i \left(\frac{e^{b^i} + e^{-b^i}}{2} \right) + \sum_{r,s,l} \alpha_{r,s}^i w_{r,l}^i x_l^i \left(\frac{e^{b^i} - e^{-b^i}}{2} \right)$$

$$= \cosh(b^i) + \sinh(b^i) \sum_{(r,s)\in\boldsymbol{y}^i} \alpha_{r,s}^i \left(\langle w_r^i, \boldsymbol{x}^i \rangle - \langle w_s^i, \boldsymbol{x}^i \rangle \right)$$

$$\leq \cosh(b^i) \ ,$$

where the first inequality follows from the convexity of the exponential function and the last inequality holds since either $\alpha_{r,s}^i > 0$ and $\left(\langle w_r^i, \boldsymbol{x}^i \rangle - \langle w_s^i, \boldsymbol{x}^i \rangle \right) < 0$, or $\alpha_{r,s}^i = 0$. Therefore we get that the objective function is lower bounded by,

$$-\log(\cosh(b^i)) + \gamma \sum_{(r,s)\in\boldsymbol{y}^i} \alpha_{r,s}^i = -\log(\cosh(b^i)) + \gamma \frac{b^i}{\|\boldsymbol{x}^i\|_\infty} \ .$$

Our particular choice of $\alpha_{r,s}^i$ implies that,

$$b^i = \|\boldsymbol{x}^i\|_\infty \sum_{(r,s)\in\boldsymbol{y}^i} \alpha_{r,s} = c^i \|\boldsymbol{x}^i\|_\infty 2 \frac{\mathbb{I}\left(W^i; (\boldsymbol{x}^i; \boldsymbol{y}^i; \boldsymbol{\chi}^i)\right)}{k(k-1)} \tag{21}$$

for $c^i \in \left[0, \frac{\log(1+\frac{\gamma}{\|\boldsymbol{x}^i\|_\infty})}{\|\boldsymbol{x}^i\|_\infty}\right]$. It can be shown that $\log(\cosh(b^i)) - \gamma b^i/\|\boldsymbol{x}^i\|_\infty \leq 0$ both for $c^i = 0$ and for $c^i = \log(1+\frac{\gamma}{\|\boldsymbol{x}^i\|_\infty})/\|\boldsymbol{x}^i\|_\infty$ (note that b^i is proportional to c^i). From the convexity of $f(b^i) = \log(\cosh(b^i)) - \gamma b^i / \|x^i\|_\infty$ it follows that $\log(\cosh(b^i)) - \gamma b^i / \|x^i\|_\infty \le 0$ for all feasible values of b^i.

We thus proved that the value of Eq. (18) is lower bounded by 0. This yields the following lower bound on Δ_i,

$$\Delta_i \ge \sum_{(r,s)\in y^i} \alpha^i_{r,s} \left(\langle w^*_r, x^i \rangle - \langle w^*_s, x^i \rangle \right) - \sum_{(r,s)\in y^i} \alpha^i_{r,s} \gamma . \tag{22}$$

We further develop the first term and get,

$$\sum_{(r,s)\in y^i} \alpha^i_{r,s} \left(\langle w^*_r, x^i \rangle - \langle w^*_s, x^i \rangle \right)$$

$$\ge \sum_{(r,s)\in y^i} \alpha^i_{r,s} \left(\gamma^* - [\gamma^* - \langle w^*_r, x^i \rangle + \langle w^*_s, x^i \rangle]_+ \right)$$

$$\ge -\sum_{\chi\in x^i} \left(\sum_{(r,s)\in \chi} \alpha^i_{r,s} \right) \max_{(r,s)\in \chi} [\gamma^* - \langle w^*_r, x^i \rangle + \langle w^*_s, x^i \rangle]_+ + \sum_{\chi\in x^i} \sum_{(r,s)\in \chi} \alpha^i_{r,s} \gamma^* . \tag{23}$$

Finally, using the upper bound of Eq. (14) we lower bound the left term in the last equation with $-\frac{2C}{k(k-1)} \mathbb{H}_{\gamma^*} \left(W^*; (x^i; y^i; \chi^i) \right)$. Thus,

$$\Delta_i \ge -2\frac{C}{k(k-1)} \mathbb{H}_{\gamma^*} \left(W^*; (x^i; y^i; \chi^i) \right) + \frac{1}{2}(\gamma^* - \gamma) \sum_{r,s} |\alpha^i_{r,s}| \tag{24}$$

Substituting Eq. (24) in Eq. (15) we get,

$$\frac{1}{2}(\gamma^* - \gamma) \sum_i \sum_{(r,s)} |\alpha^i_{r,s}| \le \log(kn) + 2\frac{C}{k(k-1)} \mathbb{H}_{\gamma^*} \left(W^*; (x^i; y^i; \chi^i) \right) ,$$

which yields the desired bound.   ∎

As in the analysis of the additive update, the bound holds true also when the the optimization problem given by Eq. (13) is *not* augmented with the additional constraints provided in Eq. (14). These additional constraints however are instrumental in the proof of the following theorem.

Theorem 2. *Assume that all the instances lie in a cube of width R ($\|x^i\|_\infty \le R$) and that $C \ge \frac{\log(1+\frac{\gamma}{R})}{R}$. Under the assumptions of Lemma 2, the cumulative loss is bounded above by,*

$$\sum_i \mathbb{I} \left(W^i; (x^i; y^i; \chi^i) \right) \le$$

$$\frac{1}{2} \frac{R k(k-1) \log(kn)}{\log\left(1+\frac{\gamma}{R}\right)(\gamma^* - \gamma)} + \frac{RC}{\log\left(1+\frac{\gamma}{R}\right)(\gamma^* - \gamma)} \mathbb{H}_{\gamma^*} \left(W^*; (x^i; y^i; \chi^i) \right) .$$

The lemma and the theorem state that for each value of γ used in the algorithm there is a feasible range of values of the margin parameter γ^*. Furthermore, if the value of γ^* is known to the algorithm in advance, then the value of the margin parameter γ can be set to provide the tightest upper bound as follows. Using the concavity of the log function we get that $\log(1 + x) \geq x$ and since we assume in Thm. 2 that $C \geq \gamma/R^2$, then the bound on the loss that is stated in the theorem becomes,

$$\frac{1}{2}\frac{Rk(k-1)\log(kn)}{(\gamma/R)(\gamma^* - \gamma)} + \frac{RC}{(\gamma/R)(\gamma^* - \gamma)}\mathbb{H}_{\gamma^*}\left(W^*;(\boldsymbol{x}^i;\boldsymbol{y}^i;\boldsymbol{\chi}^i)\right).$$

The above bound is minimized by setting $\gamma = \gamma^*/2$. Substituting this value in the bound we obtain,

$$\sum_i \mathbb{I}\left(W^i;(\boldsymbol{x}^i;\boldsymbol{y}^i;\boldsymbol{\chi}^i)\right) \leq 2\frac{R^2k(k-1)\log(kn)}{\gamma^{*2}} + 4\frac{R^2C}{\gamma^{*2}}\mathbb{H}_{\gamma^*}\left(W^*;(\boldsymbol{x}^i;\boldsymbol{y}^i;\boldsymbol{\chi}^i)\right).$$

Substituting the optimal value for C which is $\gamma^*/(2R^2)$ we finally obtain,

$$\sum_i \mathbb{I}\left(W^i;(\boldsymbol{x}^i;\boldsymbol{y}^i;\boldsymbol{\chi}^i)\right) \leq 2k(k-1)\log(kn)\frac{R^2}{\gamma^{*2}} + \frac{2}{\gamma^*}\mathbb{H}_{\gamma^*}\left(W^*;(\boldsymbol{x}^i;\boldsymbol{y}^i;\boldsymbol{\chi}^i)\right). \quad (25)$$

Before proceeding to the next section let us summarize the results obtained thus far. Similar algorithms [9,7] were designed for simple prediction problems. As a consequence the update schemes for these algorithms take closed forms. Their analyses in turn strive on the existence of an exact form solution. In this paper we address the more complex problem of category ranking for which there is no close form for the update. To analyze these algorithms the optimization problems that constitute the infrastructure for the update were augmented with additional constraints. Mathematically, these constraints are equivalent to additional *negative* slack variables in the primal optimization problem. The understanding of the semantics of these variables require further investigation. Nonetheless, this construction forces each Lagrange multipliers to attain a minimal value and distinguishes between the solutions obtained for different covers.

4   Category-Ranking Based on Bregman Divergences

The additive and multiplicative algorithms described in previous sections share a similar structure. On each iteration the online algorithms attempt to minimize the loss associated with the instantaneous category task while attempting to keep the new ranker, designated by W^{i+1}, as "close" as possible to W^i. The additive algorithm uses the square of the Euclidean distance as the means for encapsulating quantitatively the notion of closeness while the multiplicative algorithm uses the KL-divergence for that purpose. In this section we overview a unified approach that is based on Bregman divergences [2]. We would like not that while the use of the Bregman divergences in the context of category ranking problems is new, Bregman divergences have been used extensively in other learning settings (see for instance [11, 1, 4]).

A Bregman divergence is defined via a strictly convex function $F : \mathcal{X} \to \mathbb{R}$ which is defined on a closed convex set $\mathcal{X} \subseteq \mathbb{R}^n$. A Bregman function F needs to satisfy a set of constraints. We omit the description of the specific constraints and refer the reader to [3]. We further impose that F is continuously differentiable at all points of $\mathcal{X}_{\text{int}}$ (the interior of $\mathcal{X}$) which is assumed to be nonempty. The Bregman divergence that is associated with F applied to $x \in \mathcal{X}$ and $w \in \mathcal{X}_{\text{int}}$ is defined to be

$$B_F (x \| w) \overset{\text{def}}{=} F(x) - [F(w) + \nabla F(w) \cdot (x - w)] .$$

Thus, B_F measures the difference between two functions evaluated at x. The first is the function F itself and the second is the first-order Taylor expansion of F derived at w. The divergences we employ are defined via a single *scalar* convex function f such that $F(x) = \sum_{l=1}^{n} f(x_l)$, where x_l is the lth coordinate of x. The resulting Bregman divergence between x and w is thus, $B_F (x \| w) = \sum_{l=1}^{n} B_f (x_l \| w_l)$. The two divergences described in the previous section can be obtained by choosing $f(x) = (1/2) x^2$ (squared Euclidean) and $f(x) = x \log(x) - x$ (KL-divergence). For the latter we also restrict $\mathcal{X}$ to the probability simplex $\Delta_n = \{ x \mid x_l \geq 0 \, ; \sum_l x_l = 1 \}$.

We now describe an online category-ranking algorithm that can be applied with any Bregman divergence. However, the generality of the algorithm comes with a cost. Namely, the algorithm and its corresponding analysis are designed for the case where there exists a ranker W^* which is consistent with all the semi-orders that are given as feedbacks. Equipped with this assumption, the new category-ranker W^{i+1} is defined as the solution of the following problem,

$$W^{i+1} = \underset{W}{\operatorname{argmin}} \, B_F (W \| W^i) \qquad \text{s.t.} \qquad \mathbb{H}_\gamma (W; (x^i; y^i)) = 0 , \qquad (26)$$

That is, W^{i+1} is chosen among all rankers which attain a zero hinge loss on the current instance-label pair. Due to our assumption this set is not empty. The ranker that is chosen is the one whose Bregman divergence w.r.t the current ranker W^i is the smallest.

Before providing the main result of this section let us elaborate on the form of the dual of Eq. (26) and the resulting solution. Writing explicitly the constraint given in Eq. (26) we get that,

$$W^{i+1} = \underset{W}{\operatorname{argmin}} \, B_F (W \| W^i) \qquad \text{s.t.} \qquad \langle w_r, x^i \rangle - \langle w_s, x^i \rangle \geq \gamma, \ \forall (r, s) \in y^i . \quad (27)$$

The corresponding Lagrangian of this optimization problem is,

$$\mathcal{L}(W; \alpha) = \sum_{r=1}^{k} B_F (w_r \| w_r^i) + \sum_{(r,s) \in y^i} \alpha_{r,s}^i (\gamma - \langle w_r, x^i \rangle + \langle w_s, x^i \rangle) , \quad (28)$$

where $\alpha_{r,s}^i \geq 0$ (for $(r, s) \in y^i$) are Lagrange multipliers and we expanded W into its constituents w_r. To find a saddle point of $\mathcal{L}$ we first set to zero the derivative of $\mathcal{L}$ with respect to w_p for all p and get,

$$\nabla F (w_p) = \nabla F (w_p^i) + \sum_{s \, : \, (p,s) \in y^i} \alpha_{p,s}^i x^i - \sum_{r \, : \, (r,p) \in y^i} \alpha_{r,p}^i x^i . \quad (29)$$

The last equation generalizes both Eq. (6) and Eq. (12) for the Euclidean distance and the KL-divergence, respectively. As before we expand $\alpha_{r,s}$ to be defined over all r and s and get that,

$$\nabla F\left(\boldsymbol{w}_r\right) = \nabla F\left(\boldsymbol{w}_r^i\right) + \sum_s \alpha_{r,s}^i \boldsymbol{x}^i \stackrel{\text{def}}{=} \nabla F\left(\boldsymbol{w}_r^i\right) + \tau_r^i \boldsymbol{x}^i . \tag{30}$$

We thus found an *implicit* form of W^{i+1}. Substituting Eq. (30) back in the Lagrangian of Eq. (28) we obtain the dual problem,

$$\min_{\{\alpha_{r,s}^i\}} \sum_{r=1}^{k} B_F\left(\nabla F^{-1}\left(\nabla F\left(\boldsymbol{w}_r^i\right) + \sum_s \alpha_{r,s}^i \boldsymbol{x}^i\right) \| \boldsymbol{w}_r^i\right)$$

$$+ \sum_{(r,s)\in \boldsymbol{y}^i} \alpha_{r,s}^i \left(\gamma - \left\langle \nabla F^{-1}\left(\nabla F\left(\boldsymbol{w}_r^i\right) + \sum_s \alpha_{r,s}^i \boldsymbol{x}^i\right), \boldsymbol{x}^i\right\rangle\right.$$

$$\left. + \left\langle \nabla F^{-1}\left(\nabla F\left(\boldsymbol{w}_s^i\right) + \sum_r \alpha_{s,r}^i \boldsymbol{x}^i\right), \boldsymbol{x}^i\right\rangle\right),$$

$$\text{subject to:} \begin{cases} \alpha_{r,s}^i \geq 0 & (r,s) \in \boldsymbol{y}^i \\ \alpha_{s,r}^i = -\alpha_{r,s}^i & (r,s) \in \boldsymbol{y}^i \\ \alpha_{s,r}^i = 0 & \text{Otherwise} \end{cases} \tag{31}$$

where $\nabla F^{-1}(\cdot)$ is the component-wise inverse of $\nabla F(\cdot)$. It is well defined since F is strictly convex and thus ∇F is strictly monotone. It remains to describe how we set the initial ranker W^1. To be consistent with the choice of initial ranker made for the additive and multiplicative algorithms, we set $W^1 = \arg\min_W F(W)$.

The lemma below states that the cumulative sum of the dual parameters $\alpha_{r,s}^i$ is bounded. In return, this lemma can be used to derive specific loss bounds that for particular Bregman divergences.

Lemma 3. *Let $(\boldsymbol{x}^1, \boldsymbol{y}^1), \ldots, (\boldsymbol{x}^m, \boldsymbol{y}^m)$ be an input sequence for the algorithm whose update rule is described in Eq. (26) where $\boldsymbol{x}^i \in \mathbb{R}^n$ and $\boldsymbol{y}^i \in \mathcal{Y} \times \mathcal{Y}$ is a semi-order. Let $W^* \in \mathbb{R}^{n \times k}$ be a collection of k vectors which attains a positive margin $\gamma^* > 0$ on the sequence, $\gamma^* = \min_i \min_{(r,s)\in \boldsymbol{y}^i}\{\langle \boldsymbol{w}_r^*, \boldsymbol{x}^i\rangle - \langle \boldsymbol{w}_s^*, \boldsymbol{x}^i\rangle\} > 0$. Let B_F be a Bregman divergence derived from a convex function F. Then, for any value of $c > \gamma/\gamma^*$ the cumulative sum of coefficients is bounded by,*

$$\sum_i \sum_{(r,s)} |\alpha_{r,s}^i| \leq \frac{F(cW^*) - F(W^1)}{c\gamma^* - \gamma} .$$

The proof is omitted due to lack of space however we would like to discuss specific choices of Bregman divergences. If the Bregman function F is p-homogeneous, $F(a\boldsymbol{x}) = a^p F(\boldsymbol{x})$ for $p > 1$ and $W^1 = 0$ then the bound is minimized by setting, $c = \frac{\gamma}{(p-1)\gamma^*}$. In this case the bound becomes,

$$F(W^*)(p-1)\gamma^{p-1}\left(\frac{p}{(p-1)\gamma^*}\right)^p .$$

If the Bregman function F is homogeneous, $F(ax) = aF(x)$. Then the bound is minimized by setting $c \to \infty$, and we obtain that the bound on the cumulative weights is simply, $\frac{F(W^*)}{\gamma^*}$.

To conclude the paper we like to mention some open problems. First, comparing the bounds of the additive algorithm and the multiplicative algorithm we see that the bound of the additive update is k times smaller than that of the multiplicative update. This rather large gap between the two updates is not exhibited in other problems online prediction prboems. We are not sure yet whether the gap is an artifact of the analysis technique or a property of the category ranking problem. Second, currently we were not able to convert Lemma 3 into a mistake bound similar to Thm. 1and Thm. 2. We leave this problem to future research. Third, it is straightforward to employ the online updates based on Eq. (9) and Eq. (13) in a batch setting. However, it is not clear whether the additional constraints on the dual variables given in Eq. (10) and Eq. (14) can be translated into a sensible batch paradigm. The lower bounds on the weights depend on the instantaneous loss the algorithm suffers where in a batch setting this notion of temporal loss does not exist.

Acknowledgments. We are in debt to the chairs and members of program committee of COLT'05 for their constructive and thoughtful comments. This research was funded by EU Project PASCAL and by the Israeli Science Foundation grant number 522/04. Most of this work was carried out at the Hebrew University of Jerusalem.

References

1. K.S. Azoury and M.W. Warmuth. Relative loss bounds for on-line density estimation with the exponential family of distributions. *Machine Learning*, 43(3):211–246, 2001.
2. L. M. Bregman. The relaxation method of finding the common point of convex sets and its application to the solution of problems in convex programming. *USSR Computational Mathematics and Mathematical Physics*, 7:200–217, 1967.
3. Y. Censor and S.A. Zenios. *Parallel Optimization: Theory, Algorithms, and Applications*. Oxford University Press, New York, NY, USA, 1997.
4. M. Collins, R.E. Schapire, and Y. Singer. Logistic regression, AdaBoost and Bregman distances. *Machine Learning*, 47(2/3):253–285, 2002.
5. T. M. Cover and J. A. Thomas. *Elements of Information Theory*. Wiley, 1991.
6. K. Crammer. *Online Learning for Complex Categorial Problems*. PhD thesis, Hebrew University of Jerusalem, 2005. to appear.
7. K. Crammer, O. Dekel, S. Shalev-Shwartz, and Y. Singer. Online passive aggressive algorithms. In *Advances in Neural Information Processing Systems 16*, 2003.
8. K. Crammer and Y. Singer. A new family of online algorithms for category ranking. *Jornal of Machine Learning Research*, 3:1025–1058, 2003.
9. K. Crammer and Y. Singer. Ultraconservative online algorithms for multiclass problems. *Jornal of Machine Learning Research*, 3:951–991, 2003.
10. A. Elisseeff and J. Weston. A kernel method for multi-labeled classification. In *Advances in Neural Information Processing Systems 14*, 2001.
11. C. Gentile and M. Warmuth. Linear hinge loss and average margin. In *Advances in Neural Information Processing Systems 10*, 1998.
12. R. E. Schapire and Y. Singer. Improved boosting algorithms using confidence-rated predictions. *Machine Learning*, 37(3):1–40, 1999.

Margin-Based Ranking Meets Boosting in the Middle*

Cynthia Rudin[1], Corinna Cortes[2], and Mehryar Mohri[3],
and Robert E. Schapire[4]

[1] Howard Hughes Medical Institute, New York University,
4 Washington Place, Room 809, New York, NY 10003
rudin@nyu.edu
[2] Google Research, 1440 Broadway, New York, NY 10018
corinna@google.com
[3] Courant Institute, New York University, 719 Broadway,
New York, NY 10003
mohri@cs.nyu.edu
[4] Princeton University, Department of Computer Science,
35 Olden St., Princeton NJ 08544
schapire@cs.princeton.edu

Abstract. We present several results related to ranking. We give a general margin-based bound for ranking based on the L_∞ covering number of the hypothesis space. Our bound suggests that algorithms that maximize the ranking margin generalize well.

We then describe a new algorithm, Smooth Margin Ranking, that precisely converges to a maximum ranking-margin solution. The algorithm is a modification of RankBoost, analogous to Approximate Coordinate Ascent Boosting.

We also prove a remarkable property of AdaBoost: under very natural conditions, AdaBoost maximizes the exponentiated loss associated with the AUC and achieves the same AUC as RankBoost. This explains the empirical observations made by Cortes and Mohri, and Caruana and Niculescu-Mizil, about the excellent performance of AdaBoost as a ranking algorithm, as measured by the AUC.

1   Introduction

Consider the following supervised learning problem: Sylvia would like to get some recommendations for good movies before she goes to the theater. She would like a ranked list that agrees with her tastes as closely as possible, since she will see the movie closest to the top of the list that is playing at the local theater. For many pairs of movies she has seen, she will tell the learning algorithm whether she likes the first movie better than the second. This allows her to rank whichever pairs of movies she wishes, allowing for the possibility of ties between movies, and the

---

* This work is partially supported by NSF grant CCR-0325463.

P. Auer and R. Meir (Eds.): COLT 2005, LNAI 3559, pp. 63–78, 2005.
© Springer-Verlag Berlin Heidelberg 2005

possibility that certain movies cannot necessarily be compared by her, e.g, she may not compare action movies with cartoons. Another advantage of this type of scoring over real-valued scoring is that Sylvia does not need to normalize her own scores in order to compare with the rankings of another person; she just compares rankings on pairs of movies. Sylvia does not need to be consistent, since she may rank $a > b > c > a$. Each pair of movies such that Sylvia ranks the first above the second is called a "crucial pair".

The learning algorithm has access to a set of n individuals ("weak rankers", or "ranking functions") who also rank pairs of movies. The learning algorithm must combine the views of the weak rankers in order to match Sylvia's preferences, and generate a recommendation list that will generalize her views. This type of problem was studied in depth by Freund et al. [7], where the RankBoost algorithm was introduced.

In order to give some indication that an algorithm will generalize well (e.g., we want the ranking algorithm to predict movies that Sylvia will like), one often considers generalization bounds. Generalization bounds show that a small probability of error will most likely be achieved through a balance of the empirical error and the complexity of the hypothesis space. This complexity can by measured by an informative quantity, such as the VC dimension, covering number, Rademacher complexity, or a more specialized quantity, such as the bipartite rank shatter coefficient [1], which was used to derive a generalization bound specifically for the case of bipartite ranking. The "bipartite" ranking problem is a special case of the ranking problem where there are only two classes, a positive class, i.e., "good movies", and a negative class, i.e., "bad movies".

When deriving generalization bounds, it is illustrative to consider the "separable" case, where all training instances are correctly handled by the learning algorithm so the empirical error is zero. The separable case in ranking means that the algorithm's chosen ranking is consistent with all crucial pairs; the algorithm ranks the first instance in each crucial pair above the second. In the bipartite ranking problem, the separable case means that all positive instances are ranked above all negative instances, and the Area Under the ROC Curve (AUC) is exactly one.

In the separable case for classification, one important indicator of a classifier's generalization ability is the "margin", e.g., for boosting [15] and support vector machines. Although the empirical success of an algorithm depends on many factors (e.g., the type of data and how noisy it is), margin-based bounds often do provide a reasonable explanation (though not a complete understanding) of the success of many algorithms, both empirically and theoretically. Although there has been some work devoted to generalization bounds for ranking [7, 1], the bounds that we are aware of are not margin-based, and thus do not provide this useful discrimination between ranking algorithms in the separable case.

In Section 3, we provide a margin-based bound for ranking in a general setting. Our bound uses the L_∞ covering number as the complexity measure for the hypothesis space.

Since we are providing a general margin-based bound for ranking, we derive algorithms which create large margins. For the classification problem, it was proved that AdaBoost does not always maximize the margin [12]. In fact, Ada-Boost does not even necessarily make progress towards increasing the margin at every iteration. In analogy, RankBoost does not directly maximize the ranking margin, and it may not increase the margin at every iteration. In Section 4.1 we introduce a Smooth Margin Ranking algorithm, and prove that it makes progress towards increasing the "smooth" ranking margin at every iteration; this is the main step needed to prove convergence and convergence rates. This algorithm is analogous to Approximate Coordinate Ascent Boosting [14, 13] in its derivation, but the analogous proof that progress occurs at each iteration is much trickier; hence we present a sketch of this proof here.

In the bipartite ranking problem, we want our recommendation list to minimize the misranking error, e.g., the probability that a bad movie is ranked above a good movie. The empirical version of this misranking error is closely related to the AUC. RankBoost [7] minimizes an exponentiated version of this misranking error, in analogy with the classification algorithm AdaBoost, which minimizes an exponentiated version of the margins of training instances.

Although AdaBoost and RankBoost were derived analogously for the settings of classification and ranking, the parallels between these algorithms are deeper than their derivations. Cortes and Mohri [5] and Caruana and Niculescu-Mizil [3] have noted that AdaBoost experimentally seems to be very good at the bipartite ranking problem, even though it was RankBoost that was explicitly designed to solve this problem, not AdaBoost. That is, AdaBoost often achieves a large AUC. In Section 5, we show an important reason for these observations. Namely, if the weak learning algorithm is capable of producing the constant classifier, i.e., the classifier whose value is always one, then remarkably, AdaBoost and RankBoost will produce the same solution.

We proceed from the most general to the most specific. In Section 3 we provide a margin based bound for general ranking, which holds for each element of the hypothesis space. In Sections 4.1 and 4.2 we fix the form of hypothesis space to match that of RankBoost, i.e., the space of binary functions. Here, we discuss coordinate-based ranking algorithms such as RankBoost, and introduce the Smooth Margin Ranking algorithm. In Section 5, we focus on the bipartite ranking problem. Here, we discuss conditions for AdaBoost to act as a bipartite ranking algorithm by minimizing the exponentiated loss associated with the AUC. Sections 3 and 4.2 focus on the separable case, and Sections 4.1 and 5 focus on the non-separable case.

The main contributions of this paper are: 1) a margin-based ranking bound, 2) a theorem stating that our Smooth Margin Ranking algorithm makes progress at every iteration towards increasing the smooth ranking margin, and 3) conditions when AdaBoost acts as a bipartite ranking algorithm.

2   Notation

The training set, denoted by S, is $\{\mathbf{x}_i\}_{i=1,\ldots,m}$, where $\mathbf{x}_i \in \mathcal{X} \subset \mathbb{R}^N$. The set $\mathcal{X}$ may be finite or infinite. In the case of the movie ranking problem, the $\mathbf{x}_i$'s are the movies and $\mathcal{X}$ is the database. The instances $\mathbf{x}_i \in \mathcal{X}$ are chosen independently and at random (iid) from a fixed but unknown probability distribution $\mathcal{D}$ on $\mathcal{X}$. The notation $\mathbf{x} \sim \mathcal{D}$ means $\mathbf{x}$ is chosen randomly according to $\mathcal{D}$, and $S \sim \mathcal{D}^m$ means the m elements of the training set S are chosen iid according to $\mathcal{D}$.

The values of the "truth" function $\pi : \mathcal{X} \times \mathcal{X} \to \{0,1\}$, which is defined over pairs of instances, are analogous to the "labels" in classification. If $\pi(\bar{\mathbf{x}}, \tilde{\mathbf{x}}) = 1$, the pair $\bar{\mathbf{x}}, \tilde{\mathbf{x}}$ is a crucial pair, i.e., $\bar{\mathbf{x}}$ should be ranked more highly than $\tilde{\mathbf{x}}$. We require only that $\pi(\bar{\mathbf{x}}, \bar{\mathbf{x}}) = 0$, meaning $\bar{\mathbf{x}}$ cannot be ranked higher than itself, and also $\pi(\bar{\mathbf{x}}, \tilde{\mathbf{x}}) = 1$ implies $\pi(\tilde{\mathbf{x}}, \bar{\mathbf{x}}) = 0$, meaning that if $\bar{\mathbf{x}}$ is ranked higher than $\tilde{\mathbf{x}}$, that $\tilde{\mathbf{x}}$ cannot be ranked higher than $\bar{\mathbf{x}}$. (It is possible that these assumptions may be dropped.) It is possible to have $\pi(a,b) = 1$, $\pi(b,c) = 1$, and $\pi(c,a) = 1$; this forces us to be in the non-separable case. The quantity $E := \mathbb{E}_{\bar{\mathbf{x}}, \tilde{\mathbf{x}} \sim \mathcal{D}} \pi(\bar{\mathbf{x}}, \tilde{\mathbf{x}})$ is the expected fraction of pairs in the database that are crucial pairs, $0 \le E \le 1/2$. We assume that π is a deterministic (non-noisy) function, and that for each pair of training instances $\mathbf{x}_i, \mathbf{x}_k$, we receive $\pi(\mathbf{x}_i, \mathbf{x}_k)$.

Our goal is to construct a ranking function $f : \mathcal{X} \to \mathbb{R}$, which gives a real valued score to each instance in $\mathcal{X}$. We do not care about the actual values of each instance, only the relative values; for crucial pair $\bar{\mathbf{x}}, \tilde{\mathbf{x}}$, we do not care if $f(\bar{\mathbf{x}}) = .4$ and $f(\tilde{\mathbf{x}}) = .1$, only that $f(\bar{\mathbf{x}}) > f(\tilde{\mathbf{x}})$. Also, $f \in L_\infty(\mathcal{X})$ (or if $|\mathcal{X}|$ is finite, $f \in \ell_\infty(\mathcal{X})$).

In the usual setting of boosting for classification, $\forall \mathbf{x}, |f(\mathbf{x})| \le 1$, and the *margin of training instance* i (with respect to classifier f) is $y_i f(\mathbf{x}_i)$, where y_i is the classification label, $y_i \in \{-1, 1\}$ [15]. The *margin of classifier* f is the minimum margin over all training instances, $\min_i y_i f(\mathbf{x}_i)$. Intuitively, the margin tells us how much f can change before one of the training instances is misclassified; it gives us a notion of how stable the classifier is.

For the ranking setting, we define an analogous notion of margin. Here, we can normalize f so that $|f| \le 1$. The *margin of crucial pair* i,k with respect to ranking function f will be defined as $f(\mathbf{x}_i) - f(\mathbf{x}_k)$. The *margin of ranking function* f, is the minimum margin over all crucial pairs,

$$\mu_f := \min_{\{i,k \mid [\pi(\mathbf{x}_i, \mathbf{x}_k) = 1]\}} f(\mathbf{x}_i) - f(\mathbf{x}_k).$$

Intuitively, the margin tells us how much the ranking function can change before one of the crucial pairs is misranked. As with classification, we are in the separable case whenever the margin of f is positive.

3   A Margin-Based Bound for Ranking

In this section, we provide a bound which gives us an intuition for separable-case ranking and yields theoretical encouragement for margin-based ranking algorithms. The quantity we hope to minimize is analogous to the misclassification probability for classification; for two randomly chosen instances, if they are a crucial pair, we want to minimize the probability that these instances will be misranked. That is, we want to minimize:

$$\mathbb{P}_{\mathcal{D}}\{\text{misrank}_f\}:=\mathbb{P}_{\mathcal{D}}\{f(\bar{\mathbf{x}})\leq f(\tilde{\mathbf{x}})|[\pi(\bar{\mathbf{x}},\tilde{\mathbf{x}})=1]\}=\frac{\mathbb{E}_{\bar{\mathbf{x}},\tilde{\mathbf{x}}\sim\mathcal{D}}[\mathbf{1}_{[f(\bar{\mathbf{x}})\leq f(\tilde{\mathbf{x}})]}\pi(\bar{\mathbf{x}},\tilde{\mathbf{x}})]}{E}.$$

(1)

The numerator of (1) is the fraction of pairs that are both crucial and incorrectly ranked by f, and the denominator, $E:=\mathbb{E}_{\bar{\mathbf{x}},\tilde{\mathbf{x}}\sim\mathcal{D}}\pi(\bar{\mathbf{x}},\tilde{\mathbf{x}})$ is the fraction of pairs that are crucial pairs. Thus, $\mathbb{P}_{\mathcal{D}}\{\text{misrank}_f\}$ is the proportion of crucial pairs that are incorrectly ranked by f.

Since we do not know $\mathcal{D}$, we may use only empirical quantities that rely on our training sample. An empirical quantity analogous to $\mathbb{P}_{\mathcal{D}}\{\text{misrank}_f\}$ is:

$$\mathbb{P}_S\{\text{misrank}_f\} := \mathbb{P}_S\{\text{margin}_f \leq 0\} := \mathbb{P}_S\{f(\mathbf{x}_i) \leq f(\mathbf{x}_k)|[\pi(\mathbf{x}_i,\mathbf{x}_k)=1]\}$$

$$:= \frac{\sum_{i=1}^m \sum_{k=1}^m [\mathbf{1}_{(f(\mathbf{x}_i)\leq f(\mathbf{x}_k))}\pi(\mathbf{x}_i,\mathbf{x}_k)]}{\sum_{i=1}^m \sum_{k=1}^m \pi(\mathbf{x}_i,\mathbf{x}_k)}.$$

We make this definition more general, by allowing it to include a margin of $\theta \geq 0$:

$$\mathbb{P}_S\{\text{margin}_f \leq \theta\} := \mathbb{P}_S\{f(\mathbf{x}_i) - f(\mathbf{x}_k) \leq \theta|[\pi(\mathbf{x}_i,\mathbf{x}_k)=1]\}$$

$$= \frac{\sum_{i=1}^m \sum_{k=1}^m [\mathbf{1}_{(f(\mathbf{x}_i)-f(\mathbf{x}_k)\leq\theta)}\pi(\mathbf{x}_i,\mathbf{x}_k)]}{\sum_{i=1}^m \sum_{k=1}^m \pi(\mathbf{x}_i,\mathbf{x}_k)},$$

i.e., $\mathbb{P}_S\{\text{margin}_f \leq \theta\}$ is the fraction of crucial pairs in $S \times S$ with margin no larger than θ.

We want to bound $\mathbb{P}_{\mathcal{D}}\{\text{misrank}_f\}$ in terms of an empirical, margin-based term and a complexity term. The type of complexity we choose is the L_∞ covering number of the hypothesis space $\mathcal{F}$, $\mathcal{F} \subset L_\infty(\mathcal{X})$. (Upper bounds on the covering number can be calculated; see [6]). The covering number $\mathcal{N}(\mathcal{F},\sigma)$ is defined as the minimum number of balls of radius σ needed to cover $\mathcal{F}$, using the L_∞ metric. The following theorem is proved in Appendix A:

Theorem 1. For $\epsilon > 0$, $\theta \geq 0$, for all $f \in \mathcal{F}$,

$$\mathbb{P}_{S\sim\mathcal{D}^m}\left[\mathbb{P}_{\mathcal{D}}\{\text{misrank}_f\}\leq\mathbb{P}_S\{\text{margin}_f\leq\theta\}+\epsilon\right]\geq 1-\mathcal{N}\left(\mathcal{F},\frac{\epsilon\theta}{8}\right)2\exp\left[\frac{-m(\epsilon E)^2}{8}\right].$$

That is, with probability depending on m, E, θ, ϵ, and $\mathcal{F}$, the misranking probability is less than the fraction of instances with margin below θ, plus ϵ.

We have chosen to write our bound in terms of E, but we could equally well have used an analogous empirical quantity, namely $\mathbb{E}_{\mathbf{x}_i,\mathbf{x}_k\sim S}\pi(\mathbf{x}_i,\mathbf{x}_k) = \frac{1}{m(m-1)}\sum_{i=1}^m \sum_{k=1}^m \pi(\mathbf{x}_i,\mathbf{x}_k)$. This is an arbitrary decision; we cannot maximize E in practice because the data is random. Either way, the bound tells us that the margin should be an important quantity to consider in the design of algorithms.

As a special case of the theorem, we consider the case of a finite hypothesis space $\mathcal{F}$, where the covering number achieves its largest value (for any θ), i.e., $\mathcal{N}\left(\mathcal{F},\frac{\epsilon\theta}{4}\right) = |\mathcal{F}|$. Now we can solve for ϵ:

$$\delta := |\mathcal{F}| 2 \exp\left[-\frac{m(\epsilon E)^2}{8}\right] \implies \epsilon = \frac{1}{\sqrt{m}} \sqrt{\frac{8}{E^2} \left(\ln 2|\mathcal{F}| + \ln(1/\delta)\right)}.$$

This could be compared directly with Theorem 1 of Schapire et al [15]. Cucker and Smale [6] have reduced the factor ϵ^2 to a factor of ϵ in certain cases; it is possible that this bound may be tightened, especially in the case of a convex combination of weak rankers. An interesting open problem is to prove generalization bounds using Rademacher complexity or a more specialized bound analogous to those of Koltchinskii and Panchenko [10]; here the trick would be to find an appropriate symmetrization step. In any case, our bound indicates that the margin is an important quantity for generalization.

4   Coordinate-Based Ranking Algorithms

In the previous section we presented a uniform bound that holds for all $f \in \mathcal{F}$. In the following we discuss how a learning algorithm might pick one of those functions, in order to make $\mathbb{P}_{\mathcal{D}}\{\text{misrank}_f\}$ as small as possible, based on intuition gained from the bound of Theorem 1; the bound reveals the margin to be a useful quantity in the learning process, so it deserves consideration in our design of algorithms.

In Section 4.1, we discuss RankBoost's objective function $\tilde{F}$. Then, we describe a coordinate descent algorithm on this objective. In Section 4.2 we define the smooth ranking margin $\tilde{G}$, present the Smooth Margin Ranking algorithm, and prove that it makes progress towards increasing $\tilde{G}$ at each iteration and converges to a maximum margin solution.

4.1   Coordinate Descent on RankBoost's Objective

We consider the hypothesis space $\mathcal{F}$ to be the class of convex combinations of "weak" rankers $\{h_j\}_{j=1,\dots,n}$, where $h_j : X \to \{0,1\}$. We assume that if h_j is a weak ranker, that $1 - h_j$ is not chosen as a weak ranker; this assumption avoids the complicated seminorm notation in earlier work [13]. The function f is constructed as a normalized linear combination of the h_j's: $f = \sum_j \lambda_j h_j / \|\boldsymbol{\lambda}\|_1$, where $\|\boldsymbol{\lambda}\|_1 = \sum_j \lambda_j$.

We construct a structure $\mathbf{M}$, which describes how each individual weak ranker j ranks each crucial pair i, k. We define $\mathbf{M}$ element-wise as: $M_{ikj} := h_j(\mathbf{x}_i) - h_j(\mathbf{x}_k)$. Thus, $M_{ikj} \in \{-1, 0, 1\}$. Since $\mathbf{M}$ has three indices, we need to define right multiplication: $(\mathbf{M}\boldsymbol{\lambda})_{ik} := \sum_{j=1}^n M_{ikj}\lambda_j = \sum_{j=1}^n \lambda_j h_j(\mathbf{x}_i) - \lambda_j h_j(\mathbf{x}_k)$ for $\boldsymbol{\lambda} \in \mathbb{R}^n$ and left multiplication: $(\mathbf{d}^T \mathbf{M})_j := \sum_{i,k \mid [\pi(\mathbf{x}_i, \mathbf{x}_k)=1]} d_{ik} M_{ikj}$ for $\mathbf{d} \in \mathbb{R}^{\#\text{crucial}}$, where "#crucial" is the number of crucial pairs.

Just as AdaBoost can be represented as a coordinate descent algorithm on a specific objective function of $\boldsymbol{\lambda}$ (see [9]), so can RankBoost. The objective function for RankBoost is:

$$\tilde{F}(\boldsymbol{\lambda}) := \sum_{\{i,k \mid [\pi(\mathbf{x}_i, \mathbf{x}_k)=1]\}} e^{-(\mathbf{M}\boldsymbol{\lambda})_{ik}}.$$

We perform standard coordinate descent on $\tilde{F}$ to derive "Coordinate Descent RankBoost". The direction chosen at iteration t (i.e., the choice of weak ranker j_t) in the "optimal" case (where the best weak ranker is chosen at each iteration) is given by: $j_t \in \operatorname*{argmax}_{j} \left[-\frac{d\tilde{F}(\boldsymbol{\lambda}_t + \alpha \mathbf{e}_j)}{d\alpha} \Big|_{\alpha=0} \right] = \operatorname*{argmax}_{j} (\mathbf{d}_t^T \mathbf{M})_j$, where the "weights" $d_{t,ik}$ are defined over pairs of instances by: $d_{t,ik} = 0$ for non-crucial pairs, and for crucial pair i, k: $d_{t,ik} := e^{-(\mathbf{M}\boldsymbol{\lambda}_t)_{ik}}/\tilde{F}(\boldsymbol{\lambda}_t)$. One can see that the chosen weak ranker is a natural choice, namely, j_t is the most accurate weak ranker with respect to the weighted crucial training pairs.

Define $\mathcal{I}_+ := \{i, k | M_{ikj_t} = 1, \pi(\mathbf{x}_i, \mathbf{x}_k) = 1\}$ (although $\mathcal{I}_+$ is different for each t, we eliminate the subscript), also $\mathcal{I}_- := \{i, k | M_{ikj_t} = -1, \pi(\mathbf{x}_i, \mathbf{x}_k) = 1\}$. Also define $d_+ := \sum_{\mathcal{I}_+} d_{t,ik}$ and $d_- := \sum_{\mathcal{I}_-} d_{t,ik}$. The step size at iteration t is α_t, where α_t satisfies the equation for the line search along direction j_t:

$$0 = -\frac{d\tilde{F}(\boldsymbol{\lambda}_t + \alpha \mathbf{e}_{j_t})}{d\alpha}\Big|_{\alpha=\alpha_t} \quad \Rightarrow \quad \alpha_t = \frac{1}{2} \ln \frac{d_+}{d_-}. \tag{2}$$

Thus, we have derived the first algorithm, Coordinate Descent RankBoost.

RankBoost, as it is described by Freund et al. [7], is similar, but differs by the ordering of steps: the formula for α_t is calculated first (via (2)), and afterwards j_t is determined using knowledge of the formula for α_t. For RankBoost, there may not be a natural interpretation of this type of weak learning algorithm as there is for Coordinate Descent RankBoost.

It is interesting that for AdaBoost's objective function, the plain coordinate descent algorithm and the variation (choosing the coordinate with knowledge of the step size) actually turn out to both yield the same algorithm, i.e., AdaBoost.

4.2   Smooth Margin Ranking

The value of $\tilde{F}$ does not directly tell us anything about the margin, only whether the margin is positive. Using any $\boldsymbol{\lambda}$ that yields a positive margin, we can actually make $\tilde{F}$ arbitrarily small by multiplying $\boldsymbol{\lambda}$ by a large positive constant, so the objective is arbitrarily small, yet the margin may not be maximized. Actually, the same problem occurs for AdaBoost. It has been proven [12] that for certain $\mathbf{M}$'s, AdaBoost does not converge to a maximum margin solution, nor does it even make progress towards increasing the margin at every iteration. Since the calculations are identical for RankBoost, there are certain cases in which we can similarly expect RankBoost not to converge to a maximum margin solution.

In earlier work, we proposed a smooth margin function which one can maximize in order to achieve a maximum margin solution for the classification problem [13]. We also proposed a coordinate ascent algorithm on this function which makes progress towards increasing the smooth margin at every iteration. Here, we present the analogous smooth ranking function and the Smooth Margin Ranking algorithm. The smooth ranking function $\tilde{G}$ is defined as follows:

$$\tilde{G}(\boldsymbol{\lambda}) := \frac{-\ln \tilde{F}(\boldsymbol{\lambda})}{||\boldsymbol{\lambda}||}.$$

With proofs identical to those of Rudin et al. [13], one can show that:

$$\tilde{G}(\boldsymbol{\lambda}) < \mu(\boldsymbol{\lambda}) \leq \rho, \quad \text{where} \tag{3}$$

$\rho = \min_{\{\mathbf{d}| \sum_{ik} d_{ik}=1, d_{ik} \geq 0\}} \max_j (\mathbf{d}^T \mathbf{M})_j = \max_{\{\bar{\boldsymbol{\lambda}}| \sum_j \bar{\lambda}_j=1, \bar{\lambda}_j \geq 0\}} \min_i (\mathbf{M}\bar{\boldsymbol{\lambda}})_i$, i.e., the smooth ranking margin is less than the true margin, and the true margin is no greater than ρ, the min-max value of the game defined by $\mathbf{M}$ (see [8]).

We define the Smooth Margin Ranking algorithm, which is approximately coordinate ascent on $\tilde{G}$. As usual, the input to the algorithm is matrix $\mathbf{M}$. We will only define this algorithm when $\tilde{G}(\boldsymbol{\lambda})$ is positive, so that we only use this algorithm once the data has become separable; we can use RankBoost or Coordinate Descent RankBoost to get us to this point.

We will define iteration $t + 1$ in terms of the quantities known at iteration t, namely: the current value of the objective $g_t := \tilde{G}(\boldsymbol{\lambda}_t)$, the weights $d_{t,ik} := e^{-(\mathbf{M}\boldsymbol{\lambda}_t)_{ik}}/\tilde{F}(\boldsymbol{\lambda}_t)$, the direction $j_t = \operatorname*{argmax}_j (\mathbf{d}_t^T \mathbf{M})_j$, and the edge $r_t := (\mathbf{d}_t^T \mathbf{M})_{j_t}$. The choice of j_t is the same as for Coordinate Descent Rank-Boost, also see [13]. The step size α_t is chosen to obey (6) below, but we need more definitions before we state its value. We define recursive equations for $\tilde{F}$ and $\tilde{G}$, and then use these to build up to (6). We also have $s_t = \|\boldsymbol{\lambda}_t\|_1$ and $s_{t+1} = s_t + \alpha_t$, and $g_{t+1} = \tilde{G}(\boldsymbol{\lambda}_t + \alpha_t \mathbf{e}_{j_t})$.

As before, $\mathcal{I}_+ := \{i, k | M_{ikj_t} = 1, \pi(\mathbf{x}_i, \mathbf{x}_k) = 1\}$, $\mathcal{I}_- := \{i, k | M_{ikj_t} = -1, \pi(\mathbf{x}_i, \mathbf{x}_k) = 1\}$, and now, $\mathcal{I}_0 := \{i, k | M_{ikj_t} = 0, \pi(\mathbf{x}_i, \mathbf{x}_k) = 1\}$. Also $d_+ := \sum_{\mathcal{I}_+} d_{t,ik}$, $d_- := \sum_{\mathcal{I}_-} d_{t,ik}$, and $d_0 := \sum_{\mathcal{I}_0} d_{t,ik}$. So, by definition, $d_+ + d_- + d_0 = 1$. Now, r_t becomes $r_t = d_+ - d_-$. Define the factor τ_t and its "derivative" τ_t':

$$\tau_t := d_+ e^{-\alpha_t} + d_- e^{\alpha_t} + d_0, \quad \text{and} \quad \tau_t' := -d_+ e^{-\alpha_t} + d_- e^{\alpha_t}.$$

We derive a recursive equation for $\tilde{F}$, true for any α:

$$\tilde{F}(\boldsymbol{\lambda}_t + \alpha \mathbf{e}_{j_t}) = \sum_{\{i,k | \pi(\mathbf{x}_i, \mathbf{x}_k)=1\}} e^{(-\mathbf{M}\boldsymbol{\lambda}_t)_{ik}} e^{-M_{ikj_t}\alpha} = \tilde{F}(\boldsymbol{\lambda}_t)(d_+ e^{-\alpha} + d_- e^{\alpha} + d_0).$$

Thus, we have defined τ_t so that $\tilde{F}(\boldsymbol{\lambda}_{t+1}) = \tilde{F}(\boldsymbol{\lambda}_t + \alpha_t \mathbf{e}_{j_t}) = \tilde{F}(\boldsymbol{\lambda}_t)\tau_t$. We use this to write a recursive equation for $\tilde{G}$:

$$\tilde{G}(\boldsymbol{\lambda}_t + \alpha \mathbf{e}_{j_t}) = \frac{-\ln(\tilde{F}(\boldsymbol{\lambda}_t + \alpha \mathbf{e}_{j_t}))}{s_t + \alpha} = g_t \frac{s_t}{s_t + \alpha} - \frac{\ln(d_+ e^{-\alpha} + d_- e^{\alpha} + d_0)}{s_t + \alpha}.$$

For our algorithm, we set $\alpha = \alpha_t$ in the above expression:

$$g_{t+1} = g_t \frac{s_t}{s_t + \alpha_t} - \frac{\ln \tau_t}{s_t + \alpha_t} \quad \Rightarrow \quad g_{t+1} - g_t = -\frac{1}{s_{t+1}}[g_t \alpha_t + \ln \tau_t]. \tag{4}$$

With this notation we write the equation for α_t for Smooth Margin Ranking. For plain coordinate ascent, the update α^* solves:

$$0 = \left.\frac{d\tilde{G}(\boldsymbol{\lambda}_t + \alpha \mathbf{e}_{j_t})}{d\alpha}\right|_{\alpha=\alpha^*} = \frac{1}{s_t + \alpha^*}\left[-\tilde{G}(\boldsymbol{\lambda}_t + \alpha^* \mathbf{e}_{j_t}) + \left[\frac{-d\tilde{F}(\boldsymbol{\lambda}_t + \alpha \mathbf{e}_{j_t})/d\alpha\big|_{\alpha=\alpha^*}}{\tilde{F}(\boldsymbol{\lambda}_t)}\right]\right].$$

We could solve this equation numerically for α^* to get a smooth margin coordinate ascent algorithm, however, we avoid this line search. To get the update rule for Smooth Margin Ranking, we set α_t to solve:

$$0 = \frac{1}{s_t + \alpha_t}\left[-\tilde{G}(\boldsymbol{\lambda}_t) + \left[\frac{-d\tilde{F}(\boldsymbol{\lambda}_t + \alpha\mathbf{e}_{j_t})/d\alpha\big|_{\alpha=\alpha_t}}{\tilde{F}(\boldsymbol{\lambda}_t)}\right]\right] = \frac{1}{s_t + \alpha_t}\left(-g_t + \frac{-\tau_t'\tilde{F}(\boldsymbol{\lambda}_t)}{\tau_t\tilde{F}(\boldsymbol{\lambda}_t)}\right)$$

$$g_t\tau_t = -\tau_t'. \tag{5}$$

This expression can be solved analytically for α_t, which makes the algorithm as easy to implement as RankBoost:

$$\alpha_t = \ln\left[\frac{-g_t d_0 + \sqrt{g_t^2 d_0^2 + (1 + g_t)(1 - g_t)(1 + r_t - d_0)(1 - r_t - d_0)}}{(1 + g_t)(1 - r_t - d_0)}\right]. \tag{6}$$

The following theorem states that the algorithm makes significant progress towards increasing the value of $\tilde{G}$ at every iteration. An analogous statement was an essential tool for proving properties of Approximate Coordinate Ascent Boosting [13], although the proof here (for which we give a sketch) is significantly more difficult, since we cannot use the important trick used in our previous work for (the equivalent of) Lemma 1. As usual, the weak learning algorithm always achieves an edge of at least ρ for the calculation to hold.

Theorem 2.

$$g_{t+1} - g_t \geq \frac{1}{2}\frac{\alpha_t(r_t - g_t)}{s_{t+1}}.$$

Sketching the proof, we consider α_t, τ_t, d_+, and d_- as functions of three basic independent variables $r := r_t$, $g := g_t$ and, d_0, with ranges $0 < r < 1$, $0 \leq g < r$, and $0 \leq d_0 \leq 1 - r$. Define

$$\Gamma_{r,g,d_0} := \frac{-\ln\tau_t}{\alpha_t}, \quad \text{and} \quad \mathcal{B}_{r,g,d_0} := \frac{\Gamma_{r,g,d_0} - g}{r - g}.$$

Lemma 1. $\mathcal{B}_{r,g,d_0} > 1/2$.

This lemma is a monstrous calculus problem in three variables, for which the proof will be given in a longer version of this paper. Using only this lemma, we can prove the theorem directly.

Proof. (of Theorem 2) Let us unravel the notation a bit. Lemma 1 says:

$$\frac{-\ln\tau_t}{\alpha_t} = \Gamma_{r,g,d_0} > \frac{r_t + g_t}{2} \quad \Rightarrow \quad -\ln\tau_t > \frac{(r_t + g_t)\alpha_t}{2}.$$

Incorporating the recursive equation (4),

$$g_{t+1} - g_t = \frac{1}{s_{t+1}}\left[-g_t\alpha_t - \ln\tau_t\right] > \frac{\alpha_t}{s_{t+1}}\left[-g_t + \frac{(r_t + g_t)}{2}\right] = \frac{1}{2}\frac{\alpha_t(r_t - g_t)}{s_{t+1}}. \quad \square$$

Theorem 2 is the main step in proving convergence theorems, for example:

Theorem 3. *The smooth ranking margin ranking algorithm converges to a maximum margin solution, i.e.,* $\lim_{t\to\infty} g_t = \rho$.

Besides Theorem 2, the only other key step in the proof of Theorem 3 is:
Lemma 2.
$$\lim_{t\to\infty} \frac{\alpha_t}{s_{t+1}} = 0.$$
We omit the proof of Lemma 2, which uses (4), monotonicity and boundedness of the g_t sequence, and then (5).

Proof. (Of Theorem 3) The values of g_t constitute a non-decreasing sequence which is uniformly bounded by 1. Thus, a limit g_∞ exists, $g_\infty := \lim_{t\to\infty} g_t$. By (3), we know $g_t \leq \rho$ for all t. Thus, $g_\infty \leq \rho$. Suppose $g_\infty < \rho$, i.e., that $\rho - g_\infty \neq 0$. One can use an identical calculation to the one in Rudin et al. [13] to show that this assumption, together with Theorem 2 and Lemma 2 imply that $\lim_{t\to\infty} \alpha_t = 0$. Using this fact along with (5), we find:

$$g_\infty = \lim_{t\to\infty} g_t = \liminf_{t\to\infty} g_t = \liminf_{t\to\infty} \frac{-\tau_t'}{\tau_t} = \liminf_{t\to\infty} \frac{-(-d_+ e^{-\alpha_t} + d_- e^{\alpha_t})}{d_+ e^{-\alpha_t} + d_- e^{\alpha_t} + d_0} = \liminf_{t\to\infty} \frac{r_t}{1} \geq \rho.$$

This is a contradiction with the original assumption that $g_\infty < \rho$. It follows that $g_\infty = \rho$, or $\lim_{t\to\infty}(\rho - g_t) = 0$. Thus, the smooth ranking algorithm converges to a maximum margin solution. □

5   AdaBoost and RankBoost in the Bipartite Problem

In the bipartite ranking problem, every training instance falls into one of two categories, the "positive class" Y_+ and the "negative class" Y_-. Here, $\pi(\mathbf{x}_i, \mathbf{x}_k) = 1$ only when $\mathbf{x}_i \in Y_+$ and $\mathbf{x}_k \in Y_-$. Define $y_i = +1$ when $\mathbf{x}_i \in Y_+$, and $y_i = -1$ otherwise. The function $\tilde{F}$ now becomes an exponentiated version of the AUC, that is, since the step function obeys $\mathbf{1}_{x<0} \leq e^{-x}$, we have:

$$|Y_+||Y_-|(1 - \mathrm{AUC}(\boldsymbol{\lambda})) = \sum_{i\in Y_+} \sum_{k\in Y_-} \mathbf{1}_{(\mathbf{M}\boldsymbol{\lambda})_{ik}<0} \leq \sum_{i\in Y_+} \sum_{k\in Y_-} e^{-(\mathbf{M}\boldsymbol{\lambda})_{ik}} = \tilde{F}(\boldsymbol{\lambda}).$$

The AUC has been written as the Wilcoxon-Mann-Whitney statistic (see [5]).

We now show that AdaBoost minimizes RankBoost's loss function $\tilde{F}$ under a very natural condition, namely, whenever the positive and negative instances contribute equally to AdaBoost's loss function.

We define AdaBoost's matrix $\mathbf{M}^{Ada}$ element-wise by $M_{ij}^{Ada} = y_i h_j(\mathbf{x}_i)$. Each crucial pair i, k has $i \in Y_+$ and $k \in Y_-$, so elements of $\mathbf{M}$ are: $M_{ikj} = h_j(\mathbf{x}_i) - h_j(\mathbf{x}_k) = y_i h_j(\mathbf{x}_i) + y_k h_j(\mathbf{x}_k) = M_{ij}^{Ada} + M_{kj}^{Ada}$. (To change from Ada-Boost's usual $\{-1, 1\}$ hypotheses to RankBoost's usual $\{0, 1\}$ hypotheses, divide by 2.) Define vector $\mathbf{q}_{\boldsymbol{\lambda}}$ element-wise by $q_{\boldsymbol{\lambda},i} := e^{-(\mathbf{M}^{Ada}\boldsymbol{\lambda})_i}$ for $i = 1, ..., m$. Using this notation, we will write the objective functions for both AdaBoost and RankBoost. First, we define the following:

$$F_+(\lambda) := \sum_{i \in Y_+} q_{\lambda,i} \text{ and } F_-(\lambda) := \sum_{k \in Y_-} q_{\lambda,k}.$$

The objective function for AdaBoost is $F(\lambda) := F_+(\lambda) + F_-(\lambda)$. The objective function for RankBoost is: $\tilde{F}(\lambda) = F_+(\lambda)F_-(\lambda)$. Thus, the balance between the positive and negative instances is different between the algorithms.

We define "F-skew", which measures the imbalance between positive and negative instances.

$$\text{F-skew}(\lambda) := F_+(\lambda) - F_-(\lambda).$$

Theorem 4. *Assume* $\mathbf{M}^{Ada}$ *is such that* $\inf_\lambda \tilde{F}(\lambda) > 0$ *(the non-separable case). For any sequence* $\{\lambda_t\}_{t=1}^\infty$ *such that*

$$\lim_{t \to \infty} F(\lambda_t) = \inf_\lambda F(\lambda) \tag{7}$$

and $\lim_{t \to \infty} \text{F-skew}(\lambda_t) = 0$, *then*

$$\lim_{t \to \infty} \tilde{F}(\lambda_t) = \inf_\lambda \tilde{F}(\lambda). \tag{8}$$

Proof. It is possible that F or $\tilde{F}$ may have no minimizers. So, to describe (7) and (8), we use the trick from Collins et al. [4], who considered F and $\tilde{F}$ as functions of a variable where the infimum can be achieved. Define, for matrix $\bar{\mathbf{M}} \in \mathbb{R}^{\bar{m} \times n}$, the function

$$F_{\bar{\mathbf{M}}}(\lambda) := \sum_{i=1}^{\bar{m}} e^{-(\bar{\mathbf{M}}\lambda)_i}.$$

Define $\bar{\mathcal{P}} := \{\mathbf{p} | \forall i \; p_i \geq 0, \; \forall j \; (\mathbf{p}^T \bar{\mathbf{M}})_j = 0\}$ and $\bar{\mathcal{Q}} := \{\mathbf{q} | \forall i \; q_i = e^{-(\bar{\mathbf{M}}\lambda)_i}$ for some $\lambda\}$. We may thus consider $\bar{F}_{\bar{\mathbf{M}}}$ as a function of $\bar{q}$, $\bar{F}_{\bar{\mathbf{M}}}(\bar{q}) = \sum_{i=1}^{\bar{m}} \bar{q}_i$, where $\bar{q} \in \bar{\mathcal{Q}}$. We know that since all $\bar{q}_i$'s are positive, the infimum of $\bar{F}$ occurs in a bounded region of $\bar{q}$ space, which is just what we need.

Theorem 1 of Collins et al., which is taken directly from Lafferty, Della Pietra, and Della Pietra [11] implies that the following are equivalent:

1. $\bar{q}^* \in \bar{\mathcal{P}} \cap$ closure $(\bar{\mathcal{Q}})$.
2. $\bar{q}^* \in \text{argmin}_{\bar{q} \in \text{closure}(\bar{\mathcal{Q}})} \bar{F}_{\bar{\mathbf{M}}}(\bar{q})$.

Moreover, either condition is satisfied by exactly one vector $\bar{q}^*$.

The objective function for AdaBoost is $F = \bar{F}_{\mathbf{M}^{Ada}}$ and the objective for RankBoost is $\tilde{F} = \bar{F}_{\tilde{\mathbf{M}}}$, so the theorem holds for both objectives separately. For function F, denote $\bar{q}^*$ as $\mathbf{q}^*$, also $\bar{\mathcal{P}}$ as $\mathcal{P}^{Ada}$ and $\bar{\mathcal{Q}}$ as $\mathcal{Q}^{Ada}$. For function $\tilde{F}$, denote $\bar{q}^*$ as $\tilde{q}^*$, also $\bar{\mathcal{P}}$ as $\tilde{\mathcal{P}}$ and $\bar{\mathcal{Q}}$ as $\tilde{\mathcal{Q}}$. Rewriting $\mathbf{q}^* \in \mathcal{P}^{Ada}$:

$$\sum_{i \in Y_+} q_i^* M_{ij}^{Ada} + \sum_{k \in Y_-} q_k^* M_{kj}^{Ada} = 0 \; \forall j. \tag{9}$$

Define $\mathbf{q}_t$ element-wise by: $q_{t,i} := e^{-(\mathbf{M}^{Ada}\lambda_t)_i}$, for $i = 1, ..., m$ where the λ_t's are a sequence that obey (7), for example, a sequence produced by Ada-Boost. Thus, $\mathbf{q}_t \in \mathcal{Q}^{Ada}$ automatically. Since $F(\mathbf{q}_t)$ converges to the minimum of F, one can show that the sequence of $\mathbf{q}_t$'s converges to $\mathbf{q}^*$ in ℓ_p. Now define vectors $\tilde{q}_t$ element-wise by $\tilde{q}_{t,ik} := q_{t,i}q_{t,k} = \exp[-(\mathbf{M}^{Ada}\boldsymbol{\lambda}_t)_i - (\mathbf{M}^{Ada}\boldsymbol{\lambda}_t)_k] = \exp[-(\mathbf{M}\boldsymbol{\lambda}_t)_{ik}]$. Automatically, $\tilde{q}_t \in \tilde{\mathcal{Q}}$. For any pair i, k the limit of the $\tilde{q}_{t,ik}$'s is $\tilde{q}_{ik}^\infty := q_i^* q_k^*$. Thus, we need only to show $\tilde{q}^\infty = \tilde{q}^*$. We will do this by showing $\tilde{q}^\infty \in \tilde{\mathcal{P}}$; due to the uniqueness of $\tilde{q}^*$ as $\tilde{\mathcal{P}} \cap \text{closure}(\tilde{\mathcal{Q}})$, this will yield $\tilde{q}^\infty = \tilde{q}^*$.

Our assumption that the F-skew vanishes can be rewritten as:

$$\lim_{t \to \infty} [\sum_{i \in Y_+} q_{t,i} - \sum_{k \in Y_-} q_{t,k}] = 0, \quad \text{i.e.,}$$

$$\sum_{i \in Y_+} q_i^* = \sum_{k \in Y_-} q_k^*. \tag{10}$$

Consider the quantities $(\tilde{q}^{\infty T}\mathbf{M})_j$. Remember, if these quantities are zero for every j, then $\tilde{q}^\infty \in \tilde{\mathcal{P}}$ and we have proved the theorem.

$$(\tilde{q}^{\infty T}\mathbf{M})_j = (\sum_{k \in Y_-} q_k^*)(\sum_{i \in Y_+} q_i^* M_{ij}^{Ada}) + (\sum_{i \in Y_+} q_i^*)(\sum_{k \in Y_-} q_k^* M_{kj}^{Ada}).$$

Incorporating (10), which is the condition that F-skew($\mathbf{q}^*$) = 0, (11) becomes:

$$(\tilde{q}^{\infty T}\mathbf{M})_j = (\sum_{i \in Y_+} q_i^*)[\sum_{i \in Y_+} q_i^* M_{ij}^{Ada} + \sum_{k \in Y_-} q_k^* M_{kj}^{Ada}].$$

In fact, according to (9), the bracket in this expression is zero for all j. Thus, $\tilde{q}_\infty \in \tilde{\mathcal{P}}$. We have proved the theorem. $\square$

Corollary 1. *If the constant weak hypothesis $\forall \mathbf{x}$, $h_j(\mathbf{x}) = 1$ is one of the weak classifiers used to construct $\mathbf{M}^{Ada}$, and the $\{\boldsymbol{\lambda}_t\}_t$ sequence obeys (7), then*
$$\lim_{t \to \infty} \text{F-skew}(\boldsymbol{\lambda}_t) = 0, \text{ and } \{\boldsymbol{\lambda}_t\}_t \text{ thus obeys (8) by Theorem 4.}$$

That is, any algorithm which minimizes F (such as AdaBoost) solves the ranking problem whenever the weak learning algorithm is capable of producing the constant hypothesis.

Proof. Recall that $\mathbf{q}^* \in \mathcal{P}^{Ada}$. Specifically writing this condition just for the constant weak classifier yields:

$$0 = \sum_{i \in Y_+} q_i^* y_i 1 + \sum_{k \in Y_-} q_k^* y_k 1 = \sum_{i \in Y_+} q_i^* - \sum_{k \in Y_-} q_k^* = \lim_{t \to \infty} \text{F-skew}(\boldsymbol{\lambda}_t). \quad \square$$

Thus, AdaBoost and RankBoost are closely related indeed, since under this very weak condition (e.g., when the constant weak classifier is included), AdaBoost minimizes RankBoost's objective function. Given these results, it is now understandable (but still surprising) that AdaBoost performs so well as a ranking algorithm. One can directly use the convergence of the $\mathbf{q}_t$'s to show that AdaBoost produces exactly the same AUC value as RankBoost under this weak condition (in addition to the same value of the exponential loss). We expand on this in future work.

6   Conclusion

The three main results presented in this paper yield many new directions for future research. We gave a margin-based bound for general ranking. It is worth investigating the design of more specialized margin-based bounds for ranking. We described a new ranking algorithm, Smooth Margin Ranking, that maximizes the margin. It would be natural to compare the empirical performance of the Smooth Margin Ranking algorithm and RankBoost. Finally, given the AUC optimization result proved for AdaBoost, one may ask why RankBoost, or another ranking algorithm, is needed in the non-separable case? The answer may lie in the convergence rate of AdaBoost versus that of RankBoost, which we are currently studying. Our observations suggest that RankBoost (understandably) has faster convergence to a high AUC value.

References

1. Shivani Agarwal, Thore Graepel, Ralf Herbich, Sariel Har-Peled, and Dan Roth. Generalization bounds for the area under the ROC curve. *Journal of Machine Learning Research*, 6:393–425, 2005.
2. Olivier Bousquet. New approaches to statistical learning theory. *Annals of the Institute of Statistical Mathematics*, 55(2):371–389, 2003.
3. Rich Caruana and Alexandru Niculescu-Mizil. An empirical comparison of supervised learning algorithms using difference performance metrics. Technical Report TR2005-1973, Cornell University, 2005.
4. Michael Collins, Robert E. Schapire, and Yoram Singer. Logistic regression, AdaBoost and Bregman distances. *Machine Learning*, 48(1/2/3), 2002.
5. Corinna Cortes and Mehryar Mohri. AUC optimization vs. error rate minimization. In *Advances in Neural Information Processing Systems 16*, 2004.
6. Felipe Cucker and Steve Smale. On the mathematical foundations of learning. *Bull. Amer. Math. Soc.*, (39):1–49, 2002.
7. Yoav Freund, Raj Iyer, Robert E. Schapire, and Yoram Singer. An efficient boosting algorithm for combining preferences. In *Machine Learning: Proceedings of the Fifteenth International Conference*, 1998.
8. Yoav Freund and Robert E. Schapire. Adaptive game playing using multiplicative weights. *Games and Economic Behavior*, 29:79–103, 1999.
9. Jerome Friedman, Trevor Hastie, and Robert Tibshirani. Additive logistic regression: A statistical view of boosting. *The Annals of Statistics*, 38(2):337–374, April 2000.
10. Vladimir Koltchinskii and Dmitry Panchenko. Empirical margin distributions and bounding the generalization error of combined classifiers. *The Annals of Statistics*, 30(1), February 2002.
11. John D. Lafferty, Stephen Della Pietra, and Vincent Della Pietra. Statistical learning algorithms based on Bregman distances. In *Proceedings of the Canadian Workshop on Information Theory*, 1997.
12. Cynthia Rudin, Ingrid Daubechies, and Robert E. Schapire. The dynamics of AdaBoost: Cyclic behavior and convergence of margins. *Journal of Machine Learning Research*, 5:1557–1595, December 2004.

13. Cynthia Rudin, Robert E. Schapire, and Ingrid Daubechies. Analysis of boosting algorithms using the smooth margin function: A study of three algorithms. Submitted, 2004.
14. Cynthia Rudin, Robert E. Schapire, and Ingrid Daubechies. Boosting based on a smooth margin. In *Proceedings of the Sixteenth Annual Conference on Computational Learning Theory*, pages 502–517, 2004.
15. Robert E. Schapire, Yoav Freund, Peter Bartlett, and Wee Sun Lee. Boosting the margin: A new explanation for the effectiveness of voting methods. *The Annals of Statistics*, 26(5):1651–1686, October 1998.

A   Proof of Theorem 1

We owe inspiration for this proof to the works of Cucker and Smale [6], Koltchinskii and Panchenko [10], and Bousquet [2].

We define a Lipschitz function $\phi : \mathbb{R} \to \mathbb{R}$ (with Lipschitz constant $\text{Lip}(\phi)$) which acts as our loss function, and gives us the margin. We will later use the same piecewise linear definition of ϕ as Koltchinskii and Panchenko [10], but for now, we require $\forall z$, $0 \leq \phi(z) \leq 1$ and $\phi(z) = 1$ for $z < 0$. Since $\phi(z) \geq 1_{[z \leq 0]}$, we can define an upper bound for the misranking probability, namely $\mathbb{P}_\mathcal{D}\{\text{misrank}_f\} \leq \mathbb{P}_\mathcal{D}\phi_f$, where:

$$\mathbb{P}_\mathcal{D}\phi_f := \frac{\mathbb{E}_{\bar{\mathbf{x}}, \tilde{\mathbf{x}} \sim \mathcal{D}}[\phi(f(\bar{\mathbf{x}}) - f(\tilde{\mathbf{x}}))\pi(\bar{\mathbf{x}}, \tilde{\mathbf{x}})]}{\mathbb{E}_{\bar{\mathbf{x}}, \tilde{\mathbf{x}} \sim \mathcal{D}}\pi(\bar{\mathbf{x}}, \tilde{\mathbf{x}})}.$$

The empirical error associated with $\mathbb{P}_\mathcal{D}\phi_f$ is:

$$\mathbb{P}_S\phi_f := \frac{\sum_{i=1}^m \sum_{k=1}^m \phi(f(\mathbf{x}_i) - f(\mathbf{x}_k))\pi(\mathbf{x}_i, \mathbf{x}_k)}{\sum_{i=1}^m \sum_{k=1}^m \pi(\mathbf{x}_i, \mathbf{x}_k)}.$$

First, we upper bound the misranking probability by two terms: the empirical error term $\mathbb{P}_S\phi_f$, and a term characterizing the deviation of $\mathbb{P}_S\phi_f$ from $\mathbb{P}_\mathcal{D}\phi_f$ uniformly:

$$\mathbb{P}_\mathcal{D}\{\text{misrank}_f\} \leq \mathbb{P}_\mathcal{D}\phi_f = \mathbb{P}_\mathcal{D}\phi_f - \mathbb{P}_S\phi_f + \mathbb{P}_S\phi_f \leq \sup_{\bar{f} \in \mathcal{F}}(\mathbb{P}_\mathcal{D}\phi_{\bar{f}} - \mathbb{P}_S\phi_{\bar{f}}) + \mathbb{P}_S\phi_f.$$

The proof of the theorem involves an upper bound on the first term. First, define $L(f)$ as follows: $L(f) := \mathbb{P}_\mathcal{D}\phi_f - \mathbb{P}_S\phi_f$. The following lemma (for which the proof is omitted) is true for every training set S:

Lemma 3. *For any two functions $f_1, f_2 \in L_\infty(\mathcal{X})$,*

$$L(f_1) - L(f_2) \leq 4\text{Lip}(\phi)\|f_1 - f_2\|_\infty.$$

The following step is due to Cucker and Smale [6]. Let $\ell_\epsilon := \mathcal{N}\left(\mathcal{F}, \frac{\epsilon}{8\text{Lip}(\phi)}\right)$, the covering number of $\mathcal{F}$ by L_∞ disks of radius $\frac{\epsilon}{8\text{Lip}(\phi)}$. Define $f_1, f_2, ..., f_{\ell_\epsilon}$ to be the centers of such a cover, i.e., the collection of L_∞ disks D_p centered at f_p and with radius $\frac{\epsilon}{8\text{Lip}(\phi)}$ is a cover for $\mathcal{F}$. The following lemma (proof omitted) shows we do not lose too much by using f_p as a representative for disk D_p.

Lemma 4.

$$\mathbb{P}_{S\sim\mathcal{D}^m}\{\sup_{f\in D_p} L(f) \geq \epsilon\} \leq \mathbb{P}_{S\sim\mathcal{D}^m}\{L(f_p) \geq \frac{\epsilon}{2}\}.$$

Now we incorporate the fact that the training set is chosen randomly.

Lemma 5.

$$\mathbb{P}_{S\sim\mathcal{D}^m}\{L(f) \geq \epsilon/2\} \leq 2\exp\left[-\frac{m(\epsilon E)^2}{8}\right].$$

Proof. To make notation easier for this lemma, we introduce some shorthand notation:

$$\text{top}_\mathcal{D} := \mathbb{E}_{\bar{\mathbf{x}},\tilde{\mathbf{x}}\sim\mathcal{D}}\phi(f(\bar{\mathbf{x}}) - f(\tilde{\mathbf{x}}))\pi(\bar{\mathbf{x}},\tilde{\mathbf{x}}), \quad \text{bot}_\mathcal{D} := E := \mathbb{E}_{\bar{\mathbf{x}},\tilde{\mathbf{x}}\sim\mathcal{D}}\pi(\bar{\mathbf{x}},\tilde{\mathbf{x}}),$$

$$\text{top}_S := \frac{1}{m(m-1)}\sum_{i=1}^{m}\sum_{k=1}^{m}\phi(f(\mathbf{x}_i) - f(\mathbf{x}_k))\pi(\mathbf{x}_i,\mathbf{x}_k), \quad \text{bot}_S := \frac{1}{m(m-1)}\sum_{i=1}^{m}\sum_{k=1}^{m}\pi(\mathbf{x}_i,\mathbf{x}_k).$$

Since diagonal terms are $\pi(\mathbf{x}_i,\mathbf{x}_i) = 0$, $\text{top}_\mathcal{D} = \mathbb{E}_{S\sim\mathcal{D}^m}\text{top}_S$ and $\text{bot}_\mathcal{D} = \mathbb{E}_{S\sim\mathcal{D}^m}\text{bot}_S$. Thus, we can bound the difference between top_S and $\text{top}_\mathcal{D}$ using large deviation bounds; same for bot_S and $\text{bot}_\mathcal{D}$. One can show that the replacement of one instance changes top_S (or bot_S) by at most $1/m$. Thus, McDiarmid's inequality implies, for every $\epsilon_1 > 0$:

$$\mathbb{P}\{\text{top}_\mathcal{D} - \text{top}_S \geq \epsilon_1\} \leq \exp[-2\epsilon_1^2 m] \quad \text{and} \quad \mathbb{P}\{\text{bot}_S - \text{bot}_\mathcal{D} \geq \epsilon_1\} \leq \exp[-2\epsilon_1^2 m].$$

We will specify ϵ_1 in terms of ϵ later. Consider the following event:

$$\text{top}_\mathcal{D} - \text{top}_S < \epsilon_1 \quad \text{and} \quad \text{bot}_S - \text{bot}_\mathcal{D} < \epsilon_1.$$

By the union bound, this event is true with probability at least $1 - 2\exp[-2\epsilon_1^2 m]$. When the event is true, we can rearrange the equations to be a bound on $L(f)$:

$$L(f) = \frac{\text{top}_\mathcal{D}}{\text{bot}_\mathcal{D}} - \frac{\text{top}_S}{\text{bot}_S} < \frac{\text{top}_\mathcal{D}}{\text{bot}_\mathcal{D}} - \frac{\text{top}_\mathcal{D} - \epsilon_1}{\text{bot}_\mathcal{D} + \epsilon_1} =: \epsilon/2.$$

Above, we have just specified the value for ϵ_1 in terms of ϵ. Let us solve for ϵ_1:

$$\epsilon_1 = \frac{\epsilon\text{bot}_\mathcal{D}}{2 - \epsilon + 2\frac{\text{top}_\mathcal{D}}{\text{bot}_\mathcal{D}}} \geq \frac{\epsilon E}{4}.$$

Here, we have used $E := \text{bot}_\mathcal{D}$, and by definition, $\text{top}_\mathcal{D} \leq \text{bot}_\mathcal{D}$. We directly have:

$$1 - 2\exp[-2\epsilon_1^2 m] \geq 1 - 2\exp\left(-2m\left[\frac{\epsilon E}{4}\right]^2\right).$$

Therefore, from our earlier application of McDiarmid, with probability at least $1 - 2\exp\left[-\frac{m(\epsilon E)^2}{8}\right]$ the following holds: $L(f) < \epsilon/2$. $\qquad\square$

Proof. (**of Theorem** 1) Since the D_p are a cover of $\mathcal{F}$, it is true that

$$\sup_{f \in \mathcal{F}} L(f) \geq \epsilon \quad \Longleftrightarrow \quad \exists p \leq \ell_\epsilon \text{ such that } \sup_{f \in D_p} L(f) \geq \epsilon.$$

First applying the union bound, then applying Lemma 4, and then Lemma 5, we find:

$$\mathbb{P}_{S \sim \mathcal{D}^m} \left\{ \sup_{f \in \mathcal{F}} L(f) \geq \epsilon \right\} \leq \sum_{p=1}^{\ell_\epsilon} \mathbb{P}_{S \sim \mathcal{D}^m} \left\{ \sup_{f \in D_p} L(f) \geq \epsilon \right\} \leq \sum_{p=1}^{\ell_\epsilon} \mathbb{P}_{S \sim \mathcal{D}^m} \left\{ L(f_p) \geq \epsilon/2 \right\}$$

$$\leq \sum_{p=1}^{\ell_\epsilon} 2 \exp \left[-\frac{m(\epsilon E)^2}{8} \right] = \mathcal{N} \left(\mathcal{F}, \frac{\epsilon}{8\mathrm{Lip}(\phi)} \right) 2 \exp \left[-\frac{m(\epsilon E)^2}{8} \right].$$

Now, with probability at least $1 - \mathcal{N} \left(\mathcal{F}, \frac{\epsilon}{8\mathrm{Lip}(\phi)} \right) 2 \exp \left[-\frac{m(\epsilon E)^2}{8} \right]$, we have $\mathbb{P}_{\mathcal{D}}\{\mathrm{misrank}_f\} \leq \mathbb{P}_S \phi_f + \epsilon$. Let $\phi(z) = 1$ for $z \leq 0$, $\phi(z) = 0$ for $z \geq \theta$, and let $\phi(z)$ be linear in between with slope $1/\theta$. Thus, $\mathrm{Lip}(\phi) = 1/\theta$. Since $\phi(z) \leq 1$ for $z \leq \theta$, we have:

$$\mathbb{P}_S \phi_f = \frac{\sum_{i=1}^m \sum_{k=1}^m \phi(f(\mathbf{x}_i) - f(\mathbf{x}_k))\pi(\mathbf{x}_i, \mathbf{x}_k)}{\sum_{i=1}^m \sum_{k=1}^m \pi(\mathbf{x}_i, \mathbf{x}_k)} \leq \mathbb{P}_S\{\mathrm{margin}_f \leq \theta\}.$$

Thus, with probability at least $1 - \mathcal{N} \left(\mathcal{F}, \frac{\epsilon \theta}{8} \right) 2 \exp \left[- \left(\frac{m(\epsilon E)^2}{8} \right) \right]$, we have $\mathbb{P}_{\mathcal{D}}\{\mathrm{misrank}_f\} \leq \mathbb{P}_S\{\mathrm{margin}_f \leq \theta\} + \epsilon$. Thus, the theorem has been proved. $\quad\square$

Martingale Boosting

Philip M. Long[1] and Rocco A. Servedio[2,*]

[1] Center for Computational Learning Systems
[2] Department of Computer Science,
Columbia University
{plong, rocco}@cs.columbia.edu

Abstract. Martingale boosting is a simple and easily understood technique with a simple and easily understood analysis. A slight variant of the approach provably achieves optimal accuracy in the presence of random misclassification noise.

1 Introduction

Boosting [15, 7] has been an overwhelming practical success. In many applied domains, the best known algorithms use boosting. Nevertheless, some time ago, sensitivity to noise was identified as a weakness of the standard boosting techniques [6, 10, 4].

Heuristics have been proposed to combat this [14, 12]. The heuristics are based on an implicit view that noisy examples tend to be borderline cases: they penalize noisy examples roughly in proportion to how much they deviate from the norm. This view has been seen to be useful, but there are applications in which many examples are not borderline.

Some boosting algorithms have been shown to be provably noise-tolerant [17, 1, 2, 8, 9]. As in classification in general, the main approaches to theory for noise-tolerant boosting can be divided into agnostic/malicious and independent models. In the agnostic/malicious case, essentially nothing is assumed about the noise, except a limit on its rate. This may appear to be more realistic than the alternative in which the labels are assumed to be flipped independently of the sample. However, analysis of agnostic or malicious noise models is by necessity focused on the worst case; typically, in this case, noisy examples are the most extreme elements of the opposite class. Sources involving independent misclassification noise resemble applied problems more than this. Thus, analysis of learning with independent misclassification noise may be the most effective way to use theory to guide the design of boosting algorithms that are robust to noisy data other than borderline cases.

This paper is about an approach that we call *martingale boosting*. We concentrate on the problem of predicting binary classifications, say 0 and 1. As in many earlier boosting algorithms, learning proceeds incrementally in stages. In each

---

* Supported in part by NSF CAREER award CCF-0347282.

P. Auer and R. Meir (Eds.): COLT 2005, LNAI 3559, pp. 79–94, 2005.
© Springer-Verlag Berlin Heidelberg 2005

stage, examples are partitioned into bins, and a separate base classifier is chosen for each bin. An example is assigned a bin by counting the number of 1 predictions made by the appropriate base classifiers from earlier rounds. The algorithm halts after a predetermined number of rounds. In the basic version of martingale boosting, the classifier output by the algorithm processes an item to be classified in stages that correspond to the stages of training. During each stage, it applies the appropriate base classifier, and determines its final prediction by comparing the number of 1 predictions made by the chosen base classifiers with the number of 0 predictions.

Why call it martingale boosting? By choosing a separate base classifier for each bin, we can think of the algorithm as trying to push the fraction z of 1 predictions in the correct direction, whatever the current value of z.

The analysis is very simple: it proceeds by thinking of an object to be classified as taking a random walk on the number of base classifiers that predict 1. If the error rates are slightly better than random guessing on both positive and negative examples, it is easy to see that, after a few rounds, it is overwhelmingly likely that more than half the steps are in the correct direction: such examples are classified correctly by the boosted classifier.

In some cases, one can promote balanced error rates directly; for example, if decision stumps are used as base classifiers, one can easily adjust the threshold to balance the error rates on the training data. We also show that it is possible to *force* a standard weak learner to produce a classifier with balanced error rates in the cases that we need.

Martingale boosting facilitates noise tolerance by the fact that the probability of reaching a given bin depends on the *predictions* made by the earlier base classifiers, and not on the label of an example. (In particular, it does not depend on the number that are correct or incorrect, as does Boost-by-Majority [5].) The most technical aspect of the paper is to show that the reweighting to force balanced errors can be done while preserving noise-tolerance. Ideas from earlier work by Kalai and Servedio [9] are useful there.

Because it is a simple and easily understood technique that generates highly noise-tolerant algorithms, ideas from martingale boosting appear likely to be practically useful.

2   Preliminaries

Given a target concept $c : X \to \{0,1\}$ and a distribution $\mathcal{D}$ over X, we write $\mathcal{D}^+$ to denote the distribution $\mathcal{D}$ restricted to the positive examples $\{x \in X : c(x) = 1\}$. Thus, for any event $S \subseteq \{x \in X : c(x) = 1\}$ we have $\Pr_{\mathcal{D}^+}[x \in S] = \Pr_{\mathcal{D}}[x \in S]/\Pr_{\mathcal{D}}[c(x) = 1]$. Similarly, we write $\mathcal{D}^-$ to denote $\mathcal{D}$ restricted to the negative examples $\{x \in X : c(x) = 0\}$.

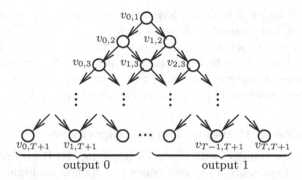

Fig. 1. The branching program produced by the boosting algorithm. Each node $v_{i,t}$ is labeled with a 0/1-valued function $h_{i,t}$; left edges correspond to 0 and right edges to 1

3   High-Level Structure of the Boosting Algorithm

The boosting algorithm works in a series of T *stages*. The hypothesis of the boosting algorithm is a layered branching program with $T+1$ layers in a grid graph structure, where layer t has t nodes (see Figure 1); we refer to the i-th node from the left in layer t as $v_{i,t}$, where i ranges from 0 to $t-1$. For $1 \leq t \leq T$, each node $v_{i,t}$ in layer t has two outgoing edges, one left edge (which is labeled with a 0) to node $v_{i,t+1}$ and one right edge (labeled with a 1) to node $v_{i+1,t+1}$. Nodes $v_{i,T+1}$ in layer $T+1$ have no outgoing edges.

Before stage t of the boosting algorithm begins, each node at levels $1, \ldots, t-1$ has been labeled with a 0/1-valued hypothesis function. We write $h_{i,j}$ to denote the hypothesis function that labels node $v_{i,j}$. In the t-th stage, hypothesis functions are assigned to each of the t nodes $v_{0,t}$ through $v_{t-1,t}$ at level t. Given an example $x \in X$ in stage t, the branching program routes the example by evaluating $h_{0,1}$ on x and then sending the example on the outgoing edge whose label is $h_{0,1}(x)$, i.e. sending it to node $v_{h_{0,1}(x),1}$. The example is routed through successive levels in this way until it reaches level t; more precisely, when example x reaches some node $v_{i,j}$ in level j, it is routed from there via the outgoing edge whose label is $h_{i,j}(x)$ to the node $v_{i+h_{i,j}(x),j+1}$. In this fashion the example x eventually reaches the node $v_{\ell,t}$ after being evaluated on $t-1$ hypotheses, where ℓ is the number of these $t-1$ hypotheses which evaluated to 1 on x.

Thus, in the t-th stage of boosting, given an initial distribution $\mathcal{D}$ over examples x, the hypotheses that have been assigned to nodes at levels $1, \ldots, t-1$ of the branching program induce t different distributions $\mathcal{D}_{0,t}, \ldots, \mathcal{D}_{t-1,t}$ corresponding to the t nodes $v_{0,t}, \ldots, v_{t-1,t}$ in layer t (a random draw x from distribution $\mathcal{D}_{i,t}$ is a draw from $\mathcal{D}$ conditioned on x reaching $v_{i,t}$). In the following sections, we will carefully specify just how the hypotheses $h_{0,t}, \ldots, h_{t-1,t}$ are generated to label the nodes $v_{0,t}, \ldots, v_{t-1,t}$ in the t-th stage of boosting; as we will see in Section 5, for the boosting algorithms that work in the standard model, it is *not* the case that $h_{i,t}$ is obtained simply by running the weak learner on distribution $\mathcal{D}_{i,t}$ and using the resulting hypothesis as $h_{i,t}$.

Once all T stages of boosting have been performed, the resulting branching program routes any example x to some node $v_{\ell,T+1}$ at level $T+1$; observe that ℓ is the number of hypotheses that evaluated to 1 out of the T hypotheses that were evaluated on x. The final classifier computed by the branching program is simple: given an example x to classify, if the final node $v_{\ell,T+1}$ that x reaches has $\ell \geq T/2$ then the output is 1, and otherwise the output is 0.

3.1   Relation to Previous Boosting Algorithms

Readers who are familiar with Freund's paper on the Boost-by-Majority algorithm [5] may experience a sense of déjà vu on looking at Figure 1, since a very similar figure appears in [5]. Indeed, both our current boosting scheme and the Boost-by-Majority algorithm can be viewed as routing an example through a branching program which has the graph structure shown in Figure 1, and both boosters work by ultimately predicting 1 or 0 according to whether the majority of T weak hypotheses evaluate to 1 or 0. However, in Boost-by-Majority, in stage t the weak learning algorithm is only invoked *once*, using a single distribution $\mathcal{D}_t$ that reweights each examples according to which node $v_{i,t}$ at level t it arrives at. Thus, in Boost-by-Majority there are only T weak hypotheses that are ever generated in the course of boosting, and each node $v_{0,t}, \ldots, v_{t-1,t}$ is labeled with the same weak hypothesis h_t; the final output is a majority vote over these T hypotheses $h_1, \ldots, h_T$. In contrast, our algorithm invokes the weak learner t *separate times* in stage t, once for each of the t distinct distributions $\mathcal{D}_{0,t}, \ldots, \mathcal{D}_{t-1,t}$ corresponding to the nodes $v_{0,t}, v_{1,t}, \ldots, v_{t-1,t}$. (We remind the reader again that as we will see in Section 5, the hypothesis $h_{i,t}$ is *not* obtained simply by running the weak learner on $\mathcal{D}_{i,t}$ and taking the resulting hypothesis to be $h_{i,t}$.) A total of $T(T+1)/2$ weak hypotheses are constructed, and any single example x only encounters T of these hypotheses in its path through the branching program.

As we will see, our algorithm has a very simple proof of correctness which seems quite different from the Boost-by-Majority proof. Moreover, the fact that our algorithm constructs a different hypothesis $h_{i,t}$ for each node $v_{i,t}$ seems to play an important role in enabling our boosting algorithm to tolerate random classification noise. We will show in Section 7 that a slight variant of our boosting algorithm can learn to any accuracy rate $1 - \epsilon < 1 - \eta$ in the presence of random classification noise at rate η; no such guarantee is given for Boost-by-Majority or any variant of it that we are aware of in the literature, and we were unable to prove such a guarantee for Boost-by-Majority. It is an interesting question for future work to determine whether Boost-by-Majority actually has (close to) this level of noise tolerance.

Another related algorithm is the "boosting by branching programs" algorithm of Mansour and McAllester [11], which we refer to as the MM algorithm. Kalai and Servedio [9] modified the MM algorithm to obtain a boosting algorithm which is robust in the presence of random classification noise.

Like the Mansour/McAllester boosting algorithm, our booster works by building a branching program. Also, as mentioned earlier, our modification and analysis of this paper's boosting algorithm to achieve random classification noise tolerance will follow the approach of Kalai & Servedio. However, there are significant differences between our boosting algorithm and this earlier work. The algorithm and analysis of [11] and [9] are based on the notion of "purity gain;" a node v is split into two descendents if each of the two labels 0 and 1 is achieved by a nonnegligible fraction of the examples that reach v, and two nodes v and w are merged if the ratio of positive to negative examples within v is similar to the ratio within w. Nodes that are pure (for some $b \in \{0, 1\}$ almost all examples that reach v are labeled with b) are "frozen" (i.e. not split any more) and assigned the label b. In contrast, in our new algorithm the label of a given terminal node in the branching program depends not on the majority vote label of examples that reach that node, but on the majority vote label of the hypotheses that are evaluated on the path to the node. In the analysis of our algorithm, progress is measured not in terms of purity gain achieved by splitting a node, but rather by the amount of "drift" in the right direction that a node imparts to the examples that reach it. (We will see, though, that notions of purity do play a role for efficiency reasons in the example oracle model implementation of the algorithm that we describe in Section 6.)

The branching program output by our algorithm has a regular structure, and is easily interpreted, arguably in contrast with the output of previous algorithms for boosting by branching programs [11, 9].

4   Boosting a Two-Sided Weak Learner

Let $c : X \to \{0, 1\}$ be the target function that we are trying to learn to high accuracy with respect to distribution $\mathcal{D}$ over X. Throughout this section the distributions $\mathcal{D}^+$ and $\mathcal{D}^-$ are defined with respect to c.

Definition 1. *A hypothesis* $h : X \to \{0, 1\}$ *is said to have* two-sided advantage γ *with respect to* $\mathcal{D}$ *if it satisfies both* $\Pr_{x \in \mathcal{D}^+}[h(x) = 1] \geq \frac{1}{2} + \gamma$ *and* $\Pr_{x \in \mathcal{D}^-}[h(x) = 0] \geq \frac{1}{2} + \gamma$.

Thus such a hypothesis performs noticeably better than random guessing both on positive examples and on negative examples. In this section we will assume that we have access to a *two-sided weak learner* that, when invoked on target concept c and distribution $\mathcal{D}$, outputs a hypothesis with two-sided advantage. (In the next section, we will perform an analysis using the usual assumption of having just a standard weak learner. That analysis can be viewed as reducing that problem to the two-side model studied here.)

We now show how the general boosting framework of Section 3 can be used to boost a two-sided weak learner to high accuracy. This is done very simply: in stage t, at each node $v_{i,t}$ we just run the two-sided weak learner on examples drawn from $\mathcal{D}_{i,t}$ (recall that this is the distribution obtained by filtering $\mathcal{D}$ to accept only those examples that reach node $v_{i,t}$), and use the resulting hypothesis, which has two-sided advantage with respect to $\mathcal{D}_{i,t}$, as the hypothesis function $h_{i,t}$ labelling node $v_{i,t}$. We refer to this boosting scheme as `Basic MartiBoost`.

The idea of the analysis is extremely simple. Let h denote the final branching program that `Basic Martiboost` constructs. We will see that a random example x drawn from $\mathcal{D}^+$ (i.e. a random positive example) is routed through h according to a random walk that is biased toward the right, and a random example x drawn from $\mathcal{D}^-$ is routed through h according to a random walk that is biased toward the left. Since h classifies example x according to whether x reaches a final node $v_{\ell,T+1}$ with $\ell \geq T/2$ or $\ell < T/2$, this will imply that h has high accuracy on both random positive examples and random negative examples.

So consider a random positive example x (i.e. x is distributed according to $\mathcal{D}^+$). For any node $v_{i,t}$, conditioned on x reaching node $v_{i,t}$ we have that x is distributed according to $(\mathcal{D}_{i,t})^+$. Consequently, by the definition of two-sided advantage we have that x goes from node $v_{i,t}$ to node $v_{i+1,t+1}$ with probability at least $1/2+\gamma$, so x does indeed follow a random walk biased to the right. Similarly, for any node $v_{i,t}$ a random negative example that reaches node $v_{i,t}$ will proceed to node $v_{i,t+1}$ with probability at least $1/2+\gamma$, and thus random negative examples follow a random walk biased to the left. Now standard bounds on random walks are easily seen to imply that if $T = O(\frac{\log 1/\epsilon}{\gamma^2})$, then the probability that a random positive example x ends up at a node $v_{\ell,T+1}$ with $\ell < T/2$ is at most ϵ. The same is true for random negative examples, and thus h has overall accuracy at least $1 - \epsilon$ with respect to $\mathcal{D}$. In more detail, we have the following theorem:

Theorem 1. *Let* $\gamma_1, \gamma_2, \ldots, \gamma_T$ *be any sequence of values between 0 and 1/2. For each value* $t = 1, \ldots, T$, *suppose that each of the* t *invocations of the weak learner on distributions* $\mathcal{D}_{i,t}$ *(with* $0 \leq i \leq t-1$) *yields a hypothesis* $h_{i,t}$ *which has two-sided advantage* γ_t *with respect to* $\mathcal{D}_{i,t}$. *Then the final output hypothesis* h *that* `Basic Martiboost` *computes will satisfy* $\Pr_{x \in \mathcal{D}}[h(x) \neq c(x)] \leq \exp\left(-(\sum_{t=1}^T \gamma_t)^2/(2T)\right)$.

Proof. As sketched above, we will begin by bounding the error rate on positive examples (a nearly identical proof will work for the negative examples).

For $t = 1, \ldots, T$ we define the 0/1 valued random variable X_t as follows: given a draw of x from $\mathcal{D}^+$, the random variable X_t takes value $h_{i,t}(x)$ where i denotes the index of the node $v_{i,t}$ that x reaches at level t of the branching program. Let the random variable Y denote $X_1 + \cdots + X_T$, so the final node at which x terminates is $v_{Y,T+1}$. Let random variables $Y_0, Y_1, \ldots, Y_T$ denote the Doob martingale sequence $Y_0 = E[Y]$ and $Y_t = E[Y|X_1, \ldots, X_t]$ for $t = 1, \ldots, T$ (see e.g. Section 4.4.3 of [13]). Note that Y_0 is a constant and Y_T equals Y.

Conditioned on x reaching node $v_{i,t}$, we have that x is distributed according to $(\mathcal{D}_{i,t})^+$, and thus for each $t = 1, \ldots, T$ the expectation $E[X_t]$ equals

$$\sum_{i=0}^{t-1} \Pr[x \text{ reaches } v_{i,t}] \cdot \Pr_{x \in (\mathcal{D}_{i,t})^+}[h_{i,t}(x) = 1] \geq \sum_{i=0}^{t-1} \Pr[x \text{ reaches } v_{i,t}] \cdot \left(\frac{1}{2} + \gamma_t\right) = \frac{1}{2} + \gamma_t,$$

so by linearity of expectation we have $E[Y] \geq \frac{T}{2} + \sum_{t=1}^T \gamma_t$. By Azuma's inequality (see e.g. Theorem 4.16 of [13]) we thus have that $\Pr_{x \in \mathcal{D}^+}[Y_T < T/2] \leq \exp\left(-\frac{(\sum_{t=1}^T \gamma_t)^2}{2T}\right)$. Recalling that Y_T equals Y and $h(x) = 0$ only if fewer than

$T/2$ of the branching program hypotheses $h_{i,t}$ that are evaluated on x yield 1, we have that $\Pr_{x \in \mathcal{D}^+}[h(x) = 0]$ equals the left-hand side of the above inequality. The same argument shows that $\Pr_{x \in \mathcal{D}^-}[h(x) = 1] \leq \exp\left(-\frac{(\sum_{t=1}^{T} \gamma_t)^2}{2T}\right)$. $\qquad \square$

Note that if we have $\gamma_t \geq \gamma$ for all t, then Theorem 1 gives the familiar bound $\Pr_{x \in \mathcal{D}}[h(x) \neq c(x)] \leq \exp(-\frac{\gamma^2 T}{2})$.

5 Boosting a Standard Weak Learner

We recall the usual definition of a weak learner.

Definition 2. *Given a target function* $c : X \rightarrow \{0,1\}$ *and a distribution* $\mathcal{D}$, *a hypothesis* $h : X \rightarrow \{0,1\}$ *is said to have* advantage γ *with respect to* $\mathcal{D}$ *if it satisfies* $\Pr_{x \in \mathcal{D}}[h(x) = c(x)] \geq \frac{1}{2} + \gamma$.

In this section we will assume that we have access to a standard weak learning algorithm which, when invoked on target concept c and distribution $\mathcal{D}$, outputs a hypothesis h which has advantage γ with respect to $\mathcal{D}$. This is the usual assumption that is made in the study of boosting, and is clearly less demanding than the two-sided weak learner we considered in the previous section. We will show how the **Basic MartiBoost** algorithm of the previous section can be modified to boost a standard weak learner to high accuracy.

For clarity of exposition, throughout this section we will consider an abstract version of the boosting algorithm in which all desired probabilities can be obtained exactly (i.e. we do not consider issues of sampling error, etc. here). We will deal carefully with these issues when we describe an example oracle model implementation of the algorithm in Section 6.

5.1 Definitions and an Easy Lemma

Let $c : X \rightarrow \{0,1\}$ be a target concept. We say that a distribution $\mathcal{D}$ over X is *balanced* if $\mathcal{D}$ puts equal weight on positive and negative examples, i.e. $\Pr_{x \in \mathcal{D}}[c(x) = 0] = \frac{1}{2}$. Given an arbitrary distribution $\mathcal{D}$ (not necessarily balanced), we write $\widehat{\mathcal{D}}$ to denote the balanced version of $\mathcal{D}$ which is an equal average of $\mathcal{D}^+$ and $\mathcal{D}^-$; i.e. for any $S \subseteq X$ we have $\Pr_{\widehat{\mathcal{D}}}[S] = \frac{1}{2}\Pr_{\mathcal{D}^+}[S] + \frac{1}{2}\Pr_{\mathcal{D}^-}[S]$.

Given a distribution $\mathcal{D}$ over X and a hypothesis $h : X \rightarrow \{0,1\}$, we define $\widehat{h}$, the balanced version of h, to be the (probabilistic) version of h described below; the key property of $\widehat{h}$ is that it outputs 0 and 1 equally often under $\mathcal{D}$. Let $b \in \{0,1\}$ be the value that h evaluates to more often, and let $r = \Pr_{x \in \mathcal{D}}[h(x) = b]$ (so $1/2 \leq r \leq 1$). Given an input $x \in X$, to evaluate $\widehat{h}$ on x we toss a biased coin which comes up heads with probability $\frac{1}{2r}$. If we get heads we output $h(x)$, and if we get tails we output $1 - b$. This ensures that $\Pr_{x \in \mathcal{D}}[\widehat{h}(x) = b] = \Pr[\text{coin is heads \& } h(x) = b] = \frac{1}{2r} \cdot r = \frac{1}{2}$.

The following simple lemma shows that if we have a weak hypothesis h that has advantage γ relative to a balanced distribution $\mathcal{D}$, then the balanced hypothesis $\widehat{h}$ has advantage at least $\gamma/2$ relative to $\mathcal{D}$.

Table 1. Each table entry gives the probability of the corresponding event under the balanced distribution $\mathcal{D}$

	$c(x) = 1$	$c(x) = 0$
$h(x) = 1$	p	q
$h(x) = 0$	$1/2 - p$	$1/2 - q$

	$c(x) = 1$	$c(x) = 0$
$h(x) = 1, \widehat{h}(x) = 1$	$\frac{p}{2r}$	$\frac{q}{2r}$
$h(x) = 1, \widehat{h}(x) = 0$	$p(1 - \frac{1}{2r})$	$q(1 - \frac{1}{2r})$
$h(x) = 0, \widehat{h}(x) = 1$	0	0
$h(x) = 0, \widehat{h}(x) = 0$	$\frac{1}{2} - p$	$\frac{1}{2} - q$

Table 2. Each table entry gives the probability of the corresponding event under the balanced distribution $\widehat{\mathcal{D}_{i,t}}$

	$h_{i,t}(x) = 0$	$h_{i,t}(x) = 1$
$c(x) = 0$	p	$1/2 - p$
$c(x) = 1$	$1/2 - p$	p

Lemma 1. *If $\mathcal{D}$ is a balanced distribution and $\Pr_{\mathcal{D}}[h(x) = c(x)] \geq \frac{1}{2} + \gamma$ then $\Pr_{\mathcal{D}}[\widehat{h}(x) = c(x)] \geq \frac{1}{2} + \frac{\gamma}{2}$.*

Proof. We may assume without loss of generality that $\Pr_{\mathcal{D}}[h(x) = 1] = r \geq \frac{1}{2}$, i.e. that $b = 1$ in the above discussion. If we let p denote $\Pr_{\mathcal{D}}[h(x) = 1 \ \& \ c(x) = 1]$ and q denote $\Pr_{\mathcal{D}}[h(x) = 1 \ \& \ c(x) = 0]$, so $p + q = r$, then the probabilities for all four possible values of h and c are given in the left side of Table 1. From the definition of $\widehat{h}$ it is straightforward to verify that the probabilities of all eight combinations of values for $h, \widehat{h}$ and c are as given in the right side of Table 1. We thus have that $\Pr_{\mathcal{D}}[\widehat{h}(x) = c(x)] = \frac{p}{2r} + q\left(1 - \frac{1}{2r}\right) + \frac{1}{2} - q = \frac{1}{2} + \frac{p-q}{2r}$. By assumption we have $\Pr_{\mathcal{D}}[h(x) = c(x)] \geq \frac{1}{2} + \gamma$, so from the left side of Table 1 we have $p - q \geq \gamma$. The claim follows since $r \leq 1$. $\square$

5.2   Boosting a Standard Weak Learner with `MartiBoost`

Our algorithm for boosting a standard weak learner, which we call `MartiBoost`, works as follows. In stage t, at each node $v_{i,t}$ we run the weak learning algorithm on the balanced version $\widehat{\mathcal{D}_{i,t}}$ of the distribution $\mathcal{D}_{i,t}$; let $g_{i,t}$ denote the hypothesis that the weak learner returns. The hypothesis $h_{i,t}$ that is used to label $v_{i,t}$ is $h_{i,t} = \widehat{g_{i,t}}$, namely $g_{i,t}$ balanced with respect to the balanced distribution $\widehat{\mathcal{D}_{i,t}}$.

The following lemma plays a key role in our proof of correctness:

Lemma 2. *We have $\Pr_{x \in (\mathcal{D}_{i,t})^+}[h_{i,t}(x) = 1] \geq \frac{1}{2} + \frac{\gamma}{2}$ and $\Pr_{x \in (\mathcal{D}_{i,t})^-}[h_{i,t}(x) = 0] \geq \frac{1}{2} + \frac{\gamma}{2}$.*

Proof. Since the original hypothesis $g_{i,t}$ that the weak learner returns when invoked with $\widehat{\mathcal{D}_{i,t}}$ has accuracy at least $\frac{1}{2} + \gamma$ with respect to $\widehat{\mathcal{D}_{i,t}}$, by Lemma 1 we have that the balanced hypothesis $h_{i,t}$ has accuracy at least $\frac{1}{2} + \frac{\gamma}{2}$ with respect to $\widehat{D_{i,t}}$. Let p denote $\Pr_{\widehat{D_{i,t}}}[h_{i,t}(x) = c(x) = 0]$. Since $\widehat{D_{i,t}}$ is a balanced distribution and $h_{i,t}$ is a balanced hypothesis, it is easy to see that all four table entries must be as given in Table 2, and thus $\Pr_{\widehat{D_{i,t}}}[h_{i,t}(x) = c(x)] = 2p \geq \frac{1}{2} + \frac{\gamma}{2}$, i.e. $p \geq \frac{1}{4} + \frac{\gamma}{4}$. But since $\widehat{D_{i,t}}$ is an equal mixture of $(D_{i,t})^+$ and $(D_{i,t})^-$, this implies that $\Pr_{x \in (D_{i,t})^+}[h_{i,t}(x) = 1] \geq (\frac{1}{4} + \frac{\gamma}{4})/\frac{1}{2} = \frac{1}{2} + \frac{\gamma}{2}$. We similarly have that $\Pr_{x \in (D_{i,t})^-}[h_{i,t}(x) = 0] \geq \frac{1}{2} + \frac{\gamma}{2}$, and the lemma is proved. $\qquad \square$

With this lemma in hand it is easy to prove correctness of `MartiBoost`:

Theorem 2. *Let $\gamma_1, \gamma_2, \ldots, \gamma_T$ be any sequence of values between 0 and $1/2$. For each value $t = 1, \ldots, T$, suppose that each of the t invocations of the weak learner on distributions $\widehat{D_{i,t}}$ (with $0 \leq i \leq t-1$) yields a hypothesis $g_{i,t}$ which has advantage γ_t with respect to $\widehat{D_{i,t}}$. Then the final branching program hypothesis h that* `MartiBoost` *constructs will satisfy $\Pr_{x \in D}[h(x) \neq c(x)] \leq \exp\left(-\frac{(\sum_{t=1}^{T} \gamma_t)^2}{8T}\right).$*

Proof. The proof is almost identical to the proof of Theorem 1. We define sequences of random variables $X_1, \ldots, X_T$ and $Y_0, \ldots, Y_T$ as before; the only difference is that (i) now we have $E[X_t] \geq \frac{1}{2} + \frac{\gamma_t}{2}$ (by Lemma 2) rather than $E[X_t] \geq \frac{1}{2} + \gamma_t$ as in the earlier proof, and (ii) the randomness is now taken over both the draw of x from D^+ and over the internal randomness of each hypothesis $h_{i,t}$ at each node in the branching program. This loss of a factor of 2 from (i) in the advantage accounts for the different constant (worse by a factor of 4) in the exponent of the bound. $\qquad \square$

6   Complexity Issues: Implementation of `MartiBoost` That Works with an Example Oracle

Thus far we have described and analyzed an abstract version of `MartiBoost` without specifying how the weak learner is actually run on the distribution $\widehat{D_{i,t}}$ at each node. One approach is to run the boosting algorithm on a fixed sample. In this case all relevant probabilities can be maintained explicitly in a look-up table, and then Theorem 2 bounds the training set accuracy of the `MartiBoost` final hypothesis over this fixed sample.

In this section we describe and analyze an implementation of the algorithm in which the weak learner runs given access to an example oracle $EX(c, D)$. As we will see, this version of the algorithm requires some changes for the sake of efficiency; in particular we will "freeze" the execution of the algorithm at nodes $v_{i,t}$ where it is too expensive to simulate $\widehat{D_{i,t}}$. We give an analysis of the time and sample complexity of the resulting algorithm which shows that it is computationally efficient and can achieve a highly accurate final hypothesis. Note that the accuracy in this case is measured with respect to the underlying distribution generating the data (and future test data).

6.1   The Model

We define weak learning in the example oracle $EX(c, D)$ framework as follows:

Definition 3. *Given a target function $c : X \to \{0, 1\}$, an algorithm A is said to be a* weak learning algorithm with advantage γ *if it satisfies the following property: for any $\delta > 0$ and any distribution $\mathcal{D}$ over X, if A is given δ and access to $EX(c, \mathcal{D})$ then algorithm A outputs a hypothesis $h : X \to \{0, 1\}$ which with probability at least $1 - \delta$ satisfies $\mathrm{Pr}_{x \in \mathcal{D}}[h(x) = c(x)] \geq \frac{1}{2} + \gamma$.*

We let $m_A(\delta)$ denote the running time of algorithm A, where we charge one time step per invocation of the oracle $EX(c, \mathcal{D})$. Thus, if we must run algorithm A using a simulated oracle $EX(c, \mathcal{D}')$ but we only have access to $EX(c, \mathcal{D})$, the runtime will be at most $m_A(\delta)$ times the amount of time it takes to simulate a draw from $EX(c, \mathcal{D}')$ given $EX(c, \mathcal{D})$.

6.2   An Idealized Version of the Oracle Algorithm

We now describe the version of MartiBoost designed to work with a sampling oracle in more detail; we call this algorithm Sampling Martiboost, or SMartiBoost. While this algorithm is intended to work with random examples, to keep the focus clear on the main ideas, let us continue for a while to assume that all required probabilities can be computed exactly. In Section 6.3 we will show that the analysis still holds if probabilities are estimated using a polynomial-size sample.

For convenience, we will use r to denote all of the random bits used by all the hypotheses $h_{i,t}$. It is convenient to think of r as an infinite sequence of random bits that is determined before the algorithm starts and then read off one at a time as needed by the algorithm (though the algorithm will use only polynomially many of them).

In stage t of SMartiBoost, all nodes at levels $t' < t$ have been labeled and the algorithm is labelling nodes $v_{0,t}, \dots, v_{t-1,t}$. Let $p_{i,t}$ denote $\mathrm{Pr}_{x \in \mathcal{D}, r}[x$ reaches $v_{i,t}]$. For each $b \in \{0, 1\}$, let $p_{i,t}^b$ denote $\mathrm{Pr}_{x \in \mathcal{D}, r}[x$ reaches $v_{i,t}$ and the label of x is $b]$, so $p_{i,t} = p_{i,t}^0 + p_{i,t}^1$. In stage t, SMartiBoost does the following for each node $v_{i,t}$:

1. If $\min_{b \in \{0,1\}} p_{i,t}^b < \frac{\epsilon}{T(T+1)}$, then the algorithm "freezes" node $v_{i,t}$ by labelling it with the bit $(1 - b)$ and making it a terminal node with no outgoing edges (so any example x which reaches $v_{i,t}$ will be assigned label $(1 - b)$ by the branching program hypothesis).
2. Otherwise, we have $\min_{b \in \{0,1\}} p_{i,t}^b \geq \frac{\epsilon}{T(T+1)}$. In this case SMartiBoost works just like MartiBoost: it runs the weak learning algorithm on the balanced version $\widehat{\mathcal{D}_{i,t}}$ of $\mathcal{D}_{i,t}$ to obtain a hypothesis $g_{i,t}$, and it labels $v_{i,t}$ with $h_{i,t} = \widehat{g_{i,t}}$, which is $g_{i,t}$ balanced with respect to $\widehat{\mathcal{D}_{i,t}}$.

The idea is that each node which is "frozen" in step (1) above contributes at most $\frac{\epsilon}{T(T+1)}$ to the error of the final branching program hypothesis; since there are at most $T(T + 1)/2$ many nodes in the branching program, the total error induced by all frozen nodes is at most $\frac{\epsilon}{2}$. On the other hand, for any node $v_{i,t}$ that satisfies condition (2) and is not frozen, the expected number of draws from

$EX(c, \mathcal{D})$ that are required to simulate a draw from $EX(c, \widehat{\mathcal{D}_{i,t}})$ is $O(\frac{T^2}{\epsilon})$, and thus we can indeed run the weak learner efficiently on the desired distributions. (We discuss computational efficiency in more detail in the next subsection where we take sampling issues into account.)

The following theorem establishes correctness of SMartiBoost:

Theorem 3. *Let* $T = \frac{8\ln(2/\epsilon)}{\gamma^2}$. *Suppose that each time it is invoked on some distribution* $\widehat{\mathcal{D}_{i,t}}$, *the weak learner outputs a hypothesis that has advantage* γ *with respect to* $\widehat{\mathcal{D}_{i,t}}$. *Then the final branching program hypothesis* h *that* SMartiBoost *constructs will satisfy* $\Pr_{x \in \mathcal{D}}[h(x) \neq c(x)] \leq \epsilon$.

Proof. Given an unlabeled instance $x \in X$ and a particular setting r of the random bits for each of the (randomized) hypotheses $h_{i,t}$ labelling nodes of the branching program, we say that (x, r) *freezes at node* $v_{i,t}$ if the path through the branching program that x takes under randomness r causes it to terminate at a node $v_{i,t}$ with $t < T + 1$ (i.e. at a node $v_{i,t}$ which was frozen by SMartiBoost). We have that $\Pr[h(x) \neq c(x)] = \Pr[h(x) \neq c(x) \ \& \ (x,r) \text{ freezes}] + \Pr[h(x) \neq c(x) \ \& \ (x,r) \text{ does not freeze}]$. This is at most $\frac{\epsilon}{2} + \Pr[h(x) \neq c(x) \ \& \ (x,r) \text{ does not freeze}]$ (here the probabilities, as in the proof of Theorem 2, are taken over the draw of x from $\mathcal{D}$ and the choice of r).

It remains to show that $\Pr[h(x) \neq c(x) \ \& \ (x,r) \text{ does not freeze}] \leq \frac{\epsilon}{2}$. As before, we first will show that $\Pr_{x \in \mathcal{D}^+}[h(x) \neq c(x) \ \& \ (x,r) \text{ does not freeze}]$ is at most $\frac{\epsilon}{2}$; the negative examples can be handled similarly.

To show that $\Pr_{x \in \mathcal{D}^+}[h(x) \neq c(x) \ \& \ (x,r) \text{ does not freeze}] \leq \frac{\epsilon}{2}$, we consider a slightly different random process than in the proof of Theorem 2. For $t = 1, \ldots, T$ we now define the $0/1$ valued random variable X'_t as follows: given a draw of x from $\mathcal{D}^+$ and a random choice of r,

- If (x, r) does not freeze at any node $v_{j,t'}$ with $t' \leq t$, then X'_t takes value $h_{i,t}(x)$ where i denotes the index of the node $v_{i,t}$ that x reaches under randomness r at level t of the branching program;
- If (x, r) freezes at some node $v_{j,t'}$ with $t' \leq t$, then X'_t takes value 1 with probability $\frac{1}{2} + \frac{\gamma}{2}$ and takes value 0 with probability $\frac{1}{2} - \frac{\gamma}{2}$.

(This part of the proof is reminiscent of [2].) It is clear that $E[X'_t \mid (x,r) \text{ freezes}$ at some node $v_{j,t'}$ with $t' \leq t] = \frac{1}{2} + \frac{\gamma}{2}$. On the other hand, if (x, r) does not freeze at any such node, then conditioned on x reaching node $v_{i,t}$ under randomness r we have that x is distributed according to $(\mathcal{D}_{i,t})^+$. It follows from Lemma 2 that $E[X'_t \mid (x,r) \text{ freezes at no node } v_{j,t'} \text{ with } t' \leq t] \geq \frac{1}{2} + \frac{\gamma}{2}$, and thus overall we have $E[X'_t] \geq \frac{1}{2} + \frac{\gamma}{2}$.

Let the random variable Y' denote $X'_1 + \cdots + X'_T$; by linearity of expectation we have $E[Y'] \geq \frac{T}{2} + \frac{T\gamma}{2}$. Let random variables $Y'_0, Y'_1, \ldots, Y'_T$ denote the Doob martingale sequence $Y'_0 = E[Y']$ and $Y'_t = E[Y'|X'_1, \ldots, X'_t]$ for $t = 1, \ldots, T$, so Y'_T is identical to Y'. By Azuma's inequality we have that $\Pr[Y'_T < T/2] \leq \exp\left(-\frac{\gamma^2 T}{8}\right)$. Now recall that if (x, r) never freezes, then the prediction $h(x)$ is determined by the majority of the values of $h_{i,t}(x)$ obtained from hypotheses $h_{i,t}$

encountered in its path through the branching program. Thus, in the particular case of positive examples, $\Pr_{x \in \mathcal{D}^+, r}[h(x) \neq c(x) \ \& \ (x, r) \text{ does not freeze}] \leq \Pr[Y_T' < T/2]$. Applying the inequality from above, bounding negative examples similarly, and recalling our choice of T, we have that $\Pr[h(x) \neq c(x) \ \& \ (x, r)$ does not freeze$] \leq \frac{\epsilon}{2}$ and the theorem is proved. $\qquad\square$

6.3   Dealing with Sampling Error

In this section we remove the assumptions that we know all required probabilities exactly, by showing that sufficiently accurate estimates of them can be obtained efficiently. We use $\tilde{O}$ below notation to hide polylogarithmic factors, and ignore the dependences on δ – which are everywhere polylogarithmic – throughout for the sake of readability.

Theorem 4. *Let $T = \Theta(\frac{\log(1/\epsilon)}{\gamma^2})$. If A is a weak learning algorithm that requires s_A many examples to construct a γ-advantage hypothesis, then* SMartiBoost *makes $O(s_A) \cdot \tilde{O}(\frac{1}{\epsilon}) \cdot poly(\frac{1}{\gamma})$ many calls to $EX(c, \mathcal{D})$ and with probability $1 - \delta$ outputs a final hypothesis h that satisfies $\Pr_{x \in \mathcal{D}}[h(x) \neq c(x)] \leq \epsilon$.*

Proof sketch. Standard sampling bounds let us estimate each $p_{i,t}^b$ and efficiently simulate $EX(c, \widehat{\mathcal{D}_{i,t}})$ for nodes $v_{i,t}$ that have some $p_{i,t}^b$ value that is not too small. Once we have run the weak learning algorithm with $EX(c, \widehat{\mathcal{D}_{i,t}})$ and it has given us its hypothesis $g_{i,t}$, we need to construct $h_{i,t}$, the randomized hypothesis obtained from $g_{i,t}$ by flipping some of its predictions in order to output 0 and 1 equally often with respect to $\widehat{\mathcal{D}_{i,t}}$. In order to do this perfectly as in Section 5.1, we would need the exact value of $r = \Pr_{x \in \widehat{\mathcal{D}_{i,t}}}[g_{i,t}(x) = b] \geq \frac{1}{2}$. While this exact value is not available to us, a straightforward generalization of Lemma 1 shows that an approximate value is good enough for our needs. $\qquad\square$

7   A Noise-Tolerant Version of SMartiBoost

In this section we show how the SMartiBoost algorithm can be modified to withstand random classification noise. We follow the approach of Kalai & Servedio [9], who showed how the branching program boosting algorithm of Mansour and McAllester can be modified to withstand random classification noise.

Given a distribution $\mathcal{D}$ and a value $0 < \eta < \frac{1}{2}$, a *noisy example oracle* is an oracle $EX(c, \mathcal{D}, \eta)$ defined as follows: each time $EX(c, \mathcal{D}, \eta)$ is invoked, it returns a labeled example $(x, b) \in X \times \{0, 1\}$ where $x \in X$ is drawn from distribution $\mathcal{D}$ and b is independently chosen to be $c(x)$ with probability $1 - \eta$ and $1 - c(x)$ with probability η. Recall the definition of noise-tolerant weak learning:

Definition 4. *Given a target function $c : X \to \{0, 1\}$, an algorithm A is said to be a noise-tolerant weak learning algorithm with advantage γ if it satisfies the following property: for any $\delta > 0$ and any distribution $\mathcal{D}$ over X, if A is given δ and access to a noisy example oracle $EX(c, \mathcal{D}, \eta)$ where $0 \leq \eta < \frac{1}{2}$, then A runs* *in time poly($\frac{1}{1-2\eta}, \frac{1}{\delta}$) and with probability at least $1 - \delta$ A outputs a hypothesis h such that* $\Pr_{x\in\mathcal{D}}[h(x) = c(x)] \geq \frac{1}{2} + \gamma$.

Ideally, we would like a boosting algorithm that can convert any noise-tolerant weak learning algorithm into a noise-tolerant strong learning algorithm that can achieve any arbitrarily low error rate $\epsilon > 0$. However, in [9] it is shown that in general it is not possible to boost the error rate ϵ down below the noise rate η.[1] They showed that a variant of the MM boosting algorithm can achieve any error rate $\epsilon = \eta + \tau$ in time polynomial in $\frac{1}{\tau}$ and the other relevant parameters. We now show that a variant of SMartiBoost has the same property.

For ease of presentation, we first give the noise-tolerant martingale boosting algorithm under the assumption that all required probabilities are obtained exactly, and then deal with sample complexity issues.

As a labeled example (x, b) proceeds through levels $1, \ldots, t-1$ of the branching program in stage t, the path it takes is completely independent of b. Thus, given a source $EX(c, \mathcal{D}, \eta)$ of noisy examples, the distribution of examples that arrive at a particular node $v_{i,t}$ is precisely $EX(c, \mathcal{D}_{i,t}, \eta)$. Once a labeled example (x, b) arrives at some node $v_{i,t}$, though, it is clear that the label b must be consulted in the "rebalancing" of the distribution $\mathcal{D}_{i,t}$ to obtain distribution $\widehat{\mathcal{D}_{i,t}}$. More precisely, the labeled examples that reach node $v_{i,t}$ are distributed according to $EX(c, \mathcal{D}_{i,t}, \eta)$, but in order to use SMartiBoost with a noise-tolerant weak learner we must simulate the *balanced* distribution $\widehat{\mathcal{D}_{i,t}}$ corrupted with random classification noise, i.e. $EX(c, \widehat{\mathcal{D}_{i,t}}, \eta')$. (As we show below, it turns out that η' need not necessarily be the same as η; it is okay to have a higher noise rate η' for the balanced oracle as long as η' is not too close to $\frac{1}{2}$.) The following lemma (Lemma 7 from [9]) shows that it is possible to do this:

Lemma 3. *Let $\tau > 0$ be any value satisfying $\eta + \frac{\tau}{2} < \frac{1}{2}$. Suppose we have access to $EX(c, \mathcal{D}, \eta)$. Let ρ denote $\Pr_{x\in\mathcal{D}}[c(x) = 1]$. Suppose that $\eta + \frac{\tau}{2} \leq \rho \leq \frac{1}{2}$ (the case where $\eta + \frac{\tau}{2} \leq 1 - \rho \leq \frac{1}{2}$ is completely analogous). Consider the following rejection sampling procedure: given a draw (x, b) from $EX(c, \mathcal{D}, \eta)$, (i) if $b = 0$ then with probability $p_r = \frac{1-2\rho}{1-\rho-\eta}$ reject (x, b), and with probability $1-p_r = \frac{\rho-\eta}{1-\rho-\eta}$ set $b' = b$ and accept (x, b'); (ii) if $b = 1$ then set b' to $1 - b$ with probability $p_f = \frac{(1-2\rho)\eta(1-\eta)}{(1-\rho-\eta)(\rho+\eta-2\rho\eta)}$ (and set b' to b with probability $1-p_f$), and accept (x, b'). Given a draw from $EX(c, \mathcal{D}, \eta)$, with probability $p_{rej} := \frac{(1-2\rho)(\rho\eta+(1-\rho)(1-\eta))}{1-\rho-\eta}$ this procedure rejects, and with probability $1 - p_{rej} = \frac{2(1-2\eta)(1-\rho)\rho}{1-\rho-\eta}$ the procedure accepts. Moreover, if the procedure accepts, then the (x, b') that it accepts is distributed according to $EX(c, \widehat{\mathcal{D}}, \eta')$ where $\eta' = \frac{1}{2} - \frac{\rho-\eta}{2(\rho+\eta-2\rho\eta)}$.*

---

[1] They showed that if cryptographic one-way functions exist, then there is no efficient "black-box" boosting algorithm that can always achieve a final error rate $\epsilon < \eta$. A black-box boosting algorithm is a boosting algorithm that can run the weak learning algorithm in a black-box fashion but cannot "inspect the code" of the weak learner. All known boosting algorithms are black-box boosters. See [9] for more discussion.

So `Noise-Tolerant SMartiBoost` works in the following way. As in Section 6.2 let $p_{i,t}$ denote $\Pr_{x \in \mathcal{D}, r}[x$ reaches $v_{i,t}]$. For $b = 0, 1$ let $q_{i,t}^b$ denote $q_{i,t}^b = \Pr_{x \in \mathcal{D}, r}[c(x) = b \mid x$ reaches $v_{i,t}] = \Pr_{x \in \mathcal{D}_{i,t}, r}[c(x) = b]$, so $q_{i,t}^0 + q_{i,t}^1 = 1$. The boosting algorithm (which takes as input a parameter $\tau > 0$, where $\eta + \tau$ is the desired final accuracy of the hypothesis; we assume WLOG that $\eta + \tau < \frac{1}{2}$) proceeds in stage t as follows: at each node $v_{i,t}$,

1. If $p_{i,t} < \frac{2\tau}{3T(T+1)}$, then the algorithm "freezes" node $v_{i,t}$ by labelling it with an arbitrary bit and making it a terminal node with no outgoing edges.
2. Otherwise, if $\min_{b \in \{0,1\}} q_{i,t}^b < \eta + \frac{\tau}{3}$, then the algorithm "freezes" node $v_{i,t}$ by making it a terminal node labeled with $(1 - b)$.
3. Otherwise the algorithm runs the noise-tolerant weak learner using $EX(c, \widehat{\mathcal{D}_{i,t}}, \eta')$ as described in Lemma 3 to obtain a hypothesis $g_{i,t}$. The balanced (with respect to $\widehat{\mathcal{D}_{i,t}}$) version of $g_{i,t}$, which we call $h_{i,t}$, is used to label node $v_{i,t}$.

Theorem 5. *Let* $T = \frac{8 \ln(3/\tau)}{\gamma^2}$. *Suppose that each time it is invoked with some oracle* $EX(c, \widehat{\mathcal{D}_{i,t}}, \eta')$, *the weak learner outputs a hypothesis* $g_{i,t}$ *with* $\Pr_{x \in \widehat{\mathcal{D}_{i,t}}}[g_{i,t}(x) = c(x)] \geq \frac{1}{2} + \gamma$. *Then the final branching program hypothesis* h *that* `Noise-Tolerant SMartiBoost` *constructs will satisfy* $\Pr_{x \in \mathcal{D}}[h(x) \neq c(x)] \leq \eta + \tau$.

Proof. As in the proof of Theorem 3, given an unlabeled instance $x \in X$ and a particular setting r of the random bits for each of the (randomized) hypotheses $h_{i,t}$ labelling nodes of the branching program, we say that (x, r) *freezes at node* $v_{i,t}$ if the path through the branching program that x takes under randomness r causes it to terminate at a node $v_{i,t}$ with $t < T + 1$ (i.e. at a node $v_{i,t}$ which was frozen by `Noise-Tolerant SMartiBoost`). We say that a node $v_{i,t}$ is *negligible* if $p_{i,t} < \frac{2\tau}{3T(T+1)}$. We have that $\Pr[h(x) \neq c(x)] = \Pr[h(x) \neq c(x)$ & (x, r) does not freeze$] + \Pr[h(x) \neq c(x)$ & (x, r) freezes at a negligible node$] + \Pr[h(x) \neq c(x)$ & (x, r) freezes at a non-negligible node$]$. Since (x, r) reaches a given negligible node $v_{i,t}$ with probability at most $\frac{2\tau}{3T(T+1)}$ and there are at most $T(T+1)/2$ many negligible nodes, $\Pr[h(x) \neq c(x)$ & (x, r) freezes at a negligible node$]$ is at most $\frac{\tau}{3}$. Consequently $\Pr[h(x) \neq c(x)]$ is at most $\frac{\tau}{3} + \Pr[h(x) \neq c(x)$ & (x, r) does not freeze$]$ plus

$$\sum_{i,t \,:\, v_{i,t} \text{ is non-negligible}} \Pr[h(x) \neq c(x) \mid (x, r) \text{ freezes at } v_{i,t}] \cdot \Pr[(x, r) \text{ freezes at } v_{i,t}].$$

Since $\Pr[h(x) \neq c(x) \mid (x, r)$ freezes at $v_{i,t}]$ equals $\Pr_{x \in \mathcal{D}_{i,t}, r}[h(x) \neq c(x)]$, by the fact that the algorithm freezes $v_{i,t}$ if $\min_{b \in \{0,1\}} q_{i,t}^b < \eta + \frac{\tau}{3}$ (case (2) above), we have that the sum above is at most $\eta + \frac{\tau}{3}$. Thus $\Pr[h(x) \neq c(x)] \leq \Pr[h(x) \neq c(x)$ & (x, r) does not freeze$] + \eta + \frac{2\tau}{3}$, so it remains to show that $\Pr[h(x) \neq c(x)$ & (x, r) does not freeze$]$ is at most $\frac{\tau}{3}$. The proof of this is identical to the proof that $\Pr[h(x) \neq c(x)$ & (x, r) does not freeze$] \leq \frac{\epsilon}{2}$ in the proof of Theorem 3 but now with $\frac{\tau}{3}$ in place of $\frac{\epsilon}{2}$. $\square$

It remains to remove the assumptions that we know all required probabilities exactly, by showing that sufficiently accurate estimates of them can be obtained efficiently via a polynomial amount of sampling. A straightforward but technical analysis (see full version for details) gives the following theorem, which establishes correctness and efficiency of the sampling-based version of Noise-Tolerant SMartiBoost:

Theorem 6. *Given any τ such that $\eta + \tau < \frac{1}{2}$, let $T = \Theta(\frac{\log(1/\tau)}{\gamma^2})$. If A is a noise-tolerant weak learning algorithm with advantage γ, then* Noise-Tolerant SMartiBoost *makes* poly$(\frac{1}{\gamma}, \frac{1}{\tau}, \frac{1}{\delta})$ *many calls to $EX(c, \mathcal{D}, \eta)$ and with probability $1 - \delta$ outputs a final hypothesis h that satisfies $\Pr_{x \in \mathcal{D}}[h(x) \neq c(x)] \leq \eta + \tau$.*

8   Conclusion

Because of its simplicity and attractive theoretical properties, we suspect martingale boosting may be useful in practice. The most likely avenue to a practically useful algorithm appears to involve repeatedly dividing the training data into bins, as opposed to using fresh examples during each stage, as is analyzed in Section 6. A generalization analysis for such an algorithm based on the syntactic complexity of the output classifier seems likely to be conservative, as was the case for boosting algorithms based on voting [16, 3]. Carrying out a meaningful formal generalization analysis is a possible topic for future research.

Because of space constraints, we have not presented a detailed computational complexity analysis. Some mileage can be gained from the fact that the base classifiers in a given stage are trained on the cells of a partition of the original dataset, possibly dividing it into small datasets.

References

[1] Shai Ben-David, Philip M. Long, and Yishay Mansour. Agnostic boosting. In *Proceedings of the 14th Annual Conference on Computational Learning Theory*, pages 507–516, 2001.
[2] N. Bshouty and D. Gavinsky. On boosting with optimal poly-bounded distributions. *Journal of Machine Learning Research*, 3:483–506, 2002.
[3] S. Dasgupta and P. Long. Boosting with diverse base classifiers. In *COLT*, 2003.
[4] T.G. Dietterich. An experimental comparison of three methods for constructing ensembles of decision trees: bagging, boosting, and randomization. *Machine Learning*, 40(2):139–158, 2000.
[5] Y. Freund. Boosting a weak learning algorithm by majority. *Information and Computation*, 121(2):256–285, 1995.
[6] Y. Freund and R. Schapire. Experiments with a new boosting algorithm. In *Proceedings of the Thirteenth International Conference on Machine Learning*, pages 148–156, 1996.
[7] Y. Freund and R. Schapire. A decision-theoretic generalization of on-line learning and an application to boosting. *Journal of Computer and System Sciences*, 55(1):119–139, 1997.

[8] Dmitry Gavinsky. Optimally-smooth adaptive boosting and application to agnostic learning. *Journal of Machine Learning Research*, 4:101–117, 2003.

[9] A. Kalai and R. Servedio. Boosting in the presence of noise. In *Proceedings of the 35th Annual Symposium on Theory of Computing (STOC)*, pages 196–205, 2003.

[10] Richard Maclin and David Opitz. An empirical evaluation of bagging and boosting. In *AAAI/IAAI*, pages 546–551, 1997.

[11] Y. Mansour and D. McAllester. Boosting using branching programs. *Journal of Computer and System Sciences*, 64(1):103–112, 2002.

[12] Llew Mason, Peter L. Bartlett, and Jonathan Baxter. Improved generalization through explicit optimization of margins. *Machine Learning*, 38(3):243–255, 2000.

[13] R. Motwani and P. Raghavan. *Randomized Algorithms*. Cambridge University Press, New York, NY, 1995.

[14] G. Rätsch, T. Onoda, and K.-R. Müller. Soft margins for AdaBoost. *Machine Learning*, 42(3):287–320, 2001.

[15] R. Schapire. The strength of weak learnability. *Machine Learning*, 5(2):197–227, 1990.

[16] R. Schapire, Y. Freund, P. Bartlett, and W. Lee. Boosting the margin: a new explanation for the effectiveness of voting methods. *Annals of Statistics*, 26(5):1651–1686, 1998.

[17] R. Servedio. Smooth boosting and learning with malicious noise. *Journal of Machine Learning Research*, 4:633–648, 2003.

The Value of Agreement, a New Boosting Algorithm*

Boaz Leskes**

University of Amsterdam, ILLC, Plantage Muidergracht 24, 1018 TV Amsterdam
bleskes@science.uva.nl

Abstract. We present a new generalization bound where the use of unlabeled examples results in a better ratio between training-set size and the resulting classifier's quality and thus reduce the number of labeled examples necessary for achieving it. This is achieved by demanding from the algorithms generating the classifiers to agree on the unlabeled examples. The extent of this improvement depends on the diversity of the learners—a more diverse group of learners will result in a larger improvement whereas using two copies of a single algorithm gives no advantage at all. As a proof of concept, we apply the algorithm, named AgreementBoost, to a web classification problem where an up to 40% reduction in the number of labeled examples is obtained.

1   Introduction

One of the simplest but popular models in machine learning is the so called *supervised learning* model. This model represents a scenario where a 'learner' is required to solve a *classification problem*. The model assumes the existence of a set of possible examples X which are divided in some way into a set of classes $\mathcal{Y} \subseteq [-1, +1]$ (often called labels). Furthermore, it is assumed that there exists a distribution P over $X \times \mathcal{Y}$, which represents the 'chance' to see a specific example and its label in real life. The learning algorithm's task is then to construct a mapping $f : X \to \mathcal{Y}$, which predicts the distribution P well, i.e., minimizes $P(\{f(x) \neq y : (x, y) \in X \times \mathcal{Y}\})$. The only information available to the learner to assist it in its task is a finite *training set* $S = \{(x_j, y_j)\}_{j=1}^{n_s}$, generated by repeatedly and independently sampling the distribution P.

Despite of the high abstraction level, many real life applications fall nicely within this model. Problems like OCR, web pages classification (as done in Internet directories) and detection of spam e-mail are only a few of many problems that fit into this scheme. In all the examples above and in many others, it is relatively hard to obtain a large sample of labeled examples. The sample has to be carefully analyzed and labeled by humans—a costly and time consuming task. However in many situations it is fairly easy to obtain unlabeled examples: examples from the example space X *without* the class that they belong to. This process can be easily mechanized and preformed by a machine, much faster then any human-plausible rate. This difference between labeled and unlabeled examples has encouraged researchers in the recent years to study the benefits that unlabeled examples may have in various learning scenarios.

---

* A full version of this paper is available on http://www.illc.uva.nl/Publications/ResearchReports/MoL-2005-02.text.pdf
** Eligible for the "Best Student Paper" award.

P. Auer and R. Meir (Eds.): COLT 2005, LNAI 3559, pp. 95–110, 2005.
© Springer-Verlag Berlin Heidelberg 2005

At first glance it might seem that nothing is to be gained from unlabeled examples. After all, unlabeled examples lack the most important piece of information—the class to which they belong. However, this is not necessarily the case. In some theoretical settings, it is beneficial to gain knowledge over the examples' marginal distribution $P(x)$ (for example in [7]). In these cases, having extra examples, with or without their label, provides this extra information. On the other hand, there exist situations (for example in [9]) where knowing $P(x)$ is not helpful and unlabeled examples do not help at all. The main goal of this sort of research is to determine the amount of information that can be extracted from unlabeled examples. However, unlabeled examples have also been used by algorithms in a more practical way: as a sort of a communication platform between two different learning algorithms. One such usage is the so called Co-Training model or strategy.

A typical example of Co-Training can be found in [5], a paper often cited with respect to unlabeled examples. In their paper, Blum and Mitchell provide both an algorithm and a theoretical framework where unlabeled examples are used to communicate an 'opinion' about an unlabeled example from one algorithm to another. As a case study, the algorithm is then applied to a web-page classification problem involving identifying courses' homepages out of a collection of web-pages.

In this Co-Training model, it is assumed that the example space can be split into two 'views' X^1 and X^2 (i.e., $X = X^1 \times X^2$) and that both views are sufficient for learning the problem. Furthermore, the theoretical framework in [5] uses a very severe assumption: for every fixed example $(\hat{x}^1, \hat{x}^2) \in X$ of non-zero probability it must hold that:

$$P\left(X^1 = \hat{x}^1 \mid X^2 = \hat{x}^2\right) = P\left(X^1 = \hat{x}^1 \mid f^2\left(X^2\right) = f^2\left(\hat{x}^2\right)\right) \tag{1}$$
$$P\left(X^2 = \hat{x}^2 \mid X^1 = \hat{x}^1\right) = P\left(X^2 = \hat{x}^2 \mid f^1\left(X^1\right) = f^1\left(\hat{x}^1\right)\right).$$

In other words, that X^1 and X^2 are conditionally independent given the label. As the authors themselves state, only four hypotheses comply with this assumption (assuming that P allows for it).

The Co-Training algorithm has been shown to produce better classifiers in the web-pages problem and in other experiments (for example, [10, 21], for more detailed analysis and limitations see [11, 14]). However, the theory presented can only be used as a motivation or a general intuition for the algorithm's success. Instead of using the training set to train only one of the learners and produce abundant newly-labeled examples for the second one, both learners are trained and subsequently label *some* unlabeled examples. These newly-labeled examples are then added to the pool of labeled examples, which is used to train the learners anew. Therefore, after being labeled, an unlabeled example assumes the same role as a labeled example: a true representation of the target function. As the authors themselves remark, this process encourages the learners to slowly *agree* on the labels of the unlabeled examples. This type of agreement is a side effect, if not a goal, of many variants of the co-training model [13, 12].

In this paper, we elaborate on this intuition and make it more precise. We show that agreement is useful and can assist in the task of learning. In other words, we present a theoretical framework where agreement between different learners has a clear advantage. Drawing upon these results, we propose a new boosting[1] algorithm—a field where our theoretical settings are especially applicable.

A similar attempt can be found in [15] where a boosting algorithm is presented, based on the above intuition. However, no proof is provided that the algorithm does result in agreeing classifiers nor for the advantage of such an agreement. A proof for the latter (in a more general settings) was provided by Dasgupta et al. in [16]. Nevertheless, for the proof to hold one still has to use the strong assumption of view-independence (Equation 1). Another example for the use of unlabeled examples in boosting can be found in [19].

2   The Value of Agreement

A typical approach in the supervised learning model is to design an algorithm that chooses a hypothesis that in some way best fits the training sample. We will show that an advantage can be gained by taking several such learning algorithms and demanding that they not only best learn the training set but also 'agree' with each other on a set of extra unlabelled examples.

The discussion below involves several learning algorithms and their accompanying hypothesis spaces. To avoid confusion, any enumeration or index that relates to different learners or hypotheses is enumerated using superscripts (typically l). All other indices, such as algorithm iterations and different examples, are denoted using a subscript.

2.1   Preliminaries

Since the learning algorithm is only given a finite sample of examples, it can only select a hypothesis based on limited information. However, the task of the algorithm is a global one. The resulting classifier f must perform well with respect to all examples in $\mathcal{X}$. The probability of error $P(\{(x,y) : f(x) \neq y\})$ must be small. In order to transfer the success of a classifier on the training set to the global case, there exist numerous *generalization bounds* (two such theorems will be given below). Typically these theorems involve some measure of the complexity or richness of the available hypothesis space. If the hypothesis space is not too rich, any hypothesis able to correctly classify the given examples cannot be to far from the target distribution. However, if H is very rich and can classify correctly any finite sample using different functions, success on a finite sample does not necessarily imply good global behavior.

As a complexity measure, we use the *Rademacher Complexity* (see [2]), which is particularly useful in the boosting scenario.

Definition 1. *Let $X_1, \ldots, X_n$ be independent samples drawn according to some distribution P on a set X. For a class of functions F, mapping X to $\mathbb{R}$, define the random variable*

$$\hat{R}_n(F) = \mathbf{E}\left[\sup_{f \in F} \left|\frac{2}{n}\sum_{i=1}^{n}\sigma_i f(X_i)\right|\right]$$

---

[1] For an excellent introduction to boosting, the reader is referred to [1].

where the expectation is taken with respect to $\sigma_1, \ldots, \sigma_n$, *independent uniform* $\{\pm 1\}$-
valued random variables. Then the Rademacher *complexity of F is* $R_n(F) = E\hat{R}_n(F)$
where the expectation is now taken over $X_1, \ldots, X_n$.

As an example, we present the following generalization bound(adapted from Theorem 3
in [1] and proved in [3]).

Theorem 1. *Let F be a class of real-valued functions from X to* $[-1, +1]$ *and let*
$\theta \in [0, 1]$. *Let P be a probability distribution on* $X \times \{-1, +1\}$ *and suppose that a
sample of N examples* $S = \{(x_1, y_1), \ldots, (x_{n_s}, y_{n_s})\}$ *is generated independently at random according to P. Then for any integer N, with probability at least* $1 - \delta$ *over samples
of length* n_s, *every* $f \in F$ *satisfies*

$$P(y \neq \text{sign}(f(x))) \leq \hat{L}^\theta(f) + \frac{2R_{n_s}(F)}{\theta} + \sqrt{\frac{\log(2/\delta)}{2n_s}}$$

where $\hat{L}^\theta(f) = \frac{1}{n_s} \sum_{i=1}^{n_s} \mathbf{I}(y_i f(x_i) \leq \theta)$ *and* $\mathbf{I}(y_i f(x_i) \leq \theta) = 1$ *if* $y_i f(x_i) \leq \theta$ *and* 0 *otherwise.*

Theorem 1 introduces a new concept named *margin*.

Definition 2. *The* margin *of a function* $h : X \to [-1, 1]$ *on an example* $x \in X$ *with a
label* $y \in \{\pm 1\}$ *is* $yh(x)$.

Margins have been used to give a new explanation to the success of boosting algorithms,
such as AdaBoost [17], in decreasing the global error long after a perfect classification
of the training examples has been achieved [4]. Typically, one would expect a learning
algorithm to eventually over-fit the training sample, resulting in an increase in global
error[2].

Theorem 1 represents a rather general type of generalization bounds. Instead of assuming that the labels are generated by one of the hypotheses in *H*, it gives a connection
between the empirical error on samples drawn from *any* distribution and the global expected error. As can be seen, the complexity of *H* plays a crucial role in this relation.
Hence, if one was able to reduce the hypothesis space *H* without harming its ability to
fit the sampled data, the resulting classifier is expected to have a smaller global error.

2.2   Formal Settings

Let $H^1, \ldots, H^L$ be a set of hypothesis spaces, each with a fitting learning algorithm, A^l.
Further suppose that all learning algorithms are forced to agree and output hypotheses
that agree with probability 1. If it is further assumed that the hypothesis that best fits the
training set belongs to every H^l (thus available to all algorithms), this scheme produces
a set of hypotheses from a potentially much *smaller* hypothesis spaces which are just as

---

[2] AdaBoost does eventually over-fit the data, if run long enough. However this happens at a
   much later stage then originally expected.

good on the training sample. Hence, the generalization capability of such hypotheses, as drawn from theorems such as Theorem 1, is potentially much better than the hypotheses outputted from any algorithm operating alone.

While the above discussion would yield the expected theoretical gain, it is very hard to implement. First, demanding that the algorithms output hypothesis that agree with probability 1 entails an ability that is unlikely to be easily available. Typically the different hypothesis spaces would consist of classifiers as different as neural networks and Bayes classifiers. It is unrealistic to demand that the hypothesis spaces will have an intersection which is rich enough to be useful to correctly classify different target distributions. While this might be feasible for $L = 2$ (such as the assumption in [5]) it is highly unlikely for a bigger number of learners. We will therefore present a more relaxed agreement demand, along with a simple way of checking it: unlabeled examples.

Definition 3.

1. *Define the* variance *of a vector in $\mathbb{R}^L$ by* $V(y^1,\ldots,y^L) = \frac{1}{L}\Sigma_{l=1}^{L}(y^l)^2 - (\frac{1}{L}\Sigma_{l=1}^{L}y^l)^2$.
2. *Furthermore, define the variance of a set of classifiers $f^1,\ldots,f^L$ to be the expected variance on examples from X, i.e., $V(f^1,\ldots,f^L) = \mathbf{E}V(f^1(x),\ldots,f^L(x))$.*

We will use the variance of a set of classifiers in the following relaxed definition of intersection as a measures of their disagreement.

Definition 4. *For any $v > 0$, define the v-intersection of a set of hypothesis spaces, $H^1,\ldots,H^L$ to be:*

$$v - \bigcap_{l=1}^{L} H^l = \left\{ f^1,\ldots,f^L : \forall l,\ f^l \in H^l,\ and\ V(f^1,\ldots,f^L) \leq v \right\}.$$

In effect, the v-intersection of $H^1,\ldots,H^L$ contains all the hypotheses whose difference with some of the members of other hypothesis spaces is hard to discover. We use this relaxed definition of intersection as the space from which the algorithms can draw their hypotheses. Note that for $v = 0$, the 0-intersection is precisely the set of hypotheses that might be outputted when the algorithms are required to agree with probability 1.

As mentioned before, unlabeled examples will be used to measure the level of agreement between the various learners. Therefore, let $U = \{u_j\}_{j=1}^{n_u}$ be a set of unlabeled examples, drawn independently from the same distribution P but without the label being available. We first show that if enough unlabeled examples are drawn, the disagreement measured on them is a good representative of the global disagreement. To this end we define a new hypothesis space $V(H^1,\ldots,H^L)$ and a target distribution $\tilde{P}$ to be used in a generalization bound resembling Theorem 1.

Definition 5.

1. *Let $V(H^1,\ldots,H^L) = \{V \circ (f^1,\ldots,f^L) : f^1 \in H^1,\ldots,f^L \in H^L\}$ where $V \circ (f^1,\ldots,f^l) : X \to [0,1]$ is defined by: $V \circ (f^1,\ldots,f^L)(x) = V(f^1(x),\ldots,f^L(x))$*
2. *Let $\tilde{P}$ be a probability distribution over $X \times [0,\infty]$ which is defined by:*

$$\forall A \subseteq X \times [0,\infty]\ \tilde{P}(A) = P(\{(x,y) \in X \times \mathcal{Y} : (x,0) \in A\}).$$

In essence, $\tilde{P}$ labels all examples in X with 0, while giving them same marginal probability as before.

Before we can use the generalizing bound, we need to establish the Rademacher complexity of the new hypothesis space $V(H^1, \ldots, H^L)$.

Lemma 1. $R_n\left(V\left(H^1, \ldots, H^L\right)\right) \leq 8\max_l R_n\left(H^l\right)$.

Proof. Using Theorem 12 from [2], which gives some structural properties of the Rademacher complexity, the result follows from the following fact: $V\left(H^1, \ldots, H^L\right) \subseteq \frac{1}{L}\sum_{l=1}^L \phi\left(H^l\right) + \left[-\phi\left(\frac{1}{L}\sum_{l=1}^L H^l\right)\right]$ where $F^1 + F^2 = \left\{f^1 + f^2 : f^1 \in F^1, f^2 \in F^2\right\}, \phi(F) = \left\{\phi \circ f : f \in F\right\}$ and $\phi(z) = z^2$. Note that ϕ is Lipschitz on $\mathcal{Y} \subseteq [-1, +1]$ with $L_\phi = 2$.

Before proving the main theorems of the section, we present the following generalization bound (adapted from [2]). This theorem allows the use of an arbitrary loss function and does not use the concepts of margins.

Theorem 2. *Consider a loss function $\mathcal{L} : \mathcal{Y} \times \mathbb{R} \to [0,1]$ and let F be a class of functions mapping X to $\mathcal{Y}$. Let $\{(x_i, y_i)\}_{i=1}^n$ be a sample independently selected according to some probability measure P. Then, for any integer n and any $0 < \delta < 1$, with probability of at least $1 - \delta$ over samples of length n, every $f \in F$ satisfies*

$$\mathbf{E}\mathcal{L}(Y, f(X)) \leq \hat{\mathbf{E}}_n \mathcal{L}(Y, f(X)) + R_n\left(\tilde{\mathcal{L}} \circ F\right) + \sqrt{\frac{8\log(2/\delta)}{n}}$$

where $\hat{\mathbf{E}}_n$ is the expectation measured on the samples and

$$\tilde{\mathcal{L}} \circ F = \{(x,y) \mapsto \mathcal{L}(y, f(x)) - \mathcal{L}(y, 0) : f \in F\}.$$

The scene is now set to give the first of the two main theorems of this section—a connection between function's agreement on a finite sample set and their true disagreement:

Theorem 3. *Let $H^1, \ldots, H^L$ be sets of functions from X to $\mathcal{Y}$ and let $U = \{u_j\}_{j=1}^{n_u}$ be a set of unlabeled examples drawn independently according to a distribution P over $X \times \mathcal{Y}$. Then for any integer n and $0 < \delta < 1$, with probability of at least $1 - \delta$ every set of functions $f^l \in H^l$, $l = 1 \ldots L$ satisfies:*

$$V(f^1, \ldots, f^L) \leq \hat{V}(f^1, \ldots, f^L) + 8\max_l R_{n_u}(H^l) + \sqrt{\frac{8\log(2/\delta)}{n_u}}$$

where $\hat{V}(f^1, \ldots, f^L)$ is the sampled expected variance, as measured on $U = \{u_j\}_{j=1}^{n_u}$.

Proof. The theorem follows directly from Theorem 2 when applied to the function set $V(H^1, \ldots, H^L)$ with $\tilde{P}$ as target distribution. The loss function is defined by $\mathcal{L}(y, z) = \min\{|y - z|, 1\}$.

Theorem 3 allows us to use a finite set of unlabeled examples to make sure (with high probability) that the classifiers selected by the learning algorithms are indeed in the desired v-intersection of the hypothesis spaces. This allows us to adapt generalization bounds to use smaller hypothesis spaces. As an example, we present an adapted version of Theorem 1.

Theorem 4. *Let $H^1, \ldots, H^L$ be a class of real-valued functions from X to $[-1, +1]$ and let $\theta \in [0, 1]$. Let P be a probability distribution on $X \times \{-1, +1\}$ and suppose that a sample of n_s labeled examples $S = \{(x_j, y_j)\}_{j=1}^{n_s}$ and n_u unlabeled examples $U = \{u_j\}_{j=1}^{n_u}$ is generated independently at random according to P. Then for any integer n_s, $\nu > 0$, $0 < \delta < 1$ and n_u such that $8 \max_l R_{n_u}(H^l) + \sqrt{\frac{8\ln(4/\delta)}{n_u}} \leq \frac{\nu}{2}$, with a probability at least $1 - \delta$, every $f^1 \in H^1, \ldots, f^L \in H^L$ whose disagreement $\hat{V}$ on U is at most $\frac{\nu}{2}$ satisfies*

$$\forall l \; P(y \neq \text{sign}(f^l(x))) \leq \hat{L}^\theta(f^l) + \frac{2 R_{n_s}\left(\nu - \bigcap_{\hat{l}} H^{\hat{l}}\right)}{\theta} + \sqrt{\frac{\log(4/\delta)}{2n_s}}$$

where $\hat{L}^\theta(f^l) = \frac{1}{n_s} \sum_{j=1}^{n_s} \mathbf{I}\left(y_i f^l(x_i) \leq \theta\right)$.

Proof. By using Theorem 3 to reduce the hypothesis space, Theorem 1 can be applied to $\nu - \bigcap_{\hat{l}} H^{\hat{l}}$. By the union bound, the probability that the procedure fails is at most $\frac{\delta}{2} + \frac{\delta}{2} = \delta$.

To conclude this section, we note that the proposed settings has the following desired property: it doesn't help to have duplicate copies of the same hypothesis space. To have any advantage, $\nu - \bigcap_{\hat{l}} H^{\hat{l}}$ must be considerably smaller then any of the base hypothesis spaces. Therefore, using only duplicate copies of the same hypothesis space $H = H^1, \ldots H^L$ gives $\nu - \bigcap_{\hat{l}} H^{\hat{l}} = H$ and hence no improvement. Furthermore, any duplicates within the set of different hypothesis spaces can be removed without changing the results.

2.3   Reduction of Labeled Examples

The previous section presented a formal setting where agreement was used to reduce the complexity of the set of possible hypotheses. The immediate implication is that training error serves as a better approximation for global true error. Therefore, for a given number of labeled examples, if the learning algorithm has produced a classifier with a low training error one can expect a lower global error. However this reduction in complexity can be also viewed from a different, though very related, point of view.

Since when given the right hypothesis space most algorithms can reduce the training error to a very low level, increasing the number of labeled examples gives a mean to decrease the two other terms in generalization bounds: the complexity of the hypothesis space and the certainty in the success of the whole procedure (δ). Using more labeled examples allows using a lower δ value without hindering the expected error of the resulting classifier (for example, Theorem 1 involves a $\sqrt{\frac{\log(2/\delta)}{2n_s}}$ term). The second result of increasing the number of labeled examples is reduction in the Rademacher complexity (or similar complexity terms). Therefore, decreasing the term relating to hypothesis space complexity, enables to use *less* labeled examples while achieving the same bound.

Algorithm 1. Agreement Boost

Denote $F\left(g^1,\ldots,g^L\right) = \sum_{l=1}^{L}\sum_{j=1}^{n_s} er\left(-y_j g^l(x_j)\right) + \eta L \sum_{j=1}^{n_u} er\left(V\left(u_j\right)\right)$ where

$V(u) = \frac{1}{L}\sum_{l=1}^{L} g^l(u)^2 - \left[\frac{1}{L}\sum_{l=1}^{L} g^l(u)\right]^2$, $\eta \in \mathbb{R}^+$ is some positive real number and $er : \mathbb{R} \to \mathbb{R}$ is some convex, strictly increasing function with continuous second derivative.

1. Set $g^l \equiv 0$ for $l = 1\ldots L$.
2. Iterate until done (counter t):
    (a) Iterate over $l = 1\ldots L$:
        i. Set $w(x_j) = er'\left(-y_j g^l(x_j)\right) y_j / Z$ for all $\left(x_j, y_j\right) \in S$ and
        $w(u_j) = 2\eta \left|\frac{1}{L}\sum_{\hat{l}=1}^{L} g^{\hat{l}}(u_j) - g^l(u_j)\right| er'\left(V(u_j)\right)/Z$ for all $u_j \in U$ where Z is a renormalization factor s.t. $\sum_{x_j} w(x_j) + \sum_{u_j} w(u_j) = 1$.

        Use $y(u_j) = sign\left(\frac{1}{L}\sum_{\hat{l}=1}^{L} g^{\hat{l}}(u_j) - g^l(u_j)\right)$ as pseudo-labels for u_j.
        ii. Receive hypothesis f_t^l from learner l using the above weights and labels.
        iii. Find $\alpha_t^l \geq 0$ that minimizes $F\left(g^1,\ldots,g^l + \alpha_t^l f_t^l,\ldots,g^L\right)$.
        iv. Set $g^l = g^l + \alpha_t^l f_t^l$.
3. Output classifier $sign(g^l)$ whose error on the samples is minimal out of the L classifiers.

To illustrate this consider Blumer et al. (Theorem 2.1.ii in [6]) concerning the simple case of consistent learners. With high probability, a sample of size $\max\left\{\frac{4}{\varepsilon}\log\frac{2}{\delta}, \frac{8d}{\varepsilon}\log\frac{13}{\varepsilon}\right\}$ is sufficient to disqualify any function in H that is too 'far' from the target $\hat{f}$. If H is made smaller, the number of functions which need to be excluded is reduced. Therefore, less labeled examples are needed in order to exclude high error functions.

Generalization bounds such as those presented before typically deal with over-fitting using the following idea: if the algorithm is given enough labeled examples it will not over-fit. Since the training sample is representative enough of target function, specializing in it does no harm. In the extreme, this leads to theorems such as the one of Blumer et al. concerning consistent learning algorithms. In the setting proposed here, the learning algorithm needs not only fit its training data but also agree with a couple of other algorithms. If the algorithms are sufficiently different, forcing them to agree inhibits their specialization on the training data, allowing to use a less representative training sample, or less labeled examples.

3   The Algorithm

In this section, we propose a new boosting algorithm named AgreementBoost (Algorithm 1), which exploits the benefits suggested by the theory presented in the previous section. Like AdaBoost, the algorithm is designed to operate in Boolean scenarios where each example can belong to one of two possible classes denoted by ± 1.

As in many boosting algorithms, AgreementBoost creates combined classifiers or ensembles. However, instead of just one such classifier, AgreementBoost creates L ensembles, one for each hypothesis space. The ensembles are constructed using L under-lying learning algorithms, one for each of the L hypothesis spaces $\{H^l\}_{l=1}^L$. At each iteration, one of the learning algorithms is presented with a weighing of both labeled and unlabeled examples in the form of a weight vector $w(x)$ and pseudo-labels for the unlabeled examples $(y(u))$. The underlying learner is then expected to return a hypoth-esis f_t^l with a near-optimal[3] edge: $\gamma = \sum\limits_{(x_j,y_j) \in S} w(x_j)y_j f^l(x_j) + \sum\limits_{u_j \in U} w(u_j)y(u_j)f^l(u_j)$.

The proposed AgreementBoost can be described as a particular instance of Any-Boost [18], a boosting algorithm allowing for arbitrary cost functions. Agreement-Boost's cost function F has been chosen to incorporate the ensembles' disagreement into the normal margin terms. This is achieved using a weighted sum of two terms: an error or margin-related term $(\sum_{l=1}^L \sum_{j=1}^{n_s} er(-y_j g^l(x_j)))$ and a disagreement term $\sum_{j=1}^{n_u} er(V(u_j))$. Despite of the fact that the these terms capture different notions, they are very similar. Both terms use the same underlying function, $er(x)$, to assign a cost to some example-related measure: The first penalizes low (negative) margins while the second condemns high variance (and hence disagreement). AgreementBoost allows for choosing any function as $er(x)$, as long as it is convex and strictly increasing. This free-dom allows for using different cost schemes and thus for future cost function analysis (as done, for example, in [18]). In the degenerate case where no unlabeled examples are used ($n_u = 0$) and e^x is used as $er(x)$, AgreementBoost is equivalent to L independent runs of AdaBoost (using the L underlying learners).

4   Proof of Convergence

In this section, we give a convergence proof for Algorithm 1. The proof considers two scenarios. The first assumes that the intersection of all $conv(H^l)$ is able to correctly classify all labeled examples using classifiers which agree on all unlabeled examples. Under this assumption, we show that the algorithm will produce classifiers, which in the limit are fully correct and agree on all unlabeled examples. In other cases, where this assumption is not valid, the algorithm will produce ensembles which minimize a function representing a compromise between correctness and agreement.

Both Mason et al. [18] and Rätsch et al. [20] provide similar convergence proofs for AnyBoost-like algorithms. While both proofs can be used (with minor modifications) in our settings, they do not fully cover both scenarios. The proof in [20] demands that the sum of the α_t^l coefficients will be bounded and thus cannot be used in cases where the theoretical assumptions hold. This can be seen easily in the case of AdaBoost, where a fully correct hypothesis will be assigned an infinite weight. While AgreementBoost will never assign an infinite weight to a hypotheses (due to the disagreement term), it is easy to come up with a similar scenario where the coefficient sum grows to infinity. In [18], Mason et al. present a theorem very similar to Theorem 5 below. However, they assume that the underlying learner performs perfectly and always returns the *best* hypothesis from the hypothesis space. Such a severe assumption is not needed in the

---

[3] For the exact definition of 'near-optimal', see Section 4.

proof presented here. Furthermore, due to the generality of AnyBoost, the result in [18] apply to the cost function alone and is not translated back to training error terms.

The proofs below are based on two assumptions concerning the learning algorithms and the hypothesis spaces. It is assumed that when presented with an example set S and a weighing $w(x)$, the underlying learning algorithms return a hypothesis f^l whose edge is at least $\delta \max_{\hat{f} \in H^l} \left(\sum_{x_j \in S} w(x_j) y_j \hat{f}(x_i) \right)$, for some $\delta > 0$. The second assumption concerns the hypothesis spaces: it is assumed that for every l and every $f^l \in H^l$ the negation of f^l is also in H^l i.e.: $f \in H^l \Rightarrow -f \in H^l$. This allows us to use absolute value in the previous assumption:

$$\sum_{x_j \in S} w(x_j) y_j f^l(x_j) \geq \delta \max_{\hat{f} \in H^l} \left| \sum_{x_j \in S} w(x_j) y_j \hat{f}(x_i) \right| \text{ for some } \delta > 0.$$

In the Lemmas and Theorems to follow, we will sometimes assume that the hypothesis spaces are finite. Due to the fact that there is only finite amount of ways to classify a finite set of examples with a ± 1 label, if some of the hypothesis spaces are infinite it will be indistinguishable when restricted to S and U. Therefore, without loss of generality, one can assume that the number of hypotheses is finite.

The convergence of the algorithm is proven taking a different point of view to the ensembles built by the algorithm. The ensembles can be seen as a mix of all possible functions in the hypothesis spaces rather then as an accumulation of hypotheses:

Definition 6.

1. *Let $H^l = \{f_i^l\}_{i \in I^l}$ be an enumeration of functions in H^l. One can rewrite the ensembles g^l built by AgreementBoost as functions from $X \times \mathbb{R}^{|H^l|}$ to $\mathbb{R}$: $g^l(x, \beta^l) = \sum_i \beta_i^l f_i^l(x)$ for $\beta^l = (\beta_1^l, \beta_2^l, \ldots) \in \mathbb{R}^{|H^l|}$ and $l = 1 \ldots L$. Further denote $\beta = (\beta^1, \ldots, \beta^L)$. Note that β_i^l is the sum of all α_t^l such that $f_t^l \equiv f_i^l$.*

2. *Let the variance of $g^1, \ldots, g^L$ on an example u be $V(u, \beta) = V\left(g^1(u, \beta^1), \ldots, g^L(u, \beta^L)\right)$.*

3. *Whenever it is clear from context what are the β parameters, $V(u)$ and $g^l(u)$ will be used for brevity.*

4. *Let $er: \mathbb{R} \to \mathbb{R}^+$ be a convex monotonically increasing function. Denoting $E(\beta) = \sum_{l=1}^L \sum_{j=1}^{n_s} er\left(-y_j g^l(x_j)\right)$ and $D(\beta) = L \sum_{j=1}^{n_u} er(V(u_j))$, the function F becomes $F(\beta) = E(\beta) + \eta D(\beta)$ for some $\eta > 0$.*

$F(\beta)$ represents a weighing between correctness and disagreement. $E(\beta)$, being a sum of loss functions penalizing negative margins, relates to the current error of the ensemble classifiers. $D(\beta)$ captures the ensembles' disagreement over the unlabeled examples.

Using the above notations and the new point of view, the edge of hypotheses becomes proportional to the partial derivative of $F(\beta)$ with respect to the corresponding coefficient. Replacing the examples' weight and labels according to the definition of AgreementBoost, we have that $\sum_{x_j \in S} w(x_j) y_j f_i^l(x_j) + \sum_{u_j \in U} w(u) y(u_j) f_i^l(u_j) = -\frac{1}{Z} \frac{\partial F}{\partial \beta_i^l}(\beta)$.

Therefore the underlying learners return hypotheses whose corresponding partial derivatives are bounded by $-\frac{\partial F}{\partial \beta_i^l}(\beta) \geq \delta \max_i -\frac{\partial F}{\partial \beta_i^l}(\beta) = \delta \max_i \left| \frac{\partial F}{\partial \beta_i^l}(\beta) \right|$. Note that this ensures that the partial derivative with respect to the returned function coefficient is non-positive and hence the choice of α_t^l in step 2.a.ii of Algorithm 1 is in fact the global optimum[4] over all $\mathbb{R}$. Since in every iteration only one coefficient is changed to a value which minimizes $F(\beta)$, Algorithm 1 is equivalent to a coordinate descent minimization algorithm (for more information about minimization algorithms see, for example, [8]).

As a last preparation before the convergence proof, we show that $F(\beta)$ is convex. Apart from having other technical advantages, this guarantees that the algorithm will not get stuck in a local minimum.

Lemma 2. *The function $F(\beta)$ is convex with respect to β.*

Lemma 3. *Let $\{\beta_n\}$ be a sequence of points generated by an iterative linear search algorithm A, i.e., $\beta_{n+1} = A(\beta_n)$ minimizing a non-negative convex function $F \in C^2$. Denote the direction in which the algorithm minimizes F in every step by $v_n = \frac{\beta_{n+1} - \beta_n}{\|\beta_{n+1} - \beta_n\|_\infty}$ and $F_n(\alpha) = F(\beta_n + \alpha v_n)$ (i.e., A minimizes $F_n(\alpha)$ in every iteration by a linear search). Then, if $\exists M, m > 0 \in \mathbb{R}^+$ such that $(\forall n) \left[m \leq \frac{d^2 F_n}{d\alpha^2}(\alpha) \leq M \right]$ for every 'feasible' α (i.e., when $F_n(\alpha) \leq F(\beta_n)$) then $\lim_{n \to \infty} \frac{dF_n}{d\alpha}(0) = 0$ and $\lim_{n \to \infty} \|\beta_{n+1} - \beta_n\|_\infty = 0$.*

Proof. The results is obtained by using a first order Tailor expansion of $F_n(\alpha)$ and bounding the remainder with m and M.

Theorem 5. *For some non-empty sets of labeled examples S and unlabeled examples U, suppose that the underlying learners are guaranteed to return a hypothesis $\hat{f}$ such that $\sum_x w(x) y_x \hat{f}(x) \geq \delta \left(\max_f \left| \sum_x w(x) y_x f(x) \right| \right)$ for some constant $\delta > 0$ and every weighing $w(x)$ of their examples. Further let $er : \mathbb{R} \to \mathbb{R}^+$ be a non constant convex monotonically increasing function such that:*

1. *$er \in C^2$ and $er'(0) > 0$.*
2. *$\exists M \in \mathbb{R}^+$ for which $er(x) \leq \max \left\{ L(|S| + \eta |U|) er(0), \frac{1}{\eta}(|S| + \eta |U|) er(0) \right\}$ implies that $er''(x) < M$.*

Then it holds that $\lim_{n \to \infty} \|\nabla F(\beta_n)\|_\infty = 0$.

Proof. We first transform the assumption with respect to $er(x)$ into the bounds necessary for Lemma 3, obtaining that $\lim_{n \to \infty} \frac{\partial F}{\partial \beta_{i_n}^{l_n}} = 0$ where l_n and i_n are the indices of the hypothesis returned by the underlying learner at iteration n. Using the assumptions with respect to the underlying learner, it follows that $(\forall i \in I^{l_n}) \left[\lim_{n \to \infty} \left| \frac{\partial F}{\partial \beta_i^{l_n}}(\beta_n) \right| = 0 \right]$. The proof is concluded using an induction on the distance of the hypothesis spaces from l_n, i.e., $H^{l_n}, H^{(l_n - 1) \mod L}, \ldots, H^{(l_n - L + 1) \mod L}$.

---

[4] This involves the convexity of $F(\beta)$ that will be discussed below.

Theorem 6. *Under the assumptions of Theorem 5 with the additional assumption that $er(x)$ is strictly monotonic and that all underlying hypothesis spaces are able to correctly classify the data using finite ensemble classifiers from the intersection of the hypothesis spaces, both the error and the disagreement of the ensemble classifiers constructed by Algorithm 1 converge to 0.*

Proof. Denote the correct classifiers as $\tilde{g}^l = \sum \tilde{\beta}_i^l f_j^l$ and by $\tilde{\beta}$ the corresponding coefficient vector $(\tilde{\beta}_1^1, \ldots, \tilde{\beta}_{|H^L|}^L)$. The correctness of the constructed classifiers is established by looking at the directional derivative $\frac{\partial F}{\partial \tilde{\beta}}$. Note that by the agreement of $\tilde{g}^l$, $\frac{\partial D}{\partial \tilde{\beta}} = 0$ and therefore $\frac{\partial F}{\partial \tilde{\beta}} = \frac{\partial E}{\partial \tilde{\beta}}$. The convergence of the disagreement term $D(\beta)$ is shown by deriving a contradiction. This is done by bounding the distance of β_n from the agreement group $B = \{\beta : \forall u \in U, V(u, \beta) = 0\}$. Suppose that a subsequence $D(\beta_{n_i}) > \varepsilon$ for some $\varepsilon > 0$. Since the tangent to a convex function is always an under estimator, the tangent to $D(\beta_{n_i})$ in the direction of B has to drop at least ε between β_{n_i} and the nearest point in B. This implies that it must have a negative slope that is bounded away from 0. However, Theorem 5 implies that the slope must converge to 0, which gives the contradiction.

5   Experiments

In this section we present a few experiments, testing the algorithm (and theory) presented in the previous sections. In these experiments, e^x was used as the loss function $er(x)$. This gives an algorithm which is very similar to AdaBoost, with the additional agreement requirement. In order to have a reference point, we compare the proposed AgreementBoost algorithm to AdaBoost, which is run separately on each of the underlying learning algorithms. In all experiments done, the η parameter is set using the following formula: $\eta = \frac{n_s}{n_u} c$, where c is some constant. This keeps the relative influence of the disagreement and training error terms in F roughly constant within a single series of experiments. This compensates for the fact that the number of labeled and unlabeled examples changes.

As a test case, we return to the problem of classifying web pages from the WebKb database presented in [5]. The WebKb database contains 1051 web pages, collected from the websites of computer science faculties of four different universities. For each web page, the database contains both the words contained in the page itself (referred to as View 1 in [5]) and words appearing in links referring to that web pages (View 2). The web pages are split into two classes: homepages of courses (230) and non-course pages (821). The goal of the learning algorithms presented in this section is to correctly classify web pages into these two classes.

In order to determine the quality of the resulting classifiers, 25% of the examples in the database were randomly selected in each experiment and held out as a test group. The experiments were repeated 20 times for each parameter set. All figures show the average result and its standard error of the mean.

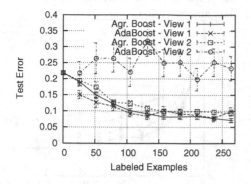

(a) Test error: Agreement Boost vs AdaBoost

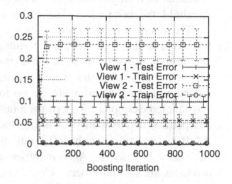

(b) Overfitting, AdaBoost, $n_s = 264$

Fig. 1. WebKb database, Naive Bayes applied to content and links

$$\eta = 1 * \frac{n_s}{264} \, , n_u = 525$$

5.1   Agreeing with the Village Fool...

The first set of experiments on the WebKb database mimics the experiments performed in [5]. The Naive Bayes algorithm is used as a single underlying learning algorithm, applied to each of the so called views: Page content and words on incoming links. This is done in a similar fashion to the toy problem, where AgreementBoost is run using the same learning algorithm on two different aspects of an example. AgreementBoost was allowed to run for 1000 iterations, using 525 unlabeled examples and setting $\eta = \frac{n_s}{264}$.

As can be seen in Figure 1, the classifiers built by AgreementBoost are roughly as good as the better of the two AdaBoost classifiers. Both AgreementBoost classifiers perform roughly the same as the AdaBoost classifier that uses the web pages' content.

One of the main assumptions used in Section 2 was that the underlying learners are all capable to produce a good classifier. However, as Figure 1(b) show, this is not the case in this experiment. While learning the links pointing to the pages produces a classifier with very low training error, it highly over-fits the data and has a very large test error. It is therefore not surprising that such a classifier has nothing to contribute. Nevertheless, AgreementBoost does seem to be able to 'choose' the better classifier. Despite of the fact that the two classifiers are forced to agree, the resulting consensus is as good as the better independent classifier.

5.2   Using a Better Learner

In light of the performance of the underlying links-based algorithm, it was replaced by a another learning algorithm which learns the web pages' content. This new underlying learner is based on a degenerate version of decision trees called tree stumps. Tree stumps consist of only one decision node, classifying an example only according to a single test. In these experiments, the web pages are classified by testing the number of instances of a single word within them. If the word has more instances then a given threshold, the web page is classified to one class and otherwise to the other.

The results of the experiments performed with the Tree Stumps algorithm are presented in Figure 2. In these experiments, 526 examples were used as unlabeled examples, allowing for up to 264 labeled examples. To perform a fair competition and to avoid over-fitting, the AdaBoost was run for only 300 iterations. As can be seen, AgreementBoost produces substantially better classifiers. On average, using the full 264 labeled example set, the tree stumps ensemble produced by AgreementBoost had 0.04 error on the test set. The naive Bayes classifier performed even better with a 0.038 test error. In comparison, the tree stumps

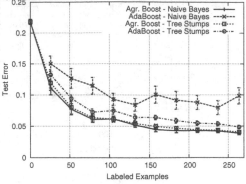

Fig. 2. Using Naive Bayes and Tree Stumps

$$\eta = 1 * \frac{n_s}{264} , n_u = 525$$

ensemble constructed by AdaBoost, which was better than the corresponding naive Bayes classifier, had a test error of 0.049.

In terms of labeled examples reduction, AgreementBoost has also produced good results. The final test error achieved by AdaBoost using the full labeled exampled set (264 examples), was already achieved by AgreementBoost's classifiers using 158 labeled examples—a reduction of 40%.

6   Conclusions and Discussion

In the first section of this paper, we have proven a new generalization bound where unlabelled examples are used to reduce the penalty corresponding to hypothesis space complexity. Demanding from the underlying learners to agree limits the amount of hypotheses at their disposal and thus reduces the complexity of their effective hypothesis spaces. However, the theorems do not allow to foresee nor to estimate the magnitude of the improvement. In the set of experiments which we have performed, a reduction of up to 40% was observed in the number of labeled examples necessary in order to achieve a desired classification error. More theoretical and experimental work is needed to better quantify this advantage.

While agreement successfully reduces the number of labeled examples, it is not without a price. Increasing the importance assigned to the learners' agreement causes a reduction in the algorithm's convergence speed. Since AgreementBoost constructs its ensembles iteratively, this results in larger and computationally more expensive classifiers. The exact trade-off between agreement weight and convergence speed is yet to be established.

When designing AgreementBoost, we have opted for simplicity and thus avoided using many of the possible improvements and modifications, many of which are non-trivial and justify new research projects. We name a few:

1. Many of the improvements of AdaBoost suggested in the literature can adapted for AgreementBoost. Modifications like regularization terms for the hypotheses weights and soft margins will probability improve that algorithm's performance.
2. For simplicity, we have kept the agreement weight (η) constant along the run. However, we suspect that changing it during the algorithm's run might lead to superior results.
3. Following previous work, we have performed all experiments using only two underlying learners. However, the theoretical framework is quite more general, allowing for an arbitrary number of underlying learners. Further experimental study involving more learners is required.

Acknowledgement. I am grateful to Leen Torenvliet, Peter Grünwald, Pieter Adriaans and Peter van Emde Boas for their time, comments and helpful insights, leading to the final version of this work.

References

1. R.Meir and G. Rätsch: An Introduction to Boosting and Leveraging. *Advanced lectures on machine learning.* Pages: 118 - 183. ISBN:3-540-00529-3.
2. P.L. Bartlett and S. Mendelson: Rademacher and Gaussian Complexities: Risk bounds and Structural Results. *The Journal of Machine Learning Research,* Vol 3. 2003. Pages 463-482.
3. V. Koltchinskii and D. Panchenko: Empirical margin distributions and bounding the generalization error of combined classifiers. *The Annals of Statistics,* 30(1), February 2002.
4. Robert E. Schapire, Yoav Freund, Peter Bartlett, and Wee Sun Lee: Boosting the margin: A new explanation for the effectiveness of voting methods. In *Machine Learning: Proceedings of the Fourteenth Fourteenth International Conference* 1997.
5. A. Blum and T. Mitchell: Combining labeled and unlabeled data with co-training. In *Proceedings of the 11th Annual Conference on Computational Learning Theory.* ACM, 1998.
6. Anselm Blumer and A. Ehrenfeucht and David Haussler and Manfred K. Warmuth: Learnability and the Vapnik-Chervonenkis dimension. *Journal of the ACM* Vol. 36, issue 4   1989.
7. K. Nigam, A. McCallum, S. Thrun, and T. Mitchell: Learning to classify text from labeled and unlabeled documents. In *Proc. of the 5th National Conference on Artificial Intelligence.* AAAI Press, 1998.
8. D. Luenberger: Introduction to Linear and Nonlinear Programming. Addison-Wesley publishing company. 1973. ISBN 0-201-04347-5.
9. T. Zhang and F. Oles, A probability analysis on the value of unlabeled data for classification problems. In *Proc. of the Int. Conference on Machine Learning,* 2000.
10. Seong-Bae Park and Byoung-Tak Zhang: Co-trained support vector machines for large scale unstructured document classification using unlabeled data and syntactic information. In *Information Processing and Management: an International Journal* Vol. 40(3), 2004.
11. Kamal Nigam and Rayid Ghani: Analyzing the effectiveness and applicability of co-training. In *Proc. of the 9th int. conference on Information and knowledge management* 2000.
12. Sally Goldman and Yan Zhou: Enhancing supervised learning with unlabeled data. In *International Joint Conference on Machine Learning,* 2000.
13. R. Hwa, M. Osborne, A. Sarkar, M. Steedman: Corrected Co-training for Statistical Parsers. In the *Proc. of the Workshop on the Continuum from Labeled to Unlabeled Data in Machine Learning and Data Mining,* International Conference of Machine Learning, Washington D.C., 2003.

14. D. Pierce and C. Cardie: Limitations of Co-Training for Natural Language Learning from Large Datasets. In *Proc. of the Conference on Empirical Methods in Natural Language Processing* 2001.
15. Michael Collins and Yoram Singer: Unsupervised models for named entity classification. In *Proc. of the Joint SIGDAT Conference on Empirical Methods in Natural Language Processing and Very Large Corpora*, 1999.
16. S. Dasgupta, Michael L. Littman, David A. McAllester: PAC Generalization Bounds for Co-training. In *Advances in Neural Information Processing Systems 14* (2001).
17. Yoav Freund and Robert E. Schapire: A decision-theoretic generalization of on-line learning and an application to boosting. *Journal of Computer and System Sciences*, 55(1), 1997.
18. L. Mason, J. Baxter, P. L. Bartlett, and M. Frean. Boosting algorithms as gradient descent in function space. *Technical report, RSISE*, Australian National University   1999.
19. K. P. Bennett and A. Demiriz and R. Maclin: Exploiting unlabeled data in ensemble methods. In *Proceedings of the eighth ACM SIGKDD int. conference on Knowledge discovery and data mining*, 2002.
20. G. Rätsch, S. Mika, and M.K. Warmuth. On the convergence of leveraging. *NeuroCOLT2 Technical Report 98*, Royal Holloway College, London, August 2001.
21. A. Levin, P. Viola and Y. Freund: Unsupervised Improvement of Visual Detectors using Co-Training. *Int. Conference on Computer Vision* (ICCV), Oct 2003, Nice, France.

A PAC-Style Model for Learning from Labeled and Unlabeled Data

Maria-Florina Balcan and Avrim Blum

Computer Science Department, Carnegie Mellon University
{ninamf, avrim}@cs.cmu.edu

Abstract. There has been growing interest in practice in using unlabeled data together with labeled data in machine learning, and a number of different approaches have been developed. However, the assumptions these methods are based on are often quite distinct and not captured by standard theoretical models. In this paper we describe a PAC-style framework that can be used to model many of these assumptions, and analyze sample-complexity issues in this setting: that is, how much of each type of data one should expect to need in order to learn well, and what are the basic quantities that these numbers depend on. Our model can be viewed as an extension of the standard PAC model, where in addition to a concept class C, one also proposes a type of compatibility that one believes the target concept should have with the underlying distribution. In this view, unlabeled data can be helpful because it allows one to estimate compatibility over the space of hypotheses, and reduce the size of the search space to those that, according to one's assumptions, are a-priori reasonable with respect to the distribution. We discuss a number of technical issues that arise in this context, and provide sample-complexity bounds both for uniform convergence and ϵ-cover based algorithms. We also consider algorithmic issues, and give an efficient algorithm for a special case of co-training.

1 Introduction

There has recently been substantial interest in using unlabeled data together with labeled data for machine learning. The motivation is that unlabeled data can often be much cheaper and more plentiful than labeled data, and so if useful information can be extracted from it that reduces the need for labeled examples, this can be a significant benefit. A number of techniques have been developed for doing this, along with experimental results on a variety of different learning problems. These include label propagation for word-sense disambiguation [23]; co-training for classifying web pages [5], parsing [15], improving visual detectors [17], and document classification [19]; transductive SVM [16] and EM [18] for text classification; graph-based methods [3, 24] and others.

The difficulty from a theoretical point of view, however, is that standard discriminative learning models do not really capture how and why unlabeled data can be of help. In particular, in the PAC model there is a complete disconnect

P. Auer and R. Meir (Eds.): COLT 2005, LNAI 3559, pp. 111–126, 2005.

between the data distribution D and the target function f being learned [6, 21]. The only prior belief is that f belongs to some class $\mathcal{C}$: even if D is known fully, any function $f \in \mathcal{C}$ is still possible. For instance, it is perfectly natural (and common) to talk about the problem of learning a concept class over the uniform distribution; but clearly in this case unlabeled data is useless — you can just generate it yourself. For learning over an unknown distribution (the standard PAC setting), unlabeled data can help somewhat, by allowing one to use distribution-specific sample-complexity bounds, but this does not seem to fully capture the power of unlabeled data in practice.

In *generative*-model settings, one *can* easily talk theoretically about the use of unlabeled data, e.g., [9, 10]. However, these results typically make strong assumptions that essentially imply that there is only one natural distinction to be made for a given (unlabeled) data distribution. For instance, a typical generative-model setting would be that we assume positive examples are generated by one Gaussian, and negative examples are generated by another Gaussian. In this case, given enough unlabeled data, we could recover the Gaussians and would need labeled data only to tell us which Gaussian is the positive one and which is the negative one.[1] This is too strong an assumption for most real-world settings. Instead, we would like our model to allow for a distribution over data (e.g., documents we want to classify) where there are a number of plausible distinctions we might want to make. In addition, we would like a general framework that can be used to model many different uses of unlabeled data.

The goal of this paper is to provide a PAC-style framework that bridges between these positions and captures many of the ways unlabeled data is typically used. We extend the PAC model in a way that allows one to express relationships that one hopes the target function and underlying distribution will possess, but without going so far as is done in generative models. We then analyze sample-complexity issues in this setting: that is, how much of each type of data one should expect to need in order to learn well, and also give a few algorithmic results.

The idea of the proposed model is to augment the notion of a *concept class* with a notion of *compatibility* between a target function and the data distribution. That is, rather than talking of "learning a concept class $\mathcal{C}$," we will talk of "learning a concept class $\mathcal{C}$ under compatibility notion χ." Furthermore, we require that the degree of compatibility be something that can be estimated from a finite sample. More specifically, we will require that χ is actually a function from $\mathcal{C} \times X$ to $[0, 1]$, where the compatibility of h with D is $\mathbf{E}_{x \in D}[\chi(h, x)]$. The degree of *in*compatibility is then something we can think of as a kind of "unlabeled error rate" that measures how a-priori unreasonable we believe some proposed hypothesis to be. For example,

Example 1 (Margins): Suppose examples are points in R^n and $\mathcal{C}$ is the class of linear separators. A natural belief in this setting is that data should be "well-

---

[1] Castelli and Cover [9, 10] do not assume Gaussians in particular, but they do assume the distributions are distinguishable, which from our perspective has the same issue.

separated": not only should the target function separate the positive and negative examples, but it should do so by some reasonable *margin* γ [16]. In this case, we could define $\chi(h, x) = 1$ if x is farther than distance γ from the hyperplane defined by h, and $\chi(h, x) = 0$ otherwise. So, the incompatibility of h with D is probability mass within distance γ of $h \cdot x = 0$. Or we could define $\chi(h, x)$ to be a smooth function of the distance of x to the separator, if we do not want to commit to a specific γ in advance. (In contrast, defining compatibility of a hypothesis based on the largest γ such that D has probability mass *exactly zero* within distance γ of the separator would *not* fit our model: it cannot be written as an expectation over individual examples and indeed one cannot distinguish "zero" from "exponentially close to zero" with a small sample.)

Example 2 (Co-training): In co-training [5], we assume examples come as pairs $\langle x_1, x_2 \rangle$, and our goal is to learn a pair of functions $\langle h_1, h_2 \rangle$. For instance, if our goal is to classify web pages, x_1 might represent the words on the page itself and x_2 the words attached to links pointing *to* this page from other pages. The hope that underlies co-training is that the two parts of the example are consistent, which then allows the co-training algorithm to bootstrap from unlabeled data.[2] In this case, we might naturally define the incompatibility of some hypothesis $\langle h_1, h_2 \rangle$ as $\mathbf{Pr}_{\langle x_1, x_2 \rangle \in D}[h_1(x_1) \neq h_2(x_2)]$.

Example 3 (Linear Separator Graph Cuts): As a special case of Example 2 above, suppose examples are *pairs* of points in R^n, $\mathcal{C}$ is the class of linear separators, and we believe the two points in each pair should both be on the *same* side of the target function (i.e., like co-training but we are requiring $h_1 = h_2$).[3] Again we can define the incompatibility of some h to be the probability mass on examples $\langle x_1, x_2 \rangle$ such that $h(x_1) \neq h(x_2)$. One thing that makes this problem interesting is that we can view examples as edges, view the data as a graph embedded in R^n, and given a set of labeled and unlabeled data, view our objective as finding a linear separator minimum *s-t* cut.

This setup allows us to analyze the ability of a finite unlabeled sample to reduce our need for labeled data, as a function of the compatibility of the target function and various measures of the "helpfulness" of the distribution. In particular, in our model we find that unlabeled data can help in several distinct ways.

---

[2] For example, *iterative co-training* uses a small amount of labeled data to get some initial information (e.g., if a link with the words "my advisor" points to a page then that page is probably a faculty member's home page) and then when it finds an unlabeled example where one half is confident (e.g., the link says "my advisor"), it uses that to label the example for training its hypothesis over the other half.

[3] As a motivating example, consider the problem of *word-sense disambiguation*: given the text surrounding some target word (like "plant") we want to determine which dictionary definition is intended (tree or factory?). Yarowsky [23] uses the fact that if a word appears twice in the same document, it is probably being used in the *same* sense both times.

- If the target function is highly compatible with D, then if we have enough unlabeled data to estimate compatibility over all $h \in C$, we can in principle reduce the size of the search space from C down to just those $h \in C$ whose estimated compatibility is high.
- By providing an estimate of D, unlabeled data can allow us to use a more refined distribution-specific notion of "hypothesis space size" such as Annealed VC-entropy [11] or the size of the smallest ϵ-cover [2], rather than VC-dimension. In fact, for natural cases (such as those above) we find that the sense in which unlabeled data reduces the "size" of the search space is best described in these distribution-specific measures.
- Finally, if the distribution is especially nice, we may find that not only does the set of compatible $h \in C$ have a small ϵ-cover, but also the elements of the cover are far apart. In that case, if we assume the target function is fully compatible, we may be able to learn from even fewer labeled examples than the $1/\epsilon$ needed just to *verify* a good hypothesis!

Our framework also allows us to address the issue of how much *unlabeled* data we should expect to need. Roughly, the "VCdim/ϵ^2" form of standard PAC sample complexity bounds now becomes a bound on the number of *unlabeled* examples we need. However, technically, the set whose VC-dimension we now care about is not C but rather a set defined by both C and χ: that is, the overall complexity depends both on the complexity of C and the complexity of the notion of compatibility (see Section 4).

Relationship to the Luckiness Framework. There is a strong connection between our approach and the luckiness framework [20]. In both cases, the idea is to define an ordering of hypotheses that depends on the data, in the hope that we will be "lucky" and find that not too many other functions are as compatible as the target. There are two main differences, however. The first is that the luckiness framework uses labeled data both for estimating compatibility and for learning: this is a more difficult task, and as a result our bounds on labeled data can be significantly better. For instance, in Example 3 above, for any non-degenerate distribution, a dataset of $n/2$ pairs can with probability 1 be completely shattered by fully-compatible hypotheses, so the luckiness framework does not help. In contrast, with a larger (unlabeled) sample, one can potentially reduce the space of compatible functions quite significantly depending on the distribution – see Section 5 and 6. Secondly, the luckiness framework talks about compatibility between a hypothesis and a *sample*, whereas we define compatibility with respect to a distribution. This allows us to talk about the amount of unlabeled data needed to estimate true compatibility. There are also a number of differences at the technical level of the definitions.

Outline of Results. We begin by describing our formal framework, and then in Section 3 we give the simplest version of our sample-complexity bounds, for the case of finite hypothesis spaces. In Section 4 we give uniform-convergence bounds for infinite hypothesis spaces. To achieve tighter bounds, in Section 5 we consider

ϵ-cover size, and give bounds that hold for algorithms that first use the unlabeled data to choose a small set of "representative" hypotheses (every compatible $h \in C$ is close to at least one of them), and then choose among the representatives based on the labeled data. In Section 6, we give our algorithmic results. We begin with a particularly simple C and χ for illustration, and then give our main algorithmic result: an efficient algorithm for learning linear separators in the Co-training model using just a *single* labeled example, under the assumption that the distribution satisfies independence given the label. In the process, we simplify the noisy halfspace learning algorithm of [4] somewhat.

2   A Formal Framework

We assume that examples (both labeled and unlabeled) come according to a fixed unknown distribution D over an instance space X, and they are labeled by some unknown target function c^*. As in the standard PAC model, a *concept class* or *hypothesis space* is a set of functions over the instance space X, and we will often make the assumption (the "realizable case") that the target function belongs to a given class C. For a given hypothesis h, the (true) error rate of h is defined as $err(h) = err_D(h) = \mathbf{Pr}_{x \in D}[h(x) \neq c^*(x)]$. For any two hypotheses $h_1, h_2 \in C$, the distance with respect to D between h_1 and h_2 is defined as $d(h_1, h_2) = d_D(h_1, h_2) = \mathbf{Pr}_{x \in D}[h_1(x) \neq h_2(x)]$. We will use $\widehat{err}(h)$ to denote the empirical error rate of h on a given labeled sample and $\hat{d}(h_1, h_2)$ to denote the empirical distance between h_1 and h_2 on a given unlabeled sample.

We define a *notion of compatibility* to be a mapping from a hypothesis h and a distribution D to $[0, 1]$ indicating how "compatible" h is with D. In order for this to be estimable from a finite sample, we require that compatibility be an expectation over individual examples.[4] Specifically, we define:

Definition 1. *A* legal notion of compatibility *is a function* $\chi : C \times X \to [0, 1]$ *where we (overloading notation) define* $\chi(h, D) = \mathbf{E}_{x \in D}[\chi(h, x)]$. *Given a sample* S, *we define* $\chi(h, S)$ *to be the empirical average over the sample.*

Definition 2. *Given compatibility notion* χ, *the* incompatibility *of h with D is* $1 - \chi(h, D)$. *We will also call this its* unlabeled error rate, $err_{unl}(h)$, *when χ and D are clear from context. For a given sample S, we use* $\widehat{err}_{unl}(h)$ *to denote the empirical average over S.*

Finally, we need a notation for the set of functions whose incompatibility is at most some given value τ.

Definition 3. *Given threshold* τ, *we define* $C_{D,\chi}(\tau) = \{h \in C : err_{unl}(h) \leq \tau\}$. *So, e.g.,* $C_{D,\chi}(1) = C$. *Similarly, for a sample S, we define* $C_{S,\chi}(\tau) = \{h \in C : \widehat{err}_{unl}(h) \leq \tau\}$

---

[4] Though one could imagine more general notions with this property as well.

3   Finite Hypothesis Spaces

We now illustrate how unlabeled data, together with a suitable compatibility notion, can reduce the need for labeled examples. We begin with the case of finite hypothesis spaces where we measure the "size" of a set of functions by just the number of functions in it. In the standard PAC model, one typically talks of either the realizable case, where we assume that $c^* \in C$, or the agnostic case where we do not. In our setting, we have the additional issue of *unlabeled* error rate, and can either make an a-priori assumption that the target function's unlabeled error is low, or else aim for a more "Occam-style" bound in which we have a stream of labeled examples and halt once they are sufficient to justify the hypothesis produced. We first give a bound for the "doubly realizable" case.

Theorem 1. *If we see m_u unlabeled examples and m_l labeled examples, where*

$$m_u \geq \frac{1}{\epsilon}\left[\ln |C| + \ln \frac{2}{\delta}\right] \quad \text{and} \quad m_l \geq \frac{1}{\epsilon}\left[\ln |C_{D,\chi}(\epsilon)| + \ln \frac{2}{\delta}\right],$$

then with probability $1 - \delta$, all $h \in C$ with $\widehat{err}(h) = 0$ and $\widehat{err}_{unl}(h) = 0$ have $err(h) \leq \epsilon$.

Proof. Notice that the probability that a given hypothesis h with $err_{unl}(h) > \epsilon$ has $\widehat{err}_{unl}(h) = 0$ is at most $(1 - \epsilon)^{m_u} < \delta/(2|C|)$ for the given value of m_u. Therefore, by the union bound, the number of unlabeled examples is sufficient to ensure that with probability $1-\delta/2$, only hypotheses in $C_{D,\chi}(\epsilon)$ have $\widehat{err}_{unl}(h) = 0$. The number of labeled examples then similarly ensures that with probability $1 - \delta/2$, none of those whose true error is at least ϵ have an empirical error of 0, yielding the theorem. $\square$

So, if the target function indeed is perfectly correct and compatible, Theorem 1 gives sufficient conditions on the number of examples needed to ensure that an algorithm that optimizes both quantities over the observed data will, in fact, achieve a PAC guarantee. To emphasize this, we will say that an algorithm efficiently PAC_{unl}-learns the pair (C, χ) if it is able to achieve a PAC guarantee using time and sample sizes polynomial in the bounds of Theorem 1.

We can think of Theorem 1 as bounding the number of labeled examples we need as a function of the "helpfulness" of the distribution D with respect to our notion of compatibility. That is, in our context, a helpful distribution is one in which $C_{D,\chi}(\epsilon)$ is small, and so we do not need much labeled data to identify a good function among them. We can get a similar bound in the situation when the target function is not fully compatible:

Theorem 2. *Given $t \in [0,1]$, if we see m_u unlabeled examples and m_l labeled examples, where*

$$m_u \geq \frac{2}{\epsilon^2}\left[\ln |C| + \ln \frac{4}{\delta}\right] \quad \text{and} \quad m_l \geq \frac{1}{\epsilon}\left[\ln |C_{D,\chi}(t + 2\epsilon)| + \ln \frac{2}{\delta}\right],$$

then with probability $1 - \delta$, all $h \in C$ with $\widehat{err}(h) = 0$ and $\widehat{err}_{unl}(h) \leq t + \epsilon$ have $err(h) \leq \epsilon$, and furthermore all $h \in C$ with $err_{unl}(h) \leq t$ have $\widehat{err}_{unl}(h) \leq t + \epsilon$.

In particular, this implies that if $err_{unl}(c^*) \leq t$ and $err(c^*) = 0$ then with high probability the $h \in C$ that optimizes $\widehat{err}(h)$ and $\widehat{err}_{unl}(h)$ has $err(h) \leq \epsilon$.

Proof. Same as Theorem 1 except apply Hoeffding bounds to the unlabeled error rates. $\qquad\square$

Finally, we give a simple Occam/luckiness type of bound for this setting. Given a sample S, let us define $\mathsf{desc}_S(h) = \ln |C_{S,\chi}(\widehat{err}_{unl}(h))|$. That is, $\mathsf{desc}_S(h)$ is the description length of h (in "nats") if we sort hypotheses by their empirical compatibility and output the index of h in this ordering. Similarly, define $\epsilon\text{-}\mathsf{desc}_D(h) = \ln |C_{D,\chi}(err_{unl}(h) + \epsilon)|$. This is an upper-bound on the description length of h if we sort hypotheses by an ϵ-approximation to the their true compatibility.

Theorem 3. *For any set S of unlabeled data, given m_l labeled examples, with probability $1 - \delta$, all $h \in C$ satisfying $\widehat{err}(h) = 0$ and $\mathsf{desc}_S(h) \leq \epsilon m_l - \ln(1/\delta)$ have $err(h) \leq \epsilon$. Furthermore, if $|S| \geq \frac{2}{\epsilon^2}[\ln|C| + \ln\frac{2}{\delta}]$, then with probability $1 - \delta$, all $h \in C$ satisfy $\mathsf{desc}_S(h) \leq \epsilon\text{-}\mathsf{desc}_D(h)$.*

The point of this theorem is that an algorithm can use observable quantities to determine if it can be confident, and furthermore if we have enough unlabeled data, the observable quantities will be no worse than if we were learning a slightly less compatible function using an infinite-size unlabeled sample.

4   Infinite Hypothesis Spaces: Uniform Convergence Bounds

To reduce notation, we will assume in the rest of this paper that $\chi(h, x) \in \{0, 1\}$ so that $\chi(h, D) = \mathbf{Pr}_{x \in D}[\chi(h, x) = 1]$. However, all our sample complexity results can be easily extended to the case that $\chi(h, x) \in [0, 1]$.

For infinite hypothesis spaces, the first issue that arises is that in order to achieve uniform convergence of *unlabeled* error rates, the set whose complexity we care about is not C but rather $\chi(C) = \{\chi_h : h \in C\}$ where we define $\chi_h(x) = \chi(h, x)$. For instance, suppose examples are just points on the line, and $C = \{h_a(x) : h_a(x) = 1 \text{ iff } x \leq a\}$. In this case, $\mathrm{VCdim}(C) = 1$. However, we could imagine a compatibility function such that $\chi(h_a, x)$ depends on some complicated relationship between the real numbers a and x. In this case, $\mathrm{VCdim}(\chi(C))$ is much larger, and indeed we would need many more unlabeled examples to estimate compatibility over all of C.

A second issue is that we need an appropriate measure for the "size" of the set of surviving functions. VC-dimension tends not to be a good choice: for instance, if we consider the case of Example 1 (margins), then even if data is concentrated in two well-separated "blobs", the set of compatible separators still has as large a VC-dimension as the entire class even though they are all very similar with respect to D. Instead, we consider the *expected* number of splits of a sample of size m drawn from D (its logarithm is *annealed VC-entropy*) which exhibits better behavior. Specifically, for any $\mathcal{C}$, we denote by $\mathcal{C}[m, D]$ the expected number of splits of m points (drawn i.i.d.) from D with concepts in $\mathcal{C}$. Also, for a given (fixed) $S \subseteq X$, we will denote by $\overline{S}$ the uniform distribution over S, and by $\mathcal{C}[m, \overline{S}]$ the expected number of splits of m points (drawn i.i.d.) from $\overline{S}$ with concepts in $\mathcal{C}$. We can now get a bound as follows:

Theorem 4. *An unlabeled sample of size*

$$m_u = \mathcal{O}\left(\frac{VCdim\left(\chi(\mathcal{C})\right)}{\epsilon^2}\log\frac{1}{\epsilon} + \frac{1}{\epsilon^2}\log\frac{2}{\delta}\right)$$

and a labeled sample of size

$$m_l > \frac{2}{\epsilon}\left[\log(2s) + \log\frac{2}{\delta}\right], \quad where \quad s = \mathcal{C}_{D,\chi}(t + 2\epsilon)[2m_l, D]$$

is sufficient so that with probability $1 - \delta$, all $h \in \mathcal{C}$ with $\widehat{err}(h) = 0$ and $\widehat{err}_{unl}(h) \leq t + \epsilon$ have $err(h) \leq \epsilon$, and furthermore all $h \in \mathcal{C}$ have $|err_{unl}(h) - \widehat{err}_{unl}(h)| \leq \epsilon$.

This is the analog of Theorem 2 for the infinite case. In particular, this implies that if $err(c^*) = 0$ and $err_{unl}(c^*) \leq t$, then with high probability the $h \in \mathcal{C}$ that optimizes $\widehat{err}(h)$ and $\widehat{err}_{unl}(h)$ has $err(h) \leq \epsilon$.

Proof Sketch: By standard VC-bounds [11, 22], the number of unlabeled examples is sufficient to ensure that with probability $1 - \delta/2$ we can estimate, within ϵ, $\mathbf{Pr}_{x \in D}[\chi_h(x) = 1]$ for all $\chi_h \in \chi(\mathcal{C})$. Since $\chi_h(x) = \chi(h, x)$, this implies we have can estimate, within ϵ, the unlabeled error rate $err_{unl}(h)$ for all $h \in \mathcal{C}$, and so the set of hypotheses with $\widehat{err}_{unl}(h) \leq t + \epsilon$ is contained in $\mathcal{C}_{D,\chi}(t + 2\epsilon)$.

The bound on the number of labeled examples follows from [11] (where it is shown that the expected number of partitions can be used instead of the maximum in the standard VC proof). This bound ensures that with probability $1 - \delta/2$, none of the functions in $\mathcal{C}_{D,\chi}(t + 2\epsilon)$ whose whose true (labeled) error is at least ϵ have an empirical (labeled) error of 0. □

We can also give a bound where we specify the number of labeled examples as a function of the *unlabeled sample*; this is useful because we can imagine our learning algorithm performing some calculations over the unlabeled data and then deciding how many labeled examples to purchase.

Theorem 5. *Given $t \geq 0$, an unlabeled sample S of size*

$$\mathcal{O}\left(\frac{\max[VCdim(\mathcal{C}), VCdim(\chi(\mathcal{C}))]}{\epsilon^2}\log\frac{1}{\epsilon} + \frac{1}{\epsilon^2}\log\frac{2}{\delta}\right)$$

is sufficient so that if we label m_l examples drawn uniformly at random from S, where

$$m_l > \frac{4}{\epsilon}\left[\log(2s) + \log\frac{2}{\delta}\right] \quad and \quad s = \mathcal{C}_{S,\chi}(t + \epsilon)[2m_l, \overline{S}]$$

then with probability $\geq 1 - \delta$, all $h \in C$ with $\widehat{err}(h) = 0$ and $\widehat{err}_{unl}(h) \leq t + \epsilon$ have $err(h) \leq \epsilon$. Furthermore all $h \in C$ have $|err_{unl}(h) - \widehat{err}_{unl}(h)| \leq \epsilon$.

Proof. Standard VC-bounds (in the same form as for Theorem 4) imply that the number of *labeled* examples m_l is sufficient to guarantee the conclusion of the theorem with "$err(h)$" replaced by "$err_{\overline{S}}(h)$" (the error with respect to $\overline{S}$) and "ϵ" replaced with "$\epsilon/2$". The number of *unlabeled* examples is enough to ensure that, with probability $\geq 1 - \delta/2$, for all $h \in C$, $|err(h) - err_{\overline{S}}(h)| \leq \epsilon/2$. Combining these two statements yields the theorem. □

So, if $err(c^*) = 0$ and $err_{unl}(c^*) \leq t$, then with high probability the $h \in C$ that optimizes $\widehat{err}(h)$ and $\widehat{err}_{unl}(h)$ has $err(h) \leq \epsilon$. If we assume $err_{unl}(c^*) = 0$ then we can use $C_{S,\chi}(0)$ instead of $C_{S,\chi}(t + \epsilon)$.

Notice that for the case of Example 1, in the worst case (over distributions D) this will essentially recover the standard margin sample-complexity bounds. In particular, $C_{S,\chi}(0)$ contains only those separators that split S with margin $\geq \gamma$, and therefore, s is no greater than the maximum number of ways of splitting $2m_l$ points with margin γ. However, if the distribution is nice, then the bounds can be much better because there may be many fewer ways of splitting S with margin γ. For instance, in the case of two well-separated "blobs" discussed above, if S is large enough, we would have just $s = 4$. We also mention that using [7, 8] we can give versions of these bounds using other complexity measures such as Rademacher averages.

5 ϵ-Cover-Based Bounds

The bounds in the previous section are for uniform convergence: they provide guarantees for *any* algorithm that optimizes well on the observed data. In this section, we consider stronger bounds based on ϵ-covers that can be obtained for algorithms that behave in a specific way: they first use the unlabeled examples to choose a "representative" set of compatible hypotheses, and then use the labeled sample to choose among these. Bounds based on ϵ-covers exist in the classical PAC setting, but in our framework these bounds and algorithms of this type are especially natural and convenient.

Recall that a set $C_\epsilon \subseteq 2^X$ is an ϵ-cover for C with respect to D if for every $c \in C$ there is a $c' \in C_\epsilon$ which is ϵ-close to c. That is, $\mathbf{Pr}_{x \in D}(c(x) \neq c'(x)) \leq \epsilon$.

To illustrate how this can produce stronger bounds, imagine examples are *pairs* of points in $\{0,1\}^n$, C is the class of linear separators, and compatibility is determined by whether both points are on the same side of the separator (i.e., the case of Example 3). Now suppose for simplicity that the target function just splits the hypercube on the first coordinate, and the distribution is uniform over pairs having the same first coordinate (so the target is fully compatible). It is not hard to show that given polynomially many unlabeled examples U and $\frac{1}{4}\log n$ labeled examples L, with high probability there will exist high-error functions consistent with L and compatible with U.[5] So, we do not yet have uniform convergence. In contrast, the cover-size of the set of functions compatible with U is constant, so ϵ-cover based bounds allow learning from just a constant number of labeled examples.

Theorem 6. *If t is an upper bound for $err_{unl}(c^*)$ and p is the size of a minimum $\epsilon - cover$ for $C_{D,\chi}(t + 4\epsilon)$, then using m_u unlabeled examples and m_l labeled examples for*

$$m_u = \mathcal{O}\left(\frac{VCdim\,(\chi(\mathcal{C}))}{\epsilon^2}\log\frac{1}{\epsilon} + \frac{1}{\epsilon^2}\log\frac{2}{\delta}\right) \;\; and \;\; m_l = \mathcal{O}\left(\frac{1}{\epsilon}\ln\frac{p}{\delta}\right),$$

we can with probability $1 - \delta$ identify a hypothesis which is 10ϵ close to c^*.

Proof Sketch: First, given the unlabeled sample U, define $H_\epsilon \subseteq \mathcal{C}$ as follows: for every labeling of U that is consistent with some h in $\mathcal{C}$, choose a hypothesis in $\mathcal{C}$ for which $\widehat{err}_{unl}(h)$ is smallest among all the hypotheses corresponding to that labeling. Next, we obtain C_ϵ by eliminating from H_ϵ those hypotheses f with the property that $\widehat{err}_{unl}(f) > t + 3\epsilon$. We then apply a greedy procedure on C_ϵ, and we obtain $G_\epsilon = \{g_1, \cdots, g_s\}$, as follows:

Initialize $H_\epsilon^1 = C_\epsilon$ and $i = 1$.

1. Let $g_i = \underset{f \in H_\epsilon^i}{\operatorname{argmin}}\; \widehat{err}_{unl}(f)$.
2. Using unlabeled data, determine H_ϵ^{i+1} by crossing out from H_ϵ^i those hypotheses f with the property that $\hat{d}(g_i, f) < 3\epsilon$.
3. If $H_\epsilon^{i+1} = \emptyset$ then set $s = i$ and stop; else, increase i by 1 and goto 1.

Our bound on m_u is sufficient to ensure that, with probability $\geq 1 - \delta/2$, H_ϵ is an ϵ-cover of $\mathcal{C}$, which implies that, with probability $\geq 1 - \delta/2$, C_ϵ is an ϵ-cover for $C_{D,\chi}(t)$. It is then possible to show G_ϵ is, with probability $\geq 1 - \delta/2$, a 5ϵ-cover for $C_{D,\chi}(t)$ of size at most p. The idea here is that by greedily creating a 3ϵ-cover of C_ϵ with respect to distribution $\overline{U}$, we are creating a 4ϵ-cover of C_ϵ with respect to D, which is a 5ϵ-cover of $C_{D,\chi}(t)$ with respect to D. Furthermore, we are doing this using no more functions than would a greedy 2ϵ-cover procedure for $C_{D,\chi}(t + 4\epsilon)$ with respect to D, which is no more than the optimal ϵ-cover of $C_{D,\chi}(t + 4\epsilon)$.

Now to learn c^* we use labeled data and we do empirical risk minimization on G_ϵ. By standard bounds [2], the number of labeled examples is enough to

---

[5] Proof: Let V be the set of all variables that (a) appear in *every* positive example of L and (b) appear in *no* negative example of L. Over the draw of L, each variable has a $(1/2)^{2|L|} = 1/\sqrt{n}$ chance of belonging to V, so with high probability V has size at least $\frac{1}{2}\sqrt{n}$. Now, consider the hypothesis corresponding to the conjunction of all variables in V. This correctly classifies the examples in L, and whp it classifies *every* other example in U negative because each example in U has only a $1/2^{|V|}$ chance of satisfying every variable in V, and the size of U is much less than $2^{|V|}$. So, this means it is compatible with U and consistent with L, even though its true error is high.

ensure that with probability $\geq 1 - \delta/2$ the empirical optimum hypothesis in G_ϵ has true error at most 10ϵ. This implies that overall, with probability $\geq 1 - \delta$, we find a hypothesis of error at most 10ϵ. $\square$

As an interesting case where unlabeled data helps substantially, consider a co-training setting where the target c^* is fully compatible *and* D satisfies the independence given the label property. As shown by [5], one can boost any weak hypothesis from unlabeled data in this setting (assuming one has enough labeled data to produce a weak hypothesis). We show here that given enough unlabeled data, in fact we can learn from just a single labeled example. Specifically it is possible to show that, for any concept classes C_1 and C_2, we have:

Theorem 7. *Assume that* $err(c^*) = err_{unl}(c^*) = 0$ *and* D *satisfies independence given the label. Then using* m_u *unlabeled examples and* m_l *labeled examples we can find a hypothesis that with probability* $1 - \delta$ *has error at most* ϵ, *provided that* $m_u = \mathcal{O}\left(\frac{1}{\epsilon} \cdot \left[(VCdim(C_1) + VCdim(C_2)) \cdot \ln\left(\frac{1}{\epsilon}\right) + \ln\left(\frac{1}{\delta}\right)\right]\right)$ *and* $m_l = \mathcal{O}(\log_{\frac{1}{\epsilon}} \frac{1}{\delta})$.

In particular, by reducing ϵ to poly(δ), we can reduce the number of labeled examples needed m_l to 1. In fact, our argument can be extended to the case considered in [1] that D^+ and D^- merely satisfy constant expansion. In section 6.2, we give an *efficient* algorithm for the case that C_1 and C_2 are the class of linear separators (though that requires true independence given the label).

6   Algorithmic Results

6.1   A Simple Computational Example

We give here a simple example to illustrate the bounds in Section 3, and for which we can give a polynomial-time algorithm that takes advantage of them. Let the instance space $X = \{0,1\}^n$, and for $x \in X$, let vars(x) be the set of variables set to 1 by x. Let C be the class of monotone disjunctions (e.g., $x_1 \vee x_3 \vee x_6$), and for $h \in C$, let vars(h) be the set of variables disjoined by h. Now, suppose we say an example x is compatible with function h if either vars$(x) \subseteq$ vars(h) or vars$(x) \cap$ vars$(h) = \phi$. This is a very strong notion of "margin": it says, in essence, that every variable is either a positive indicator or a negative indicator, and no example should contain both positive and negative indicators.

Given this setup, we can give a simple efficient PAC$_{unl}$-learning algorithm for this pair (C, χ). We begin by using our unlabeled data to construct a graph on n vertices (one per variable), putting an edge between two vertices i and j if there is any example x in our unlabeled sample with $i, j \in$ vars(x). We now use our labeled data to label the components. If the target function is fully compatible, then no component will get multiple labels (if some compnent does get multiple labels, we halt with failure). Finally, we produce the hypothesis h such that vars(h) is the union of the positively-labeled components. This is fully compatible with the unlabeled data and has zero error on the labeled data, so by Theorem 1, if the sizes of the datasets are as given in the bounds, with high probability the hypothesis produced will have error $\leq \epsilon$.

Notice that if we want to view the algorithm as "purchasing" labeled data, then we can simply examine the graph, count the number of connected components k, and then request $\frac{1}{\epsilon}[k \ln 2 + \ln \frac{2}{\delta}]$ labeled examples. (Here, $2^k = |\mathcal{C}_{S,\chi}(0)|$.) By the proof of 1, with high probability $2^k \leq |\mathcal{C}_{D,\chi}(\epsilon)|$, so we are purchasing no more than the number of labeled examples in the theorem statement.

Also, it is interesting to see the difference between a "helpful" and "non-helpful" distribution for this problem. An especially non-helpful distribution would be the uniform distribution over all examples x with $|\text{vars}(x)| = 1$, in which there are n components. In this case, unlabeled data does not help at all, and one still needs $\Omega(n)$ labeled examples (or, even $\Omega(n/\epsilon)$ if the distribution is a non-uniform as in VC-dimension lower bounds [13]). On the other hand, a helpful distribution is one such that with high probability the number of components is small, such as the case of features appearing independently given the label.

6.2   Co-training with Linear Separators

We now consider the case of co-training where the hypothesis class is the class of linear separators. For simplicity we focus first on the case of Example 3: the target function is a linear separator in R^n and each example is a *pair* of points both of which are assumed to be on the same side of the separator (i.e., an example is a line-segment that does not cross the target plane).

As in the previous example, a natural approach is to try to solve the "consistency" problem: given a set of labeled and unlabeled data, our goal is to find a separator that is consistent with the labeled examples and compatible with the unlabeled ones. Unfortunately, this consistency problem is NP-hard: given a graph G embedded in R^n with two distinguished points s and t, it is NP-hard to find the linear separator that cuts the minimum number of edges, even if the minimum is 0 [14]. For this reason, we will make an additional assumption, that the two points in an example are each drawn *independently given the label*. That is, there is a single distribution D over R^n, and with some probability p_+, two points are drawn iid from D_+ (D restricted to the positive side of the target function) and with probability $1 - p_+$, the two are drawn iid from D_- (D restricted to the negative side of the target function). Blum and Mitchell [5] have also given positive algorithmic results for co-training when (a) the two halves of an example are drawn independently given the label (which we are assuming now), (b) the underlying function is learnable via Statistical Query algorithms (which is true for linear separators by [4]), and (c) we have enough labeled data to produce a weakly-useful hypothesis on one of the halves to begin with.[6] Thus, our key contribution here is to show how we can run that algorithm

---

[6] A weakly-useful predictor is a hypothesis h such that $\mathbf{Pr}[h(x) = 1|c^*(x) = 1] > \mathbf{Pr}[h(x) = 1|c^*(x) = 0] + \epsilon$; it is equivalent to the usual notion of a "weak hypothesis" when the target function is balanced, but requires the hypothesis give more information when the target function is unbalanced.

with only *a single labeled example*. In the process, we also simplify the results of [4] somewhat.

Theorem 8. *There is a polynomial-time algorithm (in n and b, where b is the number of bits per example) to learn a linear separator under the above assumptions, using polynomially many unlabeled examples and a single labeled example.*

Proof Sketch: Assume for convenience that the target separator passes through the origin, and let us denote the separator by $c^* \cdot x = 0$. We will also assume for convenience that $p_+ \in [\epsilon/2, 1 - \epsilon/2]$; that is, the target function is not overwhelmingly positive or overwhelmingly negative (if it is, this is actually an easy case, but it makes the arguments more complicated). Define the *margin* of some point x as the distance of $x/|x|$ to the separating plane, or equivalently, the cosine of the angle between c^* and x.

We begin by drawing a large unlabeled sample $S = \{\langle x_1^i, x_2^i \rangle\}$; denote by S_j the set $\{x_j^i\}$, for $j = 1, 2$. (We describe our algorithm as working with the fixed unlabeled sample S, since we just need to apply standard VC-dimension arguments to get the desired result.) The first step is to perform a transformation T on S_1 to ensure that some reasonable $(1/poly)$ fraction of $T(S_1)$ has margin at least $1/poly$, which we can do via the Outlier Removal Lemma of [4, 12].[7] The Outlier Removal Lemma states that one can algorithmically remove an ϵ' fraction of S_1 and ensure that for the remainder, for any vector w, $\max_{x \in S_1} (w \cdot x)^2 \leq poly(n, b, 1/\epsilon') \mathbf{E}_{x \in S_1}[(w \cdot x)^2]$, where b is the number of bits needed to describe the input points. We reduce the dimensionality (if necessary) to get rid of any of the vectors for which the above quantity is zero. We then determine a linear transformation (as described in [4]) so that in that in the transformed space for all unit-length w, $\mathbf{E}_{x \in T(S_1)}[(w \cdot x)^2] = 1$). Since the maximum is bounded, this guarantees that at least a $1/poly$ fraction of the points in $T(S_1)$ have at least a $1/poly$ margin with respect to the separating hyperplane.

To avoid cumbersome notation in the rest of the discussion, we drop our use of "T" and simply use S and c^* to denote the points and separator in the transformed space. (If the distribution originally had a reasonable probability mass at a reasonable margin from c^*, then T could be the identity anyway.)

The second step is we argue that a *random* halfspace has at least a $1/poly$ chance of being a weak predictor on S_1. ([4] uses the perceptron algorithm to get weak learning; here, we need something simpler since we do not yet have any labeled data.) Specifically, consider a point x such that the angle between x and c^* is $\pi/2 - \gamma$, and imagine that we draw h at random subject to $h \cdot c^* \geq 0$ (half of the h's will have this property). Then,

$$\mathbf{Pr}_h(h(x) \neq c^*(x)|h \cdot c^* \geq 0) = (\pi/2 - \gamma)/\pi = 1/2 - \gamma/\pi.$$

---

[7] If the reader is willing to allow running time polynomial in the margin of the data set, then this part of the argument is not needed.

Since at least a $1/poly$ fraction of the points in S_1 have at least a $1/poly$ margin this implies that: small

$$\mathbf{Pr}_{h,x}[h(x) = 1|c^*(x) = 1] > \mathbf{Pr}_{h,x}[h(x) = 1|c^*(x) = 0] + 1/poly.$$

small This means that a $1/poly$ probability mass of functions h must in fact be weakly-useful predictors.

The final step of the algorithm is as follows. Using the above observation, we pick a random h, and plug it into the bootstrapping theorem of [5] (which, given unlabeled pairs $\langle x_1^i, x_2^i \rangle \in S$, will use $h(x_1^i)$ as a noisy label of x_2^i, feeding the result into an SQ algorithm), repeating this process $poly(n)$ times. With high probability, our random h was a weakly-useful predictor on at least one of these steps, and we end up with a low-error hypothesis. For the rest of the runs of the algorithm, we have no guarantees. We now observe the following. First of all, any function h with small $err(h)$ must have small $err_{unl}(h)$. Secondly, because of the assumption of independence given the label, as shown in theorem 7, the *only* functions with low unlabeled error rate are functions close to c^*, close to $\neg c^*$, close to the "all positive" function, or close to the "all negative" function.[8] So, if we simply examine all the hypotheses produced by this procedure, and pick some h with a low unlabeled error rate that is at least $\epsilon/2$-far from the "all-positive" or "all-negative" functions, then either h or $\neg h$ is close to c^*. We can now just draw a single labeled example to determine which case is which.   □

We can easily extend our algorithm to the standard co-training (where c_1^* can be different from c_2^*) as follows: we repeat the procedure in a symmetric way, and then, in order to find a good pair of functions, just try all combinations of pairs of compatible functions to find one of small unlabeled error rate, not close to "all positive", or "all negative" functions; finally use a constant number of labeled examples to produce a low error hypothesis (and here we use only one part of the example and only one of the functions in the pair).

7   Conclusions

We have provided a PAC-style model that incorporates both labeled and unlabeled data, and have given a number of sample-complexity bounds. The intent of this model is to capture many of the ways unlabeled data is typically used, and to provide a framework for thinking about when and why unlabeled data can help. The main implication of our analysis is that unlabeled data is useful if (a) we have a good notion of compatibility so that the target function indeed has a low unlabeled error rate, (b) the distribution D is *helpful* in the sense that not too many other hypotheses also have a low unlabeled error rate, and (c) we have enough *unlabeled* data to estimate unlabeled error rates well.

Our best (ϵ-cover based) bounds apply to strategies that use the unlabeled data first to select a small set of "reasonable" rules and then use labeled data

---

[8] I.e., exactly the case of the generative models we maligned at the start of this paper.

to select among them, as do our algorithms of Section 6.2. It is interesting to consider how this relates to algorithms (like the original co-training algorithm) that use labeled data first, and then use unlabeled data to bootstrap from them.

Another open problem generally would be to better understand the space of efficient algorithms in this context. In particular, even though we present two positive algorithmic results, even for fairly simple pairs (C, χ), it seems difficult to efficiently make full use of unlabeled data without additional assumptions on the distribution. A specific open problem is whether there exist efficient algorithms for the simple problem in Section 6.1 if we allow irrelevant variables. That is, we assume the set of variables is partitioned into 3 groups A, B, and C, each positive example has $|\mathsf{vars}(x) \cap A| \geq 1$ and $|\mathsf{vars}(x) \cap B| = 0$, and each negative example has $|\mathsf{vars}(x) \cap B| \geq 1$ and $|\mathsf{vars}(x) \cap A| = 0$, but we allow $|C| > 0$.

Acknowledgements. We thank Santosh Vempala for a number of useful discussions.

References

1. M. F. Balcan, A. Blum, and K. Yang. Co-training and expansion: Towards bridging theory and practice. In *NIPS*, 2004.
2. G.M. Benedek and A. Itai. Learnability with respect to a fixed distribution. *Theoretical Computer Science*, 86:377–389, 1991.
3. A. Blum and S. Chawla. Learning from labeled and unlabeled data using graph mincuts. In *Proc. ICML*, pages 19–26, 2001.
4. A. Blum, A. Frieze, R. Kannan, and S. Vempala. A polynomial-time algorithm for learning noisy linear threshold functions. *Algorithmica*, 22:35–52, 1998.
5. A. Blum and T. M. Mitchell. Combining labeled and unlabeled data with co-training. In *Proc. 11th Annual Conf. Computational Learning Theory*, pages 92–100, 1998.
6. A. Blumer, A. Ehrenfeucht, D. Haussler, and M. K. Warmuth. Learnability and the Vapnik Chervonenkis dimension. *Journal of the ACM*, 36(4):929–965, 1989.
7. S. Boucheron, O. Bousquet, and G. Lugosi. Theory of classification: a survey of recent advances. Manuscript, 2004.
8. S. Boucheron, G. Lugosi, and P. Massart. A sharp concentration inequality with applications. *Random Structures and Algorithms*, 16:277–292, 2000.
9. V. Castelli and T.M. Cover. On the exponential value of labeled samples. *Pattern Recognition Letters*, 16:105–111, 1995.
10. V. Castelli and T.M. Cover. The relative value of labeled and unlabeled samples in pattern recognition with an unknown mixing parameter. *IEEE Transactions on Information Theory*, 42(6):2102–2117, 1996.
11. L. Devroye, L. Gyorfi, and G. Lugosi. *A Probabilistic Theory of Pattern Recognition*. Springer-Verlag, 1996.
12. J. Dunagan and S. Vempala. Optimal outlier removal in high-dimensional spaces. In *Proceedings of the 33rd ACM Symposium on Theory of Computing*, 2001.
13. A. Ehrenfeucht, D. Haussler, M. Kearns, and L. Valiant. A general lower bound on the number of examples needed for learning. *Inf. and Comput*, 82:246–261, 1989.
14. A. Flaxman. Personal communication, 2003.

15. R. Hwa, M. Osborne, A. Sarkar, and M. Steedman. Corrected co-training for statistical parsers. In *ICML-03 Workshop on the Continuum from Labeled to Unlabeled Data in Machine Learning and Data Mining*, Washington D.C., 2003.
16. T. Joachims. Transductive inference for text classification using support vector machines. In *Proc. ICML*, pages 200–209, 1999.
17. A. Levin, P. Viola, and Y. Freund. Unsupervised improvement of visual detectors using co-training. In *Proc. 9th Int. Conf. Computer Vision*, pages 626–633, 2003.
18. K. Nigam, A. McCallum, S. Thrun, and T.M. Mitchell. Text classification from labeled and unlabeled documents using EM. *Mach. Learning*, 39(2/3):103–134, 2000.
19. S.-B. Park and B.-T. Zhang. Co-trained support vector machines for large scale unstructured document classification using unlabeled data and syntactic information. *Information Processing and Management*, 40(3):421 – 439, 2004.
20. J. Shawe-Taylor, P. L. Bartlett, R. C. Williamson, and M. Anthony. Structural risk minimization over data-dependent hierarchies. *IEEE Transactions on Information Theory*, 44(5):1926–1940, 1998.
21. L.G. Valiant. A theory of the learnable. *Commun. ACM*, 27(11):1134–1142, 1984.
22. V. N. Vapnik. *Statistical Learning Theory*. John Wiley and Sons Inc., 1998.
23. D. Yarowsky. Unsupervised word sense disambiguation rivaling supervised methods. In *Meeting of the Association for Computational Linguistics*, pages 189–196, 1995.
24. X. Zhu, Z. Ghahramani, and J. Lafferty. Semi-supervised learning using gaussian fields and harmonic functions. In *Proc. ICML*, pages 912–912, 2003.

Generalization Error Bounds
Using Unlabeled Data

Matti Kääriäinen

Department of Computer Science,
P.O. Box 68, FIN-00014 University of Helsinki, Finland
matti.kaariainen@cs.helsinki.fi

Abstract. We present two new methods for obtaining generalization error bounds in a semi-supervised setting. Both methods are based on approximating the disagreement probability of pairs of classifiers using unlabeled data. The first method works in the realizable case. It suggests how the ERM principle can be refined using unlabeled data and has provable optimality guarantees when the number of unlabeled examples is large. Furthermore, the technique extends easily to cover active learning. A downside is that the method is of little use in practice due to its limitation to the realizable case.

The idea in our second method is to use unlabeled data to transform bounds for randomized classifiers into bounds for simpler deterministic classifiers. As a concrete example of how the general method works in practice, we apply it to a bound based on cross-validation. The result is a semi-supervised bound for classifiers learned based on all the labeled data. The bound is easy to implement and apply and should be tight whenever cross-validation makes sense. Applying the bound to SVMs on the MNIST benchmark data set gives results that suggest that the bound may be tight enough to be useful in practice.

1 Introduction

We study an extension of the *(supervised) statistical learning model* to a model for semi-supervised learning. In the semi-supervised model, the learner gets a *labeled learning sample* $(X_1, Y_1), \ldots, (X_n, Y_n)$ and an *unlabeled learning sample* $(X_{n+1}, \ldots, X_{n+m})$. Here, the labeled examples $(X_i, Y_i) \in \mathcal{X} \times \mathcal{Y}$, $1 \le i \le n$, are independent copies of a random element (X, Y) having distribution P on $\mathcal{X} \times \mathcal{Y}$, and the unlabeled examples $X_{n+j} \in \mathcal{X}$, $1 \le j \le m$, are independent copies of X, whose distribution (the marginal distribution of P on X) we denote by P_X. Based on the (labeled and unlabeled) learning samples, the learner is supposed to pick a classifier $f \colon \mathcal{X} \to \mathcal{Y}$ with small *generalization error* $\epsilon(f) = P(f(X) \neq Y)$. In addition to the classifier, we are interested in a *generalization error bound* for it, that is, a random variable that upper bounds $\epsilon(f)$ for the learned classifier f with at least probability $1 - \delta$. The setting extends easily to learning *randomized classifiers* which will be defined formally in Section 2.

P. Auer and R. Meir (Eds.): COLT 2005, LNAI 3559, pp. 127–142, 2005.
© Springer-Verlag Berlin Heidelberg 2005

The usual motivation for studying semi-supervised learning is that in practice getting unlabeled data is often considerably easier or cheaper than getting labeled data. We are tempted to go even further and claim that in cases where the model of statistical learning theory makes sense, unlabeled data should be almost free. The reason is that if examples distributed according to P_X are hard to get, stating the goal of learning in terms of generalization performance — the expected loss on such examples — is peculiar. In such cases, it would probably be better to resort to transduction (in case the unlabeled sample to be labeled is known at the time of learning) or to state the goal of learning in terms other than generalization error. The semi-supervised model thus seems to be applicable in most of the cases in which the model of statistical learning theory is sensible. An exception to this rule is the case in which unlabeled data will be available but only after learning has taken place.

If we take the sample of unlabeled data for granted, the next question is whether and how access to it can help in learning and/or generalization error analysis. These questions have been subject to intensive research that has produced many semi-supervised learning algorithms that can be used in practice. The theoretical aspects of semi-supervised learning have received less attention, although some interesting results have been published recently [1, 2]. The value of unlabeled data to learning has been studied in restricted settings [3, 4], but to our knowledge the general question of whether unlabeled data provably helps in classifier learning has not been answered.

We prove that unlabeled data is useful in the *realizable case*, that is, when the learner is given access to a set F of classifiers that contains a *target function* f_0 for which $Y = f(X)$ (always or at least with probability 1). More specifically, we show that we can improve on the best results obtainable for *empirical risk minimization (ERM)* [5] provided we have access to a sufficiently large sample of unlabeled examples. In our second method for obtaining semi-supervised generalization error bounds we drop the assumption of the existence of a target function. The method is based on derandomizing generalization error bounds for randomized classifiers using unlabeled data. As an example of a concrete bound that can be proved using the proposed method, we transform the cross-validation estimate into a true generalization error bound for the hypothesis learned based on all the labeled data. Our empirical experiments indicate that the resulting bound applied to SVMs on the MNIST benchmark data set gives bounds comparable to cross-validation estimates. Thus, even though our second method lacks theoretical a priori optimality guarantees, it seems to provide bounds that are extremely tight in practice.

Our bounds for both the realizable and the general case are based on using the *disagreement probability* $d(f, g) = \mathbb{P}(f \neq g) = \mathbb{P}(f(X) \neq g(X))$ as a metric in the space of randomized classifiers. Variants of d have been used earlier as a basis for model selection criteria [6, 7], in providing lower bounds and estimates of the variance of the error of a hypothesis produced by a learning algorithm in a co-validation setting [1], and as an example of a distance measure that can be used in the learning by distances model [8]. To our knowledge, using d in proving generalization error bounds is original to our work. The disagreement probability d is very natural in this context, since the generalization error of a classifier is its probability of disagreeing with the target. The reason d fits the semi-supervised setting particularly well is that it can be approximated using $\hat{d}$ given by $\hat{d}(f,g) = \frac{1}{m}\sum_{j=1}^{m}[\![f(X_{n+j}) \neq g(X_{n+j})]\!]$, where the notation $[\![\phi]\!]$ means the function that has value 1 if ϕ is true and 0 otherwise. Note that $m\hat{d}(f,g)$ is the number of times f and g disagree on the unlabeled sample, so its distribution is binomial with parameters m and $d(f,g)$. Thus, one can derive confidence intervals for $d(f,g)$ given $\hat{d}(f,g)$ using the familiar techniques for binomial distributions.

2   Randomized Classifiers

In addition to standard deterministic classifiers, we work with *randomized classifiers*, also referred to as *Gibbs classifiers* in the literature. A randomized classifier f is simply a $\mathcal{Y}$-valued random variable that may depend on X but is independent of other randomized classifiers given X. In particular, the target Y is viewed as a randomized classifier. To classify an example $x \in \mathcal{X}$, a randomized classifier f chooses a label $f(x) \in \mathcal{Y}$ from the conditional distribution of f given $X = x$. A new copy of f is used each time it is applied.

In practice, a randomized classifier f is usually specified by a set of classifiers $\{f_\theta \colon \mathcal{X} \to \mathcal{Y}\}$, where the parameter θ is a realization of a random variable $\Theta = \Theta_f$ that specifies the underlying classifier to use. It is assumed that the parameters Θ_f are independent of each other and everything else. The randomized classifier corresponding to a deterministic classifier $f \colon \mathcal{X} \to \mathcal{Y}$ is simply $f(X)$. It is admittedly a bit unnatural to incorporate the distribution of X in the definition of a randomized classifier, but this choice will be technically convenient in the following. The definition of generalization error is extended to randomized classifiers f by setting $\epsilon(f) = \mathbb{P}(f \neq Y) = \mathbb{P}(f_\Theta(X) \neq Y)$.

The definition of disagreement probability $d(f,g) = \mathbb{P}(f \neq g)$ and its empirical approximation $\hat{d}(f,g)$ extend automatically to randomized classifiers. The fact that d really is a (pseudo-)metric on the space of randomized classifiers can be easily verified (also for loss functions other than the 0-1 loss). A key property of d we will take advantage of is that $\epsilon(f) = d(f,Y)$ for all randomized classifiers f, a fact first noted by Schuurmans and Southey for the special case of deterministic classifiers [6]. Thus, we can embed all the classifiers and the target into a metric space, state the goal of learning in terms of this metric, and use the metric structure of the space both in the learning process and its analysis.

Note that the distance $\hat{d}(f,g)$ between randomized classifiers f and g depends on the unlabeled data points $X_{n+j}, 1 \leq j \leq m$, and the random classifications of f and g only, so it can be computed without knowing the labels for the unlabeled points. Our strategy will be to use $\hat{d}$ to relate the generalization error of a learned classifier to that of a (randomized) classifier for which it is either known or can be tightly upper bounded. We will show how to do this in the realizable and in the general case in Sections 3 and 4, respectively.

3   The Realizable Case

In this section we present our bounds for the realizable case, discuss their properties, and outline extensions to active learning.

3.1   General Bound

Our bound for the realizable case is based on relating the learned classifier to (other) *consistent* classifiers — classifiers f for which the *empirical error* $\hat{\epsilon}(f) = \frac{1}{n} \sum_{i=1}^{n} [\![f(X_i) \neq Y_i]\!]$ is zero. The idea is that even though the target function is unknown, we know that it is among the consistent classifiers and that its generalization error is zero. Thus, if we can show that the learned classifier is not too far from any of the consistent classifiers, then it has to be close to the target function, too. Because the metric d we use for measuring distances is the disagreement probability, this implies that the generalization error of the learned classifier is bound to be close to zero as well. We will next show how to make this idea precise.

Let $F_0 = \{f \in F \mid \hat{\epsilon}(f) = 0\}$ be the set of consistent classifiers, also known as the *version space*. Here, F is the given class of classifiers that is known to contain the target f_0 by assumption, so f_0 is always in the version space. Let f be any classifier. The generalization error of f can be written as

$$\epsilon(f) = d(f, Y) = d(f, f_0).$$

Thus, the generalization error of f is simply its d-distance to f_0.

The only thing we know about f_0 is that it is by assumption consistent with the labeled data and in F_0, so the best imaginable upper bound for $d(f, f_0)$ based on the knowledge at hand is $\sup \{d(f, g) \mid g \in F_0\}$. But we do not know d, so we have to replace it by the empirical approximation $\hat{d}$ to get

$$\epsilon(f) \leq \sup_{g \in F_0} \left[\hat{d}(f, g) + (d - \hat{d})(f, g)\right] \leq \sup_{g \in F_0} \hat{d}(f, g) + \sup_{g \in F_0} (d - \hat{d})(f, g).$$

Here, only the term $\sup_{g \in F_0} (d - \hat{d})(f, g)$ depends directly on the unknown distribution P (through d). This far nothing has been assumed about f, but in order to bound the error introduced by replacing d by $\hat{d}$, one has to introduce some restrictions. A natural choice (suggested by the ERM principle) is to restrict f to be a consistent classifier chosen from F, that is, to assume $f \in F_0$. This gives

$$\epsilon(f) \leq \sup_{g \in F_0} \hat{d}(f, g) + \sup_{g', g \in F_0} (d - \hat{d})(g', g).$$

Optimizing this bound over f suggests choosing the $\hat{f} \in F_0$ whose (empirical) distance to the farthest point in F_0 is minimal (for simplicity we assume such a minimizer exists). We will call this $\hat{f}$ the *empirical center of the version space* for obvious reasons.

Putting the above reasoning together, we get the following bound for the empirical center. A similar bound without the infimum holds for any $f \in F_0$ and can be useful, e.g., if finding the empirical center is computationally hard.

Theorem 1. *Let $\hat{f}$ be the empirical center of F_0. It is always true that*

$$\epsilon(\hat{f}) \leq \inf_{f \in F_0} \sup_{g \in F_0} \hat{d}(f,g) + \sup_{g',g \in F_0} (d - \hat{d})(g',g).$$

This bound still depends on the unknown distribution P_X through the term $\sup\{(d - \hat{d})(g',g) \mid g',g \in F_0\}$. We will next show how to get rid of this dependency by using Rademacher penalization (other uniform convergence techniques familiar from generalization error analysis could have been used as well). If unlabeled data is abundant, one can also take a course similar to the hold-out bounds and use an independent sample of unlabeled data to test how close d and $\hat{d}$ really are to each other on F_0.

3.2   Concrete Bound Based on Rademacher Penalization

The idea here is to apply standard Rademacher penalization bounds to the class $\{x \mapsto [\![g'(x) \neq g(x)]\!] \mid g',g \in F_0\}$ and the sample of unlabeled data to show that the empirical expectations of these indicators (in our notation $\hat{d}$) are with high probability close to their true expectations (in our notation d). This yields an upper bound for $\sup\{(d - \hat{d})(g',g) \mid g',g \in F_0\}$, the quantity we are interested in.

Following [9], we define the Rademacher penalty $R_m(H)$ of a class H of functions from $\mathcal{X}$ to $\{0,1\}$ as follows:

$$R_m(H) = \sup_{h \in H} \left| \frac{1}{m} \sum_{j=1}^{m} \sigma_j (1 - 2h(X_{n+j})) \right|.$$

Here, the random elements X_{n+j} are independent copies of X and $\sigma_1, \ldots, \sigma_m$ is a sequence of symmetrical $\{\pm 1\}$-valued random signs independent of each other and everything else. With this definition, we have the following:

Theorem 2 ([9]). *Let H be any set of functions from $\mathcal{X}$ to $\{0,1\}$. With probability at least $1 - \delta$ (over the choice of the random signs and the $X_j s$), it is true that*

$$\sup_{h \in H} \left| \frac{1}{m} \sum_{j=1}^{m} h(X_{n+j}) - \mathbb{E}h(X) \right| \leq R_m(H) + \frac{3}{\sqrt{2}} \sqrt{\frac{\ln 2/\delta}{m}}.$$

To use this bound, H has to be independent of $X_{n+1}, \ldots, X_{n+m}$. In our case H depends on the labeled sample through F_0, but is independent of the unlabeled sample. Hence, the previous theorem can be applied, which together with Theorem 1 gives the following.

Theorem 3. *Let $\hat{f}$ be the empirical center of F_0. For all labeled learning samples, it is true with probability at least $1 - \delta$ (over the choice of the unlabeled learning sample and the Rademacher signs) that*

$$\epsilon(\hat{f}) \leq \inf_{f \in F_0} \sup_{g \in F_0} \hat{d}(f,g) + R_m(\{[\![g' \neq g]\!] \mid g',g \in F_0\}) + \frac{3}{\sqrt{2}} \sqrt{\frac{\ln(2/\delta)}{m}}.$$

This bound depends on the observed data only. Thus, the bound can be evaluated in practice if the computational problems related to evaluating the Rademacher penalty term can be overcome. If not or if one is only interested in how the bound behaves in the worst case as a function of m, one can resort to further upper bounds based on (upper bounds) for the VC dimension of $\{[\![g' \neq g]\!] \mid g', g \in F_0\}$ to get the following corollary [9, 10].

Corollary 1. *Let $\hat{f}$ be the empirical center of F_0 and let D be an upper bound for the (data-dependent) VC dimension of $\{[\![g' \neq g]\!] \mid g', g \in F_0\}$. Then with probability at least $1 - \delta$ (over the choice of the unlabeled sample) we have*

$$\epsilon(\hat{f}) \leq \inf_{f \in F_0} \sup_{g \in F_0} \hat{d}(f,g) + \sqrt{2}\sqrt{\frac{D(\ln(m/D) + 1) + \ln(2/\delta)}{m}} + \frac{3}{\sqrt{2}}\sqrt{\frac{\ln(4/\delta)}{m}}.$$

When the corollary is applicable, it implies that the error introduced by approximating d by $\hat{d}$ vanishes as the size of the unlabeled sample increases. Even though tighter bounds could be desired in practical applications, this is all we need to know in the discussion that follows.

3.3   Properties of the Bound for the Realizable Case

In this section we analyze how our bounds for the realizable case behave as a function of n and m. The general intuition is as follows. The term $\sup_{g \in F_0} \hat{d}(f, g)$ measures the amount of uncertainty about the target that remains after seeing the labeled sample. The remaining terms measure the inaccuracy introduced by approximating d by $\hat{d}$, that is, the remaining uncertainty about P_X. These two kinds of uncertainty depend on each other: The less labeled data, the larger the version space F_0, and thus the more complex the task of approximating d on F_0.

Let us first see what happens in the limit $m \to \infty$. In case the loss class $\{[\![g' \neq g]\!] \mid g', g \in F_0\}$ has finite VC dimension, we know by Corollary 1 that $(d - \hat{d})$ goes uniformly to zero on F_0. In this case, for large m, the bound reduces essentially to

$$\inf_{f \in F_0} \sup_{g \in F_0} \hat{d}(f,g) = \inf_{f \in F_0} \sup_{g \in F_0} d(f,g).$$

The best possible bound for ERM would be $\sup\{d(f,g) \mid f, g \in F_0\}$: Any smaller bound would be violated by some combinations of a consistent hypothesis f and a target g. As ERM views all $f \in F_0$ equivalently and the target may be any of the consistent functions, such a worst case situation can be realized.

In geometric terms, the lower bound for bounds for ERM is the true diameter of the version space, whereas our upper bound for the empirical center is its true radius. This simple observation immediately yields the following:

Theorem 4. *Suppose the Rademacher penalty term in Theorem 3 converges to 0 as $m \to \infty$. Then, for sufficiently large m, the bound for the empirical center is at least as good as the best possible bound for ERM and cannot be improved without additional assumptions or labeled data. The bound of Theorem 3 improves upon the best possible bound for ERM by a factor of 2 if the radius of F_0 is only half its diameter, but in case the radius equals the diameter the bounds may be equal.*

The other limiting case is when no uncertainty about the labeling remains, whence F_0 reduces to $\{f_0\}$. In this case the bound of Theorem 1 reduces to zero, irrespectively of the unlabeled learning sample. This limiting case is probably not too interesting, but it is still nice that the bound gives the correct answer.

Of course, the most interesting cases are the ones in between the extremes outlined above. Here, the exact values of $\sup\{(d - \hat{d})(g', g) \mid g', g \in F_0\}$ and its upper bounds become important. The trade-off is that the more complex F_0 is, the more unlabeled data is needed to reveal its structure, that is, to make $\sup\{(d - \hat{d})(g', g) \mid g', g \in F_0\}$ small. If F_0 is simple enough (e.g., the related class of pairs of classifiers has finite VC dimension), we know that this supremum vanishes as m increases with a speed depending on the complexity of F_0. In practice it is impossible to get or use arbitrarily large samples of unlabeled data, which makes the non-asymptotic behavior of the penalty terms important. The quest for tightest possible finite sample bounds on the deviation between $\hat{d}$ and d resembles a lot the analogous task for generalization error bounds based on uniform convergence. Unlike in the case of generalization error analysis, it seems that uniform convergence is really required here — the approximation has to be good uniformly on F_0 and not only when the distances are small.

3.4   Extensions Towards Active Learning

The only assumption on the labeled learning sample we actually used in deriving our bounds is that the labels of the examples are assigned according to the target f_0. This is enough to guarantee that $f_0 \in F_0$, which is all we need in the proofs. Hence, the bounds will remain true even if we drop the assumption that the points X_i, $1 \leq i \leq n$, are sampled from P_X. The unlabeled examples X_{n+j}, $1 \leq j \leq m$, have to be distributed according to P_X, though, since otherwise the approximation $\hat{d}$ would not necessarily converge to d.

A version of the semi-supervised model where only the unlabeled data is distributed according to P_X may be quite natural in many settings. For example, the set of examples to be labeled might be chosen by stratified sampling or in some other complex way, because one wants to focus labeling efforts to a set of points that is in some sense as informative as possible. With respect to our bounds, the efficiency of such sampling schemes can be measured in terms of the radius of the resulting version space. The less data is needed to make the radius of F_0 small, the better.

Our bounds can be used in deriving new criteria for actively selecting the points in $\mathcal{X}$ to be labeled, also. Namely, one can try to optimize the bound by selecting points to be labeled so that the *empirical radius* — the distance from the empirical center of F_0 to the farthest classifier in F_0 — decreases as much as possible when the labels are revealed. There are many variants of this active learning setting even if only label queries are considered: The learner can be forced to select all the points to be labeled before seeing any labeled examples, the learner may be allowed to query labels of points one by one in an online fashion, or the active part of learning can start only after the learner has first obtained a (randomly chosen) labeled sample as in the non-active semi-supervised setting. From a technical point of view, the choice of the setting affects the bounds only through the set on which we have to be able to guarantee that $\hat{d}$ is a good approximation to d. In the first two settings we have to have guarantees on the whole of F, while in the last setting it is enough that $\hat{d}$ and d are close to each other on the version space related to the initial non-actively chosen sample. This last case is interesting because it models a situation in which the learner is not satisfied with the bound it got with the (randomly chosen) labeled data, and tries to improve on it by querying new labels.

4   Bounds for the General Case

The results obtained in the realizable case are interesting mostly from a theoretical point of view, since the assumption that the target lies in a (simple) hypothesis class known to the learner in advance is hardly ever justifiable in practice. This limitation is not a problem of our setting only, but affects, e.g., all results obtained in the original PAC model introduced by Valiant [11]. In this section, we drop all assumptions about the existence of a target, which makes our results applicable in all situations covered by the semi-supervised learning model.

Our bounds for the general case build on bounds for randomized classifiers. The idea is to use a randomized classifier for which a good generalization bound exists as an anchoring point for the generalization error of the learned deterministic classifier. The randomized classifier together with its bound thus plays the role the target function was in in the realizable case. Randomized bounds that can be used here include, e.g., the PAC-Bayesian bounds [12], the recent bounds for ensembles of classifiers created by an online learning algorithm [13], and the progressive validation bound [14]. Test set bounds can be interpreted as a special case of this setting in which the randomized classifier is actually deterministic. Also bagging and cross-validation can be used as bases for generalization error bounds. We have worked through instances of all the above mentioned bounds, but will cover only the bound based on cross-validation in this paper.

There are many reasons for being interested in deterministic classifiers even though the bounds for randomized classifiers are often tighter. First, deterministic classifiers are nicer to work with since the predictions they give do not change randomly over time. Second, using a randomized classifier often requires storing all the underlying deterministic classifiers in memory or otherwise at hand, although at times it is possible to represent the randomized classifier in a more concise form (e.g., as a distribution of perturbations to a single deterministic classifier). In many cases the deterministic classifiers are huge and so is their number, so the memory requirements may be enormous. Third, the randomization is often introduced only to facilitate (the analysis of) generalization performance, while the underlying learning algorithm is originally designed to learn single deterministic classifiers. This is the case, e.g., with the online bound (when applied to batch algorithms) and the cross-validation bound. In such cases, aiming at bounds for the deterministic classifier learned based on all labeled data is very natural indeed.

4.1   Derandomization by Voting

Suppose f is an arbitrary randomized classifier. Let f_{vote} be the deterministic *voting classifier* related to f given by $f_{\text{vote}}(x) = \arg\max\{\mathbb{P}(f(x) = y) \mid y \in \mathcal{Y}\}$ (ties are broken arbitrarily). Replacing f by f_{vote} is a standard method of getting rid of randomness. The drawbacks of using f_{vote} instead of f are that (1) in the worst case, $\epsilon(f_{\text{vote}}) = 2\epsilon(f)$ (this is the case if f is based on fair coin tosses and the target is $1 - f_{\text{vote}}$), (2) using f_{vote} as a classifier requires storing all the classifiers underlying f in memory, and (3) one has to evaluate them all when classifying an instance. Given these, f_{vote} is probably not the classifier we are looking for. We know (1) is in general unavoidable if a deterministic approximation to f is desired, but we will show that the complexity issues (2) and (3) can be circumvented by accepting a small loss in generalization performance.

In the following theorems, the randomized classifiers f and g and the random variables α and β may depend on the labeled and unlabeled data in any way. We leave the choice of α and β intentionally open for the sake of generality. All probabilities are over the choice of data and the randomness in the classifiers.

The next Theorem is in a key role in all that follows.

Theorem 5. *Let f and g be randomized classifiers. If $\mathbb{P}(\epsilon(f) \leq \alpha) \geq 1-\delta/2$ and $\mathbb{P}(d(f,g) \leq \beta) \geq 1-\delta/2$, then $\mathbb{P}(\epsilon(g) \leq \alpha+\beta) \geq 1-\delta$, where the probabilities are over the labeled and unlabeled data as well as the randomness in the classifiers f and g.*

Proof. If f agrees with Y and g agrees with f, then g agrees with Y. Thus, g errs only if either f errs or g disagrees with f. By the assumptions, the definition of d, and the union bound, the probability for this event is at most $\alpha + \beta$.

Alternatively, one can use the triangle inequality for d and write

$$\epsilon(g) = d(g, Y) \leq d(g, f) + d(f, Y) = d(f, Y) + d(f, g) \leq \alpha + \beta,$$

where the last inequality is true with probability at least $1-\delta$ by the assumptions.
□

As a simple corollary we get the following:

Corollary 2. *Let f be a randomized classifier. If $\mathbb{P}(\epsilon(f) \leq \alpha) \geq 1 - \delta/2$ and $\mathbb{P}(d(f, f_{vote}) \leq \beta) \geq 1 - \delta/2$, then $\mathbb{P}(\epsilon(f_{vote}) < \alpha + \beta) \geq 1 - \delta$.*

In words, derandomizing f by replacing it with f_{vote} incurs a loss of at most $d(f, f_{\text{vote}})$. If f depends only on the labeled data, then $d(f, f_{\text{vote}})$ is simply the probability of the event that the classifiers f and f_{vote} (fixed after seeing the labeled data) disagree. Thus, we can use $\hat{d}(f, f_{\text{vote}})$ to obtain β. The same can be done in case of Theorem 5 if neither f nor g depend on the unlabeled data.

The next theorem shows that in case the bound for f is good, $d(f, f_{\text{vote}})$ has to be small.

Theorem 6. *For any randomized classifier f, it is true that $d(f, f_{vote}) \leq \epsilon(f)$.*

Proof. Consider the learning problem P' defined by f as follows: Choose an X according to P_X, and let $Y' = f(X)$. It is easy to see that f_{vote} is the Bayes classifier for this problem and thus has the minimal probability of misclassifying (X, Y') [15]. By the definition of Y', this probability is $d(f, f_{\text{vote}})$. Now $d(f, f_{\text{vote}}) \leq \inf_g d(f, g) \leq d(f, Y) = \epsilon(f)$, since Y can be viewed as a potential choice of g.   □

Combining this theorem with Corollary 2 gives the known result that transforming a randomized classifier to a voting classifier at most doubles the generalization error. However, it may be that $d(f, f_{\text{vote}})$ is much smaller than $\epsilon(f)$ and at least much smaller than the best bounds for $\epsilon(f)$, so Corollary 2 may provide significant improvements over the factor 2 bound.

Another interesting consequence of Theorem 6 is that if a randomized classifier f does well, it is almost deterministic in the sense that its probability of disagreeing with the deterministic classifier f_{vote} — that is, $d(f, f_{\text{vote}})$ — is small. In other words good randomized classifiers are almost deterministic on the parts of $\mathcal{X}$ with significant probability. More exactly, the expected margin of a good randomized classifier has to be large.

The classifier f_{vote} is the best deterministic approximation to f in the sense that its probability of disagreeing with f is minimal. As a corollary it also always optimizes the bound of Theorem 5. However, optimizing the distance to f (equivalently, the bound in Theorem 5) is equivalent to optimizing the generalization error only if f_{vote} happens to be the Bayes classifier for P, which needs not be the case. This and the complexity of f_{vote} motivates us to look for other choices of g in Theorem 5.

One evident choice would be the classifier g^* that minimizes $d(g, f)$ over the classifiers underlying f. By the Markov inequality, we have $d(g^*, f_{\text{vote}}) \leq d(f, f_{\text{vote}})$. Combining this with the triangle inequality, we get

$$d(f, g^*) \leq d(f, f_{\text{vote}}) + d(f_{\text{vote}}, g^*) \leq 2d(f, f_{\text{vote}}),$$

so at most a factor of 2 is lost in β by resorting to the (simple) g^* instead of the (complex) f_{vote}. A drawback is that g^* depends on the unknown d and thus has to be approximated by the classifier that optimizes $\hat{d}(g, f)$ instead. Hence, to get good bounds, we have to be able to guarantee that $\hat{d}(f, g)$ is close to $d(f, g)$ over all g underlying f that we optimize over. This can be easily accomplished by using the union bound in case the set of these g is small (at least finite), but in general one may have to resort to more complicated uniform convergence techniques.

Some bounds for randomized classifiers suggest other choices for deterministic approximations. For example, in case of the bound for the ensembles of classifiers produced by an online algorithm and the bound for cross-validation, the most natural choice is to use the classifier f_{final} learned based on all the labeled data in the role of g in Theorem 5. The next subsection is devoted to deriving such a bound for f_{final} starting from a cross-validation estimate.

4.2   A Concrete Bound Based on Cross-Validation

Cross-validation works as follows. First, the labeled data is split into k subsets or folds of equal size, where k is a parameter of the method (for simplicity, we assume that n is divisible by k). The ith fold thus consists of the points $(X_{(i-1)n/k+1}, Y_{(i-1)n/k+1}), \dots, (X_{in/k}, Y_{in/k})$, where $i = 1, \dots, k$. Then, the learning algorithm is run k times. In the ith run the examples not in fold i are used for learning and the examples in fold i for testing the learned hypothesis. This way, one gets k classifiers $f_1, \dots, f_k$ and unbiased estimates $\hat{\epsilon}_1, \dots, \hat{\epsilon}_k$ for their generalization errors $\epsilon(f_1), \dots, \epsilon(f_k)$. Here,

$$\hat{\epsilon}_i = \frac{k}{n} \sum_{j=1}^{n/k} [\![f_i(X_{(i-1)n/k+j}) \neq Y_{(i-1)n/k+j}]\!].$$

The average of these estimates is often used in assessing the performance of the classifier f_{final} — the classifier learned by the same learning algorithm that produced $f_1, \dots, f_k$, but this time based on all the labeled data. Cross-validation is widely used in practice, even though there are no guarantees that the estimates it gives are meaningful.

We now show how to transform the heuristic cross-validation estimate into a generalization error bound for f_{final} by the method presented in the previous section. Let f be the randomized classifier obtained by choosing a classifier among the classifiers f_i uniformly at random. That is, let the set of classifiers underlying f be $\{f_1, \dots, f_k\}$ and let Θ_f have uniform distribution in $\{1, \dots, k\}$.

The following generalization error bound for f that builds on tight test set bounds [16] for the underlying classifiers f_i is to our knowledge new.

Theorem 7. *Let f be the randomized classifier obtained by cross-validation as explained above. Then with probability at least $1 - \delta$ (over the choice of the labeled sample), we have*

$$\epsilon(f) \leq \frac{1}{k} \sum_{i=1}^{k} \overline{\text{Bin}}\,(\hat{\epsilon}_i, n/k, \delta/k),$$

where the inverse binomial tail [16] $\overline{\text{Bin}}\,(\hat{p}, m, \delta)$ is the p for which

$$\sum_{i=0}^{\lceil \hat{p}m \rceil} \binom{m}{i} p^i (1-p)^{m-i} = \delta.$$

Proof. For each $i = 1, \dots, k$, we have $\frac{n}{k}\hat{\epsilon}_i \sim \text{Bin}(\epsilon(f_i), \frac{n}{k})$. Thus, by definition, it is true for each i that $\epsilon(f_i) \leq \overline{\text{Bin}}\,(\hat{\epsilon}_i, n/k, \delta/k)$ with probability at least $1 - \delta/k$.

Using the definitions and the union bound, we get

$$\epsilon(f) = P(f(X) \neq Y) = \sum_{i=1}^{k} P(f(X) \neq Y | \Theta_f = i) P(\Theta_f = i)$$

$$= \frac{1}{k} \sum_{i=1}^{k} \epsilon(f_i) \leq \frac{1}{k} \sum_{i=1}^{k} \overline{\mathrm{Bin}}\left(\hat{\epsilon}_i, n/k, \delta/k\right)$$

with probability at least $1 - \delta$.   □

Combining the above bound with Theorem 5 gives the following.

Theorem 8. *Let f_{final} be the classifier learned based on all the data and let f be as above. With probability at least $1 - \delta$ (over the choice of labeled and unlabeled data and the randomization in f), we have*

$$\epsilon(f_{final}) \leq \frac{1}{k} \sum_{i=1}^{k} \overline{\mathrm{Bin}}\left(\hat{\epsilon}_i, n/k, \delta/(2k)\right) + \overline{\mathrm{Bin}}\left(\hat{d}(f, f_{final}), m, \delta/2\right).$$

Proof. Use the result of Theorem 7 (with $\delta/2$ in place of δ) to get α and choose $\beta = \overline{\mathrm{Bin}}\left(\hat{d}(f, f_{\mathrm{vote}}), m, \delta/2\right)$. The result then follows from Theorem 5.   □

The bound of Theorem 8 assumes nothing about the learning algorithm. For the bound to be tight, the algorithm has to produce hypotheses f_i with good generalization error. This is reflected to the bound by the (expectations of the) estimates $\hat{\epsilon}_i$. In addition, the algorithm has to be stable in two senses: First, the hypotheses f_i have to be relatively close to each other. Otherwise, transforming the bound for f into a bound for any deterministic classifier will incur a large loss by Theorem 6. Second, the classifier f_{final} has to be close to f, too. There are no guarantees for this in general. However, if $d(f, f_{\mathrm{final}})$ is large, using the cross-validation estimate to assess the performance of f_{final} would have been on shaky grounds anyway. Thus, the conditions required for our bound to be tight have to be true anyway in order for cross-validation to make sense.

The notion of stability required by our cross-validation bound to be tight resembles the various notions of stability studied in the learning theory literature. The connection of these notions to the generalization performance of an algorithm has received lots of attention recently. It has been shown that *training stability* (one notion of algorithmic stability) implies that the empirical and generalization errors of a learned classifier are close to each other. If the algorithm is ERM, then training stability is also necessary and sufficient for successful generalization. For this line of research, see [17] and the references therein.

The notions of algorithmic stability measure how much the error of a learned hypothesis (on a point or over the whole of $\mathcal{X}$) may change when the labeled learning sample is perturbed slightly. Estimating these stability parameters based on the observed data only may be hard, since they are often defined in terms of expectations involving the unknown distribution P. This seems to seriously limit the applicability of these stability concepts in practice. In contrast, the quantities in our bounds depend on unlabeled data only and no a priori assumptions of stability are needed. Of course, we can have no a priori guarantees on the quality of the bound either, but we hypothesize that if the algorithm is, e.g., training set stable and the bound of Theorem 7 is small, then our cross-validation bound is small, too.

4.3   Empirical Experiments with the Cross-Validation Bound

In this section we present results of experiments with the bound of Theorem 8 applied to SVMs and the MNIST dataset. The MNIST dataset consists of 60 000 labeled training examples and 10 000 labeled test examples of 28×28 gray scale images of handwritten digits from 0 to 9. We combined the training and test sets, permuted the data randomly, and used the 60 000 first examples of the permuted data set as the labeled data and forgot the labels of the remaining 10 000 examples to get a set of unlabeled data. The only preprocessing was scaling the pixel intensities to $[-1, 1]$.

As the learning algorithm, we used svmlight [18], a standard implementation of the C-SVM learning algorithm. The algorithm is capable of solving binary problems only, so we transformed the original learning problem into ten 1 vs rest problems. That is, for each $i \in \{0, \ldots, 9\}$, classifier i was provided with training examples that were labeled $+1$ if the class was i and -1 otherwise. The predictions were combined by choosing the class corresponding to the classifier whose output was the largest. All this is done internally, so that as far as the bound is concerned, the classifiers appear to be multi-class classifiers. As a kernel we used a degree 4 polynomial kernel, and chose the default value for C. The computation time required to transform the cross-validation estimate into a generalization error bound is only a few seconds on a standard PC (in addition to the time taken by the SVMs to classify the unlabeled data). In this sense transforming a cross-validation estimate into a semi-supervised bound is almost free.

Table 1 summarizes the bounds obtained for various hypotheses. The classifier f_{final} is the final multi-class SVM learned based on all labeled data. The bound

Table 1. Semi-supervised and test set bounds for (combinations of) SVMs on the MNIST data set with $n = 60\,000$, $m = 10\,000$, $k = 10$, and $\delta = 0.01$

Bound for the randomized f (Theorem 7)	2.16%
Bound for f_{vote}	2.74%
Bound for f_{final} (Theorem 8)	2.84%
Bound for the best f_i underlying f	2.89%
Empirical error of f_{final} (on the "unlabeled" data)	1.49%
Test set bound for f_{final} (on the "unlabeled" data)	1.80%

for f_{final} is almost as good as the bound for f_{vote}, and neither overshoots the exact test set bound [16] (computed by cheating and looking at the labels of the 10 000 "unlabeled" examples) by more than about a percent. This is in striking contrast with the training set bounds for f_{final} in the standard supervised setting without unlabeled data. The tightest of these bounds are applicable to two class problems only and usually even then quite loose. We did not experiment with any of these alternative bounds, but feel that it is safe to claim that they all would have been way above 100% on the multi-class learning problem at hand (for a survey on some of these bounds and their looseness, see [19]). Also note that the bound for the best f_i underlying f is worse than the bound for f_{final}. The intuitive explanation is that f_{final} has an advantage because it is learned based on all the labeled data, but it is surprising that this advantage shows up in the bounds. The test set performance of f_{vote} is slightly better than the test set performance of f, showing that derandomization may actually increase the accuracy although its effect on our bound is negative.

In summary, our initial empirical experiments seem to indicate that the proposed cross-validation bound that uses unlabeled data is considerably tighter than earlier bounds that do not require a separate labeled test set. The bound is not quite as tight as the test set bound one could use if the labels of the unlabeled sample were known, but this is to be expected as the semi-supervised bound has access to less information. In a sense, the unlabeled sample can be viewed as a cheap but still good replacement for a labeled test set.

5   Future Work

Besides applying the method presented in Section 4 to other bounds for randomized classifiers, we plan to investigate other loss functions than the 0-1 loss studied in this paper. We also plan to study the use of the bounds for model selection and other tasks. A problem with the cross-validation bound is that even though it can be used to tell how well an algorithm did on a dataset, it gives little guidance in designing algorithms that would do better. This is because the bound views the algorithm as a black box and hence cannot identify directly which of its properties are important for generalization. We hope that other bounds like the bound for ensembles of classifiers learned by an online algorithm and the PAC-Bayesian bounds may be more useful in this respect. In the realizable case, the most interesting direction seems to be pursuing the extensions to active learning and their connections to query learning and other active learning approaches.

Approximating d is only one of the possible uses of unlabeled data one can think of, and the use of d is not restricted to derandomizing classifiers. Same kinds of arguments can be used if one, e.g., wants to switch from a classifier f with a non-intelligible representation but good generalization performance (a neural network or SVM) to a classifier g with a more understandable representation (a rule set or decision tree). If $d(f, g)$ is small, then the good generalization performance of f will be inherited by the more comprehensible g. Of course, similar things can be done within a representation scheme, e.g., to find good decision tree prunings. We plan to continue working on these and other uses of unlabeled data in the near future.

Acknowledgments. I wish to thank John Langford, Jyrki Kivinen, Anssi Kääriäinen, and Taneli Mielikäinen for helpful discussions.

References

1. Madani, O., Pennock, D.M., Flake, G.W.: Co-validation: Using model disagreement to validate classification algorithms. In: NIPS 2004 Preproceedings. (2004)
2. Balcan, M.F., Blum, A.: A PAC-style model for learning from labeled and unlabeled data (2004) Draft.
3. Castelli, V., Cover, T.M.: On the exponential value of labeled samples. Pattern Recognition Letters **16** (1995) 105–111
4. Ratsaby, J., Venkatesh, S.S.: Learning from a mixture of labeled and unlabeled examples with parametric side information. In: Proceedings of the 8th Annual Conference on Computational Learning Theory (COLT'95), New York, NY, USA, ACM Press (1995) 412–417
5. Vapnik, V.N.: Statistical Learning Theory. John Wiley and Sons, New York (1998)
6. Schuurmans, D., Southey, F.: Metric-based methods for adaptive model selection and regularization. Machine Learning **42** (2002) 51–84
7. Bengio, Y., Chapados, N.: Extensions to metric-based model selection. Journal of Machine Learning Research **3** (2003) 1209–1227
8. Ben-David, S., Itai, A., Kushilevitz, E.: Learning by distances. Information and Computation **117** (1995) 240–250
9. Bartlett, P.L., Mendelson, S.: Rademacher and Gaussian complexities: Risk bounds and structural results. Journal of Machine Learning Research **3** (2002) 463–482
10. Kääriäinen, M.: Relating the Rademacher and VC bounds. Technical Report Report C-2004-57, Department of Computer Science, Series of Publications C (2004)
11. Valiant, L.G.: A theory of the learnable. Communications of the ACM **27** (1984) 1134–1142
12. McAllester, D.A.: PAC-Bayesian stochastic model selection. Machine Learning **51** (2003) 5–21
13. Cesa-Bianchi, N., Gentile, C.: Improved risk tail bounds for on-line algorithms (2004) A presentation in the (Ab)use of Bounds workshop.
14. Blum, A., Kalai, A., Langford, J.: Beating the hold-out: bounds for k-fold and progressive cross-validation. In: Proceedings of the 12th Annual Conference on Computational Learning Theory, New York, NY, ACM Press (1999) 203–208
15. Devroye, L., Györfi, L., Lugosi, G.: A Probabilistic Theory of Pattern Recognition. Volume 31 of Applications of Mathematics. Springer, Berlin Heidelberg New York (1996)
16. Langford, J.: Practical prediction theory for classification (2003) A tutorial presented at ICML 2003. Available at `http://hunch.net/~jl/projects/prediction_bounds/tutorial/tutorial.pdf`.

17. Kutin, S., Niyogi, P.: Almost-everywhere algorithmic stability and generalization error. In: Proceedings of Uncertainty in AI. (2002) 275–282
18. Joachims, T.: Making large-scale SVM learning practical. In Schölkopf, B., Burges, C., Smola, A., eds.: Advances in Kernel Methods – Support Vector Learning. MIT-Press (1999)
19. Seeger, M.: Bayesian Gaussian Process Models: PAC-Bayesian Generalisation Error Bounds and Sparse Approximations. PhD thesis, University of Edinburgh (2003)

On the Consistency
of Multiclass Classification Methods

Ambuj Tewari[1] and Peter L. Bartlett[2]

[1] Division of Computer Science, University of California, Berkeley
[2] Division of Computer Science and Department of Statistics,
University of California, Berkeley
{ambuj, bartlett}@cs.berkeley.edu

Abstract. Binary classification methods can be generalized in many
ways to handle multiple classes. It turns out that not all generalizations
preserve the nice property of Bayes consistency. We provide a necessary
and sufficient condition for consistency which applies to a large class of
multiclass classification methods. The approach is illustrated by applying
it to some multiclass methods proposed in the literature.

1   Introduction

We consider the problem of classification in a probabilistic setting: n i.i.d. pairs
are generated by a probability distribution on $\mathcal{X} \times \mathcal{Y}$. We think of y_i in a pair
(x_i, y_i) as being the *label* or *class* of the example x_i. The $|\mathcal{Y}| = 2$ case is referred
to as binary classification. A number of methods for binary classification involve
finding a real valued function f which minimizes an empirical average of the
form

$$\frac{1}{n} \sum_i \Psi_{y_i}(f(x_i)) \,. \tag{1}$$

In addition, some sort of regularization is used to avoid overfitting. Typically,
the sign of $f(x)$ is used to classify an unseen example x. We interpret $\Psi_y(f(x))$ as
being the *loss* associated with predicting the label of x using $f(x)$ when the true
label is y. An important special case of these methods is that of the so-called
large margin methods which use $\{+1, -1\}$ as the set of labels and $\phi(yf(x))$ as
the loss. Bayes consistency of these methods has been analyzed in the literature
(see [1, 4, 6, 9, 13]). In this paper, we investigate the consistency of multiclass
($|\mathcal{Y}| \geq 2$) methods which try to generalize (1) by replacing f with a vector
function $\mathbf{f}$. This category includes the methods found in [2, 5, 10, 11]. Zhang
[11, 12] has already initiated the study of these methods.

Under suitable conditions, minimizing (1) over a sequence of function classes
also approximately minimizes the "Ψ-risk" $R_\Psi(\mathbf{f}) = \mathbb{E}_{\mathcal{XY}}[\Psi_y(\mathbf{f}(x))]$. However,
our aim in classification is to find a function $\mathbf{f}$ whose probability of misclassifi-
cation $R(\mathbf{f})$ (often called the "risk" of $\mathbf{f}$) is close to the minimum possible (the
so called Bayes risk R^*). Thus, it is natural to investigate the conditions which

P. Auer and R. Meir (Eds.): COLT 2005, LNAI 3559, pp. 143–157, 2005.

guarantee that if the Ψ-risk of $\mathbf{f}$ gets close to the optimal then the risk of $\mathbf{f}$ also approaches the Bayes risk. Towards this end, a notion of "classification calibration" was defined in [1] for binary classification. The authors also gave a simple characterization of classification calibration for convex loss functions. In Section 2, we provide a different point of view for looking at classification calibration and motivate the geometric approach of Section 3.

Section 3 deals with multiclass classification and defines an analog of classification calibration (Definition 1). A necessary and sufficient condition for classification calibration is provided (Theorem 8). It is not as simple and easy to verify as in the binary case. This helps us realize that the study of multiclass classification is not a simple generalization of results known for the binary case but is much more subtle and involved. Finally, the equivalence of classification calibration and consistency of methods based on empirical Ψ-risk minimization is established (Theorem 10).

In Section 4, we consider a few multiclass methods and apply the result of Section 3 to examine their consistency. Interestingly, many seemingly natural generalizations of binary methods do not lead to consistent multiclass methods. We discuss further work and conclude in Section 5.

2   Consistency of Binary Classification Methods

If we have a convex loss function $\phi : \mathbb{R} \mapsto [0, \infty)$ which is differentiable at 0 and $\phi'(0) < 0$, then it is known [1] that any minimizer f^* of

$$\mathbb{E}_{\mathcal{X}\mathcal{Y}}[\, \phi(yf(x))\,] = \mathbb{E}_{\mathcal{X}}[\, E_{\mathcal{Y}|x}[\, \phi(yf(x))\,]\,] \tag{2}$$

yields a Bayes consistent classifier, i.e. $P(Y = +1|X = x) > 1/2 \Rightarrow f^*(x) > 0$ and $P(Y = -1|X = x) < 1/2 \Rightarrow f^*(x) < 0$. In order to motivate the approach of the next section let us work with a few examples. Let us fix an x and denote the two conditional probabilities by p_+ and p_-. We also omit the argument in $f(x)$. We can then write the inner conditional expectation in (2) as

$$p_+\,\phi(f) + p_-\,\phi(-f) \;.$$

We wish to find an f which minimizes the expression above. If we define the set $\mathcal{R} \in \mathbb{R}^2$ as

$$\mathcal{R} = \{(\phi(f), \phi(-f)) \; : \; f \in \mathbb{R}\} \;, \tag{3}$$

then the above minimization can be written as

$$\min_{\mathbf{z} \in \mathcal{R}} \; \langle \mathbf{p}, \mathbf{z} \rangle \tag{4}$$

where $\mathbf{p} = (p_+, p_-)$.

The set $\mathcal{R}$ is shown in Fig. 1(a) for the squared hinge loss function $\phi(t) = ((1-t)_+)^2$. Geometrically, the solution to (4) is obtained by taking a line whose equation is $\langle \mathbf{p}, \mathbf{z} \rangle = c$ and then sliding it (by varying c) until it just touches $\mathcal{R}$. It

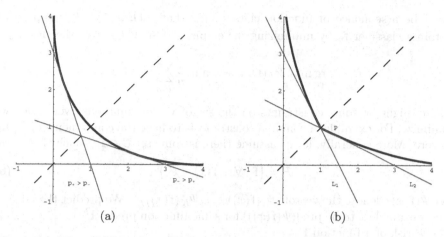

Fig. 1. (a) Squared Hinge Loss (b) Inconsistent Case (the thick curve is the set $\mathcal{R}$ in both plots)

is intuitively clear from the figure that if $p_+ > p_-$ then the line is inclined more towards the vertical axis and the point of contact is above the angle bisector of the axes. Similarly, if $p_+ < p_-$ then the line is inclined more towards the horizontal axis and the point is below the bisector. This means that $\text{sign}(\phi(-f) - \phi(f))$ is a consistent classification rule which, because ϕ is a decreasing function, is equivalent to $\text{sign}(f - (-f)) = \text{sign}(f)$. In fact, the condition $\phi'(0) < 0$ is not really necessary. For example, if we had the function $\phi(t) = ((1+t)_+)^2$, we would still get the same set $\mathcal{R}$ but will need to change the classification rule to $\text{sign}(-f)$ in order to preserve consistency.

Why do we need differentiability of ϕ at 0? Fig. 1(b) shows the set $\mathcal{R}$ for a convex loss function which is not differentiable at 0. In this case, both lines L_1 and L_2 touch $\mathcal{R}$ at P but L_1 has $p_+ > p_-$ while L_2 has $p_+ < p_-$. Thus we cannot create a consistent classifier based on this loss function. Thus the crux of the problem seems to lie in the fact that there are two distinct supporting lines to the set $\mathcal{R}$ at P and that these two lines are inclined towards different axes.

It seems from the figures that as long as $\mathcal{R}$ is symmetric about the angle bisector of the axes, all supporting lines at a given point are inclined towards the same axis except when the point happens to lie on the angle bisector. To check for consistency, we need to examine the set of supporting lines only at that point. In case the set $\mathcal{R}$ is generated as in (3), this boils down to checking the differentiability of ϕ at 0. In the next section, we deal with cases when the set $\mathcal{R}$ is generated in a more general way and the situation possibly involves more than two dimensions.

3   Consistency of Multiclass Classification Methods

Suppose we have $K \geq 2$ classes. For $y \in \{1, \ldots, K\}$, let Ψ_y be a continuous function from $\mathbb{R}^K$ to $\mathbb{R}_+ = [0, \infty)$. Let $\mathcal{F}$ be a class of vector functions $\mathbf{f} : \mathcal{X} \mapsto \mathbb{R}^K$. Let

$\{\mathcal{F}_n\}$ be a sequence of function classes such that each $\mathcal{F}_n \subseteq \mathcal{F}$. Suppose we obtain a classifier $\hat{\mathbf{f}}_n$ by minimizing the empirical Ψ-risk $\hat{R}_\Psi$ over the class $\mathcal{F}_n$,

$$\hat{\mathbf{f}}_n = \arg\min_{\mathbf{f} \in \mathcal{F}_n} \hat{R}_\Psi(\mathbf{f}) = \arg\min_{\mathbf{f} \in \mathcal{F}_n} \frac{1}{n} \sum_{i=1}^{n} \Psi_{y_i}(\mathbf{f}(x_i)) . \tag{5}$$

There might be some constraints on the set of vector functions over which we minimize. For example, a common constraint is to have the components of $\mathbf{f}$ sum to zero. More generally, let us assume there is some set $\mathcal{C} \in \mathbb{R}^K$ such that

$$\mathcal{F} = \{\mathbf{f} : \forall x, \ \mathbf{f}(x) \in \mathcal{C} \}. \tag{6}$$

Let $\Psi(\mathbf{f}(x))$ denote the vector $(\Psi_1(\mathbf{f}(x)), \dots, \Psi_K(\mathbf{f}(x)))^T$. We predict the label of a new example x to be $\mathrm{pred}(\Psi(\mathbf{f}(x)))$ for some function $\mathrm{pred} : \mathbb{R}^K \mapsto \{1, \dots, K\}$. The Ψ-risk of a function $\mathbf{f}$ is

$$R_\Psi(\mathbf{f}) = \mathbb{E}_{\mathcal{X}\mathcal{Y}}[\Psi_y(\mathbf{f}(x))] ,$$

and we denote the least possible Ψ-risk by

$$R_\Psi^* = \inf_{\mathbf{f} \in \mathcal{F}} R_\Psi(\mathbf{f}) .$$

In a classification task, we are more interested in the risk of a function $\mathbf{f}$,

$$R(\mathbf{f}) = \mathbb{E}_{\mathcal{X}\mathcal{Y}}[\mathbf{1}[\mathrm{pred}(\Psi(\mathbf{f}(x))) \neq Y]] ,$$

which is the probability that $\mathbf{f}$ leads to an incorrect prediction on a labeled example drawn from the underlying probability distribution. The least possible risk is

$$R^* = \mathbb{E}_{\mathcal{X}}[1 - \max_y p_y(x)] ,$$

where $p_y(x) = P(Y = y \mid X = x)$. Under suitable conditions, one would expect $R_\Psi(\hat{\mathbf{f}}_n)$ to converge to R_Ψ^* (in probability). It would be nice if that made $R(\hat{\mathbf{f}}_n)$ converge to R^* (in probability). In order to understand the behavior of approximate Ψ-risk minimizers, let us write $R_\Psi(\mathbf{f})$ as

$$\mathbb{E}_{\mathcal{X}\mathcal{Y}}[\Psi_y(\mathbf{f}(x))] = \mathbb{E}_{\mathcal{X}}[\mathbb{E}_{\mathcal{Y}|x}[\Psi_y(\mathbf{f}(x))]] .$$

The above minimization problem is equivalent to minimizing the inner conditional expectation for each $x \in \mathcal{X}$. Let us fix an arbitrary x for now, so we can write $\mathbf{f}$ instead of $\mathbf{f}(x)$, p_y instead of $p_y(x)$, etc. The minimum might not be achieved and so we consider the infimum of the conditional expectation above[1]

$$\inf_{\mathbf{f} \in \mathcal{C}} \sum_y p_y \Psi_y(\mathbf{f}) . \tag{7}$$

---

[1] Since p_y and $\Psi_y(\mathbf{f})$ are both non-negative, the objective function is bounded below by 0 and hence the existence of an infimum is guaranteed.

Define the subset $\mathcal{R}$ of $\mathbb{R}_+^K$ as

$$\mathcal{R} = \{(\Psi_1(\mathbf{f}), \ldots, \Psi_K(\mathbf{f})) \; : \; \mathbf{f} \in \mathcal{C}\} \; .$$

Let us define a *symmetric* set to be one with the following property: if a point $\mathbf{z}$ is in the set then so is any point obtained by interchanging any two coordinates of $\mathbf{z}$. We assume that $\mathcal{R}$ is symmetric. We can write (7) in the equivalent form

$$\inf_{\mathbf{z} \in \mathcal{R}} \langle \mathbf{p}, \mathbf{z} \rangle \; ,$$

where $\mathbf{p} = (p_1, \ldots, p_K)$. For a fixed $\mathbf{p}$, the function $\mathbf{z} \mapsto \langle \mathbf{p}, \mathbf{z} \rangle$ is a linear function and hence we do not change the infimum by taking the convex hull[2] of $\mathcal{R}$. Defining $\mathcal{S}$ as

$$\mathcal{S} = \mathrm{conv}\{(\Psi_1(\mathbf{f}), \ldots, \Psi_K(\mathbf{f})) \; : \; \mathbf{f} \in \mathcal{C}\} \; , \tag{8}$$

we finally have

$$\inf_{\mathbf{z} \in \mathcal{S}} \langle \mathbf{p}, \mathbf{z} \rangle \; . \tag{9}$$

Note that our assumption about $\mathcal{R}$ implies that $\mathcal{S}$ too is symmetric.

We now define classification calibration of $\mathcal{S}$. The definition intends to capture the property that, for any $\mathbf{p}$, minimizing $\langle \mathbf{p}, \mathbf{z} \rangle$ over $\mathcal{S}$ leads one to $\mathbf{z}$'s which enable us to figure out the index of (one of the) maximum coordinate(s) of $\mathbf{p}$.

Definition 1. *A set $\mathcal{S} \subseteq \mathbb{R}_+^K$ is classification calibrated if there exists a predictor function* $\mathrm{pred} : \mathbb{R}^K \mapsto \{1, \ldots, K\}$ *such that*

$$\forall \mathbf{p} \in \Delta_K, \quad \inf_{\mathbf{z} \in \mathcal{S} \, : \, p_{\mathrm{pred}(\mathbf{z})} < \max_y p_y} \langle \mathbf{p}, \mathbf{z} \rangle > \inf_{\mathbf{z} \in \mathcal{S}} \langle \mathbf{p}, \mathbf{z} \rangle \; , \tag{10}$$

where Δ_K is the probability simplex in $\mathbb{R}^K$.

It is easy to reformulate the definition in terms of sequences as the following lemma states.

Lemma 2. *$\mathcal{S} \subseteq \mathbb{R}_+^K$ is classification calibrated iff $\forall \mathbf{p} \in \Delta_K$ and all sequences $\{\mathbf{z}^{(n)}\}$ in $\mathcal{S}$ such that*

$$\langle \mathbf{p}, \mathbf{z}^{(n)} \rangle \to \inf_{\mathbf{z} \in \mathcal{S}} \langle \mathbf{p}, \mathbf{z} \rangle \; , \tag{11}$$

we have

$$p_{\mathrm{pred}(\mathbf{z}^{(n)})} = \max_y p_y \tag{12}$$

ultimately.

This makes it easier to see that if $\mathcal{S}$ is classification calibrated then we can find a predictor function such that any sequence achieving the infimum in (9) ultimately predicts the right label (the one having maximum probability). The following lemma shows that symmetry of our set $\mathcal{S}$ allows us to reduce the search space of predictor functions (namely to those functions which map $\mathbf{z}$ to the index of a minimum coordinate).

---

[2] If $\mathbf{z}$ is a convex combination of $\mathbf{z}^{(1)}$ and $\mathbf{z}^{(2)}$, then $\langle \mathbf{p}, \mathbf{z} \rangle \geq \min\{\langle \mathbf{p}, \mathbf{z}^{(1)} \rangle, \langle \mathbf{p}, \mathbf{z}^{(2)} \rangle\}$.

Lemma 3. *If there exists a predictor function* pred *satisfying the condition* (10) *of Definition 1 then any predictor function* pred' *satisfying*

$$\forall \mathbf{z} \in \mathcal{S}, \ z_{\mathrm{pred}'(\mathbf{z})} = \min_y z_y \tag{13}$$

also satisfies (10).

Proof. Consider some $\mathbf{p} \in \Delta_K$ and a sequence $\{\mathbf{z}^{(n)}\}$ such that (11) holds. We have $p_{\mathrm{pred}(\mathbf{z}^{(n)})} = \max_y p_y$ ultimately. In order to derive a contradiction, assume that $p_{\mathrm{pred}'(\mathbf{z}^{(n)})} < \max_y p_y$ infinitely often. Since there are finitely many labels, this implies that there is a subsequence $\{\mathbf{z}^{(n_k)}\}$ and labels M and m such that the following hold,

$$\mathrm{pred}(\mathbf{z}^{(n_k)}) = M \in \{y' : y' = \max_y p_y\} \ ,$$

$$\mathrm{pred}'(\mathbf{z}^{(n_k)}) = m \in \{y' : y' < \max_y p_y\} \ ,$$

$$\langle \mathbf{p}, \mathbf{z}^{(n_k)} \rangle \to \inf_{\mathbf{z} \in \mathcal{S}} \langle \mathbf{p}, \mathbf{z} \rangle \ .$$

Because of (13), we also have $z_M^{(n_k)} \geq z_m^{(n_k)}$. Let $\tilde{\mathbf{p}}$ and $\tilde{\mathbf{z}}$ denote the vectors obtained from $\mathbf{p}$ and $\mathbf{z}$ respectively by interchanging the M and m coordinates. Since $\mathcal{S}$ is symmetric, $\mathbf{z} \in \mathcal{S} \Leftrightarrow \tilde{\mathbf{z}} \in \mathcal{S}$. There are two cases depending on whether the inequality in

$$\liminf_k \left(z_M^{(n_k)} - z_m^{(n_k)} \right) \geq 0$$

is strict or not.

If it is, denote its value by $\epsilon > 0$. Then $z_M^{(n_k)} - z_m^{(n_k)} > \epsilon/2$ ultimately and hence we have

$$\langle \mathbf{p}, \mathbf{z}^{(n_k)} \rangle - \langle \mathbf{p}, \tilde{\mathbf{z}}^{(n_k)} \rangle = (p_M - p_m)(z_M^{(n_k)} - z_m^{(n_k)}) > (p_M - p_m)\epsilon/2$$

for k large enough. This implies $\liminf \langle \mathbf{p}, \tilde{\mathbf{z}}^{(n_k)} \rangle < \inf_{\mathbf{z} \in \mathcal{S}} \langle \mathbf{p}, \mathbf{z} \rangle$, which is a contradiction.

Otherwise, choose a subsequence[3] $\{\mathbf{z}^{(n_k)}\}$ such that $\lim(z_M^{(n_k)} - z_m^{(n_k)}) = 0$. Multiplying this with $(p_M - p_m)$, we have

$$\lim_{k \to \infty} \left(\langle \tilde{\mathbf{p}}, \tilde{\mathbf{z}}^{(n_k)} \rangle - \langle \tilde{\mathbf{p}}, \mathbf{z}^{(n_k)} \rangle \right) = 0 \ .$$

We also have

$$\lim \langle \tilde{\mathbf{p}}, \tilde{\mathbf{z}}^{(n_k)} \rangle = \lim \langle \mathbf{p}, \mathbf{z}^{(n_k)} \rangle = \inf_{\mathbf{z} \in \mathcal{S}} \langle \mathbf{p}, \mathbf{z} \rangle = \inf_{\mathbf{z} \in \mathcal{S}} \langle \tilde{\mathbf{p}}, \tilde{\mathbf{z}} \rangle = \inf_{\mathbf{z} \in \mathcal{S}} \langle \tilde{\mathbf{p}}, \mathbf{z} \rangle \ ,$$

where the last equality follows because of symmetry. This means

$$\langle \tilde{\mathbf{p}}, \mathbf{z}^{(n_k)} \rangle \to \inf_{\mathbf{z} \in \mathcal{S}} \langle \tilde{\mathbf{p}}, \mathbf{z} \rangle$$

---

[3] We do not introduce additional subscripts for simplicity.

and therefore

$$\tilde{p}_{\mathrm{pred}(\mathbf{z}^{(n_k)})} = p_M$$

ultimately. This is a contradiction since $\tilde{p}_{\mathrm{pred}(\mathbf{z}^{(n_k)})} = \tilde{p}_M = p_m$.

From now on, we assume that pred is defined as in (13). We give another characterization of classification calibration in terms of normals to the convex set $\mathcal{S}$ and its projections onto lower dimensions. For a point $\mathbf{z} \in \partial\mathcal{S}$, we say $\mathbf{p}$ is a normal to $\mathcal{S}$ at $\mathbf{z}$ if $\langle \mathbf{z}' - \mathbf{z}, \mathbf{p} \rangle \geq 0^4$ for all $\mathbf{z}' \in \mathcal{S}$. Define the set of positive normals at $\mathbf{z}$ as

$$\mathcal{N}(\mathbf{z}) = \{\mathbf{p} : \mathbf{p} \text{ is a normal to } \mathcal{S} \text{ at } \mathbf{z}\} \cap \Delta_K .$$

Definition 4. *A convex set $\mathcal{S} \subseteq \mathbb{R}_+^K$ is admissible if $\forall \mathbf{z} \in \partial\mathcal{S}, \forall \mathbf{p} \in \mathcal{N}(\mathbf{z})$, we have*

$$\mathrm{argmin}(\mathbf{z}) \subseteq \mathrm{argmax}(\mathbf{p}) \tag{14}$$

where $\mathrm{argmin}(\mathbf{z}) = \{y' : z_{y'} = \min_y z_y\}$ and $\mathrm{argmax}(\mathbf{p}) = \{y' : z_{y'} = \max_y p_y\}$.

The following lemma states that in the presence of symmetry points having a unique minimum coordinate can never destroy admissibility.

Lemma 5. *Let $\mathcal{S} \subseteq \mathbb{R}_+^K$ be a symmetric convex set, $\mathbf{z}$ a point in the boundary of $\mathcal{S}$ and $\mathbf{p} \in \mathcal{N}(\mathbf{z})$. Then $z_y < z_{y'}$ implies $p_y \geq p_{y'}$ and hence (14) holds whenever $|\mathrm{argmin}(\mathbf{z})| = 1$.*

Proof. Consider $\tilde{\mathbf{z}}$ obtained from $\mathbf{z}$ by interchanging the y, y' coordinates. It also is a point in $\partial\mathcal{S}$ by symmetry and thus convexity implies $\mathbf{z}_m = (\mathbf{z}+\tilde{\mathbf{z}})/2 \in \mathcal{S} \cup \partial\mathcal{S}$. Since $\mathbf{p} \in \mathcal{N}(\mathbf{z})$, $\langle \mathbf{z}' - \mathbf{z}, \mathbf{p} \rangle \geq 0$ for all $\mathbf{z}' \in \mathcal{S}$. Taking limits, this inequality also holds for $\mathbf{z}' \in \mathcal{S} \cup \partial\mathcal{S}$. Substituting $\mathbf{z}_m$ for $\mathbf{z}'$, we get $\langle (\tilde{\mathbf{z}} - \mathbf{z})/2, \mathbf{p} \rangle \geq 0$ which simplifies to $(z_{y'} - z_y)(p_y - p_{y'}) \geq 0$ whence the conclusion follows. □

If the set $\mathcal{S}$ possesses a unique normal at every point on its boundary then the next lemma guarantees admissibility.

Lemma 6. *Let $\mathcal{S} \subseteq \mathbb{R}_+^K$ be a symmetric convex set, $\mathbf{z}$ a point in the boundary of $\mathcal{S}$ and $\mathcal{N}(\mathbf{z}) = \{\mathbf{p}\}$ is a singleton. Then $\mathrm{argmin}(\mathbf{z}) \subseteq \mathrm{argmax}(\mathbf{p})$.*

Proof. We will assume that there exists a $y, y \in \mathrm{argmin}(\mathbf{z}), y \notin \mathrm{argmax}(\mathbf{p})$ and deduce that there are at least 2 elements in $|\mathcal{N}(\mathbf{z})|$ to get a contradiction. Let $y' \in \mathrm{argmax}(\mathbf{p})$. From the proof of Lemma 5 we have $(z_{y'} - z_y)(p_y - p_{y'}) \geq 0$ which implies $z_{y'} \leq z_y$ since $p_y - p_{y'} < 0$. But we already know that $z_y \leq z_{y'}$ and so $z_y = z_{y'}$. Symmetry of $\mathcal{S}$ now implies that $\tilde{\mathbf{p}} \in \mathcal{N}(\mathbf{z})$ where $\tilde{\mathbf{p}}$ is obtained from $\mathbf{p}$ by interchanging the y, y' coordinates. Since $p_y \neq p_{y'}$, $\tilde{\mathbf{p}} \neq \mathbf{p}$ which means $|\mathcal{N}(\mathbf{z})| \geq 2$. □

---

[4] Our sign convention is opposite to that of Rockafellar (1970) because we are dealing with minimum (instead of maximum) problems.

Lemma 7. *If $S \subseteq \mathbb{R}_+^K$ is admissible then for all $\mathbf{p} \in \Delta_K$ and all bounded sequences $\{\mathbf{z}^{(n)}\}$ such that $\langle \mathbf{p}, \mathbf{z}^{(n)} \rangle \to \inf_{\mathbf{z} \in S} \langle \mathbf{p}, \mathbf{z} \rangle$, we have $p_{\mathrm{pred}(\mathbf{z}^{(n)})} = \max_y p_y$ ultimately.*

Proof. Let $Z(\mathbf{p}) = \{\mathbf{z} \in \partial S : \mathbf{p} \in \mathcal{N}(\mathbf{z})\}$. Taking the limit of a convergent subsequence of the given bounded sequence gives us a point in ∂S which achieves the infimum of the inner product with $\mathbf{p}$. Thus, $Z(\mathbf{p})$ is not empty. It is easy to see that $Z(\mathbf{p})$ is closed. We claim that for all $\epsilon > 0$, $\mathrm{dist}(\mathbf{z}^{(n)}, Z(\mathbf{p})) < \epsilon$ ultimately. For if we assume the contrary, boundedness implies that we can find a convergent subsequence $\{\mathbf{z}^{(n_k)}\}$ such that $\forall k$, $\mathrm{dist}(\mathbf{z}^{(n_k)}, Z(\mathbf{p})) \geq \epsilon$. Let $\mathbf{z}^* = \lim_{k \to \infty} \mathbf{z}^{(n_k)}$. Then $\langle \mathbf{p}, \mathbf{z}^* \rangle = \inf_{\mathbf{z} \in S} \langle \mathbf{p}, \mathbf{z} \rangle$ and so $\mathbf{z}^* \in Z(\mathbf{p})$. On the other hand, $\mathrm{dist}(\mathbf{z}^*, Z(\mathbf{p})) \geq \epsilon$ which gives us a contradiction and our claim is proved. Further, there exists $\epsilon' > 0$ such that $\mathrm{dist}(\mathbf{z}^{(n)}, Z(\mathbf{p})) < \epsilon'$ implies $\mathrm{argmin}(\mathbf{z}^{(n)}) \subseteq \mathrm{argmin}(Z(\mathbf{p}))$[5]. Finally, by admissibility of S, $\mathrm{argmin}(Z(\mathbf{p})) \subseteq \mathrm{argmax}(\mathbf{p})$ and so $\mathrm{argmin}(\mathbf{z}^{(n)}) \subseteq \mathrm{argmax}(\mathbf{p})$ ultimately.

The next theorem provides a characterization of classification calibration in terms of normals to S.

Theorem 8. *Let $S \subseteq \mathbb{R}_+^K$ be a symmetric convex set. Define the sets*

$$S^{(i)} = \{(z_1, \dots, z_i)^T : \mathbf{z} \in S\}$$

for $i \in \{2, \dots, K\}$. Then S is classification calibrated iff each $S^{(i)}$ is admissible.

Proof. We prove the easier 'only if' direction first. Suppose some $S^{(i)}$ is not admissible. Then there exist $\mathbf{z} \in \partial S^{(i)}$ and $\mathbf{p} \in \mathcal{N}(\mathbf{z})$ and a label y' such that $y' \in \mathrm{argmin}(\mathbf{z})$ and $y' \notin \mathrm{argmax}(\mathbf{p})$. Choose a sequence $\{\mathbf{z}^{(n)}\}$ converging to $\mathbf{z}$. Modify the sequence by replacing, in each $\mathbf{z}^{(n)}$, the coordinates specified by $\mathrm{argmin}(\mathbf{z})$ by their average. The resulting sequences is still in $S^{(i)}$ (by symmetry and convexity) and has $\mathrm{argmin}(\mathbf{z}^{(n)}) = \mathrm{argmin}(\mathbf{z})$ ultimately. Therefore, if we set $\mathrm{pred}(\mathbf{z}^{(n)}) = y'$, we have $p_{\mathrm{pred}(\mathbf{z}^{(n)})} < \max_y p_y$ ultimately. To get a sequence in S look at the points whose projections are the $\mathbf{z}^{(n)}$'s and pad $\mathbf{p}$ with $K - i$ zeros.

To prove the other direction, assume each $S^{(i)}$ is admissible. Consider a sequence $\{\mathbf{z}^{(n)}\}$ with $\langle \mathbf{p}, \mathbf{z}^{(n)} \rangle \to \inf_{\mathbf{z} \in S} \langle \mathbf{p}, \mathbf{z} \rangle = L$. Without loss of generality, assume that for some j, $1 \leq j \leq K$ we have $p_1, \dots, p_j > 0$ and $p_{j+1}, \dots, p_K = 0$. We claim that there exists an $M < \infty$ such that $\forall y \leq j$, $z_y^{(n)} \leq M$ ultimately. Since $p_j z_j^{(n)} \leq L + 1$ ultimately, $M = \max_{1 \leq y \leq j}\{(L+1)/p_y\}$ works. Consider a set of labels $T \subseteq \{j+1, \dots, K\}$. Consider the subsequence consisting of those $\mathbf{z}^{(n)}$ for which $z_y \leq M$ for $y \in \{1, \dots, j\} \cup T$ and $z_y > M$ for $y \in \{j+1, \dots, K\} - T$. The original sequence can be decomposed into finitely many such subsequences corresponding to the $2^{(K-j)}$ choices of the set T. Fix T and convert the corresponding subsequence into a sequence in $S^{(j+|T|)}$ by dropping the coordinates belonging to

---

[5] For a set Z, $\mathrm{argmin}(Z)$ denotes $\cup_{\mathbf{z} \in Z} \mathrm{argmin}(\mathbf{z})$.

the set $\{j+1, \ldots, K\}$. Call this sequence $\tilde{\mathbf{z}}^{(n)}$ and let $\tilde{\mathbf{p}}$ be $(p_1, \ldots, p_j, 0, \ldots, 0)^T$. We have a bounded sequence with

$$\langle \tilde{\mathbf{p}}, \tilde{\mathbf{z}}^{(n)} \rangle \to \inf_{\tilde{\mathbf{z}} \in \mathcal{S}^{(j+|T|)}} \langle \tilde{\mathbf{p}}, \tilde{\mathbf{z}} \rangle .$$

Thus, by Lemma 7, we have $\tilde{p}_{\mathrm{pred}(\tilde{\mathbf{z}}^{(n)})} = \max_y \tilde{p}_y = \max_y p_y$ ultimately. Since we dropped only those coordinates which were greater than M, $\mathrm{pred}(\tilde{\mathbf{z}}^{(n)})$ picks the same coordinate as $\mathrm{pred}(\mathbf{z}^{(n)})$ where $\mathbf{z}^{(n)}$ is the element from which $\tilde{\mathbf{z}}^{(n)}$ was obtained. Thus we have $p_{\mathrm{pred}(\mathbf{z}^{(n)})} = \max_y p_y$ ultimately and the theorem is proved.

We will need the following lemma to prove our final theorem.

Lemma 9. *The function* $\mathbf{p} \mapsto \inf_{\mathbf{z} \in \mathcal{S}} \langle \mathbf{p}, \mathbf{z} \rangle$ *is continuous on* Δ_K.

Proof. Let $\{\mathbf{p}^{(n)}\}$ be a sequence converging to $\mathbf{p}$. If B is a bounded subset of $\mathbb{R}^K$, then $\langle \mathbf{p}^{(n)}, \mathbf{z} \rangle \to \langle \mathbf{p}, \mathbf{z} \rangle$ uniformly over $\mathbf{z} \in B$ and therefore

$$\inf_{\mathbf{z} \in B} \langle \mathbf{p}^{(n)}, \mathbf{z} \rangle \to \inf_{\mathbf{z} \in B} \langle \mathbf{p}, \mathbf{z} \rangle .$$

Let B_r be a ball of radius r in $\mathbb{R}^K$. Then we have

$$\inf_{\mathbf{z} \in \mathcal{S}} \langle \mathbf{p}^{(n)}, \mathbf{z} \rangle \le \inf_{\mathcal{S} \cap B_r} \langle \mathbf{p}^{(n)}, \mathbf{z} \rangle \to \inf_{\mathcal{S} \cap B_r} \langle \mathbf{p}, \mathbf{z} \rangle$$

Therefore

$$\limsup_n \inf_{\mathbf{z} \in \mathcal{S}} \langle \mathbf{p}^{(n)}, \mathbf{z} \rangle \le \inf_{\mathbf{z} \in \mathcal{S} \cap B_r} \langle \mathbf{p}, \mathbf{z} \rangle .$$

Letting $r \to \infty$, we get

$$\limsup_n \inf_{\mathbf{z} \in \mathcal{S}} \langle \mathbf{p}^{(n)}, \mathbf{z} \rangle \le \inf_{\mathbf{z} \in \mathcal{S}} \langle \mathbf{p}, \mathbf{z} \rangle . \tag{15}$$

Without loss of generality, assume that for some $j, 1 \le j \le K$ we have $p_1, \ldots, p_j > 0$ and $p_{j+1}, \ldots, p_K = 0$. For all sufficiently large integers n and a sufficiently large ball $B_M \subseteq \mathbb{R}^j$ we have

$$\inf_{\mathbf{z} \in \mathcal{S}} \langle \mathbf{p}, \mathbf{z} \rangle = \inf_{\mathbf{z} \in \mathcal{S}^{(j)}} \sum_{y=1}^{j} p_y z_y = \inf_{\mathbf{z} \in \mathcal{S}^{(j)} \cap B_M} \sum_{y=1}^{j} p_y z_y ,$$

$$\inf_{\mathbf{z} \in \mathcal{S}} \langle \mathbf{p}^{(n)}, \mathbf{z} \rangle \ge \inf_{\mathbf{z} \in \mathcal{S}^{(j)}} \sum_{y=1}^{j} p_y^{(n)} z_y = \inf_{\mathbf{z} \in \mathcal{S}^{(j)} \cap B_M} \sum_{y=1}^{j} p_y^{(n)} z_y .$$

and thus

$$\liminf_n \inf_{\mathbf{z} \in \mathcal{S}} \langle \mathbf{p}^{(n)}, \mathbf{z} \rangle \ge \inf_{\mathbf{z} \in \mathcal{S}} \langle \mathbf{p}, \mathbf{z} \rangle . \tag{16}$$

Combining (15) and (16), we get

$$\inf_{\mathbf{z} \in \mathcal{S}} \langle \mathbf{p}^{(n)}, \mathbf{z} \rangle \to \inf_{\mathbf{z} \in \mathcal{S}} \langle \mathbf{p}, \mathbf{z} \rangle .$$

We finally show that classification calibration of $\mathcal{S}$ is equivalent to the consistency of multiclass methods based on (5).

Theorem 10. *Let Ψ be a loss (vector) function and $\mathcal{C}$ be a subset of $\mathbb{R}^K$. Let $\mathcal{F}$ and $\mathcal{S}$ be as defined in (6) and (8) respectively. Then $\mathcal{S}$ is classification calibrated iff the following holds. For all sequences $\{\mathcal{F}_n\}$ of function classes (where $\mathcal{F}_n \subseteq \mathcal{F}$ and $\cup \mathcal{F}_n = \mathcal{F}$) and for all probability distributions P,*

$$R_\Psi(\hat{\mathbf{f}}_n) \xrightarrow{P} R_\Psi^*$$

implies

$$R(\hat{\mathbf{f}}_n) \xrightarrow{P} R^* \ .$$

Proof. ('only if') We need to prove that $\forall \epsilon > 0, \exists \delta > 0$ such that $\forall \mathbf{p} \in \Delta_K$,

$$\max_y p_y - p_{\mathrm{pred}(\mathbf{z})} \geq \epsilon \Rightarrow \langle \mathbf{p}, \mathbf{z} \rangle - \inf_{\mathbf{z} \in \mathcal{S}} \langle \mathbf{p}, \mathbf{z} \rangle \geq \delta \ . \tag{17}$$

Using this it immediately follows that $\forall \epsilon, H(\epsilon) > 0$ where

$$H(\epsilon) = \inf_{\mathbf{p} \in \Delta_K, \mathbf{z} \in \mathcal{S}} \{ \langle \mathbf{p}, \mathbf{z} \rangle - \inf_{\mathbf{z} \in \mathcal{S}} \langle \mathbf{p}, \mathbf{z} \rangle \ : \ \max_y p_y - p_{\mathrm{pred}(\mathbf{z})} \geq \epsilon \} \ .$$

Corollary 26 in [12] then guarantees there exists a concave function ξ on $[0, \infty)$ such that $\xi(0) = 0$ and $\xi(\delta) \to 0$ as $\delta \to 0^+$ and

$$R(\mathbf{f}) - R^* \leq \xi(R_\Psi(\mathbf{f}) - R_\Psi^*) \ .$$

We prove (17) by contradiction. Suppose $\mathcal{S}$ is classification calibrated but there exists $\epsilon > 0$ and a sequence $(\mathbf{z}^{(n)}, \mathbf{p}^{(n)})$ such that

$$p_{\mathrm{pred}(\mathbf{z}^{(n)})}^{(n)} \leq \max_y p_y^{(n)} - \epsilon \tag{18}$$

and

$$\left(\langle \mathbf{p}^{(n)}, \mathbf{z}^{(n)} \rangle - \inf_{\mathbf{z} \in \mathcal{S}} \langle \mathbf{p}^{(n)}, \mathbf{z} \rangle \right) \to 0 \ .$$

Since $\mathbf{p}^{(n)}$ come from a compact set, we can choose a convergent subsequence (which we still denote as $\{\mathbf{p}^{(n)}\}$) with limit $\mathbf{p}$. Using Lemma 9, we get

$$\langle \mathbf{p}^{(n)}, \mathbf{z}^{(n)} \rangle \to \inf_{\mathbf{z} \in \mathcal{S}} \langle \mathbf{p}, \mathbf{z} \rangle \ .$$

As before, we assume that precisely the first j coordinates of $\mathbf{p}$ are non-zero. Then the first j coordinates of $\mathbf{z}^{(n)}$ are bounded for sufficiently large n. Hence

$$\limsup_n \langle \mathbf{p}, \mathbf{z}^{(n)} \rangle = \limsup_n \sum_{y=1}^{j} p_y^{(n)} z_y^{(n)} \leq \lim_{n \to \infty} \langle \mathbf{p}^{(n)}, \mathbf{z}^{(n)} \rangle = \inf_{\mathbf{z} \in \mathcal{S}} \langle \mathbf{p}, \mathbf{z} \rangle \ .$$

Now (12) and (18) contradict each other since $\mathbf{p}^{(n)} \to \mathbf{p}$.

('if') If $\mathcal{S}$ is not classification calibrated then by Theorem 8 and Lemmas 5 and 6, we have a point in the boundary of some $\mathcal{S}^{(i)}$ where there are at least two normals and which does not have a unique minimum coordinate. Such a point should be there in the projection of $\mathcal{R}$ even without taking the convex hull. Therefore, we must have a sequence $\mathbf{z}^{(n)}$ in $\mathcal{R}$ such that

$$\delta_n = \langle \mathbf{p}, \mathbf{z}^{(n)} \rangle - \inf_{\mathbf{z} \in \mathcal{S}} \langle \mathbf{p}, \mathbf{z} \rangle \to 0 \tag{19}$$

and for all n,

$$p_{\mathrm{pred}(\mathbf{z}^{(n)})} < \max_y p_y \ . \tag{20}$$

Without loss of generality assume that δ_n is a monotonically decreasing sequence. Further, assume that $\delta_n > 0$ for all n. This last assumption might be violated but the following proof then goes through for δ_n replaced by $\max(\delta_n, 1/n)$. Let $\mathbf{g}_n$ be the function that maps every x to one of the pre-images of $\mathbf{z}^{(n)}$ under Ψ. Define $\mathcal{F}_n$ as

$$\mathcal{F}_n = \{\mathbf{g}_n\} \ \cup \ (\mathcal{F} \cap \{\mathbf{f} : \forall x, \langle \mathbf{p}, \Psi(\mathbf{f}(x)) \rangle - \inf_{\mathbf{z} \in \mathcal{S}} \langle \mathbf{p}, \mathbf{z} \rangle > 4\delta_n\}$$

$$\cap \{\mathbf{f} : \forall x, \forall j, |\Psi_j(\mathbf{f}(x)| < M_n\})$$

where $M_n \uparrow \infty$ is a sequence which we will fix later. Fix a probability distribution P with arbitrary marginal distribution over x and let the conditional distribution of labels be $\mathbf{p}$ for all x. Our choice of $\mathcal{F}_n$ guarantees that the Ψ-risk of $\mathbf{g}_n$ is less than that of other elements of $\mathcal{F}_n$ by at least $3\delta_n$. Suppose, we make sure that

$$P^n \left(\left| \hat{R}_\Psi(\mathbf{g}_n) - R_\Psi(\mathbf{g}_n) \right| > \delta_n \right) \to 0 \ , \tag{21}$$

$$P^n \left(\sup_{\mathbf{f} \in \mathcal{F}_n - \{\mathbf{g}_n\}} \left| \hat{R}_\Psi(\mathbf{f}) - R_\Psi(\mathbf{f}) \right| > \delta_n \right) \to 0 \ . \tag{22}$$

Then, with probability tending to 1, $\hat{\mathbf{f}}_n = \mathbf{g}_n$. By (19), $R_\Psi(\mathbf{g}_n) \to R_\Psi^*$ which implies that $R_\Psi(\hat{\mathbf{f}}_n) \to R_\Psi^*$ in probability. Similarly, (20) implies that $R(\hat{\mathbf{f}}_n) \nrightarrow R^*$ in probability.

We only need to show that we can have (21) and (22) hold. For (21), we apply Chebyshev inequality and use a union bound over the K labels to get

$$P^n \left(\left| \hat{R}_\Psi(\mathbf{g}_n) - R_\Psi(\mathbf{g}_n) \right| > \delta_n \right) \leq \frac{K^3 \|\mathbf{z}^{(n)}\|_\infty}{4n\delta_n^2}$$

The right hand side can be made to go to zero by repeating terms in the sequence $\{\mathbf{z}^{(n)}\}$ to slow down the rate of growth of $\|\mathbf{z}^{(n)}\|_\infty$ and the rate of decrease of δ_n. For (21), we use standard covering number bounds (see, for example, Section

II.6 on p. 30 in [7]).

$$P^n \left(\sup_{\mathbf{f} \in \mathcal{F}_n - \{\mathbf{g}_n\}} \left| \hat{R}_\Psi(\mathbf{f}) - R_\Psi(\mathbf{f}) \right| > \delta_n \right)$$

$$\leq 8 \exp \left(\frac{64 M_n^2 \log(2n+1)}{\delta_n^2} - \frac{n \delta_n^2}{128 M_n^2} \right)$$

Thus M_n/δ_n needs to grow slowly enough such that

$$\frac{n \delta_n^4}{M_n^4 \log(2n+1)} \to \infty \ .$$

4   Examples

We apply the results of the previous section to examine the consistency of several multiclass methods. In all these examples, the functions $\Psi_y(\mathbf{f})$ are obtained from a single real valued function $\psi : \mathbb{R}^K \mapsto \mathbb{R}$ as follows

$$\Psi_y(\mathbf{f}) = \psi(f_y, f_1, \ldots, f_{y-1}, f_{y+1}, \ldots, f_K)$$

Moreover, the function ψ is symmetric in its last $K - 1$ arguments, i.e. interchanging any two of the last $K - 1$ arguments does not change the value of the function. This ensures that the set $\mathcal{S}$ is symmetric. We assume that we predict the label of x to be $\arg\min_y \Psi_y(\mathbf{f})$.

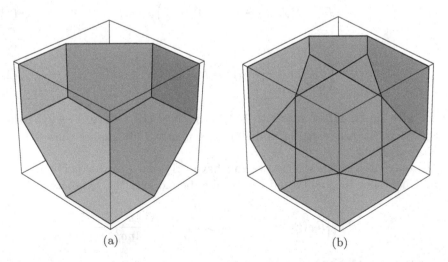

Fig. 2. (a) Crammer and Singer (b) Weston and Watkins

4.1 Example 1

The method of Crammer and Singer [3] corresponds to

$$\Psi_y(\mathbf{f}) = \max_{y' \neq y} \phi(f_y - f_{y'}), \ \mathcal{C} = \mathbb{R}^K$$

with $\phi(t) = (1 - t)_+$. For $K = 3$, the boundary of $\mathcal{S}$ is shown in Fig. 2(a). At the point $\mathbf{z} = (1, 1, 1)$, all of these are normals: $(0, 1, 1)$, $(1, 0, 1)$, $(1, 1, 0)$. Thus, there is no y' such that $p_{y'} = \max_y p_y$ for all $\mathbf{p} \in \mathcal{N}(\mathbf{z})$. The method is therefore inconsistent.

Even if we choose an everywhere differentiable convex ϕ with $\phi'(0) < 0$, the three normals mentioned above are still there in $\mathcal{N}(\mathbf{z})$ for $\mathbf{z} = (\phi(0), \phi(0), \phi(0))$. Therefore the method still remains inconsistent.

4.2 Example 2

The method of Weston and Watkins [10] corresponds to

$$\Psi_y(\mathbf{f}) = \sum_{y' \neq y} \phi(f_y - f_{y'}), \ \mathcal{C} = \mathbb{R}^K$$

with $\phi(t) = (1 - t)_+$. For $K = 3$, the boundary of $\mathcal{S}$ is shown in Fig. 2(b). The central hexagon has vertices (in clockwise order) $(1, 1, 4)$, $(0, 3, 3)$, $(1, 4, 1)$, $(3, 3, 0)$, $(4, 1, 1)$ and $(3, 0, 3)$. At $\mathbf{z} = (1, 1, 4)$, we have the following normals: $(1, 1, 0)$, $(1, 1, 1)$, $(2, 3, 1)$, $(3, 2, 1)$ and there is no coordinate which is maximum in all positive normals. The method is therefore inconsistent.

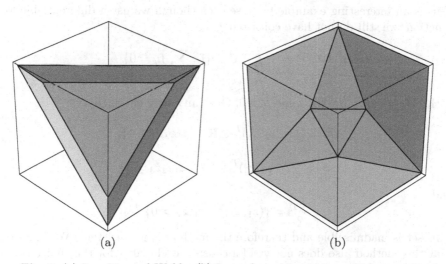

(a)   (b)

Fig. 3. (a) Lee, Lin and Wahba (b) Loss of consistency in multiclass setting

4.3   Example 3

The method of Lee, Lin and Wahba [5] corresponds to

$$\Psi_y(\mathbf{f}) = \sum_{y' \neq y} \phi(-f_{y'}), \ \mathcal{C} = \{\mathbf{f} : \sum_y f_y = 0\} \tag{23}$$

with $\phi(t) = (1-t)_+$. Fig. 3(a) shows the boundary of $\mathcal{S}$ for $K = 3$. In the general K dimensional case, $\mathcal{S}$ is a polyhedron with K vertices where each vertex has a 0 in one of the positions and K's in the rest. It is obvious then when we minimize $\langle \mathbf{p}, \mathbf{z} \rangle$ over $\mathcal{S}$, we will pick the vertex which has a 0 in the same position where $\mathbf{p}$ has its maximum coordinate. But we can also apply our result here. The set of normals is not a singleton only at the vertices. Thus, by Lemma 6, we only need to check the vertices. Since there is a unique minimum coordinate at the vertices, Lemma 5 implies that the method is consistent.

The question which naturally arises is: for which convex loss functions ϕ does (23) lead to a consistent multiclass classification method? Convex loss functions which are classification calibrated for the two class case, i.e. differentiable at 0 with $\phi'(0) < 0$, can lead to inconsistent classifiers in the multiclass setting. An example is provided by the loss function $\phi(t) = \max\{1 - 2t, 2 - t, 0\}$. Fig. 3(b) shows the boundary of $\mathcal{S}$ for $K = 3$. The vertices are $(0, 3, 3)$, $(9, 0, 0)$ and their permutations. At $(9, 0, 0)$, the set of normals includes $(0, 1, 0)$, $(1, 2, 2)$ and $(0, 0, 1)$ and therefore condition (14) is violated.

As Zhang shows in [12], a convex function ϕ differentiable on $(-\infty, 0]$ with $\phi'(0) < 0$ will yield a consistent method.

4.4   Example 4

This is an interesting example because even though we use a differentiable loss function, we still do not have consistency.

$$\Psi_y(\mathbf{f}) = \phi(f_y), \ \mathcal{C} = \{\mathbf{f} : \sum_y f_y = 0\}$$

with $\phi(t) = \exp(-\beta t)$ for some $\beta > 0$. One can easily check that

$$\mathcal{R} = \{(z_1, z_2, z_3)^T \in \mathbb{R}_+^3 : z_1 z_2 z_3 = 1\},$$

$$\mathcal{S} = \{(z_1, z_2, z_3)^T \in \mathbb{R}_+^3 : z_1 z_2 z_3 \geq 1\}$$

and

$$\mathcal{S}^{(2)} = \{(z_1, z_2)^T : z_1, z_2 > 0\} .$$

This set is inadmissible and therefore the method is inconsistent. We point out that this method also does not yield a consistent classifier for the choice $\phi(t) = (1-t)_+$.

5 Conclusion

We considered multiclass generalizations of classification methods based on convex risk minimization and gave a necessary and sufficient condition for their Bayes consistency. Our examples showed that quite often straightforward generalizations of consistent binary classification methods lead to inconsistent multiclass classifiers. This is especially the case if the original binary method was based on a non-differentiable loss function. Example 4 shows that even differentiable loss functions do not guarantee multiclass consistency. We are currently trying to find simple and sufficient differentiability conditions that would imply consistency of methods discussed in Examples 2 and 4 (like the one Zhang provides for Example 3).

Acknowledgement

We gratefully acknowledge the support of NSF under award DMS-0434383.

References

1. Bartlett, P. L., Jordan, M. I. and McAuliffe, J. D.: Large margin classifiers: Convex Loss, Low Noise and Convergence rates. In *Advances in Neural Information Processing Systems* **16** (2004)
2. Bredensteiner, E.J. and Bennett, K.P.: Multicategory Classification by Support Vector Machines. *Computational Optimization and Applications* **12** (1999) 35–46
3. Crammer, K. and Singer, Y.: On the Algorithmic Implementation of Kernel-based Vector Machines. *Journal of Machine Learning Research* **2** (2001) 265–292
4. Jiang, W.: Process Consistency for AdaBoost. *Annals of Statistics* **32**:1 (2004) 13–29
5. Lee, Y., Li, Y. and Wahba, G.: Multicategory Support Vector Machines: Theory and Application to the Classification of Microarray Data and Satellite Radiance Data. *Journal of the American Statistical Association* **99**:465 (2004) 67–81
6. Lugosi, G. and Vayatis, N.: On the Bayes-risk Consistency of Regularized Boosting Methods. *Annals of Statistics* **32**:1 (2004) 30–55
7. Pollard, D.: *Convergence of Stochastic Processes*. Springer-Verlag, New York (1984)
8. Rockafellar, R.T.: *Convex Analysis*. Princeton University Press, Princeton (1970)
9. Steinwart, I.: Consistency of Support Vector Machines and Other Regularized Kernel Classifiers. *IEEE Transactions on Information Theory* **51**:1 (2005) 128–142
10. Weston, J. and and Watkins, C.: Multi-class support vector machines. Technical Report CSD-TR-98-04, Department of Computer Science, Royal Holloway College, University of London (1998)
11. Zhang, T.: An Infinity-sample Theory For Multi-category Large Margin Classification. In *Advances in Neural Information Processing Systems* **16** (2004)
12. Zhang, T.: Statistical Analysis of Some Multi-Category Large Margin Classification Methods. *Journal of Machine Learning Research* **5** (2004) 1225–1251
13. Zhang, T.: Statistical Behavior and Consistency of Classification Methods Based on Convex Risk Minimization. *Annals of Statistics* **32**:1 (2004) 56–85

Sensitive Error Correcting Output Codes

John Langford[1] and Alina Beygelzimer[2]

[1] Toyota Technological Institute, Chicago IL 60637, USA
jl@tti-c.org
[2] IBM T. J. Watson Research Center, Hawthorne NY 10532, USA
beygel@us.ibm.com

Abstract. We present a reduction from cost-sensitive classification to binary classification based on (a modification of) error correcting output codes. The reduction satisfies the property that ϵ regret for binary classification implies l_2-regret of at most 2ϵ for cost estimation. This has several implications:

1. Any regret-minimizing online algorithm for 0/1 loss is (via the reduction) a regret-minimizing online cost-sensitive algorithm. In particular, this means that online learning can be made to work for arbitrary (i.e., totally unstructured) loss functions.
2. The output of the reduction can be thresholded so that ϵ regret for binary classification implies at most $4\sqrt{\epsilon Z}$ regret for cost-sensitive classification where Z is the expected sum of costs.
3. For multiclass problems, ϵ binary regret translates into l_2-regret of at most 4ϵ in the estimation of class probabilities. For classification, this implies at most $4\sqrt{\epsilon}$ multiclass regret.

1 Introduction

BACKGROUND: The goal of classification is to predict labels on test examples given a set of labeled training examples. Binary classification, where the number of labels is two, is the most basic learning task as it involves predicting just a single bit for each example. Due to this simplicity, binary learning is (perhaps) better understood theoretically than any other prediction task, and several empirically good binary learning algorithms exist.

Practical machine learning, on the other hand, often requires predicting more than one bit. Furthermore, each prediction may generally have a different associated loss, and ignoring this information can make the problem more difficult.[1]

---

[1] For example, consider the following problem: Given some relevant information, we must predict which of several routes to take. It is easy to design a problem where there are several paths that are typically good but occasionally very slow. If there is another path that is never the best but never slow, it may provide the best expected time of all choices. If the problem is altered into a multiclass problem of predicting the best route, this path will never be taken.

P. Auer and R. Meir (Eds.): COLT 2005, LNAI 3559, pp. 158–172, 2005.

MOTIVATION: Reductions allow us to translate performance on well-studied binary problems into performance on the more general problems arising in practice. We provide a reduction (called SECOC) from cost-sensitive classification to binary classification with the property that small regret on the created binary problem(s) implies small regret on the original cost-sensitive problem. This is particularly compelling because *any* loss function on single examples can be expressed with cost-sensitive classification. Therefore, this reduction can be used (at least theoretically) to solve a very broad set of learning problems. In addition, there is convincing empirical evidence that SECOC works well in practice, which gives further support to this style of analysis. Experiments in Section 7 show that SECOC results in superior performance on all tested multiclass learning algorithms and problems, compared to several other commonly used algorithms.

The basic SECOC reduction can be reused in several ways.

1. GENERAL ONLINE LEARNING: Any regret-minimizing online algorithm for $0/1$ loss is (via the reduction) a regret-minimizing online cost sensitive algorithm. In particular, this means that online learning can be made to work for arbitrary (i.e., totally unstructured) loss functions.
2. COST SENSITIVE CLASSIFICATION: The output of the reduction can be thresholded so that a small regret for binary classification implies a small regret for cost-sensitive classification. This implies that any consistent binary classifier is a consistent cost-sensitive classifier.
3. MULTICLASS PROBLEMS: Using the canonical embedding of multiclass classification into cost-sensitive classification, this reduction implies that small binary regret translates into small l_2 error in the estimation of class probabilities. By thresholding the estimates, we get a bound on multiclass regret. Note that this implies that *any* consistent binary classifier is (via the reduction) a consistent multiclass classifier. This is particularly important because generalization of SVMs to multiple classes have been done wrong, as shown in [8].

These applications are discussed in Section 4.

GENERAL COMMENT: It is important to understand that analysis here is orthogonal to the sample complexity analysis in, for example, PAC learning [12] or uniform convergence [14]. We consider measures over sets of examples and analyze the transformation of losses under mappings between these measures induced by the algorithms. This allows us to avoid making assumptions (which cannot be verified or simply do not hold in practice) necessary to prove sample complexity bounds. Instead, we show relative guarantees in an assumption-free setting – we bound the performance on general problems arising in practice in terms of performance on basic problems that are better understood.

CONTEXT: SECOC is a variation of error-correcting output codes (ECOC) [3]. Later, in Section 5, we show that this variation is necessary in order to satisfy a regret transform. The ECOC reduction works by learning a binary classifier, which decides membership of a label in subsets of labels. Given a sequence of subsets, each label corresponds to a binary string (or a *codeword*) defined by the inclusion of this label in the sequence of subsets. A multiclass prediction is made by finding the codeword closest in Hamming distance to the sequence of binary predictions on the test example.

For the ECOC reduction, a basic statement [5] can be made: with a good code, for all training sets, the error rate of the multiclass classifier on the training set is at most 4 times the average error rate of the individual binary classifiers. The proof of this statement is essentially the observation that there exist codes in which the distance between any two codewords is at least $\frac{1}{2}$. Consequently, at least $\frac{1}{4}$ of the classifiers must err to induce a multiclass classification error, implying the theorem.

This theorem can be generalized [2] to quantify "for all measures" rather than "for all training sets". This generalization is not as significant as it might at first seem, because the measure implicit in a very large training set can approximate other measures (and it can do so arbitrarily well when the feature space is finite). Nevertheless, it is convenient to quantify over all measures, so that the statement holds for the process generating each individual example. Since there is always some process generating examples, the result is applicable even to adversarial processes.

The weighted all pairs algorithm [2] intuitively guarantees that a small error rate on created classification problems implies a small cost-sensitive loss. The core result here is similar except that small binary *regret* implies small cost-sensitive *regret*. Regret is the error rate minus the minimum error rate. Consequently, the results here can have important implications even when, for example, the binary error induced from a multiclass problem is 0.25. SECOC does not supercede this result, however, because the regret bounds are weaker, roughly according to ϵ error rate going to $\sqrt{\epsilon}$ regret.

ECOC was modified [1] to consider margins of the binary classifiers—numbers internal to some classification algorithms that provide a measure of confidence in a binary prediction. Decoding proceeds in the same way as for ECOC except a "loss"-based[2] distance is used instead of the Hamming distance. Roughly speaking, SECOC uses the motivation behind this approach although not the approach itself. Instead of working with margins, we define binary classification problems, for which the optimal solution computes the relative expected cost (rather than the margin) of choices. This approach allows us to accomplish several things: First, we can use arbitrary classifiers rather than margin-based classifiers. We also remove the mismatch between the margin and the motivations. Optimizations of hinge loss (for SVMs) or exponential loss (for Adaboost) cause a distortion where the optimization increases the margin of small-margin examples at the expense of the margin on large-margin examples. The efficacy of Platt scaling [10] (i.e., fitting a sigmoid to a margin to get a probabilistic prediction) can be thought of as strong empirical evidence of the deficiency of margins

---

[2] "Loss" is in quotes because the notion of loss is a specification of the optimization used by the binary learning algorithm rather than the loss given by the problem, as is used in the rest of the paper.

as probability estimates. Finally, we can generalize the approach to tackle all cost-sensitive problems rather than just multiclass problems. This generalization comes at no cost in multiclass performance.

2   The SECOC Reduction

We work in an assumption-free learning setting. The SECOC reduction reduces cost-sensitive classification to importance weighted binary classification, which in turn can be reduced to binary classification using the Costing reduction [16]. We first define all the problems involved.

Definition 1. *An importance weighted binary classification problem is defined by a measure D on a set $X \times \{0, 1\} \times [0, \infty)$, where X is some arbitrary feature space, $\{0, 1\}$ is the binary label, and $[0, \infty)$ is the importance of correct classification. The goal is to find a binary classifier $b : X \to \{0, 1\}$ which minimizes the expected importance weighted loss, $E_{(x,y,i) \sim D} [iI(b(x) \neq y)]$, where $I(\cdot)$ is 1 when the argument is true and 0 otherwise.*

Cost-sensitive classification defined below is sufficiently general to express any loss function on a finite set.

Definition 2. *A cost-sensitive k-class problem is defined by a measure D on a set $X \times [0, \infty)^k$, where X is some arbitrary feature space, and the additional information $[0, \infty)^k$ is the cost of each of the k choices. The goal is to find a classifier $h : X \to \{1, ..., k\}$ which minimizes the expected cost, $E_{(x,c) \sim D} [c_{h(x)}]$.*

A cost-sensitive learning algorithm typically takes as input a sequence of training examples in $(X \times [0, \infty)^k)^*$ as advice in constructing $h(x)$.

The SECOC reduction is a cost-sensitive learning algorithm that uses a given binary learning algorithm as a black box. As with the ECOC reduction, SECOC uses a code defined by an $n \times k$ binary coding matrix M with columns corresponding to multiclass labels. For example, the columns can form a subset of any k codewords of a Hadamard code of length n, which has the property that any two distinct codewords differ in at least $n/2$ bit positions. Such codes are easy to construct when k is a power of 2. Thus, for Hadamard codes, the number n of classification problems needed is less than $2k$.

For each subset s of labels, corresponding to a row of M, we create a set of importance weighted classification problems parameterized by $t \in [t_{\min}, t_{\max}]$, where $t_{\min} = 0$ and $t_{\max} = 1$ are always correct, but significant efficiency improvements arise from appropriately chosen smaller ranges. Intuitively, the problem defined by the pair (s, t) is to answer the question "Is the cost of s greater than t times the total cost?" From the optimal solution of these problems we can compute the expected relative cost of each subset s. SECOC-Train (Algorithm 1) has the complete specification.

We write E_s to denote an expectation over s drawn uniformly from the rows of M, and E_t to denote expectation over t drawn uniformly from the interval $[t_{\min}, t_{\max}]$.

Algorithm 1. SECOC-Train (Set of k-class cost-sensitive examples S, importance weighted binary classifier learning algorithm B, range $[t_{\min}, t_{\max}]$ for t)

1. For each subset s defined by the rows of M:
   (a) For $(x, c) \in S$, let $|c| = \sum_y c_y$ and $c_s = \sum_{y \in s} c_y$.
   (b) For each t in $[t_{\min}, t_{\max}]$:
       Let $b_{st} = B(\{(x, I(c_s \geq t|c|), |c_s - |c|t|) : (x, c) \in S\})$.
2. return $\{b_{st}\}$

Algorithm 2. SECOC-Predict (classifiers $\{b_{st}\}$, example $x \in X$, label y)

return $2(t_{\min} + (t_{\max} - t_{\min})E_s E_t [I(y \in s)b_{st}(x) + I(y \notin s)(1 - b_{st}(x))]) - 1$

To make a label cost estimate, SECOC-Predict (Algorithm 2) uses a formula of the expected prediction of the subsets containing the label.

SINGLE CLASSIFIER TRICK: Multiple invocations of the oracle learning algorithm B can be collapsed into a single call using a standard trick [2, 1]. The trick is just to augment the feature space with the name of the call, and then learn a classifier b on (a random subset of) the union of all training data. With this classifier, we can define $b_{st}(x) \equiv b(\langle x, s, t \rangle)$, and all of our results hold for this single invocation classifier. The implication of this observation is that we can view SECOC-Train as a machine that maps cost-sensitive examples to importance weighted binary examples. We denote the learned binary classifier by $B(\text{SECOC-Train}(S))$.

3   The Main Theorem

Before stating the theorem, we need to define loss and regret. Given any distribution D on examples $X \times \{0, 1\} \times [0, \infty)$, the importance weighted error rate of a binary classifier b is given by

$$e(D, b) = E_{(x,y,i) \sim D} [iI(b(x) \neq y)].$$

Similarly, given any distribution D on examples $X \times [0, \infty)^k$, the cost-sensitive loss of a multiclass classifier h is given by

$$e(D, h) = E_{(x,c) \sim D} [c_{h(x)}].$$

For each of these notions of loss, the regret is the difference between the achieved performance and best possible performance:

$$r(D, h) = e(D, h) - \min_{h'} e(D, h').$$

(Note that we mean the minimum over *all* classifiers h' not over some class.) The minimum loss classifier is also known as the "Bayes optimal classifier".

We must also define how SECOC transforms its distribution D into a distribution on the learned binary classifier. To draw a sample from this distribution, we first draw a cost-sensitive sample (x, c) from D, and then apply SECOC-Train to the singleton set $\{(x, c)\}$ to get a sequence of importance weighted binary examples, one for each (s, t) pair. Now, we just sample uniformly from this set, adding the index in the sequence as a feature. We overload and denote the induced distribution by SECOC-Train(D).

Throughout the paper, for a cost vector $c \in [0, \infty)^k$ and a subset of labels $s \subseteq \{1, \ldots, k\}$, let $c_s = \sum_{y \in s} c_y$. Also let $|c| = \sum_{y=1}^{k} c_y$. The distribution $D|x$ is defined as D conditioned on x.

Theorem 1. (SECOC Regret Transform) *For all importance weighted binary learning algorithms B and cost-sensitive datasets S in $(X \times [0, \infty)^k)^*$, let $b = B(\text{SECOC-Train}(S))$. Then for all test distributions D on $X \times [0, \infty)^k$, for all labels $y \in \{1, \ldots, k\}$:*

$$E_{(x,c) \sim D} \left(\text{SECOC-Predict}(b, x, y) E_{c' \sim D|x} [|c'|] - E_{c' \sim D|x} [c'_y] \right)^2$$

$$\leq 8(t_{\max} - t_{\min})^2 r(\text{SECOC-Train}(D), b),$$

where $t_{\max} = \max_{(x,c):D(x,c)>0} \max_s(c_s/|c|)$ *and* $t_{\min} = \min_{(x,c):D(x,c)>0} \min_s(c_s/|c|)$.

This theorem relates the average regret of the created binary importance weighted classifier to the relative estimation error.

For the proof, note that the dependence on B and S can be removed by proving the theorem for all b, which is of equivalent generality.

Proof. We first analyze what happens when no regret is suffered, and then analyze the case with regret. For any s and t, let $D(s, t)$ be the distribution on $X \times \{0, 1\} \times [0, \infty)$ induced by drawing (x, c) from D and outputting $(x, I(c_s \geq t|c|), |c_s - t|c||)$.

For any choice of s and t, the optimal classifier is given by

$$b_{st}^* = \arg\min_b E_{(x,y,i) \sim D(s,t)} [iI(b(x) \neq y)]$$

$$= \arg\min_b E_{(x,c) \sim D} [|c_s - |c|t| \cdot I(b(x) \neq I(c_s \geq t|c|))].$$

For any x, the optimal value of $b(x)$ is either 0 or 1. When it is 0, the expected cost is

$$E_{c \sim D|x} \max \{(c_s - t|c|), 0\}. \tag{1}$$

Otherwise, it is

$$E_{c \sim D|x} \max \{(t|c| - c_s), 0\}. \tag{2}$$

To simplify notation, let $Z_x = E_{c \sim D|x}|c|$. Equations 1 and 2 are continuous in t; the first decreases while the second increases monotonically with t, so we need only find the single equality point to describe the optimal behavior for all t. This equality point is given by

$$E_{c \sim D|x} \max \{(c_s - t|c|), 0\} = E_{c \sim D|x} \max \{(t|c| - c_s), 0\},$$

or

$$E_{c \sim D|x}(c_s - t|c|) = 0,$$

yielding

$$t = \frac{E_{c \sim D|x}[c_s]}{Z_x},$$

and thus $b_{st}^*(x) = I(E_{c \sim D|x}[c_s] \geq tZ_x)$.

For any choice of s, we have

$$E_t[b_{st}^*(x)] = E_t I\left(E_{c \sim D|x}[c_s] \geq tZ_x\right) = \frac{\frac{E_{c \sim D|x}[c_s]}{Z_x} - t_{\min}}{t_{\max} - t_{\min}}$$

since $E_{t \in [t_{\min}, t_{\max}]} I(K \geq t) = \frac{K - t_{\min}}{t_{\max} - t_{\min}}$ for all $K \in [t_{\min}, t_{\max}]$.

Since decoding is symmetric with respect to all labels, we need analyze only one label y. Furthermore, since SECOC-Predict (Algorithm 2) is symmetric with respect to set inclusion or complement set inclusion, we can assume that y is in every subset (i.e., complementing all subsets not containing y does not change the decoding properties of the code.) Consequently,

$$\hat{c}_y = E_s E_t[b_{st}^*(x)](t_{\max} - t_{\min}) + t_{\min} = E_s \frac{E_{c \sim D|x}[c_s]}{Z_x}$$

$$= \frac{\frac{1}{2} E_{c \sim D|x}(c_y + |c|)}{Z_x} = \frac{1}{2}\left(\frac{E_{c \sim D|x}[c_y]}{Z_x} + 1\right),$$

where the third equality follows from the fact that every label other than y appears in s half the time in expectation over s. Consequently, SECOC-Predict outputs $\frac{1}{Z_x} E_{c \sim D|x}[c_y]$ for each y, when the classifiers are optimal.

Now we analyze the regret transformation properties. The remainder of this proof characterizes the most efficient way that any adversary can induce estimation regret with a fixed budget of importance weighted regret.

Examining equations 1 and 2, notice that the importance weighted loss grows linearly with the distance of tZ_x from $E_{c \sim D|x}[c_s]$, but on the other hand, each error has equal value in disturbing the expectation in SECOC-Predict (Algorithm 2). There are two consequences for an adversary attempting to disturb the expectation the most while paying the least importance weighted cost.

1) It is "cheapest" for an adversary to err on the t closest to $\frac{1}{Z_x} E_{c \sim D|x}[c_s]$ first. (Any adversary can reduce the importance weighted regret by swapping errors at larger values of $|t - \frac{1}{Z_x} E_{c \sim D|x}[c_s]|$ for errors at smaller values without altering the estimation regret.)

2) It is "cheapest" to have a small equal disturbance for each s rather than a large disturbance for a single s. (The cost any adversary pays for disturbing the overall expectation can be monotonically decreased by spreading errors uniformly over subsets s.)

Consequently, the optimal strategy for an adversary wanting to disturb the output of SECOC-Predict by Δ is to disturb the expectation for each s by $\frac{\Delta}{2(t_{\max} - t_{\min})}$. The importance weighted regret of erring (with a "1") for

$t = \frac{\Delta}{2(t_{\max}-t_{\min})} + \frac{1}{Z_x}E_{c\sim D|x}[c_s]$ can be found by subtracting equation 2 from equation 1:

$$E_{c\sim D|x}(t|\mathbf{c}| - c_s)I(c_s < t|\mathbf{c}|) - E_{c\sim D|x}(c_s - t|\mathbf{c}|)I(c_s \geq t|\mathbf{c}|)$$

$$= E_{c\sim D|x}\left(\left(\frac{\Delta}{2(t_{\max} - t_{\min})} + \frac{E_{c\sim D|x}[c_s]}{Z_x}\right)|\mathbf{c}| - c_s\right)$$

$$= \frac{\Delta}{2(t_{\max} - t_{\min})}Z_x.$$

The same quantity holds for $t = -\frac{\Delta}{2(t_{\max}-t_{\min})} + \frac{E_{c\sim D|x}[c_s]}{Z_x}$. By observation (1) above, in order for the adversary to induce an estimation error of Δ an error must occur for every $t \in \left[\frac{E_{c\sim D|x}[c_s]}{Z_x}, \frac{E_{c\sim D|x}[c_s]}{Z_x} + \frac{\Delta}{2(t_{\max}-t_{\min})}\right]$. If we consider a limit as the discretization of t goes to 0, the average regret is given by an integral of the differential regret according to:

$$\int_{u=0}^{u=\frac{\Delta Z_x}{2(t_{\max}-t_{\min})}} u\,du = \frac{\Delta^2 Z_x^2}{8(t_{\max} - t_{\min})^2}.$$

Solving for $\Delta^2 Z_x^2$ and taking an expectation over all x gives the theorem.   □

4   Applications and Corollaries

In this section we discuss various uses of SECOC to solve problems other than relative cost estimation and corollaries of the main theorem.

4.1   Reduction All the Way to Classification

The basic SECOC reduction above reduces to importance weighted binary classification. However, there are easy reductions from importance weighted binary classification to binary classification. For example, the Costing reduction [16] uses rejection sampling to alter the measure. When SECOC is composed with this reduction we get the following corollary:

Corollary 1. (SECOC Binary Regret Transform) *For any importance weighted binary learning algorithm B and cost-sensitive dataset S in $(X \times [0,\infty)^k)^*$, let $b = B(\text{Costing}(\text{SECOC-Train}(S)))$. Then for all test distributions D on $X \times [0,\infty)^k$ and all labels $y \in \{1, \ldots, k\}$:*

$$E_{(x,c)\sim D}\left(\text{SECOC-Predict}(b, x, y)E_{c'\sim D|x}[|\mathbf{c}'|] - E_{c'\sim D|x}[c'_y]\right)^2$$

$$\leq 4(t_{\max} - t_{\min})r(\text{Costing}(\text{SECOC-Train}(D)), b)E_{(x,c)\sim D}[|\mathbf{c}|]$$

Algorithm 3. SECOC-Hard-Predict (classifiers $\{b_{st}\}$, example $x \in X$)

return $\arg\min_y$ SECOC-Predict($\{b_{st}\}, x, y$)

Proof. The basic result from importance weighted analysis is that for every importance weighted test measure D, we have

$$r(D, b) = r(\text{Costing}(D), b) E_{(x,y,i) \sim D}\,[i]\,,$$

where the regret on the left is the importance weighted regret of b with respect to D, and the regret on the right is the regret with respect to the induced binary distribution.

Consequently, we need only compute an upper bound on the average importance over t and s. The average importance for fixed x and s is given by

$$\frac{1}{t_{\max} - t_{\min}} \int_{t_{\min}}^{t_{\max}} E_{\mathbf{c} \sim D|x} |t|\mathbf{c}| - c_s|\, dt.$$

This quantity is maximized (over all x and s) when $E_{\mathbf{c} \sim D|x}[c_s] = 0$. In this case the integral is $\frac{(t_{\max}-t_{\min})^2}{2(t_{\max}-t_{\min})} E_{\mathbf{c} \sim D|x}|\mathbf{c}| = \frac{(t_{\max}-t_{\min})}{2} E_{\mathbf{c} \sim D|x}|\mathbf{c}|$. Taking the expectation over x and s, we get the corollary. □

4.2   Cost Sensitive Classification

If we use the decoding function SECOC-Hard-Predict in Algorithm 3, we can choose a class in a regret transforming manner.

Corollary 2. (Hard Prediction Regret Transform) *For any importance weighted binary learning algorithm B and multiclass dataset S in $(X \times \{1,...,k\})^*$, let $b = B(\text{SECOC-Train}(S))$. Then for all test distributions D over $X \times \{1,..,k\}$:*

$$r\left(D, \text{SECOC-Hard-Predict}(b, x)\right) \le 4(t_{\max} - t_{\min}) \sqrt{2r(\text{SECOC-Train}(D), b)}$$

Proof. We can weaken Theorem 1 so that for all y:

$$E_{(x,y) \sim D} \left|\text{SECOC-Predict}(b, x, y) E_{\mathbf{c}' \sim D|x}\left[|\mathbf{c}'|\right] - E_{\mathbf{c}' \sim D|x}\left[c_y'\right]\right|$$

$$\le 2(t_{\max} - t_{\min}) \sqrt{2r(\text{SECOC-Train}(D), b)}$$

since for all X, $\sqrt{E(X)} \ge E\sqrt{X}$. When doing a hard prediction according to these outputs, our regret at most doubles because the relative cost estimate of the correct class can be increased by the same amount that the relative cost estimate of the wrong class can be decreased. □

Algorithm 4. PECOC-Train (Set of k-class multiclass examples S, importance weighted binary classifier learning algorithm B)

1. Let $S' = \{(x, \forall i \ c_i = I(i \neq y)) : (x, y) \in S\}$.
2. return SECOC-Train $\left(S', B, \left[\frac{\lfloor \frac{k}{2} \rfloor - 1}{k-1}, \frac{\lfloor \frac{k}{2} \rfloor}{k-1} \right] \right)$

Algorithm 5. PECOC-Predict (classifiers $\{b_{st}\}$, example $x \in X$, label y)

return $1 - $ SECOC-Predict($\{b_{st}\}, x, y$)$(k - 1)$

4.3   Multiclass Probability Estimation

SECOC can be used to predict the probability of class labels with the training algorithm PECOC-Train (Algorithm 4) for any k a power[3] of 2. Similarly, the prediction algorithm PECOC-Predict (Algorithm 5) is a slight modification of SECOC-Predict (Algorithm 2).

Corollary 3. (Multiclass Probability Regret Transform) *For any importance weighted binary learning algorithm B and a multiclass dataset S in $(X \times \{1, ..., k\})^*$ with k a power of 2, let $b = B(\text{PECOC-Train}(S))$. Then for all test distributions D over $X \times \{1, ..., k\}$ and all labels $y \in \{1, ..., k\}$,*

$$E_{(x,y) \sim D} \left(\text{PECOC-Predict}(b, x, y) - D(y|x) \right)^2 \leq \frac{8}{(k-1)^2} r(\text{PECOC-Train}(D), b).$$

This corollary implies that probability estimates (up to l_2 loss) are accurate whenever the classifier has small regret. When we reduce all the way to classification as in Corollary 1, the factor of $1/(k-1)^2$ disappears so the l_2 regret in class probability estimation is independent of the number of classes.

Proof. The proof just uses Theorem 1. In this case $|c| = k - 1$, $E_{c' \sim D|x} \left[c'_y \right] = 1 - D(y|x)$, and $t_{\max} - t_{\min} = \frac{1}{k-1}$.

$$E_{(x,y) \sim D} \left(\text{SECOC-Predict}(b, x, y)(k - 1) - (1 - D(y|x)) \right)^2$$

$$\leq \frac{8}{(k-1)^2} r(\text{PECOC-Train}(D), b).$$

Applying algebra finishes the corollary.   □

4.4   Multiclass Classification

When a hard prediction is made with PECOC-Hard-Predict (Algorithm 6), we achieve a simple algorithm that translates *any* consistent binary classifier into a consistent multiclass classifier.

---

[3] This limitation is not essential. See Section 6.

Algorithm 6. PECOC-Hard-Predict (classifiers $\{b_{st}\}$, example $x \in X$)

---

return $\arg\max_{y \in \{1,...,k\}}$ PECOC-Predict($\{b_{st}\}, x, y$)

Corollary 4. (Multiclass Classification Regret Transform) *For any importance weighted binary learning algorithm B and multiclass dataset S in $(X \times \{1, ..., k\})^*$ with k a power of 2, let $b = B$(PECOC-Train(S)). For all test distributions D over $X \times \{1, ..., k\}$:*

$$r\left(D, \text{PECOC-Hard-Predict}(b, x)\right) \leq \frac{4}{k-1}\sqrt{2r(\text{PECOC-Train}(D), b)}.$$

Note again that if we reduce to binary classification, the factor of $k-1$ is removed and the result is independent of the number of classes.

This guarantee can not be satisfied by ECOC (as we show in Section 5). A guarantee of this sort may be provable with other variants of ECOC (such as [1]), but this seems to be the tightest known regret transform. Since consistent generalization of binary classifiers to multiclass classifiers has historically been problematic (see [8] for a fix for SVMs), this result may be of interest.

Proof. The regret of a multiclass prediction is proportional to the difference in probability of the best prediction and the prediction made. Weakening corollary 3 gives, for all y,

$$E_{(x,y) \sim D} |\text{PECOC-Predict}(b, x, y) - D(y|x)| \leq \frac{2}{k-1}\sqrt{2r(\text{PECOC-Train}(D), b)}$$

since for all X, $\sqrt{E(X)} \geq E\sqrt{X}$. When doing a hard prediction according to these outputs, our regret at most doubles because the probability estimate of the correct class can be reduced by the same amount that the probability estimate of the wrong class increases. □

4.5 Online Learning and Loss

Notice that all basic transformations are applied to individual examples, as in line 1(b) of SECOC-Train. Consequently, the transformation can be done online. The theorems apply to any measure on (x, c), so they also apply to the uniform measure over past examples; thus online regret minimizing binary predictors can be used with SECOC to minimize cost-sensitive regret online.

In particular, this means that SECOC can be used with online learning algorithms such as weighted majority [9] in order to optimize regret with respect to *any* loss function.

Note that the notion of regret in online learning is typically defined with respect to some set of "experts" rather than the set of all possible experts as here. This distinction is not essential, because the weighted majority algorithm can be applied to an arbitrary measure over the set of all experts.

5   ECOC Can Not Transform Regret

Is it possible to get similar guarantees with ECOC? The answer is no. It is easy to show that even when ECOC is supplied with an optimal binary classifier, the reduction fails to provide an optimal multiclass classifier.

Theorem 2. (ECOC Inconsistency) *For all $k > 2$, there exists a distributions D over multiclass test examples (x, y) such that for all codes M, with $c^* = \arg\min_c r(\text{ECOC-Train}(D), c)$,*

$$r(D, \text{ECOC-Predict}(c^*)) > \frac{1}{8}$$

where ECOC-Train *and* ECOC-Predict *are as defined in the introduction.*

Proof. The proof is constructive. We choose a D which places probability on three labels: '1', '2', and '3'.

A few observations about symmetry simplify the proof. First, since only three labels have positive probability, we can rewrite any code M as a new *weighted* code M' over the three labels where each subset has a weight w_s corresponding to the number of times the subset of the three labels exists in M after projection. The second observation is that the symmetry with respect to complementarity implies that each row (and each codeword) has one '1' in it.

These observations imply that ECOC essentially uses the binary classifier to ask, "Is the probability of label $i > 0.5$?" for each $i \in \{1, 2, 3\}$. These answers are then combined with a weighted sum. If we let the probability of one label be $0.5 - \epsilon$ and the probability of the other two labels be $0.25 + \frac{\epsilon}{2}$ each, the answer to every question will be "no".

Since we have a weighted sum, the exact weighting determines the outcome (possibly with randomization to break ties). The exact distribution therefore picks a label at random to have probability $0.5 - \epsilon$, encodes that choice in the x value, and then draws the label from this associated distribution.

Under any code, the probability of predicting the label with greatest probability is at most $\frac{1}{3}$ implying a regret of $\frac{2}{3}(0.5 - \epsilon - (0.25 + \frac{\epsilon}{2}))$, which can be made arbitrarily close to $\frac{1}{6}$.   □

A margin-based version of ECOC [1] has the same lower bound whenever the coding matrices are limited to "-1" and "1" entries. This is because consistent binary classifiers might have margin 1 or -1 for each example, and the proof above holds.

However, this version of ECOC also allows "don't cares" in the coding matrix. The existence of "don't cares" allows questions of the form, "Is the probability of this label greater than that label?" In general, these are sufficiently powerful to support regret transformation consistency, with the exact quantity of regret transformation efficiency dependent on the coding matrix. We are not aware of any margin based code with "don't cares" with a better regret transform than SECOC with the Hadamard Code.

Take as an example the all-pairs code, which is consistent with margin-based ECOC. The all-pairs code creates a classifier for every pair of classes deciding (for an optimal classifier) "Is class i more probable than class j?" The problem with this question is that the classifier is applied when class i and class j each have zero probability. In this situation, an adversarial classifier can choose to report either $p_i > p_j$ or $p_j > p_i$ without paying any regret. Consequently, an adversarial binary classifier could make some label with 0 conditional probability beat all labels except for the correct label for free. This is not robust, because one error in one classifier (out of $k - 1$ active classifiers) can alter the result. Consequently, the regret transform for this code scales with k.

6   Discussion

Variants. There are several variants of the basic SECOC algorithm.

Random Code. One simple variant code is "pick a random subset s and pick a random t". This code has essentially the same analysis as the Hadamard code presented here in expectation over the random choices.

Optimal codes. For small values of k (the number of classes), it is possible to derive a better regret transform with other codes. For example, when $k = 2$ there is only one useful subset (up to symmetry in complementation), so the prediction algorithm can simply output the cost estimate for that one subset rather than 2 times the average predicted cost, minus 1. This removes a factor of 2 loosening in the last paragraph of the proof of the main theorem. When used for class probability prediction the above observation improves on the regret transform analysis of the probing algorithm [7] by a factor of $\sqrt{2}$. The reason for this improvement is (essentially) the use of a unified measure over the classification problem rather than many different measures for different problems.

Varying interval. The range of t can be made dependent on s. This is useful when embedding multiclass classification into cost-sensitive classification for k not a power of 2. Roughly speaking, allowing the range of t to vary with s eliminates the use of classifiers for which the correct prediction is "always 0" or "always 1". Eliminating these classifiers improves the regret transform by reducing the size of the set over which regret is averaged.

Clipping. Our prediction algorithms can output relative costs or probability estimates above "1" or below "0". In such cases, clipping the prediction to the interval $[0, 1]$ always reduces regret.

Why Regret Isn't Everything. Other work [2] defines a reduction with the property that small *error* on the subproblem implies small *error* on the original problem. The definition of regret we use here is superior because the theorems can apply nontrivially even on problems with large inherent noise. However, the mathematical form of the regret transforms is weaker, typically by ϵ loss changing to $\sqrt{\epsilon}$regret. Tightening the regret transform by removal of the square root seems to require a different construction.

Difficulty of Created Learning Problems. A natural concern when using any reduction is that it may create hard problems for the oracle. And in fact, learning to distinguish a random subset may be significantly harder than learning to distinguish (say) one label from all other labels, as in the One-Against-All (OAA) reduction, as observed in [1,5]. The best choice of code is a subtle affair. The method here is general and can be used with sparser coding matrices as well. Nevertheless, there is some empirical evidence in support of SECOC with Hadamard codes (presented in the next section).

7   Experimental Results

We compared the performance of SECOC, ECOC and One-Against-All (OAA) on several multiclass datasets from the UCI Machine Learning Repository [11] (ecoli, glass, pendigits, satimage, soybean, splice, vowel, and yeast). Hadamard matrices were used for both SECOC and ECOC. As oracles, we used a decision tree learner (J48), a (linear) support vector machine learner (SMO) and logistic regression (denoted LR), all available from Weka [15]. Default parameters were used for all three learners in all experiments. For datasets that do not have a standard train/test split, we used a random split with 2/3 for training and 1/3 for testing. The figures below show test error rates of SECOC plotted against those of ECOC and OAA (the axes are labeled).

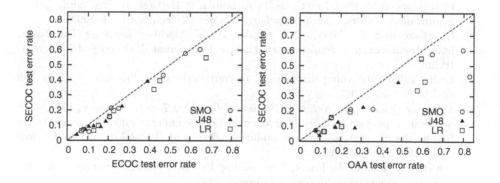

For SECOC, we used six thresholds for each row of the matrix. SECOC resulted in superior (or equal) performance on every dataset tested, for every learner used. We do not report any statistical significance tests because the assumptions they are based on are not satisfied by the datasets. Instead we report *all* experiments performed; we believe that the observed consistency across different datasets and learners gives sufficient empirical evidence in support of SECOC. The code is available from the authors.

References

1. Erin Allwein, Robert Schapire, and Yoram Singer. Reducing multiclass to binary: A unifying approach for margin classifiers. *Journal of Machine Learning Research*, 1:113–141, 2000.
2. Alina Beygelzimer, Varsha Dani, Tom Hayes, and John Langford. Reductions between classification tasks. *Electronic Colloquium on Computational Complexity*, TR04-077, 2004.
3. Thomas Dietterich and Ghulum Bakiri. Solving multiclass learning problems via error-correcting output codes. *Journal of Artificial Intelligence Research*, 2:263–286, 1995.
4. Yoav Freund and Robert Schapire. A decision-theoretic generalization of online learning and an application to boosting. *Journal of Computer and System Sciences*, 55(1), 119–139, 1997.
5. Venkat Guruswami and Amit Sahai. Multiclass learning, boosting, and error-correcting codes. In *Proceedings of the 12th Annual Conference on Computational Learning Theory (COLT)*, 145–155,1999.
6. Adam Kalai and Rocco Servedio. Boosting in the Presence of Noise. In Proceedings of the 35th Annual ACM Symposium on the Theory of Computing (STOC), 195–205, 2003.
7. John Langford and Bianca Zadrozny. Estimating class membership probabilities using classifier learners. In *Proceedings of the 10th International Workshop on Artificial Intelligence and Statistics*, 2005.
8. Yoonkyung Lee, Yi Lin, and Grace Wahba. Multicategory Support Vector Machines: Theory and Application to the Classification of Microarray Data and Satelite Radiance Data, Journal of the American Statistical Association, 99, 465 (2004) 67-81.
9. Nick Littlestone and Manfred Warmuth, The Weighted Majority Algorithm, Foundations of Computer Science, 1992.
10. John Platt. Probabilistic outputs for support vector machines and comparisons to regularized likelihood methods. In A. Smola, P. Bartlett, B. Schölkopf, and D. Schuurmans, editors, *Advances in Large Margin Classifiers*, 61–74, 1999.
11. C. Blake and C. Merz, UCI Repository of Machine Learning Databases, http://www.ics.uci.edu/~mlearn/MLRepository.html, University of California, Irvine.
12. Leslie Valiant. Learning disjunctions of conjunctions, In *Proceedings of the 9th IJCAI*, 560–566, 1985.
13. Vladimir Vapnik. *The Nature of Statistical Learning Theory*. Springer, 1995.
14. Vladimir Vapnik and Alexey Chervonenkis. On the uniform convergence of relative frequencies of event to their probabilities. *Theory of Probability and its Applications*, 16(2), 264–280, 1971.
15. Ian H. Witten and Eibe Frank, Data Mining: Practical machine learning tools with Java implementations, Morgan Kaufmann, 2000, http://www.cs.waikato.ac.nz/ml/weka/.
16. Bianca Zadrozny, John Langford, and Naoki Abe. Cost-Sensitive Learning by Cost-Proportionate Example Weighting. In *Proceedings of the 3rd IEEE International Conference on Data Mining* (ICDM) 435–442, 2003.

Data Dependent Concentration Bounds
for Sequential Prediction Algorithms

Tong Zhang

IBM T.J. Watson Research Center,
Yorktown Heights, NY, 10598, USA
tzhang@watson.ibm.com

Abstract. We investigate the generalization behavior of sequential prediction (online) algorithms, when data are generated from a probability
distribution. Using some newly developed probability inequalities, we are
able to bound the total generalization performance of a learning algorithm in terms of its observed total loss. Consequences of this analysis
will be illustrated with examples.

1 Introduction

In statistical learning, we are interested in predicting output $Y \in \mathcal{Y}$ based on ob-
servation $X \in \mathcal{X}$. Given a set of n training examples $Z_1^n = \{Z_1 = (X_1, Y_1), \dots, Z_n = (X_n, Y_n)\}$, a learning algorithm $\mathcal{A}$ produces a function $\mathcal{A}(Z_1^n; \cdot)$ on $\mathcal{X}$. With a
future example $Z_{n+1} = (X_{n+1}, Y_{n+1})$, it produces an output $\mathcal{A}(Z_1^n; X_{n+1})$, and
suffers a loss $L(\mathcal{A}(Z_1^n; X_{n+1}), Y_{n+1})$. Assume that the data are generated from
an unknown underlying probability distribution D, then the instantaneous risk
of the function produced by the algorithm is defined as the expected loss:

$$\mathbf{E}_{Z_{n+1} \sim D} \, L(\mathcal{A}(Z_1^n; X_{n+1}), Y_{n+1}).$$

In statistical learning, we assume that the training data $Z_1, \dots, Z_n$ are drawn
from the same underlying distribution D as the test data. In this paper, we are
interested in the concentration of the total instantaneous generalization risk

$$\sum_{i=1}^{n} \mathbf{E}_{Z_i} L(\mathcal{A}(Z_1^{i-1}; X_i), Y_i) \tag{1}$$

to the total empirical loss of the algorithm on the training data

$$\sum_{i=1}^{n} L(\mathcal{A}(Z_1^{i-1}; X_i), Y_i). \tag{2}$$

The former is the generalization behavior of the algorithm on the test data, and
the latter is the online performance of the algorithm on the training data. The
problem of estimating (1) in terms of (2) has been investigated in [3, 4, 10]. There

P. Auer and R. Meir (Eds.): COLT 2005, LNAI 3559, pp. 173–187, 2005.
© Springer-Verlag Berlin Heidelberg 2005

are two motivations for studying this problem. One is that this gives a probability inequality for the performance of online algorithm on future test data based on the observable "mistake" it makes on the training data. Such a concentration bound can also be used to convert many known online learning mistake bound results into PAC style probability bounds. The second motivation is somewhat different. As pointed out in [3], if we use the total empirical risk of an algorithm as a criterion to select the best learning algorithm (that is, we want to choose the algorithm with the smallest total risk), then the concentration behavior is similar to using n independent random samples. It can thus be argued that the total empirical risk of an algorithm makes better use of the data (than say, cross-validation), and thus is theoretically an attractively quantity for the purpose of model selection. We shall discuss both aspects in the paper.

The purpose of this paper is to develop data-dependent estimates of the total generalization performance (1) based on the observed total loss (2). In order to do so, we need to prove some new probability inequalities for dependent random variables that are suitable for this purpose.

2   Conditional Probability Inequalities for Sums of Dependent Random Variables

We consider a sequence of possibly dependent random variables $Z_1, Z_2, \ldots, Z_n$. For each k, Z_k may depend on the preceding random variables $Z_1, \ldots, Z_{k-1}$. Consider also a sequence of functionals $\xi_k(Z_1, \ldots, Z_k)$ ($k = 1, \ldots, n$). For example, in online mistake bound analysis, we may let $\xi_k = 1$ if a mistake is made on the k-th example, and $\xi_k = 0$ otherwise. Denote by $\mathbf{E}_{Z_k} \xi_k(Z_1, \ldots, Z_k)$ the conditional expectation of ξ_k with respect to Z_k, conditioned on $Z_1^{k-1} = \{Z_1, \ldots, Z_{k-1}\}$. Given an observed sequence $Z_1, \ldots, Z_n$, we are interested in the following two quantities:

$$s_n = \frac{1}{n} \sum_{i=1}^{n} \xi_i(Z_1, \ldots, Z_i), \quad \mu_n = \frac{1}{n} \sum_{i=1}^{n} \mathbf{E}_{Z_i} \xi_i(Z_1, \ldots, Z_i). \tag{3}$$

The first quantity is the empirical average of ξ_k, and the second quantity is the average (over k) of conditional expectation of ξ_k with respect to Z_k. We are interested in showing that s_n and μ_n are close with large probability. Note that if we let $Z_k = (X_k, Y_k)$ and $\xi_k = L(\mathcal{A}(Z_1^{k-1}; X_k), Y_k)$, then these two quantities can be interpreted as the total empirical and generalization risks of the learning algorithm $\mathcal{A}$ in equations (2) and (1).

The starting point of our analysis is the following simple equality.

Lemma 1. *Consider a sequence of random functionals* $\xi_1(Z_1), \ldots, \xi_n(Z_1, \ldots, Z_n)$. *We have*

$$\mathbf{E}_{Z_1, \ldots, Z_n} \exp \left(\sum_{i=1}^{n} \xi_i - \sum_{i=1}^{n} \ln \mathbf{E}_{Z_i} e^{\xi_i} \right) = 1.$$

Proof. We prove the lemma by induction on n. When $n = 1$, the equality is easy to verify. Assume that the claim holds for all $n \leq k$. Now for $n = k + 1$, we have

$$\mathbf{E}_{Z_1,\ldots,Z_n} \exp\left(\sum_{i=1}^{n} \xi_i - \sum_{i=1}^{n} \ln \mathbf{E}_{Z_i} e^{\xi_i}\right)$$

$$= \mathbf{E}_{Z_1,\ldots,Z_{n-1}} \left[\exp\left(\sum_{i=1}^{n-1} \xi_i - \sum_{i=1}^{n-1} \ln \mathbf{E}_{Z_i} e^{\xi_i}\right) \mathbf{E}_{Z_n} \exp(\xi_n - \ln \mathbf{E}_{Z_n} e^{\xi_n})\right]$$

$$= \mathbf{E}_{Z_1,\ldots,Z_{n-1}} \exp\left(\sum_{i=1}^{n-1} \xi_i - \sum_{i=1}^{n-1} \ln \mathbf{E}_{Z_i} e^{\xi_i}\right) = 1.$$

Note that the last equation follows from the induction hypothesis.

The following result is a direct consequence of Lemma 1, which we will use to develop more concrete concentration bounds later in the paper. In the literature, related inequalities have been used to derive conditional probability inequalities for Martingales. The technique used here simplifies and improves such results. Some tight probability bounds suitable for our purpose can be obtained as consequences of the following lemma.

Lemma 2. *Consider a sequence of random functionals $\xi_1(Z_1), \ldots, \xi_n(Z_1, \ldots, Z_n)$. Then $\forall t \geq 0$ and ρ,*

$$\Pr\left[-\sum_{i=1}^{n} \ln \mathbf{E}_{Z_i} e^{-\rho \xi_i} \geq \rho \sum_{i=1}^{n} \xi_i + t\right] \leq e^{-t}.$$

Proof. Let $\xi(\rho) = -\sum_{i=1}^{n} \ln \mathbf{E}_{Z_i} e^{-\rho \xi_i} - \rho \sum_{i=1}^{n} \xi_i$, then we have from Lemma 1: $\mathbf{E} e^{\xi(\rho)} = 1$. Now $\forall t$, we have

$$\Pr(\xi(\rho) \geq t) e^t \leq \mathbf{E} e^{\xi(\rho)} = 1.$$

Therefore $\Pr(\xi(\rho) \geq t) \leq \exp(-t)$.

Remark 1. Both in Lemma 1 and Lemma 2, the fixed size n can be replaced by a random stopping time that depends on $Z_1, \ldots, Z_n$. We can simply define $\xi_m = 0$ for $m > n$ when the sequence stops at n after seeing $Z_1, \ldots, Z_n$.

Remark 2. Given a random variable Z, the function $\ln \mathbf{E}_Z e^{-\rho Z}$ of ρ is often referred to as its logarithmic moment generating function. It is used in the large deviation literature to obtain tight asymptotic tail probability estimates. The left side of Lemma 2 is the sum of (conditional) logarithmic moment generating functions of ξ_k with respect to Z_k. The bound obtain is essentially identical to the large deviation bounds for independent variables. Therefore, we are able to translate well-known inequalities in the independent setting to the dependent setting with appropriate estimations of logarithmic moment generating functions. This is the approach we will take later on.

Based on Lemma 2, we are now ready to derive results that are direct generalizations of the corresponding cases for independent variables, using appropriate estimates of the logarithmic moment generating functions. These generalizations are the main results of this section.

2.1   Conditional Hoeffding Inequalities

For a bounded random variable $\xi \in [0, 1]$, it is well-known that its logarithmic moment generating function can be estimated as (see [9]):

$$\ln \mathbf{E} e^{-\rho \xi} \leq \ln \left[1 + (e^{-\rho} - 1) \mathbf{E} \xi \right]. \tag{4}$$

In fact, this is a simple consequence of Jensen's inequality. Using this estimate, we can obtain

Lemma 3. *Assume that $\xi_k \in [0, 1]$ for all $k = 1, \ldots, n$. Then $\forall t \geq 0$ and ρ,*

$$\Pr \left[- \ln \left[1 + \mu_n(e^{-\rho} - 1)\right] \geq \rho s_n + t \right] \leq e^{-nt},$$

where μ_n and s_n are defined in (3).

Proof. Using the concavity of logarithm, we have

$$\sum_{i=1}^{n} \ln \mathbf{E}_{Z_i} e^{-\rho \xi_i} \leq n \ln \left[\frac{1}{n} \sum_{i=1}^{n} \mathbf{E}_{Z_i} e^{-\rho \xi_i} \right].$$

Now using (4) on the right hand side of the above inequality, we obtain the result as a direct consequence of Lemma 2.

Theorem 1. *Under the conditions of Lemma 3. We have*

$$\Pr \left[\mu_n \geq \frac{\rho s_n + t}{1 - e^{-\rho}} \right] \leq e^{-nt}, \quad \Pr \left[\mu_n \geq s_n + \sqrt{t/2} \right] \leq e^{-nt}.$$

Proof. Using the fact $- \ln(1 - x) \geq x$, we obtain from Lemma 3 that with probability at most e^{-nt},

$$\mu_n(1 - e^{-\rho}) \geq \rho s_n + t.$$

This implies the first inequality.

For the second inequality, we substitute the following bound (which can be verified using Taylor expansion around $\rho = 0$; for example, see [9])

$$- \ln \left[1 + x(e^{-\rho} - 1)\right] \geq \rho x - \frac{\rho^2}{8}$$

into Lemma 3: with probability at most e^{-nt},

$$\mu_n - s_n \geq \frac{t + \rho^2/8}{\rho}.$$

Now take $\rho = \sqrt{t/8}$, we obtain the second inequality.

The second inequality is well-known [1]. We simply reproduce it here. The first inequality is superior (with any fixed ρ) when s_n is small. However, it is not tight when s_n is large. The best possible inequality can be obtained by picking the optimal ρ in Lemma 3. This is what we shall explore next.

Before introducing the next theorem, we shall introduce the following definitions: $\forall \alpha, \beta \in [0,1]$ and $t \geq 0$:

$$\mathrm{KL}(\alpha||\beta) = \alpha \ln(\alpha/\beta) + (1-\alpha)\ln((1-\alpha)/(1-\beta)),$$
$$\mathrm{KL}_2^{-1}(\alpha||t) = \sup\{\beta : \mathrm{KL}(\alpha||\beta) \leq t\}.$$

Theorem 2. *Under the conditions of Lemma 3. We have $\forall \alpha \in [0,1]$ and $t \geq 0$:*

$$\Pr\left[\mu_n \geq \mathrm{KL}_2^{-1}(\alpha||t), s_n \leq \alpha\right] \leq e^{-nt}.$$

Proof. We know from Lemma 3 that $\forall \rho \geq 0$ and $\beta \in [\alpha, 1]$, the following two inequalities hold with probability of at most e^{-nt}:

$$\mu_n \geq \beta, \quad s_n \leq \alpha, \quad -\rho\alpha - \ln\left[1 + \beta(e^{-\rho} - 1)\right] \geq t.$$

Since the claim holds for all $\rho \geq 0$, we may take the parameter ρ that maximizes the left hand side of the third inequality. That is, we take $\rho = \ln(\beta(1-\alpha)) - \ln(\alpha(1-\beta))$, and the third inequality becomes $\mathrm{KL}(\alpha||\beta) \geq t$. Now, let $\beta = \mathrm{KL}_2^{-1}(\alpha||t)$, the third inequality is trivially satisfied. We thus obtain the statement of the theorem.

The function $\mathrm{KL}_2^{-1}(\alpha||t)$ may not be intuitive at first sight. The following result gives a more intuitive form, which can be used to replace $\mathrm{KL}_2^{-1}(\alpha||t)$ in Theorem 2 as well as other theorems in the sequel.

Proposition 1. *The following bound holds for all $\alpha \in [0,1]$ and $t \geq 0$:*

$$\mathrm{KL}_2^{-1}(\alpha||t) \leq \alpha + \sqrt{2\alpha(1-\alpha)t} + 1.5(1-\alpha)t.$$

Proof. Let $\Delta\alpha = \sqrt{2\alpha(1-\alpha)t + 0.75^2(1-\alpha)^2t^2} + 0.75(1-\alpha)t$. In the following, we assume $\alpha + \Delta\alpha \leq 1$ since the bound holds trivially otherwise. Using Taylor expansion, we have

$$\mathrm{KL}(\alpha||\alpha + \Delta\alpha) = \alpha \ln\left(1 - \frac{\Delta\alpha}{\alpha + \Delta\alpha}\right) - (1-\alpha)\ln\left(1 - \frac{\Delta\alpha}{1-\alpha}\right)$$

$$\geq \alpha\left[-\frac{\Delta\alpha}{\alpha + \Delta\alpha} - \frac{\Delta\alpha^2}{2(\alpha + \Delta\alpha)^2}\frac{1 - \frac{\Delta\alpha}{3(\alpha + \Delta\alpha)}}{1 - \frac{\Delta\alpha}{(\alpha + \Delta\alpha)}}\right] - (1-\alpha)\left[-\frac{\Delta\alpha}{1-\alpha} - \frac{\Delta\alpha^2}{2(1-\alpha)^2}\right]$$

$$= \frac{\Delta\alpha^2}{2(\alpha + \Delta\alpha)} + \frac{\Delta\alpha^3}{6(\alpha + \Delta\alpha)^2} + \frac{\Delta\alpha^2}{2(1-\alpha)}$$

$$\geq \frac{\Delta\alpha^2}{2(\alpha + 0.75\Delta\alpha)} + \frac{\Delta\alpha^2}{2(1-\alpha)} \geq \frac{\Delta\alpha^2}{2(1-\alpha)(\alpha + 0.75\Delta\alpha)} = t.$$

This implies that $\mathrm{KL}_2^{-1}(\alpha||t) \leq \alpha + \Delta\alpha$.

The bound in the Theorem 2 is asymptotically best possible for large deviation probability with fixed t since it matches the large deviation lower bound for independent random variables (this claim is also true for moderate deviation when t decreases sufficiently slower than $O(1/n)$). However, in the above theorem, we require that α is chosen in advance. If we remove this condition, a slightly weaker data dependent inequality still holds. The extra penalty of the resulting deviation is no more than $O(\ln n/n) = o(1)$; consequently in the large deviation situation (with fixed t), the bound is also asymptotically the best possible. However, it might be possible to improve the extra $O(\ln n)/n$ penalty we pay for achieving data-dependency because our proof technique may be suboptimal.

The technique we use is rather standard in proving data-dependent generalization bounds in the statistical learning theory literature. The application here is new. We shall state a general result as a lemma (which will also be used later), and then use it to derive a more concrete theorem.

Lemma 4. *Under the conditions of Lemma 3. Consider a finite sequence* $0 \leq \alpha_1 \leq \cdots \leq \alpha_m = 1$, *and a sequence* $\{\Delta t_\ell\}$ *such that* $\sum_{\ell=1}^m e^{-\Delta t_\ell} \leq 1$. *Let* $\ell_*(x) : [0,1] \to \{1, \ldots, m\}$ *be any function such that* $\ell_*(x) \geq \inf\{\ell : \alpha_\ell \geq x\}$. *Then for all* $t \geq 0$, *we have*

$$\Pr\left[\mu_n \geq \mathrm{KL}_2^{-1}(\alpha_{\ell_*(s_n)} \| n^{-1}\Delta t_{\ell_*(s_n)} + t)\right] \leq e^{-nt}.$$

Proof. Let $t_\ell = t + \Delta t_\ell/n$. We obtain from Theorem 2 that for each ℓ:

$$\Pr\left[\mu_n \geq \mathrm{KL}_2^{-1}(\alpha_\ell \| t_\ell), s_n \leq \alpha_\ell\right] \leq e^{-\Delta t_\ell} e^{-nt}.$$

Take a union bound over $\ell = 1, \ldots,$, we have:

$$\Pr\left[\ell = \ell_*(s_n) : \mu_n \geq \mathrm{KL}_2^{-1}(\alpha_\ell \| t_\ell)\right]$$
$$\leq \Pr\left[\exists \ell \in \{1, \ldots, m\} : \mu_n \geq \mathrm{KL}_2^{-1}(\alpha_\ell \| t_\ell), s_n \leq \alpha_\ell\right]$$
$$\leq \sum_{\ell=1}^m e^{-\Delta t_\ell} e^{-nt} \leq e^{-nt}.$$

This proves the lemma.

Theorem 3. *Under the conditions of Lemma 3. For all* $t \geq 0$, *we have*

$$\Pr\left[\mu_n \geq \mathrm{KL}_2^{-1}(n^{-1}\lceil ns_n\rceil \| 2n^{-1}\ln(\lceil ns_n\rceil + 2) + t)\right] < e^{-nt}.$$

Proof. In Lemma 4, we take $\alpha_\ell = (\ell - 1)/n$ for $\ell = 1, \ldots, n+1$, $\Delta t_\ell = 2\ln(\ell+1)$, and $\ell_*(x) = \lceil nx\rceil + 1$.

2.2   Conditional Bennett Inequalities

In Bernstein and Bennett inequalities, the resulting bounds depend on the variance of the random variables (for example, see [2]).

These inequalities are useful for some statistical estimation problems including least squares regression and density estimation with log-loss. This is because for these problems, the variance of a random variable can be bounded by its mean: $\exists b > 0 : \mathbf{E}_{Z_k}(\xi_k - \mathbf{E}_{Z_k}\xi_k)^2 \leq b\mathbf{E}_{Z_k}\xi_k$. Probability inequalities that use variance become crucial to obtain good bounds.

Bernstein inequalities for dependent random variables have been investigated in the literature (for example, see [6, 7] and references therein). However, they were not in the form most suitable for our purpose. We shall thus derive some new bounds here that are directly applicable to statistical estimation problems. Our bounds depend on the following additional quantity:

$$\sigma_n^2 = \frac{1}{n}\sum_{i=1}^{n}\mathbf{E}_{Z_k}(\xi_k - \mathbf{E}_{Z_k}\xi_k)^2.$$

A standard estimate of moment generating function leads to the following result.

Lemma 5. *Assume that $\xi_k - \mathbf{E}_{Z_k}\xi_k \geq -1$ for each k. We have $\forall \rho > 0$:*

$$\Pr\left[\mu_n \geq \frac{e^\rho - \rho - 1}{\rho}\sigma_n^2 + s_n + \frac{t}{\rho}\right] \leq e^{-nt}.$$

Proof. Let $\tilde{\xi}_k = \xi_k - \mathbf{E}_{Z_k}\xi_k$. We start with the following estimate

$$\ln \mathbf{E}_{Z_k}e^{-\rho\tilde{\xi}_k} \leq \mathbf{E}_{Z_k}e^{-\rho\tilde{\xi}_k} - 1$$

$$= \mathbf{E}_{Z_k}\tilde{\xi}_k^2\frac{e^{-\rho\tilde{\xi}_k} + \rho\tilde{\xi}_k - 1}{\tilde{\xi}_k^2}$$

$$\leq \mathbf{E}_{Z_k}\tilde{\xi}_k^2\frac{e^\rho - \rho - 1}{1^2}.$$

The first inequality uses $\ln x \leq x - 1$. The last inequality uses the fact that $f(x) = x^{-2}(e^x - x - 1)$ is a non-decreasing function of x, and $-\rho\tilde{\xi}_k \leq \rho$. By using this estimate in Lemma 2, we obtain the desired bound.

The condition $\xi_k - \mathbf{E}_{Z_k}\xi_k \geq -1$ was considered by Bennett. It can be changed to appropriate moment conditions (in Bernstein inequalities). The proof of Lemma 5 follows a standard argument for proving Bennett bounds. This same method was also used in [7] to obtain a related bound (also see [6]). However, for statistical estimation problems, results in [7] are not directly applicable. This is because the most common application of this theorem is under the assumption that there exists a constant $b > 0$ such that $b\mathbf{E}_{Z_k}\xi_k \geq \mathbf{E}_{Z_k}(\xi_k - \mathbf{E}_{Z_k}\xi_k)^2$. Under this assumption, a more suitable bound can be derived from Lemma 5 as follows.

Theorem 4. *Assume that $\xi_k - \mathbf{E}_{Z_k}\xi_k \geq -1$ for each k. If there exists $b > 0$ such that $b\mathbf{E}_{Z_k}\xi_k \geq \mathbf{E}_{Z_k}(\xi_k - \mathbf{E}_{Z_k}\xi_k)^2$ for all k, then $\forall \alpha \geq 0$ and $t \geq 0$:*

$$\Pr\left[\mu_n \geq s_n + \sqrt{2\alpha bt} + c_b t, \quad s_n \leq \alpha\right] \leq e^{-nt},$$

where $c_b = \sqrt{(b + 2/3)b} + b + 1/3$.

Proof. It is easy to verify that for $\rho \in (0, 3)$:

$$e^\rho - \rho - 1 \leq \frac{\rho^2}{2}\sum_{u=0}^{\infty}(\rho/3)^u = \frac{\rho^2}{2(1 - \rho/3)}.$$

Using Lemma 5, for any fixed $\rho \in (0, 6/(3b + 2))$, we have with probability at least $1 - e^{-nt}$, $s_n \leq \alpha$ and

$$\mu_n < \left(1 - \frac{\rho b}{2(1 - \rho/3)}\right)^{-1}(s_n + t/\rho) \leq s_n - \alpha + \left(1 - \frac{\rho b}{2(1 - \rho/3)}\right)^{-1}(\alpha + t/\rho).$$

Since this inequality is true for all ρ, we may optimize over ρ. In particular, let $\rho^{-1} = (0.5b + 1/3) + \sqrt{0.5b(\alpha + 0.5bt + t/3)/t}$. and simplify, we obtain the theorem.

Similar to Lemma 4, we may obtain a data-dependent version of Theorem 4 with the same proof.

Lemma 6. *Under the conditions of Theorem 4. Consider a sequence $\alpha_1 \leq \alpha_2 \cdots$ and a sequence $\{\Delta t_\ell\}$ such that $\sum_\ell e^{-\Delta t_\ell} \leq 1$. Let $\ell_*(x)$ be a integer valued function such that $\ell_*(x) \geq \inf\{\ell : \alpha_\ell \geq x\}$. Then for all $t \geq 0$, we have*

$$\Pr\left[\mu_n \geq s_n + \sqrt{2b\alpha_{\ell_*(s_n)}t(s_n)} + c_b t(s_n)\right] \leq e^{-nt},$$

where $t(s_n) = t + \Delta t_{\ell_*(s_n)}/n$ and $c_b = \sqrt{(b + 2/3)b} + b + 1/3$.

Theorem 5. *Under the conditions of Theorem 4. For all $t \geq 0$, we have*

$$\Pr\left[\mu_n \geq s_n + \sqrt{2bn^{-1}\max(0, \lceil ns_n \rceil)t(s_n)} + c_b t(s_n)\right] \leq e^{-nt},$$

where $t(s_n) = t + 2n^{-1}\ln(\lceil ns_n \rceil + 2)$ and $c_b = \sqrt{(b + 2/3)b} + b + 1/3$.

Proof. In Lemma 6, we take $\alpha_\ell = (\ell - 1)/n$ for $\ell = 1, 2, \cdots$, $\Delta t_\ell = 2\ln(\ell + 1)$, and $\ell_*(x) = \lceil nx \rceil + 1$.

Note that if $\xi \in [0, 1]$, then the condition of Theorem 5 is satisfied with $b = 1$. However, Theorem 3 is tighter in this case (using Proposition 1).

3   Generalization Bounds for Some Online Algorithms

We consider two scenarios. One is classification, which requires the Hoeffding inequality developed in Section 2.1. The other is regression, which utilizes the Bennett inequality in Section 2.2.

3.1   Classification

We consider multi-category classification problem, with zero-one classification loss. We are interested in a classification function $h : \mathcal{X} \to \mathcal{Y} = \{1, \ldots, K\}$, with the classification loss

$$\mathrm{err}(h(x), y) = \begin{cases} 0 & \text{if } h(x) = y \\ 1 & \text{otherwise.} \end{cases}$$

The risk (expected classification error) of h is

$$\mathrm{err}(h) = \mathbf{E}_{(X,Y) \sim D} \mathrm{err}(h(X), Y).$$

Consider training data $Z_1^n = (Z_1, \ldots, Z_n)$ that are independently drawn from D. Consider a learning algorithm $\mathcal{A}$ that learns from the first k samples Z_1^k a classifier $\hat{h}_k(x) = \mathcal{A}(Z_1^k; x) : \mathcal{X} \to \mathcal{Y}$. We restate from Theorem 3 the following generalization bound.

Theorem 6. *Let $\hat{h}_k$ be a classifier learned from an algorithm after seeing training data $Z_1, \ldots, Z_k$. Let $\hat{M}_n = \sum_{i=1}^n \mathrm{err}(\hat{h}_{i-1}(X_i), Y_i)$ be the number of mistakes the algorithm makes online after n examples. Then with probability at most e^{-nt},*

$$\frac{1}{n} \sum_{i=1}^n \mathrm{err}(\hat{h}_i) \geq \mathrm{KL}_2^{-1}(n^{-1} \hat{M}_n || 2n^{-1} \ln(\hat{M}_n + 2) + t).$$

We may also apply the analysis to specific algorithms with known mistake bounds. For example, we may consider the multi-category perceptron algorithm [5], and obtain a margin bound accordingly. The multi-category perceptron algorithm is a natural generalization of the binary perceptron algorithm, popular in natural language processing due to its simplicity and effectiveness.

In the setting of multi-category perceptron [5], a data-point $x \in \mathcal{X}$ is represented by K vectors $\{x[1], \ldots, x[K]\}$, each corresponding to a class-label. A classifier h is represented by a linear weight vector w, with the corresponding classification rule:

$$h(x) = \arg \max_{\ell=1,\ldots,K} w^T x[\ell].$$

Let y be the true label of x. One may define the corresponding margin for the data point $z = (x, y)$ as

$$\gamma(w, z) = \frac{1}{\|w\|_2^2} \left(w^T x[y] - \max_{\ell \neq y} w^T x[\ell] \right).$$

The multi-category perceptron method maintains a weight vector starting from $w_0 = 0$. After seeing a data-point (X_i, Y_i), the algorithm uses the current weight w_{i-1} to make a prediction, which produces a label Y. We then update the weight vector as $w_i = w_{i-1} + (X_i[Y_i] - X_i[Y])$.

Assume there is a linear separator w_* for the training data $Z_1, \ldots, Z_n$ such that the margin $\inf_i \gamma(w_*, Z_i) \geq \gamma > 0$, then the standard perceptron bound can be extended to show (see [5]) that the number of mistakes that the perceptron method makes is no more than $(R/\gamma)^2$, where $R \geq \sup_{i,Y} \|X_i[Y_i] - X_i[Y]\|_2$.

Theorem 7. *Consider a linear separator* $w_*(Z_1^n)$ *for the training data* Z_1, $\ldots, Z_n$ *such that* $\inf_i \gamma(w_*, Z_i) \geq \gamma(Z_1^n) > 0$. *For all* $R(Z_1^n) \geq \sup_{i,Y} \|X_i[Y_i] - X_i[Y]\|_2$. *We have with probability of at most* e^{-nt}:

$$M = \frac{R(Z_1^n)^2}{\gamma(Z_1^n)^2} \leq n, \quad \frac{1}{n}\sum_{i=1}^n \mathrm{err}(\hat{h}_i) \geq \mathrm{KL}_2^{-1}(n^{-1}M\|2n^{-1}\ln(M+2)+t).$$

Again, Proposition 1 can be used to obtain a more intuitive bound. If the mistaken bound $R^2/\gamma^2 = O(1)$, then the generalization performance in Theorem 7 is $O(1/n)$ at constant probability $t = O(1/n)$. This can be compared to well-known batch margin bounds in the literature, which (to the author's knowledge) do not achieve the $O(1/n)$ rate under the same assumptions.

Assume further that there is a linear separator w_* that does not only separate the training data, but also all the test data. Let R and γ be defined with respect to all data, then by the data independent bound in Theorem 2, we have with probability no more than e^{-nt}:

$$\frac{1}{n}\sum_{i=1}^n \mathrm{err}(\hat{h}_i) \geq \mathrm{KL}_2^{-1}(n^{-1}R^2/\gamma^2\|t).$$

3.2   Regression

It is known that some learning problems have loss functions that satisfy the following self-bounding condition: $b\mathbf{E}L(h(X),Y) \geq \mathbf{E}L(h(X),Y)^2$ for some $b > 0$. For such problems, the Bennett inequality in Section 2.2 should be applied.

To illustrate the idea, in the following, we shall consider the least squares regression problem:

$$L(h(X),Y) = (h(X) - Y)^2,$$

where $Y \in [0,1]$. Let S be a closed convex set of functions such that $h(X) \in S$ implies that $h(X) \in [0,1]$. Let h_S be the optimal predictor in S:

$$\mathbf{E}_{X,Y}(h_S(X) - Y)^2 = \inf_{h \in S} \mathbf{E}_{X,Y}(h(X) - Y)^2.$$

We have the following inequality

Lemma 7. *Let* $Z = (X,Y)$, *and* $\Delta L_S(h,Z) = (h(X) - Y)^2 - (h_S(X) - Y)^2$. *For all* $h \in S$:

$$4\mathbf{E}_Z \Delta L_S(h,Z) \geq \mathbf{E}_Z \Delta L_S(h,Z)^2.$$

Proof. The convexity of S and optimality of h_S implies that $\forall h \in S$, the derivative of $\mathbf{E}_Z(h_S(X) + t(h(X) - h_S(X)) - Y)^2$ as a function of t is non-negative at $t = 0$. That is, $\mathbf{E}_Z(h_S(X) - Y)(h(X) - h_S(X)) \geq 0$. Therefore

$$\begin{aligned}
\mathbf{E}_Z \Delta L_S(h,Z)^2 &= \mathbf{E}_Z (h(X) - h_S(X))^2(h(X) + h_S(X) - 2Y)^2 \\
&\leq 4\mathbf{E}_Z (h(X) - h_S(X))^2 \\
&\leq 4\mathbf{E}_Z [(h(X) - h_S(X))^2 + 2(h(X) - h_S(X))(h_S(X) - Y)] \\
&= 4\mathbf{E}_Z \Delta L_S(h,Z).
\end{aligned}$$

Let $\mathcal{A}$ be a learning algorithm, and S be a set of convex functions. Assume that all hypothesis learned by $\mathcal{A}$ belong to S, we can obtain the following theorem from Theorem 5.

Theorem 8. *Let $\hat{h}_k \in S$ be a function learned from an algorithm after seeing training data $Z_1, \ldots, Z_k$. Let*

$$\hat{M}_n = \max\left(0, \sum_{i=1}^{n}(\hat{h}_{i-1}(X_i) - Y_i)^2 - \inf_{h \in S}\sum_{i=1}^{n}(h(X_i) - Y_i)^2\right).$$

Then with probability at most e^{-nt},

$$\frac{1}{n}\sum_{i=1}^{n}\mathbf{E}_Z\,(\hat{h}_i(X) - Y)^2 \geq \mathbf{E}_Z\,(\hat{h}_S(X) - Y)^2 + \frac{\hat{M}_n}{n} + \sqrt{8n^{-1}\lceil \hat{M}_n\rceil \hat{t}} + 9\hat{t},$$

where $\hat{t} = t + 2n^{-1}\ln\lceil \hat{M}_n + 2\rceil$.

Proof. We apply Theorem 5 with $\xi_k = \Delta L_S(\hat{h}_k, Z)$ and $b = 4$. We only need to note that $ns_n \leq \hat{M}_n$ and $c_b \leq 9$.

Bounds that relate the performance of an learning algorithm to the best possible performance (within a function class) is often referred to as oracle inequality in the learning theory literature. Theorem 8 can be viewed as a data-dependent oracle inequality. If $\hat{M}_n$ is small, then the total generalization performance (compared with h_S) can be faster than $O(1/\sqrt{n})$. In particular, if $\hat{M}_n = O(\ln n)$, then the performance can be as fast as $O(\ln n/n)$ with constant probability $t = O(1/n)$. The theorem can be applied to any online algorithm for least squares regression based on the observed loss. For some algorithms, it is also possible to prove data-dependent or data-independent mistake bounds for $\hat{M}_n$. Similar to Theorem 7, we may derive more specific performance bounds for these specific algorithms, assuming $\hat{M}_n$ can be bounded using some quantities that depend on the data. We shall skip the details here.

4 Expert Aggregation Algorithms

We consider learning algorithms $\mathcal{A}_\theta$ parameterized by $\theta \in \Gamma$. For notation simplicity, given a sample $Z = (X, Y)$, we let

$$L_\theta(Z_1^k; Z) = L(\mathcal{A}_\theta(Z_1^k; X), Y).$$

That is, $L_\theta(Z_1^k; \cdot)$ is the loss of the function learned by $\mathcal{A}_\theta$ using the first k training data.

In the expert framework, as in [12], we consider a prior distribution on Γ, which we denote as $d\pi_0(\theta)$. We maintain and update a distribution on Γ, and the update rule depends on a parameter η. With each sample Z_k, the distribution imposed on the experts are updated as follows:

$$d\pi_k^\eta(\theta) \sim e^{-\eta L_\theta(Z_1^{k-1}; Z_k)}\,d\pi_{k-1}^\eta(\theta),$$

where $\eta > 0$ is a fixed learning rate. We also let $\pi_0^\eta(\theta) = \pi_0(\theta)$. It follows that the distribution after seeing the first k samples Z_1^k, is the Gibbs distribution

$$d\pi_k^\eta(\theta) \sim e^{-\eta \sum_{i=1}^k L_\theta(Z_1^{i-1};Z_i)} d\pi_0(\theta). \tag{5}$$

For specific expert algorithms devised in the literature, our earlier analysis can be applied to obtain generalization bounds. In the following, we show that it is also natural to study the concentration behavior of expert aggregating algorithms directly, using tools we developed in Section 2.

Lemma 8. $\forall \eta \geq 0$, *the following inequality holds:*

$$\Pr\left[-\sum_{i=1}^n \ln \int d\pi_i^\eta(\theta) \mathbf{E}_{Z_i} e^{-\eta L_\theta(Z_1^{i-1};Z_i)} \geq M_n(\eta) \right] \leq e^{-t},$$

where

$$M_n(\eta) = -\ln \int e^{-\eta \sum_{i=1}^n L_\theta(Z_1^{i-1};Z_i)} d\pi_0(\theta).$$

Proof. If we let $\xi_k = -\ln \int d\pi_i^\eta(\theta) e^{-\eta L_\theta(Z_1^{i-1};Z_i)}$, then it is easy to verify that $\sum_{i=1}^n \xi_i = M_n$. We can now apply Lemma 2 with $\rho = 1$, and use the fact that

$$\mathbf{E}_{Z_i} e^{-\xi_i} = \int d\pi_i^\eta(\theta) \mathbf{E}_{Z_i} e^{-\eta L_\theta(Z_1^{i-1};Z_i)}.$$

The desired bound is now a direct consequence of Lemma 2.

Note that η in Lemma 8 has a similar effect of ρ in Lemma 2. If we only have one expert, then we can obtain Lemma 2 from Lemma 8. Similar to the development in Section 2, we may obtain more specific bounds from Lemma 8 using appropriate estimates of logarithmic moment generating functions.

For simplicity, we will only consider Hoeffding inequality for bounded random variables. The aggregating algorithm which we shall investigate is the performance averaged over θ with respect to the distribution π_i^η, and time steps $i = 1, \ldots, n$. This method was referred to as *Hedge* in [8], and is closely related to boosting. Its generalization performance is represented as $\mu_n(\eta)$ in the following lemma, which plays the same role of Lemma 3.

Lemma 9. *If the loss function* $L(\cdot, \cdot) \in [0, 1]$, *then*

$$\Pr\left[-\ln\left(1 + \mu_n(\eta)(e^{-\eta} - 1)\right) \geq \frac{1}{n} \ln \int e^{-\eta n s_n(\theta)} d\mu_0(\theta) + t \right] \leq e^{-nt},$$

where

$$\mu_n(\eta) = \frac{1}{n} \sum_{i=1}^n \int d\pi_i^\eta(\theta) \mathbf{E}_{Z_i} L_\theta(Z_1^{i-1}; Z_i)$$

and

$$s_n(\theta) = \frac{1}{n} \sum_{i=1}^n L_\theta(Z_1^{i-1}, Z_i).$$

Now, with a fixed learning rate η, similar to the first inequality of Theorem 1, we obtain from Lemma 9 the following generalization bound:

$$\Pr\left[\mu_n(\eta) \geq \frac{-\frac{1}{n}\ln\int e^{-\eta n s_n(\theta)}d\mu_0(\theta) + t}{1 - e^{-\eta}}\right] \leq e^{-nt}.$$

As a simple example, if we only have a finite number of experts: $|\Gamma| < \infty$, then we may take μ_0 to be the uniform distribution. This gives

$$s_n(\eta) \leq \eta \inf_{\theta \in \Gamma} s_n(\theta_\ell) + \frac{1}{n}\ln|\Gamma|.$$

We have

$$\Pr\left[\mu_n(\eta) \geq \frac{\eta \inf_{\theta \in \Gamma} s_n(\theta_\ell) + \frac{1}{n}\ln|\Gamma| + t}{1 - e^{-\eta}}\right] \leq e^{-nt}.$$

This generalization bound holds for fixed η, which may not be optimal for the observed data.

An important question is to select η based on the training data Z_1^n so as to achieve a small generalization error $\mu_n(\eta)$. This is essentially a model selection problem, which requires us to develop a data dependent bound (η depends on the training data). In order to do so, we shall use the following result to obtain a simpler representation of $M_n(\eta)$. It is a direct consequence of a convex duality, widely used in the machine learning literature in recent years. For space limitation, we skip the proof.

Proposition 2. *Consider all possible distributions π over Γ, we have*

$$-\frac{1}{n}\ln\int e^{-\eta n s_n(\theta,\eta)}d\pi_0(\theta) = \inf_\pi\left[\eta\int s_n(\theta)d\pi + \frac{1}{n}\mathrm{KL}(\pi||\pi_0)\right],$$

where $\mathrm{KL}(\pi||\pi_0) = \int \ln\frac{d\pi(\theta)}{d\pi_0(\theta)}d\pi(\theta)$.

We are now ready to present the following bound, which is similar to Theorem 2. A related bound can be found in [11].

Theorem 9. *Under the conditions of Lemma 9. We have $\forall \alpha \in [0,1]$ and $t, \delta \in [0,\infty)$:*

$$\Pr\left[\mu_n(\eta(\alpha, t+\delta)) \geq \mathrm{KL}_2^{-1}(\alpha||t+\delta), \exists\pi : \int s_n(\theta)d\pi \leq \alpha, \mathrm{KL}(\pi||\pi_0) \leq n\delta\right] \leq e^{-nt},$$

where $\eta(\alpha, u) = \ln(\mathrm{KL}_2^{-1}(\alpha||u)(1-\alpha)) - \ln(\alpha(1 - \mathrm{KL}_2^{-1}(\alpha||u)))$.

Proof. We have with probability of at most e^{-nt}, $\exists\pi$:

$$-\ln\left(1 + \mu_n(\eta)(e^{-\eta} - 1)\right) \geq \eta\int s_n(\theta)d\pi + \frac{1}{n}\mathrm{KL}(\pi||\pi_0) + t.$$

Now, let $\beta = \text{KL}_2^{-1}(\alpha||t + \delta)$. This implies that with probability at most e^{-nt}, $\exists \pi$ such that:

$$\mu_n(\eta) \geq \beta, \int s_n(\theta)d\pi \leq \alpha, \frac{1}{n}\text{KL}(\pi||\pi_0) \leq \delta,$$

$$-\ln(1 + \beta(e^{-\eta} - 1)) \geq \eta\alpha + \text{KL}(\alpha||\beta).$$

Note that the last inequality holds trivially with $\eta = \eta(\alpha, t + \delta)$. This leads to the theorem.

Using the standard union bound trick, we can obtain a version of Theorem 9 with data-dependent α and δ. The proof of the following result is a straightforward extension of that of Lemma 4. Again, due to the space limitation, we skip the proof.

Lemma 10. *Using notations of Theorem 9. Consider a set of triples $\{(\alpha_\ell, \delta_\ell, \Delta t_\ell)\}$ indexed by ℓ, where $\alpha_\ell \in [0, 1]$, $\delta_\ell \geq 0$, and $\sum_\ell e^{-\Delta t_\ell} \leq 1$. Let $\ell_*(\alpha, \delta)$ be a function such that $\alpha_\ell \geq \alpha$ and $\delta_\ell \geq \delta$. Then we have $\forall t \geq 0$:*

$$\Pr\left[\exists \pi : \ell = \ell_n(\pi), \quad \mu_n(\eta(\alpha_\ell, t_\ell)) \geq \text{KL}_2^{-1}(\alpha_\ell||t_\ell)\right] \leq e^{-nt},$$

where $\ell_n(\pi) = \ell_*(\int s_n(\theta)d\pi, \text{KL}(\pi||\pi_0)/n)$ and $t_\ell = t + \delta_\ell + \Delta t_\ell/n$.

With specific choices of $(\alpha_\ell, \delta_\ell, \Delta t_\ell)$, we can obtain the following result.

Theorem 10. *Using notations of Theorem 9. We have $\forall t \geq 0$:*

$$\Pr\left[\exists \pi : \mu_n(\eta_n^\pi) \geq \text{KL}_2^{-1}(n^{-1}\lceil ns_n^\pi\rceil||t + t_n^\pi)\right] \leq e^{-nt},$$

where

$$s_n^\pi = \int s_n(\theta)d\pi,$$

$$t_n^\pi = n^{-1}[\lceil\text{KL}(\pi||\pi_0)\rceil + 2\ln(\lceil ns_n^\pi\rceil + 2) + 2\ln(\lceil\text{KL}(\pi||\pi_0)\rceil + 2)],$$

$$\eta_n^\pi = \eta(n^{-1}\lceil ns_n^\pi\rceil, t + t_n^\pi).$$

Proof. In Lemma 10, we let ℓ be represented by a pair of positive integers (p, q) such that $\alpha_{(p,q)} = (p-1)/n$, $\delta_{(p,q)} = (q-1)/n$, $\Delta_{(p,q)} = 2\ln(p+1) + 2\ln(q+1)$. It can be easily checked that $\sum e^{-\Delta_{(p,q)}} \leq 1$. Now we can simply let $\ell_*(u, v) = (\lceil nu\rceil, \lceil nv\rceil)$ to obtain the desired result.

With constant probability $t = O(1/n)$, a convergence rate of $O(1/n)$ can be achieved when there exists a π such that $\int s_n^\pi(\theta)d\pi = O(1)$ and $\text{KL}(\pi||\pi_0) = O(1)$. The main part of t_n^π is $n^{-1}\text{KL}(\pi||\pi_0)$. By focusing on the main part, we approximately have the following bound from Theorem 10 and Proposition 1. With probability of at least $1 - e^{-nt}$, $\forall \pi$, we can appropriately chose learning rate η that depends on the data such that

$$\mu_n(\eta) < s_n^\pi + \sqrt{2s_n^\pi(1 - s_n^\pi)(t + n^{-1}\text{KL}(\pi||\pi_0))} + 1.5(1 - s_n^\pi)(t + n^{-1}\text{KL}(\pi||\pi_0)).$$

As an application, assume there are only a finite number of experts. We may just pick π_0 to be the uniform distribution and π to be concentrated on the expert with the smallest number of empirical loss such that $\text{KL}(\pi||\pi_0) = \ln|\Gamma|$ and $s_n^\pi = \inf_{\theta \in \Gamma} s_n(\theta)$.

5   Conclusion

In this paper, we considered the problem of estimating the total generalization performance of a learning algorithm based on its observed total loss. This is achieved through some newly obtained probability inequalities concerning the concentration of dependent random variables. Consequences of our analysis in classification and regression were discussed. If the observed loss is small, then the estimated generalization performance can be as fast as $O(1/n)$ with constant probability. Moreover, we showed that the technique used to prove probability inequalities for dependent variables can be naturally applied to analyze the generalization behavior of expert aggregating algorithms. In this case, by minimizing the resulting data-dependent bound, we obtain a method of choosing the learning rate η with optimal total generalization performance (according to the bound).

References

1. K. Azuma. Weighted sums of certain dependent random variables. *Tohoku Math. Journal*, 3:357–367, 1967.
2. George Bennett. Probability inequalities for the sum of independent random variables. *Journal of the American Statistical Association*, 57:33–45, 1962.
3. Avrim Blum, Adam Kalai, and John Langford. Beating the hold-out: Bounds for k-fold and progressive cross-validation. In *COLT' 99*, pages 203–208, 1999.
4. N. Cesa-Bianchi, A. Conconi, and C. Gentile. On the generalization ability of on-line learning algorithms. *IEEE Transactions on Information Theory*, pages 2050–2057, 2004.
5. Michael Collins. Discriminative training methods for hidden markov models: Theory and experiments with perceptron algorithms. In *Proc. EMNLP'02*, 2002.
6. Victor H. de la Pẽna. A general class of exponential inequalities for martingales and ratios. *The Annals of Probability*, 27:537–564, 1999.
7. David A. Freedman. On tail probabilities for martingales. *The Annals of Probability*, 3:100–118, 1975.
8. Y. Freund and R.E. Schapire. A decision-theoretic generalization of on-line learning and an application to boosting. *J. Comput. Syst. Sci.*, 55(1):119–139, 1997.
9. W. Hoeffding. Probability inequalities for sums of bounded random variables. *Journal of the American Statistical Association*, 58(301):13–30, March 1963.
10. Nick Littlestone. From on-line to batch learning. In *COLT' 89*, pages 269–284, 1989.
11. Nick Littlestone and Manfred K. Warmuth. The weighted majority algorithm. *Information and Computation*, 108:212–261, 1994.
12. Volodya Vovk. Aggregating strategies. In *COLT' 90*, pages 371–383, 1990.

The Weak Aggregating Algorithm
and Weak Mixability*

Yuri Kalnishkan and Michael V. Vyugin

Department of Computer Science, Royal Holloway,
University of London, Egham, Surrey, TW20 0EX, UK
{yura, misha}@cs.rhul.ac.uk

Abstract. This paper resolves the problem of predicting as well as the best expert up to an additive term $o(n)$, where n is the length of a sequence of letters from a finite alphabet. For the bounded games the paper introduces the Weak Aggregating Algorithm that allows us to obtain additive terms of the form $C\sqrt{n}$. A modification of the Weak Aggregating Algorithm that covers unbounded games is also described.

1 Introduction

This paper deals with the problem of prediction with expert advice. We consider the on-line prediction protocol, where outcomes $\omega_1, \omega_2, \ldots$ occur in succession while a prediction strategy tries to predict them. Before seeing an event ω_t the prediction strategy produces a prediction γ_t. We are interested in the case of a discrete outcome space, i.e., $\omega_1, \omega_2, \ldots \in \Omega$ such that $|\Omega| < +\infty$.

We use a loss function $\lambda(\omega, \gamma)$ to measure the discrepancies between predictions and outcomes. A loss function and a prediction space (a set of possible predictions) Γ specify the game, i.e., a particular prediction environment. The performance of a learner $\mathfrak{S}$ w.r.t. a game is measured by the cumulative loss suffered on the sequence of outcomes $\omega_1, \omega_2, \ldots, \omega_n$

$$\text{Loss}_{\mathfrak{S}}(\omega_1, \omega_2, \ldots, \omega_n) = \sum_{t=1}^{n} \lambda(\omega_t, \gamma_t) \ . \tag{1}$$

In the problem of prediction with expert advice we have N prediction strategies $\mathcal{E}_1, \mathcal{E}_2, \ldots, \mathcal{E}_N$ that try to predict elements of the same sequence. Their predictions become available to the merging prediction strategy $\mathfrak{M}$ every time before $\mathfrak{M}$ outputs its own prediction. The goal of $\mathfrak{M}$ is to predict nearly as well as the best expert, i.e., to suffer loss that is little bigger than the smallest of the experts' losses.

---

* An early version of this paper was published in November, 2003 as Technical Report CLRC-TR-03-01, Computer Learning Research Centre, Royal Holloway, University of London available at http://www.clrc.rhul.ac.uk/publications/techrep.htm

P. Auer and R. Meir (Eds.): COLT 2005, LNAI 3559, pp. 188–203, 2005.

This problem has been studied intensively; see, e.g., [CBFH+97, HKW98]. Papers [Vov90, Vov98] propose the Aggregating Algorithm that allows $\mathfrak{M}$ to achieve loss satisfying the inequality

$$\text{Loss}_{\mathfrak{M}}(\omega_1, \omega_2, \ldots, \omega_n) \leq c \, \text{Loss}_{\mathcal{E}_i}(\omega_1, \omega_2, \ldots, \omega_n) + a \ln N \qquad (2)$$

for all $i = 1 \ldots, N$ and all possible sequences of outcomes $\omega_1, \omega_2, \ldots, \omega_n$, $n = 1, 2, \ldots$, where the constants c and a are optimal and are specified by the game. Note that neither c nor a depend on n.

If we can take c equal to 1, the game is called mixable. It is possible to provide a geometrical characterisation of mixable games in terms of the so called sets of superpredictions. The Aggregating Algorithm fully resolves the problem of predicting as well as the best expert up to an additive constant.

There are interesting games that are not mixable, e.g., the absolute loss game introduced in Sect. 2. The Aggregating Algorithm still works for some of such games, but it only allows us to achieve values of c greater than 1.

In this paper we take a different approach to non-mixable games. We fix $c = 1$ but consider $a(n)$ that can grow when the length n of the sequence increases. We study the problem of predicting as well as the best expert up to $o(n)$ as $n \to +\infty$, where n is the length of the sequence. Sect. 3 introduces the corresponding concept of weak mixability. The main result of this paper, Theor. 1, shows that weak mixability is equivalent to a very simple geometric property of the set of superpredictions, namely, the convexity of its finite part.

If the loss function is bounded, it is possible to predict as well as the best expert up to an additive term of the form $C\sqrt{n}$, provided the finite part of the set of superpredictions is convex. This result follows from a recent paper [HP04]. We shall present our own construction, which is based on ideas from [CBFH+97].

If the game is not bounded, our construction can be applied in a different form to predict as well as the best expert up to $o(n)$.

2   Preliminaries

2.1   On-line Prediction

A *game* $\mathfrak{G}$ is a triple $\langle \Omega, \Gamma, \lambda \rangle$, where Ω is an *outcome space*, Γ is a *prediction space*, and $\lambda : \Omega \times \Gamma \to [0, +\infty]$ is a *loss function*. We assume that Ω is a finite set of cardinality $M < +\infty$; we will refer to elements of Ω as to $\omega^{(0)}, \omega^{(1)}, \ldots, \omega^{(M-1)}$. In the simplest binary case $M = 2$ and Ω may be identified with $\mathbb{B} = \{0, 1\}$. We also assume that Γ is a compact topological space and λ is continuous w.r.t. the extended topology of $[-\infty, +\infty]$. Since we treat Ω as a discrete space, the continuity of λ in two arguments is the same as continuity in the second argument. These assumption hold throughout the paper except for Remark 1, where negative losses are discussed.

The *square-loss* game, the *absolute-loss* game, and the *logarithmic* game with the outcome space $\Omega = \mathbb{B}$, prediction space $\Gamma = [0, 1]$, and loss functions $\lambda(\omega, \gamma) = (\omega - \gamma)^2$, $\lambda(\omega, \gamma) = |\omega - \gamma|$, and

$$\lambda(\omega,\gamma) = \begin{cases} -\log(1-\gamma) & \text{if } \omega = 0 \ , \\ -\log\gamma & \text{if } \omega = 1 \ , \end{cases}$$

respectively, are examples of (binary) games. A slightly different example is provided by the *simple prediction game* with $\Omega = \Gamma = \mathbb{B} = \{0,1\}$ and $\lambda(\omega,\gamma) = 0$ if $\omega = \gamma$ and $\lambda(\omega,\gamma) = 1$ otherwise.

It is essential to allow λ to accept the value $+\infty$; this assumption is necessary in order to take into account the logarithmic game as well as other unbounded games. However we impose the following restriction: if $\lambda(\omega_0,\gamma_0) = +\infty$ for some $\omega_0 \in \Omega$ and $\gamma_0 \in \Gamma$, then there is a sequence $\gamma_n \in \Gamma$ such that $\gamma_n \to \gamma_0$ and $\lambda(\omega,\gamma_n)$ is finite for all $\omega \in \Omega$ and all positive integers n. In order words, any prediction that leads to infinite loss on some outcomes can be approximated by predictions that can only lead to finite loss no matter what outcome occurs. This restriction allows us to exclude some degenerate cases and to simplify the statements of theorems.

Suppose that λ can be computed by an oracle. We assume that the oracle is capable of more than just outputting the values of λ, e.g., it can solve some simple inequalities involving λ (see Sect. 6 for more details). All natural loss functions specified by simple analytical expression satisfy these requirements.

A prediction strategy $\mathfrak{S}$ works according to the following protocol:

(1) FOR $t = 1,2,\ldots$
(2) $\mathfrak{S}$ chooses a prediction $\gamma_t \in \Gamma$
(3) $\mathfrak{S}$ observes the actual outcome $\omega_t \in \Omega$
(4) END FOR

One can identify a prediction strategy with a function from Ω^* to Γ. Over the first n trials, the strategy $\mathfrak{S}$ suffers the total loss

$$\text{Loss}_{\mathfrak{S}}^{\mathfrak{S}}(\omega_1,\omega_2,\ldots,\omega_n) = \sum_{t=1}^{n} \lambda(\omega_t,\gamma_t) \ .$$

By definition, put $\text{Loss}_{\mathfrak{S}}(\Lambda) = 0$, where Λ denotes the empty string.

2.2   Expert Advice

The problem of prediction with expert advice involve a pool of N experts $\mathcal{E}^{(1)}, \mathcal{E}^{(2)}, \ldots, \mathcal{E}^{(N)}$, which are working according to the aforementioned protocol. On trial t they output predictions $\gamma_t^{(1)}, \gamma_t^{(2)}, \ldots, \gamma_t^{(N)}$. A *merging strategy* $\mathfrak{M}$ is allowed to observe the experts' prediction before outputting its own, i.e., it works according to the following protocol:

(1) FOR $t = 1,2,\ldots$
(2) $\mathcal{E}^{(1)}, \mathcal{E}^{(2)}, \ldots, \mathcal{E}^{(N)}$ output predictions $\gamma_t^{(1)}, \gamma_t^{(2)}, \ldots, \gamma_t^{(N)} \in \Gamma$
(3) $\mathfrak{M}$ chooses a prediction $\gamma_t \in \Gamma$
(4) $\mathfrak{M}$ observes the actual outcome $\omega_t \in \Omega$
(5) END FOR

The goal of the merging strategy is to suffer loss that is not much worse than the loss of the best expert. By the best expert after trial t we mean the expert that has suffered the smallest loss over t trials.

One may think of a merging strategy as of a function

$$\mathfrak{M} : \bigcup_{N=0}^{+\infty} \bigcup_{t=1}^{+\infty} \left(\Omega^{t-1} \times \left(\Gamma^N \right)^t \right) \to \Gamma . \tag{3}$$

Here N is the number of experts and t is the number of a trial; the information available to $\mathfrak{M}$ before making a prediction on trial t consists of $t-1$ previous outcomes and t arrays each consisting of N experts' predictions.

When we speak about computability, we assume that the algorithm computing $\mathfrak{M}$ receives experts' predictions as inputs. The experts do not have to be computable in any sense. The learner has no access to their internal 'mechanics'; the only thing it knows about them is their predictions.

2.3 Geometric Interpretation of a Game

Take a game $\mathfrak{G} = \langle \Omega, \Gamma, \lambda \rangle$ such that $\Omega = \{\omega^{(0)}, \omega^{(1)}, \ldots, \omega^{(M-1)}\}$ and $|\Omega| = M$. We say that an M-tuple $(s_0, s_1, \ldots, s_{M-1}) \in (-\infty, +\infty]^M$ is a *superprediction* if there is $\gamma \in \Gamma$ such that the inequalities $\lambda(\omega^{(i)}, \gamma) \le s_i$ hold for every $i = 0, 1, 2, \ldots, M - 1$. The set of superpredictions S is an important object characterising the game.

3   Weak Mixability

One may wonder whether the learner can predict as well as the best expert up to an additive constant, i.e., to suffer loss within an additive constant range of the loss of the best expert. It is possible for the so called mixable games; for more details see [Vov90, Vov98]. Examples of mixable games include the square-loss game and the logarithmic game; the simple prediction game and the absolute-loss game are not mixable.

For non-mixable games it is not possible to predict as well as the best expert up to an additive constant. Let us relax this requirement and ask whether it is possible to predict as well as the best expert up to a larger term.

In the worst case, loss grows linearly in the length of the sequence. Therefore all terms of slower growth can be considered small as compared to loss. This motivates the following definition.

A game $\mathfrak{G}$ is *weakly mixable* if there is a function $f : \mathbb{N} \to \mathbb{R}$ such that $f(n) = o(n)$ as $n \to +\infty$ and a merging strategy $\mathfrak{M}$ such that, for every finite set of experts $\mathcal{E}^{(1)}, \mathcal{E}^{(2)}, \ldots, \mathcal{E}^{(N)}$ ($N = 1, 2, \ldots$), the inequality

$$\text{Loss}_{\mathfrak{M}}^{\mathfrak{G}}(\omega_1, \omega_2, \ldots, \omega_n) \le \text{Loss}_{\mathcal{E}^{(i)}}(\omega_1, \omega_2, \ldots, \omega_n) + f(n) \tag{4}$$

holds for all $i = 1, 2, \ldots, N$ and every finite sequence $\omega_1, \omega_2, \ldots, \omega_n \in \Omega$, $n = 1, 2, \ldots$.

The following theorem is the main result of the paper.

Theorem 1. *A game* $\mathfrak{G} = \langle \Omega, \Gamma, \lambda \rangle$ *with the set of superpredictions* S *is weakly mixable if and only if the finite part of* S, *the set* $S \cap \mathbb{R}^M$, *is convex.*

The merging strategy in the definition of weak mixability is polynomial-time computable modulo the oracle computing λ (see Sect. 6).

The examples of the weakly mixable games are the logarithmic and the square-loss game, which are also mixable, and the absolute-loss game, which is not mixable. The simple prediction game is not weakly mixable.

The rest of the paper contains the proof of the theorem. The 'only if' part follows from Theor. 2 that is proved in Appendix A.

The 'if' splits into two parts, for bounded and for unbounded games. The 'if' part for bounded games follows from [HP04]. In Sect. 4 we shall give an alternative derivation, which gives a slightly better value of the constant C in the additive term $C\sqrt{n}$. The unbounded case is described in Sect. 5.

Remark 1. Let us allow (within this remark) λ to accept negative values; they can be interpreted as 'gain' or 'reward'. If λ accepts the value $-\infty$, the expression for the total loss may include the sum $(-\infty) + (+\infty)$, which is undefined. In order to avoid this ambiguity, it is natural to prohibit λ to take the value $-\infty$. Since λ is assumed to be continuous, this implies that λ is bounded from below, i.e., there is $a > -\infty$ such that $\lambda(\omega, \gamma) \geq a$ for all values of ω and γ.

Consider another game with the loss function $\lambda'(\omega, \gamma) = \lambda(\omega, \gamma) + a$, which is nonnegative. A merging strategy working with nonnegative loss functions can be easily adapted to work with the original game: let the learner just imagine that it is playing the game with λ'. The losses w.r.t. the two games on a string $\omega_1 \omega_2 \ldots \omega_n$ will differ by an and the upper bounds of the type (4) will be preserved. On the other hand, the sets of superpredictions for the two games will differ by a shift, which preserves convexity. Therefore Theor. 1 remains true for games with loss functions bounded from below.

4   'If' Part for Bounded Games

4.1   Weak Aggregating Algorithm

In this subsection we formulate the Weak Aggregating Algorithm (WAA). Let $\mathfrak{G} = \langle \Omega, \Gamma, \lambda \rangle$ be a game such that $|\Omega| = M < +\infty$ and let N be the number of experts. Let $\Omega = \{\omega^{(0)}, \omega^{(1)}, \ldots, \omega^{(M-1)}\}$.

We describe the WAA using pseudo-code. The WAA accepts N initial normalised weights $q_1, q_2, \ldots, q_N \in [0, 1]$ such that $\sum_{i=1}^{N} q_i = 1$ and a positive number c as parameters. The role of c is similar to that of the learning rate in the theory of prediction with expert advice. Let $\beta_t = e^{-c/\sqrt{t}}$, $t = 1, 2, \ldots$.

(1) $l_1^{(i)} := 0$, $i = 1, 2, \ldots, N$
(2) FOR $t = 1, 2, \ldots$

(3) $w_t^{(i)} := q_i \beta_t^{l_t^{(i)}}$, $i = 1, 2, \ldots, N$

(4) $p_t^{(i)} := \frac{w_t^{(i)}}{\sum_{j=1}^{N} w_t^{(j)}}$, $i = 1, 2, \ldots, N$

(5)   read experts' predictions $\gamma_t^{(1)}, \gamma_t^{(2)}, \ldots, \gamma_t^{(N)}$

(6) $g_k := \sum_{j=1}^{N} \lambda\left(\omega^{(k)}, \gamma_t^{(j)}\right) p_t^{(j)}$, $k = 0, 1, \ldots, M-1$

(7)   output $\gamma_t \in \Gamma$ such that $\lambda(\omega^{(k)}, \gamma_t) \leq g_k$ for all
        $k = 0, 1, \ldots, M-1$

(8)   observe ω_t

(9) $l_{t+1}^{(i)} := l_t^{(i)} + \lambda\left(\omega_t, \gamma_t^{(i)}\right)$, $i = 1, 2, \ldots, N$

(10) END FOR

The variable $l_t^{(i)}$ stores the loss of the i-th expert $\mathcal{E}^{(i)}$, i.e., after trial t we have $l_{t+1}^{(i)} = \mathrm{Loss}_{\mathcal{E}^{(i)}}^{\mathfrak{G}}(\omega_1, \omega_2, \ldots, \omega_t)$. The values $w_t^{(i)}$ are weights assigned to experts during the work of the algorithm; they depend on the loss suffered by experts and initial weights q_i. The values $p_t^{(i)}$ are obtained by normalising $w_t^{(i)}$. Note that it is sufficient to have only one set of variables $p^{(i)}$, $i = 1, 2, \ldots, N$, one set of variables $w^{(i)}$, $i = 1, 2, \ldots, N$, and one set of variables $l^{(i)}$, $i = 1, 2, \ldots, N$ to save memory. The subscript t has been added in order to simplify referring to these variables in the proofs below.

This algorithm is applicable if the set of superpredictions S has a convex finite part $S \cap \mathbb{R}^M$. If this is the case, then the point $(g_0, g_1, \ldots, g_{M-1})$ belongs to S and thus γ_t can be found on step (7).

A game $\mathfrak{G} = \langle \Omega, \Gamma, \lambda \rangle$ is bounded if and only if λ is bounded, i.e., there is $L \in (0, +\infty)$ such that $\lambda(\omega, \gamma) \leq L$ for each $\omega \in \Omega$ and $\gamma \in \Gamma$. Examples of bounded games include the square-loss game, the absolute-loss game, and the simple prediction game. The logarithmic game is unbounded.

For bounded games the following lemma holds.

Lemma 1. *For every* $L > 0$, *every game* $\mathfrak{G} = \langle \Omega, \Gamma, \lambda \rangle$ *such that* $|\Omega| < +\infty$ *and* $\lambda(\omega, \gamma) \leq L$ *for all* $\omega \in \Omega$ *and* $\gamma \in \Gamma$, *and every finite set of experts* $\mathcal{E}^{(1)}, \mathcal{E}^{(2)}, \ldots, \mathcal{E}^{(N)}$ ($N = 1, 2, \ldots$), *the merging strategy* $\mathfrak{M}$ *following the WAA with initial weights* $q_1, q_2, \ldots, q_N \in [0, 1]$ *such that* $\sum_{i=1}^{N} q_i = 1$ *and* $c > 0$ *achieves loss satisfying*

$$\mathrm{Loss}_{\mathfrak{M}}^{\mathfrak{G}}(\omega_1, \omega_2, \ldots, \omega_n) \leq \mathrm{Loss}_{\mathcal{E}^{(i)}}(\omega_1, \omega_2, \ldots, \omega_n) + \left(cL^2 + \frac{1}{c} \ln \frac{1}{q_i}\right) \sqrt{n}$$

for every $i = 1, 2, \ldots, N$ *and every finite sequence* $\omega_1, \omega_2, \ldots, \omega_n \in \Omega$.

The proof of Lemma 1 is given in Appendix B.

Remark 2. It is easy to see that the result of Lemma 1 will still hold for a countable pool of experts $\mathcal{E}_1, \mathcal{E}_2, \ldots$ We take weights $\sum_{i=1}^{+\infty} q_i = 1$; the sums in lines (4) and (6) from the definition of the WAA become infinite but they clearly converge.

Let us take equal initial weights $q_1 = q_2 = \ldots = q_N = 1/N$ in the WAA. The additive term then reduces to $(cL^2 + (\ln N)/c)\sqrt{n}$. When $c = \sqrt{\ln N}/L$ this expression reaches its minimum. We get the following corollary.

Corollary 1. *Under the conditions of Lemma 1, there is a merging strategy $\mathfrak{M}$ achieving loss satisfying*

$$\text{Loss}_{\mathfrak{M}}^{\mathfrak{G}}(\omega_1, \omega_2, \ldots, \omega_n) \leq \text{Loss}_{\mathcal{E}^{(i)}}(\omega_1, \omega_2, \ldots, \omega_n) + 2L\sqrt{n \ln N} \ .$$

5   'If' Part for Unbounded Games

5.1   Counterexample

The WAA can be applied even in the case of an unbounded game; indeed, the only requirement is that the finite part of the set of superpredictions S is convex. However we cannot guarantee that a reasonable upper bound on the loss of the strategy using it will exist. The same applies to any strategy that uses a linear combination in the same fashion as WAA.

Indeed, consider a game with an unbounded loss function λ. Let ω_0 be such that the function $\lambda(\omega_0, \gamma)$ attains arbitrary large values.

Suppose that there are two experts $\mathcal{E}_1$ and $\mathcal{E}_2$ and on some trial they are ascribed weights $p^{(1)}$ and $p^{(2)}$ such that $p^{(2)} > 0$. Suppose that $\mathcal{E}_1$ outputs $\gamma^{(1)}$ such that $\lambda(\omega_0, \gamma^{(1)}) < +\infty$. The upper estimate on the loss of the learner in the case when the outcome ω_0 occurs is

$$g_0 = p^{(1)}\lambda(\omega_0, \gamma^{(1)}) + p^{(2)}\lambda(\omega_0, \gamma^{(2)}) \ ,$$

where $\gamma^{(2)}$ is the prediction output by $\mathcal{E}_2$. Let us vary $\gamma^{(2)}$. The weights depend on the previous behaviour of the experts and they cannot be changed. If $\lambda(\omega_0, \gamma^{(2)})$ tends to infinity, then g_0 tends to infinity and therefore the difference $g_0 - \lambda(\omega_0, \gamma^{(1)})$ tends to infinity. Thus the learner cannot compete with the first expert.

This example shows that the WAA cannot be straightforwardly generalised to unbounded games. It needs to be altered.

5.2   Approximating Unbounded Games with Bounded

The following lemma allows us to 'cut off' the infinity at a small cost.

Lemma 2. *Let $\mathfrak{G} = \langle \Omega, \Gamma, \lambda \rangle$ be a game such that $|\Omega| < +\infty$. Then for every $\varepsilon > 0$ there is $L > 0$ with the following property. For every $\gamma \in \Gamma$ there is $\gamma^* \in \Gamma$ such that $\lambda(\omega, \gamma^*) \leq L$ and $\lambda(\omega, \gamma^*) \leq \lambda(\omega, \gamma) + \varepsilon$ for all $\omega \in \Omega$.*

The proof of Lemma 2 is given in Appendix C.

We assume that the game is such that the numbers $L = L_\varepsilon$ can be computed efficiently for every ε and that γ^* can be computed efficiently given $\gamma \in \Gamma$. This is a restriction we impose on games.

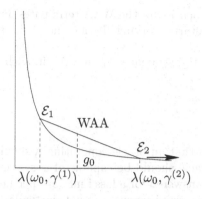

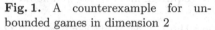

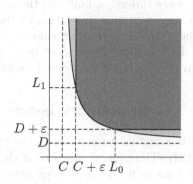

Fig. 1. A counterexample for un-bounded games in dimension 2

Fig. 2. Computing L_ε in the case of two outcomes

In the case of two outcomes $|\Omega| = 2$ computations are particularly straight-forward. See Fig. 2, where

$$C = \inf_{\gamma \in \Gamma} \lambda(\omega^{(0)}, \gamma) \text{ and } D = \inf_{\gamma \in \Gamma} \lambda(\omega^{(1)}, \gamma);$$

we can take $L_\varepsilon = \max(L_0, L_1)$. If γ is such that the point $(\lambda(\omega^{(0)}, \gamma), \lambda(\omega^{(1)}, \gamma))$ falls into the area to the right of the straight line $x = L_0$, we can take γ^* such that $(\lambda(\omega^{(0)}, \gamma^*), \lambda(\omega^{(1)}, \gamma^*)) = (L_0, D + \varepsilon)$.

5.3   Merging Experts in the Unbounded Case

Consider an unbounded game $\mathfrak{G} = \langle \Omega, \Gamma, \lambda \rangle$ and N experts $\mathcal{E}_1, \mathcal{E}_2, \ldots, \mathcal{E}_N$. Fix some $\varepsilon > 0$. Let L_ε be as above. After obtaining experts' predictions $\gamma_t^{(1)}, \gamma_t^{(2)}, \ldots, \gamma_t^{(N)}$ we can find $\gamma_t^{(1)*}, \gamma_t^{(2)*}, \ldots, \gamma_t^{(N)*}$ as in Lemma 2 and then apply the results for the bounded case to them. By proceeding in this fashion, a strategy $\mathfrak{M}$ suffers loss such that

$$\text{Loss}_{\mathfrak{M}}^{\mathfrak{G}}(\omega_1, \omega_2, \ldots, \omega_n) \leq \text{Loss}_{\mathcal{E}^{(i)}}^{\mathfrak{G}}(\omega_1, \omega_2, \ldots, \omega_n) + C_\varepsilon \sqrt{n} + \varepsilon n \qquad (5)$$

for all $i = 1, 2, \ldots, N$ and $\omega_1, \omega_2, \ldots, \omega_n \in \Omega, n = 1, 2, \ldots$, where $C_\varepsilon = 2L_\varepsilon^2 \sqrt{\ln N}$ (we are applying WAA with equal weights).

This inequality does not allow us to prove Theor. 1. In order to achieve an extra term of the order $o(n)$ we will vary ε.

Take a strictly increasing sequence of integers N_k, $k = 1, 2, \ldots$, and a sequence $\varepsilon_k > 0$, $k = 0, 1, 2, \ldots$. Consider the merging strategy $\mathfrak{M}$ defined as follows. The strategy first takes ε_0 and merges the experts' predictions using the WAA and ε_0 in the fashion described above. This continues while n, the length of the sequence of outcomes, is less than or equal to N_1. Then the strategy switches to ε_1 and applies the WAA and ε_1 until n exceeds N_2 etc (see Fig. 4). Note that each time

n passes through a limit N_i, the current invocation of the WAA terminates and a completely new invocation of the WAA starts working. It does not have to inherit anything from previous invocations.

In Appendix D we show how to choose the sequences ε_k and N_k in such a way as to achieve the desired extra term.

6   Computability Issues

In this section we summarise the properties that an oracle computing λ should satisfy. The general principle is that the oracle should be capable of answering all 'reasonable' questions that can be easily answered for a loss function specified by a simple analytical expression. Thus these requirements are not particularly restrictive.

First, the oracle should be able to evaluate the values $\lambda(\omega, \gamma)$, where $\omega \in \Omega$ and $\gamma \in \Gamma$. Secondly, given $x_1, x_2, \ldots, x_n \in [-\infty, +\infty]$, it should be able to find γ (if any) such that $\lambda(\omega^{(i)}, \gamma) \leq x_i$, $i = 1, 2, \ldots, N$. Thirdly, the oracle should be able to compute numbers L_ε and to find γ^* by $\gamma \in \Gamma$ (see Subsect. 5.2).

When we say that the oracle is supplied with a number $x \in [-\infty, +\infty]$, we assume that it is given a sequence of rational intervals I_i that shrinks to x, i.e., $x = \cap_{i=1}^{+\infty} I_i$. A rational interval is one of the intervals $[-\infty, p]$, $[p, q]$, or $[q, +\infty]$, where p and q are rational.

If we say that the oracle outputs $x \in [-\infty, +\infty]$, we mean that it outputs a sequence of rational intervals that shrinks to x. We assume that elements $\gamma \in \Gamma$ can be approximated and dealt with in a similar fashion.

Acknowledgements

We would like to thank participants of the Kolmogorov seminar on complexity theory at the Moscow State University and Alexander Shen in particular for useful suggestions that allowed us to simplify the WAA. We would also like to thank Volodya Vovk for suggesting an idea that helped us to strengthen an upper bound on the performance of WAA.

We are grateful to anonymous COLT reviewers for their detailed comments. Unfortunately, we could not incorporate all their suggestions into the conference version of the paper due to lack of space.

References

[CBFH+97] N. Cesa-Bianchi, Y. Freund, D. Haussler, D. P. Helmbold, R. E. Schapire, and M. K. Warmuth. How to use expert advice. *Journal of the ACM*, 44(3):427–485, 1997.

[HKW98]   D. Haussler, J. Kivinen, and M. K. Warmuth. Sequential prediction of individual sequences under general loss functions. *IEEE Transactions on Information Theory*, 44(5):1906–1925, 1998.

[HP04]   M. Hutter and J. Poland. Predictions with expert advice by following the
           perturbed leader for general weights. In *Algorithmic Learning Theory,
           15th International Conference, ALT 2004, Proceedings*, volume 3244 of
           Lecture Notes in Artificial Intelligence, pages 279–293. Springer, 2004.
[Vov90]   V. Vovk. Aggregating strategies. In M. Fulk and J. Case, editors, *Proceedings of the 3rd Annual Workshop on Computational Learning Theory*,
           pages 371–383, San Mateo, CA, 1990. Morgan Kaufmann.
[Vov98]   V. Vovk. A game of prediction with expert advice. *Journal of Computer
           and System Sciences*, 56:153–173, 1998.

Appendix A. Proof: 'Only If' Part

Here we will derive a statement that is slightly stronger than that required by
Theor. 1.

Theorem 2. *If a game $\mathfrak{G} = \langle \Omega, \Gamma, \lambda \rangle$, $|\Omega| = M < +\infty$, has the set of super-
predictions S such that its finite part $S \cap \mathbb{R}^M$ is not convex, then there are two
strategies $\mathfrak{S}_1$ and $\mathfrak{S}_2$ and a constant $\theta > 0$ such that for any strategy $\mathfrak{S}$ there is
a sequence $\omega_n \in \Omega$, $n = 1, 2, \ldots$, such that*

$$\max_{i=1,2} \left(\mathrm{Loss}_{\mathfrak{G}}^{\mathfrak{G}}(\omega_1, \omega_2, \ldots, \omega_n) - \mathrm{Loss}_{\mathfrak{S}_i}^{\mathfrak{G}}(\omega_1, \omega_2, \ldots, \omega_n) \right) \geq \theta n \qquad (6)$$

for all positive integers n.

If the loss function is computable, the strategies can be chosen to be computable.

Proof. We will use vector notation. If $X = (x_1, \ldots, x_n)$, $Y = (y_1, \ldots, y_n)$ and
$\alpha \in \mathbb{R}$, then $X + Y$ and αX are defined in the natural way. By $\langle X, Y \rangle$ we denote
the scalar product $\sum_{i=1}^{n} x_i y_i$.

For brevity we will denote finite sequences by bold letters, e.g., $\boldsymbol{x} = \omega_1 \ldots \omega_n \in
\Omega^n$. Let $|\boldsymbol{x}|$ be the length of $\boldsymbol{x}$, i.e., the total number of symbols in $\boldsymbol{x}$. We will
denote the number of elements equal to $\omega^{(0)}$ in a sequence $\boldsymbol{x}$ by $\natural_0 \boldsymbol{x}$, the number
of elements equal to $\omega^{(1)}$ by $\natural_1 \boldsymbol{x}$ etc. It is easy to see that $\sum_{i=0}^{M-1} \natural_i \boldsymbol{x} = |\boldsymbol{x}|$ for
every $\boldsymbol{x} \in \Omega^*$. The vector $(\natural_0 \boldsymbol{x}, \natural_1 \boldsymbol{x}, \ldots, \natural_{M-1} \boldsymbol{x})$ will be denoted by $\natural \boldsymbol{x}$.

There exists a couple of points $B_1 = \left(b_1^{(0)}, b_1^{(1)}, \ldots, b_1^{(M-1)} \right)$ and $B_2 =
\left(b_2^{(0)}, b_2^{(1)}, \ldots, b_2^{(M-1)} \right)$ such that $B_1, B_2 \in S \cap \mathbb{R}^M$ but the segment $[B_1, B_2]$ con-
necting them is not a subset of S. Let $\alpha \in (0, 1)$ be such that $C = \alpha B_1 + (1-\alpha) B_2$
does not belong to S (see Fig. 3). Since λ is continuous and Γ is compact, the
set S is closed and thus there is a small vicinity of C that is a subset of $\mathbb{R}^M \setminus S$.

Without restricting the generality one may assume that all coordinates of B_1
and B_2 are strictly positive. Indeed, the points $B_1' = B_1 + t \cdot (1, 1, \ldots, 1)$ and
$B_2' = B_2 + t \cdot (1, 1, \ldots, 1)$ belong to S for all positive t. If $t > 0$ is sufficiently

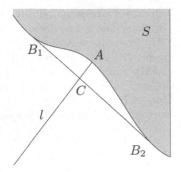

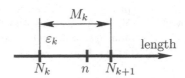

Fig. 3. The drawing for the proof of Theor. 2

Fig. 4. The sequences of N_k, M_k, and ε_k

small, then $C' = \alpha B_1' + (1 - \alpha)B_2'$ still belongs to the vicinity mentioned above and thus C' does not belong to S.

Let us draw a half-line l starting from the origin through C. Let $A = \left(a^{(0)}, a^{(1)}, \ldots, a^{(M-1)}\right)$ be the intersection of l with the boundary ∂S. Such a point really exists. Indeed, $l = \{X \in \mathbb{R}^M \mid \exists t \geq 0 : X = tC\}$. For sufficiently large t all coordinates of tC are greater than the corresponding coordinates of B_1 and thus $tC \in S$. Now let $t_0 = \inf\{t \geq 0 \mid tC \in S\}$ and $A = t_0C$. Since $C \notin S$, we get $t_0 > 1$ and thus $A = (1 + \delta)C$, where $\delta > 0$.

We now proceed to constructing the strategies $\mathfrak{S}_1$ and $\mathfrak{S}_2$. There are predictions $\gamma_1, \gamma_2 \in \Gamma$ such that $\lambda(\omega^{(i)}, \gamma_1) \leq b_1^{(i)}$ and $\lambda(\omega^{(i)}, \gamma_2) \leq b_2^{(i)}$ for all $i = 0, 1, 2, \ldots, M - 1$. Let $\mathfrak{S}_1$ be the oblivious strategy that always predicts γ_1, no matter what outcomes actually occur. Similarly, let $\mathfrak{S}_2$ be the strategy that always predicts γ_2. Without loss of generality it can be assumed that $\mathfrak{S}_1$ and $\mathfrak{S}_2$ are computable. Indeed, the points B_1 and B_2 can be replaced by computable points from their small vicinities. The definitions of $\mathfrak{S}_1$ and $\mathfrak{S}_2$ imply the inequalities

$$\mathrm{Loss}_{\mathfrak{S}_1}(\boldsymbol{x}) \leq \sum_{i=0}^{M-1} \sharp_i \boldsymbol{x} b_1^{(i)} = \langle B_1, \sharp \boldsymbol{x} \rangle \quad \text{and} \quad \mathrm{Loss}_{\mathfrak{S}_2}(\boldsymbol{x}) \leq \sum_{i=0}^{M-1} \sharp_i \boldsymbol{x} b_2^{(i)} = \langle B_2, \sharp \boldsymbol{x} \rangle \tag{7}$$

for all strings $\boldsymbol{x} \in \mathbb{B}^*$.

Now let us consider an arbitrary strategy $\mathfrak{S}$ and construct a sequence $\boldsymbol{x}_n = \omega_1\omega_2\ldots\omega_n$ satisfying the requirements of the theorem. The sequence is constructed by induction. Let $\boldsymbol{x}_0 = \Lambda$. Suppose that $\boldsymbol{x}_n$ has been constructed. Let γ be the prediction output by $\mathfrak{S}$ on the $(n + 1)$-th trial, provided the previous outcomes were elements constituting the strings $\boldsymbol{x}_n$ in the correct order. There is some $\omega^{(i_0)} \in \Omega$ such that $\lambda(\omega^{(i_0)}, \gamma) \geq a^{(i_0)}$. Indeed, if this is not true and the inequalities $\lambda(\omega^{(i)}, \gamma) < a^{(i)}$ hold for all $i = 1, 2, \ldots, M - 1$, then there is a vicinity of A that is a subset of S. This contradicts the definition of A. We let $\boldsymbol{x}_{n+1} = \boldsymbol{x}_n\omega_{i_0}$. The construction implies

$$\mathrm{Loss}_{\mathfrak{G}}(\boldsymbol{x}_n) \geq \sum_{i=0}^{M-1} \natural_i \boldsymbol{x}_n a^{(i)} = \langle A, \natural \boldsymbol{x}_n \rangle \ . \tag{8}$$

Let $\varepsilon = \min_{j=1,2; \ i=0,1,2,\ldots,M-1} b_j^{(i)} > 0$. We get $\langle B_j, \boldsymbol{x} \rangle = \sum_{i=0}^{M-1} b_j^{(i)} \natural_i \boldsymbol{x} \geq \varepsilon|\boldsymbol{x}|$ for all strings $\boldsymbol{x} \in \mathbb{B}^*$ and $j = 1,2$. Since $A = (1+\delta)(\alpha B_1 + (1-\alpha)B_2)$ we get

$$\langle A, \natural \boldsymbol{x} \rangle = (1+\delta)(\alpha \langle B_1, \natural \boldsymbol{x} \rangle + (1-\alpha)\langle B_2, \natural \boldsymbol{x} \rangle)$$
$$\geq \alpha \langle B_1, \natural \boldsymbol{x} \rangle + (1-\alpha)\langle B_2, \natural \boldsymbol{x} \rangle + \delta \varepsilon |\boldsymbol{x}|$$

for all strings $\boldsymbol{x}$. Let $\theta = \delta \varepsilon$; note that ε and δ do not depend on $\mathfrak{G}$. By combining this inequality with (7) and (8) we obtain the inequality

$$\mathrm{Loss}_{\mathfrak{G}}(\boldsymbol{x}_n) \geq \alpha \mathrm{Loss}_{\mathfrak{G}_1}(\boldsymbol{x}_n) + (1-\alpha)\mathrm{Loss}_{\mathfrak{G}_2}(\boldsymbol{x}_n) + \theta n$$

for all positive integers n.

It is easy to see that

$$\mathrm{Loss}_{\mathfrak{G}}(\boldsymbol{x}_n) - \mathrm{Loss}_{\mathfrak{G}_1}(\boldsymbol{x}_n) \geq (1-\alpha)(\mathrm{Loss}_{\mathfrak{G}_2}(\boldsymbol{x}) - \mathrm{Loss}_{\mathfrak{G}_1}(\boldsymbol{x})) + \theta n \ ,$$
$$\mathrm{Loss}_{\mathfrak{G}}(\boldsymbol{x}_n) - \mathrm{Loss}_{\mathfrak{G}_2}(\boldsymbol{x}_n) \geq \alpha(\mathrm{Loss}_{\mathfrak{G}_1}(\boldsymbol{x}) - \mathrm{Loss}_{\mathfrak{G}_2}(\boldsymbol{x})) + \theta n \ .$$

If $\mathrm{Loss}_{\mathfrak{G}_2}(\boldsymbol{x}) \geq \mathrm{Loss}_{\mathfrak{G}_1}(\boldsymbol{x})$ the former difference is greater than or equal to θn, otherwise the latter difference is greater than or equal to θn. By combining these facts we obtain (6).   □

Appendix B. Proof of Lemma 1

In this appendix we prove Lemma 1. We start with the following lemma.

Lemma 3. *Let $\mathfrak{G} = \langle \Omega, \Gamma, \lambda \rangle$ be a game such that $|\Omega| < +\infty$ and let N be the number of experts. Let the finite part of the set of superpredictions $S \cap \mathbb{R}^M$ be convex. If $\mathfrak{M}$ is a merging strategy following the WAA, then for every $t = 1, 2, \ldots$ we get*

$$\beta_t^{\mathrm{Loss}_{\mathfrak{M}}^{\mathfrak{G}}(\omega_1,\ldots,\omega_t)} \geq \beta_t^{\sum_{j=1}^{t} \alpha(j)} \sum_{i=1}^{N} q_i \beta_t^{\mathrm{Loss}_{\mathcal{E}(i)}^{\mathfrak{G}}(\omega_1,\ldots,\omega_t)}, \tag{9}$$

where

$$\alpha(j) = \log_{\beta_j} \frac{\beta_j^{\sum_{i=1}^{N} \lambda(\omega_j, \gamma_j^{(i)}) p_j^{(i)}}}{\sum_{i=1}^{N} \beta_j^{\lambda(\omega_j, \gamma_j^{(i)})} p_j^{(i)}} \tag{10}$$

for $j = 1, 2, \ldots, t$, in the notation introduced above.

Proof (of Lemma 3). The proof is by induction on t. Let us assume that (9) holds and then derive the corresponding inequality for the step $t + 1$.

The function x^α, where $0 < \alpha < 1$, is increasing in x, $x \geq 0$. If is also concave in x, $x \geq 0$. For every set of weights $p_i \in [0,1]$, $i = 1, \ldots, n$ such that $\sum_{i=1}^{n} p_i = 1$ and every array of $x_i \geq 0$, $i = 1, \ldots, n$, we get $\left(\sum_{i=1}^{n} p_i x_i\right)^\alpha \geq \sum_{i=1}^{n} p_i x_i^\alpha$.

Therefore (9) implies

$$\beta_{t+1}^{\mathrm{Loss}_{\mathfrak{M}}^{\mathfrak{G}}(\omega_1,\ldots,\omega_t)} = \left(\beta_t^{\mathrm{Loss}_{\mathfrak{M}}^{\mathfrak{G}}(\omega_1,\ldots,\omega_t)}\right)^{\log_{\beta_t}\beta_{t+1}} \tag{11}$$

$$\geq \left(\beta_t^{\sum_{j=1}^{t}\alpha(j)}\sum_{i=1}^{N} q_i \beta_t^{\mathrm{Loss}_{\mathcal{E}(i)}^{\mathfrak{G}}(\omega_1,\ldots,\omega_t)}\right)^{\log_{\beta_t}\beta_{t+1}} \tag{12}$$

$$\geq \beta_{t+1}^{\sum_{j=1}^{t}\alpha(j)}\sum_{i=1}^{N} q_i \beta_{t+1}^{\mathrm{Loss}_{\mathcal{E}(i)}^{\mathfrak{G}}(\omega_1,\ldots,\omega_t)} \tag{13}$$

Step (7) of the algorithm implies that $\lambda(\omega_{t+1}, \gamma_{t+1}) \leq \sum_{i=1}^{N} \lambda\left(\omega_{t+1}, \gamma_{t+1}^{(i)}\right) p_{t+1}^{(i)}$. By exponentiating this inequality we get

$$\beta_{t+1}^{\lambda(\omega_{t+1},\gamma_{t+1})} \geq \beta_{t+1}^{\sum_{i=1}^{N}\lambda\left(\omega_{t+1},\gamma_{t+1}^{(i)}\right)p_{t+1}^{(i)}} \tag{14}$$

$$= \frac{\beta_{t+1}^{\sum_{i=1}^{N}\lambda\left(\omega_{t+1},\gamma_{t+1}^{(i)}\right)p_{t+1}^{(i)}}}{\sum_{i=1}^{N}\beta_{t+1}^{\lambda\left(\omega_{t+1},\gamma_{t+1}^{(i)}\right)p_{t+1}^{(i)}}}\sum_{i=1}^{N}\beta_{t+1}^{\lambda\left(\omega_{t+1},\gamma_{t+1}^{(i)}\right)p_{t+1}^{(i)}} \tag{15}$$

$$= \beta_{t+1}^{\alpha(t+1)}\sum_{i=1}^{N}\beta_{t+1}^{\lambda\left(\omega_{t+1},\gamma_{t+1}^{(i)}\right)p_{t+1}^{(i)}} . \tag{16}$$

Multiplying (13) by (16) and substituting

$$p_{t+1}^{(i)} = \frac{w_{t+1}}{\sum_{j=1}^{N} w_{t+1}^{(j)}} = \frac{q_i \beta_{t+1}^{\mathrm{Loss}_{\mathcal{E}(i)}^{\mathfrak{G}}(\omega_1,\ldots,\omega_t)}}{\sum_{j=1}^{N} q_j \beta_{t+1}^{\mathrm{Loss}_{\mathcal{E}(j)}^{\mathfrak{G}}(\omega_1,\ldots,\omega_t)}}$$

completes the proof on the lemma.   □

By taking the logarithm of (9) we get

$$\mathrm{Loss}_{\mathfrak{M}}^{\mathfrak{G}}(\omega_1,\ldots,\omega_t) \leq \sum_{j=1}^{t}\alpha(j) + \log_{\beta_t}\sum_{i=1}^{N} q_i \beta_t^{\mathrm{Loss}_{\mathcal{E}(i)}^{\mathfrak{G}}(\omega_1,\ldots,\omega_t)}$$

$$\leq \sum_{j=1}^{t}\alpha(j) + \log_{\beta_t} q_i + \mathrm{Loss}_{\mathcal{E}(i)}^{\mathfrak{G}}(\omega_1,\ldots,\omega_t)$$

for every $i = 1, 2, \ldots, N$. We have $\log_{\beta_t} q_i = -\frac{\sqrt{t}}{c}\ln q_i$. It remains to estimate the first term.

Recall that L is an upper bound on λ. By applying the inequality $\ln x \leq x - 1$ we get

$$
\begin{aligned}
\alpha(t) &= \sum_{i=1}^{N} \lambda(\omega_t, \gamma_t^{(i)}) p_t^{(i)} + \frac{\sqrt{t}}{c} \ln \sum_{i=1}^{N} \beta_t^{\lambda(\omega_t, \gamma_t^{(i)})} p_t^{(i)} \\
&\leq \sum_{i=1}^{N} \lambda(\omega_t, \gamma_t^{(i)}) p_t^{(i)} + \frac{\sqrt{t}}{c} \left(\sum_{i=1}^{N} \beta_t^{\lambda(\omega_t, \gamma_t^{(i)})} p_t^{(i)} - 1 \right)
\end{aligned}
$$

By using Taylor's series with Lagrange's remainder term we obtain

$$
\beta_t^{\lambda(\omega_t, \gamma_t^{(i)})} = e^{-c\lambda(\omega_t, \gamma_t^{(i)})/\sqrt{t}} = 1 - \frac{c\lambda(\omega_t, \gamma_t^{(i)})}{\sqrt{t}} + \frac{1}{2} \left(\frac{c\lambda(\omega_t, \gamma_t^{(i)})}{\sqrt{t}} \right)^2 e^{\xi} \ ,
$$

where $\xi \in [-c\lambda(\omega_t, \gamma_t^{(i)})/\sqrt{t}, 0]$ and thus

$$
\beta_t^{\lambda(\omega_t, \gamma_t^{(i)})} \leq 1 - \frac{c\lambda(\omega_t, \gamma_t^{(i)})}{\sqrt{t}} + \frac{c^2 L^2}{2t} \ .
$$

Therefore $\alpha(t) \leq cL^2/2\sqrt{t}$ and summing yields

$$
\sum_{j=1}^{t} \alpha(j) \leq \sum_{j=1}^{t} \frac{cL^2}{2\sqrt{t}} \leq \frac{cL^2}{2} \int_0^t \frac{dx}{\sqrt{x}} = cL^2\sqrt{t} \ .
$$

This completes the proof.

Appendix C. Proof of Lemma 2

Let $|\Omega| = M$ and $\Omega = \{\omega^{(0)}, \omega^{(1)}, \ldots, \omega^{(M-1)}\}$.

For every $L > 0$ let $\Gamma_L = \{\gamma \in \Gamma \mid \lambda(\omega, \gamma) \leq L \text{ for all } \omega \in \Omega\}$ and let $P_L = \{(\lambda(\omega^{(0)}, \gamma), \lambda(\omega^{(1)}, \gamma), \ldots, \lambda(\omega^{(M-1)}, \gamma)) \mid \gamma \in \Gamma_L\}$. In other terms, $P_L = P \cap [0, L]^M$, where $P = \{(\lambda(\omega^{(0)}, \gamma), \lambda(\omega^{(1)}, \gamma), \ldots, \lambda(\omega^{(M-1)}, \gamma)) \mid \gamma \in \Gamma\}$ is the set of all 'predictions'. For every $\varepsilon > 0$ let $U_{L,\varepsilon}$ be the ε-vicinity of the set P_L, i.e., the union of all open balls of radius ε having points of P_L as their centres. Finally, let $S_{L,\varepsilon} = \{X \in [-\infty, +\infty]^M \mid X \geq Y \text{ for some } Y \in U_{L,\varepsilon}\}$.

Now fix $\varepsilon > 0$. We have $S \subseteq \bigcup_{L>0} S_{L,\varepsilon}$. Indeed, consider a point $X = (\lambda(\omega^{(0)}, \gamma), \lambda(\omega^{(1)}, \gamma), \ldots, \lambda(\omega^{(M-1)}, \gamma))$ for some $\gamma \in \Gamma$. If all coordinates of X are finite, $X \in P_L$ for some sufficiently large L. If some of the coordinates are infinite, γ can still be approximated by predictions that can only lead to finite loss and thus X belongs to some $S_{L,\varepsilon}$.

The covering $\bigcup_{L>0} S_{L,\varepsilon}$ has a finite subcovering. Indeed, let us take some $\beta \in (0,1)$ and apply the transformation $\mathfrak{B}_\beta$ specified by

$$
\mathfrak{B}_\beta(x_0, x_1, \ldots, x_{M-1}) = (\beta^{x_0}, \beta^{x_1}, \ldots, \beta^{x_{M-1}}) \ .
$$

The set $\mathfrak{B}_\beta(S)$ is a compact set and all sets $\mathfrak{B}_\beta(S_{L,\varepsilon})$ are open if considered as subsets of the space $[0, +\infty)^M$ with the standard Euclidean topology.

Therefore there is $L > 0$ such that $S \subseteq S_{L,\varepsilon}$. The lemma follows.

Appendix D. Choosing the Sequences

Take $M_0 = N_1$ and $M_j = N_{j+1} - N_j$, $j = 1, 2 \ldots$. Let a positive integer n be such that $N_k < n \le N_{k+1}$ (see Fig. 4). Applying (5) yields

$$\text{Loss}_{\mathfrak{M}}^{\mathfrak{B}}(\omega_1, \omega_2, \ldots, \omega_n) \le \text{Loss}_{\mathcal{E}^{(i)}}(\omega_1, \omega_2, \ldots, \omega_n) + \alpha(n)$$

for all $i = 1, 2, \ldots, N$, where N is the number of experts and

$$\alpha(n) = \sum_{j=0}^{k} M_j \varepsilon_j + \sum_{j=0}^{k} C_{\varepsilon_j} \sqrt{M_j} + \varepsilon_k(n - N_k) + C_{\varepsilon_k} \sqrt{n - N_k} \; ; \qquad (17)$$

note that the former two terms correspond to the previous invocations of WAA and the later two correspond to the current invocation.

We will formulate conditions sufficient for the terms in (17) to be of $o(n)$ order of magnitude. First, note that

(1) $\lim_{j \to +\infty} \varepsilon_j = 0$

is sufficient to ensure that $\varepsilon_k(n - N_k) = o(n)$ as $n \to +\infty$. Secondly, if, moreover,

(2) M_j is non-decreasing in j and

(3) ε_j is non-increasing,

then $\sum_{j=0}^{k} M_j \varepsilon_j = o(n)$. Indeed, let m be a positive integer such that $m \le k$. Condition (2) implies that $M_m \le n/(k - m + 1)$. Indeed, if $M_m > n/(k - m + 1)$, then the same holds for all M_j, $j \ge m$ and thus $\sum_{j=m}^{k} M_j > n$. We get

$$\frac{1}{n} \sum_{j=0}^{k} M_j \varepsilon_j = \frac{1}{n} \sum_{j=0}^{m} M_j \varepsilon_j + \frac{1}{n} \sum_{j=m+1}^{k} M_j \varepsilon_j$$

$$\le \frac{(m+1) M_m \varepsilon_0}{n} + \frac{\varepsilon_{m+1}}{n} \sum_{j=m+1}^{k} M_j \le \frac{(m+1)\varepsilon_0}{k - m + 1} + \varepsilon_{m+1} \; .$$

If we let $m = \sqrt{k}$, both the terms tend to 0 as k tends to $+\infty$, i.e., as $n \to +\infty$. Thirdly, similar considerations imply that if, moreover,

(4) $\lim_{j \to +\infty} M_j = +\infty$ and

(5) $C_{\varepsilon_j} \le \sqrt[8]{M_j}$, $j = 0, 1, 2, \ldots$,

then $\sum_{j=0}^{k} C_{\varepsilon_j} \sqrt{M_j} \leq \sum_{j=0}^{k} M_j / M_j^{3/8} = o(n)$.

It remains to consider the last term in (17). There are two cases, either $n - N_k \leq M_k^{3/4}$ or $n - N_k > M_k^{3/4}$. If the former case we get

$$\frac{1}{n} C_{\varepsilon_k} \sqrt{n - N_k} \leq \frac{M_k^{1/8} \sqrt{n - N_k}}{N_k} \leq \frac{M_k^{1/8} M_k^{3/8}}{M_{k-1}} = \frac{\sqrt{M_k}}{M_{k-1}} \ ,$$

while in the latter case we get

$$\frac{1}{n} C_{\varepsilon_k} \sqrt{n - N_k} \leq \frac{M_k^{1/8} \sqrt{M_k}}{M_k^{3/4}} = \frac{1}{M_k^{1/8}} \to 0$$

as $k \to +\infty$. To ensure the convergence in the former case it is sufficient to have

(6) $M_{j-1} \geq M_j^{3/4}$, $j = 1, 2, \ldots$.

Let us show that the conditions (1)–(6) are consistent, i.e., construct the sequences ε_j and M_j. Let $M_0 = \max(2, \lceil C_{\varepsilon_0}^8 \rceil)$ and $M_{j+1} = \lceil M_j^{4/3} \rceil$, $j = 0, 1, 2, \ldots$. The sequence ε_j is constructed as follows. Suppose that all ε_j have been constructed for $j \leq k$. If $C_{\varepsilon_k/2} \leq M_k^{1/8}$, we let $\varepsilon_{k+1} = \varepsilon_k/2$; otherwise we let $\varepsilon_{k+1} = \varepsilon_k$. Since $M_k \to +\infty$ and C_ε is finite for every $\varepsilon > 0$, we will be able to divide ε_k by 2 eventually and thus ensure that $\varepsilon_j \to 0$ as $j \to +\infty$.

Tracking the Best of Many Experts*

András György[1], Tamás Linder[2], and Gábor Lugosi[3]

[1] Informatics Laboratory, Computer and Automation Research Institute
of the Hungarian Academy of Sciences,
Lágymányosi u. 11, Budapest, Hungary, H-1111
gya@szit.bme.hu
[2] Department of Mathematics and Statistics,
Queen's University, Kingston, Ontario,
Canada K7L 3N6
linder@mast.queensu.ca
[3] Department of Economics, Universitat Pompeu Fabra,
Ramon Trias Fargas 25-27, 08005 Barcelona, Spain
lugosi@upf.es

Abstract. An algorithm is presented for online prediction that allows
to track the best expert efficiently even if the number of experts is exponentially large, provided that the set of experts has a certain structure
allowing efficient implementations of the exponentially weighted average
predictor. As an example we work out the case where each expert is represented by a path in a directed graph and the loss of each expert is the
sum of the weights over the edges in the path.

1 Introduction

The basic theoretical results of prediction using expert advice were pioneered by
Hannan [7] and Blackwell [2] in the 1950's and brought to the center of attention in learning theory in the 1990's by Vovk [16], Littlestone and Warmuth [11],
Cesa-Bianchi, Freund, Helmbold, Haussler, Schapire, and Warmuth [4]. These
results show that it is possible to construct algorithms for online prediction that
predict an arbitrary sequence of outcomes almost as well as the best of N experts in the sense that the cumulative loss of the predictor is at most as large
as that of the best expert plus a term proportional to $\sqrt{T \ln N}$ for any bounded
loss function, where T is the number of rounds in the prediction game. The
logarithmic dependence on the number of experts makes it possible to obtain
meaningful bounds even if the pool of experts is very large. However, the basic prediction algorithms, such as the exponentially weighted average predictor,

---

* This research was supported in part by the Natural Sciences and Engineering Re-
search Council (NSERC) of Canada, the NATO Science Fellowship of Canada, the
János Bolyai Research Scholarship of the Hungarian Academy of Sciences, Spanish
Ministry of Science and Technology and FEDER, grant BMF2003-03324, and by the
PASCAL Network of Excellence under EC grant no. 506778.

P. Auer and R. Meir (Eds.): COLT 2005, LNAI 3559, pp. 204–216, 2005.

have a computational complexity proportional to the number of experts and are therefore infeasible when the number of experts is very large.

However, in many applications the set of experts has a certain structure that may be exploited to construct efficient prediction algorithms. Perhaps the best known such example is the problem of *tracking the best expert*. In this problem there is a small number of "base" experts and the goal of the predictor is to predict as well as the best of "meta" experts defined by any sequence of $m + 1$ base experts and any partition of the time indexes up to T into $m+1$ contiguous blocks such that in block i a meta expert predicts according to the ith base expert in its defining sequence for $i = 0, \ldots, m$. If there are N base experts and the length of the prediction game is T then the total number of meta experts is $\sum_{k=0}^{m} \binom{T-1}{k} N(N-1)^k$. This problem was solved by Herbster and Warmuth [8] who exhibited computationally efficient algorithms that predict almost as well as the best of the meta experts and have regret bounds that depend on the logarithm of the number of the (meta) experts. Vovk [17] has shown that the forecasters of Herbster and Warmuth correspond to efficient implementations of the exponentially weighted forecaster run over the set of meta experts with a specific choice of the initial weights. We also refer to Auer and Warmuth [1], Bousquet and Warmuth [3], Herbster and Warmuth [9], for various extensions and powerful variants of the problem.

Another class of problems that has been investigated is when, even though no "tracking" is performed, the class of experts is very large and has a certain structure. Examples of structured classes of experts for which efficient algorithms have been constructed include prunings of decision trees (Helmbold and Schapire [5], Pereira and Singer [12]), and planar decision graphs (Takimoto and Warmuth [13]), as well as scalar quantizers for lossy data compression (György, Linder, and Lugosi [6]). These algorithms are all based on efficient implementations of the exponentially weighted average predictor. A different approach was taken by Kalai and Vempala [10] who consider Hannan's original predictor and show that it may be used to obtain efficient algorithms for a large class of problems that they call "geometric experts."

The purpose of this paper is to develop efficient algorithms to track the best expert in the case when the class of "base" experts is already very large and has some structure. Thus, in a sense, we consider a combination of the two types of problems described above. Our approach is based on a suitable modification of the original tracking algorithm of Herbster and Warmuth that allows one to apply it in the case of large, structured expert classes for which there exist efficient implementations of the exponentially weighted average prediction method. This modification is described in Section 2. In Section 3 we illustrate the method on a problem in which a base expert is associated with a path in a directed graph and the loss of a base expert is the sum of the weights over the path (that may change in every time instant). Another application involves "tracking the best quantizer" in lossy zero-delay data compression which we describe elsewhere. We also indicate how the method may be generalized to handle the tracking of general geometric experts.

2   Tracking the Best Expert: A Variation

The aim of this section is to modify the prediction algorithm of Herbster and Warmuth [8] for tracking the best expert to allow efficient implementation if the number of experts is very large. In order to handle cases in which the set of experts is not convex, we consider randomized prediction algorithms.

The online prediction problem considered in this paper is described as follows. Suppose we want to predict the sequence $y_1, \ldots, y_T$ taking values in the set $\mathcal{Y}$ of outcomes using a sequential prediction scheme. We assume that the predictor has access to a sequence $U_1, \ldots, U_T$ of independent random variables distributed uniformly over the interval $[0, 1]$. At each time instant $t = 1, \ldots, T$, the predictor observes U_t, and based on U_t and the past input values $y^{t-1} = (y_1, \ldots, y_{t-1})$ produces an "estimate" $\hat{y}_t \in \hat{\mathcal{Y}}$ of y_t, where $\hat{\mathcal{Y}}$ is the set of predictor actions that may not be the same as $\mathcal{Y}$. Then the predictor can observe the next input symbol y_t. For simplicity we assume throughout that the total number of rounds T is fixed and known to the predictor in advance.

Formally, the prediction game is defined as follows:

Parameters: number N of base experts, outcome space $\mathcal{Y}$, action space $\hat{\mathcal{Y}}$, loss function $\ell : \mathcal{Y} \times \hat{\mathcal{Y}} \to [0, 1]$, number T of rounds.

For each round $t = 1, \ldots, T$,

(1) each (base) expert forms its prediction $f_{i,t} \in \hat{\mathcal{Y}}$, $i = 1, \ldots, N$;
(2) the forecaster observes the predictions of the base experts and the random variable U_t and chooses an estimate $\hat{y}_t \in \hat{\mathcal{Y}}$;
(3) the environment reveals the next outcome $y_t \in \mathcal{Y}$.

The *cumulative loss* of the sequential scheme at time T is given by

$$L_T = \sum_{t=1}^{T} \ell(y_t, \hat{y}_t) \ .$$

The goal of the predictor is to achieve a cumulative loss (almost) as small as the best tracking of the N base experts. More precisely, to describe the loss the predictor is compared to, consider the following "m-partition" prediction scheme: The sequence of examples is partitioned into $m + 1$ contiguous segments, and on each segment the scheme assigns exactly one of the N base experts. Formally, an m-partition $\mathcal{P}(T, m, \mathbf{t}, \mathbf{e})$ of the T samples is given by an m-tuple $\mathbf{t} = (t_1, \ldots, t_m)$ such that $t_0 = 1 < t_1 < \cdots < t_m < T + 1 = t_{m+1}$, and an $(m + 1)$-vector $\mathbf{e} = (e_0, \ldots, e_m)$ where $e_i \in \{1, \ldots, N\}$. At each time instant t, $t_i \le t < t_{i+1}$, expert e_i is used to predict y_t. The cumulative loss of a partition $\mathcal{P}_{T,m,\mathbf{t},\mathbf{e}}$ is

$$L(\mathcal{P}(T, m, \mathbf{t}, \mathbf{e})) = \sum_{i=0}^{m} \sum_{t=t_i}^{t_{i+1}-1} \ell(y_t, f_{e_i,t}) = \sum_{i=0}^{m} L([t_i, t_{i+1} - 1], e_i)$$

where for any time interval I, $L(I, i) = \sum_{t \in I} \ell(y_t, f_{i,t})$ denotes the cumulative loss of expert i in I. Here and later in the paper we adopt the convention that in case a summation is empty, we define the sum to be zero (e.g., for $a > b$, $L([a, b], i) = 0$ by definition).

The goal of the predictor is to perform as well as the best partition, that is, to keep the normalized regret

$$\frac{1}{T}\left(L_T - \min_{\mathbf{t}, \mathbf{e}} L(\mathcal{P}(T, m, \mathbf{t}, \mathbf{e}))\right)$$

as small as possible (with high probability) for all possible outcome sequences.

Next we present a variation of the "fixed-share" share update algorithm of Herbster and Warmuth [8].

Algorithm 1. *Fix the positive numbers η and $\alpha < 1$, and initialize weights $w_{1,i}^s = 1/N$ for $i = 1, \ldots, N$. At time instants $t = 1, 2, \ldots, T$ let $v_t^{(i)} = w_{t,i}^s / W_t$ where $W_t = \sum_{i=1}^{N} w_{t,i}^s$, and predict $\hat{y}_t$ randomly according to the distribution*

$$\mathbb{P}\{\hat{y}_t = f_{i,t}\} = v_t^{(i)}. \tag{1}$$

After observing y_t, for all $i = 1, \ldots, N$, let

$$w_{t,i}^m = w_{t,i}^s e^{-\eta \ell(y_t, f_{i,t})} \tag{2}$$

and

$$w_{t+1,i}^s = \frac{\alpha W_{t+1}}{N} + (1 - \alpha) w_{t,i}^m \tag{3}$$

where $W_{t+1} = \sum_{i=1}^{N} w_{t,i}^m$.

Observe that $\sum_{i=1}^{N} w_{t+1,i}^s = \sum_{i=1}^{N} w_{t,i}^m = W_{t+1}$, thus there is no ambiguity in the definition of W_{t+1}. Note that equation (3) is slightly changed compared to the original algorithm of [8].

First we present a bound on the loss of the algorithm. The proof is a straightforward adaptation of the proof of [8] and therefore it is omitted.

Theorem 1. *For any positive integers m, T, real numbers $0 < \alpha < 1$, $\eta > 0$, and $\delta \in (0, 1)$, and for any sequence $y_1, \ldots, y_T$ taking values from $[0, 1]$, with probability at least $1 - \delta$, the regret L_T of Algorithm 1 can be bounded as*

$$L_T - \min_{\mathbf{t}, \mathbf{e}} L(\mathcal{P}(T, m, \mathbf{t}, \mathbf{e}))$$

$$\leq \frac{1}{\eta} \ln\left(\frac{N^{m+1}}{\alpha^m (1-\alpha)^{T-m-1}}\right) + \frac{T\eta}{8} + \sqrt{\frac{T \ln(1/\delta)}{2}}. \tag{4}$$

In particular, if $\alpha = \frac{m}{T-1}$ and $\eta = \sqrt{8 \ln \left(\frac{N^{m+1}}{\alpha^m (1-\alpha)^{T-m-1}} \right) / T}$ is chosen to mini-
mize the above bound, we have

$$L_T - \min_{\mathbf{t,e}} L(\mathcal{P}(T,m,\mathbf{t},\mathbf{e}))$$

$$\leq \sqrt{\frac{T}{2}} \sqrt{(m+1) \ln N + m \ln \frac{T-1}{m} + m} + \sqrt{\frac{T \ln(1/\delta)}{2}} \ . \qquad (5)$$

Remark. If the number of experts N is proportional to T^γ for some $\gamma > 0$, then, for any fixed $\delta > 0$, the bound in (5) is of order $\sqrt{(mT) \ln T}$ for large T, and so the normalized regret is

$$\frac{1}{T} \left(L_T - \min_{\mathbf{t,e}} L(\mathcal{P}(T,m,\mathbf{t},\mathbf{e})) \right) = O \left(\sqrt{(m/T) \ln T} \right)$$

with probability at least $1 - \delta$. That is, the rate of convergence is the same (up to a constant factor) as if we competed with the best static expert on a segment of average length.

2.1   Implementation of Algorithm 1

If the number of experts N is large, for example, $N = T^\gamma$ for some large $\gamma > 1$, then the implementation of Algorithm 1 may become computationally very hard. As it is mentioned in the introduction, for several large classes of (base) experts, efficient algorithms are known to compute the exponentially weighted average predictor when no tracking is performed. The purpose of this section is to show that, whenever such an efficient algorithm is available, the tracking forecaster can also be computed efficiently by implementing Algorithm 1 in a computationally feasible way.

The main step to this direction is an alternative expression of the weights in Algorithm 1.

Lemma 1. *For any $t = 2, \ldots, T$, the probability $v_t^{(i)}$ and the corresponding normalization factor W_t can be obtained as*

$$v_t^{(i)} = \frac{(1-\alpha)^{t-1}}{NW_t} e^{-\eta L([1,t-1],i)} + \frac{\alpha}{NW_t} \sum_{t'=2}^{t-1} (1-\alpha)^{t-t'} W_{t'} e^{-\eta L([t',t-1],i)} + \frac{\alpha}{N} \quad (6)$$

$$W_t = \frac{\alpha}{N} \sum_{t'=2}^{t-1} (1-\alpha)^{t-1-t'} W_{t'} Z_{t',t-1} + \frac{(1-\alpha)^{t-2}}{N} Z_{1,t-1} \qquad (7)$$

where $Z_{t',t-1} = \sum_{i=1}^{N} e^{-\eta L([t',t-1],i)}$ is the sum of the (unnormalized) weights assigned to the experts by the exponentially weighted prediction method for the input samples $(y_{t'}, \ldots, y_{t-1})$.

Proof. The expressions in the lemma follow directly from the recursive definition of the weights $\{w_{t,i}^s\}$. First we show that for $t = 1, \ldots, T$,

$$w_{t,i}^m = \frac{\alpha}{N} \sum_{t'=2}^{t} (1-\alpha)^{t-t'} W_{t'} e^{-\eta L([t',t],i)} + \frac{(1-\alpha)^{t-1}}{N} e^{-\eta L([1,t],i)} \tag{8}$$

$$w_{t+1,i}^s = \frac{\alpha}{N} W_{t+1} + \frac{\alpha}{N} \sum_{t'=2}^{t} (1-\alpha)^{t+1-t'} W_{t'} e^{-\eta L([t',t],i)} + \frac{(1-\alpha)^t}{N} e^{-\eta L([1,t],i)}. \tag{9}$$

Clearly, for a given t, (8) implies (9) by the definition (3). Since $w_{1,i}^s = 1/N$ for every expert i, (8) and (9) hold for $t = 1$ and $t = 2$ (for $t = 1$ the summations are 0 in both equations). Now assume that they hold for some $t \geq 2$. We show that then (8) holds for $t + 1$. By definition,

$$w_{t+1,i}^m = w_{t+1,i}^s e^{-\eta \ell(y_{t+1}, f_{i,t+1})}$$

$$= \frac{\alpha}{N} W_{t+1} e^{-\eta \ell(y_{t+1}, f_{i,t+1})} + \frac{\alpha}{N} \sum_{t'=2}^{t} (1-\alpha)^{t+1-t'} W_{t'} e^{-\eta L([t',t+1],i)}$$

$$+ \frac{(1-\alpha)^t}{N} e^{-\eta L([1,t+1],i)}$$

$$= \frac{\alpha}{N} \sum_{t'=2}^{t+1} (1-\alpha)^{t+1-t'} W_{t'} e^{-\eta L([t',t+1],i)} + \frac{(1-\alpha)^t}{N} e^{-\eta L([1,t+1],i)}$$

thus (8) and (9) hold for all $t = 1, \ldots, T$. Now (6) follows from (9) by normalization for $t = 2, \ldots, T+1$. Finally, (7) can easily be proved from (8), as for any $t = 2, \ldots, T$,

$$W_t = \sum_{i=1}^{N} w_{t-1,i}^m$$

$$= \sum_{i=1}^{N} \left(\frac{\alpha}{N} \sum_{t'=2}^{t-1} (1-\alpha)^{t-1-t'} W_{t'} e^{-\eta L([t',t-1],i)} + \frac{(1-\alpha)^{t-2}}{N} e^{-\eta L([1,t-1],i)} \right)$$

$$= \frac{\alpha}{N} \sum_{t'=2}^{t-1} (1-\alpha)^{t-1-t'} W_{t'} \sum_{i=1}^{N} e^{-\eta L([t',t-1],i)} + \frac{(1-\alpha)^{t-2}}{N} \sum_{i=1}^{N} e^{-\eta L([1,t-1],i)}$$

$$= \frac{\alpha}{N} \sum_{t'=2}^{t-1} (1-\alpha)^{t-1-t'} W_{t'} Z_{t',t-1} + \frac{(1-\alpha)^{t-2}}{N} Z_{1,t-1}.$$

$\square$

Examining formula (6), one can see that the t'-th term in the summation (including the first and last individual terms) is some multiple of $e^{-\eta L([t',t-1],i)}$. The latter expression is the weight assigned to expert i by the exponentially weighted prediction method for the last $t - t'$ samples of the sequence, that is, for $(y_{t'}, \ldots, y_{t-1})$ (the last term in the summation corresponds to the case where no previous samples of the sequence are taken into consideration). Therefore, for $t \geq 2$, the random choice (1) of a predictor can be performed in two steps. First we choose a random time τ_t, which specifies how many most recent samples we are going to use for the prediction. Then we choose the predictor according to the exponentially weighted prediction for these samples. Thus, $\mathbb{P}\{\tau_t = t'\}$ is the sum of the t'-th terms with respect to the index i in the expressions for $v_t^{(i)}$, and given $\tau_t = t'$, the probability that $\hat{y}_t = f_{i,t}$ is just the probability assigned to expert i using the exponentially weighted average prediction based on the samples $(y_{t'}, \ldots, y_{t-1})$. Hence we obtain the following algorithm.

Algorithm 2. *For $t = 1$, choose $\hat{y}_1$ uniformly from the set $\{f_{1,1}, \ldots, f_{N,1}\}$. For $t \geq 2$, choose τ_t randomly according to the distribution*

$$\mathbb{P}\{\tau_t = t'\} = \begin{cases} \frac{(1-\alpha)^{t-1}Z_{1,t-1}}{NW_t}, & \text{for } t' = 1 \\ \frac{\alpha(1-\alpha)^{t-t'}W_{t'}Z_{t',t-1}}{NW_t} & \text{for } t' = 2, \ldots, t \end{cases} \tag{10}$$

where we define $Z_{t,t-1} = N$. Given $\tau_t = t'$, choose $\hat{y}_t$ randomly according to the probabilities

$$\mathbb{P}\{\hat{y}_t = f_{i,t}|\tau_t = t'\} = \begin{cases} \frac{e^{-\eta L([t',t-1],i)}}{Z_{t',t-1}} & \text{for } t' = 1, \ldots, t-1 \\ \frac{1}{N} & \text{for } t' = t \end{cases} \tag{11}$$

The discussion preceding the algorithm shows that Algorithm 2 provides an alternative implementation of Algorithm 1.

Theorem 2. *Algorithm 1 and Algorithm 2 are equivalent in the sense that the generated predictor sequences have the same distribution. In particular, the sequence $(\hat{y}_1, \ldots, \hat{y}_T)$ generated by Algorithm 2 satisfies*

$$\mathbb{P}\{\hat{y}_t = f_{i,t}\} = v_t^{(i)} \tag{12}$$

for all t and i, where $v_t^{(i)}$ are the normalized weights generated by Algorithm 1.

It is not immediately obvious why Algorithm 2 is more efficient than Algorithm 1. However, in many cases the probabilities $\mathbb{P}\{\hat{y}_t = f_{i,t}|\tau_t = t'\}$ and normalization factors $Z_{t',t-1}$ may be computed efficiently, and in all those cases, since W_t can be obtained via the recursion formula (7), Algorithm 2 becomes feasible.

We need the following assumptions: For a given set of N (base) experts,

(a) the exponentially weighted average prediction method can be implemented in $O(g(T))$ time, that is, for time instants $t = 1, \ldots, T$, predictions $\hat{y}_1, \ldots, \hat{y}_T$

can be chosen sequentially according to the probabilities $\mathbb{P}\{\hat{y}_t = f_{i,t}\} = e^{-\eta L([1,t-1],i)}$ in $O(g(T))$ time for any $\eta > 0$;

(b) the sums of the weights $Z_{t-1} = \sum_{i=1}^{N} e^{-\eta L([1,t-1],i)}$ can be computed in $O(g(T))$ time for $t = 1, \ldots, T$.

Note that condition (b) is implied by the following two natural assumptions, which are often satisfied as byproducts of the efficient implementation of the exponentially weighted prediction method according to (a): for $t = 1, \ldots, T$,

(c_1) $\mathbb{P}\{\hat{y}_t = f_{i_t,t}\}$ can be computed for the chosen expert i_t (that is, $\hat{y}_t = f_{i_t,t}$) in $O(g(T))$ time;

(c_2) the cumulative losses $L([1,t-1], i_t)$ of the chosen experts i_t can be computed in $O(g(T))$ time.

Then Z_{t-1} can be calculated as $Z_{t-1} = e^{-\eta L([1,t-1],i_t)}/\mathbb{P}\{\hat{y}_t = f_{i_t,t}\}$.

The next theorem shows that, under assumptions (a) and (b) on the class of the base experts, Algorithm 2 can be implemented efficiently, and thus tracking can be performed with low computational complexity.

Theorem 3. *Assume that for the set of base experts conditions (a) and (b) are satisfied. Then Algorithm 2 can be implemented in $O\left(T^2 + \sum_{t=1}^{T} g(t)\right)$ time for T rounds.*

Proof. For $t = 1$ choose $\hat{y}_1$ uniformly from $\{f_{1,1}, \ldots, f_{N,1}\}$, and set $W_1 = 1$. For each $t = 2, \ldots, T$, run the exponentially weighted prediction algorithm for the base experts with the reverse set of examples $y_{t-1}, \ldots, y_1$ as input data and compute the constants $Z_{t',t-1}$ for all $t' = 1, \ldots, t-1$ in $O(g(t))$ time. Then compute W_t from $Z_{1,t-1}, \ldots, Z_{t,t-1}$ (recall that $Z_{t,t-1} = N$) and $W_1, \ldots, W_{t-1}$ according to (7) in $O(t)$ time. Then the choice of τ_t according to (10) can be performed in $O(t)$ time, and the prediction according to (11) can be chosen in $O(g(t))$ time. Thus, at time instant t, $O(g(t)) + O(t)$ computations are required, giving overall computational complexity $O(T^2 + \sum_{t=1}^{T} g(t))$. □

We illustrate the use of this algorithm in just one special case when the losses of the base experts are given by weights of a path in a directed graph. This application, that is, in a sense, a generic example, should serve as an illustration. In the full version of the paper other examples will be given.

3 Minimum Weight Path in a Directed Graph

In this section we present an application of Algorithm 2 where the constants $Z_{t',t}$ can be computed efficiently as discussed at the end of the previous section. We consider the problem of tracking the minimum-weight path of a given length in a weighted directed graph. Other efficient implementations of exponentially weighted prediction methods, such as for finding the minimum weight path (of

unrestricted length) in a weighted directed acyclic graph in Takimoto and Warmuth [14],[15], can also be combined with our tracking method in a similar way.

Formally, we have a directed graph $(\mathcal{V}, \mathcal{E})$, where $\mathcal{V}$ and $\mathcal{E}$ denote the set
of nodes and edges, respectively. Given a fixed pair of nodes s and u, let $\mathcal{R}_M$
denote the set of all directed paths of length M from s to u, let $N = |\mathcal{R}_M|$
denote the number of such paths, and assume that $\mathcal{R}_M$ is not empty (that is,
$N > 0$). We also assume that for all $z \neq u$, $z \in \mathcal{V}$, there is an edge starting
from z. (Otherwise node z is of no use in finding a path from s to u, and all
such nodes can be removed from the graph at the beginning of the algorithm in
$O(|\mathcal{V}|) + O(|\mathcal{E}|)$ time, parallel with reading the description of the graph.) At time
instants $t = 1, 2, \ldots$ the predictor picks a path $\hat{y}_t \in \mathcal{R}_M$. The cost of this path is
the sum of the weights $\delta_t(a)$ on the edges a of the path (the weights are assumed
to be nonnegative real numbers), which are revealed for each $a \in \mathcal{E}$ only after
the path has been chosen. To use our previous definition for prediction, we may
define $y_t = \{\delta_t(a)\}_{a \in \mathcal{E}}$, and the loss function as

$$\ell(y_t, \hat{y}_t) = \sum_{a \in \hat{y}_t} \delta_t(a)$$

for each pair $(y_t, \hat{y}_t)$. The cumulative loss at time instant T is given as

$$L_T = \sum_{t=1}^{T} \ell(y_t, \hat{y}_t).$$

Our goal is to perform as well as the best combination of paths (base experts)
which is allowed to change the path m times during time instants $t = 1, \ldots, T$.
As in the prediction context, such a combination is given as an m-partition
$\mathcal{P}(T, m, \mathbf{t}, \mathbf{e})$, where $\mathbf{t} = (t_1, \ldots, t_m)$ such that $t_0 = 1 < t_1 < \cdots < t_m < t_{m+1} =
T + 1$, and $\mathbf{e} = (e_0, \ldots, e_m)$, where $e_i \in \mathcal{R}_M$ (that is, expert $e \in \mathcal{R}_M$ predicts
$f_{e,t} = e$). The cumulative loss of a partition $\mathcal{P}(T, m, \mathbf{t}, \mathbf{e})$ is

$$L(\mathcal{P}(T, m, \mathbf{t}, \mathbf{e})) = \sum_{i=0}^{m} \sum_{t=t_i}^{t_{i+1}-1} \ell(y_t, e_i) = \sum_{i=0}^{m} \sum_{t=t_i}^{t_{i+1}-1} \sum_{a \in e_i} \delta_t(a).$$

Now Algorithms 1 and 2 can be used to choose the path $\hat{y}_t$ randomly at each
time instant $t = 1, \ldots, T$, and the regret

$$L_T - \min_{\mathbf{t}, \mathbf{e}} L(\mathcal{P}(T, m, \mathbf{t}, \mathbf{e}))$$

can be bounded by Theorem 1. The question is whether in this setup we can compute efficiently a path based on the exponentially weighted prediction method
and the constants $Z_{t',t}$. The following theorem gives a positive answer.

Theorem 4. *For the minimum weight path problem described in this section,
Algorithm 2 can be implemented in $O(T^2 M |\mathcal{E}|)$ time. If $\alpha = m/(T-1)$, $\delta_t(a) <
1/M$ for all time instants t and edges $a \in \mathcal{E}$, and $\eta = \sqrt{8 \ln \left(\frac{N^{m+1}}{\alpha^m (1-\alpha)^{T-m-1}} \right)} / T$,*

then the regret of the algorithm can be bounded from above, with probability at least $1 - \delta$, as

$$L_T - \min_{\mathbf{t}, \mathbf{e}} L(\mathcal{P}(T, m, \mathbf{t}, \mathbf{e}))$$

$$\leq \sqrt{\frac{T}{2}} \sqrt{(m+1) \ln N + m \ln \frac{T-1}{m} + m} + \sqrt{\frac{T \ln(1/\delta)}{2}} .$$

Proof. The bound in the theorem follows trivially from the optimized bound (5) in Theorem 1. All we need to show is that the algorithm can be implemented in $O(T^2 M |\mathcal{E}|)$ time. To do this, we show that the exponentially weighted average prediction method for T rounds can be implemented in $O(TM|\mathcal{E}|)$ time for the above described minimum weight path problem. Then the result follows by Theorem 3. In the following we modify the algorithm of György, Linder, and Lugosi [6] to choose a path $\hat{y}_t$ randomly based on $(y_1, y_2, \ldots, y_{t-1})$ (that is, based on the weights $\{\delta_j(a)\}_{a \in \mathcal{E}}, j \in [1, t-1]$) according to the probabilities

$$\mathbb{P}\{\hat{y}_t = r\} = \frac{e^{-\eta \sum_{a \in r} \Delta_{t-1}(a)}}{\sum_{r' \in \mathcal{R}_M} e^{-\eta \sum_{a \in r'} \Delta_{t-1}(a)}} \tag{13}$$

where $\Delta_{t-1}(a) = \sum_{j=1}^{t-1} \delta_j(a)$, and compute

$$Z_{t-1} = \sum_{r \in \mathcal{R}_M} e^{-\eta \sum_{a \in r} \Delta_{t-1}(a)}.$$

We show that for $t = 1, \ldots, T$, this can be done in $O(TM|\mathcal{E}|)$ time, yielding that the problem satisfies conditions (a) and (b) with $g(T) = TM|\mathcal{E}|$.

For any $z \in \mathcal{V}$ and $k = 1, \ldots, M$, let $\mathcal{R}_k^z$ denote the set of paths of length k from z to u, and let $G_{t-1}(z, k)$ denote the sum of the exponential cumulative losses in the interval $[1, t-1]$ of all paths in $\mathcal{R}_k^z$. Formally, if $\mathcal{R}_k^z$ is empty then we define $G_{t-1}(z, k) = 0$, otherwise

$$G_{t-1}(z, k) = \sum_{r \in \mathcal{R}_k^z} e^{-\eta \sum_{a \in r} \Delta_{t', t-1}(a)}. \tag{14}$$

The function $G_{t-1}(z, k)$ will prove useful in computing Z_{t-1}, as $Z_{t-1} = G_{t-1}(s, M)$, and in drawing $\hat{y}_t$ randomly for a given τ_t: Instead of computing the cumulative losses $\sum_{a \in r} \Delta_{t-1}(a)$ for all $r \in \mathcal{R}_M$ (needed by (13)), following the algorithm of [6], we can draw the path $\hat{y}_t$ by drawing its edges successively. Denote the jth node along a path $r \in \mathcal{R}_M$ by $z_{r,j}$ for $j = 0, \ldots, M$, where $z_{r,0} = s$ and $z_{r,M} = u$. Then, for any $k = 1, \ldots, M-1$, the probability that the kth node in the path $\hat{y}_t$ is z_k given that the previous nodes are $z_0, z_1, \ldots, z_{k-1}$ is given by

$$\mathbb{P}\{z_{\hat{y}_t,k} = z_k | z_{\hat{y}_t,j} = z_j, j = 0, \ldots, k-1\}$$

$$= \frac{\mathbb{P}\{z_{\hat{y}_t,j} = z_j, j = 0, \ldots, k\}}{\mathbb{P}\{z_{\hat{y}_t,j} = z_j, j = 0, \ldots, k-1\}}$$

$$= \frac{\sum_{r:z_{r,i}=z_i, i=0,\ldots,k} e^{-\eta \sum_{j=1}^{M} \Delta_{t-1}((z_{r,j-1},z_{r,j}))}}{\sum_{r:z_{r,i}=z_i, i=0,\ldots,k-1} e^{-\eta \sum_{j=1}^{M} \Delta_{t-1}((z_{r,j-1},z_{r,j}))}}$$

$$= e^{-\eta \Delta_{t-1}((z_{k-1},z_k))} \frac{G_{t-1}(z_k, M-k)}{G_{t-1}(z_{k-1}, M-k+1)}. \tag{15}$$

Therefore, given the functions Δ_{t-1} and G_{t-1}, $\hat{y}_t$ and its probability can be computed in $O(M|\mathcal{V}|)$ steps using the exponentially weighted average prediction method.

Next we show how to compute G_{t-1}. For any node $z \in \mathcal{V}$, let $\mathcal{E}(z)$ denote the set of edges starting at z. As any path of length $k \geq 2$ can be decomposed as the first edge in the path and the remaining path of length $k-1$, it is easy to see that for any $M \geq k \geq 2$, $G_{t-1}(z,k)$ can be computed recursively as

$$G_{t-1}(z,k) = \sum_{\hat{z}:(z,\hat{z})\in\mathcal{E}(z)} G_{t-1}(\hat{z}, k-1) e^{-\eta \Delta_{t-1}((z,\hat{z}))} \tag{16}$$

and

$$G_{t-1}(z,1) = \begin{cases} e^{-\eta \Delta_{t-1}((z,u))} & \text{if } (z,u) \in \mathcal{E}; \\ 0 & \text{otherwise.} \end{cases}$$

When calculating (16) for a given k, each edge is taken into consideration exactly once (and we have to do the update of G for each node). Thus, assuming that the cumulative weights $\Delta_{t-1}(a)$ are known for each edge $a \in \mathcal{E}$, the computational cost of calculating $G_{t-1}(z,k)$ for a given k is $O(|\mathcal{E}|) + O(|\mathcal{V}|) = O(|\mathcal{E}|)$ (as by assumption, $|\mathcal{E}| \geq |\mathcal{V}| - 1$). Therefore, the computational complexity of calculating $G_{t-1}(z,k)$ for all z and k, given the cumulative weights $\Delta_{t-1}(a)$ are known, is $O(M|\mathcal{E}|)$. Now as t increases from 1 to T, if we store the cumulative weights $\Delta_{t-1}(a)$ for each edge a, then only $O(|\mathcal{E}|)$ computations are needed to update the cumulative weights at the edges for each value of t. Therefore, calculating $G_{t-1}(z,k)$ for all $z \in \mathcal{V}$, $1 \leq k \leq M$, and $t = 1, \ldots, T$ requires $O(TM|\mathcal{E}|)$ computations. This shows that conditions (a) and (b) are satisfied for this problem with $g(T) = TM|\mathcal{E}|$. Applying Theorem 3 finishes the proof. □

Remarks

(i) If we assume that the graph contains no cycle with a negative weight at any time instant, then the minimum weight path (of unrestricted length) is of length at most $|\mathcal{V} - 1|$. Therefore, the algorithm can easily be modified to compete with paths of unrestricted length. All we require is an additional cycle in which M goes from 1 to $|\mathcal{V}| - 1$ to examine all possible paths. Then, in the random choice of the path, after choosing τ_t, we randomly decide the length of the path and choose a path of that length using exponential weighting. The bound on the regret remains the same as in Theorem 4; the price we pay is an increase in the complexity of the algorithm which becomes $O(T^2|\mathcal{V}|^2|\mathcal{E}|)$.

(ii) If the graph is acyclic, then the above algorithm can be simplified as there is no need to keep track the second parameter of the function G_{t-1} (this is basically an application of the weight pushing algorithm of Takimoto and Warmuth [14],[15] to the graph for the time interval $[1, t-1]$). Then the minimum weight path (of unrestricted length) can be tracked in $O(T^2 |\mathcal{E}|)$ time, while the bound on the regret still holds.

(iii) It is also possible to apply the above algorithm for tracking the best geometric expert. A geometric expert is a combination of "sub-experts" from a given set, such that the loss of a geometric expert equals the sum of the losses of its "sub-experts"; however, not all possible combinations of the "sub-experts" are allowed (for a formal definition of the problem, see Kalai and Vempala [10]). An example of the geometric expert problem is the minimum weight path problem in a graph, where the "sub-experts" are the edges and the allowed geometric (combined) experts are the paths. However, the geometric expert problem can also be treated as a special case of the minimum weight path problem, as one can easily construct a graph such that there is a one-to-one correspondence between paths of the graph (between to given nodes) and the allowed geometric experts: each edge of the graph corresponds to a "sub-expert", and each path corresponds to the geometric expert combined from the "sub-experts" corresponding to its edges. Note that usually several edges correspond to each "sub-expert". In this way it is possible to track the best geometric expert using the graph algorithms of this section. However, the complexity of the algorithm depends heavily on the number of edges of the graph, and it is not clear at all how one can create a graph with a minimum number of edges for a given set of geometric experts.

References

1. P. Auer and M.K. Warmuth. Tracking the best disjunction. *Machine Learning*, 32(2):127–150, 1998.
2. D. Blackwell. An analog of the minimax theorem for vector payoffs. *Pacific Journal of Mathematics*, 6:1–8, 1956.
3. O. Bousquet and M. K. Warmuth. Tracking a small set of experts by mixing past posteriors. *Journal of Machine Learning Research*, 3:363–396, Nov. 2002.
4. N. Cesa-Bianchi, Y. Freund, D. P. Helmbold, D. Haussler, R. Schapire, and M. K. Warmuth. How to use expert advice. *Journal of the ACM*, 44(3):427–485, 1997.
5. R.E. Schapire D.P. Helmbold. Predicting nearly as well as the best pruning of a decision tree. *Machine Learning*, 27:51–68, 1997.
6. A. György, T. Linder, and G. Lugosi. Efficient algorithms and minimax bounds for zero-delay lossy source coding. *IEEE Transactions on Signal Processing*, pages 2337–2347, Aug. 2004.
7. J. Hannan. Approximation to Bayes risk in repeated plays. In M. Dresher, A. Tucker, and P. Wolfe, editors, *Contributions to the Theory of Games*, volume 3, pages 97–139. Princeton University Press, 1957.
8. M. Herbster and M. K. Warmuth. Tracking the best expert. *Machine Learning*, pages 1–29, 1998.
9. M. Herbster and M.K. Warmuth. Tracking the best linear predictor. *Journal of Machine Learning Research*, 1:281–309, 2001.

10. A. Kalai and S. Vempala. Efficient algorithms for online decision problems. In B. Schölkopf and M. K. Warmuth, editors, *COLT 2003*, LNAI 2777, pages 26–40, Berlin–Heidelberg, 2003. Springer-Verlag.
11. N. Littlestone and M. K. Warmuth. The weighted majority algorithm. *Information and Computation*, 108:212–261, 1994.
12. F. Pereira and Y. Singer. An efficient extension to mixture techniques for prediction and decision trees. *Machine Learning*, 36:183–199, 1999.
13. E. Takimoto and M. Warmuth. Predicting nearly as well as the best pruning of a planar decision graph. *Theoretical Computer Science*, 288:217–235, 2002.
14. E. Takimoto and M. K. Warmuth. Path kernels and multiplicative updates. In J. Kivinen and R. H. Sloan, editors, *COLT 2002*, LNAI 2375, pages 74–89, Berlin–Heidelberg, 2002. Springer-Verlag.
15. E. Takimoto and M. K. Warmuth, "Path kernels and multiplicative updates," *Journal of Machine Learning Research*, vol. 4, pages 773–818, 2003.
16. V. Vovk. Aggregating strategies. In *Proceedings of the Third Annual Workshop on Computational Learning Theory*, pages 372–383, New York, 1990. Association of Computing Machinery.
17. V. Vovk. Derandomizing stochastic prediction strategies. *Machine Learning*, 35(3):247–282, 1999.

Improved Second-Order Bounds
for Prediction with Expert Advice*

Nicolò Cesa-Bianchi[1], Yishay Mansour[2,**], and Gilles Stoltz[3]

[1] DSI, Università di Milano, via Comelico 39, 20135 Milano, Italy
cesa-bianchi@dsi.unimi.it
[2] School of computer Science, Tel-Aviv University, Tel Aviv, Israel
mansour@cs.tau.ac.il
[3] DMA, Ecole Normale Supérieure, 45, rue d'Ulm, 75005 Paris, France
gilles.stoltz@ens.fr

Abstract. This work studies external regret in sequential prediction games with arbitrary payoffs (nonnegative or non-positive). External regret measures the difference between the payoff obtained by the forecasting strategy and the payoff of the best action. We focus on two important parameters: M, the largest absolute value of any payoff, and Q^*, the sum of squared payoffs of the best action. Given these parameters we derive first a simple and new forecasting strategy with regret at most order of $\sqrt{Q^*(\ln N)} + M \ln N$, where N is the number of actions. We extend the results to the case where the parameters are unknown and derive similar bounds. We then devise a refined analysis of the weighted majority forecaster, which yields bounds of the same flavour. The proof techniques we develop are finally applied to the adversarial multi-armed bandit setting, and we prove bounds on the performance of an online algorithm in the case where there is no lower bound on the probability of each action.

1 Introduction

The study of online forecasting strategies in adversarial settings has received considerable attention in the last few years in the computational learning literature and elsewhere. The main focus has been on deriving simple online algorithms that have low external regret. The external regret of an online algorithm is the difference between its expected payoff and the best payoff achievable using some strategy from a given class. Usually, this class includes a strategy, for each action, which always plays that action. In a nutshell, one can show that the average external regret per time step vanishes, and much of the research has been to both

---

* The work of all authors was supported in part by the IST Programme of the European Community, under the PASCAL Network of Excellence, IST-2002-506778.
** The work was done while the author was a fellow in the Institute of Advance studies, Hebrew University. His work was also supported by a grant no. 1079/04 from the Israel Science Foundation and an IBM faculty award.

P. Auer and R. Meir (Eds.): COLT 2005, LNAI 3559, pp. 217–232, 2005.

improve and refine the bounds. Ideally, in an adversarial setting one should be able to show that the regret with respect to any action only depends on the variance of the observed payoffs for that action. In a stochastic setting such a result seems like the most natural bound, and deriving its analogue in an adversarial setting would be a fundamental result. We believe that our results make a significant step toward this goal, although, unfortunately, fall short of completely achieving it.

In order to describe our results we first set up our model and notations, and relate them to previous works. In this paper we consider the following game-theoretic version of the prediction-with-expert-advice framework [5, 11, 13]. A forecaster repeatedly assigns probabilities to a fixed set of actions. After each assignment, the real payoff associated to each action is revealed and new payoffs are set for the next round. The forecaster's reward on each round is the average payoff of actions for that round, where the average is computed according to the forecaster's current probability assignment. The goal of the forecaster is to achieve, on any sequence of payoffs, a cumulative reward close to X^*, the highest cumulative payoff among all actions. As usual, we call regret the difference between X^* and the cumulative reward achieved by the forecaster on the same payoff sequence.

The special case of "one-sided games", when all payoffs have the same sign (they are either always non-positive or always nonnegative) has been considered by Freund and Schapire [9], and by Auer et al. [3] in a related context. These papers show that Littlestone and Warmuth's weighted majority algorithm [11] can be used as a basic ingredient to construct a forecasting strategy achieving a regret of $O(\sqrt{M|X^*|\ln N})$ in one-sided games, where N is the number of actions and M is a known upper bound on the size of payoffs. (If all payoffs are non-positive, then the absolute value of each payoff is called *loss* and $|X^*|$ is the cumulative loss of the best action.) By a simple rescaling of payoffs, it is possible to reduce the more general "signed game", in which each payoff might have an arbitrary sign, to either one of the one-sided games (note that this reduction assumes knowledge of M). However, the regret becomes $O(M\sqrt{n\ln N})$, where n is the number of game rounds. Recently, Allenberg and Neeman [2] proposed a direct analysis of the signed game avoiding this reduction. Before describing their results, we introduce some convenient notation and terminology.

Our forecasting game is played in rounds. At each time step $t = 1, 2, \ldots$ the forecaster computes an assignment $\boldsymbol{p}_t = (p_{1,t}, \ldots, p_{N,t})$ of probabilities over the N actions. Then the payoff vector $\boldsymbol{x}_t = (x_{1,t}, \ldots, x_{N,t}) \in \mathbb{R}^N$ for time t is revealed and the forecaster's reward is $\widehat{x}_t = x_{1,t}p_{1,t} + \ldots + x_{N,t}p_{N,t}$. We define the cumulative reward of the forecaster by $\widehat{X}_n = \widehat{x}_1 + \ldots + \widehat{x}_n$ and the cumulative payoff of action i by $X_{i,n} = x_{i,1} + \ldots + x_{i,n}$. For all n, let $X_n^* = \max_{i=1,\ldots,N} X_{i,n}$ be the cumulative payoff of the best action up to time n. The forecaster's goal is to keep the *regret* $X_n^* - \widehat{X}_n$ as small as possible uniformly over n.

The one-sided games, mentioned above, are the *loss game*, where $x_{i,t} \leq 0$ for all i and t, and the *gain game*, where $x_{i,t} \geq 0$ for all i and t. We call *signed game* the setup in which no assumptions are made on the sign of the payoffs. For the signed game, Allenberg and Neeman [2] show that weighted majority (used in conjunction with a doubling trick) achieves the following: on any sequence of payoffs there exists an action j such that the regret is at most of order $\sqrt{M(\ln N) \sum_{t=1}^{n} |x_{j,t}|}$, where $M = \max_{i,t} |x_{i,t}|$ is a known upper bound on the size of payoffs. Note that this bound does not relate the regret to the sum $|x_1^*| + \ldots + |x_n^*|$ of payoff sizes for the optimal action (i.e., the one achieving X_n^*). In particular, the bound $O(\sqrt{M|X_n^*| \ln N})$ for the one-sided games is only obtained if an estimate of X_n^* is available in advance.

In this paper we show new regret bounds for the signed game. Our analysis has two main advantages: first, no preliminary knowledge of the payoff size M or about the best cumulative payoff X_n^* is needed; second, our bounds are expressed in terms of sums of squared payoffs, such as $x_{i,1}^2 + \ldots + x_{i,n}^2$ and related forms. These quantities replace the larger terms $M(|x_{i,1}| + \ldots + |x_{i,n}|)$ appearing in the previous bounds. As an application of our results we obtain, without any preliminary knowledge on the payoff sequence, an improved regret bound for the one-sided games of the order of $\sqrt{(Mn - |X_n^*|)(|X_n^*|/n)(\ln N)}$.

Expressions involving squared payoffs are at the core of many analyses in the framework of prediction with expert advice, especially in the presence of limited feedback. (See, for instance, the bandit problem [3] and more generally prediction under partial monitoring [6, 7, 12]). However, to the best of our knowledge, our bounds are the first ones to explicitly include second-order information extracted from the payoff sequence. In particular, our bounds are stable under many transformations of the payoff sequence, and therefore are in some sense more "fundamental".

Some of our bounds are achieved using forecasters based on weighted majority run with a dynamic learning rate. However, we are able to obtain second-order bounds of a different flavour using a new forecaster that does not use the exponential probability assignments of weighted majority. In particular, unlike virtually all previously known forecasting schemes, the weights of this forecaster can not be represented as the gradient of an additive potential [8].

In bandit problems and, more generally, in all incomplete information problems like label-efficient prediction or prediction with partial monitoring, a crucial point is to estimate the unobserved losses. In such settings, a probability distribution is formed by using weighted averages of the cumulative estimated losses, and a common practice is to mix this probability distribution, so that the resulting distribution have all the probabilities above a certain value. Technically, this is important since it is common to divide by the probabilities (see [3, 6, 7, 10, 12]). We show that, for the algorithm of [3], using our proof technique one can simply use the original probability distribution computed with the estimates without any adjustments.

2   A New Algorithm for Sequential Prediction

We introduce a new forecasting strategy for the signed game. In Theorem 3, the main result of this section, we show that, without any preliminary knowledge of the sequence of payoffs, the regret of a variant of this strategy is bounded by a quantity defined in terms of the sums $Q_{i,n} = x_{i,1}^2 + \ldots + x_{i,n}^2$. Since $Q_{i,n} \leq M(|x_{i,1}| + \ldots + |x_{i,n}|)$, such second-order bounds are generally better than the previously known bounds (see Section 4).

Our basic forecasting strategy, which we call $\mathbf{prod}(\eta)$, has an input parameter $\eta > 0$ and maintains a set of N weights. At time $t = 1$ the weights are initialized with $w_{i,1} = 1$ for $i = 1, \ldots, N$. At each time $t = 1, 2, \ldots$, $\mathbf{prod}(\eta)$ computes the probability assignment $\boldsymbol{p}_t = (p_{1,t}, \ldots, p_{N,t})$, where $p_{i,t} = w_{i,t}/W_t$. After the payoff vector $\boldsymbol{x}_t$ is revealed, the weights are updated using the rule $w_{i,t+1} = w_{i,t}(1 + \eta x_{i,t})$. We use the notation $W_t = w_{1,t} + \ldots + w_{N,t}$. The following simple fact, whose proof is omitted, plays a key role in our analysis.

Lemma 1. *For all $z \geq -1/2$, $\ln(1 + z) \geq z - z^2$.*

Lemma 2. *Assume there exists $M > 0$ such that the payoffs satisfy $x_{i,t} \geq -M$ for $t = 1, \ldots, n$ and $i = 1, \ldots, N$. For any sequence of payoffs, for any action k, for any $\eta \leq 1/(2M)$, and for any $n \geq 1$, the cumulative reward of $\mathbf{prod}(\eta)$ is lower bounded as*

$$\widehat{X}_n \geq X_{k,n} - \frac{\ln N}{\eta} - \eta Q_{k,n} .$$

Proof. For any $k = 1, \ldots, N$, note that $x_{k,t} \geq -M$ and $\eta \leq 1/(2M)$ imply $\eta x_{k,t} \geq -1/2$. Hence, we can apply Lemma 1 to $\eta x_{k,t}$ and get

$$\ln \frac{W_{n+1}}{W_1} = -\ln N + \ln \prod_{t=1}^{n}(1 + \eta x_{k,t}) = -\ln N + \sum_{t=1}^{n} \ln(1 + \eta x_{k,t})$$

$$\geq -\ln N + \sum_{t=1}^{n} \left(\eta x_{k,t} - \eta^2 x_{k,t}^2\right) = -\ln N + \eta X_{k,n} - \eta^2 Q_{k,n} . \quad (1)$$

On the other hand,

$$\ln \frac{W_{n+1}}{W_1} = \sum_{t=1}^{n} \ln \frac{W_{t+1}}{W_t} = \sum_{t=1}^{n} \ln \left(\sum_{i=1}^{N} p_{i,t}\left(1 + \eta x_{i,t}\right)\right) \leq \eta \widehat{X}_n \quad (2)$$

where in the last step we used $\ln(1 + z_t) \leq z_t$ for all $z_t = \eta \sum_{i=1}^{N} x_{i,t} p_{i,t} \geq -1/2$. Combining (1) and (2), and dividing by $\eta > 0$, we get

$$\widehat{X}_n \geq -\frac{\ln N}{\eta} + X_{k,n} - \eta Q_{k,n}$$

which completes the proof of the lemma.   □

By choosing η appropriately, we can optimize the bound as follows.

Theorem 1. *Assume there exists $M > 0$ such that the payoffs satisfy $x_{i,t} \geq -M$ for $t = 1, \ldots, n$ and $i = 1, \ldots, N$. For any $Q > 0$, if $\mathbf{prod}(\eta)$ is run with*

$$\eta = \min\left\{1/(2M), \sqrt{(\ln N)/Q}\right\}$$

then for any sequence of payoffs, for any action k, and for any $n \geq 1$ such that $Q_{k,n} \leq Q$,

$$\widehat{X}_n \geq X_{k,n} - \max\left\{2\sqrt{Q \ln N}, 4M \ln N\right\}.$$

To achieve the bound stated in Theorem 1, the parameter η must be tuned using preliminary knowledge of a lower bound on the payoffs and an upper bound on the quantities $Q_{k,n}$. The next two results remove these requirements one by one. We start by introducing a new algorithm that, using a doubling trick over prod, avoids any preliminary knowledge of a lower bound on the payoffs.

Let prod-M(Q) be the prediction algorithm that receives a number $Q > 0$ as input parameter and repeatedly runs prod(η_r), where $\eta_r = 1/(2M_r)$ and M_r is defined below. We call epoch r the sequence of time steps when prod-M is running prod(η_r). At the beginning, $r = 0$ and prod-M(Q) runs prod(η_0), where

$$M_0 = \sqrt{Q/(4\ln N)} \quad \text{and} \quad \eta_0 = 1/(2M_0) = \sqrt{(\ln N)/Q}.$$

The last step of epoch $r \geq 0$ is the time step $t = t_r$ when $\max_{i=1,\dots,N} |x_{i,t}| > M_r$ happens for the first time. When a new epoch $r + 1$ begins, prod is restarted with parameter $\eta_{r+1} = 1/(2M_{r+1})$, where $M_{r+1} = \max_i 2^{\lceil \log_2 |x_{i,t_r}| \rceil}$. Note that $M_1 \geq M_0$ and, for each $r \geq 1$, $M_{r+1} \geq 2M_r$.

Theorem 2. *For any sequence of payoffs, for any action k, and for any $n \geq 1$ such that $Q_{k,n} \leq Q$, the cumulative reward of algorithm prod-M(Q) is lower bounded as*

$$\widehat{X}_n \geq X_{k,n} - 2\sqrt{Q \ln N} - 4M(2 + 3\ln N)$$

where $M = \max_{1 \leq i \leq N} \max_{1 \leq t \leq n} |x_{i,t}|$.

Proof. We denote by R the index of the last epoch and let $t_R = n$. If we have only one epoch, then the theorem follows from Theorem 1 applied with a lower bound of $-M_0$ on the payoffs. Therefore, for the rest of the proof we assume $R \geq 1$. Let

$$X_k^r = \sum_{s=t_{r-1}+1}^{t_r-1} x_{k,s}, \quad Q_k^r = \sum_{s=t_{r-1}+1}^{t_r-1} x_{k,s}^2, \quad \widehat{X}^r = \sum_{s=t_{r-1}+1}^{t_r-1} \widehat{x}_s,$$

where the sums are over all the time steps t in epoch r except the last one, t_r. (Here t_{-1} is conventionally set to 0.) Applying Lemma 1 to each epoch $r = 0, \dots, R$ we get that $\widehat{X}_n - X_{k,n}$ is equal to

$$\sum_{r=0}^{R}\left(\widehat{X}^r - X_k^r\right) + \sum_{r=0}^{R-1}(\widehat{x}_{t_r} - x_{k,t_r}) \geq -\sum_{r=0}^{R}\frac{\ln N}{\eta_r} - \sum_{r=0}^{R}\eta_r Q_k^r + \sum_{r=0}^{R-1}(\widehat{x}_{t_r} - x_{k,t_r}).$$

We bound each sum separately. For the first sum note that

$$\sum_{r=0}^{R}\frac{\ln N}{\eta_r} = \sum_{r=0}^{R}2M_r \ln N \leq 6M_R \ln N$$

since $M_R \geq 2^{R-r}M_r$ for each $r \geq 1$ and $M_0 \leq M_R$. For the second sum, using that the η_r decrease, we have

$$\sum_{r=0}^{R} \eta_r Q_k^r \leq \eta_0 \sum_{r=0}^{R} Q_k^r \leq \eta_0 Q_{k,n} \leq \sqrt{\frac{\ln N}{Q}} Q = \sqrt{Q \ln N} .$$

Finally,

$$\sum_{r=0}^{R-1} |\widehat{x}_{t_r} - x_{k,t_r}| \leq \sum_{r=1}^{R} 2 M_r \leq 4 M_R .$$

The resulting lower bound $2M_R(2 + 3 \ln N) + \sqrt{Q \ln N}$ implies the one stated in the theorem by noting that, when $R \geq 1$, $M_R \leq 2M$. $\square$

We now show a regret bound for the case when M and the $Q_{k,n}$ are both unknown. Let k_t^* be the index of the best action up to time t; that is, $k_t^* \in$ argmax$_k X_{k,t}$ (ties are broken by choosing the action k with minimal associated $Q_{k,t}$). We denote the associated quadratic penalty by

$$Q_t^* = Q_{k_t^*}^* = \sum_{s=1}^{t} x_{k_t^*,s}^2 .$$

Ideally, our final regret bound should depend on Q_n^*. However, note that the sequence $Q_1^*, Q_2^*, \ldots$ is not necessarily monotone, as Q_t^* and Q_{t+1}^* cannot be possibly related when the actions achieving the largest cumulative payoffs at rounds t and $t+1$ are different. Therefore, we cannot use a straightforward doubling trick, as this only applies to monotone sequences. Our solution is to express the bound in terms of the smallest nondecreasing sequence that upper bounds the original sequence $(Q_t^*)_{t \geq 1}$. This is a general trick to handle situations where the penalty terms are not monotone. Allenberg and Neeman [2] faced a similar situation, and we improve their results.

We define a new (parameterless) prediction algorithm prod-MQ in the following way. The algorithm runs in epochs using prod-M(Q) as a subroutine. The last step of epoch r is the time step $t = t_r$ when $Q_t^* > 4^r$ happens for the first time. At the beginning of each new epoch $r = 0, 1, \ldots$, algorithm prod-M(Q) is restarted with parameter $Q = 4^r$.

Theorem 3. *For any sequence of payoffs and for any $n \geq 1$, the cumulative reward of algorithm* prod-MQ *satisfies*

$$\widehat{X}_n \geq X_n^* - 8\sqrt{(\ln N) \max\left\{1, \max_{s \leq n} Q_s^*\right\}} - 12M\left(2 + \log_4 \max_{s \leq n} Q_s^*\right)(1 + \ln N)$$

where $M = \max_{1 \leq i \leq N} \max_{1 \leq t \leq n} |x_{i,t}|$.

Proof. We denote by R the index of the last epoch and let $t_R = n$. Assume that $R \geq 1$ (otherwise the proof is concluded by Theorem 2). Similarly to the proof of Theorem 2, for all epochs r and actions k introduce

$$X_k^r = \sum_{s=t_{r-1}+1}^{t_r-1} x_{k,s} , \quad Q_k^r = \sum_{s=t_{r-1}+1}^{t_r-1} x_{k,s}^2 , \quad \widehat{X}^r = \sum_{s=t_{r-1}+1}^{t_r-1} \widehat{x}_s$$

where $t_{-1} = 0$. We also denote $k_r = k^*_{t_r-1}$ the index of the best overall expert up to time $t_r - 1$ (one time step before the end of epoch r). We have that $Q^r_{k_r} \leq Q_{k_r,t_r-1} = Q^*_{t_r-1}$. Now, by definition of the algorithm, $Q^*_{t_r-1} \leq 4^r$. Theorem 2 (applied to time steps $t_{r-1} + 1, \ldots, t_r - 1$) shows that $\widehat{X}^r \geq X^r_{k_r} - \Phi(M, 4^r)$, where $\Phi(M, x) = 2\sqrt{x \ln N} + 4M(2 + 3\ln N)$. Summing over $r = 0, \ldots, R$ we get

$$\widehat{X}_n = \sum_{r=0}^{R} \widehat{X}^r + \widehat{x}_{k_r,t_r} \geq \sum_{r=0}^{R} \left(\widehat{x}_{k_r,t_r} + X^r_{k_r} - \Phi(M, 4^r) \right) . \tag{3}$$

Now, since k_1 is the index of the expert with largest payoff up to time $t_1 - 1$, we have that $X_{k_2,t_2-1} = X^1_{k_2} + x_{k_2,t_1} + X^2_{k_2} \leq X^1_{k_1} + X^2_{k_2} + M$. By a simple induction, we in fact get

$$X_{k_R,t_R-1} \leq \sum_{r=0}^{R-1} \left(X^r_{k_r} + M \right) + X^R_{k_R} . \tag{4}$$

As, in addition, X_{k_R,t_R-1} and $X_{k^*_n,n}$ may only differ by at most M, combining (3) and (4) we have indeed proven that

$$\widehat{X}_n \geq X_{k^*_n,n} - \left(2(1 + R)M + \sum_{r=0}^{R} \Phi(M, 4^r) \right) .$$

The sum over r is now bounded as follows

$$\sum_{r=0}^{R} \Phi(M, 4^r) \leq 4M(1 + R)(2 + 3\ln N) + 2^{R+1} \left(2\sqrt{\ln N} \right) .$$

The proof is concluded by noting that, as $R \geq 1$, $\sup_{s \leq n} Q^*_s \geq 4^{R-1}$ by definition of the algorithm. $\qquad\square$

3   Second-Order Bounds for Weighted Majority

In this section we derive new regret bounds for the weighted majority forecaster of Littlestone and Warmuth [11] using a time-varying learning rate. This allows us to avoid the doubling trick of Section 2 and keep the assumption that no knowledge on the payoff sequence is available to the forecaster beforehand.

Similarly to the results of Section 2, the main term in the new bounds depends on second-order quantities associated to the sequence of payoffs. However, the precise definition of these quantities makes the bounds of this section generally not comparable to the bounds obtained in Section 2.

The weighted majority forecaster using the sequence $\eta_2, \eta_3, \ldots > 0$ of learning rates assigns at time t a probability distribution $\boldsymbol{p}_t$ over the N experts defined by $\boldsymbol{p}_1 = (1/N, \ldots, 1/N)$ and

$$p_{i,t} = \frac{e^{\eta_t X_{i,t-1}}}{\sum_{j=1}^{N} e^{\eta_t X_{j,t-1}}} \qquad \text{for } i = 1, \ldots, N \text{ and } t \geq 2. \tag{5}$$

Note that the quantities $\eta_t > 0$ may depend on the past payoffs $x_{i,s}$, $i = 1,\ldots,N$ and $s = 1,\ldots,t-1$. The analysis of Auer, Cesa-Bianchi, and Gentile [4], for a related variant of weighted majority, is at the core of the proof of the following lemma (proof omitted from this extended abstract).

Lemma 3. *Consider any nonincreasing sequence $\eta_2, \eta_3, \ldots$ of positive learning rates and any sequence $\boldsymbol{x}_1, \boldsymbol{x}_2, \ldots \in \mathbb{R}^N$ of payoff vectors. Define the nonnegative function Φ by*

$$\Phi(\boldsymbol{p}_t, \eta_t, \boldsymbol{x}_t) = -\sum_{i=1}^N p_{i,t} x_{i,t} + \frac{1}{\eta_t} \ln \sum_{i=1}^N p_{i,t} e^{\eta_t x_{i,t}} = \frac{1}{\eta_t} \ln \left(\sum_{i=1}^N p_{i,t} e^{\eta_t(x_{i,t} - \widehat{x}_t)} \right)$$

Then the weighted majority forecaster (5) run with the sequence $\eta_2, \eta_3, \ldots$ satisfies, for any $n \geq 1$ and for any $\eta_1 \geq \eta_2$,

$$\widehat{X}_n - X_n^* \geq -\left(\frac{2}{\eta_{n+1}} - \frac{1}{\eta_1} \right) \ln N - \sum_{t=1}^n \Phi(\boldsymbol{p}_t, \eta_t, \boldsymbol{x}_t) \ .$$

Let Z_t be the random variable with range $\{x_{1,t}, \ldots, x_{N,t}\}$ and law $\boldsymbol{p}_t$. Note that $\mathbb{E} Z_t$ is the expected payoff $\widehat{x}_t$ of the forecaster using distribution $\boldsymbol{p}_t$ at time t. Introduce

$$\mathrm{Var}\, Z_t = \mathbb{E} Z_t^2 - \mathbb{E}^2 Z_t = \sum_{i=1}^N p_{i,t} x_{i,t}^2 - \left(\sum_{i=1}^N p_{i,t} x_{i,t} \right)^2 \ .$$

Hence $\mathrm{Var}\, Z_t$ is the variance of the payoffs at time t under the distribution $\boldsymbol{p}_t$ and the cumulative variance $V_n = \mathrm{Var}\, Z_1 + \ldots \mathrm{Var}\, Z_n$ is the main second-order quantity used in this section. The next result bounds $\Phi(\boldsymbol{p}_t, \eta_t, \boldsymbol{x}_t)$ in terms of $\mathrm{Var}\, Z_t$.

Lemma 4. *For all payoff vectors $\boldsymbol{x}_t = (x_{1,t}, \ldots, x_{N,t})$, all probability distributions $\boldsymbol{p}_t = (p_{1,t}, \ldots, p_{N,t})$, and all learning rates $\eta_t \geq 0$, we have*

$$\Phi(\boldsymbol{p}_t, \eta_t, \boldsymbol{x}_t) \leq 2\, M$$

where M is such that $|x_{i,t}| \leq M$ for all i. If, in addition, $0 \leq \eta_t |x_{i,t}| \leq 1/2$ for all $i = 1, \ldots, N$, then

$$\Phi(\boldsymbol{p}_t, \eta_t, \boldsymbol{x}_t) \leq (e-2)\eta_t \,\mathrm{Var}\, Z_t \ .$$

Proof. The first inequality is straightforward. To prove the second one we use $e^a \leq 1 + a + (e-2)a^2$ for $|a| \leq 1$. Consequently, noting that $\eta_t |x_{i,t} - \widehat{x}_t| \leq 1$ for all i by assumption, we have that

$$\Phi(\boldsymbol{p}_t, \eta_t, \boldsymbol{x}_t) = \frac{1}{\eta_t} \ln \left(\sum_{i=1}^N p_{i,t} e^{\eta_t(x_{i,t} - \widehat{x}_t)} \right)$$

$$\leq \frac{1}{\eta_t} \ln \left(\sum_{i=1}^N p_{i,t} \left(1 + \eta_t(x_{i,t} - \widehat{x}_t) + (e-2)\eta_t^2(x_{i,t} - \widehat{x}_t)^2 \right) \right) \ .$$

Using $\ln(1 + a) \leq a$ for all $a \geq -1$ and some simple algebra concludes the proof of the second inequality. $\qquad\square$

In [3] a very similar result is proven, except that there the variance is further bounded (up to a multiplicative factor) by the expectation $\widehat{x}_t$ of Z_t.

We now introduce a time-varying learning rate based on V_n. For any sequence of payoff vectors $\boldsymbol{x}_1, \boldsymbol{x}_2, \ldots$ and for all $t = 1, 2, \ldots$ let $M_t = 2^k$, where k is the smallest *nonnegative* integer such that $\max_{s=1,\ldots,t} \max_{i=1,\ldots,N} |x_{i,s}| \leq 2^k$. Now let the sequence $\eta_2, \eta_3, \ldots$ be defined as

$$\eta_t = \min\left\{ \frac{1}{2 M_{t-1}}, C\sqrt{\frac{\ln N}{V_{t-1}}} \right\} \quad \text{for } t \geq 2, \text{ with} \quad C = \sqrt{\frac{2}{e-2}\left(\sqrt{2}-1\right)}. \quad (6)$$

Note that η_t depends on the forecaster's past predictions. This is in the same spirit as the self-confident learning rates considered in [4].

We are now ready to state and prove the main result of this section.

Theorem 4. *Consider the weighted majority forecaster using the time-varying learning rate (6). Then, for all sequences of payoffs and for all $n \geq 1$,*

$$\widehat{X}_n - X_n^* \geq -4\sqrt{V_n \ln N} - 16 \max\{M, 1\} \ln N - 8 \max\{M, 1\} - M^2$$

where $M = \max_{t=1,\ldots,n} \max_{i=1,\ldots,N} |x_{i,t}|$.

Proof. We start by applying Lemma 3 using the learning rate (6), and setting $\eta_1 = \eta_2$ for the analysis,

$$\widehat{X}_n - X_n^* \geq -\left(\frac{2}{\eta_{n+1}} - \frac{1}{\eta_1}\right) \ln N - \sum_{t=1}^n \Phi(\boldsymbol{p}_t, \eta_t, \boldsymbol{x}_t)$$

$$\geq -2 \max\left\{2 M_n \ln N, (1/C)\sqrt{V_n \ln N}\right\} - \sum_{t=1}^n \Phi(\boldsymbol{p}_t, \eta_t, \boldsymbol{x}_t)$$

$$= -2 \max\left\{2 M_n \ln N, (1/C)\sqrt{V_n \ln N}\right\}$$
$$- \sum_{t \in \mathcal{T}} \Phi(\boldsymbol{p}_t, \eta_t, \boldsymbol{x}_t) - \sum_{t \notin \mathcal{T}} \Phi(\boldsymbol{p}_t, \eta_t, \boldsymbol{x}_t)$$

where C is defined in (6), and $\mathcal{T}$ is the set of times rounds $t \geq 2$ when $\eta_t|x_{i,t}| \leq 1/2$ for all $i = 1, \ldots, N$ (note that $1 \notin \mathcal{T}$ by definition). Using the second bound of Lemma 4 on $t \in \mathcal{T}$ and the first bound of Lemma 4 on $t \notin \mathcal{T}$, which in this case reads $\Phi(\boldsymbol{p}_t, \eta_t, \boldsymbol{x}_t) \leq 2M_t$, we get

$$\widehat{X}_n - X_n^* \geq -2 \max\left\{2 M_n \ln N, (1/C)\sqrt{V_n \ln N}\right\}$$
$$- (e-2) \sum_{t \in \mathcal{T}} \eta_t \operatorname{Var} Z_t - \sum_{t \notin \mathcal{T}} 2 M_t \quad (7)$$

(where $2M_1$ appears in the last sum). We first note that

$$\sum_{t \notin \mathcal{T}} M_t \leq \sum_{r=0}^{\lceil \log_2 \max\{M,1\} \rceil} 2^r \leq 2^{1+\lceil \log_2 \max\{M,1\} \rceil} \leq 4 \max\{M,1\} .$$

We now denote by T the first time step t when $V_t > M^2$. Using that $\eta_t \leq 1/2$ for all t and $V_T \leq 2M^2$, we get

$$\sum_{t \in \mathcal{T}} \eta_t \operatorname{Var} Z_t \leq M^2 + \sum_{t=T+1}^{n} \eta_t \operatorname{Var} Z_t . \tag{8}$$

We bound the sum using $\eta_t \leq C\sqrt{(\ln N)/V_{t-1}}$ for $t \geq 2$ (note that, for $t > T$, $V_{t-1} \geq V_T > M^2 > 0$). This yields

$$\sum_{t=T+1}^{n} \eta_t \operatorname{Var} Z_t \leq C\sqrt{\ln N} \sum_{t=T+1}^{n} \frac{V_t - V_{t-1}}{\sqrt{V_{t-1}}} .$$

Let $v_t = \operatorname{Var} Z_t = V_t - V_{t-1}$. Since $V_t \leq V_{t-1} + M^2$ and $V_{t-1} \geq M^2$, we have

$$\frac{v_t}{\sqrt{V_{t-1}}} = \frac{\sqrt{V_t} + \sqrt{V_{t-1}}}{\sqrt{V_{t-1}}} \left(\sqrt{V_t} - \sqrt{V_{t-1}} \right) \leq (\sqrt{2}+1) \left(\sqrt{V_t} - \sqrt{V_{t-1}} \right) . \tag{9}$$

Therefore, using that $\sqrt{2}+1 = 1/(\sqrt{2}-1)$,

$$\sum_{t=T+1}^{n} \eta_t \operatorname{Var} Z_t \leq \frac{C\sqrt{\ln N}}{\sqrt{2}-1} \left(\sqrt{V_n} - \sqrt{V_T} \right) \leq \frac{C}{\sqrt{2}-1} \sqrt{V_n \ln N} .$$

When $\sqrt{V_n} \geq 2CM_n\sqrt{\ln N}$, using $M_n \geq M$ we have that $\widehat{X}_n - X_n^*$ is at least

$$-\frac{2}{C}\sqrt{V_n \ln N} - \frac{C(e-2)}{\sqrt{2}-1}\sqrt{V_n \ln N} - 8 \max\{M, 1\} - (e-2)M^2$$

$$\geq -4\sqrt{V_n \ln N} - 8 \max\{M, 1\} - M^2$$

where we substituted the value of C and obtained a constant for the leading term equal to $2\sqrt{2(e-2)}/\sqrt{\sqrt{2}-1} \leq 3.75$. When $\sqrt{V_n} \leq 2CM_n\sqrt{\ln N}$, using $M_n \leq \max\{1, 2M\}$ we have that $\widehat{X}_n - X_n^*$ is at least

$$-8 M \ln N - \frac{C^2 4(e-2)}{\sqrt{2}-1} \max\{1/2, M\} \ln N - 8 \max\{M, 1\} - (e-2)M^2$$

$$\geq -16 \max\{M, 1\} \ln N - 8 \max\{M, 1\} - M^2 .$$

This concludes the proof.   □

4   Applications

To demonstrate the usefulness of the bounds proven in Theorems 3 and 4 we show that they lead to several improvements or extensions of earlier results.

Improvements for Loss Games. Recall the definition of quadratic penalties Q_t^* in Section 2. In case of a loss game (i.e., all payoffs are non-positive), $Q_t^* \leq ML_t^*$, where L_t^* is the cumulative loss of the best action up to time t. Therefore, $\max_{s \leq n} Q_s^* \leq ML_n^*$ and the bound of Theorem 3 is at least as good as the family of bounds called "improvements for small losses" (see, e.g., [4]), whose main term is of the form $\sqrt{ML_n^* \ln N}$. However, it is easy to exhibit examples where the new bound is far better by considering sequences of outcomes where there are some "outliers" among the $x_{i,t}$. These outliers may raise the maximum M significantly, whereas they have only little impact on the $\max_{s \leq n} Q_s^*$.

Using Translations of Payoffs. Recall that Z_t is the random variable which takes the value $x_{i,t}$ with probability $p_{i,t}$, for $i = 1, \ldots, N$. The main term of the bound stated in Theorem 4 contains $V_n = \operatorname{Var} Z_1 + \ldots + \operatorname{Var} Z_n$. Note that V_n is smaller than all quantities of the form $\sum_{t=1}^n \sum_{i=1}^N p_{i,t} (x_{i,t} - \mu_t)^2$ where $(\mu_t)_{t \geq 1}$ is any sequence of real numbers which may be chosen in *hindsight*, as it is not required for the definition of the forecaster. (The minimal value of the expression is obtained for $\mu_t = \hat{x}_t$.) This gives us a whole family of upper bounds, and we may choose for the analysis the most convenient sequence of μ_t.

To provide a concrete example, denote the effective range of the payoffs at time t by $R_t = \max_{i=1,\ldots,N} x_{i,t} - \min_{j=1,\ldots,N} x_{j,t}$ and consider the choice $\mu_t = \min_{j=1,\ldots,N} x_{j,t} + R_t/2$. The next result improves on a result of Allenberg and Neeman [2], who show a regret bound, in terms of the cumulative effective range, whose main term is $5.7\sqrt{2(\ln N)M\sum_{t=1}^n R_t}$, for a given bound M over the payoffs.

Corollary 1. *The regret of the weighted majority forecaster with variable learning rate (6) satisfies*

$$\widehat{X}_n - X_n^* \geq -2\sqrt{(\ln N)\sum_{t=1}^n R_t^2 - 16 \max\{M, 1\} \ln N - 8 \max\{M, 1\} - M^2} \ .$$

The bound proposed by Corollary 1 shows that for an effective range of M, say if the payoffs all fall in $[0, M]$, the regret is lower bounded by a quantity equal to $-2M\sqrt{n \ln N}$ (a closer look at the proof of Theorem 4 shows that the constant factor may be even equal to 1.9). The best leading constant for such bounds is, to our knowledge, $\sqrt{2}$ (see [8]). This shows that the improved dependence in the bound does not come at a significant increase in the magnitude of the leading coefficient.

Improvements for One-sided Games. The main drawback of V_n, used in Theorem 4, is that it is defined directly in terms of the forecaster's distributions p_t.

We now show how this dependence could be removed. Assume $|x_{i,t}| \leq M$ for all t and i. The following corollary of Theorem 4 reveals that weighted majority suffers a small regret in one-sided games whenever $|X_n^*|$ or $Mn - |X_n^*|$ is small (where $|x_{i,t}| \leq M$ for all t and i); that is, whenever $|X_n^*|$ is very small or very large. Improvements of the same flavour were obtained by Auer, Cesa-Bianchi, and Gentile [4] for loss games; however, their result cannot be converted in a straightforward manner to a corresponding useful result for gain games. Allenberg and Neeman [2] proved, in a gain game and for a related algorithm, a bound of the order of $11.4\sqrt{M} \min\{\sqrt{X_n^*}, \sqrt{Mn - X_n^*}\}$. That algorithm was specifically designed to ensure a regret bound of this form, and is different from the algorithm whose performance we discussed before the statement of Corollary 1. Our weighted majority forecaster achieves a better bound, even though it was not directly constructed to do so.

Corollary 2. *Consider the weighted majority forecaster using the time-varying learning rate (6). Then, for all sequences of payoffs in a one-sided game (i.e., payoffs are all non-positive or all nonnegative),*

$$\widehat{X}_n - X_n^* \geq -4\sqrt{|X_n^*|\left(M - \frac{|X_n^*|}{n}\right)\ln N} - 65\max\{1, M\}\max\{1, \ln N\} - 5M^2$$

where $M = \max_{t=1,\dots,n} \max_{i=1,\dots,N} |x_{i,t}|$.

Proof. We give the proof for a gain game. Since the payoffs are in $[0, M]$, we can write

$$V_n \leq \sum_{t=1}^{n} \left(M \sum_{i=1}^{N} p_{i,t} x_{i,t} - \left(\sum_{i=1}^{N} p_{i,t} x_{i,t}\right)^2\right) = \sum_{t=1}^{n} (M - \widehat{x}_t)\widehat{x}_t$$

$$\leq n\left(\frac{M\widehat{X}_n}{n} - \left(\frac{\widehat{X}_n}{n}\right)^2\right) = \widehat{X}_n\left(M - \frac{\widehat{X}_n}{n}\right)$$

where we used the concavity of $x \mapsto Mx - x^2$. Assume that $\widehat{X}_n \leq X_n^*$ (otherwise the result is trivial). Then, Theorem 4 ensures that

$$\widehat{X}_n - X_n^* \geq -4\sqrt{X_n^*\left(M - \frac{\widehat{X}_n}{n}\right)\ln N} - \kappa$$

where $\kappa = 16\max\{M, 1\}\ln N + 8\max\{M, 1\} + M^2$. We solve for $\widehat{X}_n$ obtaining

$$\widehat{X}_n - X_n^* \geq -4\sqrt{X_n^*\left(M - \frac{X_n^*}{n} + \frac{\kappa}{n}\right)\ln N} - \kappa - 16\frac{X_n^*}{n}\ln N.$$

Using the crude upper bound $X_n^*/n \leq M$ and performing some simple algebra, we get the desired result. $\square$

Quite surprisingly, a bound of the same form as the one shown in Corollary 2 can be derived as a Corollary of Theorem 3. The derivation uses a payoff translation technique similar to the one we discussed in the previous paragraph. However, unlike the approach presented there for the weighted majority based forecaster, here the payoffs have to be explicitly translated by the forecaster. (And each translation rule corresponds to a different forecaster.)

A simplified Algorithm for Bandit Loss Games. We close this section with a result that is not a direct consequence of Theorems 3 or 4. Rather, we derive it via an extension of Lemma 4, one of our key results at the core of the second-order analysis in Section 3.

Recall that payoffs $x_{i,t}$ in loss game are all non-positive. We use $\ell_{i,t} = -x_{i,t}$ to denote the loss of action i at time t. Similarly, $\widehat{\ell}_t = \ell_{1,t}p_{1,t} + \ldots + \ell_{N,t}p_{N,t}$ is the loss of the forecaster using $\boldsymbol{p}_t$ as probability assignment at time t. We make the simplifying assumption $\ell_{i,t} \in [0,1]$ for all i,t.

The bandit loss game (see [3] and references therein) is a loss game with the only difference that, at each time step t, the forecaster has no access to the loss vector $\boldsymbol{\ell}_t = (\ell_{1,t}, \ldots, \ell_{N,t})$. Therefore, the loss $\widehat{\ell}_t$ cannot be computed and the individual losses $\ell_{i,t}$ can not be used to adjust the probability assignment $\boldsymbol{p}_t$. The only information the forecaster receives at the end of each round t is the loss $\ell_{I_t,t}$, where I_t takes value i with probability $p_{i,t}$ for $i = 1, \ldots, N$.

In bandit problems and, more generally, in all incomplete information problems like label-efficient prediction or prediction with partial monitoring, a crucial point is to estimate the unobserved losses. In bandit algorithms based on weighted majority, this is usually done by shifting the probability distribution $\boldsymbol{p}_t$ so that all components are larger than a given threshold. Allenberg and Auer [1] apply the shifting technique to weighted majority obtaining, in bandit loss games, a regret bound of order $\sqrt{NL_n^* \ln N} + N \ln(nN) \ln n$ where L_n^* is the cumulative loss of the best action after n rounds (note that using the results of [3], derived for gain games, one would only obtain $\sqrt{Nn\ln(nN)}$). We show that *without any shifting*, a slight modification of weighted majority achieves a regret of order $N\sqrt{L_n^* \ln n} + N \ln n$. The new bound becomes better than the one by Allenberg and Auer when L_n^* is so small that $L_n^* = o((\ln n)^3)$.

The bandit algorithm, which we call EXP3LIGHT, performs the weight update $w_{i,t+1} = w_{i,t}\, e^{-\eta \widetilde{\ell}_{i,t}}$. The pseudo-losses $\widetilde{\ell}_{i,t}$ are defined by $\widetilde{\ell}_{i,t} = (\ell_{i,t}/p_{i,t})Z_{i,t}$ for $i = 1, \ldots, N$. The Bernoulli random variable $Z_{i,t}$ takes value 1 if the forecaster has drawn action i at time t; i.e., $I_t = i$.

We start with a variant of Lemma 4 for loss games (proof omitted from this extended abstract).

Lemma 5. *For all $\eta > 0$, all losses $\ell_{i,t} \geq 0$, and all sets $S_t \subseteq \{1, \ldots, N\}$,*

$$\Phi(\boldsymbol{p}_t, \eta, -\boldsymbol{\ell}_t) \leq \frac{\eta}{2} \sum_{i \in S_t} p_{i,t}\, \ell_{i,t}^2 + \sum_{i \in S_t} p_{i,t}\, \ell_{i,t} \;.$$

Lemma 5 is applied as follows (the proofs of Proposition 1 and Theorem 5 are omitted from this extended abstract).

Proposition 1. *Assume the forecaster* EXP3LIGHT *plays a bandit loss game, with losses bounded between 0 and 1. For all $\eta > 0$, the cumulative pseudo-loss of* EXP3LIGHT *satisfies*

$$\widetilde{L}_n \leq \frac{(\ln N) + N(\ln n)}{\eta} + \frac{\eta}{2} N \widetilde{L}^* + \Delta_n$$

where $\displaystyle \widetilde{L}_n = \sum_{t=1}^{n} \sum_{i=1}^{N} p_{i,t} \widetilde{\ell}_{i,t} \,, \quad \widetilde{L}_{k,n} = \sum_{t=1}^{n} \widetilde{\ell}_{k,t} \,, \quad \widetilde{L}^* = \min_{k=1,\dots,N} \widetilde{L}_{k,n} \,,$
and Δ_n *is a random variable with expectation less than* $2N$.

Theorem 5. *Consider the forecaster that runs algorithm* EXP3LIGHT *in epochs as follows. In each epoch $r = 0, 1 \dots$ the algorithm uses*

$$\eta_r = \sqrt{\frac{2\left((\ln N) + N\ln n\right)}{N 4^r}}$$

and epoch r stops whenever the pseudo-loss $\widetilde{L}^*$ in this epoch is larger than 4^r. For any bandit loss game with $\ell_{i,t} \in [0,1]$ for all i and t, the expected cumulative loss of this forecaster satisfies

$$\mathbb{E}\left[\sum_{t=1}^{n} \ell_{I_t,t}\right] - L_n^* \leq 2\sqrt{2\left((\ln N) + N\ln n\right) N \left(1 + 3L_n^*\right)}$$

$$+ (2N+1)\left(1 + \log_4(3n+1)\right) \,.$$

5   Discussion and Open Problems

Though the results of Sections 2 and 3 cannot be easily compared, the two underlying algorithms apply to loss games, gain games, as well as to signed games. In addition, note that the bounds proposed by Theorem 3 and by Theorem 4 (or, more precisely, the variant of this bound using payoffs translated by $\widehat{x}_t$) are both stable under many transformations, such as translations or changes of signs. Consequently, and most importantly, they are invariant under the change $\ell_{i,t} = M - x_{i,t}$, that converts bounded nonnegative payoffs into bounded losses, and vice versa. However, the occurrence of terms like $\max\{M, 1\}$ and M^2 makes these bounds not stable under rescaling of the payoffs. This means that if the payoffs are all multiplied by a positive number α (which may be more or less than 1), then the bounds on the regret are not necessarily multiplied by the same quantity α.

Modifying the proof of Theorem 4 we also obtained a regret bound equal to $-4\sqrt{V_n \ln N} - 16\, M \ln N - 8\, M - 2M \log M^2 / V_1$. This bound is indeed stable under rescalings and improves on Theorem 4 for instance when M much smaller than 1, or even when M is large and V_1 is not too small. We hope that the unconvenient factor $1/V_1$ could be removed soon.

A practical advantage of the weighted majority forecaster is that its update rule is completely incremental and never needs to reset the weights. This in contrast to the forecaster `prod-MQ` of Theorem 3 that uses a nested doubling trick. On the other hand, the bound proposed in Theorem 4 is not in closed form, as it still explicitly depends through V_n on the forecaster's rewards $\widehat{x}_t$. Several issues are left open. The following list mentions some of them.

- Design and analyze incremental updates for the forecaster `prod`(η) of Section 2.
- Obtain second order bounds with updates that are not multiplicative; for instance, updates based on the polynomial potentials (see [8]).
- Extend the analysis of `prod-MQ` to obtain an oracle inequality of the form

$$\widehat{X}_n \geq \max_{k=1,\ldots,N} \left(X_{k,n} - \gamma_1 \sqrt{Q_{k,n} \ln N} \right) - \gamma_2 M \ln N$$

where γ_1 and γ_2 are absolute constants. Inequalities of this form can be viewed as game-theoretic versions of the model selection bounds in statistical learning theory.

References

1. C. Allenberg-Neeman and P. Auer. Personal communication.
2. C. Allenberg-Neeman and B. Neeman. Full information game with gains and losses. Algorithmic Learning Theory, 15th International Conference, ALT 2004, Padova, Italy, October 2004, Proceedings, volume 3244 of Lecture Notes in Artificial Intelligence, pages 264-278. Springer, 2004.
3. P. Auer, N. Cesa-Bianchi, Y. Freund, and R.E. Schapire. The nonstochastic multiarmed bandit problem. *SIAM Journal on Computing*, 32:48–77, 2002.
4. P. Auer, N. Cesa-Bianchi, and C. Gentile. Adaptive and self-confident on-line learning algorithms. *Journal of Computer and System Sciences*, 64:48–75, 2002.
5. N. Cesa-Bianchi, Y. Freund, D.P. Helmbold, D. Haussler, R. Schapire, and M.K. Warmuth. How to use expert advice. *Journal of the ACM*, 3:427–485, 1997.
6. N. Cesa-Bianchi, G. Lugosi, and G. Stoltz. Minimizing regret with label efficient prediction. *IEEE Transactions on Information Theory*, to appear.
7. N. Cesa-Bianchi, G. Lugosi, and G. Stoltz. Regret minimization under partial monitoring. Submitted for journal publication, 2004.
8. N. Cesa-Bianchi and G. Lugosi. *Prediction, Learning, and Games*. Cambridge University Press, to appear.
9. Y. Freund and R.E. Schapire. A decision-theoretic generalization of on-line learning and an application to boosting. *Journal of Computer and System Sciences*, 55(1):119–139, 1997.
10. S. Hart and A. Mas-Colell. A Reinforcement Procedure Leading to Correlated Equilibrium. Economic Essays, Gerard Debreu, Wilhelm Neuefeind and Walter Trockel (editors), Springer (2001), 181-200
11. N. Littlestone and M.K. Warmuth. The weighted majority algorithm. *Information and Computation*, 108:212–261, 1994.

12. A. Piccolboni and C. Schindelhauer. Discrete prediction games with arbitrary feedback and loss. In *Proceedings of the 14th Annual Conference on Computational Learning Theory*, pages 208–223, 2001.
13. V.G. Vovk. A Game of Prediction with Expert Advice. *Journal of Computer and System Sciences*, 56(2):153–73, 1998.

Competitive Collaborative Learning

Baruch Awerbuch[1,*] and Robert D. Kleinberg[2,**]

[1] Department of Computer Science, Johns Hopkins University,
Baltimore MD 21218, USA
baruch@cs.jhu.edu
[2] Department of Mathematics, Massachusetts Institute of Technology,
Cambridge MA 02139, USA
rdk@math.mit.edu

Abstract. We develop algorithms for a community of users to make decisions about selecting products or resources, in a model characterized by two key features:

- The quality of the products or resources may vary over time.
- Some of the users in the system may be dishonest, manipulating their actions in a Byzantine manner to achieve other goals.

We formulate such learning tasks as an algorithmic problem based on the multi-armed bandit problem, but with a set of users (as opposed to a single user), of whom a constant fraction are honest and are partitioned into coalitions such that the users in a coalition perceive the same expected quality if they sample the same resource at the same time. Our main result exhibits an algorithm for this problem which converges in polylogarithmic time to a state in which the average regret (per honest user) is an arbitrarily small constant.

1 Introduction

Only a fool learns from his own mistakes. The wise man learns from the mistakes of others.

— Otto von Bismarck

It is clear that leveraging trust or shared taste enables a community of users to be more productive, as it allows them to repeat each other's good decisions while avoiding unnecessary repetition of mistakes. Systems based on this paradigm are becoming increasingly prevalent in computer networks and the applications they support. Examples include reputation systems in e-commerce (e.g. eBay, where buyers and sellers rank each other), collaborative filtering (e.g. Amazon's recommendation system, where customers recommend books to other customers), and link analysis techniques in web search (e.g., Google's PageRank, based on

---

* Supported by NSF grants ANIR-0240551 and CCR-0311795.
** Supported by a Fannie and John Hertz Foundation Fellowship.

P. Auer and R. Meir (Eds.): COLT 2005, LNAI 3559, pp. 233–248, 2005.

combining links — i.e. recommendations — of different web sites). Not surprisingly, many algorithms and heuristics for such systems have been proposed and studied experimentally or phenomenologically [5, 11, 12, 13, 15, 16, 17]. Yet well-known algorithms (e.g. eBay's reputation system, the Eigentrust algorithm [10], the PageRank [5, 13] and HITS [11] algorithms for web search) have thus far not been placed on an adequate theoretical foundation.

Our goal in this paper is to provide a theoretical framework for understanding the capabilities and limitations of such systems as a model of distributed computation. We propose a new paradigm for addressing these issues, which is inspired by online learning theory, specifically the multi-armed bandit problem [1]. Our approach aims to highlight the following challenges which confront the users of collaborative decision-making systems such as those cited above.

Malicious users. Since the Internet is open for anybody to join, the above systems are vulnerable to fraudulent manipulation by dishonest ("Byzantine") participants.

Distinguishing tastes. Agents' tastes may differ, so that the advice of one honest agent may not be helpful to another.

Temporal fluctuation. The quality of resources varies of time, so past experience is not necessarily predictive of future performance.

While our learning theory paradigm is different from prior approaches, the resulting algorithms exhibit a resemblance to algorithms previously proposed in the systems and information retrieval literature [5, 10, 11, 13] indicating that our approach may be providing a theoretical framework which sheds light on the efficacy of such algorithms in practice while suggesting potential enhancements to these algorithms.

1.1   Our Approach

The problem we will consider is a generalization of the multi-armed bandit problem studied in [1]. In that problem there is a single learner and a set Y of m *resources*. In each of T consecutive trials, the learner chooses one of the resources while the adversary chooses a cost (taking values in $[0, 1]$) for each resource; after the trial, the cost of the resource chosen by the learner is revealed, and this cost is charged to the learner. We generalize this by considering a set X of n *agents*, some of which (possibly, a majority) may be dishonest. In each trial, each of the n agents chooses a resource, and the adversary chooses a cost for each resource. Each agent then learns the cost of the resource it selected, and this cost is charged to the agent. We assume that the honest agents belong to k *coalitions*, such that agents in the same coalition who choose the same resource at the same time will perceive the same expected cost. All agents may communicate with each other between trials, to exchange information (or possibly disinformation, in the case of dishonest agents) about the costs of resources they have sampled. However, agents are unaware of which coalitions exist and which ones they belong to.

If an agent chooses to ignore the feedback from other agents, and simply runs the multi-armed bandit algorithm by itself, then the classical analysis of the multi-armed bandit algorithm [1] ensures that for any constant $\delta > 0$, if $T = \Omega(m \log m)$, then the expected average cost of the resources chosen by that agent will exceed the average cost of the best resource in hindsight by no more than δ. However, it is possible that the honest agents may require much fewer than $\Omega(m \log m)$ trials to achieve this goal, if they can find a way to pool their information without being fooled by the bad advice from dishonest agents and agents from other coalitions. Here, we show that this is in fact possible, by presenting an algorithm whose convergence time is polynomial in $k \log(n)$, assuming that a constant fraction of the agents are honest and that $m = O(n)$.

Briefly, our algorithm works by having each agent select a resource in each trial by taking a random walk on a "reputation network" whose vertex set is the set of all agents and resources. Resources are absorbing states of this random walk, while the transition probabilities at an agent x may be interpreted as the probability that x would select a given resource y, or would ask a given other agent x' for advice. When an agent learns the cost of the resource chosen in a given trial, it uses this feedback to update its transition probabilities according to the multi-armed bandit algorithm. In this way, agents will tend to raise the probability of asking for advice from other agents who have given good advice in the past. In particular, though the initial transition probabilities do not reflect the partition of the honest agents into coalitions, over time the honest agents will tend to place greater weight on edges leading to other agents in the same coalition, since the advice they receive from such agents is generally better, on average, than the advice they receive from agents in other coalitions.

1.2   Comparison with Existing Work

Above, we cited the adversarial multi-armed bandit problem [1] which forms the basis for our work, and we have indicated the ways in which our model generalizes the existing multi-armed bandit model to the setting of collaborative learning with dishonest users. Our work is also related to several other topics which we now discuss.

Collaborative filtering — spectral methods: Our problem is similar, at least in terms of motivation, to the problem of designing collaborative filtering or recommendation systems. In such problems, one has a community of users selecting products and giving feedback on their evaluations of these products. The goal is to use this feedback to make recommendations to users, guiding them to subsequently select products which they are likely to evaluate positively. Theoretical work on collaborative filtering has mostly dealt with centralized algorithms for such problems. Typically, theoretical solutions have been considered for specific (e.g., stochastic) input models [7, 8, 9, 14, 4], In such work, the goal is typically to reconstruct the full matrix of user preferences based on small set of potentially noisy samples. This is often achieved using spectral methods. In constrast, we consider a general, i.e. adversarial, input model. Matrix reconstruction techniques do not suffice in our model. Firstly, they are vulnerable to manipulation by dishonest users, as was observed in [3] and [2]. Dishonest users, who may be in the overwhelming majority, may certainly disrupt the low rank assumption which is crucial in matrix reconstruction approaches. Alternatively, they may report phony data so as to perturb the singular vectors of the matrix, directing all the agents to a particularly bad action, e.g. an unscrupulous seller.

Collaborative filtering — random sampling methods: The only known collaborative filtering algorithm which tolerates Byzantine behavior is the "Random Advice Random Sample" algorithm in [2, 3]; it achieves a logarithmic learning time. The model in [2] deals with the static case, in which bad resources are consistently bad and good resources are consistently good; the only changes in the operating environment over time occur when resources arrive or depart. The algorithm in [2] uses the notion of "recommendation": once an agent finds a good resource, it sticks to it forever and recommends it to others. As the time elapses, progressively more agents 'stick" with the good advice. The bounds on regret and convergence time in [2] are analogous to ours, and are in fact poly-logarithmically superior, to those in our Theorem 1. However, [2] does not handle costs which evolve dynamically as a function of time, and is limited to $\{0, 1\}$-valued rather than real-valued costs.

Reputation management in P2P networks: Kamvar et al [10] proposed an algorithm, dubbed *EigenTrust*, for the problem of locating resources in peer-to-peer networks. In this problem, users of a peer-to-peer network wish to select other peers from whom to download files, with the aim of minimizing the number of downloads of inauthentic files by honest users; the problem is made difficult by the presence of malicious peers who may attempt to undermine the algorithm. Like our algorithm, EigenTrust defines reputation scores using a random walk on the set of agents, with time-varying transition probabilities which are updated according to the agents' observations. Unlike our algorithm, they use a different rule for updating the transition probabilities, and they demonstrate the algorithm's robustness against a limited set of malicious exploits, as opposed to the arbitrary adversarial behavior against which our algorithm is provably robust. The problem considered here is less general than the peer-to-peer resource location problem considered in [10]; for instance, we assume that in each trial, any agent may select any resource, whereas they assume that only a subset of the resources are available (namely, those peers who claim to have a copy of the requested file). Despite these differences, we believe that our work may shed light on the efficacy of EigenTrust while suggesting potential enhancements to make it more robust against Byzantine malicious users.

The rest of this paper is organized as follows. In Section 2 we specify our precise models and results. This is followed by a section specifying a general outline of our approach. The precise specification of the main algorithm, TrustFilter, appears in Section 3. The description of the algorithm is complete except for a rather complicated subroutine, BBA, which is specified and analyzed in the following section. Finally, in Section 5, we analyze the main algorithm, modulo a random graph lemma which is proved in the full version of this paper.

2   Statements of the Problem and the Results

The operating environment consists of a set X of n agents and a set Y of m products. A subset $H \subseteq X$ of the agents are *honest*, and the rest are dishonest. Honest agents are assumed to obey the distributed protocol to be specified, and to report their observations truthfully, while dishonest agents may behave in a Byzantine manner, disobeying the protocol or reporting fictitious observations as they wish. We will assume throughout that the number of honest agents is at least αn, where $\alpha > 0$ is a parameter which may be arbitrarily small. The agents do not initially know which ones are honest and which are dishonest, nor are they assumed to know the value of α.

In each of T consecutive rounds, a cost function $C_t : X \times Y \to [0, 1]$ is given. We think of the cost $C_t(x, y)$ as agent x's perception of the cost of resource y. The costs may be set by an adaptive adversary who is allowed to choose C_t based on the agents' actions in rounds $1, \ldots, t-1$ but not on their random decisions in the present or future rounds; the adversary may also use randomization in determining C_t. Define two agents x_1, x_2 to be *consistent* if the costs $C_t(x_1, y), C_t(x_2, y)$ are random variables with the same expected value (conditional on the choices of all agents in all rounds preceding t), for all $y \in Y, 1 \leq t \leq T$.[1] We will assume that the honest agents may be partitioned into k *coalitions*, such that two agents belonging to the same coalition are consistent; the honest agents do not initially know which coalitions the other honest agents belong to.

At the beginning of each round, each agent $x \in X$ must choose a product $y = y_t(x) \in Y$. Any agent is allowed to choose any product in any round. The cost of the choice is $C_t(x, y)$, and this cost (but not the cost of any other product) is revealed to x. The agents may communicate with each other between rounds, and this communication may influence their decisions in future rounds. To simplify the exposition we will assume all messages are exchanged using a shared, synchronous, public channel. In any round t all agents (including the Byzantine dishonest agents) must commit to their message on this channel before being able to read the messages posted by other agents in round t. This public-channel assumption is for expositional clarity only: in the full version of this paper we will indicate how to achieve the same results (with slightly worse bounds) in a message-passing model where agents may only exchange messages bilaterally on point-to-point communication links, subject to the assumption that all agents can synchronize clocks and have enough time to perform $\Omega(\log n)$ communication rounds in between consecutive decision rounds. (The Byzantine agents may eavesdrop on all such communications, whereas honest agents may not eavesdrop on any message if they are not the sender or receiver.) As might be expected, some subtleties arise in the message-passing model, due to ability of the Byzantine nodes to give differing advice to different parties, and to eavesdrop on others' messages.

---

[1] The randomness of the variables $C_t(x_1, y), C_t(x_2, y)$ is due to the adversary's potential use of randomness in determining C_t.

The goal of the algorithm is to minimize the total cost incurred by honest agents. As is typical with online decision problems, we will evaluate the algorithm's performance by measuring the expected difference between the algorithm's total cost and the cost of the best assignment in which each agent chooses a single fixed product and selects this product every time. This parameter is called *regret* and will be denoted by R.

$$R = \mathbf{E} \left[\sum_{x \in H} \sum_{t=1}^{T} C_t(x, y_t(x)) - \min_{y:H \to Y} \sum_{x \in H} \sum_{t=1}^{T} C_t(x, y(x)) \right]. \tag{1}$$

The following two parameters, closely related to R, are also of interest:

- The *normalized individual regret* $\hat{R} = R/\alpha n T$ is the regret per unit time of the average honest agent. For all of the algorithms we will consider, $\hat{R}$ converges to zero as $T \to \infty$.
- The *δ-convergence time* of such an algorithm, denoted by $T(\delta)$, is defined as the minimum value of T necessary to guarantee that $\hat{R} = O(\delta)$. Here, δ is a positive constant which may be arbitrarily close to zero.

2.1   Our Results

We present a distributed algorithm, named TrustFilter, in Section 3. Let $\beta = 1 + m/n$. We will typically be interested in the case where α, β, δ are all positive constants. For ease of exposition, we will adhere to this assumption when stating the theorems in this section, absorbing such constants into the $O(\cdot)$ notation. See equations (11),(12),(13), (14) in Section 5 for bounds which explicitly indicate the dependence on α, β, and δ; in all cases, this dependence is polynomial.

Theorem 1. *Suppose the set of honest agents may be partitioned into k subsets $S_1, S_2, \ldots, S_k$, such that the agents in each subset are mutually consistent. Then the normalized regret $\hat{R}$ and δ-convergence time $T(\delta)$ of* TrustFilter *satisfy*

$$\hat{R} = O \left(k \cdot \frac{\log^4(n)}{T^{1/4}} \right) \tag{2}$$

$$T(\delta) = O(k^4 \log^{16}(n)). \tag{3}$$

The δ-convergence time bound follows from the regret bound. Typically we are interested in the case where α, β, δ, k are constants, hence we will summarize this result by saying that the algorithm has *polylogarithmic convergence time*. This is the first distributed algorithm with polylogarithmic convergence time in a dynamic environment.

3   The Algorithm TrustFilter

3.1   Intuition

As stated in the introduction, our algorithm is based on a Markov chain representing a random walk in a directed graph, whose vertices represent the set of resources and agents. We refer to this directed graph as the "reputation network." At each time, each agent picks an outgoing edge in the reputation network with appropriate probability, and then traverses this edge. If the edge leads to an agent, "advice" is sought from that agent. Else, if the edge leads to a resource, this resource is selected for sampling. Depending on the observed cost of the sampled resource, the agent updates its transition probabilities.

As an aid in developing intuition, consider the special case of this algorithm when the Markov chain is based on a random graph. Specifically, each agent picks at random a small subset of other agents and a small subset of the resources, and sets equal transition probabilities to all outgoing edges leading to members of that subset. All other outgoing probabilities are zero. Assume that agents adopt the following simple rule for updating their transition probabilities: if the agent chooses an outgoing edge and it leads to a product with cost 0, assign probability 1 permanently to that edge and probability 0 to all other edges; otherwise leave the transition probabilities unchanged. It is easy to prove, that for the static case with binary resource costs, this algorithm can be viewed as an alternative to Random Advice Random Sample algorithm in [3]; like that algorithm, it achieves logarithmic convergence time. The invariant used in the proof is the fact that the set of agents who recommend the optimal resource is growing exponentially with time. This invariant is proved by induction on time. Indeed, with high probability there is an edge in the reputation network from some honest agent to the optimal resource, and in constant time that neighboring agent will either directly sample this resource, or will stumble on an equivalent resource following advice of others. Consider the set S of honest agents who "saw the light," i.e., discovered the optimal resource. Note that the set N of neighbors of S, namely nodes with outgoing edges leading into S, is at least $|N| = |S| \cdot \rho$ where ρ is the expansion ratio of the underlying random graph. Note that within constant time, a constant fraction of agents in N will also discover the optimal resource by sampling nodes in S or following advice to other equivalent resources. Thus, within expected logarithmic time, all the agents discover the optimal resource.

Our algorithm for the case of dynamic costs looks quite different from the algorithm for static costs presented in the preceding paragraph, but it is based on the same intuition: by structuring the reputation network as a random graph, the set of honest agents who are selecting an optimal or near-optimal resource will grow exponentially over time. The main technical difference is that agents must update their transition probabilities using the multi-armed bandit algorithm, rather than shifting all of their probability mass to one outgoing edge as soon as they discover a resource with zero cost. This modification is necessary in order to deal with the fact that a resource which has zero cost at one time may not have zero cost at future times. More subtly, when agents are using the multi-armed bandit algorithm to update their transition probabilities, they must use a modification of the classical multi-armed bandit algorithm which we denote by BBA. This is because the agents do not know how many other honest agents belong to their coalition, so they must potentially consider all βn

other vertices of the reputation network as potential neighbors. (Recall from Section 2 that $\beta = (m + n)/n$, so that βn is the cardinality $X \cup Y$, the vertex set of the reputation network.) Classical multi-armed bandit algorithms, e.g. Exp3 [1], will have a convergence time of $\Omega(n \log(n))$ in such a scenario, whereas we seek a polylogarithmic convergence time. Accordingly, we present a modified bandit algorithm BBA whose salient feature is that it satisfies a significantly better bound on regret when stopped at times $T < n \log(n)$. The details of this algorithm will be explained in Section 4. For now, it is best for the reader to consider it as a black box (instantiated separately by each agent x) which outputs, at each time t, a probability distribution $\pi_t(x)$ on the set of all agents and resources. We will use the notation $\pi_t(x, y)$ to denote the probability that $\pi_t(x)$ assigns to the element $y \in X \cup Y$.

3.2   The Algorithm

Here we present an algorithm TrustFilter which solves the collaborative learning problem, establishing Theorem 1. We use, as a subroutine, the algorithm BBA whose existence is asserted by Theorem 2. We defer the specification of this subroutine until later.

At the beginning of each round t, each agent x queries its local bandit algorithm BBA(x) to obtain a probability distribution $\pi_t(x)$ on the set of agents and resources, and posts this distribution on the public channel. This enables each agent to construct an $(m + n)$-by-$(m + n)$ matrix M_t whose rows and columns are indexed by the elements of $X \cup Y$, and whose entries are given by:

$$(M_t)_{ij} = \begin{cases} \pi_t(i, j) & \text{if } i \in X \\ 1 & \text{if } i \in Y \text{ and } j = i \\ 0 & \text{if } i \in Y \text{ and } j \neq i. \end{cases}$$

We may think of M_t as the transition matrix for a Markov chain with state space $X \cup Y$, in which elements of Y are absorbing states, and the transition probabilities at an element x of X are determined by the bandit algorithm BBA(x). This Markov chain corresponds to the intuitive notion of "taking a random walk by following the advice of the bandit algorithm at each node."

The random walk starting from $x \in X$ will, with probability 1, be absorbed by some state $y \in Y$; this enables us to define a matrix A_t by

$$(A_t)_{ij} = \Pr(\text{absorbing state is } j \mid \text{starting state is } i).$$

Algebraically, A_t satisfies the equations $M_t A_t = A_t$ and $A_t \mathbf{1} = \mathbf{1}$, where $\mathbf{1}$ represents a column vector whose components are all equal to 1.

To select a product $y = y_t(x) \in Y$, x uses BBA(x) to choose a strategy $s = s_t(x) \in X \cup Y$. It then samples y randomly using the probability distribution in the row of A_t corresponding to s, learns the cost $C_t(y)$, and returns this feedback score to BBA(x). The probability distribution from which y is drawn can be determined either by computing A_t algebraically, or by simulating the random walk with transition matrix M_t starting from state s until it hits an absorbing state. We call this probability distribution on Y *harmonic measure relative to x*, by analogy with the harmonic measure defined on the boundary of a bounded domain $U \subset \mathbb{R}^d$ according the hitting probability of Brownian motion starting from a point $x \in U$.

4   The Biased Bandit Algorithm BBA

Our multi-agent learning algorithms require each agent to instantiate a single-agent learning algorithm called the *biased bandit algorithm*, or BBA, which we describe in this section. For a multi-armed bandit algorithm with strategy set $S = \{1, 2, \ldots, K\}$ (whose selection at time t is denoted by $i_t \in S$) define its *regret profile* to be the function $R(T, i)$ which specifies the algorithm's regret relative to strategy $i \in S$ at time $T \geq 1$, i.e.

$$R(T, i) = \max \left\{ \mathbf{E} \left(\sum_{t=1}^{T} C_t(i_t) - C_t(i) \right) \right\},$$

the maximum being taken over the set of all adaptive adversarial policies assigning costs C_t in $[0, 1]$. For example, the regret profile of the classical multi-armed bandit algorithm Exp3 is known to satisfy $R(T, i) = O(\sqrt{TK \log(K)})$; we call this a uniform regret profile since the value of $R(T, i)$ does not depend on i. Which *non-uniform* regret profiles are achievable by multi-armed bandit algorithms? The BBA supplies a non-trivial upper bound for this question.

Theorem 2. *Let a strategy set S of size K be given, along with positive real weights $\{w_i\}_{i \in S}$ which sum to 1. There exists a multi-armed bandit algorithm* BBA *whose regret profile satisfies*

$$R(T, i) = O\left(\frac{1}{w_i} \log^2 \left(\frac{1}{w_i} \right) T^{3/4} \right).$$

In fact, the theorem holds even if the feedback for choosing strategy i, rather than being equal to $C_t(i)$, is a random variable $X_t(i)$ (taking values in $[0, 1]$) whose conditional expectation is bounded above by $C_t(i)$. We call this the "noisy feedback model"; see Section 4.1 for details.

When the BBA algorithm is applied as a subroutine in TrustFilter, its strategy set is $S = X \cup Y$, which has $m + n$ elements. The weights assigned to these elements are a random permutation of the set

$$\left\{ \frac{1}{H_{m+n}}, \frac{1}{2H_{m+n}}, \ldots, \frac{1}{(m+n)H_{m+n}} \right\}.$$

(Here H_{m+n} represents the harmonic number $\sum_{i=1}^{m+n} 1/i$.)

One way of interpreting BBA is as an *anytime* version of the multi-armed bandit algorithm, in that it meets a non-trivial performance guarantee when stopped at any time T, even if $T \ll K$. This contrasts with traditional multi-armed bandit algorithms such as Exp3 whose performance at time $T = o(K)$ is generally indistinguishable from random guessing. The anytime guarantee for BBA can be made precise as follows. For any threshold $\lambda > 0$ let $S(\lambda) = \{i \in S : w_i \log^{-3}(1/w_i) > \lambda\}$. Theorem 2 establishes that by time T, the normalized regret of BBA relative to the strategies in $S(\delta^{-1}T^{-1/6})$ is at most δ. This set of strategies may be quite large even when $T \ll K$, and grows to encompass all of S as $T \to \infty$.

We will now describe the algorithm BBA. The high-level idea of the algorithm is to partition the strategy set into two subsets of approximately equal weight, then to further partition each of these two subsets into two pieces of approximately equal weight, and so on, building a tree $\mathfrak{T}$ whose leaves are labeled with elements of the strategy set S. We will use, as a black box, the multi-armed bandit algorithm Exp3 from [1]. An instance of Exp3 at the root of the tree is responsible for deciding whether to select a strategy from the left or right sub-tree; the task of picking a leaf of this subtree is recursively delegated to the descendants of the root. Each node z of the tree is therefore running an instance of Exp3, but gets feedback only for a random subset of the rounds, namely those in which the chosen leaf lies in its subtree. The analysis of Exp3 in models such as this, where the feedback is noisy or sporadic, is carried out in Appendix 4.1. Applying the relevant bound on Exp3's regret (Theorem 3) at each level of $\mathfrak{T}$, we will obtain the desired global upper bound on regret. A subtlety which arises in designing the algorithm is that we must ensure that each internal node z gets feedback reasonably often, which necessitates devoting a small fraction of the rounds to explicitly sampling a descendant of z.

To specify the tree $\mathfrak{T}$, we may assume without loss of generality that the weights w_i are powers of 2, say $w_i = 2^{-d_i}$. (If not, we may round each w_i down to the next-lowest power of 2, then round some of them up to restore the property that their sum is 1.) Now define $\mathfrak{T}$ to be the Huffman tree of the distribution $\{w_i\}$ [6]. This tree has the property that for any node at depth d, the combined weight of all leaves in its subtree is 2^{-d}. For a node z of depth d in $\mathfrak{T}$, let $\tilde{w}(z) = 2^{-d} \cdot d^{-2}$; note that if z is a leaf corresponding to an element i, then

$$\frac{1}{\tilde{w}(z)} = O\left(\frac{1}{w_i}\log^2\left(\frac{1}{w_i}\right)\right).$$

In the BBA algorithm, each internal node z of $\mathfrak{T}$ maintains an instance Exp3(z) of the multi-armed bandit algorithm, with a two-element strategy set identified with the two children, z_L and z_R, of z in $\mathfrak{T}$. In each round t, each internal node z chooses a child $\chi_t(z)$ according to the probability distribution supplied by Exp3(z). These choices define a mapping ℓ_t from the nodes of $\mathfrak{T}$ to the leaves of $\mathfrak{T}$, defined recursively by the rule that $\ell_t(i) = i$ for a leaf i, and $\ell_t(z) = \ell_t(\chi_t(z))$ for an internal node z. A random node $z_t \in \mathfrak{T}$ is sampled in round t according to the distribution which assigns probability $\rho(z) = T^{-1/4}\tilde{w}(z)$ to each node z other than the root r, and assigns all remaining probability mass to r. The algorithm BBA chooses strategy $i_t = \ell_t(z_t)$. Let P_t denote the path in $\mathfrak{T}$ from

z_t to i_t. After learning the cost $C_t(i_t)$, each internal node z updates Exp3(z) by attributing a feedback value $X_t(z')$ to its child $z' = \chi_t(z)$ as follows.

$$X_t(z') = \begin{cases} C_t(\ell_t(z')) & \text{if } z = z_t \\ 0 & \text{otherwise,} \end{cases}$$

4.1   Analysis of BBA

To prove Theorem 2 we must first recall some properties of the multi-armed bandit algorithm Exp3 from [1] and extend the analysis of this algorithm to a slightly more general setting, which we call the "noisy feedback model."

Theorem 3 ([1]). *For any $\varepsilon > 0$, there is a multi-armed bandit algorithm* Exp3 *with strategy set $S = \{1, 2, \ldots, K\}$ whose regret relative to strategy $i \in S$, i.e. the number*

$$R = \mathbf{E}\left(\sum_{t=1}^{T} C_t(i_t) - \sum_{t=1}^{T} C_t(i) \right),$$

satisfies $R = O(\sqrt{TK \log(K)})$.

For the applications in this paper, we actually need to work with a slight generalization of the model considered in [1]. This generalization, which we call the "noisy feedback" model, is described as follows. In each round t, in addition to specifying a cost function $C_t : S \to [0, 1]$, the adversary specifies, for each $i \in S$, a random variable $X_t(i)$ which depends only on $i_1, i_2, \ldots, i_{t-1}$ and on some random bits independent of the algorithm's random bits. This random variable takes values in $[0, 1]$ and satisfies $\mathbf{E}[X_t(i) \,\|\, \mathcal{F}_{<t}] = C_t(i)$, where $\mathcal{F}_{<t}$ denotes the σ-field generated by all random variables revealed by the algorithm and adversary prior to time t. Rather than receiving $C_t(i_t)$ as feedback, the algorithm's feedback is $X_t(i_t)$. The following easy proposition, whose proof appears in the full version of this paper, demonstrates that the regret of algorithm Exp3 is unaffected by the noisy feedback.

Proposition 1. *In the noisy feedback model, the regret R experienced by algorithm* Exp3 *relative to strategy i still satisfies $R = O(\sqrt{TK \log K})$. This bound holds regardless of whether R is defined as $R_X := \mathbf{E}\left(\sum_{t=1}^{T} X_t(i_t) - C_t(i) \right)$ or as $R_C := \mathbf{E}\left(\sum_{t=1}^{T} C_t(i_t) - C_t(i) \right)$.*

We are now ready to finish the analysis of the BBA algorithm.

Proof (Theorem 2). The analysis of BBA depends on a reduction to the noisy-feedback bandit problem defined above. If z is a node of $\mathfrak{T}$ and z' is one of its two children, define:

$$\tilde{C}_t(z') = \rho(z) C_t(\ell_t(z')).$$

Then $\tilde{C}_t(z'), X_t(z')$ take values in $[0, 1]$, and they are independent of Exp3(z)'s random choices at times $t, t+1, \ldots, T$. Moreover, recalling that $\rho(z) = \Pr(z =$

$z_t \parallel \mathcal{F}_{<t}$), we have $\mathbf{E}[X_t(z') \parallel \mathcal{F}_{<t}] = \tilde{C}_t(z')$. Therefore, $\mathsf{Exp3}(z)$ is following the algorithm $\mathsf{Exp3}$ in the noisy feedback model with cost functions $\tilde{C}_t$ and random feedback variables $X_t(z')$. Applying Proposition 1 with $K = 2$,

$$\rho(z)\mathbf{E}\left(\sum_{t=1}^{T} C_t(\ell_t(z)) - C_t(\ell_t(z'))\right) = O(\sqrt{T}).$$

This inequality holds for every edge (z, z') in $\mathfrak{T}$. Rescaling and summing over all the edges on the path P from r to i, we obtain:

$$\mathbf{E}\left(\sum_{t=1}^{T}(C_t(\ell_t(r)) - C_t(i))\right) = \sum_{(z,z')\in P}\mathbf{E}\left(\sum_{t=1}^{T}(C_t(\ell_t(z)) - C_t(\ell_t(z')))\right)$$

$$= O\left(\sum_{z\in P}\rho(z)^{-1}T^{1/2}\right)$$

$$= O\left(\sum_{z\in P}\tilde{w}(z)^{-1}T^{3/4}\right)$$

$$= O\left(\tilde{w}(i)^{-1}T^{3/4}\right)$$

$$= O\left(\frac{1}{w_i}\log^2\left(\frac{1}{w_i}\right)T^{3/4}\right). \tag{4}$$

Finally, we may account for the cost of the steps in which $z_t \neq r$ as follows:

$$\mathbf{E}\left(\sum_{t=1}^{T}C_t(i_t) - C_t(\ell_t(r))\right) \leq \sum_{t=1}^{T}\Pr(i_t \neq \ell_t(r))$$

$$\leq \sum_{t=1}^{T}\Pr(z_t \neq r)$$

$$= T \cdot \sum_{z\neq r}\rho(z) = O(T^{3/4}). \tag{5}$$

Summing the bounds (4) and (5) we obtain the desired bound on the regret of BBA:

$$R = \mathbf{E}\left(\sum_{t=1}^{T}C_t(i_t) - C_t(\ell_t(r))\right) + \mathbf{E}\left(\sum_{t=1}^{T}C_t(\ell_t(r)) - C_t(i)\right)$$

$$= O(T^{3/4}) + O\left(\frac{1}{w_i}\log^2\left(\frac{1}{w_i}\right)T^{3/4}\right)$$

$$= O\left(\frac{1}{w_i}\log^2\left(\frac{1}{w_i}\right)T^{3/4}\right).$$

5 Analysis of Algorithm **TrustFilter**

In this section we complete the analysis of algorithm TrustFilter by proving Theorem 1.

Proof (Theorem 1.). For $x \in X, s \in X \cup Y$, let

$$\tilde{C}_t(x, s) = \begin{cases} C_t(x, s) & \text{if } s \in Y \\ \mathbf{E}[C_t(x, y_t(s))] & \text{if } s \in X. \end{cases}$$

From the standpoint of agent x, the bandit algorithm BBA(x) is running in the noisy feedback model with cost functions $\tilde{C}_t(x, \cdot)$ and random feedback variables $X_t(s)$ distributed according to the cost $(C_t(x, y))$ of a random product $y \in Y$ sampled according to the harmonic measure relative to s. It follows from the analysis of BBA that for each pair of elements u, v in $H \cup Y$,

$$\mathbf{E}\left(\sum_{t=1}^{T}(\tilde{C}_t(u, u) - \tilde{C}_t(u, v))\right) = O\left(\frac{1}{w(u, v)}\log^2\left(\frac{1}{w(u, v)}\right)T^{3/4}\right). \quad (6)$$

Here $w(u, v)$ denotes the random weight assigned to strategy v by BBA(u) at initialization time. Using the fact that $1/w(u, v) = O(\beta n \log(\beta n))$, and that $\tilde{C}(u, v) = \tilde{C}(v, v)$ when u, v are consistent, we may rewrite (6) as

$$\mathbf{E}\left[\left(\sum_{t=1}^{T}\tilde{C}_t(u, u)\right) - \left(\sum_{t=1}^{T}\tilde{C}_t(v, v)\right)\right] = O\left(\frac{1}{w(u, v)}T^{3/4}\log^2(\beta n)\right), \quad (7)$$

provided that u and v are consistent. Let's introduce the following notations:

$$\bar{C}(u) = \mathbf{E}\left(\frac{1}{T}\sum_{t=1}^{T}\tilde{C}_t(u, u)\right)$$
$$B = \log^3(\beta n)T^{-1/4}$$
$$d(u, v) = (H_{m+n}w(u, v))^{-1}.$$

Then (7) may be rewritten as

$$\bar{C}(u) - \bar{C}(v) = d(u, v) \cdot O(B) \quad (8)$$

Note that for a product $y \in Y$, $\bar{C}(y)$ is simply the average cost of y, and for an agent $x \in H$, $\bar{C}(x)$ is the average cost of the products sampled by x. Let S be a consistent cluster containing x, and let $\alpha(S) = |S|/n$. Letting y^* denote a product with minimum average cost for members of S, and letting P denote a shortest path from x to y^* in the directed graph with vertex set $S \cup Y$ and edge lengths given by $d(\cdot, \cdot)$, we may sum up the bounds (8) over the edges of P to obtain

$$\bar{C}(x) - \bar{C}(y^*) = O(length(P) \cdot B) \quad (9)$$

Observe that the left side is the expected normalized regret of agent x. The random edge lengths $d(u, v)$ on the $m + n$ outgoing edges from u are simply the numbers $\{1, 2, \ldots, m + n\}$ in a random permutation. For graphs with random edge lengths specified according to this distribution, the expected distance between two given vertices is $O((\beta/\alpha) \log n)$.[2] We may conclude that the expectation of the right side of (9) is

$$O((\beta/\alpha(S)) \log(n)B) = O((\beta/\alpha(S)) \log^4(\beta n)T^{-1/4}). \tag{10}$$

It follows that the normalized regret and δ-convergence time for agents in the cluster S satisfy

$$\hat{R} = O\left(\left(\frac{\beta}{\alpha(S)}\right) \log^4(\beta n)T^{-1/4}\right) \tag{11}$$

$$T(\delta) = O\left(\left(\frac{\beta}{\alpha(S)\delta}\right)^4 \log^{16}(\beta n)\right). \tag{12}$$

Note that (12) can be interpreted as saying that the large consistent clusters learn to approximate the cost of the best resource much more rapidly than do the small clusters, which accords with one's intuition about collaborative learning. To obtain Theorem 1, we must average over the k consistent clusters $S_1, \ldots, S_k$. We may multiply the regret bound for a cluster S in (10) by the size of S, to obtain an upper bound of $O(\beta n \log^4(\beta n)T^{-1/4})$ on the aggregate regret of users in S. Summing over k such clusters, the cumulative regret of all honest users is $O(k\beta n \log^4(\beta n)T^{-1/4})$, so the normalized regret and convergence time satisfy:

$$\hat{R} = O\left(k \cdot \left(\frac{\beta}{\alpha}\right) \log^4(\beta n)T^{-1/4}\right) \tag{13}$$

$$T(\delta) = O\left(k^4 \cdot \left(\frac{\beta}{\alpha\delta}\right)^4 \log^{16}(\beta n)\right). \tag{14}$$

6   Open Problems

In this paper we have introduced and analyzed an algorithm for a simple model of collaborative learning. A key feature of our model is the presence of a large number of dishonest agents who are assumed to behave in an arbitrary Byzantine manner. However, other aspects of our model are quite idealized, and there are some very natural extensions of the model which more closely reflect the reality of collaborative learning systems such as eBay's reputation system and peer-to-peer resource discovery systems. It would be desirable to identify algorithms for some of the following extensions.

---

[2] A proof of this random graph lemma appears in the full version of this paper.

1. Study *asynchronous* collaborative learning, in which only a subset of the agents act as decision-makers in each round and the rest are inactive.
2. Study cases in which agents are constrained to choose from a proper subset of the resources, e.g. because the set of available resources is changing over time or because of limitations on the set of resources that a given agent is *ever* allowed to select.
3. Consider stronger models of collaborative filtering, by relaxing the consistency condition for two agents x_1, x_2 to belong to the same cluster. For example, consider the case where x_1, x_2 are consistent if $|C_t(x_1, y) - C_t(x_2, y)| < \varepsilon$ for all y, t, or consider the *mixture model* as in [9].
4. Study more structured collaborative decision-making problems, e.g. selecting routing paths in a network, some of whose nodes are identified with the agents.

References

1. Peter Auer, Nicolò Cesa-Bianchi, Yoav Freund, and Robert E. Schapire. Gambling in a rigged casino: the adversarial multi-armed bandit problem. In *Proceedings of the 36th Annual Symposium on Foundations of Computer Science*, pages 322–331. IEEE Computer Society Press, Los Alamitos, CA, 1995.
2. Baruch Awerbuch, Boaz Patt-Shamir, David Peleg, and Mark Tuttle. Collaboration of untrusting peers. In *Proc. of ACM conference on Electronic Commerce (EC)*, May 2004.
3. Baruch Awerbuch, Boaz Patt-Shamir, David Peleg, and Mark Tuttle. Improved recommendation systems. In *Proc. of ACM SIAM Conference on Discreet Algorithms (SODA)*, January 2005.
4. Yossi Azar, Amos Fiat, Anna Karlin, Frank McSherry, and Jared Saia. Spectral analysis of data. In *Proc. 33rd Ann. ACM Symp. on Theory of Computing (STOC)*, pages 619–626, 2001.
5. Sergey Brin and Lawrence Page. The anatomy of a large-scale hypertextual Web search engine. *Computer Networks and ISDN Systems*, 30(1–7):107–117, 1998.
6. Thomas H. Cormen, Charles E. Leiserson, and Ronald L. Rivest. *Introduction to Algorithms. 2nd Edition.* MIT Press, 2001.
7. Petros Drineas, Iordanis Kerenidis, and Prabhakar Raghavan. Competitive recommendation systems. In *Proc. 34th Ann. ACM Symp. on Theory of Computing (STOC)*, pages 82–90, 2002.
8. David Goldberg, David Nichols, Brian M. Oki, and Douglas Terry. Using collaborative filtering to weave an information tapestry. *Communications of the ACM*, 35(12):61–70, December 1992.
9. Thomas Hofmann and Jan Puzicha. Latent class models for collaborative filtering. In *Proceedings of the International Joint Conference in Artificial Intelligence (IJCAI)*, pages 688–693, 1999.
10. Sepandar D. Kamvar, Mario T. Schlosser, and Hector Garcia-Molina. The eigentrust algorithm for reputation management in p2p networks. In *Proc. 12th Int. World Wide Web Conference (WWW)*, 2003.
11. Jon Kleinberg. Finding authoritative sources in a hyperlinked environment. *J. ACM*, 46(5):604–632, 1999.

12. Pattie Maes, Robert H. Guttman, and Alexandros G. Moukas. Agents that buy and sell. *Communications of the ACM*, 42(3):81–91, 1999.
13. Lawrence Page, Sergey Brin, Rajeev Motwani, and Terry Winograd. The pagerank citation ranking: Bringing order to the web. Technical report, Stanford Digital Library Technologies Project, 1998.
14. Paul Resnick, Neophytos Iacovou, Mitesh Suchak, Peter Bergstrom, and John Riedl. Grouplens: an open architecture for collaborative filtering of netnews. In *Proceedings of the 1994 ACM Conference on Computer Supported Cooperative Work*, pages 175 – 186, October 1994.
15. Bin Yu and Munindar P. Singh. A social mechanism of reputation management in electronic communities. In *Cooperative Information Agents*, pages 154–165, 2000.
16. Giorgos Zacharia, Alexandros Moukas, and Pattie Maes. Collaborative reputation mechanisms in electronic marketplaces. In *HICSS*, 1999.
17. Oren Zamir and Oren Etzioni. Web document clustering: A feasibility demonstration. In *Research and Development in Information Retrieval*, pages 46–54, 1998.

Analysis of Perceptron-Based Active Learning

Sanjoy Dasgupta[1,*], Adam Tauman Kalai[2], and Claire Monteleoni[3,**]

[1] UCSD CSE, 9500 Gilman Drive #0114, La Jolla, CA 92093
dasgupta@cs.ucsd.edu
[2] TTI-Chicago, 1427 East 60th Street, Second Floor, Chicago, IL 60637
kalai@tti-c.org
[3] MIT CSAIL, 32 Vassar Street, Cambridge, MA 02139
cmontel@csail.mit.edu

Abstract. We start by showing that in an active learning setting, the Perceptron algorithm needs $\Omega(\frac{1}{\epsilon^2})$ labels to learn linear separators within generalization error ϵ. We then present a simple selective sampling algorithm for this problem, which combines a modification of the perceptron update with an adaptive filtering rule for deciding which points to query. For data distributed uniformly over the unit sphere, we show that our algorithm reaches generalization error ϵ after asking for just $\tilde{O}(d \log \frac{1}{\epsilon})$ labels. This exponential improvement over the usual sample complexity of supervised learning has previously been demonstrated only for the computationally more complex query-by-committee algorithm.

1 Introduction

In many machine learning applications, unlabeled data is abundant but labeling is expensive. This distinction is not captured in the standard PAC or online models of supervised learning, and has motivated the field of *active learning*, in which the labels of data points are initially hidden, and the learner must pay for each label it wishes revealed. If query points are chosen randomly, the number of labels needed to reach a target generalization error ϵ, at a target confidence level $1 - \delta$, is similar to the sample complexity of supervised learning. The hope is that there are alternative querying strategies which require significantly fewer labels.

To date, the single most dramatic demonstration of the potential of active learning is perhaps Freund et al.'s analysis of the query-by-committee (QBC) learning algorithm [7]. In their *selective sampling* model, the learner observes a stream of unlabeled data and makes spot decisions about whether or not to ask for a point's label. They show that if the data is drawn uniformly from the surface of the unit sphere in $\mathbb{R}^d$, and the hidden labels correspond perfectly to a homogeneous (i.e., through the origin) linear separator from this same distribution, then it is possible to achieve generalization error ϵ after seeing $\tilde{O}(\frac{d}{\epsilon} \log \frac{1}{\epsilon})$

---

* Funded by the NSF, under grant IIS-0347646.
** Work done primarily while at TTI-Chicago.

P. Auer and R. Meir (Eds.): COLT 2005, LNAI 3559, pp. 249–263, 2005.

points and requesting just $\tilde{O}(d \log \frac{1}{\epsilon})$ labels:[1] an exponential improvement over the usual $\tilde{O}(\frac{d}{\epsilon})$ sample complexity of learning linear separators in a supervised setting.[2] This remarkable result is tempered somewhat by the complexity of the QBC algorithm, which involves random sampling from intermediate version spaces; the complexity of the update step scales (polynomially) with the number of updates performed.

In this paper, we show how a simple modification of the perceptron update can be used to achieve the same sample complexity bounds (within $\tilde{O}$ factors), under the same streaming model and the same uniform input distribution. Unlike QBC, we do not assume a distribution over target hypotheses, and our algorithm does not need to store previously seen data points, only its current hypothesis.

Our algorithm has the following structure.

```
Set initial hypothesis v₀ ∈ ℝᵈ
For t = 0, 1, 2, . . .
    Receive unlabeled point xₜ
    Make a prediction SGN(vₜ · xₜ)
    Filtering step: Decide whether to ask for xₜ's label
    If label yₜ is requested:
        Update step: Set vₜ₊₁ based on vₜ, xₜ, yₜ
        Adjust filtering rule
    else:   vₜ₊₁ = vₜ
```

Update Step. It turns out that the regular perceptron update, that is,

$$\text{if } (x_t, y_t) \text{ is misclassified then } v_{t+1} = v_t + y_t x_t$$

cannot yield an error rate better than $\Omega(1/\sqrt{l_t})$, where l_t is the number of labels queried up to time t, no matter what filtering scheme is used. In particular:

Theorem 1. *Consider any sequence of data points $x_0, x_1, x_2, \ldots$ which is perfectly classified by some linear separator $u \in \mathbb{R}^d$. If θ_t is the angle between u and v_t, then for any $t \geq 0$, if $\theta_{t+1} \leq \theta_t$ then $\sin \theta_t \geq 1/(5\sqrt{l_t + \|v_0\|^2})$.*

This holds regardless of how the data is produced. When the points are distributed uniformly over the unit sphere, $\theta_t \geq \sin \theta_t$ (for $\theta_t \leq \frac{\pi}{2}$) is proportional to the error rate of v_t.

So instead we use a slightly modified update rule:

$$\text{if } (x_t, y_t) \text{ is misclassified then } v_{t+1} = v_t - 2(v_t \cdot x_t)x_t$$

(where x_t is assumed normalized to unit length). Note that the update can also be written as $v_{t+1} = v_t + 2y_t|v_t \cdot x_t|x_t$, since updates are only made on mistakes,

---

[1] In this paper, the $\tilde{O}$ notation is used to suppress terms in $\log d, \log \log \frac{1}{\epsilon}$ and $\log \frac{1}{\delta}$.

[2] This label complexity can be seen to be optimal by counting the number of spherical caps of radius ϵ that can be packed onto the surface of the unit sphere in $\mathbb{R}^d$.

in which case $y_t \neq \text{SGN}(v_t \cdot x_t)$, by definition. Thus we are scaling the standard perceptron's additive update by a factor of $2|v_t \cdot x_t|$ to avoid oscillations caused by points close to the hyperplane represented by the current hypothesis. The same rule, but without the factor of two, has been used in previous work [3] on learning linear classifiers from noisy data, in a batch setting. We are able to show that our formulation has the following generalization performance in a supervised (non-active) setting.

Theorem 2. *When the modified Perceptron algorithm is applied in a sequential supervised setting, with data points x_t drawn independently and uniformly at random from the surface of the unit sphere in $\mathbb{R}^d$, then with probability $1 - \delta$, after $O(d(\log \frac{1}{\epsilon} + \log \frac{1}{\delta}))$ mistakes, its generalization error is at most ϵ.*

This contrasts favorably with the $\tilde{O}(\frac{d}{\epsilon^2})$ mistake bound of the Perceptron algorithm, and a more recent variant, on the same distribution [2, 12]. As a lower bound for standard Perceptron, Theorem 1 also applies in the supervised case, as it holds for all filtering rules, including viewing all the labels. The bound on labels, $\Omega(\frac{1}{\epsilon^2})$, lower bounds mistakes as well, since the number of labels is minimized when every label yields a mistake, and thus an update.

The PAC sample complexity of the problem under the uniform distribution is $\tilde{\Theta}(\frac{d}{\epsilon})$ (lower bound [10], and upper bound [11]). Yet since not all examples yield mistakes, mistake bounds can be lower than sample bounds. A similar statement holds in the active learning case: bounds on labels can be lower than sample bounds, since the algorithms are allowed to filter which samples to label.

Filtering Step. Given the limited information the algorithm keeps, a natural filtering rule is to query points x_t when $|v_t \cdot x_t|$ is less than some threshold s_t. The choice of s_t is crucial. If it is too large, then only a miniscule fraction of the points queried will actually be misclassified – almost all labels will be wasted. On the other hand, if s_t is too small, then the waiting time for a query might be prohibitive, and when an update is actually made, the magnitude of this update might be tiny.

Therefore, we set the threshold adaptively: we start s high, and keep dividing it by two until we reach a level where there are enough misclassifications amongst the points queried. This filtering strategy makes possible our main theorem, again for data from the uniform distribution over the unit sphere in $\mathbb{R}^d$.

Theorem 3. *With probability $1 - \delta$, if the active modified Perceptron algorithm is given a stream of $\tilde{O}(\frac{d}{\epsilon} \log \frac{1}{\epsilon})$ unlabeled points, it will request $\tilde{O}(d \log \frac{1}{\epsilon})$ labels, make $\tilde{O}(d \log \frac{1}{\epsilon})$ errors (on all points, labeled or not), and have final error $\leq \epsilon$.*

2   Related Work

Our approach relates to the literature on selective sampling [7, 4]. We have already discussed query-by-committee [7], which is perhaps the strongest positive result in active learning to date. There have been numerous applications of this method and also several refinements (see, for instance, [8, 6]).

Cesa-Bianchi, Gentile, and Zaniboni [4] have recently analyzed an algorithm which conforms to roughly the same template as ours but differs in both the update and filtering rule – it uses the regular perceptron update and it queries points x_t according to a fixed, randomized rule which favors small $|v_t \cdot x_t|$. The authors make no distributional assumptions on the input and they show that in terms of worst-case hinge-loss bounds, their algorithm does about as well as one which queries *all* labels. The actual fraction of points queried varies from data set to data set. In contrast, our objective is to achieve a target generalization error with minimum label complexity, although we do also obtain a mistake bound (on both labeled and unlabeled points) under our distributional assumption.

It is known that active learning does not always give a large improvement in the sample complexity of learning linear separators. For instance, in our setting where data is distributed uniformly over the unit sphere, recent work has shown that if the target linear separator is allowed to be non-homogeneous, then the number of labels required to reach error ϵ is $\Omega(1/\epsilon)$, no matter what active learning scheme is used [5]. This lower bound also applies to learning homogeneous linear separators with respect to an arbitrary distribution.

Many active learning schemes for linear separators (or probabilistic analogues) have been proposed in the literature. Several of these are similar in spirit to our heuristic, in that they query points close to the margin, and seem to have enjoyed some empirical success; e.g., [9]. Finally, there is a rich body of theory on a related model in which it is permissible to create query points synthetically; a recent survey by Angluin [1] summarizes key results.

3   Preliminaries

In our model, all data x_t lie on the surface of the unit ball in $\mathbb{R}^d$, which we will denote as S:

$$S = \left\{ x \in \mathbb{R}^d \mid \|x\| = 1 \right\}.$$

Their labels y_t are either -1 or $+1$, and the target function is a half-space $u \cdot x \geq 0$ represented by a unit vector $u \in \mathbb{R}^d$ which classifies all points perfectly, that is, $y_t(u \cdot x_t) > 0$ for all t, with probability one.

For any vector $v \in \mathbb{R}^d$, we define $\hat{v} = \frac{v}{\|v\|}$ to be the corresponding unit vector.

Our lower bound (Theorem 1) holds regardless of how the data are generated; thereafter we will assume that the data points x_t are drawn independently from the uniform distribution over S. This implies that any hypothesis $v \in \mathbb{R}^d$ has error

$$\epsilon(v) = P_{x \in S}[\text{SGN}(v \cdot x) \neq \text{SGN}(u \cdot x)] = \frac{\arccos(u \cdot \hat{v})}{\pi}.$$

We will use a few useful inequalities for θ on the interval $(0, \frac{\pi}{2}]$.

$$\frac{4}{\pi^2} \leq \frac{1 - \cos\theta}{\theta^2} \leq \frac{1}{2}, \tag{1}$$

$$\frac{2}{\pi}\theta \leq \sin\theta \leq \theta \tag{2}$$

Equation (1) can be verified by checking that for θ in this interval, $\frac{1-\cos\theta}{\theta^2}$ is a decreasing function, and evaluating it at the endpoints.

We will also make use of the following lemma.

Lemma 1. *For any fixed unit vector a and any $\gamma \leq 1$,*

$$\frac{\gamma}{4} \leq P_{x \in S}\left[|a \cdot x| \leq \frac{\gamma}{\sqrt{d}}\right] \leq \gamma \tag{3}$$

The proof is deferred to the appendix.

4   A Lower Bound for the Perceptron Update

Consider an algorithm of the following form:

```
Pick some v₀ ∈ ℝᵈ
Repeat for t = 0, 1, 2, ...:
    Get some (x, y) for which y(vₜ · x) ≤ 0
    vₜ₊₁ = vₜ + yx
```

On any update,

$$v_{t+1} \cdot u = v_t \cdot u + y(x \cdot u). \tag{4}$$

Thus, if we assume for simplicity that $v_0 \cdot u \geq 0$ (we can always just start count when this first occurs) then $v_t \cdot u \geq 0$ always, and the angle between u and v_t is always acute. Denoting this angle by θ_t, we get

$$\|v_t\| \cos \theta_t = v_t \cdot u.$$

The update rule also implies

$$\|v_{t+1}\|^2 = \|v_t\|^2 + 1 + 2y(v_t \cdot x). \tag{5}$$

Thus $\|v_t\|^2 \leq t + \|v_0\|^2$ for all t. In particular, this means that Theorem 1 is an immediate consequence of the following lemma.

Lemma 2. *Assume $v_0 \cdot u \geq 0$ (i.e., start count when this first occurs). Then*

$$\theta_{t+1} \leq \theta_t \quad \Rightarrow \quad \sin \theta_t \geq \min\left\{\frac{1}{3}, \frac{1}{5\|v_t\|}\right\}.$$

Proof. Figure 1 shows the unit circle in the plane defined by u and v_t. The dot product of any point $x \in \mathbb{R}^d$ with either u or v_t depends only upon the projection of x into this plane. The point is misclassified when its projection lies in the shaded region. For such points, $y(u \cdot x)$ is at most $\sin \theta_t$ (point (i)) and $y(v_t \cdot x)$ is at least $-\|v_t\| \sin \theta_t$ (point (ii)).

Combining this with equations (4) and (5), we get

$$v_{t+1} \cdot u \leq v_t \cdot u + \sin \theta_t$$
$$\|v_{t+1}\|^2 \geq \|v_t\|^2 + 1 - 2\|v_t\| \sin \theta_t$$

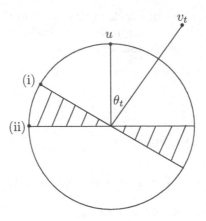

Fig. 1. The plane defined by u and v_t

To establish the lemma, we first assume $\theta_{t+1} \leq \theta_t$ and $\sin \theta_t \leq \frac{1}{5\|v_t\|}$, and then conclude that $\sin \theta_t \geq \frac{1}{3}$.

$\theta_{t+1} \leq \theta_t$ implies

$$\cos^2 \theta_t \leq \cos^2 \theta_{t+1} = \frac{(u \cdot v_{t+1})^2}{\|v_{t+1}\|^2} \leq \frac{(u \cdot v_t + \sin \theta_t)^2}{\|v_t\|^2 + 1 - 2\|v_t\| \sin \theta_t}.$$

The final denominator is positive since $\sin \theta_t \leq \frac{1}{5\|v_t\|}$. Rearranging,

$$(\|v_t\|^2 + 1 - 2\|v_t\| \sin \theta_t) \cos^2 \theta_t \leq (u \cdot v_t)^2 + \sin^2 \theta_t + 2(u \cdot v_t) \sin \theta_t$$

and using $\|v_t\| \cos \theta_t = (u \cdot v_t)$:

$$(1 - 2\|v_t\| \sin \theta_t) \cos^2 \theta_t \leq \sin^2 \theta_t + 2\|v_t\| \sin \theta_t \cos \theta_t$$

Again, since $\sin \theta_t \leq \frac{1}{5\|v_t\|}$, it follows that $(1 - 2\|v_t\| \sin \theta_t) \geq \frac{3}{5}$ and that $2\|v_t\| \sin \theta_t \cos \theta_t \leq \frac{2}{5}$. Using $\cos^2 = 1 - \sin^2$, we then get

$$\frac{3}{5}(1 - \sin^2 \theta_t) \leq \sin^2 \theta_t + \frac{2}{5}$$

which works out to $\sin^2 \theta_t \geq \frac{1}{8}$, implying $\sin \theta_t > \frac{1}{3}$.   □

The problem is that the perceptron update can be too large. In $\mathbb{R}^2$ (e.g. Figure 1), when θ_t is tiny, the update will cause v_{t+1} to overshoot the mark and swing too far to the other side of u, unless $\|v_t\|$ is very large: to be precise, we need $\|v_t\| = \Omega(1/\sin \theta_t)$. But $\|v_t\|$ grows slowly, at best at a rate of $\sqrt{t}$. If $\sin \theta_t$ is proportional to the error of v_t, as in the case of data distributed uniformly over the unit sphere, this means that the perceptron update cannot stably maintain an error rate $\leq \epsilon$ until $t = \Omega(1/\epsilon^2)$.

Inputs: dimensionality d and desired number of updates
(mistakes) M.
   Let $v_1 = x_1 y_1$ for the first example (x_1, y_1).
   For $t = 1$ to M:
      Let (x_t, y_t) be the next example with $y(x \cdot v_t) < 0$.
      $v_{t+1} = v_t - 2(v_t \cdot x_t) x_t$.

Fig. 2. The (non-active) modified Perceptron algorithm. The standard Perceptron update, $v_{t+1} = v_t + y_t x_t$, is in the same direction (note $y_t = -\mathtt{SGN}(v_t \cdot x_t)$) but different magnitude (scaled by a factor of $2|v_t \cdot x_t|$)

5 The Modified Perceptron Update

We now describe the modified Perceptron algorithm. Using a simple modification to the standard perceptron update yields the fast convergence we will prove subsequently. Unlike with standard Perceptron, this modification ensures that $v_t \cdot u$ is increasing, i.e., the error of v_t is monotonically decreasing. Another difference from the standard update (and other versions) is that the magnitude of $\|v_t\| = 1$, which is convenient for our analysis.

The modified Perceptron algorithm is shown in Figure 2. We now show that the norm of v_t stays at one. Note that $\|v_1\| = 1$ and

$$\|v_{t+1}\|^2 = \|v_t\|^2 + 4(v_t \cdot x_t)^2 \|x_t\|^2 - 4(v_t \cdot x_t)^2 = 1$$

by induction. In contrast, for the standard perceptron update, the magnitude of v_t is important and normalized vectors cannot be used.

With the modified update, the error can only decrease, because $v_t \cdot u$ only increases:

$$v_{t+1} \cdot u = v_t \cdot u - 2(v_t \cdot x_t)(x_t \cdot u) = v_t \cdot u + 2|v_t \cdot x_t||x_t \cdot u|.$$

The second equality follows from the fact that v_t misclassified x_t. Thus $v_t \cdot u$ is increasing, and the increase can be bounded from below by showing that $|v_t \cdot x_t||x_t \cdot u|$ is large. This is a different approach from previous analyses.

Blum et al. [3] used an update similar to ours, but without the factor of two. In general, one can consider modified updates of the form $v_{t+1} = v_t - \alpha(v_t \cdot x_t) x_t$. When $\alpha \neq 2$, the vectors v_t no longer remain of fixed length; however, one can verify that their corresponding unit vectors $\hat{v}_t$ satisfy

$$\hat{v}_{t+1} \cdot u = (\hat{v}_t \cdot u + \alpha |\hat{v}_t \cdot x_t||x_t \cdot u|)/\sqrt{1 - \alpha(2 - \alpha)(\hat{v}_t \cdot x_t)^2},$$

and thus any choice of $\alpha \in [0, 2]$ guarantees non-increasing error. Blum et al. used $\alpha = 1$ to guarantee progress in the denominator (their analysis did not rely on progress in the numerator) as long as $\hat{v}_t \cdot u$ and $(\hat{v}_t \cdot x_t)^2$ were bounded away from 0. Their approach was used in a batch setting as one piece of a more complex algorithm for noise-tolerant learning. In our sequential framework, we can bound $|\hat{v}_t \cdot x_t||x_t \cdot u|$ away from 0 in expectation, under the uniform distribution, and hence the choice of $\alpha = 2$ is most convenient, but $\alpha = 1$ would work as well. Although we do not further optimize our choice of the constant α, this choice itself may yield interesting future work, perhaps by allowing it to be a function of the dimension.

5.1   Analysis of (Non-active) Modified Perceptron

How large do we expect $|v_t \cdot x_t|$ and $|u \cdot x_t|$ to be for an error (x_t, y_t)? As we shall see, in d dimensions, one expects each of these terms to be on the order of $d^{-1/2} \sin \theta_t$, where $\sin \theta_t = \sqrt{1 - (v_t \cdot u)^2}$. Hence, we might expect their product to be about $(1 - (v_t \cdot u)^2)/d$, which is how we prove the following lemma.

Note, we have made little effort to optimize constant factors.

Lemma 3. *For any* v_t, *with probability at least* $\frac{1}{3}$,

$$1 - v_{t+1} \cdot u \le (1 - v_t \cdot u) \left(1 - \frac{1}{50d}\right).$$

There exists a constant $c > 0$, *such that with probability at least* $\frac{63}{64}$, *for any* v_t,

$$1 - v_{t+1} \cdot u \le (1 - v_t \cdot u) \left(1 - \frac{c}{d}\right).$$

Proof. We show only the first part of the lemma. The second part is quite similar. We will argue that each of $|v_t \cdot x_t|, |u \cdot x_t|$ is "small" with probability at most $1/3$. This means, by the union bound, that with probability at least $1/3$, they are both sufficiently large.

The error rate of v_t is θ_t/π, where $\cos \theta_t = v_t \cdot u$. Also define the error region $\xi_t = \{x \in S \,|\, \text{SGN}(v_t \cdot x) \ne \text{SGN}(u \cdot x)\}$. By Lemma 1, for an x drawn uniformly from the sphere,

$$P_{x \in S}\left[|v_t \cdot x| \le \frac{\theta_t}{3\pi\sqrt{d}}\right] \le \frac{\theta_t}{3\pi}.$$

Using $P[A|B] \le P[A]/P[B]$, we have,

$$P_{x \in S}\left[|v_t \cdot x| \le \frac{\theta_t}{3\pi\sqrt{d}} \,\bigg|\, x \in \xi_t\right] \le \frac{P_{x \in S}[|v_t \cdot x| \le \frac{\theta_t}{3\pi\sqrt{d}}]}{P_{x \in S}[x \in \xi_t]} \le \frac{\theta_t/(3\pi)}{\theta_t/\pi} = \frac{1}{3}.$$

Similarly for $|u \cdot x|$, and by the union bound the probability that $x \in \xi$ is within margin $\frac{\theta}{3\pi\sqrt{d}}$ from either u or v is at most $\frac{2}{3}$. Since the updates only occur if x is in the error region, we now have a lower bound on the expected magnitude of $|v_t \cdot x||u \cdot x|$.

$$P_{x \in S}\left[|v_t \cdot x||u \cdot x| \ge \frac{\theta_t^2}{(3\pi\sqrt{d})^2} \,\bigg|\, x \in \xi_t\right] \ge \frac{1}{3}.$$

Hence, we know that with probability at least $1/3$, $|v_t \cdot x||u \cdot x| \geq \frac{1-(v_t \cdot u)^2}{100d}$, since $\theta_t^2 \geq \sin^2 \theta_t = 1 - (v_t \cdot u)^2$ and $(3\pi)^2 < 100$. In this case,

$$1 - v_{t+1} \cdot u \leq 1 - v_t \cdot u - 2|v_t \cdot x_t||u \cdot x_t|$$
$$\leq 1 - v_t \cdot u - \frac{1-(v_t \cdot u)^2}{50d}$$
$$\leq (1 - v_t \cdot u)\left(1 - \frac{1+v_t \cdot u}{50d}\right)$$

$\square$

Finally, we give a high-probability bound, i.e. Theorem 2, stated here with proof.

Theorem 2. *With probability $1 - \delta$, after $M = O(d(\log \frac{1}{\epsilon} + \log \frac{1}{\delta}))$ mistakes, the generalization error of the modified Perceptron algorithm is at most ϵ.*

Proof. By the above lemma, we can conclude that, for any vector v_t,

$$E_{x_t \in \xi_t}[1 - v_{t+1} \cdot u] \leq (1 - v_t \cdot u)\left(1 - \frac{1}{3(50d)}\right).$$

This is because with $\geq 1/3$ probability it goes down by a factor of $1 - \frac{1}{50d}$ and with the remaining $\leq 2/3$ probability it does not increase. Hence, after M mistakes,

$$E[1 - v_M \cdot u] \leq (1 - v_1 \cdot u)\left(1 - \frac{1}{150d}\right)^M \leq \left(1 - \frac{1}{150d}\right)^M,$$

since $v_1 \cdot u \geq 0$. By Markov's inequality,

$$P\left[1 - v_M \cdot u \geq \left(1 - \frac{1}{150d}\right)^M \delta^{-1}\right] \leq \delta.$$

Finally, using (1) and $\cos \theta_M = v_M \cdot u$, we see $P[\frac{4}{\pi^2}\theta_M^2 \geq (1 - \frac{1}{150d})^M \delta^{-1}] < \delta$. Using $M = 150d \log(1/\epsilon\delta)$ gives $P[\frac{\theta_M}{\pi} \geq \epsilon] \leq \delta$ as required. $\square$

6   An Active Modified Perceptron

The active version of the modified Perceptron algorithm is shown in Figure 3. The algorithm is similar to the algorithm of the previous section, in its update step. For its filtering rule, we maintain a threshold s_t and we only ask for labels of examples with $|v_t \cdot x_t| \leq s_t$. We decrease this threshold adaptively over time, starting at $s_1 = 1/\sqrt{d}$ and reducing it by a factor of two whenever we have a run of labeled examples on which we are correct.

For Theorem 3, we select values of R, L that yield ϵ error with probability at least $1 - \delta$. The idea of the analysis is as follows:

```
Inputs: Dimensionality d, maximum number of labels L,
and patience R.
```
$v_1 = x_1 y_1$ for the first example (x_1, y_1).
$s_1 = 1/\sqrt{d}$
For $t = 1$ **to** L:
    Wait for the next example $x : |x \cdot v_t| \le s_t$ and query its label.
    Call this labeled example (x_t, y_t).
    If $(x_t \cdot v_t)y_t < 0$, **then:**
      $v_{t+1} = v_t - 2(v_t \cdot x_t)x_t$
      $s_{t+1} = s_t$
    else:
      $v_{t+1} = v_t$
    If predictions were correct on R consecutive labeled
    examples (i.e. $(x_i \cdot v_i)y_i \ge 0 \ \forall i \in \{t-R+1, t-R+2, \ldots, t\}$),
    then set $s_{t+1} = s_t/2$, **else** $s_{t+1} = s_t$.

Fig. 3. An active version of the modified Perceptron algorithm

Definition 1. *We say the tth update is "good" if,*

$$1 - v_{t+1} \cdot u \le (1 - v_t \cdot u)\left(1 - \frac{c}{d}\right).$$

(The constant c is from Lemma 3.)

1. (Lemma 4) First, we argue that s_t is not too small (we do not decrease s_t too quickly). Assuming this is the case, then 2 and 3 hold.
2. (Lemma 6) We query for labels on at least an expected $1/32$ of all *errors*. In other words, some errors may go undetected because we do not ask for their labels, but the number of mistakes total should not be much more than 32 times the number of updates we actually perform.
3. (Lemma 7) Each update is *good* (Definition 1) with probability at least $1/2$.
4. (Theorem 3) Finally, we conclude that we cannot have too many label queries, updates, or total errors, because half of our updates are good, $1/32$ of our errors are updates, and about $1/R$ of our labels are updates.

We first lower-bound s_t with respect to our error, showing that, with high probability, the threshold s_t is never too small.

Lemma 4. *With probability at least* $1 - L\left(\frac{3}{4}\right)^R$, *we have:*

$$s_t \ge \sqrt{\frac{1 - (u \cdot v_t)^2}{16d}} \text{ for } t = 1, 2, \ldots, L, \text{ simultaneously.} \tag{6}$$

Before proving this lemma, it will be helpful to show the following lemma. As before, let us define $\xi_t = \{x \in S | (x \cdot v_t)(x \cdot u) < 0\}$.

Lemma 5. *For any* $\gamma \in \left(0, \sqrt{\frac{1-(u \cdot v_t)^2}{4d}} \right]$,

$$P_{x_t \in S} \left[x_t \in \xi_t \mid |x_t \cdot v_t| < \gamma \right] \geq \frac{1}{4}$$

Proof. Let x be a random example from S such that $|x \cdot v_t| < \gamma$ and, without loss of generality, suppose that $0 \leq x \cdot v_t \leq \gamma$. Then we want to calculate the probability we err, i.e. $u \cdot x < 0$. We can decompose $x = x' + (x \cdot v_t)v_t$ where $x' = x - (x \cdot v_t)v_t$ is the component of x orthogonal to v_t, i.e. $x' \cdot v_t = 0$. Similarly for $u' = u - (u \cdot v_t)v_t$. Hence,

$$u \cdot x = (u' + (u \cdot v_t)v_t) \cdot (x' + (x \cdot v_t)v_t) = u' \cdot x' + (u \cdot v_t)(x \cdot v_t)$$

In other words, we err iff $u' \cdot x' < -(u \cdot v_t)(x \cdot v_t)$. Using $u \cdot v_t \in [0,1]$ and since $x \cdot v_t \in [0, \sqrt{(1-(u \cdot v_t)^2)/(4d)}]$, we conclude that if,

$$u' \cdot x' < -\sqrt{\frac{1-(u \cdot v_t)^2}{4d}} \tag{7}$$

then we must err. Also, let $\hat{x}' = \frac{x'}{\|x'\|}$ be the unit vector in the direction of x'. It is straightforward to check that $\|x'\| = \sqrt{1-(x \cdot v_t)^2}$. Similarly, for u we define $\hat{u}' = \frac{u'}{\sqrt{1-(u \cdot v_t)^2}}$. Substituting these into (7), we must err if, $\hat{u}' \cdot \hat{x}' < -1/\sqrt{4d(1-(x \cdot v_t))^2}$, and since $\sqrt{1-(x \cdot v_t)^2} \geq \sqrt{1-1/(4d)}$, it suffices to show that,

$$P_{x \in S} \left[\hat{u}' \cdot \hat{x}' < \frac{-1}{\sqrt{4d(1-1/(4d))}} \;\middle|\; 0 \leq x \cdot v_t \leq \gamma \right] \geq \frac{1}{4}$$

What is the probability that this happens? Well, one way to pick $x \in S$ would be to first pick $x \cdot v_t$ and then to pick $\hat{x}'$ uniformly at random from the set $S' = \{\hat{x}' \in S | \hat{x}' \cdot v_t = 0\}$, which is a unit sphere in one fewer dimensions. Hence the above probability does not depend on the conditioning. By Lemma 1, for any unit vector $a \in S'$, the probability that $|\hat{u}' \cdot a| \leq 1/\sqrt{4(d-1)}$ is at most $1/2$, so with probability at least $1/4$ (since the distribution is symmetric), the signed quantity $\hat{u}' \cdot \hat{x}' < -1/\sqrt{4(d-1)} < -1/\sqrt{4d(1-1/(4d))}$. $\square$

We are now ready to prove Lemma 4.

Proof (of Lemma 4). Suppose that condition (6) fails to hold for some t's. Let t be the smallest number such that (6) fails. By our choice of s_1, clearly $t > 1$. Moreover, since t is the smallest such number, and $u \cdot v_t$ is increasing, it must be the case that $s_t = s_{t-1}/2$, that is we just saw a run of R labeled examples (x_i, y_i), for $i = t - R, \ldots, t - 1$, with no mistakes, $v_i = v_t$, and

$$s_i = 2s_t < \sqrt{\frac{1-(u \cdot v_t)^2}{4d}} = \sqrt{\frac{1-(u \cdot v_i)^2}{4d}}. \tag{8}$$

Such an event is highly unlikely, however, for any t. In particular, from Lemma 5, we know that the probability of (8) holding for any particular i and the algorithm not erring is at most $3/4$. Thus the chance of having any such run of length R is at most $L(3/4)^R$.

Lemma 5 also tells us something interesting about the fraction of errors that we are missing because we do not ask for labels. In particular,

Lemma 6. *Given that* $s_t \geq \sqrt{(1 - (u \cdot v_t)^2)/(16d)}$, *upon the tth update, each erroneous example is queried with probability at least $1/32$, i.e.,*

$$P_{x \in S}\left[|x \cdot v_t| \leq s_t \mid x \in \xi_t\right] \geq \frac{1}{32}.$$

Proof. Using Lemmas 5 and 1, we have

$$P_{x \in S}\left[x \in \xi_t \wedge |x \cdot v_t| \leq s_t\right] \geq P_{x \in S}\left[x \in \xi_t \wedge |x \cdot v_t| \leq \sqrt{\frac{1 - (u \cdot v_t)^2}{16d}}\right]$$

$$\geq \frac{1}{4}P_{x \in S}\left[|x \cdot v_t| \leq \sqrt{\frac{1 - (u \cdot v_t)^2}{16d}}\right]$$

$$\geq \frac{1}{64}\sqrt{1 - (u \cdot v_t)^2} = \frac{1}{64}\sin\theta_t$$

$$\geq \frac{\theta_t}{32\pi}$$

For the last inequality, we have used (2). However, $P_{x \in S}[x \in \xi_t] = \theta_t/\pi$, so we are querying an error $x \in \xi_t$ with probability at least $1/32$, i.e., the above inequality implies,

$$P_{x \in S}\left[|x \cdot v_t| \leq s_t \mid x \in \xi_t\right] = \frac{P_{x \in S}\left[x \in \xi_t \wedge |x \cdot v_t| \leq s_t\right]}{P_{x \in S}[x \in \xi_t]} \geq \frac{\theta_t/(32\pi)}{\theta_t/\pi} = \frac{1}{32}.$$

$\square$

Next, we show that the updates are likely to make progress.

Lemma 7. *Assuming that* $s_t \geq \sqrt{(1 - (u \cdot v_t)^2)/(16d)}$, *a random update is good with probability at least $1/2$, i.e.,*

$$P_{x_t \in S}\left[(1 - v_{t+1} \cdot u) \leq (1 - v_t \cdot u)\left(1 - \frac{c}{d}\right) \mid |x \cdot v_t| \leq s_t \wedge x_t \in \xi_t\right] \geq \frac{1}{2}.$$

Proof. By Lemma 6, each error is queried with probability $1/32$. On the other hand, by Lemma 3 of the previous section, $63/64$ of all errors are good. Since we are querying at least $2/64$ fraction of all errors, at least half of our queried errors must be good. $\square$

We now have the pieces to guarantee the convergence rate of the active algorithm, thereby proving Theorem 3. This involves bounding both the number of labels that we query as well as the number of total errors, which includes updates as well as errors that were never detected.

Theorem 3. *With probability $1 - \delta$, using $L = O(d\log(\frac{1}{\epsilon\delta})(\log\frac{d}{\delta} + \log\log\frac{1}{\epsilon}))$ labels and making a total number of errors of $O(d\log(\frac{1}{\epsilon\delta})(\log\frac{d}{\delta} + \log\log\frac{1}{\epsilon}))$, the final error of the active modified Perceptron algorithm will be ϵ, when run with the above L and $R = O(\log\frac{d}{\delta} + \log\log\frac{1}{\epsilon})$.*

Proof. Let U be the number of updates performed. We know, by Lemma 4 that with probability $1 - L(\frac{3}{4})^R$,

$$s_t \geq \frac{\sin\theta_t}{4\sqrt{d}} \geq \frac{\theta_t}{2\pi\sqrt{d}} \tag{9}$$

for all t. Again, we have used (2). By Lemma 7, we know that for each t which is an update, either (9) fails or

$$E[1 - u \cdot v_{t+1}|v_t] \leq (1 - u \cdot v_t)\left(1 - \frac{c}{2d}\right).$$

Hence, after U updates, using Markov's inequality,

$$P\left[1 - u \cdot v_L \geq \frac{4}{\delta}\left(1 - \frac{c}{2d}\right)^U\right] \leq \frac{\delta}{4} + L\left(\frac{3}{4}\right)^R.$$

In other words, with probability $1 - \delta/4 - L(3/4)^R$, we also have

$$U \leq \frac{2d}{c}\log\frac{4}{\delta(1 - u \cdot v_L)} \leq \frac{2d}{c}\log\frac{\pi^2}{\delta\theta_L^2} = O\left(d\log\frac{1}{\delta\epsilon}\right),$$

where for the last inequality we used (1). In total, $L \leq R(U + \log_2 1/s_L)$. This is because once every R labels we either have at least one update or we decrease s_L by a factor of 2. Equivalently, $s_L \leq 2^{U-L/R}$. Hence, with probability $1 - \delta/4 - L(3/4)^R$,

$$\frac{\theta_L}{2\pi\sqrt{d}} \leq s_L \leq 2^{O(d\log(1/\delta\epsilon))-L/R}$$

Working backwards, we choose $L/R = \Theta(d\log\frac{1}{\epsilon\delta})$ so that the above expression implies $\frac{\theta_L}{\pi} \leq \epsilon$, as required. We choose,

$$R = 10\log\frac{2L}{\delta R} = \Theta\left(\log\frac{d\log\frac{1}{\epsilon\delta}}{\delta}\right) = O\left(\log\frac{d}{\delta} + \log\log\frac{1}{\epsilon}\right).$$

The first equality ensures that $L(3/4)^R \leq \delta/4$. Hence, for the L and R chosen in the theorem, with probability $1 - \frac{3}{4}\delta$, we have error $\theta_L/\pi < \epsilon$. Finally, either condition (9) fails or each error is queried with probability at least $1/32$. By the multiplicative Chernoff bound, if there were a total of $E > 64U$ errors, then with probability $\geq 1 - \delta/4$, at least $E/64 > U$ would have been caught and used as updates. Hence, with probability at most $1 - \delta$, we have achieved the target error using the specified number of labels and incurring the specified number of errors. □

7   Future Directions

The theoretical terrain of active learning is largely an unexplored wilderness. The one nontrivial scenario in which active learning has been shown to give an exponential improvement in sample complexity is that of learning a linear separator for data distributed uniformly over the unit sphere. In this paper, we have demonstrated that this particular case can be solved by a much simpler algorithm than was previously known. It is possible that our algorithm can be molded into something of more general applicability, and so it would be interesting to study its behavior under different circumstances, for instance a different distributional assumption. The uniform distribution is an impressive one to learn against because it is difficult in some ways – most of the data is close to the decision boundary, for instance – but a more common assumption would be to make the two classes Gaussian, or to merely stipulate that they are separated by a margin. How would our algorithm fare under these circumstances?

Acknowledgements

Claire Monteleoni would like to thank Adam Klivans, Brendan McMahan, and Vikas Sindhwani, for various discussions at TTI, and David McAllester for the opportunity to visit. The authors thank the anonymous reviewers for helpful comments used in revision.

References

1. D. Angluin. Queries revisited. *In Proc. 12th Int. Conference on Algorithmic Learning Theory*, LNAI,2225:12–31, 2001.
2. E. B. Baum. The perceptron algorithm is fast for nonmalicious distributions. *Neural Computation*, 2:248–260, 1997.
3. A. Blum, A. Frieze, R. Kannan, and S. Vempala. A polynomial-time algorithm for learning noisy linear threshold functions. In *Proc. 37th IEEE Symposium on the Foundations of Computer Science*, 1996.
4. N. Cesa-Bianchi, C. Gentile, and L. Zaniboni. Worst-case analysis of selective sampling for linear-threshold algorithms. In *Advances in Neural Information Processing Systems 17*, 2004.
5. S. Dasgupta. Analysis of a greedy active learning strategy. In *Advances in Neural Information Processing Systems 17*. 2004.
6. S. Fine, R. Gilad-Bachrach, and E. Shamir. Query by committee, linear separation and random walks. *Theoretical Computer Science*, 284(1):25–51, 2002.
7. Y. Freund, H. S. Seung, E. Shamir, and N. Tishby. Selective sampling using the query by committee algorithm. *Machine Learning*, 28(2-3):133–168, 1997.
8. R. Gilad-Bachrach, A. Navot, and N. Tishby. Kernel query by committee (KQBC). Technical Report 2003-88, Leibniz Center, the Hebrew University, 2003.
9. D. D. Lewis and W. A. Gale. A sequential algorithm for training text classifiers. In *Proc. of SIGIR-94, 17th ACM International Conference on Research and Development in Information Retrieval*, 1994.

10. P. M. Long. On the sample complexity of PAC learning halfspaces against the uniform distribution. *IEEE Transactions on Neural Networks*, 6(6):1556–1559, 1995.
11. P. M. Long. An upper bound on the sample complexity of PAC learning halfspaces with respect to the uniform distribution. *Information Processing Letters*, 87(5):229–23, 2003.
12. R. A. Servedio. On PAC learning using winnow, perceptron, and a perceptron-like algorithm. In *Computational Learning Theory*, pages 296 – 307, 1999.

A   Proof of Lemma 1

Let $r = \gamma/\sqrt{d}$ and let A_d be the area of a d-dimensional unit sphere, i.e. the surface of a $(d+1)$-dimensional unit ball.

$$P_x\left[|a \cdot x| \leq r\right] = \frac{\int_{-r}^{r} A_{d-2}(1-z^2)^{\frac{d-2}{2}}dz}{A_{d-1}} = \frac{2A_{d-2}}{A_{d-1}}\int_0^r (1-z^2)^{d/2-1}dz \quad (10)$$

First observe,

$$r(1-r^2)^{d/2-1} \leq \int_0^r (1-z^2)^{d/2-1}dz \leq r \quad (11)$$

For $x \in [0, 0.5]$, $1 - x \geq 4^{-x}$. Hence, for $0 \leq r \leq 2^{-1/2}$,

$$(1-r^2)^{d/2-1} \geq 4^{-r^2(d/2-1)} \geq 2^{-r^2 d}.$$

So we can conclude that the integral of (11) is in $[r/2, r]$ for $r \in [0, 1/\sqrt{d}]$. The ratio $2A_{d-2}/A_{d-1}$ can be shown to be in the range $[\sqrt{d/3}, \sqrt{d}]$ by straightforward induction on d, using the definition of the Γ function, and the fact that $A_{d-1} = 2\pi^{d/2}/\Gamma(d/2)$. □

A New Perspective on an Old Perceptron Algorithm

Shai Shalev-Shwartz[1,2] and Yoram Singer[1,2]

[1] School of Computer Sci. & Eng., The Hebrew University, Jerusalem 91904, Israel
[2] Google Inc., 1600 Amphitheater Parkway, Mountain View CA 94043, USA
{shais, singer}@cs.huji.ac.il

Abstract. We present a generalization of the Perceptron algorithm. The new algorithm performs a Perceptron-style update whenever the margin of an example is smaller than a predefined value. We derive worst case mistake bounds for our algorithm. As a byproduct we obtain a new mistake bound for the Perceptron algorithm in the inseparable case. We describe a multiclass extension of the algorithm. This extension is used in an experimental evaluation in which we compare the proposed algorithm to the Perceptron algorithm.

1   Introduction

The Perceptron algorithm [1, 15, 14] is a well studied and popular classification learning algorithm. Despite its age and simplicity it has proven to be quite effective in practical problems, even when compared to the state-of-the-art large margin algorithms [9]. The Perceptron maintains a single hyperplane which separates positive instances from negative ones. Another influential learning paradigm which employs separating hyperplanes is Vapnik's Support Vector Machine (SVM) [16]. Learning algorithms for SVMs use quadratic programming for finding a separating hyperplane attaining the maximal *margin*. Interestingly, the *analysis* of the Perceptron algorithm [14] also employs the notion of margin. However, the algorithm itself does not exploit any margin information. In this paper we try to draw a connection between the two approaches by analyzing a variant of the Perceptron algorithm, called Ballseptron, which utilizes the margin. As a byproduct, we also get a new analysis for the original Perceptron algorithm.

While the Perceptron algorithm can be used as linear programming solver [4] and can be converted to a batch learning algorithm [9], it was originally studied in the *online* learning model which is also the main focus of our paper. In online learning, the learner receives instances in a sequential manner while outputting a prediction after each observed instance. For concreteness, let $\mathcal{X} = \mathbb{R}^n$ denote our instance space and let $\mathcal{Y} = \{+1, -1\}$ denote our label space. Our primary goal is to learn a classification function $f : \mathcal{X} \to \mathcal{Y}$. We confine most of our discussion to linear classification functions. That is, f takes the form $f(\mathbf{x}) = \text{sign}(\mathbf{w}\cdot\mathbf{x})$ where $\mathbf{w}$ is a weight vector in $\mathbb{R}^n$. We briefly discuss in later sections how to use Mercer kernels with the proposed algorithm. Online algorithms work in rounds. On round t an online algorithm receives an instance $\mathbf{x}_t$ and predicts a label $\hat{y}_t$ according to its current classification function $f_t : \mathcal{X} \to \mathcal{Y}$. In our case, $\hat{y}_t = f_t(\mathbf{x}_t) = \text{sign}(\mathbf{w}_t \cdot \mathbf{x}_t)$, where $\mathbf{w}_t$ is the current weight vector used by the algorithm. The true label y_t is then revealed and the online algorithm may update

P. Auer and R. Meir (Eds.): COLT 2005, LNAI 3559, pp. 264–278, 2005.
© Springer-Verlag Berlin Heidelberg 2005

its classification function. The goal of the online algorithm is to minimize its cumulative number of prediction mistakes which we denote by ε. The Perceptron initializes its weight vector to be the zero vector and employs the update rule $\mathbf{w}_{t+1} = \mathbf{w}_t + \tau_t y_t \mathbf{x}_t$ where $\tau_t = 1$ if $\hat{y}_t \neq y_t$ and $\tau_t = 0$ otherwise.

Several authors [14, 3, 13] have shown that whenever the Perceptron is presented with a sequence of linearly separable examples, it suffers a bounded number of prediction mistakes which does not depend on the length of the sequence of examples. Formally, let $(\mathbf{x}_1, y_1), \ldots, (\mathbf{x}_T, y_T)$ be a sequence of instance-label pairs. Assume that there exists a unit vector $\mathbf{u}$ ($\|\mathbf{u}\| = 1$) and a positive scalar $\gamma > 0$ such that for all t, $y_t(\mathbf{u} \cdot \mathbf{x}_t) \geq \gamma$. In words, $\mathbf{u}$ separates the instance space into two half-spaces such that positively labeled instances reside in one half-space while the negatively labeled instances belong to the second half-space. Moreover, the distance of each instance to the separating hyperplane $\{\mathbf{x} : \mathbf{u} \cdot \mathbf{x} = 0\}$, is at least γ. We refer to γ as the margin attained by $\mathbf{u}$ on the sequence of examples. Throughout the paper we assume that the instances are of bounded norm and let $R = \max_t \|\mathbf{x}_t\|$ denote the largest norm of an instance in the input sequence. The number of prediction mistakes, ε, the Perceptron algorithm makes on the sequence of examples is at most

$$\varepsilon \leq \left(\frac{R}{\gamma}\right)^2 . \tag{1}$$

Interestingly, neither the dimensionality of $\mathcal{X}$ nor the number of examples directly effect this mistake bound. Freund and Schapire [9] relaxed the separability assumption and presented an analysis for the inseparable case. Their mistake bound depends on the *hinge-loss* attained by any vector $\mathbf{u}$. Formally, let $\mathbf{u}$ be *any* unit vector ($\|\mathbf{u}\| = 1$). The hinge-loss of $\mathbf{u}$ with respect to an instance-label pair $(\mathbf{x}_t, y_t)$ is defined as $\ell_t = \max\{0, \gamma - y_t \mathbf{u} \cdot \mathbf{x}_t\}$ where γ is a fixed target margin value. This definition implies that $\ell_t = 0$ if $\mathbf{x}_t$ lies in the half-space corresponding to y_t and its distance from the separating hyperplane is at least γ. Otherwise, ℓ_t increases linearly with $-y_t(\mathbf{u} \cdot \mathbf{x}_t)$. Let D_2 denote the two-norm of the sequence of hinge-losses suffered by $\mathbf{u}$ on the sequence of examples,

$$D_2 = \left(\sum_{t=1}^{T} \ell_t^2\right)^{1/2} . \tag{2}$$

Freund and Schapire [9] have shown that the number of prediction mistakes the Perceptron algorithm makes on the sequence of examples is at most,

$$\varepsilon \leq \left(\frac{R + D_2}{\gamma}\right)^2 . \tag{3}$$

This mistake bound does not assume that the data is linearly separable. However, whenever the data is linearly separable with margin γ, D_2 is 0 and the bound reduces to the bound given in Eq. (1). In this paper we also provide analysis in terms of the one-norm of the hinge losses which we denote by D_1 and is defined as,

$$D_1 = \sum_{t=1}^{T} \ell_t . \tag{4}$$

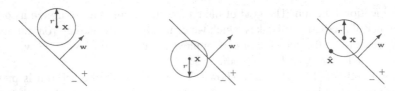

Fig. 1. An illustration of the three modes constituting the Ballseptron's update. The point $\mathbf{x}$ is labeled +1 and can be in one of three positions. Left: $\mathbf{x}$ is classified correctly by $\mathbf{w}$ with a margin greater than r. Middle: $\mathbf{x}$ is classified incorrectly by $\mathbf{w}$. Right: $\mathbf{x}$ is classified correctly but the ball of radius r is intersected by the separating hyper-plane. The point $\hat{\mathbf{x}}$ is used for updating $\mathbf{w}$

While the analysis of the Perceptron employs the notion of separation with margin, the Perceptron algorithm itself is oblivious to the absolute value of the margin attained by any of the examples. Specifically, the Perceptron does not modify the hyperplane used for classification even for instances whose margin is very small so long as the predicted label is correct. While this property of the Perceptron has numerous advantages (see for example [8]) it also introduces some deficiencies which spurred work on algorithms that incorporate the notion of margin (see the references below). For instance, if we know that the data is linearly separable with a margin value γ we can deduce that our current hyperplane is not optimal and make use of this fact in updating the current hyperplane. In the next section we present an algorithm that updates its weight vector whenever it either makes a *prediction mistake* or suffers a *margin error*. Formally, let r be a positive scalar. We say that the algorithm suffers a margin error with respect to r if the current instance $\mathbf{x}_t$ is correctly classified but it lies too close to the separating hyper-plane, that is,

$$0 < y_t \left(\frac{\mathbf{w}_t}{\|\mathbf{w}_t\|} \cdot \mathbf{x}_t \right) \leq r . \tag{5}$$

Analogously to the definition of ε, we denote by $\tilde{\varepsilon}$ the number of margin errors our algorithm suffers on the sequence of examples.

Numerous online margin-based learning algorithms share similarities with the work presented in this paper. See for instance [12, 10, 11, 2, 5]. Many of the algorithms can be viewed as variants and enhancements of the Perceptron algorithm. However, the mistake bounds derived for these algorithms are not directly comparable to that of the Perceptron, especially when the examples are not linearly separable. In contrast, under certain conditions discussed in the sequel, the mistake bound for the algorithm described in this paper is superior to that of the Perceptron. Moreover, our analysis carries over to the original Perceptron algorithm.

The paper is organized as follows. We start in Sec. 2 with a description of our new online algorithm, the Ballseptron. In Sec. 3 we analyze the algorithm using the mistake bound model and discuss the implications on the original Perceptron algorithm. Next, in Sec. 4, we describe a multiclass extension of the Ballseptron algorithm. This extension is used in Sec. 5 in which we present few experimental results that underscore some of the algorithmic properties of the Ballseptron algorithm in the light of its formal analysis. Finally, we discuss possible future directions in Sec. 6.

2   The Ballseptron Algorithm

In this section we present the Ballseptron algorithm which is a simple generalization of the classical Perceptron algorithm. As in the Perceptron algorithm, we maintain a single vector which is initially set to be the zero vector. On round t, we first receive an instance $\mathbf{x}_t$ and output a prediction according to the current vector, $\hat{y}_t = \text{sign}(\mathbf{w}_t \cdot \mathbf{x}_t)$. We then receive the correct label y_t. In case of a prediction mistake, i.e. $\hat{y}_t \neq y_t$, we suffer a unit loss and update $\mathbf{w}_t$ by adding to it the vector $y_t \mathbf{x}_t$. The updated vector constitutes the classifier to be used on the next round, thus $\mathbf{w}_{t+1} = \mathbf{w}_t + y_t \mathbf{x}_t$. In contrast to the Perceptron algorithm, we also update the classifier whenever the margin attained on $\mathbf{x}_t$ is smaller than a pre-specified parameter r. Formally, denote by $B(\mathbf{x}_t, r)$ the ball of radius r centered at $\mathbf{x}_t$. We impose the assumption that all the points in $B(\mathbf{x}_t, r)$ must have the same label as

---

PARAMETER: radius r
INITIALIZE: $\mathbf{w}_1 = \mathbf{0}$
For $t = 1, 2, \ldots$
    Receive an instance $\mathbf{x}_t$
    Predict: $\hat{y}_t = \text{sign}(\mathbf{w}_t \cdot \mathbf{x}_t)$
    If $y_t(\mathbf{w}_t \cdot \mathbf{x}_t) \leq 0$
        Update: $\mathbf{w}_{t+1} = \mathbf{w}_t + y_t \mathbf{x}_t$
    Else If $y_t(\mathbf{w}_t \cdot \mathbf{x}_t)/\|\mathbf{w}_t\| \leq r$
        Set: $\hat{\mathbf{x}}_t = \mathbf{x}_t - y_t r \mathbf{w}_t/\|\mathbf{w}_t\|$
        Update: $\mathbf{w}_{t+1} = \mathbf{w}_t + y_t \hat{\mathbf{x}}_t$
    Else // No margin mistake
        Update: $\mathbf{w}_{t+1} = \mathbf{w}_t$
    End
Endfor

Fig. 2. The Ballseptron algorithm

---

the center $\mathbf{x}_t$ (see also [6]). We now check if there is a point in $B(\mathbf{x}_t, r)$ which is misclassified by $\mathbf{w}_t$. If such a point exists then $\mathbf{w}_t$ intersects $B(\mathbf{x}_t, r)$ into two parts. We now generate a pseudo-instance, denoted $\hat{\mathbf{x}}_t$ which corresponds to the point in $B(\mathbf{x}_t, r)$ attaining the worst (negative) margin with respect to $\mathbf{w}_t$. (See Fig. 1 for an illustration.) This is obtained by moving r units away from $\mathbf{x}_t$ in the direction of $-y_t \mathbf{w}_t$, that is $\hat{\mathbf{x}}_t = \mathbf{x}_t - \frac{y_t r}{\|\mathbf{w}_t\|} \mathbf{w}_t$. To show this formally, we solve the following constrained minimization problem,

$$\hat{\mathbf{x}}_t = \underset{\mathbf{x} \in B(\mathbf{x}_t, r)}{\text{argmin}} \; y_t(\mathbf{w}_t \cdot \mathbf{x}) \; . \tag{6}$$

To find $\hat{\mathbf{x}}_t$ we recast the constraint $\mathbf{x} \in B(\mathbf{x}_t, r)$ as $\|\mathbf{x} - \mathbf{x}_t\|^2 \leq r^2$. Note that both the objective function $y_t(\mathbf{w}_t \cdot \mathbf{x})$ and the constraint $\|\mathbf{x} - \mathbf{x}_t\|^2 \leq r^2$ are convex in $\mathbf{x}$. In addition, the relative interior of the $B(\mathbf{x}_t, r)$ is not empty. Thus, Slater's optimality conditions hold and we can find $\hat{\mathbf{x}}_t$ by examining the saddle point of the problem's Lagrangian which is, $L(\mathbf{x}, \alpha) = y_t(\mathbf{w}_t \cdot \mathbf{x}) + \alpha \left(\|\mathbf{x} - \mathbf{x}_t\|^2 - r^2 \right)$. Taking the derivative of the Lagrangian w.r.t. each of the components of $\mathbf{x}$ and setting the resulting vector to zero gives,

$$y_t \mathbf{w}_t + 2\alpha(\mathbf{x} - \mathbf{x}_t) = 0 \; . \tag{7}$$

Since $y_t(\mathbf{w}_t \cdot \mathbf{x}_t) > 0$ (otherwise, we simply undergo a simple Perceptron update) we have that $\mathbf{w}_t \neq \mathbf{0}$ and $\alpha > 0$. Hence we get that the solution of Eq. (7) is $\hat{\mathbf{x}}_t = \mathbf{x}_t - (y_t/2\alpha)\mathbf{w}_t$. To find α we use the complementary slackness condition. That is, since $\alpha > 0$ we must have that $\|\mathbf{x} - \mathbf{x}_t\| = r$. Replacing $\mathbf{x} - \mathbf{x}_t$ with $-y_t \mathbf{w}_t/(2\alpha)$, the slackness condition yields that, $\frac{\|\mathbf{w}_t\|}{2\alpha} = r$ which let us express $\frac{1}{2\alpha}$ as $\frac{r}{\|\mathbf{w}_t\|}$. We thus get that $\hat{\mathbf{x}}_t = \mathbf{x}_t - \frac{y_t r}{\|\mathbf{w}_t\|} \mathbf{w}_t$. By construction, if $y_t(\mathbf{w}_t \cdot \hat{\mathbf{x}}_t) > 0$ we know that all the points in the ball of radius r centered at $\mathbf{x}_t$ are correctly classified and we set $\mathbf{w}_{t+1} = \mathbf{w}_t$.

(See also the left-most plot in Fig. 1.) If on the other hand $y_t(\mathbf{w}_t \cdot \hat{\mathbf{x}}_t) \leq 0$ (right-most plot in Fig. 1) we use $\hat{\mathbf{x}}_t$ as a pseudo-example and set $\mathbf{w}_{t+1} = \mathbf{w}_t + y_t\hat{\mathbf{x}}_t$.

Note that we can rewrite the condition $y_t(\mathbf{w}_t \cdot \hat{\mathbf{x}}_t) \leq 0$ as $y_t(\mathbf{w}_t \cdot \mathbf{x}_t)/\|\mathbf{w}_t\| \leq r$. The pseudocode of the Ballseptron algorithm is given in Fig. 2. and an illustration of the different cases encountered by the algorithm is given in Fig. 1. Last, we would like to note in passing that $\mathbf{w}_t$ can be written as a linear combination of the instances, $\mathbf{w}_t = \sum_{i=1}^{t-1} \alpha_t \mathbf{x}_t$, and therefore, $\mathbf{w}_t \cdot \mathbf{x}_t = \sum_{i=1}^{t-1} \alpha_i (\mathbf{x}_i \cdot \mathbf{x}_t)$. The inner products $\mathbf{x}_i \cdot \mathbf{x}_t$ can be replaced with an inner products defined via a Mercer kernel, $K(\mathbf{x}_i, \mathbf{x}_t)$, without any further changes to our derivation. Since the analysis in the next section does not depend on the dimensionality of the instances, all of the formal results still hold when the algorithm is used in conjunction with kernel functions.

3   Analysis

In this section we analyze the Ballseptron algorithm. Analogous to the Perceptron bounds, the bounds that we obtain do not depend on the dimension of the instances but rather on the geometry of the problem expressed via the margin of the instances and the radius of the sphere enclosing the instances. As mentioned above, most of our analysis carries over to the original Perceptron algorithm and we therefore dedicate the last part of this section to a discussion of the implications for the original Perceptron algorithm. A desirable property of the Ballseptron would have been that it does not make more prediction mistakes than the Perceptron algorithm. Unfortunately, without any restrictions on the radius r that the Ballseptron algorithm employs, such a property cannot be guaranteed. For example, suppose that the instances are drawn from $\mathbb{R}$ and all the input-label pairs in the sequence $(\mathbf{x}_1, y_1), \ldots, (\mathbf{x}_T, y_T)$ are the same and equal to $(\mathbf{x}, y) = (1, 1)$. The Perceptron algorithm makes a single mistake on this sequence. However, if the radius r that is relayed to the Ballseptron algorithm is 2 then the algorithm would make $T/2$ prediction mistakes on the sequence. The crux of this failure to achieve a small number of mistakes is due to the fact that the radius r was set to an excessively large value. To achieve a good mistake bound we need to ensure that r is set to be less than the target margin γ employed by the competing hypothesis $\mathbf{u}$. Indeed, our first theorem implies that the Ballseptron attains the same mistake bound as the Perceptron algorithm provided that r is small enough.

Theorem 1. *Let $(\mathbf{x}_1, y_1), \ldots, (\mathbf{x}_T, y_T)$ be a sequence of instance-label pairs where $\mathbf{x}_t \in \mathbb{R}^n$, $y_t \in \{-1, +1\}$, and $\|\mathbf{x}_t\| \leq R$ for all t. Let $\mathbf{u} \in \mathbb{R}^n$ be a vector whose norm is 1, $0 < \gamma \leq R$ an arbitrary scalar, and denote $\ell_t = \max\{0, \gamma - y_t \mathbf{u} \cdot \mathbf{x}_t\}$. Let D_2 be as defined by Eq. (2). Assume that the Ballseptron algorithm is run with a parameter r which satisfies $0 \leq r < (\sqrt{2} - 1)\gamma$. Then, the number of prediction mistakes the Ballseptron makes on the sequence is at most,*

$$\left(\frac{R + D_2}{\gamma} \right)^2 .$$

Proof. We prove the theorem by bounding $\mathbf{w}_{T+1} \cdot \mathbf{u}$ from below and above while comparing the two bounds. Starting with the upper bound, we need to examine three different cases for every t. If $y_t(\mathbf{w}_t \cdot \mathbf{x}_t) \leq 0$ then $\mathbf{w}_{t+1} = \mathbf{w}_t + y_t\mathbf{x}_t$ and therefore,

$$\|\mathbf{w}_{t+1}\|^2 = \|\mathbf{w}_t\|^2 + \|\mathbf{x}_t\|^2 + 2y_t(\mathbf{w}_t \cdot \mathbf{x}_t) \le \|\mathbf{w}_t\|^2 + \|\mathbf{x}_t\|^2 \le \|\mathbf{w}_t\|^2 + R^2 \ .$$

In the second case where $y_t(\mathbf{w}_t \cdot \mathbf{x}_t) > 0$ yet the Ballseptron suffers a margin mistake, we know that $y_t(\mathbf{w}_t \cdot \hat{\mathbf{x}}_t) \le 0$ and thus get

$$\|\mathbf{w}_{t+1}\|^2 = \|\mathbf{w}_t + y_t\hat{\mathbf{x}}_t\|^2 = \|\mathbf{w}_t\|^2 + \|\hat{\mathbf{x}}_t\|^2 + 2y_t(\mathbf{w}_t \cdot \hat{\mathbf{x}}_t) \le \|\mathbf{w}_t\|^2 + \|\hat{\mathbf{x}}_t\|^2 \ .$$

Recall that $\hat{\mathbf{x}}_t = \mathbf{x}_t - y_t r \mathbf{w}_t / \|\mathbf{w}_t\|$ and therefore,

$$\|\hat{\mathbf{x}}_t\|^2 = \|\mathbf{x}_t\|^2 + r^2 - 2y_t r (\mathbf{x}_t \cdot \mathbf{w}_t)/\|\mathbf{w}_t\| < \|\mathbf{x}_t\|^2 + r^2 \le R^2 + r^2 \ .$$

Finally in the third case where $y_t(\mathbf{w}_t \cdot \hat{\mathbf{x}}_t) > 0$ we have $\|\mathbf{w}_{t+1}\|^2 = \|\mathbf{w}_t\|^2$. We can summarize the three different scenarios by defining two variables: $\tau_t \in \{0,1\}$ which is 1 iff $y_t(\mathbf{w}_t \cdot \mathbf{x}_t) \le 0$ and similarly $\tilde{\tau}_t \in \{0,1\}$ which is 1 iff $y_t(\mathbf{w}_t \cdot \mathbf{x}_t) > 0$ and $y_t(\mathbf{w}_t \cdot \hat{\mathbf{x}}_t) \le 0$. Unraveling the bound on the norm of $\mathbf{w}_{T+1}$ while using the definitions of τ_t and $\tilde{\tau}_t$ gives,

$$\|\mathbf{w}_{T+1}\|^2 \le R^2 \sum_{t=1}^{T} \tau_t + (R^2 + r^2) \sum_{t=1}^{T} \tilde{\tau}_t \ .$$

Let us now denote by $\varepsilon = \sum_{t=1}^{T} \tau_t$ the number of mistakes the Ballseptron makes and analogously by $\tilde{\varepsilon} = \sum_{t=1}^{T} \tilde{\tau}_t$ the number of margin errors of the Ballseptron. Using the two definitions along with the Cauchy-Schwartz inequality yields that,

$$\mathbf{w}_{T+1} \cdot \mathbf{u} \le \|\mathbf{w}_{T+1}\| \|\mathbf{u}\| = \|\mathbf{w}_{T+1}\| \le \sqrt{\varepsilon R^2 + \tilde{\varepsilon}(R^2 + r^2)} \ . \tag{8}$$

This provides us with an upper bound on $\mathbf{w}_{T+1} \cdot \mathbf{u}$. We now turn to derive a lower bound on $\mathbf{w}_{T+1} \cdot \mathbf{u}$. As in the derivation of the upper bound, we need to consider three cases. The definition of ℓ_t immediately implies that $\ell_t \ge \gamma - y_t \mathbf{x}_t \cdot \mathbf{u}$. Hence, in the first case (a prediction mistake), we can bound $\mathbf{w}_{t+1} \cdot \mathbf{u}$ as follows,

$$\mathbf{w}_{t+1} \cdot \mathbf{u} = (\mathbf{w}_t + y_t\mathbf{x}_t) \cdot \mathbf{u} \ge \mathbf{w}_t \cdot \mathbf{u} + \gamma - \ell_t \ ,$$

In the second case (a margin error) the Ballseptron's update is $\mathbf{w}_{t+1} = \mathbf{w}_t + y_t\hat{\mathbf{x}}_t$ which results in the following bound,

$$\mathbf{w}_{t+1} \cdot \mathbf{u} = (\mathbf{w}_t + y_t\hat{\mathbf{x}}_t) \cdot \mathbf{u} = \left(\mathbf{w}_t + y_t\mathbf{x}_t - r \frac{\mathbf{w}_t}{\|\mathbf{w}_t\|} \right) \cdot \mathbf{u}$$

$$\ge \mathbf{w}_t \cdot \mathbf{u} + \gamma - \ell_t - r \left(\frac{\mathbf{w}_t}{\|\mathbf{w}_t\|} \cdot \mathbf{u} \right) \ .$$

Since the norm of $\mathbf{u}$ is assumed to be 1, by using Cauchy-Schwartz inequality we can bound $\frac{\mathbf{w}_t}{\|\mathbf{w}_t\|} \cdot \mathbf{u}$ by 1. We thus get that, $\mathbf{w}_{t+1} \cdot \mathbf{u} \ge \mathbf{w}_t \cdot \mathbf{u} + \gamma - \ell_t - r$. Finally, on rounds for which there was neither a prediction mistake nor a margin error we immediately get that, $\mathbf{w}_{t+1} \cdot \mathbf{u} = \mathbf{w}_t \cdot \mathbf{u}$. Combining the three cases while using the definitions of $\tau_t, \tilde{\tau}_t, \varepsilon$ and $\tilde{\varepsilon}$ we get that,

$$\mathbf{w}_{T+1} \cdot \mathbf{u} \ge \varepsilon\gamma + \tilde{\varepsilon}(\gamma - r) - \sum_{t=1}^{T} (\tau_t + \tilde{\tau}_t)\ell_t \ . \tag{9}$$

We now apply Cauchy-Schwartz inequality once more to obtain that,

$$\sum_{t=1}^{T} (\tau_t + \tilde{\tau}_t)\ell_t \leq \left(\sum_{t=1}^{T} (\tau_t + \tilde{\tau}_t)^2\right)^{\frac{1}{2}} \left(\sum_{t=1}^{T} (\ell_t)^2\right)^{\frac{1}{2}} = D_2\sqrt{\varepsilon + \tilde{\varepsilon}} \ .$$

Combining the above inequality with Eq. (9) we get the following lower bound on $\mathbf{w}_{T+1} \cdot \mathbf{u}$,

$$\mathbf{w}_{T+1} \cdot \mathbf{u} \geq \varepsilon\gamma + \tilde{\varepsilon}(\gamma - r) - D_2\sqrt{\varepsilon + \tilde{\varepsilon}} \ . \tag{10}$$

We now tie the lower bound on $\mathbf{w}_{T+1} \cdot \mathbf{u}$ from Eq. (10) with the upper bound from Eq. (8) to obtain that,

$$\sqrt{\varepsilon R^2 + \tilde{\varepsilon}(R^2 + r^2)} \geq \varepsilon\gamma + \tilde{\varepsilon}(\gamma - r) - D_2\sqrt{\varepsilon + \tilde{\varepsilon}} \ . \tag{11}$$

Let us now denote by $g(\varepsilon, \tilde{\varepsilon})$ the difference between the two sides of the above equation, that is,

$$g(\varepsilon, \tilde{\varepsilon}) = \varepsilon\gamma + \tilde{\varepsilon}(\gamma - r) - \sqrt{\varepsilon R^2 + \tilde{\varepsilon}(R^2 + r^2)} - D_2\sqrt{\varepsilon + \tilde{\varepsilon}} \ . \tag{12}$$

Eq. (11) implies that $g(\varepsilon, \tilde{\varepsilon}) \leq 0$ for the particular values of ε and $\tilde{\varepsilon}$ obtained by the Ballseptron algorithm. We now use the this fact to show that ε cannot exceed $((R + D_2)/\gamma)^2$. First note that if $\tilde{\varepsilon} = 0$ then g is a quadratic function in $\sqrt{\varepsilon}$ and therefore $\sqrt{\varepsilon}$ is at most the positive root of the equation $g(\varepsilon, 0) = 0$ which is $(R + D_2)/\gamma$. We thus get,

$$g(\varepsilon, 0) \leq 0 \quad \Rightarrow \quad \varepsilon \leq \left(\frac{R + D_2}{\gamma}\right)^2 \ .$$

If $\tilde{\varepsilon} \geq 1$ and $\varepsilon + \tilde{\varepsilon} \leq ((R + D_2)/\gamma)^2$ then the bound stated in the theorem immediately holds. Therefore, we only need to analyze the case in which $\tilde{\varepsilon} \geq 1$ and $\varepsilon + \tilde{\varepsilon} > ((R + D_2)/\gamma)^2$. In this case we derive the mistake bound by showing first that the function $g(\varepsilon, \tilde{\varepsilon})$ is monotonically increasing in $\tilde{\varepsilon}$ and therefore $g(\varepsilon, 0) \leq g(\varepsilon, \tilde{\varepsilon}) \leq 0$. To prove the monotonicity of g we need the following simple inequality which holds for $a > 0$, $b \geq 0$ and $c > 0$,

$$\sqrt{a + b + c} - \sqrt{a + b} = \frac{c}{\sqrt{a + b + c} + \sqrt{a + b}} < \frac{c}{2\sqrt{a}} \ . \tag{13}$$

Let us now examine $g(\varepsilon, \tilde{\varepsilon} + 1) - g(\varepsilon, \tilde{\varepsilon})$. Expanding the definition of g from Eq. (12) and using Eq. (13) we get that,

$$\begin{aligned}
g(\varepsilon, \tilde{\varepsilon} + 1) - g(\varepsilon, \tilde{\varepsilon}) &= \gamma - r - \sqrt{\varepsilon R^2 + \tilde{\varepsilon}(R^2 + r^2) + R^2 + r^2} \\
&\quad + \sqrt{\varepsilon R^2 + \tilde{\varepsilon}(R^2 + r^2)} - D_2\sqrt{\varepsilon + \tilde{\varepsilon} + 1} + D_2\sqrt{\varepsilon + \tilde{\varepsilon}} \\
&\geq \gamma - r - \frac{R^2 + r^2}{2R\sqrt{\varepsilon + \tilde{\varepsilon}}} - \frac{D_2}{2\sqrt{\varepsilon + \tilde{\varepsilon}}} \\
&= \gamma - r - \frac{R + D_2 + r^2/R}{2\sqrt{\varepsilon + \tilde{\varepsilon}}} \ .
\end{aligned}$$

We now use the assumption that $\varepsilon + \tilde{\varepsilon} > ((R + D_2)/\gamma)^2$ and that $\gamma \leq R$ to get that,

$$g(\varepsilon, \tilde{\varepsilon} + 1) - g(\varepsilon, \tilde{\varepsilon}) \geq \gamma \left(1 - \frac{r}{\gamma} - \frac{R + D_2}{2\gamma\sqrt{\varepsilon + \tilde{\varepsilon}}} - \frac{r^2}{2R(R + D_2)} \right)$$

$$> \gamma \left(1 - \frac{r}{\gamma} - \frac{1}{2} - \frac{1}{2} \left(\frac{r}{\gamma} \right)^2 \right) . \tag{14}$$

The condition that $r \leq (\sqrt{2} - 1)\gamma$ implies that the term $0.5 - r/\gamma - 0.5(r/\gamma)^2$ is strictly positive. We have thus shown that $g(\varepsilon, \tilde{\varepsilon} + 1) - g(\varepsilon, \tilde{\varepsilon}) > 0$ hence g is monotonically increasing in $\tilde{\varepsilon}$. Therefore, from Eq. (11) we get that $0 \geq g(\varepsilon, \tilde{\varepsilon}) > g(\varepsilon, 0)$. Finally, as already argued above, the condition $0 \geq g(\varepsilon, 0)$ ensures that $\varepsilon \leq ((R + D_2)/\gamma)^2$. This concludes our proof. □

The above bound ensures that whenever r is less than $(\sqrt{2} - 1)\gamma$, the Ballseptron mistake bound is as good as Freund and Schapire's [9] mistake bound for the Perceptron. The natural question that arises is whether the Ballseptron entertains any advantage over the less complex Perceptron algorithm. As we now argue, the answer is yes so long as the number of margin errors, $\tilde{\varepsilon}$, is strictly positive. First note that if $\varepsilon + \tilde{\varepsilon} \leq ((R + D_2)/\gamma)^2$ and $\tilde{\varepsilon} > 0$ then $\varepsilon \leq ((R + D_2)/\gamma)^2 - \tilde{\varepsilon}$ which is strictly smaller than the mistake bound from [9]. The case when $\varepsilon + \tilde{\varepsilon} > ((R + D_2)/\gamma)^2$ needs some deliberation. To simplify the derivation let $\beta = 0.5 - r/\gamma - 0.5\,(r/\gamma)^2$. The proof of Thm. 1 implies that $g(\varepsilon, \tilde{\varepsilon} + 1) - g(\varepsilon, \tilde{\varepsilon}) \geq \beta\gamma$. From the same proof we also know that $g(\varepsilon, \tilde{\varepsilon}) \leq 0$. We thus get that $g(\varepsilon, 0) + \tilde{\varepsilon}\beta\gamma \leq g(\varepsilon, \tilde{\varepsilon}) \leq 0$. Expanding the term $g(\varepsilon, 0) + \tilde{\varepsilon}\beta\gamma$ we get the following inequality,

$$\varepsilon\gamma - \sqrt{\varepsilon R^2} - D_2\sqrt{\varepsilon} + \tilde{\varepsilon}\beta\gamma = \varepsilon\gamma - \sqrt{\varepsilon}(R + D_2) + \tilde{\varepsilon}\beta\gamma \leq 0 . \tag{15}$$

The left-hand side of Eq. (15) is a quadratic function in $\sqrt{\varepsilon}$. Thus, $\sqrt{\varepsilon}$ cannot exceed the positive root of this function. Therefore, the number of prediction mistakes, ε, can be bounded above as follows,

$$\varepsilon \leq \left(\frac{R + D_2 + \sqrt{(R + D_2)^2 - 4\beta\gamma^2\tilde{\varepsilon}}}{2\gamma} \right)^2$$

$$\leq \frac{(R + D_2)^2 + 2(R + D_2)\sqrt{(R + D_2)^2 - 4\beta\gamma^2\tilde{\varepsilon}} + (R + D_2)^2 - 4\beta\gamma^2\tilde{\varepsilon}}{4\gamma^2}$$

$$\leq \left(\frac{R + D_2}{\gamma} \right)^2 - \beta\tilde{\varepsilon} .$$

We have thus shown that whenever the number of margin errors $\tilde{\varepsilon}$ is strictly positive, the number of prediction mistakes is smaller than $((R + D_2)/\gamma)^2$, the bound obtained by Freund and Schapire for the Perceptron algorithm. In other words, the mistake bound we obtained puts a cap on a function which depends both on ε and on $\tilde{\varepsilon}$. Margin errors naturally impose more updates to the classifier, yet they come at the expense of sheer prediction mistakes. Thus, the Ballseptron algorithm is most likely to suffer a smaller number of prediction mistakes than the standard Perceptron algorithm. We summarize these facts in the following corollary.

Corollary 1. *Under the same assumptions of Thm. 1, the number of prediction mistakes the Ballseptron algorithm makes is at most,*

$$\left(\frac{R+D_2}{\gamma}\right)^2 - \tilde{\varepsilon}\left(\frac{1}{2} - \frac{r}{\gamma} - \frac{1}{2}\left(\frac{r}{\gamma}\right)^2\right) ,$$

where $\tilde{\varepsilon}$ is the number of margin errors of the Ballseptron algorithm.

Thus far, we derived mistake bounds that depend on R, γ, and D_2 which is the square-root of the sum of the squares of hinge-losses. We now turn to an analogous mistake bound which employs D_1 instead of D_2. Our proof technique is similar to the proof of Thm. 1 and we thus confine the next proof solely to the modifications that are required.

Theorem 2. *Under the same assumptions of Thm. 1, the number of prediction mistakes the Ballseptron algorithm makes is at most,*

$$\left(\frac{R+\sqrt{\gamma D_1}}{\gamma}\right)^2 .$$

Proof. Following the proof outline of Thm. 1, we start by modifying the lower bound on $\mathbf{w}_{T+1} \cdot \mathbf{u}$. First, note that the lower bound given by Eq. (9) still holds. In addition, $\tau_t + \tilde{\tau}_t \leq 1$ for all t since on each round there exists a mutual exclusion between a prediction mistake and a margin error. We can therefore simplify Eq. (9) and rewrite it as, $\mathbf{w}_{T+1} \cdot \mathbf{u} \geq \varepsilon\gamma - \sum_{t=1}^{T} \ell_t + \tilde{\varepsilon}(\gamma - r)$. Combining this lower bound on $\mathbf{w}_{T+1} \cdot \mathbf{u}$ with the upper bound on $\mathbf{w}_{T+1} \cdot \mathbf{u}$ given in Eq. (8) we get that,

$$\varepsilon\gamma + \tilde{\varepsilon}(\gamma - r) - \sum_{t=1}^{T} \ell_t \leq \sqrt{\varepsilon R^2 + \tilde{\varepsilon}(R^2 + r^2)} . \tag{16}$$

Similar to the definition of g from Thm. 1, we define the following auxiliary function,

$$q(\varepsilon, \tilde{\varepsilon}) = \varepsilon\gamma + \tilde{\varepsilon}(\gamma - r) - \sqrt{\varepsilon R^2 + \tilde{\varepsilon}(R^2 + r^2)} - D_1 .$$

Thus, Eq. (16) yields that $q(\varepsilon, \tilde{\varepsilon}) \leq 0$. We now show that $q(\varepsilon, \tilde{\varepsilon}) \leq 0$ implies that ε cannot exceed $((R + \sqrt{\gamma D_1})/\gamma)^2$. First, note that if $\tilde{\varepsilon} = 0$ then q becomes a quadratic function in $\sqrt{\varepsilon}$. Therefore, $\sqrt{\varepsilon}$ cannot be larger than the positive root of the equation $q(\varepsilon, 0) = 0$ which is,

$$\frac{R + \sqrt{R^2 + 4\gamma D_1}}{2\gamma} \leq \frac{R + \sqrt{\gamma D_1}}{\gamma} .$$

We have therefore shown that,

$$q(\varepsilon, 0) \leq 0 \quad \Rightarrow \quad \varepsilon \leq \left(\frac{R + \sqrt{\gamma D_1}}{\gamma}\right)^2 .$$

We thus assume that $\tilde{\varepsilon} \geq 1$. Again, if $\varepsilon + \tilde{\varepsilon} \leq (R/\gamma)^2$ then the bound stated in the theorem immediately holds. We are therefore left with the case $\varepsilon + \tilde{\varepsilon} > (R/\gamma)^2$ and

$\tilde{\varepsilon} > 0$. To prove the theorem we show that $q(\varepsilon, \tilde{\varepsilon})$ is monotonically increasing in $\tilde{\varepsilon}$. Expanding the function q and using as before the bound given in Eq. (13) we get that,

$$q(\varepsilon, \tilde{\varepsilon} + 1) - q(\varepsilon, \tilde{\varepsilon}) = \gamma - r - \sqrt{\varepsilon R^2 + (\tilde{\varepsilon} + 1)(R^2 + r^2)} + \sqrt{\varepsilon R^2 + \tilde{\varepsilon}(R^2 + r^2)}$$
$$> \gamma - r - \frac{R^2 + r^2}{2\sqrt{(\varepsilon + \tilde{\varepsilon})R^2}} = \gamma - r - \frac{R + r^2/R}{2\sqrt{\varepsilon + \tilde{\varepsilon}}} .$$

Using the assumption that $\varepsilon + \tilde{\varepsilon} > (R/\gamma)^2$ and that $\gamma \leq R$ let us further bound the above as follows,

$$q(\varepsilon, \tilde{\varepsilon} + 1) - q(\varepsilon, \tilde{\varepsilon}) > \gamma - r - \frac{\gamma}{2} - \frac{\gamma r^2}{2R^2} \geq \gamma \left(\frac{1}{2} - \frac{r}{\gamma} - \frac{1}{2} \left(\frac{r}{\gamma} \right)^2 \right) .$$

The assumption that $r \leq (\sqrt{2} - 1)\gamma$ yields that $q(\varepsilon, \tilde{\varepsilon} + 1) - q(\varepsilon, \tilde{\varepsilon}) \geq 0$ and therefore $q(\varepsilon, \tilde{\varepsilon})$ is indeed monotonically increasing in $\tilde{\varepsilon}$ for $\varepsilon + \tilde{\varepsilon} > R^2/\gamma^2$. Combining the inequality $q(\varepsilon, \tilde{\varepsilon}) \leq 0$ with the monotonicity property we get that $q(\varepsilon, 0) \leq q(\varepsilon, \tilde{\varepsilon}) \leq 0$ which in turn yields the bound of the theorem. This concludes our proof.   □

The bound of Thm. 2 is similar to the bound of Thm. 1. The natural question that arises is whether we can obtain a tighter mistake bound whenever we know the number of margin errors $\tilde{\varepsilon}$. As for the bound based on D_2, the answer for the D_1-based bound is affirmative. Recall that we define the value of $1/2 - r/\gamma - 1/2(r/\gamma)^2$ by β. We now show that the number of prediction mistakes is bounded above by,

$$\varepsilon \leq \left(\frac{R + \sqrt{\gamma D_1}}{\gamma} \right)^2 - \tilde{\varepsilon}\beta . \tag{17}$$

First, if $\varepsilon + \tilde{\varepsilon} \leq (R/\gamma)^2$ then the bound above immediately holds. In the proof of Thm. 2 we have shown that if $\varepsilon + \tilde{\varepsilon} > (R/\gamma)^2$ then $q(\varepsilon, \tilde{\varepsilon} + 1) - q(\varepsilon, \tilde{\varepsilon}) \geq \beta\gamma$. Therefore, $q(\varepsilon, \tilde{\varepsilon}) \geq q(\varepsilon, 0) + \tilde{\varepsilon}\beta\gamma$. Recall that Eq. (16) implies that $q(\varepsilon, \tilde{\varepsilon}) \leq 0$ and thus we get that $q(\varepsilon, 0) + \tilde{\varepsilon}\beta\gamma \leq 0$ yielding the following,

$$\varepsilon\gamma - R\sqrt{\varepsilon} - D_1 + \tilde{\varepsilon}\beta\gamma \leq 0 .$$

The left-hand side of the above inequality is yet again a quadratic function in $\sqrt{\varepsilon}$. Therefore, once more $\sqrt{\varepsilon}$ is no bigger than the positive root of the equation and we get that,

$$\sqrt{\varepsilon} \leq \frac{R + \sqrt{R^2 + 4\gamma D_1 - 4\gamma^2\beta\tilde{\varepsilon}}}{2\gamma} ,$$

and thus,

$$\varepsilon \leq \frac{R^2 + 2R\sqrt{R^2 + 4\gamma D_1 - 4\gamma^2\beta\tilde{\varepsilon}} + R^2 + 4\gamma D_1 - 4\gamma^2\beta\tilde{\varepsilon}}{4\gamma^2}$$
$$\leq \frac{R^2 + 2R\sqrt{\gamma D_1} + \gamma D_1}{\gamma^2} - \beta\tilde{\varepsilon} ,$$

which can be translated to the bound on ε from Eq. (17).

Summing up, the Ballseptron algorithm entertains two mistake bounds: the first is based on the root of the cumulative square of losses (D_2) while the second is based directly on the cumulative sum of hinge losses (D_1). Both bounds imply that the Ballseptron would make fewer prediction mistakes than the original Perceptron algorithm so long as the Ballseptron suffers margin errors along its run. Since margin errors are likely to occur for reasonable choices of r, the Ballseptron is likely to attain a smaller number of prediction mistakes than the Perceptron algorithm. Indeed, preliminary experiments reported in Sec. 5 indicate that for a wide range of choices for r the number of online prediction mistakes of the Ballseptron is significantly lower than that of the Perceptron.

The bounds of Thm. 1 and Thm. 2 hold for any $r \leq (\sqrt{2} - 1)\gamma$, in particular for $r = 0$. When $r = 0$, the Ballseptron algorithm reduces to the Perceptron algorithm. In the case of Thm. 1 the resulting mistake bound for $r = 0$ is identical to the bound of Freund and Schapire [9]. Our proof technique though is substantially different than the one in [9] which embeds each instance in a high dimensional space rendering the problem separable. Setting r to zero in Thm. 2 yields a new mistake bound for the Perceptron with $\sqrt{\gamma D_1}$ replacing D_2 in the bound. The latter bound is likely to be tighter in the presence of noise which may cause large margin errors. Specifically, the bound of Thm. 2 is better than that of Thm. 1 when

$$\gamma \sum_{t=1}^{T} \ell_t \leq \sum_{t=1}^{T} \ell_t^2 .$$

We therefore expect the bound in Thm. 1 to be better when ℓ_t is small and otherwise the new bound is likely to be better. We further investigate the difference between the two bounds in Sec. 5.

4   An Extension to Multiclass Problems

In this section we describe a generalization of the Ballseptron to the task of multiclass classification. For concreteness we assume that there are k different possible labels and denote the set of all possible labels by $\mathcal{Y} = \{1, \ldots, k\}$. There are several adaptations of the Perceptron algorithm to multiclass settings (see for example [5, 7, 16, 17]), many of which are also applicable to the Ballseptron. We now outline one possible multiclass extension in which we associate a weight vector with each class. Due to the lack of space proofs of the mistake bound obtained by our construction are omitted. Let $\mathbf{w}^r$ denote the weight vector associated with a label $r \in \mathcal{Y}$. We also refer to $\mathbf{w}^r$ as the r'th prototype. As in the binary case we initialize each of the prototypes to be the zero vector. The predicted label of an instance $\mathbf{x}_t$ is defined as,

$$\hat{y}_t = \underset{r \in \mathcal{Y}}{\operatorname{argmax}} \, \mathbf{w}_t^r \cdot \mathbf{x}_t .$$

Upon receiving the correct label y_t, if $\hat{y}_t \neq y_t$ we perform the following update which is a multiclass generalization of the Perceptron rule,

$$\mathbf{w}_{t+1}^{y_t} = \mathbf{w}_t^{y_t} + \mathbf{x}_t \; ; \; \mathbf{w}_{t+1}^{\hat{y}_t} = \mathbf{w}_t^{\hat{y}_t} - \mathbf{x}_t \; ; \; \mathbf{w}_{t+1}^r = \mathbf{w}_t^r \; (\forall r \in \mathcal{Y} \setminus \{y_t, \hat{y}_t\}) . \quad (18)$$

In words, we add the instance $\mathbf{x}_t$ to the prototype of the correct label and subtract $\mathbf{x}_t$ from the prototype of $\hat{y}_t$. The rest of the prototypes are left intact. If $\hat{y}_t = y_t$, we check whether we still encounter a margin error. Let $\tilde{y}_t$ denote the index of the prototype whose inner-product with $\mathbf{x}_t$ is the second largest, that is,

$$\tilde{y}_t = \operatorname*{argmax}_{y \neq y_t} \left(\mathbf{w}_t^y \cdot \mathbf{x}_t \right) .$$

Analogous to the definition of $\hat{\mathbf{x}}_t$ in the binary classification problem, we define $\hat{\mathbf{x}}_t$ as the solution to the following optimization problem,

$$\hat{\mathbf{x}}_t = \operatorname*{argmin}_{\mathbf{x} \in B(\mathbf{x}_t, r)} \left(\mathbf{w}_t^{y_t} \cdot \mathbf{x} - \mathbf{w}_t^{\hat{y}_t} \cdot \mathbf{x} \right) . \tag{19}$$

Note that if $\mathbf{w}_t^{y_t} \cdot \hat{\mathbf{x}}_t > \mathbf{w}_t^{\hat{y}_t} \cdot \hat{\mathbf{x}}_t$ then all the points in $B(\mathbf{x}_t, r)$ are labeled correctly and there is no margin error. If this is the case we leave all the prototypes intact. If however $\mathbf{w}_t^{y_t} \cdot \hat{\mathbf{x}}_t \leq \mathbf{w}_t^{\hat{y}_t} \cdot \hat{\mathbf{x}}_t$ we perform the update given by Eq. (18) using $\hat{\mathbf{x}}_t$ instead of $\mathbf{x}_t$ and $\tilde{y}_t$ instead of $\hat{y}_t$. The same derivation described in Sec. 2, yields that $\hat{\mathbf{x}}_t = \mathbf{x}_t + r(\mathbf{w}_t^{\tilde{y}_t} - \mathbf{w}_t^{y_t})/\|\mathbf{w}_t^{\tilde{y}_t} - \mathbf{w}_t^{y_t}\|$. The analysis of the Ballseptron from Sec. 3 can be adapted to the multiclass version of the algorithm as we now briefly describe. Let $\{\mathbf{u}^1, \ldots, \mathbf{u}^k\}$ be a set of k prototype vectors such that $\sum_{i=1}^k \|\mathbf{u}^i\|^2 = 1$. For each multiclass example $(\mathbf{x}_t, y_t)$ define the hinge-loss of the above prototypes on this example as,

$$\ell_t = \max \left\{ 0, \max_{y \neq y_t} \left(\gamma - (\mathbf{u}^{y_t} - \mathbf{u}^y) \cdot \mathbf{x}_t \right) \right\} .$$

We now redefine D_2 and D_1 using the above definition of the hinge-loss. In addition, we need to redefine R to be $R = \sqrt{2} \max_t \|\mathbf{x}_t\|$. Using these definitions, it can be shown that slightly weaker versions of the bounds from Sec. 3 can be obtained.

5   Experimental Results

In this section we present experimental results that demonstrate different aspects of the Ballseptron algorithm and its accompanying analysis. In the first experiment we examine the effect of the radius r employed by the Ballseptron on the number of prediction mistakes it makes. We used two standard datasets: the MNIST dataset which consists of $60,000$ training examples and the USPS dataset which has 7291 training examples. The examples in both datasets are images of handwritten digits where each image belongs to one of the 10 digit classes. We thus used the multiclass extension of the Ballseptron described in the previous section. In both experiments we used a fifth degree polynomial kernel with a bias term of $1/2$ as our inner-product operator. We shifted and scaled the instances so that the average instance becomes the zero vector and the average norm over all instances becomes 1. For both datasets, we run the online Ballseptron algorithm with different values for the radius r. In the two plots on the top of Fig. 3 we depict ε/T, the number of prediction mistakes ε divided by the number of online rounds T as a function of r. Note that $r = 0$ corresponds to the original Perceptron algorithm. As can be seen from the figure, many choices of r result in a significant reduction in the number

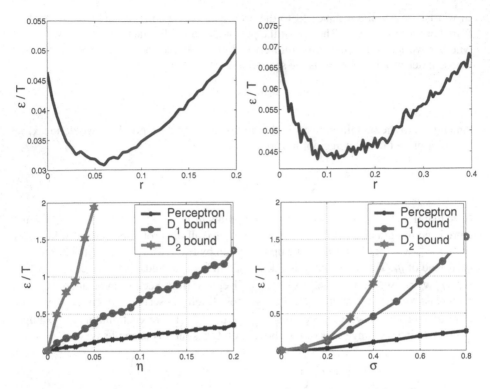

Fig. 3. Top plots: The fraction of prediction mistakes (ε/T) as a function of the radius parameter r for the MNIST (left) and USPS (right) datasets. Bottom plots: The behavior of the mistake bounds as a function of a label noise rate (left) and an instance noise rate (right)

of online prediction mistakes. However, as anticipated, setting r to be excessively large deteriorates the performance of the algorithm.

The second experiment compares the mistake bound of Thm. 1 with that of Thm. 2. To facilitate a clear comparison, we set the parameter r to be zero hence we simply confined the experiment to the Perceptron algorithm. We compared the mistake bound of the Perceptron from Eq. (3) derived by Freund and Schapire [9] to the new mistake bound given in Thm. 2. For brevity we refer to the bound of Freund and Schapire as the D_2-bound and to the new mistake bound as the D_1-bound. We used two synthetic datasets each consisting of $10,000$ examples. The instances in the two datasets, were picked from the unit circle in $\mathbb{R}^2$. The labels of the instances were set so that the examples are linearly separable with a margin of 0.15. Then, we contaminated the instances with two different types of noise, resulting in two different datasets. For the first dataset we flipped the label of each example with probability η. In the second dataset we kept the labels intact but added to each instance a random vector sampled from a 2-dimensional Gaussian distribution with a zero mean vector and a covariance matrix $\sigma^2 I$. We then run the Perceptron algorithm on each of the datasets for different values of η and σ. We calculated the mistake bounds given in Eq. (3) and in Thm. 2 for each of the datasets and for each value of η and σ. The results are depicted on the two bottom plots of Fig. 3. As can be seen from the figure, the D_1-bound is clearly tighter than the D_2-bound in the presence of label noise. Specifically, whenever the label noise level is greater than 0.03, the D_2-bound is greater than 1 and therefore meaningless. Interestingly, the D_1-bound is also slightly better than the D_2-bound in the presence of instance noise. We leave further comparisons of the two bounds to future work.

6   Discussion and Future Work

We presented a new algorithm that uses the Perceptron as its infrastructure. Our algorithm naturally employs the notion of margin. Previous online margin-based algorithms yielded essentially the same mistake bound obtained by the Perceptron. In contrast, under mild conditions, our analysis implies that the mistake bound of the Ballseptron is superior to the Perceptron's bound. We derived two mistake bounds, both are also applicable to the original Perceptron algorithm. The first bound reduces to the original bound of Freund and Schpire [9] while the second bound is new and is likely to be tighter than the first in many settings. Our work can be extended in several directions. A few variations on the proposed approach, which replaces the original example with a pseudo-example, can be derived. Most notably, we can update $\mathbf{w}_t$ based on $\hat{\mathbf{x}}_t$ even for cases where there is a prediction mistake. Our proof technique is still applicable, yielding a different mistake bound. More complex prediction problems such as hierarchical classification may also be tackled in a similar way to the proposed multiclass extension. Last, we would like to note that the Ballseptron can be used as a building block for finding an arbitrarily close approximation to the max-margin solution in a separable batch setting.

Acknowledgments

We would like to thank the COLT committee members for their constructive comments. This research was funded by EU Project PASCAL and by NSF ITR award 0205594.

References

1. S. Agmon. The relaxation method for linear inequalities. *Canadian Journal of Mathematics*, 6(3):382–392, 1954.
2. J. Bi and T. Zhang. Support vector classification with input data uncertainty. In *Advances in Neural Information Processing Systems 17*, 2004.
3. H. D. Block. The perceptron: A model for brain functioning. *Reviews of Modern Physics*, 34:123–135, 1962. Reprinted in "Neurocomputing" by Anderson and Rosenfeld.
4. A. Blum and J.D. Dunagan. Smoothed analysis of the perceptron algorithm for linear programming. In *SODA*, 2002.
5. K. Crammer, O. Dekel, S. Shalev-Shwartz, and Y. Singer. Online passive aggressive algorithms. In *Advances in Neural Information Processing Systems 16*, 2003.
6. K. Crammer, R. Gilad-Bachrach, A. Navot, and N. Tishby. Margin analysis of the LVQ algorithm. In *Advances in Neural Information Processing Systems 15*, 2002.

7. K. Crammer and Y. Singer. Ultraconservative online algorithms for multiclass problems. *Jornal of Machine Learning Research*, 3:951–991, 2003.
8. S. Floyd and M. Warmuth. Sample compression, learnability, and the Vapnik-Chervonenkis dimension. *Machine Learning*, 21(3):269–304, 1995.
9. Y. Freund and R. E. Schapire. Large margin classification using the perceptron algorithm. *Machine Learning*, 37(3):277–296, 1999.
10. C. Gentile. A new approximate maximal margin classification algorithm. *Journal of Machine Learning Research*, 2:213–242, 2001.
11. J. Kivinen, A. J. Smola, and R. C. Williamson. Online learning with kernels. In *Advances in Neural Information Processing Systems 14*. MIT Press, 2002.
12. Y. Li and P. M. Long. The relaxed online maximum margin algorithm. *Machine Learning*, 46(1–3):361–387, 2002.
13. M. Minsky and S. Papert. *Perceptrons: An Introduction to Computational Geometry*. The MIT Press, 1969.
14. A. B. J. Novikoff. On convergence proofs on perceptrons. In *Proceedings of the Symposium on the Mathematical Theory of Automata*, volume XII, pages 615–622, 1962.
15. F. Rosenblatt. The perceptron: A probabilistic model for information storage and organization in the brain. *Psychological Review*, 65:386–407, 1958. (Reprinted in *Neurocomputing* (MIT Press, 1988).).
16. V.N. Vapnik. *The Nature of Statistical Learning Theory*. Springer, 1995.
17. J. Weston and C. Watkins. Support vector machines for multi-class pattern recognition. In *Proceedings of the Seventh European Symposium on Artificial Neural Networks*, April 1999.

Fast Rates for Support Vector Machines

Ingo Steinwart and Clint Scovel

CCS-3, Los Alamos National Laboratory, Los Alamos NM 87545, USA
{ingo, jcs}@lanl.gov

Abstract. We establish learning rates to the Bayes risk for support vector machines (SVMs) using a regularization sequence $\lambda_n = n^{-\alpha}$, where $\alpha \in (0,1)$ is arbitrary. Under a noise condition recently proposed by Tsybakov these rates can become faster than $n^{-1/2}$. In order to deal with the approximation error we present a general concept called the approximation error function which describes how well the infinite sample versions of the considered SVMs approximate the data-generating distribution. In addition we discuss in some detail the relation between the "classical" approximation error and the approximation error function. Finally, for distributions satisfying a geometric noise assumption we establish some learning rates when the used RKHS is a Sobolev space.

1 Introduction

The goal in binary classification is to predict labels $y \in Y := \{-1, 1\}$ of unseen data points $x \in X$ using a training set $T = ((x_1, y_1), \ldots, (x_n, y_n)) \in (X \times Y)^n$. As usual we assume that both the training samples (x_i, y_i) and the new sample (x, y) are i.i.d. drawn from an unknown distribution P on $X \times Y$. Now given a *classifier* C that assigns to every T a function $f_T : X \to \mathbb{R}$ the prediction of C for y is sign $f_T(x)$, where we choose a fixed definition of sign$(0) \in \{-1, 1\}$. In order to "learn" from T the decision function $f_T : X \to \mathbb{R}$ should guarantee a small probability for the misclassification, i.e. sign $f_T(x) \neq y$, of the example (x, y). To make this precise the risk of a measurable function $f : X \to \mathbb{R}$ is defined by

$$\mathcal{R}_P(f) := P(\{(x, y) : \text{sign } f(x) \neq y\}),$$

and the smallest achievable risk $\mathcal{R}_P := \inf\{\mathcal{R}_P(f) \mid f : X \to \mathbb{R} \text{ measurable}\}$ is known as the *Bayes risk* of P. A function f_P attaining this risk is called a *Bayes decision function*. Obviously, a good classifier should produce decision functions whose risks are close to the Bayes risk with high probability. To make this precise, we say that a classifier is *universally consistent* if

$$\mathbb{E}_{T \sim P^n} \mathcal{R}_P(f_T) - \mathcal{R}_P \to 0 \qquad \text{for } n \to \infty. \tag{1}$$

Unfortunately, it is well known that no classifier can guarantee a convergence rate in (1) that simultaneously holds for all distributions (see [1–Thm. 7.2]). However, if one restricts considerations to suitable smaller classes of distributions

P. Auer and R. Meir (Eds.): COLT 2005, LNAI 3559, pp. 279–294, 2005.

such rates exist for various classifiers (see e.g. [2, 3, 1]). One interesting feature of these rates is that they are not faster than $n^{-1/2}$ if the considered distributions P are allowed to be noisy in the sense of $\mathcal{R}_P > 0$. On the other hand, if one restricts considerations to noise-free distributions P in the sense of $\mathcal{R}_P = 0$ then some empirical risk minimization (ERM) methods can actually learn with rate n^{-1} (see e.g. [1]). Remarkably, it was only recently discovered (see [4, 5]) that there also exists classes of noisy distributions which can be learned with rates between $n^{-1/2}$ and n^{-1}. The key property of these classes is that their noise level $x \mapsto 1/2 - |\eta(x) - 1/2|$ with $\eta(x) := P(y = 1|x)$ is well-behaved in the sense of the following definition.

Definition 1. *A distribution P on $X \times Y$ has Tsybakov noise exponent $q \in [0, \infty]$, if there exists a $C > 0$ such that for all sufficiently small $t > 0$ we have*

$$P_X \left(\{ x \in X : |2\eta(x) - 1| \leq t \} \right) \ \leq \ C \cdot t^q . \tag{2}$$

Obviously, all distributions have at least noise exponent 0. At the other extreme, (2) is satisfied for $q = \infty$ if and only if the conditional probability η is bounded away from the critical level $1/2$. In particular this shows that noise-free distributions have exponent $q = \infty$.

The aim of this work is to establish learning rates for support vector machines (SVMs) under Tsybakov's noise assumption which are comparable to the rates of [4, 5]). Therefore let us now recall these classification algorithms: let X be a compact metric space and H be a RKHS over X with continuous kernel k. Furthermore, let $l : Y \times \mathbb{R} \to [0, \infty)$ be the hinge loss which is defined by $l(y, t) := \max\{0, 1 - yt\}$. Then given a training set $T \in (X \times Y)^n$ and a regularization parameter $\lambda > 0$ SVMs solve the optimization problems

$$(\tilde{f}_{T,\lambda}, \tilde{b}_{T,\lambda}) := \arg \min_{\substack{f \in H \\ b \in \mathbb{R}}} \lambda \|f\|_H^2 + \frac{1}{n} \sum_{i=1}^{n} l\big(y_i, f(x_i) + b\big) , \tag{3}$$

or

$$f_{T,\lambda} := \arg \min_{f \in H} \lambda \|f\|_H^2 + \frac{1}{n} \sum_{i=1}^{n} l\big(y_i, f(x_i)\big) , \tag{4}$$

respectively. Furthermore, in order to control the size of the offset we always choose $\tilde{b}_{T,\lambda} := y^*$ if all samples of T have label y^*. As usual we call algorithms solving (3) *L1-SVMs with offset* and algorithms solving (4) *L1-SVMs without offset*. For more information on these methods we refer to [6].

The rest of this work is organized as follows: In Section 2 we first introduce two concepts which describe the richness of RKHSs. We then present our main result and discuss it. The following sections are devoted to the proof of this result: In Section 3 we recall some results from [7] which are used for the analysis of the estimation error, and in Section 4 we then prove our main result. Finally, the relation between the approximation error and infinite sample SVMs which is of its own interest is discussed in the appendix.

2   Definitions and Results

For the formulation of our results we need two notions which deal with the richness of RKHSs. While the first notion is a complexity measure in terms of covering numbers which is used to bound the estimation error, the second one describes the approximation properties of RKHSs with respect to distributions.

In order to introduce the complexity measure let us recall that for a Banach space E with closed unit ball B_E, the *covering numbers* of $A \subset E$ are defined by

$$\mathcal{N}(A, \varepsilon, E) := \min\left\{n \geq 1 : \exists x_1, \ldots, x_n \in E \text{ with } A \subset \bigcup_{i=1}^{n}(x_i + \varepsilon B_E)\right\}, \qquad \varepsilon > 0.$$

Given a training set $T = ((x_1, y_1), \ldots, (x_n, y_n)) \in (X \times Y)^n$ we denote the space of all equivalence classes of functions $f : X \times Y \to \mathbb{R}$ equipped with norm

$$\|f\|_{L_2(T)} := \left(\frac{1}{n}\sum_{i=1}^{n}|f(x_i, y_i)|^2\right)^{\frac{1}{2}} \tag{5}$$

by $L_2(T)$. In other words, $L_2(T)$ is a L_2-space with respect to the empirical measure of T. Note, that for a function $f : X \times Y \to \mathbb{R}$ a canonical representative in $L_2(T)$ is the restriction $f_{|T}$. Furthermore, we write $L_2(T_X)$ for the space of all (equivalence classes of) square integrable functions with respect to the empirical measure of $x_1, \ldots, x_n$. Now our complexity measure is:

Definition 2. *Let H be a RKHS over X and B_H its closed unit ball. We say that H has complexity exponent $0 < p \leq 2$ if there exists a constant $c > 0$ such that for all $\varepsilon > 0$ we have*

$$\sup_{T_X \in X^n} \log \mathcal{N}\big(B_H, \varepsilon, L_2(T_X)\big) \leq c\varepsilon^{-p}.$$

By using the theory of absolutely 2-summing operators one can show that every RKHS has complexity exponent $p = 2$. However, for meaningful rates we need complexity exponents which are strictly smaller than 2.

In order to introduce the second notion describing the approximation properties of RKHSs we first have to recall the infinite sample versions of (3) and (4). To this end let l be the hinge loss function and P be a distribution on $X \times Y$. Then for $f : X \to \mathbb{R}$ the l-risk of f is defined by $\mathcal{R}_{l,P}(f) := \mathbb{E}_{(x,y)\sim P}l(y, f(x))$. Now given a RKHS H over X and $\lambda > 0$ we define

$$(\tilde{f}_{P,\lambda}, \tilde{b}_{P,\lambda}) := \arg\min_{\substack{f \in H \\ b \in \mathbb{R}}} \left(\lambda\|f\|_H^2 + \mathcal{R}_{l,P}(f + b)\right) \tag{6}$$

and

$$f_{P,\lambda} := \arg\min_{f \in H} \left(\lambda\|f\|_H^2 + \mathcal{R}_{l,P}(f)\right) \tag{7}$$

(see [8] for the existence of these minimizers). Note that these definitions give the solutions $(\tilde{f}_{T,\lambda}, \tilde{b}_{T,\lambda})$ and $f_{T,\lambda}$ of (3) and (4), respectively, if P is an empirical distribution with respect to a training set T. In this case we write $\mathcal{R}_{l,T}(f)$ for the (empirical) l-risk.

With these notations in mind we define the *approximation error function* by

$$a(\lambda) \; := \; \lambda \|f_{P,\lambda}\|_H^2 + \mathcal{R}_{l,P}(f_{P,\lambda}) - \mathcal{R}_{l,P}, \qquad \lambda \geq 0, \qquad (8)$$

where $\mathcal{R}_{l,P} := \inf\{\mathcal{R}_{l,P}(f) \mid f : X \to \mathbb{R}\}$ denotes the smallest possible l-risk. Note that since the obvious variant of $a(.)$ that involves an *offset* is not greater than the above approximation error function, we restrict our attention to the latter. Furthermore, we discuss the relationship between $a(.)$ and the standard approximation error in the appendix.

The approximation error function quantifies how well an infinite sample L1-SVM with RKHS H approximates the minimal l-risk. It was shown in [8] that if H is dense in the space of continuous functions $C(X)$ then for *all* P we have $a(\lambda) \to 0$ if $\lambda \to 0$. However, in non-trivial situations no rate of convergence which uniformly holds for all distributions P is possible. The following definition characterizes distributions which guarantee certain polynomial rates:

Definition 3. *Let H be a RKHS over X and P be a probability measure on $X \times Y$. We say that H approximates P with exponent $0 \leq \beta \leq 1$ if there exists a constant $C > 0$ such that for all $\lambda > 0$ we have*

$$a(\lambda) \leq C\lambda^\beta .$$

Note, that H approximates every distribution P with exponent $\beta = 0$. We will see in the appendix that the other extremal case $\beta = 1$ is equivalent to the fact that the minimal l-risk can be achieved by an element $f_{l,P} \in H$.

With the help of the above notations we can now formulate our main result.

Theorem 1. *Let H be a RKHS of a continuous kernel on a compact metric space X with complexity exponent $0 < p < 2$, and let P be a probability measure on $X \times Y$ with Tsybakov noise exponent $0 \leq q \leq \infty$. Furthermore, assume that H approximates P with exponent $0 < \beta \leq 1$. We define $\lambda_n := n^{-\alpha}$ for some $\alpha \in (0,1)$ and all $n \geq 1$. If $\alpha < \frac{4(q+1)}{(2q+pq+4)(1+\beta)}$ then there exists a $C > 0$ with*

$$\mathrm{Pr}^* \Big(T \in (X \times Y)^n : \mathcal{R}_P(f_{T,\lambda_n}) \leq \mathcal{R}_P + Cx^2 n^{-\alpha\beta} \Big) \; \geq \; 1 - e^{-x}$$

for all $n \geq 1$ and $x \geq 1$. Here Pr^* is the outer probability of P^n in order to avoid measurability considerations. Furthermore, if $\alpha \geq \frac{4(q+1)}{(2q+pq+4)(1+\beta)}$ then for all $\varepsilon > 0$ there is a $C > 0$ such that for all $x \geq 1$, $n \geq 1$ we have

$$\mathrm{Pr}^* \Big(T \in (X \times Y)^n : \mathcal{R}_P(f_{T,\lambda_n}) \leq \mathcal{R}_P + Cx^2 n^{-\frac{4(q+1)}{(2q+pq+4)}+\alpha+\varepsilon} \Big) \; \geq \; 1 - e^{-x} .$$

Finally, the same results hold for the L1-SVM with offset whenever $q > 0$.

Remark 1. The best rates Theorem 1 can guarantee are (up to an ε) of the form

$$n^{-\frac{4\beta(q+1)}{(2q+pq+4)(1+\beta)}},$$

and an easy calculation shows that these rates are obtained for the value $\alpha := \frac{4(q+1)}{(2q+pq+4)(1+\beta)}$. This result has already been announced in [9] and presented in an earlier (and substantially longer) version of [7]. The main difference of Theorem 1 to its predecessors is that it does not require to choose α optimally. Finally note that unfortunately the optimal α is in terms of both q and β, which are in general not accessible. At the moment we are not aware of any method which can adaptively find the (almost) optimal values for α.

Remark 2. In [5] it is assumed that a Bayes classifier is contained in the base function classes the considered ERM method minimizes over. This assumption corresponds to a perfect approximation of P by H, i.e. $\beta = 1$, as we will see in the apppendix. If in this case we rescale the complexity exponent p from $(0, 2)$ to $(0, 1)$ and write p' for the new complexity measure our optimal rate essentially becomes $n^{-\frac{q+1}{q+p'q+2}}$. Recall that this is exactly the *form* of Tsybakov's result in [5] which is known to be optimal in a minmax sense for some specific classes of distributions. However, as far as we know our complexity measure cannot be compared to Tsybakov's and thus the above reasoning *only indicates* that our optimal rates may be optimal in a minmax sense.

Let us finally present an example which shows how the developed theory can be used to establish learning rates for specific types of kernels and distributions.

Example 1 (SVMs using Sobolev spaces). Let $X \subset \mathbb{R}^d$ be the closed unit Euclidian ball, Ω be the centered open ball of radius 3, and $W^m(\Omega)$ be the Sobolev space of order $m \in \mathbb{N}$ over Ω. Recall that $W^m(\Omega)$ is a RKHS of a continuous kernel if $m > d/2$ (see e.g. [10]). Let us write $H_m := \{f_{|X} : f \in W^m(\Omega)\}$ for the restriction of $W^m(\Omega)$ onto X endowed with the induced RKHS norm. Then (see again [10]) the RKHS H_m has complexity exponent $p := d/m$ if $m > d/2$.

Now let P be a distribution on $X \times Y$ which has geometric noise exponent $\alpha \in (0, \infty]$ in the sense of [7], and let $k_\sigma(x, x') := \exp(-\sigma^2\|x - x'\|)$, $x, x' \in \Omega$, be a Gaussian RBF kernel with associated integral operator $T_\sigma : L_2(\Omega) \to L_2(\Omega)$, where $L_2(\Omega)$ is with respect to the Lebesgue measure. Then by the results in [7–Secs. 3 & 4] there exist constants $c_d, c_{\alpha,m,d} \geq 1$ such that for all $\sigma > 0$ there exists an $f_\sigma \in L_2(\Omega)$ with $\|f_\sigma\|_{L_2(\Omega)} = c_d\sigma^d$, $\mathcal{R}_{l,P}((T_\sigma f_\sigma)_{|X}) - \mathcal{R}_{l,P} \leq c_{\alpha,m,d}\sigma^{-\alpha d}$, and $\|(T_\sigma f_\sigma)_{|X}\|_{H_m} \leq c_{\alpha,m,d}\sigma^{m-d/2}\|f_\sigma\|_{L_2(\Omega)}$. This yields a constant $c > 0$ with

$$a(\lambda) \leq c(\lambda\sigma^{2m+d} + \sigma^{-\alpha d})$$

for all $\sigma > 0$ and all $\lambda > 0$. Minimizing with respect to σ then shows that H_m approximates P with exponent $\beta := \frac{\alpha d}{(\alpha+1)d+2m}$. Consequently we can use Theorem 1 to obtain learning rates for SVMs using H_m for $m > d/2$. In particular the resulting optimal rates in the sense of Remark 1 are (essentially) of the form

$$n^{-\frac{4\alpha dm(q+1)}{(2mq+dq+4m)(2\alpha d+d+2m)}}.$$

3   Prerequisites

In this section we recall some important notions and results that we require in the proof of our main theorem. To this end let H be a RKHS over X that has a continuous kernel k. Then recall that every $f \in H$ is continuous and satisfies

$$\|f\|_\infty \le K \|f\|_H \,,$$

where we use

$$K := \sup_{x \in X} \sqrt{k(x,x)}.$$

The rest of this section recalls some results from [7] which will be used to bound the estimation error of L1-SVMs. Before we state these results we have to recall some notation from [7]: let $\mathcal{F}$ be a class of bounded measurable functions from a set Z to $\mathbb{R}$, and let $L : \mathcal{F} \times Z \to [0, \infty)$ be a function. We call L a *loss function* if $L \circ f := L(f, .)$ is measurable for all $f \in \mathcal{F}$. Moreover, if $\mathcal{F}$ is convex, we say that L is convex if $L(., z)$ is convex for all $z \in Z$. Finally, L is called *line-continuous* if for all $z \in Z$ and all $f, \hat{f} \in \mathcal{F}$ the function $t \mapsto L(tf + (1-t)\hat{f}, z)$ is continuous on $[0, 1]$. Note that if $\mathcal{F}$ is a vector space then every convex L is line-continuous. Now, given a probability measure P on Z we denote by $f_{P,\mathcal{F}} \in \mathcal{F}$ a minimizer of the L-risk

$$f \mapsto \mathcal{R}_{L,P}(f) := \mathbb{E}_{z \sim P} L(f, z).$$

If P is an empirical measure with respect to $T \in Z^n$ we write $f_{T,\mathcal{F}}$ and $\mathcal{R}_{L,T}(.)$ as usual. For simplicity, we assume throughout this section that $f_{P,\mathcal{F}}$ and $f_{T,\mathcal{F}}$ do exist. Also note that although there may exist multiple solutions we use a single symbol for them whenever no confusion regarding the non-uniqueness of this symbol can be expected. Furthermore, an algorithm that produces solutions $f_{T,\mathcal{F}}$ for all possible T is called an *empirical L-risk minimizer*.

Now the main result of this section, shown in [7], reads as follows:

Theorem 2. *Let $\mathcal{F}$ be a convex set of bounded measurable functions from Z to $\mathbb{R}$ and let $L : \mathcal{F} \times Z \to [0, \infty)$ be a convex and line-continuous loss function. For a probability measure P on Z we define*

$$\mathcal{G} := \left\{ L \circ f - L \circ f_{P,\mathcal{F}} : f \in \mathcal{F} \right\}. \tag{9}$$

Suppose we have $c \ge 0$, $0 < \alpha \le 1$, $\delta \ge 0$ and $B > 0$ with $\mathbb{E}_P g^2 \le c\,(\mathbb{E}_P g)^\alpha + \delta$ and $\|g\|_\infty \le B$ for all $g \in \mathcal{G}$. Furthermore, assume that $\mathcal{G}$ is separable with respect to $\|.\|_\infty$ and that there are constants $a \ge 1$ and $0 < p < 2$ with

$$\sup_{T \in Z^n} \log \mathcal{N}\big(B^{-1}\mathcal{G}, \varepsilon, L_2(T)\big) \le a\varepsilon^{-p} \tag{10}$$

for all $\varepsilon > 0$. Then there exists a constant $c_p > 0$ depending only on a and p such that for all $n \ge 1$ and all $x \ge 1$ we have

$$\mathrm{Pr}^* \Big(T \in Z^n : \mathcal{R}_{L,P}(f_{T,\mathcal{F}}) > \mathcal{R}_{L,P}(f_{P,\mathcal{F}}) + c_p\, \varepsilon(n, B, c, \delta, x) \Big) \le e^{-x} \,,$$

where

$$\varepsilon(n, B, c, \delta, x) := B^{\frac{2p}{4-2\alpha+\alpha p}} c^{\frac{2-p}{4-2\alpha+\alpha p}} n^{-\frac{2}{4-2\alpha+\alpha p}} + B^{\frac{p}{2}} \delta^{\frac{2-p}{4}} n^{-\frac{1}{2}} + Bn^{-\frac{2}{2+p}}$$
$$+ \left(\frac{\delta x}{n}\right)^{\frac{1}{2}} + \left(\frac{cx}{n}\right)^{\frac{1}{2-\alpha}} + \frac{Bx}{n}.$$

Let us now recall some variance bounds of the form $\mathbb{E}_P g^2 \le c \,(\mathbb{E}_P g)^\alpha + \delta$ for SVMs proved in [7]. To this end let H be a RKHS of a continuous kernel over X, $\lambda > 0$, and l be the hinge loss function. We define

$$L(f, x, y) := \lambda\|f\|_H^2 + l(y, f(x)) \tag{11}$$

and

$$L(f, b, x, y) := \lambda\|f\|_H^2 + l(y, f(x) + b) \tag{12}$$

for all $f \in H$, $b \in \mathbb{R}$, $x \in X$, and $y \in Y$. Since $\mathcal{R}_{L,T}(.)$ and $\mathcal{R}_{L,T}(.,.)$ coincide with the objective functions of the L1-SVM formulations we see that the L1-SVMs actually implement an empirical L-risk minimization in the sense of Theorem 2. Now the first variance bound from [7] does not require any assumptions on P.

Proposition 1. *Let $0 < \lambda < 1$, H be a RKHS over X, and $\mathcal{F} \subset \lambda^{-\frac{1}{2}} B_H$. Furthermore, let L be defined by (11), P be a probability measure and $\mathcal{G}$ be defined as in (9). Then for all $g \in \mathcal{G}$ we have*

$$\mathbb{E}_P g^2 \le 2\lambda^{-1}(2 + K)^2 \mathbb{E}_P g.$$

Finally, the following variance bound from [7] shows that the previous bound can be improved if one assumes a non-trivial Tsybakov exponent for P.

Proposition 2. *Let P be a distribution on $X \times Y$ with Tsybakov noise exponent $0 < q \le \infty$. Then there exists a constant $C > 0$ such that for all $\lambda > 0$, all $0 < r \le \lambda^{-1/2}$ satisfying $\tilde{f}_{P,\lambda} \in rB_H$, all $f \in rB_H$, and all $b \in \mathbb{R}$ with $|b| \le Kr + 1$ we have*

$$\mathbb{E}\left(L \circ (f, b) - L \circ (\tilde{f}_{P,\lambda}, \tilde{b}_{P,\lambda})\right)^2$$
$$\le C(Kr + 1)^{\frac{q+2}{q+1}} \left(\mathbb{E}\left(L \circ (f, b) - L \circ (\tilde{f}_{P,\lambda}, \tilde{b}_{P,\lambda})\right)\right)^{\frac{q}{q+1}} + C(Kr + 1)^{\frac{q+2}{q+1}} a^{\frac{q}{q+1}}(\lambda).$$

Furthermore, the same result holds for SVMs without offset.

4   Proof of Theorem 1

In this section we prove Theorem 1. To this end we write $f(x) \preceq g(x)$ for two functions $f, g : D \to [0, \infty)$, $D \subset (0, \infty)$, if there exists a constant $C > 0$ such that $f(x) \le Cg(x)$ holds over some range of x which usually is implicitly defined by the context. However for sequences this range is always $\mathbb{N}$. Finally we write $f(x) \sim g(x)$ if both $f(x) \preceq g(x)$ and $g(x) \preceq f(x)$ for the same range.

Since our variance bounds have different forms for the cases $q = 0$ and $q > 0$ we have to prove the theorem for these cases separately. We begin with the case $q = 0$ and an important lemma which describes a "shrinking technique".

Lemma 1. *Let H and P be as in Theorem 1. For $\gamma > -\beta$ we define $\lambda_n :=$ $n^{-\frac{1}{1+\beta+\gamma}}$. Now assume that there are constants $0 \le \rho < \beta$ and $C \ge 1$ such that*

$$\mathrm{Pr}^*\left(T \in (X \times Y)^n : \|f_{T,\lambda_n}\| \le Cx\lambda_n^{\frac{\rho-1}{2}}\right) \ge 1 - e^{-x}$$

for all $n \ge 1$, $x \ge 1$. Then there is another constant $\hat{C} \ge 1$ such that for $\hat{\rho} := \min\{\beta, \frac{\rho+\beta+\gamma}{2}, \beta+\gamma\}$ and for all $n \ge 1$, $x \ge 1$ we have

$$\mathrm{Pr}^*\left(T \in (X \times Y)^n : \|f_{T,\lambda_n}\| \le \hat{C}x\lambda_n^{\frac{\hat{\rho}-1}{2}}\right) \ge 1 - e^{-x}.$$

Proof. Let $\hat{f}_{T,\lambda_n}$ be a minimizer of $\mathcal{R}_{L,T}$ on $Cx\lambda_n^{\frac{\rho-1}{2}}B_H$, where L is defined by (11). By our assumption we have $\hat{f}_{T,\lambda_n} = f_{T,\lambda_n}$ with probability not less than $1 - e^{-x}$ since f_{T,λ_n} is unique for every training set T by the strict convexity of L. We will show that for some $\tilde{C} > 0$ and all $n \ge 1$, $x \ge 1$ the improved bound

$$\|\hat{f}_{T,\lambda_n}\| \le \tilde{C}x\lambda_n^{\frac{\hat{\rho}-1}{2}} \tag{13}$$

holds with probability not less than $1 - e^{-x}$. Consequently, $\|f_{T,\lambda_n}\| \le \tilde{C}x\lambda_n^{\frac{\hat{\rho}-1}{2}}$ will hold with probability not less than $1 - 2e^{-x}$. Obviously, the latter implies the assertion. In order to establish (13) we will apply Theorem 2 to the modified L1-SVM classifier that produces $\hat{f}_{T,\lambda_n}$. To this end we first observe that the separability condition of Theorem 2 is satisfied since H is separable and continuously embedded into $C(X)$. Furthermore it was shown in [7] that the covering number condition holds and by Proposition 1 we may choose c such that $c \sim x\lambda_n^{-1}$, and $\delta = 0$. Additionally, we can obviously choose $B \sim \lambda_n^{(\rho-1)/2}$. The term $\varepsilon(n, B, c, \delta, x)$ in Theorem 2 can then be estimated by

$$\varepsilon(n, B, c, \delta, x) \preceq x\lambda_n^{\frac{(\rho-1)p}{2+p}} \lambda_n^{-\frac{2-p}{2+p}} n^{-\frac{2}{2+p}} + x^2\lambda_n^{\frac{\rho-1}{2}} n^{-\frac{2}{2+p}} + x\lambda_n^{-1}n^{-1}$$
$$\preceq x^2\lambda_n^{\frac{p\rho+2\beta+2\gamma}{2+p}} + x^2\lambda_n^{\beta+\gamma}.$$

Now for $\rho \le \beta + \gamma$ we have $\frac{\rho+\beta+\gamma}{2} \le \frac{p\rho+2\beta+2\gamma}{2+p}$, and hence we obtain

$$\varepsilon(n, B, c, \delta, x) \preceq x^2\lambda_n^{\frac{\rho+\beta+\gamma}{2}} + x^2\lambda_n^{\beta+\gamma}.$$

Furthermore, if $\rho > \beta + \gamma$ we have both $\beta + \gamma < \frac{p\rho+2\beta+2\gamma}{2+p}$ and $\beta + \gamma < \frac{\rho+\beta+\gamma}{2}$, and thus we again find

$$\varepsilon(n, B, c, \delta, x) \preceq x^2\lambda_n^{\beta+\gamma} \sim x^2\lambda_n^{\beta+\gamma} + x^2\lambda_n^{\frac{\rho+\beta+\gamma}{2}}.$$

Now, in both cases Theorem 2 gives a constant $\tilde{C}_1 > 0$ independent of n and x such that for all $n \ge 1$ and all $x \ge 1$ the estimate

$$\lambda_n\|\hat{f}_{T,\lambda_n}\|^2 \le \lambda_n\|\hat{f}_{T,\lambda_n}\|^2 + \mathcal{R}_{l,P}(\hat{f}_{T,\lambda_n}) - \mathcal{R}_{l,P}$$
$$\le \lambda_n\|\hat{f}_{P,\lambda_n}\|^2 + \mathcal{R}_{l,P}(\hat{f}_{P,\lambda_n}) - \mathcal{R}_{l,P} + \tilde{C}_1x^2\lambda_n^{\frac{\rho+\beta+\gamma}{2}} + \tilde{C}_1x^2\lambda_n^{\beta+\gamma}$$

holds with probability not less than $1 - e^{-x}$. Furthermore, by Theorem 4 we obtain $\|f_{P,\lambda_n}\| \leq \lambda_n^{(\rho-1)/2} \leq Cx\lambda_n^{(\rho-1)/2}$ for large n which gives $f_{P,\lambda_n} = \hat{f}_{P,\lambda_n}$ for such n. With probability not less than $1 - e^{-x}$ we hence have

$$\lambda_n\|\hat{f}_{T,\lambda_n}\|^2 \leq \lambda_n\|f_{P,\lambda_n}\|^2 + \mathcal{R}_{l,P}(f_{P,\lambda_n}) - \mathcal{R}_{l,P} + \tilde{C}_1 x^2 \lambda_n^{\frac{\rho+\beta+\gamma}{2}} + \tilde{C}_1 x^2 \lambda_n^{\beta+\gamma}$$

$$\leq \tilde{C}_2 \lambda_n^{\beta} + \tilde{C}_1 x^2 \lambda_n^{\frac{\rho+\beta+\gamma}{2}} + \tilde{C}_1 x^2 \lambda_n^{\beta+\gamma}$$

for some constants $\tilde{C}_1, \tilde{C}_2 > 0$ independent of n and x. From this we easily obtain that (13) holds for *all* $n \geq 1$ with probability not less than $1 - e^{-x}$.   □

Proof (of Theorem 1 for $q = 0$). We first observe that there exists a $\gamma > -\beta$ with $\alpha = \frac{4(q+1)}{(2q+pq+4)(1+\beta+\gamma)}$. We fix this γ and define $\rho_0 := 0$ and $\rho_{i+1} := \min\{\beta, \frac{\rho_i+\beta+\gamma}{2}, \beta+\gamma\}$. Then it is easy to check that this definition gives

$$\rho_i = \min\left\{\beta, (\beta+\gamma)\sum_{j=1}^{i} 2^{-j}, \beta+\gamma\right\} = \min\left\{\beta, (\beta+\gamma)(1-2^{-i})\right\}.$$

Now, iteratively applying Lemma 2 gives a sequence of constants $C_i > 0$ with

$$\mathrm{Pr}^*\left(T \in (X \times Y)^n : \|f_{T,\lambda_n}\| \leq C_i x\lambda_n^{\frac{\rho_i-1}{2}}\right) \geq 1 - e^{-x} \qquad (14)$$

for all $n \geq 1$ and all $x \geq 1$. Let us first consider the case $-\beta < \gamma \leq 0$. Then we have $\rho_i = (\beta+\gamma)(1-2^{-i})$, and hence (14) shows that for all $\varepsilon > 0$ there exists a constant $C > 0$ such that

$$\mathrm{Pr}^*\left(T \in (X \times Y)^n : \|f_{T,\lambda_n}\| \leq Cx\lambda_n^{\frac{(1-\varepsilon)(\beta+\gamma)-1}{2}}\right) \geq 1 - e^{-x}$$

for all $n \geq 1$ and all $x \geq 1$. We write $\rho := (1-\varepsilon)(\beta+\gamma)$. As in the proof of Lemma 1 we denote a minimizer of $\mathcal{R}_{L,T}$ on $Cx\lambda_n^{\frac{\rho-1}{2}} B_H$ by $\hat{f}_{T,\lambda_n}$. We have just seen that $\hat{f}_{T,\lambda_n} = f_{T,\lambda_n}$ with probability not less than $1 - e^{-x}$. Therefore, we only have to apply Theorem 2 to the modified optimization problem which defines $\hat{f}_{T,\lambda_n}$. To this end we first see as in the proof of Lemma 1 that

$$\varepsilon(n,B,c,\delta,x) \preceq x^2 \lambda_n^{\frac{p\rho+2\beta+2\gamma}{2+p}} + x^2 \lambda_n^{\beta+\gamma} \preceq x^2 \lambda_n^{\frac{p\rho+2\beta+2\gamma}{2+p}} \preceq x^2 \lambda_n^{\beta+\gamma-\varepsilon},$$

where in the last two estimates we used the definition of ρ. Furthermore, we have already seen in the proof of Lemma 1 that $\lambda_n\|\hat{f}_{P,\lambda_n}\|^2 + \mathcal{R}_{l,P}(\hat{f}_{P,\lambda_n}) - \mathcal{R}_{l,P} \leq a(\lambda_n)$ holds for large n. Therefore, applying Theorem 2 and an inequality of Zhang (see [11]) between the excess classification risk and the excess l-risk we find that for all $n \geq 1$ we have with probability not less than $1 - e^{-x}$:

$$\mathcal{R}_P(\hat{f}_{T,\lambda_n}) - \mathcal{R}_P \leq 2\lambda_n\|\hat{f}_{T,\lambda_n}\|^2 + 2\mathcal{R}_{l,P}(\hat{f}_{T,\lambda_n}) - 2\mathcal{R}_{l,P}$$

$$\leq 2\lambda_n\|\hat{f}_{P,\lambda_n}\|^2 + 2\mathcal{R}_{l,P}(\hat{f}_{P,\lambda_n}) - 2\mathcal{R}_{l,P} + \tilde{C}_1 x^2 \lambda_n^{\beta+\gamma-\varepsilon}$$

$$\leq \tilde{C}_2 \lambda_n^{\beta+\gamma-\varepsilon}, \qquad (15)$$

where $\tilde{C}_1, \tilde{C}_2 > 0$ are constants independent of n and x. Now, from (15) we easily deduce the assertion using the definition of λ_n and γ.

Let us finally consider the case $\gamma > 0$. Then for large integers i we have $\rho_i = \beta$, and hence (14) gives a $C > 0$ such that for all $n \geq 1$, $x \geq 1$ we have

$$\Pr{}^* \left(T \in (X \times Y)^n : \|f_{T,\lambda_n}\| \leq Cx\lambda_n^{\frac{\beta-1}{2}} \right) \geq 1 - e^{-x}.$$

Proceeding as for $\gamma \leq 0$ we get $\varepsilon(n, B, c, \delta, x) \preceq x^2\lambda_n^{\frac{p\beta+2\beta+2\gamma}{2+p}} + x^2\lambda_n^{\beta+\gamma} \preceq x^2\lambda_n^\beta$, from which we easily obtain the assertion using the definition of λ_n and γ. □

In the rest of this section we will prove Theorem 1 for $q > 0$. We begin with a lemma which is similar to Lemma 1.

Lemma 2. *Let H and P be as in Theorem 1. For $\gamma > -\beta$ we define $\lambda_n :=$ $n^{-\frac{4(q+1)}{(2q+pq+4)(1+\beta+\gamma)}}$. Now assume that there are $\rho \in [0, \beta)$ and $C \geq 1$ with*

$$\Pr{}^* \left(T \in (X \times Y)^n : \|f_{T,\lambda_n}\| \leq Cx\lambda_n^{\frac{\rho-1}{2}} \right) \geq 1 - e^{-x}$$

for all $n \geq 1$ and all $x \geq 1$. Then there is another constant $\hat{C} \geq 1$ such that for $\hat{\rho} := \min\{\beta, \frac{\rho+\beta+\gamma}{2}\}$ and for all $n \geq 1$, $x \geq 1$ we have

$$\Pr{}^* \left(T \in (X \times Y)^n : \|f_{T,\lambda_n}\| \leq \hat{C}x\lambda_n^{\frac{\hat{\rho}-1}{2}} \right) \geq 1 - e^{-x}.$$

The same result holds for L1-SVM's with offset.

Proof. For brevity's sake we only prove this Lemma for L1-SVM's *with offset*. The proof for L1-SVM's without offset is almost identical.

Now, let L be defined by (12). Analogously to the proof of Lemma 1 we denote a minimizer of $\mathcal{R}_{L,T}(., .)$ on $Cx\lambda_n^{\frac{\rho-1}{2}}(B_H \times [-K-1, K+1])$ by $(\hat{f}_{T,\lambda_n}, \hat{b}_{T,\lambda_n})$. By our assumption (see [7]) we have $|\tilde{b}_{T,\lambda_n}| \leq Cx\lambda_n^{\frac{\rho-1}{2}}(K+1)$ with probability not less than $1 - e^{-x}$ for all possible values of the offset. In addition, for such training sets we have $\hat{f}_{T,\lambda_n} = \tilde{f}_{T,\lambda_n}$ since the RKHS component $\tilde{f}_{T,\lambda_n}$ of L1-SVM solutions is unique for T by the strict convexity of L in f. Furthermore, by the above considerations we may define $\hat{b}_{T,\lambda_n} := \tilde{b}_{T,\lambda_n}$ for such training sets. As in the proof of Lemma 1 it now suffices to show the existence of a $\tilde{C} > 0$ such that $\|\hat{f}_{T,\lambda_n}\| \leq \tilde{C}x\lambda_n^{\frac{\hat{\rho}-1}{2}}$ with probability not less than $1 - e^{-x}$. To this end we first observe by Proposition 2 that we may choose B, c and δ such that

$$B \sim x\lambda_n^{\frac{\rho-1}{2}}, \qquad c \sim x^{\frac{q+2}{q+1}}\lambda_n^{\frac{\rho-1}{2} \cdot \frac{q+2}{q+1}}, \qquad \text{and} \qquad \delta \sim x^{\frac{q+2}{q+1}}\lambda_n^{\frac{\rho-1}{2} \cdot \frac{q+2}{q+1} + \frac{\beta q}{q+1}}.$$

Some calculations then show that $\varepsilon(n, B, c, \delta, x)$ in Theorem 2 satisfies

$$\varepsilon(n, B, c, \delta, x) \preceq x^2\lambda_n^{\frac{\rho+\beta+\gamma}{2}} + x^2\lambda_n^{\frac{(\rho+\beta+\gamma)(2q+pq+4)+2\beta q(2-p)}{8(q+1)}}.$$

Furthermore observe that we have $\rho \leq \beta - \gamma$ if and only if $\rho + \beta + \gamma \leq \frac{(\rho+\beta+\gamma)(2q+pq+4)+2\beta q(2-p)}{4(q+1)}$. Now let us first consider the case $\rho \leq \beta - \gamma$. Then the above considerations show

$$\varepsilon(n,a,B,c,\delta,x) \preceq x^2 \lambda_n^{\frac{\rho+\beta+\gamma}{2}}.$$

Furthermore, we obviously have $\lambda_n^\beta \leq \lambda_n^{\frac{\rho+\beta+\gamma}{2}}$. As in the proof of Lemma 1 we hence find a constant $\tilde{C} > 0$ such that for all $x \geq 1$, $n \geq 1$ we have

$$\lambda \|\hat{f}_{T,\lambda_n}\|^2 \leq \tilde{C} x^2 \lambda_n^{\frac{\rho+\beta+\gamma}{2}}$$

with probability not less than $1 - e^{-x}$. On the other hand if $\rho > \beta - \gamma$ we have

$$\varepsilon(n,a,B,c,\delta,x) \preceq x^2 \lambda_n^{\frac{(\rho+\beta+\gamma)(2q+pq+4)+2\beta q(2-p)}{8(q+1)}} \leq x^2 \lambda_n^\beta,$$

so that we get $\lambda \|\hat{f}_{T,\lambda_n}\|^2 \leq \tilde{C} x^2 \lambda_n^\beta$ in the above sense.   □

Proof (of Theorem 1 for $q > 0$). By using Lemma 2 the proof in the case $q > 0$ is completely analogous to the case $q = 0$.   □

References

1. Devroye, L., Györfi, L., Lugosi, G.: A Probabilistic Theory of Pattern Recognition. Springer, New York (1996)
2. Yang, Y.: Minimax nonparametric classification—part I and II. IEEE Trans. Inform. Theory **45** (1999) 2271–2292
3. Wu, Q., Zhou, D.X.: Analysis of support vector machine classification. Tech. Report, City University of Hong Kong (2003)
4. Mammen, E., Tsybakov, A.: Smooth discrimination analysis. Ann. Statist. **27** (1999) 1808–1829
5. Tsybakov, A.: Optimal aggregation of classifiers in statistical learning. Ann. Statist. **32** (2004) 135–166
6. Schölkopf, B., Smola, A.: Learning with Kernels. MIT Press (2002)
7. Steinwart, I., Scovel, C.: Fast rates for support vector machines using Gaussian kernels. Ann. Statist. **submitted** (2004) http://www.c3.lanl.gov/~ingo/publications/ann-04a.pdf.
8. Steinwart, I.: Consistency of support vector machines and other regularized kernel machines. IEEE Trans. Inform. Theory **51** (2005) 128–142
9. Steinwart, I., Scovel, C.: Fast rates to bayes for kernel machines. In Saul, L.K., Weiss, Y., Bottou, L., eds.: Advances in Neural Information Processing Systems 17. MIT Press, Cambridge, MA (2005) 1345–1352
10. Edmunds, D., Triebel, H.: Function Spaces, Entropy Numbers, Differential Operators. Cambridge University Press (1996)
11. Zhang, T.: Statistical behaviour and consistency of classification methods based on convex risk minimization. Ann. Statist. **32** (2004) 56–134
12. Rockafellar, R.: Convex Analysis. Princeton University Press (1970)

Appendix

Throughout this section P denotes a Borel probability measure on $X \times Y$ and H denotes a RKHS of continuous functions over X. We use the shorthand $\| \cdot \|$ for $\| \cdot \|_H$ when no confusion should arise. Unlike in the other sections of this paper, here L denotes an *arbitrary* convex loss function, that is, a continuous function $L : Y \times \mathbb{R} \to [0, \infty)$ convex in its second variable. The corresponding L-risk $\mathcal{R}_{L,P}(f)$ of a function $f : X \to \mathbb{R}$ and its minimal value $\mathcal{R}_{L,P}$ are defined in the obvious way. For simplicity we also assume $\mathcal{R}_{L,P}(0) = 1$. Note that all the requirements are met by the hinge loss function. Furthermore, let us define $f_{P,\lambda}$ by replacing $\mathcal{R}_{l,P}$ by $\mathcal{R}_{L,P}$ in (7). In addition we write

$$f^*_{P,\lambda} = \arg\min \left\{ \|f\| : f \in \arg\min_{\|f'\| \leq \frac{1}{\sqrt{\lambda}}} \mathcal{R}_{L,P}(f') \right\}. \tag{16}$$

Of course, we need to prove the existence and uniqueness of $f^*_{P,\lambda}$ which is done in the following lemma.

Lemma 3. *Under the above assumptions $f^*_{P,\lambda}$ is well defined.*

Proof. Let us first show that there exists an $f' \in \lambda^{-1/2} B_H$ which minimizes $\mathcal{R}_{L,P}(.)$ in $\lambda^{-1/2} B_H$. To that end consider a sequence (f_n) in $\lambda^{-1/2} B_H$ such that $\mathcal{R}_{L,P}(f_n) \to \inf_{\|f\| \leq \lambda^{-1/2}} \mathcal{R}_{L,P}(f)$. By the Eberlein-Smulyan theorem we can assume without loss of generality that there exists an f^* with $\|f^*\| \leq \lambda^{-1/2}$ and $f_n \to f^*$ weakly. Using the fact that weak convergence in RKHS's imply pointwise convergence, Lebesgue's theorem and the continuity of L then give

$$\mathcal{R}_{L,P}(f_n) \to \mathcal{R}_{L,P}(f^*).$$

Hence there is a minimizer of $\mathcal{R}_{L,P}(.)$ in $\frac{1}{\sqrt{\lambda}} B_H$, i.e. we have

$$A := \left\{ f : f \in \arg\min_{\|f'\| \leq \frac{1}{\sqrt{\lambda}}} \mathcal{R}_{L,P}(f') \right\} \neq \emptyset.$$

We now show that there is exactly one $f^* \in A$ having minimal norm.

Existence: Let $(f_n) \subset A$ with $\|f_n\| \to \inf_{f \in A} \|f\|$ for $n \to \infty$. Like in the proof establishing $A \neq \emptyset$, we can show that there exists an $f^* \in A$ with $f_n \to f^*$ weakly, and $\mathcal{R}_{L,P}(f_n) \to \mathcal{R}_{L,P}(f^*)$. This shows $f^* \in A$. Furthermore, by the weak convergence we always have

$$\|f^*\| \leq \liminf_{n \to \infty} \|f_n\| = \inf_{f \in A} \|f\|.$$

Uniqueness: Suppose we have two such elements f and g with $f \neq g$. By convexity we find $\frac{1}{2}(f + g) \in \arg\min_{\|f\| \leq \frac{1}{\sqrt{\lambda}}} \mathcal{R}_{L,P}(f)$. However, $\|.\|_H$ is strictly convex which gives $\|\frac{1}{2}(f + g)\| < \|f\|$.   □

In the following we will define the approximation error and the approximation error function for general L. In order to also treat non-universal kernels we first denote the minimal L-risk of functions in H by

$$\mathcal{R}_{L,P,H} := \inf_{f \in H} \mathcal{R}_{L,P}(f).$$

Furthermore, we say that $f \in H$ *minimizes the L-risk in H* if $\mathcal{R}_{L,P}(f) = \mathcal{R}_{L,P,H}$. Note that if such a minimizer exists then by Lemma 3 there actually exists a unique element $f^*_{L,P,H} \in H$ minimizing the L-risk in H with $\|f^*_{L,P,H}\| \leq \|f\|$ for all $f \in H$ minimizing the L risk in H. Moreover we have $\|f_{P,\lambda}\| \leq \|f^*_{L,P,H}\|$ for all $\lambda > 0$ since otherwise we find a contradiction by

$$\lambda \|f^*_{L,P,H}\|^2 + \mathcal{R}_{L,P}(f^*_{L,P,H}) < \lambda \|f_{P,\lambda}\|^2 + \mathcal{R}_{L,P}(f_{P,\lambda}).$$

Now, for $\lambda \geq 0$ we write

$$a(\lambda) := \lambda \|f_{P,\lambda}\|^2 + \mathcal{R}_{L,P}(f_{P,\lambda}) - \mathcal{R}_{L,P,H}, \tag{17}$$

$$a^*(\lambda) := \mathcal{R}_{L,P}(f^*_{P,\lambda}) - \mathcal{R}_{L,P,H}. \tag{18}$$

Recall, that for universal kernels and the hinge loss function we have $\mathcal{R}_{L,P,H} = \mathcal{R}_{L,P}$ (see [8]), and hence in this case $a(.)$ equals the approximation error function defined in Section 2. Furthermore, for these kernels, $a^*(\lambda)$ is the "classical" approximation error of the hypothesis class $\lambda^{-1/2} B_H$. Our first theorem shows how to compare $a(.)$ and $a^*(.)$.

Theorem 3. *With the above notations we have $a(0) = a^*(0) = 0$. Furthermore, $a^*(.)$ is increasing, and $a(.)$ is increasing, concave, and continuous. In addition, we have*

$$a^*(\lambda) \leq a(\lambda) \qquad \text{for all } \lambda \geq 0,$$

and for any $h : (0, \infty) \to (0, \infty)$ with $a^*(\lambda) \leq h(\lambda)$ for all $\lambda > 0$, we have

$$a\big(\lambda h(\lambda)\big) \leq 2h(\lambda) \qquad \text{for all } \lambda > 0.$$

Proof. It is clear from the definitions (17) and (18) that $a(0) = a^*(0) = 0$ and $a^*(.)$ is increasing. Since $a(.)$ is an infimum over a family of linear increasing functions of λ it follows that $a(.)$ is also concave and increasing. Consequently $a(.)$ is continuous for $\lambda > 0$ (see [12–Thm. 10.1]), and continuity at 0 follows from the proof of [8–Prop. 3.2]. To prove the second assertion, observe that $\|f_{P,\lambda}\|^2 \leq 1/\lambda$ implies $\mathcal{R}_{L,P}(f^*_{P,\lambda}) \leq \mathcal{R}_{L,P}(f_{P,\lambda})$ for all $\lambda > 0$ and hence we find $a^*(\lambda) \leq a(\lambda)$ for all $\lambda \geq 0$. Now let $\tilde{\lambda} := h(\lambda)\|f^*_{P,\lambda}\|^{-2}$. Then we obtain

$$\tilde{\lambda}\|f_{P,\tilde{\lambda}}\|^2 + \mathcal{R}_{L,P}(f_{P,\tilde{\lambda}}) \leq \tilde{\lambda}\|f^*_{P,\lambda}\|^2 + \mathcal{R}_{L,P}(f^*_{P,\lambda}) \leq \tilde{\lambda}\|f^*_{P,\lambda}\|^2 + \mathcal{R}_{L,P,H} + h(\lambda)$$
$$\leq \mathcal{R}_{L,P,H} + 2h(\lambda).$$

This shows $a(\tilde{\lambda}) \leq 2h(\lambda)$. Furthermore we have $\lambda h(\lambda) \leq \|f^*_{P,\lambda}\|^{-2}h(\lambda) = \tilde{\lambda}$ and thus the assertion follows since $a(.)$ is an increasing function. $\qquad \square$

Our next goal is to show how the asymptotic behaviour of $a(.)$, $a^*(.)$ and $\lambda \mapsto \|f_{P,\lambda}\|$ are related to each other. Let us begin with a lemma that characterizes the existence of $f^*_{L,P,H} \in H$ in terms of the function $\lambda \mapsto \|f_{P,\lambda}\|$.

Lemma 4. *The minimizer $f^*_{L,P,H} \in H$ of the L-risk in H exists if and only if there exists a constant $c > 0$ with $\|f_{P,\lambda}\| \leq c$ for all $\lambda > 0$. In this case we additionally have $\lim_{\lambda \to 0^+} \|f_{P,\lambda} - f^*_{L,P,H}\|_H = 0$.*

Proof. Let us first assume that $f^*_{L,P,H} \in H$ exists. Then we have already seen $\|f_{P,\lambda}\| \leq \|f^*_{L,P,H}\|$ for all $\lambda > 0$, so that it remains to show the convergence. To this end let (λ_n) be a positive sequence converging to 0. By the boundedness of (f_{P,λ_n}) there then exists an $f^* \in H$ and a subsequence $(f_{P,\lambda_{n_i}})$ with $f_{P,\lambda_{n_i}} \to f^*$ weakly. This implies $\mathcal{R}_{L,P}(f_{P,\lambda_{n_i}}) \to \mathcal{R}_{L,P}(f^*)$ as in the proof of Lemma 3. Furthermore, we always have $\lambda_{n_i} \|f_{P,\lambda_{n_i}}\|^2 \to 0$ and thus

$$\mathcal{R}_{L,P,H} = \lim_{i \to \infty} \lambda_{n_i} \|f_{P,\lambda_{n_i}}\|^2 + \mathcal{R}_{L,P}(f_{P,\lambda_{n_i}}) = \mathcal{R}_{L,P}(f^*), \tag{19}$$

where the first equality can be shown as in [8] for universal kernels. In other words f^* minimizes the L-risk in H and hence we have

$$\|f_{P,\lambda_{n_i}}\| \leq \|f^*_{L,P,H}\| \leq \|f^*\| \leq \liminf_{j \to \infty} \|f_{P,\lambda_{n_j}}\|$$

for all $i \geq 1$. This shows both $\|f_{P,\lambda_{n_i}}\| \to \|f^*\|$ and $\|f^*_{L,P,H}\| = \|f^*\|$, and consequently we find $f^*_{L,P,H} = f^*$ by (19). In addition an easy calculation gives

$$\|f_{P,\lambda_{n_i}} - f^*\|^2 = \|f_{P,\lambda_{n_i}}\|^2 - 2\langle f_{P,\lambda_{n_i}}, f^* \rangle + \|f^*\|^2 \to \|f^*\|^2 - 2\|f^*\|^2 + \|f^*\|^2 = 0.$$

Now assume that $f_{P,\lambda_n} \not\to f^*_{L,P,H}$. Then there exists a $\delta > 0$ and a subsequence $(f_{P,\lambda_{n_j}})$ with $\|f_{P,\lambda_{n_j}} - f^*_{L,P,H}\| > \delta$. On the other hand applying the above reasoning to this subsequence gives a sub-subsequence converging to $f^*_{L,P,H}$ and hence we have found a contradiction.

Let us now assume $\|f_{P,\lambda}\| \leq c$ for some $c > 0$ and all $\lambda > 0$. Then there exists an $f^* \in H$ and a sequence (f_{P,λ_n}) with $f_{P,\lambda_n} \to f^*$ weakly. As in the first part of the proof we easily see that f^* minimizes the L-risk in H. $\square$

Note that if H is a universal kernel, i.e. it is dense in $C(X)$, P is an empirical distribution based on a training set T, and L is the (squared) hinge loss function then $f^*_{L,T,H} \in H$ exists and coincides with the *hard margin* SVM solution. Consequently, the above lemma shows that both the L1-SVM and the L2-SVM solutions $f_{T,\lambda}$ converge to the hard margin solution if T is *fixed* and $\lambda \to 0$.

The following lemma which shows that the function $f_{P,\lambda}$ minimizes $\mathcal{R}_{L,P}(.)$ over the ball $\|f_{P,\lambda}\| B_H$ is somewhat well-known:

Lemma 5. *Let $\lambda > 0$ and $\gamma := 1/\|f_{P,\lambda}\|^2$. Then we have $f^*_{P,\gamma} = f_{P,\lambda}$.*

Proof. We first show that $f_{P,\lambda}$ minimizes $\mathcal{R}_{L,P}(.)$ over the ball $\|f_{P,\lambda}\| B_H$. To this end assume the converse $\mathcal{R}_{L,P}(f^*_{P,\gamma}) < \mathcal{R}_{L,P}(f_{P,\lambda})$. Since we also have $\|f^*_{P,\gamma}\| \leq 1/\sqrt{\gamma} = \|f_{P,\lambda}\|$ we then find the false inequality

$$\lambda \|f^*_{P,\gamma}\|^2 + \mathcal{R}_{L,P}(f^*_{P,\gamma}) < \lambda \|f_{P,\lambda}\|^2 + \mathcal{R}_{L,P}(f_{P,\lambda}), \tag{20}$$

and consequently $f_{P,\lambda}$ minimizes $\mathcal{R}_{L,P}(.)$ over $\|f_{P,\lambda}\|B_H$. Now assume that $f_{P,\lambda} \neq f^*_{P,\gamma}$, i.e. $\|f_{P,\lambda}\| > \|f^*_{P,\gamma}\|$. Since $\mathcal{R}_{L,P}(f^*_{P,\gamma}) = \mathcal{R}_{L,P}(f_{P,\lambda})$ we then again find (20) and hence the assumption $f_{P,\lambda} \neq f^*_{P,\gamma}$ must be false. $\qquad\square$

Let us now turn to the main theorem of this section which describes asymptotic relationships between the approximation error, the approximation error function, and the function $\lambda \mapsto \|f_{P,\lambda}\|$.

Theorem 4. *The function* $\lambda \mapsto \|f_{P,\lambda}\|$ *is bounded on* $(0, \infty)$ *if and only if* $a(\lambda) \preceq \lambda$ *and in this case we also have* $a(\lambda) \sim \lambda$. *Moreover for all* $\alpha > 0$ *we have*

$$a^*(\lambda) \preceq \lambda^\alpha \qquad \text{if and only if} \qquad a(\lambda) \preceq \lambda^{\frac{\alpha}{\alpha+1}}.$$

If one of the estimates is true we additionally have $\|f_{P,\lambda}\|^2 \preceq \lambda^{-\frac{1}{\alpha+1}}$ *and* $\mathcal{R}_{L,P}(f_{P,\lambda}) - \mathcal{R}_{L,P,H} \preceq \lambda^{\frac{\alpha}{\alpha+1}}$. *Furthermore, if* $\lambda^{\alpha+\varepsilon} \preceq a^*(\lambda) \preceq \lambda^\alpha$ *for some* $\alpha > 0$ *and* $\varepsilon \geq 0$ *then we have both*

$$\lambda^{-\frac{\alpha}{(\alpha+\varepsilon)(\alpha+1)}} \preceq \|f_{P,\lambda}\|^2 \preceq \lambda^{-\frac{1}{\alpha+1}} \qquad \text{and} \qquad \lambda^{\frac{\alpha+\varepsilon}{\alpha+1}} \preceq \mathcal{R}_{L,P}(f_{P,\lambda}) - \mathcal{R}_{L,P} \preceq \lambda^{\frac{\alpha}{\alpha+1}},$$

and hence in particular $\lambda^{\frac{\alpha+\varepsilon}{\alpha+1}} \preceq a(\lambda) \preceq \lambda^{\frac{\alpha}{\alpha+1}}$.

Theorem 4 shows that if $a^*(\lambda)$ behaves essentially like λ^α then the approximation error function behaves essentially like $\lambda^{\frac{\alpha}{\alpha+1}}$. Consequently we do not loose information when considering $a(.)$ instead of the approximation error $a^*(.)$.

Proof (of Theorem 4). If $\lambda \mapsto \|f_{P,\lambda}\|$ is bounded on $(0, \infty)$ the minimizer $f^*_{L,P,H}$ exists by Lemma 4 and hence we find

$$a(\lambda) \leq \lambda\|f^*_{L,P,H}\|^2 + \mathcal{R}_{L,P}(f^*_{L,P,H}) - \mathcal{R}_{L,P,H} = \lambda\|f^*_{L,P,H}\|^2.$$

Conversely, if there exists a constant $c > 0$ with $a(\lambda) \leq c\lambda$ we find $\lambda\|f_{P,\lambda}\|^2 \leq a(\lambda) \leq c\lambda$ which shows $\|f_{P,\lambda}\| \leq \sqrt{c}$ for all $\lambda > 0$. Moreover by Theorem 3 we easily find $\lambda a(1) \leq a(\lambda)$ for all $\lambda > 0$.

For the rest of the proof we observe that Theorem 3 gives $a(\lambda) \leq a(c\lambda) \leq c\,a(\lambda)$ for $\lambda > 0$ and $c \geq 1$, and $c\,a(\lambda) \leq a(c\lambda) \leq a(\lambda)$ for $\lambda > 0$ and $0 < c \leq 1$. Therefore we can ignore arising constants by using the "$\preceq$"–notation.

Now let us assume $a^*(\lambda) \preceq \lambda^\alpha$ for some $\alpha > 0$. Then from Theorem 3 we know $a(\lambda^{1+\alpha}) \preceq \lambda^\alpha$ which leads to $a(\lambda) \preceq \lambda^{\frac{\alpha}{\alpha+1}}$. The latter immediately implies $\|f_{P,\lambda}\|^2 \preceq \lambda^{-\frac{1}{\alpha+1}}$. Conversely, if $a(\lambda) \preceq \lambda^{\frac{\alpha}{\alpha+1}}$ we define $\gamma := \|f_{P,\lambda}\|^{-2}$. By Lemma 5 we then obtain

$$a^*(\gamma) = \mathcal{R}_{L,P}(f_{P,\lambda}) - \mathcal{R}_{L,P,H} \leq a(\lambda) \preceq \lambda^{\frac{\alpha}{\alpha+1}} \preceq \|f_{P,\lambda}\|^{-2\alpha} = \gamma^\alpha.$$

Now, if $f^*_{L,P,H}$ does not exists then the function $\lambda \mapsto \|f_{P,\lambda}\|^{-2}$ tends to 0 if $\lambda \to 0$ and thus $a^*(\lambda) \preceq \lambda^\alpha$. In addition, if $f^*_{L,P,H}$ exists the assertion is trivial.

For the third assertion recall that Lemma 5 states $f_{P,\lambda} = f^*_{P,\gamma}$ with $\gamma := \|f_{P,\lambda}\|^{-2}$ and hence we find

$$a(\lambda) = \lambda\|f_{P,\lambda}\|^2 + a^*(\|f_{P,\lambda}\|^{-2}). \tag{21}$$

Furthermore, we have already seen $\|f_{P,\lambda}\|^{-2} \succeq \lambda^{\frac{1}{\alpha+1}}$, and hence we get

$$\lambda^{\frac{\alpha}{\alpha+1}} \succeq \mathcal{R}_{L,P}(f_{P,\lambda}) - \mathcal{R}_{L,P} = a^*(\|f_{P,\lambda}\|^{-2}) \succeq \|f_{P,\lambda}\|^{-2(\alpha+\varepsilon)} \succeq \lambda^{\frac{\alpha+\varepsilon}{\alpha+1}}.$$

Combining this with (21) yields the third assertion.   □

Exponential Convergence Rates in Classification

Vladimir Koltchinskii[*] and Olexandra Beznosova

Department of Mathematics and Statistics, The University of New Mexico,
Albuquerque, NM 87131-1141, USA
{vlad, beznosik}@math.unm.edu

Abstract. Let (X, Y) be a random couple, X being an observable instance and $Y \in \{-1, 1\}$ being a binary label to be predicted based on an observation of the instance. Let (X_i, Y_i), $i = 1, \ldots, n$ be training data consisting of n independent copies of (X, Y). Consider a real valued classifier $\hat{f}_n$ that minimizes the following penalized empirical risk

$$\frac{1}{n} \sum_{i=1}^{n} \ell(Y_i f(X_i)) + \lambda \|f\|^2 \to \min, \ f \in \mathcal{H}$$

over a Hilbert space $\mathcal{H}$ of functions with norm $\| \cdot \|$, ℓ being a convex loss function and $\lambda > 0$ being a regularization parameter. In particular, $\mathcal{H}$ might be a Sobolev space or a reproducing kernel Hilbert space. We provide some conditions under which the generalization error of the corresponding binary classifier $\text{sign}(\hat{f}_n)$ converges to the Bayes risk exponentially fast.

1 Introduction

Let (S, d) be a metric space and (X, Y) be a random couple taking values in $S \times \{-1, 1\}$ with joint distribution P. The distribution of X (which is a measure on the Borel σ-algebra in S) will be denoted by Π. Let (X_i, Y_i), $i \geq 1$ be a sequence of independent copies of (X, Y). Here and in what follows all random variables are defined on some probability space $(\Omega, \Sigma, \mathbb{P})$. Let $\mathcal{H}$ be a Hilbert space of functions on S such that $\mathcal{H}$ is dense in the space $C(S)$ of all continuous functions on S and, in addition,

$$\forall x, y \in S \ |f(x)| \leq \|f\| \text{ and } |f(x) - f(y)| \leq \|f\| d(x, y). \tag{1}$$

Here $\| \cdot \| = \| \cdot \|_{\mathcal{H}}$ is the norm of $\mathcal{H}$ and $\langle \cdot, \cdot \rangle = \langle \cdot, \cdot \rangle_{\mathcal{H}}$ is its inner product.

We have in mind two main examples. In the first one, S is a compact domain in $\mathbb{R}^d$ with smooth boundary. For any $s \geq 1$, one can define the following inner product in the space $C^{\infty}(S)$ of all infinitely differentiable functions in S :

$$\langle f, g \rangle_s := \sum_{|\alpha| \leq s} \int_S D^{\alpha} f D^{\alpha} g \, dx.$$

[*] Partially supported by NSF grant DMS-0304861.

P. Auer and R. Meir (Eds.): COLT 2005, LNAI 3559, pp. 295–307, 2005.

Here $\alpha = (\alpha_1, \ldots, \alpha_d)$, $\alpha_j = 0, 1, \ldots$, $|\alpha| := \sum_{i=1}^{d} \alpha_i$ and

$$D^\alpha f = \frac{\partial^{|\alpha|} f}{\partial x_1^{\alpha_1} \ldots \partial x_d^{\alpha_d}}.$$

The Sobolev space $\mathcal{H}^s(S)$ is the completion of $\left(C^\infty(S), \langle \cdot, \cdot \rangle_s \right)$. There is also a version of the definition for any real $s > 0$ that utilizes Fourier transforms. If $s > d/2 + 1$, then it follows from Sobolev's embedding theorems that conditions (1) hold with metric d being the Euclidean distance (possibly, after a proper "rescaling" of the inner product or of the metric d to make constants equal to 1).

In the second example, S is a metric compact and $\mathcal{H} = \mathcal{H}_K$ is the reproducing kernel Hilbert space (RKHS) generated by a Mercer kernel K. This means that K is a continuous symmetric nonnegatively definite kernel and $\mathcal{H}_K$ is defined as the completion of the linear span of functions $\{K_x : x \in S\}$, $K_x(y) := K(x, y)$, with respect to the following inner product:

$$\left\langle \sum_i \alpha_i K_{x_i}, \sum_j \beta_j K_{y_j} \right\rangle_K := \sum_{i,j} \alpha_i \beta_j K(x_i, y_j).$$

It is well known that $\mathcal{H}_K$ can be identified with a subset of $C(S)$ and

$$\forall f \in \mathcal{H}_K \ f(x) = \langle f, K_x \rangle_K,$$

implying that

$$|f(x)| \leq \|f\|_K \sup_{x \in S} \|K_x\|_K \text{ and } |f(x) - f(y)| \leq \|f\|_K \|K_x - K_y\|_K,$$

so again conditions (1) hold with $d(x, y) := \|K_x - K_y\|_K$ (as before, a simple rescaling is needed to ensure that the constants are equal to 1).

In binary classification problems, it is common to look for a real valued classifier $\hat{f}_n$ that solves the following penalized empirical risk minimization problem

$$\frac{1}{n} \sum_{i=1}^{n} \ell(Y_i f(X_i)) + \lambda \|f\|^2 \to \min, \ f \in \mathcal{H}, \tag{2}$$

where ℓ is a nonnegative decreasing convex loss function such that $\ell \geq I_{(-\infty, 0]}$ and $\lambda > 0$ is a regularization parameter. For instance, if ℓ is a "hinge loss", i.e. $\ell(u) = (1 - u) \vee 0$, and $\| \cdot \|$ is a RKHS-norm, this is a standard approach in kernel machines classification.

Given a real valued classifier $f : S \mapsto \mathbb{R}$, the corresponding binary classifier is typically defined as $x \mapsto \text{sign}(f(x))$, where $\text{sign}(u) = +1$ for $u \geq 0$ and -1 otherwise. The generalization error or risk of f is then

$$R_P(f) := P\{(x, y) : y \neq \text{sign}(f(x))\}.$$

It is well known that the minimium of $R_P(f)$ over all measurable functions f is attained at the regression function η defined as

$$\eta(x) := \mathbb{E}(Y|X = x).$$

The corresponding binary classifier $\mathrm{sign}(\eta(x))$ is called the Bayes classifier, the quantity $R_* := R_P(\eta)$ is called the Bayes risk and, finally, the quantity $R_P(f) - R_*$ is often referred to as the excess risk of a classifier f.

Our goal in this note is to show that under some (naturally restrictive) assumptions the expectation of the excess risk of $\hat{f}_n$ converges to 0 *exponentially fast* as $n \to \infty$. Recently, Audibert and Tsybakov [1] observed a similar phenomenon in the case of plug-in classifiers and our analysis here continues this line of work.

Denote

$$\delta(P) := \sup\{\delta > 0 : \Pi\{x : |\eta(x)| \le \delta\} = 0\}.$$

We will assume that

(a) η is a Lipschitz function with constant $L > 0$ (which, for the sake of simplicity of notations, will be assumed to be 1 in what follows):

$$|\eta(x) - \eta(y)| \le Ld(x, y).$$

(b) $\delta(P) > 0$.

These will be two main conditions that guarantee the possibilty of exponentially fast convergence rates of the generalization error to the Bayes risk. Note that condition (b), which is an extreme case of Tsybakov's low noise assumption, means that there exists $\delta > 0$ such that Π-a.e. either $\eta(x) \ge \delta$, or $\eta(x) \le -\delta$. The function η (as a conditional expectation) is defined up to Π-a.e. Condition (a) means that there exists a smooth (Lipschitz) version of this conditional expectation. Since smooth functions can not jump immediately from the value $-\delta$ to value δ, the combination of conditions (a) and (b) essentially means that there should be a wide enough "corridor" between the regions $\{\eta \ge \delta\}$ and $\{\eta \le -\delta\}$, but the probability of getting into this corridor is zero. The fact that in such situations it is possible to construct classifiers that converge to Bayes exponentially fast is essentially rather simple, it reduces to a large deviation type phenomenon, and it is even surprising that, up to our best knowledge, the possibility of such superfast convergence rates in classification has not been observed before Audibert and Tsybakov [1] (we apologize if someone, in fact, did it earlier).

Subtle results on convergence rates of the generalization error of large margin classifiers to the Bayes risk have been obtained relatively recently, see papers by Bartlett, Jordan and McAuliffe [3] and by Blanchard, Lugosi and Vayatis [5] on boosting, and papers by Blanchard, Bousquet and Massart [4] and by Scovel and Steinwart [7] on SVM. These papers rely heavily on general exponential inequalities in abstract empirical risk minimization in spirit of papers by Bartlett, Bousquet and Mendelson [2] or Koltchinskii [6] (or even earlier work by Birgé and Massart in the 90s). The rates of convergence in classification based on this general approach are at best of the order $O(n^{-1})$. In classification problems, there are many relevant probabilistic, analytic and geometric parameters to play with when one studies the convergence rates. For instance, both papers [4] and [7] deal with SVM classifiers (so, essentially, with problem (2) in the case when $\mathcal{H}$ is RKHS). In [4], the convergence rates are studied under the assumption (b) above and under some conditions on the eigenvalues of the kernel. In [7], the authors determine the convergence rates under the assumption on the entropy of the unit ball in RKHS of the same type as our assumption (3) below, under Tsybakov's low noise assumption and some additional conditions of geomeric nature. The fact that under somewhat more restrictive assumptions imposed in this paper even exponential convergence rates are possible indicates that, probably, we have not understood to the end rather subtle interplay between various parameters that influence the behaviour of this type of classifiers.

2   Main Result

We now turn to precise formulation of the results. Our goal will be to explain the main ideas rather than to give the results in the full generality, so, we will make below several simplifying assumptions.

First, we need some conditions on the loss function ℓ and to get this out of the way, we will just assume that ℓ is the so called logit loss,

$$\ell(u) = \log_2(1 + e^{-u}), \ u \in \mathbb{R}$$

(other loss functions of the same type that are decreasing, strictly convex, satisfy the assumption $\ell \geq I_{(-\infty,0]}$ and grow slower than u^2 as $u \to \infty$ will also do). We denote

$$(\ell \bullet f)(x, y) := \ell(yf(x)).$$

For a function g on $S \times \{-1, 1\}$, we write

$$Pg = \int_{S \times \{-1,1\}} g dP = \mathbb{E}\, g(X, Y).$$

Let P_n be the empirical measure based on the training data (X_i, Y_i), $i = 1, \ldots, n$. We will write

$$P_n g = \int_{S \times \{-1,1\}} g dP_n = n^{-1} \sum_{i=1}^{n} g(X_i, Y_i).$$

We use similar notations for functions defined on S. A simple and well known computation shows that the function $f \mapsto P(\ell \bullet f)$ attains its minimum at f_* defined by

$$f_*(x) = \log \frac{1 + \eta(x)}{1 - \eta(x)}.$$

We will assume in what follows that $f_* \in \mathcal{H}$. This assumption is rather restrictive. Since functions in $\mathcal{H}$ are uniformly bounded (see (1)) it means, in particular, that

η is bounded away from both $+1$ and -1. Although, there is a version of the main result below without this assumption, we are not discussing it in this note.

Next we need an assumption on so called uniform L_2-entropy of the unit ball in $\mathcal{H}$,

$$B_{\mathcal{H}} := \{f \in \mathcal{H} : \|f\| \leq 1\}.$$

Given a probability measure Q on S, let $N\left(B_{\mathcal{H}}; L_2(Q); \varepsilon\right)$ denote the minimal number of $L_2(Q)$-balls needed to cover $B_{\mathcal{H}}$. Suppose that for some $\rho \in (0, 2)$ and for some constant $A > 0$

$$\forall Q \; \forall \varepsilon > 0 : \; \log N\left(B_{\mathcal{H}}; L_2(Q); \varepsilon\right) \leq \left(\frac{A}{\varepsilon}\right)^{\rho}. \tag{3}$$

Denote $B(x, \delta)$ the open ball in (S, d) with center x and radius δ. Also, let $\mathcal{H}(x, \delta)$ be the set of all functions $h \in \mathcal{H}$ satisfying the following conditions:

$$(i) \;\; \forall y \in S \; 0 \leq h(y) \leq 2\delta$$
$$(ii) \;\; h \geq \delta \text{ on } B(x; \delta/2)$$
$$(iii) \;\; \int_{B(x;\delta)^c} h d\Pi \leq \delta \int_S h d\Pi$$

It follows from $(i) - (iii)$ that

$$\delta \Pi(B(x; \delta/2)) \leq \mathbb{E}\, h(X) \leq \frac{2\delta}{1 - \delta} \Pi(B(x; \delta)).$$

Since there exists a continuous function h such that $0 \leq h \leq \frac{3}{2}\delta$, $h \geq \frac{4}{3}\delta$ on $B(x, \delta/2)$ and $h = 0$ on $B(x, \delta)^c$, and, on the other hand, $\mathcal{H}$ is dense in $C(S)$, it is easy to see that $\mathcal{H}(x, \delta) \neq \emptyset$. Denote

$$q(x, \delta) := \inf_{h \in \mathcal{H}(x, \delta)} \|h\|.$$

The quantity $q(x, \delta)$ is, often, bounded from above uniformly in $x \in S$ by a decreasing function of δ, say by $\bar{q}(\delta)$, and this will be assumed in what follows. Often, $\bar{q}(\delta)$ grows as $\delta^{-\gamma}$, $\delta \to 0$ for some $\gamma > 0$.

Example. For instance, if $\mathcal{H} = \mathcal{H}^s(S)$ is a Sobolev space of functions in a compact domain $S \subset \mathbb{R}^d$, $s > d/2 + 1$, define

$$h(y) := \delta \varphi \left(\frac{x - y}{\delta}\right),$$

where $\varphi \in C^{\infty}(\mathbb{R}^d)$, $0 \leq \varphi \leq 2$, $\varphi(x) \geq 1$ if $|x| \leq 1/2$ and $\varphi(x) = 0$ if $|x| \geq 1$. Then h satisfies conditions (i)–(iii) (moreover, $h = 0$ on $B(x, \delta)^c$). A straightforward computation of Sobolev's norm of h shows that

$$\|h\|_{\mathcal{H}^s(S)} \leq C\delta^{1+d/2-s},$$

implying that $q(x, \delta)$ is uniformly bounded from above by $\bar{q}(\delta) = C\delta^{-\gamma}$ with $\gamma = s - \frac{d}{2} - 1$. Similar results are also true in the case of RKHS for some kernels.

Let

$$p(x, \delta) := \delta^2 \Pi(B(x, \delta/2)).$$

In what follows, $K, C > 0$ will denote sufficiently large numerical constants (whose precise values might change from place to place). Recall our assumption that $\delta(P) > 0$. In this case it is also natural to assume that for all $\delta \leq \frac{\delta(P)}{K}$ and for all x such that $|\eta(x)| \geq \delta(P)$

$$p(x, \delta) \geq \bar{p}(\delta) > 0$$

for some fixed function $\bar{p}$. This would be true, for instance, if S is a domain in $\mathbb{R}^d$ and Π has density uniformly bounded away from 0 on the set $\{x : |\eta(x)| \geq \delta(P)\}$. In this case we have for all x from this set

$$p(x, \delta) \geq c\delta^{d+2} =: \bar{p}(\delta).$$

Define now

$$r(x, \delta) := \frac{p(x, \delta)}{q(x, \delta)}.$$

Then on the set $\{x : |\eta(x)| \geq \delta(P)\}$

$$r(x, \delta) \geq \frac{\bar{p}(\delta)}{\bar{q}(\delta)}.$$

We set $U := K\left(\|f_*\| \vee L \vee 1\right)$ (here and in what follows $\vee$ stands for the maximum and $\wedge$ for the minimum) and define

$$\lambda^+ = \lambda^+(P) := \frac{1}{4U} \inf\left\{r\left(x; \frac{\delta(P)}{U}\right) : |\eta(x)| \geq \delta(P)\right\}$$

and, for a fixed $\varepsilon > K\frac{\log\log n}{n}$,

$$\lambda^- := \frac{A^{2\rho/(2+\rho)}}{n^{2/(2+\rho)}} \bigvee \varepsilon.$$

Clearly,

$$\lambda^+ \geq \frac{1}{4U} \frac{\bar{p}(\delta(P)/U)}{\bar{q}(\delta(P)/U)} > 0,$$

so, λ^+ is a positive constant. Then if n is large enough and ε is not too large, we have $\lambda^- \leq \lambda^+$.

Now, we are ready to formulate the main result.

Theorem 1. *Let $\lambda \in [\lambda^-, \lambda^+]$. Then there exists $\beta = \beta(\mathcal{H}, P) > 0$ such that*

$$\mathbb{E}\left(R_P(\hat{f}_n) - R_*\right) \leq \exp\{-\beta n\}.$$

In fact, with sufficiently large $K, C > 0$, β is equal to $C^{-1}\left(\bar{p}\left(\frac{\delta(P)}{U}\right) \wedge \varepsilon\right)$, which is positive and does not depend on n, establishing the exponential convergence rate.

3 Proof

We use a well known representation of the excess risk

$$R_P(f) - R_* = \int_{\{\mathrm{sign}(f) \neq \mathrm{sign}(\eta)\}} |\eta| d\Pi$$

to get the following bound:

$$\mathbb{E}\left(R_P(\hat{f}_n) - R_*\right) \leq$$

$$\mathbb{E} \int_{\{\hat{f}_n(x)\eta(x) \leq 0\}} |\eta(x)| \Pi(dx) = \mathbb{E} \int |\eta(x)| I_{\{\hat{f}_n(x)\eta(x) \leq 0\}} \Pi(dx) =$$

$$\int |\eta(x)| \mathbb{E} I_{\{\hat{f}_n(x)\eta(x) \leq 0\}} \Pi(dx) = \int |\eta(x)| \mathbb{P}\{\hat{f}_n(x)\eta(x) \leq 0\} \Pi(dx) \quad (4)$$

Our goal now is to bound, for a given x, $\mathbb{P}\{\hat{f}_n(x)\eta(x) \leq 0\}$. Let us assume that $\eta(x) = \delta > 0$ (the other case, when $\eta(x) < 0$, is similar). We have

$$\mathbb{P}\{\hat{f}_n(x)\eta(x) \leq 0\} = \mathbb{P}\{\hat{f}_n(x) \leq 0\} \leq$$

$$\mathbb{P}\{\hat{f}_n(x) \leq 0, \|\hat{f}_n\| \leq U\} + \mathbb{P}\{\|\hat{f}_n\| > U\}. \quad (5)$$

We start with bounding the first term. For $\delta_0 > 0$ (to be chosen later), let $h \in \mathcal{H}(x, \delta_0)$. Define

$$L_n(\alpha) := P_n(\ell \bullet (\hat{f}_n + \alpha h)) + \lambda \|\hat{f}_n + \alpha h\|^2.$$

Since $\hat{f}_n$ minimizes the functional

$$\mathcal{H} \ni f \mapsto P_n(\ell \bullet f) + \lambda \|f\|^2,$$

the function $\alpha \mapsto L_n(\alpha)$ attains its minimum at $\alpha = 0$. This function is differentiable, implying that

$$\frac{dL_n}{d\alpha}(0) = \frac{1}{n} \sum_{j=1}^{n} \ell'(Y_j \hat{f}_n(X_j)) Y_j h(X_j) + 2\lambda \langle \hat{f}_n, h \rangle = 0.$$

Assuming that $\eta(x) = \delta > 0$, $\|\hat{f}_n\| \leq U$ and $\hat{f}_n(x) \leq 0$, we need to bound from above

$$\frac{1}{n} \sum_{j=1}^{n} \ell'(Y_j \hat{f}_n(X_j)) Y_j h(X_j) + 2\lambda \langle \hat{f}_n, h \rangle,$$

trying to show that everywhere except the event of small probability the last expression is strictly negative. This would contradict the fact that it is equal to 0, implying a bound on the probability of the event $\{\hat{f}_n(x) \leq 0, \|\hat{f}_n\| \leq U\}$.

First note that

$$\frac{1}{n} \sum_{j=1}^{n} \ell'(Y_j \hat{f}_n(X_j)) Y_j h(X_j)$$

$$= \frac{1}{n} \sum_{j:Y_j=+1} \ell'(\hat{f}_n(X_j)) h(X_j) - \frac{1}{n} \sum_{j:Y_j=-1} \ell'(-\hat{f}_n(X_j)) h(X_j).$$

Note also that function ℓ' is negative and increasing, h is nonnegative and $\hat{f}_n$ is a Lipschitz function with Lipschitz norm bounded by $\|\hat{f}_n\|$. The last observation and the assumption that $\hat{f}_n(x) \leq 0$ imply that, for all $y \in B(x, \delta_0)$,

$$\hat{f}_n(y) \leq \|\hat{f}_n\|\delta_0 \leq U\delta_0$$

and, as a result,

$$\ell'(\hat{f}_n(y)) \leq \ell'(U\delta_0), \ \ell'(-\hat{f}_n(y)) \geq \ell'(-U\delta_0).$$

Also, for all $y \in S$, $|\hat{f}_n(y)| \leq \|\hat{f}_n\| \leq U$, implying that

$$|\ell'(\hat{f}_n(y))| \leq |\ell'(-U)|, \ |\ell'(-\hat{f}_n(y))| \leq |\ell'(-U)|.$$

This leads to the following upper bound:

$$\frac{1}{n}\sum_{j=1}^{n}\ell'(Y_j\hat{f}_n(X_j))Y_jh(X_j) \leq$$

$$\frac{\ell'(U\delta_0)}{n}\sum_{j:X_j\in B(x,\delta_0),Y_j=+1}h(X_j) - \frac{\ell'(-U\delta_0)}{n}\sum_{j:X_j\in B(x,\delta_0),Y_j=-1}h(X_j) +$$

$$\frac{|\ell'(-U)|}{n}\sum_{j:X_j\in B(x,\delta_0)^c}h(X_j) =$$

$$\frac{\ell'(U\delta_0)}{n}\sum_{j:X_j\in B(x,\delta_0)}\frac{1+Y_j}{2}h(X_j) - \frac{\ell'(-U\delta_0)}{n}\sum_{j:X_j\in B(x,\delta_0)}\frac{1-Y_j}{2}h(X_j) +$$

$$\frac{|\ell'(-U)|}{n}\sum_{j:X_j\in B(x,\delta_0)^c}h(X_j) =$$

$$\frac{\ell'(U\delta_0) - \ell'(-U\delta_0)}{2n}\sum_{j=1}^{n}h(X_j)I_{B(x,\delta_0)}(X_j) +$$

$$\frac{\ell'(U\delta_0) + \ell'(-U\delta_0)}{2n}\sum_{j=1}^{n}Y_jh(X_j)I_{B(x,\delta_0)}(X_j) +$$

$$\frac{|\ell'(-U)|}{n}\sum_{j=1}^{n}h(X_j)I_{B(x,\delta_0)^c}(X_j).$$

Using the fact that for logit loss ℓ'' has its maximum at 0, we get

$$\left|\frac{\ell'(U\delta_0) + \ell'(-U\delta_0)}{2} - \ell'(0)\right| \leq$$

$$\frac{|\ell'(U\delta_0) - \ell'(0)|}{2} + \frac{|\ell'(-U\delta_0) - \ell'(0)|}{2} \leq \ell''(0)U\delta_0$$

and

$$\left|\frac{\ell'(U\delta_0) - \ell'(-U\delta_0)}{2}\right| \leq \ell''(0)U\delta_0.$$

Therefore,

$$\frac{1}{n} \sum_{j=1}^{n} \ell'(Y_j \hat{f}_n(X_j)) Y_j h(X_j) \leq$$

$$\ell'(0) \frac{1}{n} \sum_{j=1}^{n} Y_j h(X_j) I_{B(x;\delta_0)}(X_j) + 2\ell''(0) U \delta_0 \frac{1}{n} \sum_{j=1}^{n} h(X_j) I_{B(x;\delta_0)}(X_j) +$$

$$\frac{|l'(-U)|}{n} \sum_{j=1}^{n} h(X_j) I_{B(x;\delta_0)^c}(X_j) =$$

$$\frac{1}{n} \sum_{j=1}^{n} \xi_j, \tag{6}$$

where $\xi, \xi_j, j \geq 1$ are i.i.d.

$$\xi := \ell'(0) Y h(X) I_{B(x,\delta_0)}(X) +$$
$$2\ell''(0) U \delta_0 h(X) I_{B(x,\delta_0)}(X) + |\ell'(-U)| h(X) I_{B(x;\delta_0)^c}(X).$$

To bound the sum of ξ_js, we will use Bernstein inequality. To this end, we first bound the expectation and the variance of ξ. We have

$$\mathbb{E}\,\xi = \ell'(0)\,\mathbb{E}\,Y h(X) I_{B(x;\delta_0)}(X) + 2\ell''(0) U \delta_0\,\mathbb{E}\,h(X) I_{B(x;\delta_0)}(X)$$
$$+|\ell'(-U)|\,\mathbb{E}\,h(X) I_{B(x;\delta_0)^c}(X).$$

Since η is Lipschitz with the Lipschitz constant L and $\eta(x) = \delta$,

$$\eta(y) \geq \delta - L\delta_0$$

for all $y \in B(x; \delta_0)$. Since also $h \in \mathcal{H}(x, \delta_0)$, we have:

$$\mathbb{E}\,Y h(X) I_{B(x;\delta_0)}(X) = \mathbb{E}\,\eta(X) h(X) I_{B(x;\delta_0)}(X)$$
$$> (\delta - L\delta_0)\,\mathbb{E}\,h(X) I_{B(x,\delta_0)}(X) \geq (\delta - L\delta_0)(1 - \delta_0)\,\mathbb{E}\,h(X),$$

$$\mathbb{E}\,h(X) I_{B(x;\delta_0)}(X) \leq \mathbb{E}\,h(X),$$

and

$$\mathbb{E}\,h(X) I_{B(x;\delta_0)^c}(X) \leq \delta_0\,\mathbb{E}\,h(X)$$

Recall that $\ell'(0) < 0$ and $\ell''(0) \geq 0$. So, the following bound for the expectation of ξ is immediate:

$$\mathbb{E}\,\xi \leq \left[\ell'(0)(\delta - L\delta_0)(1 - \delta_0) + 2\ell''(0) U \delta_0 + |\ell'(-U)|\delta_0 \right] \mathbb{E}\,h(X).$$

We will choose δ_0 small enough to make

$$[\ell'(0)(\delta - L\delta_0)(1 - \delta_0) + 2\ell''(U\delta_0) U\delta_0 + |\ell'(-U)|\delta_0] \leq -\delta_0.$$

A simple computation shows that it is enough to take

$$\delta_0 = \frac{1}{C} \frac{\delta}{U \vee L} \leq \frac{\delta}{L + 4U + 12},$$

which can be always achieved by making the numerical constant C large enough. Then the expectation satisfies the bound

$$\mathbb{E}\,\xi \leq -\delta_0 \, \mathbb{E}\, h(X).$$

As far as the variance of ξ is concerned, using an elementary bound $(a+b+c)^2 \leq 3a^2 + 3b^2 + 3c^2$, it is easy to check that

$$\mathrm{Var}(\xi) \leq C\delta_0 \, \mathbb{E}\, h(X)$$

with a sufficiently large numerical constant C. Finally, it is also straightforward that with some $C > 0$ $|\xi| \leq C\delta_0$.

Now Bernstein inequality easily yields with a sufficiently large numerical constant $C > 0$

$$\mathbb{P}\left\{ \frac{1}{n}\sum \xi_j \geq -\frac{1}{2}\delta_0 \, \mathbb{E}\, h(X) \right\} \leq 2\exp\left\{ -\frac{n\delta_0 \, \mathbb{E}\, h(X)}{C} \right\}.$$

Then, since

$$\delta_0 \, \mathbb{E}\, h(X) \geq \delta_0^2 \Pi(B(x; \delta_0/2)) = p(x, \delta_0),$$

we have with probability at least $1 - 2\exp\left\{ -\frac{np(x,\delta_0)}{C} \right\}$:

$$\frac{1}{n}\sum_{j=1}^{n} \ell'(Y_j \hat{f}_n(X_j))Y_j h(X_j) + 2\lambda\langle \hat{f}_n, h\rangle \leq$$

$$\leq -\frac{1}{2}\delta_0 \, \mathbb{E}\, h(X) + 2\lambda\langle \hat{f}_n, h\rangle \leq$$

$$\leq -\frac{1}{2}\delta_0 \, \mathbb{E}\, h(X) + 2\lambda U\|h\| \leq$$

$$\leq -\frac{1}{2}p(x, \delta_0) + 2\lambda U q(x, \delta_0) \tag{7}$$

So, if

$$\lambda < \frac{p(x, \delta_0)}{4Uq(x, \delta_0)} = \frac{r(x, \delta_0)}{4U},$$

then

$$\frac{1}{n}\sum_{j=1}^{n} \ell'(Y_j \hat{f}_n(X_j))Y_j h(X_j) + 2\lambda\langle \hat{f}_n, h\rangle < 0$$

with probability at least $1 - 2\exp\left\{ -\frac{np(x,\delta_0)}{C} \right\}$. The conclusion is that if $\eta(x) = \delta$ and $\lambda < \frac{r(x,\delta_0)}{4U}$, then

$$\mathbb{P}\left\{ \hat{f}_n(x) \leq 0, \|\hat{f}_n\| \leq U \right\} \leq 2\exp\left\{ -\frac{np(x, \delta_0)}{C} \right\}.$$

Thus, for $\lambda \leq \lambda^+$, we have

$$\mathbb{P}\left\{\hat{f}_n(x) \leq 0, \|\hat{f}_n\| \leq U\right\} \leq 2\exp\left\{-\frac{n\bar{p}(\delta_0)}{C}\right\}. \tag{8}$$

We now turn to bounding the probability $\mathbb{P}\{\|\hat{f}_n\| \geq U\}$ for a properly chosen U. This is the only part of the proof where the condition (3) on the uniform entropy of the unit ball $B_{\mathcal{H}}$ is needed. It relies heavily on recent excess risk bounds in Koltchinskii [6] as well as on some of the results in spirit of Blanchard, Lugosi and Vayatis [5] (see their Lemma 4). We formulate the bound we need in the following lemma.

Lemma 1. *Suppose that condition (3) holds and (for simplicity) that ℓ is the logit loss. Let $R \geq 1$. Then, there exists a constant $K > 0$ such that for any $t > 0$, the following event*

$$\forall f \in \mathcal{H} \text{ with } \|f\| \leq R \tag{9}$$

$$P_n(\ell \bullet f) - \inf_{\|g\| \leq R} P_n(\ell \bullet g) \leq$$

$$2\left(P(\ell \bullet f) - \inf_{\|g\| \leq R} P(\ell \bullet g)\right) + K\left(\frac{RA^{2\rho/(2+\rho)}}{n^{2/(2+\rho)}} + \frac{tR}{n}\right), \tag{10}$$

has probability at least $1 - e^{-t}$.

The argument that follows will provide a bound that is somewhat akin to some of the bounds in [7] and in [4].

Denote $E(R)$ the event of the lemma. Let $R \geq \|f_*\| \vee 1$. On the event $E(R)$, the condition $R/2 < \|\hat{f}_n\| \leq R$ implies

$$\lambda\|\hat{f}_n\|^2 \leq P_n(\ell \bullet \hat{f}_n) - \inf_{\|g\| \leq R} P_n(\ell \bullet g) + \lambda\|\hat{f}_n\|^2 =$$

$$\inf_{\|f\| \leq R}\left[P_n(\ell \bullet f) - \inf_{\|g\| \leq R} P_n(\ell \bullet g) + \lambda\|f\|^2\right] \leq$$

$$2\inf_{\|f\| \leq R}\left[P(\ell \bullet f) - \inf_{\|g\| \leq R} P(\ell \bullet g) + \lambda\|f\|^2 + K\left(\frac{RA^{2\rho/(2+\rho)}}{n^{2/(2+\rho)}} + \frac{tR}{n}\right)\right] \leq$$

$$2\left[P(\ell \bullet f_*) - \inf_{\|g\| \leq R} P(\ell \bullet g) + \lambda\|f_*\|^2\right] + 2K\left(\frac{RA^{2\rho/(2+\rho)}}{n^{2/(2+\rho)}} + \frac{tR}{n}\right) \leq$$

$$2\lambda\|f_*\|^2 + 2K\left(\frac{RA^{2\rho/(2+\rho)}}{n^{2/(2+\rho)}} + \frac{tR}{n}\right),$$

which implies that

$$\frac{R^2}{4} \leq \|\hat{f}_n\|^2 \leq 2\|f_*\|^2 + 2K\left(\frac{RA^{2\rho/(2+\rho)}}{\lambda n^{2/(2+\rho)}} + \frac{tR}{\lambda n}\right).$$

Solving this inequality with respect to R shows that on $E(R)$ the condition $R/2 \leq \|\hat{f}_n\| \leq R$ implies

$$R \leq K\left(\|f_*\| \bigvee 1 \bigvee \frac{A^{2\rho/(2+\rho)}}{\lambda n^{2/(2+\rho)}} \bigvee \frac{t}{\lambda n}\right).$$

If now $t = n\varepsilon$ and $\lambda \geq \lambda^-$, then it yields

$$R \leq K(\|f_*\| \vee 1).$$

Note that

$$P_n(\ell \bullet \hat{f}_n) + \lambda\|\hat{f}_n\|^2 \leq \ell(0)$$

(just plug in $f = 0$ in the target functional). Therefore, we have $\lambda\|\hat{f}_n\|^2 \leq \ell(0)$, or

$$\|\hat{f}_n\| \leq \sqrt{\frac{\ell(0)}{\lambda}} =: \bar{R}.$$

Define $R_k = 2^k$, $k = 0, 1, 2, \ldots, N := \log_2 \bar{R} + 1$. Note that, for our choice of λ, we have $N \leq C \log n$ with some numerical constant $C > 0$. Let $E_k := E(R_k)$. Clearly, $\mathbb{P}(E_k) \geq 1 - e^{-t}$ and, on the even E_k, the condition $R_{k-1} \leq \|\hat{f}_n\| \leq R_k$ implies

$$\|\hat{f}_n\| \leq R_k \leq K(\|f_*\| \vee 1).$$

Thus, $\|\hat{f}_n\|$ can be larger than the right hand side of the last bound only on the event $\bigcup_{k=1}^{N} E_k^c$, whose probabilty is smaller than $Ne^{-n\varepsilon}$. This establishes the following inequality:

$$\mathbb{P}\left\{\|\hat{f}_n\| \geq K(\|f_*\| \vee 1)\right\} \leq Ne^{-n\varepsilon} \leq e^{-n\varepsilon/2}, \tag{11}$$

provided that $\varepsilon \geq K\frac{\log\log n}{n}$, as it was assumed.

Combining bounds (8) and (11) and plugging the resulting bound in (5) and then in (4) easily completes the proof (subject to a minor adjustment of the constants).

Acknowledgement. The first author is very thankful to Alexandre Tsybakov for several useful and interesting conversations on the subject of the paper.

References

1. Audibert, J.–Y. and Tsybakov, A. Fast convergence rates for plug-in estimators under margin conditions. *Unpublished manuscript*, 2004.
2. Bartlett, P., Bousquet, O. and Mendelson, S. Local Rademacher Complexities. *Annals of Statistics*, 2005, to appear.
3. Bartlett, P., Jordan, M. and McAuliffe, J. Convexity, Classification and Risk Bounds. *J. American Statistical Soc.*, 2004, to appear.
4. Blanchard, G., Bousquet, O. and Massart, P. Statistical Performance of Support Vector Machines. *Preprint*, 2003, 4, 861–894.

5. Blanchard, G., Lugosi, G. and Vayatis, N. On the rates of convergence of regularized boosting classifiers. *Journal of Machine Learning Research*, 2003, 4, 861-894.
6. Koltchinskii, V. Local Rademacher Complexities and Oracle Inequalities in Risk Minimization. Preprint. *Preprint*, 2003.
7. Scovel, C. and Steinwart, I. Fast Rates for Support Vector Machines. *Preprint*, 2003.

General Polynomial Time
Decomposition Algorithms*

Nikolas List and Hans Ulrich Simon

Fakultät für Mathematik, Ruhr-Universität Bochum,
44780 Bochum, Germany
{nlist, simon}@lmi.rub.de

Abstract. We present a general decomposition algorithm that is uniformly applicable to every (suitably normalized) instance of Convex Quadratic Optimization and efficiently approaches the optimal solution. The number of iterations required to be within ε of optimality grows linearly with $1/\varepsilon$ and quadratically with the number m of variables. The working set selection can be performed in polynomial time. If we restrict our considerations to instances of Convex Quadratic Optimization with at most k_0 equality constraints for some fixed constant k_0 plus some so-called box-constraints (conditions that hold for most variants of SVM-optimization), the working set is found in linear time. Our analysis builds on a generalization of the concept of rate certifying pairs that was introduced by Hush and Scovel. In order to extend their results to arbitrary instances of Convex Quadratic Optimization, we introduce the general notion of a rate certifying q-set. We improve on the results of Hush and Scovel [8] in several ways. First our result holds for Convex Quadratic Optimization whereas the results of Hush and Scovel are specialized to SVM-optimization. Second, we achieve a higher rate of convergence even for the special case of SVM-optimization (despite the generality of our approach). Third, our analysis is technically simpler.

1 Introduction

Support vector machines (SVMs) introduced by Vapnik and co-workers [1, 29] are a promising technique for classification, function approximation, and other key problems in statistical learning theory. In this paper, we consider the optimization problems that are induced by SVMs, which are special cases of Convex Quadratic Optimization.

The difficulty of solving problems of this kind is the density of the matrix that represents the "quadratic part" of the cost function. Thus, a prohibitive amount of memory is required to store the matrix and traditional optimization algorithms

---

* This work was supported in part by the IST Programme of the European Community, under the PASCAL Network of Excellence, IST-2002-506778. This publication only reflects the authors' views. This work was furthermore supported by the Deutsche Forschungsgemeinschaft Grant SI 498/7-1.

P. Auer and R. Meir (Eds.): COLT 2005, LNAI 3559, pp. 308–322, 2005.

(such as Newton, for example) cannot be directly applied. Several authors have proposed (different variants of) a decomposition method to overcome this difficulty [25, 9, 26, 27, 21, 22, 3, 11, 16, 4, 23, 12, 10, 17, 18, 13, 7, 14, 8, 20, 19, 5]. Given an instance of Convex Quadratic Optimization, this method keeps track of a current feasible solution which is iteratively improved. In each iteration the variable indices are split into a "working set" $I \subseteq \{1, \ldots, m\}$ and its complement $J = \{1, \ldots, m\} \setminus I$. Then, the simplified instance with the variables x_i, $i \in I$, is solved, thereby leaving the values for the remaining variables x_j, $j \in J$, unchanged. The success of the method depends in a quite sensitive manner on the policy for the selection of the working set I (whose size is typically bounded by a small constant). Ideally, the selection procedure should be computationally efficient and, at the same time, effective in the sense that the resulting sequence of feasible solutions converges (with high speed) to an optimal limit point.

Our Results and their Relation to Previous Work: Hush and Scovel considered a special SVM-optimization problem that we denote as SVO in our paper. They introduced the notion of an "α-rate certifying pair" and showed that every decomposition algorithm for SVO that always inserts an α-rate certifying pair in its current working set comes within ε of optimality after $O(1/(\varepsilon\alpha^2))$ iterations. Building on a result of Chang, Hsu, and Lin [3], they presented furthermore an algorithm that constructs an $1/m^2$-rate certifying pair in $O(m \log m)$ steps.[1] Combining these results, we see that the decomposition algorithm of Hush and Scovel for problem SVO is within ε of optimality after $O(m^4/\varepsilon)$ iterations.

In this paper we present an extension of (and an improvement on) this result. We first define the general notion of an α-rate certifying q-set and show (with a simplified analysis) that it basically fits the same purpose for Convex Quadratic Optimization (denoted as CQO in our paper) as the α-rate certifying pair for SVO, where the number of iterations needed to be within ε of optimality is proportional to $q/(\varepsilon\alpha^2)$. We present a general decomposition algorithm that is uniformly applicable to every (suitably normalized) instance of CQO. Given an instance with k equality constraints and m variables, it finds an $1/m$-rate certifying $(k+1)$-set in polynomial time.[2] Combining these results, we are within ε of optimality after $O(km^2/\varepsilon)$ iterations of our decomposition algorithm. The SVM-optimization problem SVO (considered by Hush and Scovel) has only one equality constraint. Plugging in $k = 1$ in our general result, we arrive at an upper bound on the number of iterations that improves on the bound obtained by Hush and Scovel by factor m^2. The analysis of Hush and Scovel in [8] builds on an earlier analysis of conditional gradient algorithms by Dunn [6]. For this part of the analysis, we will present simpler arguments.

---

[1] Time bound $O(m \log m)$ can be improved to $O(m)$ by using the method from [28].

[2] Moreover, the algorithm can be implemented such as to find this set even in linear time when we restrict its application to instances of CQO with at most k_0 equality constraints for some fixed constant k_0. If we restrict its application to SVO, we may use the the highly efficient method from [28].

There are some alternatives to the approach with rate certifying pairs. The most prominent one is the selection of the maximally KKT-violating pairs as implemented for example in SVM^{light} [9] or LIBSVM [4]. A paper by Lin [15] seems to imply the following quite strong result for SVO (although not stating it explicitly): decomposition algorithms following the approach of maximally KKT-violating pairs are within ε of optimality after only $O(\log 1/\varepsilon)$ iterations.[3] However, the analysis is specialized to SVO. Furthermore it has to assume strict convexity of the objective function and some non-degeneracy conditions. The convergence rate is only given in terms of ε whereas the dependence on problem parameters (like, for example, m) is not clarified.

Another algorithm (related to but different from decomposition algorithms) is SimpleSVM [30] which tries to iteratively include the support vectors in the working set. Assuming strict convexity of the objective function, the authors of [30] claim a linear convergence of the method (but do neither give a complete proof nor exhibit the dependence on the various parameters explicitly). The main difference between SimpleSVM and decomposition algorithms is the size of the working set which can grow-up to the number of support vectors in the former case and is kept constant in the latter. Note that the number of support vectors is particularly large on noisy data.

There are many other papers about decomposition algorithms or related approaches that are noteworthy but cannot be mentioned properly in this abstract. The reader interested in finding more pointers to the relevant literature is referred to the full paper.

2   Preliminaries

We are mainly concerned with the problem "Convex Quadratic Optimization with box-constraints". It is denoted simply as CQO in this paper and is formally given as follows:

Definition 1 (CQO). *An instance $\mathcal{P}$ of CQO is given by*

$$\min_x f(x) = \frac{1}{2}x^\top Q x + w^\top x \text{ s.t. } Ax = b, l \leq x \leq r \ ,$$

where

- $Q \in \mathbb{R}^{m \times m}$ *is a symmetric positive semi-definite matrix over the reals and $w \in \mathbb{R}^m$, i.e., $f(x)$ is a convex quadratic cost function in m scalar variables,*
- $A \in \mathbb{R}^{k \times m}$ *and $b \in \mathbb{R}^k$ such that $Ax = b$ represents k linear equality constraints,*
- $l, r \in \mathbb{R}^m$ *and $l \leq x \leq r$ is the short-notation for the "box-constraints"*

$$\forall i = 1, \ldots, m : l_i \leq x_i \leq r_i \ .$$

---

[3] See [5] for a generalization of this result to similar but more general policies for working set selection.

In this paper, we will sometimes express $f(x')$ by means of the Taylor-expansion around x:

$$f(x') = f(x) + \nabla f(x)^\top (x' - x) + \frac{1}{2}(x' - x)^\top Q(x' - x) \ ,$$

where $\nabla f(x) = Qx + w$. For $d := x - x'$, this can be rewritten as follows:

$$f(x) - f(x') = \nabla f(x)^\top d - \frac{1}{2}d^\top Qd \ . \tag{1}$$

Note that $d^\top Qd \geq 0$ because Q is positive semi-definite.

In the sequel,

$$R(\mathcal{P}) = \{x \in \mathbb{R}^m |\ Ax = b, l \leq x \leq r\}$$

denotes the compact and convex set of feasible points for $\mathcal{P}$. The well-known first-order condition for convex function optimization[4] (valid for an arbitrary convex cost function) states that x is an optimal feasible solution iff

$$\forall x' \in R(\mathcal{P}) : \nabla f(x)^\top (x' - x) \geq 0 \ .$$

We briefly note that any instance of the *general* convex quadratic optimization problem with cost function $f(x)$, linear equality constraints, linear inequality constraints (not necessarily in the form of box-constraints) and a compact region of feasible points can be transformed into an equivalent instance of CQO because we may convert the linear inequalities into linear equations by introducing non-negative slack variables. By the compactness of the region of feasible points, we may also put a suitable upper bound on each slack variable such that finally all linear inequalities take the form of box-constraints.

We now define a subproblem of CQO, denoted as SVO in this paper, that is actually one of the most well studied SVM-optimization problems:

Definition 2 (SVO). *An instance $\mathcal{P}_0$ of SVO is given by*

$$\min_x f(x) \ \text{s.t.} \ y^\top x = 0 \ , \ l \leq x \leq r \ ,$$

where $f(x), l, r$ are understood as in Definition 1 and $y \in \{-1, 1\}^m$ is a vector whose components represent binary classification labels.

The main difference between SVO and the general problem CQO is that SVO has only a single equality constraint. Furthermore, this equality constraint is of a special form.

We are now prepared to introduce (informally) the notion of "decomposition algorithms". A *decomposition algorithm for CQO* with working sets of size at most q (where we allow that q depends on k) proceeds iteratively as follows: given an instance $\mathcal{P}$ of CQO and a feasible solution $x \in R(\mathcal{P})$ (chosen arbitrarily

---

[4] See for example [2].

in the beginning), a so-called working set $I \subseteq \{1, \ldots, m\}$ of size at most q is selected. Then x is updated by the optimal solution for the simplified instance with variables x_i, $i \in I$ (leaving the values x_j with $j \notin I$ unchanged). *Decomposition algorithms for SVO* are defined analogously. The policy for working set selection is a critical issue that we discuss in the next sections.

Notational Conventions:

- The parameters m, k, f, A, y, b, l, r are consistently used in this paper as the components of an instance of CQO or SVO. Similarly, parameter q (possibly dependent on k) always represents the (maximal) size of the working set.
- L_{max} and S_{max} are two more parameters that we associate with an instance of CQO or SVO (where L_{max} depends also on q). L_{max} denotes the largest among the eigenvalues of all the principal $(q \times q)$-submatrices of Q. S_{max} denotes the maximum side length of the box spanned by l and r, i.e., $S_{max} := \max_{1 \leq i \leq m}(r_i - l_i)$.
- For a decomposition algorithm $\mathcal{A}$, we denote the current feasible solution obtained after n iterations by x^n (such that x^0 is the feasible solution $\mathcal{A}$ starts with). The optimal feasible solution is denoted by x^*. Then

$$\Delta_n := f(x^n) - f(x^*) \tag{2}$$

denotes the difference between the value of the current solution and the optimal value.

3   Rate Certifying Sets and the Main Theorem

In section 3.1, we recall the concept of rate certifying pairs. In section 3.2, we present the new notion of rate certifying sets and state our main result, whose proof is given in sections 3.3 and 3.4.

3.1   Rate Certifying Pairs

We consider again the problem SVO from Definition 2 along with a problem instance $\mathcal{P}_0$. Let $x \in R(\mathcal{P}_0)$ be a feasible solution and $x^* \in R(\mathcal{P}_0)$ an optimal feasible solution. In the sequel, we will often use the following first-order approximation of the maximal distance (with regard to the value of the objective function) between a given point x and any other feasible solution x':

$$\sigma(x) := \sup_{x' \in R(\mathcal{P}_0)} \nabla f(x)^\top (x - x') .$$

As already noted by Hush and Scovel [8], the following holds:[5]

$$f(x) - f(x^*) \leq \nabla f(x)^\top (x - x^*) \leq \sigma(x) . \tag{3}$$

---

[5] The first inequality follows from (1) and the positive semi-definiteness of Q; the second-one is trivial.

In other words, $f(x)$ is always within $\sigma(x)$ of optimality. Note that $\sigma(x^*) = 0$ (which immediately follows from the first-order optimality condition). Thus, $\sigma(x) > 0$ if and only if x is suboptimal.

Since we are dealing with working sets whose size is bounded by a (small) parameter q, it is natural to restrict the range of x' to feasible solutions that differ from x in at most q coordinates. For $q = 2$, this leads to the following definition:

$$\sigma(x|i_1, i_2) := \sup_{x' \in R(\mathcal{P}_0): x'_i = x_i \text{ for } i \neq i_1, i_2} \nabla f(x)^\top (x - x') .$$

The following notion is crucial: (i_1, i_2) is called an α-rate certifying pair for x if

$$\sigma(x|i_1, i_2) \geq \alpha(f(x) - f(x^*)) .$$

Let α be a function in m with strictly positive values. An α-rate certifying algorithm is a decomposition algorithm for SVO that, for every m and every input instance $\mathcal{P}_0$ with m variables, always includes an $\alpha(m)$-rate certifying pair in the current working set. As mentioned already in the introduction, the main results in [8] are as follows:

Theorem 1 (Hush and Scovel [8]).

1. *Let $\mathcal{A}$ be an α-rate certifying algorithm. Consider any instance $\mathcal{P}_0$ of SVO with, say, m variables. Let L_{max} and S_{max} be the quantities associated with $\mathcal{P}_0$.[6] For sake of brevity, let $\alpha = \alpha(m)$. Then, $\mathcal{A}$ is within ε of optimality after*

$$1 + \frac{2\max\{1, 2S_{max}^2\}}{\alpha} \left(\frac{\max\{1, \alpha\Delta_0/L_{max}\}L_{max}}{\alpha\varepsilon} - 1 \right) =$$
$$O\left(\frac{L_{max}(1 + S_{max})^2}{\alpha^2\varepsilon} + \frac{\Delta_0(1 + S_{max})^2}{\alpha\varepsilon} \right)$$

   iterations.
2. *For function α given by $\alpha(m) = 1/m^2$, there exists an α-rate certifying algorithm. It constructs a working set (given $\mathcal{P}_0$ and a suboptimal feasible solution x) in $O(m \log m)$ steps (or in $O(m)$ steps when the method from [28] is applied). Furthermore, it is within ε of optimality after*

$$O\left(\frac{L_{max}(1 + S_{max})^2 m^4}{\varepsilon} + \frac{\Delta_0(1 + S_{max})^2 m^2}{\varepsilon} \right)$$

   iterations.

---

[6] See our notational conventions in section 2 for a definition (where $q = 2$).

3.2   Rate Certifying Sets

The definition of $\sigma(x)$ is easily extended to any instance $\mathcal{P}$ of CQO:

$$\sigma(x) := \sup_{x' \in R(\mathcal{P})} \nabla f(x)^\top (x - x') \ . \tag{4}$$

Clearly, inequality (3) and the subsequent comments are still valid without any change. However, since CQO deals with several equality constraints, one can in general not expect to find rate certifying *pairs*. Instead, the following general definition for $I \subseteq \{1, \dots, m\}$ will prove useful:

$$\sigma(x|I) := \sup_{x' \in R(\mathcal{P}): x'_i = x_i \text{ for } i \notin I} \nabla f(x)^\top (x - x') \ .$$

I is called an α-*rate certifying q-set* if $|I| \le q$ and

$$\sigma(x|I) \ge \alpha(f(x) - f(x^*)) \ . \tag{5}$$

Let α be a function in m with strictly positive values and let q be a function in k whose values are strictly positive integers. An (α, q)-*rate certifying algorithm* is a decomposition algorithm for CQO that, for every m, k and any problem instance $\mathcal{P}$ with m variables and k equality constraints, includes an $\alpha(m)$-rate certifying $q(k)$-set in the current working set.[7] With these notations, the following holds:

Theorem 2.   *1. Let $\mathcal{A}$ be an (α, q)-rate certifying algorithm. Consider an instance $\mathcal{P}$ of CQO with, say, m variables and k equality constraints. For sake of brevity, let $\alpha = \alpha(m)$, $q = q(k)$, and let L_{max}, S_{max} be the quantities associated with $\mathcal{P}$ and q. Then, $\mathcal{A}$ is within ε of optimality after*

$$\left\lceil \frac{2qL_{max}S^2_{max}}{\alpha^2 \varepsilon} \right\rceil + \max\left\{0, \left\lceil \frac{2}{\alpha} \ln\left(\frac{\Delta_0}{\varepsilon}\right) \right\rceil\right\} \tag{6}$$

iterations. Moreover, if $qL_{max}S^2_{max} \le \varepsilon\alpha$, then $\max\{0, \lceil 2\ln(\Delta_0/\varepsilon)/\alpha\rceil\}$ iterations (the second term in (6)) are enough.

2. For functions α, q given by $\alpha(m) = 1/m$ and $q(k) = k + 1$, there exists an (α, q)-rate certifying algorithm $\mathcal{A}$. It constructs a working set (given $\mathcal{P}$ and a suboptimal feasible solution x) in polynomial time. Moreover, if we restrict its application to instances of CQO with at most k_0 equality constraints for some fixed constant k_0, there is a linear time bound for the construction of the working set.[8]

3. The algorithm $\mathcal{A}$ from the preceding statement is within ε of optimality after

$$\left\lceil \frac{2(k+1)m^2 L_{max}S^2_{max}}{\varepsilon} \right\rceil + \max\left\{0, \left\lceil 2m \ln\left(\frac{\Delta_0}{\varepsilon}\right) \right\rceil\right\}$$

---

[7] Finding an initial feasible solution in the beginning is equivalent to solving a standard LP. For an instance of an SVM-optimization problem an initial guess usually is the zero vector.

[8] If we restrict its application to instances of SVO, we may use the the highly efficient method from [28].

iterations. Moreover, if $(k+1)L_{max}S_{max}^2 \leq \varepsilon/m$, then $\max\{0, \lceil 2m \ln(\Delta_0/\varepsilon)\rceil\}$ iterations are enough.

Clearly, the third statement in Theorem 2 follows directly from the first two statements (which will be proven in subsections 3.3 and 3.4, respectively).

A few comments on Theorem 2 are in place here. One might be tempted to think that an (α, q)-rate certifying algorithm decreases (an upper bound on) the distance between the current feasible solution and the best feasible solution (with regard to the objective value) roughly by factor $1 - \alpha$ (for $\alpha := \alpha(m)$). If such a "contraction" took place, we would be within ε of optimality after only $O(\log(1/\varepsilon)/\alpha)$ iterations. This is however spurious thinking because the σ-function is *not* concerned with this distance itself but rather with a first-order approximation of it. We will see in the proof of Theorem 2 that a run of an (α, q)-rate certifying algorithm can be decomposed into two phases. As long as the distance from the optimal value is large in comparison to (an upper bound on) the second order terms (phase 1), a contraction by factor $1 - \alpha/2$ takes place. However when we come closer to the optimal value (phase 2), the effect of the neglected second order terms becomes more significant and the convergence slows down (at least within our perhaps somewhat pessimistic analysis). Phase 1 leads to the term $\max\{0, \lceil 2\ln(\Delta_0/\varepsilon)/\alpha\rceil\}$ in (6) whereas phase 2 leads to the term $\lceil (2qL_{max}S_{max}^2)/(\alpha^2\varepsilon)\rceil$.

3.3   Proof of the 1st Statement in Theorem 2

We will use the notation introduced in Theorem 2 and consider an arbitrary iteration of the (α, q)-rate certifying algorithm $\mathcal{A}$ when it is applied on input $\mathcal{P}$. To this end, let x denote a feasible but suboptimal solution, and let x^* be the optimal feasible solution. Let I be the subset of the working set that satisfies $|I| \leq q$ and (5). Let x' be a feasible solution that satisfies $x_i = x_i'$ for every $i \notin I$ and

$$\sigma(x|I) = \nabla f(x)^\top (x - x') = \nabla f(x)^\top d , \tag{7}$$

where $d = x - x'$. Combining (5) with (7), we get

$$\nabla f(x)^\top d \geq \alpha(f(x) - f(x^*)) = \alpha\Delta , \tag{8}$$

where $\Delta = f(x) - f(x^*) \geq 0$. For some parameter $0 \leq \lambda \leq 1$ (suitably chosen later), consider the feasible solution

$$x'' = x - \lambda d$$

on the line segment between x and x'. Taylor-expansion around x allows to relate $f(x)$ and $f(x'')$ as follows:

$$f(x) - f(x'') = \lambda \nabla f(x)^\top d - \lambda^2 \frac{1}{2} d^\top Q d .$$

Note that x'' (like x') satisfies $x_i'' = x_i$ for every $i \notin I$. Thus, $x'' = x - \lambda d$ is a feasible solution that coincides with x outside the current working set. Thus, $\mathcal{A}$

(finding the optimal feasible solution that coincides with x outside the working set) achieves in the next iteration a "cost reduction" of at least $f(x) - f(x'')$.[9] x'' depends on the parameter $0 \leq \lambda \leq 1$. In the sequel, we tune parameter λ such as to obtain a "large" cost reduction. To be on the safe side, we will however perform a "pessimistic analysis" where we substitute worst case bounds for $\nabla f(x)^\top d$ and $d^\top Q d$ respectively. Clearly

$$\max_{0 \leq \lambda \leq 1} \left(\lambda \nabla f(x)^\top d - \lambda^2 \frac{1}{2} d^\top Q d \right) \geq \max_{0 \leq \lambda \leq 1} \left(\lambda B - \frac{1}{2} \lambda^2 B' \right)$$

for any lower bound B on $\nabla f(x)^\top d$ and any upper bound B' on $d^\top Q d$. According to (8), $\alpha \Delta$ can serve as a lower bound on $\nabla f(x)^\top d$. It is easily seen that the following parameter U can serve as an upper bound on $d^\top Q d$:

$$U := q L_{max} S_{max}^2 \geq d^\top Q d . \tag{9}$$

This immediately follows from the definition of L_{max} and S_{max} and from the fact that d has at most q non-zero components. We conclude from this discussion that, for every $0 \leq \lambda \leq 1$, $\mathcal{A}$ achieves in the next iteration a cost reduction of at least

$$h(\lambda) := \lambda \alpha \Delta - \frac{1}{2} \lambda^2 U .$$

It is easily seen that function $h(\lambda)$ is maximized by setting

$$\lambda := \begin{cases} 1 & \text{if } \Delta > U/\alpha \\ \alpha \Delta / U & \text{if } \Delta \leq U/\alpha \end{cases} .$$

Case 1. $\Delta > U/\alpha$. Then $\mathcal{A}$ achieves a cost reduction of at least

$$h(1) = \alpha \Delta - \frac{1}{2} U > \alpha \Delta / 2 .$$

Thus the difference $\Delta = f(x) - f(x^*)$ will shrink after the next iteration to

$$\Delta - \frac{\alpha}{2} \Delta = \Delta \left(1 - \frac{\alpha}{2} \right) ,$$

or to a smaller value, which is a proper contraction.
Case 2. $\Delta \leq U/\alpha$. Then $\mathcal{A}$ achieves a cost reduction of at least

$$h \left(\frac{\alpha \Delta}{U} \right) = \frac{\alpha^2 \Delta^2}{2U} = \gamma \Delta^2 ,$$

where

$$\gamma := \frac{\alpha^2}{2U} . \tag{10}$$

---

[9] "Achieving a cost reduction of a in the next iteration" means that the next iteration decreases the distance between the value of the current feasible solution and the value of the optimal feasible solution by at least a.

Thus, the difference $\Delta = f(x) - f(x^*)$ will shrink after the next iteration to

$$\Delta - \gamma \Delta^2$$

or to a smaller value.

Recall from (2) that sequence $(\Delta_n)_{n \geq 0}$ keeps track of the difference between the value of the current feasible solution and the value of the optimal solution. In view of the two cases described above, our pessimistic analysis obviously runs through two phases:

Phase 1. As long as $\Delta_n > U/\alpha$, we calculate with cost reduction $\alpha \Delta_n / 2$.
Phase 2. As soon as $\Delta_n \leq U/\alpha$, we calculate with cost reduction $\gamma \Delta_n^2$.

Let us first assume that $\varepsilon < U/\alpha$ (and postpone the case $\varepsilon \geq U/\alpha$ to the end of this subsection). The number of iterations in phase 1 is not larger than the smallest $n_0 \geq 0$ that satisfies the second inequality in

$$\Delta_0 \left(1 - \frac{\alpha}{2}\right)^{n_0} < \Delta_0 e^{-n_0 \alpha/2} \leq \varepsilon < \frac{U}{\alpha} ,$$

i.e.,

$$n_0 := \max\left\{0, \left\lceil \frac{2}{\alpha} \ln\left(\frac{\Delta_0}{\varepsilon}\right)\right\rceil\right\} . \tag{11}$$

In phase 2, $(\Delta_n)_{n \geq n_0}$ evolves according to

$$\Delta_{n+1} \leq \Delta_n - \gamma \Delta_n^2 = \Delta_n(1 - \gamma \Delta_n) . \tag{12}$$

Recall that $\Delta_i = f(x^i) - f(x^*) \geq 0$ for every i. As for the iterations considered in phase 2 within our analysis, we can make the stronger (pessimistic) assumption $\Delta_i > 0$.[10] Following Dunn [6], we can therefore consider the reciprocals $\delta_n := 1/\Delta_n$. Note that (12) and $\Delta_{n+1} > 0$ imply that $0 \leq \gamma \Delta_n < 1$ and so for each $n \geq n_0$ the following relation holds:

$$\delta_{n+1} - \delta_n \geq \frac{1}{\Delta_n(1 - \gamma \Delta_n)} - \frac{1}{\Delta_n} = \frac{\gamma}{1 - \gamma \Delta_n} \geq \gamma .$$

Therefore

$$\delta_n = \delta_{n_0} + \sum_{j=n_0}^{n-1} (\delta_{j+1} - \delta_j) \geq \gamma(n - n_0)$$

and consequently

$$\Delta_n = \frac{1}{\delta_n} \leq \frac{1}{\gamma(n - n_0)} .$$

It follows that $\Delta_n \leq \varepsilon$ after

$$n - n_0 := \left\lceil \frac{1}{\gamma \varepsilon} \right\rceil$$

---

[10] Otherwise phase 2 ends with the optimal solution even earlier.

iterations in phase 2. Thus the total number of iterations in both phases needed to be within ε of optimality is bounded by

$$n_0 + \left\lceil \frac{1}{\gamma\varepsilon} \right\rceil \overset{(10),(11)}{\leq} \left\lceil \frac{2U}{\alpha^2\varepsilon} \right\rceil + \max\left\{0, \left\lceil \frac{2}{\alpha} \ln\left(\frac{\Delta_0}{\varepsilon}\right) \right\rceil \right\}$$

iterations. Plugging in the definition of U from (9), we obtain (6).

Let us now finally discuss the case $U = qL_{max}S_{max}^2 \leq \varepsilon\alpha$. Since $\varepsilon \geq U/\alpha$, we come within ε of optimality during phase 1. The number of iterations required for this is the smallest n_0 that satisfies

$$\Delta_0 \left(1 - \frac{\alpha}{2}\right)^{n_0} < \Delta_0 e^{-n_0\alpha/2} \leq \varepsilon .$$

Thus, we are within ε of optimality after

$$\max\left\{0, \left\lceil \frac{2}{\alpha} \ln\left(\frac{\Delta_0}{\varepsilon}\right) \right\rceil \right\}$$

iterations. This completes the proof of the first statement in Theorem 2.

3.4   Proof of the 2nd Statement in Theorem 2

We first give a short outline of the proof. Let x be a feasible but suboptimal solution for $\mathcal{P}$. According to (3), it is sufficient to efficiently construct a working set I such that $|I| \leq k + 1$ and

$$\sigma(x|I) \geq \frac{1}{m}\sigma(x) . \tag{13}$$

To this end, we will proceed as follows. We consider auxiliary instances $\mathcal{P}_x, \mathcal{P}'_x, \mathcal{P}''_x$ of the Linear Programming Problem (denoted as LP in the sequel). The optimal values for $\mathcal{P}_x$ and $\mathcal{P}'_x$, are both shown to coincide with $\sigma(x)$. From $\mathcal{P}'_x$, we derive (basically by aggregating several equality constraints into a single-one) the instance $\mathcal{P}''_x$, whose optimal basic solution will represent a working set I of size at most $k + 1$. A comparison of the three problem instances will finally reveal that I satisfies (13).

We now move on to the technical implementation of this plan. Recall from (4) that

$$\sigma(x) = \sup_{x' \in R(\mathcal{P})} \nabla f(x)^\top(x - x') = \nabla f(x)^\top d ,$$

where $d = x - x'$. Thus $\sigma(x)$ is the optimal value of the following instance $\mathcal{P}_x$ of LP:

$$\max_d \nabla f(x)^\top d \text{ s.t. } Ad = \mathbf{0}, l \leq x - d \leq r .$$

We set

$$\mu^+ := x - l \text{ and } \mu^- := r - x$$

and split d into positive and non-positive components d^+ and d^- respectively:

$$d = d^+ - d^-, \ d^+, d^- \geq \mathbf{0}, \ \forall i = 1, \ldots, m : d_i^+ d_i^- = 0 . \tag{14}$$

With these notations, $\sigma(x)$ also coincides with the optimal value of the following instance $\mathcal{P}'_x$ of LP:

$$\max_{d^+,d^-} \begin{pmatrix} \nabla f(x) \\ -\nabla f(x) \end{pmatrix}^\top \begin{pmatrix} d^+ \\ d^- \end{pmatrix}$$

subject to

$$[A, -A] \begin{pmatrix} d^+ \\ d^- \end{pmatrix} = 0$$

$$0 \le d^+ \le \mu^+ \; , \; 0 \le d^- \le \mu^-$$

The third instance $\mathcal{P}''_x$ of LP that we consider has an additional slack variable ξ and is given as follows:

$$\max_{d^+,d^-,\xi} \begin{pmatrix} \nabla f(x) \\ -\nabla f(x) \end{pmatrix}^\top \begin{pmatrix} d^+ \\ d^- \end{pmatrix}$$

subject to

$$\forall i = 1, \ldots, m : \mu_i^- = 0 \Rightarrow d_i^- = 0 \; , \; \mu_i^+ = 0 \Rightarrow d_i^+ = 0 \tag{15}$$

$$[A, -A] \begin{pmatrix} d^+ \\ d^- \end{pmatrix} = 0 \tag{16}$$

$$\sum_{i:\mu_i^+>0} \frac{1}{\mu_i^+} d_i^+ + \sum_{i:\mu_i^->0} \frac{1}{\mu_i^-} d_i^- + \xi = 1 \tag{17}$$

$$d^+, d^- \ge 0 \; , \; \xi \ge 0 \tag{18}$$

We briefly note that we do not have to count the equality constraints in (15) because we may simply remove the variables that are set to zero from the problem instance. Recall that matrix A represents k equality constraints. Thus, $\mathcal{P}''_x$ is a linear program in canonical form with $k + 1$ equality constraints. Its optimal basic feasible solution has therefore at most $k + 1$ non-zero components. The following observations (where d, d^+, d^- are related according to (14)) are easy to verify:

1. If $\begin{pmatrix} d^+ \\ d^- \end{pmatrix}$ is a feasible solution for $\mathcal{P}'_x$ with value p, then $\frac{1}{m} \begin{pmatrix} d^+ \\ d^- \end{pmatrix}$ is a feasible solution for $\mathcal{P}''_x$ with value p/m.

2. If $\begin{pmatrix} d^+ \\ d^- \end{pmatrix}$ is a feasible solution for $\mathcal{P}''_x$ with value p, then $\begin{pmatrix} d^+ \\ d^- \end{pmatrix}$ is also a feasible solution for $\mathcal{P}'$ with value p.

Recall that $\sigma(x)$ is the value of the optimal solution for $\mathcal{P}'_x$. We may conclude from our observations that the value of the optimal solution for $\mathcal{P}''_x$, say $\sigma'(x)$, satisfies $\sigma'(x) \ge \sigma(x)/m$. Now consider an optimal basic feasible solution $\begin{pmatrix} d^+ \\ d^- \end{pmatrix}$ for $\mathcal{P}''_x$ with value $\sigma'(x)$. Let

$$I := \{i \in \{1, \ldots, m\} | \; d_i^+ \ne 0 \text{ or } d_i^- \ne 0\} \; .$$

Clearly, $|I| \leq k+1$. Since $d = d^+ - d^-$ is a feasible solution for $\mathcal{P}$ (still with value $\sigma'(x)$) that differs from x only in coordinates from I, we may conclude that

$$\sigma(x|I) \geq \sigma'(x) \geq \frac{1}{m}\sigma(x) .$$

In other words, working set I satisfies (13). The time required to compute I is dominated by the time required to solve the linear program $\mathcal{P}''_x$. This can be done in polynomial time. Since a linear program with a constant number of variables (or a linear program in standard form with a constant number of equality constraints[11]) can be solved in linear time [24], the proof for the 2nd statement of Theorem 2 is completed.

4   Conclusions and Open Problems

We have presented an analysis of a decomposition algorithm that leads to the up-to-date strongest theoretical performance guarantees within the "rate certifying pair" approach. Our analysis holds uniformly for any instance of Convex Quadratic Optimization (with box-constraints) and certainly covers most of the variants of SVM-optimization. As explained in the introduction already, there are competing approaches like, for example, the approach based on maximally KKT-violating pairs or approaches based on an iterative inclusion of support vectors. As should become clear from the introduction, none of these approaches beats the other-ones in all respects (uniform analysis for a broad variety of problems, high speed of convergence, efficient working set selection). It remains an object of future research to gain more insight (theoretically and empirically) into the (perhaps complementary) strength and weakness of the various approaches such that their combined power can be exploited to full extent.

References

1. Bernhard E. Boser, Isabelle M. Guyon, and Vladimir N. Vapnik. A training algorithm for optimal margin classifiers. In *Proceedings of the 5th Annual ACM Workshop on Computational Learning Theory*, pages 144–152, 1992.
2. Steven Boyd and Lieven Vandenberghe. *Convex Optimization*. Cambridge University Press, 2004.
3. Chih-Chung Chang, Chih-Wei Hsu, and Chih-Jen Lin. The analysis of decomposition methods for support vector machines. *IEEE Transactions on Neural Networks*, 11(4):248–250, 2000.
4. Chih-Chung Chang and Chih-Jen Lin. *LIBSVM: A library for support vector machines*, 2001. Available from http://www.csie.ntu.edu.tw/~cjlin/libsvm.
5. Pai-Hsuen Chen, Rong-En Fan, and Chih-Jen Lin. A study on SMO-type decomposition methods for support vector machines, 2005. Available from http://www.csie.ntu.edu.tw/~cjlin/papers/generalSMO.pdf.

---

[11] Such that the dual linear program has constant number of variables.

6. J. Dunn. Rates of convergence for conditional gradient algorithms near singular and non-singular extremals. *SIAM J. Control and Optimization*, 17(2):187–211, 1979.
7. Chih-Wei Hsu and Chih-Jen Lin. A simple decomposition method for support vector machines. *Machine Learning*, 46(1–3):291–314, 2002.
8. Don Hush and Clint Scovel. Polynomial-time decomposition algorithms for support vector machines. *Machine Learning*, 51(1):51–71, 2003.
9. Thorsten Joachims. Making large scale SVM learning practical. In Bernhard Schölkopf, Christopher J. C. Burges, and Alexander J. Smola, editors, *Advances in Kernel Methods—Support Vector Learning*, pages 169–184. MIT Press, 1998.
10. S. Sathiya Keerthi and E. G. Gilbert. Convergence of a generalized SMO algorithm for SVM classifier design. *Machine Learning*, 46(1–3):351–360, 2002.
11. S. Sathiya Keerthi, Shirish Krishnaj Shevade, Chiranjib Bhattacharyya, and K. R. K. Murthy. Improvements to SMO algorithm for SVM regression. *IEEE Transactions on Neural Networks*, 11(5):1188–1193, 2000.
12. S. Sathiya Keerthi, Shirish Krishnaj Shevade, Chiranjib Bhattacharyya, and K. R. K. Murthy. Improvements to Platt's SMO algorithm for SVM classifier design. *Neural Computation*, 13(3):637–649, 2001.
13. Pavel Laskov. Feasible direction decomposition algorithms for training support vector machines. *Machine Learning*, 46(1–3):315–349, 2002.
14. Shuo-Peng Liao, Hsuan-Tien Lin, and Chih-Jen Lin. A note on the decomposition methods for support vector regression. *Neural Computation*, 14(6):1267–1281, 2002.
15. Chih-Jen Lin. Linear convergence of a decomposition method for support vector machines, 2001. Available from http://www.csie.ntu.edu.tw/~cjlin/papers/linearconv.pdf.
16. Chih-Jen Lin. On the convergence of the decomposition method for support vector machines. *IEEE Transactions on Neural Networks*, 12(6):1288–1298, 2001.
17. Chih-Jen Lin. Asymptotic convergence of an SMO algorithm without any assumptions. *IEEE Transactions on Neural Networks*, 13(1):248–250, 2002.
18. Chih-Jen Lin. A formal analysis of stopping criteria of decomposition methods for support vector machines. *IEEE Transactions on Neural Networks*, 13(5):1045–1052, 2002.
19. Nikolas List. Convergence of a generalized gradient selection approach for the decomposition method. In *Proceedings of the 15th International Conference on Algorithmic Learning Theory*, pages 338–349, 2004.
20. Nikolas List and Hans Ulrich Simon. A general convergence theorem for the decomposition method. In *Proceedings of the 17th Annual Conference on Computational Learning Theory*, pages 363–377, 2004.
21. Olvi L. Mangasarian and David R. Musicant. Successive overrelaxation for support vector machines. *IEEE Transactions on Neural Networks*, 10(5):1032–1037, 1999.
22. Olvi L. Mangasarian and David R. Musicant. Active support vector machine classification. In *Advances in Neural Information Processing Systems 12*, pages 577–583. MIT Press, 2000.
23. Olvi L. Mangasarian and David R. Musicant. Lagrangian support vector machines. *Journal of Machine Learning Research*, 1:161–177, 2001.
24. Nimrod Megiddo. Linear programming in linear time when the dimension is fixed. *Journal of the Association on Computing Machinery*, 31(1):114–127, 1984.
25. Edgar E. Osuna, Robert Freund, and Federico Girosi. Training support vector machines: an application to face detection. In *Proceedings of IEEE Conference on Computer Vision and Pattern Recognition*, pages 130–136, 1997.

26. John C. Platt. Fast training of support vector machines using sequential minimal optimization. In Bernhard Schölkopf, Christopher J. C. Burges, and Alexander J. Smola, editors, *Advances in Kernel Methods—Support Vector Learning*, pages 185–208. MIT Press, 1998.

27. Craig Saunders, Mark O. Stitson, Jason Weston, Leon Bottou, Bernhard Schölkopf, and Alexander J. Smola. Support vector machine reference manual. Technical Report CSD-TR-98-03, Royal Holloway, University of London, Egham, UK, 1998.

28. Hans Ulrich Simon. On the complexity of working set selection. In *Proceedings of the 15th International Conference on Algorithmic Learning Theory*, pages 324–337, 2004.

29. Vladimir Vapnik. *Statistical Learning Theory*. Wiley Series on Adaptive and Learning Systems for Signal Processing, Communications, and Control. John Wiley & Sons, 1998.

30. S. V. N. Vishwanthan, Alexander J. Smola, and M. Narasimha Murty. SimpleSVM. In *Proceedings of the 20th International Conference on Machine Learning*, 2003.

Approximating a Gram Matrix for Improved Kernel-Based Learning

(Extended Abstract)

Petros Drineas[1] and Michael W. Mahoney[2]

[1] Department of Computer Science, Rensselaer Polytechnic Institute,
Troy, New York 12180
drinep@cs.rpi.edu
[2] Department of Mathematics, Yale University,
New Haven, CT 06520
mahoney@cs.yale.edu

Abstract. A problem for many kernel-based methods is that the amount of computation required to find the solution scales as $O(n^3)$, where n is the number of training examples. We develop and analyze an algorithm to compute an easily-interpretable low-rank approximation to an $n \times n$ Gram matrix G such that computations of interest may be performed more rapidly. The approximation is of the form $\tilde{G}_k = CW_k^+C^T$, where C is a matrix consisting of a small number c of columns of G and W_k is the best rank-k approximation to W, the matrix formed by the intersection between those c columns of G and the corresponding c rows of G. An important aspect of the algorithm is the probability distribution used to randomly sample the columns; we will use a judiciously-chosen and data-dependent nonuniform probability distribution. Let $\|\cdot\|_2$ and $\|\cdot\|_F$ denote the spectral norm and the Frobenius norm, respectively, of a matrix, and let G_k be the best rank-k approximation to G. We prove that by choosing $O(k/\epsilon^4)$ columns

$$\left\| G - CW_k^+C^T \right\|_\xi \leq \|G - G_k\|_\xi + \epsilon \sum_{i=1}^{n} G_{ii}^2,$$

both in expectation and with high probability, for both $\xi = 2, F$, and for all $k : 0 \leq k \leq \text{rank}(W)$. This approximation can be computed using $O(n)$ additional space and time, after making two passes over the data from external storage.

1 Introduction

1.1 Background

Given a collection $\mathcal{X}$ of data points, which are often but not necessarily elements of $\mathbb{R}^m$, techniques such as linear Support Vector Machines (SVMs), Gaussian Processes (GPs), Principle Component Analysis (PCA), and the related Singular Value Decomposition (SVD), identify and extract structure from $\mathcal{X}$ by

P. Auer and R. Meir (Eds.): COLT 2005, LNAI 3559, pp. 323–337, 2005.

computing linear functions, i.e., functions in the form of dot products, of the data. For example, in PCA the subspace spanned by the first k eigenvectors is used to give a k dimensional model of the data with minimal residual; thus, it provides a low-dimensional representation of the data. Such spectral analysis has a rich theoretical foundation and has numerous practical applications.

In many cases, however, there is nonlinear structure in the data (or the data, e.g. text, may not support the basic linear operations of addition and scalar multiplication). In these cases, kernel-based learning methods have proved to be quite useful [7, 27]. Kernel-based learning methods are a class of statistical learning algorithms, the best known examples of which are SVMs [7]. In this approach, data items are mapped into high-dimensional spaces, where information about their mutual positions (in the form of inner products) is used for constructing classification, regression, or clustering rules. Kernel-based algorithms exploit the information encoded in the inner product between all pairs of data items and are successful in part because there is often an efficient method to compute inner products between very complex or even infinite dimensional vectors. Thus, kernel-based algorithms provide a way to deal with nonlinear structure by reducing nonlinear algorithms to algorithms that are linear in some feature space $\mathcal{F}$ that is nonlinearly related to the original input space.

More precisely, assume that the data consists of vectors $X^{(1)}, \ldots, X^{(n)} \in \mathcal{X} \subset \mathbb{R}^m$ and let $X \in \mathbb{R}^{m \times n}$ be the matrix whose i-th column is $X^{(i)}$. In kernel-based methods, a set of features is chosen that define a space $\mathcal{F}$, where it is hoped relevant structure will be revealed, the data $\mathcal{X}$ are then mapped to the feature space $\mathcal{F}$ using a mapping $\Phi : \mathcal{X} \to \mathcal{F}$, and then classification, regression, or clustering is performed in $\mathcal{F}$ using traditional methods such as linear SVMs, GPs, or PCA. If $\mathcal{F}$ is chosen to be a dot product space and if one defines the kernel matrix, also known as the Gram matrix, $G \in \mathbb{R}^{n \times n}$ as $G_{ij} = k(x_i, x_j) = (\Phi(x_i), \Phi(x_j))$, then any algorithm whose operations can be expressed in the input space in terms of dot products can be generalized to an algorithm which operates in the feature space by substituting a kernel function for the inner product. In practice, this means presenting the Gram matrix G in place of the input covariance matrix $X^T X$. Relatedly, using the kernel k instead of a dot product in the input space corresponds to mapping the data set into a (usually) high-dimensional dot product space $\mathcal{F}$ by a (usually nonlinear) mapping $\Phi : \mathbb{R}^m \to \mathcal{F}$, and taking dot products there, i.e., $k(x_i, x_j) = (\Phi(x_i), \Phi(x_j))$. Note that for the commonly-used Mercer kernels, G is a symmetric positive semidefinite (SPSD) matrix.

The generality of this framework should be emphasized. For example, there has been much work recently on dimensionality reduction for nonlinear manifolds in high-dimensional spaces. See, e.g., Isomap, local linear embedding, and graph Laplacian eigenmap [29, 26, 4] as well as Hessian eigenmaps and semidefinite embedding [9, 30]. These methods first induce a local neighborhood structure on the data and then use this local structure to find a global embedding of the manifold in a lower dimensional space. The manner in which these different algorithms use the local information to construct the global embedding is quite different, but in [22] they are interpreted as kernel PCA applied to specially constructed Gram matrices.

This "kernel trick" has been quite successful for extracting nonlinear structure in large data sets when the features are chosen such that the structure in the data is more manifest in the feature space than in the original space. Although in many cases the features are chosen such that the Gram matrix is sparse, in which case sparse matrix computation methods may be used, in other applications the Gram matrix is dense, but is well approximated by a low-rank matrix. In this case, calculations of interest (such as the matrix inversion needed in GP prediction, the quadratic programming problem for SVMs, and the computation of the eigendecomposition of the Gram matrix) will still generally take space which is $O(n^2)$ and time which is $O(n^3)$. This is prohibitive if n, the number of data points, is large. Recent work in the learning theory community has focused on taking advantage of this low-rank structure in order to perform learning tasks of interest more efficiently. For example, in [2], several randomized methods are used in order to speed up kernel PCA. These methods have provable guarantees on the quality of their approximation and may be viewed as replacing the kernel function k by a "randomized kernel" which behaves like k in expectation. Relatedly, in [33], uniform sampling without replacement is used to choose a small set of basis training points, from which an approximation to the Gram matrix is constructed. Although this algorithm does not come with provable performance guarantees, it may be viewed as a special case of our main algorithm, and it was shown empirically to perform well on two data sets for approximate GP classification and regression. It was also interpreted in terms of the Nyström method from integral equation theory; this method has also been applied recently in the learning theory community to approximate the solution of spectral partitioning for image and video segmentation [20] and to extend the eigenfunctions of a data-dependent kernel to new data points [5, 23]. Related work taking advantage of low-rank structure includes [28, 19, 32, 6, 24, 31, 3].

1.2   Summary of Main Result

In this paper, we develop and analyze an algorithm to compute an easily-interpretable low-rank approximation to an $n \times n$ Gram matrix G. Our main result, the MAIN APPROXIMATION algorithm of Section 3.2, is an algorithm that, when given as input a SPSD matrix $G \in \mathbb{R}^{n \times n}$, computes a low-rank approximation to G of the form $\tilde{G}_k = C W_k^+ C^T$, where $C \in \mathbb{R}^{n \times c}$ is a matrix formed by randomly choosing a small number c of columns (and thus rows) of G and $W_k \in \mathbb{R}^{c \times c}$ is the best rank-k approximation to W, the matrix formed by the intersection between those c columns of G and the corresponding c rows of G. The columns are chosen in c independent random trials (and thus with replacement) according to a judiciously-chosen and data-dependent nonuniform probability distribution. The nonuniform probability distribution will be carefully chosen and will be important for the provable bounds we obtain. Let $\|\cdot\|_2$ and $\|\cdot\|_F$ denote the spectral norm and the Frobenius norm, respectively, and let G_k be the best rank-k approximation to G. Our main result, presented in a more precise form in Theorem 1, is that under appropriate assumptions:

$$\left\| G - CW_k^+ C^T \right\|_\xi \leq \| G - G_k \|_\xi + \epsilon \sum_{i=1}^n G_{ii}^2, \tag{1}$$

in both expectation and with high probability, for both $\xi = 2, F$, for all $k : 0 \leq k \leq \operatorname{rank}(W)$. This approximation can be computed in $O(n)$ space and time after two passes over the data from external storage.

1.3   Technical Report

In the interests of space, several sections have not been included in this extended abstract. For more details and discussion related to the results presented here, see the associated technical report [18]. In particular, [18] contains a discussion of the relationship between our work, recent work on Nyström-based kernel methods [33, 31, 20], and the low-rank approximation algorithm of Frieze, Kannan, and Vempala [21, 14].

2   Review of Relevant Linear Algebra

For the review of the linear algebra used in this paper, see the associated technical report [18]. Recent work in the theory of randomized algorithms has focused on matrix problems [21, 10, 1, 2, 11, 12, 13, 14, 15, 16, 17, 25]. In particular, our previous work has applied random sampling methods to the approximation of several common matrix computations such as matrix multiplication [13], the computation of low-rank approximations to a matrix [14], the computation of the CUR matrix decomposition [15], and approximating the feasibility of linear programs [16, 17]. For the review of two results from this random sampling methodology that will be used in this paper, see the associated technical report [18].

3   Approximating a Gram Matrix

Consider a set of n points in $\mathbb{R}^m$, denoted by $X^{(1)}, \ldots, X^{(n)}$, and let X be the $m \times n$ matrix whose i-th column is $X^{(i)}$. These points may be either the original data or the data after they have been mapped into the feature space. Then, define the $n \times n$ Gram matrix G as $G = X^T X$. Thus, G is a SPSD matrix and $G_{ij} = (X^{(i)}, X^{(j)})$ is the dot product between the data vectors $X^{(i)}$ and $X^{(j)}$. If G is dense but has good linear structure, i.e., is well-approximated by a low-rank matrix, then a computation of a easily-computable and easily-interpretable low-rank approximation to G, with provable error bounds, is of interest. In this section, two algorithms are presented that compute such an approximation to a Gram matrix G.

3.1   A Preliminary Nyström-Based Algorithm

In [33], a method to approximate G was proposed that, in our notation, chooses c columns from G uniformly at random and without replacement, and constructs an approximation of the form $\tilde{G} = CW^{-1}C^T$, where the $n \times c$ matrix C consists of the c chosen columns and W is a matrix consisting of the intersection of those c columns with the corresponding c rows. Analysis of this algorithm and issues such as the existence of the inverse were not addressed in [33], but computational experiments were performed and the procedure was shown to work well empirically on two data sets [33]. This method has been referred to as the Nyström method [33, 31, 20] since it has an interpretation in terms of the Nyström technique for solving linear integral equations [8]. See [18] for a full discussion.

In Algorithm 1, the PRELIMINARY APPROXIMATION algorithm is presented. It is an algorithm that takes as input an $n \times n$ Gram matrix G and returns as output an approximate decomposition of the form $\tilde{G} = CW^+C^T$, where C and W are as in [33], and where W^+ is the Moore-Penrose generalized inverse of W. The c columns are chosen uniformly at random and with replacement. Thus, the PRELIMINARY APPROXIMATION algorithm is quite similar to the algorithm of [33], except that we sample with replacement and that we do not assume the existence of W^{-1}. Rather than analyzing this algorithm (which could be done by combining the analysis of Section 3.3 with the uniform sampling bounds of [13]), we present and analyze a more general form of it, for which we can obtain improved bounds, in Section 3.2. Note, however, that if the uniform sampling probabilities are nearly optimal, in the sense that $1/n \geq \beta G_{ii}^2 / \sum_{i=1}^{n} G_{ii}^2$ for some positive $\beta \leq 1$ and for every $i = 1, \ldots, n$, then bounds similar to those in Theorem 1 will be obtained for this algorithm, with a small β-dependent loss in accuracy; see [13, 18].

Data   : $n \times n$ Gram matrix G and $c \leq n$.
Result   : $n \times n$ matrix $\tilde{G}$.
- Pick c columns of G in i.i.d. trials, uniformly at random with replacement; let $\mathcal{I}$ be the set of indices of the sampled columns.
- Let C be the $n \times c$ matrix containing the sampled columns.
- Let W be the $c \times c$ submatrix of G whose entries are $G_{ij}, i \in \mathcal{I}, j \in \mathcal{I}$.
- Return $\tilde{G} = CW^+C^T$.

Algorithm 1: The PRELIMINARY APPROXIMATION algorithm

3.2   The Main Algorithm and the Main Theorem

In [13, 14, 15, 16, 17], we showed the importance of sampling columns and/or rows of a matrix with carefully chosen nonuniform probability distributions in order to obtain provable error bounds for a variety of common matrix operations. In Algorithm 2, the MAIN APPROXIMATION algorithm is presented. It is a generalization of the PRELIMINARY APPROXIMATION algorithm that allows the column sample to be formed using arbitrary sampling probabilities. The MAIN

APPROXIMATION algorithm takes as input an $n \times n$ Gram matrix G, a probability distribution $\{p_i\}_{i=1}^n$, a number $c \leq n$ of columns to choose, and a rank parameter $k \leq c$. It returns as output an approximate decomposition of the form $\tilde{G}_k = CW_k^+C^T$, where C is an $n \times c$ matrix consisting of the chosen columns of G, each rescaled in an appropriate manner, and where W_k is a $c \times c$ matrix that is the best rank-k approximation to the matrix W, which is a matrix whose elements consist of those elements in G in the intersection of the chosen columns and the corresponding rows, each rescaled in an appropriate manner.

Data   : $n \times n$ Gram matrix G, $\{p_i\}_{i=1}^n$ such that $\sum_{i=1}^n p_i = 1$, $c \leq n$, and $k \leq c$.

Result : $n \times n$ matrix $\tilde{G}$.
- Pick c columns of G in i.i.d. trials, with replacement and with respect to the probabilities $\{p_i\}_{i=1}^n$; let $\mathcal{I}$ be the set of indices of the sampled columns.
- Scale each sampled column (whose index is $i \in \mathcal{I}$) by dividing its elements by $\sqrt{cp_i}$; let C be the $n \times c$ matrix containing the sampled columns rescaled in this manner.
- Let W be the $c \times c$ submatrix of G whose entries are $G_{ij}/(c\sqrt{p_ip_j}), i \in \mathcal{I}, j \in \mathcal{I}$.
- Compute W_k, the best rank-k approximation to W.
- Return $\tilde{G}_k = CW_k^+C^T$.

Algorithm 2: The MAIN APPROXIMATION algorithm

To implement this algorithm, two passes over the Gram matrix G from external storage and $O(n)$, i.e. sublinear in $O(n^2)$, additional space and time are sufficient (assuming that the sampling probabilities of the form, e.g., $p_i = G_{ii}^2/\sum_{i=1}^n G_{ii}^2$ or $p_i = \left|G^{(i)}\right|^2 / \|G\|_F^2$ or $p_i = 1/n$ are used). Thus, this algorithm is efficient within the framework of the Pass-Efficient model; see [13] for more details. Note that if the sampling probabilities of the form $p_i = G_{ii}^2/\sum_{i=1}^n G_{ii}^2$ are used, as in Theorem 1 below, then one may store the $m \times n$ data matrix X in external storage, in which case only those elements of G that are used in the approximation need to be computed.

In the simplest application of this algorithm, one could choose $k = c$, in which case $W_k = W$, and the decomposition is of the form $\tilde{G} = CW^+C^T$, where W^+ is the exact Moore-Penrose generalized inverse of the matrix W. In certain cases, however, computing the generalized inverse may be problematic since, e.g., it may amplify noise present in the low singular values. Note that, as a function of increasing k, the Frobenius norm bound of Theorem 2 of [18] is not necessarily optimal for $k = \text{rank}(C)$. Also, although the bounds of Theorem 1 for the spectral norm for $k \leq \text{rank}(W)$ are in general worse than those for $k = \text{rank}(W)$, the former are of interest since our algorithms hold for any input Gram matrix and we make no assumptions about a model for the noise in the data.

The sampling matrix formalism of [13] is used in the proofs of Theorem 1 in Section 3.3, and thus we introduce it here. Let us define the sampling matrix $S \in \mathbb{R}^{n \times c}$ to be the zero-one matrix where $S_{ij} = 1$ if the i-th column of A is chosen in the j-th independent random trial and $S_{ij} = 0$ otherwise. Similarly, define the rescaling matrix $D \in \mathbb{R}^{c \times c}$ to be the diagonal matrix with $D_{tt} = 1/\sqrt{cp_{i_t}}$. Then, the $n \times c$ matrix

$$C = GSD$$

consists of the chosen columns of G, each of which has been rescaled by $1/\sqrt{cp_{i_t}}$, where i_t is the label of the column chosen in the t-th independent trial. Similarly, the $c \times c$ matrix

$$W = (SD)^T GSD = DS^T GSD$$

consists of the intersection between the chosen columns and the corresponding rows, each element of which has been rescaled by with $1/c\sqrt{p_{i_t}p_{j_t}}$. (This can also be viewed as forming W by sampling a number c of rows of C and rescaling. Note, however, that in this case the columns of A and the rows of C are sampled using the same probabilities.) In Algorithm 3, the MAIN APPROXIMATION is restated using this sampling matrix formalism. It should be clear that Algorithm 3 and Algorithm 2 yield identical results.

Data   : $n \times n$ Gram matrix G, $\{p_i\}_{i=1}^n$ such that $\sum_{i=1}^n p_i = 1$, $c \le n$, and $k \le c$.

Result : $n \times n$ matrix $\tilde{G}$.
- Define the $(n \times c)$ matrix $S = \mathbf{0}_{n \times c}$;
- Define the $(c \times c)$ matrix $D = \mathbf{0}_{c \times c}$;
- **for** $t = 1, \ldots, c$ **do**
  - Pick $i_t \in [n]$, where $\mathbf{Pr}(i_t = i) = p_i$;
  - $D_{tt} = (cp_{i_t})^{-1/2}$;
  - $S_{i_t t} = 1$;

end
- Let $C = GSD$ and $W = DS^T GSD$.
- Compute W_k, the best rank-k approximation to W.
- Return $\tilde{G}_k = CW_k^+ C^T$.

Algorithm 3: The MAIN APPROXIMATION algorithm, restated

Before stating our main theorem, we wish to emphasize the structural simplicity of our main result. If, e.g., we choose $k = c$, then our main algorithm provides a decomposition of the form $\tilde{G} = CW^+C^T$:

$$\begin{pmatrix} & \\ & G & \\ & \end{pmatrix} \approx \begin{pmatrix} & \\ & \tilde{G} & \\ & \end{pmatrix} = \begin{pmatrix} & \\ & C & \\ & \end{pmatrix} (W)^+ (\, C^T \,). \tag{2}$$

Up to rescaling, the MAIN APPROXIMATION algorithm returns an approximation $\tilde{G}$ which is created from two submatrices of G, namely C and W. In the uniform sampling case, $p_i = 1/n$, the diagonal elements of the rescaling matrix D are all n/c, and these all cancel out of the expression. In the nonuniform sampling case, C is a rescaled version of the columns of G and W is a rescaled version of the intersection of those columns with the corresponding rows. Alternatively, one can view C as consisting of the actual columns of G, without rescaling, and W as consisting of the intersection of those columns with the corresponding rows, again without rescaling, in the following manner. Let $\hat{C} = GS$, let $\hat{W} = S^T G S$, and let

$$\hat{W}^+ = \hat{W}^+_{D^2, D^{-2}} = D\left(D\hat{W}D\right)^+ D \tag{3}$$

be the $\{D^2, D^{-2}\}$-weighted-$\{1,2\}$-generalized inverse of $\hat{W}$. Then, $G \approx \tilde{G} = \hat{C}\hat{W}^+\hat{C}^T$.

The following theorem states our main result regarding the MAIN APPROX-IMATION algorithm. Its proof may be found in Section 3.3.

Theorem 1. *Suppose G is an $n \times n$ SPSD matrix, let $k \leq c$ be a rank parameter, and let $\tilde{G}_k = CW_k^+C^T$ be constructed from the MAIN APPROXIMATION algorithm of Algorithm 2 by sampling c columns of G with probabilities $\{p_i\}_{i=1}^n$ such that*

$$p_i = G_{ii}^2 / \sum_{i=1}^n G_{ii}^2. \tag{4}$$

Let $r = \text{rank}(W)$ and let G_k be the best rank-k approximation to G. In addition, let $\epsilon > 0$ and $\eta = 1 + \sqrt{8 \log(1/\delta)}$. If $c \geq 64k/\epsilon^4$, then

$$\mathbf{E}\left[\left\|G - \tilde{G}_k\right\|_F\right] \leq \|G - G_k\|_F + \epsilon \sum_{i=1}^n G_{ii}^2 \tag{5}$$

and if $c \geq 64k\eta^2/\epsilon^4$ then with probability at least $1 - \delta$

$$\left\|G - \tilde{G}_k\right\|_F \leq \|G - G_k\|_F + \epsilon \sum_{i=1}^n G_{ii}^2. \tag{6}$$

In addition, if $c \geq 4/\epsilon^2$ then

$$\mathbf{E}\left[\left\|G - \tilde{G}_k\right\|_2\right] \leq \|G - G_k\|_2 + \epsilon \sum_{i=1}^n G_{ii}^2 \tag{7}$$

and if $c \geq 4\eta^2/\epsilon^2$ then with probability at least $1 - \delta$

$$\left\|G - \tilde{G}_k\right\|_2 \leq \|G - G_k\|_2 + \epsilon \sum_{i=1}^n G_{ii}^2. \tag{8}$$

Several things should be noted about this result. First, if $k \geq r = \text{rank}(W)$ then $W_k = W$, and an application of Theorem 2 of [18] leads to bounds of the form $\left\|G - \tilde{G}_r\right\|_2 \leq \epsilon \sum_{i=1}^n G_{ii}^2$, in expectation and with high probability. Second, the sampling probabilities used in Thoerem 1 may be written as $p_i = \left|X^{(i)}\right|^2 / \|X\|_F^2$, which only depend on dot products from the data matrix X. This is useful if X consists of the data after it has been mapped to the feature space $\mathcal{F}$. Finally, if the sampling probabilities were of the form $p_i = \left|G^{(i)}\right|^2 / \|G\|_F^2$ then they would preferentially choose data points that are more informative (in the sense of being longer) and/or more representative of the data (in the sense that they tend to be more well correlated with more data points). Instead the probabilities (4) ignore the correlations. As discussed in [18], this leads to somewhat worse error bounds. To the best of our knowledge, it is not known how to sample with respect to correlations while respecting the SPSD property and obtaining provably good bounds with improved error bounds. This is of interest since in many applications it is likely that the data are approximately normalized by the way the data are generated, and it is the correlations that are of interest. Intuitively, this difficulty arises since it is difficult to identify structure in a matrix to ensure the SPSD property, unless, e.g., the matrix is diagonally dominant or given in the form $X^T X$. As will be seen in Section 3.3, the proof of Theorem 1 depends crucially on the decomposition of G as $G = X^T X$.

3.3 Proof of Theorem 1

Since $G = X^T X$ it follows that both the left and the right singular vectors of G are equal to the right singular vectors of X and that the singular values of G are the squares of the singular values of X. More formally, let the SVD of X be $X = U \Sigma V^T$. Then,

$$G = V \Sigma^2 V^T = XUU^T X^T. \tag{9}$$

Now, let us consider $C_X = XSD \in \mathbb{R}^{m \times c}$, i.e., the column sampled and rescaled version of X, and let the SVD of C_X be $C_X = \hat{U} \hat{\Sigma} \hat{V}^T$. Thus, in particular, $\hat{U}$ contains the left singular vectors of C_X. We do not specify the dimensions of $\hat{U}$ (and in particular how many columns $\hat{U}$ has) since we do not know the rank of C_X. Let $\hat{U}_k$ be the $m \times k$ matrix whose columns consist of the singular vectors of C_X corresponding to the top k singular values. Instead of exactly computing the left singular vectors U of X, we can approximate them by $\hat{U}_k$, computed from a column sample of X, and use this to compute an approximation $\tilde{G}$ to G.

We first establish the following lemma, which provides a bound on $\left\|G - \tilde{G}_k\right\|_\xi$ for $\xi = 2, F$.

Lemma 1. If $\tilde{G}_k = CW_k^+ C^T$ then

$$\left\|G - \tilde{G}_k\right\|_F = \left\|X^T X - X^T \hat{U}_k \hat{U}_k X\right\|_F \tag{10}$$

$$\left\|G - \tilde{G}_k\right\|_2 = \left\|X - \hat{U}_k \hat{U}_k^T X\right\|_2^2. \tag{11}$$

Proof: Recall that $C = GSD$ and $W = (SD)^T GSD = C_X^T C_X$. Thus, $W = \hat{V} \hat{\Sigma}^2 \hat{V}$ and $W_k = \hat{V} \hat{\Sigma}_k^2 \hat{V}^T$, where $\hat{\Sigma}_k$ is the diagonal matrix with the top k singular values of C_X on the diagonal and the remainder set to 0. Then since

$C_X = XSD = \hat{U}\hat{\Sigma}\hat{V}^T$ and $W_k^+ = \hat{V}\hat{\Sigma}_k^{-2}\hat{V}^T$

$$\tilde{G}_k = GSD\,(W_k)^+\,(GSD)^T \tag{12}$$

$$= X^T\hat{U}\hat{\Sigma}\hat{V}^T\left(\hat{V}\hat{\Sigma}_k^2\hat{V}^T\right)^+\hat{V}\hat{\Sigma}\hat{U}^TX \tag{13}$$

$$= X^T\hat{U}_k\hat{U}_k^TX, \tag{14}$$

where $\hat{U}_k\hat{U}_k^T$ is a projection onto the space spanned by the top k singular vectors of W. (10) then follows immediately, and (11) follows since

$$X^TX - X^T\hat{U}_k\hat{U}_k^TX = \left(X - \hat{U}_k\hat{U}_k^TX\right)^T\left(X - \hat{U}_k\hat{U}_k^TX\right)$$

and since $\|\Omega\|_2^2 = \|\Omega^T\Omega\|_2$ for any matrix Ω.   ◇

By combining (11) with Theorem 2 of [18], we see that

$$\left\|G - \tilde{G}_k\right\|_2 \le \|X - X_k\|_2^2 + 2\left\|XX^T - C_XC_X^T\right\|_2$$

$$\le \|G - G_k\|_2 + 2\left\|XX^T - C_XC_X^T\right\|_2.$$

Since the sampling probabilities (4) are of the form $p_i = \left|X^{(i)}\right|^2 / \|X\|_F^2$, this may be combined with Theorem 1 of [18], from which, by choosing c appropriately, the spectral norm bounds (7) and (8) of Theorem 1 follow.

To establish the Frobenius norm bounds, define $E = XX^TXX^T - C_XC_X^TC_XC_X^T$. Then, we have that:

$$\left\|G - \tilde{G}_k\right\|_F^2 = \left\|X^TX\right\|_F^2 - 2\left\|XX^T\hat{U}_k\right\|_F^2 + \left\|\hat{U}_k^TXX^T\hat{U}_k\right\|_F^2 \tag{15}$$

$$\le\left\|X^TX\right\|_F^2-2\left(\sum_{t=1}^k \sigma_t^4(C_X)-\sqrt{k}\,\|E\|_F\right)+\sum_{t=1}^k\sigma_t^4(C_X)+\sqrt{k}\,\|E\|_F \tag{16}$$

$$= \left\|X^TX\right\|_F^2 - \sum_{t=1}^k\sigma_t^4(C_X) + 3\sqrt{k}\,\|E\|_F \tag{17}$$

$$\le \left\|X^TX\right\|_F^2 - \sum_{t=1}^k\sigma_t^2(X^TX) + 4\sqrt{k}\,\|E\|_F, \tag{18}$$

where (15) follows by Lemmas 1 and 2, (16) follows by Lemmas 3 and 4, and (18) follows by Lemma 5. Since

$$\left\|X^TX\right\|_F^2 - \sum_{t=1}^k\sigma_t^2(X^TX) = \|G\|_F^2 - \sum_{t=1}^k\sigma_t^2(G) = \|G - G_k\|_F^2,$$

it follows that

$$\left\|G - \tilde{G}_k\right\|_F^2 \le \|G - G_k\|_F^2 + 4\sqrt{k}\left\|XX^TXX^T - C_XC_X^TC_XC_X^T\right\|_F. \tag{19}$$

Since the sampling probabilities (4) are of the form $p_i = \left| X^{(i)} \right|^2 / \|X\|_F^2$, this may be combined with Lemma 6 and Theorem 1 of [18]. Since $(\alpha^2 + \beta^2)^{1/2} \leq \alpha + \beta$ for $\alpha, \beta \geq 0$, by using Jensen's inequality, and by choosing c appropriately, the Frobenius norm bounds (5) and (6) of Theorem 1 follow.

The next four lemmas are used to bound the right hand side of (10).

Lemma 2. *For every* $k : 0 \leq k \leq rank(W)$ *we have that:*

$$\left\| X^T X - X^T \hat{U}_k \hat{U}_k^T X \right\|_F^2 = \|X^T X\|_F^2 - 2 \left\| XX^T \hat{U}_k \right\|_F^2 + \left\| \hat{U}_k^T XX^T \hat{U}_k \right\|_F^2$$

Proof: Define $Y = X - \hat{U}_k \hat{U}_k^T X$. Then,

$$\begin{aligned}
\left\| X^T X - X^T \hat{U}_k \hat{U}_k^T X \right\|_F^2 &= \|Y^T Y\|_F^2 \\
&= \mathbf{Tr}\left(Y^T Y Y^T Y \right) \\
&= \|X^T X\|_F^2 - 2\mathbf{Tr}\left(XX^T \hat{U}_k \hat{U}_k^T XX^T \right) \\
&\quad + \mathbf{Tr}\left(\hat{U}_k^T XX^T \hat{U}_k \hat{U}_k^T XX^T \hat{U}_k \right),
\end{aligned}$$

where the last line follows by multiplying out terms and since the trace is symmetric under cyclic permutations. The lemma follows since $\|\Omega\|_F^2 = \mathbf{Tr}\left(\Omega \Omega^T \right)$ for any matrix Ω. ◇

Lemma 3. *For every* $k : 0 \leq k \leq rank(W)$ *we have that:*

$$\left| \left\| XX^T \hat{U}_k \right\|_F^2 - \sum_{t=1}^{k} \sigma_t^4(C_X) \right| \leq \sqrt{k} \left\| XX^T XX^T - C_X C_X^T C_X C_X^T \right\|_F$$

Proof: Since $\sigma_t(C_X C_X^T) = \sigma_t^2(C_X)$ and since $\hat{U}$ is a matrix consisting of the singular vectors of $C_X = XSD$, we have that

$$\begin{aligned}
\left| \left\| XX^T \hat{U}_k \right\|_F^2 - \sum_{t=1}^{k} \sigma_t^4(C_X) \right| &= \left| \sum_{t=1}^{k} \left| XX^T \hat{U}^{(t)} \right|^2 - \sum_{t-1}^{k} \left| C_X C_X^T \hat{U}^{(t)} \right|^2 \right| \\
&= \left| \sum_{t=1}^{k} \hat{U}^{(t)^T} \left(XX^T XX^T - C_X C_X^T C_X C_X^T \right) \hat{U}^{(t)} \right| \\
&\leq \sqrt{k} \left(\sum_{t=1}^{k} \left(\hat{U}^{(t)^T} (XX^T XX^T - C_X C_X^T C_X C_X^T) \hat{U}^{(t)} \right)^2 \right)^{1/2},
\end{aligned}$$

where the last line follows from the Cauchy-Schwartz inequality. The lemma then follows. ◇

Lemma 4. *For every* $k : 0 \leq k \leq rank(W)$ *we have that:*

$$\left\| \hat{U}_k^T XX^T \hat{U}_k \right\|_F^2 - \sum_{t=1}^{k} \sigma_t^4(C_X) \leq \sqrt{k} \left\| XX^T XX^T - C_X C_X^T C_X C_X^T \right\|_F$$

Proof: Recall that if a matrix U has orthonormal columns then $\left\| U^T \Omega \right\|_F \leq \left\| \Omega \right\|_F$ for any matrix Ω. Thus, we have that

$$\left\| \hat{U}_k^T X X^T \hat{U}_k \right\|_F^2 - \sum_{t=1}^k \sigma_t^4(C_X) \leq \left\| X X^T \hat{U}_k \right\|_F^2 - \sum_{t=1}^k \sigma_t^4(C_X)$$

$$\leq \left| \left\| X X^T \hat{U}_k \right\|_F^2 - \sum_{t=1}^k \sigma_t^4(C_X) \right|$$

The remainder of the proof follows that of Lemma 3.   ◇

Lemma 5. *For every* $k : 0 \leq k \leq rank(W)$ *we have that:*

$$\left| \sum_{t=1}^k \sigma_t^4(C_X) - \sigma_t^2(X^T X) \right| \leq \sqrt{k} \left\| X X^T X X^T - C_X C_X^T C_X C_X^T \right\|_F$$

Proof:

$$\left| \sum_{t=1}^k \sigma_t^4(C_X) - \sigma_t^2(X^T X) \right| \leq \sqrt{k} \left(\sum_{t=1}^k \left(\sigma_t^4(C_X) - \sigma_t^2(X^T X) \right)^2 \right)^{1/2}$$

$$= \sqrt{k} \left(\sum_{t=1}^k \left(\sigma_t(C_X C_X^T C_X C_X^T) - \sigma_t(X X^T X X^T) \right)^2 \right)^{1/2}$$

$$\leq \sqrt{k} \left\| X X^T X X^T - C_X C_X^T C_X C_X^T \right\|_F,$$

where the first inequality follows from the Cauchy-Schwartz inequality and the second inequality follows from matrix perturbation theory.   ◇

The following is a result of the BASICMATRIXMULTIPLICATION algorithm that is not found in [13], but that will be useful for bounding the additional error in (19). We state this result for a general $m \times n$ matrix A.

Lemma 6. *Suppose* $A \in \mathbb{R}^{m \times n}$, $c \in \mathbb{Z}^+$ *such that* $1 \leq c \leq n$, *and* $\{p_i\}_{i=1}^n$ *are such that* $p_k = \left| A^{(k)} \right|^2 / \left\| A \right\|_F^2$. *Construct* C *with the* BASICMATRIXMULTIPLICATION *algorithm of [13]. Then,*

$$\mathbf{E} \left[\left\| A A^T A A^T - C C^T C C^T \right\|_F \right] \leq \frac{2}{\sqrt{c}} \left\| A \right\|_F^4. \tag{20}$$

Furthermore, let $\delta \in (0,1)$ *and* $\eta = 1 + \sqrt{8 \log(1/\delta)}$. *Then, with probability at least* $1 - \delta$,

$$\left\| A A^T A A^T - C C^T C C^T \right\|_F \leq \frac{2\eta}{\sqrt{c}} \left\| A \right\|_F^4. \tag{21}$$

Proof: First note that:

$$A A^T A A^T - C C^T C C^T = A A^T A A^T - A A^T C C^T + A A^T C C^T - C C^T C C^T$$

$$= A A^T \left(A A^T - C C^T \right) + \left(A A^T - C C^T \right) C C^T.$$

Thus, by submultiplicitivity and subadditivity we have that for $\xi = 2, F$:

$$\left\| AA^T AA^T - CC^T CC^T \right\|_F \leq \left\| A \right\|_F^2 \left\| AA^T - CC^T \right\|_F + \left\| AA^T - CC^T \right\|_F \left\| C \right\|_F^2 .$$

The lemma follows since $\left\| C \right\|_F^2 = \left\| A \right\|_F^2$ when $p_k = \left| A^{(k)} \right|^2 / \left\| A \right\|_F^2$, and by applying Theorem 1 of [18].   ◇

4   Conclusion

We have presented and analyzed an algorithm that provides an approximate decomposition of an $n \times n$ Gram matrix G which is of the form $G \approx \tilde{G}_k = CW_k^+ C^T$ and which has provable error bounds of the form (1). A crucial feature of this algorithm is the probability distribution used to randomly sample columns. We conclude with two open problems related to the choice of this distribution.

First, it would be desirable to choose the probabilities in Theorem 1 to be $p_i = \left| G^{(i)} \right|^2 / \left\| G \right\|_F^2$ and to establish bounds of the form (1) in which the scale of the additional error was $\left\| G \right\|_F = \left\| X^T X \right\|_F$ rather than $\sum_{i=1}^n G_{ii}^2 = \left\| X \right\|_F^2$. This would entail extracting linear structure while simultaneously respecting the SPSD property and obtaining improved scale of error. This would likely be a corollary of a CUR decomposition [15] for a general $m \times n$ matrix A with error bounds of the form found in [15] and in which $U = W_k^+$, where W is now the matrix consisting of the intersection of the chosen columns and (in general different) rows; see [18]. This would simplify considerably the form of U found in [15] and would lead to improved interpretability. Second, we should also note that if capturing coarse statistics over the data is not of interest, but instead one is interested in other properties of the data, e.g., identifying outliers, then probabilities that depend on the data in some other manner, e.g., inversely with respect to their lengths squared, may be appropriate. We do not have provable bounds in this case.

Acknowledgments. We would like to thank Ravi Kannan for many fruitful discussions and the Institute for Pure and Applied Mathematics at UCLA for its generous hospitality.

References

1. D. Achlioptas and F. McSherry. Fast computation of low rank matrix approximations. In *Proceedings of the 33rd Annual ACM Symposium on Theory of Computing*, pages 611–618, 2001.
2. D. Achlioptas, F. McSherry, and B. Schölkopf. Sampling techniques for kernel methods. In *Annual Advances in Neural Information Processing Systems 14: Proceedings of the 2001 Conference*, pages 335–342, 2002.

3. Y. Azar, A. Fiat, A.R. Karlin, F. McSherry, and J. Saia. Spectral analysis of data. In *Proceedings of the 33rd Annual ACM Symposium on Theory of Computing*, pages 619–626, 2001.
4. M. Belkin and P. Niyogi. Laplacian eigenmaps for dimensionality reduction and data representation. *Neural Computation*, 15(6):1373–1396, 2003.
5. Y. Bengio, J.F. Paiement, P. Vincent, O. Delalleau, N. Le Roux, and M. Ouimet. Out-of-sample extensions for LLE, Isomap, MDS, eigenmaps, and spectral clustering. In *Annual Advances in Neural Information Processing Systems 16: Proceedings of the 2003 Conference*, pages 177–184, 2004.
6. C.J.C. Burges. Simplified support vector decision rules. In *Proceedings of the 13th International Conference on Machine Learning*, pages 71–77, 1996.
7. N. Cristianini and J. Shawe-Taylor. *An Introduction to Support Vector Machines and Other Kernel-based Learning Methods*. Cambridge University Press, Cambridge, 2000.
8. L.M. Delves and J.L. Mohamed. *Computational Methods for Integral Equations*. Cambridge University Press, Cambridge, 1985.
9. D.L. Donoho and C. Grimes. Hessian eigenmaps: Locally linear embedding techniques for high-dimensional data. *Proc. Natl. Acad. Sci. USA*, 100(10):5591–5596, 2003.
10. P. Drineas, A. Frieze, R. Kannan, S. Vempala, and V. Vinay. Clustering in large graphs and matrices. In *Proceedings of the 10th Annual ACM-SIAM Symposium on Discrete Algorithms*, pages 291–299, 1999.
11. P. Drineas and R. Kannan. Fast Monte-Carlo algorithms for approximate matrix multiplication. In *Proceedings of the 42nd Annual IEEE Symposium on Foundations of Computer Science*, pages 452–459, 2001.
12. P. Drineas and R. Kannan. Pass efficient algorithms for approximating large matrices. In *Proceedings of the 14th Annual ACM-SIAM Symposium on Discrete Algorithms*, pages 223–232, 2003.
13. P. Drineas, R. Kannan, and M.W. Mahoney. Fast Monte Carlo algorithms for matrices I: Approximating matrix multiplication. Technical Report YALEU/DCS/TR-1269, Yale University Department of Computer Science, New Haven, CT, February 2004.
14. P. Drineas, R. Kannan, and M.W. Mahoney. Fast Monte Carlo algorithms for matrices II: Computing a low-rank approximation to a matrix. Technical Report YALEU/DCS/TR-1270, Yale University Department of Computer Science, New Haven, CT, February 2004.
15. P. Drineas, R. Kannan, and M.W. Mahoney. Fast Monte Carlo algorithms for matrices III: Computing a compressed approximate matrix decomposition. Technical Report YALEU/DCS/TR-1271, Yale University Department of Computer Science, New Haven, CT, February 2004.
16. P. Drineas, R. Kannan, and M.W. Mahoney. Sampling sub-problems of heterogeneous Max-Cut problems and approximation algorithms. Technical Report YALEU/DCS/TR-1283, Yale University Department of Computer Science, New Haven, CT, April 2004.
17. P. Drineas, R. Kannan, and M.W. Mahoney. Sampling sub-problems of heterogeneous Max-Cut problems and approximation algorithms. In *Proceedings of the 22nd Annual International Symposium on Theoretical Aspects of Computer Science*, pages 57–68, 2005.
18. P. Drineas and M.W. Mahoney. On the Nyström method for approximating a Gram matrix for improved kernel-based learning. Technical Report 1319, Yale University Department of Computer Science, New Haven, CT, April 2005.

19. S. Fine and K. Scheinberg. Efficient SVM training using low-rank kernel representations. *Journal of Machine Learning Research*, 2:243–264, 2001.
20. C. Fowlkes, S. Belongie, F. Chung, and J. Malik. Spectral grouping using the Nyström method. *IEEE Transactions on Pattern Analysis and Machine Intelligence*, 26(2):214–225, 2004.
21. A. Frieze, R. Kannan, and S. Vempala. Fast Monte-Carlo algorithms for finding low-rank approximations. In *Proceedings of the 39th Annual IEEE Symposium on Foundations of Computer Science*, pages 370–378, 1998.
22. J. Ham, D.D. Lee, S. Mika, and B. Schölkopf. A kernel view of the dimensionality reduction of manifolds. Technical Report TR-110, Max Planck Institute for Biological Cybernetics, July 2003.
23. S. Lafon. *Diffusion Maps and Geometric Harmonics*. PhD thesis, Yale University, 2004.
24. E. Osuna, R. Freund, and F. Girosi. An improved training algorithm for support vector machines. In *Proceedings of the 1997 IEEE Workshop on Neural Networks for Signal Processing VII*, pages 276–285, 1997.
25. L. Rademacher, S. Vempala, and G. Wang. Matrix approximation and projective clustering via iterative sampling. *manuscript*.
26. S.T. Roweis and L.K. Saul. Nonlinear dimensionality reduction by local linear embedding. *Science*, 290:2323–2326, 2000.
27. B. Schölkopf, A. Smola, and K.-R. Müller. Nonlinear component analysis as a kernel eigenvalue problem. *Neural Computation*, 10:1299–1319, 1998.
28. A.J. Smola and B. Schölkopf. Sparse greedy matrix approximation for machine learning. In *Proceedings of the 17th International Conference on Machine Learning*, pages 911–918, 2000.
29. J.B. Tenenbaum, V. de Silva, and J.C. Langford. A global geometric framework for nonlinear dimensionality reduction. *Science*, 290:2319–2323, 2000.
30. K.Q. Weinberger, F. Sha, and L.K. Saul. Learning a kernel matrix for nonlinear dimensionality reduction. In *Proceedings of the 21st International Conference on Machine Learning*, pages 839–846, 2004.
31. C.K.I. Williams, C.E. Rasmussen, A. Schwaighofer, and V. Tresp. Observations on the Nyström method for Gaussian process prediction. Technical report, University of Edinburgh, 2002.
32. C.K.I. Williams and M. Seeger. The effect of the input density distribution on kernel-based classifiers. In *Proceedings of the 17th International Conference on Machine Learning*, pages 1159–1166, 2000.
33. C.K.I. Williams and M. Seeger. Using the Nyström method to speed up kernel machines. In *Annual Advances in Neural Information Processing Systems 13: Proceedings of the 2000 Conference*, pages 682–688, 2001.

Learning Convex Combinations of Continuously Parameterized Basic Kernels*

Andreas Argyriou[1], Charles A. Micchelli[2], and Massimiliano Pontil[1]

[1] Department of Computer Science, University College London,
Gower Street, London WC1E 6BT, England, UK
{a.argyriou, m.pontil}@cs.ucl.ac.uk
[2] Department of Mathematics and Statistics, State University of New York,
The University at Albany, 1400 Washington Avenue,
Albany, NY, 12222, USA

Abstract. We study the problem of learning a kernel which minimizes a regularization error functional such as that used in regularization networks or support vector machines. We consider this problem when the kernel is in the convex hull of basic kernels, for example, Gaussian kernels which are continuously parameterized by a compact set. We show that there always exists an optimal kernel which is the convex combination of at most $m + 1$ basic kernels, where m is the sample size, and provide a necessary and sufficient condition for a kernel to be optimal. The proof of our results is constructive and leads to a greedy algorithm for learning the kernel. We discuss the properties of this algorithm and present some preliminary numerical simulations.

1 Introduction

A common theme in machine learning is that a function can be learned from a finite set of input/output examples by minimizing a regularization functional which models a trade-off between an error term, measuring the fit to the data, and a smoothness term, measuring the function complexity. In this paper we focus on learning methods which, given examples $\{(x_j, y_j) : j \in \mathbb{N}_m\} \subseteq \mathcal{X} \times \mathbb{R}$, estimate a real-valued function by minimizing the regularization functional

$$Q_\mu(f, K) = \sum_{j \in \mathbb{N}_m} q(y_j, f(x_j)) + \mu \|f\|_K^2 \qquad (1)$$

where $q : \mathbb{R} \times \mathbb{R} \to \mathbb{R}_+$ is a prescribed *loss function*, μ is a positive parameter and $\mathbb{N}_m := \{1, \ldots, m\}$. The minimum is taken over $f \in \mathcal{H}_K$, a *reproducing kernel Hilbert space* (RKHS) with kernel K, see [1].

This approach has a long history. It has been studied, from different perspectives, in statistics [16], in optimal recovery [10], and more recently, has been

* This work was supported by EPSRC Grant GR/T18707/01, NSF Grant ITR-0312113 and the PASCAL European Network of Excellence.

P. Auer and R. Meir (Eds.): COLT 2005, LNAI 3559, pp. 338–352, 2005.

a focus of attention in machine learning theory, see, for example [14, 15] and references therein. The choice of the loss function q leads to different learning methods among which the most prominent have been square loss regularization and support vector machines.

As new parametric families of kernels are being proposed to model functions defined on possibly complex/structured input domains (see, for example, [14] for a review) it is increasingly important to develop optimization methods for tuning kernel-based learning algorithms over a possibly large number of kernel parameters. This motivates us to study the problem of minimizing functional (1) not only over f but also over K, that is, we consider the variational problem

$$Q_\mu(\mathcal{K}) = \inf\{Q_\mu(f, K) : f \in \mathcal{H}_K, K \in \mathcal{K}\} \tag{2}$$

where $\mathcal{K}$ is a prescribed *convex* set of kernels. This point of view was proposed in [3, 8] where the problem (2) was mainly studied in the case of support vector machines and when $\mathcal{K}$ is formed by combinations of a *finite* number of basic kernels. Other related work on this topic appears in the papers [4, 9, 11, 18].

In this paper, we present a framework which allows us to model richer families of kernels parameterized by a compact set Ω, that is, we consider kernels of the type

$$\mathcal{K} = \left\{ \int_\Omega G(\omega) dp(\omega) : p \in \mathcal{P}(\Omega) \right\} \tag{3}$$

where $\mathcal{P}(\Omega)$ is the set of all probability measures on Ω. For example, when $\Omega \subseteq \mathbb{R}_+$ and the function $G(\omega)$ is a multivariate Gaussian kernel with variance ω then $\mathcal{K}$ is a subset of the class of radial kernels. The set-up for the family of kernels in (3) is discussed in Section 2, where we also review some earlier results from [9]. In particular, we establish that if q is convex then problem (2) is equivalent to solving a saddle-point problem. In Section 3, we derive optimality conditions for problem (2). We present a necessary and sufficient condition which characterizes a solution to this problem (see Theorem 2) and show that there always exists an optimal kernel $\hat{K}$ with a *finite representation*. Specifically, for this kernel the probability measure p in (3) is an atomic measure with *at most* $m + 1$ atoms (see Theorem 1). As we shall see, this implies, for example, that the optimal radial kernel is a finite mixture of Gaussian kernels when the variance is bounded above and away from zero. We mention, in passing, that a version of our characterization also holds when Ω is locally compact (see Theorem 4). The proof of our results is constructive and can be used to derive algorithms for learning the kernel. In Section 4, we propose a greedy algorithm for learning the kernel and present some preliminary experiments on optical character recognition.

2   Background and Notation

In this section we review our notation and present some background results from [9] concerning problem (2).

We begin by recalling the notion of a kernel and RKHS $\mathcal{H}_K$. Let $\mathcal{X}$ be a set. By a *kernel* we mean a symmetric function $K : \mathcal{X} \times \mathcal{X} \to \mathbb{R}$ such that for every finite set of inputs $\mathbf{x} = \{x_j : j \in \mathbb{N}_m\} \subseteq \mathcal{X}$ and every $m \in \mathbb{N}$, the $m \times m$ matrix $K_{\mathbf{x}} := (K(x_i, x_j) : i, j \in \mathbb{N}_m)$ is positive semi-definite. We let $\mathcal{L}(\mathbb{R}^m)$ be the set of $m \times m$ positive semi-definite matrices and $\mathcal{L}_+(\mathbb{R}^m)$ the subset of positive definite ones. Also, we use $\mathcal{A}(\mathcal{X})$ for the set of all kernels on the set $\mathcal{X}$ and $\mathcal{A}_+(\mathcal{X})$ for the set of kernels K such that, for each $m \in \mathbb{N}$ and each choice of $\mathbf{x}$, $K_{\mathbf{x}} \in \mathcal{L}_+(\mathbb{R}^m)$.

According to Aronszajn and Moore [1], every kernel is associated with an (essentially) *unique* Hilbert space $\mathcal{H}_K$ with inner product $\langle \cdot, \cdot \rangle_K$ such that K is its reproducing kernel. This means that for every $f \in \mathcal{H}_K$ and $x \in \mathcal{X}$, $\langle f, K_x \rangle_K = f(x)$, where $K_x(\cdot) := K(x, \cdot)$. Equivalently, any Hilbert space $\mathcal{H}$ of real-valued functions defined everywhere on $\mathcal{X}$ such that the point evaluation functionals $L_x(f) := f(x)$, $f \in \mathcal{H}$ are continuous on $\mathcal{H}$, admits a reproducing kernel K.

Let $D := \{(x_j, y_j) : j \in \mathbb{N}_m\} \subseteq \mathcal{X} \times \mathbb{R}$ be prescribed data and y the vector $(y_j : j \in \mathbb{N}_m)$. For each $f \in \mathcal{H}_K$, we introduce the *information operator* $I_{\mathbf{x}}(f) := (f(x_j) : j \in \mathbb{N}_m)$ of values of f on the set $\mathbf{x} := \{x_j : j \in \mathbb{N}_m\}$. We let $\mathbb{R}_+ := [0, \infty)$, prescribe a nonnegative function $Q : \mathbb{R}^m \to \mathbb{R}_+$ and introduce the *regularization functional*

$$Q_\mu(f, K) := Q(I_{\mathbf{x}}(f)) + \mu \|f\|_K^2 \tag{4}$$

where $\|f\|_K^2 := \langle f, f \rangle_K$ and μ is a positive constant. Note that Q depends on y but we suppress it in our notation as it is fixed throughout our discussion. For example, in equation (1) we have, for $w = (w_j : j \in N_n)$, that $Q(w) = \sum_{j \in \mathbb{N}_m} q(y_j, w_j)$, where q is a loss function.

Associated with the functional Q_μ and the kernel K is the variational problem

$$Q_\mu(K) := \inf\{Q_\mu(f, K) : f \in \mathcal{H}_K\} \tag{5}$$

which defines a functional $Q_\mu : \mathcal{A}(\mathcal{X}) \to \mathbb{R}_+$. We remark, in passing, that all of what we say about problem (5) applies to functions Q on $\mathbb{R}^m$ which are bounded from below as we can merely adjust the expression (4) by a constant independent of f and K. Note that if $Q : \mathbb{R}^m \to \mathbb{R}_+$ is continuous and μ is a positive number then the infimum in (5) is achieved because the unit ball in $\mathcal{H}_K$ is *weakly* compact. In particular, when Q is convex the minimum is unique since in this case the right hand side of equation (4) is a *strictly* convex functional of $f \in \mathcal{H}_K$. Moreover, if f is a solution to problem (5) then it has the form

$$f(x) = \sum_{j \in \mathbb{N}_m} c_j K(x_j, x), \quad x \in \mathcal{X} \tag{6}$$

for some real vector $c = (c_j : j \in \mathbb{N}_m)$. This result is known as the *Representer Theorem*, see, for example, [14]. Although it is simple to prove, this result is remarkable as it makes the variational problem (5) amenable to computations. In particular, if Q is convex, the unique minimizer of problem (5) can be found by replacing f by the right hand side of equation (6) in equation (4) and then optimizing with respect to the vector c. That is, we have the finite dimensional variational problem

$$Q_\mu(K) := \min\{Q(K_{\mathbf{x}}c) + \mu(c, K_{\mathbf{x}}c) : c \in \mathbb{R}^m\} \tag{7}$$

where $(\cdot, \cdot)$ is the standard inner product on $\mathbb{R}^m$. For example, when Q is the square loss defined for $w = (w_j : j \in \mathbb{N}_m) \in \mathbb{R}^m$ as $Q(w) = \|w - y\|^2 := \sum_{j \in \mathbb{N}_m} (w_j - y_j)^2$ the function in the right hand side of (7) is quadratic in the vector c and its minimizer is obtained by solving a linear system of equations.

The point of view of this paper is that the functional (5) can be used as a *design criterion to select the kernel* K. To this end, we specify an arbitrary convex subset $\mathcal{K}$ of $\mathcal{A}(\mathcal{X})$ and focus on the problem

$$Q_\mu(\mathcal{K}) := \inf\{Q_\mu(K) : K \in \mathcal{K}\}. \tag{8}$$

Every input set $\mathbf{x}$ and convex set $\mathcal{K}$ of kernels determines a convex set of matrices in $\mathcal{L}(\mathbb{R}^m)$, namely $\mathcal{K}(\mathbf{x}) := \{K_\mathbf{x} : K \in \mathcal{K}\}$. Obviously, it is this set of matrices that affects the variational problem (8). For this reason, we say that the set of kernels $\mathcal{K}$ is *compact and convex* provided that for all $\mathbf{x}$ the set of matrices $\mathcal{K}(\mathbf{x})$ is compact and convex. The following result is taken directly from [9].

Lemma 1. *If $\mathcal{K}$ is a compact and convex subset of $\mathcal{A}_+(\mathcal{X})$ and $Q : \mathbb{R}^m \to \mathbb{R}$ is continuous then the minimum of (8) exists.*

The lemma requires that all kernels in $\mathcal{K}$ are in $\mathcal{A}_+(\mathcal{X})$. If we wish to use kernels K only in $\mathcal{A}(\mathcal{X})$ we may always modify them by adding *any* positive multiple of the *delta function kernel* Δ defined, for $x, t \in \mathcal{X}$, as

$$\Delta(x, t) = \begin{cases} 1, & x = t \\ 0, & x \neq t \end{cases}$$

that is, replace K by $K + a\Delta$ where a is a positive constant.

There are two useful cases of the set $\mathcal{K}$ of kernels which are compact and convex. The first is formed by the convex hull of a *finite* number of kernels in $\mathcal{A}_+(\mathcal{X})$. The second case generalizes the above one to a compact Hausdorff space Ω (see, for example, [12]) and a mapping $G : \Omega \to \mathcal{A}_+(\mathcal{X})$. For each $\omega \in \Omega$, the value of the kernel $G(\omega)$ at $x, t \in \mathcal{X}$ is denoted by $G(\omega)(x, t)$ and we assume that the function of $\omega \mapsto G(\omega)(x, t)$ is continuous on Ω for each $x, t \in \mathcal{X}$. When this is the case we say G is *continuous*. We let $\mathcal{P}(\Omega)$ be the set of all *probability measures* on Ω and observe that

$$\mathcal{K}(G) := \left\{ \int_\Omega G(\omega) dp(\omega) : p \in \mathcal{P}(\Omega) \right\} \tag{9}$$

is a compact and convex set of kernels in $\mathcal{A}_+(\mathcal{X})$. The compactness of this set is a consequence of the weak*-compactness of the unit ball in the dual space of $C(\Omega)$, the set of all continuous real-valued functions g on Ω with norm $\|g\|_\Omega := \max\{|g(\omega)| : \omega \in \Omega\}$, see [12]. For example, we choose $\Omega = [\omega_1, \omega_2]$, where $0 < \omega_1 < \omega_2$ and $G(\omega)(x, t) = e^{-\omega\|x-t\|^2}$, $x, t \in \mathbb{R}^d$, $\omega \in \Omega$, to obtain *radial kernels*, or $G(\omega)(x, t) = e^{\omega(x,t)}$ to obtain *dot product kernels*. Note that the choice $\Omega = \mathbb{N}_n$ corresponds to the first case.

Next, we establish that if the loss function $Q : \mathbb{R}^m \to \mathbb{R}$ is convex then the functional $Q_\mu : \mathcal{A}_+(\mathcal{X}) \to \mathbb{R}_+$ is convex as well, that is, the variational problem (8) is a *convex optimization problem*. To this end, we recall that the conjugate function of Q, denoted by $Q^* : \mathbb{R}^m \to \mathbb{R} \cup \{+\infty\}$, is defined, for every $v \in \mathbb{R}^m$, as

$$Q^*(v) = \sup\{(w, v) - Q(w) : w \in \mathbb{R}^m\} \tag{10}$$

and it follows, for every $w \in \mathbb{R}^m$, that

$$Q(w) = \sup\{(w, v) - Q^*(v) : v \in \mathbb{R}^m\} \tag{11}$$

see [5]. See also [17] for a nice application of the conjugate function to linear statistical models. For example, for the square loss defined above, the conjugate function is given, for every $v \in \mathbb{R}^m$, by

$$Q^*(v) = \max\left\{(w, v) - \|w - y\|^2 : w \in \mathbb{R}^m\right\} = \frac{1}{4}\|v\|^2 + (y, v).$$

Note that $Q^*(0) = -\inf\{Q(w) : w \in \mathbb{R}^m\} < \infty$ since Q is bounded from below. This observation is used in the proof of the lemma below.

Lemma 2. *If $K \in \mathcal{A}(\mathcal{X})$, $\mathbf{x}$ is a set of m points of $\mathcal{X}$ such that $K_{\mathbf{x}} \in \mathcal{L}_+(\mathbb{R}^m)$ and $Q : \mathbb{R}^m \to \mathbb{R}$ a convex function then there holds the formula*

$$Q_\mu(K) = \max\left\{-\frac{1}{4\mu}(v, K_{\mathbf{x}}v) - Q^*(v) : v \in \mathbb{R}^m\right\}. \tag{12}$$

The fact that the maximum above exists follows from the hypothesis that $K_{\mathbf{x}} \in \mathcal{L}_+(\mathbb{R}^m)$ and the fact that $Q^*(v) \geq -Q(0)$ for all $v \in \mathbb{R}^m$, which follows from equation (10). The proof of the lemma is based on a version of the von Neumann minimax theorem (see the appendix). This lemma implies that the functional $Q_\mu : \mathcal{A}_+(\mathcal{X}) \to \mathbb{R}_+$ is convex. Indeed, equation (12) expresses $Q_\mu(K)$ as the maximum of linear functions in the kernel K.

3   Characterization of an Optimal Kernel

Our discussion in Section 2 establishes that problem (8) reduces to the minimax problem

$$Q_\mu(\mathcal{K}) = -\max\{\min\{R(c, K) : c \in \mathbb{R}^m\} : K \in \mathcal{K}\} \tag{13}$$

where the function R is defined as

$$R(c, K) = \frac{1}{4\mu}(c, K_{\mathbf{x}}c) + Q^*(c), \quad c \in \mathbb{R}^m, \ K \in \mathcal{K}. \tag{14}$$

In this section we show that problem (13) admits a saddle point, that is, the minimum and maximum in (13) can be interchanged and describe the properties of this saddle point. We consider this problem in the general case that $\mathcal{K}$ is induced by a continuous mapping $G : \Omega \to \mathcal{A}_+(\mathcal{X})$ where Ω is a compact Hausdorff space, so we write $\mathcal{K}$ as $\mathcal{K}(G)$, see equation (9).

We assume that the conjugate function is differentiable everywhere and denote the gradient of Q^* at c by $\nabla Q^*(c)$.

Theorem 1. *If Ω is a compact Hausdorff topological space and $G : \Omega \to \mathcal{A}_+(\mathcal{X})$ is continuous then there exists a kernel $\hat{K} = \int_\Omega G(\omega) d\hat{p}(\omega) \in \mathcal{K}(G)$ such that $\hat{p}$ is a discrete probability measure on Ω with at most $m + 1$ atoms and, for any atom $\hat{\omega} \in \Omega$ of $\hat{p}$, we have that*

$$R(\hat{c}, G(\hat{\omega})) = \max\{R(\hat{c}, G(\omega)) : \omega \in \Omega\} \tag{15}$$

where $\hat{c}$ is the unique solution to the equation

$$\frac{1}{2\mu}\hat{K}_{\mathbf{x}}\hat{c} + \nabla Q^*(\hat{c}) = 0. \tag{16}$$

Moreover, for every $c \in \mathbb{R}^m$ and $K \in \mathcal{K}(G)$, we have that

$$R(\hat{c}, K) \le R(\hat{c}, \hat{K}) \le R(c, \hat{K}). \tag{17}$$

Proof. Let us first comment on the nonlinear equation (16). For *any* kernel $K \in \mathcal{K}(G)$ the extremal problem

$$\min\{R(c, K) : c \in \mathbb{R}^m\}$$

has a *unique* solution, since the function $c \mapsto R(c, K)$ is strictly convex and $\lim_{\|c\| \to \infty} R(c, K) = \infty$. Moreover, if we let $c_K \in \mathbb{R}^m$ be the unique minimizer, it solves the equation

$$\frac{1}{2\mu}K_{\mathbf{x}}c_K + \nabla Q^*(c_K) = 0.$$

Hence, equation (16) says that $\hat{c} = c_{\hat{K}}$.

Now let us turn to the existence of the kernel $\hat{K}$ described above. First, we note the immediate fact that

$$\max\{R(c, K) : K \in \mathcal{K}(G)\} = \max\{R(c, G(\omega)) : \omega \in \Omega\}.$$

Next, we define the function $\varphi : \mathbb{R}^m \to \mathbb{R}$ by

$$\varphi(c) := \max\{R(c, G(\omega)) : \omega \in \Omega\}, \quad c \in \mathbb{R}^m.$$

According to the definition of the conjugate function in equation (10) and the hypotheses that G is continuous and $\{G(\omega) : \omega \in \Omega\} \subseteq \mathcal{A}_+(\mathcal{X})$ we see that $\lim_{\|c\| \to \infty} \varphi(c) = \infty$. Hence, φ has a minimum. We call a minimizer $\tilde{c}$. This vector is characterized by the fact that the right directional derivative of φ at $\tilde{c}$ in all directions $d \in \mathbb{R}^m$ is nonnegative. We denote this derivative by $\varphi'_+(\tilde{c}; d)$. Using Lemma 4 in the appendix, we have that

$$\varphi'_+(\tilde{c}; d) = \max\left\{\frac{1}{2\mu}(d, G_{\mathbf{x}}(\omega)\tilde{c}) + (\nabla Q^*(\tilde{c}), d) : \omega \in \Omega^*\right\}$$

where the set Ω^* is defined as

$$\Omega^* := \{\omega : \omega \in \Omega, \ R(\tilde{c}, G(\omega)) = \varphi(\tilde{c})\}.$$

If we define the vectors $z(\omega) = \frac{1}{2\mu} G_{\mathbf{x}}(\omega)\tilde{c} + \nabla Q^*(\tilde{c})$, $\omega \in \Omega^*$, the condition that $\varphi'_+(\tilde{c}; d)$ is nonnegative for all $d \in \mathbb{R}^m$ means that

$$\max\{(z(\omega), d) : \omega \in \Omega^*\} \geq 0, \quad d \in \mathbb{R}^m.$$

Since G is continuous, the set $\mathcal{N} := \{z(\omega) : \omega \in \Omega^*\}$ is a closed subset of $\mathbb{R}^m$. Therefore, its convex hull $\mathcal{M} := co(\mathcal{N})$ is closed as well. We claim that $0 \in \mathcal{M}$. Indeed, if $0 \notin \mathcal{M}$ then there exists a hyperplane $\{c : c \in \mathbb{R}^m, (w, c) + \alpha = 0\}$, $\alpha \in \mathbb{R}$, $w \in \mathbb{R}^m$, which strictly separates 0 from $\mathcal{M}$, that is, $(w, 0) + \alpha > 0$ and $(w, z(\omega)) + \alpha \leq 0$, $\omega \in \Omega^*$, see [12]. The first condition implies that $\alpha > 0$ and, so we conclude that

$$\max\{(w, z(\omega)) : \omega \in \Omega^*\} < 0$$

which contradicts our hypothesis that $\tilde{c}$ is a minimum of φ.

By the Caratheodory theorem, see, for example, [5–Ch. 2], every vector in $\mathcal{M}$ can be expressed as a convex combination of at most $m + 1$ of the vectors in $\mathcal{N}$. In particular, we have that

$$0 = \sum_{j \in \mathbb{N}_{m+1}} \lambda_j z(\omega_j) \tag{18}$$

mm for some $\{\omega_j : j \in \mathbb{N}_{m+1}\} \subseteq \Omega^*$ and nonnegative constants λ_j with $\sum_{j \in \mathbb{N}_{m+1}} \lambda_j = 1$. Setting

$$\hat{K} := \sum_{j \in \mathbb{N}_{m+1}} \lambda_j G(\omega_j) = \int_\Omega G(\omega) d\hat{p}(\omega)$$

where $\hat{p} = \sum_{j \in \mathbb{N}_{m+1}} \lambda_j \delta_{\omega_j}$, (we denote by δ_ω the Dirac measure at ω), we can rewrite equation (18) as

$$\frac{1}{2\mu} \hat{K}_{\mathbf{x}} \tilde{c} + \nabla Q^*(\tilde{c}) = 0.$$

Hence, we conclude that $\tilde{c} = \hat{c}$ which means that

$$\min\{R(c, \hat{K}) : c \in \mathbb{R}^m\} = R(\hat{c}, \hat{K}).$$

This establishes the upper inequality in (17). For the lower inequality we observe that

$$R(\hat{c}, \hat{K}) = \int_\Omega R(\hat{c}, G(\omega)) d\hat{p}(\omega) = \sum_{j \in \mathbb{N}_{m+1}} \lambda_j R(\hat{c}, G(\omega_j)).$$

Since $\hat{c} = \tilde{c}$, we can use the definition of the ω_j to conclude for any $K \in \mathcal{K}(G)$ by equation (18) and the definition of the function φ that

$$R(\hat{c}, \hat{K}) = \varphi(\hat{c}) \geq R(\hat{c}, K). \qquad \square$$

This theorem improves upon our earlier results in [9] where only the square loss function was studied in detail. Generally, not all saddle points $(\hat{c}, \hat{K})$ of R

satisfy the properties stated in Theorem 1. Indeed, a maximizing kernel may be represented as $\hat{K} = \int_{\Omega} G(\omega) d\hat{p}(\omega)$ where $\hat{p}$ may contain more than $m + 1$ atoms or even have uncountable support (note, though, that the proof above provides a procedure for finding a kernel which is the convex combination of at most $m + 1$ kernels). With this caveat in mind, we show below that the conditions stated in Theorem 1 are necessary and sufficient.

Theorem 2. *Let $\hat{c} \in \mathbb{R}^m$ and $\hat{K} = \int_{\Omega} G(\omega) d\hat{p}(\omega)$, where $\hat{p}$ is a probability measure with support $\hat{\Omega} \subseteq \Omega$. The pair $(\hat{c}, \hat{K})$ is a saddle point of problem (13) if and only if $\hat{c}$ solves equation (16) and every $\hat{\omega} \in \hat{\Omega}$ satisfies equation (15).*

Proof. If $(\hat{c}, \hat{K})$ is a saddle point of (13) then $\hat{c}$ is the unique minimizer of the function $R(\cdot, \hat{K})$ and solves equation (16). Moreover, we have that

$$\int_{\hat{\Omega}} R(\hat{c}, G(\omega)) d\hat{p}(\omega) = R(\hat{c}, \hat{K}) = \max\{R(\hat{c}, G(\omega)) : \omega \in \Omega\}$$

implying that equation (15) holds true for every $\hat{\omega} \in \hat{\Omega}$.

On the other hand, if $\hat{c}$ solves equation (16) we obtain the upper inequality in equation (17) whereas equation (15) brings the lower inequality.   □

Theorem 1 can be specified to the case that Ω is a finite set, that is $\mathcal{K} = co(\mathcal{K}_n)$ where $\mathcal{K}_n = \{K_\ell : \ell \in \mathbb{N}_n\}$ is a prescribed set of kernels. Below, we use the notation $K_{\mathbf{x},\ell}$ for the matrix $(K_\ell)_{\mathbf{x}}$.

Corollary 1. *If $\mathcal{K}_n = \{K_j : j \in \mathbb{N}_n\} \subset \mathcal{A}_+(\mathcal{X})$ there exists a kernel $\hat{K} = \sum_{j \in \mathbb{N}_n} \lambda_j K_j \in co(\mathcal{K}_n)$ such that the set $J = \{j : j \in \mathbb{N}_n, \lambda_j > 0\}$ contains at most $\min(m + 1, n)$ elements and, for every $j \in J$ we have that*

$$R(\hat{c}, K_j) = \max\{(R(\hat{c}, K_\ell) : \ell \in \mathbb{N}_n\} \tag{19}$$

where $\hat{c}$ is the unique solution to the equation

$$\frac{1}{2\mu} \hat{K}_{\mathbf{x}} \hat{c} + \nabla Q^*(\hat{c}) = 0. \tag{20}$$

Moreover, for every $c \in \mathbb{R}^m$ and $K \in co(\mathcal{K}_n)$ we have that

$$R(\hat{c}, K) \leq R(\hat{c}, \hat{K}) \leq R(c, \hat{K}). \tag{21}$$

In the important case that $\Omega = [\omega_1, \omega_2]$ for $0 < \omega_1 < \omega_2$ and $G(\omega)$ is a Gaussian kernel, $G(\omega)(x, t) = \exp(-\omega \|x - t\|^2), x, t \in \mathbb{R}^d$, Theorem 1 establishes that a mixture of at most $m + 1$ Gaussian kernels provides an optimal kernel. What happens if we consider all possible Gaussians, that is, take $\Omega = \mathbb{R}_+$? This question is important because Gaussians generate the *whole class of radial kernels*. Indeed, we recall a beautiful result by I.J. Schoenberg [13].

Theorem 3. *Let h be a real-valued function defined on $\mathbb{R}_+$ such that $h(0) = 1$. We form a kernel K on $\mathbb{R}^d \times \mathbb{R}^d$ by setting, for each $x, t \in \mathbb{R}^d$, $K(x, t) =$*

$h(\|x - t\|^2)$. *Then K is positive definite for any d if and only if there is a probability measure p on $\mathbb{R}_+$ such that*

$$K(x,t) = \int_{\mathbb{R}_+} e^{-\omega\|x-t\|^2} dp(\omega), \quad x,t \in \mathbb{R}^d.$$

Note that the set $\mathbb{R}_+$ is *not* compact and the kernel $G(0)$ is not in $\mathcal{A}_+(\mathbb{R}^d)$. Therefore, on both accounts Theorem 1 does not apply in this circumstance. In general, we may overcome this difficulty by a limiting process which can handle kernel maps on *locally compact* Hausdorff spaces. This will lead us to an extension of Theorem 1 where Ω is locally compact. However, we only describe our approach in detail for the Gaussian case and $\Omega = \mathbb{R}_+$. An important ingredient in the discussion presented below is that $G(\infty) = \Delta$, the diagonal kernel. Furthermore, in the statement of the theorem below it is understood that when we say that $\hat{p}$ is a discrete probability measure on $\mathbb{R}_+$ we mean that $\hat{p}$ can have an atom not only at zero but also at infinity. Therefore, we can integrate any function relative to such a discrete measure over the extended positive real line provided such a function is defined therein.

Theorem 4. *Let $G : \mathbb{R}_+ \to \mathcal{A}(\mathcal{X})$ be defined as*

$$G(\omega)(x,t) = e^{-\omega\|x-t\|^2}, \quad x,t \in \mathbb{R}^d, \ \omega \in \mathbb{R}_+.$$

Then there exists a kernel $\hat{K} = \int_{\mathbb{R}_+} G(\omega)d\hat{p}(\omega) \in \mathcal{K}(G)$ such that $\hat{p}$ is a discrete probability measure on $\mathbb{R}_+$ with at most $m+1$ atoms and, for any atom $\hat{\omega} \in \mathbb{R}_+$ of $\hat{p}$, we have that

$$R(\hat{c}, G(\hat{\omega})) = \max\{R(\hat{c}, G(\omega)) : \omega \in \mathbb{R}_+\} \tag{22}$$

where $\hat{c}$ is a solution to the equation

$$\frac{1}{2\mu}\hat{K}_{\mathbf{x}}\hat{c} + \nabla Q^*(\hat{c}) = 0 \tag{23}$$

and the function Q^* is continuously differentiable. Moreover, for every $c \in \mathbb{R}^m$ and $K \in \mathcal{K}(G)$, we have that

$$R(\hat{c}, K) \leq R(\hat{c}, \hat{K}) \leq R(c, \hat{K}). \tag{24}$$

Proof. For every $\ell \in \mathbb{N}$ we consider the Gaussian kernel map on the interval $\Omega_\ell := [\ell^{-1}, \ell]$ and appeal to Theorem 1 to produce a sequence of kernels $\hat{K}_\ell = \int_{\Omega_\ell} G(\omega)d\hat{p}_\ell(\omega)$ and $\hat{c}_\ell \in \mathbb{R}^m$ with the properties described there. In particular, $\hat{p}_\ell$ is a discrete probability measure with at most $m+1$ atoms, a number *independent* of ℓ. Let us examine what may happen as ℓ tends towards infinity. Each of the atoms of $\hat{p}_\ell$ as well as their corresponding weights have subsequences which converge. Some atoms may converge to zero while others to infinity. In either case, the Gaussian kernel map *approaches a limit*. Therefore, we can extract a convergent subsequence $\{\hat{p}_{n_\ell} : \ell \in \mathbb{N}\}$ of probability measures and kernels $\{\hat{K}_{n_\ell} : \ell \in \mathbb{N}\}$ such that $\lim_{\ell \to \infty} \hat{p}_{n_\ell} = \hat{p}$, $\lim_{\ell \to \infty} \hat{K}_{n_\ell} = \hat{K}$, and $\hat{K} = \int_{\mathbb{R}_+} G(\omega) d\hat{p}(\omega)$ with the provision that $\hat{p}$ may have atoms at either zero or infinity. In either case, we replace the Gaussian by its limit, namely $G(0)$, the identically one kernel, or $G(\infty)$, the delta kernel, in the integral which defines $\hat{K}$.

To establish that $\hat{K}$ is an optimal kernel, we turn our attention to the sequence of vectors $\hat{c}_{n_\ell}$. We claim that this sequence also has a convergent subsequence. Indeed, from equation (17) for every $K = \int_{\Omega_\ell} G(\omega) dp(\omega)$, $p \in \mathcal{P}(\Omega_\ell)$ we have that

$$R(\hat{c}_{n_\ell}, K) \leq R(0, \hat{K}_{n_\ell}) = Q^*(0) < \infty.$$

Using the fact that the function Q^* is bounded below (see our comments after the proof of Lemma 2) we see that the sequence $\hat{c}_{n_\ell}$ has Euclidean norm bounded independently of ℓ. Hence, it has a convergent subsequence whose limit we call $\hat{c}$. Passing to the limit we obtain equations (23) and (24) and, so, conclude that $(\hat{c}, \hat{K})$ is a saddle point. □

We remark that extensions of the results in this section also hold true for non-differentiable convex functions Q. The proofs presented above must be modified in this general case in detail but not in substance. We postpone the discussion of this issue to a future occasion.

4   A Greedy Algorithm for Learning the Kernel

The analysis in the previous section establishes necessary and sufficient conditions for a pair $(\hat{c}, \hat{K}) \in \mathbb{R}^m \times \mathcal{K}(G)$ to be a saddle point of the problem

$$-Q_\mu(G) := \max \{\min \{R(c, K) : c \in \mathbb{R}^m\} : K \in \mathcal{K}(G)\}.$$

The main step in this problem is to compute the optimal kernel $\hat{K}$. Indeed, once $\hat{K}$ has been computed, $\hat{c}$ is obtained as the unique solution c_K to the equation

$$\frac{1}{2\mu} K_{\mathbf{x}} c_K + \nabla Q^*(c_K) = 0 \tag{25}$$

for $K = \hat{K}$.

With this observation in mind, in this section we focus on the computational issues for the problem

$$-Q_\mu(G) = \max\{g(K) : K \in \mathcal{K}(G)\} \tag{26}$$

where the function $g : \mathcal{A}_+(\mathcal{X}) \to \mathbb{R}$ is defined as

$$g(K) := \min \{R(c, K) : c \in \mathbb{R}^m\}, \quad K \in \mathcal{A}_+(\mathcal{X}). \tag{27}$$

We present a greedy algorithm for learning an optimal kernel. The algorithm starts with an initial kernel $K^{(1)} \in \mathcal{K}(G)$ and computes iteratively a sequence of kernels $K^{(t)} \in \mathcal{K}(G)$ such that

$$g(K^{(1)}) < g(K^{(2)}) < \cdots < g(K^{(s)}) \tag{28}$$

Initialization: Choose $K^{(1)} \in \mathcal{K}(G)$
For $t = 1$ to T:

1. Compute $c^{(t)} = \text{argmin}\{R(c, K^{(t)}) : c \in \mathbb{R}^m\}$ using equation (25)
2. Find $\hat{\omega} \in \Omega : (c^{(t)}, G_\mathbf{x}(\hat{\omega})c^{(t)}) > (c^{(t)}, K_\mathbf{x}^{(t)}c^{(t)})$. If such $\hat{\omega}$ does not exist terminate
3. Compute $\hat{\lambda} = \text{argmax}\{g(\lambda G(\hat{\omega}) + (1-\lambda)K^{(t)}) : \lambda \in (0,1]\}$
4. Set $K^{(t+1)} = \hat{\lambda}G(\hat{\omega}) + (1-\hat{\lambda})K^{(t)}$

Fig. 1. Algorithm to compute an optimal convex combination of kernels in the set $\{G(\omega) : \omega \in \Omega\}$

where s is the number of iterations. At each iteration t, $1 \le t \le s$, the algorithm searches for a value $\hat{\omega} \in \Omega$, if any, such that

$$(c^{(t)}, G_\mathbf{x}(\hat{\omega})c^{(t)}) > (c^{(t)}, K_\mathbf{x}^{(t)}c^{(t)}) \tag{29}$$

where we have defined $c^{(t)} := c_{K^{(t)}}$. If such $\hat{\omega}$ is found then a new kernel $K^{(t+1)}$ is computed to be the optimal convex combination of the kernels $G(\hat{\omega})$ and $K^{(t)}$, that is,

$$g(K^{(t+1)}) = \max\left\{g(\lambda G(\hat{\omega}) + (1-\lambda)K^{(t)}) : \lambda \in [0,1]\right\}. \tag{30}$$

If no $\hat{\omega} \in \Omega$ satisfying inequality (29) can be found, the algorithm terminates. The algorithm is summarized in Figure 1.

Step 2 of the algorithm is implemented with a local gradient ascent in Ω. If the value of ω found locally does not satisfy inequality (29), the smallest hyperrectangle containing the search path is removed and a new local search is started in the yet unsearched part of Ω, continuing in this way until either the whole of Ω is covered or inequality (29) is satisfied. Although in the experiments below we will apply this strategy when Ω is an interval, it also naturally applies to more complex parameter spaces, for example a compact set in a Euclidean space. Step 3 is a simple maximization problem which we solve using Newton method, since the function $g(\lambda G(\hat{\omega}) + (1 - \lambda)K^{(t)})$ is concave in λ and its derivative can be computed by applying Lemma 4. We also use a tolerance parameter ϵ to enforce a non-zero gap in inequality (29). A version of this algorithm for the case when $\Omega = \mathbb{N}_n$ has also been implemented (below, we refer to this version as the "finite algorithm"). It only differs from the continuous version in Step 2, in that inequality (29) is tested by trial and error on randomly selected kernels from $\mathcal{K}_n$.

We now show that after each iteration, either the objective function g increases or the algorithm terminates, that is, inequality (28) holds true. To this end, we state the following lemma whose proof follows immediately from Theorem 2.

Lemma 3. *Let $K_1, K_2 \in \mathcal{A}_+(\mathcal{X})$. Then, $\lambda = 0$ is not a solution to the problem*

$$\max\{g(\lambda K_1 + (1-\lambda)K_2) : \lambda \in [0,1]\}$$

if and only if $R(c_{K_2}, K_1) > R(c_{K_2}, K_2)$.

Applying this lemma to the case that $K_1 = G(\hat{\omega})$ and $K_2 = K^{(t)}$ we conclude that

$$g(K^{(t+1)}) > g(K^{(t)})$$

if and only if $\hat{\omega}$ satisfies the inequality

$$R(c^{(t)}, G(\hat{\omega})) > R(c^{(t)}, K^{(t)})$$

which is equivalent to inequality (29).

4.1   Experimental Validation

We have tested the above algorithm on eight handwritten digit recognition tasks of varying difficulty from the MNIST data-set[1]. The data are 28×28 images with pixel values ranging between 0 and 255. We used Gaussian kernels as the basic kernels, that is, $G(\sigma)(x,t) = \exp(-\|x-t\|^2/\sigma^2)$, $\sigma \in [\sigma_1, \sigma_2]$. In all the experiments, the test error rates were measured over 1000 points from the MNIST test set.

The continuous and finite algorithms were trained using the square loss and compared to an SVM[2]. In all experiments, the training set consisted of 500 points. For the finite case, we chose ten Gaussian kernels with σ's equally spaced in an interval $[\sigma_1, \sigma_2]$. For both versions of our algorithm, the starting value of the kernel was the average of these ten kernels and the regularization parameter was set to 10^{-7}. This value typically provided the best test performance among the nine values $\mu = 10^{-\ell}$, $\ell \in \{3, \ldots, 11\}$. The performance of the SVM was obtained as the best among the results for the above ten kernels and nine values of μ. This strategy slightly favors the SVM but compensates for the fact that the loss functions are different. The parameters ϵ and T of our algorithm were chosen to be 10^{-3} and 100 respectively.

Table 1 shows the results obtained. The range of σ is $[75, 25000]$ in columns 2–4, $[100, 10000]$ in columns 5–7 and $[500, 5000]$ in columns 8–10. Note that, in most cases, the continuous algorithm finds a better combination of kernels than the finite version. In general, the continuous algorithm performs better than the SVM, whereas most of the time the finite algorithm is worse than the SVM. Moreover, the results indicate that the continuous algorithm *is not affected by the range of* σ, unlike the other two methods.

Typically, the continuous algorithm requires less than 20 iterations to terminate whereas the finite algorithm may require as much as 100 iterations. Figure 2 depicts the convergence behavior of the continuous algorithm on two different tasks. In both cases $\sigma \in [100, 10000]$. The actual values of Q_μ are six orders of magnitude smaller, but they were rescaled to fit the plot. Note that, in agreement with inequality (28), Q_μ decreases and eventually converges. The misclassification error also converges to a lower value, indicating that Q_μ provides a good learning criterion.

---

[1] Available at: http://yann.lecun.com/exdb/mnist/index.html
[2] Trained using SVM-light, see: http://www.cs.cornell.edu/People/tj/svm_light

Table 1. Misclassification error percentage for the continuous and finite versions of the algorithm and the SVM on different handwritten digit recognition tasks. See text for description

Task \ Method	Cont.	Finite	SVM	Cont.	Finite	SVM	Cont.	Finite	SVM
	$\sigma \in [75, 25000]$			$\sigma \in [100, 10000]$			$\sigma \in [500, 5000]$		
odd vs. even	6.6	18.0	11.8	6.6	10.9	8.6	6.5	6.7	6.9
3 vs. 8	3.8	6.9	6.0	3.8	4.9	5.1	3.8	3.7	3.8
4 vs. 7	2.5	4.2	2.8	2.5	2.7	2.6	2.5	2.6	2.3
1 vs. 7	1.8	3.9	1.8	1.8	1.8	1.8	1.8	1.9	1.8
2 vs. 3	1.6	3.9	3.1	1.6	2.8	2.3	1.6	1.7	1.6
0 vs. 6	1.6	2.2	1.7	1.6	1.7	1.5	1.6	1.6	1.5
2 vs. 9	1.5	3.2	1.9	1.5	1.9	1.8	1.5	1.4	1.4
0 vs. 9	0.9	1.2	1.1	0.9	1.0	1.0	0.9	0.9	1.0

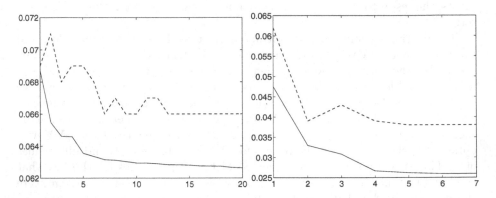

Fig. 2. Functional Q_μ (*solid line*) and misclassification error (*dotted line*) after the first iteration of the algorithm of Figure 1 for even vs. odd (*left*) and 3 vs. 8 (*right*)

5   Conclusion

We have studied the problem of learning a kernel which minimizes a convex error functional over the convex hull of prescribed basic kernels. The main contribution of this paper is a general analysis of this problem when the basic kernels are continuously parameterized by a compact set. In particular, we have shown that there always exists an optimal kernel which is a finite combination of the basic kernels and presented a greedy algorithm for learning a suboptimal kernel. The algorithm is simple to use and our preliminary findings indicate that it typically converges in a small number of iterations to a kernel with a competitive statistical performance. In the future we shall investigate the convergence properties of the algorithm, compare it experimentally to previous related methods for learning the kernel, such as those in [3, 6, 8], and study generalization error bounds for this problem. For the latter purpose, the results in [4, 18] may be useful.

References

1. N. Aronszajn. Theory of reproducing kernels. *Trans. Amer. Math. Soc.*, 686, pp. 337–404, 1950.
2. J.P. Aubin. *Mathematical Methods of Game and Economic Theory.* Studies in Mathematics and its applications, Vol. 7, North-Holland, 1982.
3. F.R. Bach, G.R.G Lanckriet and M.I. Jordan. Multiple kernels learning, conic duality, and the SMO algorithm. *Proc. of the Int. Conf. on Machine Learning*, 2004.
4. O. Bousquet and D.J.L. Herrmann. On the complexity of learning the kernel matrix. *Advances in Neural Information Processing Systems*, 15, 2003.
5. J.M. Borwein and A.S. Lewis. *Convex Analysis and Nonlinear Optimization. Theory and Examples.* CMS (Canadian Math. Soc.) Springer-Verlag, New York, 2000.
6. O. Chapelle, V.N. Vapnik, O. Bousquet and S. Mukherjee. Choosing multiple parameters for support vector machines. *Machine Learning*, 46(1), pp. 131–159, 2002.
7. M. Herbster. Relative Loss Bounds and Polynomial-time Predictions for the K-LMS-NET Algorithm. *Proc. of the 15-th Int. Conference on Algorithmic Learning Theory*, October 2004.
8. G.R.G. Lanckriet, N. Cristianini, P. Bartlett, L. El Ghaoui and M.I. Jordan. Learning the kernel matrix with semi-definite programming. *J. of Machine Learning Research*, 5, pp. 27–72, 2004.
9. C.A. Micchelli and M. Pontil. Learning the kernel function via regularization. To appear in *J. of Machine Learning Research* (see also Research Note RN/04/11, Department of Computer Science, UCL, June 2004)..
10. C. A. Micchelli and T. J. Rivlin. Lectures on optimal recovery. In Lecture Notes in Mathematics, Vol. 1129, P. R. Turner (Ed.), Springer Verlag, 1985.
11. C.S. Ong, A.J. Smola, and R.C. Williamson. Hyperkernels. *Advances in Neural Information Processing Systems*, 15, S. Becker, S. Thrun, K. Obermayer (Eds.), MIT Press, Cambridge, MA, 2003.
12. H.L. Royden. *Real Analysis.* Macmillan Publ. Company, New York, 3rd ed., 1988.
13. I.J. Schoenberg. Metric spaces and completely monotone functions. *Annals of Mathematics*, 39, pp. 811–841, 1938.
14. J. Shawe-Taylor and N. Cristianini. *Kernel Methods for Pattern Analysis.* Cambridge University Press, 2004.
15. V.N. Vapnik. *Statistical Learning Theory.* Wiley, New York, 1998.
16. G. Wahba. *Spline Models for Observational Data.* Series in Applied Mathematics, Vol. 59, SIAM, Philadelphia, 1990.
17. T. Zhang. On the dual formulation of regularized linear systems with convex risks. *Machine Learning*, 46, pp. 91–129, 2002.
18. Q. Wu, Y. Ying and D.X. Zhou. Multi-kernel regularization classifiers. *Preprint*, City University of Hong Kong, 2004.

A   Appendix

The first result we record here is a useful version of the classical von Neumann minimax theorem we have learned from [2–Ch. 7].

Theorem 5. *Let* $h : A \times B \to \mathbb{R}$ *where* A *is a closed convex subset of a Hausdorff topological vector space* X *and* B *is a convex subset of a vector space* Y*. If the function* $x \mapsto h(x, y)$ *is convex and lower semi-continuous for every* $y \in B$*, the function* $y \mapsto h(x, y)$ *is concave for every* $x \in A$ *and there exists a* $y_0 \in B$ *such that for all* $\lambda \in \mathbb{R}$ *the set* $\{x : x \in A, \, h(x, y_0) \leq \lambda\}$ *is compact then there is an* $x_0 \in A$ *such that*

$$\sup\{h(x_0, y) : y \in B\} = \sup\{\inf\{h(x, y) : x \in A\} : y \in B\}.$$

In particular, we have that

$$\min\{\sup\{h(x, y) : y \in B\} : x \in A\} = \sup\{\inf\{h(x, y) : x \in A\} : y \in B\}. \quad (31)$$

The hypothesis of lower semi-continuity means, for all $\lambda \in \mathbb{R}$ and $y \in B$, that the set $\{x : x \in A, \, h(x, y) \leq \lambda\}$ is a closed subset of A.

The next result concerns differentiation of a "max" function. Its proof can be found in [9].

Lemma 4. *Let* X *be a topological vector space,* T *a compact set and* $G(t, x)$ *a real-valued function on* $T \times X$ *such that, for every* $x \in X$ $G(\cdot, x)$ *is continuous on* T *and, for every* $t \in T$*,* $G(t, \cdot)$ *is convex on* X*. We define the real-valued convex function* g *on* X *as*

$$g(x) := \max\{G(t, x) : t \in T\}, \quad x \in X$$

and the set $M(x) := \{t : t \in T, G(t, x) = g(x)\}$*. Then the right derivative of* g *in the direction* $y \in X$ *is given by*

$$g'_+(x, y) = \max\{G'_+(t, x, y) : t \in M(x)\}$$

where $G'_+(t, x, y)$ *is the right derivative of* G *with respect to its second argument in the direction* y*.*

Proof of Lemma 2. Theorem 5 applies since $K_{\mathbf{x}} \in \mathcal{L}_+(\mathbb{R}^m)$. Indeed, we let $h(c, v) = (K_{\mathbf{x}}c, v) - Q^*(v) + \mu(c, K_{\mathbf{x}}c)$, $A = \mathbb{R}^m$, $B = \{v : Q^*(v) < \infty, v \in \mathbb{R}^m\}$ and $v_0 = 0$. Then, B is convex and, for any $\lambda \in \mathbb{R}$, the set $\{c : c \in \mathbb{R}^m, h(c, v_0) \leq \lambda\}$ is compact. Therefore, all the hypotheses of Theorem 5 hold. Consequently, using (11) in (7) we have that

$$Q_\mu(K) = \sup\{\min\{(K_{\mathbf{x}}c, v) - Q^*(v) + \mu(c, K_{\mathbf{x}}c) : c \in \mathbb{R}^m\} : v \in B\}. \quad (32)$$

For each $v \in B$, the minimum over c satisfies the equation $K_{\mathbf{x}}v + 2\mu K_{\mathbf{x}}c = 0$, implying that

$$\min\{(K_{\mathbf{x}}c, v) - Q^*(v) + \mu(c, K_{\mathbf{x}}c) : c \in \mathbb{R}^m\} = -\frac{(v, K_{\mathbf{x}}v)}{4\mu} - Q^*(v)$$

and the result follows. $\qquad\qquad\qquad\qquad\qquad\qquad\qquad\qquad\qquad\qquad\square$

On the Limitations of Embedding Methods

Shahar Mendelson

Centre for Mathematics and its Applications,
The Australian National University, Canberra,
ACT 0200, Australia
shahar.mendelson@anu.edu.au

Abstract. We show that for any class of functions H which has a reasonable combinatorial dimension, the vast majority of small subsets of the combinatorial cube can not be represented as a Lipschitz image of a subset of H, unless the Lipschitz constant is very large. We apply this result to the case when H consists of linear functionals of norm at most one on a Hilbert space, and thus show that "most" classification problems can not be represented as a reasonable Lipschitz loss of a kernel class.

1 Introduction

The aim of this article is to investigate the limitations of embedding methods (or, as we prefer to call them here, representation methods), which are commonly used in Machine Learning. Our focus is not on the statistical side, but rather on the degree by which embedding methods can be used to approximate subsets of the combinatorial cube. To be more precise, consider a class of functions H, which we call the *base class*, defined on a metric space (Ω, d_Ω), and let ϕ be a Lipschitz function with a Lipschitz constant at most L. One can represent a subset $A \subset \{-1, 1\}^n$ in H using ϕ if there are $t_1, ..., t_n \in \Omega$, such that for every $v \in A$ there is some $h_v \in H$ for which $\phi(h_v(t_j)) = v(j)$, where $v(j)$ is the j-th coordinate of v. Hence, if this is the case, we were able to represent A as a Lipschitz image (with constant at most L) of a subset of H.

In the context of Learning Theory, one should think of ϕ as a loss functional, and the question we wish to focus on is which classification problems (each problem corresponds to a subset of the combinatorial cube) can be represented in a useful manner. One could view the representation as a richness parameter of subsets of the cube. If a subset is a Lipschitz image of a subset of H (i.e. a loss class associated with a subset of H), it has to be simple.

Having this in mind, it seems likely that for a representation to be useful one needs two key ingredients. First of all, the class H has to be simple and canonical in some sense - otherwise, there is no point in using it. The second is that the Lipschitz constant of ϕ is not "too large"; if it is, the distortion caused by ϕ might make the image very rich, even if H is simple.

P. Auer and R. Meir (Eds.): COLT 2005, LNAI 3559, pp. 353–365, 2005.

The natural example in this context is margin based classifiers. For every $\gamma > 0$, define the γ margin function (which has a Lipschitz constant of $1/\gamma$) as

$$\phi_\gamma(t) = \begin{cases} 1 & \text{if } t \geq \gamma, \\ \frac{t}{\gamma} & \text{if } -\gamma < t < \gamma, \\ -1 & \text{if } t \leq -\gamma. \end{cases}$$

The base class H consists of linear functionals of norm one on a Hilbert space and ϕ is generated by the desired margin. Our question in this restricted setup is as follows.

Question 1. *Set B_{ℓ_2} to be the unit ball in the Hilbert space ℓ_2. Let $A \subset \{-1,1\}^n$, $|A| = N$ (representing a classification problem), and let $\gamma > 0$. Can one find $x_1, ..., x_n \in B_{\ell_2}$ and $x_1^*, ..., x_N^* \in B_{\ell_2}$ such that for every i, j, $x_i^*(x_j) \geq \gamma$ if $a_i(j) = 1$ and $x_i^*(x_j) \leq -\gamma$ if $a_i(j) = -1$, where $a_i(j)$ is the j-th component of the i-th element of A?*

The original motivation for this study was to understand whether embedding (or kernel) techniques using the margin or a more general loss functional could serve as a generic method in Learning Theory.

Roughly speaking, in kernel methods one embeds Ω in the unit ball of a Hilbert space using the feature map, and considers the set of linear functionals in the dual unit ball as the class of functions H. It is therefore natural to ask (though, unfortunately, this question has never been studied extensively) which classification problems can be captured as a margin loss of a kernel. Of course, a small Lipschitz constant of ϕ is translated to a large margin.

The first result (at least as far as this author is aware of) that showed the limitations of kernel methods in the context of Question 1 is due to Ben-David, Eiron and Simon [2]. They proved the remarkable fact that for every n, the vast majority of subsets of $\{-1,1\}^n$ with n elements and VC dimension at most d can not be represented for a nontrivial γ in ℓ_2. To be exact, the authors showed that for a fixed d, only a vanishing fraction (at most $\sim 2^{-cn}$) of such subsets can be represented in ℓ_2 with a margin better than $1/n^\alpha$, where $\alpha = 1/2 - 1/2d - 1/2^{d-1}$. It is easy to check that $\{-1,1\}^n$ itself is represented in ℓ_2 for $\gamma = 1/\sqrt{n}$; thus, most of the small subsets of $\{-1,1\}^n$ in the sense of VC theory are not an image of a kernel class with the margin loss - unless the margin is extremely small, i.e., close to the scale at which the entire cube is represented in ℓ_2.

The basis for this result and for others of the same flavour [4,6,9] has to do with incompatibility of structures. On one hand, one selects H to have a simple structure. On the other, there are various notions of simplicity for subsets of the combinatorial cube. Representation methods are an attempt of imposing one structure on the other. For example, the hope that kernel methods are universal in some sense, means that every reasonable classification problem (e.g. a subset of the combinatorial cube with a small VC dimension) can be represented as a reasonable Lipschitz image of a class of linear functionals. Unfortunately, it turns out that this is impossible unless the subset of the cube has a very special structure.

Not only is it impossible to find such a linear structure in most small subsets of the cube, we show here that the situation is equally bad even if one replaces the kernel class with any other simple class H. It turns out that unless H itself contains a large "cubic" structure, (and in which case, H is no longer simple), the vast majority of small subsets of the combinatorial cube are not a reasonable Lipschitz image of a subset of H. Our aim is to find the quantitative connection between the "richness" of the set H, the Lipschitz constant of the "loss" ϕ and the number of subsets of the cube that one can reconstruct using H and ϕ with such a Lipschitz constant. The richness parameter we use for H is a variant of the combinatorial dimension, and was introduced by Pajor in [11].

Definition 1. *We say that $\{t_1, ..., t_n\}$ is ε P-shattered by H if there are sets $V_+, V_- \subset \mathbb{R}$ satisfying $d(V_+, V_-) \geq \varepsilon$, such that for every $J \subset \{1, ..., n\}$ there is $h_J \in H$ for which $h_J(t_j) \in V_+$ if $j \in J$ and $h_J(t_j) \in V_-$ otherwise. We denote by $P - VC(H, \varepsilon)$ the largest cardinality of a set which is ε P-shattered by H.*

Note that this definition extends the notion of level shattering, in which $V_+ = [\alpha + \varepsilon, \infty)$ and $V_- = (-\infty, \alpha - \varepsilon]$ for some fixed α.

Here, we denote by $VC(H, \varepsilon)$ the combinatorial dimension (also known in Learning Theory literature as the *fat-shattering* dimension) of the class H at level ε.

To compare the notion of P-shattering with the standard combinatorial dimension, let us recall the definition of packing and covering numbers, which will be required throughout this article.

Definition 2. *If (Y, d) is a metric space and $K \subset Y$, then for every $\varepsilon > 0$, $N(\varepsilon, K, d)$ is the minimal number of open balls (with respect to the metric d) needed to cover K.*

A set is ε-separated with respect to a metric d if the distance between every two distinct points in the set is larger than ε. We denote the maximal cardinality of an ε-separated subset of Y by $D(\varepsilon, Y, d)$.

It is possible to show [7] that if H is a class of functions bounded by 1 then for any probability measure μ,

$$D(\varepsilon, H, L_2(\mu)) \leq \left(\frac{2}{\varepsilon}\right)^{K \cdot VC(H, c\varepsilon)}, \qquad (1.1)$$

where K and c are absolute constants.

Assume that H consists of functions bounded by 1. Then, one can verify (see the proof of Theorem 4) that if $\{t_1, ..., t_n\}$ is ε P-shattered, there is a set $H' \subset H$, $|H'| \geq 2^{cn}$ which is $\varepsilon/4$-separated in $L_2(\mu_n)$, where μ_n is the empirical measure supported on $\{t_1, ..., t_n\}$. Hence, by (1.1),

$$cn \leq \log D\left(\varepsilon/4, H, L_2(\mu_n)\right) \leq K \cdot VC(H, c'\varepsilon) \log\left(\frac{2}{\varepsilon}\right),$$

implying that for any $\varepsilon < 1$

$$P - VC(H, \varepsilon) \leq K \cdot VC(H, c\varepsilon) \log \left(\frac{2}{\varepsilon} \right),$$

for suitable absolute constants K and c.

In the reverse direction, if H is a convex and symmetric class of functions (that is, if the fact that $f \in H$ implies that $-f \in H$), then for any $\varepsilon > 0$, $VC(H, \varepsilon) \leq P - VC(H, \varepsilon)$. Indeed, in this case the combinatorial dimension can be attained by taking the fixed levels $\alpha_i = 0$ (see, e.g. [8]), and thus if a set is ε-shattered, it is also ε P-shattered.

The main result we present here connects the P-dimension of the base class H with the ability to represent "many" subsets of $\{-1, 1\}^n$ as a Lipschitz image of that class, using a function with a small Lipschitz constant. The notion of representation we focus on here is rather weak, and originated from the *soft margin*.

Definition 3. *Let H be a class of functions on Ω, and set $1/2 < \delta \leq 1$. If A is a subset of $\{-1, 1\}^n$, $|A| = N$, we say that A can be (L, δ) weakly represented in H if there are $x_1, ..., x_n \in \Omega$, $h_1, ...h_N \in H$ and $\phi : \mathbb{R} \to \mathbb{R}$ such that*

1. *$\|\phi\|_{lip} \leq L$, and*
2. *for every $1 \leq i \leq N$ there is a set $J_i \subset \{1, ..., n\}$ of cardinality $|J_i| \geq \delta n$, and for every i and $j \in J_i$, $\phi(h_i(x_j)) = a_i(j)$, where $a_i(j)$ is the j-th component of the i-th element in A.*

To formulate our main result, let (Ω^n, d_n) be the n product of Ω endowed with the metric

$$d_n(u, v) = \frac{1}{n} \sup_{h \in H} \sum_{i=1}^{n} |h(u_i) - h(v_i)|,$$

where $u = (u_1, ..., u_n)$, $v = (v_1, ..., v_n)$ and $u_i, v_i \in \Omega$. For every integer $N \leq 2^n$, the probability measure we use on the subsets of $\{-1, 1\}^n$ of cardinality N is the counting probability measure.

Theorem 1. *There exist absolute constants k and k', and for every $1/2 < \delta \leq 1$ there are constants $c(\delta), c'(\delta), c''(\delta)$ and $n_0(\delta)$ depending only on δ for which the following holds. Let H be a class of functions on Ω which are bounded by 1. For every $L > 0$, if $n \geq n_0(\delta)$, $P - VC(H, k/L) \leq c(\delta)n$ and*

$$N \geq c(\delta) \max \left\{ \frac{k'L}{n}, \frac{\log N(c'(\delta)/L, \Omega^n, d_n)}{n} \right\},$$

then with probability at least $1 - \exp(-c''(\delta)Nn)$, a set $A \subset \{-1, 1\}^n$ of cardinality N is not (L, δ) weakly represented in H.

The main novelty in Theorem 1, compared with results of a similar flavour (see, for example, [2, 4, 6, 9]), is in its nonlinear nature. Although its proof uses essentially the same ideas as in [9], what we do here goes beyond the situation where H is a class of linear functionals, which was studied in [9]. It also allows us to improve the best known estimates in what is arguably the most important case - when $H = B_{\ell_2}$.

In Section 3 we will present a detailed survey of the known estimates when $H = B_{\ell_2}$, but for now, let us formulate.

Corollary 1. *Let $H = B_{\ell_2}$, considered as a set of linear functionals on $\Omega = B_{\ell_2}$. For any $1/2 < \delta \leq 1$, if $n \geq n_0(\delta)$ and $N \geq c(\delta)n$, then with probability at least $1 - \exp(-c''(\delta)Nn)$, $A \subset \{-1,1\}^n$ with $|A| = N$ is not $(c'(\delta)\sqrt{n}, \delta)$ weakly represented in H.*

To put Corollary 1 in the right perspective, $\{-1,1\}^n$ itself is represented in B_{ℓ_2} with a constant $\sqrt{n}$. And, in fact, one can use the margin function $\phi_{1/\sqrt{n}}$ for the representation. However, by Corollary 1, for any $1/2 < \delta \leq 1$ and a slightly smaller constant (which depends on δ), the vast majority of even the very small subsets of $\{-1,1\}^n$ are not weakly represented in B_{ℓ_2}.

The rest of this article is devoted to the proofs of Theorem 1 and Corollary 1. Although it is possible to find truly nonlinear applications, (for example, when H is the set of Lipschitz functions with constant 1 on the unit ball in $\mathbb{R}^d$), we decided not to present them here, as they involve routine estimates.

We end the introduction with a notational convention. Throughout, all absolute constants are denoted by c or k. Their values may change from line to line or even within the same line. $C(\varphi)$ denotes constants which depend only on the parameter φ. For a set A, let $|A|$ be its cardinality and if A, B are subsets of a vector space, put $A + B = \{a + b | a \in A, \, b \in B\}$.

2   Proof of Theorem 1

The first step in the proof of Theorem 1 is a covering argument. Here, one shows that is suffices to control a fine enough net in (Ω^n, d_n) and a finite set of Lipschitz functions.

2.1   Covering

We shall construct a finite approximating set to the set of all "meaningful" Lipschitz functions $\phi : \mathbb{R} \to \mathbb{R}$ and all possible elements $x = (x_1, ..., x_n) \in \Omega^n$ that can be used in an (L, δ) weak representation. Since H consists of functions which are bounded by 1, it is enough to consider Lipschitz functions ϕ that map $[-1,1]$ to $[-1,1]$. Indeed, if the range of ϕ exceeds $[-1,1]$, it is possible to compose it with the retraction onto $[-1,1]$ without increasing the Lipschitz constant. For every fixed L one can identify each "legal" ϕ with the pair of nonempty subsets of $[-1,1]$, $W_+ = \{t \,|\phi(t) = 1\}$ and $W_- = \{t \,|\phi(t) = -1\}$, such that $d(W_+, W_-) > 2/L \equiv \gamma$. Divide the interval $[-1,1]$ to intervals with disjoint interiors $Y_i = [a_i, b_i]$, where $b_i = a_{i+1}$, and each Y_i has length at most $\gamma/10$. One can find such decomposition with at most cL intervals Y_i for some absolute constant c.

Recall that $A + B = \{a + b : a \in A, \, b \in B\}$, and for every ϕ, define ϕ' as follows. If Y_i intersects $W_+ + (-\gamma/100, \gamma/100)$ then $\phi' = 1$ on that set, and if it intersects $W_- + (-\gamma/100, \gamma/100)$ it is -1 on that set. On the complement, which is a finite union of intervals, define ϕ' as the linear interpolation of the boundary values at each interval. Clearly, $W_+ \subset \{\phi' = 1\}$, $W_- \subset \{\phi' = -1\}$, $\|\phi'\|_{lip} < cL$, and there are at most 3^{cL} different functions ϕ'. Denote this set of functions by Φ' and let $D_n(\varepsilon)$ be an ε cover of (Ω^n, d_n).

Lemma 1. *There exists an absolute constant k and for every $1/2 < \delta \leq 1$ there is a constant $k'(\delta)$ for which the following holds. Let $A \subset \{-1, 1\}^n$ and assume that $x = (x_1, ..., x_n) \in \Omega^n$ and ϕ can be used in an (L, δ) representation of A. If δ' satisfies $\delta' - 1/2 = (\delta - 1/2)/2$, then there are $y = (y_1, ..., y_n) \in D_n(k'(\delta)/L)$ and $\phi' \in \Phi'$ which can be used to (kL, δ') weakly represent A.*

Proof. Let $\rho > 0$ be a constant which will be specified later, set ϕ' to be as above, and put y such that $d_n(x, y) \leq \rho\gamma$ for $\gamma = 2/L$. By the definition of d_n, $\sup_{h \in H} \sum_{i=1}^{n} |h(x_i) - h(y_i)| < \rho\gamma n$. Thus, for any ρ and every $h \in H$ there is a set $J_h \subset \{1, ..., n\}$, $|J_h| \geq (1 - 1000\rho)n$, such that on J_h, $|h(x_i) - h(y_i)| < \gamma/1000$. Note that by the definition of ϕ', if $h(x_i) \in W_+$ (resp, $h(x_i) \in W_-$), then $\phi'(h(y_i)) = 1$ (resp. $\phi'(h(y_i)) = -1$).

Let $h_1, ..., h_N$ be functions that can be used to represent A. Then, since the functions can be used in a (L, δ)-weak representation, it is evident that for every i, there is a set J_i, $|J_i| \geq \delta n$ for $\delta > 1/2$ such that $\phi(h_i(x_j)) = a_i(j)$. Setting δ' by $\delta' - 1/2 = (\delta - 1/2)/2$, then for ρ sufficiently small, $|J_i \cap J_{h_i}| \geq \delta' n$, and on that intersection, $\phi'(h_i(y_j)) = a_i(j)$, as claimed. ∎

From Lemma 1 it is clear that it suffices to show that A is not represented using any $(\phi', y) \in \Phi' \times D_n(k'(\delta)/L)$, and there are at most $3^{kL} \cdot N(k'(\delta), \Omega^n, d_n)$ such pairs.

2.2 Controlling a "Rectangle"

A source of difficulty in the analysis of this problem stems in the "weakness" of the representation, namely, that one does not control every pair $h_i(x_j)$, but only a proportional set of indices for every $1 \leq i \leq N$. Next, we will show how to bypass this obstacle. We will show that there is a relatively small set $B \subset \{-1, 1\}^n$, such that for any ϕ which has a Lipschitz constant at most L and $x \in \Omega^n$, if $A \subset \{-1, 1\}^n$ is represented using (ϕ, x) then $A \subset B$. Note that the Lipschitz condition on ϕ is equivalent to having two sets, W_+ and W_- which are $2/L$ apart; on the first $\phi = 1$ and on the second $\phi = -1$.

The philosophy of the proof is as follows. Suppose that there is a "large set" $B \subset \{-1, 1\}^n$, such that for every $v \in B$ there is some $h_v \in H$ for which $\phi(h_v(x_j)) = v(j)$ on δn coordinates. If this is the case, it is possible to find a large subset of B and a large subset of $\{1, ..., n\}$ on which *for every i, j*, $\phi(h_i(x_j)) = v_i(j)$. We will show that this implies that H has a large P-shattering dimension at a scale proportional to L, in contradiction to our assumption.

The combinatorial part of the proof could be described in the following way. If one views the vectors $(h_v(x_j))_{j=1}^{n}$ as rows in a matrix, and if in each row one can control δn of the entries for $\delta > 1/2$, then if there are enough rows in the matrix, one can find a large "rectangle", or sub-matrix on which one has complete control. The exact formulation of this claim is:

Lemma 2. *For every $1/2 < \delta \leq 1$ there exist constants α, β and n_0, all depending only on δ, for which the following holds. Assume that $n \geq n_0$, that T is an $m \times n$, $\{0,1\}$-valued matrix and that each row in T has at least δn entries that are 1. If we set $\Delta = \frac{1}{2}(\delta - \frac{1}{2})(1 - \log_2(3 - 2\delta)) > 0$, and if $m \geq 2^{n(1-\Delta)}$, then T contains an (s,t) sub-matrix of 1s, for $s \geq 2^{\beta n}$, $t \geq \alpha n$, and $\alpha + \beta \geq 1 + \Delta/2$.*

The proof is based on the following estimate on the so-called "problem of Zarankiewicz".

Lemma 3. *[3] Let G be a bipartite graph with (m,n) vertices and denote by $Z(m,n,s,t)$ the maximal number of edges in G such that G does not contain an (s,t)-complete bipartite subgraph. Then,*

$$Z(m,n,s,t) \leq (s-1)^{1/t}(n-t+1)m^{1-1/t} + (t-1)m.$$

Proof of Lemma 2. Assume that $m > 2^{n(1-\Delta)}$ and define a bipartite graph in the following manner. One side consists of the rows of T and the other side is the elements of $\{1,...,n\}$. There is an edge between a the i-th row and $\{j\}$ if and only if $T_{i,j} = 1$. Using the notation of Lemma 3, the graph contains at least δmn edges. Hence, by Lemma 3, if s and t satisfy

$$\delta mn > (s-1)^{1/t}(n-t+1)m^{1-1/t} + (t-1)m \tag{2.1}$$

then G contains a complete (s,t) bipartite subgraph, which corresponds to T having an $s \times t$ sub-matrix of 1s. Setting $\alpha = \delta - 1/2$, $t - 1 = \alpha n$ and $(s-1) = 2^{\beta n}$, an easy computation shows that

$$\beta < 1 + \alpha \log_2\left(\frac{\delta - \alpha}{1 - \alpha}\right) + \frac{1}{n}\left(\log_2\left(\frac{\delta - \alpha}{1 - \alpha}\right) - \Delta n\right) \tag{2.2}$$

is enough to ensure (2.1). Note that one can choose $\beta > 0$ satisfying (2.2) such that, if $n \geq n_0$, $\alpha + \beta \geq 1 + \Delta/2$, as claimed. ∎

Theorem 2. *For every $1/2 < \delta \leq 1$ there are constants $c(\delta)$ and n_0 depending only on δ, for which the following holds. Fix $n \geq n_0$ and $L > 0$, assume that $P - VC(H, 2/L) \leq c(\delta)n$ and set $\Delta = \frac{1}{2}(\delta - \frac{1}{2})(1 - \log_2(3 - 2\delta))$. If $x = (x_1, ..., x_n) \in \Omega^n$ and ϕ is a Lipschitz function with constant at most L, there is a set $B \subset \{-1,1\}^n$, $|B| \leq 2^{n(1-\Delta)}$, such that if x and ϕ can be used to (L, δ) weakly represent A, then $A \subset B$.*

Proof. Let $c(\delta)$ be a constant which will be specified later, set n_0 to be as in Lemma 2 and assume that $P - VC(H, 2/L) \leq c(\delta)n$. Note that $v \in \{-1,1\}^n$ can be (L, δ)-weakly represented using x and ϕ if and only if there is $h_v \in H$ and $J_v \subset \{1,...,n\}$ such that $|J_v| \geq \delta n$ and for every $j \in J_v$, $\phi(h_v(x_j)) = v(j)$. Define B as the set of all such elements v, and thus, if A can be (L, δ) weakly represented using (ϕ, x) then $A \subset B$. Assume that $|B| > 2^{(1-\Delta)n}$, and define the $|B| \times n$ $\{0,1\}$-valued matrix T by $T_{i,j} = 1$, if $j \in J_{v_i}$. Applying Lemma 2 (and using its notation), T contains an (s,t) sub-matrix of 1s, where $s \geq 2^{\beta n}$, $t \geq \alpha n$ and $\alpha + \beta \geq 1 + \Delta/2$. In other words, since $n \geq n_0$, there is a set $B' \subset B$,

$|B'| \geq 2^{\beta n}$ and a set $J \subset \{1, ..., n\}$, $|J| \geq \alpha n$ such that for every $v \in B'$ there is $h_v \in H$ and for every $j \in J$, $\phi(h_v(x_j)) = v_j$.

Consider the coordinate P_J projection (restriction) of B' onto J. Since $|B'| \geq 2^{\beta n}$ and $|J| \geq \alpha n$, then $|P_J B'| \geq 2^{\beta n}/2^{n-\alpha n}$. Indeed, any point in $P_J B'$ is the image of at most $2^{n-\alpha n}$ elements in $\{-1, 1\}^n$. As $\alpha + \beta - 1 \geq \Delta/2$, it is evident that $|P_J B'| \geq 2^{n\Delta/2}$. Applying the Sauer-Shelah Lemma, there is a subset $J_1 \subset J$, such that $|J_1| \geq c(\delta)n$ and $P_{J_1} B' = P_{J_1} P_J B = \{-1, 1\}^{|J_1|}$.

Hence, for every $a \in \{-1, 1\}^{|J_1|}$ there is some $h_a \in H$ such that $\phi(h_a(x_j)) = a(j)$ for every $j \in J_1$. Because $d(\{\phi = 1\}, \{\phi = -1\}) \geq 2/L$, it follows that $P - VC(H, 2/L) \geq |J_1| = c(\delta)n$, which contradicts our assumption. ∎

Proof of Theorem 1. By Lemma 1 (and using its notation), it suffices to show that "most" subsets of the cube are not (kL, δ') weakly represented using any element from $\Phi' \times D_n(k'(\delta)/L, \Omega^n, d_n)$. The cardinality of this product set is at most $3^{cL}|D_n(k'(\delta)/L)|$ for an absolute constant c. Now, fix such a pair (ϕ, x). By the assumption of the Theorem, $P - VC(H, 2/(kL)) \leq c(\delta)n$, where $c(\delta)$ is selected as in Theorem 2, and set $\Delta' = \frac{1}{2}(\delta' - \frac{1}{2})(1 - \log_2(3 - 2\delta'))$. If $n \geq n_0(\delta')$, then by Theorem 2 applied to (kL, δ'), there is a set $B \subset \{-1, 1\}^n$ of cardinality $|B| \leq 2^{n(1-\Delta')}$, such that if x and ϕ can be used to (kL, δ') weakly represent A, then $A \subset B$.

Clearly, the probability that a random point $v \in \{-1, 1\}^n$ belongs to B is at most $|B|/2^n = 2^{-n\Delta'}$, and thus, if $|A| = N$, the probability that $A \subset B$ is at most $2^{-nN\Delta'}$. Therefore, if $3^{cL}|D_n(k'(\delta)/L)| \leq 2^{-nN\Delta'/2}$, it follows that with probability at least $1 - \exp(c'(\delta)Nn)$, A is not (L, δ) weakly represented in H. ∎

3   Application: $H = B_{\ell_2}$

A natural base class which one should consider, and which was studied in [9], is $H = B_{X^*}$ - the dual unit ball of some n-dimensional Banach space X, acting as functionals on $\Omega = B_X$. Although we do not wish to focus on this general case, as it requires some knowledge in convex geometry, let us point out several relatively easy observations. Since H consists of Lipschitz functions of norm 1 then

$$d_n(u, v) \leq \max_{1 \leq i \leq N} \sup_{h \in H} |h(u_i) - h(v_i)| \leq \max_{1 \leq i \leq N} d_\Omega(u_i, v_i).$$

Therefore,

$$N(\varepsilon, \Omega^n, d_n) \leq (N(\varepsilon, \Omega, d_\Omega))^n, \tag{3.1}$$

and for $H = B_{X^*}$, $d_\Omega(u, v) = \|u - v\|_X$. Moreover, if X is an n dimensional Banach space then by a standard volumetric estimate (see, e.g. [12]), $N(\varepsilon, \Omega, d_\Omega) \leq (3/\varepsilon)^n$, implying that

$$\frac{\log N(\varepsilon, \Omega^n, d_n)}{n} \leq cn \log(c'/\varepsilon).$$

As mentioned in the introduction, for every class of functions bounded by 1,

$$P - VC(H, \varepsilon) \leq K \cdot VC(H, c\varepsilon) \log(2/\varepsilon).$$

Hence, as long as $VC(H, 2/(kL)) \log(2L) \le c(\delta)n$, the assumption of Theorem 1 holds. It turns out that up to a $\log(n)$ factor, the "critical level" L for which this assumption is still valid is determined by a notion of distance between Banach spaces. The critical L is proportional to the so-called *Banach-Mazur distance* between X and ℓ_1^n (we refer the reader to [9] for more details). On the other hand, if L is the distance between X and ℓ_1^n, then the entire cube $\{-1, 1\}^n$ is $(L, 1)$ represented in $H = B_{X^*}$. Thus, the situation one often encounters when H is the unit ball of the dual to an n dimensional Banach space is a surprising dichotomy. For $L = d(X, \ell_1^n)$, the entire cube, and thus all its subsets can be represented in H. For a slightly smaller constant, $c(\delta)L$, the vast majority of subsets of cardinality $N \approx c'(\delta)n \log n$ are not even $(c(\delta)L, \delta)$ weakly represented in H.

The case of $H = B_{\ell_2}$ has been studied, in one form on another, by several authors. A careful examination of the proof in [2] shows that only a vanishing fraction of the subsets of $\{-1, 1\}^n$ with N elements is represented in ℓ_2 with a margin better than $c\sqrt{(\log N)/n}$ for suitable absolute constant c, as long as $N/n^2 \to \infty$. This implies that, at least when ϕ is taken from the margin function family, and as long as $L \le c\sqrt{n/\log N}$ and $N \ge cn^2$, most of the subsets of $\{-1, 1\}^n$ are not $(L, 1)$ weakly represented in B_{ℓ_2}.

A different approach, based on operator ideal theory, was used in [6] to prove that if $N \ge cn$, then with probability at least $1 - \exp(cN)$, a subset of $\{-1, 1\}^n$ with N elements is only represented in ℓ_2 with the trivial margin of $c_1/\sqrt{n}$; in other words, it improves [2] in the way N depends on n and because the restriction on L is the optimal one - $L \le c\sqrt{n}$. However, it too only applies when the Lipschitz function is taken from the margin family.

These two results are limited since they are completely Hilbertian in nature. They do not extend to the case $H = B_{X^*}$ for a non-Hilbert space X, let alone to when H is not a class of linear functionals.

In [9], the method of proof (which is essentially the same as the proof of Theorem 1) enables one to deal with weak representation by an arbitrary Lipschitz function, and to treat $H = B_{X^*}$ for a general n-dimensional Banach space. For $H = B_{\ell_2}$ it was shown that if $N \ge c(\delta)n \log n$ then with probability at least $1 - \exp(c'(\delta)Nn)$ a subset of $\{-1, 1\}^n$ of cardinality N is not (L, δ)-weakly represented in B_{ℓ_2} if $L \le c''(\delta)\sqrt{n}$. The price paid for the extension to an arbitrary Lipschitz function was that N was no longer linear in n. The main result of this section is to remove this parasitic logarithmic factor.

Although the analysis we present for B_{ℓ_2} goes beyond the Hilbertian case, it still only works under additional structural assumptions on the space X. And, though under such assumptions it is possible to remove the parasitic logarithmic factor, doing the same in the general case seems (at least to this author) a worthwhile challenge.

Theorem 3. *For every $1/2 < \delta \le 1$, there exist constants $c(\delta)$, $c'(\delta)$, $c''(\delta)$ and $n_0(\delta)$, depending only on δ, for which the following holds. For every integer $n \ge n_0$, if $L \le c(\delta)\sqrt{n}$ and $N \ge c'(\delta)n$, then with probability $1 - \exp(c''(\delta)nN)$, a set with N elements is not (L, δ) weakly represented in B_{ℓ_2}.*

Clearly, because of the structure of ℓ_2, it suffices to consider the n-dimensional Euclidean space ℓ_2^n, rather than the infinite dimensional one. Thus, $H = B_2^n$, consisting of linear functionals on $\Omega = B_2^n$.

The proof of Theorem 3 requires two preliminary steps before one can use Theorem 1. First of all, one has to identify the critical level at which $P - VC(B_{\ell_2}, \varepsilon) \leq c(\delta)n$ for the constant $c(\delta)$ appearing in Theorem 1. Then, one has to estimate $N(\varepsilon, (B_2^n)^n, d_n)$.

Lemma 4. *There exists an absolute constant c such that for every $0 < \varepsilon < 1$,*

$$P - VC(\varepsilon, B_{\ell_2}) \leq \frac{c}{\varepsilon^2}.$$

Let us mention that the same estimate holds true for the combinatorial dimension (see, e.g [8]), and thus, for this class of functions, the two dimensions are equivalent.

The proof of Lemma 4 is based on Sudakov's minoration (see, for example, [5, 12]).

Lemma 5. *There exists an absolute constant c for which the following holds. If $T \subset \ell_2^n$ then*

$$c \sup_{\varepsilon > 0} \varepsilon \sqrt{\log N(\varepsilon, T, \ell_2^n)} \leq \mathbb{E} \sup_{t \in T} \left| \sum_{i=1}^n g_i t_i \right|,$$

where $(g_i)_{i=1}^n$ are independent, standard gaussian random variables and $t = (t_1, ..., t_n)$.

Note that if μ_n is the empirical measure on $\{1, ..., n\}$ and if one views each $t \in \ell_2^n$ as a function on $\{1, ..., n\}$ in the natural way, then $\|t\|_{\ell_2^n} = \sqrt{n} \|t\|_{L_2(\mu_n)}$. Thus, by Lemma 5,

$$\sup_{\varepsilon > 0} \varepsilon \sqrt{\log N(\varepsilon, T, L_2(\mu_n))} \leq \frac{C}{\sqrt{n}} \mathbb{E} \sup_{t \in T} \left| \sum_{i=1}^n g_i t_i \right|. \tag{3.2}$$

Proof of Lemma 4. Assume that $\{x_1, ..., x_n\} \in B_{\ell_2}$ is ε P-shattered by B_{ℓ_2}. Then, there is a set $H' \subset H$, $|H'| \geq 2^{cn}$ which is $\varepsilon/4$-separated in $L_2(\mu_n)$, where μ_n is the empirical measure supported on $\{x_1, ..., x_n\}$. Indeed, each $h \in B_{\ell_2}$ can be associated with a point in $\{-1, 1\}^n$ according to whether $h(x_i) \in V_+$ or $h(x_i) \in V_-$. By a standard probabilistic argument, there is a subset of $\{-1, 1\}^n$ of cardinality 2^{cn} which is $n/4$ separated in the Hamming metric. Consider the elements in H that correspond to the separated set and let h, h' be two such elements. Thus, there is a set $I \subset \{1, ..., n\}$ of cardinality at least $n/4$ such that for every $i \in I$, if $h(x_i) \in V_+$ then $h'(x_i) \in V_-$ and vice-versa. Therefore, $\sum_{i=1}^n |h(x_i) - h'(x_i)| \geq \sum_{i \in I} |h(x_i) - h'(x_i)| \geq |I| \varepsilon$.

Let $(g_i)_{i=1}^n$ be standard independent gaussian variables. By (3.2), the fact that $\|x\|_{\ell_2} = \sup_{h \in B_{\ell_2}} h(x)$ and a standard estimate on $\mathbb{E}\| \sum_{i=1}^n g_i x_i \|_{\ell_2}$,

$$c \varepsilon \sqrt{n} \le c \sup_{\delta > 0} \delta \sqrt{\log N\left(\delta, H, L_2(\mu_n)\right)} \le \frac{1}{\sqrt{n}} \mathbb{E}_g \sup_{h \in B_{\ell_2}} \sum_{i=1}^n g_i h(x_i)$$

$$\le \frac{1}{\sqrt{n}} \mathbb{E}_g \left\| \sum_{i=1}^n g_i x_i \right\|_{\ell_2} \le 1.$$

Therefore, $n \le c/\varepsilon^2$, as claimed. ∎

To conclude the proof of Theorem 3, it remains to bound $N(\varepsilon, \Omega^n, d_n)$, and, as we already mentioned, one can take $\Omega = B_2^n$. Note that the "easy" way to upper-bound $N(\varepsilon, (B_2^n)^n, d_n)$, as presented in (3.1), leads to the superfluous $\log n$ factor, and thus a different argument is required.

Theorem 4. *There exists an absolute constant c such that for any integer n and any $\varepsilon \ge c/\sqrt{n}$, $D(\varepsilon, (B_2^n)^n, d_n) \le 2^{n^2+1}$, and thus, $N(\varepsilon, (B_2^n)^n, d_n) \le 2^{n^2+1}$.*

Before presenting the proof let us introduce the following notation. For two sets $A, B \subset \mathbb{R}^m$ let $D(A, B)$ be the maximal number of points $a_i \in A$ such that the sets $a_i + B$ are disjoint. Observe that if B is a ball of radius ε with respect to a norm $\| \ \|_X$ then $D(A, B)$ is the maximal cardinality of an ε separated subset of A with respect to d_X.

Proof of Theorem 4. Since B_2^n consists of linear functionals, then for every $u, v \in (B_2^n)^n$, $d_n(u, v) = \frac{1}{n} \sup_{h \in B_2^n} \sum_{i=1}^n |h(u_i - v_i)|$. In fact, this metric is induced by a norm on the product space $\Pi_{i=1}^n \mathbb{R}^n$,

$$\|(x_1, ..., x_n)\| = \frac{1}{n} \sup_{h \in B_2^n} \sum_{i=1}^n |h(x_i)|.$$

Consider the unit ball of this norm, which we denote by $\mathcal{K}$. Fix $\varepsilon > 0$, and observe that our aim is to find the maximal number of disjoint translates of $\varepsilon \mathcal{K}$ that are centered at points in $\mathcal{B} = \Pi_{i=1}^n B_2^n$. To that end, we use a well known volumetric argument, which we present for the sake of completeness.

Let $\mathcal{U} = \varepsilon \mathcal{K} \cap \mathcal{B}$ which is also a convex, symmetric set, and clearly, $D(\mathcal{B}, \varepsilon \mathcal{K}) \le D(\mathcal{B}, \mathcal{U})$. Let $y_1, ..., y_m$ be elements in $\mathcal{B}$ such that for every $i \ne j$, $y_i + \mathcal{U}$ and $y_j + \mathcal{U}$ are disjoint. Since $\mathcal{U} \subset \mathcal{B}$ then

$$\bigcup_{i=1}^m (y_i + \mathcal{U}) \subset 2\mathcal{B}.$$

Let $\text{vol}(A)$ be the Lebesgue measure of $A \subset \Pi_{i=1}^n \mathbb{R}^n$. Since the sets $y_i + \mathcal{U}$ are disjoint, then $\sum_{i=1}^m \text{vol}(y_i + \mathcal{U}) \le \text{vol}(2\mathcal{B}) = 2^{n^2} \text{vol}(\mathcal{B})$, and thus $m \le 2^{n^2} \text{vol}(\mathcal{B})/\text{vol}(\mathcal{U})$. To conclude the proof it is enough to show that as long as $\varepsilon \ge c/\sqrt{n}$, $\text{vol}(\mathcal{B})/\text{vol}(\mathcal{U}) \le 2$.

Let μ be the normalized volume measure on B_2^n, and set μ^n to be the product measure on $\mathcal{B}$. Therefore, if X is a random vector distributed according to μ, and if $X_1, ..., X_n$ are independent copies of X, then

$$\text{vol}(\mathcal{U}) = \text{vol}(\mathcal{B}) \cdot Pr\left((X_1, ..., X_n) \in \mathcal{U}\right).$$

Since $X_i \in B_2^n$, then

$$Pr\left((X_1, ..., X_n) \in \mathcal{U}\right) =$$

$$Pr\left((X_1, ..., X_n) \in \varepsilon\mathcal{K}\right) = Pr\left(\frac{1}{n} \sup_{h \in B_2^n} \sum_{i=1}^{n} |h(X_i)| \le \varepsilon\right),$$

and to estimate this probability we can use the uniform law of large numbers.

Note that for every $h \in B_2^n$, $c_1\sqrt{n} \le \mathbb{E}|h(X)| \le c_2\sqrt{n}$ for suitable absolute constants c_1 and c_2; this could be verified by a tedious computation, or by a representation of the volume measure on B_2^n in terms of gaussian random variables (see, for example, [12, 10] for the basic facts and [1] for representations of the volume measure on the unit balls of other ℓ_p^n spaces).

Thus, as long as $\varepsilon \ge c/\sqrt{n}$ for an appropriate $c > 0$, it suffices to estimate

$$Pr\left(\frac{1}{n} \sup_{h \in B_2^n} \left|\sum_{i=1}^{n} |h(X_i)| - \mathbb{E}|h(X)|\right| \ge \frac{c'}{\sqrt{n}}\right)$$

and to show that for a large enough c', this probability is smaller than $1/2$. And indeed, by a symmetrization argument and the contraction principle for the absolute value function (see, e.g. [5]),

$$\mathbb{E} \sup_{h \in B_2^n} \left|\frac{1}{n}\sum_{i=1}^{n} |h(X_i)| - \mathbb{E}|h(X)|\right| \le \frac{2}{n}\mathbb{E} \sup_{h \in B_2^n}\left|\sum_{i=1}^{n} \varepsilon_i h(X_i)\right| = \frac{2}{n}\mathbb{E}\left\|\sum_{i=1}^{n} \varepsilon_i X_i\right\|_{\ell_2}$$

$$\le \frac{2}{n}\mathbb{E}\left(\sum_{i=1}^{n} \|X_i\|_2^2\right)^{1/2} \le \frac{2}{\sqrt{n}},$$

and the claim follows from Chebyshev's inequality. ∎

4   Concluding Remarks

Despite several attempts to apply the method developed here to the case studied in [2], as of yet we were not able to find a unified approach to resolve both questions. The reason for that stems in the different subsets of the cube that one considers. Here, we focus on random sets with $c(\delta)n$ elements, while in [2] the authors considered subsets of cardinality n but with VC dimension at most d. Since a "typical" subset of $\{-1, 1\}^n$ with n elements has VC dimension of the order $\log n$, the sets studied in [2] can not be reached using the counting measure we use. One possible way forward could be to find a representation of the counting probability measure on the set of subsets of $\{-1,1\}^n$ with VC dimension at most d, and to combined it with Theorem 2, though finding such a representation seems highly nontrivial.

The main point of this note belongs to the *"no free lunch"* philosophy. It is natural to assume that there are no simple, universal classes of functions, which is what could be seen here. The only way one can reach most of the small subsets of the cube is if the base class itself is so rich, that it is pointless to use it in a representation.

Of course, the result presented here, much like that ones it followed, does not imply that embedding/represetation type methods are useless, as real world problems most likely do not correspond to "typical" subsets of the combinatorial cube. They have a special symmetry or a geometric structure that makes them easier to handle. Our goal should be to find the significant symmetries and to exploit them by matching the correct H to the given learning problem. The main objective in writing this article was to point out to this important, yet under-studied problem: find out which classification problems (subsets of the cube) can be represented, and by which base classes H; that is, for each H, find the subsets of the cube that have a compatible structure with that of H, and vice-versa.

References

1. F. Barthe, O. Guédon, S. Mendelson, A. Naor, A probabilistic approach to the geometry of the ℓ_p^n ball, Annals of Probability, 33 (2) 480-513, 2005.
2. S. Ben-David, N. Eiron, H.U. Simon, Limitations of learning via embeddings in Euclidean half spaces, Journal of Machine Learning Research 3, 441-461, 2002.
3. B. Bollobás, *Extremal graph theory*, Academic Press, 1978.
4. J. Forster, N. Schmitt, and H.U. Simon, Estimating the optimal margins of embeddings in Euclidean halfspaces, in *Proceedings of the 14th Annual Conference on Computational Learning Theory, 2001*, LNCS volume 2111, 402-415. Springer, Berlin, 2001.
5. M. Ledoux, M. Talagrand, *Probability in Banach spaces*, Springer, 1991.
6. N. Linial, S. Mendelson, G. Schechtman, A. Shraibman, Complexity measures of sign matrices, preprint.
7. S. Mendelson, R. Vershynin, Entropy and the combinatorial dimension, Inventiones Mathematicae, 152(1), 37-55, 2003.
8. S. Mendelson, G. Schechtman, The shattering dimension of sets of linear functionals, Annals of Probability, 32 (3A), 1746-1770, 2004.
9. S. Mendelson, Embedding with a Lipschitz function, Random Structures and Algorithms, to appear (available on the journal's web-page).
10. V.D. Milman, G. Schechtman, *Asymptotic theory of finite dimensional normed spaces*, Lecture Notes in Mathematics 1200, Springer, 1986.
11. A. Pajor, *Sous espaces ℓ_1^n des espaces de Banach*, Hermann, Paris, 1985.
12. G. Pisier, *The volume of convex bodies and Banach space geometry*, Cambridge University Press, 1989.
13. A.W. Van der Vaart, J.A. Wellner, *Weak convergence and Empirical Processes*, Springer-Verlag, 1996.

Leaving the Span

Manfred K. Warmuth[1,*] and S.V.N. Vishwanathan[2]

[1] Computer Science Department, University of California, Santa Cruz,
CA 95064, U.S.A.
manfred@cse.ucsc.edu
[2] Machine Learning Program, National ICT Australia[**],
Canberra, ACT 0200, Australia
SVN.Vishwanathan@nicta.com.au

Abstract. We discuss a simple sparse linear problem that is hard to
learn with any algorithm that uses a linear combination of the training
instances as its weight vector. The hardness holds even if we allow the
learner to embed the instances into any higher dimensional feature space
(and use a kernel function to define the dot product between the embedded instances). These algorithms are inherently limited by the fact
that after seeing k instances only a weight space of dimension k can be
spanned.

Our hardness result is surprising because the same problem can be
efficiently learned using the exponentiated gradient (EG) algorithm: Now
the component-wise logarithms of the weights are essentially a linear
combination of the training instances and after seeing k instances. This
algorithm enforces *additional constraints* on the weights (all must be
non-negative and sum to one) and in some cases these constraints alone
force the rank of the weight space to grow as fast as 2^k.

1 Introduction

Linear methods are inadequate for many learning problems. However, if linear
methods are enhanced by the *kernel trick*, then they can lead to powerful learning
methods. For this purpose, the instance domain $\mathcal{X}$ is mapped to a Reproducing
Kernel Hilbert Space (RKHS) F via a possibly non-linear embedding map Φ.
Now linear models in the feature space F can describe highly non-linear models
in the original instance space $\mathcal{X}$ and linear learning algorithms (in feature space)
can become powerful learning methods. The caveat is that this method requires a
restriction to learning algorithms whose weight vectors are linear combinations of

---

* Supported by NSF grant CCR 9821087. Part of this work was done while the first
author visited NICTA.
** mm National ICT Australia is funded by the Australian Government's Department
of Communications, Information Technology and the Arts and the Australian Research Council through Backing Australia's Ability and the ICT Center of Excellence
program.

P. Auer and R. Meir (Eds.): COLT 2005, LNAI 3559, pp. 366–381, 2005.
© Springer-Verlag Berlin Heidelberg 2005

the embedded training instances.[1] In this case, computing dot products between the weight vector and a new embedded instance reduces to efficiently computing the dot product between two embedded instances, i.e., $\langle \phi(\mathbf{x}), \phi(\tilde{\mathbf{x}}) \rangle$. This is done via the so-called *kernel function* $k(\mathbf{x}, \tilde{\mathbf{x}}) = \langle \phi(\mathbf{x}), \phi(\tilde{\mathbf{x}}) \rangle$.

In this paper the following set of conditions is called **kernel paradigm**: The weight vector (in feature space) is a linear combination of embedded training instances, the dot product of this weight vector with new instances is computed via a kernel function and the individual features (components of the embedded instances $\phi(\mathbf{x})$) are not accessed by the algorithm.

Now, consider the following *sparse linear* learning problem first discussed in Kivinen and Warmuth (1997), Kivinen et al. (1997): The instances $\mathbf{x}_t$ are the rows of an n-dimensional Hadamard matrix and the possible targets are one of the n columns of the matrix. In other words, if the target is the i-th column, then the instances are labeled by the i-th feature and this target corresponds to the standard basis vector $\mathbf{e}_i$ (This vector has a one in the i-th position and zeros elsewhere). Hadamard matrices have ± 1 entries and orthogonal rows. Therefore, as argued before in Kivinen and Warmuth (1997), Kivinen et al. (1997), this problem is hard to learn when the weight vector is required to be a linear combinations of instances: Any linear combination of past instances predicts zero on any new instance (labeled ± 1) and thus incurs constant loss.

In this paper, we show that even if the learner is allowed to embed the instances into any Euclidean space (via the use of a kernel), the above sparse linear problem is still hard to learn[2]. Any algorithm that predicts with a linear combination of the embedded instances seen so far has the property that after k instances it can only span a weight space of rank k. However, the n standard basis vectors vectors (our possible target weight vectors) form a matrix of rank n. We show that for any k training instances and any embedding into some Euclidean space (of any dimension), there always is one of the targets for which the average square loss is at least $1 - \frac{k}{n}$. Thus, after seeing half of all the instances, the average square loss is still a half.

The first question is, what is the family of algorithms that always predicts with a linear combination of the instances. The Representer Theorem and various extensions (Kimeldorf and Wahba, 1971, Schölkopf et al., 2001) provide minimization problems whose solutions are always linear combinations of instances. A more general geometric condition on the learning algorithm is given in Kivinen et al. (1997): *Any linear algorithm whose predictions are invariant with respect to a rotation of the embedded instances must predict with a weight vector that is a linear combination of the embedded instances.* However, it is important to note that our lower bounds hold for any algorithm that predicts

---

[1] The only specialized exceptions are the algorithms of Takimoto and Warmuth (2003).

[2] Our hardness result does not hold for embeddings in arbitrary dot product spaces. However, we believe that this is only a technical restriction.

with a linear combination of instances.[3] This includes algorithms that choose the coefficients of the linear combination by accessing the individual components of the embedded instances - which breaks the kernel paradigm.

Our lower bound currently only holds for linear regression with respect to the square loss. We conjecture that changing the loss function for the linear prediction algorithm does not alleviate this problem, i.e., we conjecture that for any non-negative convex loss function L, s.t. $L(y, \hat{y}) \geq 1$ whenever $|y - \hat{y}| \geq 1$, there always is one of the targets with average loss $1 - \frac{k}{n}$. Along these lines, we prove in the full paper that the lower bounds hold for the following generalization of the square loss: $L_p(y, \hat{y}) = |y - \hat{y}|^p$, for $1 < p \leq \infty$. The proof requires considerably more tools from linear algebra.

The lower bounds may be surprising because there are simple linear learning algorithms that can easily learn the above sparse linear problem. One such algorithm belongs to the Exponentiated Gradient (EG) family of algorithms which essentially have the property that the component-wise logarithms of the linear weights are a linear combination of the (embedded) training instances. By varying the coefficient of a single instance, the set of possible weight vectors reachable is already as high as the number of distinct components in the instance. Also the weight space based on k instances can contain up to 2^k standard basis vectors.

The crucial feature of the EG algorithm seems to be that it maintains constraints on the weights: the weights must be non-negative and sum to one. We can show that in some special cases these constraints alone let us reach a weight space of rank 2^k after seeing k examples. Not surprisingly, the EG algorithm, as well as any algorithm that enforces the constraints explicitly, require access to the weights of the individual features, and this breaks the kernel paradigm[4].

Following Kivinen and Warmuth (1997), the goal of this type of research is to characterize which type of linear learning algorithm is suitable for a given class of linear problems. The focus of this paper is to explore which linear prediction algorithms are suitable for sparse linear problems.

Key Open Problem: Can similar lower bounds be proven for linear thresholded predictors, i.e., now $\hat{y} = \sigma(\langle \mathbf{w}, \phi(\mathbf{x}) \rangle)$, where σ is the threshold function and $\mathbf{w}$ a linear combination of the embedded instances.

Related Work: There has been an on-going discussion of the advantages and disadvantages of kernel algorithms versus the multiplicative algorithms such as the EG algorithm and the Winnow algorithm (Littlestone, 1988). In short, multiplicative algorithms often generalize well after seeing only few examples in the case when the target is sparse. However, for harder learning problems, exponentially many weights need to be manipulated explicitly and this is too expensive

---

[3] This includes the work of Cristianini et al. (1999) that uses the EG algorithm to determine the coefficients of the linear combination.

[4] The only exceptions to this that we know of are the updates discussed in Takimoto and Warmuth (2003), where, in polynomial time exponentially many weights are updated with the EG algorithm. Curiously enough special kernels are used for this update.

((e.g., Section 9.6 of Kivinen and Warmuth, 1997) and Khardon et al. (2001)). In contrast, the kernel algorithm may converge slower for the same problems, but the kernel trick allows us to implicitly manipulate exponentially many feature weights at a low computational cost.

The embedding map can be seen as a special case of a reduction between prediction problems. For a more general notion of reduction and non-reducibility results that take the complexity of the learning problem into account see Pitt and Warmuth (1993), Warmuth (1989). Many worst-case loss bounds (e.g., Gentile and Warmuth, 1999) and generalization bounds (Schapire et al., 1998) are known to improve with the size of the margin. The goal is therefore to choose embeddings with large margins. To obtain a scaling-invariant notion of margin we must normalize the margin by the product of a pair of dual norms: the maximum p-norm of the instances and the q-norm of the target weight vector, where $\frac{1}{p} + \frac{1}{q} = 1$. In Ben-David et al. (2002) it was shown that with high probability a large fraction of the concept classes with a fixed VC dimension cannot be embedded with a 2-2-margin other than the *trivial* margin of $\frac{1}{\sqrt{n}}$, where n is the number of points. On the other hand (Forster et al., 2001) showed upper bounds on the 2-2 margin of a concept class in terms of its operator norm (the largest singular value of a matrix).

The family of algorithms whose weight vector is a linear combination of the instances seems to relate to the 2-2-margin. However, the performance of the EG algorithm seems to relate to the 1-∞-margin. For our simple Hadamard problem there is no embedding with a 2-2-margin better than $\frac{1}{\sqrt{n}}$ (the trivial 2-2-margin) (Forster et al., 2001). However, the 1-∞-margin is 1 for this problem and this seems to be the key reason why the EG algorithm does well in this case.

In this paper we prove *lower bounds* for the family of algorithms that predicts with a linear combination of the instances. However, we don't use pairs of dual norms (as was done in Kivinen and Warmuth (1997)) and we also completely bypass the concept of margins. Linear classifiers with large margins have good generalization error, but we know of no lower bounds in terms of margins (see Herbrich et al. (2005) for related experiments). Instead, we prove our lower bounds using the Singular Value Decomposition[5] (SVD) of the matrix defining the linear problem and a simple averaging argument.

2   Hadamard Matrices and SVD

We make use of properties of *Hadamard matrices* in various proofs. A Hadamard matrix is an orthogonal matrix with $\{\pm1\}$ elements. The following definition allows us to recursively define *Hadamard matrices*: When $n = 2^d$ for some d, the $n \times n$ Hadamard matrix $\mathbf{H}^n$ is given by the following recurrence:

---

[5] In Forster et al. (2001) it was shown that the 2-2 margin of a concept class is *upper bounded* by the largest singular value over n.

$$\mathbf{H}^1 = (+1) \quad \mathbf{H}^2 = \begin{pmatrix} +1 & +1 \\ +1 & -1 \end{pmatrix} \quad \mathbf{H}^4 = \begin{pmatrix} +1 & +1 & +1 & +1 \\ +1 & -1 & +1 & -1 \\ +1 & +1 & -1 & -1 \\ +1 & -1 & -1 & +1 \end{pmatrix} \quad \mathbf{H}^{2n} = \begin{pmatrix} \mathbf{H}^n & \mathbf{H}^n \\ \mathbf{H}^n & -\mathbf{H}^n \end{pmatrix}$$

We use the shorthand $\mathbf{H} = \mathbf{H}^n$, where the dimension n is understood from the context. Note that all rows of the Hadamard matrix $\mathbf{H}$ are orthogonal and of length $\sqrt{n}$.

In the *Hadamard Learning Problem*, the examples are the rows of the Hadamard matrix labeled by one of the columns. So there are n instances and n possible targets.

A matrix $\mathbf{M} \in \mathbb{R}^{n \times m}$ can be decomposed as $\mathbf{M} = \mathbf{U} \mathbf{S} \mathbf{V}^\top$ where $\mathbf{U} \in \mathbb{R}^{n \times n}$, $\mathbf{V} \in \mathbb{R}^{m \times m}$ are orthogonal and $\mathbf{S} \in \mathbb{R}^{n \times m}$ is a diagonal matrix, i.e., $S_{ij} = 0$ for $i \neq j$. Furthermore, the diagonal elements of $\mathbf{S}$ are sorted and non-negative, i.e., $S_{11} \geq S_{22} \geq \ldots \geq S_{qq} \geq 0$, where $q = \min\{m, n\}$. Henceforth, we will use s_i to denote $S_{i,i}$. If the rank r of $\mathbf{M}$ is less than q, then exactly the last $q - r$ diagonal entries are zero. Furthermore, the numbers s_i (singular values) are uniquely determined by the square roots of the eigenvalues of $\mathbf{M} \mathbf{M}^\top$. The columns of $\mathbf{U}$ are eigenvectors of $\mathbf{M} \mathbf{M}^\top$ and the columns of $\mathbf{V}$ are eigenvectors of $\mathbf{M}^\top \mathbf{M}$ (arranged in the same order as the corresponding eigenvalues s_i^2). Such a decomposition is called the Singular Value Decomposition (SVD) (e.g., Theorem 7.3.5 of Horn and Johnson, 1985). Under some mild technical assumptions, the SVD can also be extended to bounded linear operators.

The Frobenius norm of a matrix $\mathbf{M} \in \mathbb{R}^{n \times m}$ is defined as $\|\mathbf{M}\|_F = \sqrt{\sum_{i=1}^{n} \sum_{j=1}^{m} |M_{i,j}|^2}$. It is invariant under orthogonal transformations and

$$\|\mathbf{M}\|_F^2 = s_1^2 + \ldots + s_q^2 \qquad q = \min\{m, n\}. \tag{1}$$

The following theorem allows us to write the best rank-k approximation to a given matrix $\mathbf{M}$ in terms of its SVD (Page 450 (Problem 1) and Example 7.4.5, Horn and Johnson, 1985).

Theorem 1. *Let* $\mathbf{M} = \mathbf{U} \mathbf{S} \mathbf{V}^\top$ *denote the SVD of* $\mathbf{M} \in \mathbb{R}^{n \times m}$. *For* $k < r = \mathrm{rank}(\mathbf{M})$ *define* $\mathbf{M}_k = \mathbf{U} \widehat{\mathbf{S}} \mathbf{V}^\top$ *where* $\widehat{\mathbf{S}} \in \mathbb{R}^{n \times m}$ *with* $\hat{s}_i = s_i$ *for* $i = 1, \ldots, k$ *and* $\hat{s}_j = 0$ *for* $k < j \leq m$. *Then*

$$\min_{\mathrm{rank}(\widehat{\mathbf{M}})=k} \|\mathbf{M} - \widehat{\mathbf{M}}\|_F^2 = \|\mathbf{M} - \mathbf{M}_k\|_F^2 = \sum_{j=k+1}^{q} s_j^2, \qquad q = \min\{m, n\}.$$

For a Hadamard matrix $\mathbf{H}$ of dimension $n \times n$, it is easy to see that $\mathrm{rank}(\mathbf{H}) = n$ and $\mathbf{H} \mathbf{H}^\top = n \mathbf{I}$. Thus all eigenvalues of $\mathbf{H} \mathbf{H}^\top$ are equal to n and the n singular values s_i are equal to $\sqrt{n}$. The flat spectrum of the Hadamard matrix will be used later to prove our lower bounds.

3   No Embedding Leads to Small Loss

As discussed before, each of the n possible linear targets in the Hadamard Learning Problem corresponds to a standard basis vector $\mathbf{e}_i$. In our first theorem, we show that any linear combination of the instances (rows of the Hadamard matrix) in which not all instances are used is far away from all targets. So any algorithm that predicts with a linear combination of the instances cannot express any of the targets unless all examples have been observed.

Theorem 2. *Any linear combination of $k < n$ instances/rows of the n-dimensional Hadamard matrix has distance at least $\sqrt{1 - \frac{k}{n}}$ from any of the n-dimensional standard basis vectors.*

We now show that linear combinations of $k < n$ rows are not just far away from any standard basis vector, but they also have large average square loss w.r.t. any such target. In the theorem below we give lower bounds for the noise-free case, i.e., when the labels are consistent with a target (which is one of the components of the instances).

Theorem 3. *For any linear combination of k rows of the n-dimensional Hadamard matrix and any n dimensional standard basis vector, the average square loss over all n examples is at least $1 - \frac{k}{n}$.*

Next we show that a similar lower bound can be proven even if the instances can be embedded into any higher dimensional space (for instance by using a kernel function). So this lower bound applies to all algorithms that predict with a linear combination of the expanded instances. Our proof exploits the flat SVD spectrum of Hadamard matrices.

Our theorem applies to any learning algorithm that follows the following protocol: It first chooses an embedding of all n instances. It then receives a set of k embedded training instances labeled by one of the targets (i.e., we are in the noise-free case)[6]. The algorithm then produces a linear combination of the embedded training instances as its linear weight vector in feature space and is then evaluated w.r.t. the same target on all n instances.

Theorem 4. *For any embedding of the rows of the n-dimensional Hadamard matrix $\mathbf{H}$, any subset of k rows and any n linear combinations $\mathbf{w}_i$ of the embedded k rows (one per target), the following holds: If ℓ_i is the average square loss of $\mathbf{w}_i$ on the i-th target (where the average is taken over **all** n examples), then $\frac{\sum_i \ell_i}{n} \geq 1 - \frac{k}{n}$.*

The generality of the theorem might be confusing: The theorem holds for any weight vectors that are linear combinations of the k embedded *training instances*, where the coefficients of the linear combination can depend arbitrarily on the target and the training instances. In particular, the lower bound holds for the following learning model: The k training instances are drawn at random w.r.t. any distribution. If the k training instances are drawn with replacement, then the learner might end up with $k' < k$ unique instances and the lower bound

---

[6] Our results hold even if the learner embeds the instances *after* seeing the k training instances. The only restriction is that the embedding must be the same for all targets.

for those draws is then $1 - \frac{k'}{n}$ instead of $1 - \frac{k}{n}$. More discussion of probabilistic models is given in Section 5.

Note that this lower bound is weaker than the previous one in that we now average over instances *and* targets. However, since we have a lower bound on the average over targets, that same lower bound must hold for at least one of the targets. The average loss is measured w.r.t. the uniform distribution *on all* n instances. This is crucial because it disallows the case in which the algorithm predicts badly on the k training instances and well on the $n - k$ remaining test instances. Averaging over targets is also necessary because as we shall see later, for some embeddings there are linear combinations of k expanded instances that predict perfectly on k of the n targets.

Proof. Let $\phi : \mathbb{R}^n \to \mathbb{R}^m$ denote an arbitrary function that is used to map the rows of the $n \times n$ Hadamard matrix $\mathbf{H}$ to a matrix $\mathbf{Z} \in \mathbb{R}^{n \times m}$. We use $\widehat{\mathbf{H}}$ and $\widehat{\mathbf{Z}}$ to denote the sub-matrices of $\mathbf{H}$ and $\mathbf{Z}$ which contain the k rows corresponding to the training instances. The weight vector must be a linear combination of the embedded instances, i.e., the k rows of $\widehat{\mathbf{Z}}$. Let $\mathbf{w}_i = \widehat{\mathbf{Z}}^\top \mathbf{a}_i$ denote the weight vector when the instances are labeled with the i-th column of $\mathbf{H}$. We use matrix notation to combine all n learning problems into one. Let $\mathbf{A} \in \mathbb{R}^{k \times n}$ be the matrix whose columns are the coefficient vectors $\mathbf{a}_i$. All n weight vectors form the matrix $[\mathbf{w}_1, \ldots, \mathbf{w}_n] = \widehat{\mathbf{Z}}^\top \mathbf{A}$. Observe that the prediction of the algorithm on the n rows of the Hadamard matrix is given by $\mathbf{Z} \widehat{\mathbf{Z}}^\top \mathbf{A}$, while the target predictions are $\mathbf{H} \mathbf{I} = \mathbf{H}$. For the square loss we can write the total loss of the n linear classifiers as $\| \mathbf{Z} \widehat{\mathbf{Z}}^\top \mathbf{A} - \mathbf{H} \|_F^2$. The Hadamard matrix $\mathbf{H}$ has rank n while $\widehat{\mathbf{Z}}$ has rank at most k and hence $\mathbf{Z} \widehat{\mathbf{Z}}^\top \mathbf{A}$ has rank at most k. From Theorem 1 it is clear that the loss is minimized when $\mathbf{Z} \widehat{\mathbf{Z}}^\top \mathbf{A} = \mathbf{U} \widehat{\mathbf{S}} \mathbf{V}^\top$ where $\mathbf{H} = \mathbf{U} \mathbf{S} \mathbf{V}^\top$ is the SVD of $\mathbf{H}$ and $\hat{s}_i = s_i = \sqrt{n}$ for $i = 1, \ldots, k$ while $\hat{s}_{k+1} = \ldots = \hat{s}_n = 0$. The squared Frobenius norm of the residual or the total loss incurred by the algorithm is therefore $(n-k)s_n^2 = n(n-k)$. By uniformly averaging the loss over the n targets and n instances, the expected value of the loss is $1 - \frac{k}{n}$. ∎

If the hypotheses are allowed to be a bias plus a linear combination of the k chosen training instances, then the total loss of the n classifiers becomes $\| \mathbf{Z} \widehat{\mathbf{Z}}^\top \mathbf{A} + \mathbf{B} - \mathbf{H} \|_F^2$, where the bias matrix $\mathbf{B}$ is any $n \times n$ matrix with identical entries in each column. Since $\mathbf{B}$ has rank one, $\mathbf{Z} \widehat{\mathbf{Z}}^\top \mathbf{A} + \mathbf{B}$ has rank at most $k + 1$. Thus the lower bound in the above theorem changes to $1 - \frac{k+1}{n}$ instead of $1 - \frac{k}{n}$. So the lower bounds discussed in this section are not majorly affected by allowing a bias, and for the sake of simplicity we only state our results for the homogeneous case.

There is a trivial kernel that shows that the above theorem can be tight: We let the ith row of $\mathbf{H}$ map to the n-dimensional standard basis vector $\mathbf{e}_i$ (i.e., $\mathbf{Z} = \mathbf{I}$). After seeing a subset of k training instances (labeled by one of the targets), we build a hypothesis weight vector $\mathbf{w}$ as follows: w_i is set to y_i if the ith row was a training instance labeled with y_i and zero otherwise. This weight vector $\mathbf{w} \in \mathbb{R}^n$ is a linear combination of the training instances (which are all standard basis vectors $\mathbf{e}_j$ s.t. row j of $\mathbf{Z}$ is one of the k training instances). The predictions of $\mathbf{w}$ are as follows: They agree with the labels of the target on the k training instances and are zero on the remaining $n - k$ instances. We call any weight vector with the above predictions a *memorizing* weight vector. Whenever the target labels are ± 1, any memorizing weight vector has average loss $1 - \frac{k}{n}$ on the n instances. So for any of the n standard basis vectors the average loss on the n instances is exactly $1 - \frac{k}{n}$.

Note that the Hadamard matrix itself is a rotated and scaled unit matrix. So the embedding $\mathbf{Z} = \mathbf{H}$ (i.e., the identity embedding) could also be used to realize memorizing weight vectors for each target. In other words an optimal embedding for the Hadamard problem is the identity embedding (used in theorems 2 and 3). Theorem 4 shows that no kernel can lead to an improvement (when averaged over targets).

The following embedding shows that averaging over targets is necessary in the above theorem and the lower bound does not necessarily hold for the average loss w.r.t. *each* target (as was the case for the identity kernel (Theorem 3)). In this embedding $\mathbf{Z}$ consists of the first k columns of $\mathbf{H}$ (i.e., the dimension of the instances is shrunk from n down to k). Furthermore let $\widehat{\mathbf{Z}}$ be the first k rows of $\mathbf{Z}$ (in other words $\widehat{\mathbf{Z}} = \mathbf{H}(1 : k, 1 : k)$ and is nonsingular). We first define a weight vector $\mathbf{w}_i$ for each target $\mathbf{e}_i$ and then show that these weight vectors are realizable as linear combinations of the k training instances: Let $\mathbf{w}_i$ be zero if $i > k$ and $\mathbf{w}_i = \mathbf{e}_i$ otherwise. To realize these weight vectors as linear combinations of the k training instances set the coefficient vector $\mathbf{a}_i$ to zero if $i > k$ and to the ith column of $(\widehat{\mathbf{Z}}^T)^{-1}$ otherwise. Now the prediction vector $\mathbf{Z}\mathbf{w}_i$ is the ith column of $\mathbf{H}$, if $i \leq k$, and zero otherwise. In other words, using this embedding, k of the targets can be predicted perfectly (average loss 0), and the remaining $n - k$ targets have average loss 1. When we average over all n instances *and* targets, then this average is still $1 - \frac{k}{n}$ (So again the above theorem is tight). However now the average loss for each target is not lower bounded by $1 - \frac{k}{n}$, and therefore Theorem 4 cannot be strengthened as discussed above.

Note that the only fact about the Hadamard matrix that enters into the previous theorem is that its SVD spectrum is flat and it is straightforward to generalize the above theorems to arbitrary matrices. For the sake of simplicity we go back to averaging over all instances.

Corollary 1. *As in Theorem 4, but now $\mathbf{H}$ is any $n \times n$ dimensional matrix with SVD spectrum s_i. Then the lower bound on the expected square loss over all n instances changes to $\frac{1}{n^2} \sum_{i=k+1}^{n} s_i^2$. When all singular values are equal to s, then the lower bound becomes $(1 - \frac{k}{n})\frac{s^2}{n}$.*

4   Random Matrices Are Hard

Hadamard matrices seem rather special. However we will show that if the Hadamard matrix is replaced by a random ± 1 matrix, then (with high probability) the lower bound of Theorem 4 holds with slightly smaller constants. The reason for this is that the SVD spectrum of random ± 1 matrices has a heavy tail and hence when learning the columns of a random matrix, the expected loss is large for at least one column (as in Corollary 1). In Figure 1 we plot the spectrum s_i (as a function of i) of the Hadamard matrix which is a flat line at level $\sqrt{n}$, where $n = 1024$. We also plot the spectra of 500 random 1024×1024 matrices with ± 1 entries. Each such spectrum s_i is a line that is closely approximated by the linear curve $2\sqrt{n} - \frac{2i}{\sqrt{n}}$. Notice the heavy tail and low variance of the spectra: In the plot, the 500 lines become one thick line.

Recall that after seeing half of the examples, the expected square loss for the Hadamard Learning Problem is at least $\frac{1}{2}$ for at least one of the target columns (Theorem 4). When the matrix is chosen at random, then Corollary 1 implies that this loss is still about $\frac{1}{4}$.

Before we detail what is provable for random matrices we would like to discuss some related work. In Ben-David et al. (2002) it was shown that most concept classes of VC dimension d can be embedded only with a trivial 2-2 margin. This is seen as evidence that most concept classes of VC dimension d "may" be hard to learn by kernel based algorithms. (Note that random concept classes of VC dimension d might not even be *efficiently* learnable by *any* algorithm.) Furthermore, we are not aware of any formal lower bound in terms of the 2-2 margin.

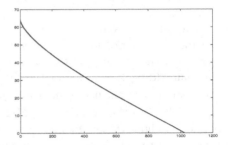

Fig. 1. The horizontal line represents the spectrum s_i (as a function of i) of the 1024 dimensional Hadamard matrix (at level $\sqrt{1024}$). The plot also contains the spectra of 500 random 1024×1024 matrices with $\{\pm 1\}$ entries. The variance of these spectra lines is small and therefore the 500 lines form one thick line

In contrast, we completely bypass the notion of the margin and give a stronger result. We define a class of *easy to learn linear problems* characterized by a random $n \times n$ matrix with ± 1 entries[7]. The instances are the rows of this matrix and the target concepts are the columns of this matrix.

In the full paper we show analytically that, with high probability, any algorithm that predicts with a linear combination of the instances cannot learn random problems of this type. By Corollary 1 it suffices to investigate the properties of the random variable $Q = \frac{1}{n^2} \sum_{i=k+1}^{n} s_i^2$. Using techniques from Davidson and Szarek (2003), Meckes (2004), we show that Q is sharply concentrated around $1 - c \cdot \frac{k}{n}$ where c is a scalar constant.

---

[7] The VC dimension of our learning problem is at most $\lg n$.

5   Probabilistic Models

In this section we prove lower bounds for the case when the training examples are chosen based on some probabilistic model.

Theorem 5. *Assume we have a uniform distribution on the n rows of the Hadamard matrix. Assume the algorithm first embeds[8] the n rows and then draws k random training examples without replacement that are all labeled by one of the n targets. It then forms its hypothesis by choosing a linear combination of the embedded k training instances.*

If ℓ_i is the expected average square loss when the target is the i-th target and the loss is averaged over **all** *n examples, then $\frac{\sum_i \ell_i}{n} \geq 1 - \frac{k}{n}$.*

Proof. Follows from Theorem 4.   ■

The lower bound on $\frac{\sum_i \ell_i}{n}$ is tight for the identity kernel and the memorizing weight vector.

Note that we always average the loss over all n instances. We believe that this is the only reasonable model for the case when the instance domain is finite. In the full paper we also develop lower bounds for the case when the loss is averaged over the $n - k$ test instances. There are no surprises but the bounds are slightly more complicated to state.

We now prove a similar theorem for the case when the training examples are drawn with replacement.

Theorem 6. *Assume we have a uniform distribution on the n rows of the Hadamard matrix. Assume the algorithm first embeds the n rows and then draws t training examples independently at random with replacement that are labeled by one of the n targets. It then forms its hypothesis by choosing the linear combination of the t embedded training instances.*

If ℓ_i is the expected average square loss when the target is the i-th target and the loss is averaged over **all** *n examples, then $\frac{\sum_i \ell_i}{n} \geq \left(1 - \frac{1}{n}\right)^t$.*

Proof. By Theorem 4 the average square loss (over all instances and targets) conditioned on the fact that k distinct training examples were drawn is at least $1 - \frac{k}{n} = \frac{n-k}{n}$. Note that $n - k$ is the number of examples *missed* in the training set. Let M be a random variable denoting the number of missed examples. By the above argument the lower bound is $\frac{E(M)}{n}$.

Clearly, $M = \sum_i M_i$, where M_i is a binary random variable indicating whether the ith example was missed, and

$$E(M) = E(\sum_i M_i) = \sum_i E(M_i) = nE(M_1) = n(1 - \frac{1}{n})^t. \qquad ■$$

---

[8] Theorem 4 guarantees that the lower bound also holds for the following protocol: The algorithm first draws k rows without replacement. It then chooses its embedding (that may depend on the chosen rows). Finally the chosen rows are labeled by one of the targets and a linear combination of the embedded k training instances is chosen as the hypothesis.

6   Rotation Invariance

Kernel algorithms are commonly motivated by weight updates derived from a "Representer Theorem" (Kimeldorf and Wahba, 1971, Schölkopf et al., 2001). This type of theorem states that if the weight vector is produced by a certain minimization problem, then it must be a linear combination of the expanded instances. In the simplest form

$$\mathbf{w} = \operatorname*{arginf}_{\mathbf{w}'} \left(\Omega(\|\mathbf{w}'\|^2) + L(\mathbf{w}') \right), \tag{2}$$

where Ω is a monotonic non-decreasing function and L is a convex real-valued loss function that only depends on the dot products between the weight vector $\mathbf{w}'$ (in feature space) and the expanded instances $\phi(\mathbf{x}_i)$.

Here, we follow Kivinen and Warmuth (1997) and first point out that there is a simple *geometric* property of an algorithm that guarantees that the algorithm produces a linear combination of the expanded instances. This property is the notion of rotation invariance of an algorithm. Representer theorems are a special case of this characterization because the objective functions (eg. (2)) used in these theorems are rotation invariant.

Representer theorems (and more generally rotation invariance) guarantee that the weight vector of an algorithm is a linear combination of the expanded instances. However, the lower bounds of our paper hold for *any* algorithm whose hypotheses are such linear combinations. This *includes* (see example at the end of section) algorithms that are not rotation invariant and algorithms that break the kernel paradigm.

We denote the examples as $(\mathbf{x}, y)$ and assume that instances $\mathbf{x}$ already lie in some expanded feature space $\mathcal{X}$ and the labels y in some label domain $\mathcal{Y} \subseteq \mathbb{R}$. For the sake of simplicity the instance domain $\mathcal{X} = \mathbb{R}^n$ for some n. An algorithm maps arbitrary sequences of examples $\langle \mathcal{S} \rangle = \{(\mathbf{x}_1, y_1), (\mathbf{x}_2, y_2), \dots, (\mathbf{x}_T, y_T)\}$ to a weight vector $\mathbf{w}(\langle \mathcal{S} \rangle)$ in the instance domain. We study the behavior of algorithms when they receive rotated sequences. If $\mathbf{U}$ is an orthonormal matrix in $\mathbb{R}^{n \times n}$, then $\langle \mathbf{U}\mathcal{S} \rangle$ denotes the sequence $\{(\mathbf{U}\mathbf{x}_1, y_1), (\mathbf{U}\mathbf{x}_2, y_2), \dots, (\mathbf{U}\mathbf{x}_T, y_T)\}$. (Note that the rotation only affects the instances.)

Theorem 7. *Let* $\langle \mathcal{S} \rangle = \{(\mathbf{x}_1, y_1), (\mathbf{x}_2, y_2), \dots, (\mathbf{x}_T, y_T)\} \subseteq \mathbb{R}^n \times \mathbb{R}$ *be any sequence of examples and let* $\mathbf{w}$ *be the input-output mapping of an algorithm from sequences of examples in* $\mathbb{R}^n \times \mathbb{R}$ *to vectors in* $\mathbb{R}^n$. *Consider the following three statements:*

1. $\mathbf{w}$ *is rotation invariant in the sense that*

$$\mathbf{w}(\langle \mathcal{S} \rangle)^\top \mathbf{x} = \mathbf{w}(\langle \mathbf{U}\mathcal{S} \rangle)^\top \mathbf{U}\mathbf{x},$$

   for all sequences $\langle \mathcal{S} \rangle$, *orthonormal matrices* $\mathbf{U} \in \mathbb{R}^{n \times n}$, *and* $\mathbf{x} \in \mathbb{R}^n$.
2. *For all* $\langle \mathcal{S} \rangle$, $\mathbf{w}(\langle \mathcal{S} \rangle)$ *must be a linear combination of the instances of* $\langle \mathcal{S} \rangle$.
3. *For all* $\langle \mathcal{S} \rangle$ *and rotation matrices* $\mathbf{U}$, $\mathbf{w}(\langle \mathbf{U}\mathcal{S} \rangle) = \mathbf{U}\mathbf{w}(\langle \mathcal{S} \rangle)$.

Now, $1 \implies 2 \wedge 3$ *and* $3 \implies 1$.

The following example shows that the implications $2 \Longrightarrow 3$ and $2 \Longrightarrow 1$ do not hold in general:

$$\mathbf{w}(\langle\, \mathcal{S}\, \rangle) = \begin{cases} \mathbf{0} & \text{if } x_{1,1} > 0 \\ \mathbf{x}_1 & \text{otherwise.} \end{cases}$$

Clearly, $\mathbf{w}(\langle\, \mathcal{S}\, \rangle)$ is a linear combination of the instances in $\langle\, \mathcal{S}\, \rangle$ and therefore Statement 2 holds for this algorithm. Choose $\mathbf{U}$ as $-\mathbf{I}$, i.e., minus the identity matrix and the first instance in $\langle\, \mathcal{S}\, \rangle$ as $\mathbf{x}_1 = (1, 0, \ldots, 0)^\top$. Now, $\mathbf{w}(\langle\, \mathcal{S}\, \rangle) = \mathbf{0}$ and $\mathbf{w}(\langle\, \mathbf{U}\mathcal{S}\, \rangle) = \mathbf{x}_1$ and therefore statements 1 and 3 are both false. Note that in this example the individual components of the instances are accessed and thus the kernel paradigm is violated. However, as long as the hypotheses produced are linear combinations, our lower bounds apply.

Even though we only defined rotation invariance in $\mathbb{R}^n$, it should be apparent that this notion can easily be generalized to arbitrary RKHS.

7   Leaving the Span with Constraints

Consider a set of k instances (rows) of the following form (Figure 2): All components are ± 1 and all 2^k bit patterns exactly appear once as a column. Assume the instances are labeled by one of the $n = 2^k$ columns (i.e., the target is one of the n standard basis vectors). Consider two algorithms: The first is any algorithm that predicts with a linear combination of the instances and the second any algorithm that produces a weight vector consistent with the examples *and* the *additional constraints* that the weights are non-negative and sum to one. For each of the algorithms, form a matrix whose columns are the n weight vectors produced by the respective algorithm as the target is varied. Clearly, the rank of the first algorithm's weight matrix is at most k (even if the instances are allowed to be embedded). However,

$$\begin{array}{cccccccc} -1 & +1 & -1 & +1 & -1 & +1 & -1 & +1 \\ -1 & -1 & +1 & +1 & -1 & -1 & +1 & +1 \\ -1 & -1 & -1 & -1 & +1 & +1 & +1 & +1 \end{array}$$

Fig. 2.   Each bit pattern appears once as a column of the $\lg n$ instances ($n = 8$).

we will show now that the rank of the second algorithms weight matrix is at least 2^k.

Lemma 1. *Assume the examples are the rows of a $k \times n$ dimensional matrix with entries ± 1 which are labeled by one of the columns of the matrix. Then any weight vector $\mathbf{w}$ that is consistent with the examples and satisfies the above additional constraints has the following property: If $w_i > 0$ then the i-th column coincides with the labels. If all columns are unique, then the $\mathbf{w}$ is always the standard basis vector that identifies the target column.*

Proof. W.l.o.g. the labels are all ones. Otherwise, multiply the corresponding instance and label by -1 and keep the weights unchanged. Now, because of the additional constraints on the weights, it is easy to see that all non-zero weights must be on columns that contain only ones. ∎

This means that the weight matrix of the second algorithm is the n-dimensional unit matrix (rank $n = 2^k$). So adding the constraint forced the rank of the weight matrix to grow exponentially with the number of examples instead of linearly.

See Figure 3 for a simple problem where imposing these additional constraints makes the weight of the consistent column grow exponentially. Maintaining constraints can be expensive. In particular, the non-negativity constraints access the individual features and this breaks the kernel paradigm.

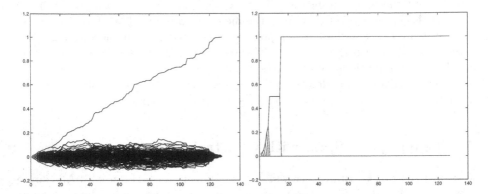

Fig. 3. The examples are the rows of a random 128×128 dimensional matrix with ± 1 entries labeled by column one. Let $\mathbf{w}^t$ be the shortest weight vector consistent with the first t examples. For $1 \leq i \leq 128$, we plot (left) the w_i^t as a function of t (x−axis). The line representing the first weight w_1^t grows roughly linearly and only after seeing all 128 examples the target weight vector $\mathbf{e}_1$ is found. On the right we have the same plot, but we enforce the additional constraints that $w_i^t \geq 0$ and $\sum_{i=1}^{n} w_i^t = 1$. Now the first weight grows much faster and the target weight vector is found much sooner

One simple algorithm that maintains the additional constraints is the Exponentiated Gradient (EG) Algorithm whose weight vector has the following *exponential form*:

$$w_i = \frac{w_i^1 \exp\left(\sum_{t=1}^{k} a_t x_i^t\right)}{Z}, \text{ where } Z = \sum_{j=1}^{n} w_j^1 \exp\left(\sum_{t=1}^{k} a_t x_j^t\right). \quad (3)$$

Here $\mathbf{w}^1$ is an initial weight vector satisfying the additional constraints. Note that $\ln w_i = \sum_{t=1}^{k} a_t x_i^t + \ln w_i^1 - \ln Z$. So except for the additional terms introduced by the initial weights and the normalization, the logarithms of the weights are a linear combination of examples [9].

If the EG algorithm is used as our second algorithm then it realizes the n standard basis vectors as follows: Set the coefficients a_t of the k examples to

---

[9] Set the nth weight to $w_n = 1 - \sum_{j=1}^{n-1} w_j$. If the initial weights are uniform then $\ln \frac{w_j}{1 - \sum_{j'=1}^{n-1} w_{j'}} = \sum_{t=1}^{k} (a_t x_j^t - a_n x_n^t)$.

$\pm\eta$ and let the learning rate η go to infinity. Each such weight vector converges to a standard basis vector, one for each of the $2^k = n$ sign patterns of the coefficients. The cost of the EG algorithm is $O(1)$ per example and feature (Kivinen and Warmuth, 1997) and again the kernel paradigm is broken because individual features are accessed.

In general, weight updates can be defined in terms of a link function[10] $\mathbf{f}$ or its associated Bregman divergence (Azoury and Warmuth, 2001). The updated weights minimize a Bregman divergence plus η times the loss on the last instance and the Bregman divergence serves as a barrier function for maintaining the constraints (e.g., Kivinen and Warmuth, 2001, Helmbold et al., 1999).

Bounds: We only sketch the bounds provable for a slightly more general version of the EG algorithm called $\mathrm{EG}^\pm$ (Kivinen and Warmuth, 1997). This algorithm maintains the constraint $\| \mathbf{w} \|_1 \leq U_1$. Assume the instances have infinity norm at most X_∞ and there is a consistent weight vector $\mathbf{u}$ s.t. $\| \mathbf{u} \|_1 \leq U_1$. (Both U_1 and X_∞ are parameters to the algorithm). One can show that after receiving k training examples drawn from any fixed distribution, the expected loss[11] of this algorithm (w.r.t. the same distributions) is $\frac{X_\infty^2 U_1^2 \ln n}{k}$ (e.g., Kivinen and Warmuth, 1997). If the learning rate is properly tuned, then these algorithms also have good bounds in the noisy case.

It is important to note that even though the bounds provable for these algorithms are messy to state, the essentials are quite simple. The weight vectors are defined using a relative entropy regularization term (in general any Bregman divergence) instead of the squared Euclidean distance used for the kernel based algorithms (which predict with a linear combination of the instances).

8 Conclusion

In Kivinen and Warmuth (1997) and Gentile and Littlestone (1999) a pair of dual norms was used to characterize the generalization performance of different families of learning algorithms. For each algorithm there are certain settings in which its bound beats the bounds of the other algorithm. In this paper we showed how the lower bounds for one important family (the one predicting with a linear combination of the instances) still hold even if the instances can be embedded into any Euclidean space.

Kernel methods are often described as "non-linear" methods because they allow the use of non-linear features. However, no matter what embedding is used, kernel methods build linear models in feature space and for some problems this is highly restrictive.

---

[10] Now $\mathbf{f}(\langle \mathcal{S} \rangle)$ is a linear combination of the (embedded) instances and $\mathbf{f}(\mathbf{w}(\langle \mathcal{S} \rangle))^\top \mathbf{x} = \mathbf{f}(\mathbf{w}(\langle \mathbf{U} \mathcal{S} \rangle))^\top \mathbf{U}\mathbf{x}$ for any orthonormal matrix $\mathbf{U}$.

[11] The bound only holds for the average weight vector: Do one pass over all k examples; starting from the initial weight vector, update the weights after each example is processed and average the resulting $k + 1$ weight vectors (e.g., Section 8 Kivinen and Warmuth, 1997).

Acknowledgments. We thank Claudio Gentile, Adam Kowalczyk, Alan Pajor and Stéphane Canu for insightful discussions.

References

K. Azoury and M. K. Warmuth. Relative loss bounds for on-line density estimation with the exponential family of distributions. *Machine Learning*, 43(3):211 – 246, 2001. Special issue on Theoretical Advances in On-line Learning, Game Theory and Boosting.

S. Ben-David, N. Eiron, and H. U. Simon. Limitations of learning via embeddings in Euclidean half-spaces. *Journal of Machine Learning Research*, 3:441 – 461, Nov. 2002.

Nello Cristianini, Colin Campbell, and John Shawe-Taylor. Multiplicative updatings for support vector learning. In *Proc. of European Symposium on Artificial Neural Networks*, pages 189 – 194, 1999.

K. R. Davidson and S. J. Szarek. Banach space theory and local operator theory. In J. Lindenstrauss and W. Johnson, editors, *Handbook of the Geometry of Banach Spaces*. North-Holland, 2003.

J. Forster, N. Schmitt, and H. U. Simon. Estimating the optimal margins of embeddings in Euclidean half spaces. In *Proc. of the 14th Annual Conference on Computational Learning Theory*, pages 402 – 415. Springer, 2001.

C. Gentile and N. Littlestone. The robustness of the *p*-norm algorithms. In *Proc. 12th Annu. Conf. on Comput. Learning Theory*, pages 1–11. ACM Press, New York, 1999.

Claudio Gentile and M. K. Warmuth. Linear hinge loss and average margin. In M. S. Kearns, S. A. Solla, and D. A. Cohn, editors, *Advances in Neural Information Processing Systems 11*, pages 225 – 231, Cambridge, MA, 1999. MIT Press.

D. P. Helmbold, J. Kivinen, and M. K. Warmuth. Relative loss bounds for single neurons. *IEEE Transactions on Neural Networks*, 10(6):1291 – 1304, Nov. 1999.

R. Herbrich, T. Graepel, and R. C. Williamson. *Innovations in Machine Learning*, chapter The Structure of Version Space. Springer, January 2005. D. Holmes and L. C. Jain Editors.

R. A. Horn and C. R. Johnson. *Matrix Analysis*. Cambridge University Press, Cambridge, 1985.

R. Khardon, D. Roth, and R. Servedio. Efficiency versus convergence of Boolean kernels for on-line learning algorithms. In *Advances in Neural Information Processing Systems 14*, pages 423–430, 2001.

G. S. Kimeldorf and G. Wahba. Some results on Tchebycheffian spline functions. *J. Math. Anal. Applic.*, 33:82 – 95, 1971.

J. Kivinen and M. K. Warmuth. Relative loss bounds for multidimensional regression problems. *Machine Learning*, 45(3):301 – 329, 2001.

J. Kivinen and M. K. Warmuth. Exponentiated gradient versus gradient descent for linear predictors. *Information and Computation*, 132(1):1 – 64, January 1997.

J. Kivinen, M. K. Warmuth, and P. Auer. The perceptron learning algorithm vs. Winnow: Linear vs. logarithmic mistake bounds when few input variables are relevant. *Artificial Intelligence*, 97(1 - 2):325 – 343, 1997.

Nick Littlestone. Learning quickly when irrelevant attributes abound: A new linear-threshold algorithm. *Machine Learning*, 2:285 – 318, 1988.

M. W. Meckes. Concentration of norms and eigenvalues of random matrices. *Journal of Functional Analysis*, 211(2):508–524, June 2004.

L. Pitt and M. K. Warmuth. The minimum consistent DFA problem cannot be approximated within any polynomial. *Journal of the ACM*, 40(1):95 – 142, 1993.

R. Schapire, Y. Freund, P. L. Bartlett, and W. S. Lee. Boosting the margin: A new explanation for the effectiveness of voting methods. *Annals of Statistics*, 26:1651 – 1686, 1998.

B. Schölkopf, R. Herbrich, and A. J. Smola. A generalized representer theorem. In *Proc. of the Annual Conference on Computational Learning Theory*, pages 416 – 426, 2001.

E. Takimoto and M. K. Warmuth. Path kernels and multiplicative updates. *Journal of Machine Learning Research*, 4:773 – 818, October 2003.

M. K. Warmuth. Towards representation independence in PAC-learning. In J. P. Jantke, editor, *Proc. of AII-89 Workshop on Analogical and Inductive Inference*, volume 397 of *Lecture Notes in Artificial Intelligence 397*, pages 78 – 103. Springer-Verlag, October 1989.

Variations on U-Shaped Learning

Lorenzo Carlucci[1,*], Sanjay Jain[2,**], Efim Kinber[3], and Frank Stephan[4,***]

[1] Department of Computer and Information Sciences, University of Delaware,
Newark, DE 19716-2586,USA and Dipartimento di Matematica,
Università di Siena, Pian dei Mantellini 44, Siena, Italy
`carlucci5@unisi.it`
[2] School of Computing, National University of Singapore,
Singapore 117543
`sanjay@comp.nus.edu.sg`
[3] Department of Computer Science, Sacred Heart University,
Fairfield, CT 06432-1000, U.S.A
`kinbere@sacredheart.edu`
[4] School of Computing and Department of Mathematics,
National University of Singapore, Singapore 117543
`fstephan@comp.nus.edu.sg`

Abstract. The paper deals with the following problem: is returning to wrong conjectures necessary to achieve full power of learning? Returning to wrong conjectures complements the paradigm of *U-shaped learning* [2, 6, 8, 20, 24] when a learner returns to old *correct* conjectures. We explore our problem for classical models of learning in the limit: **TxtEx**-learning – when a learner stabilizes on a correct conjecture, and **TxtBc**-learning – when a learner stabilizes on a sequence of grammars representing the target concept. In all cases, we show that, surprisingly, returning to wrong conjectures is sometimes necessary to achieve full power of learning. On the other hand it is not necessary to return to old "overgeneralizing" conjectures containing elements not belonging to the target language. We also consider our problem in the context of so-called *vacillatory* learning when a learner stabilizes to a finite number of correct grammars. In this case we show that both returning to old wrong conjectures and returning to old "overgeneralizing" conjectures is necessary for full learning power. We also show that, surprisingly, learners consistent with the input seen so far can be made *decisive* [2, 21] – they do not have to return to any old conjectures – wrong or right.

1 Introduction

U-shaped learning is a well-known pattern of learning behaviour in which the learner first learns the correct behaviour, then abandons it, and finally returns

---

* Supported in part by NSF grant number NSF CCR-0208616.
** Supported in part by NUS grant number R252–000–127–112.
*** Supported in part by NUS grant number R252–000–212–112.

P. Auer and R. Meir (Eds.): COLT 2005, LNAI 3559, pp. 382–397, 2005.

to the correct behaviour once again. The phenomenon of U-shaped learning has been observed by cognitive and developmental psychologists in many different cases of child development – such as language learning [6, 20, 24], understanding of temperature [24, 25] and face recognition [7]. The ability of models of human learning to accommodate U-shaped learning progressively became one of the important criteria of their adequacy; see [20, 22] and the recent [26].

Cognitive and developmental psychology deals primarily with the problem of designing models of learning that adequately accommodate U-shaped behaviour. Baliga, Case, Merkle, Stephan and Wiehagen [2] who initiated study of U-shaped learning in the context of Gold-style algorithmic learning, asked a different question: is U-shaped behaviour really *necessary* for full learning power? In particular, they showed that U-shaped behaviour is avoidable for so-called **TxtEx**-learning (explanatory learning) – when the learner stabilizes in the limit on a single correct conjecture. This result contrasts with the result by Fulk, Jain and Osherson [13] who demonstrated that U-shaped learning is necessary for the full power of so-called **TxtBc**-learners (behaviourally correct learners) that stabilize on a (possibly infinite) sequence of different grammars representing the target language. In a sequel paper [8], Carlucci, Case, Jain and Stephan investigated U-shaped behaviour with respect to the model of vacillatory (or **TxtFex**) learning, where the learner is required to stabilize on a finite number of correct conjectures. Vacillatory learning, introduced by Case [9], forms a hierarchy of more and more powerful learning criteria between **TxtEx** and **TxtBc** identification. It was shown in [8] that forbidding U-shaped behaviour for vacillatory learners makes the whole hierarchy collapse to simple **TxtEx**-learning, i.e. nullifies the extra power of allowing vacillation between a finite number of conjectures.

U-shaped learning can be viewed as a special case of a more general pattern of learning behaviour, when a learner chooses a hypothesis, then abandons it, then returns to it once again[1]. If a learner returns to a correct conjecture that the learner has previously abandoned, it is, of course, dictated by the goal of correctly learning the target concept. On the other hand, when a learner returns to a previously abandoned *wrong* conjecture, this is not desirable if a learner wants to be efficient. In this paper, we study the following question: if and when returning to wrong conjectures is necessary for the full power of learnability? In particular, we consider

(a) a model in which a learner cannot return to a previously abandoned wrong conjecture;
(b) a model in which a learner cannot return to a previously abandoned conjecture that "overgeneralizes" – more precisely, contains elements not belonging

---

[1] These two meanings of U-shaped behaviour are explicitly distinguished at the beginning of [24], the main reference for the study of U-shaped behaviour.

to the target concept.[2] The latter model is motivated by the fact that over-generalization is one of the major concerns in the study of learning behaviour [20].

We compare both models with regular types of learning in the limit and provide a full answer to the question when and how returning to wrong conjectures is necessary. The results that we obtained lead us to the following general conclusions. If we take **TxtEx** or **TxtBc** identification as a model of learning behaviour, then returning to previously abandoned wrong conjectures is necessary to achieve full power of learnability; however, it is not necessary to return to old "overgeneralizing" conjectures. On the other hand, for vacillatory identification, both returning to wrong conjectures and returning to "overgeneralizing" conjectures is necessary in a very strong sense: forbidding this kind of U-shapes collapses the whole **TxtFex**-hierarchy to simple **TxtEx**-learning. We compare more thoroughly these conclusions with results from [8] on returning to correct conjectures.

The paper has the following structure. Section 2 contains necessary notation and basic definitions. Section 3 contains definitions of all variants of previously known models of non U-shaped learning, as well as the models introduced in the present paper. In Section 4 we explore our variants of non U-shaped learning in the context of **TxtEx**-learning – when learners stabilize on one correct grammar for the target language. Firstly, we show, that, surprisingly, returning to wrong conjectures may be necessary for the full power of **TxtEx**-learning. To prove this result, we establish that learners not returning to wrong conjectures are as powerful as so-called *decisive* learners – the ones that never return to old conjectures (Theorem 7); decisive learners are known [2] to be generally weaker than general **TxtEx**-learners. On the other hand, any **TxtEx**-learner can be replaced by a learner not returning to "overgeneralizing" conjectures (Theorem 8).

In Section 5 we consider our two variants of non U-shaped learning in the context of *vacillatory* learning – when a learner stabilizes to a finite set of grammars describing the target language. We extend a result of Section 4 to show that vacillatory learners without returning to wrong conjectures do no better than just decisive **TxtEx**-learners. As for vacillatory learners not returning to "overgeneralizing" conjectures, they turn out to be doing no better than regular **TxtEx**-learners of this type. It was shown in [8] that the same collapse of the vacillatory hierarchy occurs when return to correct conjectures is forbidden. Thus, forbidding any of the three known variants of U-shaped behaviour nulli-

---

[2] A more appropriate term for this could be "partial overgeneralization", since, strictly speaking, overgeneralization means the situation when the language generated by a conjectured grammar is a proper superset of the target language [1], rather than just containing elements not in the target language. Still, we opted to use just the word "overgeneralization" to emphasize the "over the board" aspects of such type of conjectures. Note that (by Theorem 8 and 22), using the usual definition of "overgeneralization" from [1] for **NOEx** and **NOBc**, does not change these classes. However, the class **NOFex** might change.

fies the extra power of finite vacillation with respect to convergence to a single correct conjecture.

In Section 6 we explore our two variants of non U-shaped learning in the context of **TxtBc**-learnability – when learners stabilize on (potentially infinite) sequences of grammars correctly describing the target language. First, we show that there exist **TxtEx**-learnable classes of languages that cannot be learned without returning to wrong conjectures even by **TxtBc**-learners. From this Theorem and results from [2] it follows that **TxtBc**-learners not returning to correct conjectures sometimes do better than those never returning to wrong conjectures. On the other hand, we then show that, interestingly, **TxtBc**-learners not returning to wrong conjectures can sometimes do better than those never returning to right conjectures. Therefore these two forms of non U-shaped behaviour (avoiding to return to wrong conjectures and avoiding to return to correct conjectures) are of incomparable strength in the context of **TxtBc**-learning. The main result of this section is that, as in case of **TxtEx**-learnability, returning to old "overgeneralizing" conjectures can be circumvented: every **TxtBc**-learner can be replaced by one not returning to "overgeneralizing" conjectures (Theorem 22).

In Section 7 we discover a relationship between the strongest type of non U-shaped learners, that is decisive learners, and *consistent* learners [3, 21], whose conjectures are required to be consistent with the input data seen so far. Consistent learnability is known to be weaker than general **TxtEx**-learnability [3, 21]; moreover, sacrificing consistency, one can learn *pattern languages* faster than any consistent learner [18]. We show that consistent **TxtEx**-learners can be made consistent and decisive (Theorem 25). The result is surprising, since not returning to already used conjectures and being consistent with the input seen so far does not seem to be related – at least on the surface. On the other hand, some decisive learners cannot be made consistent (even if we sacrifice decisiveness).

2   Notation and Preliminaries

Any unexplained recursion theoretic notation is from [23]. The symbol $\mathcal{N}$ denotes the set of natural numbers, $\{0, 1, 2, 3, \ldots\}$. The symbols $\emptyset$, $\subseteq$, $\subset$, $\supseteq$, and $\supset$ denote empty set, subset, proper subset, superset, and proper superset, respectively. Cardinality of a set S is denoted by $\mathrm{card}(S)$. $\mathrm{card}(S) \leq *$ denotes that S is finite. The maximum and minimum of a set are denoted by $\max(\cdot)$, $\min(\cdot)$, respectively, where $\max(\emptyset) = 0$ and $\min(\emptyset) = \infty$. We let $\langle x, y \rangle = \frac{1}{2}(x + y)(x + y + 1) + y$, a standard pairing function.

By φ we denote a fixed *acceptable* programming system for the partial computable functions mapping $\mathcal{N}$ to $\mathcal{N}$ [19, 23]. By φ_i we denote the partial computable function computed by the program with number i in the φ-system. The symbol $\mathcal{R}$ denotes the set of all recursive functions, that is total computable functions. By Φ we denote an arbitrary fixed Blum complexity measure [5, 15] for the φ-system.

By W_i we denote domain(φ_i). That is, W_i is then the recursively enumerable (r.e.) subset of $\mathcal{N}$ accepted by the φ-program i. Note that all acceptable numberings are isomorphic and that one therefore could also define W_i to be the set generated by the i-th grammar. The symbol $\mathcal{E}$ will denote the set of all r.e. languages. The symbol L ranges over $\mathcal{E}$. By $\overline{L}$, we denote the complement of L, that is $\mathcal{N} - L$. The symbol $\mathcal{L}$ ranges over subsets of $\mathcal{E}$. By $W_{i,s}$ we denote the set $\{x < s \mid \Phi_i(x) < s\}$.

We now present concepts from language learning theory. A *sequence* σ is a mapping from an initial segment of $\mathcal{N}$ into $(\mathcal{N} \cup \{\#\})$. The empty sequence is denoted by Λ. The *content* of a sequence σ, denoted content(σ), is the set of natural numbers in the range of σ. The *length* of σ, denoted by $|\sigma|$, is the number of elements in σ. So, $|\Lambda| = 0$. For $n \leq |\sigma|$, the initial sequence of σ of length n is denoted by $\sigma[n]$. So, $\sigma[0]$ is Λ.

Intuitively, $\#$'s represent pauses in the presentation of data. We let σ, τ and γ range over finite sequences. We denote the sequence formed by the concatenation of τ at the end of σ by $\sigma\tau$. Sometimes we abuse the notation and use σx to denote the concatenation of sequence σ and the sequence of length 1 which contains the element x. SEQ denotes the set of all finite sequences. We let $\delta_0, \delta_1, \ldots$ denote a standard recursive 1–1 listing of all the finite sequences. We assume that $\max(\text{content}(\delta_i)) \leq i$. We let ind$(\sigma)$ denote i such that $\delta_i = \sigma$.

A *text* T for a language L [14] is a mapping from $\mathcal{N}$ into $(\mathcal{N} \cup \{\#\})$ such that L is the set of natural numbers in the range of T. $T(i)$ represents the $(i+1)$-th element in the text. The *content* of a text T, denoted by content(T), is the set of natural numbers in the range of T; that is, the language which T is a text for. $T[n]$ denotes the finite initial sequence of T with length n.

A *language learning machine from texts* [14] is an algorithmic device which computes a mapping from SEQ into $\mathcal{N}$. We note that, without loss of generality, for all criteria of learning discussed in this paper, except for consistent learning discussed in Section 7, a learner $\mathbf{M}$ may be assumed to be total.

We let $\mathbf{M}$ range over learning machines. $\mathbf{M}(T[n])$ is interpreted as the grammar (index for an accepting program) conjectured by the learning machine $\mathbf{M}$ on the initial sequence $T[n]$. We say that $\mathbf{M}$ converges on T to i, (written: $\mathbf{M}(T)\!\downarrow = i$) iff $(\forall^\infty n)[\mathbf{M}(T[n]) = i]$.

There are several criteria for a learning machine to be successful on a language. Below we define some of them.

Definition 1. (a) [10,14] $\mathbf{M}$ **TxtEx**-*identifies* a text T just in case $(\exists i \mid W_i = \text{content}(T))$ $(\forall^\infty n)[\mathbf{M}(T[n]) = i]$.
(b) [10] $\mathbf{M}$ **TxtBc**-*identifies* a text T just in case $(\forall^\infty n)[W_{\mathbf{M}(T[n])} = \text{content}(T)]$.
(c) [9] $\mathbf{M}$ **TxtFex**$_a$-*identifies* a text T just in case there exists a set D such that card$(D) \leq a$, $(\forall i \in D)[W_i = \text{content}(T)]$ and $(\forall^\infty n)[W_{\mathbf{M}(T[n])} \in D]$.

Furthermore, for $\mathbf{I} \in \{\mathbf{TxtEx}, \mathbf{TxtBc}, \mathbf{TxtFex}_a\}$: $\mathbf{M}$ **I**-*identifies an r.e. language* L (written: $L \in \mathbf{I}(\mathbf{M})$) just in case $\mathbf{M}$ **I**-identifies each text for L; $\mathbf{M}$ **I**-*identifies a class* $\mathcal{L}$ of r.e. languages (written: $\mathcal{L} \subseteq \mathbf{I}(\mathbf{M})$) just in case $\mathbf{M}$ **I**-identifies each language from $\mathcal{L}$; $\mathbf{I} = \{\mathcal{L} \subseteq \mathcal{E} \mid (\exists \mathbf{M})[\mathcal{L} \subseteq \mathbf{I}(\mathbf{M})]\}$.

[9,10,11] show that, $\mathbf{TxtEx} \subset \mathbf{TxtFex}_2 \subset \mathbf{TxtFex}_3 \subset \ldots \subset \mathbf{TxtFex}_* \subset \mathbf{TxtBc}$.

Definition 2. (a) [12] σ is said to be a *stabilizing sequence* for $\mathbf{M}$ on L iff content$(\sigma) \subseteq L$, and for all $\tau \supseteq \sigma$ such that content$(\tau) \subseteq L$, $\mathbf{M}(\sigma) = \mathbf{M}(\tau)$.

(b) [4] σ is said to be a $\mathbf{TxtEx}$-*locking sequence* for $\mathbf{M}$ on L iff σ is a stabilizing sequence for $\mathbf{M}$ on L, and $W_{\mathbf{M}(\sigma)} = L$.

(c) (Based on [4]) σ is said to be a $\mathbf{TxtBc}$-*locking sequence* for $\mathbf{M}$ on L iff content$(\sigma) \subseteq L$, and for all $\tau \supseteq \sigma$ such that content$(\tau) \subseteq L$, $W_{\mathbf{M}(\sigma)} = L$.

If $\mathbf{M}$ $\mathbf{TxtEx}$-identifies L, then there exists a $\mathbf{TxtEx}$-locking sequence for $\mathbf{M}$ on L [4]. Similar result holds for $\mathbf{TxtBc}$ and $\mathbf{TxtFex}_a$ criteria of learning.

Let INIT $= \{L \mid (\exists i)[L = \{x \mid x \leq i\}]\}$. Let $INIT_k = \{x \mid x \leq k\}$.

3   Decisive, Non U-Shaped and Related Criteria of Learning

Part (a) below gives the strongest type of non U-shaped behaviour – when a learner is not allowed to return to *any* old conjectures. Part (b) gives the definition of non U-shaped learning. Parts (c) and (d) give our two models of non U-shaped learning when a learner is not allowed to return to previously used wrong conjectures. 'NO' in part (d) stands for non-overgeneralizing.

Definition 3. (a) [21] $\mathbf{M}$ is *decisive* on text T, if there do not exist any m, n, t such that $m < n < t$, $W_{\mathbf{M}(T[m])} = W_{\mathbf{M}(T[t])}$ and $W_{\mathbf{M}(T[m])} \neq W_{\mathbf{M}(T[n])}$.

(b) [2] $\mathbf{M}$ is *non U-shaped* on text T, if there do not exist any m, n, t such that $m < n < t$, $W_{\mathbf{M}(T[m])} = W_{\mathbf{M}(T[t])} = $ content(T) and $W_{\mathbf{M}(T[m])} \neq W_{\mathbf{M}(T[n])}$.

(c) $\mathbf{M}$ is *Wr-decisive* on text T, if there do not exist any m, n, t such that $m < n < t$, $W_{\mathbf{M}(T[m])} = W_{\mathbf{M}(T[t])} \neq $ content(T) and $W_{\mathbf{M}(T[m])} \neq W_{\mathbf{M}(T[n])}$.

(d) $\mathbf{M}$ is *NO-decisive* on text T, if there do not exist m, n, t such that $m < n < t$, $W_{\mathbf{M}(T[m])} = W_{\mathbf{M}(T[t])} \nsubseteq $ content(T) and $W_{\mathbf{M}(T[m])} \neq W_{\mathbf{M}(T[n])}$.

Furthermore, $\mathbf{M}$ is decisive (non U-shaped, Wr-decisive, NO-decisive) on L if $\mathbf{M}$ is decisive (non U-shaped, Wr-decisive, NO-decisive) on each text for L.

$\mathbf{M}$ is decisive (non U-shaped, Wr-decisive, NO-decisive) on $\mathcal{L}$ if $\mathbf{M}$ is decisive (non U-shaped, Wr-decisive, NO-decisive) on each $L \in \mathcal{L}$.

We now define the learning criteria formed by placing the various constraints described above on the learner. Note that the definition used for decisive learning is class version of decisive, that is decisiveness is required to hold only for texts for the languages in the class. We do this to make it consistent with the definitions of non U-shaped, WR-decisive and NO-decisive criteria, where only the class version seems sensible.

Definition 4. (a) [21] $\mathbf{M}$ $\mathbf{DecEx}$-identifies L (written: $L \in \mathbf{DecEx}(\mathbf{M})$), iff $\mathbf{M}$ $\mathbf{TxtEx}$-identifies L, and $\mathbf{M}$ is decisive on L. $\mathbf{M}$ $\mathbf{DecEx}$-identifies $\mathcal{L}$, iff $\mathbf{M}$ $\mathbf{DecEx}$-identifies each $L \in \mathcal{L}$. $\mathbf{DecEx} = \{\mathcal{L} \mid (\exists \mathbf{M})[\mathcal{L} \subseteq \mathbf{DecEx}(\mathbf{M})]\}$.

(b) [2] $\mathbf{M}$ $\mathbf{NUShEx}$-identifies L (written: $L \in \mathbf{NUShEx}(\mathbf{M})$), iff $\mathbf{M}$ $\mathbf{TxtEx}$-identifies L, and $\mathbf{M}$ is non U-shaped on L. $\mathbf{M}$ $\mathbf{NUShEx}$-identifies $\mathcal{L}$, iff $\mathbf{M}$ $\mathbf{NUShEx}$-identifies each $L \in \mathcal{L}$. $\mathbf{NUShEx} = \{\mathcal{L} \mid (\exists \mathbf{M})[\mathcal{L} \subseteq \mathbf{NUShEx}(\mathbf{M})]\}$.

(c) **M WrEx**-identifies L (written: $L \in$ **WrEx(M)**), iff **M TxtEx**-identifies L, and **M** is Wr-decisive on L. **M WrEx**-identifies $\mathcal{L}$, iff **M WrEx**-identifies each $L \in \mathcal{L}$. **WrEx** $= \{\mathcal{L} \mid (\exists \mathbf{M})[\mathcal{L} \subseteq \mathbf{WrEx(M)}]\}$.

(d) **M NOEx**-identifies L (written: $L \in$ **NOEx(M)**), iff **M TxtEx**-identifies L, and **M** is NO-decisive on L. **M NOEx**-identifies $\mathcal{L}$, iff **M NOEx**-identifies each $L \in \mathcal{L}$. **NOEx** $= \{\mathcal{L} \mid (\exists \mathbf{M})[\mathcal{L} \subseteq \mathbf{NOEx(M)}]\}$.

One can similarly define **DecI**, **WrI**, **NOI** and **NUShI**, for $\mathbf{I} \in \{\mathbf{Fex}_*, \mathbf{Bc}\}$. It is easy to verify that for all $a \in \mathcal{N} \cup \{*\}$ and $\mathbf{I} \in \{\mathbf{Ex}, \mathbf{Fex}_a, \mathbf{Bc}\}$, (a) **DecI** $\subseteq$ **WrI** $\subseteq$ **NOI** $\subseteq$ **I**; (b) **DecI** $\subseteq$ **NUShI** $\subseteq$ **I**.

4   Explanatory Learning

Our first goal is to show that, in the context of **TxtEx**-learnability, learners not returning to wrong conjectures do no better than decisive learners. To prove this, we first establish two lemmas. We omit the proof of Lemma 5.

Lemma 5. *Suppose there exists a finite set A such that $\mathcal{L}$ does not contain any extension of A. Then $\mathcal{L} \in$ **TxtEx** $\Rightarrow \mathcal{L} \in$ **DecEx**.*

Lemma 6. *Suppose every finite set has at least two extensions in $\mathcal{L}$. Suppose $a \in \mathcal{N} \cup \{*\}$ and $\mathbf{I} \in \{\mathbf{Ex}, \mathbf{Fex}_a, \mathbf{Bc}\}$. Then, $\mathcal{L} \subseteq$ **DecI(M)** iff $\mathcal{L} \subseteq$ **WrI(M)**.*

Proof. Suppose by way of contradiction that $\mathcal{L} \subseteq$ **WrI(M)**, $\mathcal{L} \not\subseteq$ **DecI(M)**. Thus, **M** is not decisive. Let $\tau_1 \prec \tau_2 \prec \tau_3$ be such that $W_{\mathbf{M}(\tau_1)} = W_{\mathbf{M}(\tau_3)} \neq W_{\mathbf{M}(\tau_2)}$. Let L be an extension of content(τ_3) such that $W_{\mathbf{M}(\tau_1)} \neq L$ and $L \in \mathcal{L}$. Such an L exists by the hypotheses on $\mathcal{L}$. Let T be a text for L extending τ_3. Then T witnesses that **M** does not **WrI**-identify $\mathcal{L}$ since **M** returns to the wrong conjecture $W_{\mathbf{M}(\tau_1)}$ on text T. A contradiction. Lemma follows. ∎

Now we can establish one of our main results.

Theorem 7. DecEx = **WrEx**.

Proof. Suppose $\mathcal{L} \in$ **WrEx**. We consider the following cases.

Case 1: $\mathcal{L}$ contains at least two extensions of every finite set. Then by Lemma 6, $\mathcal{L}$ is in **DecEx**.

Case 2: Not Case 1. Let A' be a finite set such that $\mathcal{L}$ contains at most one extension of A'.

Case 2.1: $\mathcal{N} \in \mathcal{L}$. Then by Proposition 17 in [2], we have that $\mathcal{L} \in$ **DecEx**.

Case 2.2: $\mathcal{N} \notin \mathcal{L}$. If $\mathcal{L}$ contains no extension of A', then let $A = A'$. If $\mathcal{L}$ contains $L \neq \mathcal{N}$, $L \supseteq A'$, then let $A = A' \cup \{w\}$, where $w \notin L$. Now, $\mathcal{L}$ does not contain any superset of A. Thus, by Lemma 5, we have that $\mathcal{L} \in$ **DecEx**. ∎

As **DecEx** $\subset$ **TxtEx** [2], we conclude that some families of languages in **TxtEx** cannot be learned without returning to wrong conjectures.

However, if we allow to return to subsets of the target language (that is, wrong conjectures that do not overgeneralize), then all classes of languages in **TxtEx** become learnable, as the following result shows.

Theorem 8. TxtEx $\subseteq$ NOEx.

Proof. Suppose $\mathcal{L} \in$ **TxtEx**.

If $\mathcal{N} \in \mathcal{L}$, then $\mathcal{L} \in$ **DecEx** as shown by Baliga, Case, Merkle and Stephan [2]. So assume $\mathcal{N} \notin \mathcal{L}$. Let **M** be a machine such that, (I) **M TxtEx**-identifies $\mathcal{L} \cup$ INIT, (II) **M** is prudent[3] and (III) all texts for $L \in \mathcal{L} \cup$ INIT, start with a **TxtEx**-locking sequence for **M** on L. Note that Fulk [12] shows that this can be assumed without loss of generality. Also note that, for all k, if σ is a stabilizing sequence for **M** on $INIT_k$, then content(σ) = $INIT_k$.

For a segment σ, let $f(\sigma) = \min(\mathcal{N} - \text{content}(\sigma))$. Let $valid = \{T[m] \mid m = 0$ or $\mathbf{M}(T[m-1]) \neq \mathbf{M}(T[m])\}$. Let $consseq = \{T[m] \mid \text{content}(T[m]) \subseteq W_{\mathbf{M}(T[m])}\}$. Let $gram$ be a recursive function such that

$$
W_{gram(T[m])} = \begin{cases} \emptyset, & \\ \quad \text{if content}(T[m]) \not\subseteq W_{\mathbf{M}(T[m])}; & \\ W_{\mathbf{M}(T[m])}, & \\ \quad \text{if } T[m] \text{ is a stabilizing sequence for } W_{\mathbf{M}(T[m])}; & \\ INIT_{\langle \text{ind}(T[m]), w \rangle}, & \\ \quad \text{otherwise, for some } w \geq f(T[m]). & \end{cases}
$$

It is easy to verify that for $T[m] \in consseq$, content($T[m]$) $\subseteq W_{gram(T[m])}$.

Define **M'** as follows. $\mathbf{M'}(T[n]) = gram(T[m])$, for the largest $m \leq n$, such that $T[m]$ is valid and $W_{\mathbf{M}(T[m]),n} \supseteq$ content($T[m]$) (there exists such an m, as $m = 0$ satisfies the constraints). Note that the mapping from n to that m for which $\mathbf{M'}(T[n]) = gram(T[m])$, is monotonically non-decreasing in n.

Now suppose T is a text for $L \in \mathcal{L}$. We now show that if $W_{\mathbf{M'}(T[m'])} = W_{\mathbf{M'}(T[n'])} \neq W_{\mathbf{M'}(T[s'])}$, for $m' < s' < n'$, then $W_{\mathbf{M'}(T[m'])} \subseteq L$. So suppose m', s', n' as above are given. Suppose $\mathbf{M'}(T[m']) = gram(T[m])$, $\mathbf{M'}(T[s']) = gram(T[s])$, and $\mathbf{M'}(T[n']) = gram(T[n])$. By monotonicity of **M'** mentioned above, $m' < s' < n'$ implies $m \leq s \leq n$. If $m = n$, then we are done, as $\mathbf{M'}(T[s'])$ would also be equal to $gram(T[m])$. So assume $m < n$. As content($T[n]$) $\subseteq W_{gram(T[n])}$, and $T[n]$ is valid, we immediately have that $T[m]$ is not a stabilizing sequence for **M** on $W_{\mathbf{M}(T[m])} = W_{\mathbf{M}(T[n])} \supseteq$ content($T[n]$). Thus, $gram(T[m])$ follows the third clause in its definition. Since, $\langle \text{ind}(T[m]), \cdot \rangle \neq \langle \text{ind}(T[n]), \cdot \rangle$, for $m \neq n$, it follows that $gram(T[n])$ must follow the second clause, and thus $T[n]$ is a stabilizing sequence for $W_{\mathbf{M}(T[n])}$. As $W_{gram(T[m])}$ ($= W_{gram(T[n])}$) is in INIT, it follows that content($T[n]$) $= W_{gram(T[n])}$ (since σ being stabilizing sequence for **M** on $INIT_k$ implies that content(σ) $= INIT_k$). Thus, $W_{gram(T[m])} = W_{gram(T[n])} =$ content($T[n]$) $\subseteq L$.

It follows that **M' NOEx**-identifies $\mathcal{L}$. ∎

We now compare Theorems 7 and 8 with the following result about **NUSh**-learners from [2].

Theorem 9. [2] (a) **TxtEx $\not\subseteq$ DecBc;** (b) **TxtEx = NUShEx.**

---

[3] **M** is said to be prudent [21] iff **M TxtEx**-identifies every language W_i, such that i is in the range of **M**.

Thus, Theorem 7 implies that forbidding return to abandoned wrong conjectures is more restrictive than forbidding return to abandoned correct conjectures in the context of **TxtEx**-learning, while, from Theorem 8, the latter requirement is equivalent to forbidding to return to abandoned "overgeneralizing" conjectures. We summarize these observations in the following immediate corollary.

Corollary 10. WrEx $\subset$ NUShEx = NOEx.

5   Vacillatory Learning

In this section we show that when returning to wrong conjectures is not allowed in vacillatory learning, then the vacillatory hierarchy **TxtFex**$_1$ $\subset$ **TxtFex**$_2$ $\subset$ ... $\subset$ **TxtFex**$_*$ collapses to **TxtFex**$_1$ = **TxtEx**, so that the extra learning power given by vacillation is lost. That the same collapse occurs when returning to correct abandoned conjectures is forbidden was shown in [8].

Theorem 11. (a) **WrFex**$_*$ $\subseteq$ **TxtEx**. (b) **NOFex**$_*$ $\subseteq$ **TxtEx**.

Proof. (a) Suppose **M** **WrFex**$_*$-identifies $\mathcal{L}$.

Given a text T for a language L ($\in \mathcal{L}$), let us define an equivalence relation $E(i, j)$ as follows: If there exist n_1, n_2, n_3, n_4 such that $n_1 < n_2 < n_3 < n_4$, $\mathbf{M}(T[n_1]) = \mathbf{M}(T[n_3]) = i$ and $\mathbf{M}(T[n_2]) = \mathbf{M}(T[n_4]) = j$, then $E(i, j)$ (and $E(j, i)$) holds. Intuitively, $E(i, j)$ implies that W_i is a grammar for L iff W_j is a grammar for L. This follows by definition of **WrFex**$_*$ as either $W_i = W_j$, or both W_i and W_j are grammars for L. By taking reflexive and transitive closure of E, we get an equivalence relation.

It is easy to verify that all grammars which are output infinitely often by **M** on T are equivalent (as they will pairwise satisfy $E(\cdot, \cdot)$).

Define $\mathbf{M}'$ as follows. $\mathbf{M}'(T[n])$ first builds an approximation to E above based on $T[n]$, by setting $E(i, j)$ and $E(j, i)$ to true iff there exist n_1, n_2, n_3, n_4 such that $n_1 < n_2 < n_3 < n_4 \leq n$, $\mathbf{M}(T[n_1]) = \mathbf{M}(T[n_3]) = i$ and $\mathbf{M}(T[n_2]) = \mathbf{M}(T[n_4]) = j$. It then takes reflexive and transitive closure of E so formed. $\mathbf{M}'(T[n])$, then outputs on $T[n]$ the union of languages enumerated by members of the equivalence class of $\mathbf{M}(T[n])$.

Now for all but finitely many n, as **M** outputs a grammar for L, $\mathbf{M}'(T[n])$ will be a grammar for L. Furthermore, there will be syntactic convergence as equivalence relation E eventually stabilizes. Thus, $\mathbf{M}'$ **TxtEx**-identifies $\mathcal{L}$.

(b) Similar to part (a), except that in this case, the meaning of equivalence relation is $E(i, j)$ implies $W_i \subseteq L \Leftrightarrow W_j \subseteq L$. This follows from the definition of **NOFex**-identification as either $W_i = W_j$ or both are subsets of input language. ∎

As **TxtEx = NOEx**, we get the following result.

Corollary 12. NOFex$_*$ = NOEx.

The following corollary extends Theorem 7 from the previous section.

Corollary 13. WrFex$_*$ = DecEx.

From the above Corollaries we can conclude that, as was the case for **TxtEx**-learning, **Wr** is more restrictive than **NUSh** while **NO** is equivalent to **NUSh**. A closer look reveals a finer picture. We have shown that more learning power is lost, in the vacillatory case, by forbidding to return to abandoned wrong conjectures than by forbidding to return to correct conjectures. Also, some results from [8] seem to suggest that the necessity of returning to wrong conjectures is even *deeper* than the necessity of returning to correct conjectures, from the **TxtFex$_3$** level of the **TxtFex** hierarchy up, in the following sense. Recall the following result from [8].

Theorem 14. [8] **TxtFex$_2$ $\subseteq$ NUShBc; TxtFex$_3$ $\not\subseteq$ NUShBc.**

Thus, returning to correct conjectures is avoidable for the **TxtFex$_2$** level of the vacillatory hierarchy by shifting to the more liberal criterion of **TxtBc** identification, while there are classes learnable in the **TxtFex$_b$** sense for every $b > 2$ that cannot be learned by a **NUSh**-learner even in the **TxtBc** sense. In the next section we prove (Theorem 15) that there are **TxtEx**-learnable classes that *cannot* be **TxtBc**-learned by any **Wr**-learner. Thus, the necessity of returning to wrong abandoned conjectures is *not* avoidable by allowing infinitely many correct grammars in the limit, not even for the **TxtFex$_2$** level of the vacillatory hierarchy, while the necessity of returning to correct abandoned conjectures is so avoidable for this level of the vacillatory hierarchy.

6   Behaviourally Correct Learning

Our first result shows that, in the context of **TxtBc**-learnability, similarly to **TxtEx**-learnability, disallowing to return to wrong conjectures significantly limits the power of a learner: even **TxtEx**-learners can sometimes learn more than any **TxtBc**-learner if returning to wrong conjectures is not allowed. The reason is that the class $\mathcal{L}$ in **TxtEx $-$ DecBc** from [2] contains two distinct extensions of every finite set and thus the next theorem follows from Lemma 6.

Theorem 15. TxtEx $\not\subseteq$ WrBc.

Now we compare non U-shaped learning (when a learner cannot abandon a correct conjecture) with learning by disallowing to return to wrong conjectures. From the previous Theorem and from the fact that **TxtEx = NUShEx $\subseteq$ NUShBc**, we have the following.

Corollary 16. NUShBc $\not\subseteq$ WrBc.

We now show that, interestingly, the converse is true: **Wr** learners can sometimes do better than **NUSh** learners in the **TxtBc** setting. So **Wr** and **NUSh** are incomparable restrictions in the context of **TxtBc**-identification.

Theorem 17. WrBc $\not\subseteq$ NUShBc.

We omit the proof of above theorem. Observe that, in contrast to the case of **TxtEx** and **TxtFex**-learning, Theorem 17 implies that **WrBc** does not coincide with **DecBc**. We have in fact the following corollary of Theorem 17.

Corollary 18. DecBc $\subset$ WrBc.

Our next goal is to show that, by contrast to Theorem 15, any **TxtBc**-learner can be transformed into one that does not return to "overgeneralizing" conjectures. First, we need to establish a number of preliminary facts.

Theorem 19. (Based on [17]) *Suppose $\mathcal{L} \in$ **TxtBc**. Then there exists a machine $\mathbf{M}'$ such that $\mathbf{M}'$ **TxtBc**-identifies $\mathcal{L}$, and every text T for $L \in \mathcal{L}$ starts with a **TxtBc**-locking sequence for $\mathbf{M}'$ on L.*

Lemma 20. *Suppose $\mathbf{M}$ is given. Then there exists an r.e. set $P(\sigma)$ such that*

- *A grammar for $P(\sigma)$ can be effectively obtained from σ;*
- *If σ is a **TxtBc**-locking sequence for $\mathbf{M}$ on $W_{\mathbf{M}(\sigma)}$, then $P(\sigma)$ contains only grammars for $W_{\mathbf{M}(\sigma)}$;*
- *If σ is not a **TxtBc**-locking sequence for $\mathbf{M}$ on $W_{\mathbf{M}(\sigma)}$, then $P(\sigma)$ is either empty or contains grammars for at least two distinct languages.*

Proof. Define $P(\sigma)$ as follows. If content$(\sigma) \not\subseteq W_{\mathbf{M}(\sigma)}$, then let $P(\sigma) = \emptyset$, else let $P(\sigma) = \{\mathbf{M}(\tau) \mid \sigma \subseteq \tau, \text{content}(\tau) \subseteq W_{\mathbf{M}(\sigma)}\}$. Now if σ is a **TxtBc**-locking sequence for $\mathbf{M}$ on L, then $P(\sigma)$ consists only of grammars for L. On the other hand if σ is not a **TxtBc**-locking sequence for $\mathbf{M}$ on L, then either $P(\sigma)$ is empty or it contains grammars for at least two distinct languages. ∎

Lemma 21. *Given $\mathbf{M}$, there exists a recursive function g such that:*
(a) *If σ is a **TxtBc**-locking sequence for $\mathbf{M}$ on $W_{\mathbf{M}(\sigma)}$, then $W_{g(\sigma)} = W_{\mathbf{M}(\sigma)}$.*
(b) *If σ is not a **TxtBc**-locking sequence for $\mathbf{M}$ on $W_{\mathbf{M}(\sigma)}$, then $W_{g(\sigma)}$ is finite.*

Proof. For a finite set X and number s, let

- $CommonTime(X, s) = \max(\{t \leq s \mid (\forall p, p' \in X) W_{p,t} \subseteq W_{p',s}\})$;
- $CommonElem(X, s) = \bigcap_{p \in X} W_{p, CommonTime(X,s)}$.

Let f be a recursive function with $W_{f(X)} = \bigcup_{s \in \mathcal{N}} CommonElem(X, s)$. Here we assume that $W_{f(\emptyset)} = \emptyset$. Intuitively, $CommonTime(X, s)$ finds the largest s such that enumerations upto time $CommonTime(X, s)$ by grammars in X are included in all languages enumerated by grammars in X. $CommonElem(X, s)$ then gives intersection of elements enumerated by grammars in X upto time $CommonTime(X, s)$. Note that

(i) $\lim_{s \to \infty} CommonTime(X, s)$ is infinite iff all grammars in X are for the same language;
(ii) If $X \subseteq X'$, then $CommonTime(X, s) \geq CommonTime(X', s)$;
(iii) If $W_p \neq W_{p'}$ then for all s, $CommonTime(\{p, p'\}, s)$ is bounded by the least t such that $W_{p,t} \cup W_{p',t} \not\subseteq W_p \cap W_{p'}$.

Let Y be the set of all y such that there is an $s \geq y$, such that $y \in W_{f(X_s)}$. Note that (II) and (III) above imply that if $X_0 \subseteq X_1 \subseteq X_2 \subseteq \ldots$, $\{p, p'\} \subseteq \bigcup_{i \in \mathcal{N}} X_i$ and $W_p \neq W_{p'}$, then Y is finite. On the other hand, if all $p, p' \in \bigcup_{i \in \mathcal{N}} X_i$ are grammars for the same language, then $Y = W_p$ for any $p \in \bigcup_{i \in \mathcal{N}} X_i$.

Let P be as in Lemma 20 and let $P_s(\sigma)$ denote $P(\sigma)$ enumerated in s steps. Now let $g(\sigma)$ be such that $W_{g(\sigma)} = \bigcup_{s \in \mathcal{N}} [\{y \leq s \ \wedge \ y \in W_{f(P_s(\sigma))}\}]$. It is now easy to verify that Lemma holds.   ∎

Now we can prove one of our main results: any **TxtBc**-learner can be replaced by the one not returning to "overgeneralizing" conjectures.

Theorem 22. TxtBc $\subseteq$ NOBc.

Proof. Suppose **M TxtBc**-identifies $\mathcal{L}$. Without loss of generality (Theorem 19) assume that for any text T for $L \in \mathcal{L}$, there exists a $\sigma \subseteq T$, such that σ is a **TxtBc**-locking sequence for **M** on L. Intuitively, the proof employs two tricks. First trick (as given by g in Lemma 21) is to make sure that the infinite languages output by the learner are only on σ's which are **TxtBc**-locking sequences for the language output. This automatically ensures no semantic mind changes occur between different grammars output for the same infinite language by the learner. The second trick makes sure that finite languages output by the learner, which go beyond what is seen in the input at the time of conjecture, are for pairwise different languages. We now proceed formally.

Let g be as in Lemma 21. Let $q_0, q_1, \ldots$ be an increasing sequence of primes and $\mathbf{M}''(\sigma) = h(\sigma)$ where $W_{h(\sigma)}$ is defined as follows.

Begin $W_{h(\sigma)}$
    Enumerate content(σ)
    Loop
    Search for s such that $W_{h(\sigma)}$ enumerated upto now is a proper subset of
        $W_{g(\sigma),s}$, and card$(W_{g(\sigma),s})$ is $(q_{\text{ind}(\sigma)})^k$ for some k.
    If and when such s is found, enumerate $W_{g(\sigma),s}$.
    Forever
End

Thus, $W_{h(\sigma)}$ is $W_{g(\sigma)}$ if $W_{g(\sigma)}$ is infinite. Furthermore, if $W_{h(\sigma)}$ is finite, then it is either content(σ) or has cardinality a power of $q_{\text{ind}(\sigma)}$.

It follows that if $W_{h(\sigma)} = W_{h(\tau)}$, for $\sigma \subset \tau$, then either $W_{h(\sigma)}$ is infinite and σ is a **TxtBc**-locking sequence for **M** on $W_{g(\tau)} = W_{g(\sigma)} = W_{h(\sigma)}$, and thus, there is no semantic mind change by $\mathbf{M}''$ in between σ and τ, or $W_{h(\sigma)}$ is finite, and thus, it must be the case that $W_{h(\sigma)} = W_{h(\tau)} = $ content(τ) (otherwise, $q_{\text{ind}(\sigma)} \neq q_{\text{ind}(\tau)}$ would imply that $W_{h(\sigma)} \neq W_{h(\tau)}$).

It follows from above cases that $\mathbf{M}''$ does not return to "overgeneralizing" hypothesis. To see **TxtBc**-identification of $L \in \mathcal{L}$, let T be a text for L. Let $T[n]$ be a **TxtBc**-locking sequence for **M** on L (such an n exists by Theorem 19). Thus, $g(T[n])$ is a grammar for L. If L is finite, then without loss of generality we also assume that n is large enough such that $L \subseteq$ content$(T[n])$. Now consider any $m \geq n$. It is easy to verify that if L is infinite then $W_{h(T[m])} = W_{g(T[m])} = L$. On the other hand, if L is finite, then again $W_{h(T[m])}$ does not go beyond first step, and thus equals L.   ∎

7   Consistency

Consistency is a natural and important requirement for **TxtEx** and **TxtBc** types of learning. While for the latter, consistency requirement can be easily achieved, it is known to be restrictive for **TxtEx**-learnability [3, 21]. In this section, we establish a new interesting boundary on consistent **TxtEx**-learnability – in Theorem 25 we show that consistent **TxtEx**-learners can be made decisive (still being consistent) – contrast this result with Theorem 9(a).

Definition 23. [3, 21] **M** is said to be *consistent* on T iff, for all n, $\mathbf{M}(T[n]){\downarrow}$ and content$(T[n]) \subseteq W_{\mathbf{M}(T[n])}$.

M is said to be *consistent* on L iff, **M** is consistent on each text for L.

Definition 24. (a) [3, 21] **M ConsTxtEx**-*identifies* L iff **M** is consistent on L, and **M TxtEx**-identifies L.

(b) [3] **M ConsTxtEx**-*identifies* $\mathcal{L}$ iff **M ConsTxtEx**-identifies each $L \in \mathcal{L}$.
ConsTxtEx $= \{\mathcal{L} \mid (\exists \mathbf{M})[\mathbf{M} \text{ } \mathbf{ConsTxtEx}\text{-identifies } \mathcal{L}]\}$.

Note that for **M** to **ConsTxtEx**-identify a text T, it must be defined on each initial segment of T.[4] One can similarly define combination of consistency with decisive (called **ConsDecEx**) and other related criteria such as **ConsNUShEx**, **ConsNOEx**, **ConsWrEx**, etc. We omit proof of theorems in this section.

Theorem 25. ConsTxtEx $\subseteq$ **ConsDecEx**.

Theorem 26. NUShBc $=$ **ConsNUShBc**.

Next we show that decisive learning is stronger than consistent learning.

Theorem 27. DecEx $-$ **ConsTxtEx** $\neq \emptyset$

The proof of Theorem 22 also shows that **TxtBc** $\subseteq$ **ConsNOBc**. Thus, we have

Theorem 28. TxtBc $\subseteq$ **ConsNOBc**.

The proof of Theorem 11 also works for the case when we are considering consistent identification, so we have

---

[4] There are two other versions of consistency considered in the literature, namely $\mathcal{R}$**Cons** [16] where the learner must be total but might be inconsistent on data not belonging to the class to be learned and $\mathcal{T}$**Cons** [27] where the learner must be total and consistent on every input, whether it belongs to some language to be learnt or not. Our results also hold for $\mathcal{T}$**Cons**, however some of our results do not hold for $\mathcal{R}$**Cons**.

Theorem 29. $\mathbf{ConsWrFex_* \subseteq ConsTxtEx}$; $\mathbf{ConsNOFex_* \subseteq ConsTxtEx}$.

Corollary 30. $\mathbf{ConsWrFex_* \subseteq ConsDecEx}$; $\mathbf{ConsNOFex_* \subseteq ConsDecEx}$.

The proof of Theorem 17 shows the following as well.

Theorem 31. $\mathbf{ConsWrBc \not\subseteq NUShBc}$.

The following are open: (a) $\mathbf{ConsWrBc = WrBc}$? (b) $\mathbf{ConsDecBc = DecBc}$?

8 Conclusions

We summarize our results on the impact of the **Wr** and **NO** variants of non U-shaped behaviour and how they compare to previous results about the original notion **NUSh** from [2] and [8].

Returning to abandoned wrong conjectures turned out to be necessary for full learning power in all three of the models **TxtEx**, **TxtFex** and **TxtBc**, while returning to abandoned wrong "overgeneralizing" conjectures is necessary only for the vacillatory case and avoidable otherwise. This can be compared to results in [2] and [8] showing that returning to abandoned correct conjectures is avoidable in the **TxtEx** case while being necessary for vacillatory and behaviourally correct identification.

Also, we can conclude that forbidding to return to abandoned wrong conjectures is more restrictive than forbidding to return to correct conjectures in the **TxtEx** and in the **TxtFex** models, while the two restrictions are incomparable in the **TxtBc** case. On the other hand, forbidding to return to wrong "overgeneralizing" conjectures is equivalent to forbidding to return to correct conjectures for **TxtEx** and **TxtFex** identification.

Also, while, for the level $\mathbf{TxtFex_2}$ of the vacillatory hierarchy, the necessity of returning to correct conjectures is avoidable by shifting to the more liberal criterion of **TxtBc**-identification, the necessity of returning to wrong conjectures is *not* avoidable in this way: there are $\mathbf{TxtFex_2}$-learnable classes that cannot be **TxtBc**-learned by any **Wr** learner. This and the above observations seem to suggest that the freedom of returning to wrong abandoned conjectures is even more central for full learning power, than the freedom of returning to correct conjectures. We defer a deeper analysis of the possible significance of these results from the perspective of cognitive science to a more appropriate place.

We would like to thank Rolf Wiehagen for useful discussions, and referees of COLT'2005 for several helpful comments.

References

1. D. Angluin. Inductive inference of formal languages from positive data. *Information and Control*, 45:117–135, 1980.
2. G. Baliga, J. Case, W. Merkle, F. Stephan, and R. Wiehagen. When unlearning helps. Manuscript, http://www.cis.udel.edu/~case/papers/decisive.ps, 2005. Preliminary version of the paper appeared in ICALP, 2000.

3. J. Bārzdiņš. Inductive inference of automata, functions and programs. In *Int. Math. Congress, Vancouver*, pages 771–776, 1974.
4. L. Blum and M. Blum. Toward a mathematical theory of inductive inference. *Information and Control*, 28:125–155, 1975.
5. M. Blum. A machine-independent theory of the complexity of recursive functions. *Journal of the ACM*, 14:322–336, 1967.
6. M. Bowerman. Starting to talk worse: Clues to language acquisition from children's late speech errors. In S. Strauss and R. Stavy, editors, *U-Shaped Behavioral Growth*. Developmental Psychology Series. Academic Press, New York, 1982.
7. S. Carey. An analysis of a learning paradigm. In S. Strauss and R. Stavy, editors, *U-Shaped Behavioral Growth*. Developmental Psychology Series. Academic Press, New York, 1982.
8. L. Carlucci, J. Case, S. Jain, and F. Stephan. U-shaped learning may be necessary. Technical Report TRA11/04, School of Computing, National University of Singapore, Nov 2004.
9. J. Case. The power of vacillation in language learning. *SIAM Journal on Computing*, 28(6):1941–1969, 1999.
10. J. Case and C. Lynes. Machine inductive inference and language identification. In M. Nielsen and E. M. Schmidt, editors, *Proceedings of the 9th International Colloquium on Automata, Languages and Programming*, volume 140 of *Lecture Notes in Computer Science*, pages 107–115. Springer-Verlag, 1982.
11. J. Case and C. Smith. Comparison of identification criteria for machine inductive inference. *Theoretical Computer Science*, 25:193–220, 1983.
12. M. Fulk. Prudence and other conditions on formal language learning. *Information and Computation*, 85:1–11, 1990.
13. M. Fulk, S. Jain, and D. Osherson. Open problems in systems that learn. *Journal of Computer and System Sciences*, 49(3):589–604, 1994.
14. E. M. Gold. Language identification in the limit. *Information and Control*, 10:447–474, 1967.
15. J. Hopcroft and J. Ullman. *Introduction to Automata Theory, Languages, and Computation*. Addison-Wesley, 1979.
16. K. Jantke and H. Beick. Combining postulates of naturalness in inductive inference. *Journal of Information Processing and Cybernetics (EIK)*, 17:465–484, 1981.
17. S. Kurtz and J. Royer. Prudence in language learning. In D. Haussler and L. Pitt, editors, *Proceedings of the Workshop on Computational Learning Theory*, pages 143–156. Morgan Kaufmann, 1988.
18. S. Lange and R. Wiehagen. Polynomial time inference of arbitrary pattern languages. *New Generation Computing*, 8:361–370, 1991.
19. M. Machtey and P. Young. *An Introduction to the General Theory of Algorithms*. North Holland, New York, 1978.
20. G. Marcus, S. Pinker, M. Ullman, M. Hollander, T. Rosen, and F. Xu. *Overregularization in Language Acquisition*. Monographs of the Society for Research in Child Development, vol. 57, no. 4. University of Chicago Press, 1992. Includes commentary by Harold Clahsen.
21. D. Osherson, M. Stob, and S. Weinstein. *Systems that Learn: An Introduction to Learning Theory for Cognitive and Computer Scientists*. MIT Press, 1986.
22. K. Plunkett and V. Marchman. U-shaped learning and frequency effects in a multi-layered perceptron: implications for child language acquisition. *Cognition*, 38(1):43–102, 1991.
23. H. Rogers. *Theory of Recursive Functions and Effective Computability*. McGraw-Hill, 1967. Reprinted by MIT Press in 1987.

24. S. Strauss and R. Stavy. *U-Shaped Behavioral Growth*. Developmental Psychology Series. Academic Press, New York, 1982.
25. S. Strauss, R. Stavy, and N. Orpaz. The child's development of the concept of temperature. Manuscript, Tel-Aviv University, 1977.
26. N.A. Taatgen and J.R. Anderson. Why do children learn to say broke? a model of learning the past tense without feedback. *Cognition*, 86(2):123–155, 2002.
27. R. Wiehagen and W. Liepe. Charakteristische Eigenschaften von erkennbaren Klassen rekursiver Funktionen. *Journal of Information Processing and Cybernetics (EIK)*, 12:421–438, 1976.

Mind Change Efficient Learning

Wei Luo and Oliver Schulte

School of Computing Science, Simon Fraser University,
Vancouver, Canada
{wluoa, oschulte}@cs.sfu.ca

Abstract. This paper studies efficient learning with respect to mind changes. Our starting point is the idea that a learner that is efficient with respect to mind changes minimizes mind changes not only globally in the entire learning problem, but also locally in subproblems after receiving some evidence. Formalizing this idea leads to the notion of *uniform mind change optimality*. We characterize the structure of language classes that can be identified with at most α mind changes by some learner (not necessarily effective): A language class $\mathcal{L}$ is identifiable with α mind changes iff the accumulation order of $\mathcal{L}$ is at most α. Accumulation order is a classic concept from point-set topology. To aid the construction of learning algorithms, we show that the characteristic property of uniformly mind change optimal learners is that they output conjectures (languages) with maximal accumulation order. We illustrate the theory by describing mind change optimal learners for various problems such as identifying linear subspaces and one-variable patterns.

1 Introduction

One of the goals of computational learning theory is to design learning algorithms for which we can provide performance guarantees. Identification in the limit is a central performance goal in Gold's language learning paradigm [9]. A well-studied refinement of this notion is *identification with bounded mind changes* [8, 1]. In this paper we investigate a further refinement that we term uniform mind change optimality (UMC-optimality). Briefly, a learner is UMC-optimal if the learner achieves the best possible mind change bound not only for the entire problem, but also relative to data sequences that the learner may observe.

The general theory in this paper has two main goals. (1) To provide necessary and sufficient conditions for a language collection to be identifiable with a given (ordinal) mind-change bound by some learner (not necessarily effective). (2) To provide necessary and sufficient conditions for a learner to be UMC-optimal. The results addressing (1) help us determine when a UMC-optimal learning algorithm exists, and the results addressing (2) help us to construct optimal learning algorithms when they do exist.

We situate our study in the framework of point-set topology. Previous work has shown the usefulness of topology for learning theory [25–Ch.10], [21, 14, 4]. We show how to view a language collection as a topological space; this allows us to apply Cantor's classic concept of *accumulation order* which assigns an ordinal $\mathrm{acc}(\mathcal{L})$ to a language collection, if $\mathcal{L}$ has bounded accumulation order. We show that a language collection $\mathcal{L}$ is identifiable with mind change bound α by a learner if and only if $\mathrm{acc}(\mathcal{L}) = \alpha$.

P. Auer and R. Meir (Eds.): COLT 2005, LNAI 3559, pp. 398–412, 2005.

This result establishes a purely information-theoretic and structural necessary condition for identification with bounded mind changes. Based on the concept of accumulation order, we provide necessary and sufficient conditions for a learner to be UMC-optimal. These results show that UMC-optimality strongly constrains the conjectures of learners. We illustrate these results by analyzing various learning problems, such as identifying a linear subspace and a one-variable pattern.

The paper is organized as follows. Sect. 2 reviews standard concepts for language identification and presents our definition of mind change optimality. Then we establish the correspondence between mind change complexity and accumulation order. Sect. 4 gives necessary and sufficient conditions for a learner to be uniformly mind change optimal. Finally, we describe a general approach to constructing UMC-optimal effective learners and illustrate it with one-variable pattern languages.

2 Preliminaries: Language Identification

2.1 Standard Concepts

We employ notation and terminology from [12], [20–Ch.1], and [9]. We write $\mathbb{N}$ for the set of natural numbers: $\{0, 1, 2, ...\}$. The symbols $\subseteq, \supseteq, \subset, \supset$, and $\emptyset$ respectively stand for subset, superset, proper subset, proper superset, and the empty set. We view a language as a set of strings. We identify strings with natural numbers encoding them. Thus we define a **language** to be a subset of $\mathbb{N}$ and write L for a generic language [9–p.449]. A **language learning problem** is a collection of languages; we write $\mathcal{L}$ for a generic collection of languages. A **text** T is a mapping of $\mathbb{N}$ into $\mathbb{N} \cup \{\#\}$, where $\#$ is a symbol not in $\mathbb{N}$. (The symbol $\#$ models pauses in data presentation.) We write content(T) for the intersection of $\mathbb{N}$ and the range of T. A text T is **for** a language L iff $L = \text{content}(T)$. The initial sequence of text T of length n is denoted by $T[n]$. The set of all finite initial sequences over $\mathbb{N} \cup \{\#\}$ is denoted by SEQ. We let σ and τ range over SEQ. We write content(σ) for the intersection of $\mathbb{N}$ and the range of σ. The initial sequence of σ of length n is denoted by $\sigma[n]$.

We say that a language L is **consistent** with σ iff content$(\sigma) \subseteq L$. We write $\sigma \subset T$ or $T \supset \sigma$ to denote that text T extends initial sequence σ. For a language collection $\mathcal{L}$, the set of all finite sequences consistent with $\mathcal{L}$ is denoted by SEQ$(\mathcal{L})$ (i.e., SEQ$(\mathcal{L}) \equiv \{\sigma \in \text{SEQ} : \exists L \in \mathcal{L}. \text{content}(\sigma) \subseteq L\}$).

Examples
(1) Let $L_i \equiv \{n : n \geq i\}$, where $i \in \mathbb{N}$; we use COINIT to denote the class of languages $\{L_i : i \in \mathbb{N}\}$ [1–p.324].
(2) In the n-dimensional linear space $\mathbb{Q}^n$ over the field of rationals $\mathbb{Q}$, we can effectively encode every vector v by a natural number. Then a linear subspace of $\mathbb{Q}^n$ corresponds to a language. We write LINEAR$_n$ for the collection of all (encodings of) linear subspaces of $\mathbb{Q}^n$.

A **learner** is a function that maps a finite sequence to a language or the question mark ?, meaning "no answer for now". We normally use the Greek letter Ψ and variants to denote a learner. Our term "learner" corresponds to the term "scientist" in [20–Ch.2.1.2]. In typical applications we have available a syntactic representation for each member of the language collection $\mathcal{L}$ under investigation. In such settings we assume the existence of an index for each member of $\mathcal{L}$, that is, a function $index : \mathcal{L} \mapsto \mathbb{N}$ (cf. [10–p.18]), and we can take a **learning function** to be a function that maps a finite sequence to an index for a language (learning functions are called "scientists" in [10–Ch.3.3]). A computable learning function is a **learning algorithm**. We use the general notion of a learner for more generality and simplicity until we consider issues of computability.

Let $\mathcal{L}$ be a collection of languages. A learner Ψ **for** $\mathcal{L}$ is a mapping of SEQ into $\mathcal{L} \cup \{?\}$. Thus the learners we consider are class-preserving; for the results in this paper, this assumption carries no loss of generality. Usually context fixes the language collection $\mathcal{L}$ for a learner Ψ.

We say that a learner Ψ **identifies** a language L on a text T for L, if $\Psi(T[n]) = L$ for all but a finite number of stages n. Next we define identification of a language collection relative to some evidence.

Definition 1. *A learner Ψ identifies $\mathcal{L}$ given σ $\iff$ for every language $L \in \mathcal{L}$, and for every text $T \supset \sigma$ for L, we have that Ψ identifies L on T.*

Thus a learner Ψ identifies a language collection $\mathcal{L}$ if Ψ identifies $\mathcal{L}$ given the empty sequence Λ.

Examples

(1) The following learner Ψ_{CO} identifies COINIT: If content$(\sigma) = \emptyset$, then $\Psi_{CO}(\sigma)$:=?. Otherwise set $m := \min(\text{content}(\sigma))$, and set $\Psi_{CO}(\sigma) := L_m$.

(2) Let vectors(σ) be the set of vectors whose code numbers appear in σ. Then define $\Psi_{LIN}(\sigma) = \text{span}(\text{vectors}(\sigma))$, where span$(V)$ is the linear span of a set of vectors V. The learner Ψ_{LIN} identifies LINEAR$_n$. The problem of identifying a linear subspace of reactions arises in particle physics, where it corresponds to the problem of finding a set of conservation principles governing observed particle reactions [17, 27]. Interestingly, it appears that the theories accepted by the particle physics community match the output of Ψ_{LIN} [28, 26].

A learner Ψ **changes its mind** at some nonempty finite sequence $\sigma \in$ SEQ if $\Psi(\sigma) \neq \Psi(\sigma^-)$ and $\Psi(\sigma^-) \neq ?$, where σ^- is the initial segment of σ with σ's last element removed [7, 1]. (No mind changes occur at the empty sequence Λ.)

Definition 2 (based on [1]). *Let Ψ be a learner and c be a function that assigns an ordinal to each finite sequence $\sigma \in$ SEQ.*

1. *c is a **mind-change counter** for Ψ and $\mathcal{L}$ if $c(\sigma) < c(\sigma^-)$ whenever Ψ changes its mind at some nonempty sequence $\sigma \in$ SEQ$(\mathcal{L})$. When $\mathcal{L}$ is fixed by context, we simply say that c is a mind change counter for Ψ.*
2. *Ψ identifies a class of languages $\mathcal{L}$ **with mind-change bound** α given σ $\iff$ Ψ identifies $\mathcal{L}$ given σ and there is a mind-change counter c for Ψ and $\mathcal{L}$ such that $c(\sigma) = \alpha$.*
3. *A language collection $\mathcal{L}$ is **identifiable with mind change bound** α given σ $\iff$ there is a learner Ψ such that Ψ identifies $\mathcal{L}$ with mind change bound α given σ.*

Examples

(1) For COINIT, define a counter c_0 as follows: $c_0(\sigma) := \omega$ if $\text{content}(\sigma) = \emptyset$, where ω is the first transfinite ordinal, and $c_0(\sigma) := \min(\text{content}(\sigma))$ otherwise. Then c_0 is a mind change counter for Ψ_{CO} given Λ. Hence Ψ_{CO} identifies COINIT with mind change bound ω (cf. [1–Sect.1]).

(2) For LINEAR_n, define the counter $c_1(\sigma)$ by $c_1(\sigma) := n - \dim(\text{span}(\text{vectors}(\sigma)))$, where $\dim(V)$ is the dimension of a space V. Then c_1 is a mind change counter for Ψ_{LIN} given Λ, so Ψ_{LIN} identifies LINEAR_n with mind change bound n.

(3) Let FIN be the class of languages $\{D \subseteq \mathbb{N} : D \text{ is finite}\}$. Then a learner that always conjectures $\text{content}(\sigma)$ identifies FIN. However, there is no mind change bound for FIN [1].

2.2   Uniform Mind Change Optimality

In this section we introduce a new identification criterion that is the focus of this paper. Our point of departure is the idea that learners that are efficient with respect to mind changes should minimize mind changes not only globally in the entire learning problem but also locally after receiving specific evidence. For example, in the COINIT problem, the best global mind change bound for the entire problem is ω [1–Sect.1], but after observing initial data $\langle 5 \rangle$, a mind change efficient learner should succeed with at most 5 more mind changes, as does Ψ_{CO}. However, there are many learners that require more than 5 mind changes after observing $\langle 5 \rangle$ yet still succeed with the optimal mind change bound of ω in the entire problem.

To formalize this motivation, consider a language collection $\mathcal{L}$. If a mind change bound exists for $\mathcal{L}$ given σ, we write $\text{MC}_{\mathcal{L}}(\sigma)$ for the least ordinal α such that $\mathcal{L}$ is identifiable with α mind changes given σ. It may be natural to require that a learner should succeed with $\text{MC}_{\mathcal{L}}(\sigma)$ mind changes after each data sequence $\sigma \in \text{SEQ}(\mathcal{L})$; indeed the learner Ψ_{CO} achieves this performance for COINIT. However, in general this criterion appears too strong. The reason is the following possibility: A learner Ψ may output a conjecture $\Psi(\sigma) = L \neq ?$, then receive evidence σ inconsistent with L, and "hang on" to a refuted conjecture L until it changes its mind to L' at a future stage. This may lead to one extra mind change (from L to L') compared to the optimal number of mind changes that a learner may have achieved starting with evidence σ, for example by outputting ? until σ was observed.

A weaker requirement is that a learner Ψ has to be optimal for a subproblem $\mathcal{L}$ given σ only if $\Psi(\sigma)$ is consistent with σ. This leads us to the following definition. A conjecture $\Psi(\sigma)$ is **valid** for a sequence $\sigma \in \text{SEQ}$ if $\Psi(\sigma) \neq ?$ and $\Psi(\sigma)$ is consistent with σ.

Definition 3. *A learner Ψ is **uniformly mind change optimal** for $\mathcal{L}$ given $\sigma \in \text{SEQ}$ if there is a mind change counter c for Ψ such that (1) $c(\sigma) = \text{MC}_{\mathcal{L}}(\sigma)$, and (2) for all data sequences $\tau \supseteq \sigma$, if $\Psi(\tau)$ is valid, then $c(\tau) = \text{MC}_{\mathcal{L}}(\tau)$.*

We use the abbreviation "UMC-optimal" for "uniformly mind change optimal" (the terminology and intuition is similar to Kelly's in [15, 16]). A learner Ψ is simply UMC-optimal for $\mathcal{L}$ if Ψ is UMC-optimal given Λ.

Examples

(1) In the COINIT problem, $\text{MC}_{\mathcal{L}}(\Lambda) = \omega$, and $\text{MC}_{\mathcal{L}}(\sigma) = \min(\text{content}(\sigma))$ when content$(\sigma) \neq \emptyset$. Since c_0 is a mind change counter for Ψ_{CO}, it follows that Ψ_{CO} is UMC-optimal. Any learner Ψ such that (1) $\Psi(\sigma) = \Psi_{\text{CO}}(\sigma)$ if content$(\sigma) \neq \emptyset$ and (2) $\Psi(\sigma) = \Psi(\sigma^-)$ if content$(\sigma) = \emptyset$ is also UMC-optimal. (The initial conjecture $\Psi(\Lambda)$ is not constrained.)

(2) The learner Ψ_{LIN} is UMC-optimal. We will see that Ψ_{LIN} is the *only* learner that is both UMC-optimal and always outputs valid conjectures. Thus for the problem of inferring conservation laws, UMC-optimality coincides with the inferences of the physics community.

3 A Topological Characterization of Mind-Change Bounded Identifiability

Information-theoretical aspects of inductive inference have been studied by many learning theorists (e.g., [10] and [20]). As Jain et. al. observe [10–p.34]:

> Many results in the theory of inductive inference do not depend upon computability assumptions; rather, they are information theoretic in character. Consideration of noncomputable scientists thereby facilitates the analysis of proofs, making it clearer which assumptions carry the burden.

As an example, Angluin showed that her Condition 1 characterizes the indexed families of nonempty recursive languages inferable from positive data by computable learners [3–p.121] and that the noneffective version, Condition 2, is a necessary condition for inferability by computable learners.[1] Variants of Angluin's Condition 2 turn out to be both sufficient and necessary for various models of language identifiability by noncomputable learners ([20–Ch.2.2.2][10–Thm.3.26]). Information theoretic requirements such as Condition 2 constitute necessary conditions for computable learners, and are typically the easiest way to prove the unsolvability of some learning problems when they do apply. For example, Apsitis used the Baire topology on total recursive functions to show that $\mathbf{EX}_\alpha \neq \mathbf{EX}_{\alpha+1}$ [4–Sect.3]. On the positive side, if a sufficient condition for noneffective learnability is met, it often yields insights that lead to the design of a successful learning algorithm.

It has often been observed that point-set topology, one of the most fundamental and well-studied mathematical subjects, provides useful concepts for describing the information theoretic structure of learning problems [25–Ch.10], [21, 4, 14]. In particular, Apsitis investigated the mind change complexity of function learning problems in terms of the Baire topology [4]. He showed that Cantor's 1883 notion of accumulation order in a topological space [6] defines a natural ordinal-valued measure of complexity for function learning problems, and that accumulation order provides a lower bound on the mind change complexity of a function learning problem. We generalize Apsitis' use of topology to apply it to language collections. The following section briefly reviews the relevant topological concepts.

---

[1] Condition 2 characterizes BC-learnability for computable learners [5].

3.1   Basic Definitions in Point-Set Topology

A **topological space** over a set X is a pair $(X, \mathcal{O})$, where $\mathcal{O}$ is a collection of subsets of X, called **open sets**, such that $\emptyset$ and X are in $\mathcal{O}$ and $\mathcal{O}$ is closed under arbitrary union and finite intersection. One way to define a topology for a set is to find a base for it. A **base** $\mathcal{B}$ for X is a class of subsets of X such that

1. $\bigcup \mathcal{B} = X$, and
2. for every $x \in X$ and any $B_1, B_2 \in \mathcal{B}$ that contain x, there exists $B_3 \in \mathcal{B}$ such that $x \in B_3 \subseteq B_1 \cap B_2$.

For any base $\mathcal{B}$, the set $\{\bigcup \mathcal{C} : \mathcal{C} \subseteq \mathcal{B}\}$ is a topology for X [18–p.52]. That is, an open set is a union of sets in the base. Let $\mathcal{L}$ be a class of languages and $\sigma \in$ SEQ. We use $\mathcal{L}|\sigma$ to denote all languages in $\mathcal{L}$ that are consistent with σ (i.e., $\{L \in \mathcal{L} : L$ is consistent with $\sigma\}$); similarly $\mathcal{L}|D$ denotes the languages in $\mathcal{L}$ that include a given finite subset D. The next proposition shows that $\mathcal{B}_\mathcal{L} = \{\mathcal{L}|\sigma : \sigma \in$ SEQ$\}$ constitutes a base for $\mathcal{L}$.

Proposition 1. $\mathcal{B}_\mathcal{L} = \{\mathcal{L}|\sigma : \sigma \in$ SEQ$\}$ *is a base for* $\mathcal{L}$; *hence* $\mathcal{T}_\mathcal{L} = \{\bigcup \mathcal{S} : \mathcal{S} \subseteq \mathcal{B}_\mathcal{L}\}$ *is a topology for* $\mathcal{L}$.

The topology $\mathcal{T}_\mathcal{L}$ generalizes the **positive information topology** from recursion theory [24–p.186] if we consider the graphs of functions as languages (as in [10–Ch.3.9.2][20–Ch.2.6.2]).

Examples For the language collection COINIT we have that COINIT$|\{2,3\} = \{L_0, L_1, L_2\}$ and COINIT$|\{0\} = \{L_0\}$.

In a topological space $(X, \mathcal{T})$, a point x is **isolated** if there is an open set $O \in \mathcal{T}$ such that $O = \{x\}$. If x is not isolated, then x is an **accumulation point of** X. Following Cantor [6], we define the **derived sets** using the concept of accumulation points.

Definition 4 (Cantor). *Let* $(X, \mathcal{T})$ *be topological space.*

1. *The 0-th derived set of* X, *denoted by* $X^{(0)}$, *is just* X.
2. *For every successor ordinal* α, *the* α-*th derived set of* X, *denoted by* $X^{(\alpha)}$, *is the set of all accumulation points of* $X^{(\alpha-1)}$.
3. *For every limit ordinal* α, *the set* $X^{(\alpha)}$ *is the intersection of all* β-*th derived sets, where* $\beta < \alpha$. *That is,* $X^{(\alpha)} = \bigcap_{\beta < \alpha} X^{(\beta)}$.

We give an example from the topology of the real plane that illustrates the geometrical intuitions behind the topological concepts.

Example. Let

$$A = \{(\frac{1}{n}, \frac{1}{m}) : n, m \in \mathbb{N}\} \cup \{(\frac{1}{n}, 0) : n \in \mathbb{N}\} \cup \{(0, \frac{1}{m}) : m \in \mathbb{N}\}$$

be a set of points in the real plane $\mathbb{R}^2$ with the standard topology. We use iso(X) to denote all isolated points in X. Then iso$(A) = \{(\frac{1}{n}, \frac{1}{m}) : n, m \in \mathbb{N}\}$. Therefore

$$A^{(1)} = \{(\frac{1}{n}, 0) : n \in \mathbb{N}\} \cup \{(0, \frac{1}{m}) : m \in \mathbb{N}\}.$$

Similarly, we have $A^{(2)} = (0, 0)$, and $A^{(3)} = \emptyset$.

In the topology $\mathcal{T}_{\mathcal{L}}$, a language L is an isolated point of $\mathcal{L}$ iff there is a finite subset $D \subseteq L$ such that the observation of D entails L (i.e., $\mathcal{L}|D = \{L\}$). The derived sets of $\mathcal{L}$ can be defined inductively as shown in Def. 4. Note if $\alpha < \beta$ then $\mathcal{L}^{(\alpha)} \supseteq \mathcal{L}^{(\beta)}$. It can be shown in set theory that there is an ordinal α such that $\mathcal{L}^{(\beta)} = \mathcal{L}^{(\alpha)}$, for all $\beta > \alpha$ [13]. In other words, there must be a fix point for the derivation operation. If $\mathcal{L}$ has an empty fix point, then we say $\mathcal{L}$ is **scattered** [18–p.78]. In a non-scattered space, the nonempty fixed point is called a **perfect kernel**.

The **accumulation order of a language** L in $\mathcal{L}$, denoted by $\mathrm{acc}_{\mathcal{L}}(L)$ is the maximum ordinal α such that $L \in \mathcal{L}^{(\alpha)}$; when $\mathcal{L}$ is fixed by context, we simply write $\mathrm{acc}(L) = \alpha$. The **accumulation order of a class of languages** $\mathcal{L}$, denoted by $\mathrm{acc}(\mathcal{L})$, is the supremum of the accumulation order of all languages in it. Therefore a language collection has an accumulation order if and only if it is scattered.[2]

Examples
(1) The only isolated point in COINIT is $L_0 = \mathbb{N}$, for COINIT $|\{0\} = \{L_0\}$. Therefore COINIT$^{(1)} = \{L_i : i \geq 1\}$. Similarly L_1 is the only isolated point in COINIT$^{(1)}$; hence COINIT$^{(2)} = \{L_i : i \geq 2\}$. It is easy to verify that COINIT$^{(n)} = \{L_i : i \geq n\}$. Therefore the accumulation order of language L_i in COINIT is i and the accumulation order of COINIT is $\omega = \sup \mathbb{N}$.
(2) In LINEAR$_n = \{$linear subspaces of $\mathbb{Q}^n\}$, the only isolated point is $\mathbb{Q}^n$ itself: Let S be a set of n linearly independent points in $\mathbb{Q}^n$; then LINEAR$_n |S = \{\mathbb{Q}^n\}$. Similarly every $(n - i)$-dimensional linear subspace of $\mathbb{Q}^n$ is an isolated point in LINEAR$_n^{(i)}$. Therefore the accumulation order of LINEAR$_n$ is n.
(3) In FIN, there is *no* isolated point. This is because for every finite subset S of $\mathbb{N}$, there are infinitely many languages in FIN that are consistent with S. Therefore FIN is a perfect kernel of itself and FIN has no accumulation order.

3.2   Accumulation Order Characterizes Mind Change Complexity

In this section we show that the accumulation order of a language collection $\mathcal{L}$ is an exact measure of its mind change complexity for (not necessarily effective) learners: if $\mathrm{acc}(\mathcal{L})$ is unbounded, then $\mathcal{L}$ is not identifiable with any ordinal mind change bound; and if $\mathrm{acc}(\mathcal{L}) = \alpha$, then $\mathcal{L}$ is identifiable with a mind change bound.[3]

In a language topology, accumulation order has two fundamental properties that we apply often. Let $\mathrm{acc}_{\mathcal{L}}(\sigma) \equiv \sup\{\mathrm{acc}_{\mathcal{L}}(L) : L \in \mathcal{L}|\sigma\}$; as usual, we omit the subscript in context. A language L in $\mathcal{L}$ **has the highest accumulation order given** σ if $\mathrm{acc}_{\mathcal{L}}(L) = \mathrm{acc}_{\mathcal{L}}(\sigma)$ and for every $L' \in \mathcal{L}|\sigma$, $L' \neq L$ implies $\mathrm{acc}_{\mathcal{L}}(L') < \mathrm{acc}_{\mathcal{L}}(L)$.

Lemma 1. *Let $\mathcal{L}$ be a scattered class of languages with bounded accumulation order.*

---

[2] Accumulation order is also called scattering height, derived length, Cantor-Bendixson rank, or Cantor-Bendixson length [13].
[3] Necessary and sufficient conditions for finite mind change identifiability by learning *algorithms* appear in [19, 23].

1. *For every language $L \in \mathcal{L}$, for every text T for L, there exists a time n such that L has the highest accumulation order given $T[n]$.*
2. *For any two languages $L_1, L_2 \in \mathcal{L}$ such that $L_1 \subset L_2$ it holds that $\mathrm{acc}_{\mathcal{L}}(L_1) > \mathrm{acc}_{\mathcal{L}}(L_2)$.*

Proof. Part 2 is immediate. Part 1: For contradiction, assume there is a text T for L such that for all n, $\mathcal{L}|(T[n])$ contains some language L' such that $\mathrm{acc}(L') \geq \mathrm{acc}(L) = \alpha$. Then L is an accumulation point of $\mathcal{L}^{(\alpha)}$, the subclass of $\mathcal{L}$ that contains all languages with accumulation order less than or equal to α. Therefore $\mathrm{acc}(L) \geq \alpha + 1$, which is a contradiction. □

We now establish the correspondence between mind change complexity and accumulation order: $\mathrm{MC}_{\mathcal{L}}(\sigma) = \mathrm{acc}_{\mathcal{L}}(\sigma)$.

Theorem 1. *Let $\mathcal{L}$ be a language collection and let σ be a finite data sequence. Then there is a learner Ψ that identifies $\mathcal{L}$ given σ with mind change bound $\alpha \iff \mathrm{acc}_{\mathcal{L}}(\sigma) \leq \alpha$.*

Proof. ($\Leftarrow$) We first prove by transfinite induction the auxiliary claim (*): if there is $L_\tau \in \mathcal{L}$ that has the highest accumulation order given data sequence τ, then there is a learner Ψ_τ and a counter c_τ such that (1) $\Psi_\tau(\tau) = L_\tau$, (2) Ψ_τ identifies $\mathcal{L}$ given τ, (3) c_τ is a mind change counter for Ψ_τ given τ, and (4) $c_\tau(\tau) = \mathrm{acc}(\mathcal{L}|\tau)$. Assume (*) for all $\beta < \alpha$ and consider $\alpha = \mathrm{acc}(\mathcal{L}|\tau)$. Note that (a) if $\tau^* \supset \tau$ and there is another language $L_{\tau^*} \neq L_\tau$ that has the highest accumulation order for τ^*, then $\mathrm{acc}(\mathcal{L}|\tau^*) < \mathrm{acc}(\mathcal{L}|\tau)$. Hence by inductive hypothesis, we may choose a learner Ψ_{τ^*} and c_{τ^*} with the properties (1)–(4). Now define Ψ_τ and c_τ as follows for $\tau' \supseteq \tau$.

1. $\Psi_\tau(\tau) := L_\tau$, and $c_\tau(\tau) := \alpha$.
2. if there is a τ^* such that: $\tau \subset \tau^* \subseteq \tau'$ and there is $L_{\tau^*} \neq L_\tau$ with the highest accumulation order for τ^*, then let τ^* be the least such sequence and set $\Psi_\tau(\tau') := \Psi_{\tau^*}(\tau')$, and $c_\tau(\tau') := c_{\tau^*}(\tau')$. (Intuitively, Ψ_τ follows Ψ_{τ^*} after τ^*).
3. otherwise $\Psi_\tau(\tau') := L_\tau$ and $c_\tau(\tau') := \alpha$.

(1) and (4) are immediate. We verify (2) and (3): Let $T \supset \sigma$ be a text for a target language $L \in \mathcal{L}$. If $L = L_\tau$, then Clause 2 never applies and Ψ_τ converges to L_τ on T without any mind changes after σ. Otherwise by Lemma. 1, there is a first stage n such that Clause 2 applies at $T[n]$. Then Ψ_τ converges to L by choice of $\Psi_{T[n]}$. Also, no mind change occurs at $T[n']$ for $|\sigma| < n' < n$. By (a) and definition of $c_\tau, c_{T[n]}$, we have that $c_\tau(T[n-1]) > c_{T[n]}(T[n])$. And c_τ follows $c_{T[n]}$ after stage n. This establishes (*).

Now we construct a learner Ψ as follows for all $\tau \supseteq \sigma$.

1. if there is a τ^* such that: $\sigma \subseteq \tau^* \subseteq \tau$ and there is L_{τ^*} with the highest accumulation order for τ^*, then let τ^* be the least such sequence and set $\Psi(\tau) := \Psi_{\tau^*}(\tau)$, and $c(\tau) := c_{\tau^*}(\tau)$. (Intuitively, Ψ follows Ψ_{τ^*} after τ^*).
2. Otherwise $\Psi(\tau) :=?$ and $c(\tau) := \mathrm{acc}(\mathcal{L}|\sigma)$.

We show that Ψ identifies $\mathcal{L}$ given σ. Let $L \in \mathcal{L}$ and let $T \supset \sigma$ be any text for L. Then by Lemma 1, there is a least time n such that some language L' has the highest accumulation order for $T[n]$. So the learner Ψ converges to L by choice of $\Psi_{T[n]}$. No mind change occurs at or before $T[n]$, and $\mathrm{acc}(\mathcal{L}|\sigma) \geq \mathrm{acc}(\mathcal{L}|T[n])$; this shows that c is a mind change counter for Ψ given σ.

($\Rightarrow$) Let Ψ be a learner that identifies $\mathcal{L}$ given σ and c is a mind change counter such that $c(\sigma) = \alpha$. We prove by transfinite induction that if $\mathrm{acc}(\sigma) > \alpha$, then c is not a mind change counter for $\mathcal{L}$. Assume the claim holds for all $\beta < \alpha$ and consider α. Suppose $\mathrm{acc}(\sigma) > \alpha$; then there is $L \in \mathcal{L}|\sigma$ such that $\mathrm{acc}(L) = \alpha + 1$. Case 1: $\Psi(\sigma) = L$. Then since L is a limit point of $\mathcal{L}^{(\alpha)}$, there is L' in $\mathcal{L}^{(\alpha)}$ such that $L' \neq L$ and $\mathrm{acc}(L') = \alpha$. Let $T' \supset \sigma$ be a text for L'. Since Ψ identifies L', there is a time $n > |\sigma|$ such that $\Psi(T'[n]) = L'$. Since $\Psi(T'[n]) \neq \Psi(\sigma)$ and $\Psi(\sigma) \neq ?$, this is a mind change of Ψ, hence $c(T'[n]) < c(\sigma)$. That is, $c(T'[n]) = \beta < \alpha$. On the other hand, since $\mathrm{acc}(L') = \alpha$, we have $\mathrm{acc}(T'[n]) > \beta$. By inductive hypothesis, c is not a mind change counter for Ψ. Case 2: $\Psi(\sigma) \neq L$. Let $T \supset \sigma$ be a text for L. Since Ψ identifies L, there is a time $n > |\sigma|$ such that $\Psi(T[n]) = L$. Since $c(T[n]) \leq c(\sigma) = \alpha$ and $\mathrm{acc}(T[n]) > \alpha$, as in Case 1, c is not a mind change counter for Ψ. $\square$

Corollary 1. *Let $\mathcal{L}$ be a class of languages. Then there exists a mind-change bound for $\mathcal{L}$ if and only if $\mathcal{L}$ is scattered in the topology $\mathcal{T}_{\mathcal{L}}$.*

4   Necessary and Sufficient Conditions for Uniformly Mind Change Optimal Learners

The goal of this section is to characterize the behaviour of uniformly mind-change optimal learners. These results allow us to design mind change optimal learners and to prove their optimality. The next definition specifies the key property of uniformly MC-optimal learners.

Definition 5. *A learner Ψ is **order-driven** given σ if for all finite data sequences $\tau, \tau' \in$ SEQ($\mathcal{L}$) such that $\sigma \subseteq \tau \subset \tau'$: if (1) $\tau = \sigma$ or $\Psi(\tau)$ is valid for τ, and (2) $\mathrm{acc}_{\mathcal{L}}(\tau) = \mathrm{acc}_{\mathcal{L}}(\tau')$, then Ψ does not change its mind at τ'.*

Informally, a learner Ψ is order-driven if once Ψ makes a valid conjecture $\Psi(\tau)$ at τ, then Ψ "hangs on" to $\Psi(\tau)$ at least until the accumulation order drops at some sequence $\tau' \supset \tau$, that is, $\mathrm{acc}(\tau') < \mathrm{acc}(\tau)$. Both the learners Ψ_{CO} and Ψ_{LIN} are order-driven given Λ.

A data sequence σ is **topped** if there is a language $L \in \mathcal{L}$ consistent with σ such that $\mathrm{acc}_{\mathcal{L}}(L) = \mathrm{acc}_{\mathcal{L}}(\sigma)$. Note that if $\mathrm{acc}_{\mathcal{L}}(\sigma)$ is a successor ordinal (e.g., finite), then σ is topped. All data sequences in SEQ(LINEAR$_n$) are topped. In COINIT, the initial sequence Λ is *not* topped. As the next proposition shows, if σ is topped, the conjecture $\Psi(\sigma)$ of a UMC-optimal learner Ψ is *highly constrained*: either $\Psi(\sigma)$ is not valid, or else $\Psi(\sigma)$ must uniquely have the highest accumulation order in $\mathcal{L}|\sigma$.

Proposition 2. *Let $\mathcal{L}$ be a language collection such that $\mathrm{acc}_{\mathcal{L}}(\sigma) = \alpha$ for some ordinal α and data sequence σ. Suppose that learner Ψ is uniformly mind change optimal and identifies $\mathcal{L}$ given σ. Then*

1. Ψ is order-driven given σ.
2. for all data sequences $\tau \supseteq \sigma$, if τ is topped and $\Psi(\tau)$ is valid for τ, then $\Psi(\tau)$ is the unique language with the highest accumulation order for τ.

Proof Outline. Clause 1. Suppose that $\tau = \sigma$ or that $\Psi(\tau)$ is valid for $\tau \supset \sigma$; then $c(\tau) = \mathrm{acc}(\tau)$. If Ψ changes its mind at τ' when $\mathrm{acc}(\tau') = \mathrm{acc}(\tau)$, then $c(\tau') < c(\tau) = \mathrm{acc}(\tau')$. Hence by Theorem 1, c is not a mind change counter for Ψ.

Clause 2. Suppose for reductio that $\Psi(\tau)$ is valid for τ but $\Psi(\tau)$ does not have the highest accumulation order for τ. Then there is a language $L \in \mathcal{L}|\tau$ such that (1) $\mathrm{acc}(L) = \mathrm{acc}(\tau)$, and (2) $\mathrm{acc}(L) \geq \mathrm{acc}(\Psi(\tau))$, and (3) $L \neq \Psi(\tau)$. Choose any text $T \supset \tau$ for L. Since Ψ identifies $\mathcal{L}$, there is an $n > |\tau|$ such that $\Psi(T[n]) \neq \Psi(\tau)$ and $\mathrm{acc}(T[n]) = \mathrm{acc}(\tau)$. Hence Ψ is not order-driven. □

To illustrate, in COINIT, since the initial sequence Λ is not topped, Prop. 2 does not restrict the conjectures of UMC-optimal learners at Λ.

A learner Ψ is **regular** given σ if for all data sequences $\tau \supset \sigma$, if Ψ changes its mind at τ, then $\Psi(\tau)$ is valid. Intuitively, there is no reason for a learner Ψ to change its conjecture to an invalid one. The learners Ψ_{COINIT} and Ψ_{LIN} are regular. According to Prop. 2, being order-driven is necessary for a UMC-optimal learner. The next proposition shows that for regular learners, this property is sufficient as well.

Proposition 3. *Let $\mathcal{L}$ be a language collection such that $\mathrm{acc}(\sigma) = \alpha$ for some ordinal α and data sequence σ. If a learner Ψ identifies $\mathcal{L}$ and is regular and order-driven given σ, then Ψ is uniformly mind change optimal given σ.*

Proof. Let Ψ be regular and order-driven given σ. Define a counter c as follows for σ and $\tau \supset \sigma$.

(1) $c(\sigma) = \mathrm{acc}(\sigma)$.
(2) $c(\tau) = \mathrm{acc}(\tau)$ if $\Psi(\tau)$ is valid for τ.
(3) $c(\tau) = c(\tau^-)$ if $\Psi(\tau)$ is not valid for τ.

Clearly $c(\tau) = \mathrm{acc}(\tau)$ if $\Psi(\tau)$ is valid for τ. So it suffices to show that c is a mind change counter for Ψ. Let Ψ change its mind at $\tau \supset \sigma$. Then since Ψ is regular given σ, we have that $\Psi(\tau)$ is valid for τ and hence (a) $c(\tau) = \mathrm{acc}(\tau)$.

Case 1: There is a time n such that (1) $|\sigma| \leq n \leq \mathrm{lh}(\tau^-)$, where $\mathrm{lh}(\tau^-)$ is the length of τ^-, and (2) $\Psi(\tau^-[n])$ is valid for $\tau^-[n]$. WLOG, let n be the greatest such time. Then by the definition of c, we have that (b) $c(\tau^-[n]) = c(\tau^-)$. Since $\tau^-[n] \subset \tau$, and Ψ changes its mind at τ, and Ψ is order-driven, it follows that (c) $\mathrm{acc}(\tau^-[n]) > \mathrm{acc}(\tau)$. Also, by (2), we have that (d) $c(\tau^-[n]) = \mathrm{acc}(\tau^-[n])$. Combining (a), (b), (c) and (d), it follows that $c(\tau^-) > c(\tau)$.

Case 2: There is no time n such that $|\sigma| \leq n \leq \mathrm{lh}(\tau^-)$ and (2) $\Psi(\tau^-[n])$ is valid for $\tau^-[n]$. Then by definition of c, we have that (e) $c(\tau^-) = \mathrm{acc}(\sigma)$. And since Ψ is order-driven given σ, (f) $\mathrm{acc}(\sigma) > \mathrm{acc}(\tau)$. Combining (a), (e), and (f), we have that $c(\tau^-) > c(\tau)$.

So in either case, if Ψ changes its mind at $\tau \supset \sigma$, then $c(\tau^-) > c(\tau)$, which establishes that c is a mind change counter for Ψ given σ. Hence Ψ is UMC-optimal given σ. □

In short, Propositions 2 and 3 show that being order-driven is the key property of a uniformly mind change optimal learner.

Examples

(1) In COINIT, for any data sequence $\sigma \in$ SEQ such that content$(\sigma) \neq \emptyset$, we have that $\mathcal{L}|\sigma$ is topped and there is a unique language $L(\sigma)$ with the highest accumulation order. Since $\Psi_{CO}(\sigma) = L(\sigma)$ whenever content$(\sigma) \neq \emptyset$, the learner $\Psi_{CO}(\sigma)$ is order-driven and regular, and hence a UMC-optimal learner for COINIT by Prop. 3. But Ψ_{CO} is not the unique UMC-optimal learner: Define a modified learner Ψ_0^k by setting $\Psi_0^k(\sigma) := L_k$ if content$(\sigma) = \emptyset$, and $\Psi_0^k(\sigma) := \Psi_{CO}(\sigma)$ otherwise. Any such learner Ψ_0^k is a valid uniformly MC-optimal learner.

(2) Since LINEAR$_n$ is finite, it is a topped language collection. In fact, for all data sequences σ, the language with the highest accumulation order is given by span(vectors (σ)). Thus the learner Ψ_{LIN} is the unique uniformly MC-optimal learner for LINEAR$_n$ such that $\Psi_{LIN}(\sigma)$ is valid for all data sequences $\sigma \in$ SEQ(LINEAR$_n$).

5   Effective Uniformly Mind Change Optimal Learning

It is straightforward to computationally implement the learners Ψ_{CO} and Ψ_{LIN}. These learners have the feature that whenever they produce a conjecture L on data σ, the language L is the $\subseteq$-minimum among all languages consistent with σ. It follows immediately from Clause 2 of Lemma. 1 that Ψ_{CO} and Ψ_{LIN} always output an order-maximizing hypothesis (the language uniquely having the highest accumulation order). For many problems, e.g., COINIT and LINEAR$_n$, a language has the highest accumulation order iff it is the $\subseteq$-minimum. For such a language collection $\mathcal{L}$, if we can compute the $\subseteq$-minimum, a UMC-optimal learning algorithm for $\mathcal{L}$ can be constructed on the model of Ψ_{CO} and Ψ_{LIN}. However, these conditions are much stronger than necessary in general. In general, it suffices that we can *eventually* compute a $\subseteq$-minimum along any text. We illustrate this point by specifying a UMC-optimal learning algorithm for P_1, the languages defined by Angluin's well-known one-variable patterns [2–p.48].

Let X be a set of variable symbols and let Σ be a finite alphabet of at least two constant symbols (e.g., $0, 1, \ldots, n$). A **pattern**, denoted by p, q etc., is a finite non-null sequence over $X \cup \Sigma$. If a pattern contains exactly one distinct variable, then it is a **one-variable pattern** (e.g., x01 or 0x00x1). Following [2], we denote the set of all one-variable patterns by P_1. A **substitution** θ replaces x in a pattern p by another pattern. For example, $\theta = [x/0]$ maps the pattern xx to the pattern 00 and $\theta' = [x/xx]$ maps the pattern xx to the pattern xxxx. Substitutions give rise to a partial order $\preceq$ over all patterns. Let p and q be two patterns. We define $p \preceq q$ if there is a substitution θ such that $p = q\theta$. The **language generated by a pattern** p, denoted by $L(p)$, is the set $\{q \in \Sigma^* : q \preceq p\}$.

Angluin described an algorithm that, given a finite set S of strings as input, finds the set of one-variable patterns descriptive of S, and then (arbitrarily) selects one with the maximum length [2–Th.6.5]. A one-variable pattern p is **descriptive of a sample** S if $S \subseteq L(p)$ and for every one-variable pattern q such that $S \subseteq L(q)$, the language $L(q)$ is not a proper subset of $L(p)$ [2–p.48]. To illustrate, the pattern 1x is descriptive of the samples $\{10\}$ and $\{10, 11\}$, the pattern x0 is descriptive of the samples $\{10\}$ and $\{10, 00\}$, and the pattern x is descriptive of the sample $\{10, 00, 11\}$. We give an example (summarised in Fig. 1) to show that Angluin's algorithm is not a mind-change

Text T	:	10	00	11	0	$\cdots$
Stage n	:	1	2	3	4	$\cdots$
Patterns consistent with $T[n]$	:	1x, x0, x	x0, x	x	x	$\cdots$
Patterns descriptive of $T[n]$	:	1x, x0	x0	x	x	$\cdots$
Accumulation order of $T[n]$	:	1	1	0	0	$\cdots$
Output of Angluin's learner M_A	:	1x	x0	x	x	$\cdots$
Output of a UMC-optimal learner M	:	?	x0	x	x	$\cdots$

Fig. 1. An illustration of why Angluin's learning algorithm for one-variable patterns is not uniformly mind change optimal

optimal learner. Let x be the target pattern and consider the text $T = \langle 10, 00, 11, 0, \ldots \rangle$ for $L(\mathrm{x})$. Let us write $P_1 | S$ for the set of one-variable patterns consistent with a sample S. Then $P_1|\{10\} = \{\mathrm{1x, x0, x}\}$, $P_1|\{10, 00\} = \{\mathrm{x0, x}\}$, $P_1|\{10, 11\} = \{\mathrm{1x, x}\}$ and $P_1|\{10, 00, 11\} = \{\mathrm{x}\}$. The accumulation orders of these languages are determined as follows:

1. $\mathrm{acc}_{P_1}(L(\mathrm{x})) = 0$ since $L(\mathrm{x})$ is isolated; so $\mathrm{acc}_{P_1}(\langle 10, 00, 11 \rangle) = 0$.
2. $\mathrm{acc}_{P_1}(L(\mathrm{1x})) = 1$ since $P_1|\{10, 11\} = \{\mathrm{1x, x}\}$; so $\mathrm{acc}_{P_1}(\langle 10, 11 \rangle) = 1$.
3. $\mathrm{acc}_{P_1}(L(\mathrm{x0})) = 1$ since $P_1|\{10, 00\} = \{\mathrm{x0, x}\}$; so $\mathrm{acc}_{P_1}(\langle 10, 00 \rangle) = 1$.

Also, we have $\mathrm{acc}_{P_1}(\langle 10 \rangle) = 1$. Since for $T[1] = \langle 10 \rangle$, the one-variable patterns 1x and x0 are both descriptive of $\{10\}$, Angluin's learner M_A conjectures either 1x or x0; suppose $M_A(\langle 10 \rangle) = \mathrm{1x}$. Now let c_A be any mind change counter for M_A. Since 1x is consistent with $\langle 10 \rangle$, UMC-optimality requires that $c_A(\langle 10 \rangle) = \mathrm{acc}_{P_1}(\langle 10 \rangle) = 1$. The next string 00 in T refutes 1x, so M_A changes its mind to x0 (i.e., $M_A(T[2]) = \mathrm{x0}$), and $c_A(\langle 10, 00 \rangle) = 0$. However, M_A changes its mind again to pattern x on $T[3] = \langle 10, 00, 11 \rangle$, so c_A is not a mind change counter for M_A, and M_A is not UMC-optimal. In short, after the string 10 is observed, it is possible to identify the target one-variable pattern with one more mind change, but M_A requires two.

The issue with M_A is that M_A changes its mind on sequence $\langle 10, 00 \rangle$ even though $\mathrm{acc}_{P_1}(\langle 10 \rangle) = \mathrm{acc}_{P_1}(\langle 10, 00 \rangle) = 1$, so M_A is not order-driven and hence Proposition 2 implies that M_A is not UMC-optimal. Intuitively, an order-driven learner has to wait until the data decide between the two patterns 1x and x0. As Proposition 3 indicates, we can design a UMC-optimal learner M for P_1 by "procrastinating" until there is a pattern with the highest accumulation order. For example on text T our UMC-optimal learner M makes the following conjectures: $M(\langle 10 \rangle) = ?$, $M(\langle 10, 00 \rangle) = \mathrm{x0}$, $M(\langle 10, 00, 11 \rangle) = \mathrm{x}$.

The general specification of the UMC-optimal learning algorithm M is as follows. For a terminal $a \in \Sigma$ let $p^a \equiv p[\mathrm{x}/a]$. The proof of [2–Lemma 3.9] shows that if q is a one-variable pattern such that $L(q) \supseteq \{p^a, p^b\}$ for two distinct terminals a, b, then $L(q) \supseteq L(p)$. Thus a UMC-optimal learning algorithm M can proceed as follows.

1. Set $M(\Lambda) :=?$.
2. Given a sequence σ with $S := \text{content}(\sigma)$, check (*) if there is a one-variable pattern p consistent with σ such that $S \supseteq \{p^a, p^b\}$ for two distinct terminals a, b. If yes, output $M(\sigma) := p$. If not, set $M(\sigma) := M(\sigma^-)$.

Since there are at most finitely many patterns consistent with σ, the check (*) is effective. In fact, (*) and hence M can be implemented so that computing $M(\sigma)$ takes time linear in $|\sigma|$. Outline: Let $m = \min\{|s| : s \in S\}$. Let S^m be the set of strings in S of length m. Define $p_S(i) := a$ if $s(i) = a$ for all $s \in S^m$, and $p_S(i) := \text{x}$ otherwise for $1 \le i \le m$. For example, $p_{\{10,11,111\}} = 1\text{x}$ and $p_{\{10,01\}} = \text{x}$. Then check for all $s \in S$ if $s \in L(p_S)$. For a one-variable pattern, this can be done in linear time because $|\theta(\text{x})|$, the length of $\theta(\text{x})$, must be $\frac{|s| - term(p_S)}{|p_S| - term(p_S)}$ where $term(p_S)$ is the number of terminals in p_S. For example, if $s = 111$ and $p_S = 1\text{x}$, then $|\theta(\text{x})|$ must be 2. If p_S is consistent with S, then there are distinct $a, b \in \Sigma$ such that $\{p^a, p^b\} \subseteq S$. Otherwise no pattern p of length m is consistent with S and hence (*) fails.

6   Summary and Future Work

The topic of this paper was learning with bounded mind changes. We applied the classic topological concept of accumulation order to characterize the mind change complexity of a learning problem: A language collection $\mathcal{L}$ is identifiable by a learner (not necessarily computable) with α mind changes iff the accumulation order of $\mathcal{L}$ is at most α. We studied the properties of uniformly mind change optimal learners: roughly, a learner Ψ is uniformly mind change optimal if Ψ realizes the best possible mind change bound not only in the entire learning problem, but also in subproblems that arise after observing some data. The characteristic property of UMC-optimal learners is that they output languages with maximal accumulation order. Thus analyzing the accumulation order of a learning problem is a powerful guide to constructing mind change efficient learners. We illustrated these results in several learning problems such as identifying a linear subspace and a one-variable pattern. For learning linear subspaces, the natural method of conjecturing the least subspace containing the data is the only mind change optimal learner that does not "procrastinate" (i.e., never outputs ? or an inconsistent conjecture). Angluin's algorithm for learning a one-variable pattern is not UMC-optimal; we described a different UMC-optimal algorithm for this problem.

We outline several avenues for future work. The next challenge for pattern languages is to find a UMC-optimal algorithm for learning a general pattern with arbitrarily many variables. An important step towards that goal would be to determine the accumulation order of a pattern language $L(p)$ in the space of pattern languages. Another application is the design of UMC-optimal learners for logic programs. For example, Jain and Sharma have examined classes of logic programs that can be learned with bounded mind changes using explorer trees [12]. Do explorer trees lead to mind change optimal learning algorithms?

There are a number of open issues for the general theory of UMC-optimal learning. The proof of Theorem 1 shows that if there is any general learner that solves a learning problem $\mathcal{L}$ with α mind changes, then there is a UMC-optimal general learner for $\mathcal{L}$.

However, this may well not be the case for effective learning algorithms: Is there a language collection $\mathcal{L}$ such that there is a computable learner M that identifies $\mathcal{L}$ with α mind changes, but there is no computable UMC-optimal learner for $\mathcal{L}$? Such a separation result would show that for computable learners, UMC-optimality defines a new class of learning problems.

As the example of one-variable patterns shows, there can be a trade-off between time efficiency and producing consistent conjectures, on the one hand, and the procrastination that minimizing mind changes may require on the other (see Sect. **??**). We would like to characterize the learning problems for which this tension arises, and how great the trade-off can be.

Another project is to relate the topological concept of accumulation order to other well-known structural properties of a language collection $\mathcal{L}$. For example, it can be shown that if $\mathcal{L}$ has unbounded accumulation order (i.e., if $\mathcal{L}$ contains a nonempty perfect subset), then $\mathcal{L}$ has infinite elasticity, as defined in [29, 22]. Also, we can show that accumulation order corresponds to intrinsic complexity as defined in [7, 11], in the following sense: If $\mathcal{L}_1$ is weakly reducible to $\mathcal{L}_2$, then the accumulation order of $\mathcal{L}_2$ is at least as great as the accumulation order of $\mathcal{L}_1$. It follows immediately that COINIT $\not\leq_{weak}$ SINGLE, where SINGLE is the class of all singleton languages and has accumulation order 0, and FIN $\not\leq_{weak}$ COINIT, two results due to Jain and Sharma [11].

In sum, uniform mind change optimality guides the construction of learning algorithms by imposing strong and natural constraints; and the analytical tools we established for solving these constraints reveal significant aspects of the fine structure of learning problems.

Acknowledgments

This research was supported by a Discovery Grant from the Natural Sciences and Engineering Research Council of Canada. We would like to thank the anonymous COLT referees for their comments and suggestions.

References

1. A. Ambainis, S. Jain, and A. Sharma. Ordinal mind change complexity of language identification. *Theor. Comput. Sci.*, 220(2):323–343, 1999.
2. D Angluin. Finding patterns common to a set of strings. *J. Comput. Syst. Sci.*, 21(1):46–62, 1980.
3. D Angluin. Inductive inference of formal languages from positive data. *Information and Control*, 45(2):117–135, 1980.
4. K. Apsitis. Derived sets and inductive inference. In S. Arikawa and K. P. Jantke, editors, *Proceedings of ALT 1994*, pages 26–39. Springer, Berlin, Heidelberg, 1994.
5. G. Baliga, J. Case, and S. Jain. The synthesis of language learners. *Information and Computation*, 152:16–43, 1999.
6. G. Cantor. Grundlagen einer allgemeinen Mannigfaltigkeitslehre. In William Ewald, editor, *From Kant to Hilbert*, volume 2, pages 878–920. Oxford Science Publications, 1996.

7. R. Freivalds, E. Kinber, and C. H. Smith. On the intrinsic complexity of learning. *Inf. Comput.*, 123(1):64–71, 1995.
8. R. Freivalds and C. H. Smith. On the role of procrastination in machine learning. *Inf. Comput.*, 107(2):237–271, 1993.
9. E. Mark Gold. Language identification in the limit. *Information and Control*, 10(5):447–474, 1967.
10. S. Jain, D. Osherson, J. S. Royer, and A. Sharma. *Systems That Learn*. M.I.T. Press, 2 edition, 1999.
11. S. Jain and A. Sharma. The intrinsic complexity of language identification. *J. Comput. Syst. Sci.*, 52(3):393–402, 1996.
12. S. Jain and A. Sharma. Mind change complexity of learning logic programs. *TCS*, 284(1):143–160, 2002.
13. A. J. Jayanthan. Derived length for arbitrary topological spaces. *International Journal of Mathematics and Mathematical Sciences*, 15(2):273–277, 1992.
14. K. Kelly. *The Logic of Reliable Inquiry*. Oxford University Press, 1996.
15. K. Kelly. Efficient convergence implies Ockham's Razor. In *Proceedings of the 2002 International Workshop on Computation Models of Scientific Reasoning and Applications*, pages 24–27, 2002.
16. K. Kelly. Justification as truth-finding efficiency: How ockham's razor works. *Minds and Machines*, 14(4):485–505, 2004.
17. S. Kocabas. Conflict resolution as discovery in particle physics. *Machine Learning*, 6:277–309, 1991.
18. K. Kuratowski. *Topology*, volume 1. Academic Press, 1966. Translated by J. Jaworowski.
19. S. Lange and T. Zeugmann. Language learning with a bounded number of mind changes. In *Symposium on Theoretical Aspects of Computer Science*, pages 682–691, 1993.
20. E. Martin and D. N. Osherson. *Elements of Scientific Inquiry*. The MIT Press, Cambridge, Massachusetts, 1998.
21. E. Martin, A. Sharma, and F. Stephan. Learning, logic, and topology in a common framework. In *Proceedings of the 13th International Conference on Algorithmic Learning Theory*, pages 248–262. Springer-Verlag, 2002.
22. T. Motoki, T. Shinohara, and K. Wright. The correct definition of finite elasticity: corrigendum to identification of unions. In *Proceedings of COLT 1991*, page 375. Morgan Kaufmann Publishers Inc., 1991.
23. Y. Mukouchi. Inductive inference with bounded mind changes. In S. Doshita, K. Furukawa, K. P. Jantke, and T. Nishida, editors, *Proceedings of ALT 1992*, pages 125–134. Springer, Berlin, Heidelberg, 1993.
24. P. Odifreddi. *Classical Recursion Theory*. North-Holland, October 1999.
25. D. N. Osherson, M. Stob, and S. Weinstein. *Systems that learn: an introduction to learning theory for cognitive and computer scientists*. MIT Press, 1986.
26. O. Schulte. Automated discovery of conservation principles and new particles in particle physics. Manuscript submitted to *Machine Learning*, 2005.
27. R. Valdés-Pérez. Algebraic reasoning about reactions: Discovery of conserved properties in particle physics. *Machine Learning*, 17:47–67, 1994.
28. R. Valdés-Pérez. On the justification of multiple selection rules of conservation in particle physics phenomenology. *Computer Physics Communications*, 94:25–30, 1996.
29. K. Wright. Identification of unions of languages drawn from an identifiable class. In *Proceedings of the second annual workshop on Computational learning theory*, pages 328–333. Morgan Kaufmann Publishers Inc., 1989.

On a Syntactic Characterization of Classification with a Mind Change Bound

Eric Martin[1] and Arun Sharma[2]

[1] School of Computer Science and Engineering, National ICT Australia*,
UNSW Sydney, NSW 2052, Australia
emartin@cse.unsw.edu.au

[2] Division of Research and Commercialisation, Queensland University of Technology,
2 George street, GPO Box 2434, Brisbane QLD 4001, Australia
Arun.Sharma@qut.edu.au

Abstract. Most learning paradigms impose a particular syntax on the class of concepts to be learned; the chosen syntax can dramatically affect whether the class is learnable or not. For classification paradigms, where the task is to determine whether the underlying world does or does not have a particular property, how that property is represented has no implication on the power of a classifier that just outputs 1's or 0's. But is it possible to give a canonical syntactic representation of the class of concepts that are classifiable according to the particular criteria of a given paradigm? We provide a positive answer to this question for classification in the limit paradigms in a logical setting, with ordinal mind change bounds as a measure of complexity. The syntactic characterization that emerges enables to derive that if a possibly noncomputable classifier can perform the task assigned to it by the paradigm, then a computable classifier can also perform the same task. The syntactic characterization is strongly related to the difference hierarchy over the class of open sets of some topological space; this space is naturally defined from the class of possible worlds and possible data of the learning paradigm.

Keywords: Mind changes, difference hierarchies, normal forms.

1 Introduction

The field of Inductive inference has mainly focused on two general classes of problems: identification of a language (r.e. subset of $\mathbb{N}$) from its members (positive data), possibly together with its nonmembers (negative data) (see [5] for an overview); classification of languages w.r.t. a concept (set of languages) from

---

* National ICT Australia is funded by the Australian Government's Department of Communications, Information Technology and the Arts and the Australian Research Council through Backing Australia's Ability and the ICT Centre of Excellence Program.

P. Auer and R. Meir (Eds.): COLT 2005, LNAI 3559, pp. 413–428, 2005.

the data generated by the languages (see [4, 10]). More precisely, classification of languages w.r.t. a concept $\mathcal{C}$ requires that for all languages L, a classifier outputs 1 if L belongs to $\mathcal{C}$, and 0 otherwise, from an enumeration of the members of L. Inductive inference considers the case of limiting classification, where the correct output has to be produced in response to all but finitely many initial segments of a stream of data generated by the language to be classified. A notion of complexity is provided by considering upper bounds on the number of mind changes allowed before the sequence of outputs stabilizes to the correct output, for any order of data presentation (see [2, 1, 3]). Moreover, a distinction can be made between classification, positive classification, and negative classification: positive (respect., negative) classification requires converging to 1 (respect., 0) on streams of data for a language that belongs (respect., does not belong) to the concept, and only on those streams; hence classification is equivalent to both positive and negative classification.

In this paper we study positive classification, negative classification and classification with a bounded number of mind changes in a logical setting rather than in a numerical setting: structures play the role of languages, data can be richer—the only condition is that they can be represented by logical sentences, and the concepts themselves will be definable by logical sentences (see [8]). While it would not make sense to try and provide a syntactic characterization of classification with a mind change bound in a numerical setting, the logical setting provides the necessary expressive power for that task. When classification is cast in a logical setting, it is possible to view the task of a classifier as that of discovering the truth of the sentence that defines the concept to be learned, w.r.t. to a generalized notion of logical consequence. More precisely, classification can be formalized as the task of discovering whether a sentence φ is a generalized logical consequence of some theory which the classifier receives an enumeration of. Also, though computability is an essential feature of practical classification scenarios, the basic definitions we use make no a priori computability assumption. Indeed, one of our aims is to discover sufficient (and natural) conditions that guarantee that if classification is possible, then computable classification is possible as well. In [8] the relationship between generalized logical consequence and (possibly noncomputable) classification has been studied. Here we show that under some conditions, (possibly noncomputable) classification implies computable classification.

In [9] it is shown that a sentence is classifiable in the limit iff it is Δ_2^0; this result is generalized to a larger class of paradigms in [7]. The nontrivial direction is of course that classification implies Δ_2^0 logical complexity. The framework presented here goes a step further, and enables to also prove a similar result for classification with a bounded number of mind changes. This requires looking at links with concepts from topology, in particular the difference hierarchies over some topological space (see [6]), and defining a notion of syntactic complexity based on a new normal form: the DNF or CNF are not appropriate to establish connections with classification with a bounded number of mind changes. We proceed as follows. In Section 2 we define the notion of normal form we need. In

Section 3 we present the logical framework and its concept of generalized logical consequence, we define the classification scenario, and we introduce the fundamental topological notions. Section 4 presents the main results. We conclude in Section 5.

2   Syntax

2.1   General Notation

We fix a nonempty vocabulary $\mathcal{V}$, *i.e.*, a set of (possibly nullary) predicate and function symbols, possibly with equality. We say *structure* for $\mathcal{V}$-structure. A literal is either an atom or the negation of an atom. The presentation of the normal form that will characterize classification with a bounded number of mind changes in the kind of learning paradigm we will focus on is simpler and cleaner if we depart slightly from the usual definitions of a formula, and use a syntax that results in no loss in generality, but precisely suits our needs. This is why we (a) impose a negation normal form, and (b) define disjunction and conjunction as unary operators whose arguments are sets. More precisely, the set $\mathcal{L}^{\mathcal{V}}_{\omega\omega}$ of (finite) formulas is inductively defined as follows.

- All literals belong to $\mathcal{L}^{\mathcal{V}}_{\omega\omega}$.
- For all finite $D \subseteq \mathcal{L}^{\mathcal{V}}_{\omega\omega}$, $\bigvee D$ and $\bigwedge D$ belong to $\mathcal{L}^{\mathcal{V}}_{\omega\omega}$.
- For all $\varphi \in \mathcal{L}^{\mathcal{V}}_{\omega\omega}$ and variables x, $\exists x\varphi$ and $\forall x\varphi$ belong to $\mathcal{L}^{\mathcal{V}}_{\omega\omega}$.

In particular, $\bigvee \emptyset$ and $\bigwedge \emptyset$ are formulas, that are logically equivalent to false and true, respectively. We denote by $\mathcal{L}$ the set of closed members of $\mathcal{L}^{\mathcal{V}}_{\omega\omega}$. We refer to a member of $\mathcal{L}$ as a *sentence* and to a subset of $\mathcal{L}$ as a *theory*.

We denote by $\mathcal{L}^{\mathcal{V}}_{\omega_1\omega}$ the extension of $\mathcal{L}^{\mathcal{V}}_{\omega\omega}$ that accepts disjunctions and conjunctions of countable sets of expressions. The members of $\mathcal{L}^{\mathcal{V}}_{\omega_1\omega}$, called infinitary formulas, are needed to express some definability notions.[1] Still all results will be stated in terms of $\mathcal{L}$, whose members are finite: the role played by infinitary formulas is only indirect, in characterizing the syntactic or topological complexity of a member of $\mathcal{L}$.

We introduce a defined symbol $\sim$ that, applied to a (possibly infinitary) formula φ, abbreviates another (possibly infinitary) formula. For all $\varphi \in \mathcal{L}^{\mathcal{V}}_{\omega_1\omega}$, $\sim\varphi$ is logically equivalent to what would be $\neg\varphi$ if the application of negation were not restricted to atoms; moreover, $\sim\sim\varphi = \varphi$.

Notation 1. Given a member φ of $\mathcal{L}^{\mathcal{V}}_{\omega_1\omega}$, $\sim\varphi$ is inductively defined as follows.

- If φ is atomic then $\sim\varphi = \neg\varphi$.
- If φ is of the form $\neg\psi$ then $\sim\varphi = \psi$.
- If φ is of the form $\bigvee X$ then $\sim\varphi = \bigwedge\{\sim\psi : \psi \in X\}$.
- If φ is of the form $\bigwedge X$ then $\sim\varphi = \bigvee\{\sim\psi : \psi \in X\}$.

---

[1] The occurrence or nonoccurrence of $=$ in $\mathcal{V}$ determines whether $\mathcal{L}^{\mathcal{V}}_{\omega\omega}$ and $\mathcal{L}^{\mathcal{V}}_{\omega_1\omega}$ are languages with or without equality.

- If φ is of the form $\exists x \psi$ then $\sim\varphi = \forall x \sim\psi$.
- If φ is of the form $\forall x \psi$ then $\sim\varphi = \exists x \sim\psi$.

Given a set I and a family $(\varphi_i)_{i \in I}$ of members of $\mathcal{L}_{\omega_1\omega}^{\mathcal{V}}$, we usually write $\bigvee_{i \in I} \varphi_i$ for $\bigvee\{\varphi_i : i \in I\}$ and $\bigwedge_{i \in I} \varphi_i$ for $\bigwedge\{\varphi_i : i \in I\}$. Given $\varphi_1, \varphi_2 \in \mathcal{L}_{\omega_1\omega}^{\mathcal{V}}$, we write either $\varphi_1 \vee \varphi_2$ or $\varphi_2 \vee \varphi_1$ for $\bigvee\{\varphi_1, \varphi_2\}$; we write either $\varphi_1 \wedge \varphi_2$ or $\varphi_2 \wedge \varphi_1$ for $\bigwedge\{\varphi_1, \varphi_2\}$; $\varphi_1 \rightarrow \varphi_2$ and $\varphi_1 \leftrightarrow \varphi_2$ are also used as abbreviations.

We will need the following technical notions:

Definition 2. Let a set X of infinitary formulas be given.

- An infinitary formula that is built from X by disjunction and conjunction over finite sets is said to be *finitely positive over* X.
- A subset Y of $\mathcal{L}_{\omega_1\omega}^{\mathcal{V}}$ is said to be a *generator of* X iff X is equal to the set of closed instances of all members of Y.

2.2   Simple Normal Form

The class of ordinals is denoted by Ord. Let a subset X of $\mathcal{L}_{\omega_1\omega}^{\mathcal{V}}$ and a member φ of $\mathcal{L}_{\omega_1\omega}^{\mathcal{V}}$ be given. For all ordinals α, we say that φ is in $\Sigma_\alpha[X]$ normal form iff $\sim\varphi$ is in $\Pi_\alpha[X]$ normal form. We say that φ is in $\Pi_0[X]$ normal form iff φ is finitely positive over the set of (not necessarily closed) instances of X. Given a nonnull ordinal α, the set of infinitary formulas that are in $\Pi_\alpha[X]$ normal form is inductively defined as the set Z of all members ψ of $\mathcal{L}_{\omega_1\omega}^{\mathcal{V}}$ such that:

- ψ is in $\Sigma_\beta[X]$ normal form for some $\beta < \alpha$, or
- ψ is finitely positive over Z, or
- ψ is of the form $\bigwedge T$ for some $T \subseteq Z$, or
- ψ is of the form $\forall x \xi$ for some $\xi \in Z$.

Note that for all $\alpha, \beta \in \text{Ord}$ with $\alpha \leq \beta$ and $\beta > 1$, if φ is in $[\![\Sigma_\alpha[X] \mid \Pi_\alpha[X]]\!]$ normal form, then φ is also in $[\![\Sigma_\beta[X] \mid \Pi_\beta[X]]\!]$ normal form. On the other hand, if φ is in $[\![\Sigma_0[X] \mid \Pi_0[X]]\!]$ normal form, then φ is not necessarily in $[\![\Sigma_1[X] \mid \Pi_1[X]]\!]$ normal form. We say that φ is in simple normal form over X if φ is in $\Sigma_\alpha[X]$ or $\Pi_\alpha[X]$ normal form for some ordinal α.

We will look at learning paradigms that determine a set X such that $\Delta_2[X]$ normal form characterizes classifiability in the limit. In these paradigms, a double normal form defined from the notion of $\Sigma_1[X]$ normal form will characterize classifiability with a bounded number of mind changes. We intuitively motivate the definition of the double normal form before we define it formally.

2.3   Double Normal Form

Assume that $\mathcal{V}$ consists of the nullary predicate symbols p, q, r and s. Hence p, q, r, s are also sentences, and we can define the set $\mathcal{D}$ of *possible data* as $\{p, q, r, s\}$. Let φ be a sentence whose meaning is given by:

p	0	0	0	0	0	0	0	0	1	1	1	1	1	1	1	1
q	0	0	0	0	1	1	1	1	0	0	0	0	1	1	1	1
r	0	0	1	1	0	0	1	1	0	0	1	1	0	0	1	1
s	0	1	0	1	0	1	0	1	0	1	0	1	0	1	0	1
φ	1	1	1	1	1	0	0	0	0	1	0	1	0	1	0	0

Consider the following scenario involving a classifier. A structure $\mathfrak{M}$ is chosen, but remains unknown to the classifier, and the members of $\mathcal{D}$ that are true in $\mathfrak{M}$ are presented to the classifier, possibly with repetitions, and possibly together with an extra symbol $\natural$ that denotes 'no piece of information.' The aim is to discover in the limit whether φ is true in $\mathfrak{M}$. In response to an initial segment of the enumeration, the classifier can output either 1 (a guess that $\mathfrak{M} \models \varphi$) or 0 (a guess that $\mathfrak{M} \not\models \varphi$). A straightforward strategy that minimizes the number of mind changes is to assume that only the predicate symbols that have appeared in the enumeration are true in $\mathfrak{M}$, and output the value given by the truth table above for that particular assignment. The strategy would require to output 1 in response to $\natural$, 0 in response to $\natural, p$, and 0 in response to $\natural, p, q$—a possible sequence of data if $\mathfrak{M}$ is a model of both p and q. This suggests building a labeled forest (set of labeled trees) F over the set of subsets of $\mathcal{D}$ as follows. The roots of the members of F, if any, are labeled with the $\subseteq$-minimal members D of $\mathcal{D}$ such that the truth value of φ as given by D is equal to 1 (meaning that if all members of D get the value 1 and all members of $\mathcal{D} \setminus D$ get the value 0, then φ gets the value 1). Given a node in F labeled with D, the children of this node, if any, are labeled with the $\subseteq$-minimal members E of $\mathcal{D}$ such that $D \subset E$ and the truth value of φ as given by E differs from the truth value of φ as given by D. With our example, F consists of a unique labeled tree, namely:

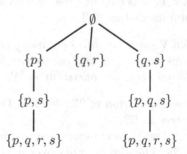

Clearly, since the height of this labeled tree is equal to 3, the strategy sketched above will produce less than 4 mind changes, and no strategy could do better. Set $\varphi_3 = \bigwedge \emptyset$, $\varphi_2 = \bigwedge\{p\} \vee \bigwedge\{q,r\} \vee \bigwedge\{q,s\}$, $\varphi_1 = \bigwedge\{p,s\} \vee \bigwedge\{p,q,s\}$, and $\varphi_0 = \bigwedge\{p,q,r,s\}$. Then φ is also logically equivalent to $\bigvee_{i\in\{1,3\}}(\varphi_i \wedge \bigwedge_{j<i} \sim\varphi_j)$. Since all members of $\mathcal{D}$ are in $\Sigma_1[\mathcal{D}]$ normal form, the previous expression will turn out to be in $\Sigma_{1,4}[\mathcal{D}]$ normal form.

More generally, let $X \subseteq \mathcal{L}^{\mathcal{V}}_{\omega_1\omega}$, $\varphi \in \mathcal{L}^{\mathcal{V}}_{\omega_1\omega}$, and a nonnull ordinal α be given. For all $\beta \in \mathrm{Ord} \setminus \{0\}$, we say that φ is in $\Pi_{\alpha,\beta}[X]$ normal form iff $\sim\varphi$ is in $\Sigma_{\alpha,\beta}[X]$ normal form. We say that φ is in $\Sigma_{\alpha,1}[X]$ normal form iff φ is in $\Sigma_\alpha[X]$

normal form. Given an ordinal β greater than 1, we say that φ is in $\Sigma_{\alpha,\beta}[X]$ normal form iff there exists a nonnull ordinal $\gamma < \beta$ such that φ is in $\Sigma_{\alpha,\gamma}[X]$ or $\Pi_{\alpha,\gamma}[X]$ normal form, or there exists a sequence $(\varphi_\gamma)_{\gamma < \beta}$ of closed infinitary formulas that are in $\Sigma_\alpha[X]$ normal form such that

$$\varphi = \bigvee_{\gamma \in I} (\varphi_\gamma \wedge \bigwedge_{\gamma' < \gamma} \sim \varphi_{\gamma'}),$$

where I is the set of all $\gamma < \beta$ whose parity is opposite to the parity of β. We say that φ is in double normal form over X if φ is in $\Sigma_{\alpha,\beta}[X]$ or $\Pi_{\alpha,\beta}[X]$ normal form for some nonnull ordinals α, β.

3   Relationships Between Learning and Topology

3.1   Learning in a Logical Setting

Let a class X be given. The class of finite sequences of members of X, including the empty sequence (), is represented by $X^\star$. Given two sets X, Y, a partial function f from X into Y, and $x, x' \in X$, we write $f(x) = f(x')$ when both $f(x)$ and $f(x')$ are defined and equal; we write $f(x) \neq f(x')$ otherwise.

We denote by $\mathcal{W}$ a set of structures[2] and by $\mathcal{D}$ a set of sentences, referred to as *possible data*. Given $T \subseteq \mathcal{L}$, $\mathrm{Mod}_{\mathcal{W}}(T)$ represents the set of models of T in $\mathcal{W}$. We put $\mathcal{P} = (\mathcal{V}, \mathcal{W}, \mathcal{L}, \mathcal{D})$, to represent the (*logical*) *paradigm* under investigation.

A structure $\mathfrak{M}$ is said to be *Henkin* iff $\mathfrak{M}$'s individuals are the nonempty sets of closed terms that they interpret; it is said to be *Herbrand* iff $\mathfrak{M}$ is Henkin and $\mathfrak{M}$'s individuals are singletons; and it is said to be *standard* if either $\mathcal{V}$ contains equality and $\mathfrak{M}$ is Henkin, or $\mathcal{V}$ is equality-free and $\mathfrak{M}$ is Herbrand. We will need the easy but fundamental result that follows.

Lemma 3. *Suppose that $\mathcal{V}$ contains infinitely many constants and $\mathcal{W}$ is the set of all standard structures over $\mathcal{V}$. Every consistent theory in which infinitely many constants in $\mathcal{V}$ do not occur is consistent in $\mathcal{W}$.*

Given a structure $\mathfrak{M}$, the $\mathcal{D}$-*diagram of* $\mathfrak{M}$, denoted $\mathrm{Diag}_{\mathcal{D}}(\mathfrak{M})$, is the set of all members of $\mathcal{D}$ that are true in $\mathfrak{M}$.

A classifier is presented with an enumeration of $\mathrm{Diag}_{\mathcal{D}}(\mathfrak{M})$ (plus possibly $\sharp$) for some possible world $\mathfrak{M}$. The aim is to discover in the limit whether φ is true in all possible worlds whose $\mathcal{D}$-diagram agrees with the $\mathcal{D}$-diagram of $\mathfrak{M}$. This corresponds to discovering in the limit whether φ is a generalized logical consequence of $\mathrm{Diag}_{\mathcal{D}}(\mathfrak{M})$, this notion being defined in the next couple of definitions.

Definition 4. Given a theory T, a $\mathcal{D}$-*minimal model of* T *in* $\mathcal{W}$ is a structure $\mathfrak{M}$ such that $\mathfrak{M} \in \mathrm{Mod}_{\mathcal{W}}(T)$ and for all $\mathfrak{N} \in \mathrm{Mod}_{\mathcal{W}}(T)$, $\mathrm{Diag}_{\mathcal{D}}(\mathfrak{N}) \not\subset \mathrm{Diag}_{\mathcal{D}}(\mathfrak{M})$.

---

[2] The requirement that $\mathcal{W}$ cannot be a proper class is mainly due to the fact that we need to consider a topology over $\mathcal{W}$; this results in no loss in generality.

Definition 5. Given a theory T, a sentence φ is a *logical consequence of T in $\mathcal{P}$*, written $T \models^{\mathcal{D}}_{\mathcal{W}} \varphi$, iff every $\mathcal{D}$-minimal model of T in $\mathcal{W}$ is a model of φ.

Suppose for instance that $\mathcal{V}$ contains a unary predicate symbol P, a constant $\overline{0}$, and a unary function symbol s. Given $n \in \mathbb{N}$, we write $\overline{n}$ to represent the term obtained from $\overline{0}$ by n applications of s. Take for $\mathcal{W}$ the set of all Herbrand structures. Put $\mathcal{D} = \{P(\overline{n}) : n \in \mathbb{N}\}$ and $\varphi = P(\overline{0}) \wedge \forall x(P(x) \leftrightarrow \neg P(s(x)))$. Then for all $\mathfrak{M} \in \mathcal{W}$, $\mathrm{Diag}_{\mathcal{D}}(\mathfrak{M}) \models^{\mathcal{D}}_{\mathcal{W}} \varphi$ iff for all $n \in \mathbb{N}$, $P(\overline{n})$ is true in $\mathfrak{M}$ just in case n is even. The task of the classification scenario is then to determine whether the extension of P in the underlying possible world represents $2\mathbb{N}$. This is a case of classification from positive data only. Putting $\mathcal{D} = \{P(\overline{n}), \neg P(\overline{n}) : n \in \mathbb{N}\}$ would formalize a classification scenario where data are both positive and negative.

When $\mathcal{P}$ captures a learning paradigm, the $\mathcal{D}$-diagrams of the members of $\mathcal{W}$ are the only theories that are legitimate starting points for logical investigation:

Definition 6. We denote $\{\mathrm{Diag}_{\mathcal{D}}(\mathfrak{M}) : \mathfrak{M} \in \mathcal{W}\}$ by $\mathcal{B}$, and refer to a member of $\mathcal{B}$ as a *possible knowledge base*.

Moreover, most classification paradigms satisfy the following notion (if not the stronger condition that distinct members of $\mathcal{W}$ have different $\mathcal{D}$-diagrams):

Definition 7. Given a possible knowledge base T and a sentence φ, we say that T *$\mathcal{D}$-minimally decides φ in $\mathcal{W}$* iff either $T \models^{\mathcal{D}}_{\mathcal{W}} \varphi$ or $T \models^{\mathcal{D}}_{\mathcal{W}} \sim\varphi$.

We use *environment* to refer to an enumeration of a possible knowledge base:

Definition 8. Given a member T of $\mathcal{B}$, an *environment for T* is any member e of $(\mathcal{D} \cup \{\sharp\})^{\mathbb{N}}$ such that for all $\varphi \in \mathcal{D}$, φ occurs in e iff φ belongs to T.

Given $\sigma \in (\mathcal{D} \cup \{\sharp\})^{*}$, denote by $\mathrm{cnt}(\sigma)$ the set of members of $\mathcal{D}$ that occur in σ. The concepts of classifier and classification, possibly with a bounded number of mind changes, are defined next, the latter using the following notion.

Definition 9. We say that a member σ of $(\mathcal{L} \cup \{\sharp\})^{*}$ is *consistent in* $\mathcal{W}$ just in case there exists a possible world $\mathfrak{M}$ such that $\mathfrak{M} \models \mathrm{cnt}(\sigma)$.

Definition 10. A *classifier* is a partial function from $(\mathcal{D} \cup \{\sharp\})^{*}$ into $\{0, 1\}$.

Definition 11. Let a sentence φ and a classifier f be given.

We say that f *positively classifies $\mathcal{B}$ in the limit following φ (in $\mathcal{P}$)* just in case for all $T \in \mathcal{B}$ and environments e for T:

- $T \models^{\mathcal{D}}_{\mathcal{W}} \varphi$ iff $\{\sigma \in (\mathcal{D} \cup \{\sharp\})^{*} : \sigma \subset e$ and $f(\sigma) = 1\}$ is cofinite.
- If $\{\sigma \in (\mathcal{D} \cup \{\sharp\})^{*} : \sigma \subset e$ and $f(\sigma) = 0\}$ is cofinite then $T \models^{\mathcal{D}}_{\mathcal{W}} \neg\varphi$.

We say that f *negatively classifies $\mathcal{B}$ in the limit following φ (in $\mathcal{P}$)* just in case for all $T \in \mathcal{B}$ and environments e for T:

- $T \models^{\mathcal{D}}_{\mathcal{W}} \neg\varphi$ iff $\{\sigma \in (\mathcal{D} \cup \{\sharp\})^* : \sigma \subset e$ and $f(\sigma) = 0\}$ is cofinite.
- If $\{\sigma \in (\mathcal{D} \cup \{\sharp\})^* : \sigma \subset e$ and $f(\sigma) = 1\}$ is cofinite then $T \models^{\mathcal{D}}_{\mathcal{W}} \varphi$.

We say that f *classifies* $\mathcal{B}$ *in the limit following* φ (*in* $\mathcal{P}$) just in case f positively and negatively classifies $\mathcal{B}$ in the limit following φ.

Note that we only consider classifiability of members of $\mathcal{L}$, which are finite, not infinitary, closed formulas—infinitary formulas play a technical role only.

Definition 12. Let a nonnull ordinal β, a sentence φ, and a classifier f be given.

Let X be the set of all $\sigma \in (\mathcal{D} \cup \{\sharp\})^*$ such that σ is consistent in $\mathcal{W}$ and $f(\tau)$ is defined for some initial segment τ of σ. We denote by R_f the binary relation over X such that for all $\sigma, \tau \in X$, $R_f(\sigma, \tau)$ holds iff $\tau \subset \sigma$ and $f(\sigma) \neq f(\tau)$.

We say that f [*positively classifies* | *negatively classifies* | *classifies*] $\mathcal{B}$ *with less than* β *mind changes following* φ (*in* $\mathcal{P}$) just in case the length of R_f is defined and smaller than or equal to β, and f [positively classifies | negatively classifies | classifies] $\mathcal{B}$ in the limit following φ.

For all ordinals β we also say 'at most β mind changes' rather than 'less than $\beta + 1$ mind changes.' If β is a limit ordinal, then converging after at most β mind changes can mean either converging after less than β mind changes, or converging after less than $\beta + 1$ mind changes. The 'less than' formulation is not only more precise than the 'at most' formulation. It is also naturally related to the topological notions that we now introduce.

3.2   Topological Definability

Some topological space is closely related to the logical notions previously introduced. It is defined as follows.

Definition 13. We denote by $\mathbb{W}$ the topological space over $\mathcal{W}$ generated by all sets of the form $\text{Mod}_{\mathcal{W}}(\varphi)$ where φ ranges over $\mathcal{D}$.

We call the sets built from $\{\text{Mod}_{\mathcal{W}}(\varphi) : \varphi \in \mathcal{D}\}$ by finite unions and finite intersections, the Π_0 *Borel* sets of $\mathbb{W}$. Their complements are the Σ_0 *Borel* sets of $\mathbb{W}$. Let $\alpha > 0$ be given. The Σ_α *Borel* sets of $\mathbb{W}$ are built from the Π_β Borel sets of $\mathbb{W}$, with $\beta < \alpha$, by countable unions. Their complements are the Π_α *Borel* sets of $\mathbb{W}$. A sentence φ can represent a Borel subset X of $\mathcal{W}$ if it is possible to obtain X from the generators of $\mathbb{W}$ using countable disjunctions and conjunctions, in such a way that the resulting representation of X can be mapped to a sentence with members of $\mathcal{D}$ replacing the generators of the topology, countable disjunctions replacing countable unions, and countable conjunctions replacing countable intersections:

Definition 14. Let a sentence φ be given.

φ is said to be [$\Sigma_0^{\mathcal{L}}$ | $\Pi_0^{\mathcal{L}}$] *Borel in* $\mathbb{W}$ iff $\text{Mod}_{\mathcal{W}}(\varphi)$ is [Σ_0 | Π_0] Borel in $\mathbb{W}$.

Let a nonnull ordinal α be given. We say that φ is [$\Sigma_\alpha^{\mathcal{L}}$ | $\Pi_\alpha^{\mathcal{L}}$] *Borel in* $\mathbb{W}$ iff there exists a set X of sentences each of which is [$\Pi_\beta^{\mathcal{L}}$ | $\Sigma_\beta^{\mathcal{L}}$] Borel in $\mathbb{W}$ for some $\beta < \alpha$ such that φ and [$\bigvee X$ | $\bigwedge X$] have the same models in $\mathcal{W}$.

Given an ordinal α, we say that φ is $\Delta_\alpha^{\mathcal{L}}$ *Borel in* $\mathbb{W}$ iff φ is both $\Sigma_\alpha^{\mathcal{L}}$ Borel and $\Pi_\alpha^{\mathcal{L}}$ Borel in $\mathbb{W}$.

The difference hierarchy introduces a further granularity in the Borel hierarchy. More precisely, every nonnull ordinal α determines a difference hierarchy, built from the Σ_α and Π_α Borel sets of $\mathbb{W}$; this hierarchy consists of sets that are all $\Delta_{\alpha+1}$ Borel in $\mathbb{W}$. We can directly define the notion of a sentence representing a set of one of the difference hierarchies:

Definition 15. Let a nonnull ordinal α and a sentence φ be given.

We say that φ is $[\![\ \Sigma_{\alpha,1}^{\mathcal{L}} \mid \Pi_{\alpha,1}^{\mathcal{L}} \ ]\!]$ *Borel in* $\mathbb{W}$ iff φ is $[\![\ \Sigma_\alpha^{\mathcal{L}} \mid \Pi_\alpha^{\mathcal{L}} \ ]\!]$ Borel in $\mathbb{W}$.

Given $\beta \in \mathrm{Ord}$ greater than 1, we say that φ is $[\![\ \Sigma_{\alpha,\beta}^{\mathcal{L}} \mid \Pi_{\alpha,\beta}^{\mathcal{L}} \ ]\!]$ *Borel in* $\mathbb{W}$ iff there exists two families $(\psi_i)_{i\in\mathbb{N}}$ and $(\varphi_i)_{i\in\mathbb{N}}$ of sentences and a family $(\beta_i)_{i\in\mathbb{N}}$ of nonnull ordinals smaller than β such that the following holds.

- For all $i \in \mathbb{N}$, ψ_i is $[\![\ \Sigma_\alpha^{\mathcal{L}} \mid \Pi_\alpha^{\mathcal{L}} \ ]\!]$ Borel in $\mathbb{W}$.
- For all $i \in \mathbb{N}$, φ_i is $[\![\ \Pi_{\alpha,\beta_i}^{\mathcal{L}} \mid \Sigma_{\alpha,\beta_i}^{\mathcal{L}} \ ]\!]$ Borel in $\mathbb{W}$.
- For all $i, j \in \mathbb{N}$, $\psi_i \wedge \psi_j \models_{\mathcal{W}} \varphi_i \leftrightarrow \varphi_j$.
- φ and $[\![\ \bigvee_{i\in\mathbb{N}}(\psi_i \wedge \varphi_i) \mid \bigwedge_{i\in\mathbb{N}}(\psi_i \vee \varphi_i) \ ]\!]$ have the same models in $\mathcal{W}$.

Given a nonnull ordinal β, we say that φ is $\Delta_{\alpha,\beta}^{\mathcal{L}}$ *Borel in* $\mathbb{W}$ iff φ is $\Sigma_{\alpha,\beta}^{\mathcal{L}}$ Borel and $\Pi_{\alpha,\beta}^{\mathcal{L}}$ Borel in $\mathbb{W}$.

We say that φ is $\mathcal{L}$-*Borel in* $\mathbb{W}$ *on level* α iff φ is $\Sigma_{\alpha,\beta}^{\mathcal{L}}$ Borel in $\mathbb{W}$ for some nonnull ordinal β.

The next proposition shows that an alternative notion of topological definability can be proposed, that follows closely the classical definition of the difference hierarchies. Since the proofs of the our main results are based directly on Definition 15, we prefer Definition 15 to Proposition 16 for a primitive expression of the notion involved. Note that the concept expressed in Definition 15 is inductive, whereas the property expressed in Proposition 16 is not.

Proposition 16. *For all nonnull* $\alpha, \beta \in \mathrm{Ord}$ *and* $\varphi \in \mathcal{L}$, φ *is* $\Sigma_{\alpha,\beta}^{\mathcal{L}}$ *Borel in* $\mathbb{W}$ *iff there exists a* $\subseteq$-*increasing sequence* $(Y_\gamma)_{\gamma<\beta}$ *of sets of sentences that are* $\Sigma_\alpha^{\mathcal{L}}$ *Borel in* $\mathbb{W}$ *such that for all* $\mathfrak{M} \in \mathcal{W}$, $\mathfrak{M} \models \varphi$ *iff* $\mathfrak{M} \models \bigvee_{\gamma<\beta} \bigvee Y_\gamma$ *and the parity of the least* $\gamma < \beta$ *such that* $\mathfrak{M} \models \bigvee Y_\gamma$ *is opposite to the parity of* β.

We will need the next technical results.

Property 17. *Let two families* $(\psi_i)_{i\in\mathbb{N}}$ *and* $(\varphi_i)_{i\in\mathbb{N}}$ *of sentences be such that for all* $i, j \in \mathbb{N}$, $\psi_i \wedge \psi_j \models_{\mathcal{W}} \varphi_i \leftrightarrow \varphi_j$. *Let* φ *be a sentence that has the same models in* $\mathcal{W}$ *as* $\bigvee_{i\in\mathbb{N}}(\psi_i \wedge \varphi_i)$. *Then for all* $i \in \mathbb{N}$, $\models_{\mathcal{W}} (\psi_i \wedge \sim\varphi) \leftrightarrow (\psi_i \wedge \sim\varphi_i)$.

Lemma 18. *Let* C *be an infinite set of constants. Assume that:*

- $\mathcal{V}$ *includes* C;
- *some subset of* $\mathcal{L}_{\omega\omega}^{\mathcal{V}\backslash C}$ *is a generator of* $\mathcal{D}$;

− $\mathcal{W}$ *is the set of standard models of a subset of* $\mathcal{L}_{\omega\omega}^{V \setminus C}$.

Let nonnull ordinals α, β *and a sentence* φ *be such that* φ *is* $[\![\ \Sigma_{\alpha,\beta}^{\mathcal{L}} \mid \Pi_{\alpha,\beta}^{\mathcal{L}} \mid \Delta_{\alpha,\beta}^{\mathcal{L}}\ ]\!]$ *Borel in* $\mathcal{W}$. *Then for all constants* c *in* C *and for all closed terms* t, $\varphi[t/c]$ *is* $[\![\ \Sigma_{\alpha,\beta}^{\mathcal{L}} \mid \Pi_{\alpha,\beta}^{\mathcal{L}} \mid \Delta_{\alpha,\beta}^{\mathcal{L}}\ ]\!]$ *Borel in* $\mathcal{W}$.

Proposition 19. *Let nonnull ordinals* α, β, *a sentence* φ, *and two families* $(\psi_i)_{i \in \mathbb{N}}$ *and* $(\varphi_i)_{i \in \mathbb{N}}$ *of sentences be such that the following holds.*

− *For all* $i \in \mathbb{N}$, ψ_i *is* $[\![\ \Sigma_{\alpha}^{\mathcal{L}} \mid \Pi_{\alpha}^{\mathcal{L}}\ ]\!]$ *Borel in* $\mathcal{W}$.
− *For all* $i \in \mathbb{N}$, φ_i *is* $[\![\ \Sigma_{\alpha,\beta}^{\mathcal{L}} \mid \Pi_{\alpha,\beta}^{\mathcal{L}}\ ]\!]$ *Borel in* $\mathcal{W}$.
− *For all* $i, j \in \mathbb{N}$, $\psi_i \wedge \psi_j \models_{\mathcal{W}} \varphi_i \leftrightarrow \varphi_j$.
− $\mathrm{Mod}_{\mathcal{W}}(\varphi)$ *is equal to* $[\![\ \mathrm{Mod}_{\mathcal{W}}(\bigvee_{i \in \mathbb{N}}(\psi_i \wedge \varphi_i)) \mid \mathrm{Mod}_{\mathcal{W}}(\bigwedge_{i \in \mathbb{N}}(\psi_i \vee \varphi_i))\ ]\!]$.

Then φ *is* $[\![\ \Sigma_{\alpha,\beta}^{\mathcal{L}} \mid \Pi_{\alpha,\beta}^{\mathcal{L}}\ ]\!]$ *Borel in* $\mathcal{W}$.

Proof. Choose two families $(\psi_{i,j})_{i,j \in \mathbb{N}}$ and $(\varphi_{i,j})_{i,j \in \mathbb{N}}$ of sentences and a family $(\beta_{i,j})_{i,j \in \mathbb{N}}$ of nonnull ordinals smaller than β such that the following holds.

i. For all $i, j \in \mathbb{N}$, $\psi_{i,j}$ is $\Sigma_{\alpha}^{\mathcal{L}}$ Borel in $\mathcal{W}$ and $\varphi_{i,j}$ is $\Pi_{\alpha,\beta_{i,j}}^{\mathcal{L}}$ Borel in $\mathcal{W}$.
ii. For all $i, j, k \in \mathbb{N}$, $\psi_{i,j} \wedge \psi_{i,k} \models_{\mathcal{W}} \varphi_{i,j} \leftrightarrow \varphi_{i,k}$.
iii. For all $i \in \mathbb{N}$, $\models_{\mathcal{W}} \varphi_i \leftrightarrow \bigvee_{j \in \mathbb{N}}(\psi_{i,j} \wedge \varphi_{i,j})$.

Let $i, i', j, j' \in \mathbb{N}$ be given, and let $\mathfrak{M}$ be a model of $\psi_i \wedge \psi_{i,j} \wedge \psi_{i'} \wedge \psi_{i',j'} \wedge \varphi_{i,j}$ in $\mathcal{W}$. Using ii, iii and the second clause in the statement of the proposition, it is immediately verified that $\mathfrak{M} \models \psi_{i,j} \wedge \varphi_{i,j}$, hence $\mathfrak{M} \models \varphi_i$, hence $\mathfrak{M}$ is a model of $\psi_i \wedge \psi_{i'} \wedge \varphi_i$, hence $\mathfrak{M} \models \varphi_{i'}$, hence $\mathfrak{M} \models \psi_{i',k} \wedge \varphi_{i',k}$ for some $k \in \mathbb{N}$, hence $\mathfrak{M} \models \psi_{i',j'} \wedge \psi_{i',k} \wedge \varphi_{i',k}$ for some $k \in \mathbb{N}$, hence $\mathfrak{M} \models \varphi_{i',j'}$. We infer that:

iv. for all $i, i', j, j' \in \mathbb{N}$, $\psi_i \wedge \psi_{i,j} \wedge \psi_{i'} \wedge \psi_{i',j'} \models_{\mathcal{W}} \varphi_{i,j} \leftrightarrow \varphi_{i',j'}$.

Moreover, iii and the third clause in the statement of the proposition imply that:

v. $\models_{\mathcal{W}} \varphi \leftrightarrow \bigvee_{i,j \in \mathbb{N}}(\psi_i \wedge \psi_{i,j} \wedge \varphi_{i,j})$.

From iv, v and i, together with the first clause in the statement of the proposition, we conclude that φ is $\Sigma_{\alpha,\beta}^{\mathcal{L}}$ Borel in $\mathcal{W}$, as wanted.

We use of the topological notions when they are technically more convenient, but thanks to the proposition below, it is possible to restate the results in the next sections in terms of classifiability with a bounded number of mind changes:

Proposition 20. *Let a sentence* φ *be* $\mathcal{D}$-*minimally decided in* $\mathcal{W}$ *by every possible knowledge base. For all nonnull ordinals* β, *the following are equivalent.*

− φ *is* $[\![\ \Sigma_{1,\beta}^{\mathcal{L}} \mid \Pi_{1,\beta}^{\mathcal{L}} \mid \Delta_{1,\beta}^{\mathcal{L}}\ ]\!]$ *Borel in* $\mathcal{W}$.
− $\mathcal{B}$ *is* $[\![\ positively\ classifiable \mid negatively\ classifiable \mid classifiable\ ]\!]$ *with less than* β *mind changes following* φ.

Example 21. Suppose that $V = \{=, \overline{0}, s, R\}$ where R is a binary predicate symbol. Let W be the set of Herbrand structures where R is interpreted as a total ordering. Let D be equal to the set of atomic sentences. Set

$$\varphi = \exists x \exists y (x \neq y \wedge R(x,y) \wedge \forall z (x = z \vee R(y,z))).$$

So φ expresses that the ordering has a first and a second element. It is easily verified that B is positively classifiable in the limit following φ, but not with any mind change bound. Let $\mathfrak{M} \in W$ have a first element, namely $\overline{4}$, and a second element, namely $\overline{2}$. So φ is a logical consequence of $\mathrm{Diag}_D(\mathfrak{M})$ in P. Then

$$\chi = \neg R(\overline{0}, \overline{2}) \wedge \neg R(\overline{1}, \overline{2}) \wedge \neg R(\overline{3}, \overline{2}) \wedge \forall x \neg R(s(s(s(s(s(x))))), \overline{2})$$

is $\Pi_1^{\mathcal{L}}$ Borel in W.

Note that for all $T \in B$, if $\{R(\overline{4}, \overline{2})\} \subseteq T$ and $T \models_W^D \chi$ then $T \models_W^D \varphi$.

4   Relationships Between Syntax and Topology

4.1   Syntactic Complexity

Having the concepts of simple and double normal form, it is then easy to define a notion of syntactic complexity, that takes into account the set W of possible worlds and a set X that will be related to the set D of possible data. More precisely, let two nonnull ordinals α, β, a set X of (not necessarily closed) formulas, and a sentence φ be given. We say that φ is $[\![\Sigma_{\alpha,\beta}^{\mathcal{L}}[X] \mid \Pi_{\alpha,\beta}^{\mathcal{L}}[X]]\!]$ in W iff $\mathrm{Mod}_W(\varphi)$ is equal to the set of models in W of a sentence which is in $[\![\Sigma_{\alpha,\beta}[X] \mid \Pi_{\alpha,\beta}[X]]\!]$ normal form. We say that φ is $\Delta_{\alpha,\beta}^{\mathcal{L}}[X]$ in W iff φ is both $\Sigma_{\alpha,\beta}^{\mathcal{L}}[X]$ and $\Pi_{\alpha,\beta}^{\mathcal{L}}[X]$ in W. If X is the set of literals, then we say $[\![\Sigma_{\alpha,\beta}^{\mathcal{L}} \mid \Pi_{\alpha,\beta}^{\mathcal{L}} \mid \Delta_{\alpha,\beta}^{\mathcal{L}}]\!]$ in W for $[\![\Sigma_{\alpha,\beta}^{\mathcal{L}}[X] \mid \Pi_{\alpha,\beta}^{\mathcal{L}}[X] \mid \Delta_{\alpha,\beta}^{\mathcal{L}}[X]]\!]$ in W. Note that in case W contains an isomorphic copy of any countable structure, a sentence is $[\![\Sigma_{\alpha,1}^{\mathcal{L}} \mid \Pi_{\alpha,1}^{\mathcal{L}} \mid \Delta_{\alpha,1}^{\mathcal{L}}]\!]$ in W iff it is $[\![\Sigma_\alpha \mid \Pi_\alpha \mid \Delta_\alpha]\!]$ in the usual sense.

4.2   From Syntactic to Topological Complexity

It is easy to verify that the topological complexity of a sentence is bounded by its syntactic complexity.

Proposition 22. *Suppose that all members of W are standard. Let X be a set formulas that subsumes D. For all nonnull ordinals α, β, all sentences that are $[\![\Sigma_{\alpha,\beta}^{\mathcal{L}}[X] \mid \Pi_{\alpha,\beta}^{\mathcal{L}}[X] \mid \Delta_{\alpha,\beta}^{\mathcal{L}}[X]]\!]$ in W, are $[\![\Sigma_{\alpha,\beta}^{\mathcal{L}} \mid \Pi_{\alpha,\beta}^{\mathcal{L}} \mid \Delta_{\alpha,\beta}^{\mathcal{L}}]\!]$ Borel in W.*

Proof. The case where $\beta = 1$ is easy, and the case where $\beta > 1$ is easily proved by induction using Proposition 16.

Corollary 23. *Suppose that W is a set of standard structures, and D contains all literals. For all $\alpha, \beta \in \mathrm{Ord} \setminus \{0\}$, all sentences that are $[\![\Sigma_{\alpha,\beta}^{\mathcal{L}} \mid \Pi_{\alpha,\beta}^{\mathcal{L}} \mid \Delta_{\alpha,\beta}^{\mathcal{L}}]\!]$ in W, are $[\![\Sigma_{\alpha,\beta}^{\mathcal{L}} \mid \Pi_{\alpha,\beta}^{\mathcal{L}} \mid \Delta_{\alpha,\beta}^{\mathcal{L}}]\!]$ Borel in W.*

4.3   From Topological to Syntactic Complexity

We have examined the easy direction of the relationship between syntactic and topological complexity. The other direction is more involved, and requires specific but natural assumptions on the vocabulary, the set of possible worlds, and the set of possible data. These assumptions will be used in Propositions 24 and 25, Corollary 26, and Proposition 27; we will discuss their intuitive meaning at the end of the section. We first state a result that deals with the Borel hierarchy, before we state and prove the corresponding result for the difference hierarchies.

Proposition 24. *Let C be an infinite set of constants. Assume that:*

- *$\mathcal{V}$ includes C;*
- *some subset X of $\mathcal{L}_{\omega\omega}^{\mathcal{V}\setminus C}$ is a generator of $\mathcal{D}$;*
- *$\mathcal{W}$ is the set of standard models of a subset of $\mathcal{L}_{\omega\omega}^{\mathcal{V}\setminus C}$.*

Then every sentence that is $\mathcal{L}$-Borel in $\mathcal{W}$, is $\Sigma_n^{\mathcal{L}}$ Borel in $\mathcal{W}$ for some $n \in \mathbb{N}$.

Moreover, for all $n \in \mathbb{N}$ and sentences φ, φ is $[\![\; \Sigma_n^{\mathcal{L}} \mid \Pi_n^{\mathcal{L}} \mid \Delta_n^{\mathcal{L}} \;]\!]$ Borel in $\mathcal{W}$ iff φ is $[\![\; \Sigma_n^{\mathcal{L}}[X] \mid \Pi_n^{\mathcal{L}}[X] \mid \Delta_n^{\mathcal{L}}[X] \;]\!]$ in $\mathcal{W}$.

In the proof of the next proposition, $\forall\varphi$ and $\exists\varphi$ denote the universal and the existential closure of φ, respectively.

Proposition 25. *Let C be an infinite set of constants. Assume that:*

- *$\mathcal{V}$ includes C;*
- *some subset X of $\mathcal{L}_{\omega\omega}^{\mathcal{V}\setminus C}$ is a generator of $\mathcal{D}$;*
- *$\mathcal{W}$ is the set of standard models of a subset of $\mathcal{L}_{\omega\omega}^{\mathcal{V}\setminus C}$.*

For all nonnull $n \in \mathbb{N}$ and sentences φ, if φ is $\mathcal{L}$-Borel in $\mathcal{W}$ on level n, then φ is $\Sigma_{n,m}^{\mathcal{L}}$ Borel in $\mathcal{W}$ for some nonnull $m \in \mathbb{N}$.

Moreover, for all nonnull $n, m \in \mathbb{N}$ and $\varphi \in \mathcal{L}$, φ is $[\![\; \Sigma_{n,m}^{\mathcal{L}} \mid \Pi_{n,m}^{\mathcal{L}} \mid \Delta_{n,m}^{\mathcal{L}} \;]\!]$ Borel in $\mathcal{W}$ iff φ is $[\![\; \Sigma_{n,m}[X] \mid \Pi_{n,m}[X] \mid \Delta_{n,m}[X] \;]\!]$ in $\mathcal{W}$.

Proof. Let $B \subseteq \mathcal{L}_{\omega\omega}^{\mathcal{V}\setminus C}$ be such that $\mathcal{W}$ is the set of standard models of B. Given a formula ψ, denote by $\widehat{\psi}$ a formula of the form $\psi[x_1/c_1, \ldots, x_k/c_k]$ where $k \in \mathbb{N}$ is the number of members of C that occur in ψ but not in φ, $c_1, \ldots, c_k$ is an enumeration of the members of C that occur in ψ but not in φ, and $x_1, \ldots, x_k$ are distinct variables that do not occur in ψ (note that $c_1, \ldots, c_k$ do not occur in B). Given a set X of formulas, set $\widehat{X} = \{\widehat{\psi} : \psi \in X\}$. Let a nonnull $n \in \mathbb{N}$ be given. We first show the following.

(∗) Let an ordinal β greater than 1, a sentence φ, a sequence $(\beta_i)_{i\in\mathbb{N}}$ of nonnull ordinals smaller than β, and two families $(\psi_i)_{i\in\mathbb{N}}$ and $(\varphi_i)_{i\in\mathbb{N}}$ of sentences be such that the following holds.
  - For all $i \in \mathbb{N}$, ψ_i is $\Sigma_n^{\mathcal{L}}$ Borel and φ_i is $\Pi_{n,\beta_i}^{\mathcal{L}}$ Borel in $\mathcal{W}$.
  - For all $i, j \in \mathbb{N}$, $\psi_i \wedge \psi_j \models_{\mathcal{W}} \varphi_i \leftrightarrow \varphi_j$.
  - $\models_{\mathcal{W}} \varphi \leftrightarrow \bigvee_{i\in\mathbb{N}} \psi_i \wedge \varphi_i$.
  Then $B \models \varphi \leftrightarrow (\exists \bigvee_{i\leq r} \widehat{\psi}_i \wedge \varphi)$ for some $r \in \mathbb{N}$.

Clearly, $\models_W \varphi \leftrightarrow \bigvee_{i \in \mathbb{N}}(\psi_i \wedge \varphi)$. Set $Y = \{\psi_i : i \in \mathbb{N}\}$. Let a finite subset D of Y be given. To prove $(*)$, it suffices to show that $B \models \varphi \rightarrow (\exists \bigvee \widehat{D} \wedge \varphi)$ for some finite subset D of Y. Suppose otherwise for a contradiction. Then $B \cup \{\varphi, \forall \sim \bigvee \widehat{D}\}$ is consistent for all finite $D \subseteq Y$. By compactness, we infer that $B \cup \{\varphi\} \cup \{\forall \sim \widehat{\psi} : \psi \in Y\}$ is consistent. Using Lemma 3, it follows that $\{\varphi\} \cup \{\forall \sim \widehat{\psi} : \psi \in Y\}$ is consistent in W. But this is in contradiction with the fact that $\models_W \varphi \rightarrow \bigvee Y$. This completes the proof of $(*)$, which implies that for all sentences φ, if φ is $\Sigma^{\mathcal{L}}_{n,\omega}$ Borel in W, then φ is $\Sigma^{\mathcal{L}}_{n,m}$ Borel in W for some nonnull $m \in \mathbb{N}$. We immediately derive that every sentence that is $\mathcal{L}$-Borel in W on level n, is $\Sigma^{\mathcal{L}}_{n,m}$ Borel in W for some nonnull $m \in \mathbb{N}$.

Let a nonnull $n \in \mathbb{N}$ be given. To complete the proof of the proposition, it suffices to show that the following holds for all nonnull $m \in \mathbb{N}$.

$(**)$ A sentence φ is $\Sigma^{\mathcal{L}}_{n,m}$ Borel in W iff there exists a sentence ψ such that $B \models \varphi \leftrightarrow \psi$ and ψ is in $\Sigma_{n,m}[X]$ normal form.

The case $m = 1$ is trivial by the choice of X. Let a nonnull $m \in \mathbb{N}$ be given, and suppose that $(**)$ has been proved for m. Let a sentence φ be given. If there exists a sentence ψ such that $B \models \varphi \leftrightarrow \psi$ and ψ is in $\Sigma_{n,m+1}[X]$ normal form, then Proposition 22 implies that φ is $\Sigma^{\mathcal{L}}_{n,m+1}$ Borel in W. Conversely, suppose that φ is $\Sigma^{\mathcal{L}}_{n,m+1}$ Borel in W. Let two families $(\psi_i)_{i \in \mathbb{N}}$ and $(\varphi_i)_{i \in \mathbb{N}}$ of sentences be such that for all $i \in \mathbb{N}$, ψ_i is $\Sigma^{\mathcal{L}}_n$ Borel in W and φ_i is $\Pi^{\mathcal{L}}_{n,m}$ Borel in W, for all $i, j \in \mathbb{N}$, $\psi_i \wedge \psi_j \models_W \varphi_i \leftrightarrow \varphi_j$, and $\models_W \varphi \leftrightarrow \bigvee_{i \in \mathbb{N}}(\psi_i \wedge \varphi_i)$. By $(*)$, let $r \in \mathbb{N}$ be such that $B \models \varphi \leftrightarrow (\exists \bigvee_{i \leq r} \widehat{\psi}_i \wedge \varphi)$. Then:

$$(\dagger) \quad B \models \varphi \leftrightarrow (\exists \bigvee_{i \leq r} \widehat{\psi}_i \wedge \sim(\exists \bigvee_{i \leq r} \widehat{\psi}_i \wedge \sim\varphi)).$$

Let Z be the set of closed instances of $\widehat{\psi}_i$, where i ranges over $\{1, \ldots, r\}$. Then $\models_W (\exists \bigvee_{i \leq r} \widehat{\psi}_i) \leftrightarrow \bigvee Z$, and we infer from Lemma 18 applied to $\alpha = 1$ that $\exists \bigvee_{i \leq r} \widehat{\psi}_i$ is $\Sigma^{\mathcal{L}}_n$ Borel in W. We now show that $\exists \bigvee_{i \leq r} \widehat{\psi}_i \wedge \sim\varphi$ is $\Sigma^{\mathcal{L}}_{n,m}$ Borel in W. Obviously:

$$(\ddagger) \quad \models_W (\exists \bigvee_{i \leq r} \widehat{\psi}_i \wedge \sim\varphi) \leftrightarrow \bigvee\{\psi \wedge (\psi \wedge \sim\varphi) : \psi \in Z\}).$$

For all $i \in \mathbb{N}$, $\psi_i \wedge \sim\varphi_i$ is clearly $\Sigma^{\mathcal{L}}_{n,m}$ Borel in W, and we derive from Property 17 that $\psi_i \wedge \sim\varphi$ is $\Sigma^{\mathcal{L}}_{n,m}$ Borel in W. Together with Lemma 18, this implies that for all $\psi \in Z$, $\psi \wedge \sim\varphi$ is $\Sigma^{\mathcal{L}}_{n,m}$ Borel in W. From this, $(\ddagger)$ and Proposition 19, we infer that $\exists \bigvee_{i \leq r} \widehat{\psi}_i \wedge \sim\varphi$ is $\Sigma^{\mathcal{L}}_{n,m}$ Borel in W. By inductive hypothesis, we can choose $p \leq m$ and a sequence $(\varphi_q)_{q < p}$ of members of X such that $B \cup \{\exists \bigvee_{i \leq r} \widehat{\psi}_i \wedge \sim\varphi\}$ has the same models as $B \cup \{\bigvee_{q \in I}(\varphi_q \wedge \bigwedge_{q' < q} \sim\varphi_{q'})\}$, where I is the set of all $q < p$ whose parity is opposite to the parity of p. Then the class of models of $B \cup \{\exists \bigvee_{i \leq r} \widehat{\psi}_i \wedge \sim\psi\}$ is the class of models in $\text{Mod}(B)$ of

$$(\exists \bigvee_{i \leq r} \widehat{\psi}_i \wedge \bigwedge_{q \leq p} \sim\varphi_q) \wedge \bigvee_{q \in J}(\varphi_q \wedge \bigwedge_{q' < q} \sim\varphi_{q'})$$

where J is the set of all $q < p$ whose parity is equal to the parity of p. This implies immediately that the models of $\exists \bigvee_{i \leq r} \widehat{\psi_i} \wedge \sim\psi$ in $\mathrm{Mod}(B)$ are the models in $\mathrm{Mod}(B)$ of some sentence which is in $\overline{\Sigma}_{n,m+1}[X]$ normal form. We conclude with (†) that $\mathrm{Mod}(B \cup \{\varphi\})$ is equal to the class of models in $\mathrm{Mod}(B)$ of some sentence that is in $\Sigma_{n,m+1}[X]$ normal form. This completes the proof of (∗∗), hence of the proposition.

Corollary 26. *Let C be an infinite set of constants. Assume that:*

- *$\mathcal{V}$ includes C;*
- *$\mathcal{D}$ is the set of closed literals;*
- *$\mathcal{W}$ is the set of standard models of a subset of $\mathcal{L}_{\omega\omega}^{\mathcal{V} \backslash C}$.*

Then for all nonnull $n, m \in \mathbb{N}$ and sentences φ, φ is $[\![\ \Sigma_{n,m}^{\mathcal{L}}\ |\ \Pi_{n,m}^{\mathcal{L}}\ |\ \Delta_{n,m}^{\mathcal{L}}\ ]\!]$ Borel in $\mathbb{W}$ iff φ is $[\![\ \Sigma_{n,m}^{\mathcal{L}}\ |\ \Pi_{n,m}^{\mathcal{L}}\ |\ \Delta_{n,m}^{\mathcal{L}}\ ]\!]$ in $\mathcal{W}$.

In the statements of Proposition 25 and Corollary 26, the members of C should be thought of as an infinite reserve of arbitrary names for arbitrary objects in the underlying world. The class of possible worlds is axiomatized: it is the class of standard models of some background knowledge that does not mention any of the arbitrary names (any of the member of C). In the statement of Proposition 25, the set of possible data can be thought of as a set of properties such that if a property applied to an object having an arbitrary name can be provided as evidence, then the same property applied to any object should also be provided as evidence.

4.4   Computable Classification

Proposition 25, together with Proposition 20, does not only provide a syntactic characterization of classifiability with a bounded number of mind changes, for a large and natural class of logical paradigms. With Lemma 3, it also proves the existence of a universal computable classifier:

Proposition 27. *Let C be an infinite set of constants. Assume that:*

- *$\mathcal{V}$ includes C;*
- *some r.e. subset X of $\mathcal{L}_{\omega\omega}^{\mathcal{V} \backslash C}$ is a generator of $\mathcal{D}$;*
- *$\mathcal{W}$ is the set of standard models of an r.e. subset of $\mathcal{L}_{\omega\omega}^{\mathcal{V} \backslash C}$;*
- *all possible knowledge bases $\mathcal{D}$-minimally decide all sentences in $\mathcal{W}$.*

Then there exists a partial recursive function F from $\mathbb{N} \times \mathcal{L} \times (\mathcal{D} \cup \{\sharp\})^{*}$ into $\{0, 1\}$ such that for all $n \in \mathbb{N}$ and $\varphi \in \mathcal{L}$, $F(n, \varphi, \cdot)$ is a classifier that $[\![$ positively classifies $|$ negatively classifies $|$ classifies $]\!]$ $\mathcal{B}$ with at most n mind changes following φ iff $\mathcal{B}$ is $[\![$ positively classifiable $|$ negatively classifiable $|$ classifiable $]\!]$ $\mathcal{B}$ with at most n mind changes following φ.

Proof. By Lemma 3, for all sentences ψ, $\psi \in \mathrm{Mod}_{\mathcal{W}}(B)$ iff $B \models \psi$, hence $\mathrm{Mod}_{\mathcal{W}}(B)$ is recursively enumerable. Hence there exists an effective procedure H

that outputs, for all $n \in \mathbb{N}$ and $\varphi \in \mathcal{L}$, a sentence ψ such that ψ is in $\Sigma_{1,n}[X]$ normal form and $\varphi \leftrightarrow \psi \in \mathrm{Mod}_{\mathcal{W}}(B)$ if such a sentence exists, or equivalently, if B is positively classifiable with at most n mind changes following φ. Moreover, it is easily verified that there exists a partial recursive function G from $\mathcal{L} \times (\mathcal{D} \cup \{\sharp\})^*$ into $\{0, 1\}$ such that for all $\psi \in \mathcal{L}$, if ψ is in $\Sigma_{1,1}[X]$ normal form then $G(\psi, \cdot)$ positively classifies B with no mind change following ψ. Using H and G, it is then easily verified that there exists a partial recursive function F from $\mathbb{N} \times \mathcal{L} \times (\mathcal{D} \cup \{\sharp\})^*$ into $\{0, 1\}$ that satisfies the claim of the proposition, together with the following property. Let a possible knowledge base T, a sentence φ, and an $n \in \mathbb{N}$ be such that $T \models_{\mathcal{W}}^{\mathcal{D}} \varphi$ and B is positively classifiable with at most n mind changes following φ. Then there exists a sentence ψ in $\Sigma_{1,n}[X]$ normal form such that $\varphi \leftrightarrow \psi \in \mathrm{Mod}_{\mathcal{W}}(B)$. Moreover, in response to longer and longer initial segments from e, $F(n, \varphi, \cdot)$ generates more and more of the sentences in $\Sigma_{1,1}[X]$ normal form from which ψ is built, assumes that the other sentences χ in $\Sigma_{1,1}[X]$ normal form from which ψ is built are such that $T \models_{\mathcal{W}}^{\mathcal{D}} \neg \chi$, and based on that assumption, determines whether $T \models_{\mathcal{W}}^{\mathcal{D}} \psi$. The answer is correct iin the limit, after at most n mind changes.

5   Conclusion

Conjunctive and disjunctive normal forms are natural canonical representations of concepts. Still they are not directly related to the notion of mind change bound in classification scenarios in a logical setting. We have shown that another normal form could provide a notion of syntactic complexity that, under general and interesting assumptions, turns out to characterize the least upper bound on the number of mind changes necessary for successful classification. A consequence of this result is that if classification is possible, then computable classification is also possible.

References

1. A. Ambainis, R. Freivalds and C. Smith: *Inductive Inference with Procrastination: Back to Definitions.* Fundamenta Informaticae. **40** pp. 1–16 (1999)
2. A. Ambainis, S. Jain and A. Sharma: *Ordinal mind change complexity of language identification.* Theoretical Computer Science. **220(2)** pp. 323–343 (1999)
3. R. Freivalds and C. Smith: *On the role of procrastination for machine learning.* Inform. Comput. **107(2)** pp. 237–271 (1993)
4. W. Gasarch, M. Pleszkoch, F. Stephan and M. Velauthapillai: *Classification using information.* Annals of Mathematics and Artificial Intelligence. Selected papers from ALT 1994 and AII 1994, vol. 23, pp. 147–168 (1998)
5. S. Jain, D. Osherson, J. Royer and A. Sharma: *Systems that learn: An Introduction to Learning Theory, Second Edition.* The MIT Press (1999)
6. A. Kechris: *Classical Descriptive Set Theory.* Graduate Texts in Mathematics 156, Springer Verlag (1994)
7. E. Martin and D. Osherson: *Elements of Scientific Inquiry.* The MIT Press (1998)

8. E. Martin, A. Sharma and F. Stephan: *Unifying Logic, Topology and Learning in Parametric Logic*. Theoretical Computer Science, special issue for ALT 2002, to appear.
9. D. Osherson, M. Stob and S. Weinstein: *A universal inductive inference machine*. Journal of Symbolic Logic, vol. 56(2), pp. 661–672 (1991)
10. F. Stephan: *On one-sided versus two-sided classification*. Archive for Mathematical Logic, vol. 40, pp. 489–513 (2001)

Ellipsoid Approximation Using Random Vectors

S. Mendelson[1] and A. Pajor[2]

[1] Centre for Mathematics and its Applications, The Australian National University, Canberra, ACT 0200, Australia
shahar.mendelson@anu.edu.au
[2] Equipe d'Analyse et Mathématiques Appliquées, Université de Marne-la-Vallée, 5, boulevard Descartes, Champs sur Marne, 77454 Marne-la-Vallée Cedex 2, France
pajor@math.univ-mlv.fr

Abstract. We analyze the behavior of a random matrix with independent rows, each distributed according to the same probability measure on $\mathbb{R}^n$ or on ℓ_2. We investigate the spectrum of such a matrix and the way the ellipsoid generated by it approximates the covariance structure of the underlying measure. As an application, we provide estimates on the deviation of the spectrum of Gram matrices from the spectrum of the integral operator.

1 Introduction

Our objective is to explore the behavior of random vectors in $\mathbb{R}^n$ (resp. ℓ_2), particularly in the context of kernel methods and kernel Principal component analysis. To be more exact, let us formulate the two questions that motivated this study (though are not necessarily the main focus here).

Question 1. *Let (Ω, μ) be a probability space and let $K : \Omega \times \Omega \to \mathbb{R}$ be a positive definite kernel. Set $T_K : L_2(\mu) \to L_2(\mu)$ to be the integral operator associated with K and μ, given by*

$$(T_K f)(t) = \int K(s,t)f(s)d\mu(s).$$

Let $t_1, ..., t_N$ be independent random variables distributed according to μ, and let $\hat{T} = \left(\frac{1}{N}K(t_i, t_j)\right)_{i,j=1}^{N}$ be the corresponding Gram matrix. Does the spectrum of $\hat{T}$ converge (in an appropriate sense) to the spectrum of T_K?

Question 1 was studied by Koltchinskii and Giné [8] for a very wide range of kernels. They showed, among other things, that if K is a finite dimensional kernel, then the spectrum of $\hat{T}$ converges to that of T in an appropriate sense as N tends to infinity, and obtained estimates on the rate of convergence, which we improve here. Let us mention that most of the effort in [8] was devoted to the study of kernels which are not trace class (that is, $\mathbb{E}K(t,t) = \infty$), for which additional arguments are required, and our results do not cover that situation.

P. Auer and R. Meir (Eds.): COLT 2005, LNAI 3559, pp. 429–443, 2005.
© Springer-Verlag Berlin Heidelberg 2005

The second question is connected to kernel PCA [11, 4]. Let X be a random vector in ℓ_2 (that is, a function from the probability space (Ω, μ) to ℓ_2), and let $X_1, ..., X_N$ be independent copies of X. Set $\{e_1, ..., e_N\}$ to be the standard unit basis in the N-dimensional Euclidean space ℓ_2^N and put $\mathcal{K}$ to be the image of the N-dimensional Euclidean ball, B_2^N, by the random operator $\Gamma : \ell_2^N \to \ell_2$ defined by $\Gamma e_i = X_i$.

For $d \leq N$, let $a_d = \inf \{\sup_{x \in \mathcal{K}} d(x, E) : E \subset \ell_2, \dim(E) = d\}$, that is, a_d is the best degree of approximation by which a d-dimensional subspace approximates the random ellipsoid $\mathcal{K}$.

Question 2. *Let E_d be the best approximating d-dimensional subspace as above. What estimates can one provide on the random variable $d(E_d, X_{N+1})$?*

In other words, the question is how close X_{N+1} is to the d-dimensional subspace that best approximates ΓB_2^N. Although we do not tackle this problem directly here, we present a method of attack which should be explored further, as explained below.

It turns out that both these questions are connected to the structure of random ellipsoids. Indeed, if $X(t)$ is a random vector in ℓ_2, it can be used to define a new Euclidean structure on its span, given by

$$\|v\|^2 = \mathbb{E}\,|\langle X, v \rangle|^2. \tag{1.1}$$

Since this norm is given by the inner product $[u, v] = \mathbb{E}\,\langle X, u \rangle \langle X, v \rangle$, its unit ball is an ellipsoid (usually called the *Binet ellipsoid*) and is denoted by $\mathcal{E}_B$.

As an example, consider the integral operator T_K. Under mild assumptions on K and Ω, by Mercer's Theorem, there is an orthonormal basis of L_2, denoted by $(\phi_i)_{i=1}^{\infty}$, such that $K(s, t) = \sum_{i=1}^{\infty} \lambda_i \phi_i(s) \phi_i(t)$ almost surely, where $(\lambda_i)_{i=1}^{\infty}$ are the eigenvalues of the integral operator T_K arranged in a non-increasing order (in fact, for our needs it is enough that the convergence is in the L_2 sense rather than almost surely, for which it suffices that K is a positive definite, square integrable kernel, and we will make these assumptions on K throughout this note). Let $X(t) = \sum_{i=1}^{\infty} \sqrt{\lambda_i} \phi_i(t) \phi_i \in \ell_2$ (here we identify $L_2(\mu)$ with ℓ_2 and (ϕ_i) with the standard basis in ℓ_2), and consider the ellipsoid

$$\mathcal{E} = \left\{ v \in \ell_2 : \sum_{i=1}^{\infty} \frac{\langle v, \phi_i \rangle^2}{\lambda_i} \leq 1 \right\}.$$

Hence, $\mathcal{E}$ is an ellipsoid with principal directions ϕ_i and the "principal lengths" are $\sqrt{\lambda_i}$. We define the polar body of $\mathcal{E}$ by

$$\mathcal{E}^\circ = \{y \in \ell_2 : \forall x \in \mathcal{E} \ |\langle x, y \rangle| \leq 1\}.$$

Let us mention that the polar of a unit ball of some finite dimensional normed space X is the unit ball of the dual space X^*. Hence, in this case $\mathcal{E}^\circ$ is simply the unit ball of dual norm to the one defined by $\mathcal{E}$. Indeed, it is easy to verify that $\mathcal{E}^\circ$ is an ellipsoid, and with respect to the norm $\|\ \|_{\mathcal{E}^\circ}$, for which $\mathcal{E}^\circ$ is its unit ball,

$$\|v\|_{\mathcal{E}^{\circ}}^{2} = \sum_{i=1}^{\infty} \lambda_i \langle v, \phi_i \rangle^2 = \mathbb{E}|\langle X(t), v \rangle|^2.$$

Thus, the Binet ellipsoid associated with $X(t)$ is the polar body of the ellipsoid $\mathcal{E}$.

In general, we define the ellipsoid $\mathcal{E}$ as the polar of $\mathcal{E}_B$. Both these ellipsoids are generated according to the covariance structure endowed by the random vector X.

Let $X_1, ..., X_N$ be independent copies of X, set $\Gamma_N : \ell_2^N \to \ell_2$ to be the random operator defined by $\Gamma_N e_i = \frac{1}{\sqrt{N}} X_i$ and denote $\hat{\mathcal{E}} = \Gamma_N B_2^N$. There are three natural questions that one can ask regarding various approximations of $\mathcal{E}$ using $\hat{\mathcal{E}}$.

1. How close are the lengths of the principal directions of $\hat{\mathcal{E}}$ to those of $\mathcal{E}$?
2. Is $\hat{\mathcal{E}}$ close to being a section of $\mathcal{E}$? (in other words, if $E = \mathrm{span}\{X_1, ..., X_N\}$, is $\hat{\mathcal{E}}$ close to $\mathcal{E} \cap E$?
3. How close is $\hat{\mathcal{E}}$ to $\mathcal{E} \cap W_N$, where W_N is the subspace of ℓ_2 spanned by the N largest principal directions of $\mathcal{E}$?

Observe that understanding these questions would lead to answers to Question 1 and Question 2. Indeed, if $X(t) = \sum_{i=1}^{\infty} \sqrt{\lambda_i}\phi_i(t)\phi_i$ is generated by the kernel K, then the lengths of the principal directions of $\hat{\mathcal{E}}$ are the square roots of the eigenvalues of the matrix $\Gamma_N^* \Gamma_N$, which is the Gram matrix $\left(\frac{1}{N}K(t_i, t_j)\right)_{i,j=1}^{N}$. On the other hand, the principal lengths of $\mathcal{E}$ are $(\sqrt{\lambda_i})_{i=1}^{\infty}$. And thus, (1) for this specific choice of the random vector $X(t)$ is simply Question 1.

Next, suppose that the answer to (3) is affirmative, and the random ellipsoid $\hat{\mathcal{E}}$ approximates the section of $\mathcal{E}$ generated by the first N principal directions. Thus, the best d-dimensional approximating subspace is close to the space spanned by the first d principal directions of $\mathcal{E}$, implying that $d(E_d, X_{N+1}) \approx d(W_d, X_{N+1})$ which can be easily estimated.

It turns out that the degree of difficulty of (1)-(3) is increasing. Roughly speaking, (1) deals with the fact that $\hat{\mathcal{E}}$ is an ellipsoid which is close to a "rotation" of $\mathcal{E} \cap W_N$, as the principal lengths of $\hat{\mathcal{E}}$ are close to the N largest of $\mathcal{E}$. On the other hand, (2) identifies $\hat{\mathcal{E}}$ as being close to a section of $\mathcal{E}$, and depends on approximating both the principal lengths *and* the principal directions. Intuitively, (3) follows from a combination of (1) and (2) (under some mild assumptions on $\mathcal{E}$); if $\hat{\mathcal{E}}$ is almost a section of $\mathcal{E}$ and has the same principal lengths as the first N largest of $\mathcal{E}$, it must be close to $\mathcal{E} \cap W_N$.

Here, we will only investigate (2) and (3) when X is a vector in $\mathbb{R}^n$ and $N > n$. In this case we will show that $\hat{\mathcal{E}}$ is a good approximation of $\mathcal{E}$ rather than of a section of $\mathcal{E}$, and (2) and (3) coincide.

The main stumbling block in the study of the singular values of the random operator Γ_N which maps e_i to $X_i/\sqrt{N}$ (or, for that matter, the singular values of the Gram matrix $\left(\frac{1}{N}\langle X_i, X_j \rangle\right)_{i,j=1}^{N}$) is that the random matrix defined by this operator has dependent entries. One can bypass this problem by considering the operator $\Gamma\Gamma^* = \sum_{i=1}^{N} X_i \otimes X_i$ (where $X_i \otimes X_i$ is the projection onto the vector X_i, that is, for any $v \in \ell_2$, $(X_i \otimes X_i)(v) = \langle X_i, v \rangle X_i$). Observe that the N

largest eigenvalues of $\Gamma\Gamma^*$ are the same as the squares of the singular values of Γ and the advantage is that $\sum_{i=1}^{N} X_i \otimes X_i$ is a sum of independent, identically distributed, operator-valued variables. One can define the average operator (also known as the covariance operator) $\Lambda = \mathbb{E}(X \otimes X)$ as the operator which satisfies for any $u, v \in \ell_2$, $\langle \Lambda u, v \rangle = \mathbb{E}\langle (X \otimes X)u, v \rangle = \mathbb{E}\langle X, u \rangle \langle X, v \rangle$, and it is standard to verify that such an operator exists under mild integrability assumptions on X.

We will investigate the way the random operator $\frac{1}{N}\sum_{i=1}^{N} X_i \otimes X_i$ deviates from the average operator Λ with respect to various operator norms. Recall that for any normed space $(E, \|\ \|_E)$, if Y is a E-valued random variable, the process $\left\| \frac{1}{N}\sum_{i=1}^{N}(Y_i - \mathbb{E}Y) \right\|_E$ is the supremum of an empirical process which is indexed by the unit ball of the dual space of E. Thus, one can apply standard tools from empirical processes theory, such as symmetrization inequalities and concentration results. Let us point out that unlike most situations studied in Learning Theory, the random vector Y we deal with here need not be bounded; thus the class of functions defined by the dual unit ball is not uniformly bounded and Talagrand's concentration inequality for empirical processes indexed by bounded classes no longer applies.

Two types of assumptions are often used to compensate for the absence of an L_∞ bound on the class of functions. The first deals with the rate of decay of the linear forms $x^*(Y)$, and the other is on the rate of decay of the norm $\|Y\|_E$. To formulate these assumptions, let us recall the notion of Orlicz norms.

Definition 1. *For a random variable V and $\alpha \geq 1$, the ψ_α norm of V is*

$$\|V\|_{\psi_\alpha} = \inf\left\{ C > 0; \ \mathbb{E}\exp\left(\frac{|V|^\alpha}{C^\alpha}\right) \leq 2 \right\}.$$

A standard argument [14] shows that if V has a bounded ψ_α norm then its tail decays faster than $2\exp(-u^\alpha/\|V\|_{\psi_\alpha}^\alpha)$. In particular, a ψ_2 random variable has a subgaussian tail and a ψ_1 variable has a sub-exponential tail. If one assumes that the linear forms decay quickly, that is, are bounded with respect to an appropriate ψ_α norm, then using the *Generic Chaining method* [13], it is possible to upper bound the expectation of the supremum of an empirical process indexed by the dual unit ball B_{E^*}, using the metric structure of the space (B_{E^*}, ψ_α). We will not explore this direction here, but rather, formulate without a proof a relatively standard result which follows from this method.

Theorem 1. *For every $K > 0$ and $0 < \delta < 1$, there exist a constant $c(K, \delta)$ for which the following holds. Let X be a random vector in ℓ_2^n and let $\mathcal{E}_B$ be its Binet ellipsoid, which is assumed to have a full rank. If, for every $v \in \ell_2^n$, $\|\langle X, v \rangle\|_{\psi_2} \leq K(\mathbb{E}|\langle X, v \rangle|^2)^{1/2} = K\|v\|_{\mathcal{E}_B}$, then for any $0 < \varepsilon < 1$ and $N \geq c(K, \delta)n/\varepsilon^2$, with probability at least $1 - \delta$, every $v \in \mathbb{R}^n$ satisfies,*

$$(1 - \varepsilon)\|v\|_{\mathcal{E}_B} \leq \left(\frac{1}{N}\sum_{i=1}^{N}\langle X_i, v \rangle^2 \right)^{1/2} \leq (1 + \varepsilon)\|v\|_{\mathcal{E}_B}. \tag{1.2}$$

Theorem 1 gives an equivalence between the ellipsoid $\hat{\mathcal{E}}^\circ$, which is the polar of $\Gamma_N B_2^N$, and the Binet ellipsoid. Unfortunately, such a result has several intrinsic limitations. First of all, the degree of approximation it provides is possibly too strong for our goals, in the following sense. Let $\lambda_1^{1/2}, ..., \lambda_n^{1/2}$ be the n (nonzero) singular values of Γ_N. Then, for any $v \in \mathbb{R}^n$, $\|v\|_{\mathcal{E}_B}^2 = \sum_{i=1}^n \lambda_i v_i^2$, and if many of the λ_is are very small, one can have vectors on the ℓ_2^n unit sphere, but with a small ellipsoid norm. Since Theorem 1 states that $\mathcal{E}_B \subset (1+\varepsilon)\hat{\mathcal{E}}^\circ$ and $\hat{\mathcal{E}}^\circ \subset (1+\varepsilon)\mathcal{E}_B$, its assertion is more restrictive than, say,

$$\mathcal{E}_B \subset \hat{\mathcal{E}}^\circ + \varepsilon B_2^n \quad \text{and} \quad \hat{\mathcal{E}}^\circ \subset \mathcal{E}_B + \varepsilon B_2^n, \tag{1.3}$$

where $A + B = \{a + b \ : \ a \in A, \ b \in B\}$. Equation (1.3) implies that each point in $\mathcal{E}_B$ can be written as a sum of a point in the random ellipsoid and a point with a small Euclidean norm and vice-versa, which would suffice in many applications.

The price one pays for the strong degree of approximation in Theorem 1 is that the bound holds only when the number of sample points N is of the order of the dimension n. And, there is no advantage if the singular values of Γ_N are small. This perhaps helps to explain the remark we made - that to see how well the random ellipsoid approximates the deterministic one is intrinsically more difficult if one selects this strong sense of approximation, because the fact that one has many "small" principal directions does not play to ones advantage.

The second problem with this approach is that the ψ_2 assumption on the linear forms $\langle X, v \rangle$ is very difficult to check, and is often not even true. In certain problems in convex geometry one can verify such an assumption, but in general, it is too much to hope for. Moreover, even in geometric scenarios, a more realistic assumption is a ψ_1 condition rather than a ψ_2 condition, which makes the analysis of the problem much more difficult, and Theorem 1 is no longer true as stated (see [2, 12, 3] for more details).

The approach we take here is to assume that probability that $\|X\|$ is large decays quickly (though $\|X\|$ need not be bounded) rather than the linear forms. In the context of integral operators, the motivation for this type of assumption is clear, since $\|X(t)\|_2^2 - K(t, t)$. Thus, one only has to consider the decay properties of the diagonal of the kernel. To that end, in most of the results we present, we require the following assumption:

Assumption 1. *Let X be a random vector in ℓ_2^n (resp. ℓ_2). Assume that*

1. *There is some $\rho > 0$ such that for every θ of norm 1, $\left(\mathbb{E}|\langle X, \theta \rangle|^4\right)^{1/4} \leq \rho$.*
2. *Set $Z = \|X\|$. Then $\|Z\|_{\psi_\alpha} < \infty$ for some $\alpha \geq 1$.*

In other words, the assumptions we make are on the fourth moment of linear forms $\langle X, \theta \rangle$, and (which is the more important part), on the decay properties of $\|X\|$. The first assumption follows if the second one is verified (and with essentially the same constant), using a Cauchy-Schwarz inequality and the fact that the L_p norm is upper bounded by the ψ_α norm, although in some cases one can obtain a better estimate on ρ.

1.1   Some Preliminaries

To derive tail estimates for $\left\| \frac{1}{N} \sum_{i=1}^{N} X_i \otimes X_i - \mathbb{E}(X \otimes X) \right\|_{2 \to 2}$ (where $\| \ \|_{2 \to 2}$ is the operator norm from ℓ_2 to ℓ_2), we shall use a well known symmetrization theorem [14] that originated in the works of Kahane and Hoffman-Jørgensen. Recall that a Rademacher random variable is a random variable taking values ± 1 with probability $1/2$.

Theorem 2. *Let Z be a stochastic process indexed by a set F and let N be an integer. For every $i \leq N$, let $\mu_i : F \to \mathbb{R}$ be arbitrary functions and set $(Z_i)_{i \leq N}$ to be independent copies of Z. Under mild topological conditions on F and (μ_i) ensuring the measurability of the events below, for any $x > 0$,*

$$\beta_N(x) Pr \left(\sup_{f \in F} \left| \sum_{i=1}^{N} Z_i(f) \right| > x \right) \leq 2 Pr \left(\sup_{f \in F} \left| \sum_{i=1}^{N} \varepsilon_i \left(Z_i(f) - \mu_i(f) \right) \right| > \frac{x}{2} \right),$$

where $(\varepsilon_i)_{i=1}^{N}$ are independent Rademacher random variables and

$$\beta_N(x) = \inf_{f \in F} Pr \left(\left| \sum_{i=1}^{N} Z_i(f) \right| < \frac{x}{2} \right).$$

Observe that in the case of the ℓ_2 operator norm, the supremum of an empirical process is taken with respect to $\mathcal{U}$ - the set of tensors $v \otimes w$, where v and w are vectors in the unit Euclidean ball, in which case, $\| X \otimes X - \Lambda \|_{2 \to 2} = \sup_{U \in \mathcal{U}} \langle X \otimes X - \Lambda, U \rangle$. The next corollary follows from a standard estimate on $\beta_N(x)$, and its proof is omitted.

Corollary 1. *Let X be a random vector which satisfies Assumption 1 and let $X_1, ..., X_N$ be independent copies of X. Then,*

$$Pr \left(\left\| \sum_{i=1}^{N} (X_i \otimes X_i - \Lambda) \right\|_{2 \to 2} > xN \right) \leq 4 Pr \left(\left\| \sum_{i=1}^{N} \varepsilon_i X_i \otimes X_i \right\|_{2 \to 2} > \frac{xN}{2} \right),$$

provided that $x \geq c\sqrt{\rho^4/N}$, for some absolute constant c.

Thanks to the symmetrization argument and to the fact that for every empirical process

$$\mathbb{E} \sup_{f \in F} \left| \sum_{i=1}^{N} (f(X_i) - \mathbb{E}f) \right| \leq 2 \mathbb{E}_{X \times \varepsilon} \sup_{f \in F} \left| \sum_{i=1}^{N} \varepsilon_i f(X_i) \right|,$$

it is enough to analyze the way operators of the form $\sum_{i=1}^{N} \varepsilon_i x_i \otimes x_i$ behave for a fixed set $x_1, ..., x_N$ in $\mathbb{R}^n$, or more generally, in ℓ_2.

Remark 1. *Observe that even if $x_i \in \ell_2$, in order to compute the operator norm of $\sum_{i=1}^{N} \varepsilon_i x_i \otimes x_i$, it suffices to restrict the operator to the span of $x_1, ..., x_N$, and thus we can assume that $x_i \in \ell_2^d$ for $d = \min\{N, n\}$.*

We will use several operator norms in what follows - all of which are connected to the singular values of an operator between two Hilbert spaces. The next definition is presented only in the finite dimensional case, but it has an obvious infinite dimensional analog.

Definition 2. *For $1 \leq p < \infty$, let C_p^d be the space of operators on $\mathbb{R}^d$, endowed with the norm $\|T\|_{C_p^n} = \left(\sum_{i=1}^n s_j^p(T) \right)^{1/p}$, where $s_j(T)$ is the j-th singular value of T. The space C_p^d is called the p-th Schatten class of $\mathbb{R}^d$.*

Note that C_2^d is the space of operators on $\mathbb{R}^d$ with the Hilbert-Schmidt norm. Also, for $p = \infty$, C_p^d is the standard ℓ_2 operator norm, and it is easy to verify that for $p = \log d$, $\|T\|_{2 \to 2} \leq \|T\|_{C_p^d} \leq e \|T\|_{2 \to 2}$.

The following inequality plays a central role in our analysis and is due to Lust-Piquard (see [9] for an exposition of that, and other results of a similar flavor). The estimate on the constant B_p was established by Rudelson [12].

Theorem 3. *There exists an absolute constant C, and for every $2 \leq p < \infty$ there is a constant B_p depending only on p, which satisfies $B_p \leq C\sqrt{p}$, for which the following holds. Let $y_1, ..., y_N$ be operators on $\mathbb{R}^d$, and denote*

$$
A = \max \left\{ \left\| \left(\sum_{i=1}^N y_i^* y_i \right)^{1/2} \right\|_{C_p^d}, \left\| \left(\sum_{i=1}^N y_i y_i^* \right)^{1/2} \right\|_{C_p^d} \right\}.
$$

Then,

$$
A \leq \left(\mathbb{E}_\varepsilon \left\| \sum_{i=1}^N \varepsilon_i y_i \right\|_{C_p^d}^p \right)^{1/p} \leq B_p A.
$$

We will use Theorem 3 for $y_i = x_i \otimes x_i$, and, as in Remark 1, without loss of generality, $y_i \in C_p^d$, for $d = \min\{n, N\}$. One can verify that in this case, $A = \left\| \left(\sum_{i=1}^N \|x_i\|^2 x_i \otimes x_i \right)^{1/2} \right\|_{C_p^d}$, and thus, for $p \geq 2$,

$$
A \leq \left(\mathbb{E} \left\| \sum_{i=1}^N \varepsilon_i x_i \otimes x_i \right\|_{C_p^d}^p \right)^{1/p} \leq C\sqrt{p} A \tag{1.4}
$$

The final preliminary result we require is Lidskii's inequality, on the differences of the sequences of the singular values of symmetric operators. For an operator T, denote by $\mu(T)$ the vector of singular values of T, arranged in a non-increasing order. Recall that for a vector $v \in \mathbb{R}^d$, and $1 \leq p < \infty$, $\|v\|_{\ell_p^d} = \left(\sum_{i=1}^d |v_i|^p \right)^{1/p}$ and for $p = \infty$, $\|v\|_\infty = \max_{1 \leq i \leq d} |v_i|$ (with obvious analogs for $d = \infty$).

Theorem 4. *[7] Let A and B be symmetric operators on $\mathbb{R}^d$. Then, for every $1 \leq p \leq \infty$, $\|\mu(A) - \mu(B)\|_{\ell_p^d} \leq \|\mu(A - B)\|_{\ell_p^d}$.*

The two most interesting cases here are $p = 2$ and $p = \infty$. For $p = 2$ it follows that the Euclidean distance between the vectors $\mu(A)$ and $\mu(B)$ is bounded by the Hilbert-Schmidt norm of $A - B$. For $p = \infty$, $\|\mu(A) - \mu(B)\|_{\ell_\infty^d} \leq \|A - B\|_{2 \to 2}$.

2   Results

Let us begin with two estimates on the singular values of $\Gamma_N : \ell_2^N \to \ell_2$ defined by $\Gamma_N e_i = \frac{1}{\sqrt{N}} X_i$. Clearly, the nonzero eigenvalues of $\Gamma_N \Gamma_N^* = \frac{1}{N} \sum_{i=1}^N X_i \otimes X_i$, denoted by $\hat{\lambda}_1 \geq \hat{\lambda}_2 \geq ...$, are the same as the nonzero eigenvalues of the Gram matrix $\left(\frac{1}{N} \langle X_i, X_j \rangle \right)_{i,j=1}^N$. As a notational convention, we will extend the finite vector $(\hat{\lambda}_1, ..., \hat{\lambda}_N)$ to an infinite one, by adding 0 in the $N + 1$ component and beyond. Thus, one can consider the ℓ_2 and ℓ_∞ norms of the difference $\lambda - \hat{\lambda}$.

Our aim is to compare the eigenvalues of $\Gamma_N \Gamma_N^*$ to those of the average operator $\mathbb{E}(X \otimes X)$ (denoted by $\lambda_1 \geq \lambda_2 \geq ...$) with respect to the two norms. Since both $\sum_{i=1}^N X_i \otimes X_i$ and $\mathbb{E}(X \otimes X)$ are symmetric, and as long as $\mathbb{E}(X \otimes X)$ is in the appropriate Schatten class, then by Theorem 4 and approximating $\mathbb{E}(X \otimes X)$ by a finite dimensional operator, it follows that

$$\|\lambda - \hat{\lambda}\|_\infty = \sup_i \left| \lambda_i - \hat{\lambda}_i \right| \leq \left\| \frac{1}{N} \sum_{i=1}^N X_i \otimes X_i - \mathbb{E}(X \otimes X) \right\|_{2 \to 2},$$

$$\|\lambda - \hat{\lambda}\|_2 = \left(\sum_{i=1}^\infty |\lambda_i - \hat{\lambda}_i|^2 \right)^{1/2} \leq \left\| \frac{1}{N} \sum_{i=1}^N X_i \otimes X_i - \mathbb{E}(X \otimes X) \right\|_{C_2}.$$

The following bounds the expectation of the two norms of $\frac{1}{N} \sum_{i=1}^N X_i \otimes X_i - \mathbb{E}(X \otimes X)$. Its first part is a minor extension to a result due to Rudelson [12].

Theorem 5. *There exists an absolute constant C for which the following holds. Let X be a random vector in ℓ_2^n (resp. ℓ_2), set $d = \min\{N, n\}$ put $Q_N = (\mathbb{E} \max_{1 \leq i \leq N} \|X_i\|^2)^{1/2}$, recall that $\Lambda = \mathbb{E}(X \otimes X)$ and set $T = \frac{1}{N} \sum_{i=1}^N X_i \otimes X_i - \Lambda$. Then,*

$$\mathbb{E} \|T\|_{2 \to 2} \leq C \max \left\{ \frac{\log d}{N} Q_N^2, \ \min \left\{ \|\Lambda\|_{2 \to 2}, \sqrt{\frac{\log d}{N}} \|\Lambda\|_{2 \to 2}^{1/2} Q_N \right\} \right\}.$$

Also, if $\mathbb{E} \|X\|^4 < \infty$, then, $\mathbb{E} \|T\|_{C_2} \leq \frac{C}{\sqrt{N}} \left(\mathbb{E} \|X\|^4 \right)^{1/2}$.

Remark 2. *It follows from a standard integration argument (see, e.g. [14]) that if Z is a random variable with a bounded ψ_α norm, and if $Z_1, ..., Z_N$ are independent copies of Z then*

$$\left\| \max_{1 \leq i \leq N} Z_i \right\|_{\psi_\alpha} \leq C \|Z\|_{\psi_\alpha} \log^{1/\alpha} N$$

for an absolute constant C. Hence, for any integer p,

$$\left(\mathbb{E}\max_{1\leq i\leq N}|Z_i|^p\right)^{1/p} \leq Cp^{1/\alpha}\|Z\|_{\psi_\alpha}\log^{1/\alpha}N. \tag{2.1}$$

In particular, if $Z = \|X\|$ has a bounded ψ_α norm, then one can bound Q_N using $\|Z\|_{\psi_\alpha}$.

Proof of Theorem 5. Because the first part of the claim is an easy extension of a result from [12] we omit its proof. Some of the ideas required are also used in the proof of Theorem 7, below.

Turning to the second part of the claim, using a symmetrization argument, Hölder's inequality and applying Theorem 3 for $Y_i = X_i \otimes X_i$, it follows that

$$\mathbb{E}\left\|\frac{1}{N}\sum_{i=1}^{n}X_i\otimes X_i - \mathbb{E}(X\otimes X)\right\|_{C_2} \leq \frac{1}{N}\mathbb{E}_X\left(\mathbb{E}_\varepsilon\left\|\sum_{i=1}^{N}\varepsilon_iX_i\otimes X_i\right\|_{C_2}^2\right)^{1/2}$$

$$\leq \frac{C}{N}\mathbb{E}_X\left(\left\|\left(\sum_{i=1}^{N}\|X_i\|^2X_i\otimes X_i\right)^{1/2}\right\|_{C_2}\right).$$

Let $U_i = \|X_i\|X_i$ and set $(\hat{\mu}_i)_{i=1}^{N}$ to be the singular values of the symmetric operator $\sum_{i=1}^{N}U_i\otimes U_i$. Since the nonzero singular values of $\sum_{i=1}^{N}U_i\otimes U_i$ are the same as that of $(\langle U_i, U_j\rangle)_{i,j=1}^{N}$, then $\sum_{i=1}^{N}\hat{\mu}_i = \sum_{i=1}^{N}\|U_i\|^2 = \sum_{i=1}^{N}\|X_i\|^4$. Hence,

$$\left\|\left(\sum_{i=1}^{N}U_i\otimes U_i\right)^{1/2}\right\|_{C_2} = \left(\sum_{i=1}^{N}\hat{\mu}_i\right)^{1/2} = \left(\sum_{i=1}^{N}\|X_i\|^4\right)^{1/2},$$

from which the claim follows. ∎

It is possible to obtain estimates (which are probably suboptimal) on higher moments of $\left\|\frac{1}{N}\sum_{i=1}^{N}X_i\otimes X_i - \mathbb{E}(X\otimes X)\right\|_{2\to2}$, and thus establish a deviation inequality, even when $\|X\|$ is not bounded. Of course, if $\|X\|$ is a bounded variable, one can apply Talagrand's concentration inequality for uniformly bounded empirical processes. To prove the desired deviation inequality in the unbounded case, one uses a "high moment" analog of the first part of Theorem 5, which builds on Theorem 3 and on Rudelson's approach from [12].

Theorem 6. *There exists an absolute constant c such that for any integers n and N, any $x_1, ..., x_N \in \mathbb{R}^n$ and any $p \geq 1$,*

$$\left(\mathbb{E}_\varepsilon\left\|\sum_{i=1}^{N}\varepsilon_ix_i\otimes x_i\right\|_{2\to2}^p\right)^{\frac{1}{p}} \leq c\max\{\sqrt{\log d},\sqrt{p}\}\left\|\sum_{i=1}^{N}x_i\otimes x_i\right\|_{2\to2}^{1/2}\max_{1\leq i\leq N}\|x_i\|,$$

where $(\varepsilon_i)_{i=1}^{N}$ are independent Rademacher random variables and $d=\min\{N,n\}$.

Note that this moment inequality immediately leads to a ψ_2 estimate on the random variable $\left\| \sum_{i=1}^{N} \varepsilon_i x_i \otimes x_i \right\|_{2 \to 2}$.

Corollary 2. *There exists an absolute constant c such that for any integers n and N, any $x_1, ..., x_N \in \mathbb{R}^n$ and any $t > 0$,*

$$Pr\left(\left\{ \left\| \sum_{i=1}^{N} \varepsilon_i x_i \otimes x_i \right\|_{2 \to 2} \geq t \right\} \right) \leq 2 \exp\left(-\frac{t^2}{\Delta^2} \right),$$

where $\Delta = c\sqrt{\log d} \left\| \sum_{i=1}^{N} x_i \otimes x_i \right\|_{2 \to 2}^{1/2} \max_{1 \leq i \leq N} \|x_i\|$ and $d = \min\{N, n\}$.

Let us formulate and prove the desired tail estimate.

Theorem 7. *There exists an absolute constant c for which the following holds. Let X be a random vector in ℓ_2^n (resp. ℓ_2) which satisfies Assumption 1 and set $Z = \|X\|$, $\Lambda = \mathbb{E}(X \otimes X)$ and $\beta = (1 + 2/\alpha)^{-1}$. For any integers n and N let $d = \min\{N, n\}$,*

$$A_{d,N} = \|Z\|_{\psi_\alpha} \frac{\sqrt{\log d}(\log N)^{1/\alpha}}{\sqrt{N}} \quad \text{and} \quad B_{d,N} = \frac{\rho^2}{\sqrt{N}} + \|\Lambda\|_{2 \to 2}^{1/2} A_{d,N}.$$

Then, for $1 \leq p < \infty$,

$$\left(\mathbb{E} \left\| \frac{1}{N} \sum_{i=1}^{N} (X_i \otimes X_i) - \Lambda \right\|_{2 \to 2}^{p} \right)^{1/p} \leq cp^{\frac{1}{\beta}} \max\left\{ \frac{\rho^2}{\sqrt{N}} + \|\Lambda\|_{2 \to 2}^{1/2} A_{d,N}, A_{d,N}^2 \right\},$$

and thus,

$$\left(\mathbb{E} \left(\sup_i |\hat{\lambda}_i - \lambda_i| \right)^p \right)^{1/p} \leq cp^{\frac{1}{\beta}} \max\left\{ \frac{\rho^2}{\sqrt{N}} + \lambda_1^{1/2} A_{d,N}, A_{d,N}^2 \right\}.$$

In particular, for any $x > 0$

$$Pr\left(\left\| \sum_{i=1}^{N} (X_i \otimes X_i) - \Lambda \right\|_{2 \to 2} \geq xN \right) \leq \exp\left(-\left(\frac{cx}{\max\{B_{d,N}, A_{d,N}^2\}} \right)^\beta \right),$$

and the same tail estimate holds for $\sup_i \left| \lambda_i - \hat{\lambda}_i \right|$.

Proof. Consider the random variables

$$S = \left\| \frac{1}{N} \sum_{i=1}^{N} \varepsilon_i X_i \otimes X_i \right\|_{2 \to 2} \quad \text{and} \quad V = \left\| \frac{1}{N} \sum_{i=1}^{N} (X_i \otimes X_i - \Lambda) \right\|_{2 \to 2}.$$

It follows from Corollaries 1 and 2 that for any $t \geq c\sqrt{\rho^4/N}$,

$$Pr(V \geq t) \leq 4Pr(S \geq t/2) = 4\mathbb{E}_X Pr_\varepsilon(S \geq t/2 | X_1, ..., X_N)$$

$$\leq 8\mathbb{E}_X \exp\left(-\frac{t^2 N^2}{\Delta^2} \right),$$

where $\Delta = c\sqrt{\log d} \left\| \sum_{i=1}^{N} X_i \otimes X_i \right\|_{2 \to 2}^{1/2} \max_{1 \leq i \leq N} \|X_i\|$ for some absolute constant c. Setting c_0 to be the constant from Corollary 1, then by Fubini's Theorem and dividing the region of integration to $t \leq c_0 \sqrt{\rho^4/N}$ (in this range one has no control on $Pr(V \geq t)$) and $t > c_0 \sqrt{\rho^4/N}$, it is evident that

$$
\begin{aligned}
\mathbb{E}V^p &= \int_0^\infty pt^{p-1} Pr(V \geq t) \, dt \\
&\leq \int_0^{c_0\sqrt{\rho^4/N}} pt^{p-1} dt + 8\,\mathbb{E}_X \int_0^\infty pt^{p-1} \exp\left(-\frac{t^2 N^2}{\Delta^2}\right) dt \\
&\leq \left(c_0\sqrt{\rho^4/N}\right)^p + c^p p^{p/2} \mathbb{E}_X \left(\frac{\Delta}{N}\right)^p
\end{aligned}
$$

for some new absolute constant c.

The second term is bounded by

$$
c^p \left(\frac{p\log n}{N}\right)^{\frac{p}{2}} \mathbb{E}\left(\left\| \frac{1}{N}\sum_{i=1}^N X_i \otimes X_i \right\|_{2\to2}^{\frac{p}{2}} \max_{1\leq i\leq N} \|X_i\|^p\right)
$$

$$
\leq c^p \left(\frac{p\log n}{N}\right)^{\frac{p}{2}} \mathbb{E}\left(\left(\left\| \frac{1}{N}\sum_{i=1}^N X_i \otimes X_i - \Lambda \right\|_{2\to2} + \|\Lambda\|_{2\to2}\right)^{\frac{p}{2}} \max_{1\leq i\leq N} \|X_i\|^p\right)
$$

$$
\leq c^p \left(\frac{p\log n}{N}\right)^{\frac{p}{2}} \left(\mathbb{E}\left(V + \|\Lambda\|_{2\to2}\right)^p\right)^{\frac{1}{2}} \left(\mathbb{E}\max_{1\leq i\leq N}\|X_i\|^{2p}\right)^{\frac{1}{2}}
$$

for some new absolute constant c. Hence, setting $Z = \|X\|$ and applying Assumption 1 and (2.1), we arrive at

$$
(\mathbb{E}V^p)^{\frac{1}{p}} \leq c\frac{\rho^2}{\sqrt{N}} + cp^{\frac{1}{\alpha}+\frac{1}{2}}\left(\frac{\log n}{N}\right)^{\frac{1}{2}}(\log^{\frac{1}{\alpha}} N)\|Z\|_{\psi_\alpha}\left((\mathbb{E}V^p)^{\frac{1}{p}} + \|\Lambda\|_{2\to2}\right)^{\frac{1}{2}},
$$

for some absolute constant c. Set $A_{d,N} = \left(\frac{\log d}{N}\right)^{\frac{1}{2}}(\log^{1/\alpha} N)\|Z\|_{\psi_\alpha}$ and $\beta = (1+2/\alpha)^{-1}$. Thus,

$$
(\mathbb{E}V^p)^{\frac{1}{p}} \leq c\frac{\rho^2}{\sqrt{N}} + cp^{\frac{2}{\beta}}\|\Lambda\|_{2\to2}^{\frac{1}{2}} A_{d,N} + cp^{\frac{2}{\beta}} A_{d,N} (\mathbb{E}V^p)^{\frac{1}{2p}},
$$

implying that $(\mathbb{E}V^p)^{\frac{1}{p}} \leq cp^{\frac{1}{\beta}} \max\left\{\frac{\rho^2}{\sqrt{N}} + \|\Lambda\|_{2\to2}^{1/2} A_{d,N}, A_{d,N}^2\right\}$.

Therefore, $\|V\|_{\psi_\beta} \leq c\max\left\{B_{d,N}, A_{d,N}^2\right\}$, from which the estimate of the Theorem follows by a standard argument. ∎

Let us give an example of how the previous theorem can be used to compare the spectrum of the integral operator T_K with that of the Gram matrix.

Corollary 3. *Let* $K : \Omega \times \Omega \to \mathbb{R}$ *be a positive definite kernel, such that* $\|K\|_{\psi_\alpha} < \infty$ *for some* $\alpha \geq 1$. *If* (λ_i) *is the spectrum of the integral operator (arranged in a non-increasing order) and* $(\hat{\lambda}_i)$ *is the spectrum of the Gram matrix* $\left(\frac{1}{N}K(t_i, t_j)\right)_{i,j=1}^{N}$ *also arranged in a non-increasing order, then*

1. For $1 \leq p < \infty$,

$$\left(\mathbb{E}\sup_i \left|\lambda_i - \hat{\lambda}_i\right|^p\right)^{1/p} \leq$$

$$cp^{1+2/\alpha}\|K(t,t)\|_{\psi_{\alpha/2}} \max\left\{\frac{\sqrt{\log d}\log^{1/\alpha} N}{\sqrt{N}}, \frac{\log d \log^{2/\alpha} N}{N}\right\}.$$

2. If $\mathbb{E}K^2(t,t) < \infty$ *then* $\mathbb{E}\|\lambda - \hat{\lambda}\|_2 \leq C\left(\frac{\mathbb{E}K^2(t,t)}{N}\right)^{1/2}$.

Note that the second part of Corollary 3 generalizes and improves the following Lemma (Lemma 4.1) from [8].

Lemma 1. *Let* $K(x,y) = \sum_{i=1}^{R}\lambda_i\phi_i(x)\phi_i(y)$ *for* $R < \infty$, *and set* $\xi^2(R) = \sum_{1\leq i,j\leq R}(\lambda_i^2 + \lambda_j^2)\mathbb{E}\phi_i^2\phi_j^2$. *Then,*

$$\mathbb{E}\delta_2^2(\lambda, \hat{\lambda}) \leq \frac{\xi^2(R)}{N} - 2\frac{\sum_{i=1}^{R}\lambda_i^2}{N},$$

where for $u, v \in \ell_2$ $\delta_2(u,v) = \inf_\pi \|u - \pi(v)\|_{\ell_2}$, π *is a permutation of* $\{1, ...\}$ *and* $\pi(v) = (v_{\pi(1)}, ...)$.

Our result extends this lemma in several ways. First of all, ours is an infinite dimensional result. Second, for every finite dimensional kernel, $\xi^2(R) \geq \mathbb{E}K^2(t,t)$, and finally, $\delta_2(\lambda, \hat{\lambda}) \leq \|\lambda - \hat{\lambda}\|_2$.

Corollary 3 is different from the results in [15], where the difference between the empirical trace and the actual one, and between the "tails" of the traces $\sum_{d+1}^{\infty}\lambda_i$ and $\sum_{d+1}^{\infty}\hat{\lambda}_i$ were established, rather than the ℓ_∞ and ℓ_2 distances of the vectors of the singular values, as in Corollary 3.

2.1 Approximation by Ellipsoids

Turning to (2), we will see how, for a finite dimensional vector X, the random operator Γ_N (defined by $\Gamma_N e_i = \frac{1}{\sqrt{N}}X_i$) approximates the polar of the Binet ellipsoid (the latter is generated by the covariance structure of X and was defined in (1.1)). Such an approach could be helpful in the analysis of Question 2. Indeed, if $\Gamma_N B_2^N$ asymptotically converges to $\mathcal{E}_B^\circ$, then its principal directions must converge to the principal directions of $\mathcal{E}_B^\circ$, and thus, the best d-approximating subspace of $\Gamma_N B_2^N$ will coincide in the limit with the space spanned by the d largest principal directions of $\mathcal{E}_B^\circ$.

Fix an integer n, let X be a random vector in ℓ_2^n, set $\mathcal{E}_B$ to be the Binet ellipsoid generated by X, and put (ψ_i) to be the orthonormal basis of the principal directions of $\mathcal{E}_B$. Without loss of generality, assume that $\mathcal{E}_B$ has full rank. Then, $X = \sum_{i=1}^{n} \langle X, \psi_i \rangle \psi_i$, the covariance operator can be represented in the basis (ψ_i) by the matrix $A = \mathrm{diag}(\lambda_1, ..., \lambda_n)$, and it is standard to verify that $\mathcal{E}_B = A^{-1/2} B_2^n$. Set $Y = A^{-1/2} X$, and observe that Y is an isotropic vector; that is, for every $y \in \ell_2^n$, $\mathbb{E} |\langle Y, y \rangle|^2 = \|y\|_{\ell_2^n}^2$. The question of how well $\mathcal{K} = \{\sum_{i=1}^{n} a_i Y_i : \sum_{i=1}^{n} a_i^2 \le 1\}$ approximates a multiple of the Euclidean ball has been thoroughly studied (see, e.g., [10, 6, 2, 12, 3]) under various assumptions on the vector Y. To that end, one has to show that for every $y \in B_2^n$,

$$\left| \frac{1}{N} \sum_{i=1}^{N} \langle Y_i, y \rangle^2 - 1 \right| \le \delta. \qquad (2.2)$$

By duality, (2.2) is equivalent to

$$(1 - \delta') \sqrt{N} B_2^n \subset \mathcal{K} \subset (1 + \delta') \sqrt{N} B_2^n$$

for a suitable δ', that is, to

$$(1 - \delta') A^{1/2} B_2^n \subset \Gamma_N B_2^n \subset (1 + \delta') A^{1/2} B_2^n,$$

implying that, $\Gamma_N B_2^n$ is equivalent to the dual of the Binet ellipsoid. One can verify that $\sup_{\{y : \|y\| = 1\}} \left| \frac{1}{N} \sum_{i=1}^{N} \langle Y, y \rangle^2 - 1 \right| \le \delta$ if and only if all the singular values of the random operator $e_i \to Y_i / \sqrt{N}$ satisfy $|\mu_i - 1| \le \delta$. Therefore, it suffices to show that, with high probability,

$$\left\| \frac{1}{N} \sum_{i=1}^{N} Y_i \otimes Y_i - \mathrm{Id} \right\|_{2 \to 2} \le \delta,$$

which is the question we studied in the previous section.

Note that to apply Theorem 5, it suffices to control the decay of the ℓ_2^n norm of the random vector $A^{-1/2} X$, which is

$$\left\| A^{-1/2} X \right\|_2^2 = \sum_{j=1}^{n} \frac{1}{\lambda_j} \langle X_i, \psi_j \rangle^2 = \sum_{j=1}^{n} \frac{\langle X_i, \psi_j \rangle^2}{\mathbb{E} |\langle X, \psi_j \rangle|^2}.$$

Define $f_j = \frac{\langle X, \psi_j \rangle}{(\mathbb{E} |\langle X, \psi_j \rangle|^2)^{1/2}}$, observe that $(f_i)_{i=1}^{n}$ are orthonormal with respect to $L_2(\mu)$ and that $\left\| A^{-1/2} X \right\|_2^2 = \sum_j f_j^2$.

The next corollary can be derived from Theorem 5.

Corollary 4. *There exists an absolute constant c for which the following holds. Let Y be an isotropic random vector in ℓ_2^n, put $Y_1, ..., Y_N$ to be independent copies of Y and set $Q_N = \left(\mathbb{E} \max_{1 \le i \le N} \|Y_i\|_2^2 \right)^{1/2}$. If $\frac{Q_N^2 \log n}{N} \le 1$ then*

$$\mathbb{E} \left\| \frac{1}{N} \sum_{i=1}^{N} Y_i \otimes Y_i - \mathrm{Id} \right\|_{2 \to 2} \le c \cdot Q_N \sqrt{\frac{\log n}{N}}.$$

From the corollary applied to the random vector $Y = A^{-1/2}X$, it follows that if $Z = \|Y\|_2$ and $\|Z\|_{\psi_2} \leq c\sqrt{n}$ then for $\delta = c \cdot Q_N \sqrt{\log n/N} \leq c\sqrt{n/N} \log n$, with high probability,

$$(1 - \delta)\mathcal{E}_B^\circ \subset \Gamma_N B_2^N \subset (1 + \delta)\mathcal{E}_B^\circ.$$

Example. Let K be a finite dimensional, continuous kernel and set (ϕ_i) to be its Mercer basis. Then, $\langle X(t), \phi_i \rangle = \sqrt{\lambda_i}\phi_i(t)$, $f_i(t) = \phi_i(t)$, and $Y = (\phi_i(t))_{i=1}^n$. Assume that the eigenfunctions are bounded by M (such a bound always exists because each eigenfunction is bounded by Mercer's Theorem, and there is a finite number of eigenfunctions). Thus , $Z \equiv \|Y\|_2 \leq M\sqrt{n}$ and the same holds for Q_N. Therefore, if $N \geq c(M)n \log n$, $\Gamma_N B_2^N$ is a good approximation of the ellipsoid $\{\sum_{i=1}^n a_i \sqrt{\lambda_i}\phi_i : \sum_{i=1}^n a_i^2 \leq 1\}$.

2.2   Some Remarks

The assumption that $\|Z\|_{\psi_\alpha} \leq c\sqrt{n}$ is the best that one can hope for. Indeed, $\|Z\|_{\psi_\alpha} \geq c_\alpha \left(\mathbb{E}Z^2\right)^{1/2} \geq c_\alpha\sqrt{n}$. It also says something about the geometry of the random vector, since it implies that it is impossible for many of the functions f_i to be "peaked" at the same place. The most extreme case in which this condition holds is when the functions $\langle X, \psi_i \rangle$ are supported on disjoint sets of measure $1/n$, which implies that X is always in the direction of one of the ψ_is. More generally, the condition means that the random vector X can not have a components "much larger" than $\sqrt{\lambda_j}$ in many of the directions ψ_j simultaneously. For example, if $A = \{i : |\langle X, \psi_j \rangle| \geq \sqrt{t\lambda_j}\}$, then by the ψ_α assumption,

$$Pr\left(\{|A| \geq k\}\right) \leq Pr\left(\left\{\sum_{i=1}^n f_j^2 \geq kt\right\}\right) \leq 2\exp\left(-c\left(\frac{kt}{n}\right)^{\alpha/2}\right).$$

Let us mention that such an assumption on the random vector is not that far-fetched. First of all, if $\mathcal{E}$ is an n dimensional ellipsoid in $L_2(\mu)$, one can find orthonormal vectors ϕ_i and positive scalars θ_i, such that

$$\mathcal{E} = \left\{\sum_{i=1}^n a_i \sqrt{\theta_i}\phi_i : \sum_{i=1}^n a_i^2 \leq 1\right\}$$

and $\sum_{i=1}^n \phi_i^2 = n$ pointwise. This basis is a simple example of the so-called *Lewis basis*, which has many applications in convex geometry (see, for example, [5]). Hence, one can approximate any ellipsoid by the random ellipsoid $\Gamma_N B_2^N$ using $X(t) = \sum_{i=1}^n \sqrt{\theta_i}\phi_i(t)\phi_i$.

The second remark we wish to make is that if Y is an isotropic vector in $\mathbb{R}^n$ which distributed according to a log-concave measure, and if $Z = \|Y\|$, then $\|Z\|_{\psi_2} \leq c\sqrt{n}$. This fact was shown in [3], and generalized the analogous result for a random point selected from a convex body, due to Alesker [1].

To conclude, because this notion of approximation is very strong, one must impose restrictive conditions on the random vector X which also depend on the structure of the eigenfunctions. Perhaps a possible way of improving the rate of $\sqrt{n/N}\log n$ is to consider a weaker notion of approximation, namely that $\hat{\mathcal{E}} \subset \mathcal{E} + \delta B_2^n$ and $\mathcal{E} \subset \hat{\mathcal{E}} + \delta B_2^n$. It seems likely that for this notion of approximation, one could use the fact that $\mathcal{E}$ has small eigenvalues and obtain a better bound. The disadvantage is that the analysis of this question could be difficult, because one has to simultaneously control three different Euclidean structures (of $\mathcal{E}$, $\hat{\mathcal{E}}$ and B_2^n), and thus we leave it open for further investigation.

References

1. S. Alesker, ψ_2 estimates for the Euclidean norm on a convex body in isotropic position, Operator Theory Adv. Appl. 77, 1-4 1995.
2. J. Bourgain, Random points in isotropic convex bodies, in Convex Geometric Analysis (Berkeley, CA, 1996) Math. Sci. Res. Inst. Publ. 34 (1999), 53-58.
3. A.A. Giannopoulos, V.D. Milman, Concentration property on probability spaces, Adv. Math. 156, 77-106, 2000.
4. R. Herbrich, *Learning kernel classifiers*, MIT Press, 2002.
5. W.B. Johnson, G. Schechtman: Finite dimensional subspaces of L_p, in *Handbook of the Geometry of Banach Spaces, Vol 1* (W.B. Johnson, J. Lindenstrauss eds.), North Holland, 2001.
6. R. Kannan, L. Lovász, M. Simonovits, Random walks and $O^*(n^5)$ volume algorithm for convex bodies, Random structures and algorithms, 2(1) 1-50, 1997.
7. T. Kato, *A short introduction to perturbation theory for linear operators*, Springer-Verlag, 1982.
8. V. Koltchinskii, E. Giné, Random matrix approximation of spectra of integral operators. Bernoulli, 6 (2000) 113-167.
9. F. Lust-Piquard, G. Pisier, Non-commutative Khinchine and Paley inequalities, Ark. Mat. 29, 241-260, 1991.
10. V.D. Milman, A. Pajor, Isotropic position and inertia ellipsoids and zonoids of the unit ball of a normed n-dimensional space, Lecture notes in mathematics 1376, 64-104, Springer, 1989.
11. B. Schölkopf, A.J. Smola, *Learning with kernels*, MIT Press, 2002.
12. M. Rudelson, Random vectors in the isotropic position, Journal of Functional Analysis, 164, 60-72, 1999.
13. M. Talagrand, *The generic chaining*, forthcoming.
14. A.W. Van der Vaart, J.A. Wellner, *Weak convergence and Empirical Processes*, Springer-Verlag, 1996.
15. L. Zwald, O. Bousquet, G. Blanchard, Statistical properties of kernel principal component analysis, in *Proceedings of COLT 2004, J. Shawe-Taylor and Y. Singer (Eds)*, LNAI 3120, 594-608, Springer-Verlag 2004.

The Spectral Method
for General Mixture Models

Ravindran Kannan[1], Hadi Salmasian[1], and Santosh Vempala[2]

[1] Yale University, New Haven CT 06511, USA
kannan@cs.yale.edu, hadi.salmasian@yale.edu
[2] MIT, Cambridge MA 02139, USA
vempala@math.mit.edu

Abstract. We present an algorithm for learning a mixture of distributions based on spectral projection. We prove a general property of spectral projection for arbitrary mixtures and show that the resulting algorithm is efficient when the components of the mixture are logconcave distributions in $\Re^n$ whose means are separated. The separation required grows with k, the number of components, and $\log n$. This is the first result demonstrating the benefit of spectral projection for *general* Gaussians and widens the scope of this method. It improves substantially on previous results, which focus either on the special case of spherical Gaussians or require a separation that has a considerably larger dependence on n.

1 Introduction

Mixture models are widely used for statistical estimation, unsupervised concept learning, text and image classification etc. [11, 17]. A finite mixture model for an unknown distribution is a weighted combination of a finite number of distributions of a known type. The problem of learning or estimating a mixture model is formulated as follows. We assume that we get samples from a distribution F on $\Re^n$ which is a mixture (convex combination) of unknown distributions $F_1, F_2, \ldots, F_k$, with (unknown) mixing weights $w_1, w_2, \ldots, w_k > 0$ i.e., $F = \sum_{i=1}^{k} w_i F_i$ and $\sum_{i=1}^{k} w_i$. The goal is to (a) classify the sample points according to the underlying distributions and (b) estimate essential parameters of the components, such as the mean and covariance matrix of each component. This problem has been widely studied, particularly for the special case when each F_i is a Gaussian.

One algorithm that is often used is the EM (Expectation-Maximization) algorithm. It is quite general, but does not have guarantees on efficiency and could even converge to an incorrect or suboptimal classification. A second known technique, from statistics, projects the sample points to a random low-dimensional subspace and then tries to find the right classification by exploiting the low dimensionality and exhaustively examining all possible classifications. The trouble is that two different densities may overlap after projection — the means of the

P. Auer and R. Meir (Eds.): COLT 2005, LNAI 3559, pp. 444–457, 2005.

projected densities may coincide (or get closer), making it hard to separate the samples.

In this paper, we investigate the method known as spectral projection, i.e., the representation of the data in the subspace spanned by its top k principal components. We present our results following a discussion of the relevant literature.

1.1   Recent Theoretical Work

There has been progress in recent years in finding algorithms with rigorous theoretical guarantees [3, 2, 4, 19], mostly for the important special case of learning mixtures of Gaussians. These algorithms assume a separation between the means of each pair of component distributions which depends on the variances of the two distributions and also on n and k. For a component F_i of the mixture let μ_i denotes its mean and σ_i denote the maximum standard deviation along any direction in $\Re^n$. In order for the classification problem to have a well-defined (unique) solution with high probability, any two components i, j must be separated by $\sigma_i + \sigma_j$ times a logarithmic factor; if the separation is smaller than this, then the distributions overlap significantly and some of the samples have a good chance of coming from more than one component. Dasgupta [3] showed that if each mixing weight is $\Omega(1/k)$ and the variances are within a bounded range, then a separation of (the Ω^* notation suppresses logarithmic terms and error parameters)

$$|\mu_i - \mu_j| = (\sigma_i + \sigma_j)\Omega^*(n^{1/2})$$

is enough to efficiently learn the mixture.

Shortly thereafter, this result was improved by Dasgupta and Schulman [4] and Arora and Kannan [2] who reduced the separation required to

$$|\mu_i - \mu_j| = (\sigma_i + \sigma_j)\Omega^*(n^{1/4}).$$

In [4], the algorithm used is a variant of EM (and requires some technical assumptions on the variances), while the result of [2] works for general Gaussians using distance-based classification. The idea is that at this separation, it is possible to examine just the pairwise distances of the sample point and infer the right classification with high probability.

The dependence on n is critical; typically n represents the number of attributes and is much larger than k, the size of the model. Further, the underlying method used in these papers, namely, distance-based classification, inherently needs such a large separation that grows with n [2].

In [19], a spectral algorithm was used for the special case of spherical Gaussians and the separation required was reduced to

$$|\mu_i - \mu_j| = (\sigma_i + \sigma_j)\Omega^*(k^{1/4}).$$

Since k is usually a constant and much less than n, this is a substantial improvement for the spherical case. The algorithm uses a projection of the sample to the subspace spanned by the top k singular vectors of the distribution (i.e., the singular vectors of a matrix, each of whose rows is one of the iid samples drawn according to the mixture), also called the SVD subspace. The idea there is that the SVD subspace of a mixture of spherical Gaussians *contains* the means of the k components. Hence, after projection to this subspace the separation between the means is preserved. On the other hand each component is still a Gaussian and the dimension is only k, and so the separation required is only a function of k. Further, even for a sample, the SVD subspace is "close" to the means and this is used in the algorithm.

1.2   New Results

Given the success of the spectral method for spherical Gaussians, a natural question is whether it can be used for more general distributions, in particular for nonspherical Gaussians. At first sight, the method does not seem to be applicable. The property that the SVD subspace of the distribution contains the means is clearly false for nonspherical Gaussians, e.g., see Figure 1. In fact, the SVD subspace can be orthogonal to the one spanned by the means and so using spectral methods might seem hopeless.

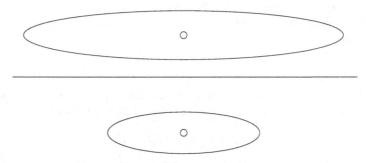

Fig. 1. The SVD subspace W, the plane that minimizes the average squared distance, might miss the means of the components entirely

The key insight of this paper is that this example is misleading and while the SVD subspace does not contain the means, it is always *close* (in an average sense) to the means of the distributions (Theorem 1). As a result, upon projection to this subspace, the inter-mean distances are approximately preserved "on average". Moreover, this property is true for a mixture of *arbitrary* distributions.

It is then a reasonable idea to project the sample to the SVD subspace to reduce the dimensionality. To identify individual components in this subspace, we need them to remain nonoverlapping. If the mixture is arbitrary, then even though the means are separated on average, the samples could intermingle. To overcome this, we assume that the component distributions are logconcave.

A function $f : \Re^n \to \Re_+$ is logconcave if its logarithm is concave, i.e., for any two points $x, y \in \Re^n$ and any $\lambda \in [0, 1]$,

$$f(\lambda x + (1 - \lambda)y) \geq f(x)^\lambda f(y)^{1-\lambda}.$$

These functions have many useful properties, e.g., the product, minimum and convolution of two logconcave functions are also logconcave [5, 10, 15]. Logconcave densities are a powerful generalization of Gaussians. Besides Gaussians, many other common probability measures, like the exponential family and the uniform measure over a convex set are logconcave. So, for example, one component of a mixture could be a Gaussian while another is the uniform distribution over a cube. The following properties make these distributions suitable for our purpose: (a) the projection of a logconcave distribution remains logconcave (b) the distance of a random point from the mean has an exponential tail.

In Section 3, we give an iterative spectral algorithm that identifies one component of the mixture in each iteration. It should be emphasized that there are many possible alternatives for identifying the components *after* projection (e.g., the EM algorithm) and we expect they will also benefit from the enhancement provided by projection. For the post-projection algorithm presented here, we assume that each mixing weight is at least ε and the pairwise separation satisfies

$$|\mu_i - \mu_j| = (\sigma_i + \sigma_j)\Omega^*(k^{\frac{3}{2}}/\varepsilon^2).$$

More precisely, our algorithm only requires a lower bound ε, a probability of error δ, an upper bound k, and a sample set from an n-dimensional mixture distribution of size $\Omega(\frac{n}{\varepsilon}\log^5(nk/\delta))$ which satisfies the given separation, and it classifies all but a fixed number with probability at least $1 - \delta$ (Theorem 3). It is easy to see that it requires time polynomial in $n, \varepsilon, \log(\frac{1}{\delta})$. The means and covariance matrices of the components can be estimated using $O(\frac{n}{\varepsilon}\log^5(nk/\delta))$ samples (Theorem 2). For the special case of Gaussians, $O(n\log^3(n/\delta)/\varepsilon)$ samples suffice. Table 1 presents a comparison of algorithms for learning mixtures (logarithmic terms are suppressed).

Table 1. Comparison

Authors	Separation	Assumptions	Method
Dasgupta [3]	$n^{\frac{1}{2}}$	Gaussians, bounded variances and $w_i = \Omega(1/k)$	Random projection
Dasgupta-Schulman [4]	$n^{\frac{1}{4}}$	Spherical Gaussians	EM+distances
Arora-Kannan [2]	$n^{\frac{1}{4}}$	Gaussians	Distances
Vempala-Wang [19]	$k^{\frac{1}{4}}$	Spherical Gaussians	Spectral projection
This paper	$\frac{k^{\frac{3}{2}}}{\varepsilon^2}$	Logconcave distributions	Spectral projection

1.3   Notation

A mixture F has k components $F_1, \ldots, F_k$. We denote their mixing weights by $w_1, \ldots, w_k$ and their means by $\mu_1, \ldots \mu_k$. The maximum variance of F_i in any direction is denoted by σ_i^2. For any subspace W, we denote the maximum variance of F_i along any direction in W by $\sigma_{i,W}^2$.

Let S be a set of iid samples S from F. One can think of S as being picked as follows: first i is picked from $\{1, 2, \ldots, k\}$ with probability w_i (unknown to the algorithm); then a sample is picked from F_i. We can partition S as $S = S_1 \cup S_2 \cup \ldots \cup S_k$ where each S_i is from F_i (note: this partition of S is unknown to the algorithm). For each i, we denote by μ_i^S the sample mean, i.e.,

$$\mu_i^S = \frac{1}{|S_i|} \sum_{x \in S_i} x.$$

For a subspace V and a vector x, we write $d(x, V)$ for the orthogonal distance of x from V.

For any set of points S, we can form a matrix A whose rows are the points in S. The subspace spanned by the top k right singular vectors of A will be called the *SVD subspace* of S. For any subspace W, we denote the maximum variance of a set of sample points in $S = S_1 \cup \ldots \cup S_k$ which belong to S_i along any direction in W by $\hat{\sigma}_{i,W}^2(S)$.

2   The SVD Subspace

In this section, we prove an important property of spectral projection. The theorem says that the SVD subspace of a sample is close to the means of the samples from each component of the mixture, where "close" is in terms of the sample variances. Note that the theorem holds for *any* mixture. In the analysis of our algorithm, we will apply it only to mixtures of logconcave distributions.

Theorem 1. *Let* $S = S_1 \cup S_2 \ldots \cup S_k$ *be a sample from a mixture* F *with* k *components such that* S_i *is from the ith component* F_i *and let* W *be the SVD subspace of* S. *For each* i, *let* μ_i^S *be the mean of* S_i *and* $\hat{\sigma}_{i,W}^2(S)$ *be the maximum variance of* S_i *along any direction in* W. *Then,*

$$\sum_{i=1}^k |S_i| d(\mu_i^S, W)^2 \leq k \sum_{i=1}^k |S_i| \hat{\sigma}_{i,W}^2(S).$$

Proof. Let M be the span of $\mu_1^S, \mu_2^S, \ldots, \mu_k^S$. For $x \in \Re^n$, write $\pi_M(x)$ for the projection of x onto M and $\pi_W(x)$ for the projection of x onto W.

Using the facts that μ_i^S is the average of $x \in S_i$ and $\mu_i^S \in M$, we write

$$\sum_{x \in S} |\pi_M(x)|^2 = \sum_{i=1}^k \sum_{x \in S_i} |\pi_M(x) - \mu_i^S|^2 + \sum_{i=1}^k |S_i||\mu_i^S|^2$$

$$\geq \sum_{i=1}^k |S_i||\mu_i^S|^2$$

$$= \sum_{i=1}^k |S_i||\pi_W(\mu_i^S)|^2 + \sum_{i=1}^k |S_i| d(\mu_i^S, W)^2. \tag{1}$$

On the other hand,

$$\sum_{x \in S} |\pi_W(x)|^2 = \sum_{i=1}^{k} \sum_{x \in S_i} |\pi_W(x - \mu_i^S)|^2 + \sum_{i=1}^{k} |S_i| |\pi_W(\mu_i^S)|^2$$

$$\leq k \sum_{i=1}^{k} |S_i| \hat{\sigma}_{i,W}^2(S) + \sum_{i=1}^{k} |S_i| |\pi_W(\mu_i^S)|^2. \qquad (2)$$

It is well-known that the SVD subspace maximizes the sum of squared projections among all subspaces of rank at most k (alternatively, it minimizes the sum of squared distances to the subspace; see e.g. [7]). From this, we get

$$\sum_{x \in S} |\pi_W(x)|^2 \geq \sum_{x \in S} |\pi_M(x)|^2.$$

Using this, the RHS of (2) is at least the RHS of (1) and the theorem follows. □
    The same proof also yields an inequality for the entire distribution:

$$\sum_{i=1}^{k} w_i d(\mu_i, W)^2 \leq k \sum_{i=1}^{k} w_i \sigma_i^2.$$

Here W is the SVD subspace of the entire distribution (subspace spanned by the top k principal components of the distribution).
    Although we will apply the inequality only for logconcave component distributions, it suggests a benefit for spectral projection more generally. The inequality puts a lower bound on the average squared distance between component means after projection; if the means are well-separated to begin with, they continue to be, in an average sense. On the other hand, the distance of a point from the mean of its distribution can only shrink upon projection, thus magnifying the ratio of inter-component distance to intra-component distance. This aspect is studied further along with empirical results in [20].

3   An Iterative Spectral Algorithm

In this section, we describe the algorithm. It follows the method suggested by Theorem 1, namely, to project on the SVD subspace and to try to identify components in that subspace. However, since pairwise distances are only preserved in an average sense, it is possible that some means are very close to each other in the projected subspace and we cannot separate the corresponding samples. To get around this, we will show that all "large" components remain well-separated from the rest and there is at least one large component. We identify this component, filter it from the sample and repeat. For technical reasons (see below), the samples used to compute the SVD are discarded. The input to the algorithm below is a set of N iid samples and a parameter $N_0 < N$.

Algorithm.

Repeat while there are samples left:

1. For a subset S of size N_0, find the k-dimensional SVD subspace W.
2. Discard S and project the rest, T, to the subspace W.
3. For each projected point p:
   --- Find the closest $\varepsilon N/2$ points. Let this set be $T(p)$ with mean $\mu(p)$.
   --- Form the matrix $A(p)$ whose rows are x-$\mu(p)$ for each x in $T(p)$. Compute the largest singular value $\sigma(p)$ of $A(p)$ (Note: this is the maximum standard deviation of $T(p)$ over all directions in W).
4. Find a point p_0 for which $\sigma(p_0)$ is maximum. Let T_0 be the set of all points of T whose projection to W is within distance $\frac{\sqrt{k}\log N}{\varepsilon}\sigma(p)$ of p_0.
5. Label T_0 as one component; estimate its mean and covariance matrix.
6. Delete T_0 from T.

In Step 3 of the algorithm, for any point p, the top singular value $\sigma(p)$ of $A(p)$ can also be expressed as follows:

$$\sigma(p)^2 = \max_{v\in W, |v|=1} \frac{1}{|T_p|}\sum_{q\in T_p}|q\cdot v|^2 - \left(\frac{1}{|T_p|}\sum_{q\in T_p}q\cdot v\right)^2.$$

This value is an estimate of the maximum variance of the entire subsample of the component to which p belongs.

There is a technical issue concerning independence. If we use the entire sample to compute the SVD subspace W, then the sample is not independent from W. So we use a subset S to compute the SVD subspace in each iteration and discard it. The rest of the sample, i.e., the part not used for SVD computation is classifed correctly with high probability. The size of the subset S in each iteration is N_0.

We can state guarantees for the algorithm in two different ways. The first is a guarantee that the estimated means and covariances are approximations of the means and covariances of individual components. Recall that the covariance matrix of a distribution G with mean μ is $\mathsf{E}_G((x-\mu)(x-\mu)^T)$, the matrix whose ij'th is the covariance of the ith and jth coordinates of a random point x drawn from G.

Theorem 2. *For* $0 < \eta < 1$, *let*

$$N_0 = C\frac{n}{\varepsilon\eta^2}\log^5\left(\frac{n}{\eta\delta}\right).$$

Suppose that have have $2kN_0$ iid samples from a mixture F of k logconcave distributions in $\Re^n$, with mixing weights at least ε and the means separated as

$$\forall i,j \quad |\mu_i - \mu_j| \geq 1024(\sigma_i + \sigma_j) \left(\frac{k^{\frac{3}{2}}}{\varepsilon^2} \right) \log 2kN_0.$$

Then the iterative spectral algorithm with this setting of N_0 finds approximations $\mu_1', \ldots, \mu_k'$ to the means and $A_1, \ldots, A_k$ to the covariance matrices such that with probability at least $1 - \delta$, for $1 \leq i \leq k$,

$$|\mu_i - \mu_i'| \leq \eta \sigma_i \quad and \quad \left\| A_i^{-1} \mathsf{E}_{F_i} \left((x - \mu_i)(x - \mu_i)^T \right) - I \right\|_F \leq \eta$$

where $\| \cdot \|_F$ is the Frobenius norm, the square root of the sum of the squares of all the entries.

A second guarantee is when we have N samples and the separation grows with $\log N$. In this case, we can classify all but kN_0 samples.

Theorem 3. *Suppose we have N iid samples from a mixture F of k logconcave distributions with mixing weights at least ε and the means of the components separated as*

$$\forall i,j \quad |\mu_i - \mu_j| \geq 1024(\sigma_i + \sigma_j) \left(\frac{k^{\frac{3}{2}}}{\varepsilon^2} \right) \log N.$$

Then, for any $0 < \delta < 1$, with

$$N_0 = C \frac{n}{\varepsilon} \log^5 \frac{n}{\delta},$$

the iterative spectral algorithm correctly classifies $N - 2kN_0$ samples with probability at least $1 - \delta$ (a subset of $2kN_0$ samples are used by the algorithm and discarded).

We will prove Theorem 3 in the next section. The proof of Theorem 2 is very similar.

4   Analysis

4.1   Preliminaries

We begin with some properties of logconcave distributions, paraphrased from [12, 13]. The proof of the first uses a theorem from [16] (see also [6]).

Lemma 1. *Let $0 < \eta < 1$ and $y_1, \ldots, y_m$ be iid samples from a logconcave distribution G in $\Re^n$ whose mean is the origin. There is an absolute constant C such that for*

$$m > C \frac{n}{\eta^2} \log^5 \left(\frac{n}{\eta \delta} \right)$$

with probability at least $1 - \delta$, for any vector $v \in R^n$,

$$(1 - \eta)\mathsf{E}_G((v^T y)^2) \leq \frac{1}{m} \sum_{i=1}^{n} (v^T y_i)^2 \leq (1 + \eta)\mathsf{E}_G((v^T y)^2).$$

Lemma 2. *Let F be any logconcave distribution in $\Re^n$ with mean μ and second moment $\mathsf{E}_F(|X - \mu|^2) = R^2$. There is an absolute constant c such that for any $t > 1$,*
$$\Pr(|X - \mu| > tR) < e^{-ct}.$$

Lemma 3. *Let $f : \Re \to \Re_+$ be a logconcave density function with variance σ^2. Then*
$$\max_{\Re} f(x) \leq \frac{1}{\sigma}.$$

4.2   Sample Properties

Assume that $N > 2kN_0$. If T is the subset of samples that are not used for SVD computation, then there is a partition T as $T = T_1 \cup T_2 \cup \ldots \cup T_k$ where T_i is the set of samples from F_i.

Lemma 4. *With probability at least $1 - \delta/4k$, for every $i \in \{1, 2, \ldots, k\}$,*

a. *$w_i|T| - \frac{\varepsilon}{4}|T| \leq |T_i| \leq w_i|T| + \frac{\varepsilon}{4}|T|$.*
b. *$|\mu_i - \mu_i^T| \leq \frac{\sigma_i}{4}$.*
c. *For any subspace W, $\frac{7}{8}\sigma_{i,W} \leq \hat{\sigma}_{i,W}^2(T) \leq \frac{8}{7}\sigma_{i,W}^2$.*

Proof. a. Follows easily from a Chernoff bound [14].
  b. For any fixed $|T_i|$, the random variable $\mu_i^T = \frac{1}{|T_i|} \sum_{x \in T_i} x$ is a convolution of logconcave distributions and hence is also logconcave. Its variance is $n\sigma_i^2/|T_i|$. We apply Lemma 2 to this distribution to get the bound.
  c. Follows immediately from Lemma 1.
                                                                                                    □

In our proof, we would like to apply Theorem 1. However, the theorem holds for the sample S that is used to compute the SVD subspace. The next lemma derives a similar bound for an independent sample T that is not used in the SVD computation.

Lemma 5. *Suppose $T = T_1 \cup \ldots \cup T_k$ is the set of sample points not used for the SVD computation in the algorithm. Then we have*

$$\sum_{i=1}^{k} |T_i| d(\mu_i^S, W)^2 \leq 2k \sum_{i=1}^{k} |T_i| \hat{\sigma}_i^2 \tag{3}$$

where $\hat{\sigma}_i^2 = \hat{\sigma}_{i,W}^2(T)$ is the maximum variance of T_i along any direction in W.

Proof. First, we apply Theorem 1 to S. Then, using Lemma 4(a), we can relate $|T_i|$ to $|S_i|$ and we have

$$\sum_{i=1}^{k} |T_i| d(\mu_i^S, W) \le \frac{3}{2} k \sum_{i=1}^{k} |T_i| \hat{\sigma}_{i,W}^2(S).$$

Next, Lemma 1 implies that

$$\hat{\sigma}_{i,W}^2(S) \le \frac{7}{6} \sigma_{i,W}^2.$$

Finally, we use the lower bound in Lemma 4(c) to get the desired inequality.   □

4.3   Proof of Theorem 3

We will prove the following claim: With probability at least $1 - (\delta/2k)$, the algorithm identifies one component exactly in any one iteration. We will prove the claim for the first iteration and it will follow inductively for all subsequent iterations.

Let $T = T_1 \cup T_2 \cup \ldots \cup T_k$ be the partition of the current sample T according to the components F_i. For each i, recall that μ_i^T is the sample mean and define $\hat{\mu}_i^T$ to be the projection of μ_i^T to the subspace spanned by W. Similarly, we have μ_i^S and $\hat{\mu}_i^S$. For convenience, we write $\hat{\sigma}_{i,W}(T)^2$ as $\hat{\sigma}_i^2$. Let

$$\alpha = 1024 \frac{k^{\frac{3}{2}}}{\varepsilon^2} \log N \quad \text{and} \quad \beta = \frac{\varepsilon^3}{8096k}.$$

We say that a component F_r is *large* if the following condition holds:

$$|T_r|\hat{\sigma}_r^2 \ge \beta \max_i |T_i|\hat{\sigma}_i^2. \tag{4}$$

The proof is based on the next two lemmas.

Lemma 6. *For any large component F_r, for every $i \ne r$,*

$$|\hat{\mu}_i^T - \hat{\mu}_r^T| > \frac{\alpha}{8}(\sigma_i + \sigma_r).$$

Proof. Let $d_r = d(\mu_r^S, W)$. For any large component r satisfying (4), by (3),

$$|T_r|d_r^2 \le 2k \sum_i |T_i|\hat{\sigma}_i^2 \le \frac{2k^2}{\beta}|T_r|\hat{\sigma}_r^2. \tag{5}$$

Thus,

$$d_r^2 \le \frac{2k^2}{\beta}\hat{\sigma}_r^2 \le \frac{\alpha^2}{16}\hat{\sigma}_r^2.$$

Next, let

$$R = \{i \ne r \ : \ |\hat{\mu}_i^S - \hat{\mu}_r^S| \le \frac{\alpha}{4}(\sigma_i + \sigma_r)\}.$$

Then, by the assumed separation, for each $i \in R$, we must have (using Lemma 4b)

$$d_i = d(\mu_i^S, W) \geq |\mu_i - \mu_r| - |\mu_i - \mu_i^S| - |\mu_r - \mu_r^S| - d_r - |\hat{\mu}_i^S - \hat{\mu}_r^S|$$
$$\geq \frac{\alpha}{3}\sigma_r \geq \frac{\alpha}{4}\hat{\sigma}_r.$$

Therefore, using (5),

$$\frac{2k^2}{\beta}|T_r|\hat{\sigma}_r^2 \geq 2k \sum_{i=1}^{k} |T_i|\hat{\sigma}_i^2 \geq \sum_{i=1}^{k} |T_i|d_i^2$$

$$\geq \sum_{i \in R} |T_i|d_i^2 \geq \sum_{i \in R} |T_i|\frac{\alpha^2}{16}\hat{\sigma}_r^2.$$

As a result,

$$\sum_{i \in R} |T_i| \leq \frac{32k^2}{\alpha^2\beta}|T_r| < \frac{\varepsilon}{2}|T|.$$

However, since each $|T_i| \geq \frac{\varepsilon}{2}|T|$ (by Lemma 4(a)), this implies that R is empty. To complete the lemma, we note that by Lemma 4(b), for any j,

$$|\hat{\mu}_j^T - \hat{\mu}_j^S| \leq |\mu_j^T - \mu_j^S| \leq |\mu_j^T - \mu_j| + |\mu_j - \mu_j^S| \leq 2\sigma_j,$$

and then use triangle inequality.   □

Lemma 7. *Let $p \in T_i$. With probability at least $1 - \delta/4k$,*

$$\sigma(p)^2 \leq 16k\hat{\sigma}_i^2.$$

Further, if i is a large component, then

$$\sigma(p)^2 \geq \frac{w_i^2}{512}\hat{\sigma}_i^2.$$

Proof. By Lemma 2, within a radius of $\sqrt{2k}\sigma_{i,W}$ of any point p from T_i, there will be at least $\varepsilon N/2$ points from the same component. Even if some points from other components are within this distance of p, they cannot increase $\sigma(p)$ beyond this value. To complete the proof, we use Lemma 4(c).

For the second inequality, note that by Lemma 6 the set of samples used to compute $\sigma(p)$ are all from T_i. If v is the direction in W for which the distribution F_i has maximum variance, then Lemma 3 implies that for

$$H = \{x \in \Re^n : \mu^{T(p)} \cdot v - \frac{\varepsilon}{8}\sigma_{i,W} \leq v.x \leq \mu^{T(p)} \cdot v + \frac{\varepsilon}{8}\sigma_{i,W}\}$$

we have $F_i(H) \leq \frac{1}{\sigma_{i,W}} \times 2\frac{\varepsilon\sigma_{i,W}}{8} = \frac{\varepsilon}{4}$.

Now we apply VC-dimension techniques (see [9]). Suppose $|T_i| > \frac{1}{\varepsilon}$. This is guaranteed by Lemma 4a. Since the VC-dimension of intervals on a line is 2, with probability $1 - \frac{\delta}{4}$ the following statement is true:

- For any interval I along the direction v, if $H_I = \{x \in \Re^n : x \cdot v \in I\}$, then

$$|\frac{|T_i \cap H_I|}{|T_i|} - F_i(H_I)| \leq \frac{\varepsilon}{8}.$$

Therefore $|T(p) \cap H| \leq \frac{3\varepsilon}{8}|T_i| \leq \frac{3}{4} \times \frac{\varepsilon|T_i|}{2} \leq \frac{3|T(p)|}{4}$. This means that at least $\frac{|T(p)|}{4}$ samples in $T(p)$ are out of the strip H, i.e. they are at least as far as $\frac{\varepsilon}{8}\sigma_{i,W}$ apart from $\mu^{T(p)}$ in the direction of v. Hence, using Lemma 4c,

$$\sigma(p)^2 \geq \frac{1}{|T(p)|} \sum_{x \in T(p)} (x \cdot v - \mu^{T(p)} \cdot v)^2$$

$$\geq \frac{1}{|T(p)|} \times \frac{|T(p)|}{4} \times (\frac{\varepsilon}{8}\sigma_{i,W})^2$$

$$\geq \frac{\varepsilon^2}{256}\sigma_{i,W}^2 \geq \frac{\varepsilon^2\hat{\sigma}_i^2}{512}$$

which completes the proof.

$\square$

We continue with the proof of Theorem 3. By Lemma 2, and the first part of Lemma 7, if the point p_0 in Step 4 that maximizes $\sigma(p)$ is from a component r satisfying (4), then the set of samples identified is entirely from T_r. Next we will show that the point p_0 in step (4) must indeed be from a large component. Let r be the component for which $|T_r|\hat{\sigma}_r^2$ is maximum. Take any $p \in T_i$ for an i which is not large, i.e.,

$$|T_i|\hat{\sigma}_i^2 < \beta|T_r|\hat{\sigma}_r^2. \tag{6}$$

Therefore,

$$\hat{\sigma}_i^2 \leq \beta\frac{|T_r|}{|T_i|}\hat{\sigma}_r^2 \leq \frac{\beta}{\varepsilon}\hat{\sigma}_r^2.$$

By Lemma 7,

$$\sigma(p)^2 < 16k\hat{\sigma}_i^2 \leq \frac{16k\beta}{\varepsilon}\hat{\sigma}_r^2 = \frac{\varepsilon^2}{512}\hat{\sigma}_r^2.$$

On the other hand, for any point $q \in T_r$,

$$\sigma(q)^2 \geq \frac{\varepsilon^2}{512}\hat{\sigma}_r^2 > \sigma(p)^2.$$

Hence the point p_0 chosen in step 4 will be from a large component.

Now by Lemma 4, the number of samples we have in T_0 is enough to estimate the mean and covariance matrix. Finally, using these estimates, by Lemma 2, the set T_0 contains all the sample points from a single component with high probability.

5   Concluding Remarks

As pointed out by a referee, the dimensionality of the SVD subspace can be reduced as $k, k-1, \ldots$, in successive iterations of the algorithm.

From the example in Figure 1.2, it is not hard to see that spectral projection requires a separation between means that grows with the largest variance of individual components. Following the preliminary version of our results [18, 8], Achlioptas and McSherry [1] have improved the polynomial dependence on k and ε using a more sophisticated algorithm *after* projection. It remains an open problem to learn (nonspherical) Gaussians at smaller separation. The near-disjointness of Gaussian components (e.g., total variation distance nearly 1 for two Gaussians), and thus their learnability, is implied by the assumption that the distance between two means is of the order of the variance *in the direction of* the line joining the means. Spectral projection fails at such a small separation and a different technique will have to be used.

On the other hand, the main technique used in this paper is fairly easy to implement and commonly used in practice for many applications. In [20], Vempala and Wang present empirical evidence and propose an explanation for why the method is effective for real data where the assumption that the components are Gaussian (or logconcave) might not be valid.

Finally, most guarantees for spectral methods assume that the data is generated from some restricted model such as a random model. Our algorithm is also for "random" data, but the distributions considered are more general. Spectral projection seem to be well-suited for such models and our result can be viewed as further evidence of this.

Acknowledgement. We thank the NSF (awards ITR-0312354 and ITR-0312339) and the Sloan foundation.

References

1. D. Achlioptas and F. McSherry: On Spectral Learning of Mixtures of Distributions, this proceedings.
2. S. Arora, R. Kannan. Learning mixtures of arbitrary Gaussians. *Proc. 33st ACM STOC*, 2001.
3. S. DasGupta: Learning mixtures of Gaussians. *Proc. of FOCS*, 1999.
4. S. DasGupta, L. Schulman: A two-round variant of EM for Gaussian mixtures. *Uncertainty in Artificial Intelligence*, 2000.
5. A. Dinghas: Über eine Klasse superadditiver Mengenfunktionale von Brunn–Minkowski–Lusternik-schem Typus, *Math. Zeitschr.* **68**, 111–125, 1957.
6. A. A. Giannopoulos and V. D. Milman: Concentration property on probability spaces. Adv. Math. 156(1), 77–106, 2000.
7. G. Golub and C. Van Loan, *Matrix Computations*, Johns Hopkins University Press, 1989.
8. R. Kannan, H. Salmasian and S. Vempala: The Spectral Method for Mixture Models. ECCC Tech. Rep. 067, 2004.
9. M. Kearns and U. Vazirani: An Introduction to Computational Learning Theory, MIT Press, 1994.
10. L. Leindler: On a certain converse of Hölder's Inequality II, *Acta Sci. Math. Szeged* 33 (1972), 217–223.
11. B. Lindsay. *Mixture models: theory, geometry and applications.* American Statistical Association, Virginia 1995.

12. L. Lovász and S. Vempala: Logconcave functions: Geometry and Efficient Sampling Algorithms, *Proc. of FOCS*, 2003.
13. L. Lovász and S. Vempala: The Geometry of Logconcave Functions and an $O^*(n^3)$ sampling algorithm, Microsoft Research Tech. Report MSR-TR-2003-04.
14. R. Motwani and P. Raghavan: Randomized Algorithms, Cambridge University Press, 1995.
15. A. Prékopa: Logarithmic concave measures and functions, *Acta Sci. Math. Szeged* 34 (1973), 335–343.
16. M. Rudelson: Random vectors in the isotropic position, *J. Funct. Anal.* **164** (1999), 60–72.
17. D.M. Titterington, A.F.M. Smith, and U.E. Makov. *Statistical analysis of finite mixture distributions,* Wiley, 1985.
18. S. Vempala: On the Spectral Method for Mixture Models, IMA workshop on Data Analysis and Optimization, 2003. http://www.ima.umn.edu/talks/workshops/5-6-9.2003/vempala/vempala.html
19. S. Vempala and G. Wang: A spectral algorithm for learning mixtures of distributions, *Proc. of FOCS*, 2002; J. Comput. System Sci. 68(4), 841–860, 2004.
20. S. Vempala and G. Wang: The benefit of spectral projection for document clustering. *Proc. of the 3rd Workshop on Clustering High Dimensional Data and its Applications*, SIAM International Conference on Data Mining, 2005.

On Spectral Learning
of Mixtures of Distributions

Dimitris Achlioptas[1] and Frank McSherry[2]

[1] Microsoft Research, One Microsoft Way, Redmond WA 98052, USA
[2] Microsoft Research, 1065 La Avenida, Mountain View CA 94043, USA
{optas, mcsherry}@microsoft.com

Abstract. We consider the problem of learning mixtures of distributions via spectral methods and derive a characterization of when such methods are useful. Specifically, given a mixture-sample, let $\overline{\mu}_i, \overline{C}_i, \overline{w}_i$ denote the empirical mean, covariance matrix, and mixing weight of the samples from the i-th component. We prove that a very simple algorithm, namely spectral projection followed by single-linkage clustering, properly classifies every point in the sample provided that each pair of means $\overline{\mu}_i, \overline{\mu}_j$ is well separated, in the sense that $\|\overline{\mu}_i - \overline{\mu}_j\|^2$ is at least $\|\overline{C}_i\|_2(1/\overline{w}_i + 1/\overline{w}_j)$ plus a term that depends on the concentration properties of the distributions in the mixture. This second term is very small for many distributions, including Gaussians, Log-concave, and many others. As a result, we get the best known bounds for learning mixtures of arbitrary Gaussians in terms of the required mean separation. At the same time, we prove that there are many Gaussian mixtures $\{(\mu_i, C_i, w_i)\}$ such that each pair of means is separated by $\|C_i\|_2(1/w_i + 1/w_j)$, yet upon spectral projection the mixture collapses completely, i.e., all means and covariance matrices in the projected mixture are identical.

Keywords: learning mixtures of distributions, spectral methods, singular value decomposition, gaussians mixtures, log-concave and concentrated distributions.

1 Introduction

A mixture of k distributions $D_1, \ldots, D_k$ with mixing weights $w_1, \ldots, w_k$, where $\sum_i w_1 = 1$, is the distribution in which each sample is drawn from D_i with probability w_i. Learning mixtures of distributions is a classical problem in statistics and learning theory (see [4, 5]). Perhaps the most studied case is that of learning Gaussian mixtures. In such a mixture, each constituent distribution is a multivariate Gaussian, characterized by a mean vector $\mu_i \in \mathbb{R}^d$ and an arbitrary covariance matrix $C_i = R_i R_i^T \in \mathbb{R}^{d \times d}$. That is, a sample from the i-th Gaussian is a vector $\mu_i + R_i x$, where $x \in \mathbb{R}^d$ is a vector whose components are i.i.d. $N(0,1)$ random variables. We let $\sigma_i^2 = \|C_i\|$ denote the maximum directional variance of each Gaussian, where $\| \cdot \|$ denotes the matrix spectral norm.

P. Auer and R. Meir (Eds.): COLT 2005, LNAI 3559, pp. 458–469, 2005.
© Springer-Verlag Berlin Heidelberg 2005

We begin with discussing some earlier works on learning Gaussian mixtures, which serve as the motivation (and canonical model) for our work. A generally fruitful approach to learning mixtures of Gaussians is to start by projecting the samples onto a low dimensional space. This idea, originated in non-parametric statistics in the 60s, is motivated by the fact that reducing the dimensionality of the host space, dramatically reduces the number of potential component separators, thus affording a more complete search among them. Moreover, it is well-known that the projection of a Gaussian mixture onto a fixed subspace is also a Gaussian mixture, one in which the means and mixing weights behave in the obvious way, while the covariance matrices get transformed to new matrices of no greater maximum directional variance.

Dasgupta [2] pioneered the idea of projecting Gaussian mixtures onto *random* low-dimensional subspaces. For a typical subspace, the separation of each mean μ_i from the other means shrinks at the same rate as $\mathbf{E}[\|R_i x\|^2]$, i.e., in proportion to the reduction in dimension. Thus, the random projection's main feature is to aid clustering algorithms that are exponential in the dimension. But, in order for a mixture to not collapse under a typical projection the separation between means μ_i, μ_j needs to grow as $(\sigma_i + \sigma_j) \times d^{1/2}$, i.e., not only must the Gaussians not touch but, in fact, they must be pulled further and further apart as their dimensionality grows.

In [3], Dasgupta and Schulman reduced this requirement to $(\sigma_i + \sigma_j) \times d^{1/4}$ for spherical Gaussians by showing that, in fact, under this conditions the EM algorithm can be initialized so as to learn the μ_i in only two rounds. Arora and Kannan [1] combined random projections with sophisticated distance-concentration arguments in the context of learning mixtures of general Gaussians. In their work, the separation of means is not the only relevant parameter and their results apply to many cases where a worst-case mixture with the given separation characteristics is not learnable by any algorithm. That said, the worst case separation required by the results in [1] is also $(\sigma_i + \sigma_j) \times d^{1/4}$.

Rather than projecting the mixture onto a random subspace, we could dream of projecting it onto the subspace spanned by the mean vectors. This would greatly enhance the "contrast" in the projected mixture since $\mathbf{E}[\|R_i x\|^2]$ is reduced as before, but the projected means remain fixed and, thus, at the same distance. Recently, Vempala and Wang [6] did just this, by exploiting the fact that in the case of *spherical* Gaussians, as the number of samples grows, the subspace spanned by the top singular vectors of the data set converges to the subspace spanned by the mean vectors. This allowed them to give a very simple and elegant algorithm for learning spherical Gaussians which works as long as each pair of means μ_i, μ_j is separated by $(\sigma_i + \sigma_j) \times k^{1/4}$, i.e., a length independent of the original dimensionality.

Unfortunately, for non-spherical Gaussians the singular vector subspace does not in general convergence to the subspace spanned by the means. Vempala and Wang [6] observed this and asked if spectral projections can be useful for distributions that are not weakly isotropic, e.g. non-spherical Gaussians. In recent related work, Kannan, Salmasian, and Vempala [8] show how to use spectral projections to learn mixtures of Log-concave distributions in which each pair of means μ_i, μ_j is separated by, roughly, $k^{3/2}(\sigma_i + \sigma_j)/w_{\min}^2$.

Here, we show that combining spectral projection with single-linkage clustering gives a method for recursively dissecting mixtures of concentrated distributions, e.g., Gaussian mixtures, when each pair of means μ_i, μ_j in the mixture is separated by $(\sigma_i + \sigma_j)(1/w_i + 1/w_j)^{1/2}$, plus a term describing the concentration of the constituent distributions. For example, for Gaussian mixtures this second term is of order $(\sigma_i + \sigma_j)(k + (k \log n)^{1/2})$.

At the same time, we also provide a lower bound that demonstrate that for spectral projection, separation in excess of $(\sigma_i + \sigma_j)(1/w_i + 1/w_j)^{1/2}$ is mandatory. That is, we prove that for any set of mixing weights $w_1, \ldots, w_k$, there is an arrangement of *identical* Gaussians, with maximal directional variance σ where every pair of means μ_i, μ_j is separated by $\sigma(1/w_i + 1/w_j)^{1/2}$, yet upon spectral projection the mixture collapses completely, i.e., all means and covariance matrices in the projected mixture are identical. Thus, with the exception of the concentration term, our upper and lower bounds coincide.

We should mention briefly an important difference of our approach as compared to much previous work. Given as input some $k' \geq k$, our algorithm recursively subdivides the data set using cuts that respect mixture boundaries whenever applied to mixtures with at least two components present. Unlike previous work, our algorithm does not terminate with a partition of the input samples into k sets, but instead continues subdivision, returning a hierarchy that describes many legitimate k-partitions for varying values of k. This subdivision tree admits simple dynamic programming algorithms that can reconstruct k-partitions minimizing a variety of loss functions, which we discuss later in further detail. Importantly, it gives the flexibility to explore several values of k in a uniform manner. Computing each cut in this tree reduces to computing the top k singular vectors of a sample submatrix followed by a Minimum Spanning Tree computation on the corresponding projected sample. As a result, a naive implementation of our algorithm runs in time $O(kd^3n^2)$. If one is a bit more careful and performs the MST computations on appropriately large subsamples, the running time becomes linear in n, specifically $O(n(k^2d^2 + d^3)/w_{\min})$.

2   Our Techniques and Results

From this point on, we adopt the convention of viewing the data set as a collection of samples with hidden labels, rather than samples from a pre-specified mixture of distributions. This will let us describe sufficient conditions for correct clustering that are independent of properties of the distributions. Of course, we must eventually determine the probability that a specific distribution yields samples with the requisite properties, but deferring this discussion clarifies the results, and aids in their generality.

Our exposition uses sample statistics: $\overline{\mu}_i$, $\overline{\sigma}_i$, and $\overline{w}_i$. These are the empirical analogues of μ_i, σ_i, and w_i, computed from a $d \times n$ matrix of labeled samples A. We also use $\overline{n}_i$ to denote the number of samples in the mixture with label i.

The advantages of sample statistics are twofold: i) they allow for more concise and accurate proofs, and ii) they yield pointwise bounds that may be applied to arbitrary sets of samples. We will later discuss the convergence of the sample statistics to their distributional equivalents, but for now the reader may think of them as equivalent.

2.1   Spectral Projection and Perturbation

We start our analysis with an important tool from linear algebra: the optimal rank k column projection. For every matrix A and integer k, there exists a rank k projection matrix P_A such that for any other matrix X of rank at most k,

$$\|A - P_A A\| \leq \|A - X\| . \tag{1}$$

The matrix P_A is spanned by the top k left singular vectors of A, read from A's singular value decomposition.

Our key technical result is that the sample means $\bar{\mu}_i$ are only slightly perturbed when projected through P_A. We use the notation $\bar{\sigma}^2 = \sum_i \bar{w}_i \bar{\sigma}_i^2$ for the weighted maximum directional variance.

Theorem 1. *For any set A of labeled samples, for all i, $\|\bar{\mu}_i - P_A \bar{\mu}_i\| \leq \bar{\sigma}/\bar{w}_i^{1/2}$.*

Proof. Let $x_i \in \{0, 1/\bar{n}_i\}^n$ be the scaled characteristic vector of samples in A with label i, i.e., $x_i^q = 1/\bar{n}_i$ iff the q-th sample has label i. Thus, $\bar{\mu}_i = A x_i$ and

$$\|\bar{\mu}_i - P_A \bar{\mu}_i\| = \|(A - P_A A)x_i\| < \|A - P_A A\| \|x_i\| \leq \|A - P_A A\|/\bar{n}_i^{1/2} . \tag{2}$$

Let B be the $d \times n$ matrix that results by replacing each sample (column) in A by the empirical mean of its component. B has rank at most k, and so by (1)

$$\|A - P_A A\| \leq \|A - B\| . \tag{3}$$

Write $D = A - B$ and let D_j be the $d \times \bar{n}_j$ submatrix of samples with label j, so that $\|D_j D_j^T / \bar{n}_j\| = \bar{\sigma}_j^2$. Then

$$\|D\|^2 = \|DD^T\| = \|\sum_j D_j D_j^T\| \leq \sum_j \|D_j D_j^T\| = \sum_j \bar{\sigma}_j^2 \bar{n}_j = \bar{\sigma}^2 n . \tag{4}$$

Combining (2),(3) and (4) we get $\|\bar{\mu}_i - P_A \bar{\mu}_i\| \leq \bar{\sigma}(n/\bar{n}_i)^{1/2} = \bar{\sigma}/\bar{w}_i^{1/2}$.   □

Theorem 1 and the triangle inequality immediately imply that for every i, j the separation of $\bar{\mu}_i, \bar{\mu}_j$ is reduced by the projection onto P_A by no more than

$$\|(\bar{\mu}_i - \bar{\mu}_j) - P_A(\bar{\mu}_i - \bar{\mu}_j)\| \leq \bar{\sigma}(1/\bar{w}_i^{1/2} + 1/\bar{w}_j^{1/2}) . \tag{5}$$

In Theorem 2 below we sharpen (5) slightly (representing an improvement of no more than a factor of $\sqrt{2}$). As we will prove in Section 4, the result of Theorem 2 is *tight*.

Theorem 2. *For any set A of labeled samples, for all i, j, $\|(\overline{\mu}_i - \overline{\mu}_j) - P_A(\overline{\mu}_i - \overline{\mu}_j)\| \leq \overline{\sigma}(1/\overline{w}_i + 1/\overline{w}_j)^{1/2}$.*

Proof. Analogously to Theorem 1, we now choose $x_{ij} \in \{0, 1/\overline{n}_i, -1/\overline{n}_j\}^n$ so that $\overline{\mu}_i - \overline{\mu}_j = A x_{ij}$ and $\|x_{ij}\| = (1/\overline{n}_i + 1/\overline{n}_j)^{1/2}$. Recall that by (3) and (4) we have $\|(A - P_A A)\| \leq \overline{\sigma} n^{1/2}$. Thus,

$$
\begin{aligned}
\|(\overline{\mu}_i - \overline{\mu}_j) - P_A(\overline{\mu}_i - \overline{\mu}_j)\| &= \|(A - P_A A)x_{ij}\| \\
&\leq \|A - P_A A\|(1/\overline{n}_i + 1/\overline{n}_j)^{1/2} \\
&= \overline{\sigma}(1/\overline{w}_i + 1/\overline{w}_j)^{1/2} .
\end{aligned}
$$

$\square$

2.2   Combining Spectral Projection and Single-Linkage

We now describe a simple partitioning algorithm combining spectral projection and single-linkage that takes as input a training set A, a set to separate B, and a parameter k. The algorithm computes an optimal rank k projection for the samples in A which it applies to the samples in B. Then, it applies single-linkage to the projected samples, i.e., it computes their minimum spanning tree and removes the longest edge from it.

Separate(A, B, k):

1. Construct the Minimum Spanning Tree on $P_A B$ with respect to the 2-norm.
2. Cut the longest edge, and return the connected components.

Separate will be the core primitive we build upon in the following sections, and so it is important to understand the conditions under which it is guaranteed to return a proper cut.

Theorem 3. *Assume that A, B are sets of samples containing the same set of labels and that the sample statistics of A satisfy, with $i = \arg\max_i \overline{\sigma}_i$,*

$$
\forall j \neq i : \quad \|\overline{\mu}_i - \overline{\mu}_j\| > \overline{\sigma}_i(1/\overline{w}_i + 1/\overline{w}_j)^{1/2} + 4 \max_{x_u \in B} \|P_A(x_u - \overline{\mu}_u)\| . \quad (6)
$$

*If B contains at least two labels, then **Separate**(A, B, k) does not separate samples of the same label.*

Proof. The proof idea is that after projecting B on P_A, the samples in B with label i will be sufficiently distant from all other samples so that the following is true: all intra-label distances are shorter than the shortest inter-label distance involving label i. As a result, by the time an inter-label edge involving label i is added to the Minimum Spanning Tree, the samples of each label already form a connected component.

By the triangle inequality, the largest intra-label distance is at most

$$
\|P_A(x_i - x_j)\| \leq 2 \max_{x_v \in B} \|P_A(x_v - \overline{\mu}_v)\| . \quad (7)
$$

On the other hand, also by the triangle inequality, all inter-label distances are at least

$$\|P_A(x_i - x_j)\| \geq \|P_A(\overline{\mu}_i - \overline{\mu}_j)\| - 2 \max_{x_v \in B} \|P_A(x_v - \overline{\mu}_v)\| . \tag{8}$$

To bound $\|P_A(\overline{\mu}_i - \overline{\mu}_j)\|$ from below we first apply the triangle inequality one more time to get (9). We then bound the first term in (9) from below using (6) and the second term using Theorem 2, thus getting

$$\|P_A(\overline{\mu}_i - \overline{\mu}_j)\| \geq \|\overline{\mu}_i - \overline{\mu}_j\| - \|(I - P_A)(\overline{\mu}_i - \overline{\mu}_j)\| \tag{9}$$

$$> (\overline{\sigma}_i - \overline{\sigma})(1/\overline{w}_i + 1/\overline{w}_j)^{1/2} + 4 \max_{x_v \in B} \|P_A(x_v - \overline{\mu}_v)\| . \tag{10}$$

As $\overline{\sigma}_i \geq \overline{\sigma}$, combining (8) and (10) we see, by (7), that all inter-label distances involving label i have length exceeding the upper bound on intra-label distances.

$\square$

2.3 k-Partitioning the Full Sample Set

Given two sets of samples A, B and a parameter k, **Separate** bisects B by projecting it onto the optimal rank k subspace of A and applying single-linkage clustering. Now, we show how to use **Separate** recursively and build an algorithm **Segment** which on input A, B, k outputs a full k-partition of B. To classify n sample points from a mixture of distributions we simply partition them at random into two sets X, Y and invoke **Segment** twice, with each set being used once as the training set and once as the set to be partitioned.

Applying **Separate** recursively is non-trivial. Imagine that we are given sets A, B meeting the conditions of Theorem 3 and by running **Separate**(A, B, k) we now have a valid bipartition $B = B_1 \cup B_2$. Recall that one of the conditions in Theorem 3 is that the two sets given as input to **Separate** contain the same set of labels. Therefore, if we try to apply **Separate** to either B_1 or B_2 using A as the training set we are guaranteed to not meet that condition! Another, more technical, problem is that we would like each recursive invocation to succeed or fail independently of the rest. Using the same training set for all invocations introduces probabilistic dependencies among them that are very difficult to deal with.

To address these two problems we will need to be a bit more sophisticated in our use of recursion: given sets A, B rather than naively running **Separate**(A, B, k), we will instead first subsample A to get a training set A_1 and then invoke **Separate**$(A_1, A \cup B - A_1, k)$. The idea is that if A_1 is big enough it will have all the good statistical properties of A (as demanded by Theorem 3) and **Separate** will return a valid bipartition of $A \cup B - A_1$. The benefit, of course, is that each part of B will now be accompanied by the subset of $A - A_1$ of same labels. Therefore, we can now simply discard A_1 and proceed to apply the same idea to each of the two returned parts, as we know which points in each part came from A and which came from B.

Our algorithm **Segment** will very much follow the above idea, the only difference being that rather than doing subsampling with each recursive call we will fix a partition of $A = A_1 \cup \cdots \cup A_k$ at the outset and use it throughout the recursion. More specifically, we will think of the execution of **Segment** as a full binary tree with $2^k - 1$ nodes, each of which will correspond to an invocation of **Separate**. In each level $1 \leq \ell \leq k$ of the tree, all invocations will use A_ℓ as the training set and they will partition some subset of $A_{\ell+1} \cup \cdots \cup A_k \cup B$. So, for example, at the second level of the tree, there will be two calls to **Separate**, both using A_2 as the training set and each one partitioning the subset of $A \cup B - A_1$ that resulted by the split at level 1. Clearly, one of these two parts can already consist of samples from only one label, in which case the invocation at level 2 will produce a bipartition which is arbitrary (and useless). Nevertheless, as long as these are the only invocations in which samples with the same label are split, there exists a subset of k nodes in the tree which corresponds exactly to the labels in B. As we will see, we will be able to identify this subset in time $O(k^2 \min(n, 2^k))$ by dynamic programming.

Formally, **Segment** takes as input a sample set $S \subseteq A \cup B$ and a parameter ℓ indicating the level. Its output is the hierarchical partition of S as captured by the binary tree mentioned above. To simplify notation below, we assume that the division of A into $A_1, \ldots, A_k$ is known to the algorithm.

Segment(S, ℓ)
1. Let $[L, R] = $ **Separate**$(A_\ell \cap S, S \setminus A_\ell, k)$.
2. If $\ell < k$ invoke **Segment**$(L, \ell + 1)$ and **Segment**$(R, \ell + 1)$.

To state the conditions that guarantee the success of **Segment** we need to introduce some notation. For each i, ℓ, let $\overline{\mu}_i^\ell$, $\overline{\sigma}_i^\ell$, and $\overline{w}_i^\ell$ be the sample statistics associated with label i in A_ℓ. For each vector $\mathbf{v} \subseteq \{1, \ldots, k\}$ let $A_\ell^{\mathbf{v}}$ denote the set of samples from A_ℓ with labels from $\mathbf{v}$, and let $B_\ell^{\mathbf{v}}$ denote the set of samples from $\bigcup_{m > \ell} A_m \cup B$ with labels from $\mathbf{v}$. Finally, we say that a hierarchical clustering is *label-respecting* if for any set of at least two labels, the clustering does not separate samples of the same label.

Theorem 4. *Assume that $A_1, \ldots, A_k$ and B each contain the same set of labels and that for every pair $(\ell, \mathbf{v})$, with $i = \arg\max_{i \in \mathbf{v}} \overline{\sigma}_i^\ell$, we have:*

$$\forall j \in \mathbf{v} - i: \quad \|\overline{\mu}_i^\ell - \overline{\mu}_j^\ell\| \geq \overline{\sigma}_i^\ell (1/\overline{w}_i^\ell + 1/\overline{w}_j^\ell)^{1/2} + 4 \max_{x_u \in B_\ell^{\mathbf{v}}} \|P_{A_\ell^{\mathbf{v}}}(x_u - \overline{\mu}_u^\ell)\| .$$

The hierarchical clustering **Segment**$(A \cup B, 1)$ *produces will be label-respecting.*

Proof. The proof is inductive, starting with the inductive hypothesis that in any invocation of **Segment**(S, ℓ) where S contains at least two labels, the set S equals $B_{\ell-1}^{\mathbf{v}}$ for some $\mathbf{v}$. Therefore, we need to prove that **Separate**$(A_\ell \cap S, S \setminus A_\ell, k) = $ **Separate**$(A_\ell^{\mathbf{v}}, B_\ell^{\mathbf{v}}, k)$ will produce sets L and R that do not share labels.

For every $(\mathbf{v}, \ell)$, if $i = \arg\max_{i \in \mathbf{v}} \overline{\sigma}_i^\ell$, our assumed separation guarantees that label i satisfies

$$\forall j \in \mathbf{v} - i: \quad \|\overline{\mu}_i^\ell - \overline{\mu}_j^\ell\| \geq \overline{\sigma}_i^\ell (1/\overline{w}_i^\ell + 1/\overline{w}_j^\ell)^{1/2} + 4 \max_{x_u \in B_\ell^{\mathbf{v}}} \|P_{A_\ell^{\mathbf{v}}}(x_u - \overline{\mu}_u^\ell)\| .$$

While the above separation condition refers to the sample statistics of A_ℓ, when we restrict our attention to A_ℓ^y, the samples means and standard deviations do not change and the sample mixing weights only increase. Therefore, the requirements of Theorem 3 hold for A_ℓ^y, B_ℓ^y concluding the proof.   □

Given the hierarchical clustering generated by **Segment** we must still determine which set of $k-1$ splits is correct. We will, in fact, solve a slightly more general problem. Given an arbitrary function scoring subsets of B, $score : 2^B \to \mathbb{R}$, we will find the k-partition of the samples with highest total (sum) score. For many distributions, such as Gaussians, there are efficient estimators of the likelihood that a set of data was generated from the distribution and such estimators can be used as the score function. For example, in cross training log-likelihood estimators, the subset under consideration is randomly partitioned into two parts. First, the parameters of the distribution are learned using one part and then the likelihood of the other part given these parameters is computed.

We will use dynamic programming to efficiently determine which subset set of $k - 1$ splits corresponds to a k-partition for which the sum of the scores of its parts is highest. As one of the options in the $k-1$ splits by labels, our result will score at least as high as the latent partition. The dynamic program computes, for every node S in the tree and integer $i \le k$, the quantity $opt(S, i)$, the optimal score gained by budgeting i parts to the subset S. If we let $S = L \cup R$ be the cut associated with S, the dynamic program is defined by the rules

$$opt(S, 1) = score(S) \text{ and } opt(S, i) = \max_{j < i}[opt(L, j) + opt(R, i - j)] .$$

We are ultimately interested in $opt(B, k)$ which we can be computed efficiently in a bottom up fashion in time $O(k^2 \min(n, 2^k))$.

Finally, all of the techniques that we have used to partition B can be used to partition A. We can divide B into k sets $B_1, \dots B_k$ to use as training in the classification of A. For all but the most obtuse sets of samples, a random partition into A and B will yield samples for which $\|\overline{\mu}_i^A - \overline{\mu}_j^B\|$ is minimized at $i = j$ allowing us to merge the partition of A with the partition of B. We avoid stating a theorem generally about the combination of these three steps, but do so in the next section with concrete distributions.

3   Results for Gaussian, Log-Concave, and Concentrated Mixtures

We now examine how our results apply to specific distributions, such as Gaussian and Log-concave distributions, as well as a more general class that we define below. In fact, we will start with the more general class, and instantiate the other two from it.

First, we say that a distribution x is f-concentrated for a function $f : \mathbb{R} \to \mathbb{R}$ if for every unit vector v

$$\Pr\left[|v^T(x - \mathbf{E}[x])| > f(\delta)\right] \le \delta . \tag{11}$$

In words, when we project the distribution onto any fixed line, a random sample will be within $f(\delta)$ of the mean with probability $1 - \delta$. Second, we say that a distribution is *g-convergent* for a function $g : \mathbb{R} \to \mathbb{R}$ if a sample of size $g(\delta)$ with probability $1 - \delta$ satisfies

$$\|\overline{\mu} - \mu\| \leq \sigma/8 \quad \text{and} \quad \sigma/2 \leq \overline{\sigma} \leq 2\sigma , \tag{12}$$

where $\overline{\mu}$ and $\overline{\sigma}^2$ denote the sample mean and the sample maximum directional variance, respectively.

Before proceeding, we prove an extension of f-concentration to low dimensional projections:

Lemma 1. *Let x be a distribution that is f-concentrated. For any fixed k dimensional projection P,*

$$\Pr\left[\|P(x - \mathbf{E}[x])\| > k^{1/2} f(\delta/k)\right] \leq \delta .$$

Proof. Given any set of k orthogonal basis vectors $v_1, \ldots, v_k$ for the space associated with P, we can write $P = \sum_i v_i v_i^T$. As the v_i are orthonormal, we can use the Pythagorean equality

$$\|P(x - \mathbf{E}[x])\|^2 \;=\; \|\sum_i v_i v_i^T (x - \mathbf{E}[x])\|^2 \;=\; \sum_i |v_i^T(x - \mathbf{E}[x])|^2 . \tag{13}$$

Taking a union bound, the probability that any of the k terms in the last sum exceeds $f(\delta/k)^2$ is at most δ, giving a squared distance of at most $k f(\delta/k)^2$ and completing the proof. □

With these definitions in hand, we now state and prove a result about the classification of concentrated, convergent distributions.

Theorem 5. *Consider any mixture of k distributions where each distribution i is f_i-concentrated and g_i-convergent. Assume that A contains at least*

$$k \times \max_i \left(\left(g_i(\delta/k^2) + 8\log(k^2/\delta)\right) w_i^{-1} \right)$$

samples from the mixture and that B contains n samples. If

$$\forall i, \forall j \neq i: \quad \|\mu_i - \mu_j\| > 4\sigma_i(1/w_i + 1/w_j)^{1/2} + 4k^{1/2} \max_{\sigma_v < 4\sigma_i} f_v\left(\frac{\delta}{nk2^k}\right)$$

then with probability at least $1 - 3\delta$, the hierarchical clustering produced by **Segment**$(A \cup B, 1)$ *will be label-respecting.*

Proof. We argue that with probability $1 - 3\delta$ the sets $A_1, \ldots, A_k, B$ meet the conditions of Theorem 4.

As A is broken uniformly into $A_1, \ldots, A_k$, each of these k sets will contain a number of samples that is at least $\max_i \left(g_i(\delta/k^2)/w_i + 8\log(k^2/\delta)/w_i\right)$. Importantly, the first term is sufficient to ensure that with probability $1 - \delta$ each of the mixtures in each of A_ℓ have "converged", in the sense of (12). The second term ensures that with probability $1 - \delta$ we have $\overline{w}_i^\ell \geq w_i/2$ for each i, ℓ.

Given these bounds relating the sample statistics to their limits, and letting $s = \frac{\delta}{nk2^k}$ to simplify notation, the assumed separation of $\|\mu_i - \mu_j\|$ ensures that for all ℓ, for all i, and for all $j \neq i$,

$$\|\overline{\mu}_i^\ell - \overline{\mu}_j^\ell\| > \overline{\sigma}_i^\ell (1/\overline{w}_i^\ell + 1/\overline{w}_j^\ell)^{1/2} + 4 \max_{\sigma_u < 4\sigma_i} \left(k^{1/2} f_u(s) + \|\mu_u - \overline{\mu}_u^\ell\| \right) \quad (14)$$

As there are at most $k2^k$ matrices A_ℓ^v, the f_i-concentration of the distributions ensures that with probability at least $1 - \delta$, for all $A_\ell^\mathsf{v}, B_\ell^\mathsf{v}$

$$\max_{x_u \in B_\ell^\mathsf{v}} \|P_{A_\ell^\mathsf{v}}(x_u - \mu_u)\| \leq k^{1/2} \max_{j \in \mathsf{v}} f_j(s) \ . \quad (15)$$

By the triangle inequality and submultiplicativity,

$$\max_{x_u \in B_\ell^\mathsf{v}} \|P_{A_\ell^\mathsf{v}}(x_u - \overline{\mu}_u^\ell)\| \leq \max_{j \in \mathsf{v}} \left(k^{1/2} f_j(s) + \|\mu_j - \overline{\mu}_j^\ell\| \right) \ . \quad (16)$$

Now, for each ℓ, v, from (12) we have that for any $\overline{\sigma}_j^\ell \leq \overline{\sigma}_i^\ell$, it is the case that $\sigma_j \leq 4\sigma_i$. Specifically, considering $i = \arg\max_{i \in \mathsf{v}} \overline{\sigma}_i^\ell$ we have that

$$\max_{j \in \mathsf{v}} \left(k^{1/2} f_j(s) + \|\mu_j - \overline{\mu}_j^\ell\| \right) \leq \max_{\sigma_u \leq 4\sigma_i} \left(k^{1/2} f_u(s) + \|\mu_u - \overline{\mu}_u^\ell\| \right) \ . \quad (17)$$

Combining (15), (16), and (17) with (14), we see that for all ℓ, v, if we let $i = \arg\max_{i \in \mathsf{v}} \overline{\sigma}_i^\ell$, then

$$\forall j \in \mathsf{v} - i \quad \|\overline{\mu}_i^\ell - \overline{\mu}_j^\ell\| > \overline{\sigma}_i^\ell (1/\overline{w}_i^\ell + 1/\overline{w}_j^\ell)^{1/2} + 4 \max_{x_u \in B_\ell^\mathsf{v}} \|P_{A_\ell^\mathsf{v}}(x_u - \overline{\mu}_u^\ell)\| \ .$$

$\square$

3.1   Gaussian and Log-Concave Mixtures

We now show that for mixtures of both Gaussian and Log-concave distributions, **Segment** produces a hierarchical clustering that is label-respecting, as desired. From this, using dynamic programming as discussed in Section 2.3, we can efficiently find the k-partition that maximizes any scoring function which scores each part independently of the others. For example, in the case of Gaussians, this allows us to find a k-partition with cross-training log-likelihood at least as high as the latent partition in time $O(k^2 \min(n, 2^k))$.

Theorem 6. *Consider any mixture of k Gaussian distributions with parameters $\{(\mu_i, \sigma_i, w_i)\}$ and assume that $n \gg k(d + \log k)/w_{\min}$ is such that*

$$\forall i \, \forall j : \quad \|\mu_i - \mu_j\| \geq 4\sigma_i(1/w_i + 1/w_i)^{1/2} + 4\sigma_i(k \log(nk) + k^2)^{1/2} \ .$$

*Let A and B each contain n samples from the mixture and partition $A = A_1 \cup \ldots \cup A_k$ randomly. With probability that tends to 1 as $n \to \infty$, the hierarchical clustering produced by **Segment**$(A \cup B, 1)$ will be label-respecting.*

Proof. Standard results show that any Gaussian is f-concentrated for $f(\delta) = \sigma(2\log(1/\delta))^{1/2}$. Using techniques from Soshnikov [7] describing concentration of the median of σ_i^ℓ for various sample counts, one can show that a d-dimensional Gaussian with maximum directional variance σ^2 is g-convergent for $g(\delta) = cd\log(1/\delta)$ for a universal constant c.   □

A recent related paper of Kannan et al. [8] shows that Log-concave distributions, those for which the logarithm of the probability density function is concave, are also reasonably concentrated and convergent.

Theorem 7. *Given a mixture of k Log-concave distributions with parameters $\{(\mu_i, \sigma_i, w_i)\}$ assume that for some fixed $n \gg k(d(\log d)^5 + \log k)/w_{\min}$ the following holds:*

$$\forall i \,\forall j : \quad \|\mu_i - \mu_j\| \geq 4\sigma_i(1/w_i + 1/w_i)^{1/2} + 4\sigma_i k^{1/2}(\log(nk) + k) \ .$$

*Let A and B each contain n samples from the mixture and partition $A = A_1 \cup \ldots \cup A_k$ randomly. With probability that tends to 1 as $n \to \infty$, the hierarchical clustering produced by **Segment**$(A \cup B, 1)$ will be label-respecting.*

Proof. Lemma 2 of [8] shows that any Log-concave distribution is f-concentrated for $f(\delta) = \sigma\log(1/\delta)$. Lemma 4 of [8] shows that for any Log-concave distribution there is a constant c such that the distribution is g-convergent for $g(\delta) = cd(\log(d/\delta))^5$.   □

4   Lower Bounds

We now argue that for any set of mixing weights $w_1, \ldots, w_k$, there is an arrangement of *identical* Gaussians for which spectral projection is not an option. This also demonstrates that the bound in Theorem 1 is tight.

Theorem 8. *For any $\sum_i w_i = 1$, there exists a mixture of Gaussians with $\|C_i\| = \sigma^2$ satisfying*

$$\|\mu_i - \mu_j\| = \sigma(1/w_i + 1/w_j)^{1/2} \tag{18}$$

for which the optimal rank k subspace for the distribution is arbitrary.

Proof. We choose the μ_i to be mutually orthogonal and of norm $\sigma/w_i^{1/2}$. To each we assign the common covariance matrix $C = \sigma^2 I - \sum_i w_i \mu_i \mu_i^T$. The optimal rank k subspace for the distribution is the optimal rank k subspace for the expected outer product of a random sample x from the mixture which is

$$\mathbf{E}[xx^T] \;=\; \sum_i w_i \mu_i \mu_i^T + \sum_i w_i C \;=\; \sigma^2 I \ .$$

Since the identity matrix favors no dimensions for its optimal approximation, the proof is complete.   □

Remark: The theorem above only describes a mixture for which there is no preference for a particular subspace. By diminishing the norms of the μ_i ever so slightly, we can set the optimal rank k subspace arbitrarily and ensure that it does not intersect the span of the means.

Remark: One can construct counterexamples with covariance matrices of great generality, so long as they discount the span of the means $\sum_i w_i \mu_i \mu_i^T$, and promote some other k dimensions. In particular, the $d - 2k$ additional dimensions can have 0 variance, demonstrating that the maximum variance $\sigma^2 = \|C\|_2^2$ is the parameter of interest, as opposed to the average variance $\|C\|_F^2/d$, or any other function that depends on more than the first k singular values of C.

Remark: If one is willing to weaken Theorem 8 slightly by dividing the RHS of (18) by 2, then we can take as the common covariance matrix $C = 2\sigma^2 I - \sum_i w_i \mu_i \mu_i^T$, which has eccentricity bounded by 2. Bounded eccentricity was an important assumption of Dasgupta [2], who used random projections, but we see here that it does not substantially change the lower bound.

References

1. S. Arora and R. Kannan, Learning mixtures of arbitrary Gaussians, In Proc. *33rd ACM Symposium on Theory of Computation*, 247–257, 2001.
2. S. Dasgupta, Learning mixtures of Gaussians, In Proc. *40th IEEE Symposium on Foundations of Computer Science*, 634–644, 1999.
3. S. Dasgupta, L. Schulman, A 2-round variant of EM for Gaussian mixtures, In Proc. *16th Conference on Uncertainty in Artificial Intelligence*, 152–159, 2000.
4. B. Lindsay, Mixture models: theory, geometry and applications, *American Statistical Association*, Virginia, 2002.
5. D.M. Titterington, A.F.M. Smith, and U.E. Makov, *Statistical analysis of finite mixture distributions*, Wiley, 1985.
6. S. Vempala and G. Wang, A Spectral Algorithm of Learning Mixtures of Distributions, In Proc. *43rd IEEE Symposium on Foundations of Computer Science*, 113–123, 2002.
7. A. Soshnikov, A Note on Universality of the Distribution of the Largest Eigenvalues in Certain Sample Covariance Matrices, *J. Stat. Phys.*, v.108, Nos. 5/6, pp. 1033–1056, (2002)
8. H. Salmasian, R. Kannan, S. Vempala, The Spectral Method for Mixture Models, In *Electronic Colloquium on Computational Complexity (ECCC)* (067), 2004.

From Graphs to Manifolds – Weak and Strong Pointwise Consistency of Graph Laplacians

Matthias Hein[1], Jean-Yves Audibert[2], and Ulrike von Luxburg[3]

[1] Max Planck Institute for Biological Cybernetics, Tübingen, Germany
[2] CERTIS, ENPC, Paris, France
[3] Fraunhofer IPSI, Darmstadt, Germany

Abstract. In the machine learning community it is generally believed that graph Laplacians corresponding to a finite sample of data points converge to a continuous Laplace operator if the sample size increases. Even though this assertion serves as a justification for many Laplacian-based algorithms, so far only some aspects of this claim have been rigorously proved. In this paper we close this gap by establishing the strong pointwise consistency of a family of graph Laplacians with data-dependent weights to some weighted Laplace operator. Our investigation also includes the important case where the data lies on a submanifold of $\mathbb{R}^d$.

1 Introduction

In recent years, methods based on graph Laplacians have become increasingly popular. In machine learning they have been used for dimensionality reduction [1], semi-supervised learning [12], and spectral clustering (see [11] for references). The usage of graph Laplacians has often been justified by their relations to the continuous Laplace operator. Most people believe that for increasing sample size, the Laplace operator on the similarity graph generated by a sample converges in some sense to the Laplace operator on the underlying space. It is all the more surprising that rigorous convergence results for the setting given in machine learning do not exist. It is only for some cases where the graph has certain regularity properties such as a grid in $\mathbb{R}^d$ that results are known.

In the more difficult setting where the graph is generated randomly, only some aspects have been proven so far. The approach taken in this paper is first to establish the convergence of the discrete graph Laplacian to a continuous counterpart ("variance term"), and in a second step the convergence of this continuous operator to the continuous Laplace operator ("bias term"). For compact submanifolds in $\mathbb{R}^d$ the second step has already been studied by Belkin [1] for Gaussian weights and the uniform measure, and was then generalized to general isotropic weights and general densities by Lafon [7]. Belkin and Lafon show that the bias term converges pointwise for $h \to 0$, where h is the bandwidth of isotropic weights. However, the convergence of the variance term was left open in [1] and [7].

P. Auer and R. Meir (Eds.): COLT 2005, LNAI 3559, pp. 470–485, 2005.

The first work where, in a slightly different setting, both limit processes have been studied together is Bousquet et al. [3]. Using the law of large numbers for U-statistics, the authors studied the convergence of the regularizer $\Omega_n(f) = \langle f, L_n f \rangle$ for sample size $n \to \infty$ (where $f \in \mathbb{R}^n$ and L_n is the unnormalized graph Laplacian on n sample points). Then taking the limit for the bandwidth $h \to 0$ they arrived at a weighted Laplace operator in $\mathbb{R}^d$. The drawback of this approach is that the limits in n and h are not taken simultaneously.

In contrast to this work, in [11] the bandwidth h was kept fixed while the large sample limit $n \to \infty$ of the graph Laplacian (normalized and unnormalized) was considered. In this setting, the authors show strong convergence results of graph Laplacians to certain limit integral operators, which then even imply the convergence of the eigenvalues and eigenfunctions of the graph Laplacian.

The goal of this paper is to surpass the limitations of previous approaches. We study the convergence of both bias and variance term, where the limits $n \to \infty$ and $h \to 0$ are taken simultaneously. The main achievement of this paper is Theorem 3, where the strong pointwise consistency of the normalized graph Laplacian with varying data dependent weights as introduced in [4] is shown. The limit operator is in general a weighted Laplace-Beltrami operator. Based on our analysis we argue against using the unnormalized graph Laplacian.

We would like to mention that after submission of our manuscript, we learned that a result related to a special case of Theorem 2 has been proven independently by Belkin and Niyogi in their parallel COLT paper [2] and has been announced in [8] (see Section 4 for a short discussion).

Theorem 3 is proven as follows. In section 2 we introduce general graph Laplacians. Then in Section 3, we establish the first step of Theorem 3, namely the convergence of the bias term in the general case where the data lies on a submanifold M in $\mathbb{R}^d$. We prove that the difference between the weighted Laplace-Beltrami operator and its kernel-based approximation goes to zero when the bandwidth $h \to 0$. Then in Section 4 we show that the variance term, namely the difference between the normalized graph Laplacian and the kernel-based approximation, is small with high probability if $nh^{d+4}/\log n \to \infty$. Plugging both results together we arrive at the main result in Theorem 3.

2   The Graph Laplacian

In this section we define the graph Laplacian on an undirected graph. To this end one has to introduce Hilbert spaces H_V and H_E of functions on the vertices V resp. edges E, define a difference operator d, and then set the graph Laplacian as $\Delta = d^* d$. This approach is well-known in discrete potential theory and was independently introduced in [13]. In many articles, graph Laplacians are used without explicitly mentioning d, H_V and H_E. This can be misleading since there always exists a whole family of choices for d, H_V and H_E which all yield the same graph Laplacian.

Hilbert Space Structure on the Vertices V and the Edges E: Let (V, W) be a graph, where V denotes the set of vertices with $|V| = n$, and W is a positive, symmetric $n \times n$ similarity matrix, that is $w_{ij} = w_{ji}$ and $w_{ij} \geq 0$, $i, j = 1, \ldots, n$. We say that there is an (undirected) edge from i to j if $w_{ij} > 0$. Moreover, the degree function d is defined as $d_i = \sum_{j=1}^n w_{ij}$. We assume here that $d_i > 0$, $i = 1, \ldots, n$. That means that each vertex has at least one edge. The inner products on the function spaces $\mathbb{R}^V$ resp. $\mathbb{R}^E$ are defined as $\langle f, g \rangle_V = \sum_{i=1}^n f_i \, g_i \, \chi(d_i)$ and $\langle F, G \rangle_E = \frac{1}{2} \sum_{i,j=1}^n F_{ij} \, G_{ij} \, \phi(w_{ij})$, where $\chi : \mathbb{R}_+^* \to \mathbb{R}_+^*$, $\phi : \mathbb{R}_+^* \to \mathbb{R}_+^*$, and $\mathbb{R}_+^* = \{x \in \mathbb{R} | x > 0\}$. By our assumptions on the graph both inner products are well-defined. Let $\mathcal{H}(V, \chi) = (\mathbb{R}_V, \langle \cdot, \cdot \rangle_V)$ and $\mathcal{H}(E, \phi) = (\mathbb{R}^E, \langle \cdot, \cdot \rangle_E)$.

The Difference Operator d and its Adjoint d^*: We define the difference operator $d : \mathcal{H}(V, \chi) \to \mathcal{H}(E, \phi)$ as follows:

$$\forall \, e_{ij} \in E, \qquad (df)(e_{ij}) = \gamma(w_{ij})(f(j) - f(i)),$$

where $\gamma : \mathbb{R}_+^* \to \mathbb{R}_+^*$. In the case of a finite graph (i.e., $|V| < \infty$) d is always a bounded operator. The adjoint operator d^* is defined by $\langle df, u \rangle_E = \langle f, d^*u \rangle_V$, for any $f \in H(V, \chi), u \in \mathcal{H}(E, \phi)$. It is straightforward to derive

$$(d^*u)(l) = \frac{1}{2\chi(d_l)} \sum_{i=1}^n \gamma(w_{il}) \phi(w_{il})(u_{il} - u_{li}).$$

The two terms in the right hand side of Equation (1) can be interpreted as the outgoing resp. ingoing flow.

The General Graph Laplacian: The operator $\Delta : \mathcal{H}(V, \chi) \to \mathcal{H}(V, \chi)$ defined as $\Delta = d^*d$ is obviously self-adjoint and positive semi-definite:

$$\langle f, \Delta g \rangle_V = \langle df, dg \rangle_E = \langle \Delta f, g \rangle_V, \quad \langle f, \Delta f \rangle_V = \langle df, df \rangle_E \geq 0.$$

Using the definitions of the difference operator d and its adjoint d^* we can directly derive the graph Laplacian:

$$(\Delta f)(l) = (d^*df)(l) = \frac{1}{\chi(d_l)} \left[f(l) \sum_{i=1}^n \gamma(w_{il})^2 \phi(w_{il}) - \sum_{i=1}^n f(i) \gamma(w_{il})^2 \phi(w_{il}) \right].$$

The following operators are usually defined as the 'normalized' and 'unnormalized' graph Laplacian Δ_{nm} resp. Δ_{unm}:

$$(\Delta_{\mathrm{nm}} f)(i) = f(i) - \frac{1}{d_i} \sum_{j=1}^n w_{ij} f(j), \quad (\Delta_{\mathrm{unm}} f)(i) = d_i f(i) - \sum_{j=1}^n w_{ij} f(j).$$

We observe that there exist several choices of χ, γ and ϕ which result in Δ_{nm} or Δ_{unm}. Therefore it can cause confusion if one speaks of the 'normalized' or 'unnormalized' graph Laplacian without explicitly defining the corresponding Hilbert spaces and the difference operator. We just note that one can resolve this ambiguity at least partially if one not only asks for consistency of the graph Laplacian but also for consistency of $\mathcal{H}_V$. Unfortunately, due to space restrictions we cannot further elaborate on this topic.

3   The Weighted Laplacian and Its Approximations

The Laplacian is one of the most prominent operators in mathematics. Nevertheless, most books either deal with the Laplacian in $\mathbb{R}^d$ or the Laplace-Beltrami operator on a manifold M. Not so widely used is the weighted Laplacian on a manifold. This notion is useful when one studies a manifold with a measure, in our case the probability measure generating the data, which in the following we assume to be absolutely continuous wrt the natural volume element of the manifold[1]. In this section we show how the weighted Laplacian can be approximated pointwise by using kernel-based averaging operators. The main results are Theorem 1 and Corollary 1.

Approximations of the Laplace-Beltrami operator based on averaging with the Gaussian kernel have been studied in the special case of the uniform measure on a compact submanifold without boundary in Smolyanov et al.[9, 10] and Belkin [1]. Belkin's result was then generalized by Lafon [7] to general densities and to a wider class of isotropic, positive definite kernels. Whereas the proof of Theorem 1 in [7] applies for compact hypersurfaces[2] in $\mathbb{R}^d$, a proof for general compact submanifolds using boundary conditions is stated in [4]. In this section, we will prove Theorem 1 for general submanifolds M, including the case where M is not compact and without the assumptions of positive definiteness of the kernel nor with any boundary conditions[3]. Especially for dimensionality reduction the case of low-dimensional submanifolds in $\mathbb{R}^d$ is important. Notably, the analysis below also includes the case where due to noise the data is only concentrated around a submanifold. In this section we will use the Einstein summation convention.

Definition 1 (Weighted Laplacian). *Let (M, g_{ab}) be a Riemannian manifold with measure P, where P has a density p with respect to the natural volume element $dV = \sqrt{\det g}\, dx$ and let Δ_M be the Laplace-Beltrami operator on M. Then we define the s-th weighted Laplacian Δ_s as*

$$\Delta_s := \Delta_M + \frac{s}{p}g^{ab}(\nabla_a p)\nabla_b = \frac{1}{p^s}g^{ub}\nabla_a(p^s\nabla_b) = \frac{1}{p^s}\mathrm{div}(p^s\,\mathrm{grad}). \tag{1}$$

In the family of weighted Laplacians there are two cases which are particularly interesting. The first one, $s = 0$, corresponds to the standard Laplace-Beltrami operator. This notion is interesting if one only wants to use properties of the geometry of the manifold, but not of the data generating probability measure. The second case, $s = 1$, corresponds to the weighted Laplacian $\Delta_1 = \frac{1}{p}\nabla^a(p\nabla_a)$.

---

[1] Note that the case when the probability measure is absolutely continuous wrt the Lebesgue measure on $\mathbb{R}^d$ is a special case of our setting.

[2] A hypersurface is a submanifold of codimension 1.

[3] Boundary conditions are hard to transfer to the graph setting.

This operator can be extended to a self-adjoint operator[4] in $L_2(M, p \, dV)$, which is the natural function space on M given $P = p \, dV$.

Let us introduce the following notations: $C^k(M)$ is the set of C^k-functions on M with finite norm[5] given by $\|f\|_{C^k(M)} = \sup_{\sum_{i=1}^m l_i \leq k, \, x \in M} \left| \frac{\partial^{|\sum_{i=1}^m l_i|}}{\partial (x^1)^{l_1} \ldots \partial (x^m)^{l_m}} f(x) \right|$. $B(x, \epsilon)$ denotes a ball of radius ϵ. To bound the deviation of the extrinsic distance in $\mathbb{R}^d$ in terms of the intrinsic distance in M we define for each $x \in M$ the *regularity radius* $r(x)$ as

$$r(x) = \sup\{r > 0 \mid \|i(x) - i(y)\|_{\mathbb{R}^d}^2 \geq \frac{1}{2} d_M^2(x, y), \quad \forall y \in B_M(x, r)\}. \tag{3}$$

Assumption 1 $- \, i : M \to \mathbb{R}^d$ *is a smooth, isometric embedding*[6],
- *The boundary ∂M of M is either smooth or empty,*
- *M has a bounded second fundamental form,*
- *M has bounded sectional curvature,*
- *for any $x \in M$, $r(x) > 0$, and r is continuous,*
- *for any $x \in M$, $\delta(x) := \inf\limits_{y \in M \backslash B_M(x, \frac{1}{3} \min\{\text{inj}(x), r(x)\})} \|i(x) - i(y)\|_{\mathbb{R}^d} > 0$, where*

$\text{inj}(x)$ *is the injectivity radius at x* [7].

The first condition ensures that M is a smooth submanifold of $\mathbb{R}^d$ with the metric induced from $\mathbb{R}^d$ (this is usually meant when one speaks of a submanifold in $\mathbb{R}^d$). The next four properties guarantee that M is well behaved. The last condition ensures that if parts of M are far away from x in the geometry of M, they do not come too close to x in the geometry of $\mathbb{R}^d$. In order to emphasize the distinction between extrinsic and intrinsic properties of the manifold we always use the slightly cumbersome notations $x \in M$ (intrinsic) and $i(x) \in \mathbb{R}^d$ (extrinsic). The reader who is not familiar with Riemannian geometry should keep in mind that locally, a submanifold of dimension m looks like $\mathbb{R}^m$. This becomes apparent if one uses normal coordinates. Also the following dictionary between terms of the manifold M and the case when one has only an open set in $\mathbb{R}^d$ (i is then the identity mapping) might be useful.

Manifold M	open set in $\mathbb{R}^d$
g_{ij} , $\sqrt{\det g}$	δ_{ij} , 1
natural volume element	Lebesgue measure
Δ_s	$\Delta_s = \sum_{i=1}^d \frac{\partial^2 f}{\partial (z_i)^2} + \frac{s}{p} \sum_{i=1}^d \frac{\partial p}{\partial z^i} \frac{\partial f}{\partial z^i}$

---

[4] When M is compact, connected and oriented and for any $f, g \in C^\infty(M)$ vanishing on the boundary, by the first Green identity, we have

$$\int_M f(\Delta_s g) \, p^s dV = \int_M f\left(\Delta g + \frac{s}{p} \langle \nabla p, \nabla g \rangle\right) p^s dV = -\int_M \langle \nabla f, \nabla g \rangle \, p^s dV. \tag{2}$$

[5] We refer to Smolyanov et al.[9] for the technical details concerning this definition.

[6] i.e. the Riemannian metric g_{ab} on M is induced by $\mathbb{R}^d$, $g_{ab}^M = i_* g_{ab}^{\mathbb{R}^d}$, where $g_{ab}^{\mathbb{R}^d} = \delta_{ab}$.

[7] Note that the injectivity radius $\text{inj}(x)$ is always positive.

The kernels used in this paper are always isotropic, that is they can be written as functions of the norm in $\mathbb{R}^d$. Furthermore we make the following assumptions on the kernel function k:

Assumption 2   – $k : \mathbb{R}_+ \to \mathbb{R}$ *is measurable, non-negative and non-increasing,*
  – $k \in C^2(\mathbb{R}_+)$, *that is in particular k and $\frac{\partial^2 k}{\partial x^2}$ are bounded,*
  – k, $|\frac{\partial k}{\partial x}|$ *and* $|\frac{\partial^2 k}{\partial x^2}|$ *have exponential decay: $\exists c, \alpha, A \in \mathbb{R}_+$ such that for any $t \geq A$, $f(t) \leq ce^{-\alpha t}$, where $f(t) = \max\{k(t), |\frac{\partial k}{\partial x}|(t), |\frac{\partial^2 k}{\partial x^2}|\}$.*

Also let us introduce the helpful notation[8] $k_h(t) = \frac{1}{h^m} k\left(\frac{t}{h^2}\right)$, where we call h the bandwidth of the kernel. Let us now define our kernel-based averaging operators similar to Lafon [7][9]. We define the h-averaged density as:

$$p_h(x) = \int_M k_h\left(\|i(x) - i(y)\|_{\mathbb{R}^d}^2\right) p(y)\sqrt{\det g}\, dy.$$

Note that the distance used in the kernel function is the distance in the ambient space $\mathbb{R}^d$. In this paper we use a family of measure-dependent kernels parameterized by $\lambda \geq 0$ introduced in [4] defined as:

$$\tilde{k}_{\lambda,h}\left(\|i(x) - i(y)\|_{\mathbb{R}^d}^2\right) := \frac{k_h\left(\|i(x) - i(y)\|_{\mathbb{R}^d}^2\right)}{[p_h(x)p_h(y)]^\lambda}.$$

Let $\tilde{d}_{\lambda,h}(x) = \int_M \tilde{k}_{\lambda,h}\left(\|i(x) - i(y)\|_{\mathbb{R}^d}^2\right) p(y)\sqrt{\det g}\, dy.$

Definition 2 (Kernel-based approximation of the Laplacian). *We introduce the following kernel-based averaging operator $A_{\lambda,h}$:*

$$(A_{\lambda,h}f)(x) = \frac{1}{\tilde{d}_{\lambda,h}(x)} \int_M \tilde{k}_{\lambda,h}\left(\|i(x) - i(y)\|_{\mathbb{R}^d}^2\right) f(y)p(y)\sqrt{\det g}\, dy \qquad (4)$$

and the approximation of the Laplacian $\Delta_{\lambda,h}f := \frac{1}{h^2}\left(f - A_{\lambda,h}f\right)$.

A very useful tool in the proof of our main theorems is the following Proposition of Smolyanov et al.[9], which locally relates the extrinsic distance in $\mathbb{R}^d$ with the intrinsic distance $d_M(x, y)$ of the manifold.

Proposition 1. *Let $i : M \to \mathbb{R}^d$ be an isometric embedding of the smooth m-dimensional Riemannian manifold M into $\mathbb{R}^d$. Let $x \in M$ and V be a neighborhood of 0 in $\mathbb{R}^m$ and let $\Psi : V \to U$ provide normal coordinates of a neighborhood U of x, that is $\Psi(0) = x$. Then for all $y \in V$:*

$$\|y\|_{\mathbb{R}^m}^2 = d_M^2(x, \Psi(y)) = \|(i \circ \Psi)(y) - i(x)\|_{\mathbb{R}^d}^2 + \frac{1}{12}\|\Pi(\dot{\gamma}, \dot{\gamma})\|_{T_x\mathbb{R}^d}^2 + O(\|x\|_{\mathbb{R}^m}^5)$$

where Π is the second fundamental form of M and γ the unique geodesic from x to $\Psi(y)$ such that $\dot{\gamma} = y^i \partial_{y^i}$.

---

[8] In order to avoid problems with differentiation the argument of the kernel function will be the squared norm.

[9] But note that we do not require the kernel to be positive definite and we integrate with respect to the natural volume element.

The volume form $dV = \sqrt{\det g_{ij}(y)}dy$ of M satisfies in normal coordinates

$$dV = \left(1 + \frac{1}{6}R_{iuvi}\, y^u y^v + O(\|y\|^3_{\mathbb{R}^m})\right)dy$$

in particular $(\Delta\sqrt{\det g_{ij}})(0) = -\frac{1}{3}R$, where R is the scalar curvature (i.e., $R = g^{ik}g^{jl}R_{ijkl}$).

The following proposition describes the asymptotic expression of the convolution parts in the averaging operators $A_{\lambda,h}$. This result is interesting in itself since it shows the interplay between intrinsic and extrinsic geometry of the submanifold if one averages locally. The proof is similar to that of [10], but we now use general kernel functions, which makes the proof a little bit more complicated. We define $C_1 = \int_{\mathbb{R}^m} k(\|y\|^2)dy < \infty, \quad C_2 = \int_{\mathbb{R}^m} k(\|y\|^2)y_1^2 dy < \infty.$

Proposition 2. *Let M and k satisfy Assumptions 1 and 2. Furthermore let P have a density p with respect to the natural volume element and $p \in C^3(M)$. Then for any $x \in M\backslash\partial M$, there exists an $h_0(x) > 0$ for any $f \in C^3(M)$ such that for all $h < h_0(x)$,*

$$\int_M k_h\left(\|i(x) - i(y)\|^2_{\mathbb{R}^d}\right)f(y)p(y)\sqrt{\det g}\, dy = C_1 p(x)f(x)$$

$$+ \frac{h^2}{4}C_2\left(p(x)f(x)\left[-R + \frac{1}{2}\left\|\sum_a \Pi(\partial_a, \partial_a)\right\|^2_{T_{i(x)}\mathbb{R}^d}\right] + 2(\Delta_M(pf))(x)\right) + O(h^3),$$

where $O(h^3)$ is a function depending on x, $\|f\|_{C^3}$ and $\|p\|_{C^3}$.

Proof: See appendix.   □

Now we are ready to formulate the asymptotic result for the operator $\Delta_{\lambda,h}$, which extends the result of Lafon mentioned before.

Theorem 1. *Let M and k satisfy Assumptions 1 and 2. Furthermore let k now have compact support on $[0, R^2]$[10] and let P have a density p with respect to the natural volume element which satisfies $p \in C^3(M)$ and $p(x) > 0$, for any $x \in M$. Then for any $\lambda \geq 0$, for any $x \in M\backslash\partial M$, there exists an $h_1(x) > 0$ for any $f \in C^3(M)$ such that for all $h < h_1(x)$,*

$$(\Delta_{\lambda,h}f)(x) = -\frac{C_2}{2C_1}\left((\Delta_M f)(x) + \frac{s}{p(x)}\langle\nabla p, \nabla f\rangle_{T_x M}\right) + O(h^2)$$

$$= -\frac{C_2}{2C_1}(\Delta_s f)(x) + O(h^2), \tag{5}$$

where Δ_M is the Laplace-Beltrami operator of M and $s = 2(1 - \lambda)$.

Proof: The need for compactness of the kernel k comes from the fact that the modified kernel $\tilde{k}$ depends on $p_h(y)$. Now we can use the Taylor expansion of Proposition 2 for $p_h(y)$ only for h in the interval $(0, h_0(y))$. Obviously it can

---

[10] That means $k(t) = 0$, if $t > R^2$.

happen that $h_0(y) \to 0$ when we approach the boundary. Therefore, when we have to control $h_0(y)$ over the whole space M, the infimum could be zero, so that the estimate holds for no h. By restricting the support of the kernel k to a compact set $[0, R^2]$, it can be directly seen from the proof of Proposition 2 that $h_0(y)$ has the form $h_0(y) = \epsilon(y)/R$, where $\epsilon(y) = \frac{1}{3}\min\{r(y), \mathrm{inj}(y)\}$. Now $h_0(x)$ is continuous since $r(x)$ is continuous by assumption and $\mathrm{inj}(x)$ is continuous on the compact subset $\overline{B(x, 2\epsilon)}$, see [6][Prop. 2.1.10]. Therefore we conclude that since $h_0(y)$ is continuous on $\overline{B(x, 2\epsilon)}$ and $h_0(y) > 0$, $h_1(x) = \inf_{y \in \overline{B(x, 2\epsilon)}} h_0(y) > 0$. Then for the interval $(0, h_1(x))$ the estimate for $p_h(y)$ holds uniformly over the whole ball $B(x, \epsilon)$. That is, using the definition of $\tilde{k}$ as well as Proposition 2 and the expansion $\frac{1}{(a+h^2 b)^\lambda} = \frac{1}{a^\lambda} - \lambda\frac{h^2 b}{a^{\lambda+1}} + O(h^4)$ we get for $h \in (0, h_1(x))$ that

$$\int_M \tilde{k}_{\lambda,h}\left(\|i(x) - i(y)\|^2\right) f(y)p(y)\sqrt{\det g}\, dy$$

$$= \frac{1}{p_h^\lambda(x)} \int_{B(x,\epsilon)} k_h\left(\|i(x) - i(y)\|^2\right) f(y)$$

$$\left[\frac{C_1 p(y) - \lambda/2 C_2 h^2(p(y)S + \Delta p)}{C_1^{\lambda+1} p(y)^\lambda} + O(h^3)\right] \sqrt{\det g}\, dy \qquad (6)$$

where the $O(h^3)$-term is continuous on $B(x, \epsilon)$ and we have introduced the abbreviation $S = \frac{1}{2}[-R + \frac{1}{2}\|\sum_a \Pi(\partial_a, \partial_a)\|^2_{T_{i(x)}\mathbb{R}^d}]$. Using $f(y) = 1$ we get

$$\tilde{d}_{\lambda,h}(x) = \frac{1}{p_h^\lambda(x)} \int_{B(x,\epsilon)} k_h\left(\|i(x) - i(y)\|^2\right)$$

$$\left[\frac{C_1 p(y) - \lambda/2 C_2 h^2(p(y)S + \Delta p)}{C_1^{\lambda+1} p(y)^\lambda} + O(h^3)\right] \sqrt{\det g}\, dy \qquad (7)$$

as an estimate for $\tilde{d}_{\lambda,h}(x)$. Now using Proposition 2 again we arrive at:

$$\Delta_{\lambda,h}f = \frac{f - A_{\lambda,h}f}{h^2} = \frac{1}{h^2}\frac{\tilde{d}_{\lambda,h}f - \tilde{d}_{\lambda,h}A_{\lambda,h}f}{\tilde{d}_{\lambda,h}}$$

$$= -\frac{C_2}{2 C_1}\left(\Delta_M f + \frac{2(1-\lambda)}{p}\langle\nabla p, \nabla f\rangle\right) + O(h^2)$$

where all $O(h^2)$-terms are finite on $B(x, \epsilon)$ since p is strictly positive. □

Note that the limit of $\Delta_{\lambda,h}$ has the opposite sign of Δ_s. This is due to the fact that the Laplace-Beltrami operator on manifolds is usually defined as a negative definite operator (in analogy to the Laplace operator in $\mathbb{R}^d$), whereas the graph Laplacian is positive definite. But this varies through the literature, so the reader should be aware of the sign convention. From the last lines of the previous proof, it is easy to deduce the following result for the unnormalized case. Let

$$(\Delta'_{\lambda,h}f)(x) = \frac{1}{h^2}\left(\tilde{d}_{\lambda,h}(x)f(x) - \int_M \tilde{k}_{\lambda,h}\left(\|i(x) - i(y)\|^2\right) f(y)p(y)\sqrt{\det g}\, dy\right). \qquad (8)$$

Corollary 1. *Under the assumptions of Theorem 1, for any $\lambda \geq 0$, any $x \in M \backslash \partial M$, any $f \in C^3(M)$ there exists an $h_1(x) > 0$ such that for all $h < h_1(x)$,*

$$(\Delta'_{\lambda,h} f)(x) = -p(x)^{1-2\lambda} \frac{C_2}{2C_1^\lambda} (\Delta_s f)(x) + O(h^2), \quad \text{where} \quad s = 2(1-\lambda). \quad (9)$$

This result is quite interesting. We observe that in the case of a uniform density it does not make a difference whether we use the unnormalized or the normalized approximation of the Laplacian. However, as soon as we have a non-uniform density, the unnormalized one will converge only up to a function to the Laplacian, except in the case $\lambda = \frac{1}{2}$ where both the normalized and unnormalized approximation lead to the same result. This result confirms the analysis of von Luxburg et al. in [11], where the consistency of spectral clustering was studied. There the unnormalized Laplacian is in general not consistent since it has a continuous spectrum. Obviously the limit operator $\Delta'_{\lambda,h} = -p^{1-2\lambda} \frac{C_2}{2C_1^\lambda} \Delta_s$ has also a continuous spectrum even if Δ_s is compact since it is multiplied with $p^{1-2\lambda}$.

4   Strong Pointwise Consistency of Graph Laplacians

In the last section we identified certain averaging operators $\Delta_{\lambda,h}$ which in the limit $h \to 0$ converge pointwise to the corresponding Laplacian Δ_s, where $s = 2(1-\lambda)$. In this section we will provide the connection to the normalized graph Laplacian $\Delta_{\lambda,n,h}$ with data-dependent weights $\tilde{w}_\lambda(X_i, X_j)$ defined as

$$\tilde{w}_\lambda(X_i, X_j) = \frac{k\left(\|i(X_i) - i(X_j)\|^2 / h^2\right)}{[d(X_i)d(X_j)]^\lambda}, \quad \lambda \geq 0 \quad (10)$$

where $d(X_i) = \sum_{r=1}^n k(\|i(X_i) - i(X_r)\|^2 / h^2)$. Note that the weights are not multiplied with $1/h^m$, as it was usual for the kernel function in the last section. There are two reasons for this. The first one is that this factor would lead to infinite weights for $h \to 0$. The second and more important one is that this factor cancels for the normalized Laplacian. This is very important in the case where the data lies on a submanifold of unknown dimension m, since then also the correct factor $\frac{1}{h^m}$ would be unknown. Note also that for the unnormalized Laplacian this factor does not cancel if $\lambda \neq \frac{1}{2}$. This means that for $\lambda \neq \frac{1}{2}$ the unnormalized Laplacian cannot be consistently estimated if the data lies on a proper submanifold of unknown dimension, since the estimate in general blows up or vanishes. Therefore we will consider only the normalized graph Laplacian in the following and for simplicity omit the term 'normalized'.

The graph Laplacian is defined only for functions on the graph, but it is straightforward to extend the graph Laplacian to an estimator of the Laplacian for functions defined on the whole space by using the kernel function,

$$(\Delta_{\lambda,h,n} f)(x) = \frac{1}{h^2} (f - A_{\lambda,h,n} f)(x) := \frac{1}{h^2} \left(f(x) - \frac{1}{\tilde{d}_\lambda(x)} \sum_{j=1}^n \tilde{w}_\lambda(x, X_j) f(X_j) \right),$$

$$(11)$$

where $\tilde{d}_\lambda(x) = \sum_{r=1}^{n} \tilde{w}_\lambda(x, X_i)$. The factor $\frac{1}{h^2}$ comes from introducing an $\frac{1}{h}$-term in the definition of the derivative operator d on the graph. It is natural to introduce this factor since we want to estimate a derivative. Especially interesting is the form of the second term of the graph Laplacian for $\lambda = 0$ where the weights are not data-dependent. In this case, this term can be identified with the Nadaraya-Watson regression estimate. Therefore, for $\lambda = 0$ we can adapt the proof of pointwise consistency of the Nadaraya-Watson estimator of Greblicki, Krzyzak and Pawlak [5] and apply it to the graph Laplacian. The following Lemma will be useful in the following proofs.

Lemma 1. *Let $X_1, \dots, X_n$ be n i.i.d. random vectors in $\mathbb{R}^d$ with law P, which is absolutely continuous with respect to the natural volume element dV of a submanifold $M \subset \mathbb{R}^d$ satisfying Assumption 1. Let p denote its density, which is bounded, continuous and positive $p(x) > 0$, for any $x \in M$. Furthermore let k be a kernel with compact support on $[0, R^2]$ satisfying Assumption 2. Let $x \in M \backslash \partial M$, define $b_1 = \|k\|_\infty \|f\|_\infty$, $b_2 = C \|k\|_\infty \|f\|_\infty^2$, where C is a constant depending on x, $\|p\|_\infty$ and $\|k\|_\infty$. Then for any $f \in C^3(M)$,*

$$\mathrm{P}\Big(\Big|\frac{1}{n}\sum_{i=1}^{n} k_h(\|i(x) - i(X_i)\|^2)f(X_i) - \int_M k_h(\|i(x) - i(y)\|^2)f(y)p(y)\sqrt{\det g}\, dy\Big| \geq \epsilon\Big)$$

$$\leq 2\exp\left(-\frac{nh^m\epsilon^2}{2b_2 + 2b_1\epsilon/3}\right)$$

Now the proof of pointwise consistency in the case $\lambda = 0$ is straightforward.

Theorem 2 (Weak and strong pointwise consistency for $\lambda = 0$). *Let $X_i \in \mathbb{R}^d$, $i = 1, \dots, n$ be random vectors drawn i.i.d. from the probability measure P on $M \subset \mathbb{R}^d$, where M satisfies Assumption 1 and has $\dim M = m$. Furthermore let P be absolutely continuous with respect to the volume element dV with density $p \in C^3(M)$ and $p(x) > 0$, $\forall x \in M$, and let $\Delta_{0,h,n}$ be the graph Laplacian in (11) with weights of the form (10), where k has compact support on $[0, R^2]$. Then for every $x \in M \backslash \partial M$ and for every function $f \in C^3(M)$, if $h \to 0$ and $nh^{m+4} \to \infty$*

$$\lim_{n\to\infty} (\Delta_{0,h,n}f)(x) = -\frac{2\,C_1}{C_2}(\Delta_2 f)(x) \quad \text{in probability.}$$

If even $nh^{m+4}/\log n \to \infty$, then almost sure convergence holds.

Proof: We rewrite the estimator $\Delta_{0,h,n}f$ in the following form

$$(\Delta_{0,h,n}f)(x) = \frac{1}{h^2}\left[f(x) - \frac{(A_{0,h}\,f)(x) + B_{1n}}{1 + B_{2n}}\right] \tag{12}$$

where

$$(A_{0,h}\,f)(x) = \frac{\mathbb{E}_Z\, k_h(\|i(x) - i(Z)\|^2)f(Z)}{\mathbb{E}_Z\, k_h(\|i(x) - i(Z)\|^2)}$$

$$B_{1n} = \frac{\frac{1}{n}\sum_{j=1}^{n} k_h(\|i(x) - i(X_j)\|^2)f(X_j) - \mathbb{E}_Z\, k_h(\|i(x) - i(Z)\|^2)f(Z)}{\mathbb{E}_Z\, k_h(\|i(x) - i(Z)\|^2)}$$

$$B_{2n} = \frac{\frac{1}{n}\sum_{j=1}^{n} k_h(\|i(x) - i(X_j)\|^2) - \mathbb{E}_Z\, k_h(\|i(x) - i(Z)\|^2)}{\mathbb{E}_Z\, k_h(\|i(x) - i(Z)\|^2)}$$

In Theorem 1 we have shown that

$$\lim_{h \to 0}(\Delta_{0,h}f)(x) = \lim_{h \to 0}\frac{1}{h^2}\left[f(x) - (A_{0,h}\,f)(x)\right] = -\frac{2\,C_1}{C_2}(\Delta_2 f)(x) \tag{13}$$

Let $hR \le \mathrm{inj}(x)$, then $\mathbb{E}_Z \, k_h(\|i(x) - i(Z)\|^2) \ge K \inf_{y \in B_M(x,hR)} p(y)$, where K is a constant and using Lemma 1 we get with $d_2 = \frac{\|f\|_\infty^2}{(K \inf_{y \in B_M(x,hR)} p(y))^2}$, $d_1 = \frac{\|f\|_\infty}{K \inf_{y \in B_M(x,\epsilon)} p(y)}$:

$$P(|B_{1n}| \ge h^2 t) \le \exp\left(-\frac{nh^{m+4}\,t^2}{2\,\|k\|_\infty\,(d_2 + t\,d_1/3)}\right),$$

Note that since p is continuous and p is strictly positive the infimum is achieved and positive. The same analysis can be done for B_{2n}, where we do not have to deal with the $1/h^2$-factor. This shows convergence in probability. Complete convergence (which implies almost sure convergence) can be shown by proving for all $t > 0$ the convergence of the series $\sum_{n=0}^{\infty} P\left(|B_{1n}| \ge h^2 t\right) < \infty$. A sufficient condition for that is $nh^{d+4}/\log n \to +\infty$ when $n \to \infty$. $\square$

Under the more restrictive assumption that the data is sampled from a uniform probability measure on a compact submanifold we learned that Belkin and Niyogi have independently proven the convergence of the unnormalized graph Laplacian in [2]. It is clear from Theorem 1 and Corollary 1 that in the case of a uniform measure the limit operators for normalized and unnormalized graph Laplacian agree up to a constant. However, as mentioned before the unnormalized graph Laplacian has the disadvantage that in order to get convergence one has to know the dimension m of the submanifold M, which in general is not the case.

Lemma 2. *Let $X_i \in \mathbb{R}^d$, $i = 1,\ldots,n$ be random vectors drawn i.i.d. from the probability measure P on $M \subset \mathbb{R}^d$, where M satisfies Assumption 1 and has $\dim M = m$. Furthermore let P be absolutely continuous with respect to the volume element dV with continuous density $p(x)$. Let $k(\|x - y\|^2)$ be a bounded kernel with compact support on $[0, R^2]$. Let $\lambda \ge 0$, $x \in M$ with $p(x) > 0$, $f \in C(M)$ and $n \ge 2$. Then there exists a constant $C > 1$ such that for any $0 < \varepsilon < 1/C$, $0 < h < \frac{1}{C}$ with probability at least $1 - Cne^{-\frac{nh^m \varepsilon^2}{C}}$, we have*

$$|(A_{\lambda,h,n}f)(x) - (A_{\lambda,h}f)(x)| \le \varepsilon.$$

Proof: For sufficiently large C, the assertion of the lemma is trivial for $\varepsilon < \frac{2\|k\|_\infty}{(n-1)h^m}$. So we will only consider $\frac{2\|k\|_\infty}{(n-1)h^m} \le \varepsilon \le 1$. The idea of the proof is to use deviation inequalities to show that the empirical terms, which are expressed as a sum of i.i.d. random variables, are close to their expectations. Then we can prove that the empirical term

$$(A_{\lambda,h,n}f)(x) = \frac{\sum_{j=1}^{n} k_h(\|i(x) - i(X_j)\|^2)f(X_j)[d(X_j)]^{-\lambda}}{\sum_{r=1}^{n} k_h(\|i(x) - i(X_r)\|^2)[d(X_r)]^{-\lambda}} \tag{14}$$

is close to the term $(A_{\lambda,h}f)(x)$. Consider the event $\mathcal{E}$ for which we have

$$
\begin{cases}
\text{for any } j \in \{1,\ldots,n\}, \ \left|\frac{d(X_j)}{n-1} - p_h(X_j)\right| \le \varepsilon \\
\left|\frac{d(x)}{n} - p_h(x)\right| \le \varepsilon \\
\left|\frac{1}{n}\sum_{j=1}^{n} k_h(\|i(x)-i(X_j)\|^2)[p_h(X_j)]^{-\lambda} - \int_M k_h(\|i(x)-i(y)\|^2)[p_h(y)]^{-\lambda}p(y)\sqrt{\det g}\,dy\right| \le \varepsilon \\
\left|\frac{1}{n}\sum_{j=1}^{n} \frac{k_h(\|i(x)-i(X_j)\|^2)f(X_j)}{[p_h(X_j)]^{\lambda}} - \int_M \frac{k_h(\|i(x)-i(y)\|^2)f(y)}{[p_h(y)]^{\lambda}}p(y)\sqrt{\det g}\,dy\right| \le \varepsilon \\
\left|\frac{1}{n}\sum_{j=1}^{n} k_h(\|i(x)-i(X_j)\|^2)f(X_j) - \int_M k_h(\|i(x)-i(y)\|^2)f(y)p(y)\sqrt{\det g}\,dy\right| \le \varepsilon
\end{cases}
$$

We will now prove that for sufficiently large C, the event $\mathcal{E}$ holds with probability at least $1 - Cne^{-\frac{nh^m\varepsilon^2}{C}}$. For the second assertion defining $\mathcal{E}$, we use Lemma 1 (with $N = n - 1$ and the conditional probability wrt X_j for a given $1 \le j \le d$) to obtain that for $\varepsilon \le 1$,

$$
\mathrm{P}\left(\left|\tfrac{1}{n-1}\sum_{i\ne j} k_h(\|i(x)-i(X_i)\|^2) - p_h(x)\right| \ge \varepsilon \Big| X_j\right) \le 2e^{-\frac{(n-1)h^m\varepsilon^2}{C}}.
$$

First integrating wrt to the law of X_j and then using an union bound we get

$$
\mathrm{P}\left(\left|\tfrac{1}{n-1}\sum_{i\ne j} k_h(\|i(x)-i(X_i)\|^2) - p_h(x)\right| \ge \varepsilon\right) \le 2e^{-\frac{(n-1)h^m\varepsilon^2}{C}} \quad \text{and}
$$

$$
\mathrm{P}\left(\text{for any } j \in \{1,\ldots,n\}, \ \left|\tfrac{d(X_j)}{n-1} - \tfrac{k_h(0)}{n-1} - p_h(X_j)\right| \le \varepsilon\right) \ge 1 - 2ne^{-\frac{(n-1)h^m\varepsilon^2}{C}}.
$$

Therefore for $\frac{2\|k\|_\infty}{(n-1)h^m} \le \varepsilon \le 1$ we have[11]

$$
\mathrm{P}\left(\text{for any } j \in \{1,\ldots,n\}, \ \left|\tfrac{d(X_j)}{n-1} - p_h(X_j)\right| \le \varepsilon\right) \ge 1 - 2ne^{-\frac{(n-1)h^m\varepsilon^2}{C}}.
$$

Similarly we can prove that for $\frac{2\|k\|_\infty}{nh^m} \le \varepsilon \le 1$ with probability at least $1 - 2e^{-Cnh^m\varepsilon^2}$, the third assertion defining $\mathcal{E}$ holds. For the three last assertions, a direct application of Lemma 1 shows that they also hold with high probability. Finally, combining all these results, we obtain that for $\frac{2\|k\|_\infty}{(n-1)h^m} \le \varepsilon \le 1$, the event $\mathcal{E}$ holds with probability at least $1 - Cne^{-\frac{nh^m\varepsilon^2}{C}}$. Let us define

$$
\begin{cases}
\mathcal{A} := \int_M k_h(\|i(x)-i(y)\|^2)f(y)[p_h(y)]^{-\lambda}p(y)\sqrt{\det g}\,dy \\
\hat{\mathcal{A}} := \frac{1}{n}\sum_{j=1}^{n} k_h(\|i(x)-i(X_j)\|^2)f(X_j)\left[\tfrac{d(X_j)}{n-1}\right]^{-\lambda} \\
\mathcal{B} := \int_M k_h(\|i(x)-i(y)\|^2)[p_h(y)]^{-\lambda}p(y)\sqrt{\det g}\,dy \\
\hat{\mathcal{B}} := \frac{1}{n}\sum_{j=1}^{n} k_h(\|i(x)-i(X_j)\|^2)\left[\tfrac{d(X_j)}{n-1}\right]^{-\lambda}
\end{cases}
$$

and let us now work only on the event $\mathcal{E}$. Let $p_{\min} = p(x)/2$ and $p_{\max} = 2p(x)$. By continuity of the density, for C large enough and any $h < 1/C$, the density satisfies $0 < p_{\min} \le p \le p_{\max}$ on the ball $B_M(x, 2hR)$. So for any $y \in B_M(x, hR)$,

---

[11] We recall that the value of the constant C might change from line to line.

there exists a constant $D_1 > 0$ such that $D_1 p_{\min} \leq p_h(y) \leq D_1 \sqrt{2} p_{\max}$. Using the first order Taylor formula of $[x \mapsto x^{-\lambda}]$, we obtain that for any $\lambda \geq 0$ and $a, b > \beta$, $\left|a^{-\lambda} - b^{-\lambda}\right| \leq \lambda \beta^{-\lambda-1} |a - b|$. So we can write

$$
\begin{aligned}
|\hat{\mathcal{B}} - \mathcal{B}| &\leq \left| \tfrac{1}{n} \textstyle\sum_{j=1}^{n} k_h(\|i(x) - i(X_j)\|^2) \left(\left[\tfrac{d(X_j)}{n-1}\right]^{-\lambda} - [p_h(X_j)]^{-\lambda} \right) \right| \\
&\quad + \left| \tfrac{1}{n} \textstyle\sum_{j=1}^{n} k_h(\|i(x) - i(X_j)\|^2) [p_h(X_j)]^{-\lambda} - \mathcal{B} \right| \\
&\leq \left| \tfrac{d(x)}{n} \right| \lambda (D_1 p_{\min})^{-\lambda-1} \varepsilon + \varepsilon \\
&\leq \left| \tfrac{d(x)}{n} - p_h(x) \right| \lambda (D_1 p_{\min})^{-\lambda-1} \varepsilon + p_h(x) \lambda (D_1 p_{\min})^{-\lambda-1} \varepsilon + \varepsilon \\
&\leq \lambda (D_1 p_{\min})^{-\lambda-1} \varepsilon + \sqrt{2} D_1 p_{\max} \lambda (C_1 p_{\min})^{-\lambda-1} \varepsilon + \varepsilon := C' \varepsilon
\end{aligned}
$$

Similarly we prove that $|\hat{\mathcal{A}} - \mathcal{A}| \leq C'' \varepsilon$. Let $\zeta := \tfrac{1}{2} \tfrac{D_1 p_{\min}}{(\sqrt{2} D_1 p_{\max})^{\lambda}}$. We have $\mathcal{B} \geq 2\zeta$. Let us introduce $\varepsilon_0 := \min\{\tfrac{\zeta}{C'}, 1\}$. For $\tfrac{2\|k\|_\infty}{(n-1)h^m} \leq \varepsilon \leq \varepsilon_0$, we have also $\hat{\mathcal{B}} \geq \zeta$. Combining the last three results, we obtain that there exists $D_2 > 0$ such that

$$
\left| \tfrac{\mathcal{A}}{\mathcal{B}} - \tfrac{\hat{\mathcal{A}}}{\hat{\mathcal{B}}} \right| \leq \tfrac{|\mathcal{A} - \hat{\mathcal{A}}|}{\hat{\mathcal{B}}} + \mathcal{A} \tfrac{|\mathcal{B} - \hat{\mathcal{B}}|}{\mathcal{B} \hat{\mathcal{B}}} \leq \tfrac{C'' \varepsilon}{\zeta} + D_2 p_{\max} (C_1 p_{\min})^{-\lambda} \tfrac{C' \varepsilon}{2\zeta^2} \leq C \varepsilon.
$$

Noting that $A_{\lambda,h} f = \mathcal{A}/\mathcal{B}$ and $A_{\lambda,h,n} f = \hat{\mathcal{A}}/\hat{\mathcal{B}}$, we have proved that there exists a constant $C > 1$ such that for any $0 < \varepsilon < 1/C$

$$
|(A_{\lambda,h,n} f)(x) - (A_{\lambda,h} f)(x)| \leq C \varepsilon
$$

with probability at least $1 - Cne^{-\frac{nh^m \varepsilon^2}{C}}$. This leads to the desired result.   □

Combining Lemma 2 with Theorem 1 we arrive at our main theorem.

Theorem 3 (Weak and strong pointwise consistency). *Let $X_i \in \mathbb{R}^d$, $i = 1, \ldots, n$ be random vectors drawn i.i.d. from the probability measure P on $M \subset \mathbb{R}^d$, where M satisfies Assumption 1 and has $\dim M = m$. Let P be absolutely continuous with respect to the volume element dV with density $p \in C^3(M)$ and p strictly positive. Let $\Delta_{\lambda,h,n}$ be the graph Laplacian in (11) with weights of the form (10), where k has compact support on $[0, R^2]$ and satisfies Assumption 2. Define $s = 2(1 - \lambda)$. Then, for every $x \in M \backslash \partial M$ and for every function $f \in C^3(M)$, if $h \to 0$ and $nh^{m+4}/\log n \to \infty$*

$$
\lim_{n \to \infty} (\Delta_{\lambda,h,n} f)(x) = -\frac{2 C_1}{C_2} (\Delta_s f)(x) \quad \textit{almost surely.}
$$

Proof: The proof consists of two steps. By Theorem 1 the bias term converges.

$$
\lim_{h \to 0} \left| (\Delta_{\lambda,h} f)(x) - \left[-\left(\frac{2 C_1}{C_2} \Delta_s f \right)(x) \right] \right| \to 0. \tag{15}
$$

Next we consider the variance term $|(\Delta_{\lambda,h,n} f)(x) - (\Delta_{\lambda,h} f)(x)|$. We have

$$
|(\Delta_{\lambda,h,n} f)(x) - (\Delta_{\lambda,h} f)(x)| = \frac{1}{h^2} |(A_{\lambda,h,n} f)(x) - (A_{\lambda,h} f)(x)|.
$$

Up to the factor $1/h^2$ this is the term studied in Lemma 2, so that we get under the conditions stated there:

$$P\left(\left|(\Delta_{\lambda,h,n}f)(x) - (\Delta_{\lambda,h}f)(x)\right| \geq \epsilon\right) \leq C n e^{-\frac{nh^{m+4}\epsilon^2}{C}}$$

Then, using the same technique as in Theorem 2, one shows complete convergence for $nh^{m+4}/\log n \to \infty$, which implies almost sure convergence. □

This theorem states conditions for the relationship of the sample size n and the bandwidth h for almost sure convergence. It is unlikely that this rate can be improved (up to the logarithmic factor), since the rates for estimating second derivatives in nonparametric regression are the same. Another point which cannot be underestimated is that we show that the rate that one gets only depends on the intrinsic dimension m of the data (that is the dimension of the submanifold M). This means that even if one has data in a very high-dimensional Euclidean space $\mathbb{R}^d$ one can expect to get a good approximation of the Laplacian if the data lies on a low-dimensional submanifold. Therefore, our proof provides a theoretical basis for all algorithms performing dimensionality reduction using the graph Laplacian. Another point is that one can continuously control the influence of the probability distribution with the parameter λ and even eliminate it in the case $\lambda = 1$. The conditions of this theorem are very mild. We only require that the submanifold is not too much twisted and that the kernel is bounded and compact. Note that in large scale practical applications, compactness of the kernel is necessary for computational reasons anyway.

Acknowledgments

We would like to thank Olaf Wittich for his help with [9, 10] and Bernhard Schölkopf for helpful comments and support.

References

[1] M. Belkin. *Problems of Learning on Manifolds*. PhD thesis, University of Chicago, 2003. http://www.people.cs.uchicago.edu/~misha/thesis.pdf.

[2] M. Belkin and P. Niyogi. Towards a theoretical foundation for Laplacian-based manifold methods. to appear in the Proc. of COLT, 2005.

[3] O. Bousquet, O. Chapelle, and M. Hein. Measure based regularization. In *Advances in Neural Information Processing Systems*, volume 16, 2003.

[4] S. Coifman and S. Lafon. Diffusion maps. Preprint, Jan. 2005, to appear in Applied and Computational Harmonic Analysis, 2005.

[5] W. Greblicki, A. Krzyzak, and M. Pawlak. Distribution-free pointwise consistency of kernel regression estimate. *Annals of Statistics*, 12:1570–1575, 1984.

[6] W. Klingenberg. *Riemannian Geometry*. De Gruyter, 1982.

[7] S. S. Lafon. *Diffusion Maps and Geometric Harmonics*. PhD thesis, Yale University, 2004. http://www.math.yale.edu/~sl349/publications/dissertation.pdf.

[8] P. Niyogi.   Learning functional maps on Riemannian submani-
     folds.   Talk presented at IPAM workshop on multiscale struc-
     tures in the analysis of high-dimensional data, 2004.   available at
     http://www.ipam.ucla.edu/publications/mgaws3/mgaws3_5188.pdf.

[9] O. G. Smolyanov, H. von Weizsäcker, and O. Wittich. Brownian motion on a man-
     ifold as limit of stepwise conditioned standard Brownian motions. In *Stochastic
     processes, physics and geometry: new interplays, II*, 2000.

[10] O. G. Smolyanov, H. von Weizsäcker, and O. Wittich. Chernoff's theorem and dis-
     crete time approximations of Brownian motion on manifolds. Preprint, available
     at http://lanl.arxiv.org/abs/math.PR/0409155, 2004.

[11] U. von Luxburg, M. Belkin, and O. Bousquet. Consistency of spectral clustering.
     Technical Report 134, Max Planck Institute for Biological Cybernetics, 2004.

[12] D. Zhou, O. Bousquet, T. N. Lal, J. Weston, and B. Schölkopf. Learning with
     local and global consistency. In *NIPS 16*, 2004.

[13] D. Zhou, B. Schölkopf, and T. Hofmann. Semi-supervised learning on directed
     graphs. In *NIPS 17*, 2005.

A   Appendix: Proof of Proposition 2

The following lemmas are needed in the proof of the asymptotics of $A_{\lambda,h}$.

Lemma 3. *If the kernel $k : \mathbb{R} \to \mathbb{R}$ satisfies the assumptions in Assumption 2,*

$$\int_{\mathbb{R}^m} \frac{\partial k}{\partial x}(\|u\|^2) u^i u^j u^k u^l du = -\frac{1}{2} C_2 \left[\delta^{ij}\delta^{kl} + \delta^{ik}\delta^{jl} + \delta^{il}\delta^{jk} \right]. \tag{16}$$

Lemma 4. *Let k satisfy Assumption 2 and let V_{ijkl} be a given tensor. Assume
now $\|z\|^2 \geq \|z\|^2 + V_{ijkl} z^i z^j z^k z^l + \beta \|z\|^5 \geq \frac{1}{2} \|z\|^2$ on $B(0, r_{\min}) \subset \mathbb{R}^m$. Then
there exists a constant C and a $h_0 > 0$ such that for all $h < h_0$ and for all
$f \in C^3(B(0, r_{\min}))$*

$$\left| \int_{B(0,r_{\min})} k_h \left(\frac{\|z\|^2 + V_{ijkl} z^i z^j z^k z^l + \beta \|z\|^5}{h^2} \right) f(z) dz \right.$$
$$\left. - \left(C_1 f(0) + C_2 \frac{h^2}{2} \left[(\Delta f)(0) - f(0) \sum_{i,k}^m V_{iikk} + V_{ikik} + V_{ikki} \right] \right) \right| \leq C h^3. \tag{17}$$

To prove Proposition 2, let $\epsilon = \frac{1}{3} \min\{\mathrm{inj}(x), r(x)\}$[12], where ϵ is positive by the
assumptions on M. Then we decompose M in $M = B(x, \epsilon) \cup (M \backslash B(x, \epsilon))$ and
integrate separately. The integral over $M \backslash B(x, \epsilon)$ can be estimated by using the
definition of $\delta(x)$ (see Assumption 1) and the fact that k is non-increasing:

$$\int_{M \backslash B(x,\epsilon)} k_h \left(\|i(x) - i(y)\|_{\mathbb{R}^d}^2 \right) f(y) p(y) \sqrt{\det g} \, dy \leq \frac{1}{h^m} k \left(\frac{\delta(x)^2}{h^2} \right) \|f\|_\infty$$

---

[12] The factor $1/3$ is needed in Theorem 1.

Since $\delta(x)$ is positive by the assumptions on M and k decays exponentially, we can make the upper bound smaller than h^3 for small enough h. Now we deal with the integral over $B(x, \epsilon)$. Since ϵ is smaller than the injectivity radius $\mathrm{inj}(x)$, we can introduce normal coordinates $z = \exp^{-1}(y)$ with origin $0 = \exp^{-1}(x)$ on $B(x, \epsilon)$, so that we can write the integral over $B(x, \epsilon)$ as:

$$\int\limits_{B(0,\epsilon)} k_h \left(\frac{\|z\|^2 - \frac{1}{12}\sum_{\alpha=1}^{d} \frac{\partial^2 i^\alpha}{\partial z^a \partial z^b} \frac{\partial^2 i^\alpha}{\partial z^u \partial z^v} z^a z^b z^u z^v + O(\|z\|^5)}{h^2} \right) p(z) f(z) \sqrt{\det g}\, dz$$

(18)

by using our assumption that $pf\sqrt{\det g}$ is in $C^3(B(0, \epsilon))$. Therefore we can apply Lemma 4 and compute the integral in (18) which results in:

$$\left[p(0)f(0)\left(C_1 + C_2 \frac{h^2}{24} \sum_{\alpha=1}^{d} \frac{\partial^2 i^\alpha}{\partial z^a \partial z^b} \frac{\partial^2 i^\alpha}{\partial z^c \partial z^d} \left[\delta^{ab}\delta^{cd} + \delta^{ac}\delta^{bd} + \delta^{ad}\delta^{bc} \right] \right) \right.$$
$$\left. + C_2 \frac{h^2}{2} \Delta_M (pf\sqrt{\det g})\Big|_0 + O(h^3) \right],$$

(19)

where we have used that the Laplace-Beltrami operator Δ_M in normal coordinates z^i at 0 is given as $\Delta_M f\big|_x = \sum_{i=1}^{m} \frac{\partial^2 f}{\partial (z^i)^2}\big|_0$. The second term in the above equation can be evaluated using the Gauss equations, see [10–Proposition 6].

$$\sum_{\alpha=1}^{d} \frac{\partial^2 i^\alpha}{\partial z^a \partial z^b} \frac{\partial^2 i^\alpha}{\partial z^c \partial z^d} \left[\delta^{ab}\delta^{cd} + \delta^{ac}\delta^{bd} + \delta^{ad}\delta^{bc} \right] = -2R + 3 \left\| \sum_{j=1}^{m} \Pi(\partial_{z^j}, \partial_{z^j}) \right\|^2_{T_{i(x)}\mathbb{R}^d}$$

where R is the scalar curvature. Plugging this result into (19) and using from Proposition 1, $\Delta_M \sqrt{\det g}\big|_0 = -\frac{1}{3}R$, finishes the proof.

Towards a Theoretical Foundation
for Laplacian-Based Manifold Methods

Mikhail Belkin and Partha Niyogi

The University of Chicago, Department of Computer Science
{misha, niyogi}@cs.uchicago.edu

Abstract. In recent years manifold methods have attracted a considerable amount of attention in machine learning. However most algorithms in that class may be termed "manifold-motivated" as they lack any explicit theoretical guarantees. In this paper we take a step towards closing the gap between theory and practice for a class of Laplacian-based manifold methods. We show that under certain conditions the graph Laplacian of a point cloud converges to the Laplace-Beltrami operator on the underlying manifold. Theorem 1 contains the first result showing convergence of a random graph Laplacian to manifold Laplacian in the machine learning context.

1 Introduction

Manifold methods have become increasingly important and popular in machine learning and have seen numerous recent applications in data analysis including dimensionality reduction, visualization, clustering and classification. The central modeling assumption in all of these methods is that the data resides on or near a low-dimensional submanifold in a higher-dimensional space. It should be noted that such an assumption seems natural for a data-generating source with relatively few degrees of freedom.

However in almost all modeling situations, one does not have access to the underlying manifold but instead approximates it from a point cloud. The most common approximation strategy in these methods it to construct an adjacency graph associated to a point cloud. Most manifold learning algorithms then proceed by exploiting the structure of this graph. The underlying intuition has always been that since the graph is a proxy for the manifold, inference based on the structure of the graph corresponds to the desired inference based on the geometric structure of the manifold. However few theoretical results are available to justify this intuition.

In this paper we take the first steps towards a theoretical foundation for manifold-based methods in learning. An important and popular class of learning methods makes use of the graph Laplacian for various learning applications. It is worth noting that in almost all cases, the graph itself is an empirical object, constructed as it is from sampled data. Therefore any graph-theoretic technique is only applicable, when it can be related to the underlying process generating the data. This is an implicit assumption, which is rarely formalized in the literature.

P. Auer and R. Meir (Eds.): COLT 2005, LNAI 3559, pp. 486–500, 2005.

We will show that under certain conditions the graph Laplacian is directly related to the manifold Laplace-Beltrami operator and converges to it as data goes to infinity.

This paper presents and extends the unpublished results obtained in [1]. A version of Theorem 1 showing empirical convergence of the graph Laplacian to the manifold Laplacian was stated in [19].

1.1   Prior Work

Many manifold and graph-motivated learning methods have been recently proposed, including [22, 27, 3, 12] for visualization and data representation, [30, 29, 9, 23, 4, 2, 26] for partially supervised classification and [25, 28, 24, 18, 14] among others for spectral clustering. A discussion of various spectral methods and their out-of-sample extensions is given in [5].

The problem of estimating geometric and topological invariants from point cloud data has recently attracted some attention. Some of the recent work includes estimating geometric invariants of the manifold, such as homology [31, 20], geodesic distances [6], and comparing point clouds using Gromov-Hausdorff distance [15].

In particular, we note the closely related Ph.D. thesis of Lafon, [16], which generalized the convergence results from [1] to the important case of an arbitrary probability distribution on a manifold. Those results are further generalized and presented with an empirical convergence theorem in the parallel COLT paper [13].

We also note [17], where convergence of a class of graph Laplacians and the associated spectral objects, such as eigenfunctions and eigenvalues, is shown, which in particular, implies consistency of normalized spectral clustering. However connections to geometric objects, such as the Laplace-Beltrami operator, are not considered in that work.

Finally we point out that while the parallel between the geometry of manifolds and the geometry of graphs is well-known in spectral graph theory and in certain areas of differential geometry (see, e.g., [10]) the exact nature of that parallel is usually not made precise.

2   Notation and Preliminaries

Before we can formulate the main result we need to fix some notation. In general, we denote vectors and points on a manifold with bold letters and one-dimensional quantities with ordinary letters. Matrices will be denoted by capital letters, operators on functions by bold capital letters.

A weighted graph $G = (V, E)$ is a set of vertices $v_1, \ldots, v_n \in V$ and weighted edges connecting these vertices represented by an adjacency matrix W. W is a symmetric matrix with nonnegative entries. Recall that the *Laplacian* matrix of a weighted graph G is the matrix $L = D - W$, where D is a diagonal matrix $D(i, i) = \sum_j W(i, j)$.

Given a set of points $\mathcal{S}_n = \{\mathbf{x}_1, \ldots, \mathbf{x}_n\}$ in $\mathbb{R}^k$, we construct a graph G, whose vertices are data points. We put $W_n^t(i,j) = e^{-\frac{\|\mathbf{x}_i - \mathbf{x}_j\|^2}{4t}}$. We will denote the corresponding graph Laplacian by $L_n^t = D_n^t - W_n^t$. Note that we suppress the dependence on $\mathcal{S}_n$ to simplify notation.

We may think of L_n^t as an operator on functions, defined on the graph of data points. If $f : V \to \mathbb{R}$

$$L_n^t f(\mathbf{x}_i) = f(\mathbf{x}_i) \sum_j e^{-\frac{\|\mathbf{x}_i - \mathbf{x}_j\|^2}{4t}} - \sum_j f(\mathbf{x}_j) e^{-\frac{\|\mathbf{x}_i - \mathbf{x}_j\|^2}{4t}}$$

This operator can be naturally extended to an integral operator (with respect to the empirical measure of the dataset) on functions in $\mathbb{R}^k$:

$$\mathbf{L}_n^t(f)(\mathbf{x}) = f(\mathbf{x}) \sum_j e^{-\frac{\|\mathbf{x} - \mathbf{x}_j\|^2}{4t}} - \sum_j f(\mathbf{x}_j) e^{-\frac{\|\mathbf{x} - \mathbf{x}_j\|^2}{4t}}$$

Of course, we have $\mathbf{L}_n^t f(\mathbf{x}_i) = L_n^t f(\mathbf{x}_i)$. We will call $\mathbf{L}_n^t$ the *Laplacian operator associated to the point cloud* $\mathcal{S}_n$.

3   Main Result

Our main contribution is to establish a connection between the graph Laplacian associated to a point cloud and the Laplace-Beltrami operator on the underlying manifold from which the points are drawn.

Consider a compact[1] k-dimensional differentiable manifold $\mathcal{M}$ isometrically embedded in $\mathbb{R}^N$. We will assume that the data is sampled from a uniform distribution in the induced measure on $\mathcal{M}$.

Given data points $\mathcal{S}_n = \{\mathbf{x}_1, \ldots, \mathbf{x}_n\}$ in $\mathbb{R}^N$ sampled i.i.d. from this probability distribution we construct the associated Laplacian operator $\mathbf{L}_n^t$. Our main result shows that for a fixed function $f \in C^\infty(\mathcal{M})$ and for a fixed point $\mathbf{p} \in \mathcal{M}$, after appropriate scaling the operator $\mathbf{L}_n^t$ converges to the true Laplace-Beltrami operator on the manifold.

Theorem 1. *Let data points* $\mathbf{x}_1, \ldots, \mathbf{x}_n$ *be sampled from a uniform distribution on a manifold* $\mathcal{M} \subset \mathbb{R}^N$ *Put* $t_n = n^{-\frac{1}{k+2+\alpha}}$, *where* $\alpha > 0$ *and let* $f \in C^\infty(\mathcal{M})$. *Then there is a constant* C, *s.t. in probability,*

$$\lim_{n \to \infty} C \frac{(4\pi t_n)^{-\frac{k+2}{2}}}{n} \mathbf{L}_n^{t_n} f(\mathbf{x}) = \Delta_{\mathcal{M}} f(\mathbf{x})$$

Without going into full details we then outline the proof of the following

---

[1] It is possible to provide weaker but more technical conditions, which we will not discuss here.

Theorem 2. *Let data points* $\mathbf{x}_1, \ldots, \mathbf{x}_n$ *be sampled from a uniform distribution on a compact manifold* $\mathcal{M} \subset \mathbb{R}^N$. *Let* $\mathcal{F}$ *be the space of functions* $f \in C^\infty(\mathcal{M})$, *such that* Δf *is Lipschitz a fixed Lipschitz constant. Then there exists a sequence of real numbers* $t_n \to 0$, *and a constant* C, *such that in probability*

$$\lim_{n \to \infty} \sup_{\substack{\mathbf{x} \in \mathcal{M} \\ f \in \mathcal{F}}} \left| C \frac{(4\pi t_n)^{-\frac{k+2}{2}}}{n} \mathbf{L}_n^{t_n} f(\mathbf{x}) - \Delta_{\mathcal{M}} f(\mathbf{x}) \right| = 0$$

This stronger uniform result (with, however, a potentially worse rate of convergence) will in our opinion lead to consistency results for various learning algorithms in the future work.

3.1   Laplace Operator and the Heat Equation

We will now recall some results on the heat equation and its connection to the Laplace-Beltrami operator and develop some intuitions about the methods used in the proof.

Now we need to recall some results about the heat equation and heat kernels. Recall that the *Laplace operator* in $\mathbb{R}^k$ is defined as

$$\Delta f(\mathbf{x}) = \sum_i \frac{\partial^2 f}{\partial x_i^2}(\mathbf{x})$$

We say that a sufficiently differentiable function $u(\mathbf{x}, t)$ satisfies the *heat equation* if

$$\frac{\partial}{\partial t} u(\mathbf{x}, t) - \Delta u(\mathbf{x}, t) = 0 \tag{1}$$

The heat equation describes diffusion of heat with the initial distribution $u(\mathbf{x}, t)$. The solution to the heat equation is given by a semi-group of heat operators $\mathbf{H}^t$. Given an initial heat distribution $f(\mathbf{x})$, $\mathbf{H}^t(f)$ is the heat distribution at time t.

It turns out that this operator is given by convolution with the heat kernel, which for $\mathbb{R}^k$ is the usual Gaussian.

$$\mathbf{H}^t f(\mathbf{x}) = \int_{\mathbb{R}^k} f(\mathbf{y}) H^t(\mathbf{x}, \mathbf{y}) d\mathbf{y}$$

$$H^t(\mathbf{x}, \mathbf{y}) = (4\pi t)^{-\frac{k}{2}} e^{-\frac{\|\mathbf{x} - \mathbf{y}\|^2}{4t}}$$

We summarize this in the following

Theorem 3 (Solution to the heat equation in $\mathbb{R}^k$). *Let* $f(\mathbf{x})$ *be a sufficiently differentiable bounded function. We then have*

$$\mathbf{H}^t f = (4\pi t)^{-\frac{k}{2}} \int_{\mathbb{R}^k} e^{-\frac{\|\mathbf{x} - \mathbf{y}\|^2}{4t}} f(\mathbf{y}) d\mathbf{y} \tag{2}$$

$$f(\mathbf{x}) = \lim_{t \to 0} \mathbf{H}^t f(\mathbf{x}) = (4\pi t)^{-\frac{k}{2}} \int_{\mathbb{R}^k} e^{-\frac{\|\mathbf{x} - \mathbf{y}\|^2}{4t}} f(\mathbf{y}) d\mathbf{y} \tag{3}$$

The function $u(\mathbf{x}, t) = \mathbf{H}^t f$ *satisfies the heat equation*

$$\frac{\partial}{\partial t}u(\mathbf{x},t) - \Delta u(\mathbf{x},t) = 0$$

The heat equation is the key to approximating the Laplace operator. Recalling that a Gaussian integrates to 1, we observe that

$$-\Delta f(\mathbf{x}) = \frac{\partial}{\partial t}\mathbf{H}^t f(\mathbf{x})\Big|_{t=0} =$$

$$\lim_{t\to 0}\frac{1}{t}\left((4\pi t)^{-\frac{k}{2}}\int_{\mathbb{R}^k}e^{-\frac{\|\mathbf{x}-\mathbf{y}\|^2}{4t}}f(\mathbf{y})dy - f(\mathbf{x})(4\pi t)^{-\frac{k}{2}}\int_{\mathbb{R}^k}e^{-\frac{\|\mathbf{x}-\mathbf{y}\|^2}{4t}}d\mathbf{y}\right)$$

This quantity can easily be approximated from a point cloud[2] $\mathbf{x}_1,\ldots,\mathbf{x}_n$ by computing the empirical version of the integrals involved:

$$\hat{\Delta}f(\mathbf{x}) = \frac{1}{t}\frac{(4\pi t)^{-\frac{k}{2}}}{n}\left(f(\mathbf{x})\sum_i e^{-\frac{\|\mathbf{x}_i-\mathbf{x}\|^2}{4t}} - \sum_i e^{-\frac{\|\mathbf{x}_i-\mathbf{p}\|^2}{4t}}f(\mathbf{x}_i)\right) =$$

$$\frac{(4\pi t)^{-\frac{k+2}{2}}}{n}\mathbf{L}_n^t(f)(\mathbf{p})$$

This intuition can be easily turned into a convergence result for $\mathbb{R}^k$.

Extending this analysis to an arbitrary manifold, however, is not as straightforward as it might seem at first blush. The two principal technical issues are the following:

1. With some very rare exceptions we do not know the exact form of the heat kernel $H_{\mathcal{M}}^t(\mathbf{x},\mathbf{y})$.
2. Even the asymptotic form of the heat kernel requires knowing the geodesic distance between points in the point cloud. However we can only observe distances in the ambient space $\mathbb{R}^N$.

Remarkably both of these issues can be overcome as certain intrinsic quantities (scalar curvature) make an appearance and ultimately cancel out in the final computation!

4   Proof of the Main Results

4.1   Basic Differential Geometry

Before we proceed further, let us briefly review some basic notions of differential geometry. Assume we have a compact[3] differentiable k-dimensional submanifold

---

[2] We are ignoring the technicalities about the probability distribution for the moment. It is not hard however to show that it is sufficient to restrict the distribution to some open set containing the point $\mathbf{x}$.

[3] We assume compactness to simplify the exposition. A weaker condition will suffice as noted above.

of $\mathbb{R}^N$ with the induced Riemannian structure. That means that we have a notion of *length* for curves on $\mathcal{M}$. Given two points $\mathbf{x}, \mathbf{y} \in \mathcal{M}$ the *geodesic distance* $\mathrm{dist}_{\mathcal{M}}(\mathbf{x}, \mathbf{y})$ is the length of the shortest curve connecting $\mathbf{x}$ and $\mathbf{y}$. It is clear that $\mathrm{dist}_{\mathcal{M}}(\mathbf{x}, \mathbf{y}) \geq \|\mathbf{x} - \mathbf{y}\|$.

Given a point $\mathbf{p} \in \mathcal{M}$, one can identify the *tangent space* $T_{\mathbf{p}}\mathcal{M}$ with an affine subspace of $\mathbb{R}^N$ passing through $\mathbf{p}$. This space has a natural linear structure with the origin at $\mathbf{p}$. Furthermore it is possible to define the *exponential map* $\exp_{\mathbf{p}} : T_{\mathbf{p}}\mathcal{M} \to \mathcal{M}$. The key property of the exponential map is that it takes lines through origin in $T_{\mathbf{p}}\mathcal{M}$ to geodesics passing through $\mathbf{p}$. The exponential map is a local diffeomorphism and produces a natural system of coordinates for some neighborhood of $\mathbf{p}$. The Hopf-Rinow theorem (see, e.g., [11]) implies that a compact manifold is *geodesically complete*, i.e. that any geodesic can be extended indefinitely which, in particular, implies that there exists a geodesic connecting any two given points on the manifold.

The Riemannian structure on $\mathcal{M}$ induces a measure corresponding to the *volume form*, which we will denote as μ. For a compact $\mathcal{M}$ total volume of $\mathcal{M}$ is guaranteed to be finite, which gives rise to the canonical *uniform* probability distribution on $\mathcal{M}$.

Before proceeding with the main proof we state one curious property of geodesics, which will be needed later. It concerns the relationship between $\mathrm{dist}_{\mathcal{M}}(\mathbf{x}, \mathbf{y})$ and $\|\mathbf{x} - \mathbf{y}\|$. The geodesic and chordal distances are shown pictorially in Fig. 1. It is clear that when $\mathbf{x}$ and $\mathbf{y}$ are close, the difference between these two quantities is small. Interestingly, however, this difference is smaller than one (at least the authors) would expect initially. It turns out (cf. 7) that when the manifold is compact

$$\mathrm{dist}_{\mathcal{M}}(\mathbf{x}, \mathbf{y}) = \|\mathbf{x} - \mathbf{y}\| + O(\|\mathbf{x} - \mathbf{y}\|^3)$$

In other words chordal distance approximates geodesic distance up to order three. This observation and certain consequent properties of the geodesic map make the approximations used in this paper possible.

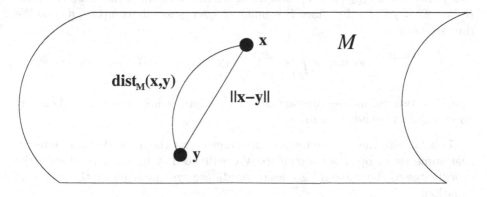

Fig. 1. Geodesic and chordal distance

The Laplace-Beltrami operator $\Delta_{\mathcal{M}}$ is a second order differential operator. The family of diffusion operators $\mathbf{H}^t_{\mathcal{M}}$ satisfies the following properties:

$$\Delta_{\mathcal{M}}\mathbf{H}^t_{\mathcal{M}}(f) = \frac{\partial}{\partial t}\mathbf{H}^t_{\mathcal{M}}(f) \quad \text{Heat Equation}$$

$$\lim_{t \to 0}\mathbf{H}^t_{\mathcal{M}}(f) = f \qquad \delta\text{-family property}$$

It can be shown (see, e.g., [21]) that $\mathbf{H}^t_{\mathcal{M}}(f)$ is an integral operator, a convolution with the *heat kernel*. Our proof hinges on the fact that in geodesic coordinates the heat kernel can be approximated by a Gaussian for small values of t and the observations about the geodesics above.

4.2   Main Proof

We will now proceed with the proof of the main theorem.

First we note that the quantities

$$\int_{\mathcal{M}} e^{-\frac{\|\mathbf{p}-\mathbf{x}\|^2}{4t}} f(\mathbf{x})\, d\mu_{\mathbf{x}}$$

and

$$f(\mathbf{p})\int_{\mathcal{M}} e^{-\frac{\|\mathbf{p}-\mathbf{x}\|^2}{4t}}\, d\mu_{\mathbf{x}}$$

can be empirically estimated from the point cloud.

We will show how the Laplace-Beltrami operator can be estimated using these two empirical quantities. This estimate will provide a connection to $\mathbf{L}^t_n$.

The main theorem will be proved in several steps.

Lemma 1. *Given any open set* $\mathcal{B} \subset \mathcal{M}$, $\mathbf{p} \in \mathcal{B}$, *for any* $l \in N$,

$$\int_{\mathcal{B}\subset\mathcal{M}} e^{-\frac{\|\mathbf{p}-\mathbf{y}\|^2}{4t}} f(\mathbf{y})\, d\mu_{\mathbf{y}} - \int_{\mathcal{M}} e^{-\frac{\|\mathbf{p}-\mathbf{y}\|^2}{4t}} f(\mathbf{y})\, d\mu_{\mathbf{y}} = o(t^l)$$

as $t \to 0$.

Proof. Let $d = \inf_{\mathbf{x}\notin\mathcal{B}} \|\mathbf{p} - \mathbf{x}\|^2$ and let M be the measure of the complement to $\mathcal{B}$, i.e., $M = \mu(\mathcal{M} - \mathcal{B})$. Since $\mathcal{B}$ is open and $\mathcal{M}$ is locally compact, $d > 0$. We thus see that

$$\left| \int_{\mathcal{B}} e^{-\frac{\|\mathbf{p}-\mathbf{y}\|^2}{4t}} f(\mathbf{y})\, d\mu_{\mathbf{y}} - \int_{\mathcal{M}} e^{-\frac{\|\mathbf{p}-\mathbf{y}\|^2}{4t}} f(\mathbf{y})\, d\mu_{\mathbf{y}} \right| \le M \sup_{\mathbf{x}\in\mathcal{M}} (|f(\mathbf{x})|)e^{-\frac{d^2}{4t}}$$

The first two terms are constant and $e^{-\frac{d^2}{4t}}$ approaches zero faster then any polynomial as t tends to zero.

This Lemma allows us to replace the integral over the manifold by an integral over some small open set around $\mathbf{p}$. We will need it in order to change the coordinates to the standard geodesic coordinate system given by the following equation:

$$\mathbf{y} = \exp_{\mathbf{p}}(\mathbf{x})$$

Given a function $f : \mathcal{M} \to \mathbb{R}$, we rewrite it in geodesic coordinates by putting $\tilde{f}(\mathbf{x}) = f(\exp(\mathbf{x}))$.

We will need the following key statement relating the Laplace-Beltrami operator and the Euclidean Laplacian:

Lemma 2.

$$\Delta_{\mathcal{M}} f(\mathbf{p}) = \Delta_{\mathbb{R}^k} \tilde{f}(0) \tag{4}$$

Proof. See, e.g., [21], page 90.

This allows one to reduce Laplace-Beltrami operator to a more easily analyzed Laplace operator on $\mathbb{R}^k$.

Since $\exp_{\mathbf{p}} : T\mathcal{M}_{\mathbf{p}} = \mathbb{R}^k \to \mathcal{M}$ is a locally invertible, we can choose an open $\tilde{\mathcal{B}} \subset \mathbb{R}^k$, s.t. $\exp_{\mathbf{p}}$ is a diffeomorphism onto its image $\mathcal{B} \subset \mathcal{M}$.

Lemma 3. *The following change of variable formula holds:*

$$\int_{\mathcal{B}} e^{-\frac{\|\mathbf{p}-\mathbf{y}\|^2}{4t}} f(\mathbf{y}) \, d\mu_{\mathbf{y}} = \int_{\tilde{\mathcal{B}}} e^{-\frac{\phi(\mathbf{x})}{4t}} \tilde{f}(\mathbf{x}) \det(d\exp(\mathbf{x})) \, d\mathbf{x} \tag{5}$$

where $\phi(\mathbf{x})$ is a function, such that $\phi(\mathbf{x}) = \|\mathbf{x}^2\| + O(\|\mathbf{x}^4\|)$.

Proof. We obtain the result by applying the usual change of variable formula for manifold integrals and observing the relationship between geodesic and chordal distances from Lemma 7.

Lemma 4. *There exists a constant C, such that*

$$\frac{\partial}{\partial t} \left((4\pi t)^{-\frac{k}{2}} \int_{\mathcal{B}} e^{-\frac{\|\mathbf{p}-\mathbf{y}\|^2}{4t}} f(\mathbf{y}) \, d\mu_{\mathbf{y}} \right) \bigg|_0 = \Delta_{\mathcal{M}} f(\mathbf{p}) + \frac{1}{3} ks(\mathbf{p})f(\mathbf{p}) + Cf(\mathbf{p}) \tag{6}$$

Proof. We first use Eq. 5 from the previous Lemma to rewrite the integral in the geodesic normal coordinates. We then apply Eq. 12 to obtain

$$\frac{\partial}{\partial t} \left((4\pi t)^{-\frac{k}{2}} \int_{\mathcal{B}} e^{-\frac{\|\mathbf{p}-\mathbf{y}\|^2}{4t}} f(\mathbf{y}) \, d\mu_{\mathbf{y}} \right) \bigg|_0 = \Delta_{\mathbb{R}^k} (\tilde{f} \det(d\exp_{\mathbf{p}}))(0) + C\tilde{f}(0) \tag{7}$$

From the asymptotics of the exponential map (Eq. 10), we know that

$$|\Delta_{\mathbb{R}^k} \det(d\exp_{\mathbf{p}}(\mathbf{x}))| = \frac{s(\mathbf{p})}{3} + O(\|\mathbf{x}\|)$$

Using properties of the Laplacian and recalling that $\tilde{f}(0) = f(\mathbf{p})$ yields and that $\det(d\exp_{\mathbf{p}}(\mathbf{x}))|$ has no terms of degree 1 in its Taylor expansion at 0, we have

$$\Delta_{\mathbb{R}^k} (\tilde{f} \det(d\exp_{\mathbf{p}}))(0) = \Delta_{\mathbb{R}^k} \tilde{f}(0) + \frac{1}{3} ks(\mathbf{p})f(\mathbf{p})$$

Noticing that by Eq. 4 $\Delta_{\mathbb{R}^k} \tilde{f}(0) = \Delta_{\mathcal{M}} f(\mathbf{p})$, we obtain the result.

Thus we get the following

Lemma 5.

$$\lim_{t \to 0} (4\pi t)^{-\frac{k+2}{2}} \left(\int_{\mathcal{M}} e^{-\frac{\|\mathbf{p}-\mathbf{y}\|^2}{4t}} f(\mathbf{p}) \, d\mu_{\mathbf{y}} - \int_{\mathcal{M}} e^{-\frac{\|\mathbf{p}-\mathbf{y}\|^2}{4t}} f(\mathbf{y}) \, d\mu_{\mathbf{y}} \right) = \Delta_{\mathcal{M}} f(\mathbf{p})$$

Proof. Consider the constant function $g(\mathbf{y}) = f(\mathbf{p})$. By applying the Eq. 6 to this function we obtain

$$\frac{\partial}{\partial t} \left((4\pi t)^{-\frac{k}{2}} \int_{\mathcal{B}} e^{-\frac{\|\mathbf{p}-\mathbf{y}\|^2}{4t}} f(\mathbf{p}) \, d\mu_{\mathbf{y}} \right) \bigg|_{0} = \frac{1}{3} ks(\mathbf{p}) f(\mathbf{p}) + C f(\mathbf{p}) \qquad (8)$$

To simplify the formulas put $A(t) = (4\pi t)^{-\frac{k+2}{2}} \int_{\mathcal{M}} e^{-\frac{\|\mathbf{p}-\mathbf{y}\|^2}{4t}} f(\mathbf{y}) \, d\mu_{\mathbf{y}}$. Using the δ-family property of the heat kernel, we see that

$$A(0) = \lim_{t \to 0} (4\pi t_n)^{-\frac{k}{2}} \int_{\mathcal{B}} e^{-\frac{\|\mathbf{p}-\mathbf{y}\|^2}{4t}} f(\mathbf{p}) \, d\mu_{\mathbf{y}} = f(\mathbf{p})$$

From the definition of the derivative and Eqs. 6,8 we obtain

$$\Delta_{\mathcal{M}} f(\mathbf{p}) = \lim_{t \to 0} \frac{A(t) - A(0)}{t} =$$

$$\lim_{t \to 0} (4\pi t_n)^{-\frac{k+2}{2}} \left(\int_{\mathcal{M}} e^{-\frac{\|\mathbf{p}-\mathbf{y}\|^2}{4t}} f(\mathbf{p}) \, d\mu_{\mathbf{y}} - \int_{\mathcal{M}} e^{-\frac{\|\mathbf{p}-\mathbf{y}\|^2}{4t}} f(\mathbf{y}) \, d\mu_{\mathbf{y}} \right)$$

Theorem 4. *Let data points* $\mathbf{x}_1, \ldots, \mathbf{x}_n$ *be sampled in i.i.d. fashion from a uniform distribution on a compact submanifold* $\mathcal{M} \subset \mathbb{R}^N$. *Fix* $\mathbf{p} \in \mathcal{M}$. *Let* $\mathbf{L}_n^{t_n}$ *be the associated operator. Put* $t_n = n^{-\frac{1}{k+2+\alpha}}$, *where* $\alpha > 0, \alpha \in \mathbb{R}$. *Then in probability*

$$\lim_{n \to \infty} (4\pi t_n)^{-\frac{k+2}{2}} \mathbf{L}_n^{t_n} f(\mathbf{x}) = \frac{\Delta_{\mathcal{M}} f(\mathbf{p})}{\mathrm{vol}(\mathcal{M})}$$

Proof. Recall that (the extension of) the graph Laplacian $\mathbf{L}_n^t$ applied to f at $\mathbf{p}$ is

$$\mathbf{L}_n^t f(\mathbf{p}) = \frac{1}{n} \left(\sum_{i=1}^n e^{-\frac{\|\mathbf{p}-\mathbf{x}_i\|^2}{4t}} f(\mathbf{p}) - \sum_{i=1}^n e^{-\frac{\|\mathbf{p}-\mathbf{x}_i\|^2}{4t}} f(\mathbf{x}_i) \right)$$

We note that $\mathbf{L}_n^t f(\mathbf{p})$ is the empirical average of n independent random variables with the expectation

$$\mathbb{E} \mathbf{L}_n^t f(\mathbf{p}) = \left(f(\mathbf{p}) \int_{\mathcal{M}} e^{-\frac{\|\mathbf{p}-\mathbf{y}\|^2}{4t}} \, d\mathbf{y} - \int_{\mathcal{M}} f(\mathbf{y}) e^{-\frac{\|\mathbf{p}-\mathbf{y}\|^2}{4t}} \, d\mathbf{y} \right) \qquad (9)$$

By an application of Hoeffding's inequality 6, we have

$$\mathbb{P} \left[(4\pi t)^{-(k+2)/2} |\mathbf{L}_n^t f(\mathbf{p}) - \mathbb{E} \mathbf{L}_n^t f(\mathbf{p})| > \epsilon \right] \leq e^{-\epsilon^2 n (4\pi t)^{(k+2)}}$$

Choosing t as a function of n by letting $t = t_n = \left(\frac{1}{n}\right)^{\frac{1}{k+2+\alpha}}$, where $\alpha > 0$, we see that for any fixed $\epsilon > 0$

$$\lim_{n \to \infty} \mathbb{P} \left[(4\pi t_n)^{-(k+2)/2} |\mathbf{L}_n^{t_n} f(\mathbf{p}) - \frac{1}{n} \mathbb{E} \mathbf{L}_n^{t_n} f(\mathbf{p})| > \epsilon \right] = 0.$$

Noting that by Lemma 5 and Eq. 9

$$\lim_{n \to \infty} (4\pi t_n)^{-\frac{1}{(k+2)/2}} \, \mathbf{L}_n^{t_n} = \frac{\Delta_{\mathcal{M}} f(\mathbf{p})}{\text{vol}(\mathcal{M})}$$

we obtain the theorem.

5   Uniform Convergence

For a fixed function f, let

$$A_f(t) = (4\pi t)^{-\frac{k+2}{2}} \left(\int_{\mathcal{M}} e^{-\frac{\|\mathbf{p}-\mathbf{y}\|^2}{4t}} f(\mathbf{p}) \, d\mu_{\mathbf{y}} - \int_{\mathcal{M}} e^{-\frac{\|\mathbf{p}-\mathbf{y}\|^2}{4t}} f(\mathbf{y}) \, d\mu_{\mathbf{y}} \right)$$

Its empirical version from the point cloud is simply

$$\hat{A}_f(t) = (4\pi t)^{-\frac{k+2}{2}} \frac{1}{n} \sum_{i=1}^{n} e^{-\frac{\|\mathbf{p}-\mathbf{y}\|^2}{4t}} (f(\mathbf{p}) - f(\mathbf{x}_i)) = \frac{-(4\pi t)^{\frac{k+2}{2}}}{n} \mathbf{L}_n^t f(\mathbf{p})$$

By the standard law of large numbers, we have that $\hat{A}_f(t)$ converges to $A_f(t)$ in probability. One can easily extend this uniformly over all functions in the following proposition

Proposition 1. *Let F be the space of functions $f \in C^{\infty}(\mathcal{M})$, such that Δf is Lipschitz with Lipschitz constant C. For each fixed t, we have*

$$\lim_{n \to \infty} \mathbb{P} \left[\sup_{f \in F} |\hat{A}_f(t) - A_f(t)| > \epsilon \right] = 0$$

Proof. Let $F_\gamma \subset F$ be a γ-net in F in the L_∞ topology (guaranteed by the Sobolev embedding theorem) and let $N(\gamma)$ be the size of this net. This guarantees that for any $f \in F$, there exists $g \in F_\gamma$ such that $\|f - g\|_\infty < \gamma$. By a standard union bound over the finite elements of F_γ, we have

$$\lim_{n \to \infty} \mathbb{P} \left[\sup_{g \in F_\gamma} |\hat{A}_g(t) - A_g(t)| > \frac{\epsilon}{2} \right] = 0$$

Now for any $f \in F$, we have that

$$|\hat{A}_f(t) - A_f(t)| \le |\hat{A}_f(t) - \hat{A}_g(t) + \hat{A}_g(t) + A_g(t) - A_g(t) - A_f(t)|$$

$$\le |\hat{A}_f(t) - \hat{A}_g(t)| + |\hat{A}_g(t) - A_g(t)| + |A_g(t) - A_f(t)|$$

It is easy to check that for $\gamma = \frac{\epsilon}{4}(4\pi t)^{\frac{k+2}{2}}$, we have

$$|\hat{A}_f(t) - A_f(t)| < \frac{\epsilon}{2} + \sup_{g \in F_\gamma} |\hat{A}_g(t) - A_g(t)|$$

Therefore

$$\mathbb{P}\left[\sup_{f \in F} |\hat{A}_f(t) - A_f(t)| > \epsilon\right] \leq \mathbb{P}\left[\sup_{g \in F_\gamma} |\hat{A}_g(t) - A_g(t)| > \frac{\epsilon}{2}\right]$$

Taking limits as n goes to infinity, the result follows.

Now we note from Lemma 5 that for each $f \in F$, we have

$$\lim_{t \to 0}(A_f(t) - \Delta_{\mathcal{M}} f(p)) = 0$$

By an analog of the Arzela-Ascoli Theorem, the uniform convergence over a ball in a suitable Sobolev space over a compact domain can be shown, i.e.,

$$\lim_{t \to 0} \sup_{f \in F}(A_f(t) - \Delta_{\mathcal{M}} f(p)) = 0$$

Therefore, from Proposition 1 and the above fact, we see that there exists a monotonically decreasing sequence t_n such that $\lim_{n \to \infty} t_n = 0$ for which the following theorem is true.

Theorem 5. *Let data points* $\mathbf{x}_1, \ldots, \mathbf{x}_n$ *be sampled from a uniform distribution on a compact manifold* $\mathcal{M} \subset \mathbb{R}^N$ *and let* $\mathcal{F}_C$ *be the space of functions* $f \in C^\infty(\mathcal{M})$, *such that* Δf *is Lipschitz with Lipschitz constant* C. *Then there exists a sequence of real numbers* t_n, $t_n \to 0$, *such that in probability*

$$\lim_{n \to \infty} \sup_{f \in \mathcal{F}_C} \left|\frac{(4\pi t_n)^{-\frac{k+2}{2}}}{n} \mathbf{L}_n^{t_n} f(\mathbf{x}) - \Delta_{\mathcal{M}} f(\mathbf{x})\right| = 0$$

A similar uniform convergence bound can be shown using the compactness of $\mathcal{M}$ and leads to Theorem 2.

6   Auxiliary and Technical Lemmas

6.1   Exponential Map and Geodesics

Lemma 6. *Asymptotics for the derivative of the* exp.

$$|\Delta_{\mathbb{R}^k} \det(d \exp_{\mathbf{p}}(\mathbf{x}))| = \frac{s(\mathbf{p})}{3} + O(\|\mathbf{x}\|) \tag{10}$$

where $s(\mathbf{p})$ *is the scalar curvature of* $\mathcal{M}$ *at* $\mathbf{p}$.

Proof. This fairly standard result of differential geometry follows from properties of Jacobi fields. While the proof goes beyond the scope of this paper, cf. the discussion on page 115 in [11]. The result above follows from Eq. 6 together with some basic linear algebra after writing the curvature tensor in the geodesic normal coordinates.

Lemma 7.
$$\| \exp_{\mathbf{p}}(\mathbf{x}) \|^2 = \| \mathbf{x} - \mathbf{p} \|^2 + O(\| \mathbf{x} - \mathbf{p} \|^4)$$

Proof. The geodesic distance from a fixed point $\mathbf{x} \in \mathcal{M}^k$ as a function of $\mathbf{y}$ can be written as
$$\mathrm{dist}_{\mathcal{M}^k}(\mathbf{x}, \mathbf{y}) = \| \mathbf{y} - \mathbf{x} \| + O(\| \mathbf{y} - \mathbf{x} \|^3)$$
where $\| \mathbf{y} - \mathbf{x} \|$ is the ordinary norm in $\mathbb{R}^N$. Thus the geodesic distance can be approximated by Euclidean distance in the ambient space up to terms of order three. We outline the proof. We first prove the statement for the curve length in $\mathbb{R}^2$. Let $f(x)$ be a differentiable function. Without the loss of generality we can assume that $f(0) = 0$, $f'(0) = 0$. Therefore $f(x) = ax^2 + O(x^3)$. Now the length of the curve along the graph of $f(x)$ is given by

$$\mathrm{dist}_{\mathcal{M},0}(t) = \int_0^t \sqrt{1 + (f')^2}\, dx$$

We have $\sqrt{1 + (f')^2} = 1 + 2ax^2 + O(x^3)$. Thus

$$\int_0^t \sqrt{1 + (f')^2}\, dx = t + \frac{2}{3}at^3 + O(t^4)$$

Similarly, we can also see that segment of the line connecting the point t to the origin is equal in length to both the curve length and to t up to some terms of order 3.

In general, we can take a section of the manifold by a 2-dimensional plane through $\mathbf{x}$ and $\mathbf{y}$, such that the plane intersects the manifold at a curve. It is not hard to see, that such a plane always exists.

It is clear that the length of the geodesic is bounded from below by the length of the line segment connecting $\mathbf{x}$ to the $\mathbf{y}$ and from above by the length of the curve formed by intersection of the plane and $\mathcal{M}^k$. By applying the case of $\mathbb{R}^2$, we see that the latter is equal to $\| \mathbf{x} - \mathbf{y} \|$ plus order three terms, which implies the statement.

6.2   Technical Results in $\mathbb{R}^k$

Lemma 8. *Let $\mathcal{B} \subset \mathbb{R}^k$ be an open set, such that $\mathbf{x} \in \mathcal{B}$. Then as $t \to 0$*

$$\int\limits_{\mathbb{R}^k - \mathcal{B}} (4\pi t)^{-\frac{k}{2}} e^{-\frac{\| \mathbf{x} - \mathbf{y} \|^2}{4t}}\, dx = o\left(\frac{1}{t} e^{-\frac{1}{t}} \right)$$

Proof. Without a loss of generality we can assume that $\mathbf{x} = 0$. There exists a cube C_s with side s, such that $0 \in C_s \in \mathcal{B}$. We have $\int\limits_{\mathbb{R}^k - \mathcal{B}} (4\pi t)^{-\frac{k}{2}} e^{-\frac{\| \mathbf{z} \|^2}{4t}}\, dx <$

$\int\limits_{\mathbb{R}^k - C_s} (4\pi t)^{-\frac{k}{2}} e^{-\frac{\| \mathbf{z} \|^2}{4t}}\, dx$. Using the standard substitution $\mathbf{z} = \frac{\| \mathbf{z} \|}{\sqrt{t}}$, we can rewrite the last integral as

$$\int\limits_{\mathbb{R}^k - C_s} (4\pi t)^{-\frac{k}{2}} e^{-\frac{\| \mathbf{z} \|^2}{4t}}\, dx = \int\limits_{\mathbb{R}^k - C_{\frac{s}{\sqrt{t}}}} (4\pi)^{-\frac{k}{2}} e^{-\frac{\| \mathbf{z} \|^2}{4}}\, d\mathbf{z}$$

The last quantity is the probability that all coordinates of a standard multivariate Gaussian are greater than than $\frac{s}{\sqrt{t}}$ in absolute value and is therefore equal to $2 - 2(1 - \mathrm{Erf}(\frac{s}{\sqrt{t}}))^k < 2k - 2k\,\mathrm{Erf}\left(\frac{s}{\sqrt{t}}\right)$. Applying a well-known inequality $1 - \mathrm{Erf}(t) < \frac{1}{t\exp(t^2)}$ yields the statement.

Lemma 9. *Let $\phi : \mathbb{R}^k \to \mathbb{R}^k$ be a differentiable function such that $\phi(\mathbf{x}) = \mathbf{x} + O(\mathbf{x}^3)$, i.e. the Taylor expansion for each coordinate of ϕ does not have any terms of degree 2, $[\phi(\mathbf{x})]_i = x_i + O(\|\mathbf{x}\|^3)$ at the origin. Then for any open set $\mathcal{B}$ containing the origin the following two expressions hold (the first one is true even if ϕ has terms of degree 2.*

$$f(0) = \lim_{t\to 0}(4\pi t)^{-\frac{n}{2}} \int_{\mathcal{B}\subset R^k} e^{-\frac{\phi(\mathbf{y})^2}{4t}} f(\mathbf{y})\,d\mathbf{y} \tag{11}$$

$$\Delta f(0) = -\frac{\partial}{\partial t}\left((4\pi t)^{-\frac{n}{2}}\int_{\mathcal{B}\subset R^k} e^{-\frac{\phi(\mathbf{y})^2}{4t}}f(\mathbf{y})\,d\mathbf{y}\right)\bigg|_0 + Cf(0) \tag{12}$$

C here is a constant depending only on ϕ.

Proof. We will concentrate on proving formula (12), formula (11) is a corollary of the computation below. From the previous Lemma, it can be easily seen that the set $\mathcal{B}$ can be replaced by the whole space R^k. For simplicity we will show the formula when $n = 1$. The case of arbitrary n is no different but requires rather cumbersome notation. We can write $f(y) = a_0 + a_1 y + a_2 y^2 + \dots$ and $\phi(y) = y + b_0 y^3 + \dots$. Put $y = \sqrt{t}x$. Changing the variable, we get:

$$\frac{1}{\sqrt{t}}\int_{\mathbb{R}} e^{-\frac{\phi(y)^2}{4t}} f(y)dy = \frac{1}{\sqrt{t}}\int_{\mathbb{R}} e^{-\frac{ty^2 + t^2 b_0 y^4 + \dots}{4t}} f(\sqrt{t}y)\sqrt{t}dy =$$

$$= \int_{\mathbb{R}} e^{-\frac{y^2 + tb_0 y^4 + o(t)}{4}} f(\sqrt{t}y)dy$$

Note that $e^{-\frac{y^2 + tb_0 y^4 + o(t)}{4}} = e^{-\frac{y^2}{4}} e^{-\frac{tb_0 y^4 + o(t)}{4}} = e^{-\frac{y^2}{4}}(1 - t\frac{b_0}{4}y^4 + o(t))$. Thus the previous integral can be written as

$$\int_{\mathbb{R}} e^{-\frac{x^2}{4}}\left(1 - t\frac{b_0}{4}x^4 + o(t)\right) f(\sqrt{t}x)dx$$

$$= \int_{\mathbb{R}} e^{-\frac{x^2}{4}}\left(1 - t\frac{b_0}{4}x^4 + o(t)\right)\left(a_0 + a_1\sqrt{t}x + a_2 tx^2 + o(t)\right) dx$$

$$= \int_{\mathbb{R}} e^{-\frac{x^2}{4}}\left(a_0 + a_1\sqrt{t}x + t(a_2 x^2 - a_0\frac{b_0}{4}x^4) + o(t)\right) dx$$

Note that the second term $a_1\sqrt{t}x$ is an odd function in x and therefore $\int_{\mathbb{R}} e^{-\frac{x^2}{4}} a_1\sqrt{t}xdx = 0$.
Thus

$$\frac{\partial}{\partial t}\left(\frac{1}{2\sqrt{t\pi}}\int_{\mathbb{R}} e^{-\frac{y^2 + y^4\phi(y)}{4t}} f(y)dy\right)\bigg|_0 = \frac{1}{2\sqrt{\pi}}\int_{\mathbb{R}} e^{-\frac{x^2}{4}} a_2 x^2 dx - \frac{1}{2\sqrt{\pi}}\int_{\mathbb{R}} e^{-\frac{x^2}{4}}\frac{b_0}{4}x^4 dx$$

The first integral in the sum is exactly the Laplacian of f at 0, $\Delta f(0) = \frac{1}{2\sqrt{\pi}} \int_{\mathbb{R}} e^{-\frac{x^2}{4}} a_2 x^2 dx$. The second summand depends only on the value $a_0 = f(0)$ and the function ϕ, which completes the proof.

6.3   Probability

Theorem 6 (Hoeffding). *Let* $X_1, \ldots, X_n$ *be independent identically distributed random variables, such that* $|X_i| \leq K$. *Then*

$$P\left\{ \left| \frac{\sum_i X_i}{n} - \mathbb{E}X_i \right| > \epsilon \right\} < 2 \exp\left(-\frac{\epsilon^2 n}{2K^2} \right)$$

Acknowledgements

We thank Matthias Hein for pointing out an error in Claim 4.2.6. in [1] and an earlier version of Lemma 6.

References

1. M. Belkin, *Problems of Learning on Manifolds*, The University of Chicago, Ph.D. Dissertation, 2003.
2. M. Belkin, P. Niyogi, *Using Manifold Structure for Partially Labeled Classification*, NIPS 2002.
3. M. Belkin, P. Niyogi. (2003). *Laplacian Eigenmaps for Dimensionality Reduction and Data Representation*, Neural Computation, Vol. 15, No. 6, 1373-1396.
4. M. Belkin, P. Niyogi, V. Sindhwani, *On Manifold Regularization*, AI Stats 2005.
5. Y. Bengio, J.-F. Paiement, P. Vincent, O. Delalleau, N. Le Roux, M. Ouimet, *Out-of-Sample Extensions for LLE, Isomap, MDS, Eigenmaps, and Spectral Clustering*, NIPS 2003.
6. M. Bernstein, V. de Silva, J.C. Langford, J.B. Tenenbaum, *Graph approximations to geodesics on embedded manifolds*, Technical Report, 2000.
7. O. Bousquet, O. Chapelle, M. Hein, *Measure Based Regularization*, NIPS 2003.
8. Y. Bengio, J-F. Paiement, and P. Vincent, *Out-of-Sample Extensions for LLE, Isomap, MDS, Eigenmaps, and Spectral Clustering*, NIPS 2003.
9. Chapelle, O., J. Weston and B. Schoelkopf, *Cluster Kernels for Semi-Supervised Learning*, NIPS 2002.
10. F. R. K. Chung. (1997). *Spectral Graph Theory*. Regional Conference Series in Mathematics, number 92.
11. M. do Carmo, *Riemannian Geometry*, Birkhauser, 1992.
12. D. L. Donoho, C. E. Grimes, *Hessian Eigenmaps: new locally linear embedding techniques for high-dimensional data*, Proceedings of the National Academy of Arts and Sciences vol. 100 pp. 5591-5596.
13. M. Hein, J.-Y. Audibert, U. von Luxburg, *From Graphs to Manifolds – Weak and Strong Pointwise Consistency of Graph Laplacians*, COLT 2005, (to appear).
14. M. Meila, J. Shi, *Learning segmentation by random walks*, NIPS 2000.
15. F. Memoli, G. Sapiro, *Comparing Point Clouds*, IMA Technical Report, 2004.

16. S. Lafon, *Diffusion Maps and Geodesic Harmonics*, Ph. D. Thesis, Yale University, 2004.
17. U. von Luxburg, M. Belkin, O. Bousquet, *Consistency of Spectral Clustering*, Max Planck Institute for Biological Cybernetics Technical Report TR 134, 2004.
18. A. Ng, M. Jordan, Y. Weiss, *On Spectral Clustering: Analysis and an Algorithm*, NIPS 2001.
19. P. Niyogi, *Estimating Functional Maps on Riemannian Submanifolds from Sampled Data*, http://www.ipam.ucla.edu/publications/mgaws3/mgaws3_5188.pdf, presented at IPAM Workshop on Multiscale structures in the analysis of High-Dimensional Data, 2004.
20. P. Niyogi, S. Smale, S. Weinberger, *Finding the Homology of Submanifolds with High Confidence from Random Samples*, Univ. of Chicago Technical Report TR-2004-08, 2004.
21. S. Rosenberg, *The Laplacian on a Riemannian Manifold*, Cambridge University Press, 1997.
22. Sam T. Roweis, Lawrence K. Saul. (2000). *Nonlinear Dimensionality Reduction by Locally Linear Embedding*, Science, vol 290.
23. A. Smola and R. Kondor, *Kernels and Regularization on Graphs*, COLT/KW 2003.
24. J. Shi, J. Malik, *Normalized Cuts and Image Segmentation*, IEEE Transactions on Pattern Analysis and Machine Intelligence, 22, 8, 2000.
25. D. Spielman, S. Teng, *Spectral partitioning works: planar graphs and finite element meshes*, FOCS 1996.
26. Martin Szummer, Tommi Jaakkola, *Partially labeled classification with Markov random walks*, NIPS 2001.
27. J.B.Tenenbaum, V. de Silva, J. C. Langford. (2000). *A Global Geometric Framework for Nonlinear Dimensionality Reduction*, Science, Vol 290.
28. R. Kannan, S. Vempala, A. Vetta, *On Clusterings - Good, Bad and Spectral*, Technical Report, Computer Science Department, Yale University, 2000.
29. D. Zhou, O. Bousquet, T.N. Lal, J. Weston and B. Schoelkopf, *Learning with Local and Global Consistency*, NIPS 2003.
30. X. Zhu, J. Lafferty and Z. Ghahramani, *Semi-supervised learning using Gaussian fields and harmonic functions*, ICML 2003.
31. A. Zomorodian, G. Carlsson, *Computing persistent homology*, 20th ACM Symposium on Computational Geometry, 2004.

Permutation Tests for Classification

Polina Golland[1], Feng Liang[2], Sayan Mukherjee[2,3], and Dmitry Panchenko[4]

[1] Computer Science and Artificial Intelligence Laboratory,
[2] Institute of Statistics and Decision Sciences,
[3] Institute for Genome Sciences and Policy, Duke University,
Durham, NC 27708, USA
[4] Department of Mathematics, Massachusetts Institute of Technology,
Cambridge, MA 02139, USA
pollina@csail.mit.edu, {feng, sayan}@stat.duke.edu
panchenk@math.mit.edu

Abstract. We describe a permutation procedure used extensively in classification problems in computational biology and medical imaging. We empirically study the procedure on simulated data and real examples from neuroimaging studies and DNA microarray analysis. A theoretical analysis is also suggested to assess the asymptotic behavior of the test. An interesting observation is that concentration of the permutation procedure is controlled by a Rademacher average which also controls the concentration of empirical errors to expected errors.

1 Introduction

Many scientific studies involve detection and characterization of predictive patterns in high dimensional measurements, which can often be reduced to training a binary classifier or a regression model. Examples of this type of data include medical image studies and gene expression analysis. Image-based clinical studies of brain disorders attempt to detect neuroanatomical changes induced by diseases, as well as predict development of the disease. The goals of gene expression analysis include classification of the tissue morphology and prediction of the treatment outcome from DNA microarray data. Data in both fields are characterized by high dimensionality of the input space (thousands of features) and small datasets (tens of independent examples), typical of many biological applications.

A basic question is in this setting is how can one have any modicum of faith in the accuracy of the trained classifier. One approach to this problem would be to estimate the test error on a hold-out set – or by applying a cross-validation procedure, such as a jackknife [2] – which, in conjunction with a variance-based convergence bound, provides a confidence interval for the expected error. Small sample sizes render this approach ineffective as the variance of the error on a hold-out set is often too large to provide a meaningful estimate on how close we are to the true error. Applying variance-based bounds to the cross-validation error estimates produces misleading results as the cross-validation iterations are

P. Auer and R. Meir (Eds.): COLT 2005, LNAI 3559, pp. 501–515, 2005.

not independent, causing us to underestimate the variance. Classical generalization bounds are also not appropriate in this regime due to the high dimensionality and small sample size. In addition, even if a consistent algorithm is used that produces a classifier with low variance the data itself may have no structure. Neither cross-validation nor classical generalization bounds address this issue.

Recently, several research groups, including ours, proposed using permutation tests [10, 8] to assess the reliability of the classifier's accuracy via a notion of statistical significance [7, 16, 13, 15, 6]. Intuitively, statistical significance is a measure of how likely the observed accuracy would be obtained by chance, only because the training algorithm identified some pattern in the high-dimensional data that happened to correlate with the class labels as an artifact of a small data set size. A significant classifier would reject the null hypothesis that the features and the labels are independent, that is, there is no difference between the two classes. The cross-validation error or the test error on a hold-out set is used as a test statistic that measures how different the two classes are with respect to the family of classifiers we use in training, and its distribution under the null hypothesis is estimated by permuting the labels.

A notion of statistical significance or of variance does not always add more information to the classification problem than the classification error. For example, for a fixed classifier [9] shows that statistical significance estimates carry at most as much information as the classification error. This is due to the fact that a fixed classifier can be modeled as a Bernoulli distribution and the variance will be determined by the mean, which is an estimate of the classifiers accuracy. However, this will not hold for a family of classifiers, the family needs to be restricted to control the variance and for a uniform law of large numbers to hold.

The objective of this paper is to examine with some care permutation tests for classification both empirically and theoretically so as to provide users with some practical recommendations and suggest a theoretical basis to the procedure. The remaining of the paper is organized as follows. The next section describes the permutation procedure to estimate statistical significance of classification results. Section 3 applies the procedure to simulated data as well as real data from the fields of brain imaging and gene expression analysis and offers practical guidelines for applying the procedure. In Section 4, we suggest a theoretical analysis of the procedure that leads to convergence bounds governed by similar quantities to those that control standard empirical error bounds, closing with a brief discussion of open questions.

2   Permutation Test for Classification

In two-class comparison hypothesis testing, the differences between two data distributions are measured using a dataset statistic

$$T : (\mathbb{R}^n \times \{-1, 1\})^l \mapsto \mathbb{R},$$

such that for a given dataset $S = \{(\mathbf{x}_k, y_k)\}_{k=1}^l$, where $\mathbf{x}_k \in \mathbb{R}^n$ are observations and $y_k \in \{-1, 1\}$ are the corresponding class labels, $T(\mathbf{x}_1, y_1, \ldots, \mathbf{x}_l, y_l)$ is a measure of the similarity of the subsets $\{\mathbf{x}_k|y_k=1\}$ and $\{\mathbf{x}_k|y_k=-1\}$. The null hypothesis typically assumes that the two conditional probability distributions are identical, $p(\mathbf{x}|y=1) = p(\mathbf{x}|y=-1)$, or equivalently, that the data and the labels are independent, $p(\mathbf{x}, y) = p(\mathbf{x})p(y)$. The goal of the hypothesis test is to reject the null hypothesis at a certain level of significance α which sets the maximal acceptable probability of false positive (declaring that the classes are different when the null hypothesis is true). For any value of the statistic, the corresponding *p-value* is the highest level of significance at which the null hypothesis can still be rejected.

The test statistics used in this paper are training errors, cross-validation errors, or jackknife estimates. Here we give as an example the jackknife estimate

$$T(\mathbf{x}_1, y_1, \ldots, \mathbf{x}_l, y_l) = \frac{1}{l} \sum_{i=1}^{l} I(f_{S^i}(x_i) \neq y_i),$$

where S^i is the dataset with the ith sample removed and f_{S^i} is the function obtained by the classification algorithm given the dataset S^i and $I(\cdot)$ is the indicator function.

Suppose we have chosen an appropriate statistic T and the acceptable significance level α. Let Π_l be the set of all permutations of the samples $(\mathbf{x}_i)_{i=1}^l$, where for the permutation π, $\mathbf{x}_i^\pi$ is the i-th sample after permutation. The permutation test procedure is described as follows:

- Repeat M times (with index $m = 1, \ldots, M$):
  - sample a permutation π^m from a uniform distribution over Π_l,
  - compute the statistic value for this permutation of samples

$$t^m = T(\mathbf{x}_1^m, y_1, \ldots, \mathbf{x}_l^m, y_l).$$

- Construct an empirical cumulative distribution (ecdf)

$$\hat{P}(T < t) = \frac{1}{M} \sum_{m=1}^{M} \Theta(t - t^m),$$

where the step function $\Theta(x - y) = 1$ if $x \geq y$ and otherwise is 0.

- Compute $t_0 = T(\mathbf{x}_1, y_1, \ldots, \mathbf{x}_l, y_l)$ and the corresponding p-value $\hat{p}_0 = \hat{P}(t_0)$. If $\hat{p}_0 \leq \alpha$, then reject the null hypothesis.

Ideally, we would like to use the entire set of permutations Π_l to calculate the corresponding p-value p_0, but it might be not feasible for computational reasons. Instead, we resort to sampling from Π_l and use Monte Carlo methods to approximate p_0. The Monte Carlo approximation $\hat{p}_0$ has a standard deviation given by $\sqrt{\frac{p_0(1-p_0)}{M}}$ [3]. Since p_0 is unknown in practice, the corresponding upper bound $\frac{1}{2\sqrt{M}}$ is often used to determine the number of iterations required to achieve desired prevision of the test.

3   Application of the Test

In this section, we demonstrate the procedure on simulated data and then on two different examples, a study of changes in the cortical thickness due to Alzheimer's disease using MRI scans for measurement and a discrimination between two types of leukemia based on DNA microarray data. For a more extensive exposition over various datasets see [12].

The simulated data was generated as follows: 160 samples were generated from two normal distributions in $\mathbb{R}^2$ with means $(\pm 1, 0)$ and identity covariance with half the samples drawn from each distribution. Samples from group one were assigned a label $y = +1$ with probability p and $y = -1$ with probability $(1 - p)$. The opposite was done for group two. The probability $p \in [0, .5]$ denotes the noise level. We used linear discriminant analysis to train the classifier. The results are shown in Figures (1, 2, 3) for training error, leave-one-out error, and test error (the hold-out set is 20 samples per group), respectively. The black lines in the graphs plot the ecdfs of various errors for 5000 permutations of the data. As the noise parameter p is scanned over $\{.1, .2, .3, .4, .5\}$ the value of the unpermuted statistic, the red bar, shifts right. The value at which the red bar meets the black line determines the p-value (given in the caption for each figure). When the noise level increases, that is, the labels and features become more independent, the p-value increases as shown in those figures.

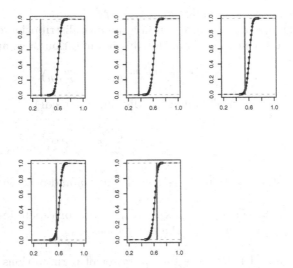

Fig. 1. Training error: p-values $= \{0.0002, 0.0002, 0.0574, 0.1504, 0.8290\}$

For the real dataset we used linear Support Vector Machines [19] to train a classifier, and jackknifing (i.e., sampling without replacement) for cross-validation. The number of cross-validation iterations was 1,000, and the number of permutation iterations was 10,000.

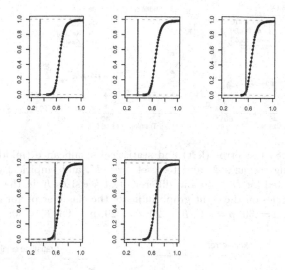

Fig. 2. Leave-one-out error: p-values $= \{0.0002, 0.0002, 0.0430, 0.1096, 0.7298\}$

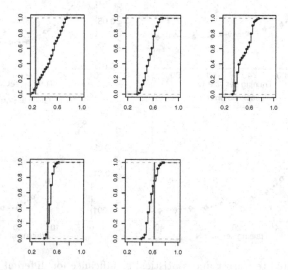

Fig. 3. Test error: p-values $= \{0.0764, 0.0012, 0.0422, 0.1982, 0.7594\}$

The first example compares the thickness of the cortex in 50 patients diagnosed with dementia of the Alzheimer type and 50 normal controls of matched age [5, 4]. The dimensionality of the input space was $300,000$.

The statistic and its null distribution as a function of training set and hold-out set size is plotted in Figure (4). Every point in the first two graphs is characterized by a corresponding training set size N and hold-out set size K, drawn from the original dataset. It is not surprising that increasing the number of training examples improves the robustness of classification as exhibited by both the ac-

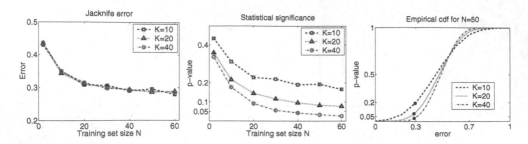

Fig. 4. Estimated test error (left) and statistical significance (middle) computed for different training set sizes N and test set sizes K, and empirical error distribution (right) constructed for $N = 50$ and different test set sizes K in the cortical thickness study. Filled circles on the right graph indicate the classifier performance on the true labels ($K = 10$: $e = .30$, $p = .19$; $K = 20$: $e = .29$, $p = .08$; $K = 40$: $e = .29$, $p = .03$)

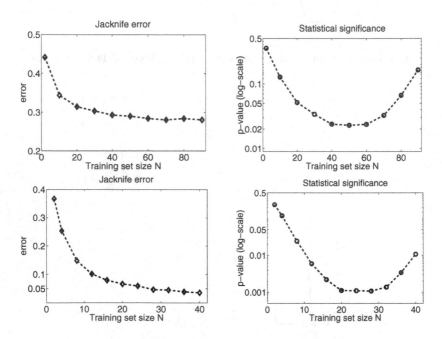

Fig. 5. Estimated test error and statistical significance for different training set sizes N for (top) the cortical thickness study and (bottom) the leukemia morphology study. Unlike the experiments in Figure (4), all of the examples unused in training were used to test the classifier. The p-values are shown on a logarithmic scale

curacy and the significance estimates. By examining the left graph, we conclude that at approximately $N = 40$, the accuracy of the classification saturates at 71% ($e = .29$). After this point decreasing the number of hold-out samples does not significantly affect the estimated classification error, but does substantially decrease the statistical significance of the same error value. The right graph in Figure (4) illustrates this point for a particular training set size of $N = 50$.

Figure (5) shows the estimated classification error and the corresponding p-values that were estimated using all of the examples left out in the training step in the hold-out set. While the error graph looks very similar to that in Figure (4), the behavior of significance estimates is quite different. The p-values originally decrease as the training set size increases, but after a certain point, they start growing. Two conflicting factors control p-value estimates as the number of training examples increases: improved accuracy of the classification, which causes the point of interest to slide to the left – and as a result, down – on the ecdf curve, and the decreasing number of test examples, which causes the ecdf curve to become more shallow.

The second example compares DNA microarray expression data from two types of leukemia acute myeloid leukemia (AML) and acute lymphoblastic leukemia (ALL) [7, 16]. The data set contains 48 samples of AML and 25 samples of ALL. The dimensionality of the input space was $7, 129$. Figure 5 shows the results for this study. The cross-validation error reduces rapidly as we increase the number of training examples, dropping below 5% at $N = 26$ training examples. The p-values also decrease very quickly as we increase the number of training examples, achieving minimum of $.001$ at $N = 28$ training examples. Like the previous example, the most statistically significant result lies in the range of relatively slow error change.

4   A Theoretical Motivation for the Permutation Procedure

The point of the permutation procedure is to examine if a classifier selected from a family of classifiers given a dataset is predictive. By predictive we mean that the dependence relationship between y and $\mathbf{x}$ learned by the classifier is significantly different from the independent one. In the examples shown previously in the paper we used the training error as well as the leave-one-out or cross-validation error as the statistic used in the permutation procedure. Our theoretical motivation will focus on the training error. We will remark on generalizations to the leave-one-out error.

In Section 4.2 we relate the concentration of the permutation procedure to p-values and comment on generalizing the proof to account for the leave-one-out error as the statistic used in the permutation procedure. In Section 4.3 we note that for classifiers finite VC dimension is a necessary and sufficient condition for the concentration of the permutation procedure.

4.1   Concentration of the Permutation Procedure

We are given a class of classifiers $\mathcal{C}$. Since there are only two classes, any classifier $c \in \mathcal{C}$ can be regarded as a subset of $\mathbb{R}^n$ to which class label $\{+1\}$ is assigned. Without loss of generality we will assume $\emptyset \in \mathcal{C}$. Assume there is an unknown concept c_0: $y = +1$, if $\mathbf{x} \in c_0$ and $y = -1$, otherwise. For a permutation $\boldsymbol{\pi}$ of the training data, the smallest training error on the permuted set is

$$e_l(\boldsymbol{\pi}) = \min_{c \in \mathcal{C}} P_l(c \triangle c_0) \tag{1}$$

$$= \min_{c \in \mathcal{C}} \left[\frac{1}{l} \sum_{i=1}^{l} I(\mathbf{x}_i \in c, \mathbf{x}_i^{\pi} \notin c_0) + I(\mathbf{x}_i \notin c, \mathbf{x}_i^{\pi} \in c_0) \right],$$

where $\mathbf{x}_i$ is the i-th sample and $\mathbf{x}_i^{\pi}$ is the i-th sample after permutation. For a fixed classifier $c \in \mathcal{C}$ the average error is

$$\mathbb{E}P_l(c \triangle c_0) = \left(1 - \frac{1}{l}\right) [P(c)(1 - P(c_0)) + (1 - P(c))P(c_0)] +$$
$$\frac{1}{l}[P(c) + P(c_0) - 2P(c \cap c_0)],$$

where the expectation is taken over the data $\mathbf{x}$ and permutations $\boldsymbol{\pi}$. As l gets large the average error is approximately $P(c)(1 - P(c_0)) + (1 - P(c))P(c_0)$ and since we can assume $P(c_0) \leq 1/2$ taking $c = \emptyset$ minimizes the average error at $P(c_0)$. We later refer to $P(c_0)$ as the random error because, a classifier such as $c = \emptyset$ is not informatively at all. Our goal is to show that under some complexity assumptions on class $\mathcal{C}$ the smallest training error $e_l(\boldsymbol{\pi})$ is close to the random error $P(c_0)$.

Minimizing (1) is equivalent to the following maximization problem

$$\max_{c \in \mathcal{C}} \left[\frac{1}{l} \sum_{i=1}^{l} I(\mathbf{x}_i \in c)(2I(\mathbf{x}_i^{\pi} \in c_0) - 1) \right],$$

since

$$e_l(\boldsymbol{\pi}) = P_l(\mathbf{x} \in c_0) - \max_{c \in \mathcal{C}} \left[\frac{1}{l} \sum_{i=1}^{l} I(\mathbf{x}_i \in c)(2I(\mathbf{x}_i^{\pi} \in c_0) - 1) \right],$$

and $P_l(\mathbf{x} \in c_0)$ is the empirical measure of the target concept. We would like to show that $e_l(\boldsymbol{\pi})$ is close to the random error $P(\mathbf{x} \in c_0)$ and give rates of convergence. We will do this by bounding the process

$$G_l(\boldsymbol{\pi}) = \sup_{c \in \mathcal{C}} \left[\frac{1}{l} \sum_{i=1}^{l} I(\mathbf{x}_i \in c)(2I(\mathbf{x}_i^{\pi} \in c_0) - 1) \right]$$

and using the fact that, by Chernoff's inequality, $P_l(\mathbf{x} \in c_0)$ is close to $P(\mathbf{x} \in c_0)$:

$$\mathbb{P}\left(P(\mathbf{x} \in c_0) - P_l(\mathbf{x} \in c_0) \leq \sqrt{\frac{2P(c_0)(1 - P(c_0))t}{l}} \right) \geq 1 - e^{-t}. \tag{2}$$

Theorem 1. *If the concept class $\mathcal{C}$ has VC dimension V then with probability* $1 - Ke^{-t/K}$

$$G_l(\boldsymbol{\pi}) \leq K \min \left(\sqrt{\frac{V \log l}{l}}, \frac{V \log l}{l(1 - 2P(c_0))^2} \right) + \sqrt{\frac{Kt}{l}}.$$

Remark. The second quantity in the above bound comes from the application of Chernoff's inequality similar to (2) and, thus, has a "one dimensional nature" in a sense that it doesn't depend on the complexity (VC dimension) of class $\mathcal{C}$. An interesting property of this result is that if $P(c_0) < 1/2$ then first term that depends on the VC dimension V will be of order $\frac{V \log l}{l}$ which, ignoring the "one dimensional terms", gives the zero-error type rate of convergence of $e_l(\pi)$ to $P(\mathbf{x} \in c_0)$. Combining this theorem and equation (2) we can state that with probability $1 - Ke^{-t/K}$.

$$P(\mathbf{x} \in c_0) \leq P_l(\mathbf{x} \in c_0) + K \min\left(\sqrt{\frac{V \log l}{l}}, \frac{V \log l}{l(1 - 2P(c_0))^2}\right) + \sqrt{\frac{Kt}{l}}.$$

Throughtout this paper K designates a constant the value of which can change over the equations.

In order to prove Theorem 1, we require several preliminary results. We first prove the following useful lemma.

Lemma 1. *It is possible to construct on the same probability space two i.i.d Bernoulli sequences $\varepsilon = (\varepsilon_1, \ldots, \varepsilon_n)$ and $\varepsilon' = (\varepsilon'_1, \ldots, \varepsilon'_n)$ such that ε is independent of $\varepsilon'_1 + \ldots + \varepsilon'_n$ and $\sum_{i=1}^{n} |\varepsilon_i - \varepsilon'_i| = |\sum_{i=1}^{n} \varepsilon_i - \sum_{i=1}^{n} \varepsilon'_i|$.*

Proof. For $k = 0, \ldots, n$, let us consider the following probability space $\mathcal{E}_k$. Each element w of $\mathcal{E}_k$ consists of two coordinates $w = (\varepsilon, \pi)$. The first coordinate $\varepsilon = (\varepsilon_1, \ldots, \varepsilon_n)$ has the marginal distribution of an i.i.d. Bernoulli sequence. The second coordinate π implements the following randomization. Given the first coordinate ε, consider a set $\mathcal{I}(\varepsilon) = \{i : \varepsilon_i = 1\}$ and denote its cardinality $m = \text{card}\{\mathcal{I}(\varepsilon)\}$. If $m \geq k$, then π picks a subset $\mathcal{I}(\pi, \varepsilon)$ of $\mathcal{I}(\varepsilon)$ with cardinality k uniformly, and if $m < k$, then π picks a subset $\mathcal{I}(\pi, \varepsilon)$ of the complement $I^c(\varepsilon)$ with cardinality $n - k$ also uniformly. On this probability space $\mathcal{E}_k$, we construct a sequence $\varepsilon' = \varepsilon'(\varepsilon, \pi)$ in the following way. If $k \leq m = \text{card}\{\mathcal{I}(\varepsilon)\}$ then we set $\varepsilon'_i = 1$ if $i \in \mathcal{I}(\pi, \varepsilon)$ and $\varepsilon'_i = -1$ otherwise. If $k > m = \text{card}\{\mathcal{I}(\varepsilon)\}$ then we set $\varepsilon'_i = -1$ if $i \in \mathcal{I}(\pi, \varepsilon)$ and $\varepsilon'_i = 1$ otherwise. Next, we consider a space $\mathcal{E} = \cup_{k \leq n} \mathcal{E}_k$ with probability measure $\mathbb{P}(\mathcal{A}) = \sum_{k=0}^{n} B(n, p, k)\mathbb{P}(\mathcal{A} \cap \mathcal{E}_k)$, where $B(n, p, k) = \binom{n}{k}p^k(1 - p)^{n-k}$. On this probability space the sequence ε and ε' will satisfy the conditions of the lemma. First of all, $X = \varepsilon'_1 + \ldots + \varepsilon'_n$ has binomial distribution since by construction $\mathbb{P}(X = k) = \mathbb{P}(\mathcal{E}_k) = B(n, p, k)$. Also, by construction, the distribution of ε' is invariant under the permutation of coordinates. This, clearly, implies that ε' is i.i.d. Bernoulli. Also, obviously, ε is independent of $\varepsilon'_1 + \ldots + \varepsilon'_n$. Finally, by construction $\sum_{i=1}^{n} |\varepsilon_i - \varepsilon'_i| = |\sum_{i=1}^{n} \varepsilon_i - \sum_{i=1}^{n} \varepsilon'_i|$. □

Definition 1. *Let $u > 0$ and let $\mathcal{C}$ be a set of classifiers. Every finite set of concepts $c_1, \ldots, c_n$ with the property that for all $c \in \mathcal{C}$ there is a c_j such that*

$$\frac{1}{l}\sum_{i=1}^{l} |c_j(x_i) - c(x_i)|^2 \leq u$$

is called a u-cover with respect to $||\cdot||_{L_2(\mathbf{x}_l)}$. *The covering number* $\mathcal{N}(\mathcal{C}, u, \{\mathbf{x}_1, ..\mathbf{x}_l\})$ *is the smallest number for which the above holds.*

Definition 2. *The uniform metric entropy is* $\log \mathcal{N}(\mathcal{C}, u)$ *where* $\mathcal{N}(\mathcal{C}, u)$ *is the smallest integer for which*

$$\forall l, \quad \forall (\mathbf{x}_1, ..., \mathbf{x}_l), \quad \mathcal{N}(\mathcal{C}, u, \{\mathbf{x}_1, ..\mathbf{x}_l\}) \leq \mathcal{N}(\mathcal{C}, u).$$

Lemma 2. *The following holds with probability greater than* $1 - Ke^{-t/K}$

$$G_l(\boldsymbol{\pi}) \leq \sup_r \left[K \frac{1}{\sqrt{l}} \int_0^{\sqrt{\mu_r}} \sqrt{\log \mathcal{N}(u, \mathcal{C})} du - \frac{\mu_r}{2} (1 - 2P(c_0)) + \sqrt{\frac{\mu_r(t + 2\log(r + 1))}{l}} \right]$$

$$+ 2\sqrt{\frac{2tP(c_0)(1 - P(c_0))}{l}},$$

where $\mu_r = 2^{-r}$ *and* $\log \mathcal{N}(\mathcal{C}, u)$ *is the uniform metric entropy for the class* $\mathcal{C}$.

Proof. The process

$$G_l(\boldsymbol{\pi}) = \sup_{c \in \mathcal{C}} \left[\frac{1}{l} \sum_{i=1}^l I(\mathbf{x}_i \in c)(2I(\mathbf{x}_i^\pi \in c_0) - 1) \right].$$

can be rewritten as

$$G_l(\boldsymbol{\pi}) = \sup_{c \in \mathcal{C}} \left[\frac{1}{l} \sum_{i=1}^l I(\mathbf{x}_i \in c)\varepsilon_i \right],$$

where $\varepsilon_i = 2I(\mathbf{x}_i^\pi \in c_0) - 1 = \pm 1$ are Bernoulli random variables with $P(\varepsilon_i = 1) = P(c_0)$. Due to permutations the random variables (ε_i) depend on $(\mathbf{x}_i)$ only through the cardinality of $\{\mathbf{x}_i \in c_0\}$. By lemma 1 we can construct a random Bernoulli sequence (ε_i') that is independent of $\mathbf{x}$ and for which

$$G_l(\boldsymbol{\pi}) \leq \sup_{c \in \mathcal{C}} \left[\frac{1}{l} \sum_{i=1}^l I(\mathbf{x}_i \in c)\varepsilon_i' \right] + \left| \frac{1}{l} \sum_{i=1}^l \varepsilon_i - \frac{1}{l} \sum_{i=1}^l \varepsilon_i' \right|.$$

We first control the second term

$$\left| \frac{1}{l} \sum_{i=1}^l \varepsilon_i - \frac{1}{l} \sum_{i=1}^l \varepsilon_i' \right| \leq \left| \frac{1}{l} \sum_{i=1}^l \varepsilon_i' - (2P(c_0) - 1) \right| + \left| \frac{1}{l} \sum_{i=1}^l \varepsilon_i - (2P(c_0) - 1) \right|,$$

then using Chernoff's inequality twice we get with probability $1 - 2e^{-t}$

$$\left| \frac{1}{l} \sum_{i=1}^l \varepsilon_i - \frac{1}{l} \sum_{i=1}^l \varepsilon_i' \right| \leq 2\sqrt{\frac{2tP(c_0)(1 - P(c_0))}{l}}.$$

We block concepts in $\mathcal{C}$ into levels

$$\mathcal{C}_r = \left\{ c \in \mathcal{C} : \frac{1}{l} \sum_{i=1}^{l} I(\mathbf{x}_i \in c) \in (2^{-r-1}, 2^{-r}] \right\}$$

and denote $\mu_r = 2^{-r}$. We define the processes

$$R(r) = \sup_{c \in \mathcal{C}_r} \left[\frac{1}{l} \sum_{i=1}^{l} I(\mathbf{x}_i \in c) \varepsilon_i' \right],$$

and obtain

$$\sup_{c \in \mathcal{C}} \left[\frac{1}{l} \sum_{i=1}^{l} I(\mathbf{x}_i \in c) \varepsilon_i' \right] \leq \sup_r R(r).$$

By Talagrand's convex hull inequality on the two point space [17], we have for each level r

$$\mathbb{P}_{\varepsilon'} \left(R(r) \leq \mathbb{E}_{\varepsilon'} \sup_{c \in \mathcal{C}_r} \left[\frac{1}{l} \sum_{i=1}^{l} I(\mathbf{x}_i \in c) \varepsilon_i' \right] + \sqrt{\frac{\mu_r t}{l}} \right) \geq 1 - K e^{-t/K}.$$

Note that for this inequality to hold, the random variables (ε') need only be independent, they do not need to be symmetric. This bound is conditioned on a given $\{\mathbf{x}_i\}_{i=1}^{l}$ and by taking the expectation w.r.t. $\{\mathbf{x}_i\}$ we get,

$$\mathbb{P} \left(R(r) \leq \mathbb{E}_{\varepsilon'} \sup_{c \in \mathcal{C}_r} \left[\frac{1}{l} \sum_{i=1}^{l} I(\mathbf{x}_i \in c) \varepsilon_i' \right] + \sqrt{\frac{\mu_r t}{l}} \right) \geq 1 - K e^{-t/K}.$$

If, for each r, we set $t \to t + 2\log(r+1)$, we can write

$$\mathbb{P} \left(\forall r \; R(r) \leq \mathbb{E}_{\varepsilon'} \sup_{c \in \mathcal{C}_r} \left[\frac{1}{l} \sum_{i=1}^{l} I(\mathbf{x}_i \in c) \varepsilon_i' \right] + \sqrt{\frac{\mu_r(t + 2\log(r+1))}{l}} \right)$$

$$\geq 1 - \sum_{r=0}^{\infty} \frac{1}{(r+1)^2} e^{-t/4} \geq 1 - 2 e^{-t/4}.$$

Using standard symmetrization techniques we add and subtract an independent sequence ε_i'' such that $\mathbb{E}\varepsilon_i'' = \mathbb{E}\varepsilon_i' = (2P(c_0) - 1)$:

$$\mathbb{E}_{\varepsilon'} \sup_{c \in \mathcal{C}_r} \left[\frac{1}{l} \sum_{i=1}^{l} I(\mathbf{x}_i \in c) \varepsilon_i' \right]$$

$$\leq \mathbb{E}_{\varepsilon'} \sup_{c \in \mathcal{C}_r} \left[\frac{1}{l} \sum_{i=1}^{l} I(\mathbf{x}_i \in c) \varepsilon_i' - \frac{1}{l} \sum_{i=1}^{l} I(\mathbf{x}_i \in c) \mathbb{E}\varepsilon_i'' + \frac{1}{l} \sum_{i=1}^{l} I(\mathbf{x}_i \in c)(2P(c_0) - 1) \right]$$

$$\leq \mathbb{E}_{\varepsilon' \varepsilon''} \sup_{c \in \mathcal{C}_r} \left[\frac{1}{l} \sum_{i=1}^{l} I(\mathbf{x}_i \in c)(\varepsilon' - \varepsilon'') \right] - (1 - 2P(c_0)) \inf_{c \in \mathcal{C}_r} \left(\frac{1}{l} \sum_{i=1}^{l} I(\mathbf{x}_i \in c) \right)$$

$$\leq 2\mathbb{E}_{\eta_i} \sup_{c \in \mathcal{C}_r} \left[\frac{1}{l} \sum_{i=1}^{l} I(\mathbf{x}_i \in c) \eta_i \right] - \frac{\mu_r(1 - 2P(c_0))}{2},$$

where $\eta_i = (\varepsilon_i' - \varepsilon_i'')/2$ takes values $\{-1, 0, 1\}$ with probability $P(\eta_i = 1) = P(\eta_i = -1)$. One can easily check that the random variables η_i are subgaussian, i.e.

$$\mathbb{P}\left(\sum_{i=1}^{l} \eta_i a_i > t\right) \leq e^{-\frac{t^2}{2\sum_{i=1}^{l} a_i^2}},$$

which is the only prerequisite for the chaining method. Thus, one can write Dudley's entropy integral bound, [18]

$$\mathbb{E}_{\eta_i} \sup_{c \in \mathcal{C}_r} \left[\frac{1}{l}\sum_{i=1}^{l} I(\mathbf{x}_i \in c)\eta_i\right] \leq K\frac{1}{\sqrt{l}} \int_0^{\sqrt{\mu_r}} \sqrt{\log \mathcal{N}(u, \mathcal{C})} du.$$

We finally get

$$\mathbb{P}\left(\forall r \ R(r) \leq K\frac{1}{\sqrt{l}} \int_0^{\sqrt{\mu_r}} \sqrt{\log \mathcal{N}(u, \mathcal{C})} du + \sqrt{\frac{\mu_r(t + 2\log(r+1))}{l}} - \frac{\mu_r(1 - 2P(c_0))}{2}\right)$$

$$\geq 1 - 2e^{-t/4}.$$

This completes the proof of Lemma 2. $\square$

Proof of Theorem 1. For a class with VC dimension V, it is well known that [18]

$$\frac{1}{\sqrt{l}} \int_0^{\sqrt{\mu_r}} \sqrt{\log \mathcal{N}(u, \mathcal{C})} du \leq K\sqrt{\frac{V\mu_r \log \frac{2}{\mu_r}}{l}}.$$

Since without loss of generality we only need to consider $\mu_r > 1/l$, it remains to apply lemma 2 and notice that

$$\sup_r \left[K\sqrt{\frac{V\mu_r \log l}{l}} - \frac{\mu_r}{2}(1 - 2P(c_0))\right] \leq K\min\left(\sqrt{\frac{V\log l}{l}}, \frac{V\log l}{l(1 - 2P(c_0))^2}\right).$$

All other terms that do not depend on the VC dimension V can be combined to give $\sqrt{Kt/l}$. $\square$

4.2 Relating p-Values to Concentration and the Leave-One-Out Error as the Permutation Statistic

The result of the previous section states that for VC classes the training error concentrates around $q = \min\{P(y = 1), P(y = -1)\}$.

We can relate this concentration result to the p-value computed by the permutation procedure. The purpose of this is to give a theoretical justification for the empirical procedure outlined in section 2. We do not recommend replacing the empirical procedure with the theoretical bound in practical applications. We assume the statistic used in the permutation procedure is the training error

$$\tau = \frac{1}{l}\sum_{i=1}^{l} I(f_S(x_i) \neq y_i),$$

and f_S is the function obtained by the classification algorithm given the dataset S. If we were given the distribution of the training errors over random draws and random label permutations we would have the distribution under the null hypothesis $P_{null}(\xi)$ and the p-value of the statistic τ would simply be $P_{null}(\xi \leq \tau)$. In the empirical procedure outlined in section 2 we used an empirical estimate $\hat{P}(\xi)$ to computed the p-value.

The results of section 4.1 give us a bound of the deviation of the training error of the permuted data from $P(c_0)$ under the null hypothesis, namely,

$$\mathbb{P}\left(|e_l(\boldsymbol{\pi}) - P(c_0)| \geq \varepsilon\right) \leq Ke^{-\varepsilon^2 \mathcal{O}(l)}, \tag{3}$$

where $\mathcal{O}(l)$ ignores $\log l$ terms. We assume that we know $P(c_0)$, otherwise it can be accurately estimated by a frequency count of $y = \pm 1$. We can bound the p-value by setting $|t - P(c_0)| = \varepsilon$ and computing $Ke^{-\varepsilon^2 \mathcal{O}(l)}$.

The difference between the p-value computed using the inequality (3) and that outlined in section 2 is the later is a one-sided test and is based upon empirical approximations rather than bounds. A one-sided test can be derived from the results in section 4.1 in a similar fashion as the two-sided test.

We can also use the leave-one-out error as the statistic used in the permutation procedure

$$\tau = \frac{1}{l}\sum_{i=1}^{l} I(f_{S^i}(x_i) \neq y_i),$$

where S^i is the dataset with the ith sample removed and f_{S^i} is the function obtained by the classification algorithm given the dataset S^i. In this case, for certain algorithms we can make the same theoretical arguments for the leave-one-out estimator as we did for the training error since with high probability the training error is close to the leave-one-out error.

Proposition 1. *If independent of measure* $\mu(\mathbf{x}, y)$ *with probability greater than* $1 - Ke^{-t/K}$

$$\left|\frac{1}{l}\sum_{i=1}^{l} I(f_{S^i}(x_i) \neq y_i) - \frac{1}{l}\sum_{i=1}^{l} I(f_S(x_i) \neq y_i)\right| \leq K\sqrt{\frac{t \log l}{l}},$$

then the leave-one-out estimate on the permuted data will concentrate around $P(c_0)$ *with the same rates of convergence as the training error.*

The proof is obvious in that if the deviation between the leave-one-out estimator and the training error is of the same order as that of the deviation between the training error and $P(c_0)$ and both hold with exponential probability then we can simply replace the leave-one-out error with the training error and maintain the same rate of convergence.

The condition in Proposition 1 holds for empirical risk minimization on a VC class in the realizable setting [11] and for Tikhonov regularization with Lipschitz loss functions [1].

4.3   A Necessary and Sufficient Condition for the Concentration of the Permutation Procedure

In this section we note that for a class of classifiers finite VC dimension is a necessary and sufficient condition for the concentration of the training error on the permuted data.

The proof of lemma 2 makes no assumptions of the class $\mathcal{C}$ except that it is a class of indicator functions and the bounds used in the proof are tight in that the equality can be achieved under certain distributions. A step in the proof of the lemma involved upper-bounding the Rademacher process by Dudley's entropy integral. The assumptions on the class $\mathcal{C}$ are introduced to control the Rademacher process in the inequality in lemma 2. For finite VC dimension the process can be upper bounded by $\mathcal{O}\left(\sqrt{\frac{1}{l}}\right)$ using Dudley's entropy integral which proves sufficiency. The Rademacher process can also be lower bounded by a function of the metric entropy by Sudakov minorization [18]. If $\mathcal{C}$ has infinite VC dimension this lower bound is a constant and the process does not concentrate which proves necessity.

5   Open Problems

The following is a list of open problems related to this methodology:

1. *Leave-one-out error and training error.* In the theoretical motivation, we relate the leave-one-out error to the training error for certain algorithms. The result would be stronger if proposition 1 held for VC classes in the nonrealizable setting.
2. *Feature selection.* Both in neuroimaging studies and in DNA microarray analysis, finding the features which most accurately classify the data is very important. Permutation procedures similar to the one described in this paper have been used to address this problem [7, 16, 14]. It would be very interesting to extend the type of analysis here to the feature selection problem.

References

1. O. Bousquet and A. Elisseeff. Stability and generalization. *Journal Machine Learning Research*, 2:499–526, 2002.
2. B. Efron. *The Jackknife, The Bootstrap, and Other Resampling Plans.* SIAM, Philadelphia, PA, 1982.
3. Bradley Efron and Robert Tibshirani. *An introduction to the bootstrap.* Chapman & Hall Ltd, 1993.
4. B. Fischl and A.M. Dale. Measuring the thickness of the human cerebral cortex from magnetic resonance images. *PNAS*, 26:11050–11055, 2000.
5. B. Fischl, M.I. Sereno, R.B.H. Tootell, and A.M. Dale. High-resolution intersubject averaging and a coordinate system for the cortical surface. *Human Brain Mapping*, 8:262–284, 1999.

6. P. Golland and B. Fischl. Permutation tests for classification: Towards statistical significance in image-based studies. In *IPMI'2003: The 18th International Conference on Information Processing and Medical Imaging*, volume LNCS 2732, pages 330–341, 2003.
7. T.R. Golub, D. Slonim, P. Tamayo, C. Huard, M. Gaasenbeek, J.P. Mesirov, H. Coller, M.L. Loh, J.R. Downing, M.A. Caligiuri, C. D. Bloomfield, and E. S. Lander. Molecular Classification of Cancer: Class discovery and class prediction by gene expression monitoring. *Science*, 286:531–537, 1999.
8. P. Good. *Permutation Tests: A Practical Guide to Resampling Methods for Testing Hypothesis*. Springer-Verlag, 1994.
9. T. Hsing, S. Attoor, and E. Dougherty. Relation between permutation-test p values and classifier error estimates. *Machine Learning*, 52:11–30, 2003.
10. M.G. Kendall. The treatment of ties in ranking problems. *Biometrika*, 33:239–251, 1945.
11. S. Kutin and P. Niyogi. Almost-everywhere algorithmic stability and generalization error. Technical report TR-2002-03, University of Chicago, 2002.
12. S. Mukherjee, P. Golland, and D. Panchenko. Permutation tests for classification. AI Memo 2003-019, Massachusetts Institute of Technology, 2003.
13. S. Mukherjee, P. Tamayo, S. Rogers, R. Rifkin, A. Engle, C. Campbell, T.R. Golub, and J.P. Mesirov. Estimating dataset size requirements for classifying dna microarray data. *Journal Computational Biology*, 10(2):119–142, 2003.
14. T.E. Nichols and A.P. Holmes. Nonparametric permutation tests for functional neuroimaging: A primer with examples. *Human Brain Mapping*, 15:1–25, 2001.
15. S. Pomeroy, P. Tamayo, M. Gaasenbeek, L. Sturlia, M. Angelo, j. Y. H. Kim M. E. McLaughlin, L. C. Goumnerova, P. M. Black, C. Lauand J. C. Lau, J. C. Allen, D. Zagzag, M. M. Olson, T. Curran, C. Wetmore, J. A. Biegel, T. Poggio, S. Mukherjee, R. Rifkin, A. Califano, G. Stolovitzky, D. N. Louis, J. P. Mesirov, E. S. Lander, and T. R. Golub. Prediction of embryonal tumor outcome based on gene expression. *Nature*, 415:436–442, 2002.
16. D. Slonim, P. Tamayo, J.P. Mesirov, T.R. Golub, and E. Lander. Class prediction and discovery using gene expression data. In *Proceedings of the Fourth Annual Conference on Computational Molecular Biology (RECOMB)*, pages 263–272, 2000.
17. M. Talagrand. Concentration of measure and isoperimetric inequalities in product spaces. *Publications Mathématiques de l'I.H.E.S.*, 81:73–205, 1995.
18. A. van der Vaart and J. Wellner. *Weak convergence and Empirical Processes With Applications to Statistics*. Springer-Verlag, 1996.
19. V.N. Vapnik. *Statistical Learning Theory*. John Wiley & Sons, 1998.

Localized Upper and Lower Bounds for Some Estimation Problems

Tong Zhang

IBM T.J. Watson Research Center, Yorktown Heights, NY 10598
tzhang@watson.ibm.com

Abstract. We derive upper and lower bounds for some statistical estimation problems. The upper bounds are established for the Gibbs algorithm. The lower bounds, applicable for all statistical estimators, match the obtained upper bounds for various problems. Moreover, our framework can be regarded as a natural generalization of the standard minimax framework, in that we allow the performance of the estimator to vary for different possible underlying distributions according to a pre-defined prior.

1   Introduction

The purpose of this paper is to derive upper and lower bounds for some prediction problems in statistical learning. The upper bounds are obtained for the Gibbs algorithm. The lower bounds are obtained from some novel applications of well-known information theoretical inequalities (specifically, data-processing theorems). We show that the upper bounds and lower bounds have very similar forms, and match under various conditions.

In statistical prediction, we have input space $\mathcal{X}$ and output space $\mathcal{Y}$, and a space of predictors $\mathcal{G}$. For any $X \in \mathcal{X}$, $Y \in \mathcal{Y}$, and any predictor $\theta \in \mathcal{G}$, we incur a loss $L_\theta(X, Y) = L_\theta(Z)$, where $Z = (X, Y) \in \mathcal{Z} = \mathcal{X} \times \mathcal{Y}$. Consider a probability measure D on $\mathcal{Z}$. Our goal is to find θ from a random sample $\hat{Z}$ from D, such that the loss $\mathbf{E}_Z L_\theta(Z)$ is small, where $\mathbf{E}_Z$ is the expectation with respect to D.

In the standard learning theory, we consider n random samples instead of one sample. The two formulations are in fact equivalent. To see this, consider $X = \{X_1, \ldots, X_n\}$ and $Y = \{Y_1, \ldots, Y_n\}$. Let $L_\theta(Z) = \sum_{i=1}^n L_{i,\theta}(X_i, Y_i)$. If $Z_i = (X_i, Y_i)$ are independent random variables, then it follows that $\mathbf{E}_Z L_\theta(Z) = \sum_{i=1}^n \mathbf{E}_{Z_i} L_{i,\theta}(X_i, Y_i)$. We shall thus focus on the one-sample case first without loss of generality.

In this paper, we consider randomized estimators. They are defined with respect to a prior π on $\mathcal{G}$, which is a probability measure on $\mathcal{G}$. For a randomized estimation method, given sample $\hat{Z}$ from D, we select θ from $\mathcal{G}$ based on a sample-dependent probability measure $d\hat{\pi}_{\hat{Z}}(\theta)$ on $\mathcal{G}$, In this paper, we shall call such a sample-dependent probability measure as a *posterior randomization measure* (or simplified as posterior). The word posterior in this paper is not

P. Auer and R. Meir (Eds.): COLT 2005, LNAI 3559, pp. 516–530, 2005.

necessarily the Bayesian posterior distribution in the traditional sense. For notational simplicity, we also use the symbol $\hat{\pi}$ to denote $\hat{\pi}_{\hat{Z}}$. The randomized estimator associated with a posterior randomization measure is thus completely determined by its posterior $\hat{\pi}$. Its *posterior averaging risk* is the averaged risk of the randomized estimator drawn from this posterior randomization measure, which can be defined as

$$\mathbf{E}_{\theta \sim \hat{\pi}} \mathbf{E}_Z L_\theta(Z) = \mathbf{E}_Z \int L_\theta(Z) d\hat{\pi}(\theta).$$

In this paper, we are interested in estimating this average risk for an arbitrary posterior $\hat{\pi}$. The statistical complexity of this randomized estimator $\hat{\pi}$ will be measured by its *KL-entropy* respect to the prior, which is defined as:

$$D_{KL}(\hat{\pi}||\pi) = \int_{\mathcal{G}} \ln \frac{d\hat{\pi}(\theta)}{d\pi} d\hat{\pi}(\theta), \tag{1}$$

assuming it exists.

2   Analysis of the Gibbs Algorithm

Theoretical properties of the Gibbs algorithm have been studied by various researchers. In particular, some bounds obtained in this paper are related (but not identical) to independently obtained results in [3]. The main technical tool used here, based on the following lemma, is simpler and more general. See [8, 9] for its proof.

Lemma 1. *Consider randomized estimation, where we select posterior $\hat{\pi}$ on $\mathcal{G}$ based on $\hat{Z}$, with π a prior. Consider a real-valued function $L_\theta(Z)$ on $\mathcal{G} \times \mathcal{Z}$.*

$$c(\alpha) = \ln \mathbf{E}_{\theta \sim \pi} \mathbf{E}_Z^\alpha e^{-L_\theta(Z)},$$

then $\forall t$, the following event holds with probability at least $1 - \exp(-t)$:

$$-(1 - \alpha) \mathbf{E}_{\theta \sim \hat{\pi}} \ln \mathbf{E}_Z e^{-L_\theta(Z)} \leq \mathbf{E}_{\theta \sim \hat{\pi}} L_\theta(\hat{Z}) + D_{KL}(\hat{\pi}||\pi) + c(\alpha) + t.$$

Moreover, we have the following expected risk bound:

$$-(1 - \alpha) \mathbf{E}_{\hat{Z}} \mathbf{E}_{\theta \sim \hat{\pi}} \ln \mathbf{E}_Z e^{-L_\theta(Z)} \leq \mathbf{E}_{\hat{Z}} \left[\mathbf{E}_{\theta \sim \hat{\pi}} L_\theta(\hat{Z}) + D_{KL}(\hat{\pi}||\pi) \right] + c(\alpha).$$

If we choose $\alpha = 0$ in Lemma 1, then $c(\alpha) = 0$. However, choosing $\alpha \in (0, 1)$ is useful for some parametric problems, where we would like to obtain a convergence rate of the order $O(1/n)$. In such cases, the choice of $\alpha = 0$ would lead to a rate of $O(\ln n / n)$, which is suboptimal.

We shall consider the case of n iid samples $\hat{Z} = (\hat{Z}_1, \ldots, \hat{Z}_n) \in \mathcal{Z} = \mathcal{Z}_1 \times \cdots \times \mathcal{Z}_n$, where $\mathcal{Z}_1 = \cdots = \mathcal{Z}_n$. The loss function is $L_\theta(\hat{Z}) = \rho \sum_{i=1}^n \ell_\theta(\hat{Z}_i)$, where ℓ is a function on $\mathcal{G} \times \mathcal{Z}_1$ and $\rho > 0$ is a constant. The Gibbs algorithm is a randomized estimator $\hat{\pi}_\rho$ defined as:

$$d\hat{\pi}_\rho = \frac{\exp(-\rho \sum_{i=1}^n \ell_\theta(\hat{Z}_i))}{\mathbf{E}_{\theta \sim \pi} \exp(-\rho \sum_{i=1}^n \ell_\theta(\hat{Z}_i))} \, d\pi. \tag{2}$$

It is not difficult to verify that it minimizes the right hand side of Lemma 1 among all probability distributions on $\mathcal{G}$:

$$\hat{\pi}_\rho = \arg \inf_{\hat{\pi}} \left[\rho \mathbf{E}_{\theta \sim \hat{\pi}} \sum_{i=1}^n \ell_\theta(\hat{Z}_i) + D_{KL}(\hat{\pi} \| \pi) \right]. \tag{3}$$

Lemma 2. *Define resolvability*

$$r_\rho = -\frac{1}{\rho n} \ln \mathbf{E}_{\theta \sim \pi} e^{-\rho n \mathbf{E}_{Z_1} \ell_\theta(Z_1)}.$$

Then $\forall \alpha \in [0, 1)$, the expected generalization performance of the Gibbs algorithm (2) can be bounded as

$$-\mathbf{E}_{\hat{Z}} \mathbf{E}_{\theta \sim \hat{\pi}_\rho} \ln \mathbf{E}_{Z_1} e^{-\rho \ell_\theta(Z_1)} \leq \frac{\rho}{1 - \alpha} \left[r_\rho + \frac{1}{\rho n} \ln \mathbf{E}_{\theta \sim \pi} \mathbf{E}_{Z_1}^{\alpha n} e^{-\rho \ell_\theta(Z_1)} \right].$$

Proof. We obtain from (3)

$$\mathbf{E}_{\hat{Z}} \left[\rho \mathbf{E}_{\theta \sim \hat{\pi}_\rho} \sum_{i=1}^n \ell_\theta(\hat{Z}_i) + D_{KL}(\hat{\pi}_\rho \| \pi) \right]$$

$$\leq \inf_{\pi'} \mathbf{E}_{\hat{Z}} \left[\rho \mathbf{E}_{\theta \sim \pi'} \sum_{i=1}^n \ell_\theta(\hat{Z}_i) + D_{KL}(\pi' \| \pi) \right]$$

$$\leq \inf_{\pi'} \left[\rho n \mathbf{E}_{\theta \sim \pi'} \mathbf{E}_{\hat{Z}_i} \ell_\theta(\hat{Z}_i) + D_{KL}(\pi' \| \pi) \right] = \rho n r_\rho.$$

Let $L_\theta(\hat{Z}) = \rho \sum_{i=1}^n \ell_\theta(\hat{Z}_i)$. Substituting the above bound into the right hand side of the second inequality of Lemma 1, and using the fact that $\mathbf{E}_Z e^{-L_\theta(Z)} = \mathbf{E}_{Z_1}^n e^{-\rho \ell_\theta(Z_1)}$, we obtain the desired inequality.

Theorem 1. *Consider the Gibbs algorithm in (2). Assume there exist positive constants K such that $\forall \theta$:*

$$\mathbf{E}_{Z_1} \ell_\theta(Z_1)^2 \leq K \mathbf{E}_{Z_1} \ell_\theta(Z_1).$$

Under either of the following conditions:

- *Bounded loss: $\exists M \geq 0$ s.t. $-\inf_{\theta, Z_1} \ell_\theta(Z_1) \leq M$; let $\beta_\rho = 1 - K(e^{\rho M} - \rho M - 1)/(\rho M^2)$.*

– *Bernstein loss:* $\exists M, b > 0$ *s.t.* $\mathbf{E}_{Z_1}(-\ell_\theta(Z_1))^m \leq m! M^{m-2} K b \mathbf{E}_{Z_1} \ell_\theta(Z_1)$ *for all* $\theta \in \mathcal{G}$ *and integer* $m \geq 3$; *let* $\beta_\rho = 1 - K\rho(1 - \rho M + 2b\rho M)/(2 - 2\rho M)$.

Assume we choose a sufficiently small ρ *such that* $\beta_\rho > 0$. *Let the (true) expected loss of* θ *be* $R(\theta) = \mathbf{E}_{Z_1} \ell_\theta(Z_1)$, *then the expected generalization performance of the Gibbs algorithm is bounded by*

$$\mathbf{E}_{\hat{Z}} \mathbf{E}_{\theta \sim \hat{\pi}_\rho} R(\theta) \leq \frac{1}{(1-\alpha)\beta_\rho} \left[r_\rho + \frac{1}{\rho n} \ln \mathbf{E}_{\theta \sim \pi} e^{-\alpha \rho \beta_\rho n R(\theta)} \right], \qquad (4)$$

where r_ρ *is the resolvability defined in Lemma 2.*

Proof. (Sketch) Under the bounded-loss condition, we can use the following moment generating function estimate:

$$\ln \mathbf{E}_{Z_1} e^{-\rho \ell_\theta(Z_1)} \leq -\rho \mathbf{E}_{Z_1} \ell_\theta(Z_1) + \frac{e^{\rho M} - \rho M - 1}{M^2} \mathbf{E}_{Z_1} \ell_\theta(Z_1)^2$$

$$\leq -\left(\rho - \frac{K}{M^2}(e^{\rho M} - \rho M - 1) \right) \mathbf{E}_{Z_1} \ell_\theta(Z_1) = -\rho \beta_\rho \mathbf{E}_{Z_1} \ell_\theta(Z_1).$$

Now substitute this bound into Lemma 2, and simplify, we obtain the desired result. The proof is similar for the Bernstein-loss condition (with appropriate logarithmic moment generating function estimate). $\qquad \blacksquare$

Remark 1. Since $(e^x - x - 1)/x \to 0$ as $x \to 0$, we know that the first condition $\beta_\rho > 0$ can be satisfied as long as we pick a sufficiently small ρ. In fact, using the inequality $(e^x - x - 1)/x \leq 0.5xe^x$ (when $x \geq 0$), we may also take $\beta_\rho = 1 - 0.5\rho K e^{\rho M}$ in the first condition of Theorem 1.

We shall now study consequences of (4) under some general conditions on the local prior structure $\pi(\epsilon) = \pi(\{\theta : R(\theta) \leq \epsilon\})$ around the best achievable parameter. For some specific forms of local prior conditions, convergence rates can be stated very explicitly.

Theorem 2. *If (4) holds with a non-negative function* $R(\theta)$, *then*

$$\mathbf{E}_{\hat{Z}} \mathbf{E}_{\theta \sim \hat{\pi}_\rho} R(\theta) \leq \frac{\Delta(\alpha \beta_\rho, \rho n)}{(1-\alpha)\beta_\rho \rho n},$$

where

$$\Delta(a, b) = \ln \inf_{u,v} \left[\sup_{\epsilon \leq u} \frac{\max(0, \pi(\epsilon/a) - v)}{\pi(\epsilon)} + \inf_\epsilon \frac{v + (1-v)\exp(-bu)}{\pi(\epsilon)e^{-b\epsilon}} \right],$$

and $\pi(\epsilon) = \pi(\{\theta : R(\theta) \leq \epsilon\})$.

Proof. We have

$$r_\rho = -\frac{1}{\rho n} \ln \mathbf{E}_{\theta \sim \pi} e^{-\rho n R(\theta)} = -\frac{1}{\rho n} \ln \underbrace{\int \pi(\epsilon/(\rho n)) e^{-\epsilon} d\epsilon}_{A}.$$

Similarly, the second term on the right hand side of (4) is

$$\frac{1}{\rho n}\ln \mathbf{E}_{\theta\sim\pi}e^{-\alpha\rho\beta_\rho nR(\theta)} = \frac{1}{\rho n}\ln\int\pi(\epsilon/(\alpha\beta_\rho\rho n))\,e^{-\epsilon}d\epsilon$$

$$\le\frac{1}{\rho n}\ln\left[\underbrace{\int_0^{\rho nu}\left(\pi(\epsilon/(\alpha\rho\beta_\rho n))-v\right)e^{-\epsilon}d\epsilon}_{B}+\underbrace{\left(v+(1-v)e^{-\rho nu}\right)}_{C}\right].$$

To finish the proof, we only need to show that $(B+C)/A \le e^{\Delta(\alpha\beta_\rho,\rho n)}$.

Consider arbitrary real numbers u and v. From the expressions, it is easy to see that $B/A \le \sup_{\epsilon\le u}\frac{\max(0,\pi(\epsilon/(\alpha\beta_\rho))-v)}{\pi(\epsilon)}$. Moreover, since $A \ge \sup_\epsilon(\pi(\epsilon)e^{-\rho n\epsilon})$, we have $C/A \le C/\sup_\epsilon(\pi(\epsilon)e^{-\rho n\epsilon})$. Combining these inequalities, we have $(B+C)/A \le e^{\Delta(\alpha\beta_\rho,\rho n)}$. The desired bound is now a direct consequence of (4).

In the following, we give two simplified bounds, one with global entropy, which gives correct rate of convergence for non-parametric problems. The other bound is a refinement that uses localized entropy, useful for parametric problems. They direct consequences of Theorem 2.

Corollary 1 (Global Entropy Bound). *If (4) holds, then*

$$\mathbf{E}_{\hat{Z}}\,\mathbf{E}_{\theta\sim\hat{\pi}_\rho}R(\theta) \le \frac{\inf_\epsilon[\rho n\epsilon - \ln\pi(\epsilon)]}{\beta_\rho\rho n} \le \frac{2\bar{\epsilon}_{global}}{\beta_\rho},$$

where $\pi(\epsilon) = \pi(\{\theta : R(\theta)\le\epsilon\})$ and $\bar{\epsilon}_{global} = \inf\left\{\epsilon : \epsilon \ge \frac{1}{\rho n}\ln\frac{1}{\pi(\epsilon)}\right\}$.

Proof. For the first inequality, we take $v = 1$ in Theorem 2, and let $\alpha \to 0$. For the second inequality, we simply note from the definition of $\bar{\epsilon}_{global}$ that $\inf_\epsilon[\rho n\epsilon - \ln\pi(\epsilon)] \le 2\rho n\bar{\epsilon}_{global}$.

Corollary 2 (Local Entropy Bound). *If (4) holds, then*

$$\mathbf{E}_{\hat{Z}}\,\mathbf{E}_{\theta\sim\hat{\pi}_\rho}R(\theta) \le \frac{\bar{\epsilon}_{local}}{(1-\alpha)\beta_\rho},$$

where $\pi(\epsilon) = \pi(\{\theta : R(\theta)\le\epsilon\})$, and

$$\bar{\epsilon}_{local} = \frac{2}{\rho n} + \inf\left\{\frac{\epsilon}{\alpha\beta_\rho} : \epsilon \ge \sup_{\epsilon'\in[\epsilon,2u]}\frac{\alpha\beta_\rho}{\rho n}\ln\left[\frac{\pi(\epsilon'/(\alpha\beta_\rho))}{\pi(\epsilon')}+\frac{\exp(-\rho nu)}{\pi(u)}\right]\right\}.$$

Proof. For the first inequality, we simply take $u = u_2$ and $v = \pi(u_1/(\alpha\beta_\rho))$ in Theorem 2, and use the following bounds

$$\sup_{\epsilon\le u}\frac{\max(0,\pi(\epsilon/(\alpha\beta_\rho))-v)}{\pi(\epsilon)} \le \sup_{\epsilon\in[u_1,u_2]}\frac{\pi(\epsilon/(\alpha\beta_\rho))}{\pi(\epsilon)},$$

$$\frac{v}{\sup_\epsilon(\pi(\epsilon)e^{-\rho n\epsilon})} \le \frac{v}{ve^{-\rho nu_1/(\alpha\beta_\rho)}} = \exp\left(\frac{\rho nu_1}{\alpha\beta_\rho}\right),$$

$$\frac{(1-v)\exp(-\rho nu)}{\sup_\epsilon(\pi(\epsilon)e^{-\rho n\epsilon})} \le \frac{\exp(-\rho nu_2)}{\pi(u_2/2)e^{-\rho nu_2/2}} = \frac{\exp(-\rho nu_2/2)}{\pi(u_2/2)}.$$

For the second inequality, we let $u_2 = 2u$ and $u_1/(\alpha\beta_\rho) = \bar{\epsilon}_{local} - \ln 2/(\rho n)$. Then by the definition of $\bar{\epsilon}_{local}$, we have $\sup_{\epsilon \in [u_1, u_2]} \frac{\pi(\epsilon/(\alpha\beta_\rho))}{\pi(\epsilon)} + \exp(\frac{\rho n u_1}{\alpha\beta_\rho}) + \frac{\exp(-\rho n u_2/2)}{\pi(u_2/2)} \leq 2\exp(\frac{\rho n u_1}{\alpha\beta_\rho}) = \exp(\rho n \bar{\epsilon}_{local})$. This gives the second inequality.

Remark 2. By letting $u \to \infty$ in the definition of $\bar{\epsilon}_{local}$, we can see easily that $\bar{\epsilon}_{local} \leq \ln 2/(\rho n) + \bar{\epsilon}_{global}/(\alpha\beta_\rho)$. Therefore using the localized complexity $\bar{\epsilon}_{local}$ is always better (up to a constant) than using $\bar{\epsilon}_{global}$. If the ratio $\pi(\epsilon/(\alpha\beta_\rho))/\pi(\epsilon)$ is much smaller than $\pi(\epsilon)$, the localized complexity can be much better than the global complexity.

In the following, we consider three cases of local prior structures, and derive the corresponding rates of convergence. Comparable lower-bounds are given in Section 4.

2.1   Non-parametric Type Local Prior

It is well known that for standard nonparametric families such as smoothing splines, etc, the ϵ-entropy often grows at the order of $O(\epsilon^{-r})$ for some $r > 0$. We shall not list detailed examples here, and simply refer the readers to [5, 6, 7] and references there-in. Similarly, we assume that there exists constants C and r such that the prior $\pi(\epsilon)$ satisfies the condition:

$$C_1\epsilon^{-r} \leq \ln \frac{1}{\pi(\epsilon)} \leq C_2\epsilon^{-r}.$$

This implies that $\bar{\epsilon}_{global} \leq (C_2/(\rho n))^{1/(1+r)}$. It is easy to check that $\bar{\epsilon}_{local}$ is the same order of $\bar{\epsilon}_{global}$ when $C_1 > 0$. Therefore, for prior that behaves non-parametrically around the truth, it does not matter whether we use global complexity or local complexity.

2.2   Parametric Type Local Prior

For standard parametric families, the prior π has a density with an underlying dimensionality d: $\pi(\epsilon) = O(\epsilon^{-d})$. We may assume that the following condition holds:

$$C_1 + d\ln\frac{1}{\epsilon} \leq \ln\frac{1}{\pi(\epsilon)} \leq C_2 + d\ln\frac{1}{\epsilon}.$$

This implies that $\bar{\epsilon}_{global}$ is of the order $d\ln n/n$. However, we have

$$\bar{\epsilon}_{local} \leq \frac{\ln 2 + C_2 - C_1 - d\ln(\alpha\beta_\rho)}{\rho n},$$

which is of the order $O(d/n)$ for large d. In this case, we obtain a better rate of convergence using localized complexity measure.

2.3   Singular Local Prior

It is possible to obtain a rate of convergence faster than $O(1/n)$. This cannot be obtained with either $\bar{\epsilon}_{global}$ or $\bar{\epsilon}_{local}$, which are of the order no better than n^{-1}.

The phenomenon of faster than $O(1/n)$ convergence rate is related to super-efficiency and hence can only appear at countably many isolated points.

To see that it is possible to obtain faster than $1/n$ convergence rate (super efficiency) in our framework, we only consider the simple case where

$$\sup_{\epsilon \leq 2u} \frac{\pi(\epsilon/(\alpha\beta_\rho))}{\pi(\epsilon)} = 1.$$

That is, we have a point-like prior mass at the truth with zero density around it (up to a distance of $2u$). In this case, we can apply Corollary 2 with $u_1 = -\infty$ and $u_2 = 2u$, and obtain

$$\mathbf{E}_{\hat{Z}} \mathbf{E}_{\theta \sim \hat{\pi}_\rho} R(\theta) \leq \frac{\ln\left[1 + \frac{\exp(-\rho n u)}{\pi(u)}\right]}{(1-\alpha)\beta_\rho \rho n}.$$

This gives an exponential rate of convergence. Clearly this example can be generalized to the case that a point is not completely isolated from its neighbor.

3   Some Examples

We focus on consequences and applications of Theorem 1. Specifically, we give two important examples for which (4) holds with some positive constants α, ρ, and β_ρ.

3.1   Conditional Density Estimation

Conditional density estimation is very useful in practical applications. It includes the standard density estimation problem widely studied in statistics as a special case. Moreover, many classification algorithms (such as decision trees or logistic regression) can be considered as conditional density estimators.

Let $Z_1 = (X_1, Y_1)$, where X_1 is the input variable, and Y_1 is the output variable. We are interested in estimating the conditional density $p(Y_1|X_1)$. In this framework, we assume (with a slight abuse of notation) that each parameter θ corresponds to a conditional density function: $\theta(Z_1) = p(Y_1|\theta, X_1)$. In density estimation, we consider negative log loss function $-\ln\theta(Z_1)$. Our goal is to find a randomized conditional density estimator θ from the data, such that the expected log-loss $-\mathbf{E}_{Z_1} \ln\theta(Z_1)$ is as small as possible.

In this case, the Gibbs estimator in (2) becomes

$$d\hat{\pi}_\rho \propto \prod_{i=1}^{n} \theta(\hat{Z}_i)^\rho d\pi, \tag{5}$$

which corresponds to the Bayesian posterior distribution when $\rho = 1$. Lemma 2 can be directly applied since the left hand side can be interpreted as a (Hellinger-like) distance between distributions. This approach has been taken in [8]. However, in this section, we are interested in using the log-loss on the left-hand side.

We further assume that θ is defined on a domain $\mathcal{G}$ which is a closed convex density class. However, we do not assume that $\mathcal{G}$ contains the true conditional density. We also let $\theta_{\mathcal{G}}$ be the optimal density in $\mathcal{G}$ with respect to the log loss:

$$\mathbf{E}_{Z_1} \ln \frac{1}{\theta_{\mathcal{G}}(Z_1)} = \inf_{\theta \in \mathcal{G}} \mathbf{E}_{Z_1} \ln \frac{1}{\theta(Z_1)}.$$

In the following, we are interested in a bound which compare the performance of the randomized estimator (5) to the best possible predictor $\theta_{\mathcal{G}} \in \mathcal{G}$, and thus define

$$\ell_\theta(Z_1) = \ln \frac{\theta_{\mathcal{G}}(Z_1)}{\theta(Z_1)}.$$

In order to apply Theorem 1, we need the following variance bound. We skip the proof due to the space limitation.

Proposition 1. *If there exists a constant $M_{\mathcal{G}} \geq 0$ such that $-M_{\mathcal{G}} \mathbf{E}_{Z_1} \ell_\theta(Z_1)^2 \leq \mathbf{E}_{Z_1} \ell_\theta(Z_1)^3$. Then $\mathbf{E}_{Z_1} \ell_\theta(Z_1)^2 \leq \frac{8 M_{\mathcal{G}}}{3} \mathbf{E}_{Z_1} \ell_\theta(Z_1)$.*

Using this result, we obtain the following theorem from Theorem 1.

Theorem 3. *Consider the estimator (5) for conditional density estimation (under log-loss). Then $\forall \alpha \in [0,1)$, inequality (4) holds with $R(\theta) = \mathbf{E}_{Z_1} \ln \frac{\theta_{\mathcal{G}}(Z_1)}{\theta(Z_1)}$ under either of the following two conditions:*

- $\sup_{\theta_1, \theta_2 \in \mathcal{G}, Z_1} \ln \frac{\theta_1(Z_1)}{\theta_2(Z_1)} \leq M_{\mathcal{G}}$: *we pick ρ such that $\beta_\rho = (11 \rho M_{\mathcal{G}} + 8 - 8 e^{\rho M_{\mathcal{G}}}) / (3 \rho M_{\mathcal{G}}) > 0$.*
- $\forall \theta \in \mathcal{G}$ *and* $m \geq 3$, $\mathbf{E}_{Z_1} (\ln \frac{\theta(Z_1)}{\theta_{\mathcal{G}}(Z_1)})^m \leq m! M_{\mathcal{G}}^{m-2} b \mathbf{E}_{Z_1} (\ln \frac{\theta(Z_1)}{\theta_{\mathcal{G}}(Z_1)})^2$: *we pick ρ such that $\beta_\rho = 1 - 8 b \rho M_{\mathcal{G}} (1 - \rho M_{\mathcal{G}} + 2 b \rho M_{\mathcal{G}}) / (1 - \rho M_{\mathcal{G}}) > 0$.*

Proof. Under the first condition, using Proposition 1, we may take $K = 8/3 M_{\mathcal{G}}$ and $M = M_{\mathcal{G}}$ in Theorem 1 (bounded loss case). Under the second condition, using Proposition 1, we may take $K = 16 M_{\mathcal{G}} b$ and $M = M_{\mathcal{G}}$ in Theorem 1 (Bernstein loss case).

Similar to the remark after Theorem 1, we may also let $\beta_\rho = (3 - 4 \rho M_{\mathcal{G}} e^{\rho M_{\mathcal{G}}})/3$ under the first condition of Theorem 3. The second condition involves moment inequalities that needs to be verified for specific problems. It applies to certain unbounded conditional density families such as conditional Gaussian models with bounded variance. We shall discuss a related scenario in the least squares regression case. Note that under Gaussian noise with identical variance, the conditional density estimation using the log-loss is equivalent to the estimation of conditional mean using least squares regression.

Since for log-loss, (4) holds under appropriate boundedness or moment assumptions on the density family, consequences in Section 2 applies. As we shall show in Section 4, similar lower bounds can be derived.

3.2   Least Squares Regression

Let $Z_1 = (X_1, Y_1)$, where X_1 is the input variable, and Y_1 is the output variable. We are interested in predicting Y_1 based on X_1. We assume that each parameter θ corresponds to a predictor: $\theta(X_1)$. The quality of the predictor is measured by the mean squared error $\mathbf{E}_{Z_1}(\theta(X_1) - Y_1)^2$. In this framework, the Gibbs estimator in (2) becomes

$$\hat{\pi}_\rho \propto \exp\left[-\rho \sum_{i=1}^n (\theta(X_i) - Y_i)^2\right]. \tag{6}$$

We further assume that θ is defined on a domain $\mathcal{G}$, which is a closed convex function class. Let $\theta_\mathcal{G}$ be the optimal predictor in $\mathcal{G}$ with respect to the least squares loss:

$$\mathbf{E}_{Z_1}(\theta_\mathcal{G}(X_1) - Y_1)^2 = \min_{\theta \in \mathcal{G}} \mathbf{E}_{Z_1}(\theta(X_1) - Y_1)^2.$$

In the following, we are interested in comparing the performance of the randomized estimator (5) to the best possible predictor $\theta_\mathcal{G} \in \mathcal{G}$. Define

$$\ell_\theta(Z_1) = (\theta(X_1) - Y_1)^2 - (\theta_\mathcal{G}(X_1) - Y_1)^2.$$

We have the following proposition. Again, we skip the proof due to the limitation of space.

Proposition 2. Let $A_\mathcal{G} = \sup_{X_1, \theta \in \mathcal{G}} |\theta(X_1) - \theta_\mathcal{G}(X_1)|$ and $\sup_{X_1, \theta \in \mathcal{G}} \mathbf{E}_{Y_1|X_1} |\theta(X_1) - Y_1|^m \leq m! B_\mathcal{G}^{m-2} M_\mathcal{G}$ for $m \geq 2$. Then we have:

$$\mathbf{E}_{Z_1}(-\ell_\theta(Z_1))^m \leq m!(2A_\mathcal{G}B_\mathcal{G})^{m-2}4M_\mathcal{G}\mathbf{E}_{Z_1}\ell_\theta(Z_1).$$

The moment estimates can be combined with Theorem 1, and we obtain the following theorem.

Theorem 4. *Consider the estimator (6) for least squares regression. Then $\forall \alpha \in [0, 1)$, inequality (4) holds with $R(\theta) = \mathbf{E}_{Z_1}(\theta(X_1) - Y_1)^2 - \mathbf{E}_{Z_1}(\theta_\mathcal{G}(X_1) - Y_1 Z)^2$, under either of the following conditions:*

- *$\sup_{\theta \in \mathcal{G}, Z_1}(\theta(X_1) - Y_1)^2 \leq M_\mathcal{G}$: we pick ρ such that $\beta_\rho = (5\rho M_\mathcal{G} + 4 - 4e^{\rho M_\mathcal{G}})/(\rho M_\mathcal{G}) > 0$.*
- *Proposition 2 holds for all integer $m \geq 2$: we pick small ρ such that $\beta_\rho = 1 - 4M_\mathcal{G}\rho/(1 - 2A_\mathcal{G}B_\mathcal{G}\rho) > 0$.*

Proof. Under the first condition, using Proposition 2, we have $M_\mathcal{G} \leq \sup_{\theta \in \mathcal{G}, Z_1} (\theta(X_1) - Y_1)^2$. We may thus take $K = 4M_\mathcal{G}$ and $M = M_\mathcal{G}$ in Theorem 1 (bounded loss case). Under the second condition, using Proposition 2, we can let $K = 8M_\mathcal{G}$, $M = 2A_\mathcal{G}B_\mathcal{G}$ and $b = 1/2$ in Theorem 1 (Bernstein loss case).

The theorem applies to unbounded regression problems with exponentially decaying noise such as Gaussian noise. For example, the following result holds.

Corollary 3. *Assume that there exists function $y_0(X)$ such that*

- *For all X_1, the random variable $|Y_1 - y_0(X_1)|$, conditioned on X_1, is dominated by the absolute value of a zero-mean Gaussian random variable[1] with standard deviation σ.*
- *$\exists$ constant $b > 0$ such that $\sup_{X_1} |y_0(X) - \theta(X_1)| \leq b$.*

If we also choose A such that $A \geq \sup_{X_1, \theta \in \mathcal{G}} |\theta(X_1) - \theta_{\mathcal{G}}(X_1)|$, then (4) holds with $\beta_\rho = 1 - 4\rho(b + \sigma)^2/(1 - 2A(b + \sigma)\rho) > 0$.

4   Lower Bounds

The purpose of this section is to prove some lower bounds which hold for arbitrary statistical estimators. Our goal is to match these lower bounds to the upper bounds proved earlier (at least for certain problems), which implies that the Gibbs algorithm is near optimal.

Upper bounds we obtained in previous sections are for every possible realization of the underlying distribution. It is not possible to obtain a lower bound for any specific realization since we can always design an estimator that picks a parameter that achieves the best possible performance under this particular distribution. However, such an estimator will not work well for a different distribution. Therefore as far as lower bounds are concerned, we are interested in the performance averaged over a set of underlying distributions.

In order to obtain lower bounds, we associate each parameter θ with a probability distribution $q_\theta(x, y)$ so that we can take samples $Z_i = (X_i, Y_i)$ from this distribution. In addition, we shall design the map in such a way that the optimal parameter under this distribution is θ. For (conditional) density estimation, the map is the density itself. For regression, we associate each predictor θ with a conditional Gaussian distribution with constant variance and the conditional mean given by the prediction $\theta(X_1)$ of each input X_1.

We consider the following scenario: we put a prior π on θ, which becomes a prior on the distribution $q_\theta(x, y)$. Assume that we are interested in estimating θ, under a loss function $\ell_\theta(Z_1)$, then the quantity

$$R_\theta(\theta') = \mathbf{E}_{Z_1 \sim q_\theta} \ell_{\theta'}(Z_1)$$

is the true risk between an estimated parameter θ' and the true distribution parameter θ. The average performance of an arbitrary randomized estimator $\hat{\theta}(Z)$ can thus be expressed as

$$\mathbf{E}_{\theta \sim \pi} \mathbf{E}_{Z \sim q_\theta(Z)} R_\theta(\hat{\theta}(Z)), \tag{7}$$

where Z consists of n independent samples $Z = \{(X_1, Y_1), \ldots, (X_n, Y_n)\}$ from the underlying density. In this section, we are mainly interested in obtaining a

---

[1] That is, conditioned on X_1, the moments of $|Y_1 - y_0(X_1)|$ with respect to Y_1 are no larger than the corresponding moments of the dominating Gaussian random variable.

lower bound for any possible estimator, so that we can compare this lower bound to the upper bound for the Gibbs algorithm developed earlier.

Note that (7) only gives one performance measure, while the upper bound for the Gibbs method is specific for every possible truth q_θ. It is thus useful to study the best local performance around any possible θ with respect to the underlying prior π. To address this issue, we observe that for every partition of the θ space into the union of disjoint small balls B_k, we may rewrite (7) as

$$\sum_j \pi(B_k) \mathbf{E}_{\theta \sim \pi_{B_k}} \mathbf{E}_{Z \sim q_\theta(Z)} R_\theta(\hat{\theta}(Z)),$$

where for each small ball B_k, the localized prior is defined as:

$$\pi_{B_k}(A) = \frac{\pi(A \cap B_k)}{\pi(B_k)}.$$

Therefore, instead of bounding the optimal Bayes risk with respect to the global prior π in (7), we shall bound the optimal risk with respect to a local prior π_B for a small ball B around any specific parameter θ, which gives a more refined performance measure. In this framework, if for some small local ball π_B, the Gibbs algorithm has performance not much worse than the best possible estimator, then we can say that it is *locally near optimal*.

The main theorem in our lower bound analysis is presented below. Related techniques appeared in [2, 4, 7].

Theorem 5. *Consider an arbitrary randomized estimator $\hat{\theta}(Z)$ that takes value in $B' \subset \mathcal{G}$, where Z consists of n independent samples $Z = \{(X_1, Y_1), \ldots, (X_n, Y_n)\}$ from some underlying density q_θ, then for all non-negative functions $R_\theta(\theta')$, we have*

$$\mathbf{E}_{\theta \sim \pi_B} \mathbf{E}_{Z \sim q_\theta(Z)} R_\theta(\hat{\theta}(Z)) \geq 0.5 \sup \left\{ \epsilon : \inf_{\theta' \in B'} \ln \frac{1}{\pi_B(\{\theta : R_\theta(\theta') < \epsilon\})} \geq 2n\Delta_B + 4 \right\},$$

where $\Delta_B = \mathbf{E}_{\theta \sim \pi_B} \mathbf{E}_{\theta' \sim \pi_B} D_{KL}(q_\theta(Z_1) \| q_{\theta'}(Z_1))$.

Proof. The joint distribution of (θ, Z) is given by $\prod_{i=1}^n q_\theta(Z_i) d\pi_B(\theta)$. Denote by $I(\theta, Z)$ the mutual information between θ and Z. Now let Z' be a random variable independent of θ and with the same marginal of Z, then by definition, the mutual information can be regarded as the KL-divergence between the joint distributions of (θ, Z) and (θ, Z'), which we write (with a slight abuse of notation) as:

$$I(\theta, Z) = D_{KL}((\theta, Z) \| (\theta, Z')).$$

Now consider an arbitrary estimator $\hat{\theta} : \mathcal{Z} \to B'$. By the data processing theorem for KL-divergence (that is, processing does not increase KL-divergence), with input $(\theta, Z) \in \mathcal{G} \times \mathcal{Z}$ and binary output $\mathbf{1}(R_\theta(\hat{\theta}(Z)) \leq \epsilon)$, we obtain

$$D_{KL}(\mathbb{1}(R_\theta(\hat{\theta}(Z)) \leq \epsilon) \| \mathbb{1}(R_\theta(\hat{\theta}(Z')) \leq \epsilon))$$
$$\leq D_{KL}((\theta, Z) \| (\theta, Z')) = I(\theta, Z)$$
$$= \mathbf{E}_{\theta_1 \sim \pi_B} \mathbf{E}_{Z \sim q_{\theta_1}}(Z) \ln \frac{q_{\theta_1}(Z)}{\mathbf{E}_{\theta_2 \sim \pi_B} q_{\theta_2}(Z)}$$
$$\leq \mathbf{E}_{\theta_1 \sim \pi_B} \mathbf{E}_{Z \sim q_{\theta_1}}(Z) \mathbf{E}_{\theta_2 \sim \pi_B} \ln \frac{q_{\theta_1}(Z)}{q_{\theta_2}(Z)}$$
$$= n \mathbf{E}_{\theta_1 \sim \pi_B} \mathbf{E}_{\theta_2 \sim \pi_B} D_{KL}(q_{\theta_1} \| q_{\theta_2}) = n \Delta_B.$$

The second inequality is a consequence of Jensen's inequality and the concavity of logarithm.

Now let $p_1 = P(R_\theta(\hat{\theta}(Z)) \leq \epsilon)$ and $p_2 = P(R_\theta(\hat{\theta}(Z')) \leq \epsilon)$, then the above inequality can be rewritten as:

$$D_{KL}(p_1 \| p_2) = p_1 \ln \frac{p_1}{p_2} + (1 - p_1) \ln \frac{1 - p_1}{1 - p_2} \leq n \Delta_B.$$

Since $\hat{\theta}(Z')$ is independent of θ, we have

$$p_2 \leq \sup_{\theta' \in B'} \pi_B(\{\theta : R_\theta(\theta') \leq \epsilon\}).$$

Now we consider any ϵ such that $\sup_{\theta' \in B'} \pi_B(\{\theta : R_\theta(\theta') < \epsilon\}) \leq 0.25 e^{-2n\Delta_B}$. This implies that $p_2 \leq 0.25 e^{-2n\Delta_B} \leq 0.25$.

We now show that in this case, $p_1 \leq 1/2$. Since $D_{KL}(p_1 \| p_2)$ is increasing in $[p_2, 1]$, we only need to show that $D_{KL}(0.5 \| p_2) \geq n\Delta_B$. This easily follows from the inequality

$$D_{KL}(0.5 \| p_2) \geq 0.5 \ln \frac{0.5}{p_2} + 0.5 \ln \frac{0.5}{1} \geq n\Delta_B.$$

Now, we have shown that $p_1 \leq 0.5$, which implies that $P(R_\theta(\hat{\theta}(Z)) \geq \epsilon) \geq 0.5$. Therefore we have $\mathbf{E}_{\theta \sim \pi_B} \mathbf{E}_{Z \sim q_\theta(Z)} R_\theta(\hat{\theta}(Z)) \geq 0.5\epsilon$.

Theorem 5 has a form that resembles Corollary 2. In the following, we state a result which shows the relationship more explicitly.

Corollary 4 (Local Entropy Lower Bound). *Under the notations of Theorem 5. Consider a reference point $\theta_0 \in \mathcal{G}$, and balls $B(\theta_0, \epsilon) \subset \mathcal{G}$ which contains θ_0 and indexed by $\epsilon > 0$, such that*

$$\sup_{\theta_1, \theta_2 \in B(\theta_0, \epsilon)} D_{KL}(q_\theta(Z_1) \| q_{\theta'}(Z_1)) \leq \epsilon.$$

Given $u > 0$, consider $\underline{\epsilon}(\theta_0, u)$ which satisfies:

$$\underline{\epsilon}(\theta_0, u) = \sup_{\epsilon > 0} \left\{ \epsilon : \inf_{\theta' \in B'} \ln \frac{\pi(B(\theta_0, u\epsilon))}{\pi(\{\theta : R_\theta(\theta') < \epsilon\} \cap B(\theta_0, u\epsilon))} \geq 2nu\epsilon + 4 \right\},$$

then locally around θ_0, we have

$$\mathbf{E}_{\theta \sim \pi_{B(\theta_0, u \leq (\theta_0, u))}} \mathbf{E}_{Z \sim q_\theta(Z)} R_\theta(\hat{\theta}(Z)) \geq 0.5 \underline{\epsilon}(\theta_0, u).$$

The definition of $B(\theta_0, \epsilon)$ requires that within the $B(\theta_0, \epsilon)$ ball, the distributions q_θ are nearly indistinguishable up to a scale of ϵ, when measured by their KL-divergence. Corollary 4 implies that the local performance of an arbitrary statistical estimator cannot be better than $\underline{\epsilon}(\theta_0, u)/2$. The bound in Corollary 4 will be good if the ball $\pi(B(\theta_0, \epsilon))$ is relatively large. That is, there are many distributions that are statistical nearly indistinguishable (in KL-distance). Therefore the bound of Corollary 4 is similar to Corollary 2, but the localization is within a small ball which is statistically nearly indistinguishable (rather than the $R(\cdot)$ localization for the Gibbs estimator). From an information theoretical point of view, this difference is rather intuitive and clearly also necessary since we allow arbitrary statistical estimators (which can simply estimate the specific underlying distribution q_θ if they are distinguishable).

It follows that if we want the upper bound in Corollary 2 to match the lower bound in Corollary 4, we need to design a map $\theta \to q_\theta$ such that locally around θ_0, a ball with small $R(\cdot)$ risk is also small information theoretically in terms of the KL-distance between q_θ and q_{θ_0}. Consider the following two types of small R balls:

$$B_1(\theta, \epsilon) = \{\theta' : R_\theta(\theta') < \epsilon\}, \quad B_2(\theta, \epsilon) = \{\theta' : R_{\theta'}(\theta) < \epsilon\}.$$

Now assume that we can find a map $\theta \to q_\theta$ such that locally around θ_0, q_θ within a small B_1-ball is also small in the information theoretical sense (small KL-distance). That is, we have for some $c > 0$ that

$$\sup\{D_{KL}(q_\theta(Z_1) \| q_{\theta'}(Z_1)) : \theta, \theta' \in B_1(\theta_0, c\epsilon)\} \leq \epsilon. \tag{8}$$

For problems such as density estimation and regression studied in this paper, it is easy to design such a map (under mild conditions such as the boundedness of the loss). We shall not go into the details for verifying specific examples of (8). Now, under this condition, we can take

$$\underline{\epsilon}(\theta_0, u) = \sup_{\epsilon > 0} \left\{ \epsilon : \inf_{\theta' \in B'} \ln \frac{\pi(B_1(\theta_0, cu\epsilon))}{\pi(B_2(\theta', \epsilon) \cap B_1(\theta_0, cu\epsilon))} \geq 2nu\epsilon + 4 \right\}.$$

As a comparison, according to Corollary 2, the Gibbs method at θ_0 gives an upper bound of the following form (which we simplify to focus on the main term) with some constant $u' \in (0, 1)$:

$$\bar{\epsilon}_{local} \leq \frac{2}{\rho n} + \inf \left\{ \epsilon : \rho n \epsilon \geq \sup_{\epsilon' \geq \epsilon} \ln \frac{\pi(B_1(\theta_0, \epsilon'))}{\pi(B_1(\theta_0, u'\epsilon'))} \right\}.$$

Essentially, the local upper bound for the Gibbs algorithm is achieved at $\bar{\epsilon}_{local}$ such that

$$n\bar{\epsilon}_{local} \sim \sup_{\epsilon' \geq \bar{\epsilon}_{local}} \ln \frac{\pi(B_1(\theta_0, \epsilon'))}{\pi(B_1(\theta_0, u'\epsilon'))},$$

where we use $\sim$ to denote approximately the same order, while the lower bound in Corollary 4 implies that (let $u' = 1/(cu)$):

$$n\underline{\epsilon} \sim \inf_{\theta' \in B'} \ln \frac{\pi(B_1(\theta_0, \underline{\epsilon}))}{\pi(B_2(\theta', u'\underline{\epsilon}) \cap B_1(\theta_0, \underline{\epsilon}))}.$$

From this, we see that our upper and lower bounds are very similar. There are two main differences which we outline below.

- In the lower bound, for technical reasons, B_2 appears in the definition of the local entropy. In order to argue that the difference does not matter, we need to assume that the prior probabilities of B_1 and B_2 are of the same order.
- In the lower bound, we use the smallest local entropy in a neighbor of θ_0, While in the upper bound we use the largest local entropy at θ_0 across different scales. This difference is not surprising since the lower bound is with respect to the average in a small neighborhood of θ_0.

Both differences are relatively mild and somewhat expected. We consider two situations which parallel Section 2.1 and Section 2.2.

4.1   Non-parametric Type Local Prior

Similar to Section 2.1, we assume that for some sufficiently large constant v: there exist $0 < C_1 < C_2$ such that

$$C_2 \epsilon^{-r} \leq \inf_{\theta' \in B'} \ln \frac{1}{\pi(B_2(\theta', \epsilon) \cap B_1(\theta_0, v\epsilon))}, \quad \ln \frac{1}{\pi(B_1(\theta_0, v\epsilon))} \leq C_1 \epsilon^{-r},$$

which measures the order of global entropy around a small neighborhood of θ_0. Now under the condition (8) and let $u = v/c$, Corollary 4 implies that

$$\underline{\epsilon} \geq \sup \left\{ \epsilon : 2un\epsilon + 4 \leq (C_2 - C_1)\epsilon^{-r} \right\}.$$

This implies that $\underline{\epsilon}$ is of the order $n^{-1/(1+r)}$, which matches the order of the Gibbs upper bound $\bar{\epsilon}_{global}$ in Section 2.1.

4.2   Parametric Type Local Prior

Similar to Section 2.2, we assume that for some sufficiently large constant v: there exist $0 < C_1 < C_2$ such that

$$C_2 + d\ln \frac{1}{\epsilon} \leq \inf_{\theta' \in B'} \ln \frac{1}{\pi(B_2(\theta', \epsilon) \cap B_1(\theta_0, v\epsilon))}, \quad \ln \frac{1}{\pi(B_1(\theta_0, v\epsilon))} \leq C_1 + d\ln \frac{1}{\epsilon}.$$

which measures the order of global entropy around a small neighborhood of θ_0. Now under the condition (8) and let $u = v/c$, Corollary 4 implies that

$$\underline{\epsilon} \geq \sup \left\{ \epsilon : 2c^{-1}n\epsilon \leq C_2 - C_1 - 4 \right\}.$$

That is, we have a convergence rate of the order $1/n$, which matches the parametric upper bound $\bar{\epsilon}_{local}$ for the Gibbs algorithm in Section 2.2.

5   Discussions

In this paper, we established upper and lower bounds for some statistical estimation problems. Our upper bound analysis is based on a simple information theoretical inequality, which can be used to analyze randomized estimation methods such as Gibbs algorithms. The resulting upper bounds rely on the local prior decaying rate in some small ball around the truth. Moreover, we are able to obtain lower bounds that have similar forms as the upper bounds. For some problems (such as density estimation and regression), the upper and lower bounds match under mild conditions. This suggests that both of our upper bound and lower bound analysis are relatively tight.

This work can be regarded as an extension of the standard minimax framework since we allow the performance of the estimator to vary for different underlying distributions, according to the pre-defined prior. The framework we study here is closely related to the concept of adaption in the statistical literature. At the conceptual level, both seek to find locally near optimal estimators around any possible true underlying distribution within the class.

This paper also shows that in theory, the Gibbs algorithm is better behaved than (possibly penalized) empirical risk minimization that picks an estimator to minimize the (penalized) empirical risk. In particular, for certain problems such as density estimation and regression, the Gibbs algorithm can achieve the best possible convergence rate under relatively mild assumptions on the prior structure. However, it is known that for non-parametric problems, empirical risk minimization can lead to sub-optimal convergence rate if the covering number grows too rapidly (or in our case, prior decays too rapidly) when ϵ (the size of the covering ball) decreases [1].

References

1. Lucien Birgé and Pascal Massart. Rates of convergence for minimum contrast estimators. *Probab. Theory Related Fields*, 97(1-2):113–150, 1993.
2. R.E. Blahut. Information bounds of the Fano-Kullback type. *IEEE Transactions on Information Theory*, 22:410–421, 1976.
3. Olivier Catoni. A PAC-Bayesian approach to adaptive classification. Available online at http://www.proba.jussieu.fr/users/catoni/homepage/classif.pdf.
4. Te Sun Han and Sergio Verdú. Generalizing the Fano inequality. *IEEE Transactions on Information Theory*, 40:1247–1251, 1994.
5. S.A. van de Geer. *Empirical Processes in M-estimation*. Cambridge University Press, 2000.
6. Aad W. van der Vaart and Jon A. Wellner. *Weak convergence and empirical processes*. Springer Series in Statistics. Springer-Verlag, New York, 1996.
7. Yuhong Yang and Andrew Barron. Information-theoretic determination of minimax rates of convergence. *The Annals of Statistics*, 27:1564–1599, 1999.
8. Tong Zhang. Learning bounds for a generalized family of Bayesian posterior distributions. In *NIPS 03*, 2004.
9. Tong Zhang. On the convergence of MDL density estimation. In *COLT 2004*, pages 315–330, 2004.

Improved Minimax Bounds on the Test and Training Distortion of Empirically Designed Vector Quantizers*

András Antos

Informatics Laboratory, Research Division,
Computer and Automation Research Institute of the Hungarian
Academy of Sciences, H-1518 Lágymányosi u.11,
Budapest, Hungary
antos@szit.bme.hu

Abstract. It is shown by earlier results that the minimax expected (test) distortion redundancy of empirical vector quantizers with three or more levels designed from n independent and identically distributed data points is at least $\Omega(1/\sqrt{n})$ for the class of distributions on a bounded set. In this paper, a much simpler construction and proof for this are given with much better constants. There are similar bounds for the training distortion of the empirically optimal vector quantizer with three or more levels. These rates, however, do not hold for a one-level quantizer. Here the two-level quantizer case is clarified, showing that it already shares the behavior of the general case. Given that the minimax bounds are proved using a construction that involves discrete distributions, one suspects that for the class of distributions with uniformly bounded continuous densities, the expected distortion redundancy might decrease as $o(1/\sqrt{n})$ uniformly. It is shown as well that this is not so, proving that the lower bound for the expected test distortion remains true for these subclasses.

1 Introduction

Designing empirical vector quantizers is an important problem in data compression. In many practical situations we do not have a good source model in hand, but we are able to collect source samples, called also the training data, to get information on the source distribution. Here our aim is to design a quantizer with a given rate, based on these samples, whose expected distortion on the source distribution is as close to the distortion of an optimal quantizer (that is, one with minimum distortion) of the same rate as possible.

One approach to this problem is, for example, the empirical distortion minimization, supported by the idea that if the samples are from the real source, then a quantizer that performs well on the training data (i.e., that has small training distortion) should have a good performance on this source, as well. In

---

* This research was supported in part by the NATO Science Fellowship.

P. Auer and R. Meir (Eds.): COLT 2005, LNAI 3559, pp. 531–544, 2005.

fact, Pollard [1], [2] showed that this method is consistent under general conditions on the source μ when the training sample is n consecutive elements of a stationary and ergodic sequence drawn according to this source. He proved that the mean-squared error (MSE) $D(\mu, q_n^*)$ of the empirically optimal quantizer q_n^* (when applied to the true source) tends almost surely (a.s.) to the optimum MSE $D^*(\mu)$ achieved by an optimal quantizer. It is also shown there that the training distortion $D(\mu_n, q_n^*)$ of q_n^* tends as well to $D^*(\mu)$ a.s., that is, $D(\mu_n, q_n^*)$ is a strongly consistent estimate of $D^*(\mu)$, however $\mathbf{E}D(\mu_n, q_n^*) \leq D^*(\mu)$.

These consistency results do not inform us about the number of training samples required to ensure that the test or training distortion of q_n^* is close to the optimum MSE. To answer this question one usually studies the rates of the convergences above, that is, gives upper bounds for the distortion redundancy $D(\mu, q_n^*) - D^*(\mu)$ and for $D^*(\mu) - D(\mu_n, q_n^*)$ for finite sample sizes. It was shown by Linder $et\ al.$ [3] (see also [4],[5]) that the expected distortion redundancy $J(\mu, q_n^*) = \mathbf{E}D(\mu, q_n^*) - D^*(\mu)$ as well as $D^*(\mu) - \mathbf{E}D(\mu_n, q_n^*)$ can be bounded as $O(1/\sqrt{n})$ uniformly for all distributions over a given bounded region. These results have several extensions; see, for example, [6], [7], and [8].

In case of one-level quantizing, the only code point of q_n^* is the average of the samples, and it is easy to show that $J(\mu, q_n^*) = D^*(\mu) - \mathbf{E}D(\mu_n, q_n^*) = O(1/n)$ uniformly for all distributions over a given bounded region, that is, the convergences rate of both the test and the training distortion are much faster than the general $O(1/\sqrt{n})$ rate.

However, it is known that for three or more quantization levels, the $O(1/\sqrt{n})$ upper bounds on $J(\mu, q_n^*)$ and $D^*(\mu) - \mathbf{E}D(\mu_n, q_n^*)$ are tight in the minimax sense: It is shown in [9] for these cases that for any empirical quantizer design algorithm, that is, when the resulting quantizer q_n is an arbitrary function of the samples, and for any n large enough, there is a distribution in the class of distributions over a bounded region such that $J(\mu, q_n) = \mathbf{E}D(\mu, q_n) - D^*(\mu) \geq c_0/\sqrt{n}$. These "bad" distributions used in the proof are supported on finitely many atoms, but the proof is really complicated, which also leads to losses in the constants. As [9] words: "The constant c_0 of the theorem is rather small [...], and it can probably be improved upon at the expense of a more complicated analysis." However, in Theorem 1 of this paper, we give an even simpler and much shorter proof for this minimax lower bound with about 10^7-times better constant c_0.

For the training distortion of q_n^*, Linder [4] showed for three or more quantization levels that there is a distribution in the class of distributions over a bounded region such that for all sample size large enough $D^*(\mu) - \mathbf{E}D(\mu_n, q_n^*) = \Omega(1/\sqrt{n})$.

However, the above lower bounds in [9] and [4] leave open the case of two-level quantizers. We prove in Theorems 2 and 3 for the test and training distortion, respectively, that in this case we already get the same lower rates as in the general (at least three-level) case.

Based on certain considerations, one might think that for the class of distributions over a bounded region with uniformly bounded continuous densities, $J(\mu, q_n^*) = O(1/n^\alpha)$ uniformly, where $\alpha > 1/2$ constant. We also show that this is not so proving that the lower bound for the expected distortion redundancy remains true restricting ourselves to these type of distribution classes.

The rest of the paper is organized as follows. In Sect. 2 we give the necessary definitions and earlier results in details. In Sect. 3 we present our lower bound results. Section 4 contains the proofs of some theorems.

2   Empirical Vector Quantizer Design

Nearest Neighbor Quantizers. A d-dimensional N-*level vector quantizer* ($N \geq 1$ is an integer) is a measurable mapping $q : \mathcal{R}^d \to \mathcal{C}$, where the *codebook* $\mathcal{C} = \{y_1, \ldots, y_N\} \subset \mathcal{R}^d$ is a collection of N distinct d-vectors, called the *code points*. The quantizer is completely characterized by its codebook and the sets $S_i = \{x \in \mathcal{R}^d : q(x) = y_i\}$, $i = 1, \ldots, N$ called the *partition cells* (as they form a partition of $\mathcal{R}^d$) via the rule $q(x) = y_i$, if $x \in S_i$. The set $\{S_1, \ldots, S_N\}$ is called the partition of q.

The performance of the quantizer q, when quantizing a random vector $X \in \mathcal{R}^d$ with distribution μ called the *source*, is measured by the *expected distortion* (or mean-squared error)

$$D(\mu, q) \stackrel{\text{def}}{=} \mathbf{E}\{\|X - q(X)\|^2\}$$

where $\| \cdot \|$ denotes the Euclidean norm. Throughout this paper we assume $\mathbf{E}\{\|X\|^2\} < \infty$, thus the distortion is finite. The goal of quantization is to find quantizers with a given number of code points that have minimum distortion. We define the optimum distortion by

$$D^*(\mu) \stackrel{\text{def}}{=} \inf_{q \in \mathcal{Q}_N} D(\mu, q)$$

where $\mathcal{Q}_N$ denotes the set of all N-level quantizers. If $D(\mu, q^*) = D^*(\mu)$ then $q^* \in \mathcal{Q}_N$ is called *optimal*.

A quantizer q is called a *nearest neighbor* quantizer, if it satisfies

$$\|x - q(x)\| = \min_{y_i \in \mathcal{C}} \|x - y_i\|, \qquad \text{for all } x \in \mathcal{R}^d .$$

It is well known (see, e.g., [2]) that it suffices to consider nearest neighbor quantizers when searching for an optimal quantizer. Thus any optimal quantizer can be assumed to be nearest neighbor, and so finding an optimal quantizer is equivalent to finding its codebook. Using this, it is proved in [2] that there always exists an optimal quantizer.

Empirical Design. In many situations, the distribution μ is unknown, and the only available information about it is in the form of *training data*, that is, a sequence $X_1^n \stackrel{\text{def}}{=} X_1, \ldots, X_n$ of n independent and identically distributed (i.i.d.) copies of X. It is assumed that X_1^n and X are also independent. The training data is used to construct an *empirically designed* quantizer $q_n(\cdot) = q_n(\cdot, X_1, \ldots, X_n)$, which is a random function depending on the training sample. The goal is to produce such quantizers with performance approaching $D^*(\mu)$. The performance of q_n in quantizing X is measured by the *test distortion*

$$D(\mu, q_n) = \mathbf{E}\{\|X - q_n(X)\|^2 | X_1^n\} = \int_{\mathcal{R}^d} \|x - q_n(x)\|^2 \, \mu(dx) \ .$$

Note that $D(\mu, q_n)$ is a random variable.

Also of interest is the *training distortion* (or empirical distortion) of any q, defined as its distortion in quantizing the training data

$$D(\mu_n, q) = \frac{1}{n} \sum_{i=1}^{n} \|X_i - q(X_i)\|^2$$

where μ_n is the *empirical distribution* corresponding to the training data defined by

$$\mu_n(A) = \frac{1}{n} \sum_{i=1}^{n} I_{\{X_i \in A\}}$$

for every Borel set $A \subset \mathcal{R}^d$, where I_E denotes the indicator function of the event E. Note that although q is a deterministic mapping, the training distortion $D(\mu_n, q)$ is also a random variable depending on the training data X_1^n.

We define an *empirically optimal vector quantizer* (which is a specific empirically designed quantizer) as a quantizer q_n^* that minimizes the training distortion:

$$q_n^* \overset{\text{def}}{=} \arg\min_{q \in \mathcal{Q}_N} D(\mu_n, q) \ .$$

q_n^* is an optimal quantizer for μ_n. Note that q_n^* always exists (although it is not necessarily unique), and we can assume that it is a nearest neighbor quantizer.

It is well known that $\{q_n^*; n = 1, 2, \ldots\}$ is consistent in the sense that $\lim_{n \to \infty} D(\mu, q_n^*) = D^*(\mu)$ a.s. for any $N \geq 1$ [1],[2]. Similarly, it is also shown that $D(\mu_n, q_n^*)$ is a strongly consistent estimate of $D^*(\mu)$, that is, $\lim_{n \to \infty} D(\mu_n, q_n^*) = D^*(\mu)$ a.s. However the training distortion is always optimistically biased, that is, $\mathbf{E}D(\mu_n, q_n^*) < D^*(\mu)$ (unless $\mathbf{E}D(\mu_n, q_n^*) = D^*(\mu) = 0$).

Finite Sample Upper Bounds. To determine the number of samples needed to achieve a given level of distortion, the finite sample behavior of the *expected distortion redundancy*

$$J(\mu, q_n) \overset{\text{def}}{=} \mathbf{E}D(\mu, q_n) - D^*(\mu)$$

has to be analyzed.

Denote the closed ball of radius r centered at $x \in \mathcal{R}^d$ by $S(x, r)$ and, in particular, let $S = S(0, 1)$. Let $\mathcal{P}(1)$ denote the family of distributions supported on S. From this point, we assume that $\mu \in \mathcal{P}(1)$, hence μ is supported on

S, that is, $\mathbf{P}\{\|X\| \leq 1\} = 1$. (One can generalize the results to cases when $\mathbf{P}\{\|X\| \leq T\} = 1$ for some fixed $T < \infty$ by straightforward scaling, see, e.g., [5].)

It is of interest how fast $J(\mu, q_n^*)$ converges to 0. To our knowledge the best accessible upper bound concerning its dependence on n, N, and d, can be obtained by combining results of [3] with recent developments of [4], implying:

$$0 \leq J(\mu, q_n^*) \leq 2C_1 \sqrt{\frac{Nd}{n}}$$

for all $n \geq 1$ and $\mu \in \mathcal{P}(1)$, where $C_1 = 96$. The result in [4] also implies an upper bound on the size of the bias of $D(\mu_n, q_n^*)$:

$$0 \leq D^*(\mu) - \mathbf{E}D(\mu_n, q_n^*) \leq C_1 \sqrt{\frac{Nd}{n}}$$

for all $n \geq 1$ and $\mu \in \mathcal{P}(1)$. (Sometimes this bound is referred to as a *lower* bound on $\mathbf{E}D(\mu_n, q_n^*)$.)

Minimax Lower Bounds. A natural question is whether there exists a method, perhaps different from empirical distortion minimization, which provides an empirically designed quantizer with substantially smaller test distortion. In case of $N = 1$, it is easy to check that $J(\mu, q_n^*) = \mathbf{Var}X/n$. Similarly, for the training distortion $D^*(\mu) - \mathbf{E}D(\mu_n, q_n^*) = \mathbf{Var}X/n$. Thus the convergence rate is $O(1/n)$ in both cases, substantially faster than the $O(1/\sqrt{n})$ rate above. However, for $N \geq 3$ lower bounds in [9] and [4] show that the $O(1/\sqrt{n})$ convergence rate above cannot be improved in the following sense (Φ denotes the standard normal distribution function):

Proposition 1 (Bartlett, Linder, and Lugosi [9]). *If $N \geq 3$, then for any empirically designed N-level quantizer q_n trained on $n \geq n_0 = 16N/(3\Phi(-2)^2) \approx 10305N$ samples, we have*

$$\sup_{\mu \in \mathcal{P}(1)} J(\mu, q_n) \geq CN^{-2/d} \sqrt{\frac{N}{n}}$$

where $C = \Phi(-2)^4 2^{-12}/\sqrt{6} \approx 2.67 \cdot 10^{-11}$.

The construction and the proof in [9] is extremely complicated, which also leads to losses in the constants. In what follows, we give a much simpler construction and a shorter proof for Proposition 1 with about 10^7-times better constant C and better n_0.

A somewhat similar lower bound on the bias of the training distortion of empirically optimal quantizers is the following:

Proposition 2 (Linder [4]). *If $N \geq 3$, then there exists a distribution $\mu \in \mathcal{P}(1)$ such that for all training set size $n \geq n_0 = 2N/3$*

$$D^*(\mu) - \mathbf{E}D(\mu_n, q_n^*) \geq cN^{-2/d} \sqrt{\frac{N}{n}}$$

where $c = 2^{-8}/3$.

This is often referred to as an *upper* bound on $\mathbf{E}D(\mu_n, q_n^*)$. Note that this Proposition holds only for one empirically designed quantizer, the empirically optimal one, but on the other hand, it gives also an *individual* rate in the sense, that it provides a fix distribution for all n.

3   Main Results

Improved Minimax Lower Bounds. First we state the improved versions of Proposition 1:

Theorem 1. *Proposition 1 holds also with* $n_0 = 8N$ *and* $C = \frac{211}{360^2\sqrt{3}}\Phi(-0.92) \approx 1.68 \cdot 10^{-4}$.

The idea behind our proof and its differences from the one in [9] are best illustrated by the special case $d = 1$, $N = 6$. Assume that μ is concentrated on four pairs of points: $(-1, -1 + \Delta)$, $(-1/3, -1/3 + \Delta)$, $(1/3 - \Delta, 1/3)$, and $(1 - \Delta, 1)$, such that $\mu(-1) = \mu(-1 + \Delta) = (1 + u_1\delta)/8$, $\mu(1) = \mu(1 - \Delta) = (1 - u_1\delta)/8$, $\mu(-1/3) = \mu(-1/3 + \Delta) = (1 + u_2\delta)/8$, and $\mu(1/3) = \mu(1/3 - \Delta) = (1 - u_2\delta)/8$, where $u_1, u_2 \in \{-1, +1\}$. This gives four distributions. Then if Δ is sufficiently small, the code points of the 6-level optimal quantizer consist of $\{-1 + \Delta/2, 1 - \Delta, 1\}$ if $u_1 = -1$ or $\{-1, -1 + \Delta, 1 - \Delta/2\}$ if $u_1 = 1$, plus $\{-1/3 + \Delta/2, 1/3 - \Delta, 1/3\}$ if $u_2 = -1$ or $\{-1/3, -1/3 + \Delta, 1/3 - \Delta/2\}$ if $u_2 = -1$. Therefore, an empirical quantizer should "learn" from the data which of the four distributions generates that. This leads to a hypothesis testing problem for u_1 and u_2 whose error may be approximated through inequalities for the binomial distribution. Proper choice of Δ and δ provides the desired $\Omega(1/\sqrt{n})$ lower bound for the expected distortion redundancy. The idea is the same for general case.

For the four distributions above, the weights are $(1 - \delta)/8$ and $(1 + \delta)/8$, and exactly two of the pairs have mass $(1 - \delta)/4$. In the original proof in [9], for the $N = 6$ case, all the $\binom{4}{2} = 6$ distributions with this property were involved. In the general case, this meant an exponentially (in N) larger distribution class and more involved parameterization than in our proof, led to expressions which were really difficult to handle, and resulted in significant loss in the constants. Our simplified proof is somewhat suggested also by ideas in [4–Proof of Theorem 1]. Although our result gives an improvement only in the constant factor of the lower bound and thus it leaves the gap compared to the upper bound, we conjecture that it is sharp in respect of the factor $N^{-2/d}$ and that the upper bound might be improved in this respect.

Note that, as a special case of Theorem 1 for $N = 3$, we can get the following constants by careful analysis (see also [5]):

Corollary 1. *For any empirically designed 3-level quantizer q_n trained on $n \geq n_0 = 9$ samples,*

$$\sup_{\mu \in \mathcal{P}(1)} J(\mu, q_n) \geq \frac{C}{\sqrt{n}}$$

where $C = 3\Phi(-7/\sqrt{54})/80 \approx 6.39 \cdot 10^{-3}$.

Two-Level Quantizers. The results so far leave open the $N = 2$ case. In the following, we prove that in this case we already get the same rates as in the general case of $N \geq 3$. Thus, as soon as the criterion function (the expected distortion of nearest neighbor quantizers as a function of the code vectors) is not convex, the rate is slower than for $N = 1$ when the criterion function is convex. This requires some modification of the constructions in the proofs of Propositions 1 and 2. For the test distortion, we have:

Theorem 2. *Corollary 1 holds also for* $N = 2$ *with* $n_0 = 25$ *and* $C = \frac{1557}{30625} \Phi(-\frac{7}{\sqrt{54}}) \approx 8.66 \cdot 10^{-3}$.

The idea behind the proof and its differences from the $N = 3$ case is the following: In the proof for $N = 3$, μ was concentrated on four (two pairs) of points. Now assume that μ is concentrated on three points: -1, 0, and 1, such that $\mu(0) = 0.4$, $\mu(-1) = 0.3 + u\delta/2$ and $\mu(1) = 0.3 - u\delta/2$, where u is either -1 or $+1$. Then the code points of the 2-level optimal quantizer consist of $\{-\frac{3-5\delta}{7-5\delta}, 1\}$ if $u = -1$, and $\{-1, \frac{3-5\delta}{7-5\delta}\}$ if $u = 1$. Though these depend on δ, they remain in a small interval distinguishing sharply the two cases. Thus, though the family of sensible quantizers are richer now, we can proceed similarly to the $N \geq 3$ case. For a detailed proof, see the forthcoming full version.

For the training distortion, we have:

Theorem 3. *Proposition 2 holds also for* $N = 2$ *with* $n_0 = 1$ *and* $c = 1/24$.

Continuous Distributions. Certain considerations suggest that for classes of more regularized distributions a faster uniform rate of convergence can be achieved for $J(\mu, q_n)$ for some empirical quantizer q_n. For example, [10–Theorem 2, Corollary 1] and their proofs imply $O(\log n/n)$ uniform rate of $J(\mu, q_n^*)$ for a class of scalar distributions with continuous densities supported on S such that

(*) there is a fixed $\epsilon > 0$ that for all these densities the second derivative matrices of the criterion function have only eigenvalues greater than ϵ at each optimal codebook.

(Note that, under similar smoothness assumptions, Chou [11] pointed out that $D(\mu, q_n^*) - D^*(\mu)$ decreases as $O(1/n)$ in probability based on an asymptotic normality result of Pollard [12].) On the other hand, approximating the discrete distributions used in the proof of Proposition 1 by higher and higher density function peaks would lead to an unbounded sequence of densities. Considering this, one might think that the ugly technical condition (*) can be omitted in proving faster uniform convergence rates, that is, for example, for the class $\mathcal{D}_K$ of distributions with continuous densities supported on S and bounded by $K > 0$, there is a sequence $\{a_n\} = o(1/\sqrt{n})$ depending only on N, d, and K such that for all $n \geq 1$ and $\mu \in \mathcal{D}_K$,

$$J(\mu, q_n^*) \leq a_n \ .$$

Here we show that, surprisingly, this conjecture is false, moreover it fails for any empirical quantizer q_n, proving that Proposition 1 remains true restricting ourselves for the case $\mu \in \mathcal{D}_K$. For simplicity, this is given only for the special case $d = 1$ and $N = 3$. The basic idea is the same for the general case.

Theorem 4. *If $K \geq 12/5$ then Corollary 1 holds with $C = \frac{3}{80}(1 - \frac{6}{5K})^2 \Phi(-\frac{7}{\sqrt{54}})$ $\approx 6.39 \cdot 10^{-3} \left(1 - \frac{6}{5K}\right)^2$ also if the supremum is taken over only $\mathcal{D}_K$.*

For the limit $K \to \infty$, we get

Corollary 2. *Corollary 1 holds also if the supremum is taken over only for $\mu \in \mathcal{P}(1)$ with continuous densities.*

Theorem 4 might be surprising, also because replacing the atoms by intervals of a density, the cell interval boundaries of the quantizers can split them anywhere, which seems to be an essential difference compared to the discrete case. The idea behind the proof is the following: Introduce $h = 3/(10K)$. Note that $h \leq 1/8$ for $K \geq 12/5$. In contrast with the discrete case, where μ was concentrated on the set $\{-1, -1/2, 1/2, 1\}$, here assume instead that μ is concentrated on the set

$$A = [-1, -1 + 2h] \cup [-1/2 - 2h, -1/2] \cup [1/2, 1/2 + 2h] \cup [1 - 2h, 1] \quad (1)$$

such that $\mu([-1, -1+2h]) = \mu([-1/2-2h, -1/2]) = (1+u\delta)/4$ and $\mu([1/2, 1/2+ 2h]) = \mu([1-2h, 1]) = (1-u\delta)/4$, where u is either -1 or $+1$, and the distribution inside all of these intervals have a symmetric continuous density vanishing at the end points. Then the code points of the 3-level optimal quantizer consist of $\{-3/4, 1/2+h, 1-h\}$ if $u = -1$, and $\{-1+h, -1/2-h, 3/4\}$ if $u = 1$. Using small (but n-independent) h, we can assure that none of the cell interval boundaries of the sensible quantizers actually splits any interval of the support A, thus we can proceed similarly to the discrete case. See the forthcoming full version for a detailed proof which uses the following lemma:

Lemma 1. *If $h \leq 1/8$ and $\delta \leq 1/4$ then for any 3-level scalar quantizer q there exists a 3-level nearest neighbor scalar quantizer q' whose two cell interval boundaries do not intersect the support A in (1) and, in particular, one of these boundaries is in $(-1/2, 1/2)$, such that for $u = \pm 1$, $D(\mu_u, q') \leq D(\mu_u, q)$.*

4   Proofs

Proof of Theorem 1. For the sake of simplicity, we assume that N is divisible by 3. (This assumption is clearly insignificant, see [4–proof of Theorem 1] for an argument.) Certainly,

$$\sup_{\mu \in \mathcal{P}(1)} J(\mu, q_n) \geq \sup_{\mu \in \mathcal{D}} J(\mu, q_n) \quad (2)$$

where $\mathcal{D} \subseteq \mathcal{P}(1)$ is any restricted class. Define $\mathcal{D}$ as follows: each member of $\mathcal{D}$ is concentrated on the set of $4k = 4N/3$ fixed points $\{z_i, z_i' \in S : i = 1, \ldots, 2k\}$, where $z_i' = z_i + (\Delta, 0, 0, \ldots, 0)$ and $0 < \Delta \leq 1/4$. The positions of $z_1, \ldots, z_{2k}$

satisfy the property that the distance between any two of them is greater than 3Δ. The members of $\mathcal{D}$ are parameterized by the sign vectors $u = (u_1, \ldots, u_k) \in \{-1, +1\}^k$. For $1 \leq i \leq k$, denote z_{k+i} and z'_{k+i} also by y_i and y'_i, respectively, and define $u_{k+i} = -u_i$. For $0 < \delta \leq 1/2$ and $i = 1, \ldots, k$, set

$$\mu_u(\{z_i\}) \stackrel{\text{def}}{=} \mu_u(\{z'_i\}) \stackrel{\text{def}}{=} \frac{1 + u_i \delta}{4k}$$

$$\mu_u(\{y_i\}) \stackrel{\text{def}}{=} \mu_u(\{y'_i\}) \stackrel{\text{def}}{=} \frac{1 - u_i \delta}{4k} \ .$$

(The total mass adds up to one.) Let $\mathcal{D}$ contain all such distributions. Thus $|\mathcal{D}| = 2^k$ and $N = 3k$.

Let $\mathcal{Q}^*$ denote the collection of N-level nearest neighbor quantizers q such that for each $1 \leq i \leq k$, q has code points either at z_i, z'_i, and $(y_i + y'_i)/2$, or at $(z_i + z'_i)/2$, y_i, and y'_i. Then for each μ_u the essentially unique optimal N-level quantizer is in $\mathcal{Q}^*$. It is easy to see that for all u,

$$D^*(\mu_u) = \min_{q \in \mathcal{Q}^*} D(\mu_u, q) = \frac{\Delta^2}{8}(1 - \delta) \ .$$

Let $\mathcal{Q}$ denote the collection of N-level nearest neighbor quantizers q such that for some k values of $i \in \{1, \ldots, 2k\}$, q has code points at both z_i and z'_i, and for the remaining k values of i, q has a single code point at $(z_i + z'_i)/2$. Note that $\mathcal{Q} \supseteq \mathcal{Q}^*$. One can show that for any N-level quantizer q there is a $q' \in \mathcal{Q}$ such that

$$D(\mu_u, q') \leq D(\mu_u, q), \qquad \text{for all } u \ . \tag{3}$$

See [9–Appendix, Proof of Step 3] for a proof.

Let $\mathcal{Q}^{(n)}$ denote the family of empirically designed quantizers q_n such that for every fixed $x_1, \ldots, x_n$, we have $q_n(\cdot, x_1, \ldots, x_n) \in \mathcal{Q}$. Then (3) implies that it is enough to take the infimum over $\mathcal{Q}^{(n)}$, that is,

$$\inf_{q_n} \sup_{\mu \in \mathcal{P}(1)} J(\mu, q_n) \geq \inf_{q_n} \max_{u \in \{-1, 1\}^k} J(\mu_u, q_n) = \inf_{q_n \in \mathcal{Q}^{(n)}} \max_{u \in \{-1, 1\}^k} J(\mu_u, q_n) \ . \tag{4}$$

Any $q_n \in \mathcal{Q}^{(n)}$ can be represented by the 3-tuple $(A_n, A'_n, \{u_{n,i}\}_{i \leq k})$, where A_n, A'_n, and $\{u_{n,i}\}$ are determined by q_n (and thus depend on the data X_1^n) the following way:

- $A_n = \{i \leq k : (z_i + z'_i)/2 \text{ (exclusive) or } (y_i + y'_i)/2 \text{ is code point of } q_n\}$,
- $A'_n = \{i \leq k : \text{all of } z_i, z'_i, y_i, y'_i \text{ are code points of } q_n\}$,
- $u_{n,i} = \begin{cases} +1 \text{ if } z_i \text{ and } z'_i \text{ are code points of } q_n \\ -1 \text{ otherwise} \end{cases} \quad (i = 1, \ldots, k)$.

Note that $2|A'_n| + |A_n| = k$. For any u and $q_n \in \mathcal{Q}^{(n)}$,

$$D(\mu_u, q_n) - D^*(\mu_u) = \frac{\Delta^2 \delta}{4k} \left(|A'_n| + \sum_{i \in A_n} I_{\{u_{n,i} \neq u_i\}} \right)$$

$$= \frac{\Delta^2 \delta}{4k} \left(\sum_{i \leq k, i \notin A_n} \frac{1}{2} + \sum_{i \in A_n} I_{\{u_{n,i} \neq u_i\}} \right)$$

$$= \frac{\Delta^2 \delta}{4k} \sum_{i=1}^{k} \left(I_{\{i \notin A_n\}} \frac{1}{2} + I_{\{i \in A_n\}} I_{\{u_{n,i} \neq u_i\}} \right)$$

$$\geq \frac{\Delta^2 \delta}{4k} \sum_{i=1}^{k} \frac{1}{2} I_{\{u_{n,i} \neq u_i\}} = \frac{\Delta^2 \delta}{8k} \sum_{i=1}^{k} I_{\{u_{n,i} \neq u_i\}}$$

and thus

$$\max_{u \in \{-1,1\}^k} J(\mu_u, q_n) \geq \frac{\Delta^2 \delta}{8k} \max_{u \in \{-1,1\}^k} \sum_{i=1}^{k} \mathbf{P}\{u_{n,i} \neq u_i\} . \tag{5}$$

We write $X_1^n(u)$ for X_1^n to indicate how the samples depend on u, and use randomization such that u is replaced by a vector $U = (U_1, \ldots, U_k) \in \{-1, +1\}^k$ of i.i.d. zero mean random signs. Then for any $q_n \in \mathcal{Q}^{(n)}$,

$$\max_{u \in \{-1,+1\}^k} \sum_{i=1}^{k} \mathbf{P}\{u_{n,i}(X_1^n(u)) \neq u_i\} \geq \mathbf{E} \left\{ \sum_{i=1}^{k} \mathbf{P}\{u_{n,i}(X_1^n(U)) \neq U_i | U\} \right\}$$

$$\geq \sum_{i=1}^{k} \mathbf{P}\{u_{n,i}(X_1^n(U)) \neq U_i\} . \tag{6}$$

Here $\mathbf{P}\{u_{n,i}(X_1^n(U)) \neq U_i\}$ is the error probability of the classification problem of whether U_i is -1 or $+1$ based on the observation $X_1^n(U)$, and thus it is not less than the corresponding optimal error probability, which is given by the following formula (see, e.g., [13]):

$$\inf_{u_{n,i}} \mathbf{P}\{u_{n,i}(X_1^n(U)) \neq U_i\} \geq \mathbf{E}\{\min(\mathbf{P}\{U_i = 1 | X_1^n\}, \mathbf{P}\{U_i = -1 | X_1^n\})\}$$

$$= \mathbf{E}\{\min(\mathbf{P}\{U_1 = 1 | X_1^n\}, \mathbf{P}\{U_1 = -1 | X_1^n\})\} \tag{7}$$

by symmetry. Let $M = |\{j \leq n : X_j \in \{z_1, z_1'\}\}|$ and $\bar{M} = |\{j \leq n : X_j \in \{y_1, y_1'\}\}|$. It is easy to check that $(M, \bar{M})$ is a sufficient statistics of X_1^n for U_1, and that if $M \leq$ (or $\geq$) $\bar{M}$ then $\mathbf{P}\{U_1 = 1 | M, \bar{M}\} \leq$ (or $\geq$) $\mathbf{P}\{U_1 = -1 | M, \bar{M}\}$, respectively. Thus

$$\mathbf{E}\{\min(\mathbf{P}\{U_1 = 1 | X_1^n\}, \mathbf{P}\{U_1 = -1 | X_1^n\})\}$$

$$= \mathbf{E}\{\min(\mathbf{P}\{U_1 = 1 | M, \bar{M}\}, \mathbf{P}\{U_1 = -1 | M, \bar{M}\})\}$$

$$\geq \mathbf{E}\{I_{\{M \leq \bar{M}\}} \min(\mathbf{P}\{U_1 = 1 | M, \bar{M}\}, \mathbf{P}\{U_1 = -1 | M, \bar{M}\})\}$$

$$= \mathbf{E}\{I_{\{M \leq \bar{M}\}} \mathbf{P}\{U_1 = 1 | M, \bar{M}\}\} \tag{8}$$

$$= \mathbf{P}\{M \leq \bar{M}, U_1 = 1\}$$

$$= \frac{1}{2} \mathbf{P}\{M \leq \bar{M} | U_1 = 1\} .$$

From (4)–(8) we conclude that

$$\inf_{q_n} \sup_{\mu \in \mathcal{P}(1)} J(\mu, q_n) \geq \frac{\Delta^2 \delta}{16} \mathbf{P}\{M \leq \bar{M} | U_1 = 1\} . \tag{9}$$

Let $B = M + \bar{M}$, which has binomial distribution with parameters $(n, 1/k)$ for any u. Now

$$\mathbf{P}\{M \leq \bar{M} | U_1 = 1\} = \mathbf{P}\{\bar{M} \geq B/2 | U_1 = 1\} \tag{10}$$
$$= \mathbf{E}\{\mathbf{P}\{\bar{M} \geq B/2 | U_1 = 1, B\} | U_1 = 1\} .$$

Note that given $U_1 = 1$ and B, $\bar{M}$ has binomial distribution with parameters B and $p = (1 - \delta)/2$. We lower bound the above probability using an inequality by Slud [14] which states that for all $Bp \leq l \leq B(1 - p)$,

$$\mathbf{P}\{\bar{M} \geq l | U_1 = 1, B\} \geq \Phi\left(-\frac{l - Bp}{\sqrt{Bp(1-p)}}\right) . \tag{11}$$

For $1/\delta \leq B \leq 9/(25\delta^2)$, the choice $l = \lceil B/2 \rceil$ satisfies the conditions of Slud's inequality, and for $\delta < 0.1$ we obtain

$$\mathbf{P}\{\bar{M} \geq B/2 | U_1 = 1, B\} \geq \mathbf{P}\{\bar{M} \geq \lceil B/2 \rceil | U_1 = 1, B\}$$
$$\geq \Phi\left(-\frac{\lceil B/2 \rceil - B(1-\delta)/2}{\sqrt{B(1-\delta^2)/4}}\right)$$
$$\geq \Phi\left(-\frac{1 + B\delta}{\sqrt{B(1-\delta^2)}}\right) \tag{12}$$
$$\geq \Phi\left(-\frac{1 + 3\sqrt{B}/5}{\sqrt{B(1 - 9/(25B))}}\right) = \Phi\left(-\frac{5 + 3\sqrt{B}}{\sqrt{25B - 9}}\right)$$
$$\geq \Phi\left(-\frac{5 + 3\sqrt{11}}{\sqrt{25 \cdot 11 - 9}}\right) > \Phi(-0.92)$$

where we used the conditions $\delta \leq 3/(5\sqrt{B})$ and $B \geq 1/\delta > 10$ above. Hence, using that B and U_1 are independent,

$$\mathbf{P}\{M \leq \bar{M} | U_1 = 1\} \geq \mathbf{E}\left\{ I_{\{\frac{1}{\delta} \leq B \leq \frac{9}{25\delta^2}\}} \Phi(-0.92) \Big| U_1 = 1\right\}$$
$$= \Phi(-0.92) \mathbf{P}\left\{\frac{1}{\delta} \leq B \leq \frac{9}{25\delta^2}\right\} . \tag{13}$$

For $n \geq 24k = 8N$, letting

$$\delta = \frac{12}{25}\sqrt{\frac{k}{n}} \quad (< 0.1) \tag{14}$$

by Chebyshev's inequality

$$\mathbf{P}\left\{\frac{1}{\delta} \le B \le \frac{9}{25\delta^2}\right\} = \mathbf{P}\left\{\frac{25}{12}\sqrt{\frac{n}{k}} \le B \le \frac{25}{16}\frac{n}{k}\right\}$$

$$\ge \mathbf{P}\left\{\frac{7}{16}\frac{n}{k} \le B \le \frac{25}{16}\frac{n}{k}\right\} = 1 - \mathbf{P}\left\{|B - \mathbf{E}B| > \frac{9}{16}\frac{n}{k}\right\}$$

$$\ge 1 - \frac{n/k(1 - 1/k)}{\frac{9^2}{16^2}\frac{n^2}{k^2}} \ge 1 - \frac{16^2 k}{9^2 n} \tag{15}$$

$$\ge 1 - \left(\frac{2}{3}\right)^5 = \frac{211}{243} .$$

Combining (9), (13)–(15), we obtain

$$\inf_{q_n} \sup_{\mu \in \mathcal{P}(1)} J(\mu, q_n) \ge \frac{211\Delta^2}{8100}\Phi(-0.92)\sqrt{\frac{k}{n}}$$

where $0 < \Delta \le 1/4$ such that there exist $z_1, \ldots, z_{2k} \in S$ with distance at least 3Δ between any two of them and with each $z_i' \in S$. The latter is ensured if each $z_i \in S(0, 3/4) \subseteq S(0, 1 - \Delta)$. Thus, we need a lower bound for the cardinality of the maximal 3Δ-packing of $S(0, 3/4)$. It is well known (e.g., [15]) that this is lower bounded by the cardinality of the minimal 3Δ-covering of $S(0, 3/4)$, which is clearly bounded below by the ratio of the volume of $S(0, 3/4)$ and that of $S(0, 3\Delta)$, that is, by $(1/4\Delta)^d$. Hence $2k$ points can be packed in $S(0, 3/4)$ as long as $2k \le (1/4\Delta)^d$, thus the choice

$$\Delta = \frac{1}{4(2k)^{1/d}}$$

satisfies the required property. Resubstitution of this value and $2k = 2N/3$ proves the theorem. □

Proof of Theorem 3. Define $\mu \in \mathcal{P}(1)$ as the uniform distribution concentrated on three fixed points $\{-1, 0, 1\}$. It is easy to see that there are exactly two optimal 2-level quantizers for μ; with codebooks

$$\mathcal{C}_1 = \{-1/2, 1\} \quad \text{and} \quad \mathcal{C}_2 = \{-1, 1/2\}$$

respectively. Consequently, $D^*(\mu) = 1/6$.

Let M and $\bar{M}$ be the number of training data points falling on -1 and 1, respectively. Let q_n be the training set dependent 2-point nearest neighbor quantizer whose codebook is $\mathcal{C}_1$ if $M < \bar{M}$ and $\mathcal{C}_2$ if $M \ge \bar{M}$. Then the expected training distortion of q_n is

$$\mathbf{E}D(\mu_n, q_n) = \mathbf{E}\left\{\frac{1}{n}\sum_{j=1}^{n}(X_j - q_n(X_j))^2\right\}$$

$$= \frac{1}{4n} \mathbf{E}\{n - \max(M, \bar{M})\} \tag{16}$$

$$= \frac{1}{4} - \frac{1}{4n} \mathbf{E}\{\max(M, \bar{M})\} \ .$$

Since the empirically optimal quantizer q_n^* minimizes the training distortion over all 2-point quantizers, we have

$$\mathbf{E}D(\mu_n, q_n) \geq \mathbf{E}D(\mu_n, q_n^*) \ .$$

Therefore, using (16) and that $\mathbf{E}M = \mathbf{E}\bar{M} = n/3$, we can lower bound the difference $D^*(\mu) - \mathbf{E}D(\mu_n, q_n^*)$ as

$$D^*(\mu) - \mathbf{E}D(\mu_n, q_n^*) \geq \frac{1}{6} - \frac{1}{4} + \frac{1}{4n} \mathbf{E}\{\max(M, \bar{M})\}$$

$$= -\frac{1}{12} + \frac{1}{4n} \mathbf{E}\left\{ \frac{M + \bar{M}}{2} + \frac{|\bar{M} - M|}{2} \right\} \tag{17}$$

$$= -\frac{1}{12} + \frac{1}{12} + \frac{\mathbf{E}\{|\bar{M} - M|\}}{8n} = \frac{\mathbf{E}\{|\sum_{j=1}^{n} X_j|\}}{8n} \ .$$

We lower bound the the last expectation using the following inequality: for any random variable Z with finite fourth moment,

$$\mathbf{E}|Z| \geq \frac{(\mathbf{E}\{Z^2\})^{3/2}}{(\mathbf{E}\{Z^4\})^{1/2}} \tag{18}$$

(see [16–p. 194] or [13–Lemma A.4]). Since X_j's are independent, identically distributed, and have zero mean, we have

$$\mathbf{E}\left\{ \left(\sum_{j=1}^{n} X_j \right)^2 \right\} = n\mathbf{E}\{X_1^2\} = 2n/3 \ .$$

On the other hand, expanding $(\sum_{j=1}^{n} X_j)^4$ yields

$$\mathbf{E}\left\{ \left(\sum_{j=1}^{n} X_j \right)^4 \right\} = n\mathbf{E}\{X_1^4\} + 3n(n-1)(\mathbf{E}\{X_1^2\})^2$$

$$= \frac{2n}{3} + 3n(n-1)\frac{4}{9}$$

$$= \frac{2n(2n-1)}{3}$$

$$\leq 4n^2/3 \ .$$

Hence (18) gives

$$\mathbf{E}\left\{ \left| \sum_{j=1}^{n} X_j \right| \right\} \geq \frac{(2n/3)^{3/2}}{(4n^2/3)^{1/2}} = \frac{\sqrt{2n}}{3} \ .$$

Combining this with (17), we conclude that for all $n \geq 1$,

$$D^*(\mu) - \mathbf{E}D(\mu_n, q_n^*) \geq \frac{1}{12\sqrt{2}} \frac{1}{\sqrt{n}} \; . \qquad \qquad \square$$

References

1. Pollard, D.: Strong consistency of k-means clustering. Annals of Statistics **9** (1981) 135–140
2. Pollard, D.: Quantization and the method of k-means. IEEE Transactions on Information Theory **IT-28** (1982) 199–205
3. Linder, T., Lugosi, G., Zeger, K.: Rates of convergence in the source coding theorem, in empirical quantizer design, and in universal lossy source coding. IEEE Transactions on Information Theory **40** (1994) 1728–1740
4. Linder, T.: On the training distortion of vector quantizers. IEEE Trans. Inform. Theory **IT-46** (2000) 1617–1623
5. Linder, T.: Learning-theoretic methods in vector quantization. In Györfi, L., ed.: Principles of nonparametric learning. Number 434 in CISM Courses and Lectures. Springer-Verlag, Wien, New York (2002) 163–210
6. Linder, T., Lugosi, G., Zeger, K.: Empirical quantizer design in the presence of source noise or channel noise. IEEE Trans. Inform. Theory **IT-43** (1997) 612–623
7. Merhav, N., Ziv, J.: On the amount of side information required for lossy data compression. IEEE Trans. Inform. Theory **IT-43** (1997) 1112–1121
8. Zeevi, A.J.: On the performance of vector quantizers empirically designed from dependent sources. In Storer, J., Cohn, M., eds.: Proceedings of Data Compression Conference, DCC'98, Los Alamitos, California, IEEE Computer Society Press (1998) 73–82
9. Bartlett, P., Linder, T., Lugosi, G.: The minimax distortion redundancy in empirical quantizer design. IEEE Transactions on Information Theory **IT-44** (1998) 1802–1813
10. Antos, A., Györfi, L., György, A.: Improved convergence rates in empirical vector quantizer design. In: Proceedings 2004 IEEE International Symposium on Information Theory, IEEE, IEEE Information Theory Society (2004) 301 (Chicago, IL, June 28–July 2, 2004.) Full paper submitted.
11. Chou, P.A.: The distortion of vector quantizers trained on n vectors decreases to the optimum as $O_p(1/n)$. In: Proceedings 1994 IEEE International Symposium on Information Theory. IEEE, IEEE Information Theory Society (1994) 457 (Trondheim, Norway, June 27–July 1, 1994.).
12. Pollard, D.: A central limit theorem for k-means clustering. Annals of Probability **10** (1982) 919–926
13. Devroye, L., Györfi, L., Lugosi, G.: A Probabilistic Theory of Pattern Recognition. Number 31 in Applications of Mathematics, Stochastic Modelling and Applied Probability. Springer-Verlag, New York (1996)
14. Slud, E.V.: Distribution inequalities for the binomial law. Annals of Probability **5** (1977) 404–412
15. Kolmogorov, A.N., Tikhomirov, V.M.: ϵ-entropy and ϵ-capacity of sets in function spaces. Translations of the American Mathematical Society **17** (1961) 277–364
16. Devroye, L., Györfi, L.: Nonparametric Density Estimation: The L_1 View. John Wiley, New York (1985)

Rank, Trace-Norm and Max-Norm

Nathan Srebro[1] and Adi Shraibman[2]

[1] University of Toronto Department of Computer Science,
Toronto ON, Canada
[2] Hebrew University Institute of Computer Science,
Jerusalem, Israel
nati@cs.toronto.edu, adidan@cs.huji.ac.il

Abstract. We study the rank, trace-norm and max-norm as complexity measures of matrices, focusing on the problem of fitting a matrix with matrices having low complexity. We present generalization error bounds for predicting unobserved entries that are based on these measures. We also consider the possible relations between these measures. We show gaps between them, and bounds on the extent of such gaps.

1   Introduction

Consider the problem of approximating a noisy (or partially observed) target matrix Y with another matrix X. This problem arises often in practice, e.g. when analyzing tabulated data such as gene expressions, word counts in a corpus of documents, collections of images, or user preferences on a collection of items.

A common general scheme for solving such problems is to select a matrix X that minimizes some combination of the *complexity* of X and the *discrepancy* between X and Y. The heart of the matter is the choice of the measure of complexity for X and the measure of discrepancy between X and Y.

The most common notion of complexity of a matrix in such tasks is its rank (as in PCA, Latent Semantic Analysis, the Aspect Model and a variety of other factor models and generalizations of these approaches). Recently, the *trace-norm* and *max-norm* were suggested as alternative measures of complexity with strong connections to maximum-margin linear classification [1]. Whereas bounding the rank corresponds to constraining the *dimensionality* of each row of U and V in a factorization $X = UV'$, bounding the trace-norm and max-norm corresponds to constraining the *norms* of rows of U and V (average row-norm for the trace-norm, and maximal row-norm for the max-norm). Unlike low-rank factorizations, such constraints lead to *convex* optimization problems.

In this paper we study the rank, trace-norm and max-norm as measures of matrix complexity, concentrating on the implications to the problem mentioned above.

We begin by considering the problem of predicting unknown entries in a partially observed matrix Y (as in collaborative prediction). We assume the prediction is made by choosing a matrix X for which some combination of the

P. Auer and R. Meir (Eds.): COLT 2005, LNAI 3559, pp. 545–560, 2005.

discrepancy between X and Y on the one hand, and the complexity of X on the other hand, is minimized. We present generalization error bounds for general measures of discrepancy and for the cases where the complexity measure for X is either rank (Section 3.1, repeating a previous analysis [2]), trace-norm or max-norm (Sections 3.2 and 3.3, elaborating on and proving previously quoted bounds [1]). We make no assumptions about the matrix Y, other than that the observed entries are chosen at random. The bounds, and the complexity measures used to obtain them (cardinality, pseudodimension and Rademacher complexity), are insightful in comparing the three measures of matrix complexity we are considering.

In addition to results about generic measures of discrepancy, we also specifically consider binary target matrices: For $Y \in \pm 1^{n \times m}$, we study the minimum rank, max-norm and (normalized) trace-norm of a matrix X such that $X_{ij} Y_{ij} \geq 1$ for all i, j. We refer to these as the dimensional-complexity $\mathrm{dc}(Y)$, max-complexity $\mathrm{mc}(Y)$ and trace-complexity $\mathrm{tc}(Y)$ of a binary matrix Y.

We study relations between the three matrix complexity measures. Matrices that can be approximated by a matrix of low max-norm can also be approximated by a matrix with low rank. In Section 4 we show this for general measures of discrepancy, generalizing previous results [3,4] for binary target matrices. But this relationship is not reversible: We give examples of explicit binary matrices with low dimensional-complexity that have high max-complexity. Previously, examples in which the max-complexity is a polynomial function of the dimensional-complexity [5], or where the dimensional-complexity is constant but the max-complexity is logarithmic in the matrix size [4] have been shown. We present an explicit construction establishing that the max-complexity is not bounded by any polynomial of the dimensional-complexity and the logarithm of the matrix size.

Similarly we give examples of matrices with low trace-complexity but high dimensional-complexity and max-complexity. This gap is related to a requirement for uniform sampling of observed entries, which we show to be necessary for generalization error bounds based on the trace-norm but not on the max-norm or rank. We also show that the gap we obtain is the largest possible gap, establishing a first lower bound on the trace-complexity in terms of the max-complexity or dimensional-complexity (Section 5).

Embedding Classifiers as Linear Separators. The dimensional-complexity and max-complexity have been studied in the context of embedding concept classes as low-dimensional, or large-margin, linear separators. A concept class $\mathcal{H} = \{h : \Phi \to \pm 1\}$ of binary valued functions can be represented as a $|\Phi| \times |\mathcal{H}|$ matrix Y, with $Y_{\phi,h} = h(\phi)$. The dimensional-complexity of Y is the minimum d such that each $\phi \in \Phi$ can be embedded as a point $u_\phi \in \mathbb{R}^d$ and each classifier $h \in \mathcal{H}$ can be embedded as a separating homogeneous hyperplane determined by its normal $v_h \in \mathbb{R}^d$, such that $h(\phi) = \mathrm{sign}\, v_h' u_\phi$. The max-complexity is the smallest M such that Φ can be embedded as points and $\mathcal{H}$ as linear separators in an infinite dimensional unit ball, where all separators separate with a margin of at least $1/M$, i.e. $\frac{|v_h' u_\phi|}{|v_h|} \geq 1/M$. Studying linear separators (in particular using kernel methods) as a generic approach to classification leads one to ask what concept classes can or cannot be embedded as low-dimensional or large-margin linear separators; that is, what matrices have high dimensional-complexity and max-complexity [4, 6].

These questions are existential questions, aimed at understanding the limits of kernel-based methods. Here, the concept class of interest is the class of matrices themselves, and we apply much of the same techniques and results in order to understand the performance of a concrete learning problem.

2   Preliminaries

Notation. For vectors, $|v|_p$ is the l_p norm and $|v| = |v|_2$. For matrices, $\|X\|_{\mathrm{Fro}} = \sqrt{\sum_{ij} X_{ij}^2}$ is the Frobenius norm; $\|X\|_2 = \max_{|u|=|v|=1} u'Xv$ is the spectral norm and is equal to the maximum singular value of X; $\|X\|_{2\to\infty} = \max_{|u|_2=1} |Xu|_\infty = \max_i |X_i.|$ is the maximum row norm of X; $|X|_\infty = \max_{ij} |X_{ij}|$.

Discrepancy. We focus on element-wise notions of discrepancy between two $n \times m$ matrices Y and X: $\mathcal{D}(X;Y) = \frac{1}{nm} \sum_{ij} g(X_{ij}; Y_{ij})$, where $g(x; y)$ is some loss function. The *empirical* discrepancy for a subset $S \subset [n] \times [m]$ of the observed entries of Y is $\mathcal{D}_S(X;Y) = \frac{1}{|S|} \sum_{ij \in S} g(X_{ij}; Y_{ij})$. The discrepancy relative to a distribution $\mathcal{P}$ over entries in the matrix (i.e. over $[n] \times [m]$) is $\mathcal{D}_\mathcal{P}(X;Y) = \mathbf{E}_{ij \sim \mathcal{P}}[g(X_{ij}; Y_{ij})]$.

Since the norms are scale-sensitive measures of complexity, the scale in which the loss function changes is important. This is captured by Lipschitz continuity: A loss function $g : \mathbb{R} \times Y \to \mathbb{R}$ is L-Lipschitz if for every y, x_1, x_2, $|g(x_1; y) - g(x_2; y)| \leq L|x_1 - x_2|$.

For the special case of binary target matrices $Y \in \{\pm 1\}^{n \times m}$, the discrepancy with respect to the sign-agreement zero-one error is the (normalized) Hamming distance between $\mathrm{sign}\, X$ and $\mathrm{sign}\, Y$. It will be useful to consider the set of matrices whose sign patterns agree with the target matrix: $\mathrm{SP}(Y) = \{X | \mathrm{sign}\, X = \mathrm{sign}\, Y\}$. For scale-dependent (e.g. norm-based) complexity measures of X, considering the signs of entries in X is no longer enough, and their magnitudes must also be bounded. We consider $\mathrm{SP}^1(Y) = \{X | \forall_{ij} X_{ij} Y_{ij} \geq 1\}$, corresponding to a *margin* sign-agreement error.

Complexity. The **rank** of a matrix X is the minimum k such that $X = UV'$, $U \in \mathbb{R}^{n \times k}$, $V \in \mathbb{R}^{m \times k}$. The *dimensional-complexity* of a sign matrix is:

$$\mathrm{dc}(Y) \doteq \min\{\mathrm{rank}\, X | X \in \mathrm{SP}(Y)\} = \min\{\mathrm{rank}\, X | X \in \mathrm{SP}^1(Y)\} \qquad (1)$$

The **max-norm** (also known as the γ_2-norm [7]) of a matrix X is given by:

$$\|X\|_{\max} \doteq \min_{X=UV'} \|U\|_{2\to\infty} \|V\|_{2\to\infty} \qquad (2)$$

While the rank constrains the dimensionality of rows in U and V, the max-norm constrains the norms of all rows in U and V. The **max-complexity** for a sign matrix Y is $\mathrm{mc}(Y) \doteq \min\{\|X\|_{\max} | X \in \mathrm{SP}^1(Y)\}$

The **trace-norm**[1] $\|X\|_\Sigma$ is the sum of the singular values of X (i.e. the roots of the eigenvalues of XX^t).

Lemma 1. $\|X\|_\Sigma = \min_{X=UV'} \|U\|_{Fro} \|V\|_{Fro} = \min_{X=UV'} \frac{1}{2}(\|U\|^2_{Fro}+\|V\|^2_{Fro})$

While the max-norm constrains the maximal norm of the rows in U and V, the trace-norm constrains the *sum* of the norms of the rows in U and V. That is, the max-norm constrains the norms uniformly, while the trace-norm constrains them on average. The **trace-complexity** of a sign matrix Y is $\mathrm{tc}(Y) \doteq \min\{\|X\|_\Sigma/\sqrt{nm}|X \in \mathrm{SP}^1(Y)\}$.

Since the maximum is greater than the average, the trace-norm is bounded by the max-norm: $\|X\|_\Sigma/\sqrt{nm} \le \|X\|_{\max}$ and $\mathrm{tc}(Y) \le \mathrm{mc}(Y)$. In Section 5 we see that there can be a large gap between $\|X\|_\Sigma/\sqrt{nm}$ and $\|X\|_{\max}$.

Extreme Values. For any sign matrix $Y, 1 \le \mathrm{tc}(Y) \le \mathrm{mc}(Y) \le \|Y\|_{\max} \le \sqrt{n}$. Rank-one sign matrices Y have $\mathrm{dc}(Y) = \mathrm{mc}(Y) = \mathrm{tc}(Y) = 1$ and are the only sign matrices for which any of the three quantities is equal to one. To obtain examples of matrices with high trace-complexity, note that:

Lemma 2. *For any* $Y \in \{\pm1\}^{n\times m}$, $\mathrm{tc}(Y) \ge \sqrt{nm}/\|Y\|_2$.

Proof. Let $X \in \mathrm{SP}(Y)$ s.t. $\|X\|_\Sigma = \sqrt{nm}\mathrm{tc}(Y)$, then by the duality of the spectral norm and the trace-norm, $\|X\|_\Sigma \|Y\|_2 \ge \sum_{ij} X_{ij}Y_{ij} \ge nm$. □

An example of a sign matrix with low spectral norm is the Hadamard matrix $H_p \in \{\pm1\}^{2^p \times 2^p}$, where H_{ij} is the inner product of i and j as elements in $GF(2^p)$. Using $\|H_p\|_2 = 2^{p/2}$ we get $\mathrm{mc}(H_{\log n}) = \mathrm{tc}(H_{\log n}) = \sqrt{n}$ [5]. Although counting arguments prove that for any n, there exist $n\times n$ sign matrices for which $\mathrm{dc}(Y) > n/11$ (Lemma 3 below, following Alon *et al* [8] who give a slightly weaker bound), the Hadamard matrix, for which it is known that $\sqrt{n} \le \mathrm{dc}(H_{\log n}) \le n^{0.8}$ [6], is the most extreme known concrete example.

3   Generalization Error Bounds

Consider a setting in which a random subset S of the entries of Y is observed. Based on the observed entries Y_S we would like to predict unobserved entries in Y. This can be done by fitting a low-complexity matrix X to Y_S and using X to predict unobserved entries. We present generalization error bounds on the overall discrepancy in terms of the observed discrepancy. The bounds do *not* assume any structure or probabilistic assumption on Y, and hold for any (adversarial) target matrix Y. What is assumed is that the sample S is chosen at random.

We are interested in predicting unobserved entries not only as an application of matrix learning (e.g. when predicting a user's preferences based on preferences of the user and other users, or completing missing experimental data), but also as a conceptual learning task where the different measures of complexity can

---

[1] Also known as the *nuclear norm* and the *Ky-Fan n-norm*.

arbitrary source distribution	⇔	target matrix Y
random training set	⇔	random set S of observed entries
hypothesis	⇔	concept matrix X
training error	⇔	observed discrepancy $\mathcal{D}_S(X;Y)$
generalization error	⇔	true discrepancy $\mathcal{D}(X;Y)$

Fig. 1. Correspondence with post-hoc bounds on the generalization error for standard feature-based prediction tasks

be compared and related. Even when learning is done for some other purpose (e.g. understanding structure or reconstructing a latent signal), the ability of the model to predict held-out entries is frequently used as an ad-hoc indicator of its fit to the true underlying structure. Bounds on the generalization ability for unobserved entries can be used as a theoretical substitute to such measures (with the usual caveats of using generalization error bounds).

The Pseudodimension and the Rademacher Complexity. To obtain generalization error bounds, we consider matrices as functions from index pairs to entry values, and calculate the pseudodimension of the class of low-rank matrices and the Rademacher complexity of the classes of low max-norm and low trace-norm matrices. Recall that:

Definition 1. *A class $\mathcal{F}$ of real-valued functions* pseudo-shatters *the points $x_1, \ldots, x_n$ with thresholds $t_1, \ldots, t_n$ if for every binary labeling of the points $(s_1, \ldots, s_n) \in \{+, -\}^n$ there exists $f \in \mathcal{F}$ s.t. $f(x_i) \leq t_i$ iff $s_i = -$. The* pseudodimension *of a class $\mathcal{F}$ is the supremum over n for which there exist n points and thresholds that can be shattered.*

Definition 2. *The* empirical Rademacher complexity *of a class $\mathcal{F}$ over a specific sample $S = (x_1, x_2, \ldots)$ is given by: $\hat{R}_S(\mathcal{F}) = \frac{2}{|S|} \mathbf{E}_\sigma \left[\sup_{f \in \mathcal{F}} |\sum_i \sigma_i f(x_i)| \right]$, where the expectation is over the uniformly distributed random signs σ_i.*

The Rademacher complexity with respect to a distribution D is the expectation, over a sample of $|S|$ points drawn i.i.d. from D: $R_{|S|}^D(\mathcal{F}) = \mathbf{E}_S \left[\hat{R}_S(\mathcal{F}) \right]$.

It is well known how to obtain Generalization error bounds in terms of the pseudodimension and Rademacher complexity. Our emphasis is on calculating the pseudodimension and the Rademacher complexity. We do not present the tightest possible bounds in terms of these measures.

3.1 Low-Rank Matrices

Generalization error bounds for prediction with low-rank matrices can be obtained by considering the number of sign configurations of low-rank matrices [2] (following techniques introduced in [8]):

Lemma 3 ([9]). $|\{Y \in \{\pm 1\}^{n \times m} | dc(Y) \leq k\}| \leq (8em/k)^{k(n+m)}$

This bound is tight up to a multiplicative factor in the exponent: for $m > k^2$, $|\{Y \in \{\pm 1\}^{n \times m} | dc(Y) \le k\}| \ge m^{\frac{1}{2}(k-1)n}$.

Using the bound of Lemma 3, a union bound of Chernoff bounds yields a generalization error bound for the zero-one sign agreement error (since only signs of entries in X are relevant). Generalization error bounds for other loss functions can be obtained by using a similar counting argument to bound the pseudodimension of the class $\mathcal{X}^k = \{X | \operatorname{rank} X \le k\}$. To do so, we need to bound not only the number of sign configurations of such matrices, but the number of sign configurations relative to any threshold matrix T:

Lemma 4 ([2]). $\forall_{T \in \mathbb{R}^{n \times m}} |\{\operatorname{sign}(X - T) | \operatorname{rank} X \le k\}| \le \left(\frac{8em}{k}\right)^{k(n+m)}$

Corollary 1. $pseudodimension(\mathcal{X}^k) \le k(n + m) \log \frac{8em}{k}$

Theorem 1 ([2]). *For any monotone loss function bounded by M, any $n \times m$ matrix Y, any distribution $\mathcal{P}$ of index pairs (i, j), $n, m > 2$, $\delta > 0$ and integer k, with probability at least $1 - \delta$ over choosing a set S of $|S|$ index pairs according to $\mathcal{P}$, for all matrices X with $\operatorname{rank} X \le k$:*

$$\mathcal{D}_{\mathcal{P}}(X; Y) < \mathcal{D}_S(X; Y) + 6\sqrt{\frac{k(n+m)\log\frac{8em}{k}\log\frac{M|S|}{k(n+m)} - \log\delta}{|S|}}$$

3.2   Low Trace-Norm Matrices

In order to calculate the Rademacher complexity of the class $\mathcal{X}[M] = \{X | \|X\|_\Sigma \le M\}$, we observe that this class is convex and that any unit-trace-norm matrix is a convex combination of unit-norm rank-one matrices $X = \sum D_{aa}(U_{\cdot a} V_{\cdot a}')$, where $X = UDV'$ is the SVD and $U_{\cdot a}, V_{\cdot a}$ are columns of U, V. Therefore, $\mathcal{X}[1] = \operatorname{conv}\mathcal{X}_1[1]$, where $\mathcal{X}_1[1] \doteq \{uv' \mid u \in \mathbb{R}^n, v \in \mathbb{R}^m, |u| = |v| = 1\}$ is the class of unit-norm rank-one matrices. We use the fact that the Rademacher complexity does not change when taking convex combinations, and calculate the Rademacher complexity of $\mathcal{X}_1[1]$. We first analyze the empirical Rademacher complexity for any fixed sample S, possibly with repeating index pairs. We then bound the average Rademacher complexity for a sample of $|S|$ index pairs drawn uniformly at random from $[n] \times [m]$ (with repetitions).

The Empirical Rademacher Complexity. For an empirical sample $S = \{(i_1, j_1), (i_2, j_2), \ldots\}$ of $|S|$ index pairs, the empirical Rademacher complexity of rank-one unit-norm matrices is the expectation:

$$\hat{R}_S(\mathcal{X}_1[1]) = \mathbf{E}_\sigma \left[\sup_{|u|=|v|=1} \left| \frac{2}{|S|} \sum_{\alpha=1}^{|S|} \sigma_\alpha u_{i_\alpha} v_{j_\alpha} \right| \right] \tag{3}$$

where σ_α are uniform ± 1 random variables. For each index pair (i, j) we will denote by s_{ij} the number of times it appears in the empirical sample S, and consider the random variables $\sigma_{ij} = \sum_{\alpha \text{ s.t. } (i_\alpha, j_\alpha)=(i,j)} \sigma_\alpha$.

Since the variables σ_α are independent, $\mathbf{E}[\sigma_{ij}^2] = s_{ij}$, and we can calculate:

$$\hat{R}_S(\mathcal{X}_1[1]) = \mathbf{E}_\sigma \left[\sup_{|u|,|v|=1} \left| \frac{2}{|S|} \sum_{i,j} \sigma_{ij} u_i v_j \right| \right] = \frac{2}{|S|} \mathbf{E}_\sigma \left[\sup_{|u|,|v|=1} |u'\sigma v| \right] = \frac{2\mathbf{E}_\sigma[\|\sigma\|_2]}{|S|}$$

where σ is an $n \times m$ matrix of σ_{ij}.

The Rademacher complexity is equal to the expectation of the spectral norm of the random matrix σ (with a factor of $\frac{2}{|S|}$). Using the Frobenius norm to bound the spectral norm, we have:

$$\hat{R}_S(\mathcal{X}_1[1]) \leq \frac{2}{|S|} \mathbf{E}_\sigma[\|\sigma\|_{\text{Fro}}] \leq \frac{2}{|S|} \sqrt{|S|} = \frac{2}{\sqrt{|S|}} \tag{4}$$

As a supremum over all sample sets S, this bound is tight: consider a sample of $|S|$ index pairs, all in the same column. The rank-one unit-norm matrix attaining the supremum would match the signs of the matrix with $\pm 1/\sqrt{|S|}$ yielding an empirical Rademacher complexity of $2/\sqrt{|S|}$. The form of (4) is very disappointing, and does not lead to meaningful generalization error bounds.

Even though the empirical Rademacher complexity for a specific sample might be very high, in what follows we show that the *expected* Rademacher complexity, for a uniformly chosen sample, is low. Using the Frobenius norm to bound the Spectral norm of σ will no longer be enough, and in order to get a meaningful bound we must analyze the expected spectral norm more carefully.

Bounding $\mathbf{E}_\sigma[\|\sigma\|_2]$. In order to bound the expected spectral norm of σ, we apply Theorem 3.1 of [10], which bounds the expected spectral norm of matrices with entries of fixed magnitudes but random signs in terms of the maximum row and column magnitude norms. If S contains no repeated index pairs ($s_{ij} = 0$ or 1), we are already in this situation, as the magnitudes of σ are equal to s. When some index pairs are repeated, we consider a different random matrix, $\tilde{\sigma}_{ij} = \epsilon_{ij} s_{ij}$, where ϵ_{ij} are i.i.d. unbiased signs. Using $\tilde{\sigma}$ instead of σ gives us an upper bound on the empirical Rademacher complexity (Lemma 12 from the Appendix). Applying Theorem 3.1 of [10] to $\tilde{\sigma}_{ij}$, we obtain:

$$\hat{R}_S(\mathcal{X}_1[1]) \leq \frac{2}{|S|} \mathbf{E}_\epsilon[\|\tilde{\sigma}\|_2] \frac{2}{|S|} \leq K(\ln m)^{\frac{1}{4}} \left(\max_i |s_i.| + \max_j |s._j| \right) \tag{5}$$

where $|s_i.|$ and $|s._j|$ are norms of row and column vectors of the matrix s, and K is the absolute constant guaranteed by Theorem 3.1 of [10].

Bounding the Row and Column Norms. For the worst samples, the norm of a single row or column vector of s might be as high as $|S|$, but for random uniformly drawn samples, we would expect the row and column norms to be roughly $\sqrt{|S|/n}$ and $\sqrt{|S|/m}$. To make this estimate precise we proceed in two steps[2]. We first use Bernstein's inequality to bound the maximum value of s_{ij},

---

[2] We assume here $nm > |S| > n \geq m > 3$. See [9] for more details.

uniformly over all index pairs: $\Pr_S(\max_{ij} s_{ij} > 9\ln n) \leq \frac{1}{|S|}$. When the maximum entry in s is bounded, the norm of a row can be bounded by the square root of the number of observations in the row. In the second step we use Bernstein's inequality again to bound the expected maximum number of observations in a row (similarly column) by $6(\frac{|S|}{n} + \ln|S|)$. Combining these results we can bound the Rademacher complexity, for a random sample set where each index pair is chosen uniformly and independently at random:

$$
\begin{aligned}
R_{|S|}^{\text{uniform}}(\mathcal{X}_1[1]) &= \mathbf{E}_S\left[\hat{R}_S(\mathcal{X}_1[1])\right] \\
&\leq \Pr\left(\max_{ij} s_{ij} > 9\ln n\right)\sup_S \hat{R}_S(\mathcal{X}_1[1]) + \mathbf{E}_S\left[\hat{R}_S(\mathcal{X}_1[1])\,\Big|\,\max_{ij} s_{ij} \leq 9\ln n\right] \\
&\leq \frac{1}{|S|}\cdot\frac{2}{\sqrt{|S|}} + \frac{2}{|S|}K(\ln m)^{\frac{1}{4}}\mathbf{E}_S\left[\max_i |s_i.| + \max_j |s._j|\,\Big|\,\max_{ij} s_{ij} \leq 9\ln n\right] \\
&\leq \frac{2}{|S|^{3/2}} + \frac{2K(\ln m)^{\frac{1}{4}}}{|S|}\sqrt{9\ln n}\left(\sqrt{6(\frac{|S|}{n} + \ln|S|)} + \sqrt{6(\frac{|S|}{m} + \ln|S|)}\right) \quad (6)
\end{aligned}
$$

Taking the convex hull, scaling by M and rearranging terms:

Theorem 2. *For some universal constant K, the expected Rademacher complexity of matrices of trace-norm at most M, over uniform samplings of index pairs is at most (for $|S|/\ln n \geq n \geq m$): $R_{|S|}^{\text{uniform}}(\mathcal{X}[M]) \leq K\frac{M}{\sqrt{nm}}\sqrt{\frac{(n+m)\ln^{3/2} n}{|S|}}$*

Applying Theorem 2 of [11][3]:

Theorem 3. *For any L-Lipschitz loss function, target matrix Y, $\delta > 0$, $M > 0$ and sample sizes $|S| > n\log n$, and for a uniformly selected sample S of $|S|$ entries in Y, with probability at least $1-\delta$ over the sample selection, the following holds for all matrices $X \in \mathbb{R}^{n \times m}$ with $\frac{\|X\|_\Sigma}{\sqrt{nm}} \leq M$:*

$$
\mathcal{D}(X;Y) < \mathcal{D}_S(X;Y) + KL\sqrt{\frac{M^2(n+m)\ln^{3/2}n - \log\delta}{|S|}}
$$

Where K is a universal constant that does not depend on Y, n, m, the loss function, or any other quantity.

3.3   Low Max-Norm Matrices

Since the max-norm gives us a bound on the trace-norm, we can apply Theorems 2 and 3 also to matrices of bounded max-norm. However, when the max-norm is

---

[3] By bounding the zero-one sign-agreement error with the 1-Lipschitz function $g(x,y) = \max(0, \min(yx - 1, 1))$, which in turn is bounded by the margin sign-agreement error, generalization error bounds in terms of the margin can be obtained from bounds in terms of the Lipschitz constant.

bounded it is possible to obtain better bounds, avoiding the logarithmic terms, and more importantly, bounds that hold for *any* sampling distribution.

As we did for low trace-norm matrices, we bound the Rademacher complexity of low max-norm matrices by characterizing the unit ball of the max-norm $\mathcal{B}_{\max} = \{X \mid \|X\|_{\max} \leq 1\}$ as a convex hull. Unlike the trace-norm unit ball, we cannot exactly characterize the max-norm unit ball as a convex hull. However, using Grothendiek's Inequality we can bound the unit ball with the convex hull of rank-one sign matrices $\mathcal{X}_{\pm} = \{X \in \{\pm 1\}^{n \times m} \mid \operatorname{rank} X = 1\}$.

Theorem 4 (Grothendieck's Inequality [12–page 64]). *There is an absolute constant $1.67 < K_G < 1.79$ such that the following holds: Let A_{ij} be a real matrix, and suppose that $\left| \sum_{i,j} A_{ij} s_i t_j \right| \leq 1$ for every choice of reals with $|s_i|, |t_j| \leq 1$ for all i, j. Then $\left| \sum_{i,j} a_{ij} \langle x_i, y_j \rangle \right| \leq K_G$, for every choice of unit vectors x_i, y_j in a real Hilbert space.*

Corollary 2. $\operatorname{conv} \mathcal{X}_{\pm} \subset \mathcal{B}_{\max} \subset K_G \operatorname{conv} \mathcal{X}_{\pm}$

Proof. Noting that the dual norm to the max-norm is:

$$\|A\|^*_{max} = \max_{\|B\|_{\max} \leq 1} \langle A, B \rangle = \max_{x_i, y_j \in \mathbb{R}^k : |x_i|, |y_j| \leq 1} \sum_{i,j} a_{ij} x_i' y_j. \tag{7}$$

where the maximum is over any k, we can restate Grothendieck's inequality as $\|A\|^*_{max} \leq K_G \|A\|_{\infty \to 1}$ where $\|A\|_{\infty \to 1} = \max_{s_i, t_j \in \mathbb{R} : |s_i|, |t_j| \leq 1} \sum_{i,j} a_{ij} s_i t_j$. We also have $\|A\|_{\infty \to 1} \leq \|A\|^*_{max}$, and taking the duals:

$$\|A\|^*_{\infty \to 1} \geq \|A\|_{max} \geq K_G \|A\|^*_{\infty \to 1} \tag{8}$$

We now note that $\|A\|_{\infty \to 1} = \max_{B \in \mathcal{X}_{\pm}} \langle A, B \rangle$ and so $\mathcal{X}_{\pm}$ is the unit ball of $\|A\|^*_{\infty \to 1}$ and (8) establishes the Corollary.   □

The class of rank-one sign matrices is a finite class of size $|\mathcal{X}_{\pm}| = 2^{n+m-1}$, and so its empirical Rademacher complexity (for any sample) can be bounded by $\hat{R}_S(\mathcal{X}_{\pm}) < \sqrt{7 \frac{2(n+m) + \log |S|}{|S|}}$ [9]. Taking the convex hull of this class and scaling by $2M$ we have (for $2 < |S| < nm$):

Theorem 5. *The Rademacher complexity of matrices of max-norm at most M, for any index-pair distribution, is bounded by[4]: $R_{|S|}(\mathcal{X}^{\max}[M]) \leq 12M \sqrt{\frac{n+m}{|S|}}$*

Theorem 6. *For any L-Lipschitz loss function, any matrix Y, any distribution $\mathcal{P}$ of index pairs (i, j), $n, m > 2$, $\delta > 0$ and $M > 0$, with probability at least $1 - \delta$ over choosing a set S of $|S|$ index pairs according to $\mathcal{P}$, for all matrices X with $\|X\|_{\max} \leq M$:*

$$\mathcal{D}_{\mathcal{P}}(X; Y) < \mathcal{D}_S(X; Y) + 17 \sqrt{\frac{M^2(n+m) - \log \delta}{|S|}}$$

---

[4] For large enough n, m, the constant 12 can be reduced to $K_G \sqrt{8 \ln 2} < 4.197$.

4   Between the Max-Norm and the Rank

We have already seen that the max-norm bounds the trace-norm, and so any low max-norm approximation is also a low trace-norm approximation. Although the max-norm does not bound the rank (e.g. the identity matrix has max-norm one but rank n), using random projections, a low max-norm matrix can be approximated by a low rank matrix [3]. Ben David et al [4] used this to show that $dc(Y) = O(mc^2(Y) \log n)$. Here, we present a slightly more general analysis, for any Lipschitz continuous loss function.

Lemma 5. *For any $X \in R^{n \times m}$ and any $\|X\|_{\max} > \epsilon > 0$, there exists X' such that $|X - X'|_\infty < \epsilon$ and $\operatorname{rank} X \le 9(\|X\|_{\max}/\epsilon)^2 \log(3nm)$.*

Proof. Set $M = \|X\|_{\max}$ and let $X = UV'$ with $\|U\|_{2 \to \infty}^2 = \|V\|_{2 \to \infty}^2 = M$. Let $A \in \mathbb{R}^{k \times d}$ be a random matrix with independent normally distributed entries, then for any u, v with $u' = Au$ and $v' = Av$ we have [3]:

$$\Pr\left(1 - \varepsilon\right)|u - v|^2 \le |u' - v'|^2 \le (1 + \varepsilon)|u - v|^2 \ge 1 - 2e^{-k(\varepsilon^2 - \varepsilon^3)/4} \quad (9)$$

Set $\varepsilon = \frac{2\epsilon}{3M}$ and $k = 4\ln(3nm)/\varepsilon^2 = 9(M/\epsilon)^2 \ln(3nm)$. Taking a union bound over all pairs (U_i, V_j) of rows of U and V, as well as all pairs $(U_i, 0)$ and $(V_j, 0)$, we get that with positive probability, for all i, j, $|U_i' - V_j'|^2$, $|U_i'|^2$ and $|V_j'|^2$ are all within $(1 \pm \varepsilon)$ of $|U_i - V_j|^2$, $|U_i|^2 \le M$ and $|V_j|^2 \le M$, respectively. Expressing $U_i' V_j'$ in terms of these norms yields $U_i V_j - 3M\varepsilon/2 \le U_i' V_j' \le U_i V_j + 3M\varepsilon/2$, and so $|UV' - X|_\infty \le 3M\varepsilon/2 = \epsilon$ and $\operatorname{rank} UV \le k = 9(M/\epsilon)^2 \ln(3nm)$.   □

Corollary 3. *For any L-Lipschitz continuous loss function, any matrices X, Y, and any $\|X\|_{\max} > \epsilon > 0$, there exists X' such that $\mathcal{D}(X'; Y) \le \mathcal{D}(X; Y) + \epsilon$ and $\operatorname{rank} X' \le 9 \|X\|_{\max}^2 (L/\epsilon)^2 \log(3nm)$.*

Corollary 4. *For any sign matrix Y, $dc(Y) \le 10mc^2(Y) \log(3nm)$.*

Proof. For $X \in \mathrm{SP}^1(Y)$, setting $\epsilon = \sqrt{0.9}$ ensures $\operatorname{sign} X' = \operatorname{sign} X = Y$.   □

Using Lemma 5 and Theorem 1 it is possible to obtain a generalization error bound similar to that of Theorem 6, but with additional log-factors. More interestingly, Corollary 4 allows us to bound the number of matrices with low max-complexity[5]:

Lemma 6. $\log |\{Y \in \{\pm1\}^{n \times m} | mc(Y) \le M\}| < 10M^2(n+m) \log(3nm) \log(\frac{m}{M^2})$

Noting that $Y \in \{\pm1\}^{n \times m}$ with at most M "1"s in each row has $mc(Y) \le M$ establishes that this bound is tight up to logarithmic factors:

Lemma 7. *For $M^2 < n/2$, $\log |\{Y \in \{\pm1\}^{n \times n} | mc(Y) \le M\}| \ge M^2 n \log(n/M^2)$*

---

[5] A tighter analysis, allowing the random projection to switch a few signs, can reduce the bound to $40M^2(n+m) \log^2(m/M^2)$.

A Gap Between dc(Y) and mc(Y). We have seen that dc(Y) can be bounded in terms of $\mathrm{mc}^2(Y)$ and that both yield similar generalization error bounds. We now consider the inverse relationship: can $\mathrm{mc}^2(Y)$ be bounded in terms of dc(Y)?

The Hadamard matrix $H_p \in \mathbb{R}^{n \times n}$ ($n = 2^p$) is an example of a matrix with a polynomial gap between $\mathrm{mc}^2(H_p) = n$ and $\sqrt{n} \leq \mathrm{rank}(H_p) < n^{0.8}$. This gap still leaves open the possibility of a weaker polynomial bound. The triangular matrix $T_n \in \{\pm 1\}^{n \times n}$ with $+1$ on and above the diagonal and -1 below it, exhibits a non-polynomial gap: $\mathrm{dc}(T_n) = 2$ while $\mathrm{mc}(T_n) = \theta(\log n)$ [5–Theorem 6.1]. But we may ask if there is a polynomial relation with logarithmic factors in n. In order to show that mc(Y) is not polynomially bounded by dc(Y), even with poly $\log n$ factors, we examine tensor exponents[6] of triangular matrices (note that $H_1 = T_2$, and so $H_p = T_2^{\otimes p}$, up to row and column permutations).

Theorem 7. *For any $r > 0$, there exists an $n \times n$ sign matrix Y such that $\mathrm{mc}(Y) > (\mathrm{dc}(Y)\log(n))^r$.*

To prove the Theorem, we will use the following known results:

Lemma 8. *For any four matrices A, B, C, D: $(A \otimes B)(C \otimes D) = (AC) \otimes (BD)$.*

Theorem 8 ([5–Theorem 4.1]). *Let Y be a sign matrix, and let $Y = UDV$ be its SVD. If the matrix UV has the same signs as Y then $\frac{\|Y\|_\Sigma}{\sqrt{nm}} \leq \mathrm{mc}(Y)$. If in addition all the rows of the matrix $U\sqrt{D}$, and all the columns of the matrix $\sqrt{D}V$ have equal length, then $\frac{\|Y\|_\Sigma}{\sqrt{nm}} = \mathrm{mc}(Y)$.*

Theorem 9 ([5]). *Denote by T_n the triangular $n \times n$ matrix and $T_n = UDV$ its SVD decomposition, then UV is signed as T_n and all the rows of the matrix $U\sqrt{D}$, and all the columns of the matrix $\sqrt{D}V$ have equal length.*

Proof of Theorem 7. To prove the theorem we first show that if two matrices A and B satisfy the properties that are guarantied by Theorem 9 for triangular matrices, then the tensor product $A \otimes B$ also satisfies this properties. And thus tensor products of triangular matrices have these properties. This follows from the following applications of Lemma 8:

1. Let $U_A D_A V_A = A$ and $U_B D_B V_B = B$ be the SVD of A and B respectively, then $(U_A \otimes U_B)(D_A \otimes D_B)(V_A \otimes V_B)$ is the SVD of $A \otimes B$, since if v_A is a eigenvector of AA^t with eigenvalue μ_A and v_B is an eigenvector of BB^t with eigenvalue μ_B then

$$(A \otimes B)(A \otimes B)^t(v_A \otimes v_B) = (AA^t) \otimes (BB^t)(v_A \otimes v_B)$$
$$= (AA^t v_A) \otimes (BB^t v_B) = \mu_A v_A \otimes \mu_B v_B = \mu_A \mu_B (v_A \otimes v_B).$$

Thus $v_A \otimes v_B$ is an eigenvector of $(A \otimes B)(A \otimes B)^t$ with eigenvalue $\mu_A \mu_B$.

---

[6] $A \otimes B$ and $A^{\otimes p}$ denotes tensor products and exponentiation.

2. If the matrix $U_A V_A$ has the same signs as A, and the matrix $U_B V_B$ as the same signs as B then the matrix $(U_A \otimes U_B)(V_A \otimes V_B) = (U_A V_A) \otimes (V_A V_B)$ has the same signs as $A \otimes B$, since the sings of the tensor product is determined only by the signs of the matrices in the product.

3. If the rows of $U_A \sqrt{D_A}$ have equal length and so does the rows of $U_B \sqrt{D_B}$, and equivalently the columns of $\sqrt{D_A} V_A$ and $\sqrt{D_B} V_B$, then the rows of the matrix $(U_A \otimes U_B)\sqrt{D_A \otimes D_B}$, and the columns of the matrix $\sqrt{D_A \otimes D_B}(V_A \otimes V_B)$ have equal length, since rows (equiv. columns) of $P \otimes Q$ are tensor products of rows (equiv. columns) in P and Q.

For any $t > 0$ and integer $p > 0$, let $k = 2^{2^t}$ and $n = 2^{p2^t}$ and consider $T_k^{\otimes p} \in \{\pm 1\}^{n \times n}$. By the above considerations and Theorems 8 and 9, $\mathrm{mc}(T_k^{\otimes p}) = \mathrm{mc}(T_k)^p \geq (c2^t)^p$ for some $c > 0$, while $\mathrm{dc}(T_k^{\otimes p}) = \mathrm{dc}(T_k)^p \leq 2^p$. For any $r > 0$ we can choose $t = p > \max(6r, -2 \log c)$ and so:

$$(\mathrm{dc}(T_k^{\otimes p}) log(n))^r \leq 2^{r(p+t+\log p)} < 2^{2tp} < 2^{p(t+\log c)} \leq \mathrm{mc}(T_k^{\otimes p}) \qquad \square$$

Matrices with Bounded Entries. We note that a large gap between the max-complexity and the dimensional-complexity is possible only when the low-rank matrix realizing the dimensional-complexity has entries of vastly varying magnitudes: For a rank-k matrix X with entries bounded by R, Awerbuch and Kleinberg's *Barycentric spanner* [13] construction can be used to obtain a factorization $X = UV', U \in R^{n \times k}, V \in R^{m \times k}$, such that the entries of U and V are bounded by $\sqrt{R}$. This establishes that $\|X\|_{\max} \leq |X|_\infty \operatorname{rank} X$. Now, if $X \in \mathrm{SP}(Y)$ with $\operatorname{rank} X = k$ and $\frac{\max_{ij}|X_{ij}|}{\min_{ij}|X_{ij}|} \leq R$, we can scale X to obtain $X' \in \mathrm{SP}^1(Y)$ with $\|X'\|_{\max} \leq |X'|_\infty \operatorname{rank} X' \leq Rk$.

5   Between the Trace-Norm and the Max-Norm or Rank

The generalization error bounds highlight an important distinction between the trace-norm and the other two measures: the trace-norm is an *on average* measure of complexity, and leads to generalization error bounds only with respect to a uniform sampling distribution. This is not an artifact of the proof techniques. To establish this, consider:

Lemma 9. *For any $k < n$ and $Y \in \{\pm 1\}^{n \times n}$ such that $Y_{ij} = 1$ for $i > k$ or $j > k$ (i.e. except on the leading $k \times k$ submatrix): $tc(Y) \leq \|Y\|_\Sigma /n \leq k^{3/2}/n + \sqrt{2}$*

Proof. Write $Y = X_1 + X_2$ where X_1 is 0 on the leading $k \times k$ submatrix and 1 elsewhere: $\|Y\|_\Sigma \leq \|X_1\|_\Sigma + \|X_2\|_\Sigma \leq \sqrt{\operatorname{rank} X_1} \|X_1\|_{\mathrm{Fro}} + \sqrt{\operatorname{rank} X_2} \|X_2\|_{\mathrm{Fro}} \leq \sqrt{kk} + \sqrt{2}n$. $\qquad \square$

Corollary 5. $|\{Y \in \{\pm 1\}^{n \times n} | tc(Y) \leq M\}| \geq 2^{((M-\sqrt{2})n)^{4/3}}$

Consider fitting an $n \times n$ binary target matrix, where entries are sampled only in the leading $n^{2/3} \times n^{2/3}$ submatrix. A matrix X with $\|X\|_\Sigma / n < 3$ is sufficient to get all possible values in the submatrix, and so even with $|S| = \Theta(n^{4/3})$ we cannot expect to generalize even when $\|X\|_\Sigma / n$ is constant.

Using Lemma 9 we can also describe matrices Y with large gaps between $\mathrm{tc}(Y)$ and both $\mathrm{mc}(Y)$ and $\mathrm{dc}(Y)$. An $n \times n$ sign matrix with a Hadamard matrix in the leading $k \times k$ subspace and ones elsewhere provides an example where $\mathrm{mc}(Y) = \Theta((\mathrm{tc}(Y)n)^{1/3})$, e.g. $\mathrm{tc}(Y) < 3$ and $\mathrm{tc}(Y) = n^{1/3}$. Counting arguments ensure a similar gap with $\sqrt{\mathrm{dc}(Y)}$. We show that this gap is tight:

Theorem 10. *For every $n \times n$ sign matrix Y, $\mathrm{mc}(Y) \leq 3(\mathrm{tc}(Y)n)^{1/3}$.*

Recall that $1 \leq \mathrm{tc}(Y) \leq \mathrm{mc}(Y) \leq \sqrt{n}$. The bound in meaningful even for matrices with large $\mathrm{tc}(Y)$, up to $\sqrt{n}/27$. To prove the Theorem, we first show:

Lemma 10. *Let $X \in \mathbb{R}^{n \times n}$ with $\|X\|_\Sigma = M$, then X can be expressed as $X = B + R + C$, where $\|B\|_{\max} \leq (M^{1/3}$, R has at most $M^{2/3}$ rows that are non-zero and C has at most $M^{2/3}$ columns that are non-zero. Furthermore, for every i, j, at most one of B_{ij}, R_{ij} and C_{ij} is non-zero.*

Proof. Let $X = UV'$ be a decomposition of X s.t. $\|U\|_{\mathrm{Fro}}^2 = \|V\|_{\mathrm{Fro}}^2 = M$. At most $M^{2/3}$ of the rows of U and $M^{2/3}$ of the rows of V have squared norms greater than $M^{1/3}$. Let $R_{ij} = X_{ij}$ when $|U_i|^2 > M^{1/3}$ and zero otherwise. Let $C_{ij} = X_{ij} - R_{ij}$ when $|V_j|^2 > M^{1/3}$, zero otherwise. Let $B = X - R - C$. Zeroing the rows of U and V with squared norms greater than $M^{1/3}$ leads to a factorization of B with maximal squared row-norm $M^{1/6}$, establishing $\|B\|_{\max} \leq M^{1/3}$.   □

To prove the Theorem, let $X \in \mathrm{SP}^1(Y)$ with $\mathrm{tc}(Y) = \|X\|_\Sigma / n$ and let $X = B + R + C$ as in Lemma 10, and note that $B + \mathrm{sign}\,R + \mathrm{sign}\,C \in \mathrm{SP}^1(Y)$ ($\mathrm{sign}\,R, \mathrm{sign}\,C$ are zero where R, C are zero). Writing $(\mathrm{sign}\,R) = I(\mathrm{sign}\,R)$ establishes $\|\mathrm{sign}\,R\|_{\max} \leq \|I\|_{2\to\infty} \|\mathrm{sign}\,R\|_{2\to\infty} = 1\sqrt{\|X\|_\Sigma^{2/3}} = \|X\|_\Sigma^{1/3}$ and similarly $\|\mathrm{sign}\,C\|_{\max} \leq \|X\|_\Sigma^{1/3}$. Using the convexity of the max-norm:

$$\mathrm{mc}(Y) \leq \|B + \mathrm{sign}\,R + \mathrm{sign}\,C\|_\Sigma \leq 3\|X\|_\Sigma^{1/3} = 3(n\mathrm{tc}(Y))^{1/3}   □$$

Since $\mathrm{dc}(Y) = O(\mathrm{mc}^2(Y)\log(n))$, Theorem 10 also provides a tight (up to log factors) bounds on the possible gap between dc and tc.

Using Lemma 6, Theorem 10 provides a non-trivial upper bound on the number of sign matrices with low trace-complexity, but a gap of $\sqrt[3]{M^2/n}$ still remains between this upper bound and the lower bound of Corollary 5:

Corollary 6. $\log |\{Y | \mathrm{tc}(Y) \leq M\}| < 7M^{2/3}n^{5/3}\log(3nm)\log(n/M^2)$

6   Discussion

The initial motivation for the study reported here was to obtain a better understanding and a theoretical foundation for "Maximum Margin Matrix Factorization" (MMMF) [1], i.e. learning with low trace-norm and low max-norm matrices. We see as the main product of this study not the generalization error bounds as numerical bounds, but rather the relationships between the three measures, and the way in which they control the "complexity", as measured in terms of their generalization ability. The generalization error bounds display the similar roles of rank X, $\|X\|_{\max}^2$ and $\|X\|_\Sigma^2 /nm$ in controlling complexity and highlight the main difference between the trace-norm and the other two measures. We note the interesting structure of the two hierarchies of classes of low dimensional-complexity and max-complexity matrices: Any class of matrices with bounded max-complexity is a subset of a class of matrices with bounded dimensional-complexity of "roughly" the same size (logarithm of size differs only by logarithmic factors). But this class of bounded dimensional-complexity matrices includes matrices with very high max-complexity.

Open Issues. Although we show that the dimensional-complexity can not bound the max-complexity, it might still be the case that changing a few entries of a low-dimensional-complexity matrix is enough to get to to a low-max-complexity matrix. Beyond sign matrices, we can ask whether for any X and ϵ there exists X' with $\|X'\|_{\max}^2 \leq O(\operatorname{rank} X (1/\epsilon)^2 \operatorname{poly} \log n)$ and $\delta(X, X') \leq \epsilon$ for some error measure δ. Theorem 7 precludes this possibility for $\delta(X, X') = |X - X'|_\infty$, but it is possible that such a relationship holds for, e.g., $\delta(X, X') = \frac{1}{nm} \sum_{ij} |X_{ij} - X'_{ij}|$. Such results might tell us that when enough discrepancy is allowed, approximating with the rank is not very different then approximating with the max-norm. On the other hand, it would be interesting to understand if, for example, the matrices $T_t^{\otimes p}$ do not have any low max-norm matrix in their vicinity.

Throughout the paper we have largely ignored log-factors, but these can be very significant. For example, tighter bounds on the number of low max-complexity matrices can help us understand questions like the median max-complexity over all matrices.

References

1. Srebro, N., Rennie, J., Jaakkola, T.: Maximum margin matrix factorization. In: Advances In Neural Information Processing Systems 17. (2005)
2. Srebro, N., Alon, N., Jaakkola, T.: Generalization error bounds for collaborative prediction with low-rank matrices. In: Advances In Neural Information Processing Systems 17. (2005)
3. Arriaga, R.I., Vempala, S.: An algorithmic theory of learning: Robust concepts and random projection. In: Proc. of the 40th Foundations of Computer Science. (1999)
4. Ben-David, S., Eiron, N., Simon, H.U.: Limitations of learning via embeddings in euclidean half spaces. JMLR **3** (2002) 441–461
5. Forster, J., Schmitt, N., Simon, H.U., Suttorp, T.: Estimating the optimal margins of embeddings in euclidean half spaces. Machine Learning **51** (2003) 263–281
6. Forster, J., Simon, H.U.: On the smallest possible dimension and the largest possible margin of linear arrangements representing given concept classes uniform distribution. In: Proceedings of the 13th International Conference on Algorithmic Learning Theory, Springer-Verlag (2002) 128–138

7. Linial, N., Mendelson, S., Schechtman, G., Shraibman, A.: Complexity measures of sign matrices. www.cs.huji.ac.il/~nati/PAPERS (2004)
8. Alon, N., Frankl, P., Rödel, V.: Geometrical realization of set systems and probabilistic communication complexity. In: Proceedings of the 26th Annual Symposium on the Foundations of Computer Science (FOCS). (1985) 227–280
9. Srebro, N.: Learning with Matrix Factorization. PhD thesis, Massachusetts Institute of Technology (2004)
10. Seginer, Y.: The expected norm of random matrices. Comb. Probab. Comput. **9** (2000) 149–166
11. Panchenko, D., Koltchinskii, V.: Empirical margin distributions and bounding the generalization error of combined classifiers. Annals of Statistics **30** (2002)
12. Pisier, G.: Factorization of linear operators and geometry of Banach spaces. Volume 60. Conference Board of the Mathemacial Sciences (1986)
13. Awerbuch, B., Kleinberg, R.: Adaptive routing with end-to-end feedback: Distributed learning and geometric approaches. In: Proceedings of the 36th ACM Symposium on Theory of Computing (STOC). (2004)

A   Consolidating Signs of Repeated Points

We show that for any function class and distribution, the Rademacher complexity can be bounded from above by consolidating all random signs corresponding to the same point into a single sign. We first show that consolidating a single sign can only increase the Rademacher complexity:

Lemma 11. *For any function class $\mathcal{F}$ and sample $S = (x_1, \ldots, x_n)$ with $x_1 = x_2$:*

$$\mathbf{E}_\sigma \left[\sup_{f \in \mathcal{F}} \left| \sum_{i=1}^n \sigma_i f(x_i) \right| \right] \leq \mathbf{E}_\sigma \left[\sup_{f \in \mathcal{F}} \left| \sigma_2 2 f(x_2) + \sum_{i=3}^n \sigma_i f(x_i) \right| \right]$$

where σ_i are i.i.d. unbiased signs.

Proof. We first note that removing x_1, x_2 can only decrease the expectation:

$$\mathbf{E}_\sigma \left[\sup_{f \in \mathcal{F}} \left| \sum_{i=1}^n \sigma_i f(x_i) \right| \right] = \mathbf{E}_{\sigma_{3:n}} \left[\mathbf{E}_{\sigma_{1,2}} \left[\sup_{f \in \mathcal{F}} \left| \sigma_1 f(x_1) + \sigma_2 f(x_2) + \sum_{i=3}^n \sigma_i f(x_i) \right| \right] \right]$$

$$\geq \mathbf{E}_{\sigma_{3:n}} \left[\sup_{f \in \mathcal{F}} \left| \mathbf{E}_{\sigma_{1,2}} \left[\sigma_1 f(x_1) + \sigma_2 f(x_2) \right] + \sum_{i=3}^n \sigma_i f(x_i) \right| \right] = \mathbf{E}_{\sigma_{3:n}} \left[\sup_{f \in \mathcal{F}} \left| \sum_{i=3}^n \sigma_i f(x_i) \right| \right]$$

Using this inequality we can now calculate:

$$\mathbf{E}_\sigma \left[\sup_{f \in \mathcal{F}} \left| \sum_{i=1}^n \sigma_i f(x_i) \right| \right] \leq \frac{1}{2} \mathbf{E}_\sigma \left[\sup_{f \in \mathcal{F}} \left| \sum_{i=1}^n \sigma_i f(x_i) \right| \right]$$

$$+ \frac{1}{2} \mathbf{E}_\sigma \left[\sup_{f \in \mathcal{F}} \left| \sigma_2 2 f(x_2) + \sum_{i=3}^n \sigma_i f(x_i) \right| \right]$$

Subtracting the first term on the right-hand side from the original left-hand side gives us the desired inequality.   □

By iteratively consolidating identical sample points, we get:

Lemma 12 (Sign Consolidation). *For any function class $\mathcal{F}$ and sample $S = (x_1, \ldots, x_n)$, denote by s_x the number of times a sample appears in the class, and let σ_x be i.i.d. unbiased random signs. Then:*

$$\mathcal{R}_S(\mathcal{F}) \leq \mathbf{E}_\sigma \left[\sup_{f \in \mathcal{F}} \left| \frac{2}{|S|} \sum_{x \in S} \sigma_x s_x f(x) \right| \right]$$

Learning a Hidden Hypergraph

Dana Angluin and Jiang Chen

Department of Computer Science, Yale University
{angluin, criver}@cs.yale.edu

Abstract. We consider the problem of learning a hypergraph using
edge-detecting queries. In this model, the learner may query whether a
set of vertices induces an edge of the hidden hypergraph or not. We show
that an r-uniform hypergraph with m edges and n vertices is learnable
with $O(2^{4r} m \cdot poly(r, \log n))$ queries with high probability. The queries
can be made in $O(min(2^r r^2 \log^2 n, r^3 \log^3 n))$ rounds. We also give an
algorithm that learns a non-uniform hypergraph whose minimum edge
size is r_1 and maximum edge size is r_2 using $O(f_1(r_1, r_2) \cdot m^{(r_2 - r_1 + 2)/2} \cdot poly(\log n))$ queries with high probability, and give a lower bound of
$\Omega(f_2(r_1, r_2) \cdot m^{(r_2 - r_1 + 2)/2})$ for this class of hypergraphs, where f_1 and
f_2 are functions depending only on r_1 and r_2. The queries can also be
made in $O(min(2^{r_2} r_2^2 \log^2 n, r_2^3 \log^3 n))$ rounds.

1 Introduction

A hypergraph $H = (V, E)$ is given by a set of vertices V and a set of edges
E, which is a subset of the power set of V ($E \subseteq 2^V$). The dimension of
a hypergraph H is the cardinality of the largest set in E. H is said to be
r-uniform if E contains only sets of size r. In this paper, we are interested
in learning a hidden hypergraph use *edge-detecting* queries of the following
form

$$Q_H(S) : \textit{does } S \textit{ include at least one edge of } H?$$

where $S \subseteq V$. The query $Q_H(S)$ is answered 1 or 0, indicating whether S contains all vertices of at least one edge of H or not. We abbreviate $Q_H(S)$ to
$Q(S)$ whenever the choice of H is clear from the context. This type of query
may be motivated by the following scenario. We are given a set of chemicals, some groups of chemicals of which react and others don't. When multiple chemicals are combined in one test tube, a reaction is detectable if and
only if at least one group of chemicals in the tube react. Considerable effort
[1, 2, 3, 4, 5] has been devoted to the case when the underlying network is a
graph. Among them, Grebinski and Kucherov [5], Alon *et al.*[2] and Beigel
et al.[4] study the case when the underlying networks are Hamiltonian cy-
cles or matchings, which have specific applications to genome sequencing. In
this application, DNA sequences are aligned according to the reactions that

P. Auer and R. Meir (Eds.): COLT 2005, LNAI 3559, pp. 561–575, 2005.
© Springer-Verlag Berlin Heidelberg 2005

involve the two ends of pairs of DNA sequences in certain experimental settings. The reaction graph can be characterized as either a Hamiltonian cycle or path (if you consider each DNA sequence as a vertex) or a matching (if you consider each end of a DNA sequence as a vertex). Implementations of some of these algorithms are in practical use. Angluin and Chen [3] generalize the problem to general reaction graphs and show general graphs are efficiently learnable. In this work, we consider a more general problem when the chemicals react in groups of size more than 2, i.e. the underlying reaction network is a hypergraph. In [3], Angluin and Chen give an adaptive algorithm which takes $O(\log n)$ queries per edge, where n is the number of vertices. This is nearly optimal as we can easily show using an information-theoretic argument. As a matter of fact, with the same information-theoretic argument, we can show that linear dependency on the number of edges is optimal for learning hypergraphs with bounded number of edges and bounded dimension as well. However, the lower bound is not achievable for the class of hypergraphs with bounded number of edges and bounded dimension. It is shown in [3] that $\Omega((2m/r)^{r/2})$ edge-detecting queries are required to learn a general hypergraph of dimension r and with m edges. In the heart of the construction of [3], edges of size 2 are deliberately arranged to hide an edge of size r. The discrepancy in sizes of different coexisting edges is the main barrier for the learner. However, this lower bound does not deny efficient algorithms for classes of hypergraphs whose edges sizes are close. In particular, the question whether there is a learning algorithm for uniform hypergraphs using queries only linear in the number of edges is still left open, which is the main subject of this paper.

In this paper, we are able to answer this question affirmatively. Let n be the number of vertices and m be the number of edges in the hypergraph. We show that an r-uniform hypergraph is learnable with $O(2^{4r} m \cdot poly(r, \log n) \cdot \log(1/\delta))$ queries with probability at least $1 - \delta$.

We also obtain results for learning the class of hypergraphs that is slightly non-uniform. Formally speaking,

Definition 1. *A hypergraph is (r_1, r_2)-uniform, where $r_1 \leq r_2$, if its minimum and maximum edge sizes are r_1 and r_2 respectively.*

The class of hypergraphs used in the construction of the lower bound in [3] is in fact $(2, r)$-uniform. Therefore, they show that $\Omega((2m/r)^{r/2})$ edge-detecting queries are required to learn a $(2, r)$-uniform hypergraph. Based on this result, we show by a simple reduction that $\Omega(f_2(r_1, r_2) \cdot m^{(r_2 - r_1 + 2)/2})$ queries are required to learn the class of (r_1, r_2)-uniform hypergraphs, where f_2 is a function that depends only on r_1 and r_2. On the other hand, we extend the algorithm that learns uniform hypergraphs to learning the class of (r_1, r_2)-uniform hypergraphs with $O(f_1(r_1, r_2) \cdot m^{(r_2 - r_1 + 2)/2} \cdot poly(\log n) \cdot \log(1/\delta))$ queries with probability at least $1 - \delta$, where f_1 depends only on r_1 and r_2. The upper bound and lower bound have the same dependence of m.

Another important issue studied in the literature is the parallelism of algorithms. Since the queries are motivated by experiment design scenario, it is desirable that experiments can be conducted in parallel. Alon *et al.*[2] and Alon *et al.*[1] give lower and upper bounds for 1-round algorithms for certain types of graphs. Beigel *et al.*[4] describe an 8-round algorithm for learning a matching. Angluin and Chen [3] give a 5-round algorithm for learning a general graph. In this paper, we show that in our algorithm for r-uniform hypergraphs, queries can be made in $O(min(2^r r^2 \log^2 n, r^3 \log^3 n))$ rounds, and in our algorithm for (r_1, r_2)-uniform hypergraphs, queries can be made in $O(min(2^{r_2} r_2^2 \log^2 n, r_2^3 \log^3 n))$ rounds.

In the paper, we also introduce an interesting combinatorial object, which we call an *independent covering family*. Basically, an independent covering family of a hypergraph is a collection of independent sets that cover all non-edges. An interesting observation is that the set of negative queries of any algorithm that learns a hypergraph drawn from a class of hypergraphs that is closed under the operation of adding an edge is an independent covering family of that hypergraph. Note both the class of r-uniform hypergraphs and the class of (r_1, r_2)-uniform hypergraphs are closed under the operation of adding an edge. This implies that the query complexity of learning the hypergraph is bounded below by the minimum size of its independent covering families. In the opposite direction, we give a subroutine to find one arbitrary edge from a hypergraph. With the help of this subroutine, we show that if we can construct small-sized independent covering families for some class of hypergraphs, we are able to obtain an efficient learning algorithm for it. In this paper, we give a randomized construction of an independent covering family of size $O(r2^{2r} m \log n)$ for an r-uniform hypergraphs with m edges. This yields a learning algorithm using queries quadratic in m, which is further improved to give an algorithm using queries linearly in m.

As mentioned in [3] and some other papers, the hypergraph learning problem may also be viewed as the problem of learning a monotone disjunctive normal form (DNF) boolean formula using membership queries only. Each vertex of H is represented by a variable and each edge by a term containing all variables associated with the vertices of the edge. A membership query assigns 1 or 0 to each variable, and is answered 1 if the assignment satisfies at least one term, and 0 otherwise, that is, if the set of vertices corresponding to the variables assigned 1 contains all vertices of at least one edge of H. An r-uniform hypergraph corresponds to a monotone r-DNF. An (r_1, r_2)-uniform hypergraph corresponds to a monotone DNF whose terms are of sizes in the range of $[r_1, r_2]$. Thus, our results apply also to learning the corresponding classes of monotone DNF formulas using membership queries.

The paper is organized as follows. In section 3, we formally define the concept of independent covering family and give a randomized construction of independent covering families for general r-uniform hypergraphs. In section 4, we show how to efficiently find an arbitrary edge in a hypergraph and give a simple learning algorithm using queries quadratic in the number of edges. In section 5, we give an algorithm that learns r-uniform hypergraphs using queries linear in the number of edges. Finally, we give upper and lower bounds for learning the class of (r_1, r_2)-uniform hypergraphs in section 6.

2   Preliminaries

Let $H = (V, E)$ be a hypergraph. In this paper, we assume that edges do not contain each other, as there is no way to detect the existence of the edges that contain other edges using edge-detecting queries. A subset of V is an *independent set* of H if it contains no edge of H. We use the term *non-edge* to denote any set that is a candidate edge in some class of hypergraphs but is not an edge in the target hypergraph. For example, in an r-uniform hypergraph, any r-set that is not an edge is a non-edge. In an (r_1, r_2)-uniform hypergraph, any set of size in the range of $[r_1, r_2]$ that is not an edge is a non-edge. The *degree* of a set χ in a hypergraph H denoted as $d_H(\chi)$ is the number of edges of H that contain χ. In particular, $d_H(\emptyset) = |E|$ is the number of all edges in H.

Throughout the paper, we omit the ceiling and floor signs whenever they are not crucial.

3   An Independent Covering Family

Definition 2. An independent covering family *of a hypergraph H is a collection of independent sets of H such that every non-edge not containing an edge is contained in one of these independent sets, i.e. the independent covering family covers all the non-edges that does not contain an edge.*

When H is a uniform hypergraph, the above only requires that every non-edge is contained in one of the independent sets in the independent covering family. An example is shown below.

Example 1. Let $V = [1, 6]$. Let $H = (V, \{\{1, 2, 3\}, \{4, 5, 6\}, \{2, 4, 5\}\})$ be a 3-uniform hypergraph.

$$\mathcal{F} = \{\{1, 2, 4, 6\}, \{1, 2, 5, 6\}, \{1, 3, 4, 5\}, \{1, 3, 4, 6\}, \{2, 3, 4, 6\}, \{2, 3, 5, 6\}\}$$

is an independent covering family of H. As we can easily verify, all sets in $\mathcal{F}$ are independent sets. And every 3-set except $\{1, 2, 3\}, \{4, 5, 6\}, \{2, 4, 5\}$ is contained in some set in $\mathcal{F}$.

The concept of independent covering families is central in this paper. This can be appreciated from two aspects.

First, we observe that if the target hypergraph is drawn from a class of hypergraphs that is closed under the operation of adding an edge (e.g. the class of all r-uniform hypergraphs), the set of negative queries of any algorithm that learns it is an independent covering family of this hypergraph. This is because if there is a non-edge not contained in any of the sets on which these negative queries are made, we will not be able to distinguish between the target hypergraph and the hypergraph with this non-edge being an extra edge. Therefore, the minimum size of independent covering families bounds the query complexity from below. Furthermore, any learning algorithm gives a construction of an independent covering family of the target hypergraph. Therefore, in order to learn the hypergraph, we have to be able to construct an independent covering family for it.

Second, although the task of constructing an independent covering family seems substantially easier than that of learning, since the hypergraph is known in the construction task, we show that efficient construction of small-sized independent covering families yields an efficient learning algorithm. In section 4, we will show how to find an arbitrary edge out of a hypergraph of dimension r using $O(r \log n)$ queries. Imagine a simple algorithm in which at each iteration we maintain a sub-hypergraph of the target hypergraph which contains edges that we have found, and construct an independent covering family for it and ask queries on all the sets in the family. If there is a set whose query is answered positively, we can find at least one edge out of this set. The edge must be a new edge as the set is an independent set of the sub-hypergraph that we have found. We repeat this process until there is no edges left, or in other words we have collected all the edges in the target hypergraph, in which case the independent covering family we construct is a proof of this fact. Suppose that we can construct an independent covering family of size at most $f(m)$ for any hypergraph with at most m edges. The above algorithm learns this class of hypergraphs using only $O(f(m) \cdot m \cdot r \log n)$ queries.

In the rest of this section, we give a randomized construction of an linear-sized (linear in the number of edges) independent covering family of an r-uniform hypergraph which succeeds with probability at least $1/2$. By the standard probabilistic argument, the construction proves the existence of an independent covering family of size linear in the number of edges for any uniform hypergraph. This construction leads to a quadratic algorithm described in section 4, and is also a central part of our main algorithm given in section 5.

Our main theorem in this section is as follows.

Theorem 1. *Any r-uniform hypergraph with m edges has an independent covering family of size $O(r2^{2r} m \log n)$.*

Before giving the construction, we introduce some notation and definitions. Let $p_H(\chi) = 1/(2^{r+1} d_H(\chi))^{1/(r-|\chi|)}$, where $\chi \subseteq V$. We will call $p_H(\chi)$ the *discovery probability* of χ. We say that

Definition 3. *χ is minimal if it has the minimum discovery probability among its subsets. i.e. $\forall \chi' \subset \chi, p_H(\chi) < p_H(\chi')$.*

Definition 4. *A (χ, p)-sample is a random set of vertices that contains χ and contains each other vertex independently with probability p.*

We will abbreviate (χ, p)-sample as χ-sample when the choice of p is clear or not important in the context. We call a vertex set *relevant* if it is contained in at least one hyperedge in the hypergraph. Similarly, a vertex is *relevant* if it is contained in at least one hyperedge in the hypergraph.

In the construction, we draw $(\chi, p_H(\chi))$-samples independently for each relevant set χ. Each $(\chi, p_H(\chi))$-sample deals only with non-edges that contain χ.

Let us take look at the probability that a $(\chi, p_H(\chi))$-sample P_χ covers some non-edge $z \supseteq \chi$ while excluding all edges. Due to our choice of $p_H(\chi)$,

$$Pr[z \subseteq P_\chi] = p_H(\chi)^{r-|\chi|} = \frac{1}{2^{r+1}d_H(\chi)}$$

If we draw $2^{r+1}d_H(\chi)$ many χ-samples, the probability that z is covered by at least one χ-sample is $\Omega(1)$. However, a $(\chi, p_H(\chi))$-sample that covers z may not be an independent set. If z contains a high degree set χ', sampling with probability $p_H(\chi)$ may not be sufficient to exclude all the edges that contain χ' with reasonable probability. But since we will also draw $(\chi', p_H(\chi'))$-samples, it is reasonable to hope that a $(\chi', p_H(\chi'))$-sample has better chance of success in dealing with z. In fact, in our construction, we show that the set of χ-samples, where $\chi \subseteq z$ has the minimum discovery probability among all relevant subsets of z, has an independent set that covers z w.h.p. Thus, we only need to draw samples for those sets that are minimal.

The construction is given below.

Algorithm 1 Construction of an independent covering family of an r-uniform hypergraph H

1: $\mathcal{F}_H \leftarrow$ a set containing $4(\ln 2 + r\ln n) \cdot 2^r d_H(\chi)$ $(\chi, p_H(\chi))$-samples drawn independently for every minimal relevant set χ.
2: Output the family of independent sets of $\mathcal{F}_H$.

Lemma 1. $\mathcal{F}_H$ contains an independent covering family of H with probability at least $1/2$.

Proof. Suppose z is a non-edge and χ is a subset of z with the minimum discovery probability. It is easy to see that χ is minimal. Let P_χ be a χ-sample. As argued before,

$$Pr[z \subseteq P_\chi] = \frac{1}{2^{r+1}d_H(\chi)}$$

Since χ has the minimum discovery probability among all subsets of z, the degree of any subset $\chi' \subseteq z$ is at most $1/(2^{r+1}p_H(\chi)^{r-|\chi'|})$. By the union bound,

$$Pr[P_\chi \text{ is independent}|z \subseteq P_\chi] \geq 1 - \sum_{\chi' \subseteq z} d_H(\chi')p_H(\chi)^{r-|\chi'|}$$

$$\geq 1 - \sum_{\chi' \subseteq z} \frac{1}{2^{r+1}p_H(\chi)^{r-|\chi'|}}p_H(\chi)^{r-|\chi'|}$$

$$\geq 1/2$$

The probability that a χ-sample contains z and is independent is at least $1/(2^{r+2}d_H(\chi))$. The probability that such a χ-sample exists in $\mathcal{F}_H$ is at least $1-2n^{-r}$. Thus, the probability that every non-edge is contained in some negative sample in $\mathcal{F}_H$ is at least $1 - \binom{n}{r}/(2n^r) \geq 1/2$. $\square$

Since the size of $\mathcal{F}_H$ is bounded by $\sum_\chi 4(\ln 2 + r\ln n) \cdot 2^r d_H(\chi) = O(r2^{2r}m\log n)$, using a standard probabilistic argument, this proves Theorem 1.

4   A Simple Quadratic Algorithm

In this section, we give an algorithm that finds an arbitrary edge in a hypergraph of dimension r using only $r \log n$ edge-detecting queries. Combining this with a slightly modified version of the construction in the previous section, we obtain an algorithm using queries quadratic in m that learns r-uniform hypergraphs with m edges w.h.p.

4.1   Find One Edge

We start with a simpler task, finding just one relevant vertex in the hypergraph. The algorithm is shown in Algorithm 2.

Algorithm 2 FIND-ONE-VERTEX

1: $S = V, A = V$.
2: **while** $|A| > 1$ **do**
3:     Divide A arbitrarily into A_1 and A_2, such that $|A_1| = \lceil |A|/2 \rceil$, $|A_2| = \lfloor |A|/2 \rfloor$.
4:     **if** $Q(S \backslash A_1) = 0$ **then**
5:         $A = A_1$.
6:     **else**
7:         $A = A_2, S = S \backslash A_1$.
8:     **end if**
9: **end while**
10: Output the element in A.

Lemma 2. *FIND-ONE-VERTEX finds one relevant vertex in a non-empty hypergraph with n vertices using at most $\log n$ edge-detecting queries.*

Proof. First we show that the following conditions hold for each iteration. These conditions guarantee that A contains at least one relevant vertex.

$$Q(S) = 1, Q(S \backslash A) = 0$$

Since we assume that the hypergraph is non-empty, the above conditions clearly hold for our initial assignment of S and A. Let's assume $Q(S) = 1$ and $Q(S \backslash A) = 0$ at the beginning of an iteration. There are two cases:

Case 1: $Q(S \backslash A_1) = 0$, clearly the conditions hold for S and A_1.
Case 2: $Q(S \backslash A_1) = 1$, since $Q((S \backslash A_1) \backslash A_2) = Q(S \backslash (A_1 \cup A_2)) = Q(S \backslash A) = 0$, the conditions hold for $S \backslash A_1$ and A_2.

Since the size of A halves at each iteration, after at most $\log n$ iterations, A has exactly one relevant vertex. The algorithm takes at most $\log n$ edge-detecting queries in total, as it makes one query each iteration.   □

With the help of FIND-ONE-VERTEX, we are able to find one edge from a non-empty hypergraph, which is not necessarily uniform.

Lemma 3. *There is a deterministic adaptive algorithm that finds one hyperedge in a non-empty hypergraph of dimension r with n vertices using $r \log n$ edge-detecting queries.*

Proof. When $r = 1$, the problem is exactly the problem of finding one relevant vertex and hence solvable using $\log n$ queries. Assume inductively the lemma is true when $r = k-1$. When $r = k$, we first find one relevant vertex v using FIND-ONE-VERTEX, in the meantime we also obtain a set S such that $Q(S) = 1$ and $Q(S \setminus \{v\}) = 0$. Thus S contains only hyperedges incident with v. Consider the induced $(k-1)$-uniform hypergraph on S with v removed. By inductive assumption, we are able to find one hyperedge e_{k-1} in the induced hypergraph using $(k-1) \log n$ queries. $e_{k-1} \cup \{v\}$ is a hyperedge in the original hypergraph. The query complexity is therefore $k \log n$ as desired.   □

We will refer to the algorithm described in Lemma 3 as *FIND-ONE-EDGE*.

4.2   A Quadratic Algorithm

Let $H = (V, E)$ be the hypergraph the algorithm has found so far. Let $\delta' = \delta/m$. An algorithm that learning a uniform hypergraph with probability at least $1 - \delta$ is given in Algorithm 3.

Algorithm 3 A Quadratic Algorithm

1: $e \leftarrow$ FIND-ONE-EDGE(V). $E \leftarrow \{e\}$.
2: **repeat**
3:     $F_H \leftarrow 4(\ln \frac{1}{\delta'} + r \ln n) \cdot 2^r d_H(\chi)$ $(\chi, p(\chi))$-samples drawn independently for every minimal relevant set χ in H.
4:     Make queries on sets on F_H that are independent in H.
5:     Call FIND-ONE-EDGE on one positive sample if there exist any. Let e be the edge found.
6:     $E \leftarrow E \cup \{e\}$.
7: **until** no new edge found

In the algorithm we draw $4(\ln(1/\delta') + r \ln n) \cdot 2^r d_H(\chi)$ χ-samples. Using essentially the same argument as in section 3, we can guarantee that F_H contains an independent covering family with probability at least $1 - \delta'$. Since the algorithm takes at most m iterations, the algorithm succeeds with probability at least $1 - \delta$. The query complexity of this algorithm is $O(2^{2r} m^2 \cdot poly(r, \log n) \cdot \log 1/\delta)$.

5   A Linear-Query Algorithm

Reconstructing an independent covering family at the discovery of every new edge is indeed wasteful. In this section we show how to modify the quadratic algorithm to obtain an algorithm using queries only linear in the number of edges. Our algorithm is optimal in the dependency on m. Moreover, the queries can be made in $O(min(r^2 2^r \log^2 n, r^3 \log^3 n))$ parallel rounds.

Before we begin to describe our algorithm, we introduce some notation and make some definitions. First we reduce the discovery probabilities. Let

$$p_H(\chi) = 1/(2^{r+|\chi|+2} d_H(\chi))^{1/(r-|\chi|)}$$

Let the *best discovery probability* of χ be the minimum discovery probability among all its subsets. That is,

$$p_H^*(\chi) = \min_{\chi' \subseteq \chi} p_H(\chi')$$

Definition 5. *Let $\rho(\chi, p)$ be the probability that a (χ, p)-sample is positive, where χ is a vertex set of size less than r.*

Remark 1. $\rho(\chi, p)$ is continuous and monotonic increasing [3].

Definition 6. *Let $p_\chi = \min \{p | \rho(\chi, p) = 1/2^{r+1}\}$ be the* threshold probability *of χ.*

Remark 2. Due to the fact that $\rho(\chi, 0) = 0$, $\rho(\chi, 1) = 1$ and that $\rho(\chi, p)$ is continuous and monotonic increasing, the threshold probability uniquely exists.

In the quadratic algorithm, an "obvious" improvement we can make is that instead of calling FIND-ONE-EDGE on one positive samples, we can call it on all positive samples. It is plausible that it will yield more edges. However, there is no guarantee that different calls to FIND-ONE-EDGE will output different edges. For instance, if two sets contain the same edge, in the worst case, calls to FIND-ONE-EDGE on these two sets will produce the same edge. We use several standard tricks to circumvent this obstacle. In fact, the family of samples constructed here is more complex that that used in section 4, so as to ensure w.h.p. that the algorithm will make a certain amount of progress at each iteration. By doing so, we are able to reduce the number of iterations from m to $O(min(2^r r \log n, r^2 \log^2 n))$, hence reduce the number of queries.

First of all, the sampling probabilities are halved in order to accommodate more edges. More precisely, imagine that we draw $(\chi, 0.5p(\chi))$-samples instead of $(\chi, p(\chi))$-samples in the quadratic algorithm. At any iteration, take a look at a sample drawn several iterations ago, which the quadratic algorithm did not call FIND-ONE-EDGE on. Such a sample will still have reasonable probability of excluding all the edges that have been found, as long as the degree of χ has not been increased by a factor of $2^{r-|\chi|}$ or equivalently the discovery probability of χ has not been decreased by half.

Second, the algorithm draws samples for all relevant sets instead of just minimal relevant sets. Roughly speaking, the smaller the discovery probability of a relevant set in the target hypergraph the more important it is to the algorithm. However, the hypergraph that have been found at each iteration may be far from the target hypergraph. Hence the algorithm is not able tell the potential importance of each relevant sets. Therefore, the algorithm draws samples for all relevant sets. The algorithm uses the best discovery probability for each relevant set so as to exclude the edges that have been found with reasonable probability.

Finally, besides samples that are drawn proportional to degrees, the algorithm also draws samples proportional to contributions of each relevant set. The idea is simple. Draw more samples for those relevant sets that are more likely to produce a new edge. The algorithm maintains a *contribution* counter $c(\chi)$ for each relevant set χ, which records the number of new edges that χ-samples have produced. As we have already said, different calls to FIND-ONE-EDGE at each iteration may output the same edge. As all calls to FIND-ONE-EDGE at each iteration are made in parallel, it is not clear which sample each new edge should be attributed to. To solve this problem, the algorithm process the calls to FIND-ONE-EDGE sequentially in an arbitrary order. We say that a call to FIND-ONE-EDGE produces a new edge if it outputs an edge that is not output by any previous calls in this order. Similarly we say that a sample P produces a new edge if it is positive and FIND-ONE-EDGE(P) outputs a new edge.

Therefore, $\mathcal{F}_H$ consists of two parts: $\mathcal{F}_H^1$ and $\mathcal{F}_H^2$. In $\mathcal{F}_H^1$, the algorithm draws samples proportional to the contribution of each relevant set. $\mathcal{F}_H^2$ is closer to that of $\mathcal{F}_H$ in the section 4. Intuitively, the algorithm uses samples in $\mathcal{F}_H^1$ to find edges while samples in $\mathcal{F}_H^2$ are mainly used to cover non-edges of H. $\mathcal{F}_H^2$ not only gives a short proof when H is the target hypergraph, but also finds important relevant sets efficiently. Discovering important relevant sets is essential simply because the algorithm may not be able to find an edge or cover a non-edge if all its important relevant subsets are not known. Note at beginning of the algorithm, the only known relevant set is $\emptyset$. The design of $\mathcal{F}_H^2$ guarantees that if the contribution of the most important subset of an edge or a non-edge stops doubling, a more important relevant subset of the edge or non-edge will be discovered w.h.p.

Let $H = (V, E)$ be the hypergraph the algorithm has found so far. δ' is a parameter we will decide later. The algorithm named LINEAR-QUERY is shown in Algorithm 4. At each iteration, the algorithm operates in two phases, the query phase and computation phase. In the query phase, the algorithm draws random samples and make queries on them. Queries in this phase can be made in $r \log n + 1$ parallel rounds. In the computation phase, the algorithm processes the query results of the query phase to update the contribution counter of each set.

We will show that the algorithm terminates in $O(min(r2^r \log n, r^2 \log^2 n))$ iterations w.h.p. Since $\sum_\chi d_H(\chi) \leq 2^r m$ and $\sum_\chi c(\chi) \leq (2^r + 1)m$ (note that $c(\chi)$ is one more than the number of new edges χ-samples in $\mathcal{F}_H^1$ produce), the number of queries made at each iteration is at most $O(r2^{4r} m \log(1/\delta') \log n)$. Therefore, the total number of queries will be linear in the number of edges w.h.p. as desired.

Consider some iteration of the algorithm. Let H_0 be the hypergraph the algorithm has found at the beginning of the iteration. Let z be an edge that has not yet been found. Suppose χ has the minimum threshold probability among all

---

Algorithm 4 LINEAR-QUERY

1: $e \leftarrow$ FIND-ONE-EDGE(V).
2: $E \leftarrow \{e\}$. $c(\emptyset) \leftarrow 1$.
3: **repeat**
   QUERY PHASE
4:    Let $\mathcal{F}_H^1$ be a family that for every known relevant set χ contains $c(\chi) \cdot 2^{r+2} \ln \frac{1}{\delta'}$
      $(\chi, 0.5 p_H^*(\chi))$-samples.
5:    Let $\mathcal{F}_H^2$ be a family that for every known relevant set χ contains $2^{3r+3} d_H(\chi) \ln \frac{1}{\delta'}$
      $(\chi, 0.25 p_H^*(\chi))$-samples.
6:    Let $\mathcal{F}_H = \mathcal{F}_H^1 \cup \mathcal{F}_H^2$. Make queries on sets in F_H that are independent in H.
7:    Call FIND-ONE-EDGE on all positive samples.
   COMPUTATION PHASE
8:    For each relevant set χ, divide χ-samples in $\mathcal{F}_H^1$ in $c(\chi)$ groups of size $2^{r+2} \ln \frac{1}{\delta'}$.
9:    Process the samples in $\mathcal{F}_H^1$ group by group in an arbitrary order. Increase $c(\chi)$
      by the number of new edges that χ-samples produce. Add newly found edges to
      E.
10:   Process the samples in $\mathcal{F}_H^2$ in an arbitrary order. Add newly found edges to E.
11:   For every newly found relevant set χ, $c(\chi) \leftarrow 1$.
12: **until** no new edge is found

---

relevant subsets of z. χ can be either *active*, in which case a group of χ-samples likely to hit an edge or *inactive* otherwise. Formally speaking,

Definition 7. *We say that χ is active if $\rho(\chi, 0.5 p_{H_0}^*(\chi)) \geq 1/2^{r+1}$ and inactive otherwise.*

The following two assertions serve as the goals for each iteration.

Assertion 1. *Consider one group of χ-samples $\mathcal{G}$ in $\mathcal{F}_{H_0}^1$. Let H be the hypergraph the algorithm has found before this group is processed. If χ is active, either $p_H^*(\chi) < 0.5 p_{H_0}^*(\chi)$ or $\mathcal{G}$ will produce a new edge.*

Assertion 2. *If χ is inactive, at the end of this iteration, either z has been found or a new subset of z whose threshold probability is at most $0.5 p_\chi$ has been found relevant (a set is found relevant if an edge that contains it is found).*

The following two lemmas show that both assertions hold w.h.p.

Lemma 4. *Assertion 1 is true with probability at least $1 - \delta'$.*

Proof. If $p_H^*(\chi) \geq 0.5 p_{H_0}^*(\chi)$, the probability a $(\chi, 0.5 p_{H_0}^*(\chi))$-sample contains an edge in H is at most

$$\sum_{\chi' \subseteq \chi} d_H(\chi')(0.5 p_{H_0}^*(\chi))^{r-|\chi'|} \leq \sum_{\chi' \subseteq \chi} d_H(\chi') p_H^*(\chi)^{r-|\chi'|} \leq \frac{2^{|\chi|}}{2^{r+|\chi|+2}} = \frac{1}{2^{r+2}}$$

Since $\rho(\chi, 0.5 p_{H_0}^*(\chi))) \geq 1/2^{r+1}$, the probability that a $(\chi, 0.5 p_{H_0}^*(\chi))$-sample is positive but contains no edge in H is at least $1/2^{r+1} - 1/2^{r+2} = 1/2^{r+2}$. Recall that $\mathcal{G}$ contains $2^{r+2} \ln(1/\delta')$ $(\chi, 0.5 p_{H_0}^*(\chi))$-samples. Therefore, with probability at least $1 - \delta'$ there exists at least one such $(\chi, 0.5 p_{H_0}^*(\chi))$-sample in $\mathcal{G}$, which will produce a new edge. $\square$

Lemma 5. *Assertion 2 is true with probability at least* $1 - \delta'$.

Proof. Let $\chi^* \subseteq \chi$ have the minimum discovery probability among all subsets of χ at the beginning of the iteration. Therefore, $p_{H_0}(\chi^*) = p^*_{H_0}(\chi)$ by the definition. We have $\rho(\chi, 0.5p_{H_0}(\chi^*)) < 1/2^{r+1}$ and hence $0.5p_{H_0}(\chi^*) < p_\chi$ due to the fact $\rho(\chi, p)$ is monotonic increasing in p. Let A_χ be the collection of all subsets of z whose threshold probabilities are at least $0.5p_\chi$. Thus,

$$\forall \chi' \in A_\chi, \rho(\chi', 0.25p_{H_0}(\chi^*)) < \rho(\chi', 0.5p_\chi) \leq \rho(\chi', p_{\chi'}) = 1/2^{r+1}.$$

Let P_{χ^*} be a χ^*-sample. We have

$$Pr[z \subseteq P_{\chi^*}] = (0.25p_{H_0}(\chi^*))^{r-|\chi^*|} = \frac{1}{2^{r+|\chi^*|+2+2r-2|\chi^*|}d_{H_0}(\chi^*)} \geq \frac{1}{2^{3r+2}d_{H_0}(\chi^*)}$$

and

$$Pr[\exists \text{ an edge } e \subseteq P_{\chi^*}, e \cap z \in A_\chi | z \subseteq P_{\chi^*}] \leq \sum_{\chi' \in A_\chi} \rho(\chi', 0.25p_{H_0}(\chi^*)) \leq 1/2.$$

With probability at least $1/(2^{3r+3}d_{H_0}(\chi^*))$, P_{χ^*} contains no edge whose intersection with z is in A_χ. The probability that there exists such a P_{χ^*} in $\mathcal{F}^2_{H_0}$ is at least $1 - \delta'$, as we draw at least $2^{3r+3}d_{H_0}(\chi^*)\ln(1/\delta')$ $(\chi^*, 0.25p_{H_0}(\chi^*))$-samples.

Suppose indeed P_{χ^*} is such a sample. If P_{χ^*} contains only one edge, namely z, z will be found. Otherwise, FIND-ONE-EDGE(P_{χ^*}) produces an edge whose intersection with z has threshold probability at most $0.5p_\chi$. Since χ has the minimum threshold probability among all known relevant subsets of z, we find a new relevant subset of z. □

Let H_1 be the hypergraph that has been found at the end of the iteration. Let $c_{H_0}(\chi)$ and $c_{H_1}(\chi)$ be the values of $c(\chi)$ at the beginning and end of the iteration respectively. The following lemma is easy to verify.

Lemma 6. *At each iteration, if no assertion is violated, one of the following two events happens.*

1. *either* $c_{H_1}(\chi) \geq 2c_{H_0}(\chi)$ *or* $p^*_{H_1}(\chi) < 0.5p^*_{H_0}(\chi)$.
2. *either* z *has been found or a new subset of* z *whose threshold probability is at most* $0.5p_\chi$ *has been found relevant.*

Proof. There are two cases:

- χ is active:
  If every group of χ-samples yields a new edge, $c(\chi)$ at least doubles during the iteration. Otherwise, there is a group of queries that doesn't yield a new edge. Suppose H is the hypergraph that has been found when this happens.

By Assertion 1, we have $p_H^*(\chi) < 0.5p_{H_0}^*(\chi)$. Clearly, $p_{H_1}^*(\chi) \le p_H^*(\chi) < 0.5p_{H_0}^*(\chi)$.

- χ is inactive:
  This is direct consequence of Assertion 2. □

The minimum and maximum possible values for both discovery probabilities and threshold probabilities are $1/(2^{2r+1}m)$ and $1/2$ respectively. The minimum and maximum possible values for $c(\chi)$ are 1 and $m + 1$. And there are at most 2^r subsets of z. It follows that

Corollary 1. *Assuming no assertion is violated, the algorithm terminates in* $O(min(r2^r \log n, r^2 \log^2 n))$ *iterations.*

Now we bound the total number of assertions we need to satisfy before the algorithm succeeds. There is one assertion of type 1 for each group of queries. The total number is bounded by $\sum_\chi c(\chi) = O(2^r m)$ per iteration. There is one assertion of type 2 associated with every edge per iteration. The total number is bounded by m per iteration. Thus the total number of assertions we need to satisfy before the algorithm succeeds is bounded by $O(r^2 2^r m \log^2 n)$. Choose $\delta' = \Theta(\delta/(r^2 2^r m \log^2 n))$ and the algorithm will succeed with probability at least $1 - \delta$. Since queries at each iteration are made in $O(r \log n)$ paralle rounds, it follows that

Theorem 2. *With probability at least* $1 - \delta$, *LINEAR-QUERY learns an r-uniform hypergraph with m edges and n vertices, using $O(2^{4r} m \cdot poly(r, \log n) \cdot \log(1/\delta))$ queries, in $O(min(r^2 2^r \log^2 n, r^3 \log^3 n))$ parallel rounds.*

6   Non-uniform Hypergraphs

In this section, we extend our results to learning (r_1, r_2)-uniform hypergraphs. The following theorem is proved in [3].

Theorem 3. $\Omega((2m/r)^{r/2})$ *edge-detecting queries are required to identify a hypergraph drawn from the class of all $(2, r)$-uniform hypergraphs with n vertices and m edges.*

We show that by a simple reduction this gives us a lower bound for general (r_1, r_2)-uniform hypergraphs.

Theorem 4. $\Omega((2m/(r_2 - r_1 + 2))^{(r_2-r_1+2)/2})$ *edge-detecting queries are required to identify a hypergraph drawn from the class of all (r_1, r_2)-non-uniform hypergraphs with n vertices and m edges.*

Proof (Proof sketch). Given a $(2, r_2 - r_1 + 2)$-uniform hypergraph $H = (V, E)$. Let $H' = (V \cup V', E')$ be an (r_1, r_2)-uniform hypergraph, where $|V'| = r_1 - 2$, $V' \cap V = \phi$ and $E' = \{e \cup V'|e \in E\}$. Any algorithm that learns H' can be converted to learn H with the same number of queries. □

We now show that a modified version of LINEAR-QUERY gives an upper bound which is optimal in terms of the dependency on m.

Theorem 5. *There is a randomized algorithm that learns an (r_1, r_2)-uniform hypergraph with m edges and n vertices with probability at least $1 - \delta$, using $O(2^{r_2^2} m^{(r_2 - r_2 + 2)/2} \cdot poly(2^{r_2}, \log n) \cdot \log(1/\delta))$ queries. Furthermore, the queries can be made in $O(min(2^{r_2} r_2^2 \log^2 n, r_2^3 \log^3 n))$ rounds.*

Proof. We have been choosing the discovery probability for χ to be inversely proportional to the $(r - |\chi|)$th root of $d(\chi)$ for r-uniform hypergraphs. It is so chosen that a χ-sample has good chance of excluding edges that contain χ. In non-uniform hypergraphs, the edges are not of the same size any more. We need to set new discovery probabilities, while the purpose remains as before. In other words, we would like to choose p such that $\sum_{e \in E, e \supseteq \chi} p^{|e \backslash \chi|} \leq 1/2^{r+2}$. Similarly, we would like to choose p to be inversely proportional to wth root of $d(\chi)$, where $w = min_{e \supseteq \chi} |e \backslash \chi|$. When $|\chi| < r_1$, the minimum size of $e \backslash \chi$ is $r_1 - |\chi|$. When $|\chi| \geq r_1$, the minimum size is 1. However, the case when $|e \backslash \chi| = 1$ is special. Let P_χ be a (χ, p)-sample for a set χ of size that does not contain an edge. In order to exclude e from P_χ, we have to exclude the vertex in $e \backslash \chi$. On the other hand, if we exclude all the vertices whose union with χ contains an edge, we can easily exclude all the corresponding edges from P_χ. Therefore, we can construct a *modified* (χ, p)-sample by removing from a (χ, p)-sample those vertices whose union with χ contains an edge of the known hypergraph H. The new algorithm draws only modified samples. In the modified samples, we need only consider the edge e such that $|e \backslash \chi| \geq 2$. Therefore, we define the new discovery probability as below.

$$p_H(\chi) = \begin{cases} 1/(2^{r_2 + |\chi| + 2} d_H(\chi))^{1/(r_1 - |\chi|)}, & \text{if } |\chi| \leq r_1 - 2 \\ 1/(2^{r_2 + |\chi| + 2} d_H(\chi))^{1/2}, & \text{otherwise} \end{cases}$$

In the modified algorithm we will use r_2 whenever r is used. It differs from LINEAR-QUERY only in step 4 and 5. $\mathcal{F}_H^1$ is constructed as before but with the new discovery probabilities and modified samples. $\mathcal{F}_H^2$ consists of $2(4/p_H(\chi))^{r_2 - |\chi|} \ln(1/\delta')$ modified $(\chi, 0.25 p_H(\chi))$-samples. Note that the discovery probabilities are chosen as if all the edges were of minimum size, while the numbers of samples drawn in $\mathcal{F}_H^2$ are chosen as if all the non-edges of H (or potential edges in the target hypergraph) were of the maximum size. It is easy to verify that Assertion 1 and Assertion 2 are still true with probability at least $1 - \delta'$. Therefore, we have the same bound on the number of iterations w.h.p, which is at most $O(min(2^{r_2} r_2 \log n, r_2^2 \log^2 n))$. It is easy to see the number of samples in $\mathcal{F}_H^2$ dominates. At each iteration, the number of χ-samples in $\mathcal{F}_H^2$ is at most

$$2(4/p_H(\chi))^{r_2 - |\chi|} \ln(1/\delta') = \begin{cases} O(2^{r_2^2} d_H(\chi)^{\frac{r_2 - |\chi|}{r_1 - |\chi|}} \cdot \log(1/\delta)) & \text{if } |\chi| \leq r_1 - 2 \\ O(2^{r_2^2} d_H(\chi)^{\frac{r_2 - r_1 + 2}{2}} \cdot \log(1/\delta)) & \text{otherwise} \end{cases}$$

Note that $(r_2 - |\chi|)/(r_1 - |\chi|)$ is at most $(r_2 - r_1 + 2)/2$ when $|\chi| \leq r_1 - 2$. The number of modified χ-samples we draw in the algorithm is bounded by $O(2^{r_2^2} d_H(\chi)^{(r_2 - r_1 + 2)/2} \cdot poly(2^{r_2}, \log n) \cdot \log(1/\delta))$. Because $\sum_\chi d_H(\chi) \leq 2^{r_2} m$

and $\forall \chi, d_H(\chi) \leq m$, we have $\sum_\chi d_H(\chi)^{(r_2-r_1+2)/2} \leq 2^{r_2} m^{(r_2-r_1+2)/2}$. Therefore, the new algorithm uses $O(2^{r_2} m^{(r_2-r_1+2)/2} \cdot poly(2^{r_2}, \log n) \cdot \log(1/\delta))$ queries, and the queries can be made in $O(min(2^{r_2} r_2^2 \log^2 n, r_2^3 \log^3 n))$ rounds.   □

Acknowledgement

The authors would like to thank the referees for helpful comments.

References

1. Alon, N., Asodi, V.: Learning a hidden subgraph. In: 31st International Colloquium on Automata, Languages and Programming. (2004) 110–121
2. Alon, N., Beigel, R., Kasif, S., Rudich, S., Sudakov, B.: Learning a hidden matching. In: The 43rd Annual IEEE Symposium on Foundations of Computer Science. (2002) 197–206
3. Angluin, D., Chen, J.: Learning a hidden graph using O(log n) queries per edge. In: The 17th Annual Conference on Learning Theory, Springer (2004) 210–223
4. Beigel, R., Alon, N., Kasif, S., Apaydin, M.S., Fortnow, L.: An optimal procedure for gap closing in whole genome shotgun sequencing. In: RECOMB. (2001) 22–30
5. Grebinski, V., Kucherov, G.: Optimal query bounds for reconstructing a Hamiltonian Cycle in complete graphs. In: Fifth Israel Symposium on the Theory of Computing Systems. (1997) 166–173

On Attribute Efficient and Non-adaptive Learning of Parities and DNF Expressions

Vitaly Feldman[*]

Harvard University, Cambridge, MA 02138
vitaly@eecs.harvard.edu

Abstract. We consider the problems of attribute-efficient PAC learning of two well-studied concept classes: parity functions and DNF expressions over $\{0,1\}^n$.

We show that attribute-efficient learning of parities with respect to the uniform distribution is equivalent to decoding high-rate random linear codes from low number of errors, a long-standing open problem in coding theory.

An algorithm is said to use membership queries (MQs) *non-adaptively* if the points at which the algorithm asks MQs do not depend on the target concept. We give a deterministic and a fast randomized attribute-efficient algorithms for learning parities by non-adaptive MQs.

Using our non-adaptive parity learning algorithm and a modification of Levin's algorithm for locating a weakly-correlated parity due to Bshouty *et al.*, we give the first non-adaptive and attribute-efficient algorithm for learning DNF with respect to the uniform distribution. Our algorithm runs in time $\tilde{O}(ns^4/\epsilon)$ and uses $\tilde{O}(s^4/\epsilon)$ non-adaptive MQs where s is the number of terms in the shortest DNF representation of the target concept. The algorithm also improves on the best previous algorithm for learning DNF (of Bshouty *et al.*).

1 Introduction

The problems of PAC learning parity functions and DNF expressions are among the most fundamental and well-studied problems in machine learning theory. Along with running time efficiency, an important consideration in the design of learning algorithms is their *attribute efficiency*. A class $\mathcal{C}$ of Boolean functions is said to be *attribute-efficiently learnable* if there is an efficient algorithm which can learn any function $f \in \mathcal{C}$ using a number of examples which is polynomial in the "size" (description length) of the function f to be learned, rather than in n, the number of attributes in the domain over which learning takes place. Attribute-efficiency arises naturally from a ubiquitous practical scenario in which the total number of potentially influential attributes is much larger than the number of

---

[*] Supported by grants from the National Science Foundation NSF-CCF-9877049, NSF-CCF-0432037, and NSF-CCF-0427129.

P. Auer and R. Meir (Eds.): COLT 2005, LNAI 3559, pp. 576–590, 2005.

relevant attributes (i.e., the attributes on which the concept actually depends), whereas examples are either scarce or expensive to get.

Learning of DNF expressions and attribute-efficient learning of parities from random examples with respect to the uniform distribution are both long-standing challenges in learning theory. Lack of substantial progress on these questions has resulted in attempts to solve them in stronger learning models. The most well-studied such model is one in which a *membership query oracle* is given to the learner in addition to the example oracle. The learning algorithm may query this oracle for a value of the target function at any point of its choice. Jackson gave the first algorithm that learns DNF from membership queries (MQs) under the uniform distribution [13] and later Bshouty, Jackson and Tamon gave a more efficient and attribute-efficient algorithm for learning DNF in the same setting [4]. The first algorithm for attribute-efficient learning of parities using MQs is due to Blum, Hellerstein and Littlestone [1], and their result was later refined by Uehara *et al.* [19].

A number of later works gave learning algorithms for DNF expressions in models where the learning algorithm is more passive than in the MQ model [15, 2, 5]. A restricted model of membership queries, which addresses some of the disadvantages of the MQ model, is the model in which MQs are asked non-adaptively. An algorithm is said to use MQs *non-adaptively* (in our context we will often call it non-adaptive for brevity) if the queries of the algorithm do not depend on the target concept. In other words the learning algorithm can be split into two stages. The first stage, given the learning parameters, generates a set S of queries for the membership oracle. The second one, given the answers to the queries in S, produces a hypothesis (without further access to the oracle). An immediate advantage of this model (over the usual MQ) is the fact that the queries to the membership oracle can be parallelized. This, for example, is crucial in DNA sequencing and other biological applications where tests are very time-consuming but can be parallelized (*cf.* [7, 6] and references therein). Another advantage of a non-adaptive learner is that the same set of points can be used to learn numerous concepts. This seems to be happening in human brain where a single example can be used in learning of several different concepts and hence systems that aim to reproduce learning abilities of the human brain need to possess this property [21, 22, 23]. It is important to note that in the two practical applications mentioned above, attribute-efficiency is also a major concern. It is therefore natural to ask: which classes can be PAC learned attribute-efficiently by non-adaptive MQs? We refer to this model of learning as *ae.naMQ learning*. This question was first explicitly addressed by Damaschke [6] who proved that any function of r variables is ae.naMQ learnable when it is represented by the truth table of the function (requiring $r \log n + 2^r$ bits). Later Guijarro *et al.* gave an algorithm for learning functions of at most $\log n$ variables in the decision tree representation [11]. But the question remains open for numerous other representations used in learning theory.

1.1   Our Results

We first establish the equivalence between attribute-efficient learning of parities from random uniform examples [1] and decoding high-rate random linear codes from low number of errors. The latter is a long-standing open problem in coding theory widely believed intractable. Thus we may consider this equivalence as a new evidence of the hardness of attribute-efficient learning of parities from random examples only.

We show how a similar equivalence yields an efficient deterministic algorithm that learns parities from $r \log n$ non-adaptive MQs improving on the algorithm by Uehara *et al.* [19]. We also give a fast randomized algorithm for ae.naMQ learning of parities.

We give the first ae.naMQ algorithm for learning DNF expressions with respect to the uniform distribution. It runs in time $\tilde{O}(ns^4/\epsilon)$ and uses $\tilde{O}(s^4 \log^2 n/\epsilon)$ MQs (where s is the DNF-size of the target concept). The algorithm improves on the $\tilde{O}(ns^6/\epsilon^2)$-time and $\tilde{O}(ns^4 \log n/\epsilon^2)$-query algorithm of Bshouty *et al.* Our improvement is achieved via an application of our randomized ae.naMQ algorithm for learning parities and two independent modifications of the algorithm by Bshouty *et al.*

1.2   Previous Results

Blum *et al.* were the first to ask whether parities are learnable attribute-efficiently (in the related *on-line mistake-bound* model) [1]. They also presented the first algorithm to learn parity functions attribute-efficiently using MQs. Their algorithm is based on the following approach. First all the relevant attributes are identified and then a simple (not attribute-efficient) algorithm restricted to the relevant variables is used to learn the concept. Since then other algorithms were proposed for attribute-efficient identification of relevant variables [3, 12]. All the algorithms are based on a binary search for a relevant variable given a positive and a negative example. Binary search and the fact that queries in the second stage depend on the variables identified in the first stage only allows for the construction of adaptive algorithms via this approach. Uehara *et al.* gave several algorithms for attribute-efficient learning of parities that again used adaptiveness in an essential way [19]. Among other results they gave the first attribute-efficient deterministic algorithm for learning parities using $O(r^4 \log n)$ MQs where r denotes the number of relevant variables.

Little previous work has been published on attribute-efficient learning of parities from random examples. Indeed, the first non-trivial result in this direction has only recently been given by Klivans and Servedio [17]. They prove that parity functions on at most k variables are learnable in polynomial time using $O(n^{1-\frac{1}{k}} \log n)$ examples.

Efficient learning of unrestricted DNF formulas under the uniform distribution begins with a famous result by Jackson [13]. The algorithm, while polynomial-time, is somewhat impractical due to the $\tilde{O}(ns^{10}/\epsilon^{12})$ bound on running time. By substantially improving the key components of Jackson's algorithm the works of Freund [9], Bshouty *et al.* [4], and Klivans and Servedio [16] resulted in an algorithm that learns DNF in time $\tilde{O}(ns^6/\epsilon^2)$ and uses $\tilde{O}(ns^4/\epsilon^2)$ MQs[1]. This algorithm is non-adaptive but also not attribute-efficient. Using the algorithm for identification of relevant variables by Bshouty and Hellerstein mentioned above Bshouty *et al.* gave an attribute-efficient version of their algorithm running in time $\tilde{O}(rs^6/\epsilon^2 + n/\epsilon)$ and using $\tilde{O}(rs^4 \log n/\epsilon^2)$ adaptive MQs.

2   Preliminaries

General. For vectors $x, y \in \{0,1\}^n$ we denote by $x|y$ the vector obtained by concatenating x with y; by $x \oplus y$ the vector obtained by bitwise XOR of x and y; by $[k]$ the set $\{1, 2, \ldots, k\}$; by e_i a vector with 1 in i-th position and zeros in the rest; by x_i the i-th element of vector x; by M_i the i-th column of matrix M; and define $x_{[i,j]} = x_i|x_{i+1}|\cdots|x_j$. Dot product $x \cdot y$ of vectors $x, y \in \{0,1\}^n$ denotes $\sum_i x_i y_i$ (mod 2) or simply vector product xy^T over $\mathbf{GF}(2)$ (with vectors being row vectors by default). By $\mathtt{wt}(x)$ we denote the Hamming weight of x and we define $\mathtt{dist}(x, y) = \mathtt{wt}(x \oplus y)$.

To analyze accuracy and confidence of estimates produced by random sampling besides the more standard Chernoff and Hoeffding bounds, we use Bienaymé-Chebyshev's inequality for pairwise independent samples.

Lemma 1 (Bienaymé-Chebyshev). *Let* $X_1, \ldots, X_m$ *be pairwise independent random variables all with mean* μ *and variance* σ^2. *Then for any* $\lambda \geq 0$,

$$\mathbf{Pr}\left[\left|\frac{1}{m}\sum_{i=1}^{m} X_i - \mu\right| \geq \lambda\right] \leq \frac{\sigma^2}{m\lambda^2} \ .$$

We study learning of Boolean functions on the Boolean cube $\{0,1\}^n$. Our Boolean functions take values $+1$ (true) and -1 (false). Our main interest are the classes of parity functions and DNF expressions. Parity function $\chi_a(x)$ for a vector $a \in \{0,1\}^n$ is defined as $\chi_a(x) = (-1)^{a \cdot x}$. We refer to the vector associated with a parity function as its *index*. We denote the concept class of parity functions $\{\chi_a \mid a \in \{0,1\}^n\}$ by PAR and the class of all the parities on at most k variables by PAR(k). We represent a parity function by listing all the variables on which it depends. This representation for a parity on k variables requires $\theta(k \log n)$ bits.

For the standard DNF representation and any Boolean function f we denote by DNF-size(f) the number of terms in a DNF representation of f with the minimal number of terms. In context of learning DNF this parameter is always denoted s. The uniform distribution over $\{0,1\}^n$ is denoted $\mathcal{U}$.

Boolean Linear Codes. By saying that C is a *random* $[N, K]_2$ *code* we mean that C is defined by choosing randomly, uniformly and independently K vectors in $\{0,1\}^N$ that form the basis of C. Alternatively, we can say that the generator

---

[1] Bshouty *et al.* claimed sample complexity $\tilde{O}(ns^2/\epsilon^2)$ but this was in error as explained in Remark 11.

matrix G of C was chosen randomly with each entry equal to 1 with probability $1/2$ independently of others. We denote this distribution by $\mathcal{U}_{K \times N}$.

Standard definitions of the PAC model and the Fourier transform are omitted (*cf.* [2]).

Learning by Non-adaptive Membership Queries. We say that an algorithm $\mathcal{A}$ uses MQs *non-adaptively* if it can be split into two stages. The first stage, given all the parameters of learning, (n, ϵ and δ) and a bound on the size of the target concept, generates a set of points $S \subseteq \{0,1\}^n$. The second stage, given the answers from $\text{MEM}(c)$ on points in S, i.e. the set $\{(x, c(x)) \mid x \in S\}$, computes a hypothesis (or, in general, performs some computation). Neither of the stages has any other access to $\text{MEM}(c)$. We note that in the general definition of PAC learning we did not assume that size of the target concept (or a bound on it) is given to the learning algorithm. When learning with adaptive queries a good bound can be found via the "guess-and-double" technique but for adaptive algorithms we will assume that this bound is always given. Clearly the same "guess-and-double" technique can be used to produce a sequence of independent and non-adaptive executions of the learning algorithm.

3   Attribute-Efficient Learning of Parities

In this section we would like to show that there exist non-adaptive and attribute-efficient algorithms for learning of parity functions and also to give evidence that without MQs the problem is likely to be hard. Unlike in the rest of the paper in this section we will use parities as $0, 1$ functions. To emphasize this we use $\dot{\chi}$ instead of χ.

Theorem 2. *Assume that there exists an algorithm* RandDec *that for a randomly chosen* $[N, K]_2$ *code* C *and any* $y \in \{0,1\}^N$ *such that* $\exists x \in \{0,1\}^K$, $\text{dist}(C(x), y) \leq E$, *runs in polynomial (in N) time and, with probability at least* $1/2$ *(over the choice of C and the random choices of* RandDec*), finds x. Then* $PAR(E)$ *over* $\{0,1\}^K$ *is efficiently learnable from* $O((N-K)\log(1/\delta))$ *random examples.*

Proof. Let $\dot{\chi}_c \in PAR(E)$ be the target function. We first choose randomly and uniformly vectors $v^1, v^2, \ldots, v^K \in \{0,1\}^K$ and assume (for simplicity) that the obtained vectors span $\{0,1\}^K$. We then ask for $N - K$ random examples from $\text{EX}_{\mathcal{U}}(\dot{\chi}_c)$. We denote them by $(w^1, a_1), \ldots, (w^{N-K}, a_{N-K})$. Let V be the matrix formed by taking vectors $v^1, v^2, \ldots, v^K$ as its columns, that is $V_{i,j} = v_i^j$ and let W be the matrix formed similarly by taking vectors $w^1, w^2, \ldots, w^{N-K}$ as its columns. Let $G = (V \mid VW)$ and let $y = (0^K, a_1, a_2, \ldots, a_{N-K})$. By the definition of W, $(cV^{-1})G = (c|a_1|a_2|\cdots|a_{N-K})$ and therefore $\text{dist}(cV^{-1}G, y) \leq E$. All the entries of G are random and independent and therefore with probability at least $1/2$, RandDec will return $t = cV^{-1}$. Consequently we can obtain c with probability at least $1/2$. By repeating this procedure $\log(1/\delta)$ times we will get the target function with the desired probability.

Now we examine the case that $v^1, v^2, \ldots, v^K$ do not span $\{0,1\}^K$. With probability at least $2/3$, the rank of V is at least $K-1$ (the proof of this simple lemma is omitted due to space limitations). Let U be full rank $K \times K$ matrix such that $V = UR$ and R is in row echelon form. Let $G = (V \mid UW)$ (all the entries are still randomly and independently chosen). Without loss of generality assume that first $K-1$ columns of R are equal to those of identity matrix I_K. Let $b = \dot{\chi}_c(R_K)$. Then $cU^{-1}G = (c_1 \mid \cdots \mid c_{K-1} \mid b \mid a_1 \mid \cdots \mid a_{N-K})$. We can therefore try to decode as before for 2 possibilities of b. That is, for each $b \in \{0,1\}$ we try to decode vector $(0^{K-1} \mid b \mid a_1 \mid \cdots \mid a_{N-K})$. The probability that RandDec fails is $< 1/2$ and therefore the probability of failure when the rank of V is at least $K-1$ is $< 3/4$. Therefore with probability at least $1/4$ this procedure will return c.   □

Interestingly, the opposite direction is also true. Attribute-efficient learning of parities implies efficient decoding of random linear codes from relatively low number of errors.

Theorem 3. *Assume that there exists an algorithm $\mathcal{A}$ that efficiently learns $PAR(k)$ using at most $t(k, \log n, \log(1/\delta))$ queries and $k \cdot t(k, \log n, 2) = o(n)$. Then there exists an algorithm RandDec that for a randomly chosen $[N, K]_2$ code C with $K = n$ and $N = n + t(k, \log n, 2)$ and any $y \in \{0,1\}^N$ such that $\exists x \in \{0,1\}^K$, $\mathrm{dist}(C(x), y) \leq k$, runs in polynomial (in N) time and, with probability at least $1/2$, (over the choice of C and the random choices of RandDec) finds x.*

Proof. The idea of the reduction is to split the positions of code in two parts. The first large part has information about the message and is corrupted by at most k errors. The other small part does not have errors and is used to locate the errors by providing the parity of indices with errors on random examples.

Let G be the random generator matrix of C. We choose a random set of indices $I \subset [N]$ of size K. Let V be a $K \times K$ matrix formed by taking all columns of G with indices in I, and W by taking the columns with indices not in I. Let $G' = (V \mid W)$. From definition of G' it is G with its columns permuted. We denote this permutation by σ and let y' be y with the order of its bits permuted by σ ($y'_{\sigma(i)} = y_i$). As in the proof of Theorem 2, we assume for simplicity that V has full rank (the more general case is handled as in the proof of Theorem 2 and we omit it for brevity). The standard form generator matrix of C permuted by σ is $H = (I_K \mid V^{-1}W)$. The reduction is based on this matrix as it was done in the proof of Theorem 2.

For each i let $a_i = y'_{K+i} \oplus (y'_{[1,K]} \cdot (V^{-1}W_i))$ or in, equivalently in the vector form, $a = y'_{[K+1,N]} \oplus (y'_{[1,K]}V^{-1}W)$. We run $\mathcal{A}(n, k, \delta = 1/4)$. When $\mathcal{A}$ requests i-th example we return $(V^{-1}W_i, a_i)$. It is clear that $V^{-1}W_i$'s are uniformly and independently distributed over $\{0,1\}^n$. Let $\dot{\chi}_{c_h}$ be parity function returned by $\mathcal{A}$. RandDec returns $(y'_{[1,K]} \cdot c_h)V^{-1}$.

To see that RandDec defined as above will find the message we denote by J the set of indices in which xG differs from y (i.e., has errors). Expected size of $J \cap ([N] \backslash I)$ equals $(N-K)|J|/N \leq kt(k, \log n, 2)/N = o(1)$. Therefore with probability at least $1 - o(1)$ the size of this intersection is zero, i.e., all the errors have occurred in indices in I and none in $[N] \backslash I$. Let c be the vector in $\{0,1\}^K$ such that $c_i = 1$ iff $i \in \sigma(J)$ and let $z = xV$. By the definition of z and c,

$$zV^{-1}G' = xG' = (y'_{[1,K]} \oplus c)|y'_{[K+1,N]} \ .$$

On the other hand

$$zV^{-1}G' = z(I \mid V^{-1}W) = z|zV^{-1}W \ .$$

We can therefore derive that $z = y'_{[1,K]} \oplus c$ and

$$y'_{[K+1,N]} = zV^{-1}W = (y'_{[1,K]} \oplus c)V^{-1}W = (y'_{[1,K]}V^{-1}W) \oplus (cV^{-1}W).$$

This implies that

$$a = y'_{[K+1,N]} \oplus (y'_{[1,K]}V^{-1}W) = cV^{-1}W$$

or, in other words, the examples that were supplied to $\mathcal{A}$ correspond to parity $\dot{\chi}_c$ on columns of $V^{-1}W$. Hence with probability at least $3/4$, $c_h = c$. Given c, we know that $x = zV^{-1} = (y'_{[1,K]} \oplus c)V^{-1}$ which is exactly the output of RandDec.

□

Notice that for $k = n^{\Omega(1)}$ the trivial Gram-Schmidt algorithm is attribute-efficient. It is therefore natural to expect that this case will not yield any non-trivial decoding procedure. On the other hand, for $k = n^{o(1)}$ any attribute-efficient algorithm will satisfy the condition $kt(k, \log n, 2) = o(n)$ and hence will give a non-trivial error-correcting algorithm. The algorithm of Klivans and Servedio [17], while not attribute-efficient, gives an algorithm that corrects up to k errors for random codes of rate $\frac{1}{1+O(n^{-\frac{1}{k}} \log n)}$ where k is $o(\frac{\log n}{\log \log n})$.

A straightforward simplification of Theorems 2 and 3 also implies equivalence of linear binary codes with efficient error-correcting decoding procedure to ae.naMQ learning of parities. From this equivalence together with BCH or Reed-Solomon codes we obtain the following result (the proof is omitted due to space limitations).

Theorem 4. *For each $k \leq n$ there exists a deterministic algorithm that ae.naMQ learns the class $PAR(k)$. It asks $k \log n$ MQs and runs in time $O(n^3)$.*

We next present a simple randomized algorithm.

Theorem 5. *For each $k \leq n$ there exists an algorithm that ae.naMQ learns the class $PAR(k)$ in time $O(nk \log(n/\delta))$ and asks $O(k \log(n/\delta))$ MQs.*

Proof. Let χ_c be the target concept (such that $\mathbf{wt}(c) \leq k$). We define $\mathcal{D}_{\frac{1}{t}}$ to be the product distribution such that for each i, $\mathbf{Pr}[x_i = 1] = \frac{1}{t}$. Let us draw a point x randomly according to distribution $\mathcal{D}_{\frac{1}{4k}}$. Then for each $i \leq n$

$$\mathbf{Pr}_{\mathcal{D}_{\frac{1}{4k}}}[x_i = 1 \text{ and } \dot{\chi}_c(x) = 1] = \mathbf{Pr}_{\mathcal{D}_{\frac{1}{4k}}}[\dot{\chi}_c(x) = 1 \mid x_i = 1] \, \mathbf{Pr}_{\mathcal{D}_{\frac{1}{4k}}}[x_i = 1]$$

$$= \frac{1}{4k} \mathbf{Pr}_{\mathcal{D}_{\frac{1}{4k}}}[\dot{\chi}_c(x) = 1 \mid x_i = 1] \ .$$

Our second observation is that for any set of indices $B \subseteq [n]$ and the corresponding parity function $\dot{\chi}_b$,

$$\mathbf{Pr}_{\mathcal{D}_{\frac{1}{4k}}}[\dot{\chi}_b(x) = 1] \le 1 - \mathbf{Pr}_{\mathcal{D}_{\frac{1}{4k}}}[\forall i \in B, \ x_i = 0] = 1 - (1 - \frac{1}{4k})^{|B|} \le \frac{|B|}{4k} .$$

We now assume that $c_i \ne 1$ and therefore does not influence $\dot{\chi}_c$. Then by the second observation

$$\mathbf{Pr}_{\mathcal{D}_{\frac{1}{4k}}}[\dot{\chi}_c(x) = 1 \mid x_i = 1] = \mathbf{Pr}_{\mathcal{D}_{\frac{1}{4k}}}[\dot{\chi}_c(x) = 1] \le \frac{k}{4k} \le 1/4 .$$

Now assume that $c_i = 1$ and let $c' = c \oplus e_i$. Then $\dot{\chi}_c(x) = 1$ if and only if $\dot{\chi}_{c'}(x) = 0$ and $\dot{\chi}_{c'}(x)$ is independent of x_i. Therefore

$$\mathbf{Pr}_{\mathcal{D}_{\frac{1}{4k}}}[\dot{\chi}_c(x) = 1 \mid x_i = 1] = \mathbf{Pr}_{\mathcal{D}_{\frac{1}{4k}}}[\dot{\chi}_{c'}(x) = 0 \mid x_i = 1]$$

$$= 1 - \mathbf{Pr}_{\mathcal{D}_{\frac{1}{4k}}}[\dot{\chi}_{c'}(x) = 1] \ge 1 - \frac{k-1}{4k} > 3/4 .$$

Hence estimation of $\mathbf{Pr}_{\mathcal{D}_{\frac{1}{4k}}}[x_i = 1 \text{ and } \dot{\chi}_c(x) = 1]$ within the half of the expectation can be used to find out whether $c_i = 1$. By taking $\alpha k \log(n/\delta)$ independent samples[2] with respect to $\mathcal{D}_{\frac{1}{4k}}$ (for some constant $\alpha \ge 32 \ln 2$) we will get that each estimate is correct with probability at least $1 - \delta/n$ and therefore we will discover c with probability at least $1 - \delta$. The running time of resulting algorithm is clearly $O(nk \log(n/\delta))$.   □

4   Weak Parity Learning

The original Jackson's algorithm for learning DNF expressions with respect to the uniform distribution is based on a procedure that weakly learns DNF with respect to the uniform distribution [13]. The procedure for weak learning is essentially an algorithm that, given a Boolean function f finds one of its heavy Fourier coefficients, if one exist. Jackson's algorithm is based on a technique by Goldreich and Levin for finding a heavy Fourier coefficient [10]. Bshouty, Jackson, and Tamon used a later algorithm by Levin [18] to give a significantly faster weak learning algorithm [4]. Below we briefly describe Levin's algorithm with improvements by Bshouty et al. . Detailed proofs of all the statements and smaller remarks can be found in the paper by Bshouty et al. [4](Sect. 4) (we follow their definitions and notation to simplify the reference).

A Fourier coefficient $\hat{f}(a)$ of a function $f : \{0,1\}^n \to \{-1,+1\}$ is said to be θ-heavy if $|\hat{f}(a)| \ge \theta$.

---

[2] It is important to use the multiplicative and not the additive form of Chernoff bounds to get linear dependence on k.

Definition 6 (Weak Parity Learning). *Given $\theta > 0$ and access to MEM(f) for a Boolean function f that has at least one θ-heavy Fourier coefficient the weak parity learning problem consists of finding the index a $\theta/3$-heavy Fourier coefficient of f.*

We will only consider algorithms for weak parity learning that are efficient, that is, produce the result with probability at least $1 - \delta$ in time polynomial in n, θ^{-1} and $\log(1/\delta)$. In addition we are interested in weak parity learning algorithms that are attribute-efficient.

Definition 7 (Attribute-Efficient Weak Parity Algorithm). *Attribute-efficient weak parity algorithm is an algorithm that given k, θ, δ, and MEM(f) for f that has a θ-heavy Fourier coefficient of degree at most k efficiently solves weak parity learning problem and asks polynomial in $k, \log n, \theta^{-1}$, and $\log(1/\delta)$ number of MQs.*

Attribute-efficient weak learning of DNF can be obtained from attribute-efficient weak parity algorithm via the following lemma by Bshouty and Feldman.

Lemma 8 ([2](Lemma 18)). *For any Boolean function f of DNF-size s and a distribution $\mathcal{D}$ over $\{0,1\}^n$ there exists a parity function χ_a such that*

$$|\mathbf{E}_{\mathcal{D}}[f\chi_a]| \geq \frac{1}{2s+1} \text{ and } \mathtt{wt}(a) \leq \log((2s+1)L_\infty(2^n\mathcal{D})) .$$

Levin's algorithm is based on estimating a Fourier coefficient $\hat{f}(a)$ by sampling f on randomly-chosen pairwise independent points. More specifically, the following pairwise independent distribution is generated. For a fixed k, a random m-by-n 0-1 matrix R is chosen and the set $Y = \{pR \mid p \in \{0,1\}^m - \{0^m\}\}$ is formed. Bienaymé-Chebyshev's inequality implies that

$$\mathbf{Pr}_R\left[|\frac{\sum_{x \in Y} f(x)\chi_a(x)}{2^m - 1} - \hat{f}(a)| \geq \gamma\right] \leq \frac{1}{(2^m - 1)\gamma^2} \tag{1}$$

Therefore using a sample for $m = \log(9\rho^{-1}\theta^{-2} + 1)$, $\sum_{x \in Y} f(x)\chi_a(x)$ will, with probability at least $1 - \rho$, approximate $\hat{f}(a)$ within $\theta/3$.

On the other hand, $\sum_{x \in Y} f(x)\chi_a(x)$ is a summation over all (but one[3]) elements of a linear subspace of $\{0,1\}^n$ and therefore can be seen as a Fourier coefficient of f restricted to the subspace Y. That is, if we define $f_R(p) = f(pR)$ then, by definition of Fourier transform, for every $z \in \{0,1\}^m$

$$\widehat{f_R}(z) = 2^{-m} \sum_{p \in \{0,1\}^m} f_R(p)\chi_z(p) .$$

This together with equality $\chi_a(pR) = \chi_{aR^T}(p)$ implies that $\hat{f}(a)$ is approximated by $\widehat{f_R}(aR^T)$ (with probability at least $1 - \rho$).

---

[3] The value at 0^m does not influence the estimation substantially and therefore can be offset by slightly increasing the size of sample space Y [4].

All the coefficients $\widehat{f_R}(z)$ can be computed exactly in time $|Y|\log|Y|$ via the FFT algorithm giving estimations to all the Fourier coefficients of f.

Another key element of the weak parity algorithm is the following equation. For $c \in \{0,1\}^n$ let $f_c(x) = f(x \oplus c)$. Then

$$\widehat{f_c}(a) = 2^{-n} \sum_{x \in \{0,1\}^n} f(x \oplus c)\chi_a(x) = 2^{-n} \sum_{x \in \{0,1\}^n} f(x)\chi_a(x \oplus c) = \hat{f}(a)\chi_a(c) .$$

$$(2)$$

Assuming that $\hat{f}(a) \geq \theta$ estimation of $\hat{f}(a)$ within $\theta/3$ (when successful) has the same sign as $\hat{f}(a)$. Similarly we can obtain the sign of $\widehat{f_c}(a)$. The sign of the product $\hat{f}(a)\widehat{f_c}(a)$ then is equal to $\chi_a(c)$. This gives a way to make MQs for χ_a using the values $\widehat{f_{c,R}}(aR^T)$ for a random R and leads to the following result.

Theorem 9. *Let $\mathcal{B}(k,\delta)$ be an ae.naMQ algorithm for learning parities that runs in time $t(n,k,\log(1/\delta))$ and uses $q(\log n, k, \log(1/\delta))$ MQs. Then there exists an attribute-efficient weak parity learning algorithm $\texttt{WeakDNF}-\mathcal{U}(\theta, \mathbf{k}, \delta)$ that runs in time $\tilde{O}\left(\theta^{-2} \cdot t(n,k,2) \cdot q(\log n, k, 2)\right)$ and asks $\tilde{O}\left(\theta^{-2} \cdot q^2(\log n, k, 2)\right)$ non-adaptive MQs.*

Proof. Let S be the set of MQs for execution of $\mathcal{B}(k, 1/4)$. Choose randomly a m-by-n matrix R for $m = \log\left(9\theta^{-2} \cdot 4 \cdot (q(\log n, k, 2) + 1) + 1\right)$ and compute the Fourier transforms of f_R and $f_{y,R}$ for each $y \in S$.

Then, for each $z \in \{0,1\}^m$ such that $|\widehat{f_R}(z)| \geq 2\theta/3$, we run $\mathcal{B}(k, 1/4)$ with the answer to MQ $y \in S$ equal to $\texttt{sign}(\widehat{f_R}(z)\widehat{f_{y,R}}(z))$ (here the non-adaptiveness of parity learning algorithm is essential). If the output of $\mathcal{B}(k, 1/4)$ is a parity function on at most k variables we add it to the set of hypotheses H.

By Lemma 1, for a such that $|\hat{f}(a)| \geq \theta$ and $\text{wt}(a) \leq k$, with probability at least $1 - \frac{1}{4(q(\log n, k, 2)+1)}$, each of the estimations $\widehat{f_{y,R}}(aR^T)$ for $y \in S \cup \{0^k\}$ will be within $\theta/3$ of $\hat{f}_y(a)$. In particular, all of them will have the right sign with probability at least $3/4$. When all the signs used for $\mathcal{B}$'s MQs are correct, $\mathcal{B}(k, 1/4)$ succeeds with probability at least $3/4$. Therefore a will pass the magnitude test and will be added as a possible hypothesis with probability at least $1/2$. On the other hand for any $\hat{f}(b) \leq \theta/3$ it will not pass the magnitude test with probability at least $1 - \frac{1}{4(q(\log n, k, 2)+1)} \geq 3/4$. Therefore by repeating this procedure $O(\log(1/\delta))$ times (for independent R's and S's) we will find a $\theta/3$-heavy coefficient with probability at least $1 - \delta$. It can be easily verified that time and sample complexity of the algorithm are as stated and its MQs are non-adaptive. $\square$

Another way to see Theorem 9 is as a way to convert an ae.naMQ algorithm for learning parities to an attribute-efficient algorithm for learning parities with malicious noise (with respect to $\mathcal{U}$) of rate arbitrarily close to $1/2$. This follows from the fact that a parity function χ_c corrupted by noise of rate η has Fourier coefficient on c of weight at least $1 - 2\eta$.

We can now use the randomized parity learning algorithm and Theorems 8, 9 to get an algorithm for weakly learning DNF with the following properties.

Theorem 10. *There exist an algorithm* WeakDNF-$\mathcal{U}$ *that for a Boolean function* f *of DNF-size* s *given* n, s, δ, *and access to* $MEM(f)$, *with probability at least* $1 - \delta$, *finds a* $(\frac{1}{2} - \Omega(\frac{1}{s}))$-*approximator to* f *with respect to* $\mathcal{U}$. *Furthermore,* WeakDNF-$\mathcal{U}$ *runs in time* $\tilde{O}\left(ns^2\right)$ *and asks* $\tilde{O}\left(s^2 \log^2 n\right)$ *non-adaptive MQs.*

The previous weak learning algorithm by Bshouty *et al.* requires $\tilde{O}\left(ns^2\right)$ MQs and runs in time[4] $\tilde{O}\left(ns^2\right)$.

5   Learning DNF Expressions

Jackson's DNF learning paper gives a way to use a weak DNF learning algorithm with respect to the uniform distribution to obtain a (strong) DNF learning algorithm. It consists of generalizing a weak parity algorithm to work for any real-valued function (and not only Boolean functions). An important property of the generalized algorithm is that its running time depends polynomially on the L_∞ norm of the function. This algorithm is then used with a boosting algorithm that produces distributions that are *polynomially-close* to the uniform distribution; that is, the distribution function is bounded by $p2^{-n}$ where p is a polynomial in learning parameters (such boosting algorithms are called *p-smooth*). In Jackson's result Freund's boost-by-majority algorithm [8] is used to produce distribution functions bounded by $O(\epsilon^{-(2+\rho)})$ (for arbitrarily small constant ρ). More recently, Klivans and Servedio have observed [16] that a later Freund's algorithm [9] produces distribution functions bounded by $\tilde{O}(\epsilon)$, thereby improving the dependence of running time and sample complexity on ϵ. This improvement together with improved weak DNF learning algorithm due to Bshouty *et al.* gives DNF learning algorithm that runs in (ns^6/ϵ^2) time and has sample complexity of $\tilde{O}(ns^4/\epsilon^2)$.

Remark 11. Bshouty *et al.* claimed sample complexity of $\tilde{O}(ns^2/\epsilon^2)$ based on erroneous assumption that sample points for weak DNF learning can be reused across boosting stages. A distribution function $\mathcal{D}_i$ in i-th stage depends on hypotheses produced in previous stages. The hypotheses depend on random sample points and therefore in i-th stage the same set of sample points cannot be considered as chosen randomly and independently of $\mathcal{D}_i$ [14]. This implies that new and independent points have to be sampled for each boosting stage and increases the sample complexity of the algorithm by Bshouty *et al.* by a factor of $O(s^2)$.

We now briefly describe the generalization of weak parity learning and the boosting step, stressing only the points relevant to our improvements. Let f be the target DNF expression of size s. Lemma 8 states that f has an $\Omega(1/s)$-correlated parity of degree bounded by $O\left(\log\left(sL_\infty(2^n\mathcal{D})\right)\right)$. This implies that function $f(x)2^n\mathcal{D}(x)$ has an $\Omega(1/s)$-heavy Fourier coefficient of degree bounded

---

[4] The running time bound is based on use of a membership query oracle, that given any two vectors $x, y \in \{0,1\}^n$, passed to it "by reference", returns $f(x \oplus y)$ in $O(1)$ time.

by $O\left(\log\left(sL_\infty(2^n\mathcal{D})\right)\right)$. Therefore one can expect that weak parity algorithm WeakDNF-$\mathcal{U}$ applied to function $f2^n\mathcal{D}$ should find the desired parity. By revisiting the proof of Theorem 9 we can see that the only concern is Equation 1 in which we used the fact that the random variable $f(y) \in \{-1,+1\}$ has variance $\sigma^2 \le 1$. This is likely to be wrong for random variable $f(y)2^n\mathcal{D}(y)$. Instead we can derive that (expectations are by default for x chosen randomly from $\mathcal{U}$)

$$\sigma^2 = \mathbf{Var}(f(x)2^n\mathcal{D}(x)) = \mathbf{E}[(f(x)2^n\mathcal{D}(x))^2] - \mathbf{E}^2[f(x)2^n\mathcal{D}(x)] \qquad (3)$$
$$\le L_\infty(2^n\mathcal{D}(x))\mathbf{E}[2^n\mathcal{D}(x)] - \mathbf{E}^2[2^n\mathcal{D}(x)] < L_\infty(2^n\mathcal{D}(x)) \qquad (4)$$

This bound on variance relies essentially on the fact that $\mathcal{D}(x)$ is a distribution[5] and is better than $L_\infty^2(2^n\mathcal{D}(x))$ bound for an unrestricted function $\mathcal{D}(x)$ that was used in analysis of previous weak DNF learning algorithms [13, 4]. The only thing that has to be done to offset this higher variance is to use larger sample space (by $L_\infty(2^n\mathcal{D}(x))$ times). This yields the following weak DNF learning result.

Theorem 12. *There exist an algorithm* WeakDNF *that for a Boolean function f of DNF-size s and any distribution $\mathcal{D}(x)$, given n, s, δ, and access to $MEM(f)$, with probability at least $1 - \delta$, finds a $(\frac{1}{2} - \Omega(\frac{1}{s}))$-approximator to f with respect to $\mathcal{D}$. Furthermore,* WeakDNF

- *runs in time $\tilde{O}\left(ns^2L_\infty(2^n\mathcal{D}(x)) + t_\mathcal{D}\right)$ where $t_\mathcal{D}$ is a bound on the time required to estimate $\mathcal{D}(x)$ on all the points used as MQs of* WeakDNF;
- *asks $\tilde{O}\left(s^2\log^2 n \cdot L_\infty(2^n\mathcal{D}(x))\right)$ non-adaptive MQs;*
- *returns a parity function on at most $O(\log(s \cdot L_\infty(2^n\mathcal{D}(x)))$ variables or its negation.*

Our next observation specifically addresses the bound $t_\mathcal{D}$. Evaluation of distribution function $\mathcal{D}_i(x)$ at boosting stage i usually involves evaluation of $i - 1$ previous hypotheses on x and therefore, in a general case, for a sample of size q will require $\Omega(i \cdot q)$ steps making the last stages of boosting noticeably slower. We show that, in fact, for most known boosting methods the complexity of boosting a weak learner based on Levin's algorithm (in particular the weak learning algorithm by Bshouty *et al.* and WeakDNF) can be significantly reduced. The idea is to use the fact that most boosting algorithms compose weak hypotheses linearly, the samples come from a linear subspace of low dimension, and parities are linear functions.

Lemma 13. *Let $\{c_1, c_2, \ldots, c_i\}$ be a set of vectors in $\{0,1\}^n$ of Hamming weight at most w; $\bar{\alpha} \in \mathbb{R}^i$ be a real-valued vector, and R be a m-by-n 0-1 matrix. Then the set of pairs*

$$S = \{\langle p, \sum_{j \le i} \alpha_j \chi_{c_j}(pR)\rangle \mid p \in \{0,1\}^m\}$$

can be computed in time $\tilde{O}(i \cdot w \log n + 2^m)$.

---

[5] Actual $\mathcal{D}(x)$ given to a weak learner will be equal to $c\mathcal{D}'(x)$ where $\mathcal{D}'(x)$ is a distribution and c is a constant in $[2/3, 4/3]$ [4]. This modifies the bound above by a small constant factor.

Proof. We define $g(x) = \sum_{j \leq i} \alpha_j \chi_{c_j}(x)$ and for $p \in \{0,1\}^m$ we define $g_R(p) = g(pR)$ (as in Sect. 4). Our goal is to find the values of function g on all the points of some k-dimensional subspace of $\{0,1\}^n$. The function is given as a linear combination of parities, or in other words, we are given its Fourier transform. Hence the problem is simply to compute the inverse Fourier transform or g. This task can be performed in $O(k2^k)$ steps using the FFT algorithm. Naturally, the transform has to be done from the Fourier coefficients of g_R and not g (as we are given). But the relation between the complete and restricted transforms is simple and follows from the formula below.

$$g_R(p) = \sum_{j \leq i} \alpha_j \chi_{c_j}(pR) = \sum_{j \leq i} \alpha_j \chi_{c_j R^T}(p) = \sum_{z \in \{0,1\}^m} \left[\left(\sum_{j \leq i;\ c_j R^T = z} \alpha_j \right) \chi_z(p) \right]$$

Hence $\widehat{g_R}(z) = \sum_{j \leq i;\ c_j R^T = z} \alpha_j$. To compute the Fourier transform of g_R we need to compute $c_j R^T$ for each $j \leq i$ and sum the ones that correspond to the same z. Given that each c_j is of Hamming weight w, $c_j R^T$ can be computed in $O(wm \log n)$ steps. Therefore the computation of the Fourier transform and the inversion using the FFT algorithm will take $O(i \cdot w \log n + m2^m)$ steps. $\square$

Corollary 14. *Let $\{b_1 \chi_{c_1}, b_2 \chi_{c_2}, \ldots, b_i \chi_{c_i}\}$ be a set of hypotheses returned by* WeakDNF *in i stages of a certain L-smooth boosting algorithm ($b_j \in \{-1, +1\}$ is a sign of χ_{c_j}); $\bar{\alpha} \in \mathbb{R}^i$ be a real-valued vector; and W be a set of queries for the $(i+1)$-th execution of* WeakDNF. *Then the set of pairs*

$$S = \{\langle y, \sum_{j \leq i} \alpha_j b_j \chi_{c_j}(z) \rangle \mid z \in W\}$$

can be computed in time $\tilde{O}(i + s^2 L \log^2 n)$.

Proof. As can be seen from the proof of Theorem 9, WeakDNF asks queries on set $Y = \{pR \mid p \in \{0,1\}^m\}$ for a randomly chosen R and $2^m = \tilde{O}(s^2 L \log^2 n)$ to compute the Fourier transform of $(f2^n \mathcal{D}_{i+1})_R$ and then for each query y of ae.naMQ parity learning algorithm it computes the Fourier transform of $(f2^n \mathcal{D}_{i+1})_{y,R}$ by asking queries on points in the set $Y_y = \{z \oplus y \mid z \in Y\}$. The set Y_y is a subset of linear subspace of dimension $m + 1$ spanned by the rows of R and vector y. Therefore by using Lemma 13 on subspace Y and then on each Y_y we can compute the set S in $\tilde{O}(i + s^2 L \log^2 n)$ time. $\square$

To apply these observations to the computation of distribution function $\mathcal{D}_i$ generated while learning DNF we need to look closer at Freund's boosting algorithm B_{Comb} [9, 16]. It is based on a combination of two other boosting algorithms. The first one F1 is used to boost from accuracy $\frac{1}{2} - \gamma$ to accuracy $1/4$. The output of the first booster is used as a weak learner by the second boosting algorithm B_{Filt}. Each of the executions of F1 has $O(\gamma^{-2})$ stages and B_{Filt} has $O(\log(1/\epsilon))$ stages. Accordingly, the distribution function can be decomposed into $\mathcal{D}_{i,j}(x) = \mathcal{D}_i^{\text{Filt}} \cdot \mathcal{D}_j^{\text{F1}}$. In both boosting algorithms by Freund the weight of a point equals to $w_i(N(x))/\alpha$ where $N(x)$ is the number of previous hypotheses that are correct on x, w_i is a certain real-valued function, and α is a normalization factor independent of x. Therefore the only information about the previous hypotheses that is needed to compute $\mathcal{D}_j^{\text{F1}}$ is the number of them that are correct on x. Let $b_1\chi_{c_1}, b_2\chi_{c_2}, \ldots, b_{j-1}\chi_{c_{j-1}}$ be the hypotheses generated by previous stages of F1. Then $N(x) = \frac{f(x)(\sum_{l \le j-1} b_l\chi_{c_l}(x)) + j - 1}{2}$, that is, given $\sum_{l \le j-1} b_l\chi_{c_l}(x)$ and $f(x)$, $N(x)$ can be computed in $O(1)$ steps. Therefore Cor. 14 implies that $\mathcal{D}_j^{\text{F1}}(x)$ for all the points needed by WeakDNF can be computed in $\tilde{O}(s^2 \log^2 n/\epsilon)$ steps (values of f for all the points in the sample are available in WeakDNF).

Let $h_1, h_2, \ldots, h_{i-1}$ be the previous hypotheses needed for computation of $\mathcal{D}_i^{\text{Filt}}$. For each $l \le i - 1$, h_l is output of F1 or a random coin flip. Majority of $O(s^2)$ parities (or their negations) is simply the sign of their sum. Hence by Cor. 14, $h_l(x)$ for all the points in the sample for WeakDNF can be computed in $\tilde{O}(s^2 \log^2 n/\epsilon)$ time. B_{Filt} has $O(\log(1/\epsilon))$ stages and therefore all the previous hypotheses can be computed in $\tilde{O}(s^2/\epsilon)$ time and consequently $\mathcal{D}_i^{\text{Filt}}(x)$ can be computed in $\tilde{O}(s^2/\epsilon)$ time.

Altogether we have obtained a learning algorithm for DNF expressions with the following properties.

Theorem 15. *There exists an algorithm* AENALearnDNF *that for any Boolean function f of DNF-size s, given n, s, ϵ, δ and access to MEM(f), with probability at least $1 - \delta$, finds an ϵ-approximator to f with respect to $\mathcal{U}$. Furthermore,* AENALearnDNF *runs in time $\tilde{O}(ns^4/\epsilon)$ and asks $\tilde{O}(s^4 \log^2 n/\epsilon)$ non-adaptive MQs.*

The improvements to the algorithm by Bshouty *et al.* are summarized below.

- The use of attribute-efficient weak learning improves the total sample complexity from $\tilde{O}(ns^4/\epsilon^2)$ to $\tilde{O}(s^4 \log^2 n/\epsilon^2)$ and the same running time is achieved without assumptions on the MQ oracle (see Theorem 10).
- Faster computation of distribution functions used in boosting improves the total running time from $\tilde{O}(ns^6/\epsilon^2)$ to $\tilde{O}(ns^4/\epsilon^2)$ (see Corollary 14).
- Tighter estimation of variance improves the dependence of running time and sample complexity on ϵ from $1/\epsilon^2$ to $1/\epsilon$ (3).

Acknowledgments

We thank Leslie Valiant for his advice and encouragement of this research. We are grateful to Jeffrey Jackson for discussions and clarifications on the DNF learning algorithm of Bshouty *et al.* We also thank Alex Healy, Dmitry Gavinsky and anonymous COLT reviewers for valuable comments and proofreading of the earlier version of this paper.

References

[1] A. Blum, L. Hellerstein, and N. Littlestone. Learning in the presence of finitely or infinitely many irrelevant attributes. *JCSS*, 50:32–40, 1995.

[2] N. Bshouty and V. Feldman. On using extended statistical queries to avoid membership queries. *Journal of Machince Learning Research*, 2:359–395, 2002.

[3] N. Bshouty and L. Hellerstein. Attribute efficient learning with queries. *Journal of Computer and System Sciences*, 56:310–319, 1998.

[4] N. Bshouty, J. Jackson, and C. Tamon. More efficient PAC learning of DNF with membership queries under the uniform distribution. In *Proceedings of COLT '99*, pages 286–295, 1999.

[5] N. Bshouty, E. Mossel, R. O'Donnell, and R. Servedio. Learning DNF from random walks. In *Proceedings of FOCS '03*, pages 189–199, 2003.

[6] P. Damaschke. Adaptive versus nonadaptive attribute-efficient learning. In *Proceedings of STOC '98*, pages 590–596. ACM Press, 1998.

[7] M. Farach, S. Kannan, E. Knill, and S. Muthukrishnan. Group testing problems in experimental molecular biology. In *Proceedings of Sequences '97*, 1997.

[8] Y. Freund. Boosting a weak learning algorithm by majority. In *Proceedings of the Third Annual Workshop on Computational Learning Theory*, pages 202–216, 1990.

[9] Y. Freund. An improved boosting algorithm and its implications on learning complexity. In *Proceedings of the Fifth Annual Workshop on Computational Learning Theory*, pages 391–398, 1992.

[10] O. Goldreich and L. Levin. A hard-core predicate for all one-way functions. In *Proceedings of STOC '89*, pages 25–32, 1989.

[11] D. Guijarro, V. Lavin, and V. Raghavan. Exact learning when irrelevant variables abound. In *Proceedings of EuroCOLT '99*, pages 91–100, 1999.

[12] D. Guijarro, J. Tarui, and T. Tsukiji. Finding relevant variables in PAC model with membership queries. *Lecture Notes in Artificial Intelligence*, 1720:313 – 322, 1999.

[13] J. Jackson. An efficient membership-query algorithm for learning DNF with respect to the uniform distribution. In *Proceedings of STOC '94*, pages 42–53, 1994.

[14] J. Jackson. Personal communication, 2004.

[15] J. Jackson, E. Shamir, and C. Shwartzman. Learning with queries corrupted by classification noise. In *Proceedings of the Fifth Israel Symposium on the Theory of Computing Systems*, page 45. IEEE Computer Society, 1997.

[16] A. Klivans and R. Servedio. Boosting and hard-core set construction. *Machine Learning*, 51(3):217–238, 2003.

[17] A. Klivans and R. Servedio. Toward attribute efficient learning of decision lists and parities. In *Proceedings of COLT '04*, pages 234–248, 2004.

[18] L. Levin. Randomness and non-determinism. *Journal of Symbolic Logic*, 58(3):1102–1103, 1993.

[19] R. Uehara, K. Tsuchida, and I. Wegener. Optimal attribute-efficient learning of disjunction, parity, and threshold functions. In *Proceedings of EuroCOLT '97*, pages 171–184, 1997.

[20] L. Valiant. A theory of the learnable. *Communications of the ACM*, 27(11):1134–1142, 1984.

[21] L. Valiant. *Circuits of the Mind*. Oxford University Press, 1994.

[22] L. Valiant. A neuroidal architecture for cognitive computation. *Journal of ACM*, 47(5):854–882, 2000.

[23] L. Valiant. Knowledge infusion (unpublished manuscript). 2005.

Trading in Markovian Price Models

Sham M. Kakade and Michael Kearns

Department of Computer and Information Science,
University of Pennsylvania,
Philadelphia, PA 19104

Abstract. We examine a Markovian model for the price evolution of a
stock, in which the probability of local upward or downward movement
is arbitrarily dependent on the current price itself (and perhaps some
auxiliary state information). This model directly and considerably generalizes many of the most well-studied price evolution models in classical
finance, including a variety of random walk, drift and diffusion models.
Our main result is a "universally profitable" trading strategy — a single fixed strategy whose profitability competes with the optimal strategy
(which knows all of the underlying parameters of the infinite and possibly
nonstationary Markov process).

1 Introduction

We examine a Markovian model for the price evolution of a stock, in which
the probability of local upward or downward movement is arbitrarily dependent
on the current price itself (and perhaps some auxiliary state information). Our
main result is a "universally profitable" trading strategy — a single fixed strategy whose profitability competes with the optimal strategy (which knows all
of the underlying parameters of the infinite and possibly nonstationary Markov
process). While we shall make this statement more precise shortly, our strategy
is provably profitable whenever the optimal strategy has significant profits.

The strategy itself is efficient and simple, and employs a "best expert" weighting scheme (Cesa-Bianchi et al. [1997]) over two substrategies — one of which
attempts to do rudimentary learning from past observations (which may be extremely sparse), and one of which tries to spot significant directional trends
in price. Our main technical contribution is a proof that in our model, one of
these two strategies must always have a profit that compares favorably with the
optimal strategy.

There are several motivations for the model we introduce. The language of
Wall Street and finance is riddled with suggestions that the dynamics of price
movement may depend strongly on price itself. Professionals and articles discuss
"support" and "resistance" levels for a stock — specific prices or ranges of prices
below or above which the market will apparently not let the share price fall or
rise, respectively. The field of technical analysis is dominated by price patterns
whose appearance is thought to signal future behavior. The common notion of

P. Auer and R. Meir (Eds.): COLT 2005, LNAI 3559, pp. 606–620, 2005.

price uptrends or downtrends is predicated on a series of price levels in which the directional bias is nonzero.

There are also many less speculative reasons price dynamics may change dramatically with price. For example, one might expect there to be support for the share price at the level at which market capitalization (share price times number of outstanding shares, which is essentially the cost of buying the entire company) equals the liquid assets of the company. Similarly, many investors become uncomfortable if the ratio of the share price to a company's earnings (P/E ratio) becomes excessively large compared to its sector average. Note that in these cases there may be many factors aside from price influencing trading behavior (market cap, P/E) — but such factors may nevertheless lead to different price dynamics at different prices.

From the perspective of related literature on trading algorithms, we are particularly interested in price models that fall in between the highly adversarial assumptions typical of competitive analysis and universal portfolio work in computer science (Cover and Ordentlich [1996], Blum and Kalai [1999], El-Yaniv et al. [2001], Helmbold et al. [1996]), and the strong statistical assumptions typical of classical finance random walk and diffusion models and their generalizations (reviewed in Section 3). Our model and result can be thought of as exhibiting a "sweet spot" in the pantheon of price models, in the sense that it contains an extremely rich range of statistical behaviors, yet still permits a universally profitable trading strategy.

We emphasize from the outset that while our model is a gross oversimplification of all the complexities that enter into real-world price formation, it directly and considerably generalizes many of the most well-studied price evolution models in classical finance, including a variety of random walk, drift and diffusion models (see Section 3). To our knowledge, our model has not been explicitly considered before in the finance literature, especially in an algorithmic and learning context.

The outline of the paper follows. In Section 2, we provide the formal definition of our model and the optimal trading strategy that knows the process parameters. In Section 3, we briefly review some of the most common price evolution models in the finance and computer science literatures and relate our model to these. In Section 4, we discuss a number of interesting properties of the model and give simulation results for a particular instance that demonstrates these properties. Section 5 contains our main result. In Section 6 we generalize our result to permit simple extensions of the state.

2   Model and Definitions

In the most basic version of our model, the probabilistic dynamics of directional price movement depend only on the current price. More precisely, we assume that for every integer p between $-\infty$ and $+\infty$, there is a *bias* value $\epsilon(p) \in [-\frac{1}{2}, \frac{1}{2}]$. The interpretation of this bias is as follows: if the price at time t is p_t, then with probability $\frac{1}{2} + \epsilon(p_t)$ we have $p_{t+1} = p_t + 1$, and with probability $\frac{1}{2} - \epsilon(p_t)$ we have $p_{t+1} = p_t - 1$. Note that in this model, $|p_{t+1} - p_t| = 1$ always; it will be clear that all of our results hold with only slight degradation in a more general setting in which p_{t+1} must only remain in a bounded range around p_t, including the possibility of no movement. In our model, price movements are additive, prices are always integer values, and negative prices are allowed for convenience, as all that will matter are the profits made from price movements. (In the long version of this paper we will discuss a generalization of our results when p_t represents the log price. For this case, the price remains positive.) Without loss of generality, we always assume the initial price p_1 is 0.

The complete probabilistic dynamics of price movement at all possible prices are given by the infinite vector of biases $\epsilon(p)$ for all integers p, which we shall denote simply by ϵ. A model in our class is thus a countably infinite-state Markov process. (Note that $\epsilon = \mathbf{0}$ corresponds to an unbiased random walk.) We emphasize that this Markov process may be nonstationary and non-recurrent — an infinite walk may never return to its origin, and may forever visit new prices.

In this paper, we will be concerned with trading algorithms that have no a priori information about ϵ, yet can compete with the optimal algorithm that knows the full vector of biases. In order to make such comparisons, it is necessary to somehow limit the amount of risk the optimal algorithm can assume. For instance, if $\epsilon(p) = 1/2$ for some price p, so upward movement at price p is a certainty, the "optimal" algorithm should purchase an infinite number of shares. We shall thus limit our attention to trading strategies whose share position (number of shares owned (*long*) or owed (*short*)) at any time is at most 1. Other restrictions are possible, but this one has especially natural properties.

With this restriction, then, the optimal algorithm $A_{\mathrm{opt}} = A_{\mathrm{opt}}(\epsilon)$ is straightforward. If the current price is p_t and $\epsilon(p_t) > 0$, then A_{opt} buys one share; and if $\epsilon(p_t) < 0$ then A_{opt} sells (shorts) 1 share. If $\epsilon(p_t) = 0$, then A_{opt} takes no action. Whichever action A_{opt} takes at time t, at the next time step $t+1$, A_{opt} reverses its action by selling the share bought or buying the share sold at time t, and then repeating the process on p_{t+1}. Thus after each time step, A_{opt} either earns +1 (if it bought a share and the price rose, or it sold a share and the price fell), or loses -1. Thus, we can view A_{opt} as an algorithm for 1-step binary prediction of price movements on the probabilistic sequence of prices. Note that if the price enters a long period of upwards price movement (for example) that A_{opt} correctly predicts, then A_{opt} will be repeatedly buying a share, selling it at the next step and immediately buying another share, etc. This behavior is formally equivalent to buying a single share and holding it for the same period.

For any given bias vector ϵ and number of steps T, we let $\boldsymbol{p} = (p_1, p_2, \ldots, p_T)$ be a random variable that is a sequence of T prices generated according to ϵ. Without loss of generality, we assume $p_1 = 0$. For any trading algorithm A and price sequence $\boldsymbol{p}$, we let $V(A, \boldsymbol{p})$ denote the total amount earned or lost by A on $\boldsymbol{p}$ divided by T (so that earnings are normalized to per-step averages) and $V(A, \epsilon, T) = \mathbf{E}_{\epsilon,T}[V(A, \boldsymbol{p})]$ is thus the expected per-step earnings or losses of A over T-step sequences $\boldsymbol{p}$ distributed according to ϵ. We consider both cases where A may or may not have knowledge of T. We limit ourselves to only consider algorithms A which limit their share position to at most 1 share, and so it is easy to see that $V(A, \epsilon, T)$ is between -1 and 1. We note that $V(A, \epsilon, T)$ can be highly dependent on the specific value of T, since we are in an infinite-state Markov process: larger values of T may cause us to visit new price levels whose dynamics are entirely unlike those seen on smaller time scales.

With these definitions, it is easy to show that $V(A_{\text{opt}}, \epsilon, T)$ is in fact the optimal expected value among all trading algorithms whose position is at most 1 share at all times, which we shall thus also denote with the shorthand $V^*(\epsilon, T)$. Note that $V^*(\epsilon, T) \in [0, 1]$ always.

For any sequence p, we define $\#(p)$ to denote the number of *unique* prices appearing in p. Thus $\mathbf{E}_{\epsilon, T}[\#(p)]$ is the expected number of unique prices, and $\mathbf{E}_{\epsilon, T}[\#(p)/T]$ is the expected fraction of steps that are first visits to some price. This expectation will play a crucial role in our analysis.

3   Related Models

There is a rich history of mathematical models for the evolution of price time series. Perhaps the most basic and well-studied of these are variants of standard random walk or diffusion processes, often referred to in the literature as *Wiener processes*. Among others, this category includes pure unbiased random walks of price and random walks with overall upward or downward drifts (for instance, to model the overall growth of the securities markets historically). Perhaps the most general in this line of models is the *Ito process*, in which the instantaneous drift and variance may depend arbitrarily on both the current price and the time. A good overview of all of these models can be found in Hull [1993].

Our model can be viewed as being considerably more general than a Wiener process with drift, but considerably less general than a general Ito process. In particular, it will be easy to see that our results do not hold in the latter model. Broadly speaking, if the price process is allowed to depend arbitrarily on time, it is impossible to compete with the profitability of an omniscient party that knows exactly the nature of this time dependence.

The popularity of the various random walk models stems in part from their consistency with broader economic theory, most notably the Efficient Market Hypothesis (EMH), the thesis that individual trader rationality should drive all (expected) profit and arbitrage opportunities out of the market for a stock (or at least all those opportunities beyond those implied by consistent long-term growth, inflation, or drift). However, a long line of relatively recent works have carefully questioned and refuted random walk models and their variants, primarily on the basis of observed conflicts between historical price data and model predictions (Lo and MacKinlay [1999]). Some of these studies have suggested behavioral explanations for the deviations between historical prices and the EMH, which are certainly in the spirit of our model, where the market may react differently to different prices for psychological reasons.

The extensive field of *technical analysis* (Murphy [1999]), which suggests that certain price (and other) patterns may presage market behavior, is also clearly at odds with the EMH, at least in its strongest form. The long-term statistical profitability of certain technical indicators has been argued based on historical data (Brock et al. [1992]). The implicit assumptions of many technical strategies is that price dynamics are largely determined by the current price and some simple auxiliary state information (such as whether the recent price has shown an uptrend or downtrend, or the high and low prices over some recent time window). While our basic model permits only the current price as the Markovian state, in Section 6 we generalize our main result to hold for simple generalizations that incorporate many common technical indicators.

As noted in the Introduction, our model is also considerably more specialized (in terms of the allowed price behavior) than the worst-case price models often examined in computer science and related fields (Cover and Ordentlich [1996], Blum and Kalai [1999], El-Yaniv et al. [2001], Helmbold et al. [1996]). Indeed, in such models, one could never prove that *any* fixed collection of strategies always contained one competing with the optimal strategy that knew the price generation process. The precise point of our model and result is the introduction of a more limited but still quite powerful statistical model for price evolution, along with the proof that a fixed and simple strategy that mixes rudimentary learning and trend-spotting must always be competitive.

4   Properties of the Model, and an Example

Let us now enumerate a few properties (or in some cases, non-properties) of our model that are noteworthy and that distinguish it from some of the more classical models discussed in Section 3:

- As already noted, setting all $\epsilon(p) = 0$ yields a standard (additive) random walk, while all $\epsilon(p) = \alpha$ for some nonzero α yields a random walk with drift.
- One can also program rich mixtures of uptrends, downtrends, unbiased random walks, support and resistance levels, and other features in a single instance of our model.
- While our model does not allow the detailed specification of time-dependent events (and indeed, our main result would not hold in models such as a general Ito process), one can program rich temporal behaviors *in expectation*. We shall see examples shortly.
- None of the standard random variables of interest — such as the price after T steps, the maximum and minimum prices over T steps, or the profitability of fixed trading strategies — are (necessarily) unimodal in distribution or sharply peaked around their means.
- The optimal per-step profitability $V^*(\epsilon, T)$ may be nonmonotonic in T.

We now examine a concrete instance of our model. Since all we are concerned with is the additive movements of the price, without loss of generality we assume that the initial price is zero. Now consider the following instance of our model, which will be shown in simulation in Figures 1 through 3.

- For $p = -25, \ldots, 25$, $\epsilon(p) = 0$. Thus, on either side of the initial price, there is a bounded region of unbiased random walk.
- For $p = 26, \ldots, 40$, $\epsilon(p) = 0.1$. Thus, above the random walk region around the initial price, there is a small region of uptrend.
- For $p > 40$, $\epsilon(p) = -0.1$. Thus, above the uptrend there is an infinite region of probabilistic resistance to further upward movement.
- For $p = -100, \ldots, -26$, $\epsilon(p) = -0.1$. Thus, below the random walk region around the initial price, there is a large but bounded region of downtrend.
- For $p < -101$, $\epsilon(p) = 0$. Thus, below the downtrend there is an infinite region of unbiased random walk.

Figures 1 through 3 each show 16 randomly sampled time series from the model ϵ described above. Each figure shows samples from one of the four time scales $T = 100, 1000, 10000$. Horizontal lines are used to delineate the different regimes of price behavior enumerated above. All of the behaviors identified at the beginning of this section are clearly exhibited, and are discussed in the figure captions.

5   Main Result

In this section, we develop our main result: a trading strategy that knows nothing about the underlying model parameters ϵ, but whose per-step profitability can be provably related to $V^*(\epsilon, T)$. While the analysis is rather involved, the strategy itself and the intuition behind it are appealingly simple and are now sketched briefly.

The key to the analysis is the quantity $\mathbf{E}_{\epsilon,T}[\#(p)/T]$, the expected fraction of first visits to prices. The first insight is that if this expectation is "small", then we make "enough" repeat visits to prices to obtain a slight advantage in estimating the biases. For the final result to work out, we must show that this intuition holds even when the average number of visits per state is far too small (such as a constant) to apply concentration inequalities such as the Chernoff bound.[1] Essentially, while we may not have large enough samples to assert an advantage in estimating the bias of any *particular* price, we prove that an advantage exists *on average* across the prices visited. In this case a rather rudimentary learning strategy fares well.

The second insight is that if $\mathbf{E}_{\epsilon,T}[\#(p)/T]$ is "large", the price must be following a strong trend that is driven by an overall directional bias, and cannot be easily reversed *on a comparable time scale* (even though it may be reversed on much longer time scales). In this case a simple trend-following or momentum strategy is profitable.

The challenge in the analysis is to make these intuitions precise, and to prove that competing with optimal is possible for all values of $\mathbf{E}_{\epsilon,T}[\#(p)/T]$. In Sec-

---

[1] Roughly speaking, if the bias vector ϵ is such that the model behaves in a manner similar to a random walk, yet still permitting profit by the optimal algorithm, the number of visits to a price will usually not be frequent enough to obtain a benefit from using concentration inequalities.

tion 5.1 we provide the analysis for the case of "small" values for $\mathbf{E}_{\epsilon,T}[\#(\boldsymbol{p})/T]$, and in Section 5.2 we consider the case of large values. Section 5.3 stitches the pieces together to give our main result, which we now state:

Theorem 1. *(Main Result) Let $\gamma > 0$, and let T' satisfy $T'e^{-\gamma^2 T'/100} < \gamma/32$ (which is satisfied for $T' = \Omega((1/\gamma^2)\ln(1/\gamma))$). There exists an algorithm A_{master}, taking input γ, such that for all ϵ and $T \geq T'$, as long as $V^*(\epsilon, T) \geq 2\sqrt{\gamma}$, we have*

$$V(A_{\text{master}}(\gamma), \epsilon, T) \geq \frac{\gamma}{4}V^*(\epsilon, T) - \sqrt{2\ln(2)/T}. \tag{1}$$

Let us interpret this result briefly. If the profitability of the optimal algorithm is too small (quantified as being below $2\sqrt{\gamma}$), we simply "give up" and are not competitive. The parameter γ thus provides a trade-off to the user of A_{master}. Smaller values of γ will cause the lower bound on $V(A_{\text{master}}, \epsilon, T)$ to take effect at smaller values of $V^*(\epsilon, T)$, but the competitive ratio (which is essentially $\gamma/4$) degrades accordingly. Larger values of γ cause us to not compete at all for a wider range of $V^*(\epsilon, T)$, but give a better competitive ratio when $V^*(\epsilon, T)$ is sufficiently large.

Note also that Theorem 1 provides an "anytime" result, in that the strategy A_{master} is competitive *simultaneously* on all time scales, and does not require T as an input. This is important in light of the fact that $V^*(\epsilon, T)$ may be nonmonotonic in T.

The remainder of this section is devoted to developing A_{master} and proving Theorem 1.

5.1   A Statistical Strategy

We now define a simple trading algorithm that makes minimal use of past observations. We shall denote this algorithm A_{stat}. If the current price p_t is being visited for the first time (that is, time t is the earliest appearance of price p_t in the sequence $\boldsymbol{p}$), A_{stat} makes no trade. In this case, after p_{t+1} is revealed, A_{stat} stores a *first-visit record* consisting of the price p_t along with an indication of whether p_{t+1} went up or down from p_t.

If t is *not* the first time price p_t has been visited, then A_{stat} looks up the first-visit record for p_t and trades according to this record — that is, if after the first visit to p_t the price went up, A_{stat} buys one share, otherwise it sells one share, respectively. To obey the 1-share position limit, at time $t + 1$ A_{stat} sells off or buys back the position it accumulated and repeats the process on p_{t+1}.

Thus, A_{stat} is the algorithm that makes perhaps the least possible use of statistical history, simply predicting that what happened after the very first visit to a price will continue to happen. Obviously, it would make more intuitive sense to collect statistics on *all* the visits to a given price, and trade based on these cumulative statistics. But it turns out that A_{stat} must operate with sample sizes that are far too small to usefully apply large-deviation bounds such as the Chernoff inequality. Thus we cannot provide a general bound in which our expected value is a linear fraction of the optimal value. Instead, we compete against the square of the optimal value (which we conjecture is the best possible). More formally, we have:

Theorem 2. *(Statistical Strategy) For any biases ϵ and any T,*

$$V(A_{\text{stat}}, \epsilon, T) \geq V^*(\epsilon, T)^2 - \mathbf{E}_{\epsilon,T}[\#(\boldsymbol{p})/T]. \tag{2}$$

Proof. Let us first write down an explicit expression for the T-step optimal value $V^*(\epsilon, T)$. At each time step t, the optimal algorithm examines the bias $\epsilon(p_t)$ to decide how to trade. Abusing notation slightly, let us denote $\epsilon(t) = \epsilon(p_t)$ when t is a time value and not a price value and thus there is no risk of confusion. The expected profit of A_{opt} at time t is then

$$\left(\frac{1}{2} + |\epsilon(t)|\right)(+1) + \left(\frac{1}{2} - |\epsilon(t)|\right)(-1) = 2|\epsilon(t)|. \tag{3}$$

Now recall that $V^*(\epsilon, T) = \mathbf{E}_{\epsilon,T}[V(A_{\text{opt}}, \boldsymbol{p})]$. Since $V(A_{\text{opt}}, \boldsymbol{p})$ is a sum of T 1-step returns, by linearity of expectation we may write

$$V^*(\epsilon, T) = \frac{1}{T} \sum_{t=1}^{T} \sum_{\boldsymbol{p}:|\boldsymbol{p}|=t} \Pr_{\epsilon,t}[\boldsymbol{p}](2|\epsilon(t)|) \tag{4}$$

where each inner sum over sequences $\boldsymbol{p}$ of length $t \leq T$ is the expected profit of A_{opt} on the step t.

Let us now analyze the 1-step expected profit of algorithm A_{stat} at time t. If t is the first visit to the price p_t in the sequence $\boldsymbol{p}$, then the profit of A_{stat} is 0. Otherwise, the profit depends on whether the first visit to p_t revealed the correct or incorrect sign of $\epsilon(p_t)$. More precisely, the expected return of A_{stat} on non-first visits to p_t may be written

$$\left(\frac{1}{2} + |\epsilon(t)|\right)(2|\epsilon(t)|) + \left(\frac{1}{2} - |\epsilon(t)|\right)(-2|\epsilon(t)|) = 4|\epsilon(t)|^2. \tag{5}$$

The logic here is that with probability $\frac{1}{2} + |\epsilon(t)|$, the first visit to p_t reveals the correct sign of the bias, in which case on all subsequent visits, A_{stat} will behave the same as A_{opt} and receive $2|\epsilon(t)|$ in expected profits; and with probability $\frac{1}{2} - |\epsilon(t)|$, the first visit to p_t reveals the incorrect sign, in which case on all subsequent visits, A_{stat} will receive $-2|\epsilon(t)|$. Thus the expectation is taken over *both* the randomization on the current visit to p_t, and the randomization on the first visit.

We would now like to apply this observation on the 1-step profit of A_{stat} to obtain an expression for $V(A_{\text{stat}}, \epsilon, T)$; the main challenge is in dealing with the dependencies introduced by conditioning on the number of visits to each price level. The following inequality can be shown (details omitted):

$$V(A_{\text{stat}}, \epsilon, T) \geq \frac{1}{T} \sum_{t=1}^{T} \sum_{\boldsymbol{p}:|\boldsymbol{p}|=t} \Pr_{\epsilon,t}[\boldsymbol{p}](4|\epsilon(t)|^2) - \mathbf{E}_{\epsilon,T}[\#(\boldsymbol{p})/T] \tag{6}$$

Combining Equation (4) and Equation (6), we now have:

$$V(A_{\text{stat}}, \epsilon, T) - V^*(\epsilon, T)^2 \geq$$

$$\frac{4}{T} \sum_{t=1}^{T} \sum_{p:|p|=t} \Pr_{\epsilon,t}[p] |\epsilon(t)|^2 - \left(\frac{2}{T} \sum_{t=1}^{T} \sum_{p:|p|=t} \Pr_{\epsilon,t}[p] |\epsilon(t)| \right)^2 - \mathbf{E}_{\epsilon,T}[\#(p)/T] \quad (7)$$

It remains to show that the first two terms are positive.

Recall that each $\epsilon(t) = \epsilon(p_t)$ is actually the bias at some price level p_t. Let us define for each price q

$$w(q) = \frac{1}{T} \sum_{t=1}^{T} \sum_{p:|p|=t, p(t)=q} \Pr_{\epsilon,t}[p]. \quad (8)$$

It is easy to see that since the price must remain in the range $[-T, T]$ on sequences of length at most T, the values $w(-T), \ldots, w(T)$ sum to 1 and are all positive, and thus can be interpreted as a distribution. The first two terms in Equation (7) may be rewritten as

$$4 \left(\sum_{q=-T}^{T} w(q) |\epsilon(q)|^2 - \left(\sum_{q=-T}^{T} w(q) |\epsilon(q)| \right)^2 \right) \quad (9)$$

This difference is non-negative as desired, by the convexity of the function $f(x) = x^2$. (Interestingly, note that this difference has the form of the variance of $\epsilon(q)$ with respect to the distribution $w(q)$.) $\qquad \square$

5.2   A Momentum Strategy

We now turn attention to a strategy that will succeed for large values of the quantity $\mathbf{E}_{\epsilon,T}[\#(p)/T]$. For any given values of γ and T, the momentum strategy $A_{\text{mom}}(\gamma, T)$ can be described as follows:

1. For all $p \in (-\gamma T/4, \gamma T/4)$, take no action.
2. For all $p \geq \gamma T/4$, purchase one share and sell it back at the next time step.
3. For all $p \leq -\gamma T/4$, sell one share and purchase it back at the next time step.

Note this strategy uses knowledge of the time T; however, this dependency can be removed (details omitted) to yield an algorithm that is competitive on all time scales simultaneously.

The following definitions will be necessary in our analysis of A_{mom}. For the remainder of this subsection, p will denote a price sequence of length T for some fixed T. Let $\max(p)$ ($\min(p)$, respectively) be the maximum (minimum, respectively) price reached on p. Let $\text{drop}(p)$ be the absolute value of the difference between $\max(p)$ and the *smallest* price reached on p *after* the first visit to $\max(p)$. Thus, $\text{drop}(p)$ measures the "fall" from the high price. Similarly, we define rise($\boldsymbol{p}$) to be the absolute value of the difference between min($\boldsymbol{p}$) and the *largest* price reached on $\boldsymbol{p}$ *after* the first visit to min($\boldsymbol{p}$).

A_{mom} enjoys the following performance guarantee.

Theorem 3. *(Momentum Strategy) Let $\gamma > 0$, and let T' satisfy $T'e^{-\gamma^2 T'/48} < \gamma/16$. If $T > T'$ and if either $\mathbf{E}_{\epsilon,T}[\max(\boldsymbol{p})/T] \geq \gamma$ or $\mathbf{E}_{\epsilon,T}[|\min(\boldsymbol{p})/T|] \geq \gamma$ then*

$$V(A_{\mathrm{mom}}(\gamma, T), \epsilon, T) \geq \frac{\gamma}{2} \geq \frac{\gamma}{2} V^*(\epsilon, T) \tag{10}$$

Note that unlike the guarantee for A_{stat}, A_{mom} must be run for a time larger than some threshold time. Essentially, this time is the time long enough to discover the trend. Also, note that we always must have either $\mathbf{E}_{\epsilon,T}[\max(\boldsymbol{p})] \geq \mathbf{E}_{\epsilon,T}[\#(\boldsymbol{p})]/2$ or $\mathbf{E}_{\epsilon,T}[|\min(\boldsymbol{p})|] \geq \mathbf{E}_{\epsilon,T}[\#(\boldsymbol{p})]/2$.

At the heart of the proof of Theorem 3 is the following simple probabilistic lemma. The lemma essentially states that if the price makes large moves on some time scale, then with high probability it cannot return to its starting value on a comparable time scale.

Lemma 1. *For any constant $a > 0$, we have*

1. *For all ϵ, T and $z \geq aT$, $\mathrm{Pr}_{\epsilon,T}[\max(\boldsymbol{p}) = z$ and $\mathrm{drop}(\boldsymbol{p}) \geq aT/2] \leq e^{-a^2 T/12}$.*
2. *For all ϵ, T and $z \leq -aT$, $\mathrm{Pr}_{\epsilon,T}[\min(\boldsymbol{p}) = z$ and $\mathrm{rise}(\boldsymbol{p}) \geq aT/2] \leq e^{-a^2 T/12}$.*

Proof. (Sketch) We sketch only Part 1, as Part 2 is entirely symmetric. First let us suppose that among the biases $\epsilon(0), \ldots, \epsilon(z)$ there are more than $aT/4$ which are negative. In this case we show that the probability of $\max(\boldsymbol{p})$ even reaching the price z is small. In order for the price to reach z, it clearly must "get through" these negative biases — in other words, the price must have a net upwards movement of at least $aT/4$ even when restricted only to those visits to prices with negative bias. If we modify all of these negative biases to be equal to 0 (unbiased), we can clearly only *increase* the probability that $\max(\boldsymbol{p})$ reaches the price z.

We can thus bound $\mathrm{Pr}_{\epsilon,T}[\max(\boldsymbol{p}) = z]$ by the probability that in T independent flips of a fair coin, we would see an excess of heads over tails of at least $aT/4$. By the standard Chernoff bound, the probability of seeing such an excess in T flips is at most $e^{-(a^2/2)^2 T/3} = e^{-a^2 T/12}$. Since the probability of $\max(\boldsymbol{p})$ even reaching z has been thus bounded, the lemma holds in this case.

Otherwise, we must have that at most $aT/4$ of the biases $\epsilon(0), \ldots, \epsilon(z)$ are negative. In this case we show that $\mathrm{Pr}_{\epsilon,T}[\mathrm{drop}(\boldsymbol{p}) \geq aT/2]$ is small. Since the price can drop by a net amount of at most $aT/4$ when restricted only to visits to prices with negative biases, in order to drop by a total of at least $aT/2$, it must drop a further net amount of at least $aT/4$ when restricted only to visits to prices with positive biases. Using a similar argument, it is straightforward to see that this probability is bounded by $e^{-a^2 T/12}$. $\square$

Lemma 1 is used to prove the following result (and a similar result holds in terms of $\mathbf{E}_{\epsilon,T}[\min(\boldsymbol{p})/T]$).

Lemma 2. *Let $\gamma > 0$, and let T' be such that $T'e^{-\gamma^2 T'/48} < \gamma/16$. If $T > T'$, then for any biases ϵ*

$$V(A_{\mathrm{mom}}(\gamma, T), \epsilon, T) \geq \mathbf{E}_{\epsilon,T}[\max(\boldsymbol{p})/T] - \gamma/2 \qquad (11)$$

Proof. (Sketch) First, using an argument that is similar to the proof of the Markov inequality, one can show:

$$\sum_{x > \gamma T/4} \Pr_{\epsilon,T}[\max(\boldsymbol{p}) = x](x - \gamma T/4) \geq \mathbf{E}_{\epsilon,T}[\max(\boldsymbol{p})] - \gamma T/4. \qquad (12)$$

Informally, this summation is the expected profit from the cases in which the maximum price exceeds $\gamma T/4$, conditioned on the subsequent drop being at most $\gamma T/4$.

Now one can use Lemma 1 to show that the value of A_{mom} is close to the above. This argument is somewhat involved and is included in the long version of this paper. □

Theorem 3 follows from Lemma 2 under the assumption that $\mathbf{E}_{\epsilon,T}[\max(\boldsymbol{p})] > \gamma T$, and noting that $V^*(\epsilon, T) \leq 1$.

5.3   Putting the Pieces Together

Theorems 2 and 3 establish that for any biases ϵ and any T, *at least one* of the two strategies A_{stat} and A_{mom} must have an expected profit that compares "favorably" with that of the optimal algorithm that knows ϵ. We now wish to define a *single* strategy accomplishing this same criterion. Of course, one way of doing this is to have a strategy that simply flips a fair coin at the outset of trading to decide wether to use A_{stat} or A_{mom} for the duration of the sequence, at a cost of a factor of 2 in our expected return in comparison to $V^*(\epsilon, T)$. While this cost is insignificant in light of the other constant factors we are already absorbing, we prefer to apply the so-called "experts" methods of worst-case on-line analysis. When we generalize our results to permit the biases ϵ to depend on an underlying state variable more complex than just the current price, the experts methodology will be necessary.

In order to apply the experts framework, it is important to recall the observation made in Section 2 that our trading model can really be viewed as an instance of on-line binary prediction. We view trading strategies (and A_{stat}, A_{mom} and the optimal trading algorithm in particular) as making a series of trades or predictions, each of which wins or loses immediately. We can thus immediately apply the on-line weighting scheme of Cesa-Bianchi et al. [1997] to the strategies A_{stat} and A_{mom} (in this case, an especially small set of experts); let us call the resulting strategy A_{master}, since it can be viewed as a "master" strategy allocating capital between the two subordinate strategies. Combining Theorem 16 of Cesa-Bianchi et al. [1997] with Theorems 2 and 3 allows one to show that

$$V(A_{\mathrm{master}}, \epsilon, T) \geq \min\left(V^*(\epsilon, T)^2 - \gamma, \frac{\gamma}{4}V^*(\epsilon, T)\right) - \sqrt{2\ln(2)/T} \qquad (13)$$

always holds. Notice that this lower bound may actually be near zero for small values of $V^*(\epsilon, T)$. From this equation, Theorem 1 follows.

6   Extending the State

So far we have focused exclusively on a model in which the directional bias of the price movement may depend arbitrarily on the current price itself. In this section we generalize our results to a considerably richer class of models, in which the directional bias $\epsilon = \epsilon(p, s)$ may depend on both price p and some auxiliary information s. For example, one might posit that a more realistic model for price dynamics is that the directional bias depends not only on the current price, but also on whether the current price was arrived at from below or above. We can model this by letting the probability that $p_{t+1} = p_t + 1$ be $\frac{1}{2} + \epsilon(p_t, s_t)$, where $\epsilon(p_t, s_t) \in [-\frac{1}{2}, \frac{1}{2}]$ and $s_t \in \{0, 1\}$ equals 1 if $p_t = p_{t-1} + 1$ (uptrend) and 0 if $p_t = p_{t-1} - 1$ (downtrend). We again have an infinite Markov process, but with the Markovian state now being the pairs (p, s) rather than just p alone. We will continue to use the notation ϵ to denote the infinite set of biases $\epsilon(p, s)$ for all integer prices p and binary trend indicators s.

We now outline why the results of Section 5 continue to hold with some additional machinery, after which we will provide a more general and formal statement. Let $\boldsymbol{p}$ be the sequence of prices p_t, and let $\boldsymbol{s}$ be the corresponding sequence of auxiliary values s_t. Let us define $\#(\boldsymbol{p}, \boldsymbol{s})$ to be the number of *unique* states (p_t, s_t) visited on $(\boldsymbol{p}, \boldsymbol{s})$. Then it is easily verified that Theorem 2 holds with $\mathbf{E}_{\epsilon, T}[\#(\boldsymbol{p})/T]$ replaced by $\mathbf{E}_{\epsilon, T}[\#(\boldsymbol{p}, \boldsymbol{s})/T]$. In this case, the obvious modification of strategy A_{stat} — namely, to always trade according to the observed behavior of the price on the *first* visit to state (p, s) — permits an identical analysis.

The extension of Theorem 3 is slightly more involved. In particular, in our new model Lemma 1 simply no longer holds — we can now easily "program" behavior that (for example) causes the price to deterministically rise to some price and then deterministically fall back to its starting value. In the price-only model, such behavior was excluded by Lemma 1, which states that the probability of the conjunction of a steep rise in price and a subsequent drop is exponentially small.

However, in the new model it remains true that if $\mathbf{E}_{\epsilon, T}[\#(\boldsymbol{p}, \boldsymbol{s})/T]$ is larger than γ, then either $\mathbf{E}_{\epsilon, T}[\max(\boldsymbol{p})]$ or $\mathbf{E}_{\epsilon, T}[\min(\boldsymbol{p})]$ must be large — namely, one of them must be at least $\gamma T/4$ (as opposed to $\gamma T/2$ in the price-only model). This is because for every n unique *states* we visit, we must visit at least $n/2$ unique *prices* as well, since for each price p there are only two associated states $(p, 0)$ and $(p, 1)$. To exploit this, despite the fact that Lemma 1 no longer holds, we make richer use of the Cesa-Bianchi et al. [1997] results. For each $1 \leq i \leq T$, we introduce two simple trading strategies, A_{+i} and A_{-i}. Strategy A_{+i} buys a single share at the outset of trading, and sells it back if and only if the price reaches the value i above its starting point. Strategy A_{-i} sells a single share at the outset of trading, and buys it back if and only if the price reaches the value i below its starting point. If either $\mathbf{E}_{\epsilon,T}[\max(\boldsymbol{p})]$ or $\mathbf{E}_{\epsilon,T}[\min(\boldsymbol{p})]$ is at least $\gamma T/4$, then clearly the expected maximum per-step profit among the strategies $\{A_{+i}, A_{-i}\}_{1 \leq i \leq T}$ is at least $\gamma/4$.

The new overall algorithm is thus to apply the weighting scheme of Cesa-Bianchi et al. [1997] to the strategies $\{A_{+i}, A_{-i}\}_{1 \leq i \leq T}$ along with the strategy A_{stat}. Regardless of the value of $\mathbf{E}_{\epsilon,T}[\#(\boldsymbol{p}, \boldsymbol{s})/T]$, one of these $2T+1$ strategies will be profitable.

To generalize the analysis above, note that the only property we required of the state space (p, s) is that each possible price p has only a "small" number of possible extensions s (2 in the analysis above). This motivates the following definition: for any price p, let us define $\kappa(p)$ to be $|\{(p, s) \in S\}|$, where S is the set of possible states. For instance, in the example above, for any given p, only the states $(p, 0)$ and $(p, 1)$ are possible, so $\kappa(p) = 2$ always. We then define $\kappa_{\max} = \max_p\{\kappa(p)\}$. Note that $\kappa_{\max}$ can be finite and small even though an infinite number of values of s are possible as we range over all values of p. For example, if s is defined to be the maximum price in the last ℓ time steps, then for any p, there are at most 2ℓ possible values for s; but the domain of s is all the integers.

Let $A_{\text{general}}(T)$ refer to this more general algorithm which takes T as an input and which weights the strategies A_{stat} and $\{A_{+i}, A_{-i}\}_{1 \leq i \leq T}$ as discussed above. Then we have the following theorem.

Theorem 4. *(Main Result, Extended State) Let $\kappa_{\max}$ be as defined above. Let $\gamma > 0$, and let T' be such that $T'e^{-\gamma^2 T'/100} < \gamma/32$ (which is satisfied for $T' = \Omega((1/\gamma^2)\ln(1/\gamma)))$. If $T \geq T'$, then for any ϵ and as long as*

$$V^*(\epsilon, T) \geq 2\sqrt{(\gamma^2/4\kappa_{\max}) + 4\gamma} \tag{14}$$

we have

$$V(A_{\text{general}}(T), \epsilon, T) \geq \frac{\gamma}{2\kappa_{\max}}V^*(\epsilon, T) - \sqrt{2\ln(T)/T}. \tag{15}$$

Note that this differs from the price-only result of Theorem 1 in that our competitive ratio is now proportional to $\gamma/\kappa_{\max}$ rather than γ, and the regret term $\sqrt{2\ln(T)/T}$ of the weighting scheme now has $\ln(T)$ replacing $\ln(2)$. Also, this result is not anytime since A_{general} takes as input the time T.

Thus for constant $\kappa_{\max}$, our bound essentially suffers only a constant factor degradation.

Acknowledgments

We give to warm thanks to Adam Kalai and Sebastian Seung for valuable discussions on the material presented here. We also thank the reviewers for their numerous helpful comments and suggestions.

References

A. Blum and A. Kalai. Universal portfolios with and without transaction costs. *Machine Learning*, 35(3):193–205, 1999.

A. Brock, J. Lakonishok, and B. Lebaron. Simple technical trading rules and the stochastic properties of stock returns. *Journal of Finance*, (47):1731–1764, 1992.

Nicolo Cesa-Bianchi, Yoav Freund, David Haussler, David P. Helmbold, Robert E. Schapire, and Manfred K. Warmuth. How to use expert advice. *J. ACM*, 44(3): 427–485, 1997. ISSN 0004-5411.

T. Cover and E. Ordentlich. Universal portfolios with side information. *IEEE Transactions on Information Theory*, 42(2), 1996.

R. El-Yaniv, A. Fiat, R. M. Karp, and G. Turpin. Optimal search and one-way trading online algorithms. *Algorithmica*, 30:101–139, 2001.

David P. Helmbold, Robert E. Schapire, Yoram Singer, and Manfred K. Warmuth. On-line portfolio selection using multiplicative updates. In *International Conference on Machine Learning*, pages 243–251, 1996. URL citeseer.ist.psu.edu/article/helmbold98line.html.

J. Hull. *Options, Futures, and Other Derivative Securities*. Prentice Hall, 1993.

A. Lo and A.C. MacKinlay. *A Non-Random Walk Down Wall Street*. Princeton University Press, 1999.

J. Murphy. *Technical Analysis of the Financial Markets*. New York Institute of Finance, 1999.

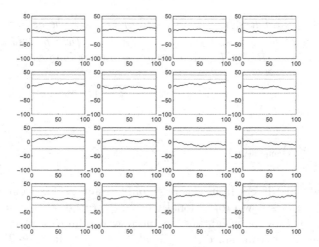

Fig. 1. 16 sampled walks of length $T = 100$ from the model described in Section 4. On this short time scale, with high probability, the walk remains in the unbiased region between $p = -25$ and $p = 25$

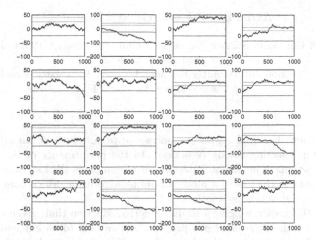

Fig. 2. 16 sampled walks of length $T = 1000$. Most walks either enter the uptrend region above $p = 25$ and are lifted to the resistance level at $p = 40$ (plot in row 1, column 3, denoted $(1,3)$ in the sequel), or enter the downtrend region below $p = -25$ (plot $(1,2)$). Some walks enter the uptrend or downtrend only very late (plot $(2,1)$), or do not even leave the unbiased region (plot $(3,1)$)

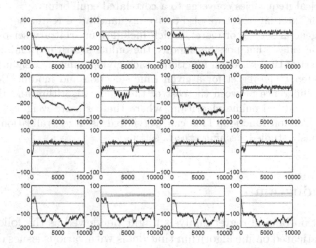

Fig. 3. 16 sampled walks of length $T = 10000$. Now all walks either traverse the uptrend and remain near the $p = 40$ resistance level, or traverse the downtrend and follow an unbiased random walk below $p = -100$, the bottom of the downtrend region. On this time scale, some of the uptrend walks are starting to show "cracks" in the form of dips back into the original unbiased region (plots $(2,2)$, $(2,4)$ and $(3,2)$). Eventually these cracks will pull the price back through the original unbiased region and into the downtrend; asymptotically, all walks eventually spend most of their lives in the lower unbiased region below $p = -100$

From External to Internal Regret

Avrim Blum[1],* and Yishay Mansour[2],**

[1] School of Computer Science, Carnegie Mellon University,Pittsburgh, PA 15213
avrim@cs.cmu.edu
[2] School of Computer Science, Tel-Aviv University, Israel
mansour@cs.tau.ac.il

Abstract. External regret compares the performance of an online algorithm, selecting among N actions, to the performance of the best of those actions in hindsight. Internal regret compares the loss of an online algorithm to the loss of a modified online algorithm, which consistently replaces one action by another.

In this paper, we give a simple generic reduction that, given an algorithm for the external regret problem, converts it to an efficient online algorithm for the internal regret problem. We provide methods that work both in the *full information* model, in which the loss of every action is observed at each time step, and the *partial information* (bandit) model, where at each time step only the loss of the selected action is observed. The importance of internal regret in game theory is due to the fact that in a general game, if each player has sublinear internal regret, then the empirical frequencies converge to a correlated equilibrium.

For external regret we also derive a quantitative regret bound for a very general setting of regret, which includes an arbitrary set of modification rules (that possibly modify the online algorithm) and an arbitrary set of time selection functions (each giving different weight to each time step). The regret for a given time selection and modification rule is the difference between the cost of the online algorithm and the cost of the modified online algorithm, where the costs are weighted by the time selection function. This can be viewed as a generalization of the previously-studied *sleeping experts* setting.

1 Introduction

The motivation behind regret analysis might be viewed as the following: we design a sophisticated online algorithm that deals with various issues of uncertainty and decision making, and sell it to a client. Our online algorithm runs for some

---

* This work was supported in part by NSF grants CCR-0105488 and IIS-0312814.
** The work was done while the author was a fellow in the Institute of Advance studies, Hebrew University. This work was supported in part by the IST Programme of the European Community, under the PASCAL Network of Excellence, IST-2002-506778, by a grant no. 1079/04 from the Israel Science Foundation and an IBM faculty award. This publication only reflects the authors' views.

P. Auer and R. Meir (Eds.): COLT 2005, LNAI 3559, pp. 621–636, 2005.

time and incurs a certain loss. We would like to avoid the embarrassment that our client will come back to us and claim that in *retrospect* we could have incurred a much lower loss if we used his simple alternative policy π. The regret of our online algorithm is the difference between the loss of our algorithm and the loss using π. Different notions of regret quantify differently what is considered to be a "simple" alternative policy.

At a high level one can split alternative policies into two categories. The first consists of alternative policies that are independent from the online algorithm's action selection, as is done in *external regret*. External regret, also called the *best expert* problem, compares the online algorithm's cost to the best of N actions in retrospect [19, 15, 24, 17, 18, 6]. This implies that the simple alternative policy performs the same action in all time steps, which indeed is quite simple. Nonetheless, one important application of external regret to online algorithm analysis is a general methodology of developing online algorithms whose performance matches that of an optimal static offline algorithm by modeling the possible static solutions as different actions.

The second category are those alternative policies that consider the online sequence of actions and suggest a simple modification to it, such as "every time you bought IBM, you should have bought Microsoft instead." This notion is captured by *internal regret* [13]. Specifically, internal regret allows one to modify the online action sequence by changing every occurrence of a given action i by an alternative action j. Specific low internal regret algorithms were derived in [20, 12, 13, 14, 7], where the use of the approachability theorem [4] has played an important role in some of the algorithms [20, 12, 14].

One of the main contributions of our work is to show a simple online way to efficiently convert any external regret algorithm into an *internal* regret algorithm. Our guarantee is somewhat stronger than internal regret and we call it *swap regret*, which allows one to *simultaneously* swap multiple pairs of actions. (If there are N actions total, then swap-regret is bounded by N times the internal regret.) Using known results for external regret we can derive a swap regret bound of $O(N\sqrt{T\log N} + N\log N)$, and with additional optimization we are able to reduce this regret bound to $O(\sqrt{NT\log N} + N\log N\log T)$. We also show an $\Omega(\sqrt{NT})$ lower bound for the case of randomized online algorithms against an adaptive adversary.

The importance of internal regret is due to its tight connection to correlated equilibria [3]. For a general-sum game of any finite number of players, a distribution Q over the joint action space is a correlated equilibrium if every player would have zero internal regret when playing it. In a repeated game scenario, if each player uses an action selection algorithm whose internal regret is sublinear in T, then the empirical distribution of the players actions converges to a correlated equilibrium (see, e.g. [20]). In fact, we point out that the deviation from a correlated equilibrium is bounded exactly by the average swap regret of the players.

We also extend our internal regret results to the *partial information model*, also called the *adversarial multi-armed bandit* (MAB) problem [2]. In this model,

the online algorithm only gets to observe the loss of the action actually selected, and does not see the losses of the actions not chosen. For example, if
you are driving in rush-hour traffic and need to select which of several routes to
take, you only observe the travel time on the route actually taken. If we view
this as an online problem, each day selecting which route to take on that day,
then this fits the MAB setting. Furthermore, the route-choosing problem can
be viewed as a general-sum game: your travel time depends on the choices of
the other drivers as well. Thus, if *every* driver uses a low internal-regret algorithm, then traffic patterns will converge to a correlated equilibrium. For the
MAB problem, our combining algorithm requires additional assumptions on the
base external-regret MAB algorithm: a smoothness in behavior when the actions
played are taken from a somewhat different distribution than the one proposed
by the algorithm. Luckily, these conditions are satisfied by existing external-
regret MAB algorithms such as that of Auer et al. [2]. For the multi-armed
bandit setting, we derive an $O(\sqrt{N^3 T \log N} + N^2 \log N)$ swap-regret bound.
Thus, after $T = O(\frac{1}{\epsilon^2} N^3 \log N)$ rounds, the empirical distribution on the history is an ϵ-correlated equilibrium. (The work of [21] also gives a multi-armed
bandit algorithm whose internal regret is sublinear in T, but does not derive
explicit bounds.)

One can also envision broader classes of regret. Lehrer [23] defines a notion of
wide range regret that allows for arbitrary action-modification rules, which might
depend on history, and also Boolean time selection functions (which determine
which subset of times is relevant). Using the approachability theorem [4], he
shows a scheme that in the limit achieves no regret (regret is sublinear in T).
While [23] derives the regret bounds in the limit, we derive finite-time regret
bounds for this setting. We show that for any family of N actions, M time
selection functions and K modification rules, the maximum regret with respect to
any selection function and modification rule is bounded by $O(\sqrt{TN \log(MK)} + N \log(MK))$. Our model also handles the case where the time selection functions
are not Boolean, but rather reals in $[0, 1]$.

This latter result can be viewed as a generalization of the *sleeping experts*
setting of [5, 16]. In the sleeping experts problem, we again have a set of experts,
but on any given time step, each expert may be awake (making a prediction)
or asleep (not predicting). This is a natural model for combining a collection
of if-then rules that only make predictions when the "if" portion of the rule is
satisfied, and this setting has had application in domains ranging from man-
aging a calendar [5] to text-categorization [11] to learning how to formulate
web search-engine queries [10]. By converting each such sleeping-expert into a
pair ⟨expert, time-selection function⟩, we achieve the desired guarantee that for
each sleeping-expert, our loss *during the time that expert was awake* is not much
more than its loss in that period. Moreover, by using non-Boolean time-selection
functions, we can naturally handle prediction rules that have varying degrees
of confidence in their predictions and achieve a confidence-weighted notion of
regret.

We also study the case of deterministic Boolean prediction in the setting of time selection functions. We derive a deterministic online algorithm whose number of weighted errors, with respect to any time selection function from our class of M selection functions is at most $3OPT + 1 + 2\log M$, where OPT is the best constant prediction for that time selection function. (For lack of space, the proof is omitted in this extended abstract.)

Recent Related Work. It was brought to our attention [25] that comparable results can be achieved based on independent work appearing in the journal version of [26]: specifically, the results regarding the relation between external and internal regret [27] and the multi-armed bandit setting [8]. In comparison to [27], we are able to achieve a better swap regret guarantee in polynomial time (a straightforward application of [27] to swap regret would require time-complexity $\Omega(N^N)$; alternatively, they can achieve a good internal-regret bound in polynomial time, but then their swap regret bound becomes worse by a factor of $\sqrt{N}$). On the other hand, work of [27] is applicable to a wider range of loss functions, which also capture scenarios arising in portfolio selection. We should stress that the above techniques are very different from the techniques proposed in our work.

2   Model and Preliminaries

We assume an adversarial online model where there are N available actions $\{1, \ldots, N\}$. At each time step t, an online algorithm H selects a distribution p^t over the N actions. After that, the adversary selects a loss vector $\ell^t \in [0,1]^N$, where $\ell_i^t \in [0,1]$ is the loss of the i-th action at time t. In the *full information model*, the online algorithm receives the loss vector ℓ^t and experiences a loss $\ell_H^t = \sum_{i=1}^N p_i^t \ell_i^t$. In the *partial information model*, the online algorithms receives $(\ell_{k^t}^t, k^t)$, where k^t is distributed according to p^t, and $\ell_H^t = \ell_{k^t}^t$ is its loss. The loss of the i-th action during the first T time steps is $L_i^T = \sum_{t=1}^T \ell_i^t$, and the loss of H is $L_H^T = \sum_{t=1}^T \ell_H^t$. The aim for the external regret setting is to design an online algorithm that will be able to approach the best action, namely, to have a loss close to $L_{min}^T = \min_i L_i^T$. Formally we would like to minimize the external regret $R = L_H^T - L_{min}^T$.

We introduce a notion of a *time selection* function. A time selection function I is a function over the time steps mapping each time step to $[0,1]$. That is, $I : \{1, \ldots, T\} \to [0,1]$. The loss of action j using time-selector I is $L_{j,I}^T = \sum_t I(t)\ell_j^t$. Similarly we define $L_{H,I}$, the loss of the online algorithm H with respect to time selection function I, as $L_{H,I}^T = \sum_t I(t)\ell_H^t$, where ℓ_H^t is the loss of H at time t. This notion of experts with time selection is very similar to the notion of "sleeping experts" studied in [16]. Specifically, for each action j and time selection function I, one can view the pair (j, I) as an expert that is "awake" when $I(t) = 1$ and "asleep" when $I(t) = 0$ (and perhaps "partially awake" when $I(t) \in (0,1)$).

We also consider modification rules that modify the actions selected by the online algorithm, producing an alternative strategy we will want to compete against. A *modification rule* F has as input the history and an action choice and outputs a (possibly different) action. (We denote by F^t the function F at time t, including any dependency on the history.) Given a sequence of probability distributions p^t used by an online algorithm H, and a modification rule F, we define a new sequence of probability distributions $f^t = F^t(p^t)$, where $f_i^t = \sum_{j:F^t(j)=i} p_j^t$. The loss of the modified sequence is $L_{H,F} = \sum_t \sum_i f_i^t \ell_i^t$. Similarly, given a time selection function I and a modification rule F we define $L_{H,I,F} = \sum_t \sum_i I(t) f_i^t \ell_i^t$.

In our setting we assume a finite class of N actions, $\{1, \ldots, N\}$, a finite set $\mathcal{F}$ of K modification rules, and a finite set $\mathcal{I}$ of M time selection function. Given a sequence of loss vectors, the regret of an online algorithm H with respect to the N actions, the K modification rules, and the M time selection functions, is

$$R_H^{\mathcal{I},\mathcal{F}} = \max_{I \in \mathcal{I}} \max_{F \in \mathcal{F}} \{L_{H,I} - L_{H,I,F}\}.$$

Note that the external regret setting is equivalent to having a single time-selection function ($I(t) = 1$ for all t) and a set $\mathcal{F}^{ex}$ of N modification rules F_i, where F_i always outputs action i. For internal regret, the set $\mathcal{F}^{in}$ consists of $N(N-1)$ modification rules $F_{i,j}$, where $F_{i,j}(i) = j$ and $F_{i,j}(i') = i'$ for $i' \neq i$. That is, the internal regret of H is

$$\max_{F \in \mathcal{F}^{in}} \{L_H - L_{H,F}\} = \max_{i,j} \sum_t p_i^t (\ell_i^t - \ell_j^t).$$

We define a slightly extended class of internal regret which we call *swap regret*. This case has $\mathcal{F}^{sw}$ include all N^N functions $F : \{1, \ldots, N\} \to \{1, \ldots, N\}$, where the function F swaps the current online action i with $F(i)$ (which can be the same or a different action).

A few simple relationships between the different types of regrets: since $\mathcal{F}^{ex} \subseteq \mathcal{F}^{sw}$ and $\mathcal{F}^{in} \subseteq \mathcal{F}^{sw}$, both external and internal regret are upper-bounded by swap-regret. Also, swap-regret is at most N times larger than internal regret. On the other hand, even with $N = 3$, there are simple examples which separate internal and external regret [26].

2.1   Correlated Equilibria and Swap Regret

We briefly sketch the relationship between correlated equilibria [3] and swap regret.

Definition 1. *A general-sum game $\langle M, (A_i), (s_i) \rangle$ has a finite set M of m players. Player i has a set A_i of N actions and a loss function $s_i : A_i \times (\times_{j \neq i} A_j) \to [0, 1]$ that maps the action of player i and the actions of the other players to a real number. (We have scaled losses to $[0, 1]$)*

The aim of each player is to minimize its loss. A correlated equilibrium [3] is a distribution P over the joint action space with the following property. Imagine a correlating device draws a vector of actions a using distribution P over $\times A_i$, and gives player i the action a_i from a. (Player i is not given any other information regarding a.) The probability distribution P is a correlated equilibria if for each player it is its best response to play the suggested action (provided that the other players do not deviate).

We now define an ϵ-correlated equilibrium.

Definition 2. *A joint probability distribution P over $\times A_i$ is an ϵ-correlated equilibria if for every player j and for any function $F : A_j \rightarrow A_j$, we have $E_{a\sim P}[s_j(a_j, a^{-j})] \leq E_{a\sim P}[s_j(F(a_j), a^{-j})] + \epsilon$, where a^{-j} denotes the joint actions of the other players.*

The following theorem relates the empirical distribution of the actions performed by each player, their swap regret and the distance from a correlated equilibrium (see also, [12, 13, 20]).

Theorem 1. *Let $G =< M, (A_i), (s_i) >$ be a game and assume that for T time steps each player follows a strategy that has swap regret of at most $R(T, N)$. The empirical distribution Q of the joint actions played by the players is an $(R(T, N)/T)$-correlated equilibrium, and the loss of each player equals, by definition, its expected loss on Q.*

The above states that the payoff of each player is its payoff in some approximate correlated equilibrium. In addition, it relates the swap regret to the distance from a correlated equilibria. Note that if the average swap regret vanishes then the procedure converges, in the limit, to a correlated equilibria (see [20, 12, 14]).

3   Generic Reduction from External to Swap Regret

We now give a black-box reduction showing how any algorithm A achieving good external regret can be used as a subroutine to achieve good swap regret as well. The high-level idea is as follows. We will instantiate N copies of the external-regret algorithm. At each time step, these algorithms will each give us a probability vector, which we will combine in a particular way to produce our own probability vector p. When we receive a loss vector ℓ, we will partition it among the N algorithms, giving algorithm A_i a fraction p_i (p_i is our probability mass on action i), so that A_i's belief about the loss of action j is $\sum_t p_i^t \ell_j^t$, and matches the cost we would incur putting i's probability mass on j. In the proof, algorithm A_i will in some sense be responsible for ensuring low regret of the $i \rightarrow j$ variety. The key to making this work is that we will be able to define the p's so that the sum of the losses of the algorithms A_i on their own loss vectors matches our overall true loss.

To be specific, let us formalize what we mean by an external regret algorithm.

Definition 3. *An algorithm A has external regret $R(L_{min}, T, N)$ if for any sequence of T losses ℓ^t such that some action has total loss at most L_{min}, for any action $j \in \{1, \ldots, N\}$ we have*

$$L_A^T = \sum_{t=1}^{T} \ell_A^t \le \sum_{t=1}^{T} \ell_j^t + R(L_{min}, T, N) = L_j^T + R(L_{min}, T, N)$$

We assume we have N algorithms A_i (which could all be identical or different) such that A_i has external regret $R_i(L_{min}, T, N)$. We combine the N algorithms as follows. At each time step t, each algorithm A_i outputs a distribution q_i^t, where $q_{i,j}^t$ is the fraction it assigns action j. We compute a vector p such that $p_j^t = \sum_i p_i^t q_{i,j}^t$. That is, $p = pQ$, where p is the row-vector of our probabilities and Q is the matrix of $q_{i,j}$. (We can view p as a stationary distribution of the Markov Process defined by Q, and it is well known such a p exists and is efficiently computable.) For intuition into this choice of p, notice that it implies we can consider action selection in two equivalent ways. The first is simply using the distribution p to select action j with probability p_j. The second is to select algorithm A_i with probability p_i and then to use algorithm A_i to select the action (which produces distribution pQ).

When the adversary returns ℓ^t, we return to each A_i the loss vector $p_i \ell^t$. So, algorithm A_i experiences loss $(p_i^t \ell^t) \cdot q_i^t = p_i^t (q_i^t \cdot \ell^t)$.

Now we consider the guarantee that we have for algorithm A_i, namely, for any action j,

$$\sum_{t=1}^{T} p_i^t (q_i^t \cdot \ell^t) \le \sum_{t=1}^{T} p_i^t \ell_j^t + R_i(L_{min}, T, N) \qquad (1)$$

If we sum the losses of the N algorithms at any time t, we get $\sum_i p_i^t (q_i^t \cdot \ell^t) = p^t Q^t \ell^t$, where p^t is the row-vector of our probabilities, Q^t is the matrix of $q_{i,j}^t$, and ℓ^t is viewed as a column-vector. By design of p^t, we have $p^t Q^t = p^t$. So, the sum of the perceived losses of the N algorithms is equal to our actual loss $p^t \ell^t$.

Therefore, summing equation (1) over all N algorithms, the left-hand-side sums to L_H^T and so we have that for any function $F : \{1, \ldots, N\} \to \{1, \ldots, N\}$,

$$L_H^T \le \sum_{i=1}^{N} \sum_{t=1}^{T} p_i^t \ell_{F(i)}^t + \sum_{i=1}^{N} R_i(L_{min}, T, N).$$

We have therefore proven the following theorem.

Theorem 2. *For any N algorithms A_i with regret R_i, for every function $F : \{1, \ldots, N\} \to \{1, \ldots, N\}$, the above algorithm satisfies*

$$L_H \le L_{H,F} + \sum_{i=1}^{N} R_i(L_{min}, T, N),$$

i.e., the swap-regret of H is at most $\sum_{i=1}^{N} R_i(L_{min}, T, N)$.

A typical *optimized experts algorithm* [24, 17, 2, 6] will have $R(L_{min}, T, N) = O(\sqrt{L_{min} \log N} + \log N)$. (Alternatively, Corollary 4 can be also used to deduce the above bound.) We can immediately derive the following corollary.

Corollary 1. *Using an optimized experts algorithm as the A_i, for every function $F : \{1, \ldots, N\} \to \{1, \ldots, N\}$, we have that*

$$L_H \leq L_{H,F} + O(N\sqrt{T \log N} + N \log N)$$

We can perform a slightly more refined analysis of the bound by having L^i_{min} be the minimum loss for an action in A_i. Since $\sum_{i=1}^N \sqrt{L^i_{min}} \leq \sum_{i=1}^N L^i_{min}$, and this is bounded by T since we scaled the losses given to algorithm A_i at time t by p^t_i, this implies the worst case regret is $O(\sqrt{TN \log N} + N \log N)$. The only problem is that algorithm A_i needs to "know" the value of L^i_{min} to set its internal parameters correctly. One way to avoid this is to use an adaptive method [1]. We can also avoid this problem using the standard doubling approach of starting with $L_{min} = 1$ and each time our guess is violated, we double the bound and restart the online algorithm. The external regret of such a resetting optimized experts algorithm would be

$$\sum_{j=1}^{\log L_{min}} O(\sqrt{2^j \log N} + \log N) = O(\sqrt{L_{min} \log N} + \log L_{min} \log N).$$

Going back to our case of N multiple online algorithms A_i, we derive the following,

Corollary 2. *Using resetting optimized experts algorithms as the A_i, for every function $F : \{1, \ldots, N\} \to \{1, \ldots, N\}$, we have that*

$$L_H \leq L_{H,F} + O(\sqrt{TN \log N} + N \log N \log T)$$

One strength of the above general reduction is it ability to accommodate new regret minimization algorithms. For example, using the algorithm of [9] one can get a more refined regret bound, which depends on the second moment.

3.1   Lower Bounds for Swap Regret

Notice that while good algorithms for the experts problem achieve external regret roughly $O(\sqrt{T \log N})$, our swap-regret bounds are roughly $O(\sqrt{TN \log N})$. Or, to put it another way, for external regret one can achieve regret ϵT by time $T = O(\epsilon^{-2} \log N)$, whereas we need $T = O(\epsilon^{-2} N \log N)$ to achieve swap-regret ϵT (or an ϵ-correlated equilibrium). A natural question is whether this is best possible. We give here a partial answer.

First, one tricky issue is that for a given stochastic adversary, the optimal policy for minimizing loss may *not* be the optimal policy for minimizing swap-regret. For example, consider a process in which losses are generated by an almost unbiased coin, with slight biases so that the optimal policy for minimizing loss uses each action T/N times. Because of the variance of the coin flips, in retrospect, most actions can be swapped with an expected gain of $\Omega(\sqrt{(T \log N)/N})$ each, giving a total swap-regret of $\Omega(\sqrt{TN \log N})$ for this policy. However, a policy that just picks a single fixed action would have swap-regret only $O(\sqrt{T \log N})$ even though its expected loss is higher.

We show a lower bound of $\Omega(\sqrt{TN})$ on swap regret, but in a different model. Specifically, we have defined swap regret with respect to the *distribution* p^t produced by the player, rather that the actual action a_t selected from that distribution. In the case that the adversary is oblivious (does not depend on the player's action selection) then the two models have the same expected regret. However we will consider a *dynamic* adversary, whose choices may depend on the player's action selection in previous rounds. In this setting (dynamic adversary *and* regret defined with respect to the action selected from p^t rather than p^t itself) we derive the following theorem.

Theorem 3. *There exists a dynamic adversary such that for any randomized online algorithm A, the expected swap regret of A is $(1-\lambda)\sqrt{TN}/128$, for $T \geq N$ and $\lambda = NTe^{-cN}$ for some constant $c > 0$.*

Proof. (sketch) The adversary behaves as follows. At each time step t, for any action that has been played less than $8T/N$ times by A, the adversary flips a fair coin to set its loss to 0 or 1 (call these *random-loss* actions). However, once an action has been played $8T/N$ times by A, then its loss is 1 from then on (call these *1-loss* actions). Note that at most $N/8$ actions ever become 1-loss actions.

Now, if A in expectation plays 1-loss actions more than $1/4$ of the time, then A will incur such a high loss that it will even have a large *external* regret. Specifically, A will have an expected loss at least $5T/8$, whereas with high probability there will exist some action of total loss at most $T/2$, and this gap exceeds the bounds of the theorem. On the other hand, if A plays random-loss actions at least $3/4$ of the time, then there must be a large number (at least $N/16$) actions that are played at least $T/(4N)$ times by A. However, in the subset of T_i time-steps that A plays some action i, there is a high probability that some other action has loss only $\frac{1}{2}T_i - \frac{1}{4}\sqrt{T_i}$, even if A were able to choose which actions to make 1-loss actions (and thereby remove from consideration) after the fact. On the other hand, A's expected loss is $\frac{1}{2}T_i$. Thus, A has expected swap-regret at least $(N/16)(\frac{1}{4}\sqrt{T/(4N)}) = \sqrt{TN}/128$. The $(1 - \lambda)$ factor is to guarantee that the realized values are close to their expected value, with high probability.   □

4   Reducing External to Swap Regret in the Partial Information Model

In the full information setting the learner gets, at the end of each time step, full information on the costs of all the actions. In the partial information (bandit) model, the learner gets information only about the action that was selected. In some applications this is a more plausible model regarding the information the learner can observe.

The reduction in the partial information model is similar to the one of the full information model, but with a few additional complications. We are given N

partial information algorithms A_i. At each time step t, each algorithm A_i gives a distribution q_i^t. Our master online algorithm combines them to some distribution p^t which it uses. Given p^t it receives a feedback, but now this includes information only regarding one action, i.e., it receives $(\ell_{k^t}^t, k^t)$, where k^t is distributed according to p^t. We take this feedback and distribute to each algorithm A_i a feedback (b_i^t, k^t), such that $\sum_i b_i^t = \ell_{k^t}^t$. The main technical difficulty is that now the action selected, k^t, is distributed according to p^t and not q_i^t. (For example, it might be that A_i has $q_{i,j}^t = 0$ but it receives a feedback about action j. From A_i's point of view this is impossible! Or, more generally, A_i might start noticing it seems to have a very bad random-number generator.) For this reason, for the reduction to work we need to make a stronger assumption about the guarantees of the algorithms A_i, which luckily is implicit in the algorithms of [2]. Our main result is summarized in the following theorem.

Theorem 4. *Given a multi-arm bandit algorithm satisfying Lemma 1 below (such as the algorithm of [2]), it can be converted to a master online algorithm Int_MAB, such that for every function $F : \{1, \ldots, N\} \to \{1, \ldots, N\}$, we have that*

$$E_{p^t}[L_{Int\_MAB}] \leq E_{p^t}[L_{Int\_MAB,F}] + N \cdot R^{MAB}(T, T, N)$$

where $R^{MAB}(C, T, N) = O(\sqrt{CN \log N} + N \log N)$.

Proof. Since results of [2] are stated in terms of maximizing gain rather then minimizing loss we will switch to this notation, and later derive the loss minimization results.

At each time step t the multi-arm bandit algorithm A_i gives a *selection distribution* q_i^t over actions, and given all the selection distributions we compute an *action distribution* p^t. We would like to keep two sets of gains, one is the *real gain*, denoted by b_i^t, and the other is the gain that the MAB algorithm A_i observes $g_{A_i}^t$. Given the action distribution p^t the adversary selects a vector of real gains b_i^t. Our MAB algorithm Int_MAB receives a single feedback $(b_{k^t}^t, k^t)$ where k^t is a random variable that with probability p_j^t equals j. Given b^t it returns to each A_i the pair $(g_{A_i}^t, k^t)$, where the observed gain $g_{A_i}^t$ is based on b^t, p^t and q_i^t. Note that k^t is distributed according to p^t, which may not equal q_i^t: it is for this reason we need to use an MAB algorithm that satisfies Lemma 1.

In order to specify our MAB algorithm, Int_MAB, we need to specify how it selects the action distribution p^t and the observed gains $g_{A_i}^t$. At each time step t, each algorithm A_i outputs a selection distribution q_i^t, where $q_{i,j}^t$ is the probability it assigns action j. We compute an action distribution p^t such that $p_j^t = \sum_i p_i^t q_{i,j}^t$. That is, $p = pQ$, where p is the row-vector of our probabilities and Q is the matrix of $q_{i,j}$. Given p^t the adversary returns a real gain $(b_{k^t}^t, k^t)$, namely, the real gain is of our algorithm $b_{k^t}^t$. We return to each algorithm A_i an observed gain of $g_{A_i}^t = p_i^t b_{k^t}^t q_{i,k^t}/p_{k^t}^t$. (In general, define $g_{i,j}^t = p_i^t b_j^t q_{i,j}^t/p_j^t$, where $b_j^t = 0$ if $j \neq k^t$.) First, we will show that $\sum_{i=1}^N g_{A_i}^t = b_{k^t}^t$ and that $g_{A_i}^t \in [0,1]$. From the property of the distribution p^t we have that,

$$\sum_{i=1}^{N} g_{A_i}^t = \sum_{i=1}^{N} \frac{p_i^t b_{k^t}^t q_{i,k^t}}{p_{k^t}^t} = \frac{p_{k^t}^t b_{k^t}^t}{p_{k^t}^t} = b_{k^t}^t.$$

This shows that we distribute our real gain between the algorithms A_i, namely that the sum of the observed gains equals the real gain. In addition, it bounds the observed gain that each algorithm A_i receives. Namely, $0 \le g_{A_i}^t \le b_{k^t}^t \le 1$.

In order to describe the guarantee that each external regret multi-arm bandit algorithm A_i has, for our application, we need the following additional definition. At time t let $X_{i,j}^t$ be a random variable such that $X_{i,j}^t = g_{i,j}^t/q_{i,j}^t = p_i^t b_j^t/p_j^t$ if $j = k^t$ and $X_{i,j}^t = 0$ otherwise. The expectation of $X_{i,j}^t$ is

$$E_{k^t \sim p^t}[X_{i,j}^t] = p_j^t \frac{p_i^t b_j^t}{p_j^t} = p_i^t b_j^t$$

Lemma 1 ([2]). *There exists a multi-arm bandit algorithm, A_i, such that for any sequence of observed gains $g_{i,j}^t \in [0,1]$, for any sequence of selected actions k^t, and any action r and parameter $\gamma \in (0,1]$, the expected observed gains is bounded by,*

$$G_{A_i,g^t} \equiv \sum_{t=1}^{T} g_{A_i}^t \equiv \sum_{t=1}^{T} g_{k^t}^t \ge (1-\gamma) \sum_{t=1}^{T} X_{i,r}^t - \frac{N \ln N}{\gamma} - \frac{\gamma}{N} \sum_{t=1}^{T} \sum_{j=1}^{N} X_{i,j}^t \quad (2)$$

We now use Lemma 1. Note, in Auer et al. [2] the action distribution is identical to the selection distribution, i.e. $p^t = q^t$, and the observed and real gain are identical, i.e., $g^t = b^t$. Auer et al. [2] derive the external regret bound by taking the expectation with respect to the action distribution (which is identical to the selection distribution). In our case we will like to separate the real gain from the observed gain.

Let the total observed gain of algorithm A_i be $G_{A_i} = \sum_{t=1}^{T} g_{A_i}^t = \sum_{t=1}^{T} g_{i,k^t}^t$. Since we distribute our gain between the A_i, i.e., $\sum_{i=1}^{N} g_{A_i}^t = b_{Int\_MAB}^t$, we have that $B_{Int\_MAB} = \sum_{t=1}^{T} b_{Int\_MAB}^t = \sum_{i=1}^{N} G_{A_i}$. Since $g_{i,j}^t \in [0,1]$, by Lemma 1, this implies that for any action r we have

$$E_{p^t}[G_{A_i}] \ge (1-\gamma) \sum_{t=1}^{T} E_{p^t}[X_{i,r}^t] - \frac{N \ln N}{\gamma} - \frac{\gamma}{N} \sum_{t=1}^{T} \sum_{j=1}^{N} E_{p^t}[X_{i,j}^t]$$

$$= (1-\gamma) \sum_{t=1}^{T} p_i^t b_r^t - \frac{N \ln N}{\gamma} - \frac{\gamma}{N} \sum_{t=1}^{T} \sum_{j=1}^{N} p_i^t b_j^t$$

$$\ge (1-\gamma) B_{i,r} - \frac{N \ln N}{\gamma} - \frac{\gamma}{N} \sum_{j=1}^{N} B_{i,j}$$

$$\ge B_{i,r} - O(\sqrt{B_{max} N \ln N} + N \ln N) = B_{i,r} - R^{MAB}(B_{max}, N, T)$$

where $B_{i,r} = \sum_{t=1}^{T} p_i^t b_r^t$, $B_{max} = \max_{i,j} B_{i,j}$ and $\gamma = \min\{\sqrt{(N \ln N)/B_{max}}, 1\}$.

Note that the expected benefit of our algorithm is $E[B_{Int\_MAB,b^t}] = \sum_{i=1}^N$ $B_{i,i}$. For the regret we like to compare the gain of $B_{i,i}$ to that of $B_{i,r}$, which is the change in our benefit if each time we play action r rather than i. For swap regret, we compare our expected benefit to that of $\sum_{i=}^N B_{i,F(i)}$, for some function F. Therefore, we have that for any function $F : \{1, \ldots, N\} \to \{1, \ldots, N\}$,

$$E_{p^t}[B_{Int\_MAB}^T] = \sum_{i=1}^N E_{p^t}[G_{A_i}] \geq \sum_{i=1}^N B_{i,F(i)} - N \cdot R^{MAB}(B_{max}, T, N).$$

For the case of losses let $b_j^t = 1 - c_j^t$. Then $B_{MAB} = T - L_{MAB}$ and we derive Theorem 4.   □

5   External Regret with Time-Selection Functions

We now present a simple online algorithm that achieves a good external regret bound in the presence of time selection functions, generalizing the *sleeping experts* setting. Specifically, our goal is for each action a, and each time-selection function I, that our total loss during the time-steps selected by I is not much more than the loss of a during those time steps (or more generally, the losses weighted by I when $I(t) \in [0, 1]$). The idea of the algorithm is as follows. Let $R_{a,I}$ be the regret of our algorithm with respect to action a and time selection function I. That is, $R_{a,I} = \sum_t I(t)(\ell_H^t - \ell_a^t)$. Let $\tilde{R}_{a,I}$ be a less-strict notion of regret in which we multiply our loss by some $\beta < 1$, that is, $\tilde{R}_{a,I} = \sum_t I(t)(\beta \ell_H^t - \ell_a^t)$. What we will do is give to each action a and time selection function I a weight $w_{a,I}$ that is exponential in $\tilde{R}_{a,I}$. We will prove that the sum of our weights never increases, and thereby be able to easily conclude that none of the $\tilde{R}_{a,I}$ can be too large.

Specifically, for each of the N actions and the M time selection functions we maintain a weight $w_{a,I}^t$. We update these weights using the rule $w_{a,I}^{t+1} = w_{a,I}^t \beta^{I(t)(\ell_a^t - \beta \ell_H^t)}$, where ℓ_H^t is the loss of our online algorithm H at time t. (Initially, $w_{a,I}^0 = 1$.) Equivalently, $w_{a,I}^t = \beta^{-\tilde{R}_{a,I}^t}$, where $\tilde{R}_{a,I}^t$ is the "less-strict" regret mentioned above up to time t.

At time t we define $w_a^t = \sum_I I(t) w_{a,I}^t$, $W^t = \sum_a w_a^t$ and $p_a^t = w_a^t / W^t$. Our distribution over actions at time t is p^t.

Claim. At any time t we have $0 \leq \sum_{a,I} w_{a,I}^t \leq NM$.

Proof. Initially, at time $t = 0$, the claim clearly holds. Observe that at time t we have the following identity,

$$W^t \ell_H^t = W^t \sum_a p_a^t \ell_a^t = \sum_a w_a^t \ell_a^t = \sum_a \sum_I I(t) w_{a,I}^t \ell_a^t. \tag{3}$$

For the inductive step we show that the sum of the weights can only decrease. Note that for any $\beta \in [0, 1]$, for $x \in [0, 1]$ we have $\beta^x \leq 1 - (1 - \beta)x$, and for $x \in [-1, 0]$ we have $\beta^x \leq 1 + (1 - \beta)|x|/\beta$.

$$\sum_a \sum_I w_{a,I}^{t+1} = \sum_a \sum_I w_{a,I}^t \beta^{I(t)(\ell_a^t - \beta \ell_H^t)}$$

$$\leq \sum_a \sum_I w_{a,I}^t (1 - (1-\beta)I(t)\ell_a^t)(1 + (1-\beta)I(t)\ell_H^t)$$

$$\leq (\sum_a \sum_I w_{a,I}^t) - (1-\beta)(\sum_{a,I} w_{a,I}^t \ell_a^t) + (1-\beta)(\sum_{a,I} I(t)w_{a,I}^t \ell_H^t)$$

$$= (\sum_a \sum_I w_{a,I}^t) - (1-\beta)W^t \ell_H^t + (1-\beta)W^t \ell_H^t \quad \text{(using eqn. (3))}$$

$$= (\sum_a \sum_I w_{a,I}^t). \qquad \square$$

Corollary 3. *For every action a and time selection I we have*

$$w_{a,I}^t = \beta^{L_{a,I} - \beta L_{H,I}} \leq MN,$$

where $L_{H,I} = \sum_t I(t)\ell_H^t$ is the loss of the online algorithm with respect to time-selection function I.

A simple algebraic manipulation of the above implies the following theorem

Theorem 5. *For every action a and every time selection function $I \in \mathcal{I}$ we have*

$$L_{H,I} \leq \frac{L_{a,I} + (\log NM)/\log(1/\beta)}{\beta}$$

We can optimize for β in advance, or do it dynamically using [1], establishing:

Corollary 4. *For every action a and every time selection function $I \in \mathcal{I}$ we have*

$$L_{H,I} \leq L_{a,I} + O(\sqrt{L_{min} \log NM} + \log MN),$$

where $L_{min} = \max_I \min_a \{L_{a,I}\}$.

6   Arbitrary Time Selection and Modification Rules

In this section we combine the techniques from Sections 3 and 5 to derive a regret bound for the general case where we assume that there is a finite set $\mathcal{I}$ of M time selection functions, and a finite set $\mathcal{F}$ of K modification rules. Our goal is to design an algorithm such that for any time selection function $I \in \mathcal{I}$ and any $F \in \mathcal{F}$, $L_{H,I}$ is not too much larger than $L_{H,I,F}$.

We maintain at time t, a weight $w_{j,I,F}^t$ per action j, time selection I and modification rule F. Initially $w_{j,I,F}^0 = 1$. We set

$$w_{j,I,F}^{t+1} = w_{j,I,F}^t \beta^{p_j^t I(t)(\ell_{F(j)}^t - \beta \ell_{H,j}^t)},$$

where $W_{j,F}^t = \sum_I I(t)w_{j,I,F}^t$, $W_j^t = \sum_F W_{j,F}^t$, and $\ell_{H,j}^t = \sum_F W_{j,F}^t \ell_{F(j)}^t / W_j^t$.

We use the weights to define a distribution p^t over actions as follows. We select a distribution p^t such that

$$p_i^t = \sum_{j=1}^{N} p_j^t \sum_{F:F(j)=i} W_{j,F}^t / W_j^t.$$ (4)

I.e., p is the stationary distribution of the associated Markov chain. Notice that the definition of p implies that the loss of H at time t can either be viewed as $\sum_i p_i^t \ell_i^t$ or as $\sum_j p_j^t \sum_F (W_{j,F}^t/W_j^t)\ell_{F(j)}^t = \sum_j p_j^t \ell_{H,j}^t$. The following Claim, whose proof is omitted, bounds the magnitude of the weights.

Claim. For every action j, at any time t we have $0 \leq \sum_{I,F} w_{j,I,F}^t \leq MK$

The following theorem (proof omitted) derives the general regret bound.

Theorem 6. *For every time selection $I \in \mathcal{I}$ and modification rule $F \in \mathcal{F}$, we have that*

$$L_{H,I} \leq L_{H,I,F} + O(\sqrt{TN \log MK} + N \log MK)$$

7   Conclusion and Open Problems

In this paper we give general reductions by which algorithms achieving good external regret can be converted to algorithms with good internal (or swap) regret, and in addition develop algorithms for a generalization of the sleeping experts scenario including both real-valued time-selection functions and a finite set of modification rules.

A key open problem left by this work is whether it is possible to achieve swap-regret that has a logarithmic or even sublinear dependence on N. Specifically, for *external* regret, existing algorithms achieve regret ϵT in time $T = O(\frac{1}{\epsilon^2} \log N)$, but our algorithms for swap-regret achieve regret ϵT only by time $T = O(\frac{1}{\epsilon^2} N \log N)$. We have shown that sublinear dependence is not possible in against an adaptive adversary with swap-regret defined with respect to the actions actually chosen from the algorithm's distribution, but we do not know whether there is a comparable lower bound in the distributional setting (where swap-regret is defined with respect to the distributions p^t themselves), which is the model we used for all the algorithms in this work. In particular, an algorithm with lower dependence on N would imply a more efficient (in terms of number of rounds) procedure for achieving an approximate correlated equilibrium.

References

1. Peter Auer, Nicolò Cesa-Bianchi, and Claudio Gentile. Adaptive and self-confident on-line learning algorithms. *JCSS*, 64(1):48–75, 2002. A preliminary version has appeared in Proc. 13th Ann. Conf. Computational Learning Theory.

2. Peter Auer, Nicolò Cesa-Bianchi, Yoav Freund, and Robert E. Schapire. The nonstochastic multiarmed bandit problem. *SIAM Journal on Computing*, 32(1):48–77, 2002.

3. R. J. Aumann. Subjectivity and correlation in randomized strategies. *Journal of Mathematical Economics*, 1:67–96, 1974.

4. D. Blackwell. An analog of the mimimax theorem for vector payoffs. *Pacific Journal of Mathematics*, 6:1–8, 1956.

5. A. Blum. Empirical support for winnow and weighted-majority based algorithms: results on a calendar scheduling domain. *Machine Learning*, 26:5–23, 1997.

6. Nicolò Cesa-Bianchi, Yoav Freund, David P. Helmbold, David Haussler, Robert E. Schapire, and Manfred K. Warmuth. How to use expert advice. In *STOC*, pages 382–391, 1993. Also, *Journal of the Association for Computing Machinery*, 44(3): 427-485 (1997).

7. Nicolò Cesa-Bianchi and Gábor Lugosi. Potential-based algorithms in on-line prediction and game theory. *Machine Learning*, 51(3):239–261, 2003.

8. Nicolò Cesa-Bianchi, Gábor Lugosi, and Gilles Stoltz. Regret minimization under partial monitoring. unpublished manuscript, 2004.

9. Nicolò Cesa-Bianchi, Yishay Mansour, and Gilles Stoltz. Improved second-order bounds for prediction with expert advice. In *COLT*, 2005.

10. W. Cohen and Y. Singer. Learning to query the web. In *AAAI Workshop on Internet-Based Information Systems*, 1996.

11. W. Cohen and Y. Singer. Context-sensitive learning methods for text categorization. *ACM Transactions on Information Systems*, 17(2):141–173, 1999.

12. D. Foster and R. Vohra. Calibrated learning and correlated equilibrium. *Games and Economic Behavior*, 21:40–55, 1997.

13. D. Foster and R. Vohra. Asymptotic calibration. *Biometrika*, 85:379–390, 1998.

14. D. Foster and R. Vohra. Regret in the on-line decision problem. *Games and Economic Behavior*, 29:7–36, 1999.

15. Dean P. Foster and Rakesh V. Vohra. A randomization rule for selecting forecasts. *Operations Research*, 41(4):704–709, July–August 1993.

16. Y. Freund, R. Schapire, Y. Singer, and M. Warmuth. Using and combining predictors that specialize. In *Proceedings of the 29th Annual Symposium on Theory of Computing*, pages 334–343, 1997.

17. Yoav Freund and Robert E. Schapire. A decision-theoretic generalization of on-line learning and an application to boosting. In *Euro-COLT*, pages 23–37. Springer-Verlag, 1995. Also, JCSS 55(1): 119-139 (1997).

18. Yoav Freund and Robert E. Schapire. Adaptive game playing using multiplicative weights. *Games and Economic Behavior*, 29:79–103, 1999. A preliminary version appeared in the Proceedings of the Ninth Annual Conference on Computational Learning Theory, pages 325–332, 1996.

19. J. Hannan. Approximation to bayes risk in repeated plays. In M. Dresher, A. Tucker, and P. Wolfe, editors, *Contributions to the Theory of Games*, volume 3, pages 97–139. Princeton University Press, 1957.

20. S. Hart and A. Mas-Colell. A simple adaptive procedure leading to correlated equilibrium. *Econometrica*, 68:1127–1150, 2000.

21. S. Hart and A. Mas-Colell. A reinforcement procedure leading to correlated equilibrium. In Wilhelm Neuefeind Gerard Debreu and Walter Trockel, editors, *Economic Essays*, pages 181–200. Springer, 2001.

22. Mark Herbster and Manfred K. Warmuth. Tracking the best expert. In *International Conference on Machine Learning*, pages 286–294, 1995.

23. E. Lehrer. A wide range no-regret theorem. *Games and Economic Behavior*, 42:101–115, 2003.
24. Nick Littlestone and Manfred K. Warmuth. The weighted majority algorithm. *Information and Computation*, 108:212–261, 1994.
25. Gilles Stoltz. Private communication.
26. Gilles Stoltz and Gábor Lugosi. Internal regret in on-line portfolio selection. In *COLT*, 2003. To appear in Machine Learning Journal.
27. Gilles Stoltz and Gábor Lugosi. Learning correlated equilibria in games with compact sets of strategies. submitted to Games and Economic Behavior, 2004.

Separating Models of Learning from Correlated and Uncorrelated Data

Ariel Elbaz, Homin K. Lee, Rocco A. Servedio*,
and Andrew Wan

Department of Computer Science,
Columbia University
{arielbaz, homin, rocco, atw12}@cs.columbia.edu

Abstract. We consider a natural framework of learning from correlated data, in which successive examples used for learning are generated according to a random walk over the space of possible examples. Previous research has suggested that the Random Walk model is more powerful than comparable standard models of learning from independent examples, by exhibiting learning algorithms in the Random Walk framework that have no known counterparts in the standard model. We give strong evidence that the Random Walk model is indeed more powerful than the standard model, by showing that if any cryptographic one-way function exists (a universally held belief in public key cryptography), then there is a class of functions that can be learned efficiently in the Random Walk setting but not in the standard setting where all examples are independent.

1 Introduction

It is a commonly held belief in machine learning that having access to correlated data – for example, having random data points that differ only slightly from each other – is advantageous for learning. However, we are not aware of research that rigorously validates this belief from the vantage point of the abilities and limitations of computationally efficient learning. Our work is motivated by this disparity.

We study a natural model of learning from correlated data, by considering a framework in which the learning algorithm has access to successive examples that are generated by a *random walk*. We give strong evidence that learning is indeed easier, at least for some problems, in this framework of correlated examples than in the standard framework in which no correlations exist between successive examples.

---

* Supported in part by NSF CAREER award CCF-0347282 and a Sloan Foundation Fellowship.

P. Auer and R. Meir (Eds.): COLT 2005, LNAI 3559, pp. 637–651, 2005.

1.1   Background

In the well-known Probably Approximately Correct (PAC) learning model introduced by Valiant [16], a learning algorithm is given access to a source $EX_\mathcal{D}(c)$ of labelled examples each of which is drawn *independently* from a fixed probability distribution $\mathcal{D}$ over the space of possible instances. The goal of the learning algorithm is to construct (with high probability) a high-accuracy hypothesis for the target concept c with respect to $\mathcal{D}$.

Aldous and Vazirani [1] introduced and studied a variant of the PAC learning model in which successive examples are generated according to a Markov process, i.e. by taking a random walk on an (exponentially large) graph. Subsequent work by Gamarnik [8] extended this study to infinite Markov chains and gave bounds on the sample complexity required for learning in terms of the VC dimension and certain mixing properties of the underlying Markov chain. Neither [1] nor [8] considered computational issues for learning algorithms in the Random Walk framework.

In this paper we consider an elegant model of learning from Random Walk examples that is well suited for computational analyses. This model was introduced by Bartlett, Fischer and Höffgen [2] and subsequently studied by Bshouty *et al.* [6]. In this framework (described in detail in Section 2), successive examples for the learning algorithm are produced sequentially according to an unbiased random walk on the Boolean hypercube $\{0,1\}^n$. The PAC goal of constructing a high-accuracy hypothesis for the target concept with high probability (where accuracy is measured with respect to the stationary distribution of the random walk, i.e. the uniform distribution on $\{0,1\}^n$) is unchanged. This is a natural way of augmenting the model of uniform distribution PAC learning over the Boolean hypercube (which has been extensively studied, see e.g. [4, 5, 7, 12, 13, 14, 15, 17] and references therein) with the ability to exploit correlated data.

Bartlett *et al.* gave polynomial-time learning algorithms in this model for several concept classes including Boolean threshold functions in which each weight is either 0 or 1, parities of two monotone conjunctions over $x_1, \ldots, x_n$, and Disjunctive Normal Form (DNF) formulas with two terms. These learning algorithms are *proper*, meaning that in each case the learning algorithm constructs a hypothesis representation that belongs to the class being learned. Since proper learning algorithms were not known for these concept classes in the standard uniform distribution model, this gave the first circumstantial evidence that having access to random walk examples rather than uniform independent examples might bestow a computational advantage.

More recently, Bshouty *et al.* [6] gave a polynomial-time algorithm for learning the unrestricted class of all polynomial-size DNF formulas over $\{0,1\}^n$ in the Random Walk model. Since no comparable polynomial-time algorithms are known in the standard uniform distribution model (and their existence is a well-studied open question for which an affirmative answer would yield a $1000 prize, see [3]), this gives stronger evidence that the Random Walk model is strictly more powerful than the normal uniform distribution model. Thus, it is natural to now ask whether the perceived superiority of random walk learning over uniform distribution learning can be rigorously established under some widely accepted hypothesis about efficient computation.[1]

1.2   Our Results

In this work we give such a separation, under a generic cryptographic hardness assumption, between the Random Walk model and the uniform distribution model. Our main result is a proof of the following theorem:

Theorem 1. *If any cryptographic one-way function exists, then there is a concept class over $\{0,1\}^n$ that is PAC learnable in $poly(n)$ time in the Random Walk model but is not PAC learnable in $poly(n)$ time in the standard uniform distribution model.*

We emphasize that the separation established by Theorem 1 is computational rather than information-theoretic. It will be evident from our construction that the concept class of Theorem 1 has $poly(n)$ VC dimension, and thus the class can be learned using $poly(n)$ many *examples* even in the distribution-independent PAC learning model; the difficulty is in obtaining a *polynomial-time* algorithm.

We remind the reader that while the existence of any one-way function is a stronger assumption than the assumption that P$\neq$NP (since at this point it is conceivable that P$\neq$NP but one-way functions do not exist), it is an almost universally accepted assumption in cryptography and complexity theory. (In particular, the existence of one-way functions is the weakest of the many assumptions on which the entire field of public-key cryptography is predicated.) We also remind the reader that all known representation-independent computational hardness results in learning theory (where any efficiently evaluatable hypothesis representation is allowed for the learning algorithm, as is the case in Theorem 1 above) rely on cryptographic hardness assumptions rather than complexity-theoretic assumptions such as P$\neq$NP.

The rest of the paper is structured as follows: Section 2 gives necessary definitions and background from cryptography and the basics of our random walk model. Section 3 gives a partial separation, and in Section 4 we show how the construction from Section 3 can be used to achieve a total separation and prove Theorem 1.

2   Preliminaries

2.1   Notation

We denote by $[n]$ the set $\{1,\ldots,n\}$. For an n-bit string $r \in \{0,1\}^n$ and an index $i \in [n]$, the i-th bit of r is denoted $r[i]$. We write $\mathcal{U}$ to denote the uniform distribution on $\{0,1\}^n$.

---

[1] Note that it is necessary to make some computational hardness assumption in order to separate these two learning models. It is easy to see that if P=NP, for instance, then the concept class of all polynomial-size Boolean circuits would be efficiently learnable in both these models (as well as far weaker models), and essentially all considerations about the computational complexity of learning would become trivial.

2.2   Learning Models

Recall that a concept class $\mathcal{C} = \cup_{n \in \mathbb{N}} \mathcal{C}_n$ is a collection of Boolean functions where each $f \in \mathcal{C}_n$ maps $\{0,1\}^n \to \{0,1\}$. A *uniform example oracle* for f is an oracle $EX_U(f)$ which takes no inputs and, when invoked, outputs a pair $\langle x, f(x) \rangle$ where x is drawn uniformly and independently from $\{0,1\}^n$ at each invocation.

Definition 1 (PAC learning). *A concept class $\mathcal{C}$ is uniform distribution PAC-learnable if there is an algorithm A with the following property: for any n, any target concept $f \in \mathcal{C}_n$, and any $\epsilon, \delta > 0$, if A is given access to oracle $EX_U(f)$ then A runs for $poly(n, \frac{1}{\epsilon}, \frac{1}{\delta})$ time steps and with probability $1 - \delta$ outputs a Boolean circuit h such that $\Pr_{x \in \mathcal{U}}[h(x) \neq c(x)] \leq \epsilon$.*

In the (uniform) Random Walk model studied in [2, 6], a *random walk* oracle is an oracle $EX_{RW}(f)$ which, at its first invocation, outputs an example $\langle x, f(x) \rangle$ where x is drawn uniformly at random from $\{0,1\}^n$. Subsequent calls to $EX_{RW}(f)$ yield examples generated according to a uniform random walk on the hypercube $\{0,1\}^n$. That is, if x is the i-th example, the $i + 1$-st example is x', where x' is chosen by uniformly selecting one of the n bits of x and flipping it.

Definition 2 (PAC learning in the Random Walk model). *A concept class $\mathcal{C}$ is PAC-learnable in the Random Walk model if there is an algorithm A that satisfies Definition 1 above but with $EX_{RW}(f)$ in place of $EX_U(f)$.*

As in [6], it is convenient for us to work with a slight variant of the Random Walk oracle which is of equivalent power; we call this the *updating Random Walk* oracle and denote it by $EX_{URW}(f)$. If the last example generated by $EX_{URW}(f)$ was $x \in \{0,1\}^n$, the updating Random Walk oracle chooses a uniform index $i \in [n]$, but instead of flipping the bit $x[i]$ it replaces $x[i]$ with a uniform random bit from $\{0,1\}$ (i.e. it flips the bit with probability $1/2$ and leaves x unchanged with probability $1/2$) to obtain the new example x'. We say that such a step *updates* the i-th bit position.

An easy argument given in [6] shows that the Random Walk oracle can efficiently simulate the updating Random Walk oracle and vice versa, and thus any concept class that is efficiently learnable from one oracle is also efficiently learnable from the other. We introduce the updating Random Walk oracle because it is easy to see (and well known) that the updating random walk on the hypercube mixes rapidly. More precisely, we have the following fact which will be useful later:

Fact 1. *Let $\langle x, f(x) \rangle$ be a labeled example that is obtained from $EX_{URW}(f)$, and let $\langle y, f(y) \rangle$ be the labeled example that $EX_{URW}(f)$ outputs $n \ln \frac{n}{\delta}$ draws later. Then with probability at least $1 - \delta$, the two strings x, y are uniformly and independently distributed over $\{0,1\}^n$.*

Proof. Since it is clear that x and y are each uniformly distributed, the only thing to check for Fact 1 is independence. This follows since y will be independent of x if and only if all n bit positions are updated in the $n \ln \frac{n}{\delta}$ draws between x

and y. For each draw, the probability that a particular bit is not updated is $(1 - \frac{1}{n})$. Thus after $n \ln \frac{n}{\delta}$ draws, the probability that any bit of r has not been updated is at most $n(1 - \frac{1}{n})^{n \ln \frac{n}{\delta}} \leq \delta$. This yields the fact.   ∎

Note that Fact 1 implies that any concept class C that is uniform distribution PAC-learnable is also PAC-learnable in the Random Walk model, since we can obtain independent uniform random examples in the Random Walk model with essentially just a $\Theta(n \log n)$ slowdown.

2.3   Background from Cryptography

We write R_n to denote the set of all 2^{2^n} Boolean functions from $\{0,1\}^n$ to $\{0,1\}$. We refer to a function f chosen uniformly at random from R_n as a *truly random function*. We write D^f to denote a probabilistic polynomial-time (p.p.t.) algorithm D with black-box oracle access to the function f.

Informally, a one-way function is a function $f : \{0,1\}^n \to \{0,1\}^n$ that is computable by a poly(n) time algorithm but is hard to invert in the sense that no poly(n)-time algorithm can successfully compute f^{-1} on a nonnegligible fraction of outputs of f. (See [9] for a detailed definition and discussion of one-way functions.) In a celebrated result, Håstad *et al.* [11] showed that if any one-way function exists, then *pseudorandom function families* must exist as well.

Definition 3. *A* pseudorandom function family *[10] is a collection of functions* $\{f_s : \{0,1\}^{|s|} \to \{0,1\}\}_{s \in \{0,1\}^*}$ *with the following two properties:*

1. *(efficient evaluation) there is a deterministic algorithm which, given an n-bit seed s and an n-bit input x, runs in time poly(n) and outputs $f_s(x)$;*
2. *(pseudorandomness) for all polynomials Q, all p.p.t. oracle algorithms D, and all sufficiently large n, we have that*

$$\left| \Pr_{f \in R_n} [D^f(1^n) \text{ outputs } 1] - \Pr_{s \in \{0,1\}^n} [D^{f_s}(1^n) \text{ outputs } 1] \right| < \frac{1}{Q(n)}.$$

The argument 1^n indicates that the "distinguisher" algorithm D must run in poly(n) time steps since its input is of length n. Intuitively, condition (2) above states that a pseudorandom function cannot be distinguished from a truly random function by any polynomial-time algorithm that has black-box access to the pseudorandom function with an inverse polynomial advantage over random guessing.

3   A Partial Separation

3.1   A First Attempt

It is clear that in the Random Walk model a learning algorithm will get many pairs of examples that are adjacent vertices of the Hamming cube $\{0,1\}^n$, whereas this will not be the case for a learner in the standard uniform distribution model (with high probability, a set of poly(n) many independent uniform examples from $\{0,1\}^n$ will contain no pair of examples that have Hamming distance less than $n/2 - O(\sqrt{n \log n})$. Thus, in attempting to separate the random walk model from the standard uniform distribution model, it is natural to try to construct a concept class using pseudorandom functions f_s but altered in such a way that seeing the value of the function on adjacent inputs gives away information about the seed s.

One natural approach is the following: given a pseudorandom function family $\{f_s : \{0,1\}^k \to \{0,1\}\}_{s \in \{0,1\}^k}$, one could define a concept class of functions $\{f'_s : \{0,1\}^k \times \{0,1\}^{\log k} \times \{0,1\} \to \{0,1\}\}_{s \in \{0,1\}^k}$ as follows:

$$f'_s(x, i, b) = \begin{cases} f_s(x) & \text{if } b = 0 \\ f_s(x) \oplus s[i] & \text{if } b = 1 \end{cases}$$

where x is a k-bit string, i is a $(\log k)$-bit string encoding an integer between 1 and k, and b is a single bit. A learning algorithm in the Random Walk model will be able to obtain all bits $s[1], \ldots, s[k]$ of the seed s (by waiting for pairs of successive examples $(x, i, b), (x, i, 1 - b)$ in which the final bit b flips for all k possible values of i), and will thus be able to exactly identify the target concept. However, even though a standard uniform distribution learner will not obtain any pair of inputs that differ only in the final bit b, it is not clear how to show that no algorithm in the standard uniform distribution model can learn the concept class to high accuracy. Such a proof would require one to show that any polynomial-time uniform distribution learning algorithm could be used to "break" the pseudorandom function family $\{f_s\}$, and this seems difficult to do. (Intuitively, this difficulty arises because the $b = 1$ case of the definition of f'_s "mixes" bits of the seed with the output of the pseudorandom function.) Thus, we must consider alternate constructions.

3.2 A Partial Separation

In this section we describe a concept class and prove that it has the following two properties: (1) A randomly chosen concept from the class is indistinguishable from a truly random function to any polynomial-time algorithm which has an $EX_U(\cdot)$ oracle for the concept (and thus no such algorithm can learn to accuracy $\epsilon = \frac{1}{2} - \frac{1}{\text{poly}(n)}$); (2) However, a Random Walk algorithm with access to $EX_{RW}(\cdot)$ can learn any concept in the class to accuracy $\frac{3}{4}$. In the next section we will extend this construction to fully separate the Random Walk model from the standard uniform model and thus prove Theorem 1.

Our construction uses ideas from Section 3.1; as in the construction proposed there, the concepts in our class will reveal information about the seed of a pseudorandom function to learning algorithms that can obtain pairs of points with only the last bit flipped. However, each concept in the class will now be defined by *two* pseudorandom functions rather than one; this will enable us to prove that the class is indeed hard to learn in the uniform distribution model (but will also prevent a Random Walk learning algorithm from learning to high accuracy).

Let $\mathcal{F}$ be a family of pseudorandom functions $\{f_r : \{0,1\}^k \to \{0,1\}\}_{r \in \{0,1\}^k}$. We construct a concept class $\mathcal{G} = \{g_{r,s} : r, s \in \{0,1\}^k\}$, where $g_{r,s}$ takes an n-bit input that we split into four parts for convenience. As before, the first k bits x give the "actual" input to the function, while the other parts determine the mode of function that will be applied.

$$g_{r,s}(x, i, b, y) = \begin{cases} f_s(x) & \text{if } y = 0, b = 0 \\ f_s(x) \oplus r[i] & \text{if } y = 0, b = 1 \\ f_r(x) & \text{if } y = 1 \end{cases} \tag{1}$$

Here b and y are one bit and i is $\log k$ bits to indicate which bit of the seed r is exposed. Thus half of the inputs to $g_{r,s}$ are labeled according to f_r, and the other half are labeled according to either f_s or $f_s \oplus r[i]$ depending on the value of b.

The following lemma establishes that $\mathcal{G}$ is not efficiently PAC-learnable under the uniform distribution, by showing that a random function from $\mathcal{G}$ is indistinguishable from a truly random function to any algorithm which only has $EX_U(\cdot)$ access to the target concept. (A standard argument shows that an efficient PAC learning algorithm can be used to obtain an efficient distinguisher simply by running the learning algorithm and using its hypothesis to predict a fresh random example. Such an approach must succeed with high probability for any function from the concept class by virtue of the PAC criterion, but no algorithm that has seen only poly(n) many examples of a truly random function can predict its outputs on fresh examples with probability nonnegligibly greater than $\frac{1}{2}$.)

Lemma 1. *Let $g_{r,s} : \{0,1\}^n \to \{0,1\}$ be a function from $\mathcal{G}$ chosen by selecting r and s uniformly at random from $\{0,1\}^k$, where k satisfies $n = k + \log k + 2$. Let f be a truly random function. Then for any $\epsilon = \Omega(\frac{1}{\text{poly}(n)})$, no p.p.t. algorithm can distinguish between having oracle access to $EX_U(g_{r,s})$ versus oracle access to $EX_U(f)$ with success probability greater than $\frac{1}{2} + \epsilon$.*

Proof. The proof is by a hybrid argument. We will construct two intermediate functions, h_r and h'_r. We will show that $EX_U(g_{r,s})$ is indistinghable from $EX_U(h_r)$, $EX_U(h_r)$ from $EX_U(h'_r)$, and $EX_U(h'_r)$ from $EX_U(f)$. It will then follow that $EX_U(g_{r,s})$ is indistinguishable from $EX_U(f)$.

Consider the function

$$h_r(x, i, b, y) = \begin{cases} f(x) & \text{if } y = 0, b = 0 \\ f(x) \oplus r[i] & \text{if } y = 0, b = 1 \\ f_r(x) & \text{if } y = 1 \end{cases} \tag{2}$$

Here we have simply replaced f_s with a truly random function. We claim that no p.p.t. algorithm can distinguish oracle access to $EX_U(g_{r,s})$ from oracle access to $EX_U(h_r)$; for if such a distinguisher D existed, we could use it to obtain an algorithm D' to distinguish a randomly chosen $f_s \in \mathcal{F}$ from a truly random function in the following way. D' picks r at random from $\{0,1\}^k$ and runs D, answering D's queries to its oracle by choosing i, b and y at random, querying its own oracle to receive a bit q, and outputting q when both y and b are 0, $q\oplus r[i]$ when $y = 0$ and $b = 1$, and $f_r(x)$ when $y = 1$. It is easy to see that if D'''s oracle is for a truly random function $f \in \mathcal{R}$ then this process perfectly simulates access to $EX_U(h_r)$, and if D'''s oracle is for a randomly chosen $f_s \in \mathcal{F}$ then this process perfectly simulates access to $EX_U(g_{r,s})$ for r, s chosen uniformly at random.

We now consider the intermediate function

$$h'_r(x,i,b,y) = \begin{cases} f(x) & \text{if } y = 0 \\ f_r(x) & \text{if } y = 1 \end{cases}$$

and argue that no p.p.t. algorithm can distinguish oracle access to $EX_U(h_r)$ from access to $EX_U(h'_r)$. When $y = 1$ or both $y = 0$ and $b = 0$, both h_r and h'_r will have the same output. Otherwise, if $y = 0$ and $b = 1$ we have that $h_r(x,i,b,y) = f(x) \oplus r_i$ whereas $h'_r(x,i,b,y) = f(x)$. Now, it is easy to see that an algorithm with *black-box query access* to h_r can easily distinguish h_r from h'_r (simply because flipping the penultimate bit b will always cause the value of h_r to flip but will only cause the value of h'_r to flip half of the time). But for an algorithm that only has oracle access to $EX_U(\cdot)$, conditioned on never receiving the same string x twice (a condition that fails to hold only with negligible – in fact, inverse exponential – probability), it is easy to see that whether the oracle is for h_r or h'_r, each output value that the algorithm sees on inputs with $y = 0$ and $b = 1$ will be a fresh independent uniform random bit. (This is simply because a random function f can be viewed as tossing a coin to determine its output on each new input value, so no matter what $r[i]$ is, XORing it with $f(x)$ yields a fresh independent uniform random bit.)

Finally, it follows from the definition of pseudorandomness that no p.p.t. algorithm can distinguish oracle access to $EX_U(h'_r)$ from access to $EX_U(f)$. We have thus shown that $EX_U(g_{r,s})$ is indistinghable from $EX_U(h_r)$, $EX_U(h_r)$ from $EX_U(h'_r)$, and $EX_U(h'_r)$ from $EX_U(f)$. It follows that $EX_U(g_{r,s})$ is indistinguishable from $EX_U(f)$, and the proof is complete.   ∎

We now show that $g_{r,s}$ is learnable to accuracy $\frac{3}{4}$ in the Random Walk model.

Lemma 2. *There is an algorithm A with the following property: for any $\delta > 0$ and any concept $g_{r,s} \in \mathcal{G}$, if A is given access to a Random Walk oracle $EX_{RW}(g_{r,s})$ then A runs in time $poly(n, \log(1/\delta))$ and with probability at least $1 - \delta$, algorithm A outputs an efficiently computable hypothesis h such that $\Pr_U[h(x) \neq g_{r,s}(x)] \leq \frac{1}{4}$.*

Proof. As described in Section 2, for convenience in this proof we will assume that we have an updating Random Walk oracle $EX_{URW}(g_{r,s})$.

We give an algorithm that, with probablity $1 - \delta$, learns all the bits of r. Once the learner has obtained r she outputs the following (randomized) hypothesis h:

$$h(x,i,b,y) = \begin{cases} \$ & \text{if } y = 0 \\ f_r(x) & \text{if } y = 1 \end{cases}$$

where $ denotes a random coin toss at each invocation. Note that h incurs zero error relative to $g_{r,s}$ on inputs that have $y = 1$, and has error rate exactly $\frac{1}{2}$ on inputs that have $y = 0$. Thus the overall error rate of h is exactly $\frac{1}{4}$.

We now show that with probability $1 - \delta$ (over the random examples received from $EX_{URW}(g_{r,s})$) the learner can obtain all of r after receiving $T = O(n^2 k \cdot \log^2(n/\delta))$ many examples from $EX_{URW}(g_{r,s})$. The learner does this by looking at pairs of successive examples; we show (Fact 4 below) that after seeing $t = O(nk \cdot \log(k/\delta))$ pairs, each of which is independent from all other pairs, we obtain all of r with probability at least $1 - \frac{\delta}{2}$. To get t independent pairs of successive examples, we look at blocks of $t' = O(n \log(tn/\delta))$ many consecutive examples, and use only the first two examples from each such block. By Fact 1 we have that for a given pair of consecutive blocks, with probability at least $1 - \frac{\delta}{2t}$ the first example from the second block is random even given the pair of examples from the first block. A union bound over the t blocks gives total failure probability at most $\frac{\delta}{2}$ for independence, and thus an overall failure probability of at most δ.

We have the following simple facts:

Fact 2. *If the learner receives two consecutive examples $w = (x, i, 0, 0), w' = (x, i, 1, 0)$ and the corresponding labels $g_{r,s}(w), g_{r,s}(w')$, then the learner can obtain the bit $r[i]$.*

Fact 3. *For any $j \in [k]$, given a pair of consecutive examples from $EX_{URW}(g_{r,s})$, a learning algorithm can obtain the value of $r[j]$ from this pair with probability at least $\frac{1}{4kn}$.*

Proof. By Fact 2, if the first example is $w = (x, i, b, y)$ with $i = j$, $y = 0$ and the following example differs in the value of b, then the learner obtains $r[j]$. The first example (like every example from $EX_{URW}(g_{r,s})$) is uniformly distributed and thus has $i = j$, $y = 0$ with probability $\frac{1}{2k}$. The probability that the next example from $EX_{URW}(g_{r,s})$ flips the value of b is $\frac{1}{2n}$. ∎

Fact 4. *After receiving $t = 4kn \cdot \log(k/\delta')$ independent pairs of consecutive examples as described above, the learner can obtain all k bits of r with probability at least $1 - \delta'$.*

Proof. For any $j \in [k]$, the probability that $r[j]$ is not obtained from a given pair of consecutive examples is at most $(1 - \frac{1}{4kn})$. Thus after seeing t independent pairs of consecutive examples, the probability that any bit of r is not obtained is at most $k(1 - \frac{1}{4kn})^t$. This yields the fact. ∎

Thus the total number of calls to $EX_{URW}(g_{r,s})$ that are required is

$$T = t \cdot t' = O(nk \log(k/\delta)) \cdot O(n \log(tn/\delta)) = O(n^2 k \log^2(n/\delta)).$$

Since $k = O(n)$, Lemma 2 is proved. ∎

4   A Full Separation

We would like to have a concept class for which a Random Walk learner can output an ϵ-accurate hypothesis for any $\epsilon > 0$. The drawback of our construction in Section 3.2 is that a Random Walk learning algorithm can only achieve a particular fixed error rate $\epsilon = \frac{1}{4}$. Intuitively, a Random Walk learner cannot achieve accuracy better than $\frac{3}{4}$ because on half of the inputs the concept's value is essentially determined by a pseudorandom function whose seed the Random Walk learner cannot discover. It is not difficult to see that for any given $\epsilon = \frac{1}{\text{poly}(n)}$, by altering the parameters of the construction we could obtain a concept class that a Random Walk algorithm can learn to accuracy $1 - \epsilon$ (and which would still be unlearnable for a standard uniform distribution algorithm). However, this would give us a different concept class for each ϵ, whereas what we require is a single concept class that can be learned to accuracy ϵ for each $\epsilon > 0$.

In this section we present a new concept class $\mathcal{G}'$ and show that it achieves this goal. The idea is to string together many copies of our function from Section 3.2 in a particular way. Instead of depending on two seeds r, s, a concept in $\mathcal{G}'$ is defined using k seeds $r_1, \ldots, r_k$ and $k - 1$ subfunctions $g_{r_1, r_2}, g_{r_2, r_3}, \ldots, g_{r_{k-1}, r_k}$. These subfunctions are combined in a way that lets the learner learn more and more of the seeds $r_1, r_2, \ldots$, and thus learn to higher and higher accuracy, as she receives more and more examples.

4.1   The Concept Class $\mathcal{G}'$

We now describe $\mathcal{G}'$ in detail. Each concept in $\mathcal{G}'$ is defined by k seeds $r_1, \ldots, r_k$, each of length k. The concept $g'_{r_1, \ldots, r_k}$ is defined by

$$g'_{r_1, \ldots, r_k}(x, i, b, y, z) = \begin{cases} g_{r_{\alpha(z)}, r_{\alpha(z)+1}}(x, i, b, y) & \text{if } \alpha(z) \in \{1, \ldots, k-1\} \\ f_{r_k}(x) & \text{if } \alpha(z) = k \end{cases}$$

As in the previous section x is a k-bit string, i is a $\log k$-bit string, and b and y are single bits. The new input z is a $(k-1)$-bit string, and the value $\alpha(z) \in [k]$ is defined as the index of the leftmost bit in z that is 1 (for example if $z = 0010010111$ then $\alpha(z) = 3$); if $z = 0^{k-1}$ then $\alpha(z)$ is defined to be k. By this design, the subfunction $g_{r_j, r_{j+1}}$ will be used on a $1/2^j$ fraction of the inputs to g'. Note that g' maps $\{0, 1\}^n$ to $\{0, 1\}$ where $n = 2k + \log k + 1$.

4.2   Uniform Distribution Algorithms Cannot Learn $\mathcal{G}'$

We first show that $\mathcal{G}'$ is not efficiently PAC-learnable under the uniform distribution. This is implied by the following lemma:

Lemma 3. *Let $g'_{r_1, \ldots, r_k} : \{0, 1\}^n \to \{0, 1\}$ be a function from $\mathcal{G}'$ chosen by selecting $r_1, \ldots, r_k$ uniformly at random from $\{0, 1\}^k$, where k satisfies $n = 2k + \log k + 1$. Let f be a truly random function. Then for any $\epsilon = \Omega(\frac{1}{\text{poly}(n)})$, no p.p.t. algorithm can distinguish between having access to $EX_U(g'_{r_1, \ldots, r_k})$ versus access to $EX_U(f)$ with success probability greater than $\frac{1}{2} + \epsilon$.*

Proof. Again we use a hybrid argument. We define the concept classes $\mathcal{H}(\ell) = \{h_{r_1,\ldots,r_\ell;f} : r_1,\ldots,r_\ell \in \{0,1\}^k, f \in \mathcal{R}_k\}$ for $2 \leq \ell \leq k$. Each function $h_{r_1,\ldots,r_\ell;f}$ takes the same n-bit input (x,i,b,y,z) as $g'_{r_1,\ldots,r_k}$. The function $h_{r_1,\ldots,r_\ell;f}$ is defined as follows:

$$h_{r_1,\ldots,r_\ell;f}(x,i,b,y,z) = \begin{cases} g_{r_{\alpha(z)},r_{\alpha(z)+1}}(x,i,b,y) & \text{if } \alpha(z) < \ell \\ f(x) & \text{otherwise.} \end{cases}$$

Here as before, the value $\alpha(z) \in [k]$ denotes the index of the leftmost bit of z that is one (and we have $\alpha(z) = k$ if $z = 0^{k-1}$).

We will consider functions that are chosen uniformly at random from $\mathcal{H}(\ell)$, i.e. $r_1,\ldots,r_\ell$ are chosen randomly from $\{0,1\}^k$ and f is a truly random function from $\mathcal{R}_k$. Using Lemma 1, it is easy to see that for a distinguisher that is given only oracle access to $EX_U(\cdot)$, a random function from $\mathcal{H}(2)$ is indistinguishable from a truly random function from $\mathcal{R}_n$. We will now show that, for $2 \leq \ell < k$, if a random function from $\mathcal{H}(\ell)$ is indistinguishable from a truly random function then the same is true for $\mathcal{H}(\ell+1)$. This will then imply that a random function from $\mathcal{H}(k)$ is indistinguishable from a truly random function.

Let $h_{r_1,\ldots,r_{\ell+1}}$ be taken randomly from $\mathcal{H}(\ell+1)$ and f be a truly random function from $\mathcal{R}_n$. Suppose we had a distinguisher D that distinguishes between a random function from $\mathcal{H}(\ell+1)$ and a truly random function from $\mathcal{R}_n$ with success probability $\frac{1}{2} + \epsilon$, where $\epsilon = \Omega(\frac{1}{\text{poly}(n)})$. Then we can use D to obtain an algorithm D' for distinguishing a randomly chosen $f_s \in \mathcal{F}$ from a randomly chosen function $f \in \mathcal{R}_k$ in the following way. D' first picks strings $r_1,\ldots,r_\ell$ at random from $\{0,1\}^k$. D' then runs D, simulating its oracle in the following way. At each invocation, D' draws a random (x,i,b,y,z) and behaves as follows:

- If $\alpha(z) < \ell$, then D' outputs $\langle (x,i,b,y,z), g_{r_{\alpha(z)},r_{\alpha(z)+1}}(x,i,b,y) \rangle$.
- If $\alpha(z) = \ell$, then D' calls its oracle to obtain $\langle x', \beta \rangle$. If $y = b = 0$ then D' outputs $\langle (x',i,b,y,z), \beta \rangle$. If $y = 0$ but $b = 1$ then D' outputs $\langle (x',i,b,y,z), \beta \oplus r_\ell[i] \rangle$. If $y = 1$ then D' outputs $\langle (x',i,b,y,z), f_{r_\ell}(x) \rangle$.
- If $\alpha(z) > \ell$, D' outputs the labelled example $\langle (x,i,b,y,z), r(x) \rangle$ where $r(x)$ is a fresh random bit for each x. (The pairs $(x,r(x))$ are stored, and if any k-bit string x is drawn twice – which is exponentially unlikely in a sequence of poly(n) many draws – D' uses the same bit $r(x)$ as before.)

It is straightforward to check that if D''s oracle is $EX_U(f_s)$ for a random $f_s \in \mathcal{F}$, then D' simulates an oracle $EX_U(h_{r_1,\ldots,r_{\ell+1}})$ for D, where $h_{r_1,\ldots,r_{\ell+1}}$ is drawn uniformly from $\mathcal{H}(\ell+1)$. On the other hand, we claim that if D''s oracle is $EX_U(f)$ for a random $f \in \mathcal{R}_k$, then D' simulates an oracle that is indistinguishable from $EX_U(h_{r_1,\ldots,r_\ell})$ for D, where $h_{r_1,\ldots,r_\ell}$ is drawn uniformly from $\mathcal{H}(\ell)$. Clearly the oracle D' simulates is identical to $EX_U(h_{r_1,\ldots,r_\ell})$ for $\alpha(z) \neq \ell$. For $\alpha(z) = \ell$, D' simulates the function h_{r_ℓ} as in Equation 2 in the proof of Lemma 1, which is indistinguishable from a truly random function as proved in the lemma.

Thus the success probability of the distinguisher D' is the same as the probability that D succeeds in distinguishing $\mathcal{H}(\ell+1)$ from $\mathcal{H}(\ell)$. Recall that $\mathcal{H}(\ell)$ is indistinguishable from a truly random function, and that D succeeds in distinguishing $\mathcal{H}(\ell + 1)$ from a truly random function with probability at least $\frac{1}{2} + \epsilon$ by assumption. This implies that D' succeeds in distinguishing a randomly chosen $f_s \in \mathcal{F}$ from a randomly chosen function $f \in \mathcal{R}_k$ with probability at least $\frac{1}{2} + \epsilon - \frac{1}{\omega(\text{poly}(n))}$, but this contradicts the pseudorandomness of $\mathcal{F}$.

Finally, we claim that for any p.p.t. algorithm, having oracle access to a random function from $\mathcal{H}(k)$ is indistinguishable from having oracle access to a random function from $\mathcal{G}'$. To see this, note that the functions $h_{r_1,\ldots,r_\ell;f}$ and $g'_{r_1,\ldots,r_\ell}$ differ only on inputs (x, i, b, y, z) that have $\alpha(z) = k$, i.e. $z = 0^{k-1}$ (on such inputs the function $g_{r_1,\ldots,r_\ell}$ will output $f_{r_k}(x)$ whereas $h_{r_1,\ldots,r_\ell;f}$ will output $f(x)$). But such inputs are only a $\frac{1}{2^{\Omega(n)}}$ fraction of all possible inputs, so with overwhelmingly high probability a p.p.t. algorithm will never receive such an example.   ∎

4.3   Random Walk Algorithms Can Learn $\mathcal{G}'$

The following lemma completes the proof of our main result, Theorem 1.

Lemma 4. *There is an algorithm B with the following property: for any $\epsilon, \delta > 0$, and any concept $g_{r_1,\ldots,r_k} \in \mathcal{G}'$, if B is given access to a Random Walk oracle $EX_{RW}(g_{r_1,\ldots,r_k})$, then B runs in time $\text{poly}(n, \log(1/\delta), 1/\epsilon)$ and can with probability at least $1 - \delta$ output a hypothesis h such that $\Pr_U[h(x) \neq g_{r_1,\ldots,r_k}(x)] \leq \epsilon$.*

Proof. The proof is similar to that of Lemma 2. Again, for convenience we will assume that we have an updating Random Walk oracle $EX_{URW}(g_{r_1,\ldots,r_k})$. Recall from Lemma 2 that there is an algorithm A that can obtain the string r_j with probability at least $1 - \delta'$ given $t' = O(nk \cdot \log(n/\delta'))$ independent pairs of successive random walk examples

$$\Big(\langle w, g_{r_j, r_{j+1}}(w) \rangle, \langle w', g_{r_j, r_{j+1}}(w') \rangle \Big).$$

Algorithm B works in a sequence of v stages. In stage j, the algorithm simply tries to obtain t' independent example pairs for $g_{r_j, r_{j+1}}$ and then uses Algorithm A. Assuming the algorithm succeeds in each stage, after stage v algorithm B has obtained $r_1, \ldots, r_v$. It follows directly from the definition of $\mathcal{G}'$ that given $r_1, \ldots, r_v$, Algorithm B can construct a hypothesis that has error at most $\frac{3}{2^{v+2}}$ (see Figure 1) so we may take $v = \log \frac{1}{\epsilon} + 1$ to obtain error at most ϵ. (Note that this implicitly assumes that $\log \frac{1}{\epsilon} + 1$ is at most k; we deal with the case $\log \frac{1}{\epsilon} + 1 > k$ at the end of the proof.)

If the learner fails to obtain $r_1, \ldots, r_v$, then either:

1. Independence was not achieved between every pair of examples;
2. Algorithm B fails to acquire t' pairs of examples for $g_{r_j, r_{j+1}}$ in some stage j; or
3. Algorithm B acquires t' pairs of examples for $g_{r_j, r_{j+1}}$ but Algorithm A fails to obtain r_j in some stage j.

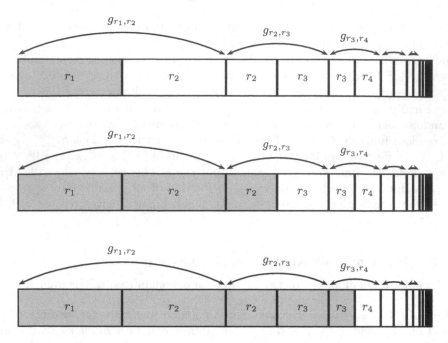

Fig. 1. Stages 1, 2 and 3 of Algorithm B. Each row represents the output values of $g'_{r_1,\ldots,r_k}$. After stage j the algorithm "knows" $r_1,\ldots,r_j$ and can achieve perfect accuracy on the shaded region

We choose the total number of examples so that each of these probabilities is bounded by $\delta/3$ to achieve an overall failure probability of at most δ.

As will be clear from the analysis of cases (2) and (3) below, in total Algorithm B will use $4 \cdot 2^{v+1}t'$ pairs of examples in stages 1 through v, where t' will be bounded later. Each pair of examples is obtained by using the first two examples from a block of $s = O(n \log(v \cdot 2^{v+1}t'n/\delta))$ many consecutive examples from the updating Random Walk oracle. With this choice of s, the same argument as in the proof of Lemma 2 shows that the total failure probability for independence is at most $\frac{\delta}{3}$.

We bound (2) assuming full independence between all pairs of examples. In stage j, Algorithm B uses $4 \cdot 2^j t'$ pairs of examples. Observe that each pair of examples has both examples from $g_{r_j,r_{j+1}}$ with probability at least $2^{-(j+1)}$. By a Chernoff bound, the probability that less than t' of the example pairs in stage j are from $g_{r_j,r_{j+1}}$ is at most $e^{-\frac{t'}{8}}$. Thus the overall probability of failure from condition (2) is at most $ve^{-\frac{t'}{8}}$ which is at most $\delta/3$ for $t' \geq \ln(3v/\delta)$.

We bound (3) assuming full independence between all pairs of examples as well. In stage j, we know by Fact 4 that after seeing $t' = O(nk \log(3vk/\delta))$ pairs of examples for $g_{r_j,r_{j+1}}$, the probability of failing to obtain r_j is at most $\delta/3v$. Hence the overall failure probability from condition (3) is at most $\frac{\delta}{3}$.

We thus may take $t' = O(nk \log(3vk/\delta))$ and achieve an overall failure probability of δ for obtaining $r_1,\ldots,r_v$. It follows that the overall number of examples required from the updating Random Walk oracle is $\text{poly}(2^v, n, \log \frac{1}{\delta}) = \text{poly}(n, \frac{1}{\epsilon}, \log \frac{1}{\delta})$, which is what we required.

Finally, we observe that if $\log \frac{1}{\epsilon} + 1 > k$, since $k = \frac{n}{2} - O(\log n)$ a $\text{poly}(\frac{1}{\epsilon})$-time algorithm may run for, say, $2^{\frac{5}{2}n}$ time steps and thus build an explicit truth table for the function. Such a table can be used to exactly identify each seed $r_1, \ldots, r_k$ and output an exact representation of the target concept.   ∎

Acknowledgements

We warmly thank Tal Malkin for helpful discussions.

References

[1] D. Aldous and U. Vazirani. A Markovian extension of Valiant's learning model. In *Proceedings of the Thirty-First Symposium on Foundations of Computer Science*, pages 392–396, 1990.

[2] P. Bartlett, P. Fischer, and K.U. Höffgen. Exploiting random walks for learning. *Information and Computation*, 176(2):121–135, 2002.

[3] A. Blum. Learning a function of r relevant variables (open problem). In *Proceedings of the 16th Annual Conference on Learning Theory and 7th Kernel Workshop*, pages 731–733, 2003.

[4] A. Blum, M. Furst, J. Jackson, M. Kearns, Y. Mansour, and S. Rudich. Weakly learning DNF and characterizing statistical query learning using Fourier analysis. In *Proceedings of the Twenty-Sixth Annual Symposium on Theory of Computing*, pages 253–262, 1994.

[5] N. Bshouty, J. Jackson, and C. Tamon. More efficient PAC learning of DNF with membership queries under the uniform distribution. In *Proceedings of the Twelfth Annual Conference on Computational Learning Theory*, pages 286–295, 1999.

[6] N. Bshouty, E. Mossel, R. O'Donnell, and R. Servedio. Learning DNF from Random Walks. In *Proceedings of the 44th IEEE Symposium on Foundations on Computer Science*, pages 189–198, 2003.

[7] N. Bshouty and C. Tamon. On the Fourier spectrum of monotone functions. *Journal of the ACM*, 43(4):747–770, 1996.

[8] D. Gamarnik. Extension of the PAC framework to finite and countable Markov chains. In *Proceedings of the 12th Annual Conference on Computational Learning Theory*, pages 308–317, 1999.

[9] O. Goldreich. *Foundations of Cryptography: Volume 1, Basic Tools*. Cambridge University Press, New York, 2001.

[10] O. Goldreich, S. Goldwasser, and S. Micali. How to construct random functions. *Journal of the Association for Computing Machinery*, 33(4):792–807, 1986.

[11] J. Hastad, R. Impagliazzo, L. Levin, and M. Luby. A pseudorandom generator from any one-way function. *SIAM Journal on Computing*, 28(4):1364–1396, 1999.

[12] J. Jackson. An efficient membership-query algorithm for learning DNF with respect to the uniform distribution. *Journal of Computer and System Sciences*, 55:414–440, 1997.

[13] J. Jackson, A. Klivans, and R. Servedio. Learnability beyond AC^0. In *Proceedings of the 34th ACM Symposium on Theory of Computing*, 2002.

[14] M. Kharitonov. Cryptographic hardness of distribution-specific learning. In *Proceedings of the Twenty-Fifth Annual Symposium on Theory of Computing*, pages 372–381, 1993.

[15] N. Linial, Y. Mansour, and N. Nisan. Constant depth circuits, Fourier transform and learnability. *Journal of the ACM*, 40(3):607–620, 1993.

[16] L. Valiant. A theory of the learnable. *Communications of the ACM*, 27(11):1134–1142, 1984.

[17] K. Verbeurgt. Learning DNF under the uniform distribution in quasi-polynomial time. In *Proceedings of the Third Annual Workshop on Computational Learning Theory*, pages 314–326, 1990.

Asymptotic Log-Loss of Prequential Maximum Likelihood Codes

Peter Grünwald[1] and Steven de Rooij[2]

[1] CWI Amsterdam
Peter.Grunwald@cwi.nl
www.grunwald.nl
[2] CWI Amsterdam
S.de.Rooij@cwi.nl
www.cwi.nl/~rooij

Abstract. We analyze the Dawid-Rissanen *prequential maximum likelihood codes* relative to one-parameter exponential family models $\mathcal{M}$. If data are i.i.d. according to an (essentially) *arbitrary* P, then the redundancy grows at rate $\frac{1}{2}c\ln n$. We show that $c = \sigma_1^2/\sigma_2^2$, where σ_1^2 is the variance of P, and σ_2^2 is the variance of the distribution $M^* \in \mathcal{M}$ that is closest to P in KL divergence. This shows that prequential codes behave quite differently from other important universal codes such as the 2-part MDL, Shtarkov and Bayes codes, for which $c = 1$. This behavior is undesirable in an MDL model selection setting.

1 Introduction

Universal coding lies at the basis of on-line prediction algorithms for data compression and gambling purposes. It has been extensively studied in the COLT community, typically under the name of 'sequential prediction with log loss', see, for example [8, 1, 3]. It also underlies Rissanen's theory of MDL (minimum description length) learning [2, 9] and Dawid's theory of prequential model assessment [6]. Roughly, a code is *universal* with respect to a set of candidate codes $\mathcal{M}$ if it achieves small *redundancy*: it allows one to encode data using not many more bits than the optimal code in $\mathcal{M}$. The redundancy is very closely related to the *expected regret*, which is perhaps more widely known within the COLT community – see Section 4. The main types of universal codes are the *Shtarkov* or *NML* code, the *Bayesian mixture* code, the *2-part MDL code* and the *prequential maximum likelihood (ML) code*, also known as the 'ML plug-in code' or the 'predictive MDL code' [2, 9]. This code was introduced independently by Rissanen [14] and by Dawid [6], who proposed it as a probability forecasting strategy rather than directly as a code. The main ideas are explained in Section 2. Here we study the case where no code in $\mathcal{M}$ corresponds to the data-generating distribution P, for the wide class of 1-parameter exponential families $\mathcal{M}$. We find that then the redundancy of the prequential code can be quite different from that of the other methods: the redundancies are $\frac{1}{2}c\ln n + O(1)$. Under

P. Auer and R. Meir (Eds.): COLT 2005, LNAI 3559, pp. 652–667, 2005.
© Springer-Verlag Berlin Heidelberg 2005

regularity conditions on P and $\mathcal{M}$, we find $c = 1$ for Bayes, NML and 2-part codes, whereas for the prequential ML codes, we can get any $c > 0$, depending on P and $\mathcal{M}$.

Relevance: As discussed in Section 5, the result has interesting consequences for parameter estimation and practical data compression. The most important and surprising consequence is for MDL learning and model selection, where our result implies that the prequential ML code may behave suboptimally *even if one of the models under consideration is correct after all!*

Contents. In Section 2 we informally state and explain our result. Section 3 contains the formal statement of our main result (Theorem 1), as well as a proof. Section 4 provides Theorem 2, which implies that a version of our result still holds if 'redundancy' is replaced by 'expected regret'. We discuss further issues, including relevance of the result and related work, in Section 5. Section 6 states and proves various lemma's needed in the proofs of Theorem 1 and 2. We provide a lot more discussion, and discuss the proofs in much greater detail, in the technical report [10].

2   Main Result, Informally

Suppose $\mathcal{M} = \{M_\theta : \theta \in \Theta\}$ is a k-dimensional parametric family of distributions, which we use to model some distribution P from which we sample i.i.d. outcomes $Z_1, Z_2, \ldots$ A code is *universal* for $\mathcal{M}$ if it is almost as efficient at coding the outcomes from P as the best element of $\mathcal{M}$. (We use codes and distributions interchangeably.) The *redundancy* of a universal code U with respect to P is defined as

$$\mathcal{R}_U(n) := E_P[L_U(Z_1, \ldots, Z_n)] - \inf_{\theta \in \Theta} E_P[-\ln M_\theta(Z_1, \ldots, Z_n)], \qquad (1)$$

where L_U is the length function of U and $M_\theta(Z_1, \ldots, Z_n)$ denotes the probability mass or density of $Z_1, \ldots, Z_n$ under distribution M_θ; these and other notational conventions are detailed in Section 3. Often, P is assumed to be an element of the model. If such is the case, then by the information inequality [5] the second term is minimized for $M_\theta = P$, so that

$$\mathcal{R}_U(n) = E_P[L_U(Z_1, \ldots, Z_n)] - E_P[-\ln P(Z_1, \ldots, Z_n)], \qquad (2)$$

We use nats rather than bits as units of information to simplify equations; a nat can be thought of as the amount of information needed to distinguish between e rather than 2 alternatives. Thus, (2) can be interpreted as the expected number of additional nats one needs to encode n outcomes if one uses the code U instead of the optimal (Shannon-Fano) code with lengths $-\ln P(Z_1, \ldots, Z_n)$. A good universal code achieves small redundancy (or regret, see Section 4) for all or 'most' $P \in \mathcal{M}$.

The four major types of universal codes, Bayes, NML, 2-part and prequential ML, all achieve redundancies that are (in an appropriate sense) close to optimal. Specifically, under regularity conditions on $\mathcal{M}$ and its parameterization, these four types of universal codes all satisfy, for all $P \in \mathcal{M}$,

$$\mathcal{R}(n) = \frac{k}{2} \ln n + O(1), \tag{3}$$

where the $O(1)$ may depend on θ and the universal code used. (3) is the famous 'k over 2 log n formula', refinements of which lie at the basis of most practical approximations to MDL learning, see [9].

In this paper we consider the case where the data are i.i.d. according to an *arbitrary* P not necessarily in the model $\mathcal{M}$. It is now appropriate to rename the redundancy to *relative* redundancy, since we measure the number of nats we lose relative to the best element in the model, rather than relative to the generating distribution P. The definition (1) remains unchanged. It can no longer be rewritten as (2) however: Assuming it exists and is unique, let M_{θ^*} be the element of $\mathcal{M}$ that minimizes KL divergence to P:

$$\theta^* := \arg\min_{\theta \in \Theta} D(P \| M_\theta) = \arg\min_{\theta \in \Theta} E_P[-\ln M_\theta(Z)],$$

where the equality follows from the definition of the KL divergence [5]. Then the relative redundancy satisfies

$$\mathcal{R}_U(n) = E_P[L_U(Z_1, \ldots, Z_n)] - E_P[-\ln M_{\theta^*}(Z_1, \ldots, Z_n)]. \tag{4}$$

It turns out that for the NML, 2-part MDL and Bayes codes, the relative redundancy (4) with $P \notin \mathcal{M}$, still satisfies (3), at least under conditions on $\mathcal{M}$ and P (Section 4). In this paper, we show for the first time that (3) does *not* hold for the prequential ML code. The prequential ML code U works by sequentially predicting Z_{i+1} using a (slightly modified) ML or Bayesian MAP estimator $\hat{\theta}_i = \hat{\theta}(z^i)$ based on the past data, that is, the first i outcomes $z^i = z_1, \ldots, z_i$. The total codelength $L_U(z^n)$ on a sequence z^n is given by the sum of the individual 'predictive' codelengths (log losses): $L_U(z^n) = \sum_{i=0}^{n-1}[-\ln M_{\hat{\theta}_i}(z_{i+1})]$. In our main theorem, we show that if L_U denotes the prequential ML code length, and $\mathcal{M}$ is a regular one-parameter exponential family ($k = 1$), then

$$\mathcal{R}_U(n) = \frac{1}{2} \frac{\text{var}_P X}{\text{var}_{M_{\theta^*}} X} \ln n + O(1), \tag{5}$$

where X is the sufficient statistic of the family. Example 1 below illustrates the phenomenon. Note that if $P \in \mathcal{M}$, then $M_{\theta^*} = P$ and (5) becomes the familiar expression. The result holds as long as $\mathcal{M}$ and P satisfy a mild condition that is stated and discussed in the next section. Section 5 discusses the consequences of this result for compression, estimation and model selection, as well as its relation to the large body of earlier results on prequential ML coding.

Example 1. Let $\mathcal{M}$ be the family of Poisson distributions, parameterized by their mean μ. Since neither the NML universal code nor Jeffreys' prior are defined for this model it is attractive to use the prequential ML code as a universal code for this model. The ML estimator $\hat{\mu}_i$ is the empirical mean of $z_1, \ldots, z_i$.

Suppose $Z, Z_1, Z_2, \ldots$ are i.i.d. according to a degenerate P with $P(Z = 4) = 1$. Since the sample average is a sufficient statistic for the Poisson family, $\hat{\mu}_i$ will be equal to 4 for all $i \geq 1$. On the other hand, μ^*, the parameter (mean) of the distribution in $\mathcal{M}$ closest to P in KL-divergence, will be equal to 4 as well. Thus the redundancy (4) of the prequential ML code is given by

$$\mathcal{R}_U(n) = -\ln M_{\hat{\mu}_0}(4) + \ln M_4(4) + \sum_{i=1}^{n-1} [-\ln M_4(4) + \ln M_4(4)] = O(1),$$

assuming an appropriate definition of $\hat{\mu}_0$. In the case of the Poisson family, we have $Z = X$ in (5). Thus, since $\mathrm{var}_P Z = 0$, this example agrees with (5).

Now suppose data are i.i.d. according to some P_τ, with $P_\tau(Z = z) \propto (z+1)^{-3}$ for all z smaller than τ, and $P_\tau(Z = z) = 0$ for $z \geq \tau$. It is easy to check that, for $\tau \to \infty$, the entropy of P_τ converges to a finite constant, but the variance of P_τ tends to infinity. Thus, by choosing τ large enough, the regret obtained by the Poisson prequential ML code can be made to grow as $c \log n$ for arbitrarily large c.

Example 2. The Hardy-Weinberg model deals with genotypes of which the alleles are assumed independently Bernoulli distributed according to some parameter p. There are four combinations of alleles, usually denoted 'aa', 'AA', 'aA', 'Aa'; but since 'aA' and 'Aa' result in the same genotype, the Hardy-Weinberg model is defined as a probability distribution on three outcomes. We model this by letting X be a random variable on the underlying space, that maps 'aA' and 'Aa' to the same value: $X(aa) = 0$, $X(aA) = X(Aa) = \frac{1}{2}$ and $X(AA) = 1$. Then $P(X = 0) = (1-p)^2$, $P(X = \frac{1}{2}) = 2p(1-p)$ and $P(X = 1) = p^2$. The Hardy-Weinberg model is an exponential family with sufficient statistic X. To see this, note that for any parameter $p \in [0, 1]$, we have $EX = \mu = P(A) = p$, so we can parameterize the model by the mean of X. The variance of the distribution with parameter μ is $\frac{1}{2}\mu(1 - \mu)$. Now suppose that we code data in a situation where the Hardy-Weinberg model is *wrong* and the genotypes are in fact distributed according to $P(X = \frac{1}{2}) = P(X = 1) = \frac{1}{2}$ and $P(X = 0) = 0$, such that mean and variance of X are $\frac{3}{4}$ and $\frac{2}{32}$ respectively. The closest distribution in the model has the same mean (since the mean is a sufficient statistic), and variance $\frac{3}{32}$. Thus the prequential ML code will achieve an asymptotic regret of $\frac{1}{3}\ln n$ rather than $\frac{1}{2}\ln n$ (up to $O(1)$).

3   Main Result, Formally

In this section, we define our quantities of interest and we state and prove our main result. Throughout this text we use nats rather than bits as units of information. Outcomes are capitalized if they are to be interpreted as random variables instead of instantiated values. A sequence of outcomes $z_1, \ldots, z_n$ is abbreviated to z^n. We write E_P as a shorthand for $E_{Z \sim P}$, the expectation of Z under distribution P. When we consider a sequence of n outcomes independently distributed $\sim P$, we use E_P even as a shorthand for the expectation of $(Z_1, \ldots, Z_n)$ under the n-fold product distribution of P. Finally, $P(Z)$ denotes the probability mass function of P in case Z is discrete-valued, and it denotes the density of P, in case Z takes its value in a continuum. When we write 'density function of Z', then, if Z is discrete-valued, this should be read as 'probability mass function of Z'. Note however that in our main result, Theorem 1 below, we do not assume that the data-generating distribution P admits a density.

Let $\mathcal{Z}$ be a set of outcomes, taking values either in a finite or countable set, or in a subset of k-dimensional Euclidean space for some $k \geq 1$. Let $X : \mathcal{Z} \to \mathbb{R}$ be a random variable on $\mathcal{Z}$, and let $\mathcal{X} = \{x \in \mathbb{R} : \exists z \in \mathcal{Z} : X(z) = x\}$ be the range of X. Exponential family models are families of distributions on $\mathcal{Z}$ defined relative to a random variable X (called 'sufficient statistic') as defined above, and a function $h : \mathcal{Z} \to [0, \infty)$. Let $Z(\eta) := \int_{z \in \mathcal{Z}} e^{-\eta X(z)} h(z) dz$ (the integral to be replaced by a sum for countable $\mathcal{Z}$), and $\Theta_\eta := \{\eta \in \mathbb{R} : Z(\eta) < \infty\}$.

Definition 1 (Exponential family). *The* single parameter exponential family [12] *with* sufficient statistic X *and* carrier h *is the family of distributions with densities* $M_\eta(z) := \frac{1}{Z(\eta)} e^{-\eta X(z)} h(z)$, *where* $\eta \in \Theta_\eta$. Θ_η *is called the* natural parameter space. *The family is called* regular *if* Θ_η *is an open interval of* $\mathbb{R}$.

In the remainder of this text we only consider single parameter, regular exponential families with a 1-to-1 parameterization, but this qualification will henceforth be omitted. Examples include the Poisson, geometric and multinomial families, and the model of all Gaussian distributions with a fixed variance or mean.

The statistic $X(z)$ is sufficient for η [12]. This suggests reparameterizing the distribution by the expected value of X, which is called the *mean value parameterization*. The function $\mu(\eta) = E_{M_\eta}[X]$ maps parameters in the natural parameterization to the mean value parameterization. It is a diffeomorphism (it is one-to-one, onto, infinitely often differentiable and has an infinitely often differentiable inverse) [12]. Therefore the mean value parameter space Θ_μ is also an open interval of $\mathbb{R}$. We note that for some models (such as Bernoulli and Poisson), the parameter space is usually given in terms of the a non-open set of mean-values (e.g., $[0,1]$ in the Bernoulli case). To make the model a regular exponential family, we have to restrict the set of parameters to its own interior. Henceforth, whenever we refer to a standard statistical model such as Bernoulli or Poisson, we assume that the parameter set has been restricted in this sense.

We are now ready to define the prequential ML model. This is a distribution on infinite sequences $z_1, z_2, \ldots \in \mathcal{Z}^\infty$, recursively defined in terms of the distributions of Z_{n+1} conditioned on $Z^n = z^n$, for all $n = 1, 2, \ldots$, all $z^n = (z_1, \ldots, z_n) \in \mathcal{Z}^n$. In the definition, we use the notation $x_i := X(z_i)$.

Definition 2 (Prequential ML model). *Let* Θ_μ *be the mean value parameter domain of an exponential family* $\mathcal{M} = \{M_\mu \mid \mu \in \Theta_\mu\}$. *Given* $\mathcal{M}$ *and constants* $x_0 \in \Theta_\mu$ *and* $n_0 > 0$, *we define the* prequential ML model U *by setting, for all* n, *all* $z^{n+1} \in \mathcal{Z}^{n+1}$:

$$U(z_{n+1} \mid z^n) = M_{\hat{\mu}(z^n)}(z_{n+1}),$$

where $U(z_{n+1} \mid z^n)$ is the density/mass function of z_{n+1} conditional on $Z^n = z^n$,

$$\hat{\mu}(z^n) := \frac{x_0 \cdot n_0 + \sum_{i=1}^n x_i}{n + n_0},$$

and $M_{\hat{\mu}(z^n)}(\cdot)$ is the density of the distribution in $\mathcal{M}$ with mean $\hat{\mu}(z^n)$.

We henceforth abbreviate $\hat{\mu}(z^n)$ to $\hat{\mu}_n$. We usually refer to the prequential ML model in terms of the corresponding codelength function

$$L_U(z^n) = \sum_{i=0}^{n-1} L_U(z_{i+1} \mid z_i) = \sum_{i=0}^{n-1} -\ln M_{\hat{\mu}_i}(z_{i+1}).$$

To understand this definition, note that for exponential families, for any sequence of data, the ordinary maximum likelihood parameter is given by the average $n^{-1} \sum x_i$ of the observed values of X [12]. Here we define our prequential model in terms of a slightly modified maximum likelihood estimator that introduces a 'fake initial outcome' x_0 with multiplicity n_0 in order to avoid infinite code lengths for the first few outcomes (a well-known problem called by Rissanen the "inherent singularity" of predictive coding [16, 10]) and to ensure that the prequential ML code of the first outcome is well-defined. In practice we can take $n_0 = 1$ but our result holds for any $n_0 > 0$. The justification of our modification to the ML estimator is discussed further in Section 5 and in [10].

Theorem 1 (Main result). *Let $X, X_1, X_2, \ldots$ be i.i.d. $\sim P$, with $E_P[X] = \mu^*$. Let $\mathcal{M}$ be a single parameter exponential family with sufficient statistic X and μ^* an element of the mean value parameter space. Let U denote the prequential ML model with respect to $\mathcal{M}$. If $\mathcal{M}$ and P satisfy Condition 1 below, then*

$$\mathcal{R}_U(n) = \frac{\operatorname{var}_P X}{\operatorname{var}_{M_{\mu^*}} X} \frac{1}{2} \ln n + O(1). \tag{6}$$

To reconcile this with (5), note that M_{μ^*} is the element of $\mathcal{M}$ achieving smallest expected codelength, i.e. it achieves $\inf_{\mu \in \Theta_\mu} D(P \| M_\mu)$ [12].

Condition 1 *We require that the following holds both for $T := X$ and $T := -X$:*

- *If T is unbounded from above then there is a $k \in \{4, 6, \ldots\}$ such that the first k moments of T exist under P and that $\frac{d^4}{d\mu^4} D(M_{\mu^*} \| M_\mu) = O\left(\mu^{k-6}\right)$.*
- *If T is bounded from above by a constant g then $\frac{d^4}{d\mu^4} D(M_{\mu^*} \| M_\mu)$ is polynomial in $1/(g - \mu)$.*

The condition implies that Theorem 1 can be applied to most single-parameter exponential families that are relevant in practice. To illustrate, in [10] we have explicitly computed the fourth derivative of the divergence for a number of exponential families: the Poisson, geometric, Normal, Bernoulli, exponential and Pareto families; all parameters beside the mean are treated as fixed values. As can be seen from [10–Figure 1], for these exponential families, our condition applies whenever the fourth moment of P exists. We explain the need for Condition 1 directly after the proof of Theorem 1:

Proof. (of Theorem 1) Here we only give the proof for the special case that $X = Z$, i.e. the sufficient statistic of $\mathcal{M}$ is equal to the observed outcome. Extension to the general case is trivial, see [10]. Thus, in the proof of Theorem 1 as well as all the Lemmas and Propositions it makes use of, it is implicitly understood that $X = Z$. The proof relies on Lemma 2 (Section 6), which has a complicated and lengthy proof. But as we shall see, once one takes Lemma 2 for granted, the proof becomes quite straightforward:

We abbreviate $\delta_i = \hat{\mu}_i - \mu^*$ and $\frac{d^k}{d\mu^k} D(M_{\mu^*} \| M_\mu) = D^{(k)}(\mu)$. That is, $D^{(k)}(\mu)$ is the k-th derivative of the function $f(\mu) := D(M_{\mu^*} \| M_\mu)$. The proof is based on a Taylor expansion of the KL divergence $D(M_{\mu^*} \| M_{\hat{\mu}_i})$ around μ^*:

$$D(M_{\mu^*} \| M_{\hat{\mu}_i}) = 0 + \delta_i D^{(1)}(\mu^*) + \frac{\delta_i^2}{2} D^{(2)}(\mu^*) + \frac{\delta_i^3}{6} D^{(3)}(\mu^*) + \frac{\delta_i^4}{24} D^{(4)}(\mu)$$

The last term is the remainder term of the Taylor expansion, in which $\mu \in [\mu^*, \hat{\mu}_i]$. The second term $D^{(1)}(\mu^*)$ is zero, since $D(\mu^* \| \mu)$ has its minimum at $\mu = \mu^*$ [12]. As is well-known [12], for exponential families the term $D^{(2)}(\mu)$ coincides precisely with the Fisher information $I(\mu)$ evaluated at μ. Another standard result [12] for the mean-value parameterization says that for all μ,

$$I(\mu) = \frac{1}{\operatorname{var}_{M_\mu} X}. \tag{7}$$

Therefore:

$$D(M_{\mu^*} \| M_{\hat{\mu}_i}) = \frac{1}{2} \delta_i^2 / \operatorname{var}_{M_{\mu^*}}(X) + \frac{1}{6} \delta_i^3 D^{(3)}(\mu^*) + \frac{1}{24} \delta_i^4 D^{(4)}(\mu) \tag{8}$$

We now compute the expected sum of (8), where $\hat{\mu}_i$ (and therefore δ_i) is a random variable that takes on values according to P, while μ^* is fixed. We get:

$$\sum_{i=0}^{n-1} \mathop{E}_{\hat{\mu}_i \sim P} [D(M_{\mu^*} \| M_{\hat{\mu}_i})] = \frac{1}{2\operatorname{var}_{M_{\mu^*}}(X)} \sum_{i=0}^{n-1} E_P [\delta_i^2] + R(n), \tag{9}$$

where the remainder term $R(n)$ is given by

$$R(n) = \sum_{i=0}^{n-1} \mathop{E}_{\hat{\mu}_i \sim M^*} \left[\frac{1}{6} \delta_i^3 D^{(3)}(\mu^*) + \frac{1}{24} \delta_i^4 D^{(4)}(\mu) \right] \tag{10}$$

where μ and δ_i are random variables depending on $\hat{\mu}_i$ and i. Theorem 1 now follows by rewriting the term on the left and the two terms on the right in (9):

1. Lemma 1 (Section 6) shows that $\mathcal{R}_U(n) = \sum_{i=0}^{n-1} E_{\hat{\mu}_i \sim P} [D(M_{\mu^*} \| M_{\hat{\mu}_i})]$, so that the left-hand side of (9) is equal to the left-hand side of (6).
2. Lemma 2 (Section 6) shows that $R(n) = O(1)$.
3. To evaluate the remaining term $\frac{1}{2\operatorname{var}_{M_{\mu^*}}(X)} \sum_{i=0}^{n-1} E_P [\delta_i^2]$ in (9), note that $\hat{\mu}_i$ is almost the ML estimator. This suggests that each term in the sum

$\sum_{i=0}^{n-1} E_P [\delta_i{}^2]$ should be almost equal to the variance of the ML estimator, which is $\mathrm{var} X / i$. Because of the slight modification that we made to the estimator, the variance becomes $\mathrm{var} X / (i+1) + O((i+1)^{-2})$ (this is easy to verify; an explicit proof is given as Theorem 5 in [10]). We then get:

$$\sum_{i=0}^{n-1} E_P \left[(\hat{\mu}_i - \mu^*)^2 \right] = \sum_{i=0}^{n-1} O\left((i+1)^{-2} \right) + \mathrm{var}_P(X) \sum_{i=0}^{n-1} (i+1)^{-1}$$
$$= O(1) + \mathrm{var}_P(X) \ln n, \tag{11}$$

so that Theorem 1 follows with items (1) and (2) above.

Discussion. Lemma 1 follows relatively easily by rewriting the sum using the chain rule for relative entropy and the fact that X is a sufficient statistic. The truly difficult part of the proof is Lemma 2. It involves infinite sums of expectations over unbounded fourth-order derivatives of the KL divergence. To make this work, we (1) slightly modify the ML estimator by introducing the initial fake outcome x_0. And (2), we need to impose Condition 1. To understand it, consider the case $T = X$, X unbounded from above. The condition essentially expresses that, as $\hat{\mu}$ increases to infinity, the fourth order Taylor-term does not grow too fast. Similarly, if X is bounded from above by g, the condition ensures that the fourth-order term grows slowly enough as $\hat{\mu} \uparrow g$. The same requirements are imposed for decreasing $\hat{\mu}$.

4   Redundancy vs. Regret

The 'goodness' of a universal code relative to a model $\mathcal{M}$ can be measured in several ways: rather than using redundancy (as we did here), one can also choose to measure codelength differences in terms of *regret*, where one has a further choice between *expected regret* and *worst-case regret* [2]. Here we only discuss the implications of our result for the expected regret measure.

Let $\mathcal{M} = \{M_\theta \mid \theta \in \Theta\}$ be a family of distributions parameterized by Θ. Given a sequence $z^n = z_1, \ldots, z_n$ and a universal code U for $\mathcal{M}$ with lengths L_U, the *regret* of U on sequence z^n is defined as

$$L_U(z^n) - \inf_{\theta \in \Theta} [-\ln M_\theta(z^n)]. \tag{12}$$

Note that if the (unmodified) ML estimator $\hat{\theta}(z^n)$ exists, then this is equal to $L_U(z^n) + \ln M_{\hat{\theta}(z^n)}(z^n)$. Thus, one compares the codelength achieved on z^n by U to the best possible that could have been achieved on that particular z^n, using any of the distributions in $\mathcal{M}$. Assuming $Z_1, Z_2, \ldots$ are i.i.d. according to some (arbitrary) P, one may now consider the expected regret

$$\widehat{\mathcal{R}}_U(n) := E_P[L_U(Z^n) - \inf_{\theta \in \Theta} [-\ln M_\theta(Z^n)]],$$

To quantify the difference with redundancy, consider the function

$$d(n) := \inf_{\theta \in \Theta} E_P[-\ln M_\theta(Z^n)] - E_P \left[\inf_{\theta \in \Theta} [-\ln M_\theta(Z^n)] \right],$$

and note that for any universal code, $\mathcal{R}_U(n) - \widehat{\mathcal{R}}_U(n) = d(n)$. In case $P \in \mathcal{M}$, then under regularity conditions on $\mathcal{M}$ and its parameterization, it can be shown [4] that $\lim_{n \to \infty} d(n) = \frac{k}{2}$ where k is the dimension of $\mathcal{M}$. In our case, where P is not necessarily in $\mathcal{M}$, we have the following :

Theorem 2. *Let $\mathcal{X}$ be finite. Let P, M_μ and μ^* be as in Theorem 1. Then*

$$\lim_{n \to \infty} d(n) = \frac{1}{2} \frac{\mathrm{var}_P X}{\mathrm{var}_{M_{\mu^*}} X}. \tag{13}$$

For lack of space we have to omit the proof. It can be found in [10]. Note that the previous result for one-dimensional models $\mathcal{M}$ with $P \in \mathcal{M}$, $d(n) \to 1/2$, is a special case of (13). We conjecture that, under a condition similar to Condition 1, the same result still holds for general, not necessarily finite or countable or bounded $\mathcal{X}$, but at the time of writing this submission we did not yet find the time to sort out the details. In any case, our result is sufficient to show that in some cases (namely, if $\mathcal{X}$ is finite), we have

$$\widehat{\mathcal{R}}_U(n) = \frac{1}{2} \frac{\mathrm{var}_P X}{\mathrm{var}_{M_{\mu^*}} X} \ln n + O(1),$$

so that, up to $O(1)$-terms, the redundancy and the regret of the prequential ML code behave in the same way.

Incidentally, Theorem 2 can be used to substantiate the claim we made in Section 2, which stated that the Bayes (equipped with a strictly positive differentiable prior), NML and 2-part codes still achieve relative redundancy of $\frac{1}{2} \ln n$ if $P \neq \mathcal{M}$, at least if $\mathcal{X}$ is finite. Let us informally explain why this is the case. It is easy to show that Bayes, NML and (suitably defined) 2-part codes achieve regret $\frac{1}{2} \ln n + O(1)$ for *all* sequences $z_1, z_2, \ldots$ such that $\hat{\theta}(z^n)$ is bounded away from the boundary of the parameter space M, for all large n [2, 9]. It then follows using, for example, the Chernoff bound that these codes must also achieve expected regret $\frac{1}{2} \ln n + O(1)$ for *all* distributions P on $\mathcal{X}$ that satisfy $E_P[X] = \mu^* \in \Theta_\mu$. Theorem 2 then shows that they also achieve relative redundancy $\frac{1}{2} \ln n + O(1)$ for *all* distributions P on $\mathcal{X}$ that satisfy $E_P[X] = \mu^* \in \Theta_\mu$. We omit further details.

5 Discussion

1. Variations of Prequential Coding. As discussed in [10], in order to apply the prequential ML code, either the ML estimator has to be slightly modified, or, [6], the first few outcomes have to be ignored. While our modification of the ML estimator can be re-interpreted in terms of the second, more common solution to the 'startup problem', it has an additional advantage: our modified ML estimators are equivalent to (a) Bayesian MAP estimators with a conjugate prior, and (b) Bayesian mean estimators resulting from a variation of conjugate priors. Thus, for a large class of priors, our result continues to hold if one uses 'prequential Bayes MAP' or 'prequential Bayes mean' rather than prequential ML coding [10]. Rissanen's *predictive MDL* code behaves differently for unordered data, but our result implies that Rissanen's scheme cannot achieve redundancy $\frac{1}{2} \ln n + O(1)$ for arbitrary P either [10]. In fact, we conjecture:

Conjecture 1. Let $\mathcal{M}$ be a regular exponential family with sufficient statistic X and let $\mathcal{P}$ be the set of distributions on $\mathcal{Z}$ such that $E_P[X^4]$ exists. There exists *no "in-model" estimator* such that the corresponding prequential code achieves redundancy $\frac{1}{2} \ln n + O(1)$ for all $P \in \mathcal{P}$.

Here, by an *in-model estimator* we mean an algorithm that takes as input any sample of arbitrary length and outputs an $M \in \mathcal{M}$. Let us contrast this with "out-model estimators": fix some prior on the parameter set Θ_μ and let $P(\mu \mid z_1, \ldots, z_{n-1})$ be the Bayesian posterior with respect to this prior and data $z_1, \ldots, z_{n-1}$. One can think of the Bayesian predictive distribution $P(z_n \mid z_1, \ldots, z_{n-1}) := \int_{\mu \in \Theta_\mu} M_\mu(z_n) P(\mu \mid z_1, \ldots, z_{n-1}) d\mu$ as an *estimate* of the distribution of Z, based on data $z_1, \ldots, z_{n-1}$. But unlike estimators as defined in the conjecture above, the resulting *Bayesian predictive estimator* will in general not be a member of $\mathcal{M}$, but rather of its convex closure: we call it an *out-model estimator*. The redundancy of the Bayesian universal model is equal to the *accumulated Kullback-Leibler (KL) risk* of the Bayesian predictive estimator [10]. Thus, the accumulated KL risk of the Bayesian predictive estimator is $\frac{1}{2} \ln n + O(1)$ even under misspecification. Thus, if our conjecture above holds true, then in-model estimators behave in a fundamentally different way from out-model estimators in terms of their asymptotic risk.

Example 3. The well-known Laplace and Krichevsky-Trofimov estimators for the Bernoulli model [9] define prequential ML models according to Definition 2: they correspond to $x_0 = 1/2, n_0 = 2$, and $x_0 = 1/2, n_0 = 1$ respectively. Yet, they also correspond to Bayesian predictive distributions with uniform prior or Jeffreys' prior respectively. This implies, for example, that the codelength achieved by the Bayesian universal model with Jeffreys' prior and the prequential ML model with $x_0 = 1/2, n_0 = 1$ must *coincide*. We claimed before that the expected regret for a Bayesian universal model is $\frac{1}{2} \log n + O(1)$ if data are i.i.d. $\sim P$, for essentially all distributions P. This may seem to contradict our result which says that the expected regret of the prequential ML model can be $0.5c \log n + O(1)$ with $c \neq 1$ if $P \notin \mathcal{M}$. But there really is no contradiction: since the Bernoulli model happens to contain all distributions P on $\{0, 1\}$, we cannot have $P \notin \mathcal{M}$ so Theorem 1 indeed says that $c = 1$ no matter what P we choose. But with more complicated models such as the Poisson or Hardy-Weinberg model, it is quite possible that $P \notin \mathcal{M}$. Then the Bayesian predictive distribution will *not* coincide with any prequential ML model and we can have $c \neq 1$.

2. Practical Relevance. We just discussed the theoretical relevance of Theorem 1. But, as discussed in [10], it also has important practical consequences for data compression and MDL model selection. We first consider data compression. Our result indicates that the redundancy can be both larger and smaller than $\frac{1}{2} \ln n$, depending on the variance of the 'true' P. In practical data compression tasks, it is often the case that $P \notin \mathcal{M}$. Then, the prequential ML can behave either better or worse than the Bayesian code, depending on the situation. Let us now consider the interesting case of *MDL model selection* (which is not the same as ¿data compression!) between two non-overlapping parametric models $\mathcal{M}_1$ and $\mathcal{M}_2$ where one of the two models is *correct*: we observe some data z^n generated by a distribution from either $\mathcal{M}_1$ or $\mathcal{M}_2$. We pick the model such that the corresponding prequential codelength of z^n is minimized. Without loss of generality, assume $P \in \mathcal{M}_1$. Then P cannot be in $\mathcal{M}_2$. By Theorem 1, the prequential codelength relative to $\mathcal{M}_1$ is approximately equal to the Bayesian codelength, whereas relative to $\mathcal{M}_2$ the codelengths are quite different. It follows that prequential ML model selection will behave differently from Bayesian model selection. In [7] we performed some model selection experiments between the Poisson and geometric model. The results strongly suggest that the prequential ML codes typically behave worse (and never better!) than the Bayesian or NML codes; we provide a theoretical explanation for this phenomenon (but no formal proof) in [7]. These experiments thus show that *under misspecification our result is relevant even in a well-specified context!*

3. Related Work.

There are a plethora of results concerning the redundancy and/or the regret for the prequential ML code, for a large variety of models including multivariate exponential families, ARMA processes, regression models and so on. Examples are [15, 11, 17, 13]. In all these papers it is shown that either the regret or the redundancy grows as $\frac{k}{2} \ln n + o(\ln n)$, either in expectation or almost surely. [13] even evaluates the remainder term explicitly. The reason that these results do not contradict ours, is that they invariably concern the case where the generating P is in $\mathcal{M}$, so that automatically $\text{var}_{M^*}(X) = \text{var}_P(X)$.

6   Proofs

Lemma's 1 and 2, used in the proof of Theorem 1, are stated and proved, respectively, in Section 6.1 and 6.2. But we first provide some general results about deviations between average and mean, on which the proofs of Lemma 2 and Theorem 2 are based.

Theorem 3. *Suppose* $X, X_1, X_2, \ldots$ *are i.i.d. with mean 0. If the first* $k \in \mathbb{N}$ *moments of* X *exist, then we have Then* $E\left[\left(\sum_{i=1}^{n} X_i\right)^k\right] = O\left(n^{\lfloor \frac{k}{2} \rfloor}\right)$.

Remark. It follows as a special case of Theorem 2 of [18] that $E\left[\left|\sum_{i=1}^{n} X_i\right|^k\right] = O(n^{\frac{k}{2}})$ which almost proves this theorem and which is in fact sufficient for our purposes, as can be seen from the proof of Lemma 2. The advantage of Theorem 3 over Theorem 2 of [18] is that Theorem 3 has an elementary proof. Unfortunately, we had to omit this proof for lack of space. It can be found in [10].

Theorem 4. *Let* $X, X_1, \ldots$ *be i.i.d., let* $\hat{\mu}_n := (n_0 \cdot x_0 + \sum_{i=1}^{n} X_i)/(n + n_0)$ *and* $\mu^* = E[X]$. *If the first* k *moments of* X *exist, then* $E[(\hat{\mu}_n - \mu^*)^k] = O(n^{-\lceil \frac{k}{2} \rceil})$.

Proof. We define $Y_i := X_i - \mu^*$; this can be seen as a new sequence of i.i.d. random variables with mean 0, and $y_0 := x_0 - \mu^*$. Rewrite $E\left[(\hat{\mu}_n - \mu^*)^k\right]$ as

$$E\left[\left(n_0 y_0 + \sum_{i=1}^{n} Y_i\right)^k\right](n + n_0)^{-k} = O\left(n^{-k}\right)\sum_{p=0}^{k}\binom{k}{p}(n_0 y_0)^p E\left[\left(\sum_{i=1}^{n} Y_i\right)^{k-p}\right]$$

$$= O\left(n^{-k}\right)\sum_{p=0}^{k}\binom{k}{p}(n_0 y_0)^p \cdot O\left(n^{\lfloor\frac{k-p}{2}\rfloor}\right),$$

where in the last step we used Theorem 3. We sum $k + 1$ terms of which the term for $p = 0$ grows fastest in n, so the expression is $O(n^{-\lceil\frac{k}{2}\rceil})$ as required.

Theorem 5. *Let $X, X_1, \ldots$ be i.i.d. random variables, define $\hat{\mu}_n := (n_0 \cdot x_0 + \sum_{i=1}^{n} X_i)/(n + n_0)$ and $\mu^* = E[X]$. Let $k \in \{0, 2, 4, \ldots\}$. If the first k moments exists then $P(|\hat{\mu}_n - \mu^*| \geq \delta) = O\left(n^{-\lceil\frac{k}{2}\rceil}\delta^{-k}\right)$.*

Proof. Using Markov's inequality and Theorem 4 we get:
$$P(|\hat{\mu}_n - \mu^*| \geq \delta) = P\left((\hat{\mu}_n - \mu^*)^k \geq \delta^k\right) \leq E\left[(\hat{\mu}_n - \mu^*)^k\right]\delta^{-k} = O\left(n^{-\frac{k}{2}}\delta^{-k}\right).$$

6.1   Lemma 1: Redundancy for Exponential Families

Lemma 1. *Let U be a prequential ML model and $\mathcal{M}$ be an exponential family as in Theorem 1. We have $\mathcal{R}_U(n) = \sum_{i=0}^{n-1} E_{\hat{\mu}_i \sim P}\left[D(M_{\mu^*} \| M_{\hat{\mu}_i})\right]$.*

Proof. We have:

$$\arg\inf_{\mu} E_P\left[-\ln M_\mu(X^n)\right] = \arg\inf_{\mu} E_P\left[\ln\frac{M_{\mu^*}(X^n)}{M_\mu(X^n)}\right] = \arg\inf_{\mu} D(M_{\mu^*} \| M_\mu).$$

In the last step we used Proposition 1 below. The divergence is minimized when $\mu = \mu^*$ [12], so we find that (the last step following again from Proposition 1):

$$\mathcal{R}_U(n) = E_P[-\ln U(X^n)] - E_P[-\ln M_{\mu^*}(X^n)] = E_P\left[\ln\frac{M_{\mu^*}(X^n)}{U(X^n)}\right]$$

$$= E_P\left[\sum_{i=0}^{n-1}\ln\frac{M_{\mu^*}(X_i)}{M_{\hat{\mu}_i}(X_i)}\right] = \sum_{i=0}^{n-1} E_P\left[\ln\frac{M_{\mu^*}(X_i)}{M_{\hat{\mu}_i}(X_i)}\right] = \sum_{i=0}^{n-1}\mathop{E}_{\hat{\mu}_i \sim P}\left[D(M_{\mu^*} \| M_{\hat{\mu}_i})\right].$$

Proposition 1. *Let $X \sim P$ with mean μ^*, and let M_μ index an exponential family with sufficient statistic X, so that M_{μ^*} exists. We have:*
$$E_P\left[-\ln\frac{M_{\mu^*}(X)}{M_\theta(X)}\right] = D(M_{\mu^*} \| M_\theta).$$

Proof. Let $\eta(\cdot)$ denote the function mapping parameters in the mean value parameterization to the natural parameterization. (It is the inverse of the function $\mu(\cdot)$ which was introduced in the discussion of exponential families.) By working out both sides of the equation we find that they both reduce to $\eta(\mu^*)\mu^* + \ln Z(\eta(\mu^*)) - \eta(\theta)\mu^* - \ln Z(\eta(\theta))$.

6.2   Lemma 2: Convergence of the Sum of the Remainder Terms

Lemma 2. *Let $R(n)$ be defined as in (10). Then $R(n) = O(1)$.*

Proof. We omit irrelevant constants and the term for the first outcome, which is well-defined because of our modification of the ML estimator. We abbreviate $\frac{d^k}{d\mu^k}D(M_{\mu^*}\|M_\mu) = D^{(k)}(\mu)$ as in the proof of Theorem 1. First we consider the third order term. We write $E_{\delta_i \sim P}$ to indicate that we take the expectation over data which is distributed according to P, of which δ_i is a function. We use Theorem 4 to bound the expectation of δ_i^3; under the condition that the first three moments exist, which is assumed to be the case, we obtain,

$$\sum_{i=1}^{n-1} E_{\delta_i \sim P}\left[\delta_i^3 D^{(3)}(\mu^*)\right] = D^{(3)}(\mu^*)\sum_{i=1}^{n-1}E[\delta_i^3] = D^{(3)}(\mu^*)\sum_{i=1}^{n-1}O(i^{-2}),$$

which is $O(1)$, since the constants implicit in $O(\cdot)$ are the same across terms.

The fourth order term is more involved, because $D^{(4)}(\mu)$ is not necessarily constant across terms. To compute it we first distinguish a number of regions in the value space of δ_i: let $\Delta_- = (-\infty, 0)$ and let $\Delta_0 = [0, a)$ for some constant value $a > 0$. If the individual outcomes X are bounded on the right hand side by a value g then we require that $a < g$ and we define $\Delta_1 = [a, g)$; otherwise we define $\Delta_j = [a + j - 1, a + j)$ for $j \geq 1$. Now we must establish convergence of:

$$\sum_{i=1}^{n-1} E_{\delta_i \sim P}\left[\delta_i^4 D^{(4)}(\mu)\right] = \sum_{i=1}^{n-1}\sum_j P(\delta_i \in \Delta_j) E_{\delta_i \sim P}\left[\delta_i^4 D^{(4)}(\mu) \mid \delta_i \in \Delta_j\right]$$

If we can establish that the sum converges for all regions Δ_j for $j \geq 0$, then we can use a symmetrical argument to establish convergence for Δ_- as well, so it suffices if we restrict ourselves to $j \geq 0$. First we show convergence for Δ_0. In this case, the basic idea is that since the remainder $D^{(4)}(\mu)$ is well-defined over the interval $\mu^* \leq \mu < \mu^* + a$, we can bound it by its extremum on that interval, namely $m := \sup_{\mu \in [\mu^*, \mu^* + a)} \left|D^{(4)}(\mu)\right|$. Now we get:

$$\left|\sum_{i=1}^{n-1} P(\delta_i \in \Delta_0)E\left[\delta_i^4 D^{(4)}(\mu) \mid \delta_i \in \Delta_0\right]\right| \leq \left|\sum_{i=1}^{n-1} 1 \cdot E\left[\delta_i^4 \left|D^{(4)}(\mu)\right|\right]\right|,$$

which is less or equal than $\left|m\sum_i E\left[\delta_i^4\right]\right|$. Using Theorem 4 we find that $E[\delta_i^4]$ is $O(i^{-2})$, the sum of which converges. Theorem 4 requires that the first four moments of P exist, but this is guaranteed to be the case: either the outcomes are bounded from both sides, in which case all moments necessarily exist, or the existence of the required moments is part of the condition on the main theorem.

Now we distinguish between the unbounded and bounded cases. First we assume X is unbounded from above. In this case, we must show convergence of:

$$\left|\sum_{i=1}^{n-1}\sum_{j=1}^{\infty} P(\delta_i \in \Delta_j)E\left[\delta_i^4 D^{(4)}(\mu) \mid \delta_i \in \Delta_j\right]\right|$$

We bound this expression from above. The δ_i in the expectation is at most $a + j$. Furthermore $D^{(4)}(\mu) = O(\mu^{k-6})$ by assumption on the main theorem, where $\mu \in [a + j - 1, a + j)$. Depending on k, both boundaries could maximize this function, but it is easy to check that in both cases the resulting function is $O(j^{k-6})$. So we get:

$$\cdots \leq \sum_{i=1}^{n-1} \sum_{j=1}^{\infty} P(|\delta_i| \geq a + j - 1)(a + j)^4 O(j^{k-6})$$

Since we know from the condition on the main theorem that the first $k \geq 4$ moments exist, we can apply Theorem 5 to find that $P(|\delta_i| \geq a + j - 1) = O(i^{-\lceil \frac{k}{2} \rceil}(a + j - 1)^{-k}) = O(i^{-\frac{k}{2}})O(j^{-k})$ (since k has to be even); plugging this into the equation and simplifying we obtain $\sum_i O(i^{-\frac{k}{2}}) \sum_j O(j^{-2})$. For $k \geq 4$ this expression converges.

Now we consider the case where the outcomes are bounded from above by g. This case is more complicated, since now we have made no extra assumptions as to existence of the moments of P. Of course, if the outcomes are bounded from both sides, then all moments necessarily exist, but if the outcomes are unbounded from below this may not be true. To remedy this, we map all outcomes into a new domain in such a way that all moments of the transformed variables are guaranteed to exist. Any constant x^- defines a mapping $g(x) := \max\{x^-, x\}$. We define the random variables $Y_i := g(X_i)$, the initial outcome $y_0 := g(x_0)$ and the mapped analogues of μ^* and $\hat{\mu}_i$, respectively: $\mu^\dagger$ is defined as the mean of Y under P and $\tilde{\mu}_i := (y_0 \cdot n_0 + \sum_{j=1}^{i} Y_j)/(i + n_0)$. Since $\tilde{\mu}_i \geq \hat{\mu}_i$, we can bound:

$$\left| \sum_i P(\delta_i \in \Delta_1) E\left[\delta_i^4 D^{(4)}(\mu) \mid \delta_i \in \Delta_1\right] \right| \leq \sum_i P(\hat{\mu}_i - \mu^* \geq a) \sup_{\delta_i \in \Delta_1} \left| \delta_i^4 D^{(4)}(\mu) \right|$$

$$\leq \sum_i P(|\tilde{\mu}_i - \mu^\dagger| \geq a + \mu^* - \mu^\dagger) g^4 \sup_{\delta_i \in \Delta_1} \left| D^{(4)}(\mu) \right| \quad (14)$$

By choosing x^- small enough, we can bring $\mu^\dagger$ and μ^* arbitrarily close together; in particular we can choose x^- such that $a + \mu^* - \mu^\dagger > 0$ so that application of Theorem 5 is safe. It reveals that the summed probability is $O(i^{-\frac{k}{2}})$ for any even $k \in \mathbb{N}$. Now we bound $D^{(4)}(\mu)$ which is $O((g - \mu)^{-m})$ for some $m \in \mathbb{N}$ by the condition on the main theorem. Here we use that $\mu \leq \hat{\mu}_i$; the latter is maximized if all outcomes equal the bound g, in which case the estimator equals $g - n_0(g - x_0)/(i + n_0) = g - O(i^{-1})$. Putting all of this together, we get $\sup |D^{(4)}(\mu)| = O((g - \mu)^{-m}) = O(i^m)$; if we plug this into the equation we obtain:

$$\cdots \leq \sum_i O(i^{-\frac{k}{2}}) g^4 O(i^m) = g^4 \sum_i O(i^{m-\frac{k}{2}})$$

This converges if we choose $k \geq 6m$. We can do this because the construction of $g(\cdot)$ ensures that all moments exist, and therefore certainly the first $6m$.

7   Conclusion and Future Work

We established two theorems about the relative coding redundancy. The two theorems combined state, essentially, that the expected regret of exponential family models behaves differently for the prequential plug-in universal code than for the Bayes, NML/Shtarkov and 2-part codes. This has consequences for coding, for MDL model selection, and for the behavior of the Kullback-Leibler risk. We conjecture that a similar result holds if the prequential code is not based on the ML but any other asymptotically consistent estimator, as long as each estimate is required to lie in the model $\mathcal{M}$. In future work, we hope to extend Theorem 2 to general 1-parameter exponential families with arbitrary sample spaces.

Acknowledgment. This work was supported in part by the IST Program of the European Community, under the PASCAL Network of Excellence, IST-2002-506778. This publication only reflects the authors' views.

References

1. K. Azoury and M. Warmuth. Relative loss bounds for on-line density estimation with the exponential family of distributions. *Machine Learning*, 43(3), 2001.
2. A. Barron, J. Rissanen, and B. Yu. The minimum description length principle in coding and modeling. *IEEE Trans. Inf. Theory*, 44(6):2743–2760, 1998.
3. N. Cesa-Bianchi and G. Lugosi. Worst-case bounds for the logarithmic loss of predictors. *Journal of Machine Learning*, 43(3):247–264, 2001.
4. B.S. Clarke and A.R. Barron. Information-theoretic asymptotics of Bayes methods. *IEEE Trans. Inf. Theory*, IT-36(3):453–471, 1990.
5. T.M. Cover and J.A. Thomas. *Elements of Information Theory*. Wiley, 1991.
6. A.P. Dawid. Present position and potential developments: Some personal views, statistical theory, the prequential approach. *Journal of the Royal Statistical Society, Series A*, 147(2):278–292, 1984.
7. S. de Rooij and P. Grünwald. An empirical study of MDL model selection with infinite parametric complexity. Available at the CoRR arXiv at http://xxx.lanl.gov/abs/cs.LG/0501028abs.cs.LG/0501028, 2005.
8. Y. Freund. Predicting a binary sequence almost as well as the optimal biased coin. In *Proc. Ninth Annual Conf. on Comp. Learning Theory (COLT' 96)*, 1996.
9. P. Grünwald. MDL tutorial. In P. Grünwald, J. Myung, and M. Pitt, editors, *Advances in Minimum Description Length*. MIT Press, 2005.
10. P. Grünwald and S. de Rooij. Asymptotic log–loss of prequential maximum likelihood codes. Available at the CoRR arXiv at http://xxx.lanl.gov/, 2005.
11. E.M. Hemerly and M.H.A. Davis. Strong consistency of the PLS criterion for order determination of autoregressive processes. *Ann. Statist.*, 17(2):941–946, 1989.
12. R. Kass and P. Vos. *Geometric Foundations of Asymptotic Inference*. Wiley, 1997.
13. L. Li and B. Yu. Iterated logarithmic expansions of the pathwise code lengths for exponential families. *IEEE Trans. Inf. Theory*, 46(7):2683–2689, 2000.
14. J. Rissanen. Universal coding, information, prediction and estimation. *IEEE Trans. Inf. Theory*, 30:629–636, 1984.

15. J. Rissanen. A predictive least squares principle. *IMA Journal of Mathematical Control and Information*, 3:211–222, 1986.
16. J. Rissanen. *Stochastic Complexity in Statistical Inquiry*. World Scientific, 1989.
17. C.Z. Wei. On predictive least squares principles. *Ann. Statist.*, 20(1):1–42, 1990.
18. P. Whittle. Bounds for the moments of linear and quadratic forms in independent variables. *Theory of Probability and its Applications*, V(3), 1960.

Teaching Classes with High Teaching Dimension Using Few Examples

Frank J. Balbach

Institut für Theoretische Informatik, Universität zu Lübeck,
Ratzeburger Allee 160, 23538 Lübeck, Germany
balbach@tcs.uni-luebeck.de

Abstract. We consider the Boolean concept classes of 2-term DNF and 1-decision lists which both have a teaching dimension exponential in the number n of variables. It is shown that both classes have an average teaching dimension linear in n. We also consider learners that always choose a *simplest* consistent hypothesis instead of an *arbitrary* consistent one. Both classes can be taught to these learners by efficient teaching algorithms using only a linear number of examples.

1 Introduction

In learning from examples, a learner typically knows only little about the source of these examples. In addition, the learner is required to learn from all such sources, regardless of their quality. Even in the query model [1, 2], the burden of learning rests almost exclusively on the part of the learner, because the oracle, although answering truthfully, is assumed to behave adversarially whenever possible. Helpful teachers who are honestly interested in the learner's success have been studied in several ways, though.

Within the inductive inference paradigm, Freivalds, Kinber, and Wiehagen [7] and Jain, Lange, and Nessel [15] developed a model in which the learner is provided with good examples chosen by an implicitly given teacher.

Jackson and Tomkins [14] as well as Goldman and Mathias [10, 17] defined models of teacher/learner pairs where teachers and learners are constructed explicitly. The requirement to construct both learners and teachers leads to the problem of collusion. For preventing the teacher to simply encode the target concept, all models mentioned so far use some kind of adversary who disturbs the teaching process and makes it more challenging. Angluin and Kriķis' [3, 4] model prevents collusion by giving incompatible hypothesis spaces to teacher and learner. This makes simple encoding of the target concept impossible.

A different notion of helpful teacher was introduced by Goldman, Rivest, and Shapire [8, 11] and Goldman and Kearns [9], and independently by Shinohara and Miyano [20]. Here, a teacher is an algorithm that, given a target concept c from a concept class $\mathcal{C}$, produces a sequence of examples for c. It is different from the aforementioned models in that now the teacher is considered successful if its examples force *every* consistent learning algorithm to output the target concept.

P. Auer and R. Meir (Eds.): COLT 2005, LNAI 3559, pp. 668–683, 2005.

This is equivalent to saying that c must be the only concept in $\mathcal{C}$ consistent with the teacher's examples.

The minimum number of examples necessary to teach a concept c is called its teaching dimension [9] (or key size [20], or specification number [5]). The maximum teaching dimension over all concepts in $\mathcal{C}$ is the teaching dimension of $\mathcal{C}$. This value has been studied as a measure for the difficulty to teach $\mathcal{C}$ [13].

The following example shows that this measure does not always capture our intuition. Consider the concept class consisting of all singleton concepts and the empty concept. To successfully teach the empty concept, a teacher has to rule out all singleton concepts. This can only be done by providing *all* negative examples. The teaching dimension then is the maximum possible which does not properly reflect the easy teachability one would expect from this class.

Two reasons for this implausible result are obvious. First, the teaching dimension of the class is determined by the worst case teaching dimension over all concepts. Easily learnable concepts are not taken into account. Second, the teacher has to teach all consistent learners and among them there are unreasonable ones. In the above example, as long as the teacher leaves out at least one negative example, there is a learner outputting a singleton concept containing a left out example. This clearly is not a plausible learner and one can expect to simplify teaching by requiring learners to be a little more "sensible."

In this paper, we take a look at the two obvious remedies. First, we consider the average teaching dimension instead of the worst case teaching dimension. This has been done previously by Anthony, Brightwell and Shawe-Taylor [5] for the class of linearly separable Boolean functions and by Kuhlmann [16] for classes of VC-dimension 1.

Second, we restrict the class of admissible learners by imposing an additional constraint besides that of consistency, namely that of preferring simple hypotheses over complex ones. This principle, well known as *Occam's Razor*, is of such great importance in learning theory that frequently the process of learning is even equated with finding a simple hypothesis. To apply this principle, we first assign a complexity to each concept. We then admit only those learners who output consistent hypotheses of least complexity.

Note that restricting the admissible learners in such a way presents a middle course between teaching *all* learners and teaching only *one* learner.

Our presentation focuses on two concept classes: 2-term DNF and 1-decision lists. In the monotone variant both classes have already been studied by Goldman and Kearns [9] who proved their teaching dimension to be linear in the number of Boolean variables. The general (non-monotone) variants are easily seen to have a teaching dimension exponential in the number of variables and are therefore well suited objects for our study.

As we shall see, both classes exhibit another questionable property of the teaching dimension. After introducing natural complexity measures for the concepts, one finds that with growing complexity the teaching dimension decreases. This undesired phenomenon disappears when the learners obey the *Occam's Razor* principle.

2   Notations and Definitions

Let $X_n = \{0,1\}^n$ be the set of all assignments to n Boolean variables. We consider *concepts* $c\colon X_n \to \{0,1\}$, or equivalently $c \subseteq X_n$, and *concept classes* $\mathcal{C}_n \subseteq 2^{X_n}$. Elements from X_n are called *instances* and pairs $(x,y) \in X_n \times \{0,1\}$ of an instance and a Boolean value are called *examples*. A concept c is *consistent* with a set $S = \{(x_1,y_1),\ldots,(x_m,y_m)\}$ of examples if $c(x_i) = y_i$ for all $i = 1,\ldots,m$.

A set S of examples is a *teaching set* [9, 20] for c with respect to $\mathcal{C}$ if c is the only concept in $\mathcal{C}$ consistent with S. The *teaching dimension* of c is defined as the size of its smallest teaching set: $TD(c) = \min\{|S|: S$ is teaching set for c wrt $\mathcal{C}\}$. The teaching dimension of $\mathcal{C}$ is defined as the maximum teaching dimension over all concepts: $TD(\mathcal{C}) = \max\{TD(c) : c \in \mathcal{C}\}$. Finally, we define the *average teaching dimension* $\overline{TD}(\mathcal{C}) = \frac{1}{|\mathcal{C}|}\sum_{c\in\mathcal{C}} TD(c)$.

A teacher providing a teaching set for c makes sure that every consistent learner outputting only hypotheses from $\mathcal{C}$ successfully learns c from the given examples. We now restrict the class of learners that must be successful to those that output consistent hypotheses from $\mathcal{C}$ of minimal complexity.

Let $K\colon \mathcal{C} \to \mathbb{N}$ map each concept to a natural number interpreted as its complexity. A *K-learner* is now required to output a consistent hypothesis with minimal complexity among all consistent hypotheses. In order to teach a concept c to those K-learners, a teacher has to provide enough examples to rule out all concepts with complexity less or equal to $K(c)$.

We call a set S of examples a *K-set* for c if c is consistent with S and for all $c' \in \mathcal{C} \setminus \{c\}$ consistent with S, $K(c') > K(c)$. The *K-dimensions* are defined as: $KD(c) = \min\{|S| : S$ is K-set for c wrt $\mathcal{C}\}$ and $KD(\mathcal{C}) = \max\{KD(c) : c \in \mathcal{C}\}$. It is clear from the definitions that the K-dimension depends on the measure K.

Let $\mathcal{D}_n$ be the class of all concepts representable by a *1-decision list* [19] over n variables. A 1-decision list is a list $D = \langle(\ell_1,b_1),\ldots,(\ell_m,b_m),(*,b_{m+1})\rangle$ of *nodes* consisting of literals ℓ_i and *labels* $b_i \in \{0,1\}$. A node (ℓ,b) is called *positive* if $b = 1$, *negative* otherwise. The node $(*,b)$ is the *default node*. The concept c_D represented by D is defined by: $c_D(x) = b_j$ for the minimum $j \le m$ such that x satisfies ℓ_j and $c_D(x) = b_{m+1}$ if no such j exists. We say (ℓ,b) *absorbes* an instance x, if ℓ is the first literal in D satisfied by x. We define the *length* of a decision list as the number of nodes (not counting the default node), i.e., $len(D) = m$ and the *length* of a concept $c \in \mathcal{D}_n$ as the length of its shortest decision list: $len(c) = \min_{c=c_D} len(D)$.

Let $\mathcal{C}_n^k$ be the class of all concepts representable by a *k-term DNF*, that is a disjunction of no more than k monomials over n variables. Note that $\mathcal{C}_n^k \supset \mathcal{C}_n^{k-1} \supset \cdots \supset \mathcal{C}_n^0 = \{\emptyset\}$.

We use Boolean variables $v_1,\ldots,v_n$ and denote by v^0 or $\bar{v}$ negative literals, and by v^1 or v positive literals. A monomial over n variables is represented by a string $M \in \{0,1,*\}^n$, where the i-th character of M is denoted by $M[i]$. $M[i] = 0,1,*$ specifies whether v_i occurs negated, unnegated, or not at all. One yields the set of satisfying assignments by replacing every $*$ with arbitrary values from $\{0,1\}$. Every monomial, except for the contradictory one, can be represented this way. Sometimes we identify M with the set of its satisfying assignments. Note that $M_1 \subseteq M_2$ iff for all i, $M_1[i] = M_2[i]$ or $M_2[i] = *$.

When we consider two monomials M_1, M_2 we say that they have a *strong difference at i* if $\{0,1\} \ni M_1[i] \neq M_2[i] \in \{0,1\}$. They have a *weak difference at i* if either $M_1[i] = *$ and $M_2[i] \in \{0,1\}$ or $M_2[i] = *$ and $M_1[i] \in \{0,1\}$. Two weak differences, at positions i and j, are said to be *of the same kind* if $M_q[i] = M_q[j] = *$ for a $q \in \{1,2\}$, that is if both $*$ occur in the same monomial; they are called *of different kind* otherwise.

For a string $M \in \{0,1,*\}^n$ we denote by $M[\frac{*}{0}]$ and $M[\frac{*}{1}]$ the string resulting from substitution of all $*$ by 0 and 1, respectively. Strings $s, s' \in \{0,1\}^n$ are called *neighbors* if they differ in only one bit and *i-neighbors* if they differ only in the i-th bit. For $z \in \{0,1\}$ we define $\bar{z} = 1 - z$.

3   Average Teaching Dimension

In this section we show that 2-term DNFs as well as 1-decision lists have a linear average teaching dimension, although their teaching dimension is 2^n. A similar result was given by Anthony et. al. [5] who prove an n^2 upper bound for the average teaching dimension of linearly separable concepts.

3.1   2-Term DNF

We start by looking at the simpler class of 1-term DNF (monomials). Goldman and Kearns [9] showed the class of monomials (without the empty concept) to have a teaching dimension of $n + 1$. Adding the empty concept does not change the teaching dimension of the non-empty concepts since their optimal teaching sets always contain a positive example that rules out the empty concept. The empty concept has a teaching dimension of 2^n since each of the 2^n singleton concepts is contained in $\mathcal{C}_n^1$ and one example can only rule out one such concept. There are 3^n non-empty concepts representable by monomials and therefore

$$\overline{TD}(\mathcal{C}_n^1) \leq \frac{2^n + 3^n \cdot (n+1)}{3^n + 1} \leq \left(\frac{2}{3}\right)^n + n + 1 \leq n + 2 \ .$$

If we turn towards the 2-term DNF, we have a similar situation. The empty concept has a teaching dimension of 2^n. Concepts representable as monomial have a teaching dimension wrt $\mathcal{C}_n^2$ at least as large as the number of negative examples (i. e., not satisfying instances), hence $TD(c) > 2^{n-1}$ for $c \in \mathcal{C}_n^1$.

To prove an average teaching dimension linear in n we have to show two things about the remaining concepts in $\mathcal{C}_n^2 \setminus \mathcal{C}_n^1$ (the *true 2-term DNF*), namely that they are numerous enough and that their teaching dimension is at most linear in n.

We start with the latter. The basic idea is similar to teaching a single monomial M (cf. [9]). We provide two complementary positive examples per monomial. They ensure that a monomial P consistent with them must at least encompass M. All neighbors of an arbitrary positive example that do not satisfy the monomial are then chosen as negative examples. They ensure that P cannot be a proper superset of M.

Things are more complicated with two monomials, since they need not to be disjoint and, furthermore, many concepts in $\mathcal{C}_n^2$ can be represented by more than one 2-term DNF.

Lemma 1. *Let M_1, M_2 be two monomials and let $c \in \mathcal{C}_n^2 \setminus \mathcal{C}_n^1$ be represented by the 2-term DNF $M_1 \vee M_2$. Then $TD(c) \leq 2n + 4$.*

Proof. In the following we distinguish five cases according to the number and kind of differences between M_1 and M_2 (see Fig. 1).

Case 1. M_1 and M_2 have at least two strong differences.
By symmetry, without loss of generality we can assume two strong differences occuring at position 1 and 2: $* \neq M_1[1] \neq M_2[1] \neq *$ and $* \neq M_1[2] \neq M_2[2] \neq *$.

First we define a set $S = S^+ \cup S^-$ of cardinality at most $4 + 2n$ and then we show that S is a teaching set for $M_1 \vee M_2$.

Let $s_1 = M_1[\frac{*}{0}]$, $s_1' = M_1[\frac{*}{1}]$, $s_2 = M_2[\frac{*}{0}]$, $s_2' = M_2[\frac{*}{1}]$. Then $S^+ = \{(s_1, 1), (s_1', 1), (s_2, 1), (s_2', 1)\}$. S^- consists of all neighbors of s_1 or s_2 that neither satisfy M_1 nor M_2 and thus can serve as negative examples. Obviously, $|S| \leq 4 + 2n$.

In order to show that S is a teaching set, we consider a 2-term DNF consistent with S with monomials P_1, P_2. We assume without loss of generality that s_1 satisfies P_1.

Claim: $s_1, s_1' \in P_1 \setminus P_2$ and $s_2, s_2' \in P_2 \setminus P_1$.
First, we show $s_2, s_2' \notin P_1$. Suppose $s_2 \in P_1$. From $s_1, s_2 \in P_1$, $s_1[1] \neq s_2[1]$ and $s_1[2] \neq s_2[2]$ we get that $P_1[1] = P_2[2] = *$. Then P_1 also contains the 1-neighbor

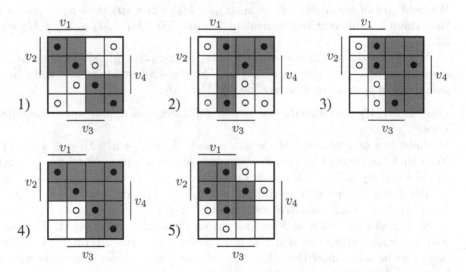

Fig. 1. Karnaugh diagrams of five 2-term DNFs over four variables according to the five cases distinguished in Lemma 1. Positive instances are marked by a gray background. Examples included in the teaching set are marked by a circle

s of s_1. On the other hand, $s \notin M_1 \vee M_2$ and hence $s \in S^-$. Thus P_1 is satisfied by a negative example, a contradiction. This proves the claim.

Analogously one can show that $s_2' \notin P_1$. This implies $s_2, s_2' \in P_2$. In a symmetric way one proves $s_1, s_1' \notin P_2$.

The Claim implies $P_1[i] = *$ for all i with $M_1[i] = *$ and $P_1[i] \supseteq M_1[i]$ for all other i. It remains to show that $P_1[i] = M_1[i]$ for all i with $M_1[i] \neq *$ and analogously for P_2 and M_2.

Suppose there is an i such that $P_1[i] = * \neq M_1[i]$. Let s be the i-neighbor of s_1. Then $s \in P_1 \setminus M_1$. Additionally $s \notin M_2$, since s certainly differs from M_2 at the first or second bit (not necessarily at both, since one of them could be i). Thus, $s \in S^-$ and since P_1 is consistent with S^-, $s \in P_1$ cannot be true, a contradiction.

By the same arguments, one shows that $P_2[i] = M_2[i]$ for all i with $M_2[i] \neq *$. We have now proved $P_1 = M_1$ and $P_2 = M_2$, hence S is a teaching set for c.

We will not present Cases 2 to 5 in full length, but confine ourselves to defining teaching sets of size at most $2n + 4$.

Case 2. M_1, M_2 have one strong difference and two weak differences of different kind.

Without loss of generality $M_1 = z_1 * z_3 \mu_1$ and $M_2 = \bar{z}_1 z_2 * \mu_2$ with $\mu_1, \mu_2 \in \{0, 1, *\}^*$ and $z_1, z_2, z_3 \in \{0, 1\}$.

We define the positive examples as $s_1 = z_1 \bar{z}_2 z_3 \mu_1 [\frac{*}{0}]$, $s_1' = z_1 z_2 z_3 \mu_1 [\frac{*}{1}]$, $s_2 = \bar{z}_1 z_2 \bar{z}_3 \mu_2 [\frac{*}{0}]$ and $s_2' = \bar{z}_1 z_2 z_3 \mu_2 [\frac{*}{1}]$. The negative examples are again all neighbors of s_1 or s_2 that do not satisfy $M_1 \vee M_2$.

Case 3. M_1, M_2 have one strong difference, at least two weak differences of the same kind, and no differences of different kind.

Without loss of generality $M_1 = z_1 z_2 z_3 \mu_1$, $M_2 = \bar{z}_1 * * \mu_2$ with $\mu_1 \subseteq \mu_2$. Note that there is a different but equivalent 2-term DNF: $M_1 \vee M_2 \equiv \widehat{M}_1 \vee M_2$ with $\widehat{M}_1 := * z_2 z_3 \mu_1$.

We define the positive examples as $s_1 = z_1 z_2 z_3 \mu_1 [\frac{*}{0}]$, $s_1' = z_1 z_2 z_3 \mu_1 [\frac{*}{1}]$, $s_2 = \bar{z}_1 \bar{z}_2 z_3 \mu_2 [\frac{*}{0}]$ and $s_2' = \bar{z}_1 z_2 \bar{z}_3 \mu_2 [\frac{*}{1}]$. The negative examples are again those neighbors of s_1 or s_2 that do not satisfy $M_1 \vee M_2$.

Case 4. M_1, M_2 have exactly one strong difference and exactly one weak difference.

Without loss of generality $M_1 = z_1 z_2 \mu$ and $M_2 = \bar{z}_1 * \mu$ with $\mu \in \{0, 1, *\}^*$. Note that the concept has three equivalent representations. With $m_1 = z_1 z_2 \mu$, $\widehat{M}_1 = * z_2 \mu$, $m_2 = \bar{z}_1 \bar{z}_2 \mu$, $\widehat{M}_2 := \bar{z}_1 * \mu$ we have $m_1 \vee \widehat{M}_2 \equiv \widehat{M}_1 \vee \widehat{M}_2 \equiv \widehat{M}_1 \vee m_2$.

We define five positive examples as $z_1 z_2 \mu [\frac{*}{0}]$, $z_1 z_2 \mu [\frac{*}{1}]$, $\bar{z}_1 \bar{z}_2 \mu [\frac{*}{0}]$, $\bar{z}_1 \bar{z}_2 \mu [\frac{*}{1}]$, $\bar{z}_1 z_2 \mu [\frac{*}{0}]$, and a single negative example by $z_1 \bar{z}_2 \mu [\frac{*}{0}]$.

So far all cases with at least one strong difference are covered. The cases without strong difference still remain. Since among true 2-term DNF neither term can be subterm of the other, we only need to consider situations with at least two weak differences of different kind.

Some of these cases are already covered. Case 4 treats the case of exactly two differences of different kind (and otherwise identical terms), Case 3 treats the case of exactly two differences of different kind plus exactly one more weak difference. Thus, only the following case remains.

Case 5. M_1, M_2 have at least two disjoint pairs of weak differences of different kind.
Without loss of generality, $M_1 = z_1 z_2 * * \mu_1$ and $M_2 = * * z_3 z_4 \mu_2$.

We define the positive examples $s_1 = z_1 z_2 \bar{z}_3 z_4 \mu_1[\begin{smallmatrix}*\\0\end{smallmatrix}]$, $s_1' = z_1 z_2 z_3 \bar{z}_4 \mu_1[\begin{smallmatrix}*\\1\end{smallmatrix}]$, $s_2 = \bar{z}_1 z_2 z_3 z_4 \mu_2[\begin{smallmatrix}*\\0\end{smallmatrix}]$ and $s_2' = z_1 \bar{z}_2 z_3 z_4 \mu_2[\begin{smallmatrix}*\\1\end{smallmatrix}]$. As negative examples we use all neighbors of s_1 or s_2 that do not satisfy $M_1 \vee M_2$.   □

Theorem 2. $TD(\mathcal{C}_n^2 \setminus \mathcal{C}_n^1) \leq 2n + 4$.

Proof. Lemma 1 presents a complete distinction of cases for the class $\mathcal{C}_n^2 \setminus \mathcal{C}_n^1$ and in each case the teaching dimension is bounded by $2n + 4$.   □

The previous lemma proves a bound for the teaching dimension not only with respect to $\mathcal{C}_n^2 \setminus \mathcal{C}_n^1$, but in fact with respect to $\mathcal{C}_n^2$. The next lemma provides bounds for the number of concepts in $\mathcal{C}_n^2 \setminus \mathcal{C}_n^1$.

Lemma 3. $\frac{1}{3} \cdot 9^n \leq |\mathcal{C}_n^2 \setminus \mathcal{C}_n^1| \leq \frac{2}{3} \cdot 9^n$ *for all* $n \geq 10$.

Proof. All 2-term DNFs of the form considered in Case 1 of Lemma 1 represent pairwise different concepts (modulo permutation of the monomials). Each such DNF can be described by the number i of strong differences ($2 \leq i \leq n$), their kind (two possibilities: 0/1 or 1/0), and the kind of the positions without strong differences ($n - i$ positions with seven possibilities each: 0/0, 1/1, 0/*, 1/*, */*, */0, */1). The number of concepts represented by such 2-term DNFs is thus $\frac{1}{2} \cdot \sum_{i=2}^{n} \binom{n}{i} \cdot 2^i \cdot 7^{n-i} = \frac{1}{2} \cdot (9^n - 7^n - 2n \cdot 7^{n-1})$ which proves the lower bound.

There are $(3^n + 1)^2$ syntactically different 2-term DNFs of which the $3^n + 1$ ones with two identical monomials do not represent true 2-term DNFs. The remaining $3^n(3^n+1)$ 2-term DNFs represent $\frac{1}{2} \cdot 3^n(3^n+1) = \frac{1}{2}(9^n+3^n)$ concepts. This number is therefore an upper bound for $|\mathcal{C}_n^2 \setminus \mathcal{C}_n^1|$. We omit the details.   □

The above proof actually shows the number of true 2-term DNF concepts to be asymptotically equal to $\frac{1}{2} \cdot 9^n$. We are now ready to calculate the average teaching dimension of $\mathcal{C}_n^2$.

Theorem 4. $\overline{TD}(\mathcal{C}_n^2) \leq 4n + 10$ *for all* $n \geq 10$.

Proof. The teaching dimension of the 3^n+1 concepts in $\mathcal{C}_n^1$ can be upper-bounded by 2^n and that of the other concepts by $2n + 4$. Therefore for almost all n

$$\overline{TD}(\mathcal{C}_n^2) \leq \frac{(3^n + 1) \cdot 2^n + \frac{2}{3} \cdot 9^n \cdot (4 + 2n)}{(3^n + 1) + \frac{1}{3} \cdot 9^n} \leq \frac{9^n + 9^n \cdot (4 + 2n)}{\frac{1}{2} \cdot 9^n} = 4n + 10. \quad \square$$

3.2   1-Decision Lists

The class of 1-decision lists has a teaching dimension of 2^n (cf. [14]). We use a result from Anthony *et. al.* [5] which gives an upper bound for the teaching dimension of decision lists in dependence of their length.

Lemma 5. $TD(c) \leq (len(c) + 1) \cdot 2^{n-len(c)}$ for all $c \in \mathcal{D}_n$.

The teaching dimension of the concepts grows roughly exponentially as their length decreases. In this section we show that the number of concepts of a certain length grows faster, thus leading to a small average teaching dimension. We denote the number of length m concepts in $\mathcal{D}_n$ by A_m^n.

As usual we assume decision lists to be in reduced form, i. e., each variable occurs at most once (either negated or not) and the default node and its predecessor (if any) have different labels. It is known that a 1-decision list can be transformed into an equivalent reduced 1-decision list in linear time (cf. [10]) and that reduced decision lists are of minimal length (see [21]).

Both properties persist if we further restrict decision lists to end in a positive node and a negative default node. We call these lists *normal form decision lists* (NFDL). Note that only concepts of length at least one can be represented by an NFDL. Every reduced decision list either is an NFDL or can be transformed into one by inverting the default label and the last node's label and literal.

In order to determine A_m^n it suffices to count the number of inequivalent NFDLs of length m. To do so, we first derive an equivalence criterion for NFDLs.

It is clear that if consecutive nodes with the same label are permuted, the represented concept remains the same. However, the converse is not true, even when only NFDLs are considered. For example, the decision lists $\langle (v_1, 0), (v_2, 1), (*, 0) \rangle$ and $\langle (\bar{v}_2, 0), (\bar{v}_1, 1), (*, 0) \rangle$ are equivalent, but cannot be transformed into one another by permuting consecutive nodes with the same label.

One way to yield a converse of the statement is to allow permutations of the last (positive) node with one of its negative predecessors. In order to prove this, we need some definitions.

Definition 6. *Let D be an NFDL with label sequence $b_1, \ldots, b_m$. The segments of D are the longest sequences of consecutive nodes with the same label. There is one exception in case $m \geq 2$: The last node never forms a segment of its own, but is always attached to the next to last node's segment.*

A segment is homogenous *if all nodes in it have the same label, otherwise it is* inhomogenous.

Some examples of label sequences with marked segment boundaries are: $|000|11|0001|$, $|11|0|1|0|111|$, $|0|11|00|11|01|$. Note that the segmentation is unique and that inhomogenous segments can only occur last.

Definition 7. *Two segments $G = \langle (x_1^{\alpha_1}, b_1), \ldots, (x_r^{\alpha_r}, b_r) \rangle$ and $H = \langle (y_1^{\beta_1}, b_1), \ldots, (y_r^{\beta_r}, b_r) \rangle$ are* equivalent *$(G \equiv H)$, if there is a permutation π, such that*

(1) $\forall i : x_i = y_{\pi(i)}$ and   (2) $\forall i : \alpha_i = \begin{cases} \beta_{\pi(i)}, & \text{if } b_i = b_{\pi(i)}, \\ 1 - \beta_{\pi(i)}, & \text{if } b_i \neq b_{\pi(i)}. \end{cases}$

For homogenous segments the definition is equivalent to $\{x_1^{\alpha_1}, \ldots, x_r^{\alpha_r}\} = \{y_1^{\beta_1}, \ldots, y_r^{\beta_r}\}$. Two inhomogenous segments are equivalent if they contain the same variables and each variable that occurs in the positive node of one segment has its sign inverted if it occurs in a negative node in the other segment.

The next lemma which presents an equivalence criterion for NFDLs shows that Definitions 6 and 7 are indeed useful.

Lemma 8. *Two decision lists D and E in normal form are equivalent if and only if their label sequences are equal and for their segmentations $D = D_1, \ldots, D_r$ and $E = E_1, \ldots, E_r$, $D_i \equiv E_i$ for all i.*

Proof. For the if part, let $D = D_1, \ldots, D_r$ and $E = E_1, \ldots, E_r$ be two NFDLs with equal label sequences and equivalent segments. Let $1 \leq i \leq r$. We prove

Claim 1. For all instances $z \in \{0,1\}^n$ both segments, D_i and E_i, behave equivalently, that is they either classify z in the same way (positive or negative) or they don't classify z at all.

Proof. First, we consider homogenous segments D_i, E_i with label b. If z satisfies a literal in D_i then it also satisfies a literal in E_i and hence both segments classify z as b. If z does not satisfy any literal in D_i, the same is true for E_i and neither segment classifies z.

Next, consider inhomogenous segments $D_i = \langle (\ell_1, 0), \ldots, (\ell_{s-1}, 0), (\ell_s, 1) \rangle$ and E_i. Since such segments can only occur at the end of an NFDL, each z is classified by E_i and D_i (or by the negative default node common to both lists). If z is classified positive by D_i it passes all nodes $\ell_1, \ldots, \ell_{s-1}$ and is absorbed by the last node $(\ell_s, 1)$. Now consider the permutation π from the definition of $D_i \equiv E_i$. If π lets ℓ_s in its place, z still reaches ℓ_s and is classified as positive. If, however, ℓ_s is exchanged with some literal ℓ_j ($j \neq s$), then the signs of ℓ_s and ℓ_j are both inverted and hence z still passes all negative nodes (in particular $(\bar{\ell}_s, 0)$), reaches the last node $(\bar{\ell}_j, 1)$, and is classified as positive. The same arguments show that if z is classified as positive by E_i than also by D_i. This proves Claim 1.

Now it is easy to prove by induction that an instance z reaches a segment D_i iff it reaches the corresponding segment E_i. And since D_i and E_i behave equivalently, D and E must be equivalent.

For the only if part, let D, E be two equivalent NFDLs. Let $b_1, \ldots, b_m$ be the label sequence of D. The number of instances classified as positive by D is $\sum_{i=1}^{m} b_i 2^{n-i}$. Since E is equivalent to D, it must have the same number of positive instances and therefore the same label sequence. Hence both lists are segmented into the same number of segments, $D = D_1, \ldots, D_r$ and $E = E_1, \ldots, E_r$, and corresponding segments are of equal length.

It remains to prove $D_i \equiv E_i$ for all $i \leq r$. We show:

Claim 2. If the instances reaching D_i are the same as those reaching E_i then $E_i \equiv D_i$ and the instances leaving D_i are the same as those leaving E_i.

Proof. Let Z be the set of instances reaching both D_i and E_i. First we consider homogenous segments, $D_i = \langle (x_1^{\alpha_1}, b), \ldots, (x_s^{\alpha_s}, b) \rangle$ and $E_i = \langle (y_1^{\beta_1}, b), \ldots, (y_s^{\beta_s}, b) \rangle$ with $b \in \{0, 1\}$. Let $\langle (y^\beta, \bar{b}) \rangle$ be the first node after E_i in E.

Suppose that there is a literal x^α in D_i, but not in E_i. Since none of the variables $x_1, \ldots, x_s, y_1, \ldots, y_s, y$ appears in one of the first $i - 1$ segments (D and E are NFDLs), for each assignment to these variables there must be an instance in Z. Let z be an assignment satisfying y^β and x^α, but no one of $y_j^{\beta_j}$

for all j. This z is then classified as b by D and as $\bar{b}$ by E, a contradiction. It follows that every literal in D_i is also contained in E_i, that is both segments are permutations of each other.

Now let D_i and E_i be inhomogenous. Then both segments come last in their decision list, i.e. $i = r$. The classification of the instances in Z by D depends only on the variables in D_r and all these variables are indeed relevant. Therefore E_r must contain the same variables.

It remains to show Condition (2) of the definition of $E_r \equiv D_r$. Let x^α be the literal in the last node of D_r. If x^α remains the last node after permuting (i.e., in E_r) its sign has to remain unchanged. Otherwise all instances in Z classified as positive by D_r would be classified differently by E_r. The other literals in D_r have to keep their sign as well.

If x is moved to a negative node in E_r, it has to appear as $x^{1-\alpha}$. Otherwise all instances in Z satisfying x^α would be classified as negative by E_r, although there is such an instance classified as positive by D_r. Additionally, all other literals in D_r (except the one moved to the last position) keep their sign. Suppose there is a literal ℓ occuring as $\bar{\ell}$ in E_r. Then we choose an instance $z \in Z$ satisfying ℓ and classified as positive by D_r. This z would then be classified as negative by E_r. Altogether $E_r \equiv D_r$. This proves Claim 2.

Since all instances in $\{0,1\}^n$ reach D_1 and E_1, Claim 2 can be used to prove by induction that $D_i \equiv E_i$ for all i. $\qquad\square$

Now that we can use Lemma 8 to recognize inequivalent NFDLs, we can analyze A_m^n more closely.

Lemma 9. *For all n and $2 \leq m \leq n$, $A_m^n \geq 2(n - m + 1) \cdot A_{m-1}^n$.*

Proof. Let $n \geq 2$ and $2 \leq m \leq n$. We consider A_{m-1}^n pairwise inequivalent NFDLs of length $m - 1$ and prove that each of them can be extended to an NFDL of length m in $2(n-m+1)$ ways such that all extended lists are mutually inequivalent.

We first consider the case $m = 2$ which somewhat differs from the general case. An NFDL of length 1 consists of exactly one positive node $(v_j^\alpha, 1)$ (with negative default). We get $2(n-1)$ NFDL of length 2 by prepending the positive nodes $(v_i, 1)$ or $(\bar{v}_i, 1)$ for each $i \neq j$. This yields $n - 1$ distinct concepts since in every new list the two nodes can be permuted without changing the represented concept. Similarly we get $n-1$ concepts by prepending the *negative* nodes $(v_i, 0)$ or $(\bar{v}_i, 0)$ for $i \neq j$. Each of the former $n - 1$ new concepts is different from each of the latter $n - 1$ ones since a segment with labels $1, 1$ cannot be equivalent to one with labels $0, 1$ (Lemma 8). This proves $A_2^n \geq 2(n-1) \cdot A_1^n$.

Now let $m > 2$. Let D be an NFDL of length $m - 1$ and let b_1 be the label of the first node. D contains exactly $m - 1$ different variables, hence there are $n - m + 1$ variables left. By prepending each of these variables (negated or not) as nodes with label $\bar{b}_1$ we get $2(n - m + 1)$ new NFDLs of length m.

The prepended node certainly forms a segment of its own, because its label is different from that of the second node. (The first node cannot form an inhomogenous segment with the second in the case $m > 2$.)

In this way we get $2(n - m + 1) \cdot A_{m-1}^n$ NFDLs of length m. These are all mutually inequivalent since they either differ in their first segment, or if their first nodes are equal they are extension of two already inequivalent NFDLs. □

The following corollary relates the number of NFDLs of a certain length to the total number $\sum_{m'=1}^n A_{m'}^n$ of NFDLs.

Corollary 10. For $n \geq 2$ and $1 \leq m \leq n$: $\sum_{m'=1}^n A_{m'}^n \geq 2^{n-m} \cdot (n - m)! \cdot A_m^n$.

Theorem 11. The average teaching dimension of $\mathcal{D}_n$ is linear in n.

Proof. We first prove the statement for the concept class of NFDLs. Then we argue that the inclusion of the missing concepts, $\emptyset$ and X_n, does not matter.

Using Lemma 5 we bound the average teaching dimension from above by

$$\frac{\sum_{m=1}^n (m + 1)2^{n-m} \cdot A_m^n}{\sum_{m=1}^n A_m^n} = \sum_{m=1}^n (m + 1)2^{n-m} \cdot \frac{A_m^n}{\sum_{m'=1}^n A_{m'}^n} .$$

Now we apply Corollary 10 to the fraction and get a new upper bound of

$$\sum_{m=1}^n (m + 1)2^{n-m} \cdot \frac{1}{2^{n-m} \cdot (n - m)!} = \sum_{m=1}^n \frac{m + 1}{(n - m)!} = \sum_{m=0}^{n-1} \frac{n + 1 - m}{m!} .$$

To see that this value grows linearly in n, we divide by n and obtain

$$\frac{1}{n} \sum_{m=0}^{n-1} \frac{n + 1 - m}{m!} \leq \frac{n + 1}{n} \sum_{m=0}^{n-1} \frac{1}{m!}$$

which converges to Euler's number as $n \to \infty$.

Since $|\mathcal{D}_n|$ grows faster than 2^n, the two missing concepts amount only to a fraction of less than 2^{1-n} of all concepts. Their teaching dimension of 2^n increases the average teaching dimension therefore by less than 2. □

Given Theorems 11 and 4, we conclude that 1-decision lists and 2-term DNFs are rather simple to teach despite their high teaching dimension. We are now going to judge the classes' teachability again, but in a different way.

4 Complexity Based Learners

We begin with a simple general fact. Let $\mathcal{C}$ be a concept class and let $K: \mathcal{C} \to \mathbb{N}$ be a complexity measure. Such a K implies a partitioning of $\mathcal{C}$: $\mathcal{C}^{=k} = \{c \in \mathcal{C} : K(c) = k\}$. Additionally we define $\mathcal{C}^{\leq k} = \{c \in \mathcal{C} : K(c) \leq k\}$. A teacher who wants to teach a concept $c \in \mathcal{C}^{=k}$ to K-learners has to give enough examples to uniquely specify c among all the concepts in $\mathcal{C}^{\leq k}$. Concepts with higher K-value need not be ruled out by the examples. The following lemma is therefore obvious.

Lemma 12. For all $c \in \mathcal{C}^{=k}$, $KD(c) = TD(c)$, where the teaching dimension is taken with respect to $\mathcal{C}^{\leq k}$.

4.1   2-Term DNF

There are many natural ways to measure the complexity of concepts representable by k-term DNF. Here we shall use the minimal number of terms necessary to represent a concept. Formally, $K(c) = 0$, if $c = \emptyset$, $K(c) = 1$, if $c \in \mathcal{C}_n^1 \setminus \{\emptyset\}$, $K(c) = 2$, if $c \in \mathcal{C}_n^2 \setminus \mathcal{C}_n^1$. It is possible to use results from Sect. 3.1 to calculate the K-dimension of $\mathcal{C}_n^2$.

Theorem 13. $KD(\mathcal{C}_n^2) \leq 2n + 4$.

Proof. If we denote the set of 2-term DNF by $\mathcal{C}_n$, we have, with the notations introduced above, $\mathcal{C}_n^{=0} = \mathcal{C}_n^0$, $\mathcal{C}_n^{\leq 1} = \mathcal{C}_n^1$, $\mathcal{C}_n^{\leq 2} = \mathcal{C}_n^2$. In order to apply Lemma 12, we have to compute several teaching dimensions.

- $TD(\emptyset) = 1$ wrt $\mathcal{C}_n^0$, hence $KD(\emptyset) = 1$;
- For $c \in \mathcal{C}_n^{=1}$, $TD(c) \leq n + 1$ wrt $\mathcal{C}_n^{\leq 1}$ (see beginning of Sect. 3.1), hence $KD(c) \leq n + 1$;
- For $c \in \mathcal{C}_n^{=2}$, $TD(c) \leq 2n + 4$ wrt $\mathcal{C}_n^{\leq 2}$ (see reasoning after Theorem 2), hence $KD(c) \leq 2n + 4$. $\qquad\square$

The last theorem, when compared to $TD(\mathcal{C}_n^2) = 2^n$, illustrates that teaching concepts to complexity based learners can be significantly simpler in terms of the number of examples. Another point in favor of the K-learners is that now more complex concepts (as measured by K) are harder to teach (as measured by the number of examples). In contrast, the teaching dimension for $\mathcal{C}_n^{=0}$, $\mathcal{C}_n^{=1}$, and $\mathcal{C}_n^{=2}$ is 2^n, at least 2^{n-1}, and at most $2n + 4$, respectively, and hence decreases as the concepts become more complex.

The greater plausibility comes at almost no cost regarding computational complexity on the part of the teacher. From Lemma 1 one can easily build an efficient teaching algorithm T computing K-sets for 2-term DNF concepts.

One can argue, however, that there is a cost on the part of the learner. The learner has not only to find a consistent hypothesis, but a *minimal* one. This can be an intractable problem. In fact, finding an *arbitrary* consistent 2-term DNF is already NP complete (cf. [18]).

On the other hand, K-learners only have to solve the problem of finding minimal consistent hypotheses restricted to those example sets provided by the teacher. The teacher T, for instance, outputs example sets from which the target concept can be inferred efficiently.

The number of positive examples determines whether a 0-, 1-, or 2-term DNF has to be learned. In the only non-trivial case, 2-term DNF, there are at most five positive examples and at most 30 ways to select two pairs of them. For each such selection the learner computes the minimum monomial for each pair and checks the resulting 2-term DNF for consistency with all examples. The learner then outputs the first consistent 2-term DNF it encounters.

4.2   1-Decision Lists

A natural measure of complexity for 1-decision lists is their length. We thus define for $c \in \mathcal{D}_n$: $K(c) = len(c)$. The next theorem describes K-sets for 1-decision lists.

v_1	v_2	v_3	v_4	v_5	v_6	v_7	$*$
+	−	−	−	+	+	+	−
0	0	0	0	0	0	0,	−
0	0	0	0	0	0	1,	+
0	0	0	0	0	1	0,	+
0	0	0	0	1	0	0,	+
0	0	0	1	1	1	1,	−
0	0	1	0	1	1	1,	−
0	1	0	0	1	1	1,	−
1	1	1	1	1	1	1,	+

v_1	v_2	v_3	v_4	v_5	v_6	v_7	$*$
+	+	+	−	−	−	−	+	−
0	0	0	0	0	0	0,	−
0	0	0	0	0	0	1,	+
0	0	0	0	0	1	1,	−
0	0	0	0	1	0	1,	−
0	0	0	1	0	0	1,	−
0	0	1	1	1	1	0,	+
0	1	0	1	1	1	0,	+
1	0	0	1	1	1	0,	+

Fig. 2. K-sets for two 1-decision lists. Positive nodes and examples are marked with $+$, negative ones by $−$. Each row corresponds to one example. A 1 or 0 specifies whether or not the instance satisfies the node's literal

Theorem 14. $KD(\mathcal{D}_n) \leq n+1$ and for all $c \in \mathcal{D}_n$: $KD(c) \leq len(c) + 1$.

Proof. It suffices to show $KD(c) \leq len(c)+1$ for all $c \in \mathcal{D}_n$. To teach the concepts $\emptyset$ and X_n to K-learners one arbitrary example suffices, because these concepts are representable by length 0 decision lists.

Let $c \in \mathcal{D}_n$ be representable by an NFDL D with segments $D_1, \ldots, D_r$. We define a set S of examples containing exactly one example for each node in D, including the default node. We will not present a formal proof that S is a K-set, but we shall give reasons for this during the construction of S (see also Fig. 2).

We start at the end of D. For the default node we include an arbitrary instance reaching the default node. Now, assume the last segment, D_r, is homogenous (with label 1). For each node $(\ell, 1)$ in D_r we include exactly one example, namely one that satisfies only ℓ and therefore reaches the node. With these examples included, we ensure that nodes of the form $(\bar{\ell}, 1)$ or $(\ell, 0)$ or $(\bar{\ell}, 0)$ are not consistent with S. Besides $(\ell, 1)$ only nodes with variables not occurring in D_r are possible. An NFDL consistent with S as defined so far therefore contains only nodes from D_r plus some nodes with irrelevant variables.

D_{r-1} is homogenous with label 0. For each node $(\ell, 0)$ in D_{r-1} we include a 0-classified instance that satisfies only ℓ among the literals in D_{r-1} and satisfies all literals in D_r. The other literals in D remain unsatisfied. This ensures two things. First, for $(\ell, 0)$ in D_{r-1}, nodes of the form $(\bar{\ell}, 0)$ or $(\ell, 1)$ or $(\bar{\ell}, 1)$ are inconsistent with S. Second, nodes with variables from D_r are inconsistent as well. To see the latter, assume a node $(\ell, 1)$ in D_r. It is inconsistent with S since there is a positive example satisfying ℓ and a negative one. This also excludes $(\ell, 0)$. Similarly, $(\bar{\ell}, 0)$ and $(\bar{\ell}, 1)$ are inconsistent with S as witnessed by the negative default node's example that satisfies $\bar{\ell}$ and by a positive example satisfying $\bar{\ell}$ from the set of examples for D_r.

An NFDL E consistent with S defined so far starts with nodes from D_{r-1}. Each such node removes exactly one example from the D_{r-1} set. Only when *all* these examples are removed, and hence all nodes from D_{r-1} have been selected, the nodes from D_r become elligible. In addition, nodes with irrelevant variables can occur at arbitrary positions of E. They do not remove any examples.

If we proceed in this manner for all other segments $D_{r-2}, \ldots, D_1$ we get a set S with $len(D) + 1$ examples. From the above reasoning it follows that an NFDL E consistent with S consists of segments $E_1, \ldots, E_r$ such that each E_i contains all nodes from D_i plus zero or more nodes with irrelevant variables. A shortest such E obviously contains exactly zero irrelevant nodes and is therefore equivalent to D (Lemma 8). But then S is a K-set for D.

A very similar, but slightly more complicated, reasoning applies in case of an inhomogenous segment D_r.   □

A comparison between teaching 1-decision lists to arbitrary learners (Sect. 3.2) and teaching them to complexity based learners (Theorem 14) shows that the latter yields again more plausible results. Teaching decision lists to K-learners requires much less examples and moreover the difficulty of teaching grows as the complexity of the concepts increases (cf. Lemma 5).

Furthermore, a teacher T producing the K-sets defined in Theorem 14 can be realized as a polynomial time algorithm.

Similar to the situation with 2-term DNFs, one can object that it is probably intractable to even approximate the *shortest* consistent 1-decision list (cf. [12]), whereas it is possible to find an *arbitrary* consistent 1-decision list efficiently (cf. [19, 6]). Thus, once again K-learners face a much harder problem.

Another similarity to teaching 2-term DNFs is, however, that the problem for the K-learners becomes efficiently solvable if it is restricted to those examples actually given by the teacher. In fact, Rivest's algorithm [19] does find a minimal hypothesis when taught by T.

We can interpret this as a teacher whose good examples enable the learner to solve an otherwise intractable learning problem.

Finally, we want to demonstrate a relation between teaching K-learners and the *trusted information teaching model* of Jackson and Tomkins [14]. In this model the teacher provides not only a set of examples, but also additional information about the target. The size of this additional information must be logarithmic in the size of the target concept. Since $K(c)$ is the representation size of a $c \in \mathcal{D}_n$, the teacher is allowed to add $\log K(c)$ bits of information and can thus communicate the length of c to the learner.

The learner, on the other hand, is required not only to produce a correct hypothesis, but also to detect whether its input was given by the "true" teacher or by an adversary. A small modification of Rivest's algorithm, which after producing a hypothesis h on input sample S simulates the true teacher on h and compares $T(h)$ with S, does both in polynomial time.

Corollary 15. *The concept class of 1-decision lists is polynomially teachable with trusted information.*

From previous results it only follows that 1-decision lists are not polynomially teachable without trusted information and that they are teachable by a computationally unbounded teacher with trusted information (cf. [14]). In some sense, Corollary 15 completes the teachability results for 1-decision lists in the trusted information model.

Conclusion. A closer look at two concept classes with worst case teaching dimension has revealed that they are not as hard to teach as their teaching dimension suggests. The average teaching dimension and the K-dimension, which are both linear, seem to be more appropriate measures of teachability since they properly reflect our intuition that both classes should be easily teachable.

Acknowledgments. The author heartily thanks the anonymous referees for many valuable comments.

References

1. D. Angluin. Queries and concept learning. *Machine Learning*, 2(4):319–342, 1988.
2. D. Angluin. Queries revisited. In *ALT 2001, Proceedings*, volume 2225 of *Lecture Notes in Artificial Intelligence*, pages 12–31. Springer, 2001.
3. D. Angluin and M. Kriķis. Teachers, learners and black boxes. In *Proceedings COLT 1997*, pages 285–297. ACM Press, New York, NY, 1997.
4. D. Angluin and M. Kriķis. Learning from different teachers. *Machine Learning*, 51(2):137–163, 2003.
5. M. Anthony, G. Brightwell, and J. Shawe-Taylor. On specifying boolean functions by labelled examples. *Discrete Applied Mathematics*, 61(1):1–25, 1995.
6. T. Eiter, T. Ibaraki, and K. Makino. Decision lists and related Boolean functions. *Theoretical Computer Science*, 270(1–2):493–524, 2002.
7. R. Freivalds, E. B. Kinber, and R. Wiehagen. On the power of inductive inference from good examples. *Theoretical Computer Science*, 110(1):131–144, 1993.
8. S. Goldman. *Learning Binary Relations, Total Orders, and Read-Once Formulas*. PhD thesis, MIT Dept. of Electr. Engineering and Computer Science, Sept. 1990.
9. S. A. Goldman and M. J. Kearns. On the complexity of teaching. *J. of Comput. Syst. Sci.*, 50(1):20–31, 1995.
10. S. A. Goldman and H. D. Mathias. Teaching a smarter learner. *J. of Comput. Syst. Sci.*, 52(2):255–267, 1996.
11. S. A. Goldman, R. L. Rivest, and R. E. Schapire. Learning binary relations and total orders. *SIAM J. Comput.*, 22(5):1006–1034, Oct. 1993.
12. T. Hancock, T. Jiang, M. Li, and J. Tromp. Lower bound on learning decision lists and trees. *Inform. Comput.*, 126(2):114–122, 1996.
13. T. Hegedüs. Generalized teaching dimensions and the query complexity of learning. In *Proceedings COLT 1995*, pages 108–117. ACM Press, New York, NY, 1995.
14. J. Jackson and A. Tomkins. A computational model of teaching. In *Proceedings COLT 1992*, pages 319–326. ACM Press, New York, NY, 1992.
15. S. Jain, S. Lange, and J. Nessel. Learning of r.e. languages from good examples. In *ALT '97, Proceedings*, volume 1316 of *LNAI*, pages 32–47. Springer, 1997.
16. C. Kuhlmann. On teaching and learning intersection-closed concept classes. In *Proceedings EuroCOLT '99*, volume 1572 of *LNAI*, pages 168–182. Springer, 1999.
17. H. D. Mathias. A model of interactive teaching. *J. of Comput. Syst. Sci.*, 54(3): 487–501, 1997.
18. L. Pitt and L. G. Valiant. Computational limitations on learning from examples. *J. ACM*, 35(4):965–984, 1988.

19. R. L. Rivest. Learning decision lists. *Machine Learning*, 2:229–246, 1987.
20. A. Shinohara and S. Miyano. Teachability in computational learning. *New Generation Computing*, 8(4):337–348, 1991.
21. H. U. Simon. Learning decision lists and trees with equivalence-queries. In *Euro-COLT '95, Proceedings*, number 904 in LNAI, pages 322–336. Springer, 1995.

Optimum Follow the Leader Algorithm

Dima Kuzmin and Manfred K. Warmuth

University of California - Santa Cruz

Consider the following setting for an on-line algorithm (introduced in [FS97]) that learns from a set of experts: In trial t the algorithm chooses an expert with probability p_i^t. At the end of the trial a loss vector[1] $L^t \in [0, R]^n$ for the n experts is received and an expected loss of $\sum_i p_i^t L_i^t$ is incurred. A simple algorithm for this setting is the *Hedge* algorithm which uses the probabilities $p_i^t \sim \exp^{-\eta L_i^{<t}}$. This algorithm and its analysis is a simple reformulation of the randomized version of the Weighted Majority algorithm (WMR) [LW94] which was designed for the absolute loss. The total expected loss of the algorithm is close to the total loss of the best expert $L_* = \min_i L_i^{\leq T}$. That is, when the learning rate is optimally tuned based on L_*, R and n, then the total expected loss of the Hedge/WMR algorithm is at most

$$L_* + \sqrt{2}\sqrt{L_* R \log n} + O(\log n).$$

The factor of $\sqrt{2}$ is in some sense optimal [Vov97].

A new randomized algorithm for choosing the expert was given in [KV05]: *perturb* the losses of the experts by adding noise ν_i to $L_i^{<t}$ and then choose the expert with minimum perturbed loss. This *Following the Perturbed Leader* (FPL) algorithm has the same total expected loss bound except that the $\sqrt{2}$ factor is replaced by **2**.

So the first question is whether there is an alternate way to perturb the losses in FPL which realizes WMR (with the optimal factor on the second term). In FPL the noise parameters of the additive noise only depend on the overall learning rate. But if you replace the entire loss $L_i^{<t}$ by a randomized loss depending on the learning rate **and** $L_i^{<t}$, then WMR can be realized:

Lemma 1. *Let Z_i be independent exponential random variables with parameters $\lambda_i = e^{-\eta L_i^{<t}}$ and $I = \arg\min_i Z_i$. Then $P(I = i) \sim \exp^{-\eta L_i^{<t}}$.*

Proof. $\min_i Z_i$ is an exponential random variable with parameter $\sum_i \lambda_i$ and $P(I = i) = \frac{\lambda_i}{\sum_j \lambda_j}$. □

However we know of no efficient implementation of WMR for the following representative application introduced in [TW03]: We have a directed graph with a source and a sink. The experts are the acyclic source to sink paths and the loss of a path is *additive* in the sense that it is the sum of the losses of its edges. The goal is again to incur loss close the best expert/path.

It is easy to implement the original FPL algorithm [KV05] (which has the worse constant): the loss of each edge is perturbed by some additive noise and

---

[1] It suffices to require that $(\max_i L_i^t - \min_i L_i^t) \leq R$.

P. Auer and R. Meir (Eds.): COLT 2005, LNAI 3559, pp. 684–686, 2005.
© Springer-Verlag Berlin Heidelberg 2005

the algorithm predicts with the path of minimum loss. However, we don't know how to implement WMR without computing the following type of quantity: the sum of acyclic paths from a start vertex to the sink. In [TW03] this problem is avoided by enlarging the set of path experts to *all* source to sink paths[2]. With the enlarged pool of experts, the path weights can be summed via dynamic programming.

So the natural open problem is whether there is a way to perturb the losses of the edges so that choosing the shortest path realizes WMR. That is, does there exist a distribution D, parameterized by L, satisfying the following two conditions.

1. If $Z_1 \sim D(L_1), \ldots, Z_n \sim D(L_n)$ are independent random variables, then

$$P(\arg\min(Z_1, \ldots, Z_n) = i) \sim \exp^{-L_i}$$

2. If $Z_1 \sim D(L_1)$ and $Z_2 \sim D(L_2)$ are independent random variables, then

$$Z_1 + Z_2 \sim D(L_1 + L_2)$$

There are many distributions that satisfy one of the two properties (e.g. the exponential satisfies 1 and the gamma satisfies 2). The first condition seems to correspond to closure of the distribution under the minimum operation. Specifically, all the distributions that we know to satisfy 1, also satisfy $\min(Z_1, \ldots, Z_n) \sim D(e^{-L_1} + \ldots + e^{-L_n})$. We did not however establish formally whether closure under minimum and condition 1 are equivalent.

The solution has to avoid the following caveat. Consider for instance a case where losses of all edges (and paths) are zero. Then choosing a shortest path yields a random variable whose parameter is related to the number of paths. So if the parameter can be *accurately* estimated by sampling, then this solves a #P-complete problem [Val79].

Essentially, the original FPL is efficient if an expert with minimum perturbed loss can be found efficiently. Is the same true for Hedge/WMR which has the optimum constant before the square root term? Or, what is the best constant achievable by any algorithm that efficiently computes the minimum w.r.t. a perturbed loss?

References

[FS97]   Yoav Freund and Robert E. Schapire. A decision-theoretic generalization of on-line learning and an application to boosting. *Journal of Computer and System Sciences*, 55(1):119–139, August 1997.

[KV05]   Adam Kalai and Santosh Vempala. Efficient algorithms for online decision problems. *J. Computer System Sci*, 2005. To appear.

[LW94]   N. Littlestone and M. K. Warmuth. The weighted majority algorithm. *Information and Computation*, 108(2):212–261, 1994.

---

[2] It suffices to consider paths of length at most ℓ, where ℓ is the longest acyclic path from the source to the sink.

[TW03]   E. Takimoto and M. K. Warmuth. Path kernels and multiplicative updates. *Journal of Machine Learning Research*, 4:773–818, October 2003.

[Val79]   Leslie Valiant. The complexity of enumeration and reliability problems. *SIAM Journal on Computing*, 8:410–421, 1979.

[Vov97]   V. Vovk. A game of prediction with expert advice. *J. Computer System Sci*, 1997.

The Cross Validation Problem

John Langford

TTI-Chicago
jl@hunch.net

1 The Method

K-fold cross validation is a commonly used technique which takes a set of m examples and partitions them into K equal-size sets (folds) of size m/K. For each set, a classifier is trained on the other sets.

2 The Problem

Assume only that samples are drawn iid from a distribution D on classification example $X \times \{0,1\}$ where X is a feature and $\{0,1\}$ is a label. Derive a classifier from the K classifiers with a lower true error rate bound than other approaches (discussed in section 3). The bound should have the form: For all learning algorithms A, number of sets K,

$$\Pr_{S \sim D^m} (e(D, h) \leq f(S, h, h_1, ..., h_K)) \geq 1 - \delta$$

where h is the classifier derived from the cross validation process on m examples producing classifiers $h_1, ..., h_K$, f is the bound (a computable function), and $e(D, h) = \Pr_{(x,y) \sim D}(h(x) \neq y)$ is the true error rate of h.

3 Past Work

1. Devroye, Rogers, and Wagner analyzed cross validation and found algorithm specific bounds for nearest neighbor and space partitioning algorithms. Much of this is documented here [1].
2. Michael Kearns and Dana Ron [2] analyzed cross validation and found that under additional stability assumptions the bound for the classifier which learns on all the data is not much worse than for a test set of size m/K.
3. Avrim Blum, Adam Kalai, and John Langford [3] analyzed cross validation and found that you can do at least as well as a test set of size m/K using the randomized classifier which draws uniformly from the K learned classifiers.
4. Yoshua Bengio and Yves Grandvalet [4] analyzed cross validation and concluded that there was no unbiased estimator of variance.
5. Matti Kaariainen [5] noted that you can safely derandomize a stochastic classifier (such as one that randomizes over the K sets) using unlabeled data without additional assumptions.

P. Auer and R. Meir (Eds.): COLT 2005, LNAI 3559, pp. 687–688, 2005.

4   Some Extreme Cases to Sharpen Intuition

1. Suppose on every set the learned classifier is the same. Then, the cross-validation error should behave something like a test set of size m. This is radically superior to a test set of size m/K. Behavior like this is often observed in practice.
2. Consider leave-one-out cross validation. Suppose we have a "learning" algorithm that uses the classification rule "always predict the parity of the labels on the training set". Suppose the learning problem is defined by a distribution which picks y=1 with probability 0.5. Then, with probability 0.5, all leave-one-out errors will be 0 and otherwise 1 (like a single coin flip). This example suggests that incorporating information about the stochastic difference between the classifier may yield a tighter bound.

5   Impact

On any individual problem, solving this might have only have a small impact due to slightly improved judgement of success. But, because cross validation is used very extensively, the overall impact of a good solution might be very significant.

References

1. Luc Devroye, Laszlo Gyorfi, and Gabor Lugosi, "A Proabibilistic Theory of Pattern Recognition", Springer, 1996.
2. Michael Kearns and Dana Ron, "Algorithmic Stability and Sanity-Check Bounds for Leave-One-Out Cross-Validation", Neural Computation 11(6), pages 1427-1453. 1999.
3. Avrim Blum, Adam Kalai, and John Langford, "Beating the Holdout: Bounds for KFold and Progressive Cross-Validation", COLT 1999, pages 203-208.
4. Yoshua Bengio and Yves Grandvalet "No unbiased estimator of the variance of K-fold cross-validation", Journal of Machine Learning Research, 5, 1089-1105, 2004.
5. Matti Kaariainen, "Generalization Error Bounds Using Unlabeled Data", COLT 2005.

Compute Inclusion Depth of a Pattern

Wei Luo

School of Computing Science, Simon Fraser University,
Vancouver, Canada
wluoa@cs.sfu.ca

1   Problem Description

We define a concept of *inclusion depth* (see Definition 1) to capture mind-change complexity [3, 1] of pattern identification problems [2]. Our basic question is whether the inclusion depth for any pattern is computable. We conjecture a combinatorial characterization that, if true, leads to a linear time algorithm to compute inclusion depth.

Let X be a set of variable (e.g., $x_1, x_2, \dots$) and Σ be a finite set of alphabet containing at least two symbols (e.g., $\{0, 1\}$). A **pattern**, denoted by p, q etc., is a finite non-null sequence over $X \cup \Sigma$. The **language** of a pattern p with alphabet Σ, denoted by $L_\Sigma(p)$, is the set of ground strings that are consequences of p by substituting each variable in p with a string in Σ^+. For example, if $\Sigma = \{0, 1\}$, strings 010 and 10110 are in $L_\Sigma(x_1 x_2 x_1)$, but $1010 \notin L_\Sigma(x_1 x_2 x_1)$.

Definition 1. *The **inclusion depth** of a pattern p with alphabet Σ, denoted by $\mathrm{ID}_\Sigma(p)$, is the length of the longest inclusion chain connecting the language of the universal pattern $L_\Sigma(x_1)$ and the language $L_\Sigma(p)$.*

For example, if $p = 0x_1 1$ and $\Sigma = \{0, 1\}$, then

$$L_\Sigma(x_1) \supset L_\Sigma(x_1 x_2) \supset L_\Sigma(x_1 1) \supset L_\Sigma(x_1 x_2 1) \supset L_\Sigma(0x_1 1)$$

is an inclusion chain connecting $L_\Sigma(x_1)$ and $L_\Sigma(0x_1 1)$; it is routine though tedious to verify that there exists no longer inclusion chain connecting the two. Thus the inclusion depth $\mathrm{ID}_\Sigma(0x_1 1)$ is equal to 4.

Question 1.   Is there an algorithm to compute $\mathrm{ID}_\Sigma(p)$ for any pattern p and any alphabet Σ? If yes, is there a polynomial time algorithm?

Question 2.   Is it true that, for every alphabet Σ with at least two symbols,

$$\mathrm{ID}_\Sigma(p) = 2|p| - \#\mathrm{var}(p) - 1 \tag{1}$$

where $|p|$ is the length (number of variables and constants) of p and $\#\mathrm{var}(p)$ the number of *distinct* variables in p. If the answer to this question is yes, then we have a linear time algorithm that computes inclusion depth using Eq. (1), and hence a positive answer to Question 1.

P. Auer and R. Meir (Eds.): COLT 2005, LNAI 3559, pp. 689–690, 2005.

2   Motivation

Inclusion depth captures the mind change complexity of the pattern identification problem given some initial evidence. If there exists an algorithm to compute the inclusion depth of a pattern, then we can use it to compute the mind change bound[1] of a pattern identification problem given some initial evidence. Moreover, we can construct a uniformly mind-change optimal learner [6].

3   Partial Solution and Difficulties

It is known that pattern inclusion is undecidable [5]. However, to compute the inclusion depth, we may not need to decide inclusion for any two patterns.

Intuitively, patterns with longer length are more constrained, and so are patterns with fewer distinct variables. With observing some shorter examples, this suggests a conjecture that for a pattern p, the inclusion depth $\mathrm{ID}(p)$ is related to the length $|p|$ and the number of distinct variables $\#\mathrm{var}(p)$ by Eq. (1). To prove this equation, it suffices to establish the following conjecture.

Conjecture 1. Let p and q be two patterns. If $L(p) \subset L(q)$, then

$$2|p| - \#\mathrm{var}(p) > 2|q| - \#\mathrm{var}(q). \tag{2}$$

To see why the reference to alphabet Σ is dropped, note that if $L_\Sigma(p) \subseteq L_\Sigma(q)$, then for every $\Sigma' \subseteq \Sigma$, we have that $L_{\Sigma'}(p) \subseteq L_{\Sigma'}(q)$. Therefore, we need to consider only the case that Σ contains exactly two symbols.

Exhaustive computation of my program shows that Eq. (2) holds for patterns of the length less than or equal to 7; computation for longer patterns has been computationally impractical for us. Therefore, if two patterns p and q form a counterexample to Eq. (2), one of them must be longer than 7.

References

1. A. Ambainis, S. Jain, and A. Sharma. Ordinal mind change complexity of language identification. *Theor. Comput. Sci.*, 220(2):323–343, 1999.
2. D Angluin. Finding patterns common to a set of strings. *J. Comput. Syst. Sci.*, 21(1):46–62, 1980.
3. R. Freivalds and C. H. Smith. On the role of procrastination in machine learning. *Inf. Comput.*, 107(2):237–271, 1993.
4. E. Mark Gold. Language identification in the limit. *Information and Control*, 10(5):447–474, 1967.
5. T. Jiang, A. Salomaa, K. Salomaa, and S. Yu. Inclusion is undecidable for pattern languages. In A. Lingas, R. Karlsson, and S. Carlsson, editors, *ICALP93*, volume 700 of *LNICS*, pages 301–312, 1993.
6. W. Luo and O. Schulte. Mind change efficient learning. to appear in COLT 2005.

---

[1] In problems of learning languages with positive data, **mind-change bound** [1] measures the worst-case number of mind-changes a learner has to make before it converges to the correct answer in the sense defined by Gold in [4].

Author Index

Lecture Notes in Artificial Intelligence (LNAI)

Vol. 3264: G. Paliouras, Y. Sakakibara (Eds.), Grammatical Inference: Algorithms and Applications. XI, 291 pages. 2004.

Vol. 3259: J. Dix, J. Leite (Eds.), Computational Logic in Multi-Agent Systems. XII, 251 pages. 2004.

Vol. 3257: E. Motta, N.R. Shadbolt, A. Stutt, N. Gibbins (Eds.), Engineering Knowledge in the Age of the Semantic Web. XVII, 517 pages. 2004.

Vol. 3249: B. Buchberger, J.A. Campbell (Eds.), Artificial Intelligence and Symbolic Computation. X, 285 pages. 2004.

Vol. 3248: K.-Y. Su, J. Tsujii, J.-H. Lee, O.Y. Kwong (Eds.), Natural Language Processing – IJCNLP 2004. XVIII, 817 pages. 2005.

Vol. 3245: E. Suzuki, S. Arikawa (Eds.), Discovery Science. XIV, 430 pages. 2004.

Vol. 3244: S. Ben-David, J. Case, A. Maruoka (Eds.), Algorithmic Learning Theory. XIV, 505 pages. 2004.

Vol. 3238: S. Biundo, T. Frühwirth, G. Palm (Eds.), KI 2004: Advances in Artificial Intelligence. XI, 467 pages. 2004.

Vol. 3230: J.L. Vicedo, P. Martínez-Barco, R. Muñoz, M. Saiz Noeda (Eds.), Advances in Natural Language Processing. XII, 488 pages. 2004.

Vol. 3229: J.J. Alferes, J. Leite (Eds.), Logics in Artificial Intelligence. XIV, 744 pages. 2004.

Vol. 3228: M.G. Hinchey, J.L. Rash, W.F. Truszkowski, C.A. Rouff (Eds.), Formal Approaches to Agent-Based Systems. VIII, 290 pages. 2004.

Vol. 3215: M.G.. Negoita, R.J. Howlett, L.C. Jain (Eds.), Knowledge-Based Intelligent Information and Engineering Systems, Part III. LVII, 906 pages. 2004.

Vol. 3214: M.G.. Negoita, R.J. Howlett, L.C. Jain (Eds.), Knowledge-Based Intelligent Information and Engineering Systems, Part II. LVIII, 1302 pages. 2004.

Vol. 3213: M.G.. Negoita, R.J. Howlett, L.C. Jain (Eds.), Knowledge-Based Intelligent Information and Engineering Systems, Part I. LVIII, 1280 pages. 2004.

Vol. 3209: B. Berendt, A. Hotho, D. Mladenic, M. van Someren, M. Spiliopoulou, G. Stumme (Eds.), Web Mining: From Web to Semantic Web. IX, 201 pages. 2004.

Vol. 3206: P. Sojka, I. Kopecek, K. Pala (Eds.), Text, Speech and Dialogue. XIII, 667 pages. 2004.

Vol. 3202: J.-F. Boulicaut, F. Esposito, F. Giannotti, D. Pedreschi (Eds.), Knowledge Discovery in Databases: PKDD 2004. XIX, 560 pages. 2004.

Vol. 3201: J.-F. Boulicaut, F. Esposito, F. Giannotti, D. Pedreschi (Eds.), Machine Learning: ECML 2004. XVIII, 580 pages. 2004.

Vol. 3194: R. Camacho, R. King, A. Srinivasan (Eds.), Inductive Logic Programming. XI, 361 pages. 2004.

Vol. 3192: C. Bussler, D. Fensel (Eds.), Artificial Intelligence: Methodology, Systems, and Applications. XIII, 522 pages. 2004.

Vol. 3191: M. Klusch, S. Ossowski, V. Kashyap, R. Unland (Eds.), Cooperative Information Agents VIII. XI, 303 pages. 2004.

Vol. 3187: G. Lindemann, J. Denzinger, I.J. Timm, R. Unland (Eds.), Multiagent System Technologies. XIII, 341 pages. 2004.

Vol. 3176: O. Bousquet, U. von Luxburg, G. Rätsch (Eds.), Advanced Lectures on Machine Learning. IX, 241 pages. 2004.

Vol. 3171: A.L.C. Bazzan, S. Labidi (Eds.), Advances in Artificial Intelligence – SBIA 2004. XVII, 548 pages. 2004.

Vol. 3159: U. Visser, Intelligent Information Integration for the Semantic Web. XIV, 150 pages. 2004.

Vol. 3157: C. Zhang, H. W. Guesgen, W.K. Yeap (Eds.), PRICAI 2004: Trends in Artificial Intelligence. XX, 1023 pages. 2004.

Vol. 3155: P. Funk, P.A. González Calero (Eds.), Advances in Case-Based Reasoning. XIII, 822 pages. 2004.

Vol. 3139: F. Iida, R. Pfeifer, L. Steels, Y. Kuniyoshi (Eds.), Embodied Artificial Intelligence. IX, 331 pages. 2004.

Vol. 3131: V. Torra, Y. Narukawa (Eds.), Modeling Decisions for Artificial Intelligence. XI, 327 pages. 2004.

Vol. 3127: K.E. Wolff, H.D. Pfeiffer, H.S. Delugach (Eds.), Conceptual Structures at Work. XI, 403 pages. 2004.

Vol. 3123: A. Belz, R. Evans, P. Piwek (Eds.), Natural Language Generation. X, 219 pages. 2004.

Vol. 3120: J. Shawe-Taylor, Y. Singer (Eds.), Learning Theory. X, 648 pages. 2004.

Vol. 3097: D. Basin, M. Rusinowitch (Eds.), Automated Reasoning. XII, 493 pages. 2004.

Vol. 3071: A. Omicini, P. Petta, J. Pitt (Eds.), Engineering Societies in the Agents World. XIII, 409 pages. 2004.

Vol. 3070: L. Rutkowski, J. Siekmann, R. Tadeusiewicz, L.A. Zadeh (Eds.), Artificial Intelligence and Soft Computing - ICAISC 2004. XXV, 1208 pages. 2004.

Vol. 3068: E. André, L. Dybkjær, W. Minker, P. Heisterkamp (Eds.), Affective Dialogue Systems. XII, 324 pages. 2004.

Vol. 3067: M. Dastani, J. Dix, A. El Fallah-Seghrouchni (Eds.), Programming Multi-Agent Systems. X, 221 pages. 2004.

Vol. 3066: S. Tsumoto, R. Słowiński, J. Komorowski, J.W. Grzymała-Busse (Eds.), Rough Sets and Current Trends in Computing. XX, 853 pages. 2004.

Vol. 3065: A. Lomuscio, D. Nute (Eds.), Deontic Logic in Computer Science. X, 275 pages. 2004.

Vol. 3060: A.Y. Tawfik, S.D. Goodwin (Eds.), Advances in Artificial Intelligence. XIII, 582 pages. 2004.

Vol. 3056: H. Dai, R. Srikant, C. Zhang (Eds.), Advances in Knowledge Discovery and Data Mining. XIX, 713 pages. 2004.

Vol. 3055: H. Christiansen, M.-S. Hacid, T. Andreasen, H.L. Larsen (Eds.), Flexible Query Answering Systems. X, 500 pages. 2004.

Vol. 3048: P. Faratin, D.C. Parkes, J.A. Rodríguez-Aguilar, W.E. Walsh (Eds.), Agent-Mediated Electronic Commerce V. XI, 155 pages. 2004.

Vol. 3040: R. Conejo, M. Urretavizcaya, J.-L. Pérez-de-la-Cruz (Eds.), Current Topics in Artificial Intelligence. XIV, 689 pages. 2004.